P9-BZM-162

<u>EXACTLY THE WORD YOU NEED—</u>
<u>WHEN YOU NEED IT MOST</u>

With our extensive crossword definitions section, twenty comprehensive special reference sections, and our exclusive "Word Finder," *The Dell Crossword Dictionary* ends your down-and-across search for stumpers like these:

    1. Temple birds
    2. Addams Family handyman?
    3. Belted hunter
    4. Nice name?
    5. Cassino cash

Answers:

    1. Owls (See Colleges and Universities.)
    2. Thing
    3. Orion (Look up "hunter.")
    4. Nom (Look up "French words.")
    5. Lira (See Nations Information, Italy.)

THE DELL CROSSWORD DICTIONARY

ORIGINALLY COMPILED BY
KATHLEEN RAFFERTY

REVISED, UPDATED, AND EXPANDED BY
WAYNE ROBERT WILLIAMS

Delta
Trade Paperbacks

THE DELL CROSSWORD DICTIONARY
A Delta Book

PUBLISHING HISTORY
Delta trade paperback edition published January 1996
Delta trade paperback reissue edition / November 2006

Published by
Bantam Dell
A Division of Random House, Inc.
New York, New York

All rights reserved
Copyright © 1950, 1960, 1984, 1994 by Dell Publishing
Copyright © renewed 1978 by Dell Publishing

Delta is a registered trademark of Random House, Inc.,
and the colophon is a trademark of Random House, Inc.

ISBN-13: 978-0-385-31515-9
ISBN-10: 0-385-31515-5

Printed in the United States of America
Published simultaneously in Canada

www.bantamdell.com

BVG 29 28 27 26 25 24 23 22 21 20

ABOUT THIS BOOK . . .

Kathleen Rafferty compiled and edited *The Dell Crossword Dictionary* 44 years ago. It continues to this day to be the crossword puzzle solver's ultimate reference source.

It was designed to be a portable book in which one could find the answers to put into those few remaining unfilled squares and complete every crossword. Although much has changed in the world of crossword puzzles in the last 44 years, completely filling in every square in a puzzle is still the solver's goal.

Crossword puzzles have evolved over the years. They have improved along with the skills of the people constructing them. Most contemporary constructors try to avoid using obscure, obsolete, and archaic words. The emphasis has shifted from puzzles full of little-known words to puzzles with clever clues for interesting and challenging words. However, one person's interesting word may be another person's obscure word. The need for a reference source to help solve crossword puzzles remains.

This book is many reference books combined into a single, easy-to-carry volume. It is a dictionary, thesaurus, almanac, encyclopedia, gazetteer, word finder, and much more. This new edition, while maintaining its convenient size, has been expanded to include more information. This was accomplished by reorganizing the material and eliminating redundancies. Many new facts have been added and some outdated information has been removed.

The format of the book remains the same. There are still three basic sections: Clues & Definitions, Special Sections, and the Word Finder. (For more information on Clues & Definitions and the Word Finder, see the introductions on pages 8 and 247.) One important change in this edition concerns alphabetization. The original dictionary used the word-by-word alphabetizing method. In this book the method used is letter-by-letter. This method is the one used in most dictionaries. When alphabetizing single words, both methods are the same. In this book, however, there are many multi-word items alphabetized and it is here where the difference between the two methods comes into play. In the letter-by-letter method, alphabetization progresses letter by letter and stops when you reach a comma. Spaces between words, hyphens, and abbreviation periods are disregarded. When two or more items are identical up to the comma, the words following the commas are used to alphabetize them.

The Special Sections have been greatly expanded in this new edition of *The Dell Crossword Dictionary*. The largest single addition is the Name Finder. The names of thousands of famous people are cross-referenced by first and last names. When you know a person's first name but not his last, the Name Finder is the only reference source you need. As an additional helpful feature, each name is accompanied by a code letter to indicate the person's profession. (See page 136 for an introduction to the Name Finder.)

The Special Sections that you have relied on in the past have been updated and expanded. Many new ones have been added, including: Animals, Constellations & Stars, Sports Teams, and more.

All three- and four-letter words found in the Clues & Definitions section and every one of the Special Sections are cross-referenced from the Word Finder.

It is impossible to pack more information into a book which is already full. Some things had to be removed. Deciding what to keep, what to eliminate, and what to add has not been easy. The goal in creating this edition was to make the "ultimate reference source" even better for you, the crossword puzzle solver.

All the Best,

Wayne Robert Williams

CONTENTS

CLUES & DEFINITIONS

Crossword Puzzle clues and definitions are arranged alphabetically letter by letter, as explained in the introduction. Each clue is accompanied by a word or words in capital letters. These are some possible answers to the clue.

That is simple enough, however, the clue in the crossword puzzle you are solving will not always be expressed in the same way as it is listed here. To attempt to list all the different ways that constructors and editors might choose to write a clue would be a daunting task indeed.

A logical method has been determined to avoid the redundancy of listing the same clues over and over in different wordings. This space would be better used by more clues for other answer words. In general, clues are listed with the primary word of a clue first. This results in many inverted clues of the type "deer, red." The clue in the puzzle you are solving may read "Red deer," but you won't find it listed both ways here. Space is at a premium. Of course, exceptions abound. It is not always easy to determine which is the primary word in a clue. Many clues are still listed more than once with slightly different wording.

When your clue is a single word, you may find your answer word immediately. Then again, perhaps not. The English language is full of synonyms. Constructors and editors often stretch their imaginations to the limit. Don't give up if your answer is not listed with the clue word when you find it. Try looking up some of the answer words listed with the clue word. This may lead you to the correct answer.

If the answer you are seeking is not in this section you may find it in one of the other sections of this book. Become familiar with the information in the Special Sections. By fully utilizing all of the sections of this book, you should be able to find the answers for most clues.

A

a Aare, city on the.......BERN; BERNE
Aaron, brother of.................MOSES
Aaron, sister of....................MIRIAM
Aaron, son of.......................NADAB
abaca, top-quality.................LUPIS
abandon........QUIT, STOP; LEAVE,
............YIELD; DESIST, MAROON
abandoned..........LEFT; FORLORN
abate.............EBB; WANE; LETUP;
............................LESSEN, RELENT
abbess, Middle Eastern.........AMMA
abbreviations.............See page 235.
abdominal.......................VENTRAL
Abel, brother/killer of...............CAIN
abhor.................SCORN, SNEER;
.......................DESPISE, DISDAIN
abhorrent.........FOUL, MEAN, VILE;
...............NASTY, SORRY; FILTHY
Abie, love of.............................ROSE
Abijah, son of..............................ASA
ability...................CRAFT, KNACK,
.................MIGHT, SKILL; TALENT
abject...............BASE; WRETCHED
able to.......................................CAN
"___ Abner".............................LI'L
abode of the dead.................HELL;
...........................HADES, SHEOL
b Abominable Snowman............YETI
abound................TEEM; CRAWL,
......................SWARM; BRISTLE
abounding.............RIFE; REPLETE
about......................ANENT, CIRCA
about so....................................YAY
above..........................OVER, UPON
abrade.....................RUB; CHAFE
Abraham, brother of.....................
..........................HARAN, NAHOR
Abraham, father of.............TERAH
Abraham, nephew of.................LOT
Abraham, son of................ISAAC;
..................................ISHMAEL
Abraham, wife of................SARAH
abrogate.............ANNUL; CANCEL,
..........................REPEAL; VITIATE
abscond.....................FLEE, SKIP;
......................DECAMP, ESCAPE
absence, permit for.............EXEAT
absent...............OFF, OUT; AWAY,
...........................GONE; MISSING
absolute....PURE; SHEER, TOTAL,
.........UTTER; ARRANT; PERFECT
absolve sins.......................SHRIVE
absorb.............SOP; SOAK, SUCK
absorbed.................RAPT; INTENT
SUBTLE abstruse...........DEEP; ESOTERIC
Absyrtus, father of.............AEETES
abundant...........AMPLE; COPIOUS

abuse.................RAIL; MISUSE, c
...................REVILE; MISTREAT
abut.........MEET; BOUND, TOUCH,
............VERGE; ADJOIN, BORDER
abyss...........GULF, HOLE; CHASM
Abyssinia....................See Ethiopia.
accent.....................TONE; STRESS
accent, Irish......................BROGUE
access............ENTRY; ENTREE
accommodate......FIT; HOLD, SUIT,
.................TUNE; FAVOR, HOUSE,
.............PUT UP; ATTUNE, OBLIGE
___ accompli.............................FAIT
accomplished............DID; SKILLED
according to..............................A LA
accost.....................HAIL; GREET
account entry.............ITEM; DEBIT;
..................................CREDIT
accumulate.........AMASS, HOARD;
........ACCRUE, GARNER, GATHER
accumulation............FUND, MASS
accustomed............USED, WONT;
......USUAL; ENURED; REGULAR,
..................ROUTINE; HABITUAL
Achilles, advisor of...........NESTOR
Achilles, father of...............PELEUS
Achilles, mother of.............THETIS
Achilles, victim of.............HECTOR; d
..................................TROILUS
acid radical.......................ACETYL
acids...................AMINO, BORIC
acknowledge.............OWN; AVOW;
.............ADMIT, ALLOW, GRANT
acorns, dried....................CAMATA
acquiesce.........AGREE; ACCEDE,
......ACCEPT, ASSENT; CONSENT
acquire................GET, WIN; GAIN,
............LAND, REAP; OBTAIN
acronyms.................See page 235.
across.............OVER; SPANNING
act......DEED, FEAT, POSE, SHAM,
................SHOW; FEIGN, STAGE
active..........SPRY; AGILE, BRISK,
.............PEPPY; LIVELY; DYNAMIC
actor......................PARTY; PLAYER
actor, bad...............HAM; EMOTER
actors, group of.................TROUPE
actor's hint...............................CUE
actor's valet...................DRESSER
actual.......................REAL, TRUE;
....................EXTANT; FACTUAL
actual being.............................ESSE
actuality.................FACT; BEING
adage......SAW; MAXIM; BYWORD,
.......................SAYING; PROVERB
Adam, mate of.............EVE; LILITH
Adam, grandson of.................ENOS

9

ADDING BEADS - ABACI
ANCIENT CITY ON AEGEAN - LYDIA

Adam, son of / aircraft, motorless

a

Adam, son of ....ABEL, CAIN, SETH
adapt ....FIT; SUIT; ADJUST,
.........................TAILOR; FASHION
Addams Family butler ....LURCH
Addams Family cousin ....ITT
Addams Family hand ....THING
adder, common ....ASP
addict ....USER
addition ....ADDENDUM
addition to a bill ....RIDER
add on ....AFFIX, ANNEX;
....ATTACH
adept .....ABLE; EXPERT, MASTER
adequate..................FAIR; AMPLE;
....ENOUGH
adhere..........BOND, KEEP, OBEY;
.................CLING, STICK; CLEAVE
adhesive........GUM; GLUE; PASTE
adjust..........FIX, SET; SUIT, TUNE;
.............ADAPT; ATTUNE, TAILOR
adjutant ....AIDE; SECOND
adjutant bird.HURGILA, MARABOU
admonish.............CHIDE, SCOLD;
....................REBUKE; UPBRAID
adolescence ....TEENS, YOUTH;
....NONAGE
adorable ....CUTE
Adriana, servant of ....LUCE
Adriatic seaport.....................BARI
adroit...........DEFT, NEAT; SLICK;

b

.............CLEVER, FACILE, NIMBLE
adulterate ....DOPE, LOAD;
.......................DEBASE, DOCTOR
advantage .....EDGE, JUMP, ODDS,
....SAKE; FAVOR, START; PROFIT
advisor, female ....EGERIA
Aeëtes, daughter of ....MEDEA
Aegeus, wife of..................MEDEA
Aeneas, wife of ....CREUSA
Aeneid author........VERGIL, VIRGIL
aerial bomb, guidable............AZON;
....RAZON
Aesir gods ....TYR; FREY, LOKI,
........ODIN, THOR; FRIGG, FREYA,
..............BRAGI, WODEN; BALDER
Aeson, half-brother of..........PELIAS
Aeson, son of ....JASON
affectionate..............FOND, WARM;
............................LOVING, TENDER
affirm ....AVER; POSIT; ASSERT
affirmative ....AYE, YEA, YEP,
..............YES; OKAY, SURE, YEAH
afflict..............PAIN, RACK; CURSE
affluence ....EASE; RICHES,
....WEALTH
affray ....BRAWL, FIGHT, MELEE
Afghan title ....AMIR, KHAN
afresh ....ANEW; AGAIN
African bast fiber.........................IYO
Afr. bustard variety ....KORI

c

Afr. cattle breed ....SANGA
Afr. cereal grass......................TEFF
Afr. cotton garment ....TOB; TOBE
Afr. ground squirrel ....XERUS
Afr. hornbill............................TOCK
Afr. milletlike grass................FUNDI
Afr. plant ....ALOE
Afr. ravine ....DONGA
Afr. scrubby tree ....BITO
Afr. soldier............................ASKARI
Afr. tableland .....KAROO; KARROO
Afr. thorn-bush stockade ....BOMA
Afr. worm ....LOA
Afrikaans ....TAAL
Afrikaner ....BOER
aft ....REAR; ASTERN
after awhile ....ANON
aftermath ....ROWEN; EFFECT,
.......................RESULT; OUTCOME
afterward ....THEN
again............................BIS; ANEW;
.....................AFRESH, ENCORE
against ....CON; ANTI; CONTRA,
....................VERSUS; ABUTTING
agalloch ....ALOESWOOD
Agamemnon, brother ofMENELAUS
Agamemnon, daughter ofELECTRA
Agamemnon, parents of...AEROPE,
....ATREUS
Agamemnon, son of........ORESTES
agate stone......................ACHATE
agave fiber ......TULA; ISTLE, IXTLE
age ....EON, ERA; RIPEN;
..........................MATURE, PERIOD
aged ....OLD; ANILE; SENILE
agency ....MEANS; MEDIUM
agent........................REP; FACTOR
aggregate ....ALL, SUM; MASS;
..........TOTAL; GARNER, GATHER
agitate ....MOVE, STIR;
.................CHURN, SHAKE, SHIFT
agitated state ....FUNK, SNIT
agitation............DITHER, FLURRY,
.........................TUMULT; TURMOIL
agnomen ....NAME; EPITHET
agree .....GIBE; ASSENT, CONCUR
agreement.MISE, PACT; ACCORD,
....TREATY; CONCORD, ENTENTE
agriculture goddess ....CERES;
......................VACUNA; DEMETER
Agrippina, son of....................NERO
ahead ....EARLY; LEADING
aid ....ABET, HAND, HELP;
............ASSIST, RELIEF, SUCCOR
Aïda's love......................RADAMES
aim ....END; GOAL, MARK;
.........INTENT, OBJECT, TARGET
air....AURA, MOOD, TUNE, WIND
air-conditioning abbreviation .....BTU
aircraft, motorless ....GLIDER

d

ALLA BREVE (handwritten)

a airfoil, vertical ....FIN
Air Force mascot ....FALCON
air passage................FLUE, VENT
airplane ....JET; FLIGHT
airport, Boston ....LOGAN
airport, Chicago ....OHARE
airport, Washington D.C. ...DULLES
airport marker ....PYLON
airship....................................BLIMP
air supply ....AERATOR
airy........GAUZY, LIGHT; BREEZY,
................JAUNTY; VAPOROUS
ait ....ISLE
Ajax, father of ....TELAMON
akin ....COGNATE, RELATED
alarm............FEAR; ALERT, PANIC
.........SCARE; TOCSIN; WARNING
alas ....ACH, HEU, OCH
alas, Irish..........OHONE; OCHONE
Alaska glacier ....MUIR
alb: archaic..........................AUBE
albatross, sooty ....NELLY
Alceste composer ....GLUCK
alcohol, solid....................STEROL
alcoholic drink ....GIN, RUM, RYE;
........GROG, OUZO, RAKI; VODKA;
.....BRANDY, COGNAC, GRAPPA,
...PERNOD, SCOTCH; BOURBON,
....................WHISKEY, TEQUILA
Alcott heroine .....AMY, MEG; BETH
b alcove..................NICHE; RECESS
alder tree, Scot. ....ARN
ale, sour..............................ALEGAR
ale, strong ....NOG; NOGG
ale mug ....TOBY
alert ....WARN
alewife.....POMPANO; MENHADEN
Alexandrian theologian ....ARIUS
Alexander, erroneous victory site of.
....ARBELA
Alexander, father of ....PHILIP
Alexander, tutor of........ARISTOTLE
Alexander, victory site of........IRBIL,
....................ISSUS; GRANICUS
Alexander's kingdom .....MACEDON
alfalfa ....LUCERN; LUCERNE
Alfonso's queen ....ENA
alga, Jap. food ....NORI;
....................LAVER; AMANORI
alga, one-celled..................DIATOM
algae, fan-shaped..............PADINA
algarroba tree ....CAROB
Algerian governor ....DEY
Algonquian language ....CREE
Ali Baba's word ....SESAME
alienate........................ESTRANGE;
..............................DISAFFECT
align..............ALLY, LINE; RANGE;
....................LEAGUE; FEDERATE
alkali ....LYE, REH; USAR

PART A (handwritten)

alkaloid, stimulating........CAFFEINE **c**
allanite ....CERINE
allay ...EASE, CALM, LULL; QUIET,
..............STILL; SETTLE, SOOTHE
allegory, religious ....PARABLE
Aleppo resident....................SYRIAN
alleviate ....EASE; ALLAY;
....................LESSEN; ASSUAGE
alley ....MIB, MIG; LANE
Alley Oop, girlfriend of...........OOLA
alliance .....PACT; UNION; LEAGUE
alliance, Pac. ....SEATO
alliance, Western ....NATO
alligator, S. A. ....CAIMAN
alligator in "Pogo" ....ALBERT
alligator pear ....AVOCADO
allot ....GIVE, METE; ASSIGN
allotment ....LOT; PART; QUOTA,
..........SHARE; RATION; PORTION
allow..............LET; ADMIT; PERMIT,
....................SUFFER; SANCTION
allowance ....LOT; ODDS, PART;
..............QUOTA, SHARE; RATION
alloy ....MIX
alloy, aluminum-copper........DURAL
alloy, copper-tin...............BRONZE,
....OROIDE
alloy, copper-zinc................BRASS,
....OROIDE
alloy, iron-nickel ....INVAR
alloy, lead-tin ....CALIN, TERNE **d**
alloy, nickel-copper ....MONEL
alloy, non-ferrous .....TULA; NIELLO
allspice ....PIMENTO
allure ....DRAW, PULL; CHARM,
..............TEMPT; APPEAL, ENTICE
allusion ....HINT
almond-flavored drink ....ORGEAT
almost ...ABOUT, ANEAR; NEARLY
alms box or chest..................ARCA
aloe ....AGAVE
aloe derivative ....ALOIN
aloe fiber ....PITA
alone ....BUT; ONLY, SOLO
alone on stage...........SOLA; SOLUS
along........................WITH; BESIDE
alp..PEAK
Alp, Fr. ....BLANC
alpaca ....PACO
alphabet, Arabic ....AYN, DAD, DAL,
....JIM, KAF, KHA, LAM, MIM, NUN,
..QAF, SAD, SIN, THA, WAW, ZAY;
............ALIF, DHAL, SHIN; GHAYN
alphabet, Greek (in order) ...ALPHA,
................BETA, GAMMA, DELTA,
................EPSILON, ZETA, ETA,
................THETA, IOTA, KAPPA,
..LAMBDA, MU, NU, XI, OMICRON,
..PI, RHO, SIGMA, TAU, UPSILON,
..................PHI, CHI, PSI, OMEGA

ANCIENT ALPHABET - RUNIC
ANGLE OF FIRST ORDER: SERAPH
AMESLAN - ASL (AM. SIGN LANG.)

alphabet, Hebrew / annul

a alphabet, Hebrew............HET, KAF,
............MEM, NUN, SIN, TAV, VAV,
............YOD; AYIN, BETH, KOPH,
..........RESH, SHIN, TETH; ALEPH,
..............GIMEL, LAMED, SADHE,
............ZAYIN; DALETH, SAMEKH
alphabet, spoken (in order) .ALPHA,
............BRAVO, CHARLIE, DELTA,
............ECHO, FOX-TROT, GOLF,
........HOTEL, INDIA, JULIET, KILO,
............LIMA, MIKE, NOVEMBER,
............OSCAR, PAPA, QUEBEC,
............ROMEO, SIERRA, TANGO,
.....UNIFORM, VICTOR, WHISKEY,
............X-RAY, YANKEE, ZULU
Alps ....TYROL
Alps pass ....CENIS
Altar constellation ....ARA
altar end of a church.............APSE
altar screen ....REREDOS
altar shelf ....GRADIN;
............GRADINE, RETABLE
altar side curtain ....RIDDEL
altar top ....MENSA
alternate ....FILL-IN, ROTATE;
............STAND-IN
alternatives....................ORS
alumni....................GRADS
always..............E'ER; EVER
amadou ....PUNK
b amass ....HOARD;
............GARNER, GATHER
amateur ....TYRO; NOVICE
Amazon cetacean genus ....INIA
Amazon region people............TUPI
Amazon tributary.............APA, ICA;
..............JURUA, NEGRO, PURUS
............XINGU; JAPURA;
............MADEIRA, TAPAJOS
ambassador ....ENVOY; LEGATE
amend ....ALTER; REVISE
amends, make ....ATONE
ament....................IDIOT, MORON
American, to a Brit. ....YANK
Amer. nighthawk ....PISK
Amer. patriot..............HALE, OTIS;
............ALLEN; REVERE
ammunition ....AMMO, SHOT
ammunition wagon..........CAISSON
among............MID; AMID; AMIDST
Amon-Re, wife of....................MUT
amorous stare....................LEER
amphibian genus......HYLA; ANURA
amphitheater....................ARENA
amulet ....CHARM; FETISH
amuse....................DIVERT
analyze ....ASSAY; DISSECT
analyze grammatically ....PARSE
ancestral spirit, P. I. ....ANITO
ancestral spirits, Rom. ....LARES

c anchor....................FIX, TIE;
............MOOR; KEDGE
anchor part ....FLUKE
anchovy sauce....................ALEC
ancient....................OLD; AGED
ancient times..............ELD; YORE
and....................TOO; ALSO,
............PLUS, WITH
Andes' cold higher region ......PUNA
Andes grass ....ICHU
Andes mountain basin ....HOYA
andiron....................DOG
and not....................NOR
Andromache, husband of..HECTOR
Andy Capp, wife of....................FLO
anecdotes..................ANA; TALES
anent............ABOUT; BESIDE
anesthetic ....GAS; ETHER
Angel of Death ....AZREAL
anger............IRE; WRATH; ENRAGE
anger, fit of..............SNIT; PIQUE;
............TEMPER
angle ....BEND, BIAS, TURN,
............VIEW; SLANT; OUTLOOK
angle, 57°....................RADIAN
angle of a leafstalk ....AXIL
Anglo-Saxon god of peace ....ING
A.-S. king....................INE
A.-S. letter..........EDH, ETH; YOGH
A.-S. slave....................ESNE
d angry....................HOT, MAD;
............SORE; IRATE
animal, draft....................OXEN
animal, giraffelike..............OKAPI
animal, undersized ....RUNT
animal and plant life ....BIOTA
animal body....................SOMA
animal's leg on coat of arms..GAMB
animals of an area ....FAUNA
animal sound.......BAY, LOW, MOO;
........BARK, BRAY, HOWL, ROAR,
........YAWP, YELP, YOWL; BLEAT,
..............GRUNT, NEIGH, SNORT
animal trail......RUN; SLOT; SPOOR
animated: music ....ANIME
ankle(s) ....TARSI, TALUS;
............TARSUS
Annapolis student.................PLEBE
annas, sixteen ....RUPEE
annatto seeds or tree.......ACHIOTE
anneal ....TEMPER; TOUGHEN
annex ....ADD, ELL; WING;
............ATTACH
annihilate....................DESTROY
announce....CALL, PAGE; HERALD
annoy....................IRK, TRY, VEX;
............RILE; PEEVE, TEASE
annuity, form of ....TONTINE
annul....................UNDO, VOID;
............CANCEL, REVOKE

12

ANIMATION FRAMES: CELS
AMBROSIA OF IMMORTALITY: AMRITA

a anoint.................OIL; ANELE
another......................NEW; AGAIN
answer, have the...........KNOW
ant...................EMMET; PISMIRE
ant, stinging.........................KELEP
Antarctic bird................PENGUIN
antecedent......PRIOR, ANCESTOR
antelope.........................GNU, KOB;
.........GUIB, KOBA, KUDU, ORYX,
.................POKU, PUKU, TORA;
.........................ADDAX, BONGO,
.............ELAND, ORIBI; RHEBOK
antelope, Indian.......SASIN; NILGAI
antelope, large Afr.............IMPALA
antelope, Siberian...............SAIGA
antelope, small Afr.............DUIKER
antelope, tawny.....................ORIBI
antenna..................HORN, PALP;
.............................AERIAL, FEELER
anthracite.............................COAL
anthracite, inferior quality.......CULM
anti-aircraft fire........................FLAK
antic...........DIDO; CAPER, PRANK
antiseptic...CLEAN, IODIN, SALOL;
..................CRESOL, IODINE
antitoxin(s)...............SERA; SERUM
antler point....SNAG, TINE; PRONG
anvil, small..........................TEEST
anvil of the ear.....................INCUS
anxiety.....CARE; ANGST, WORRY
b aoudad.................................ARUI
apathy..............ENNUI; PHLEGM
aperture...........GAP; HOLE, SLOT,
.........VENT; OPENING, ORIFICE
aphasia, motor.....ALALIA, MUTISM
aphorism.....................SAW; RULE;
.........................ADAGE, MAXIM
Aphrodite, lover of.................ARES;
.............................ANCHISES
Aphrodite, mother of.............DIONE
Aphrodite, son of...............AENEAS
Aphrodite to Romans...........VENUS
apiece.................................EACH
apocopate...........................ELIDE
Apocrypha, books of the.......TOBIT;
.................BARUCH, DANIEL,
.................ESDRAS, ESTHER,
.................JUDITH, WISDOM;
.........MANASSEH; MACCABEES
Apollo, birthplace of.............DELOS
Apollo, mother of....LETO; LATONA
Apollo, sacred valley of........TEMPE
Apollo, sister of...DIANA; ARTEMIS
Apollo, son of..............................ION
Apostles................................JOHN,
.........JUDE (THADDEUS); JAMES,
.................JUDAS, PETER, SIMON;
.........ANDREW, PHILIP, THOMAS
......(DIDYMUS); MATTHEW (LEVI);
.........MATTHIAS; BARTHOLOMEW

apparent................CLEAR, PLAIN; *c*
.................PATENT; EVIDENT,
.................VISIBLE; MANIFEST
apparition.............BOGY; GHOST,
.........SHADE, SPOOK; SHADOW,
.........................SPIRIT, WRAITH;
.................PHANTOM, SPECTER
appear.........LOOK, LOOM, SEEM;
.................ARISE, ISSUE; EMERGE
appearance...............LOOK, MIEN;
.................IMAGE; ADVENT,
.................ASPECT; ARRIVAL
appease................................CALM;
.................PACIFY, SOOTHE;
.................PLACATE, SATISFY
appellation.................NAME; TITLE
append.....................ADD; ANNEX
appendage.......ARM; FORK, LIMB;
.............................BRANCH
appendage, caudal...................TAIL
appetizer.........................CANAPE
applaud..............................CLAP
applause, thunderous............ROAR
apple....................ROME; PIPPIN
apple acid.........................MALIC
applelike tree.....................SORB
apples, crushed.................POMACE
apple seed................................PIP
apple tree genus.................MALUS
appoint.........GEAR, MAKE, NAME
apportion.................GIVE, METE; *d*
.................ALLOT, ALLOW;
.................ASSIGN; ALLOCATE
appraise....RATE; ASSAY, GAUGE,
.................JUDGE, VALUE; ASSESS
apprise......TELL; ADVISE, NOTIFY
approach.........NEAR, PLAN, TACK
appropriate...........APT, FIT; RIGHT
approve.....................OKAY, PASS
approved................................OK'D
approves..............................OK'S
apricot, Jap.............................UME
apricot, Korean.....................ANSU
apricots, Afr. dried..............MEBOS
apropos.....GERMANE; RELEVANT
apteryx................................KIWI
aptitude........BENT, GIFT; FLAIR,
.........KNACK; TALENT; FACULTY
aquamarine.........................BERYL
Arab......................GAMIN; SEMITE
Arab cloak, sleeveless............ABA
Arab drink, beerlike....BOSA, BOZA
Arab state of bliss....................KEF
Arabian chief....................SAYYID
Arabian chieftain..........AMIR, EMIR
Arabian domain................EMIRATE
Arabian judge.....CADI, KADI, QADI
"Arabian Nights" dervish..........AGIB
Arabian nomad..................BERBER
Arabian Sea gulf....................ADEN

13 *ARABIAN SEA FEEDER - INDUS*

Arabic alphabet / asceticism, Hindu

a
Arabic alphabet..........See alphabet.
Arabic jinni, evil.....AFRIT; AFREET,
..........................AFRITE, EFREET
Arabic script..........NESKI; NESKHI,
.....................................NASKHI
Arabic script, angular ....CUFIC,
.....................................KUFIC
arachnid.........MITE, TICK; SPIDER
Arawakan language.............TAINO
arbiter.................JUDGE; UMPIRE;
.....................................REFEREE
arch, pointed...........OGEE; OGIVE;
.....................................LANCET
archangel............URIEL; MICHAEL
archbishop........................PRIMATE
Archbishop of Canterbury..BECKET
archer, famous Gr. ....TEUCER
archer, famous Swiss..............TELL
archer in Eng. ballad.............CLYM
archetype.......MASTER; ORIGINAL
archfiend..............................SATAN
architect's drawing, full-scale..........
.....................................EPURE
architectural style................DORIC,
..........IONIC; GOTHIC; GEORGIAN
Arctic.......NORTH, POLAR; FRIGID
Arctic AF base.......................THULE
Arctic dog.........HUSKY; SAMOYED
Arctic gull genus....................XEMA
Arctic plain.........................TUNDRA

b
ardor...........FIRE, ZEAL; FERVOR;
.....................................PASSION
areca.....................................BETEL
arene derivative........................ARYL
Ares, mother of......................HERA
Ares, sister of...........................ERIS
ares, ten..............................DECARE
Argo crewman..............MOPSUS,
.........................TIPHYS; ANCAEUS
.........................POLYDEUCES
Argonauts, leader of the.......JASON
Argonauts, ship of the...........ARGO
argument.........ROW; CASE, SPAT;
.................FIGHT, POINT; DEBATE
arhat...................................LOHAN
aria.........AIR; SOLO, SONG, TUNE
arias.......................................SOLI
aridity, having........................XERIC
Arikara people..........................REE
arise............DAWN, FLOW; BEGIN,
..........START; APPEAR, EMERGE
arista..AWN
Ark's landing place............ARARAT
armadillo, Braz. ..TATU; DASYPUS
armadillo, six-banded........PELUDO
armadillo, small.....................PEBA
armadillo, three-banded........APAR
armadillo, twelve-banded TATOUAY
armor, body......................CUIRASS
armor, buttocks...................CULET

c
armor, chain............................MAIL
armor, horse...........................BARD
armor, leg............................GREAVE
armor, Rom. cuirass...........LORICA
armor, thigh.........CUISSE, TUILLE
armor, throat......................GORGET
armor bearer...................ARMIGER
army.......HOST; CROWD, FLOCK;
.....................LEGION; MULTITUDE
army group...........................CADRE
army provisioner................SUTLER
aromatic herb.....DILL, MINT, SAGE
aromatic seed.........ANISE, CUMIN
aromatic substance...........BALSAM
aromatic weed.....................TANSY
around........BACK, OVER; ABOUT,
.....................ROUND; THROUGH
arouse........STIR; WAKEN; EXCITE
arpeggio...........................ROULADE
arraign............ACCUSE, CHARGE,
.....................INDICT; INCULPATE
arrange.........................FIX, SET
arrangement.......ORDER; LAYOUT
array..............LOT, SET; GROUP
arrest.................NAB; BUST, HALT,
.....................STOP; COLLAR
arrest writ...........................CAPIAS
arris.............................PIEN; PIEND
arrow...................DART; POINTER
arrow, fit string to an..............NOCK

d
arrowroot.....................................PIA
arrowshaped...................HASTATE
arroyo, broad....................HONDO
arsenic trisulfide...........ORPIMENT
art.............CRAFT, GUILE, KNACK
Artemis, mother of................LETO
Artemis, twin of.................APOLLO
Artemis, victim of.................ORION
artery, largest.....................AORTA
artery of the neck...........CAROTID
artful........SLY; DEFT, FOXY, WILY
arthritis, form of.....................GOUT
Arthur, foster brother of............KAY
Arthurian lady............ENID; ELAINE
article.......................THE; ITEM
articulated joint....................HINGE
artifice............PLOY; FEINT, TRICK, _RUSE_
artificial fishing fly..................HERL
artificial language.....................IDO
artless...................................NAIVE
art medium, diluted..............WASH
art movement.......................DADA
art with acid, create.............ETCH
artwork, pasted..............COLLAGE
arum plant...TARO; AROID, CALLA
Aryan...................MEDE, SLAV
asafetida..............................HING
ascent.......CLIMB, GRADE, SLOPE
ascetic, ancient...................ESSENE
asceticism, Hindu.................YOGA

ATHOS-PORTHOS

a ascorbic acid .... VITAMIN C
ash seed .... SAMARA
ashy pale .... LIVID
Asia Minor, ancient city in ...... MYRA
Asia Minor region .... AEOLIA
Asiatic evergreen .... BAGO
askew .... AWRY; CROOKED
aspect .CAST, FACE, LOOK, VIEW;
.... ANGLE, SLANT; VISAGE
ass, wild .... KIANG; ONAGER
assail .... HIT; ABUSE, BESET;
.... REVILE, STRIKE
Assam hills .... NAGA
assault .... STORM; ATTACK
assault, prolonged .... SIEGE
assayer .... TESTER
assaying cup .... CUPEL
assemble ...CALL, MEET; MUSTER
assembly ...... GROUP; CONGRESS
assembly, A.-S. GEMOT; GEMOTE
assembly, Hawaiian .... HUI
assembly, S. Afr. Boer .... RAAD
assert .... AVER, AVOW, HOLD;
.... CLAIM; ALLEGE; DECLARE
assess .... TAX; LEVY; VALUE
assets, liquid .... CASH
asseverate .... AVER
assimilate .... ABSORB, DIGEST
assistance .... AID; HAND; HELP;
.... RELIEF, SUCCOR
b assistant .... AIDE
assistant, military .... ADC
associate .... ALLY, CHUM, MATE
association, trade .... GUILD
assuage .... CALM, EASE;
.... ALLAY; SOFTEN;
.... SOOTHE; RELIEVE
asterisk .... STAR
astern .... AFT; ABAFT
astringent .... SOUR; ACERB,
.... ACRID, HARSH;
.... BITTER; ACERBIC
astringent fruit .... SLOE
asylum .... HAVEN; REFUGE
Atahualpa, King .... INCA
Atalanta, husband of .... MILANION
atap palm .... NIPA
atelier .... STUDIO
Athabaskan language .... HUPA
Athamas, daughter of .... HELLE
Athamas, first wife of .... NEPHELE
Athamas, second wife of .... INO
Athamas, son of .... PHRIXUS
Athena .... PALLAS
Athena, Rom. .... MINERVA
Athena, title of .... ALEA
Athenian .... ATTIC
Athenian demagogue .... CLEON
Athens, first king of .... CECROPS
Athens, last king of .... CODRUS

c atom, parts of an .... GLUON,
.... QUARK; PROTON; NEURON
atomic number .... See page 245.
atomic physicists .... BOHR, RABI,
.... UREY; FERMI, PAULI
atomic submarines .... SKATE,
.... SARGO; TRITON; NAUTILUS
at once: pharmacy .... STAT
attach .... FIX; CLIP, MOOR
attack .... HIT; PLAN,
.... TACK; COURSE
attack, mock .... FEINT
attempt .... TRY; STAB;
.... TRIAL; EFFORT
attendant, hunter's .... GILLY; GILLIE
attention .... HEED, MARK, NOTE
attention-getting sound .... AHEM
attest .... SWEAR; VERIFY
attic .... LOFT; GARRET
Attica resident-alien .... METIC
Attila .... ATLI; ETZEL
Attila's followers .... HUNS
attitude .... POSE; STANCE
Attorney General, Clinton's .... RENO
attribute .... TRAIT;
.... CREDIT, IMPUTE
attune .... FIX, SET; ADJUST
auction .... SALE
audience .... GATE; PUBLIC;
.... HEARING
d auditory .... OTIC; AURAL
auger .... BORER
augment .... WAX; GROW; SWELL
augur .... DIVINE; PROPHESY
augury .... OMEN; PORTEND
auk, razor-billed .... ALCA
auricle .... EAR
auricular .... OTIC; EARED
aurochs .... URUS; WISENT
aurora .... EOS; DAWN
auspices .... AEGIS
Australasian harrier-hawk ...... KAHU
Austral. shrub genus .... HOYA
Austral. boomerang .... KILEY,
.... KYLIE
Austral. cockatoo .... GALAH
Austral. gum tree .... KARRI;
.... TUART, KARRI
Austral. marsupial ..... TAIT; KOALA;
.... NUMBAT, WOMBAT;
.... KANGAROO
Austral. timber tree .... PENDA
author .... MAKER, WRITE
author, boys' .... ALGER, HENTY
author, nature stories .... SETON
author, unknown .... ANON
authoritative .... TRUE; VALID;
.... MIGHTY; OFFICIAL
authority .... POWER, RIGHT
automaton .... ROBOT

15

a

automaton, Jewish legend ..GOLEM
ave ....HAIL
avena...................................OAT
avenge ....REPAY
avenger: Heb. ....GOEL
average ....PAR; MEAN;
.........................NORM; USUAL;
...............COMMON, MEDIAN
averse ....LOATH
Avernal ....INFERNAL
Avernus...............................HELL
Avesta division ....YASHT
avid.........KEEN; EAGER; GREEDY
avifauna(e) ...BIRD; BIRDS, ORNIS
___ Aviv...................................TEL
avocado, Mex. ....COYO

avoid..........DUCK, SHUN; DODGE,
............ELUDE, EVADE; ESCAPE
avouch...........AVER, AVOW, HOLD
await judgment ....PEND
aware, be ....KNOW
aweto ....WERI
awkward ....BULKY, INEPT;
........CLUMSY, GAUCHE, UNEASY
awn ....ARISTA
awned.............................ARISTATE
awry ....AMISS, WRONG
axilla ....ALA
axillary ....ALAR
axis deer ....CHITAL; CHEETAL
Ayatollah's predecessor........SHAH
Aztec spear.......................ATLATL

c

B

Babism founder........................BAB
Babist....................................BABI
babul tree pods ....GARAD
baby carriage ....PRAM
Babylonia, part of ....SUMER
Babylonian's neighbor ......ELAMITE
Bacchanalian cry..................EVOE
bacchante ....MAENAD

b Bacchus, follower of............SATYR
Bacchus, son of ....COMUS
back, of the......................DORSAL
backbone ....CHINE, SPINE
back door.........................POSTERN
back of the neck ....NAPE
back talk ....GUFF, SASS
backward ....FRO
bacon, cover meat with ....BARD
bacteria-free ....ASEPTIC
badge, Jap. family ....MON
badger....................................BAIT
badgerlike animal ....RATEL
badgers, Old World...........MELES
baffle ....BALK, FOIL;
..............STUMP; STYMIE,
.................THWART; CONFOUND
bagatelle ....TRIFLE
bag net...................................FYKE
bagpipe hole LILL
bagpipe pipe ....DRONE; CHANTER
bagpipe sound ....SKIRL
bailiff, old Eng. ....REEVE
baize fabric.........DOMET; DOMETT
baker bird......................HORNERO
baking chamber............KILN, OAST
balance...............................REST;
.......................POISE; OFFSET,
.......................STASIS, STEADY
balance, sentence............PARISON

Balance, The ....LIBRA
balancing weight ....BALLAST
Balder, killer of ....LOKI
Balder, wife of...................NANNA
baldness..........................ALOPECIA
ball, yarn or thread................CLEW
ballad.......................................LAY
ballet jump...............................JETE
ballet skirt ....TUTU
ballet turn ....FOUETTE
balloon basket ....NACELLE
balm of Gilead..................BALSAM
balsalike wood ....BONGO
balsam ....FIR; TOLU; RESIN
Balt ....ESTH
Baltic Finn ....VOD
Balto-Slav ....LETT
Baluchistan people ....MARI, REKI
Bambi author.....................SALTEN
Bambi rabbit ....THUMPER
Bambi's cousin ....GOBO
bamboo.................................REED
bamboo shoots, pickled.......ACHAR
banal ....BLAND, INANE,
............................VAPID; CLICHE,
...........................JEJUNE; INSIPID
banana, kind of..............PLANTAIN
banana, Polynesian....................FEI
banana genus ....MUSA
band..............BELT, BEVY, GANG,
........GIRD, PACK, RING; CORPS,
.............GROUP, STRIA, TROOP;
........................LEAGUE, STRIPE
band: Arch. ....FASCIA
band, muscle or nerve ....TAENIA
bandages, inferior ....BATT
bandicoot ....RAT
banish......EXILE, EXPEL; DEPORT

d

BAMBI AUNT'ENA

BARRELS:
COOPER - FIXER/MAKER
ADZE
CRUZE } STAVE: SIDE SLAT
PLANER

a bank................HEAP, HILL, LUMP,
................MASS, PILE; MOUND,
................STACK; DEPOSIT
bank of a river, of the .....RIPARIAN,
................LITTORAL
bankrupt ....BUST
bank shot................CAROM
bank transaction................LOAN
banner........FLAG, JACK; COLORS,
................ENSIGN; PENNANT;
................STANDARD, STREAMER
banter ....JEST, JOSH; CHAFF
Bantu language ....ILA
Bantu people................GOGO
Bantu-speaking people ......PONDO;
................MPONDO
baptismal basin ....FONT
baptism font................LAVER
bar................ROD; STOP; BLOCK,
................COURT, SHAFT;
................IMPEDE; OBSTRUCT
bar, legally ....ESTOP
bar, topmast ....FID
barb, feather ....HERL
barbarian ....BOOR; YAHOO;
................VULGAR
Barbary ape ....MAGOT
barber ....SHAVER, TONSOR
Barber of Seville................FIGARO
Barbie's boyfriend................KEN
b bare................BALD, MERE, NUDE;
............NAKED, STRIP; EXPOSE,
................REVEAL, SIMPLE
bargain ..BUY; DEAL, PACT, SALE;
................DICKER, HAGGLE
barge, heavy ....HOY
bark............BAY, YAP, YIP; SNAP
bark, lime tree ....BAST; BASTE
bark, medicinal ....COTO;
................CORTEX
bark, paper mulberry ....TAPA
bark, rough exterior................ROSS
barking................LATRANT
bark remover................ROSSER
barometric line ....ISOBAR
barracuda ....SENET; SENNET
barracuda, small ....SPET
barrelmaker................COOPER
barrel slat ....STAVE
barren land................USAR
Bartered Bride, The character................
................HANS, MUFF; AGNES;
................KEZAL, MARIE, MISHA
base................LOW; FOOT, MEAN,
................ROOT, VILE; CHEAP;
................SORDID; SQUALID
base, arch. ....SOCLE; PLINTH
base, attached at the ....SESSILE
baseball equipment................BAT;
................BALL, MITT

baseball error ....MUFF   *c*
baseball hit................BUNT
baseball hose? ....SOX
baseball team ....NINE
bashful ....COY, SHY; TIMID
basin, broad structural ....TALA
basis................ROOT; REASON;
................FOOTING
basket................GOAL; SCORE
basketball team................FIVE
Basse-Normandie city............CAEN
bath cake ....SOAP
baton................STICK
batrachian................FROG, TOAD
batter ....RAM; BEAT, DRUB,
................MAUL; PUMMEL
battery plate ....GRID
battle................ANZIO, CRECY;
................ACTIUM, MIDWAY,
................VERDUN; BULL RUN,
................IWO JIMA; HASTINGS,
................NORMANDY
battle, Amer. Rev............CONCORD
battle, Civil War ....SHILOH
battle, King Arthur's last ....CAMLAN
battle, WW I ....MARNE;
................SOMME, YPRES
battle-ax ....TWIBILL
"Battle Hymn of the Republic" writer
................HOWE
bauble ....BEAD   *d*
bay ....COVE, HOWL;
................BIGHT, INLET
bay tree ....LAUREL
bay window ....ORIEL
bazaar........FAIR; SOUK; MARKET
beach................SHORE; STRAND
beach cabin................CABANA
beads, prayer................ROSARY
beak ....NEB, NIB; BILL
beam................RAY; SMILE, STRUT
bean................SOY, URD; LIMA
bean, field ....PINTO
bean, kidney ....HARICOT
bean, pleasant-smelling.......TONKA
bean, poisonous................CALABAR
bean tree ....CATALPA
bear................CARRY, FETCH,
................STAND, YIELD;
................STOMACH; TOLERATE
bear, Australian................KOALA
bear constellation................URSA
bearded seal ....MAKLUK
beard of grain ....AWN; ARISTA
bearing................MIEN; HEADING
bearing plate ....GIB
bear's-ear................AURICULA
bear witness........VOUCH; ATTEST
beast of burden................ASS;
................BURRO, LLAMA

BEG: CADES

beat / bill, soft part of a

a beat ....WHIP; METER, PULSE;
...........................THROB, THUMP;
........................HAMMER, THRASH
beater, mortar ....RAB
Beatles, the ....JOHN (LENNON),
...................PAUL (McCARTNEY);
........................RINGO (STARR);
...............GEORGE (HARRISON)
Beatles' record label ....APPLE
beat rapidly ....PANT; THROB
beat up ....LICK
beaver oil ....CASTOR
beaver skin ....PLEW
beche-de-mer ....TREPANG
beckon .....COURT, TEMPT; INVITE
bed...................................COT, KIP;
..............................DOSS; FLOOR;
................BOTTOM, PALLET
Bedouin headband cord ....AGAL
bee, male ....DRONE
beechnuts, fallen ....MAST
beefwood, Australian............BELAH
beefwood, Polynesian ....TOA
beehive, straw ....SKEP
bee house.................HIVE; APIARY
beer.............................ALE; BOCK,
.............MEAD, SUDS; LAGER,
.......................STOUT; PORTER
beer ingredient ....HOPS, MALT
beer mug ....STEIN
b bees, of ....APIAN
Beethoven, birthplace of........BONN
beetle ....DOR
beetle, click ....ELATER
beetle, sacred...................SCARAB
bee tree ....LINDEN; BASSWOOD
befall......................................HAP
before ......ERE, PRE; EVER, ONCE
beget ....SIRE; SPAWN;
....FATHER
Beggar's Opera dramatist ....GAY
begin ....OPEN; START;
..................................EMBARK
beginner ....TIRO, TYRO
beginning ....BASIC; INITIAL;
...................................GENESIS
beginning at.........................FROM
behind ....AFT; AFTER; ASTERN
behold! ....ECCE; VOILA
beige shade ....ECRU
being ....ENTITY
being, abstract ....ESSE; ENTIA
being, essential.......................ENS
belch ....BURP
beleaguerment ....SIEGE
Belem's state........................PARA
belief..........CREED, FAITH, TENET
believe ....CREDIT
believe, formerly...................TROW
bell, alarm ....TOCSIN

bell, sound of a.......................TOLL   *c*
bellow.......................BAWL, YELL
bellowing ....AROAR
bell's tongue ....CLAPPER
bell tower.....BELFRY; CAMPANILE
below: naut. ....ALOW
belt.....................HIT; GIRD, SASH,
.................................ZONE; CLOUT
belt, sword or bugle ....BALDRIC
bench ....PEW; SETTLE
bend ....SNY; FLEX, GENU;
........................STOOP; FLEXURE
benediction ..BENISON; BLESSING
benefactor ....PATRON
benefit ....BOON; AVAIL
Bengal people ....KOL; KOHL
Ben Hur, author of ....WALLACE
Ben Hur's rival.................MESSALA
Benjamin, firstborn of ....BELA
bent.....................ARCED, BOWED;
.....................ANGLED, TALENT;
...............................CROOKED
Beowulf monster.............GRENDEL
bequeath.................................WILL
Bermuda grass ....DOOB
Bern's river.....................AAR; AARE
berserk ....AMOK, WILD
beseech ....PRAY; ENTREAT
besides .....TOO, YET; ALSO, ELSE
bestow ....AWARD; CONFER
betel leaf concoction.....PAN; BUYO   *d*
betel nut ....BONGA
betel palm ....ARECA; PINANG
betoken ....DENOTE
betroth, formerly....................AFFY
bevel ....SLANT
bevel a ship's timber.............SNAPE
bevel out ....REAM
bevel to join ....MITER
beverage..............DRINK, QUAFF;
.....................LIQUOR; POTABLE
beverage, Australian ....KAVA
beverage, hot wine and lemon ....
...................................NEGUS
beverage, malt ....BEER
beverage, Mex. ....CHIA
beverage, Paraguayan...........MATE
Bible......................See page 196.
bicarbonate ....SODA
bice blue ....AZURITE
bicker...................................CAVIL
bicycle built for two ....TANDEM
biddy......................................HEN
Big Apple ....NYC
big casino ....TEN
Bihar India, city in..................GAYA
bikini top ....BRA
bile ....GALL
bill ....DUN, NEB; BEAK; CHECK
bill, soft part of a....................CERE

US BIBLE: ARV
BIBLICAL LION: ARI

BINARY COMPOUND: OXIDE
SMALL BIRD: TOMTIT
SMALL SONG BIRD: VIREO

a billiard shot..............BANK; BREAK,
.................CAROM, MASSE
bill of fare...............MENU; CARTE
billow.......BULGE, SURGE, SWELL
binary digits.............................BITS
bind...................TAPE, WRAP;
..................PINCH, SWATH
biography.............LIFE; MEMOIRS
bird.....................AUK, KEA, MEW,
.............OWL, TIT; CHAT, COOT,
........DOVE, DUCK, ERNE, GULL,
............HAWK, IBIS, KITE, KIWI,
.........LARK, LOON, MERL, RAIL,
.........SMEW, SORA, SWAN, TEAL,
....TERN, WREN; BOOBY, CRAKE,
..CRANE, EAGLE, EGRET, FINCH,
.............GOOSE, GREBE, HERON,
............MACAW, MURRE, OUZEL,
......PEWIT, PIPIT, ROBIN, SNIPE,
.....STILT, STORK, SWIFT, VIREO;
........ARGALA, AVOCET, BARBET,
.....CANARY, CONDOR, CUCKOO,
........CURLEW, DARTER, DUNLIN,
......GANNET, GROUSE, HOOPOE,
.........LINNET, MAGPIE, MARTIN,
.........ORIOLE, OSPREY PETREL,
.........PIGEON, PLOVER, PUFFIN,
.........SHRIKE, THRUSH, TOUCAN,
..................TOWHEE, TURKEY,
bird, Arctic..........BRANT; FULMAR
b bird, black ....ANI, CROW,
..................ROOK; RAVEN
bird, blue.................................JAY
bird, extinct................MOA; DODO
bird, flightless.............EMU; EMEU,
......................KIWI, RHEA, WEKA;
......................OSTRICH, PENGUIN
bird, hunting......................FALCON
bird, mythical...........................ROC
bird, S.A. game.....................GUAN
bird, talking ....MYNA;
........................MYNAH; PARROT
bird, unfledged......................EYAS
bird, US national ....EAGLE
bird, web-footed........DUCK, LOON;
.....................................GOOSE
bird, West Indies ....TODY
bird flesh ....FOWL
bird house ....COTE
bird in Pers. poetry.............BULBUL
bird life ....ORNIS
bird's beak ....NEB, NIB
bird's cry ....CAW, COO;
...........................CHIRP, TWEET
birds of a region.................ORNIS;
......................................AVIFAUNA
biretta....................................CAP
birth, at....................................NEE
birth, of ....NATAL
birthmark.MOLE; NEVUS; NAEVUS

birthmarks............................NEVI c
birthstones ....January-GARNET
.....................February-AMETHYST
....................March-BLOODSTONE
...............................April-DIAMOND
..............................May-EMERALD
..............June-PEARL (alexandrite)
...........................July-RUBY
.........August-SARDONYX (peridot)
...................September-SAPPHIRE
............October-OPAL (tourmaline)
.............November-TOPAZ (citrine)
....December-TURQUOISE (zircon)
birthwort, Eur. ....CLEMATIS
bishop ....PRELATE
bishop of Rome......................POPE
bishopric.................................SEE
bishop's attendant............VERGER
bishop's hat.......................MITER
bishop's title, Eastern ....ABBA
Bismarck sinker....................HOOD
bistro...................................CAFE
bite..................NIP; EDGE, GNAW;
..........................STING; MORSEL
bitter............ICY; ACRID; ACERBIC
bitter drug ....ALOE
bitter vetch ....ERS
bivalve mollusk......CLAM; MUSSEL
bivouac ....CAMP
bizarre ....OUTRE
black...............JET; EBON, INKY; d
...............EBONY, RAVEN, SABLE
black and blue.......................LIVID
blackbird.....CROW, MERL; RAVEN
blackbird, Eur. ....OUZEL
black buck of India ....SASIN
black cuckoo ....ANI
blackfish.........TAUTOG: TAUTAUG
black measles ....ESCA
Blackmore heroine.............LORNA
Black Sea arm......................AZOV
blacksmith's block.................ANVIL
blacksnake ....RACER
blackthorn fruit.....................SLOE
blanch....................PALE; BLEACH;
................................ETIOLATE
blanket, horse ....MANTA
blanket, S.A. ....PONCHO,
..................................SERAPE
blast-furnace stone ....TYMP
blaubok ....ETAAC
bleach....................PALE; BLANCH;
................................ETIOLATE
bleaching vat ....KIER
bleak.......GRIM; HARSH; GLOOMY
bled.......................................RAN
blemish .....FLAW; FAULT; DEFECT
blesbok ....NUNNI
bless ....SAIN; THANK; HALLOW
bless: Yidd. ....BENSH

19

a blessing..BOON; GRACE; THANKS
blight..........DASH; BLAST, WRECK
blind cetacean......................SUSU
blind god, Teutonic .HOTH; HODER
blind in falconry ....SEEL
blindness........................CECITY
blister ....BLEB; EXCORIATE
block ....BAR; CLOG; IMPEDE
blockhead..........ASS; DOLT, JERK
block of wood..........................NOG
blood, liquid part of.............SERUM
bloodcurdling..........GORY; SCARY
blood of the gods.................ICHOR
blood pigment........................HEME
blood sucker....................LEECH
blood-sucking parasite ....TICK
blood vessel...........................VEIN
blood vessel, main..............AORTA
bloody....................................GORY
blouse, long.........................TUNIC
blow ....GUST, JOLT, PUFF,
.............SWAT; BLAST; EXPLODE
blow, heavy ....THUD
blubber, strip ....FLENSE
blue....................SAD; RACY
Bluebeard, wife of ....FATIMA
bluebonnet ....LUPINE
blue bull of India ....NILGAI
blue color.................NAVY; SMALT
blue dye ....WOAD
b "Blue Eagle"............................NRA
blue flag ....IRIS
blue-footed petrel....................TITI
bluegrass, Kentucky................POA
blue gray ....MERLE, SLATE
blue-green ....AQUA, BICE,
.............................TEAL; EMAIL
blue mineral ....IOLITE
blue-pencil...........................EDIT
blue pointer shark.................MAKO
bluff ....FOOL; COZEN, TRICK
bluish-white metal...................ZINC
blunder ....ERR
blunt.............CURT, DULL; GRUFF
blurt out ....BLAT
blush ....FLUSH; REDDEN
boa, ringed ....ABOMA
boast........................BRAG, CROW,
.............................HAVE; VAUNT
boastful air ....PARADO
boat.ARK, HOY, TUB, TUG; DORY,
.......PUNT, YAWL; CANOE, SKIFF,
..........SLOOP; CAIQUE, CUTTER,
.........DINGHY, DUGOUT, GALLEY;
......................PINNACE, PIRAGUA
boat, back of a ....STERN
boat, Chin. ....SAMPAN
boat, dispatch........................AVISO
boat, fishing...................DOGGER;
...............................CORACLE

boat, flat-bottomed .SCOW; BARGE   **c**
boat, freight ....LIGHTER
boat, Inuit.................KAYAK, UMIAK
boat, It. ....GONDOLA
boat, mail ....PACKET
boat, Malay ....PROA
boat, Nile ....SANDAL
boat, North Sea...................COBLE
boat, racing ....SCULL, SHELL
boat, river ....BARGE, FERRY
boat, three-oared ....RANDAN
boat deck ....POOP; ORLOP
boat front.....................BOW; PROW
boatswain ....BO'S'N
bobbin ....PIRN, REEL; SPOOL
Bobbsey Twins ....NAN; BERT
bobwhite...............................COLIN
bodice support......................BUSK
body ....BULK; CORPUS
body, trunk of the ....TORSO
body, zoological....................SOMA
body of laws............CODE; CODEX
body of people ......CORPS, FORCE
Boer general ....BOTHA
bog...........................FEN; MIRE,
.....................QUAG; MARSH
boil ....MOIL, STEW;
........................CHURN; SEETHE
boil down..........................DECOCT
Bolero composer.................RAVEL
boll weevil ....PICUDO   **d**
Bolshevik leader ....LENIN
bolt....................RUN; GULP; SCOOT
bombastic.......TURGID; OROTUND
bombyx.......................SILKWORM
bond ....TIE; PACT; STICK;
............................ADHERE
Bond movie ....DR. NO
bondsman.............SERF; VASSAL
bondsman's money ....BAIL
bone: Gr. ....OSTE
bone, ankle........................TALUS
bone, arm ....ULNA
bone, breast ....STERNUM
bone, ear ....ANVIL, INCUS;
.....................STAPES, HAMMER;
.............MALLEUS, STIRRUP
bone, jaw ....MANDIBLE
bone, leg....FEMUR, TIBIA; FIBULA
bone, of...........................OSTEAL
bone, pelvic ....ILIUM
bone, skull........NASAL; MASTOID;
............PARIETAL, TEMPORAL
bones ....OSSA
bone scraper....................XYSTER
bonnet monkey ....MUNGA
bonnyclabber.......................SKYR
bony ....OSTEAL
book......TOME; PRIMER, VOLUME
bookbinding style..................YAPP

20

BRAGI'S WIFE: IDUN

a
bookkeeping entry..DEBIT; CREDIT
booklet....................BROCHURE
book of devotions............MISSAL
book of feasts, Cath. ....ORDO
book of hours......................HORA
book of maps....................ATLAS
book palm ....TALIERA
boom times ....UPS
boor.............OAF; CLOD, LOUT
boot.................................KICK
boot, Inuit sealskin ....KAMIK
booth................KIOSK, STALL;
.............................CUBICLE
booty ....LOOT, PELF, SWAG
booty, take ....REAVE
borax, crude ....TINCAL
Borden calf........................ELMO
Borden cow.......................ELSIE
border ....RIM; ABUT, BRIM,
.......................EDGE; VERGE
bore ....TIRE; WEARY; CALIBER
bore, tidal.........................EAGRE
boredom...........................ENNUI
boredom indication ....YAWN
born ....NEE
borough ....BURG
bosh ....ROT, POSH
boss......HEAD; ORDER; HONCHO
boss on a shield ....UMBO
botanist ....GRAY; MENDEL
b botch...FLUB, HASH, MESS, MUFF
bother ....ADO, BUG, NAG,
.........VEX; FUSS, TO-DO; PEEVE,
................TEASE; HARASS,
............MOLEST, PESTER
bottle, glass ....CARAFE
bottle, liquor......................FLASK
bottle, oil and vinegar ....CRUET
bottom, river or sea................BED
boundary...............EDGE; MARCH;
.............................BORDER
bounder ....CAD
bounds ....AMBIT, JUMPS
bouquet...........................AROMA
Bovary, Madame ....EMMA
bovine animal.COW; BULL; STEER
bovines ....COWS, OXEN;
............STEER; CATTLE
bow, Oriental ....SALAAM
bower ....ARBOR
bowfin ....AMIA; MUDFISH
bowling alley ....LANE
bowling score........SPARE; STRIKE
box............................BIN; CUFF;
.....................SPAR; CHEST
box, ecclesiastic ....ARCA
box, metal ....CANISTER
boxfish ....CHAPIN
boxing decision ....TKO
boxing glove, Rom. ....CESTUS

boxing weapon ....FIST *c*
box-opener ....PANDORA
box sleigh ....PUNG
boy ....LAD; TYKE; YOUTH
"Boy King" ....TUT
BPOE member ....ELK
brace ....TWO; PAIR; TRUSS
bracer................................TONIC
brag ....BOAST, VAUNT
brahma bull...........................ZEBU
Brahman rules ....SUTRA
braid ....PLAIT, QUEUE
brain layer ....OBEX
brain opening.......................PYLA
brain ridge(s) ....GYRI; GYRUS
brain tissue(s) ....TELA; TELAE
branch ....ARM; LIMB, TWIG
branched ....RAMOSE
branches: biol. ....RAMI
branchia ....GILL
brant, common....................QUINK
brassard ....ARMBAND
brassie.................................CLUB
Brave Bulls author..................LEA
brawl................MELEE; FRACAS
Brazilian nutritious drink ....ASSAI
Braz. red...........................ROSET
Braz. heron ....SOCO
Braz. rubber tree ....ULE; HULE
Braz. tree ....APA; ANDA
Brazos, city on the ....WACO *d*
breach ....GAP; RIFT;
.........................CLEFT; HIATUS
bread, hard crisp ....RUSK
break..........................REST, SNAP;
...........................PAUSE, SPLIT
breakers ....SURF
breakwater.............PIER; BARRIER
breast ....BUST; BOSOM
breath, audible ....SIGH
breathe rapidly...........GASP, PANT
breathing, harsh ...RALE; STRIDOR
breath of life, Hindu ....PRANA
breech-cloth, Polynesian ....MALO
breed ....REAR, SIRE;
.............................BEGET, RAISE
breeding establishment..........FARM
Bremen's river....................WESER
breviary ....SUMMARY
brewer's vat ....TUN
brewing, one ....GYLE
bribe ....SOP; GRAFT
brick, sun-dried....................ADOBE
brick carrier ....HOD
bricklayer ....MASON
bridal wreath ....SPIREA
bridge ....SPAN
bridge, floating ....PONTOON
bridge, Mississippi.................EADS
bridge call ....BID; PASS

21

BRING OUT: ELICIT
BUDDIST THAI: LAO

a bridge holding .... TENACE
bridge maneuver .... FINESSE
bridge part .... TRESTLE
brief .... CURT; TERSE
brigand .... LATRON
Brigham Young U. site .... PROVO
bright .... APT; NITID,
.... SMART, VIVID
bright-colored fish ..... BOCE, OPAH,
.... TANG; TETRA; WRASSE
brilliance .... ECLAT
bring .... TOTE
brisk: music .... ALLEGRO
bristle .... SETA
bristly .... SETOSE
Britain, ancient .... CELT, PICT
Brit. conservative .... TORY
Briton, ancient .... CELT
Britons, ancient tribe of .... ICENI
broadbill duck .... SCAUP
broadcast .... AIR
broken seed coats .... BRAN
Brontë heroine .... EYRE
bronze Roman money .... AES
brood .... FRET, MOPE;
.... WORRY; LITTER
brook, small .... RILL
broom of twigs .... BESOM
brothel keeper .... BAWD; MADAM
brother .... FRA; FRIAR
b brown .... TAN; SEPIA;
.... UMBER, RUSSET,
.... SIENNA, SORREL
brown, dull yellowish .... DRAB
brown, pale .... ECRU
brown, yellowish .... BRAN;
.... ALOMA, PABLO
Browning poem, girl in a .... PIPPA
brown sugar, low-grade ..... PANELA
brow of a hill: Scot. .... SNAB
browse .... LOOK; GRAZE
Brünhilde, mother of...ERDA; ERDE
brusque .... BLUNT, TERSE
Brythonic .... CORNISH
Brythonic sea god .... LER
bubble in glass .... BLEB
Buddha's birth country .... INDIA
Buddha's sacred tree .... PIPAL
Buddha's title .... GAUTAMA
Buddhist liturgical language ..... PALI
Buddhist monk .... LAMA
Buddhist monk in Nirvana ....
.... ARHAT, LOHAN
Buddhist sacred city .... LHASA
Buddhist sacred mountain ...... OMEI
Buddhist scripture .... SUTRA
Buddhist sect ... SOTO .... ZEN
Buddhist shrine .... DAGOBA
buds, pickled .... CAPERS
buffalo, Indian .... ARNA

c buffalo pea .... VETCH
buffet .... SLAP, TOSS
buffoon .... FOOL; CLOWN;
.... JESTER, MUMMER
build .... ERECT
building wing .... ELL
bulb, edible .... SEGO; CAMASS
bulblike stem .... CORM
bulk .... HEFT, MASS
bull, sacred Eg. .... APIS
bullet size .... CALIBER
bull fighter ..... TORERO; MATADOR
bullring .... CORRIDA
bullring cheer .... OLE
bully .... HECTOR
bulrush .... TULE
Bulwer-Lytton heroine .... IONE
bunch .... TUFT; GROUP
bunch grass .... STIPA
bundle .... BALE, PACK; PACKET
bundle of twigs .... FAGOT
bundling machine .... BALER
bungle .... BOTCH
bungling action .... MUFF
bunting .... FLAGS
buoy .... MARKER
buoy, kind of .... CAN, NUN, NUT;
.... BELL, SPAR
buoyancy .... FLOTAGE
burbot .... LING
d Burchell's zebra .... DAUW
burden .... LOAD, ONUS; WEIGHT
burglar .... YEGG
burial place .... TOMB; CRYPT
Burmese capital, ancient .... AVA
burn .... BLAZE, STING;
.... SCORCH
burn incense .... CENSE
burning bush: Biblical .... WAHOO
burning desire? .... ARSON
burnish .... RUB
burrowing animal ...... MOLE; RATEL
bury .... INTER
bushel quarter .... PECK
bushy clump: Brit. .... TOD
business .... TRADE
business symbol .... LOGO
buss .... KISS
Bus Stop playwright .... INGE
bustle .... ADO; TO-DO
but .... YET; ONLY; STILL
but also .... NAY
butcher's frame .... GAMBREL
butter, Indian .... GHEE
butterfly .... PAPAW, SATYR,
.... SNOUT; CALIGO,
.... IDALIA; BUCKEYE
butterfly's kin .... MOTH
butter tree .... SHEA
butter tub .... FIRKIN

BRIT JAIL: GAOL
BRITTANY PORT: BREST
BRIT UNDERSHIRT: VEST
BRIT. REF. VOLUME: O.E.D
BRIT RAINCOAT: MAC

BRIT LAST LETTER: ZED
BRIT MONEY: QUID

a buttocks..........PRAT, RUMP, TUSH
button, detachable..................STUD
bygone days ....AGO; YORE

Byron poem ....LARA c
Byzantine ....INTRICATE
Byzantine capital ....NICAEA

C

C, mark under a ....CEDILLA
caama, S. Afr. ....FOX
cabal ....PLOT;
..................COTERIE, PLOTTERS
cabaret, small.......................BOITE
cabbage ....KAIL, KALE
cabbage, type of ....SAVOY
cabinet, open ....ETAGERE
cactus fruit, edible ....COCHAL
Caddoan Indian ....REE
cadence count...............HEP, HUP
Cadmus, daughter of ....INO
Caen's river ....ORNE
Caesar, slayer of ....CASCA;
...................BRUTUS; CASSIUS
Cain, brother of.....................ABEL
Cain, land of............................NOD
Cain, son of.......................ENOCH
Cain, victim of.......................ABEL
cake, rich ....TORTE
calamity ....WOE; DISASTER
b calcium oxide..........................LIME
calf meat ....VEAL
caliber...............BORE; DIAMETER
calico horse.........................PINTO
California, southern.................BAJA
California base or fort..............ORD
California motto ....EUREKA
California wine county ....NAPA
caliph ....ALI, IMAM
call ....CRY, DUB;
..........................WAKEN; MUSTER
call forth.................EVOKE; ELICIT
calling ....METIER; VOCATION
Calliope, sister of.................ERATO
Callisto, son of ....ARCAS
Call of the Wild, The dogs.....BUCK;
....SPITZ
call to cows ....SOOK
calm ....COOL, EVEN; QUIET,
..............STILL; GENTLE, PLACID,
....SERENE, SETTLE; TRANQUIL
calorie...................................THERM
calumniate.......MALIGN; SLANDER
calumny ....LIBEL; SLANDER
Calvinist....................GENEVAN
calyx leaf ....SEPAL
cam ....TAPPET
cambric.............................PERCALE
cambric grass ....RAMIE
came down with ....GOT

camel, female ....NAGA
camel, Indian ....OONT
camel hair cloth or robe ....ABA
Camelot lady ....ENID
cameo stone ....ONYX
camera lens............................ZOOM
camera platform ....DOLLY
Camille dramatist ....DUMAS
Canada goose ....OUTARDE
canal, Afr. ....SUEZ
canal, Canadian.............WELLAND
canal, Eur. ....KIEL
canal, Latin Amer. ....PANAMA
canal, New York ....ERIE
canal bank ....BERM
canary yellow......................MELINE
canasta collection ....SEVENS
canasta play.........................MELD
cancel.........DELE; ANNUL, ERASE
candid ....OPEN; FRANK
candidates, list of...................SLATE
candle ....DIP; TEST; TAPER d
candle element ....WICK
candle holder ....SCONCE;
....................................GIRANDOLE
candlelight ....GLIM
candlenut tree ....AMA
candle wick, snuffed.............SNAST
cane....................................RATTAN
canine animal ....DOG, FOX;
..................WOLF; DINGO, HYENA
Canio, wife of......................NEDDA
cannabis..................HEMP; GRASS
canna plant.........................ACHIRA
cannon ....BIT; MORTAR
canoe, Central Amer. ....BONGO,
....BUNGO
canoe, Malay ....PROA
canoe, Maori seagoing ....WAKA
canon ....LAW; CODE
canonical hour ....SEXT; LAUDS;
.............................NONES, PRIME;
.........................MATINS, TIERCE
canopy ....COPE; TESTER
cant ....TILT; ARGOT,
..........................IDIOM, SLANT
cant hook ....PEAVEY
Cantique de Noel composer..ADAM
canvas........DUCK, TUKE; SAILS
canvasback duck ....SCAUP
canvas piece ....TARP

CALLED: VCLEPT
CAMPUS GRIND: WONK
ANCIENT CALCULATOR: ABACUS

CAPEK PLAY: RUR
CAROLINA RAIL: SORA
CARPENTER'S GROOVE: DADO

canvas shelter / catchword

a

canvas shelter ....TENT
cape ....COD, MAY;
...........................HORN, NESS
cape, fur......................PALATINE
cape, Pope's ....FANON, ORALE
Capek character................ROBOT
caper.............DIDO, LEAP; ANTIC
caprice ....WHIM; FANCY
captain, Melville's ....AHAB
captain, Muslim ship's ...RAIS, REIS
captain's boat ....GIG
capture ....BAG, NAB,
.............................NET; SEIZE
capucine ....MELINE
car ....AUTO; COUPE,
.........................SEDAN; VEHICLE
car, classic ....REO
caracallike animal ....LYNX
caravel of Columbus ...NINA; PINTA
carbolic acid ....PHENOL
carbon, powdery ....SOOT
card................ACE; JACK, KING,
.............TREY; DEUCE, JOKER,
...........................KNAVE, QUEEN
card game..........GIN, LOO; BRAG;
.............MONTE, OMBRE, POKER,
.........RUMMY, WHIST; BRIDGE,
........CASINO, ECARTE, EUCHRE,
.....HEARTS; BEZIQUE, CANASTA,
....................PIQUET; PINOCHLE;
b PINOCHLE..................SOLITAIRE
card game, gambling ....FARO
card game, three-handed ....SKAT
card in Euchre, high ....BOWER
card-reader's card................TAROT
cards, high.......................HONORS
card wool ....TUM; TEASE
care, anxious....................CARK
careen.............LEAN, TILT; LURCH
career ....CALLING
care for ....LIKE, LOVE,
.........................RECK, TEND
caress.......................PET; TOUCH
cargo.............LOAD; PORTAGE
cargo, load...........................LADE
Carmen composer ....BIZET
carnation ....PINK
carnelian ....SARD
carol ....NOEL
Caroline Islands group ....TRUK
carol singer, Eng. ....WAIT
carom..........BOUNCE; RICOCHET
carousal .....ORGY; BINGE, SPREE
carouse ....REVEL
carp...............................CAVIL
carp, Jap. ....KOI
carp, red-eyed ....RUDD
carpet, Afghan ....HERAT
carpet, Caucasian .....BAKU, KUBA;
....................SHIRVAN; KARISTAN

carpet, Indian ....AGRA   c
carpet, Pers. ....SEHNA, SENNA
carriage ....GIG; DRAY,
.........HACK, MIEN, PRAM, SADO,
.............TRAP; BUGGY, COACH,
............COUPE, POISE, SULKY;
........CALASH, FIACRE, HANSOM,
.....................LANDAU, SURREY,
.................TROIKA; BEARING,
.................CARIOLE, DROSHKY,
.................HACKNEY, PHAETON
carriage, Fr. ....FIACRE
carried away ....GAGA
Carroll heroine ....ALICE
carrot-family plant.................ANISE
carrot ridges ....JUGA
carry ....LUG; TOTE
carry over water ....FERRY
cart, heavy ....DRAY
carte ....MENU
Carthage, of ....PUNIC
Carthage, queen of ....DIDO
cartograph ....MAP
Casablanca characters ....SAM;
............................ILSA, RICK
case, grammatical..............DATIVE
case, needle ....ETUI
cask ....KEG, TUB, TUN
cassava ....JUCA, YUCA
cassia leaves ....SENNA
caste, cattle rearing.................AHIR   d
caste, gardener......................MALI
caste, low ....KOLI, PARIAH
caste, Tamil merchant ....CHETTY
caster ....CRUET; ROLLER
casting mold.............................DIE
cast metal ....INGOT
cast off ....MOLT, SHED
Castor, killer of........................IDAS
Castor, mother of..................LEDA
castor bean poison................RICIN
cat................MANX, PUSS; KITTY,
.............TABBY; CALICO, KITTEN,
.....................MOUSER, TOMCAT;
.................BURMESE, CHESHIRE,
..........................SIAMESE
cat, Afr. ....CIVET, GENET
cat, Amer. ....PUMA;
.................COUGAR, OCELOT
cat, castrated male ....GIB
cat, spotted.........PARD; MARGAY,
.............................OCELOT
cat, tailless.......................MANX
catalog ....LIST; RECORD
catalufa ....SCAD
catapult...........................ONAGER
cataract ....FALLS
catch ....NAB; HOOK, SNAG,
.........................TRAP; SNARE
catchword ....CUE; SLOGAN

24

CAVITY: FOSSA
CAVITIES IN BONE: ANTRA
CHAIR DESIGNER: EAMES

a caterpillar, N. Z. ....WERI; AWETO
catfish, armor-plated ....DORAD
cat genus ....FELIS
cathedral ....MINSTER
cathedral, Fr. ....CHARTRES
cathedral city, Eng. ....ELY
cathedral passage ....SLYPE
Catholic, Eastern....UNIAT; UNIATE
Catholic tribunal ....ROTA
catkin ....AMENT
cat's cry..................MEW; MEOW;
.........................MIAOU, MIAOW
cat's-paw...DUPE, TOOL; STOOGE
cattail ....TULE
cattle, largest type of ....GAUR
cattle breed..........ANGUS, DEVON;
........DEXTER, JERSEY, SUSSEX;
..............GUERNSEY, HEREFORD,
...............LONGHORN, HOLSTEIN
cattleman........COWBOY, DROVER
Caucasian wild goat ....TUR
Caucasian language....ANDI, AVAR
Caucasian Muslim ....LAZ
Caucasus people .....SVAN; OSSET
caucho tree....................ULE; HULE
caudal appendage...................TAIL
caulk lightly..........................CHINSE
cause ....MOTIVE, REASON;
....CRUSADE
caustic ....ACERBIC, CUTTING,
b ....MORDANT; SCATHING
caustic poison ....PHENOL
cauterize................................SEAR
cauterizing agent ....MOXA
caution ....CARE, HEED, WARN;
.............................ALERT; REGARD
cautious ....WARY; CHARY
Cavalleria Rusticana heroine..LOLA
cavalryman, Pol. ....UHLAN
cavalryman, Turk. or Alg. ....
............................SPAHI; SPAHEE
cave explorer..............SPELUNKER
cavern................................GROTTO
caviar.....................................ROE
caviar fish ....SHAD; STURGEON
cavil........................CARP; OBJECT
cavity, sinus ....ANTRUM
cavity in a rock............VUG; VUGG;
...............................VUGH; GEODE
cavy, spotted ....PACA
cavy, wild..........................APEREA
cease............HALT, STOP; AVAST
Cecrops, daughter of ....HERSE
cedar, Himalayan..............DEODAR
celebrated ....FAMED, NOTED;
.................EMINENT; RENOWNED
ceiling, build a ....CEIL
cell, reproductive...............GAMETE
cella ....NAOS
cellular substance ....LININ

Celt..............................GAEL *c*
Celt, legendary ....ITH; MILED
Celtic ....ERSE, MANX; WELSH
Celtic church center ....IONA
Celtic land measure ....COLP;
....................................COLLOP
cement ....LUTE; PUTTY;
..................................SOLDER
cenobite................................MONK
cenote ....WELL
censure..................BLAME, FAULT
center.............HUB; CORE; HEART
center, farthest away from ...DISTAL
center, toward ....ENTAD
centerpiece...................EPERGNE
centesimal unit.......................GRAD
centessimi, 100 ....LIRA
central ....KEY, MID; PIVOTAL
central line ....AXIS
central points ....FOCI
century plant ....AGAVE, YUCCA
century plant fiber ....PITA
cereal, cooked ....FARINA
cereal grain or grass ......OAT, RYE;
...............................WHEAT; MILLET
cereal grass, E. Indian..........MAND
.............................RAGI; RAGGEE
cereal spike...................COB, EAR
ceremonial chamber, Pueblo ...KIVA
Ceres, mother of.....................OPS
certificate, money..............SCRIP *d*
cerulean ....AZURE; SKY-BLUE
cervine animal........................DEER
cesspool ....SUMP
cetacean..................ORC; WHALE;
.................NARWHAL; PORPOISE
Ceylon ....SRI LANKA
Ceylonese fishing boat...........DONI;
...................................DHONI
Ceylonese langur...................MAHA
chafe ....RUB; FRET, GALL
chaff...............................BANTER
chaffinch..................CHINK, SPINK
chain, form into a ....CATENATE
chain, nautical ....TYE
chair.........................HEAD, SEAT
chair, portable ....SEDAN
chair part ....RUNG; SPLAT
chaise ....GIG
chalcedony ....ONYX; AGATE;
.....................JASPER; CAT'S-EYE
chalcedony, red...................SARD
chalice, ecclesiastical......................
...................AMA; AMULA, CALIX
chalice, holy ....GRAIL
chalice veil, Eastern church......AER
chalky silicate.......................TALC
challenge ....DARE, DEFY
chamber ....ROOM; CAMERA
chance ....HAP, LOT; LUCK

25

chances / choler

a chances ....LOTS, ODDS
chancy ....IFFY; RISKY
change ....FLUX, VARY; ALTER
change: music ....MUTA
change the decor.................REDO
channel, television ....ABC, AMC,
.BBC, CBC, CBS, CNN, HBO, MTV,
.NBC, PBS, TBS, TNT, USA; ESPN
Channel Islands ....SARK; JERSEY;
.............ALDERNEY, GUERNSEY
channel marker ....BUOY
channels................MEDIA, STRIA
chant...............................INTONE
chanticleer ....COCK
chantry..............................CHAPEL
chaos ....MESS; SNARL
Chaos, son of ....EREBUS
chapel, private ....ORATORY
chapel, sailor's ....BETHEL
chaperon, Sp. ....DUENA
chaplet ....ANADEM, WREATH
character ....NATURE, SYMBOL
characteristic ....TRAIT
charge ....FEE; COST;
......................DEBIT; INDICT
charged particle ....ION
charger................................STEED
charge solemnly ....ADJURE
chariot race site...............CIRCUS
charity ....ALMS
b Charlemagne, father of ....PEPIN
charm, magic ....JUJU; SPELL;
.....................AMULET, GRI-GRI
Charon's payment.................OBOL
Charon's river ....STYX
chart ....MAP
Charybdis, partner of..........SCYLLA
chasm ....ABYSS
chaste..................PURE; VESTAL
Chateaubriand heroine ....ATALA
chatter ....GAB, YAP; PRATE
chatterbox ....PIET; MAGPIE
cheat...............CON; BILK; COZEN
cheater's notes ....CRIB, PONY
check............REIN, STEM; BRAKE
cheek, lower ....JOWL
cheek bone ....MALAR
cheer...........OLE, RAH; BRAVO
cheerless ....SAD; DRAB
cheese ....BLEU, BRIE, EDAM;
...........GOUDA, GRANA; ROMANO
..................BOURSIN, CHEDDAR,
..................GRUYERE, RICOTTA;
.............MUENSTER, PARMESAN
cheeselike ....CASEOUS
chela.................................CLAW
chemical compound.............AMIDE,
........AMINE, ESTER, IMIDE, IMINE
chemical salt ....ESTER, NITER
chemist's pot ....ALUDEL

cherish ....FOSTER; TREASURE c
cherry red ....CERISE
chess finale ....MATE
chess move ....CASTLE
chess piece ....KING, PAWN,
............................ROOK; QUEEN;
...................BISHOP, KNIGHT
chess situation...................CHECK
chestnut, sweet Eur. ....MARRON
chest sound ....RALE
chew............BITE, GNAW; CHOMP
chewink ....TOWHEE
chide..............SCOLD; BERATE
chief ....HEAD, MAIN; LEADER
chief, Native Amer. ....SACHEM
chilblain ....KIBE
child ....KID, TOT;
.......................BABE, BABY, TYKE
child, unruly ....BRAT
child of the streets ....GAMIN
child's seat ....LAP
Chilean timber tree ....PELU;
....KOWHAI
Chilean volcano ....LASCAR,
....LLAIMA
chills and fever .....AGUE; MALARIA
chimney pipe...........................FLUE
China grass ....RHEA
China in poetry ....CATHAY
Chin. boat ....JUNK
Chin. chairman.....................MAO d
Chin. character (longevity).....SHOU
Chin. dynasty...........HAN, SUI, YIN;
.......................CH'IN, CHOU, HSIA;
..........................MING, SUNG,
...................T'ANG, TSIN, YUAN;
.........CH'ING, SHANG; MANCHU
Chin. flour............................MEIN
Chin. idol............................JOSS
Chin. people, ancient ....SERES
Chin. plant ....UDO; GINSENG
Chin. poet ....LI PO
Chin. secret society ....TONG
Chin. silk cloth ....PONGEE
Chin. stringed instrument ....KIN
Chin. warehouse ....HONG
Chin. wormwood paste ....MOXA
Chin. yellow ....SIL
chinin ....COYO
chinook salmon......................TYEE
chip ....NICK
chipmunk..........................HACKEE
chipmunks, cartoon ......CHIP, DALE
chip of stone..........SPALL; GALLET
chirp ....TWEET; TWITTER
chocolate source ....CACAO
choice ....BEST, FINE; CREAM,
.................ELECT, ELITE; SELECT
choke ....GAG; RETCH
choler ....IRE; BILE, RAGE

choose / clear

a choose ....OPT; PICK; ELECT
chop ....AXE, CUT, HEW, LOP
chopped ....HEWN
chop up....................MINCE
chord, three-toned................TRINE
chore ....JOB; DUTY
Chosen nation ....KOREA
Christmas ......NOEL, XMAS, YULE
Christmas scene ....CRECHE
chromosome positions.............LOCI
chronicles ....ANNALS
chrysalis ....PUPA
chrysanthemum................MUM
chrysanthemum, Jap. ....KIKU
church, Scot. ....KIRK
church bench ....PEW
church calendar....................ORDO
church center ....NAVE
church contribution ....TITHE
church council ....SYNOD
church court ....ROTA
church dignitary.................POPE;
....................BISHOP, PRIEST;
...............PRELATE; CARDINAL
church dish................PATEN
church leader ....ELDER
church part................APSE, NAVE
church property ....GLEBE
church reader ....LECTOR
church recess ....APSE
b church vessel ....AMA, PYX;
.............................AMULA
church worker ..SEXTON, VERGER
cibola...................................ONION
cicatrix ....SCAR
cigar...................CLARO, SMOKE;
...................CORONA, STOGIE;
.........................CHEROOT
cigarette: Brit. slang.................FAG
cigarfish.............................SCAD
cinchona bark.................QUININE
cincture ....BELT
cinnamon, kind of................CASSIA
cipher ....ZERO
cipher system ....CODE
Circe, home of...................AEAEA
circle...............LOOP, RING
circle of light ....HALO; NIMBUS
circle segment ....ARC
circuit..............LAP; AMBIT, ORBIT
circular motion ....GYRE
circular plate ....DISK
circular turn ....LOOP
circular saw ....EDGER
circumference measure ...
.....................GIRT; GIRTH
Cisco Kid's horse ....DIABLO
cistern ....BAC, VAT
cite....................QUOTE
Citizen Kane sled ....ROSEBUD

citrus fruit ....LIME; LEMON; c
................................ORANGE
city, of a ....CIVIC, URBAN
city, Philistines'..................EKRON
City, Queen ....CINCINNATI
City of a Hundred Towers......PAVIA
City of Bridges ....BRUGES
City of God ....HEAVEN
City of Kings ....LIMA
City of Lights ....PARIS
City of Luxury ....SYBARIS
City of Masts....................LONDON
City of Rams ....CANTON
City of Refuge ....MEDINA
City of Saints...............MONTREAL
City of the Prophet ....MEDINA
City of the Seven Hills ......ROME
City of the Violet Crown.....ATHENS
City of Victory ....CAIRO
city political division...............WARD
city slicker ....DUDE
civet, Asiatic ....ZIBET; ZIBETH
civet, lesser........................RASSE
civetlike animal ....GENET
Civil War commander.............LEE;
.................POPE; EWELL, GRANT,
.......................MEADE, SCOTT,
.........SYKES; CUSTER, HOOKER;
....................FORREST, JACKSON
civil wrong ....TORT
claim.................ASSERT, DEMAND d
clam, razor.........................SOLEN
clamor................................DIN; NOISE
clan...................GEN; SEPT; TRIBE
clan, Gr. ....GENOS
clan leader ....ALDER
clarinet socket ....BIRN
clash ....JAR; COLLIDE
clasp.....................GRIP, HOLD,
...............HOOK; GRASP; CLENCH;
.................................EMBRACE
class.............ILK; CASTE, GENUS;
.................GENERA; SPECIES
classifieds ....ADS
classify..........RANK, RATE, SORT,
............................TYPE; GRADE
claw.............NAIL; CHELA, TALON
claw, ornamental.................GRIFFE
clay ....ARGIL, LOESS
clay, baked ....TILE
clay, porcelain ....KAOLIN
clay, potter's ....ARGIL
clayey soil .....BOLE, MALM, MARL;
.................................GAULT
clay mineral ....NACRITE
clay molding plate ....DOD
clay-pigeon shooting ....SKEET
clay plug ....BOTT
cleansing agent ....BORAX
clear ....NET, RID; LUCID; LIMPID

27

cleave / collect

a
cleave ....REND, RIVE;
.................................CLING, SPLIT
cleaving tool ....FROE
Clemenceau's nickname ....TIGRE
clement..............................MILD
Cleopatra's attendant ....IRAS
Cleopatra's needle...........OBELISK
Cleopatra's serpent.................ASP
clergyman........................ABBE;
.........................CANON, PADRE,
.......................VICAR; CURATE,
.....................PRIEST, RECTOR
clergyman, Coptic ....ANBA
cleric, opposite of ....LAIC
clerical cap ....BIRETTA
clerical seats ....SEDILIA
clever ....APT; ARCH
click beetle ....ELATER
climb ....SCALE; ASCENT
climbing pepper ....BETEL
climbing plant ......IVY; VINE; LIANA
cling ....STICK; ADHERE
clingfish ....SUCKER
Clio, sister of....................ERATO
clip............................CUT, MOW;
.............................SNIP; SHEAR
clique...................................SET
cloak ....WRAP; CAPOTE,
..................................MANTLE
cloak, woman's ....DOLMAN

b
clock, shipshaped ....NEF
clogs, wooden ....PATTENS
cloister......................MONASTERY
Cloister Hearth author ......READE
close............................NEAR, NIGH,
................................SEAL, SHUT
closing measure in music ......CODA
cloth ....FABRIC
cloth, apronlike ....BIB
cloth, old wool.................CHEYNEY
clothe ....TOG; VEST
clothes moth ....TINEA
clothing ....DUDS, GARB, GEAR,
................................TOGS; RAIMENT
cloth made from bark ....TAPA
cloth measure, former...............ELL
cloth scrap ....RAG
cloud................CIRRUS, NIMBUS;
.....................CUMULUS, STRATUS
cloud, luminous ....NIMBUS
cloudiness ....FOG; FILM, HAZE,
..................MIST, MURK; BRUME
clouds, broken......................RACK
cloudy..................DULL; LOWERY
clout.............HIT; SWAT; WHACK
clown.............APER, GOOF, ZANY;
.............................JOKER; JESTER
cloy ....PALL, SATE
club, shaped like a...........CLAVATE
clumsy.................INEPT; OAFISH

c
cluster ....TUFT
cluster of fibers ....NEP
cluster pine.....................PINASTER
coach, Turk. ....ARABA
coach dog...................DALMATIAN
coagulate.......................GEL; CLOT
coagulated substance............CRUD
coal, heat-treated.................COKE
coal, live ....EMBER
coal, size of ....EGG, NUT, PEA
coal cart ....CORF
coal dust ....COOM, SMUT, SOOT
coalition ....UNION, MERGER
coal refuse.................CULM, SLAG
coal scuttle ....HOD
coarse ....CRUDE, ROUGH;
.....................................GRITTY
coastal bird ....GULL, TERN
coastal region of India...........GHAT
coat ....LAYER
coat, animal...FUR; PELT; PELAGE
coat, soldier's ....TUNIC
coat with alloy ....TERNE
cob ....SWAN
cobbler...............................SUTOR
cobra, Eg. ....HAJE
cobra, Hindu ....NAGA
cobra, hoodless ....MAMBA
cocaine source ....COCA
cockatoo, Australian ....GALAH
cockboat ....TUG
coconut, dried....................COPRA
coconut fiber ....COIR
cocoon insect ....PUPA
cod, young ....SCROD
code........................LAW; CIPHER
code breaker........................KEY
codfish, small Eur. ....POOR
codfish, of ....GADOID
Coeus, daughter of ....LETO
coffee ....JAVA
coffee, brew........................PERK
coffee and chocolate ....MOCHA
coffee cup stand ....ZARF
coffin stand ....BIER
cognizant ....AWARE
cognomen.............NAME; EPITHET
cohere ....BOND; STICK; CLEAVE
coil ....WIND; TWINE, TWIST
coin, cut edges of ....NIG
coin, reverse side of ....VERSO
coincide.....................JIBE; AGREE
coin money ....MINT
colander..............................SIEVE
cold ....ALGID, GELID;
.....................................FRIGID
cold mountain wind of Peru ....PUNA
coldwater trout ....CISCO
cole ___ ....SLAW
collect....................AMASS; GARNER

d

28

a collection of sayings ....ANA
college common ....QUAD
college entrance exams..........SATS
college organization, briefly ....FRAT
colleges ....See page 200.
colloquialism ....IDIOM
colonize ....SETTLE
colonnade, Gr. ....STOA
color ....HUE; SHADE;
....REDDEN
color, change ....DYE; TINT
color, splash of ....BLOB
Colorado park.......................ESTES
colorless.............................DRAB
color slightly ....TINT; TINGE
columbite, variety of...........DIANITE
Columbus, birthplace of ......GENOA
Columbus, port of.................PALOS
Columbus, ship of ....NINA; PINTA
column, Gr. ....DORIC, IONIC
column, Buddhist.....................LAT
columns, arranged in ....TABULAR
coma ....TRANCE
combat, knight's ....JOUST
combat scene ....ARENA
comb horses......................CURRY
combination ....BLEND, UNION
comb wool..............CARD; TEASE
come back.........................RECUR
comedian's foil ....STOOGE
b come down with.....................GET
comedy ....FARCE
Comedy of Errors servant ......LUCE
come forth............ISSUE; EMERGE
comfort.................EASE; SOLACE;
....CONSOLE
command..............SWAY; ORDER;
.........................SKILL; BEHEST;
.......................BIDDING, MASTERY
commander, Eg. ....SIRDAR
command to horses.................GEE,
.................................HAW, HUP
commercial award, TV..............CLIO
commission, military ....BREVET
commodity.......................STAPLE
common ....VULGAR; GENERAL
common man.........................PLEB
commonplace ....BANAL, TRITE
commotion........ADO; STIR, TO-DO
commune, Dutch ....EDE
communion cup......................AMA
communion dish ....PATEN
communion table ....ALTAR
commute................................RIDE
compact.......LEAN; SPARE, THICK
companion....PAL; MATE; SPOUSE
company ....FIRM; GUEST
company image ....LOGO
comparative conjunction ....THAN
compassion................PITY, RUTH

c compass direction ....EBN, EBS,
.........ENE, ESE, NBE, NBW, NNE,
.........NNW, SBE, SBW, SSE, SSW,
.............WBN, WBS, WNW, WSW
compel...................MAKE; FORCE;
........................COERCE, OBLIGE
compendium.................SYLLABUS
compensate ....PAY; REPAY;
....OFFSET
competed...............................RAN
competent ....ABLE
complacent.........................SMUG
complain ....BEEF; GRIPE,
....................WHINE; GROUCH;
.....................................GRUMBLE
complete ....ALL; FULL;
.............................TOTAL, WHOLE
comply ....MIND, OBEY
composition ....ESSAY, THEME
composition, musical ....OPUS;
.........ETUDE, MOTET, RONDO,
.........................SUITE; SONATA;
.............CONCERTO, SYMPHONY
computer, load a ....BOOT
computer chip ....ROM;
.............................PROM; EPROM
computer choices ....MENU
computer input......................DATA
computer operator.................USER
computer terminals...................PCS
d comrade-in-arms ....ALLY
conceal ....HIDE, MASK, VEIL
concede ....OWN; AVOW, GIVE;
.................ADMIT, GRANT, YIELD
conceive............VISION; PICTURE
concern ......CARE, FIRM; REGARD
concerning.............................IN RE;
.......................ABOUT, ANENT
concert halls..........................ODEA
conch ....SHELL
conciliate ....ATONE
conciliatory gift.........................SOP
concise ....BRIEF,
.........................SHORT, TERSE
concluding passage: music ...CODA
concoct.................................BREW
concur ....JIBE; AGREE
condescend............DEIGN, STOOP
condiment....SALT; CURRY, SPICE
condition ....STATE; STATUS
condition in agreement ....PROVISO
conduct.................LEAD; GUIDE
conductor ....MAESTRO
conductor's stick ....BATON
conduit ....MAIN; DRAIN,
....SEWER
cone filled with explosives .PETARD
cone of silver ....PINA
confabulate.......CHAT, CHIN, TALK
confection ....CANDY; COMFIT

confection, nut / cornmeal

a confection, nut ....PRALINE
confederate ....ALLY
Confederate soldier ....REB
confederation...................LEAGUE
conference...................PALAVER
confess ....AVOW; ADMIT
confession of faith ....CREDO
confidence ....FAITH, TRUST
confine...................PEN; CAGE
confined...................PENT
confront ....FACE, MEET
confused, make...................ADDLE
confusion ....MESS; BABEL
congealed dew...................RIME
conger ....EEL
congregate ....MEET; GATHER
coniferous tree......FIR, YEW; PINE;
...................CEDAR; SPRUCE
conjunction ....AND, BUT, NOR
connect ....JOIN, LINK; UNITE
connected series of writings.......
...................CATENA
connecting strip of land....ISTHMUS
connection ....NEXUS
connective tissue ....FASCIA
connubial ....MARITAL
conquer ....BEAT, BEST;
...................MASTER
conqueror of Mexico ....CORTES
...................CORTEZ
b Conrad's *Victory* heroine ....LENA
conscript...........DRAFT; DRAFTEE
consecrate...................BLESS
consecrated ....HOLY; OBLATE
consecrated places, Gr. ....HIERA
consequence.RESULT; OUTCOME
Conservative, Brit. ....TORY
consider ....DEEM, RATE;
...................TREAT; REGARD
consonant, hard ....FORTIS
consonant, unaspirated ....LENIS
consonant, voiceless ....SURD
conspire ....PLOT
Constantine, birthplace of ....NIS
constellations............See page 207.
constrictor...................BOA; ABOMA
container ....BOX, CAN, JAR, TIN,
......TUB, URN, VAT; CASE, CASK,
...........PAIL, SACK, VASE; CRATE
contemporary, briefly ....MOD
contempt, show ....SNEER
contend ....VIE; COPE
contest ....BOUT
contest, ancient Gr. ....AGON
contingencies ....IFS
continue ....LAST; ENDURE
contort ....WARP; TWIST
contraction, poetic ....E'EN, 'ERE,
...........O'ER, OFT, 'TIL, 'TIS;
...................NE'ER, 'TWAS

c contraction, pronoun.....HE'D, HE'S,
...................I'LL, IT'S, I'VE, WE'D;
.........HE'LL, IT'LL, SHE'D, SHE'S,
...................WE'LL, WE'RE,
...............WE'VE, YOU'D; SHE'LL,
.........THEY'D, YOU'LL, YOU'RE;
...................THEY'LL, THEY'RE
contradict ....DENY; REBUT
...................NEGATE
contrition ....REMORSE
contrive ....MAKE; DEVISE
control...................REIN; STEER
conundrum.........ENIGMA, RIDDLE
convert to Judaism ....GER
convex moldings...................TORI
convoy...................ESCORT
coney ....PIKA; RABBIT
cook...................CHEF
cook food...................FRY; BAKE,
...................BOIL, STEW; BROIL,
...................ROAST, SAUTE
cook in cream ....SHIRR
cooking pot ....OLLA
cool ....ICE
copal ....ANIME, ELEMI
copper ....CENT
Copperfield, Mrs. ....DORA
copper yellow...................MELINE
copse ....HOLT
copse, prairie...................MOTTE
copy ....APE, FAX; MODEL;   **d**
...................ECTYPE
coral element ....POLYP
cord ....LINE, ROPE, WIRE
cord, Bedouin's...................AGAL
cordage fiber...................COIR, ERUC,
...........FERU, HEMP, IMBE, JUTE;
...................ABACA, SISAL
cordage tree ....SIDA
Cordelia, father of ....LEAR
core ....PITH; HEART
core, casting mold ....COPE, DRAG;
...................NOWEL
cork, extract of ....CERIN
cork, shallow ....SHIVE
Cork County port ....COBH
cork helmet...................TOPI; TOPEE
corkwood ....BALSA
corm...................BULB
cormorant, Afr. ....DUIKER
corn, hulled ....HOMINY
cornbread...................PONE
corn crake bird ....RAIL
corner ....NOOK, TREE; ANGLE;
...................RECESS
cornerstone ....QUOIN
corn extract ....ZEIN
cornice support ....ANCON
corn lily ....IXIA
cornmeal ....MASA

a cornmeal drink ....POSOL;
...............POSOLE, POZOLE
cornu ....HORN
corolla part ....PETAL
coronation stone, Scot. ......SCONE
corpulent ....FAT; OBESE
correct..............FIX; TRUE; RIGHT
correlative ....NOR
correspond....JIBE; AGREE, TALLY
corridor.............................HALL
corrode ....EAT; RUST
corrupt ....VENAL; VITIATE
corrupt with money ....BRIBE
corsair ....PIRATE
corset bone ....BUSK
cortege ....RETINUE
corundum ....EMERY
cos lettuce ....ROMAINE
Cossack ....TATAR
Cossack chief.................ATAMAN,
....HETMAN
cosset ....PET; PAMPER
costa ....RIB
coterie ....SET
cotillion attendee...................DEB
cotton, SW US.....................PIMA
cotton fabric ....LAWN;
...............DENIM; MADRAS
cotton fabric, coarse ....SURAT
cotton flannel ....DOMET; DOMETT
b cotton gum tree................TUPELO
cotton machine ....GIN
cotton tree ....SIMAL
cottonwood.......................ALAMO
cougar ....PUMA; PANTHER
council, ecclesiastical ....SYNOD
council, A.-S. king's ....WITAN
counsel.............................REDE
counselor.........................MENTOR
count ....TOTAL; NUMBER
counter ....BAR; COMPUTER
counter current.....................EDDY
countermand ....REVOKE
counterpart........MATCH; VIS-A-VIS
countersink ....REAM
counting frame ABACI.ABACUS
country bumpkin.......RUBE; YOKEL
county: Danish......................AMT
county: Eng. ....SHIRE
county: Swed. ....LAN
couple ....TWO; PAIR
courage ....HEART, NERVE,
..............PLUCK; METTLE, SPIRIT
course ....WAY; ROAD, TACK
course, complete.............CYCLE
course, meal ....SALAD, ENTREE
course, part of a ....LAP, LEG
course, school: Abbr. .....ALG, BIO,
................LIT, SCI; CHEM, TRIG
court.......................................WOO

court, A.-S. ....GEMOT; GEMOTE c
court, church ....ROTA
court, inner ....PATIO; ATRIUM
court, old Eng. ....LEET
court action ....SUIT
court cry ....OYES, OYEZ
court hearing..........................OYER
courtly ....AULIC
court order ....ARRET
court panel ....JURY
court proceeding ....TRIAL
courtship area, grouse's...........LEK
Cousteau's ship ....CALYPSO
cover, take ....HIDE
cover, took ....HID
covey ....BEVY; BROOD
cow.......BOSSY, BULLY; HECTOR
coward ....CRAVEN
cowboy, S. A. ....GAUCHO
cowboy's leg covering ....CHAPS
cowboy's nickname ....TEX: BUCK
cowfish....................................TORO
cowl ....HOOD
cows ....KINE
cow shelter ....BYRE
coxcomb.....................FOP; DANDY
coy ....SHY; TIMID; FLIRTY
coypu ....NUTRIA
cozy ....SNUG; HOMEY
cozy spot ....DEN; NEST
crab genus.........................MAJA d
crack ....SNAP; CHINK; CREVICE
crackpot ....NUT: LOONY
craft.........................ART; TRADE
craftsman...........................ARTISAN
crafty.......SLY; CAGY, FOXY, WILY
craggy hill ....TOR
cramp....................................KINK
crane, ship's ....DAVIT
cranial nerves ....VAGI
crape fern ....TODEA
cravat.......................................TIE
crave ....ASK, BEG; LONG; DESIRE
craw ....MAW; CROP
crayon ....CHALK; PASTEL
craze....................FAD; MANIA
crazy.............LOCO, WILD; LOONY
cream ....ELITE
created.................................MADE
credit transfer system ....GIRO
creek ....KILL, RILL
creep along ....INCH
creeper ....IVY
Cremona craftsman ....AMATI
crescent moon's point ....CUSP
crescent-shaped ....LUNATE
crescent-shaped figure..........LUNE
crescent-shaped mark .....LUNULA
crest ....TOP; COMB, PEAK
crest, mountain ....ARETE

Cretan princess / custody

a
Cretan princess................ARIADNE
crew.........................GANG, TEAM
cribbage pin or score.............PEG
cribbage term ....NOB; NOBS
cricket ....GRIG
cricket field parts..........ONS; OFFS
cricket term ....BYE; OVER;
....YORKER
Crimean river......................ALMA
criminal................................FELON
crimp ....CURL
crimson ....RED
cringe and flatter..................FAWN
crippled ....HALT, LAME
criticize ....CARP, ZING; CAVIL
crocodile of India................GAVIAL
Croesus, land of ....LYDIA
crony ....PAL; CHUM; BUDDY
crooked...................AWRY, BENT
crookneck squash ....CUSHAW
crooner.............VALLEE; SINATRA
crop ....MAW; CRAW
crops, raise ....FARM
cross ....SPAN; IRATE;
....TRAVERSE
cross, crude wooden ....ROOD
cross, Eg. ....ANKH
crossbeam ....TRAVE
crossbill bird ....LOXIA
cross-examine ....GRILL
b cross hairs ....RETICLE
cross oneself ....SAIN
crosspiece....................BAR; RUNG
cross stroke ....SERIF
cross threads ....WEFT, WOOF
crow ....BRAG, ROOK; CRAKE
crow, Brit. ....JACKDAW
crowd................PRESS; THRONG
crown ....CAP; PATE; TIARA;
....DIADEM
crown, pope's triple ....TIARA
crown of Osiris ....ATEF
crucial point..........................CRUX
crucible.................TRIAL; ORDEAL
crucifixion letters ....INRI
crude ....RAW; ROUGH;
....COARSE
crude metal ....ORE
cruel person ....SADIST
cruet........................AMA; CASTER
cruising ....ASEA
crumbled, easily ....FRIABLE
Crusader's foe ....SARACEN
crush ....MASH; SUBDUE
crustacean ....CRAB; ISOPOD,
.....................SHRIMP; LOBSTER
cry ....SOB; HOWL, MOAN, WAIL,
.............................WEEP; LAMENT
cry, mournful.........................YOWL
cry, Australian ....COOEE

cry for silence in court ....OYES,
....OYEZ
crystal-clear ....PELLUCID
Cuban dance ....CONGA;
....HABANERA
Cuban secret police ....PORRA
cubic decimeter....................LITER
cubicle ....CELL; STALL
cubic measure ....CORD
cubic meter ....STERE
cubitus ....ULNA
cuckold...........................RAM, TUP
cuckoo, black colonial ....ANI
cuckoo, Oriental ....KOEL, KOIL
cuckoopint ....ARUM
cucumber ....CUKE, PEPO
cud ....QUID; RUMEN
cuddly...................................CUTE
cudgel........................CLUB, DRUB;
....STAVE, STICK
cue ....HINT
cue, music...........................PRESA
cuirass, Rom. ....LORICA
cull ....GLEAN; SELECT
culmination ....END; ACME,
....APEX, PEAK
cultivate land ......HOE; PLOW, TILL
culture medium ....AGAR
cunning.......................SLY; WILY;
....SHARP, SLICK
cup, assaying......................CUPEL
cupbearer of the gods ....HEBE;
....GANYMEDE
Cupid........................AMOR, EROS
cupola...................................DOME
cup stand of metal, coffee ......ZARF
cup to hold a gem ....DOP; DOPP
cur...........................DOG; MUTT
curassow ....MITU
curdling powder.................RENNET
cure......................................HEAL
cure-all ....ELIXIR; PANACEA
curl ....COIL, FRIZ, WIND;
....FRIZZ
currency ....See page 213.
curse ....CUSS
curt ....TERSE; BRUSQUE
curve ....ARC, BOW, ESS;
....BEND; SINUS
curved in........................CONCAVE
curved out ....CONVEX
curved plank ....SNY
cushion.................PAD; HASSOCK
Cushitic lang. ....KAFA, SAHO;
....GALLA, KAFFA
custard ....FLAN
custard apple ....ANNONA
custard cake.......................ECLAIR
Custer's horse VIC
custody ....CHARGE

CZAR'S EDICTS: UKASES

a custom.....................LAW; WONT;
..................HABIT, USAGE
customer ....PATRON
customs ....MORES
cut ....HEW, LOP, MOW;
.............DOCK, HACK, KERF;
.............REAP, SLIT, SNEE;
.........SEVER, SHEAR; CLEAVE
cut, deep ....GASH
cut down ....FELL
cut of beef ....RIB; LOIN, RUMP;
............CHUCK, FLANK, PLATE,
..........ROUND, SHANK, STEAK

cut out ....EXCISE **c**
cutting tool ....ADZ, AXE,
................HOB, SAW
cuttlefish ....SQUID
cuttlefish fluid ....INK
cylinder................................TUBE
cylinder, moving.................PISTON
cylindrical ....TERETE
cyma ....GOLA
Cymbeline, daughter of .....IMOGEN
Cymru.................................WALES
Cymry................................WELSH
cyst ....WEN

D-DAY CRAFT: LST
DC ADVISORS: NSC
DAWN SONGS: AUBADES

D

Dadaist ....ARP; ERNST, GROSZ,
...................TZARA; DUCHAMP
Daedalus, son of ....ICARUS
dagger.........DIRK, SNEE; BODKIN
dagger, Scot. ....SKEAN
dagger, thin.....................STILETTO
daily.................................DIURNAL
dais.................................ESTRADE
daisy, type of ....MOON; OXEYE;
....................................SHASTA
Dallas sch. ....SMU
b dam....................................WEIR
dam, US ....OAHE; HOOVER;
............FORT PECK, OROVILLE
damage........HARM, HURT; INJURY
Damascus river...................ABANA
Damon, friend of.............PYTHIAS
damp........WET; DANK; MOIST
damselfish.....................PINTANO
dance ......HOP, JIG; FRUG, PONY,
....REEL; GALOP, GAVOT, POLKA,
................RUMBA, TANGO, TWIST
dance, Israeli ....HORA
dance, school ....HOP; PROM
dance, stately old ....MINUET,
......................................PAVANE
dance company....................A.B.T.;
...........................KIROV; BOLSHOI;
...............................MOISEYEV
dancer/choreographer ....AILEY,
....................HINES, KELLY, PETIT,
..........THARP; ALONSO, ASHTON,
........BEJART, BOLGER, CASTLE,
........DUNCAN, FOKINE, GRAHAM,
.........VALOIS, VEREEN; ASTAIRE,
....................DE MILLE, FONTEYN,
....................JOFFREY, MARKOVA,
.....................NUREYEV, PAVLOVA
dance step ....PAS; CHASSE;
.........................GLISSADE
dancing girl, Eg. ....ALMA

dancing girl, Jap. ....GEISHA
dandy ....FOP; DUDE, TOFF
Danish astronomer ....BRAHE
Danish king......KNUT; CANUTE
Danish physicist....................BOHR
dank ....WET; DAMP; MOIST
Dante's patron ....SCALA
Danube, city on the ....ULM;
.............................LINZ, WIEN
Danube, old name of ....ISTER
Danube tributary ....INN, OLT;
...................................ISAR, PRUT **d**
daring ....BOLD; BRAVE
dark ....DIM; INKY; BLACK,
............DUSKY, MURKY; GLOOMY
dark and threatening, appear.LOUR
dark wood........................EBONY
Darwin's ship ....BEAGLE
___ Darya River ....AMU
dash.......BRIO, DART, ELAN, FLIT,
.................HINT; SCOOT; HASTEN
date, Rom. ....IDES; NONES
date, specific........................DAY
David Copperfield character ....
....................DORA, HEEP; DARTLE
David's captain ....JOAB
David's commander.............AMASA
David's daughter ....TAMAR
David's father.......................JESSE
David's son ....SOLOMON
David's wife ....MICHAL
dawn: poetically ....MORN
dawn goddess ....EOS; AURORA
day: Heb. ....YOM
day, specified ....DATE
Dayak people........................IBAN
Dayak short sword ....PARANG
daybreak ....DAWN
daydream ....REVERIE
day's march.........................ETAPE
dead ....LATE, NUMB; DEFUNCT

a dead, abode of the ....HELL;
..................HADES, SHEOL
deadly..................FATAL; LETHAL
deadly sins, seven................ENVY,
..................LUST; ANGER, PRIDE,
..................SLOTH; GLUTTONY;
..................COVETOUSNESS
dealer........MONGER; MERCHANT
dealer, cloth ....DRAPER
dearth ....WANT
death deity, Rom. ....MORS
death notice, briefly ....OBIT
death rattle............................RALE
debauchee ....RAKE, ROUE
debris, rocky ....SCREE
debts, have........................OWE
decade ....TEN
decamp............ELOPE, LEAVE
decay ....ROT; SPOIL;
..................PUTREFY
decay, dental ....CARIES
deceit...........SHAM, WILE; FRAUD,
..................GUILE; DUPLICITY
deceive........................BILK, DUPE,
..................FOOL, GULL; TRICK;
..................MISLEAD; HOODWINK
decelerate ....SLOW; RETARD
deception ....HOAX
decibels, ten ....BEL
decimal unit..........................TEN
b deck, ship's ....POOP; ORLOP
declaim ....RANT, RAVE;
..................ORATE; RECITE
declaration in whist............MISERE
declare ....AVER, AVOW;
..................STATE; AVOUCH
declare, in card games............MELD
decline ....EBB; SINK, WANE;
..................REFUSE
declivity ....SCARP, SLOPE
decorate ....DECK; ADORN
decorated wall part ....DADO
decorous ....STAID; DEMURE
decoy ....LURE; PLANT
decrease ....EBB; WANE;
..................LESSEN, RECEDE
decree ....ACT; FIAT; CANON,
..................EDICT; ORDAIN
decree, Russ. ....UKASE
decree of a court...............ARRET
deduce ....INFER, JUDGE;
..................GATHER; CONCLUDE
deed ....ACT; GESTE; EXPLOIT
deeds....................................ACTA
deep-fat fried ....RISSOLE
deer, Andean ....PUDU
deer, Asian.......................SAMBAR
deer, barking......................KAKAR,
..................KAKUR; MUNTJAC
deer, female........DOE, ROE; HIND

c deer, Indian...........................AXIS
deer, Jap. ....SIKA
deer, Kashmir..................HANGUL
deer, male ....BUCK, STAG
deer, red ....ROE; HART
deer, S. A. ....GEMUL;
..................GUEMAL, HUEMUL
deer, spotted........KAKAR; CHITAL
deer, young ....FAWN
deerlike ....CERVINE
deer track............................SLOT
defamation ....LIBEL
defeat............BEST, ROUT; CRUSH
defeat in chess....................MATE
defect..........................FLAW, LACK
deference ....RESPECT
defiant shout...........................YAH
defraud ....BILK, GULL; CHEAT
defy ....DARE; CHALLENGE
degrade...............ABASE, LOWER;
..................DEBASE
degrading...........................MENIAL
degree ....GRADE, STAGE
degree, ultimate ....NTH
deity ....GOD
delay ....LAG; STAY; DALLY;
..................TARRY; DETAIN; HOLDUP
delicate ....FINE
delicate pattern, having a ....LACY
delight.......................JOY; CHEER;
..................PLEASE, RELISH
demand ....NEED; CLAIM; INSIST
demeanor....................AIR; MIEN;
..................STYLE; MANNER;
..................BEARING, CONDUCT
Demeter, daughter of.............CORA
Demeter's other name ....IOULO
demigod................................HERO.
demolish ....RAZE, RUIN; FLATTEN
demolish: Brit. ....RASE
demon ....IMP; DEVIL; FIEND
demon, Muslim ....DJINN, JINNI;
..................DJINNI
demonstrative pronoun ....THAT,
..................THIS, WHOM;
..................THESE, THOSE
den ....DIVE, LAIR; HAUNT
denary ....TEN
denial ....NAY; REFUSAL;
..................NEGATION
Dennis the Menace's dog.......RUFF
denomination.........................SECT
denote ....MEAN, SHOW;
..................INDICATE
dense ....CRASS, THICK; STUPID
dental tool ....SCALER
deny ....NEGATE; GAINSAY
depart.................DIE; QUIT; LEAVE
departed.........GONE, LEFT, WENT
departure ....EXODUS

34

DESIDERATA: NEEDS
"DIES IRAE"
DESERT: BIOMÉ
DESERT GULLY: WADI

a dependent............WARD; CHARGE
depict........LIMN, SHOW; RENDER
depict sharply.....................ETCH
deplore ....RUE; REGRET,
...................REPENT; CENSURE,
...................................CONDEMN
deposit, alluvial.......DELTA, GEEST
deposit, caked ....CRUD
deposit, clayey ....MARL
deposit, geyser ....SINTER
deposit, mineral ....ORE; LODE
deposit, river ....ALLUVIUM
depravity ....VICE
depressed ....LOW, SAD; DOWN
depressed state.....................FUNK
depression ....DENT; FOVEA
deprivation.............................LOSS
depute ....APPOINT; DELEGATE
deputy ....AGENT; SECOND
derby ....BOWLER
deride.....................GIBE, MOCK;
...................SCOFF, TAUNT
derrick ....CRANE; STEEVE
descendant ....SCION
descendants, male side ....GENS
desert, Afr. ....NAMIB; NUBIAN,
...................SAHARA; KALAHARI
desert, Asian .....LUT; GOBI, THAR;
...................KARA-KUM
desert, Australian ....GIBSON
b desert, California ....MOJAVE
desert, Chilean ....ATACAMA
desert date.............................BITO
deserter.................................RAT
desert plant ....AGAVE; CACTUS
deserve ....EARN; MERIT
design....................IDEA, PLAN;
...........MOTIF; LAYOUT, SCHEME
desire ....YEN; URGE,
...................WANT, WISH; CRAVE
desire, strong....................HUNGER
desirous ....FAIN
desolate ....BLEAK, WASTE
despoil....................................RUIN
despot ....TYRANT; DICTATOR
dessert............PIE; CAKE; SWEET;
...................MOUSSE, TRIFLE
destiny ....DOOM, FATE; KARMA
destroy ....RAZE, RUIN;
...........LEVEL, SMASH, WRECK
detail ....FACT, ITEM; POINT
detain ....SEIZE; ARREST
detection device....RADAR, SONAR
detective ....TEC; DICK
determination ....WILL; RULING
determine .....RULE; JUDGE, LIMIT;
...................DECIDE; RESOLVE
detest ....HATE; LOATHE
dethrone ....OUST; DEPOSE
detonator ....CAP; FUZE

devaluate ....LOWER; REDUCE   c
deviate ....ERR, VEER; STRAY;
...................WANDER; DIVERGE
devil ....DEMON, SATAN
devilfish ....MANTA
Devon river ....EXE
devotee ....FAN
devotion, nine-day ....NOVENA
devoutness ....PIETY
dewlap....................................JOWL
dexterity ....SKILL; AGILITY
diadem...................................TIARA
diagonal ....BIAS
dialect........IDIOM, LINGO; PATOIS
diamond, industrial ....BORT
Diana....................................ARTEMIS
Diana, mother of ....LATONA
diaper ....DIDY
diaphanous...............THIN; SHEER
diatribe ....SCREED; HARANGUE
Dickens, illustrator of ....PHIZ
Dickens character ....PIP, TIM;
...................DORA, GAMP, HEEP;
...............DROOD, FAGIN; DORRIT
Dickens pseudonym ....BOZ
die away ....FADE, FAIL
Die Fledermaus girl ....ADELE
"Dies ___ ".................................IRAE
diet...FARE
differ..................VARY; DISAGREE
difference, solar/lunar year ..EPACT   d
different ....OTHER; DIVERS
difficulty....................RUB; RIGOR;
...................STRIFE; TROUBLE
dig ....GRUB; DELVE
dignitary................................VIP
dike ....LEVEE
dilatory.....................SLOW; TARDY
dilemma ....FIX, JAM; SPOT
dilute ....THIN; WATER
dim, become ....BLEAR; DARKLE
diminish.....................EBB; ABATE;
....REDUCE
dingle ....DALE, DELL, GLEN
dinner jacket ....TUX; TUXEDO
Dioscuri.............CASTOR, POLLUX
dip ....DAP; DUNK, LADE
diplomacy ....TACT
diplomat ....ENVOY; CONSUL;
...................ATTACHE
dipping in water ....BATH
direct ....LEAD; FRANK, GUIDE;
...................LINEAL; FIRSTHAND
direct a helmsman ....CONN
direct attention ....REFER
dirge.....................LINOS, LINUS
dirigible ....BLIMP
dirk ....SNEE; DAGGER
dirty lock of wool ....FRIB
disable ....CRIPPLE

a disappear gradually ....FADE;
....EVANESCE
disapproval, express......BOO; HISS
disavow ....DENY; RECANT
disburse ....PAY; DEAL; SPEND
discernment ....WIT; ACUMEN
discharge.................EMIT, FIRE,
................................SACK; SHOOT
disciple ....APOSTLE
disciple in India ....CHELA
disciplinarian ....MARTINET
disclaim ....DENY
disclose ....BARE; REVEAL
disconcert ....FAZE; ABASH;
....................CHAGRIN, MORTIFY
discord................CLASH; DISSENT
discourse ....HOMILY, SPEECH
discourse, art of.............RHETORIC
discover ....SEE, SPY;
................................FIND; LEARN
discriminate ....SECERN
discussion ....TALK
discussion group ....FORUM
disease, fungal ....ERGOT
disease, grape-vine..............ESCA;
................ERINEUM, ERINOSE
disease, imaginary................CRUD
disease, plant..........SMUT; SCALD
disease, skin.............POX; ECZEMA
disease, tropical...................SPRUE
b disease spreader.................GERM;
................VECTOR; CARRIER
disembark............................LAND
disencumber ....RID
disengage..........................FREE
disfigure.................MAR; DEFACE
disgrace ....SHAME; IGNOMINY
disguise..........MASK, VEIL; CLOAK
....................COVER; COSTUME
dish ....PLATE
dish, Hawaiian ....POI
dish, highly seasoned.............OLIO,
....OLLA
dish, hominy ....POSOL;
................POSOLE, POZOLE
dish, Hung. ....GOULASH
dish, It. ....PASTA; RAVIOLI;
................GNOCCHI, LASAGNA
dish, main ....ENTREE
dish, meat.............STEW; RAGOUT
dish, Mex. ....TAMALE
dish, stemmed ....COMPOTE
dishearten ....LET DOWN;
................................DISPIRIT
dishonor...........SHAME; OBLOQUY
disinclined.........................AVERSE
disinfectant ....CRESOL, PHENOL
disk, ice hockey.....................PUCK
disk, metal ....PATEN
dislocate ....MOVE, SLIP; SHAKE

c dismal........................SAD; BLEAK;
........................DREARY, GLOOMY
dismantle ....RAZE; LEVEL;
....DESTROY
dismay ....DAUNT,
................SHAKE, SHOCK;
................APPALL, HORRIFY
dismiss ....FIRE; REFUSE,
................................REJECT
dismiss from a job ....AXE, CAN
dismounted.............................ALIT
disorder ....MESS; CHAOS;
................ANARCHY, TURMOIL
disorderly retreat....................ROUT
disparaging ....SNIDE
disparaging remark................SLUR
dispatch....................SEND; HASTE
dispatch a dragon ....SLAY
dispatch boat........................AVISO
dispelled ....GONE
display........................AIR; SHOW;
................................ARRAY; EVINCE
display area, bird's.....LEK; BOWER
display proudly....................VAUNT
displease ....OFFEND
disposed ....APT; GIVEN;
................PRONE; LIABLE;
................LIKELY; INCLINED
disposition ....MOOD; TEMPER
dispossess ....ROB; STRIP; DIVEST
d disprove ....BELIE; REFUTE
disputable ....MOOT
dissertation ......THESIS; TREATISE
dissonant ....ATONAL
distance, to or from a.............AFAR
distant ....FAR, YON;
................YOND; REMOTE
distilling vessel................MATRASS
distinctive air ....AURA, MIEN;
................................CACHET
distress signal......................SOS
distribute ....DEAL, SORT;
................GROUP, SHARE, STREW
district............AREA, ZONE; REGION
disturb........................VEX; FRET;
................ANNOY, UPSET;
................RUFFLE; DERANGE
disturbance................FUSS, STIR;
................UPROAR, RUMPUS,
................................TUMULT
ditch............FOSS, RINE; FOSSE,
........SHUCK; TRENCH; DISCARD
ditch, water-filled...................MOAT
ditto ....SAME
divan....................................SOFA
dive ....DEN; HEADER
dive bomber ....STUKA
diverge ....FORK; STRAY;
................SWERVE; DEVIATE
diverse.................MIXED; VARIED

36

DOLLAR: SIMOLEON BUCK
DOLPHIN GENUS: INIA

a divest ....ROB; STRIP;
..................EXPOSE; DEPRIVE
divide ....FORK; BREAK,
.............SEVER, SPLIT; BRANCH;
..................................SEPARATE
Divine Comedy author ....DANTE
divine favor ....GRACE
divine revelation, Heb. ....TORAH
divine utterance ....ORACLE
divinity ....DEITY
divorce, Muslim ....TALAK
"Dixie" composer ....EMMETT
___ *dixit* ....IPSE
dizzy, be ....SWIM
DNA element ....CODON
docile ....MEEK, TAME; GENTLE
Dr. Jekyll's other self ....HYDE
doctrine ....DOGMA, TENET
documents, wicker box for ....
....HANAPER
doe ....HIND; FEMALE
dog ....CANIS; CANINE
dog, breed of ....PUG; CHOW;
............BOXER; HOUND, HUSKY,
............SPITZ; BEAGLE, BORZOI,
..........BRIARD, COLLIE, POODLE,
.....................SALUKI, SETTER;
.....................SPANIEL, TERRIER
dog, Cracker Jacks ....BINGO
dog, Greyfriars' ....BOBBY
b dog, Hungarian ....PULI; KUVASZ
dog, John Brown's ....RAB
dog, RCA Victor ....NIPPER
dog, Sputnik ....LAIKA
dog, Welsh ....CORGI
dog, wild Australian ....DINGO
dog, wild Indian ....DHOLE
dog-fisher ....OTTER
dog in movies ....ASTA, TOTO;
...............................BENJI; LASSIE;
...................................RIN TIN TIN
dog in the *Odyssey* ....ARGOS
dogma ....TENET
dog salmon ....KETA
dog sound ....YIP; BARK, RUFF
...............WOOF, YELP; GROWL
dog star ....SIRIUS
dogwood ....CORNEL
dole ....RELIEF; WELFARE
dolphin ....DORADO
dolt ....ASS, OAF;
.......................CLOD; DUNCE
domain ....AREA; FIELD, REALM
Dombey's suitor, Miss..........TOOTS
dome, small ....CUPOLA
domestic ....MAID; LOCAL
domesticated ....TAME
dominion ....RULE, SWAY;
..............................POWER, TITLE;
.....................................COMMAND

domino ....CAPE, MASK c
Don Carlos, princess in ....EBOLI
Don Juan, mother of ....INEZ
donkey...........ASS; MOKE; BURRO
donkey's call ....BRAY
doom ....CONDEMN,
....DESTINE
door ....ENTRY; PORTAL
doorkeeper, Masonic ....TILER
door part ....JAMB, SASH,
...............................SILL; LINTEL
door section......................PANEL
dorado ....CUIR, DOLPHIN
dormant ....ASLEEP, LATENT
dormouse, large Eur. ....LOIR
dots, paint with ....STIPPLE
dotted with (figures) ....SEME
double ....DUAL, TWIN;
....BINARY
double-curved molding ....CYMA,
....GOLA
double dagger ....DIESIS
double salt ....ALUM
double tooth ....MOLAR
doubletree ....EVENER
dowel...................................PIN
down ....SAD; FUZZ; EIDER
down, facing ....PRONE
down quilt ....DOVET
drag...........LUG, TOW, TUG; HAUL
drain...................SAP; SEWER; d
....DEPLETE
Dravidian language.....MALE, NAIR,
.............TODA; NAYAR, TAMIL
draw ....TIE; PULL; DEPICT,
....SKETCH
draw forth ....EDUCE
draw from...........................DERIVE
drawing curve ....SPLINE
drawing room ....SALON
draw out ....ATTENUATE
draw tight ....FRAP
dreadful ....DIRE
Dream Girl playwright ....RICE
dregs......................LEES; DROSS
drench ....WET; SOAK;
............................DOUSE, SOUSE
dress ....GARB; CLOTHE
dress, ball ....GOWN
dressed..................................CLAD
dried up ....SERE
drift ....FLOW; MOUND; INTENT
drill ....BORE; TRAIN
drill piece ....BIT
drink ....SIP; GULP; SWIG;
..............................QUAFF; IMBIBE;
.....................................BEVERAGE
drink, almond-flavored ......ORGEAT
drink, Christmas .....NOG; WASSAIL
drink, fermented honey ....MEAD

37

drink, hot / dynasty, Italian

a
drink, hot........................TODDY
drink, hot milk ....POSSET
drink, palm ....NIPA
drink, rum or gin and spices.........
....BUMBO
drink, small ....NIP, PEG, SIP;
.............................DRAM, SLUG
drink, soft ....ADE, POP; SODA
drink, whiskey ....STINGER
drinking bowl, large ....MAZER
drinking vessel......................CUP;
....................MUG; TOBY; JORUM,
.......................STEIN; TANKARD
drink of liquor ....NIP; BRACER
drink of the gods...............NECTAR
drive ....RUN; PROD, PUSH,
.............ROAD; IMPEL, PILOT,
....................VIGOR; PROPEL,
....................THRUST; CRUSADE
drive away ....SHOO; DISPEL
drive back ....REPEL; REPULSE
drivel ....DROOL; SLAVER
driver, reckless ....JEHU
drizzle..........MIST; SMUR; MIZZLE
droll ....ZANY; COMIC, FUNNY
dromedary, swift................MEHARI
drone ....BEE, BUM, DOR, HUM
droop ....SAG; FLAG, LOLL,
.......................WILT; SLOUCH
drooping ....ALOP
b
drop ....DAB; DRAM,
.................FALL; DEPTH, LOWER,
.......................SLUMP; CANCEL,
...................PLUNGE; GLOBULE
drop, one ....MINIM
dropsy...........EDEMA; ANASARCA
dross................................SLAG;
..................SPRUE; SCORIA
drought-tolerant legume ....GUAR
drove ....HERD, RODE
drove of horses.....................ATAJO
drowse ....NOD
drudge ....SLOG, TOIL; GRIND
drug ....DOPE; OPIATE
drum, small.........TABOR; TABRET
drumbeat ....TATTOO;
....................................RAT-A-TAT
drumbeat, double ....FLAM
drum-call to arms ....RAPPEL
drunkard ....SOT; LUSH, WINO,
.......................RUMMY, SOUSE,
.........TOPER; BARFLY, BOOZER;
....................TIPPLER, TOSSPOT
drunk driving: Abbr. ....DUI, DWI
dry ....ARID
dry, as wine................SEC; BRUT;
...................................SECCO
dry-goods dealer ....DRAPER
dry riverbed...........................WADI
dub ....NAME; KNIGHT

c
duck ....STOOP; CROUCH
duck, Arctic ....EIDER
duck, breed of ....PEKIN, ROUEN;
..................................MALLARD
duck, diving.........................SMEW
duck, fresh-water ....TEAL
duck, male ....DRAKE
duck, N. Amer. ....COOT
duck, ring-necked scaup ....DOGY
duck, river....................SHOVELER
duck, sea ....EIDER, SCAUP;
....................................SCOTER
duck eggs, Chin. ....PIDAN
duck lure.............................DECOY
duct, anatomical ....VAS; VASA
dude ....FOP; DANDY
dueling, prove a claim by ....
..................................DERAIGN
dugout canoe..................PIROGUE
dugout canoe with outrigger BANCA
duke's domain ....DUCHY
dulcimer ....CIMBALOM
dulcimer, Pers. ....SANTIR
dull ....DRY, LOGY;
..............BLUNT, PROSY; BORING
dullard ....OAF; BOOR, DODO
dull color.........DUN; DRAB; TERNE
dull finish ....MATTE
dull silk fabric ....GROS
Dumas hero ....ATHOS;
....................ARAMIS; PORTHOS;
..................................D'ARTAGNAN
dunderhead.....BOZO, FOOL, JERK
dung beetle ....DOR; SCARAB
dunlin bird ....STIB
dupe........................USE; SUCKER
duration........................SPAN, TIME
dusk..........................EVE; SUNSET
dusky ....DIM; DARK; SWART
Dutch cheese.......................EDAM
Dutch coin, old.......................DOIT
Dutch commune ....EDE
Dutch courage ....LIQUOR
Dutch painter ....HALS; STEEN
duty.......................CHORE; TARIFF
dwarf...........RUNT; STUNT, TROLL
dwell...........................BIDE, LIVE
dwelling ....ABODE
dye, blue ....WOAD
dye, indigo..............................ANIL
dye, red..................AURIN, EOSIN;
.................................ANNATTO
dye, yellow ....WELD, WOLD
dye gum ....KINO
dyes, any ....FUCI
dyes containing nitrogen..........AZO
dyewood tree............................TUI
dynamite inventor ....NOBEL
dynasty, first Chin. ....HSIA
dynasty, It. ....SAVOY

c (right margin)
d (right margin)

E

a eager..........AGOG, AVID; ARDENT
eagle, sea...................ERN; ERNE
eagle of the Bible...................GIER
eagle's nest...............AERY, EYRY;
...................AERIE, EYRIE
eaglestone...........................AETITE
ear...................LUG; HANDLE
ear, of the.................OTIC; AURAL
earache.............................OTALGIA
ear canal...............................SCALA
ear cavity.......................UTRICLE
ear inflammation...................OTITIS
earnest...............GRAVE, SOBER,
..........STAID; PLEDGE, SOMBER;
...................SERIOUS, SINCERE
Earp brothers...................WYATT;
...................MORGAN, VIRGIL
ear prominence...............TRAGUS
ear shell..........ORMER; ABALONE
ear stone.........OTOLITE, OTOLITH
earth.................DIRT, LOAM, SOIL
earth, fine-grained.................CLAY
earth, wet.....................BOG, MUD;
...................MIRE, MUCK
earth deposit in rock cavities.GUHR
earthenware maker...........POTTER
earthly...........................TERRENE
b Earth personified.........GAEA, GAIA
earthquake........SEISM; TEMBLOR
earthquake shock...............TREMOR
East.........ASIA; LEVANT, ORIENT
Easter...................PASCH
Eastern Catholic.....UNIAT; UNIATE
Eastern Orthodox synod.....SOBOR
E. Indian dye tree.................DHAK
E. Indian fruit.....................DURIAN
E. Indian herb...............PIA; SOLA;
...................TOPEE; SESAME
E. Indian red dye root...........CHAY,
...............CHOY; CHAYA, CHOYA
E. Indian palm......................NIPA
E. Indian tanning tree............AMLA;
...................EMBLIC
E. Indian term of address......SAHIB
E. Indian timber tree......SAL; TEAK
E. Indian tree, large...............SIRIS;
...................LEBBEK
east of Eden country...............NOD
east wind...................EURUS
easy....................LAX; COZY,
...................SOFT; FACILE,
...................GENTLE, SMOOTH
easy gait...............................LOPE
easy job.................SNAP; CINCH,
...................SINECURE
eat...................SUP; DINE
eat away...............................ERODE

eaten away.........................EROSE c
eating away...................CAUSTIC,
...................ERODENT
eating dirt or clay........GEOPHAGY
eccentric person.........GINK, KOOK
eccentric piece, rotating...........CAM
ecclesiastic.....................PRELATE
ecru...................BEIGE
edge...................HEM, LIP, RIM;
...................HONE, WHET; BLADE,
...................BRINK, STING;
...................BORDER; ADVANTAGE
edging...................PICOT
edging, make...........................TAT
edible mushroom...................CEPE
edible root.........OCA, YAM; TARO;
...................CASSAVA
edict........LAW; DECREE, NOTICE
Edison's middle name.............ALVA
edit...................REVISE, REDACT
Edomite city...............PAU
Edomite king...........................BELA
educated....................LETTERED,
...................LITERATE
educe...................EVOKE; ELICIT
eel, marine...................CONGER
eel, small...................GRIG
eel, young...................ELVER d
eelworm...................NEMA
effeminate mannerisms.........CAMP
effervescence...................FIZZ
effervescent, make............AERATE
effigy...................IDOL; DUMMY
effluvium.................AURA; VAPOR;
...................MIASMA
effort..........CHORE, PAINS, TRIAL
effusive...................GUSHING
eft...................NEWT
egg...................OVUM
egg, fertilized...................ZOON
egg, insect...................NIT
egg dish...................OMELET
egg drink...................NOG
eggs...................OVA, ROE
eggs, fertilized...................ZOA
egg-shaped...................OVAL;
...................OVATE, OVOID
egg white, raw...................GLAIR
ego...................SELF
Egyptian bird...................IBIS
Eg. capital, former............THEBES
Eg. Christian...................COPT
Eg. city, ancient...................SAIS
Eg. cobra...................HAJE
Eg. crown...................ATEF
Eg. god of pleasure...................BES
Eg. king...........MENES; RAMSES
SETI

39

ELECTRA's BRO : ORESTES
EMANCIPATE : MANUMIT
END (PREFIX) : TELO

Egyptian paper / engender

a Eg. paper *PAPYRI* ....PAPYRUS
Eg. Pharaoh, briefly ....TUT
Eg. sacred bird ....IBIS
Eg. sacred bull ....APIS
eight ....OCTAD, OCTET
eight days after feast ....UTAS
eight notes.....................OCTAVE
Eire legislature ....DAIL
eject ....EMIT, OUST, SPEW
elaborate ....ORNATE
Elam's capital ....SUSA
eland ....ANTELOPE
Elbe tributary ....EGER, ISER
elbow.......................ANCON
El Cid's horse ....BABIECA
El Cid's sword ....COLADA
elder ....SENIOR
eldest, in law ....EIGNE
electric catfish ....RAAD
electric force unit ....VOLT
electric reluctance unit ....REL
electric unit..................AMP, MHO,
.............................OHM; FARAD,
.........................HENRY; AMPERE
electrified particle....................ION
electrode.........ANODE; CATHODE
electromagnet ....RELAY
electron tube.....................TRIODE;
.............................KLYSTRON
elegance.............................GRACE
b elegant..........................FINE, POSH
elegist.................................POET
elements, chemical...See page 245.
elemi ....ANIME, COPAL
elephant, flying ....DUMBO
elephant, Indian....................HATHI
elephant prod.....................ANKUS
elevated ground ....MESA
elevated ground, slightly.....RIDEAU
elevation of mind...........ANAGOGE
elevator, Brit. ....LIFT
elf ....PIXIE; SPRITE
Elia ....LAMB
elicit ....EDUCE
elide ....DELE, OMIT, SLUR
eliminate ....RID; DELETE,
....REMOVE
Elixir of Love, The heroine ....ADINA
elk, Amer. ....MOOSE; WAPITI
elk hide...............................LOSH
elliptical ....OVAL; OVOID
elm seed ....SAMARA
elongated ....PROLATE
else ....OTHER; OTHERWISE
elude....................DODGE, EVADE
elude with sudden turns ....JINK
emanation ....AURA
embankment.....DAM; BUND, DIKE;
....LEVEE
embellish ....GILD; ADORN

embellished, overly ....ORNATE c
ember...........................ASH; COAL
emblem ....BADGE; INSIGNIA
emblem of authority ....MACE
embrace ....HUG; CLASP;
.......................EMBODY, TAKE ON;
....SQUEEZE
emend.....................................EDIT
emerald ....BERYL; SMARAGD
emerge........LOOM; ARISE, ISSUE
emetic ....IPECAC
eminent....................................NOTED
emit....................................VENT
emmer ....SPELT
emmet ....ANT
emphasis ....ACCENT, STRESS
empire....................................REALM
employ...............USE; HIRE; PLACE
employees ....STAFF; PERSONNEL
employer ....BOSS, USER
emporium..................MART; STORE
empty ....BARE, IDLE,
...................VAIN, VOID; CLEAR;
.......................HOLLOW, VACANT
emulate ....COPY; MODEL;
.....................FOLLOW; PATTERN
enamelware ....LIMOGES
enchantress ....CIRCE, MEDEA
encircle.........................GIRD, RING
encircled area.................ENCLAVE
encircling band......................ZONE d
enclose ....HEM; CAGE,
.............................COOP, RING
enclosure ......PEN; YARD; ATRIUM
encomium..........PRAISE; TRIBUTE
encompass ....CIRCLE, ENGIRD
encounter ....MEET; CLASH,
....RUN-IN
encountered ....MET
encourage...........CHEER; FOSTER
end ....TIP; GOAL, REAR,
.....................................STOP, TAIL;
.................CEASE; FINALE, FINISH
end: music ....FINE
endearment ....HON; BABE,
.................BABY; DEAR; HONEY,
.....................SUGAR; DARLING
endeavor ....TRY; ESSAY; EFFORT
ending, comparative ....-IER, -IOR
ending, superlative ....-EST
endow....................ENDUE; INVEST
end result ....PRODUCT
endure ....BEAR, LAST; ABIDE
energy ....PEP, VIM, ZIP; FORCE
...............POWER, STEAM, VIGOR
energy unit ....ERG, RAD
engage ....HIRE, MESH; PLEDGE
engaged ....BUSY
engender ....MAKE; SPAWN;
....EFFECT

40

OLD ENG. LETTER: EDH
ENTOMB: INURN, INTER

a engine, fixed part of an ......STATOR
engine, gun the ....REV
engine, rotary ....TURBINE
English daisy ....GOWAN
Eng. dramatist ....SHAW; ORTON,
......................PEELE; DRYDEN,
....................STOREY; SHERIDAN
Englishman in India ....RAJ
Eng. poet ....GRAY; AUDEN,
SCOT.........BLAKE, BYRON, CAREW,
..........DONNE, ELIOT; SPENDER;
.......COLERIDGE; WORDSWORTH
Eng. royal house .....YORK; TUDOR
Eng. spa ....BATH; MARGATE
Eng. spy ....ANDRE
Eng. statesman ....EDEN, PITT
engraver's tool ....BURIN
engrossed..........................RAPT
enigma ....PUZZLE, RIDDLE
enlarge ....GROW;
..................SWELL; DILATE,
...............EXPAND; MAGNIFY
enlarge a hole ....REAM
enmity..........ANIMUS; ANIMOSITY
Enoch, father of ....CAIN
ensign ....FLAG
ensnare ....NET; TRAP
entangle ....WEB; SNARL
enter ....BEGIN; ENROLL,
................TAKE UP; PENETRATE
b entertain ....AMUSE; DIVERT
enthusiasm ....ELAN; ARDOR,
...........VERVE; SPIRIT; PASSION
enthusiastic................AVID; RABID
entice ....BAIT, LURE,
................TOLE; TEMPT; ALLURE
entrance ....DOOR, GATE; PORTAL
entrance, ceremonial ....ARCH
entrance, mine ....ADIT
entreat ....PRAY; PLEAD
entry, single ....ITEM
entwine ....WEAVE; ENLACE
enumerate ....LIST; COUNT
envelop ....WRAP; ENFOLD
environment...........SCENE; MILIEU
envoy ....AGENT
envoy, pope's...................LEGATE
envy ....COVET;
................BEGRUDGE
epic poetry.............EPOS; EPOPEE
epoch...................AGE, ERA; TIME;
.................................PERIOD
equal ....TIE; EVEN, PEER
equality ....PAR; PARITY
equilibrium ....STASIS; BALANCE
equine ....ASS; HORSE, ZEBRA
equip ....FIT, RIG; GEAR;
................OUTFIT; FURNISH
equitable ....EVEN, FAIR, JUST
equivocate ....HEDGE; PALTER

c era...............................AGE; TIME;
..........................EPOCH; PERIOD
eradicate ....ERASE, PURGE
erase ......UNDO; CLEAR; REMOVE
erect ....REAR; RAISE; UPRIGHT
ergo ....HENCE
ergs, ten million ....JOULE
Eris, brother of.....................ARES
ermine, summer ....STOAT
Eros ....CUPID
erotic................................SEXY
errand boy ....PAGE
error ....SLIP; LAPSE; MISCUE
error in print........................TYPO
error list ....ERRATA
Esau.................................EDOM
Esau, brother of ....JACOB
Esau, father-in-law of ....ELON
Esau, grandson of ....OMAR
Esau, home of ....SEIR
Esau, wife of ....ADAH
escape ....FLEE; DODGE,
..................ELUDE; DECAMP,
.................FLIGHT; EVASION
eschew...............................SHUN
escutcheon band ....FESS
Eskimo ....See Inuit.
esoteric ....DEEP; PROFOUND
Esperanto, modified.................IDO
espy ....SEE, SPY; SIGHT;
................................GLIMPSE
esquire ....ARMIGER
essay ....TRY; TEST; PAPER,
.......................THEME; ATTEMPT;
................................ENDEAVOR
essence, rose ....ATTAR
essential part ....CORE, PITH
establish ....BASE; FOUND
established value ....PAR
estate, landed ....MANOR
estate manager ....STEWARD
esteem ....HONOR, PRIZE
ester, hydroid acid ....IODINE
ester, oleic acid................OLEATE
estimate ....RATE; GAUGE;
................................RECKON
estrade...............................DAIS
estuary ....RIA
Eternal City...........................ROME
eternity...........AGE, EON; INFINITY
ether compound ....ESTER
ethereal.........AIRY; FILMY; SHEER
Ethiopian Christian language .GEEZ
Eth. Danakil people ....AFAR
Eth. king's title ....NEGUS
Eth. prince ....RAS
Ethiopic ....GEEZ
eucalyptus eater................KOALA
eucalyptus secretion....LAAP, LERP
eucalyptus tree ....YATE

d

41

a Eucharist case ....PYX
Eucharist cloth ....FANON
Eucharist spoon ....LABIS
Eucharist wafer ....HOST
eulogy...........................ELOGE
euphemistic oath .....DANG, DARN,
.........DRAT, GOSH, HECK, JEEZ
euphorbia......................SPURGE
eureka red.......................PUCE
Euripedes play ....MEDEA;
.............BACCHAE, ORESTES;
..........................ALCESTIS
European iris ....ORRIS
Eur. kite................GLED; GLEDE
Eur. porgy ....PARGO
Eurydice, husband of .....ORPHEUS
Eurytus, daughter of ....IOLE
evade ......DODGE, ELUDE, SHIRK
evaluate ....RATE; ASSESS
evangelist.................LUKE, MARK
Evans, Mary Ann ....ELIOT
Eve, grandson of..................ENOS
even.................TIE; FLAT; EQUAL,
............LEVEL, PLANE; STEADY;
......................UNVARYING
even if.............................THOUGH
evening party...................SOIREE
evening prayers ....VESPERS
ever...........................ALWAYS
evergreen ....FIR, YEW; PINE;

b ....CAROB, CEDAR, OLIVE,
.........SAVIN; CALABA, LAUREL,
........................SABINE, SPRUCE
evergreen bean ....CAROB
evergreen genus ....OLAX
evict.................................OUST
evident..................CLEAR, PLAIN;
....................PATENT; VISIBLE
evil...........................BAD, MAL
evil god, Eg. ....SET; SETH
evil intent, in law....DOLUS, FRAUD
evil spirit, Hindu ....ASURA
evolve............UNFOLD; DEVELOP
exacerbate....................IRRITATE
exact..........................EVEN, TRUE;
.........BLEED; DEMAND, EXTORT,
.........SQUARE, STRICT; PRECISE
examine ....QUIZ, TEST, VIEW;
............ASSAY, CHECK; INSPECT
excavate ....DIG; PION; DREDGE
excavated..............................DUG
excavation, mine ....PIT; STOPE
exceed............TOP; BEST; OUTDO
exceedingly: music ....TRES
excellence..............MERIT; VIRTUE
excellent..................A-ONE; PRIME
except..........................BUT; SAVE
excess ....GLUT; LUXUS, SPARE;
....................NIMIETY, SURPLUS
excess of solar year.............EPACT

c exchange premium, discount..AGIO
exchequer....................FISC, FISK
excite ....ELATE, ROUSE;
.........................AROUSE
excited ....AGOG; MANIC
excitement, public ....FUROR
exclamation ....ACH, A-HA, BAH,
.........FIE, HAH, HEY, HOI, HUH,
.........OCH, O-HO, PAH, TCH, TSK,
.....TUT, UGH, WOW, YOW; ALAS,
.................PHEW, WHOA; ALACK
exclamation, Fr. ....HEIN
exclamation, Ger. ....HOCH
exclamation, Irish ....ADAD,
.............AHEY; ARRAH; OCHONE
exclamation, It....................UFA
exclamation, Scot. ....OCH
exclamation of disdain ....POOH
exclamation of disgust ....PISH
exclamation of pain .....OUCH, YIPE
exclamation of relief ....WHEW
exclamations of delight ...AHS, OHS
exclamations of doubt ....HAHS
exclude ....BAR; DEBAR;
......................EXCEPT; PROHIBIT
exclusive ....SOLE; FANCY;
..........CHOICE, SELECT, SINGLE
exclusive group ....ELITE
exclusively ....ONLY
excoriate...................DRUB, FRET,

d ....LASH; CHAFE;
.................ABRADE, SCATHE
excrement ....DUNG; MANURE
excuse ....PLEA; REMIT, SPARE
execrated ....CURST, SWORE
exemplar...........MODEL; PATTERN
exertion ....DINT
exhaust.........SAP; TIRE; DEPLETE
exigency ....NEED
exist...................................LIVE
existing ....ALIVE, BEING
exit ....LEAVE; DEPART,
......................................EGRESS
___ ex machina....................DEUS
expand ....GROW; DILATE;
..................DISTEND, ENLARGE
expanse ....SEA; SWEEP;
....................SPREAD; BREADTH
expatriate ....EXILE
expectation ....HOPE
expedite ....EASE;
.........................HURRY; HASTEN
expedition............................SAFARI
experienced emotions ....FELT
expert ....ADEPT;
.................MASTER, WIZARD
expiate ....ATONE
explain ....SOLVE; DEFINE
explode ....POP; BLOW; BURST,
......................ERUPT; DEBUNK

a exploit ....USE; DEED,
........................FEAT; STUNT
explorer Ericson ....LEIF
explosive letters ....TNT
explosive sound ....BOOM
expose........................AIR; BARE,
........................SHOW; DISPLAY
expression, local ....IDIOM
expressionless................WOODEN
expunge....DELE; ERASE; DELETE
extend ....GROW; SWELL,
........WIDEN; EXPAND, SPREAD;
................LENGTHEN, ELONGATE
extensive..............AMPLE, BROAD
extent..................RANGE, REACH,
........................SCOPE; DEGREE,
....................LENGTH; MEASURE
external covering.......HIDE, HUSK,
................PEEL, PELT, RIND, SKIN
extirpate ....CLEAR, ERASE
extort.......BLEED, EXACT, GOUGE

extra ....NEW; MORE, VERY; c
................ADDED, OTHER, SPARE
extract ....DRAW; ELICIT
extraneous ....ALIEN; FOREIGN
extra page ....INSERT
extreme ....ULTRA
exudate plant .....GUM, LAC; RESIN
exude...............EMIT, OOZE, REEK
exult ....CROW; ELATE, GLORY
eye ....ORB, SEE; GLIM, OGLE
eye, of the ....OPTIC
eye cosmetic ......KOHL; MASCARA
eye inflammation..........STY; IRITIS
eyelash(es) ....CILIA; CILIUM
eye layer................................UVEA
eye of a bean ....HILUM
eye of an insect ....STEMMA;
................................OCELLUS
eye part ....IRIS; CORNEA, RETINA
eye socket ....ORBIT
eye-worm, Afr. ....LOA

F

Fabian Soc. member G.B.S.; SHAW
fable ....MYTH, TALE, YARN;
........................STORY; LEGEND
b Fables in Slang author..............ADE
fable writer ....AESOP
fabled ....LEGENDARY
fabric.....BAFT DUCK, LAWN, SILK,
.......TAPA, TUKE; CREPE, MOIRE,
.............ORLON, RAYON; CANVAS
fabric, angora....................MOHAIR
fabric, bleeding ....MADRAS
fabric, camel's hair.............CAMLET
fabric, coarse cotton ....SURAT
fabric, corded ....REP; REPP;
....PIQUE
fabric, cotton ....LENO, MULL;
................DENIM, MANTA, SCRIM;
........................CALICO, CRETON,
....................NANKIN, PENANG;
................NANKEEN; CRETONNE
fabric, curtain ....NET; SCRIM
fabric, feltlike........................BAIZE
fabric, figured ....DAMASK;
....PAISLEY
fabric, fuzzy ....FELT
fabric, knitted ....TRICOT
fabric, light wool ....ALPACA
fabric, lustrous ....POPLIN, SATEEN
fabric, mourning..................CRAPE
fabric, net...............TULLE; MALINE
fabric, plaid............MAUD; TARTAN
fabric, printed.......................BATIK
fabric, ribbed ....CORD; PIQUE

fabric, satin ....PEKIN; ETOILE
fabric, sheer....................GAUZE;
....................................ORGANZA
fabric, silk ....SURAH; PONGEE, d
....................................SAMITE
fabric, stiff ....WIGAN
fabric, striped.......DORIA; MADRAS
fabric, thick............................DRAB
fabric, thick silk ....GROS
fabric, twilled wool ....SERGE
fabric, upholstery ....BROCATEL;
................................BROCATELLE
fabric, velvetlike finished......PANNE
fabric, wool ....FELT; SERGE;
................MERINO; STAMMEL
fabric, worsted..................ETAMINE
fabricate ....MAKE
fabric from remnants ....MUNGO
fabric stretcher..................TENTER
face ....DIAL, LOOK, MEET;
............FRONT; FACADE, VISAGE
facet, gem ....BEZEL, CULET
face with stone ....REVET
facile ....EASY
facing of a glacier................STOSS
fact......................DATUM; DETAIL
faction.............SECT, SIDE; CABAL
factor.......................PART; DETAIL
factory................................PLANT
faculty .....KNACK, RIGHT; TALENT
fade ....DIE, DIM; WITHER
Faerie Queene iron man ......TALUS
Faerie Queene lady.................UNA

FARM CART; WAIN
FANON ! ~~CRACK~~ OR ALE

Faerie Queene writer / FDR's dog

a *Faerie Queene* writer ......SPENSER
failure........................DUD; BUST,
.......................FLOP; DEFEAT
fainting.....................SYNCOPE
fair ....JUST; CLEAR;
.......................IMPARTIAL
fairway, piece of the ....DIVOT
fairy ....ELF, FAY; PERI;
.......................PIXIE; SPRITE
fairy king.....................OBERON
fairy queen...............MAB; TITANIA
faith, article of ....TENET
faithful ....TRUE; LOYAL;
.......................STAUNCH
falcon.................SAKER; MERLIN
falcon, Asian ....LAGGAR, LUGGAR
falcon, female ....LANNER
falcon, Indian ....SHAHIN
falcon, male ....SAKERET
fall.............DROP, PLOP; SPILL
fallacy.................ERROR; IDOLUM
fallacies ....IDOLA
fall back ....RETREAT
fallow deer ....ADDRA
fall short........................FAIL
false excuse .....LIE; SUBTERFUGE
false friend..........IAGO; TRAITOR
false fruit of a rose ....HIP
false god ....IDOL
Falstaff's follower ....NYM
b fame.................ECLAT, KUDOS;
.......................RENOWN, REPUTE
famed ....NOTED
familiar.............BRAZEN, VERSED;
.......................ROUTINE; INTIMATE
family, Ferrara ....ESTE
family, Florentine ....MEDICI
family, Genoese...................DORIA
family member..............DAD, MOM,
.................POP, SIS; AUNT, MAMA,
.................PAPA; UNCLE; COUSIN
famous...GREAT, KNOWN, NOTED
fan ....ROOTER; SUPPORTER
fan, swinging.......PUNKA; PUNKAH
fanatical.................RABID, ULTRA;
.......................EXTREME, RADICAL
fancy.............IDEA, WHIM; SWANK
fancy dresser.................FOP; DUDE
fanfare ....TANTARA
fare ....DIET, FEND, FOOD;
.............GET BY, SHIFT; MANAGE
farewell........AVE; VALE; SO LONG
farewell, Brit. ....TA-TA
farinaceous ....MEALY
farinaceous food...................SAGO;
.......................SALEP; FARINA
farm, tenant ....CROFT
farmer ....GRANGER
farmer, Soviet.......................KULAK
farm group ....GRANGE

farmyard, S. Afr. ....WERF *c*
Faroe Islands magistrate ......FOUD,
.......................FOWD
Farouk, father of....................FUAD
fashion.........FORM, MAKE, MODE,
.......................MOLD; MODEL; STYLE
fasten ....PIN; BOLT, LOCK, NAIL,
......SEAL, TACK; RIVET; ATTACH
fasten: naut. ....BELAY; BATTEN
fastener...............NUT, PIN; BRAD,
.............CLIP, HASP, NAIL, SNAP,
.......................STUD; CLASP, RIVET;
.......................CLEVIS, COTTER
fastener, wire....................STAPLE
fastener, wood.........................FID,
.......................PEG; DOWEL
fastening.............................LATCH
fastening post: naut. ....BITT;
.......................BOLLARD
fastidious.............................FUSSY,
.......................PICKY; DAINTY
fast month ....RAMADAN
fast period, Rom. Cath. ....LENT
fat ....LARD, OILY,
.............SUET; OBESE, STOUT,
.......................THICK; PORTLY
fat, animal...................TALLOW
fat, liquid part of...................OLEIN
fat, of........................SEBACEOUS
fat, solid part of................STEARIN
fatal...............................DEADLY, *d*
.......................LETHAL, MORTAL
fate ....LOT; DOOM; KISMET
fateful.............................DIRE
Fate in Gr. mythology...........MOIRA
Fates, The Three ....CLOTHO;
.................ATROPOS; LACHESIS
father .....DAD, POP; SIRE; BEGET,
.............DADDY, PADRE; PRIEST
father: Arabic ....ABU; ABOU
father: Heb. ....ABBA
father's side kinship..........AGNATE
fathom ....GRASP,
.......................PROBE, SOUND
fatigue.........TIRE; DRAIN, WEARY
Fatima, husband of....................ALI
fatty ....ADIPOSE
fatty gland secretion ....SEBUM
fatuous...............................INANE
faucet ....TAP; COCK; SPIGOT
fault finder ....MOMUS
faulty ....BAD; FLAWED
faux pas ....ERROR, GAFFE
favor ....GAIN; GRACE, HONOR
favorable vote ....AYE, YES
favorite ....PET; IDOL
fawn color.............................FAON
fawning favorite ....MINION
FDR's coin ....DIME
FDR's dog ....FALA

44

a fear ....DREAD; HORROR,
...................PHOBIA, TERROR
fearful ....DIRE; AWFUL; AGHAST
feast................DEVOUR, RELISH,
...................SPREAD; BANQUET
Feast of Lanterns (Jap.) ....BON
Feast of Tabernacles (Heb.) ....
...................................SUKKOT
feather ......PENNA, PINNA, PLUME
feathered scarf ....BOA
feather grass........................STIPA
feather palms ....EJOO;
...................................GOMUTI
feathers, molt ....|................MEW
feathers, soft...........DOWN; EIDER
federal agent..........G-MAN, T-MAN
federal agents.........G-MEN, T-MEN
feeble.....................PUNY, WEAK;
...........FAINT, MUTED; TENUOUS
feel .....|.....................AIR; GROPE,
...................SENSE, THINK,
...........TOUCH, YEARN; FINGER
...........INTUIT, HANDLE; BELIEVE
feeler.............PALP; ANTENNA
feet, having ....PEDATE
feet, of ....PEDAL
feign...........................ACT; FAKE,
...................SHAM; PUT ON
feline ....CAT
fellow ....BUB, BUD, GUY, JOE,
b ....LAD, MAC, PAL;
...................CHAP, CHUM, GENT;
...................BLOKE, BUDDY
female....GAL; DAME, DOLL, GIRL,
...................LADY, LASS; BROAD,
...........CHICK, WENCH, WOMAN
female insect........................GYNE
fence, steps over a................STILE
fence, sunken and hidden.....HA-HA
fence of shrubs...................HEDGE
fence of stakes ....PALISADE
fencing guard position ....SIXTE;
...................OCTAVE, QUARTE,
...................QUINTE, TIERCE,
...................SECONDE, SEPTIME
fencing hit ....PUNTO
fencing sword ....EPEE, FOIL;
...........................SABER
fencing term ....TOUCHE
fencing thrust .....LUNGE; REMISE;
...................PASSADO, RIPOSTE
ferment ....YEAST
fern, climbing ....NITO
fern, edible.............................TARA
fern "seed".............................SPORE
fern spore cluster(s) ....SORI;
...........................SORUS
Ferrara patron of the arts........ESTE
ferrum....................................IRON
ferryman ....CHARON

fertilizer ....MARL; GUANO; c
...................................MANURE
fertilizer, banned ....DDT
fertilizer ingredient................UREA
fervent........KEEN; FIERY; ARDENT
fervor...........ZEAL, ZEST; ARDOR
fester.........ROT; DECAY; RANKLE
festival ....FAIR, FETE,
...................................GALA; FIESTA
festival, Creek Indian...........BUSK
festival, Gr. ....AGON; DELIA
fetal membrane ....CAUL
fetish...................OBI; JUJU, OBIA,
..............ZEMI; CHARM; GRI-GRI
fetter............GYVE, IRON; CHAIN;
..................SHACKLE; HANDCUFF
feudal benefice ....FEU
feudal estate ....FEUD, FIEF
feudal land ....BENEFICE
feudal tenant ....VASSAL
fever, intermittent.................AGUE;
...................................TERTIAN
feverish ....FEBRILE
fez ....TARBOOSH
fiber ....PITA; RAFFIA,
...................STAPLE, THREAD
fiber, bark ...TAPA; OLONA, TERAP
fiber, cordage ....COIR, FERU,
...................HEMP, IMBE, JUTE;
...................ABACA, SISAL
fiber, hat or basket ....DATIL d
fiber, textile ....SABA
fiber, woody ....BAST
fiberboard substance ......BAGASSE
fiber from palms ....ERUC
fiber knot...................................NEP
fiber plant......ISTLE, IXTLE, RAMIE
fiber plant, Braz. ....CAROA;
...................................PINGUIN
fiber plant, E. Indian ....SUNN
fibers, knotted ....NOIL
fiddle, medieval ....GIGA; GIGUE
fiddler crab genus.....................UCA
field...................LEA; ACRE, AREA;
..............CROFT, REALM; DOMAIN
field deity........................PAN; FAUN
field stubble ....ROWEN
fight ....FRAY; MELEE; BATTLE
fight, two-man........................DUEL
figurative usage ....TROPE
figure ....SOLID
figure, five-sided ....PENTAGON
figure, four-sided ....TETRAGON
figure, multi-sided...........POLYGON
figure, oval ....ELLIPSE
figure, six-sided.............HEXAGON
figure, ten-sided ....DECAGON
figure of speech ....TROPE;
...................SIMILE; METAPHOR
figure with equal angles.....ISOGON

a Fijian chestnut ....RATA
Fijian sarong....................SULU
filament ....HAIR; FIBER
filament, plant...............ELATER
filament of flax ....HARL; HARLE
filch.............STEAL, SWIPE
file ....ROW; LINE, RANK, TIER;
..................QUEUE; COLUMN
file, coarse..............................RASP
file, three-square single-cut...........
....................................CARLET
filefish..................................LIJA
filled completely ....SATED;
...............................REPLETE
fillet ....BONE, ORLE, ORLO
fillip ....PROD, PUSH, SPUR
film, green ....PATINA
film yeast ....FLOR
filthy.......................................VILE
filthy lucre.............................PELF
finale: music..................CODA
finch...............LINNET, SISKIN
finch, Eur. ....TARIN, SERIN
finch, S. Afr. ....FINK
find fault ....CARP; CAVIL
fine, as a line......................LEGER
fine, punish by ....AMERCE
fine, record of ....ESTREAT
finesse................ART; SKILL
finger....................DIGIT, THUMB,

b ....TOUCH; PINKIE;
...............MINIMUS, POINTER
finger cymbals ....CASTANETS
finger inflammation..............FELON;
..............................WHITLOW
fingerless glove ....MITT; MITTEN
finger nail half-moon ....LUNULA
fingerprint pattern ....WHORL
finger-throwing game ....MORA
finisher..................EDGER, ENDER
finishing tool......................REAMER
Finland, in Finnish................SUOMI
Finnish steam bath ....SAUNA
firearm........................GUN; RIFLE;
..................MAUSER, PISTOL;
...............CARBINE; REVOLVER
fire basket (torch) ....CRESSET
fire bullet............................TRACER
firecracker.......................PETARD
fired clay ....TILE
firedog ....ANDIRON
fire god ....VULCAN
fire opal, Fr. ....GIRASOL
fireplace ....GRATE,
....................INGLE; HEARTH
fireplace side shelf ....HOB
firewood bundle ....FAGOT
fireworks.................GERB; GERBE
firm ....FAST; STEADY;
...............COMPANY, STAUNCH

firmament.................................SKY
firn ....NEVE
firs' genus, true ....ABIES
first...........................PRIME; INITIAL
first, went...............................LED
first appearance ....DEBUT
firstborn ....ELDEST, SENIOR
firstborn, in law.....................EIGNE
first day of the month, Rom. ....CAL,
....................................KAL; CALENDS
First Ladies, US ....See page 190.
first miracle site ....CANA
first part in a duet ....PRIMO
first place, took ....WON
first principles ....ABCS
first-rate ....ACE; A-ONE
fish...........ANGLE, TRAWL, TROLL
fish, alligator ....GAR
fish, ancient.........................ELOPS
fish, aquarium ......GUPPY, LOACH,
...........MOLLY, TETRA; GOURAMI
fish, Atl. ....TAUTOG;
...............ESCOLAR, TAUTAUG
fish, bait ....CHUB
fish, boned.........................FILLET
fish, bony ....CARP; TELEOST
fish, butterfly ....BLENNY,
.....................................CHITON
fish, carplike...............DACE, RUDD
fish, Caspian Sea........STERLET
fish, codlike .....CUSK, HAKE, LING,
...............................TUSK
fish, colorful ....BOCE, OPAH
fish, cyprinoid ....IDE; ORFE
fish, dolphin.................MAHI-MAHI
fish, elongated.......EEL, GAR; PIKE
fish, flat ....DAB, RAY; SOLE;
.............................BRILL, FLUKE;
.............................FLOUNDER
fish, Florida freshwater......TARPON
fish, game ....BASS; TROUT
fish, garden pond ....KOI
fish, Great Lakes ....CISCO, PERCH
fish, group of.......SHOAL; SCHOOL
fish, Hawaiian ....AKU
fish, herringlike ....SHAD
fish, hook for...............................GIG;
.............................GAFF; DRAIL
fish, linglike ....COD
fish, mackerellike ....CERO;
.............................TINKER
fish, nest-building.................ACARA
fish, N. Z. ....IHI
fish, parasitic ....REMORA
fish, perchlike ....DARTER
fish, piece of ....FILLET
fish, silvery ....MULLET
fish, sparoid...........................SARGO
fish, spiny ....GOBY; PERCH
fish, sucker...........PEGA; REMORA

46

a fish, tropical ....GUASA,
.......................SARGO, SNOOK;
.......................ROBALO; GROUPER
fish, young ....FRY
fish by trolling ....DRAIL
fish cleaner ....SCALER
fish eggs..............................ROE
fisherman's hut, Orkney ....SKEO
fish from a boat....................TROLL
fishhook line-leader ....SNELL
fishhook point ....BARB
fishing line ....SNELL, TRAWL
fishing line cork ....BOB; BOBBIN
fishing line, multihooked ....SPILLER
fishing trip, Scot. herring......DRAVE
fish net ....SEINE, TRAWL;
.............................SPILLER
fish-pitching prong........PEW; GAFF
fish-poison tree ....BITO
fish sauce ....ALEC
fish sign ....PISCES
fish sperm ....MILT
fish trap ....WEIR
fish whisker ....BARBEL
fish with bait on the surface .....DAP,
.....................................DIB
fissure ....RIFT, RIMA;
...............BREAK, CHINK, CLEFT,
.........................CRACK, SPLIT
fissures, full of ....RIMOSE

b fist..........................NEAF; NIEVE
fit............APT; RIPE, SUIT; ADAPT
fit for cultivation ....ARABLE
fit of sulks..............FUNK, HUFF
fit of temper..............SNIT; PIQUE
fit to drink........................POTABLE
five, group of....................PENTAD
five-dollar bill ....FIN, VEE
five-franc piece ....ECU
five of trump ....PEDRO
fixed charge ....FEE
fix or fixed............................SET
flaccid ....LIMP
flag................TIRE; ENSIGN
flag, military.......................GUIDON
flag's corner ....CANTON
flank..................................SIDE
flap..................................TAB
flaring edge ....LIP; FLANGE
flat ....DRAB, DULL, EVEN;
.....................LEVEL, PLANE,
.....................STALE; INSIPID
flat-bottomed boat.....DORY, PUNT,
.....................SCOW; BARGE
flatten ....LEVEL; SMOOTH
flatter ....SUIT; BECOME;
.....................................BLANDISH
flattery, Irish....................BLARNEY
flavor...........LACE, TANG; AROMA,
.........................SAPOR; SEASON

flax, soak............................RET
flee........................LAM, RUN; BOLT
fleece ....WOOL; SWINDLE
fleet............FAST, NAVY; ARMADA
fleet, merchant..................ARGOSY
fleur-de-lis ....LILY
flexible ....AGILE;
.....................PLIANT, SUPPLE
flight, Mohammed's ....HEJIRA
flightless birds, of ....RATITE
flight organ ....WING
Flintstones characters ....DINO,
.........................FRED; BETTY,
.........................WILMA; BAM BAM,
.........................BARNEY; PEBBLES
flip ....SCAN, SKIM, TOSS
flit ....FLY, GAD; FLUTTER
float ....BUOY, RAFT, WAFT
floating ....NATANT
floating masses of weeds ......SUDD
floating wreckage ....FLOTSAM
flock, small............................COVEY
flock of fowl in flight ....SKEIN
flock of quail..........................BEVY
flock of swans.......................BANK
flog ....BEAT, LASH, WHIP
flood ....SEA; EAGRE,
.........................SPATE; DELUGE,
.........................FRESHET, TORRENT
floodgate ....CLOW; SLUICE
floor covering ....MAT, PAD, RUG;
.....................................CARPET
flora and fauna ....BIOTA
floral leaf ....BRACT, SEPAL
Florentine family ....MEDICI
Florida tree ....MABI
flounder ....DAB; SOLE; FLUKE;
.........................PLAICE, WALLOW
flourish, musical ....ROULADE
flour sieve ....BOLTER
flow ....RUN; FLUX
flower, Easter........................LILY
flower, fall ....ASTER; COSMOS
flower, field ....GOWAN
flower, new ....BUD
flower, Oriental......................LOTUS
flower, showy ....CALLA
flower cluster ....CYME; ANADEM,
.....................................RACEME
flower holder...........................VASE
flower part ....PETAL, SEPAL;
.........................CARPEL, SPADIX
flower spike ....AMENT
flow out ....EMIT; SPILL
fluctuate ....WAVER
fluent ....GLIB
fluff of yarn ....LINT
fluid(s), medical ....SERA; SERUM
fluidity unit ....RHE
flume ....SHUTE; SLUICE

MERBIT

FOREARM BONE: ULNA
FOREIGN STUDENT SUBJ.: ESL

flunk / forgiving

a

flunk................................FAIL
flushed................................RED
flute, ancient............................TIBIA
flute, small ....FIFE
flutter...................FLAP, LUFF,
...................WAVE; HOVER
fly ....SOAR, WING;
...................GLIDE; AVIATE
fly, Afr. ....TSE-TSE
fly, artificial...................HARL
fly, small ....GNAT; MIDGE
fly agaric....................AMANITA
flycatcher............ALDER, PEWEE;
...................PHOEBE
flying ....VOLANT
Flying Dutchman girl ....SENTA
flying fox....................KALONG
flying lemur....................COLUGO
flying saucer ....UFO
foam....................SUDS; LATHER
fodder, store ....ENSILE
fodder building ....SILO
fog....................DAZE, HAZE,
...................MIST, MURK; GLOOM;
...................STUPOR; OBSCURE
foist...................FOB; IMPOSE
fold...................PLY; RUGA; PLEAT;
...................CREASE, DOUBLE
folded like a fan.................PLICATE
fold of skin ....PLICA

b

folds, arrange in...................DRAPE
folio ....PAGE
folk dance, Slavic ....KOLO
folklore monster...................TROLL
folkways ....MORES
follow ....DOG; TAIL;
...........ENSUE, TRACE; COMPLY,
...................PURSUE, SHADOW
foment...................ABET
fondle ....PET; CARESS
font...................LAVER, STOUP
food...................EATS, FARE, MEAT,
...................MENU; MANNA; ALIMENT
food, bit of...................ORT
food, provide with.................CATER
food, soft...................PAP
food, unappetizing ....SLOP
food for animals ....FORAGE
food forbidden Israelites ....TREF;
...................TEREFA; TEREFAH
food of the gods.................AMRITA;
...................AMBROSIA
fool ....ASS; DOLT, DUPE,
...................JERK; SIMP; BLUFF,
...................COZEN, IDIOT, NINNY, TRICK
foolish............DAFT, ZANY; INANE,
...................SILLY; ASININE
fool's bauble ....MAROTTE
fool's gold...................PYRITE
foot, animal's ....PAD, PAW

c

foot, Gr. poetic ....IONIC
foot, having a ....PEDATE
foot, poetic............IAMB; ANAPEST
foot, two-syllable..........SPONDEE;
...................TROCHEE
foot, verse ....DACTYL
footless...................APOD; APODAL
footlike structure ....PES
foot part, horse's ....PASTERN
foot soldier ....PEON
foot soldier, Irish .....KERN; KERNE
footstalk, leaf or flower.........STRIG
footstool...................MORA, POUF;
...................HASSOCK, OTTOMAN
for...................PRO
forage plant ....ALSIKE,
...................LUCERN; ALFALFA
forage plant, Indian.............GUAR
foramen...................PORE
foray ....RAID
forbidden ....TABU; TABOO;
...................BANNED
Forbidden City...................LHASA
forbidding ....STERN
force...................VIM; CREW, TEAM;
...........CORPS, POWER; COERCE,
.......COMPEL, DURESS, ENERGY;
...................PRESSURE
force, unit of ....DYNE
foreboding ....OMEN
forefather ....SIRE
forehead...................BROW
forehead, of the ....METOPIC
foreigner in Hawaii ....HAOLE
foreign in origin ....EXOTIC
foreign trade discount ....AGIO
foremost part.................BOW, VAN;
...................FRONT
foremost segment of an insect........
...................ACRON
foreordain ....DESTINE
foreshadow ....BODE
forest, Braz. ....MATTA
forestall ....AVERT, DETER;
...................PREVENT
forest clearing ....GLADE
forest ox ....ANOA
forests, of ....SYLVAN;
...................NEMORAL
forest warden ....RANGER
foretell............AUGUR; PREDICT
foretoken ....OMEN
forever, in poetry ....ETERNE
for fear that...................LEST
forfeit ....DROP, LOSE
forgetfulness fruit ....LOTUS
forgetfulness water.............LETHE
forgive ....REMIT; EXCUSE,
...................PARDON
forgiving ....CLEMENT

d

48

a forgo ....WAIVE, YIELD;
....ABANDON
formation, military ....ECHELON
former ....ERST
formerly....................................ONCE
formic acid source....................ANT
formula...........RECIPE; EQUATION
forsaken ....LORN
for shame ....FIE
fort ....REDAN; CITADEL
fort, US military...............DIX, ORD;
....................KNOX, SILL; BLISS,
.....................BRAGG; EUSTIS
forth ....OUT
forthwith.....................................NOW
fortification........REDAN; REDOUBT
fortification, ditchside.........ESCARP
fortification, slope ....TALUS
fortification of felled trees ....ABATIS
fortified place, Irish............LIS; LISS
fortify ....ARM, MAN
forward ....PERT; AHEAD,
........................SASSY; FOSTER;
..................PROMOTE, REROUTE
foul-smelling................OLID; FETID
...........................REEKY; FOETID
found ....ESTABLISH
foundation ....BASE; BASIS
four, group of ....TETRAD
four-inch measure ....SPAN
b fourth estate.........................PRESS
fowl ....HEN; CAPON, POULT
fowl's gizzard, etc. ....GIBLET
fox, Afr. desert....................FENNEC
fox, S. Afr. ....ASSE; CAAMA
fox-hunters' coats ....PINKS
Fox River tribe ....SAUK
fraction..................PART; DECIMAL
Fra Diavolo composer ....AUBER
fragment of pottery ....SHARD
fragrant ....SCENTED;
................................REDOLENT
frail piece ....WISP
frame, supporting............TRESTLE
framework ....TRUSS
France, once ....GAUL
franchise ....VOTE; CHARTER
Franciscan ....MINORITE
frank..OPEN;
....................CANDID, HONEST
Frankenstein's assistant ....IGOR
frankincense ....OLIBANUM
fraud ....SHAM
fraught......................................LADEN
fray ....MELEE
free..........RID; GRATIS; UNLOOSE
freebooter................................PIRATE
freedman in Kentish law........LAET
freedom, briefly ....LIB
free-for-all ....FRAY; MELEE

c freeman, A.-S. ....CEORL
freight car ....GONDOLA
French art group ....DADA; FAUVES
Fr. artist....................DORE, DUFY,
...............GROS; COROT, DEGAS,
...........MANET, MONET; BRAQUE,
.......................RENOIR; CHAGALL,
.......................MATISSE, UTRILLO
Fr. author ....SUE; GIDE, HUGO,
.....................LOTI, ZOLA; CAMUS,
............................DUMAS, RENAN,
............................VERNE; RACINE,
.......................SARTRE; COCTEAU
Fr. business abbreviation..........CIE
Fr. chalk ....TALC
Fr. coin, old ....SOU
Fr. detective force.............SURETE
Fr. dramatist ....RACINE
Fr. ecclesiastical city ....SENS
Fr. explorer.........CABOT; CARTIER
Fr. exclamation ....HEIN
Fr. fort, Battle of Verdun.........VAUX
Fr. general..............FOCH; HOCHE
................GAMELIN; DEGAULLE
Fr.-Ger. region.......................SAAR
Fr. historic provinces ....FOIX,
....................NICE; ANJOU, AUNIS,
.............BEARN, BERRY, CORSE,
........................MAINE; ALSACE,
........................ARTOIS, MARCHE,
.........................POITOU, SAVOIE
Fr. lace-making town ....CLUNY
Fr. marshal................NEY; MURAT
Fr. meat dish ....SALMI
Fr. months (in order)........JANVIER,
.......................FEVRIER, MARS,
..........................AVRIL, MAI,
.............JUIN, JUILLET, AOUT,
..............SEPTEMBRE, OCTOBRE,
..............NOVEMBRE, DECEMBRE
Fr. philosopher ....COMTE
Fr. premier, former................LAVAL
Fr. priest ....ABBE, PERE
Fr. pronoun ....CES, ILS, MES,
................TOI, UNE; ELLE; ELLES
Fr. psychologist ....BINET
Fr. revolutionary ....MARAT
Fr. sculptor ....RODIN
Fr. singer ....PIAF; SABLON
Fr. soldier ....POILU
Fr. soprano ....PONS; CALVE
Fr. statesman ....COTY
FRENCH WORDS:
after ....APRES
again ....ENCORE
airplane............................AVION
alas ....HELAS
all ....TOUS, TOUT
among ....ENTRE
arm...................................BRAS

EYE! OEIL
TO BE! ETRE
FRENCH ARTIST: ARP, COROT

French words (article / read)

a FRENCH WORDS: *continued*

article	LAS, LES, UNE
at the home of	CHEZ
aunt	TANTE
baby	BEBE
back	DOS
bacon	LARD
bath	BAIN
be, to	ETRE
beach	GREVE, PLAGE
beast	BETE
before	AVANT
between	ENTRE
bitter	AMER
black	NOIR
blue	AZUR, BLEU
bridge	PONT
but	MAIS
cabbage	CHOU
cake	GATEAU
carefully groomed	SOIGNE
carriage	FIACRE; VOITURE
case or box	ETUI
chicken	POULET; POUSSIN
child	ENFANT
cloud	NUE; NUAGE
cock (rooster)	COQ
cup	COUPE, TASSE
dance, formal	BAL
daughter	FILLE

b

dear	CHER
deed	FAIT
devil	DEMON; DIABLE
dirty	SALE
donkey	ANE; BAUDET
down with	A BAS
dream	REVE; SONGE
duke	DUC
dungeon	CACHOT
east	EST
egg	OEUF
enamel	EMAIL
encore!	BIS
equal	EGAL
evening	SOIR
evil	MAL
father	PERE
fear	PEUR
finally	ENFIN
fingering	DOIGTE
fire	FEU
five	CINQ
friend, female	AMIE
friend, male	AMI
friends	AMIS
game(s)	JEU; JEUX
gift	DON; CADEAU
God	DIEU
good	BON
good-bye	ADIEU; AU REVOIR

c

gravy	JUS
gray	GRIS
ground	TERRE
hall	SALLE
handle	ANSE; MANCHE
head	CHEF, TETE
health	SANTE
here	ICI
his	SES
hour	HEURE
house	MAISON
husband	MARI; EPOUX
idea	IDEE
in	DANS
is	EST
island	ILE
kind	SORTE
king	ROI
lamb	AGNEAU
land	TERRE
laugh	RIRE
laughter	RISEE
law	LOI; DROIT
leather	CUIR
left	GAUCHE
lily	LIS
little	PEU; EXIGU
lively	GAI, VIF; VIVANT
lodging place	GITE
low	BAS

d

maid	BONNE
mail	POSTE
mask, black velvet	LOUP
me	MOI
milk	LAIT
mine	A MOI
mother	MERE
mount	MONT
museum	MUSEE
nail	CLOU; ONGLE
name	NOM
near	PRES; PROCHE
night	NUIT
no	NON
nose	NEZ
nothing	RIEN; NEANT
on	SUR
one	UNE
our	NOUS
out	HORS; DEHORS
over	SUR
pork	PORC
pout	MOUE
pretty	JOLI; JOLIE
queen	REINE
quickly	VITE
rabbit	LAPIN
railway station	GARE
raw	CRU
read	LIRE

50

FRET: REPINE

a FRENCH WORDS: *continued*
rifle range............................TIR
riot..............................EMEUTE
river...........................RIVIERE
roast....................ROTI; ROTIR
salt........................SEL; SALE
school.............ECOLE, LYCEE
sea......................MER; MARIN
senior.............................AINE
servant........................BONNE
she................................ELLE
sheath............................ETUI
sheep.......................MOUTON
shelter.............................ABRI
shine...............LUIRE; LUSTRE
shooting match....................TIR
sickness...................MALADIE
silk................................SOIE
small...................MENU; PETIT
soldier..........................SOLDAT
some...............................DES
son..................................FILS
soul or spirit.....................AME
spring..................PRINTEMPS
star.............................ETOILE
state...............................ETAT
storm...........................ORAGE
summer............................ETE
there!.............................VOILA
they....................ILS; ELLES

b thirty.............................TRENTE
thou................................TOI
too much.........................TROP
towards...........................VERS
under..............................SOUS
upon.................................SUR
us...................................NOUS
very...............................TRES
vineyard..........................VIGNE
wall..................................MUR
water(s).............EAU; EAUX
wave.................ONDE; VAGUE
well.................................BIEN
wine..................................VIN
winter...........................HIVER
with................................AVEC
without..........................SANS
wolf................................LOUP
woods............................BOIS
yes..................................OUI
yesterday.......................HIER
you....................TOI; VOUS
your..............................VOTRE
frenzied........................AMOK
frequently....................OFTEN
fresh.................NEW; NOVEL
freshet............FLOOD, SPATE
freshwater worm...........NAID, NAIS
Freud, translator of..............BRILL
Freudian concepts.................IDS

Freudian stage....................ANAL *c*
friar...........................FRA; MONK
friar, mendicant.................SERVITE
friction-reduction device............GIB
Friendly Islands....................TONGA
friends.................CIRCLE, CLIQUE
friendship.............................AMITY
frigate bird, Hawaiian........IOA, IWA
Frigg, husband of.................ODIN
fright............FEAR; DREAD, PANIC
frighten..................ALARM, SCARE
frill, neck....................RUFF; JABOT
fringe benefit...........................PERK
fringe of curls or bangs...FRISETTE
frisk.............................PLAY, ROMP;
......................................SEARCH
frog genus.............................RANA
frogs, of.............................RANINE
frolic...............LARK, PLAY, ROMP;
..............CAPER, SPORT, SPREE
from head-to-foot..........CAP-A-PIE
front.........................HEAD, FORE;
......................FACADE, FACING
frontier post...........................FORT
frontiersman......BOONE; CARSON;
.................................CROCKETT
frost.....................ICE; HOAR, RIME
froth......................FOAM; SPUME
frown...............GLARE, SCOWL;
...................................GLOWER
frugal.............THRIFTY, PRUDENT *d*
fruit...................FIG; IMBU, LIME,
..........PEAR, PLUM, UGLI; APPLE,
..............BERRY, CACAO, GRAPE,
.................GUAVA, ICACO, ILAMA,
.............LEMON, OLIVE, PEACH,
DRUPE.............PRUNE; BANANA,
..........DAMSON, DURIAN, FEIJOA,
............JUJUBE, LITCHI, LOQUAT,
....................MEDLAR, ORANGE,
..............PIPPIN, QUINCE, RAISIN,
...................SAPOTE; TANGELO
fruit, Afr..................AKEE; ACKEE
fruit, decay of overripe...........BLET
fruit, dry.............................ACHENE
fruit, fleshy.............................POME
fruit, hard-shelled.......NUT; GOURD
fruit, interior of a..........PITH, PULP
fruit, lemonlike....................CITRON
fruit, plumlike........................SLOE
fruit, pulpy.................UVA; DRUPE
fruit, southern.....................PAPAW
fruit, tropical...........DATE; MANGO
fruit, vine.............................MELON
fruit, yellow tropical..........PAPAYA
fruit dish.........................COMPOTE
fruiting spike.............................EAR
fruit of a maple.................SAMARA
frustrate............STYMIE, THWART
fry lightly...............................SAUTE

fuel / garment, priest's

a fuel ....GAS, LOG, OIL;
..........................COAL, COKE
fuel, rocket ....LOX
fuel, turf................................PEAT
fuel ship ....TANKER
Fugard heroine ....LENA
fugue theme ....DUX
fulcrum, oar's ....THOLE
full...............................PLENARY
Fulton's steamboat ......CLERMONT
fume ....REEK; SMOKE
fun................................SPORT
function ....USE; ROLE, WORK
function, trigonometric ....SINE;
..........................COSINE, SECANT
fundamental ....BASIC
funeral bell ....KNELL

c funeral music ....DIRGE
funeral notice ....OBIT
funeral oration.....................ELOGE
funeral pile............................PYRE
fungus ....AGARIC
fungus, edible....MOREL; TRUFFLE
fungus, white-spored........AMANITA
fur, in Heraldry ....VAIR
Furies, Gr. ....ERINYES
Furies, Rom. ....DIRAE
Furies, the.....ALECTO; MAGAERA;
..........................TISIPHONE
furlongs, eight ....MILE
furtive ....SLY; SNEAKY
fury ....IRE
furze ....WHIN; GORSE
fuss ....ADO; TO-DO; BOTHER

G

GAGE BOOK: ELENI
GADDED.: SWANNED
GAME TABLE COVER: BAIZE
TAKE AWAY GAME: NIM
GAME AUTHORITY: HOYLE

gabi ....TARO
gadget ....GIZMO
Gaelic ....ERSE; CELTIC
Gaelic poem, division of a......DUAN
gaff ....SPAR
gain.......GET, WIN; EARN; PROFIT
gait ....LOPE, PACE, TROT;
b ....CANTER, GALLOP
Galahad, mother of ....ELAINE
Galatea's beloved...................ACIS
Galilee town ....CANA
gallery, art.............................SALON
gallery, open.....................LOGGIA
galley...............................BIREME;
.................TRIREME, UNIREME
galley, fast.......................DROMOND
gallop, rapid ....TANTIVY
gallop slowly ....LOPE
gal of song.............................SAL
Galsworthy heroine ....IRENE
Galway Bay isles....................ARAN
gamble..................BET; RISK;
..................WAGER; CHANCE,
..................HAZARD; VENTURE
gambling, legal: Abbr. ....OTB
gambling game, bingolike ......KENO
gambling location ....CASINO
gambol.................DIDO; CAPER
game ....FUN; PLAY; SPORT;
FARO....PLUCKY; GALLANT, VALIANT
game, Basque...................PELOTA
game, dice ....LUDO
game, equipmentless ....TAG
game, guessing ....MORA; CANUTE
gamecock.............................STAG
gamekeeper......................RANGER
game of skill..............POOL; CHESS

d game piece ....MAN
gaming cubes ....DICE
Ganda dialect ....SOGA
Ganges boat........................PUTELI
gangplank ....RAMP
gangrene precursor..............NOMA
gangster.........MUG; HOOD, THUG
gangster's gal......................MOLL
gap ....HIATUS, LACUNA
gap, hedge.............MUSE; MEUSE
gardening tool ....HOE;
.......................RAKE; SPADE
garden invader ....WEED
garden plot...............................BED
garland ....LEI; ANADEM;
..................................CHAPLET
garment...........COAT, ROBE, SLIP;
.................CLOAK, DRESS, SHIFT,
..................SHIRT, SKIRT, TUNIC;
..................BLOUSE, JACKET
garment, Anglican bishop's........
.................................CHIMERE
garment, Arab ....ABA
garment, fitted ....REEFER;
..................................LEOTARD
garment, Hindu ....SARI; BANYAN
garment, Jewish high priest's........
.................................EPHOD
garment, loose ....CYMAR; CAMISE
garment, Malay.................SARONG
garment, Muslim women's ......IZAR
garment, N. Afr. ....HAIK; HAICK
garment, outer................CAPOTE;
..................................PALETOT
garment, Polynesian...........PAREU
garment, priest's ....ALB; COPE;
.................AMICE, STOLE

52

GEMSBOK: ORYX

a garment, rain ....PONCHO
garment, Renaissance........SIMAR,
....SYMAR
garment, scarflike ....TIPPET
garment, Turk. ....DOLMAN
garment, woman's.............BODICE,
....MANTUA
garnishment ....LIEN
garret ....ATTIC
gas............................FUEL; BLAST
gas, charge with ....AERATE
gas, inert ....ARGON, XENON
gas, radioactive.....RADON, NITON
gas apparatus.................AERATOR
gas for colored lights ....NEON
gastropod ....WHELK; LIMPET
gate..PORTAL
gate, water ....SLUICE
gateway...................................PYLON
gateway, Buddhist temple ...TORAN
gateway, Chin. commemorative......
....PAI-LOU
gateway, Jap. ....TORII
gateway, Pers. ....DAR
gateway, Shinto shrine ....TORII
gather ....MASS; AMASS,
.........................GLEAN; ACCRUE,
.....................GARNER, MUSTER
gather in bundles...............SHEAVE
gaucho's device........BOLA; BOLAS
b Gaul, ancient people of ....REMI
gaunt....................................THIN;
.............................SPARE; SKINNY
gazelle ....ARIEL
gazelle, Afr. ....ADMI, MOHR;
...............ADDRA, KORIN, MHORR
gazelle, Asian ....AHU
gazelle, Pers.........................CORA
gazelle, Tibetan......................GOA
gear ....RIG; EQUIP;
...................OUTFIT, TACKLE
gear-shift position ....PARK
gear tooth...............................COG
gear wheels, smaller of two .PINION
gee whiz ....GOSH; GOLLY
Gelderland city.......................EDE
gelid ....ICY; COLD
gem ....JADE, ONYX, OPAL,
..................RUBY, SARD; AGATE,
...........PEARL; GARNET, SPINEL;
...................EMERALD, PERIDOT
Gemini's immortal half ....POLLUX
Gemini's mortal half ....CASTOR
gem weight ....CARAT
gender..........................SEX; MALE;
.....................FEMALE, NEUTER
genealogy representation ....TREE
generation ....AGE
genetic letters ....DNA, RNA
genie, Eg. ....HAPI

gentle ....EASY, MEEK,   c
................MILD, TAME; DOCILE,
..........................PACIFY, TENDER
genuflect................................KNEEL
geode ....VUG; VUGG, VUGH
geological epoch....................BALA,
..........ECCA, LIAS, MUAV; ERIAN,
........UINTA; EOCENE; PLIOCENE
geological formation ....TERRAIN
geological vein angle ....HADE
geometrical line ....LOCUS;
....SECANT
geometric solid ....CONE,
..............................CUBE; PRISM
geometry rule ....THEOREM
geophagy ....PICA
Geraint, wife of ....ENID
germ ....BUG; VIRUS;
....MICROBE
Germanic gods.......................TIU;
.............................DONAR, WODEN
German admiral.....................SPEE
Ger. article ....DAS, DER, EIN
Ger. bacteriologist ....KOCH
Ger. conjunction ....UND
Ger.-Czech region ....SUDETEN
Ger. district of old ....GAU
Ger. dive bomber ....STUKA
Ger. emperor...........................OTTO
Ger. highway...............AUTOBAHN
Ger. industrial valley ....RUHR   d
Ger. John ....HANS
Ger. landscape painter ....ROOS
Ger. name prefix ....VON
Ger. philosopher.......KANT; HEGEL
Ger. physicist............OHM; ERMAN
Ger. theologian......................ARND
Ger. title ....VON; GRAF; PRINZ
Ger. toast................................HOCH
GERMAN WORDS:
A................................EIN; EINE
above ....UBER
again ....WIEDER
alas...................ACH; WEHE
ass or donkey ....ESEL
beer...................................BIER
blood..................................BLUT
count...................................GRAF
eat ....ESSEN
eight ....ACHT
evening............................ABEND
everything.........................ALLES
four.....................................VIER
gentleman..........................HERR
hall....................................SAAL
hall, great ....AULA
heaven ....HIMMEL
hunter ....JAGER
I...ICH
ice ....EIS

53 BLUE: BLAU
GER. CHIEF: OBER

a GERMAN WORDS: *continued*
iron....................EISEN
league..................BUNDNIS
love....................LIEBE
mind...................GEMUT
Mrs. ....FRAU
nation or people ....VOLK
never...................NIE
new ....NEU
no ....NEIN
noble ....EDEL
old ....ALT
one ....EIN; EINE
out ....AUS
soft...................LEISE
song...................LIED
spirit ....GEIST
state ....STAAT
steel ....STAHL
storm...................STURM
stress...................DRANG
than...................ALS
the...................DAS, DER, DIE
three...................DREI
thunder...................DONNER
town ....STADT
us ....UNS
very ....ECHT, SEHR
with ....MIT
without...................OHNE

b you.........IHR, SIE; DICH, EUCH
your..................IHR; DEIN,
..................EUER, EURE, IHRE
germfree ....ASEPTIC; ANTISEPTIC
get by, barely ....EKE
get out! ....SCAT, SHOO; SCRAM
ghastly...................DIRE, GRIM;
...........AWFUL, LURID; MACABRE;
...................GRUESOME
ghost...................SHADE, SPOOK;
...................SHADOW, SPIRIT,
...................WRAITH; SPECTER
ghost, Indian...............BHUT
giant...........HUGE; JUMBO, TITAN
giant, Norse...................YMIR
giant, rock-throwing bronze ..TALOS
giant killed by Apollo ....OTUS
Giant ranch ....REATA
giants, Biblical.............ANAK, EMIM
gibbon, Malay...................LAR
gift ....TALENT; PRESENT
gift giver ....DONOR
gift recipient...................DONEE
gig ....NAPPER
Gilgit language ....SHINA
gills, four ....PINT
gilt...................DORE
gin...................TRAP
gingerbread tree ....DOOM
ginkgo tree ....ICHO

giraffelike animal ....OKAPI *c*
girasol ....OPAL
girder...................TRUSS
girdle...................OBI; CEST, SASH
girl ....FOX, GAL, SIS; CHIT,
........DAME, MAID, MISS; BROAD,
..............CHICK, HONEY; MAIDEN
Girl Scouts founder ....LOW
girth, saddle ....CINCH
gist...................NUB; PITH
give, legally ....REMISE
give up ....CEDE; WAIVE, YIELD
glacial chasm...................CREVASSE
glacial pinnacle ....SERAC
glacial snow field........FIRN, NEVE
glacial stage, last Eur. ....WURM
glacial trough...................DORR
gladly, once...................FAIN
gland ....PINEAL; ADRENAL,
...................THYROID
glass...................LENS; MIRROR
glass, blue...................SMALT
glass, bubble in...................BLEB
glass, partly fused ..FRIT; PARISON
glass, super-transparent ....UVIOL
glass-furnace mouth...........BOCCA
glass ingredient ....SILICON
glassmaker ....GLAZIER
glassmaker's oven...................LEHR
glassy ....HYALINE
glazier's tack ....BRAD *d*
gleam...................GLINT
glide...................SKIM, SLIP;
...................SKATE, SLIDE
globe...................ORB; SPHERE
gloomy...................DARK, DOUR,
...................GLUM, GRUM; MURKY;
...................DREARY, SULLEN
"Gloomy Dean" ....INGE
glove...................MITT
glove leather ....KID; NAPA; SUEDE
glower ....LOUR; SCOWL
glowing...................ROSY; RUDDY;
...................ARDENT
glut...................CLOY, SATE;
...................GORGE; EXCESS;
...................SURFEIT, SURPLUS
gnarl...................KNUR
gnat, small...................MIDGE
gnome...................GREMLIN
gnome in Germanic folklore ....
...................KOBOLD
go...............RUN; WEND; DEPART
goad ....PROD, SPUR, URGE;
...........IMPEL; INCITE; PROVOKE
goal ....AIM, END;
...................SCORE; TARGET
goa powder...................ARAROBA
goat, Alpine mountain ....IBEX
goat, Asian ....JAGLA, SEROW

WOODEN GOBLET: MAZER
GRANT'S OPPONENT: R.E.LEE
"GOOD EARTH" HEROINE: OLAN

goat, wild ....TAHR, THAR
goat antelope, Himalayan....GORAL
goat god................................PAN
goatsucker, large ....POTOO
gob ....TAR, WAD; LUMP;
..........CLUMP; SAILOR, SEAMAN
go back................REVERT
goblet, medieval ....HANAP
goblin ....PUCK
goby, small ....MAPO
Gods and Goddesses ....
..............................See page 198.
Goethe heroine ....MIGNON
Goethe work ....FAUST; EGMONT
golconda ....MINE
gold, of................................AURIC
golden ....AUREATE
Golden Fleece keeper ....AEETES
Golden Fleece seeker..........JASON
golden oriole ....PIROL
golden oriole, Eur. ....LORIOT
golden-touch king ....MIDAS
gold leaf, imitation ....ORMOLU
golf attendant ....CADDY; CADDIE
golf ball holder..........................TEE
golf ball position.........................LIE
golf club ....IRON, WOOD;
.........................BAFFY, CLEEK,
..............SPOON, WEDGE;
..........DRIVER, MASHIE, PUTTER;
........................BRASSIE, NIBLICK
golf club, part...............TOE; HEEL;
..............................HOSEL, SHAFT
golf course, part............TEE; TRAP;
..........GREEN, ROUGH; BUNKER,
........................DOGLEG; FAIRWAY
golf hole ....CUP
golf score......PAR; BOGIE, EAGLE;
..................................BIRDIE
golf shot ....CHIP, HOOK, LOFT,
.........PUTT; DRIVE, PITCH, SLICE
golf stroke, ground-striking ....BAFF
gomuti ....ARENGA
gondolier's song.........BARCAROLE
gone ....OUT; AWAY; PASSED
gone by.............AGO; PAST, YORE
gonfalon ....BANNER
"Good Queen Bess" ....ORIANA
goods ....WARES;
.................THINGS; EFFECTS
goose, male ....GANDER
goose, sea ....SOLAN
goose, wild...........................BRANT
gooseberry...............................FABE
goose call ....HONK
goose genus ....ANSER
gorge ....GLUT; CHASM;
..........................RAVINE; SATIATE
Gorgons, The..MEDUSA, STHENO;
....EURYALE

Gorgons' parent ....CETO;
....................................PHORCYS
gorse......................WHIN; FURZE
Gottfried, sister of ....ELSA
gourd rattle ....MARACA
gourmet...........................EPICURE
government patronage..........PORK
governor, Pers. ....SATRAP
governor, Turk. ....BEY
grace ....ADORN; PRAYER
graceful...................................EASY;
........................FLUID; ELEGANT
Graces, aka ....CHARITES
Graces, father of The ....ZEUS
Graces, mother of The EURYNOME
Graces, The.........AGLAIA, THALIA;
........................EUPHROSYNE
grackle ....DAW; MYNAH
grade ....MARK, RANK,
....................RATE, STEP; CLASS,
.......................SCORE; CALIBER
grade, mediocre......................CEE
gradient ....SLOPE
graduation attire ....CAP; GOWN
Graf ___ ....SPEE
graft ....FIX; BRIBE; SCION
grain ....OAT, RYE;
.................SEED, WALE; DURRA,
................SPELT, WHEAT; MILLET
grain, coarse ....SAMP
grain, ground.......................GRIST
grain beetle larva ....CADELLE
grain husk ....BRAN
grain stalks ....HAULM
grammatically dissect ....PARSE
grampus ....ORC
grange ....FARM
grant .....CEDE; AWARD; CONFER;
....................CONCEDE; TRANSFER
granular snow ....FIRN, NEVE
grape ....UVA; MUSCAT
..................CATAWBA, CONCORD
grape, white ....MALAGA
grape disease........................ESCA
grapefruit ....POMELO
grape genus ....VITIS
grape juice ....MUST
grape juice, unfermented ....STUM
grape refuse ....MARC
Grapes of Wrath, The family ..JOAD
grape syrup ....DIBS, SAPA
graphite ....KISH; KEESH
grasp ....SEE, GRIP;
..............RANGE, SEIZE; CLENCH,
........................CLUTCH, FATHOM
grass ....BENT, HEMP,
..........................REED; SEDGE;
....................DARNEL; TIMOTHY
grass, Andes ....ICHU
grass, blue ....POA

55

GREEK CONFLICT: AGON
CATEGORIZED GROUPS: TAXA
GREENSWARD: SOD/TURF

ANCIENT GREEK WT: MINA
GUDRUN'S VICTIM: ATLI
GREEK CROSS: TAU
OLDER COIN: OBOL
ARS GRATIA ARTIS

grass, range / gullible person

a
grass, range ....GRAMA
grass, sour ....SORREL
grasshopper...................GRIG
grassland..SWARD.....SAVANNAH
grasslands, S. Afr. ....VELDT
grasslands, western ....RANGE
grass stem ....CULM
grass tuft......................HASSOCK
grate ....JAR; RASP; SCRAPE
gratify.....................SATE; PLEASE
grating ....GRILLE
gratuitous....................FREE
gratuity........................TIP
grave ....DIRE; SOBER, STAID;
..................SEVERE, SOMBER
gravestone(s)........STELE; STELAE
Gray, botanist ....ASA
gray, mole ....TAUPE
gray and black plaid ....MAUD
grayish ....ASHEN
grayish-brown............DUN; TAUPE
grayish-reddish brown ....KAFFA
gray kingbird ....PIPIRI
gray parrot, Afr. ....JAKO
graze ....SKIM, SKIP;
...................BRUSH, CAROM;
.................GLANCE; RICOCHET
grease.......................OIL; LARD
greater ....MORE; MAJOR
Greece ....HELLAS

b
greedy...........AVID; PIGGISH
Greek ....HELLENE
Greek alphabet ....See alphabet.
Gr. amphora ....PELIKE
Gr. assembly ....AGORA
Gr. athletic contest ....AGON
Gr. author ....ZENO; AESOP;
..............HOMER, PLATO, TIMON;
.........HESIOD, PINDAR, SAPPHO,
.....STRABO, THALES; PLUTARCH
Gr. city ....POLIS
Gr. city, ancient........ELIS; SPARTA
Gr. colony in Asia Minor ....IONIA
Gr. column ....DORIC, IONIC
Gr. commonalty ....DEMOS
Gr. community ....DEME
Gr. dialect ....AEOLIC
Gr. festival city....................NEMEA
Gr. garment ....CHITON
Gr. goddess of night ....NYX
Gr. hero ....AJAX; JASON
Gr. market place ....AGORA
Gr. mythical flyer.................ICARUS
Gr. pastoral poet ....BION
Gr. patriarch ....ARIUS
Gr. priest ....MYST
Gr. quadrennial festival..........DELIA
Gr. sculptor ....PHIDIAS
Gr. shield ....PELTA
Gr. township ....DEME

c
green ....BICE, JADE; BERYL,
..............FRESH, OLIVE; RESEDA;
..............EMERALD, UNTRIED
green, pale grayish ....CELADON
Green Bay tribe ....SAUK
green chalcedony...............JASPER
green cheese...................SAPSAGO
green chrysolite...............PERIDOT
Green Hornet's valet ....KATO
green in heraldry ....VERT
Greenland town ....ETAH; THULE
Green Mansions bird-girl.........RIMA
Green Mountain hero............ALLEN
greeting.........AVE; HAIL; SALUTE
grief...DOLOR.....WOE; SORROW
grimalkin ....CAT
grinding tooth ....MOLAR
groom, Indian.....SAIS, SICE, SYCE
groove ....RUT; GRIND; ROUTINE
grooved ....LIRATE; STRIATE
grope ....FEEL
gross.........................CRASS
grotesque figure ....MAGOT
ground grain ....MEAL
groundhog......................MARMOT
groundnut ....SOJA; APIOS
group...........BAND, BODY, CREW,
.................TEAM; BATCH, CROWD;
...............ASSORT, GATHER
grouper................................MERO

d
grouse......................PTARMIGAN
grove of trees ....COPSE
grow ....WAX; RAISE;
....................................INCREASE
growl ....GNAR; SNARL
grub...................FOOD; LARVA
grudge ....SPITE
gruel, maize......................ATOLE
gruesome ....GRISLY; MACABRE
guard ....SENTRY
Gudrun, husband of.................ATLI
guenon monkey......................MONA
guest house ....INN
Guinea tree ....MORA
guide ....LEAD; PILOT, STEER
guiding rule ....MOTTO
Guido's note ....E LA
guild of merchants ....HANSE
guillemot ....COOT; MURRE
guilty...........NOCENT; CULPABLE
guinea fowl, young.................KEET
guinea pig ....CAVY
gulf, Med. ....TUNIS
gulf, southeast Asian ....TONKIN
gulf of the Ionian Sea ....ARTA
gull ....MEW; SKUA;
.................TERN, XEMA
gullet ....MAW; CRAW
gullible person...............SAP; DUPE;
.................CHUMP; SUCKER

GUITAR GADGET: CAPO
GULF OF CELEBES SEA: MORO
GREEK DESTINY: MOIRA
MODERN GREEK: DEMOTIC

a *Gulliver's Travels* author ....SWIFT
Gulliver's Travels race ......YAHOOS
gulls, of.................................LARINE
gully, Afr. ....DONGA
gulp...SWIG
gum ....RESIN; BALATA
gum, astringent ....KINO
gum arabic.........................ACACIA
gumbo....................................OKRA
gum resin ....ELEMI, LOBAN,
....MYRRH

gum tree, Central Amer. ....TUNO   c
gun: slang ....GAT, ROD;
.............................IRON; PIECE;
..................HEATER, ROSCOE
gun-barrel cleaner ....SWAB
gusto ....ZEST; RELISH
guy-rope ....STAY, VANG
gymnastics move ....KIP
gypsum, kind of ....GESSO;
....SELENITE
gypsy ....ROM; ROMANY

H

H.............................AITCH
habit ....RUT; WONT; USAGE
habitation ....LIFE; ABODE
habituate ....INURE
habituated ....USED
hackney coach: Fr. ....FIACRE
had been ....WAS
Hades....................DIS; HELL;
..................ORCUS, PLUTO,
..............SHEOL; TARTARUS
Hades, area near ....EREBUS
Hades ferryman................CHARON
Hades river..............STYX; LETHE;
b ....ACHERON
hag ....CRONE, WITCH
haggard...................WAN; GAUNT;
....DRAWN
Haggard novel ....SHE
hail..................AVE; LAUD;
..............EXTOL, GREET;
.............SALUTE; ORIGINATE
hail, naut. ....AHOY; AVAST
hair, animal........FUR; MANE, PELT
hair, false.............RUG, WIG; FALL;
....TOUPEE
hair, remove....................DEPILATE
hair, rigid...............................SETA
hair, quantity of.....................CURL,
.................HANK, LOCK; BANGS,
...........................SHOCK, TRESS
hairdo ....AFRO, COIF; SHAG;
.................BANGS, BRAID, PLAIT;
.................CHIGNON, PAGEBOY
hair dressing...................POMADE
hair knot.................BUN; CHIGNON
hairnet.................................SNOOD
hair shirt...............................CILICE
hair splitter............................PART
hairy ....COMOSE, PILOSE
Haitian voodoo deity ....LOA
Halcyone, husband of ....CEYX
half ....MOIETY
half-boot.................................PAC

half dozen.................................SIX
halfpenny, Brit. ....MAG
half-way ....MID
hallow ....BLESS
halo .....AURA; CORONA, NIMBUS;
....................AUREOLA, AUREOLE
halt ....LAME, STOP; CEASE
Ham, son of ....CUSH
Hamite ....BERBER, SOMALI
Hamite people of Eth. ....SAHO
Hamitic language.......AGAO, AGAU
hamlet..........BURG, DORP, TOWN
Hamlet's castle ....ELSINORE
Hamlet's friend................HORATIO   d
Hamlet's jester ....YORICK
Hamlet's love ....OPHELIA
hammer ....KEVEL; POUND
hammer, heavy ....MAUL
hammer, large ....SLEDGE
hammer, lead....................MADGE
hammer, tilt ....OLIVER
hammerhead part...................PEEN
hamper ....CRAMP; FETTER;
....TRAMMEL
hand ....AID, PUD; MANUS
hand, clenched........................FIST
hand, whist ....TENACE
handbill ....FLIER
handcuff.............................MANACLE
handle ....EAR, LUG, PAW;
.....................ANSA, HILT, KNOB;
.............HELVE, TREAT; MANAGE
handle, scythe....................SNATH,
.....................SNEAD; SNATHE
handle roughly ....MAUL
hand of cards, abandon a.......FOLD
handsome man ......HUNK; ADONIS
handwriting ....SCRIPT
handwriting on the wall ....MENE,
...........MENE, TEKEL, UPHARSIN
hang ....LOOM;
......................HOVER; DANGLE,
....................IMPEND; SUSPEND

a hang fire ....PEND, SLOW
hankering ....YEN; ITCH
Hannibal's defeat, site of ....ZANA
Hannibal victory, site of a .CANNAE
happen ....OCCUR; BEFALL,
....................BETIDE, CHANCE
happening ....EVENT
harangue ....RANT, RAVE;
....................TIRADE; DIATRIBE
Haran, son of ....LOT
harass ....NAG; BESET; PESTER
harbinger ....HERALD
harbor ....BAY; COVE,
....................PORT; HAVEN;
....................REFUGE; SHELTER
harden ....GEL, SET; INURE
hardwood ......ASH, OAK; HICKORY
Hardy heroine ....TESS
hare, immature ....LEVERET
hare genus ....LEPUS
harem ....ZENANA; SERAGLIO
harem guard ....EUNUCH
harem room ....ODA
harlot of Jericho ....RAHAB
harm ....BANE, HURT;
....................DAMAGE, INJURE
harmony................TUNE; ACCORD;
....................BALANCE, CONCORD
harp, ancient triangular ......TRIGON
Harp constellation....................LYRA
b harp guitar key ....DITAL
Harpies, The.....AELLO; CELAENO,
....................OCYPETE; PODARGE
harrow ....LOOT; PLUNDER
harrow blade........................DISC
Harrow's rival ....ETON
hartebeest ....TORA; KAAMA
harvest ....REAP
harvest goddess ....OPS
hashish ....KEF; KEEF,
....................KHAT; BHANG
hasty pudding ....SEPON
hat....................FEZ, TAM; BERET,
..............BUSBY, DERBY, TOQUE;
......BOATER, BONNET, BOWLER,
........CALASH, CAPOTE, CASTOR,
......CLOCHE, FEDORA, MOBCAP;
....................PILLBOX, STETSON
hat, straw.TOYO; MILAN; PANAMA
hat, sun....................................TERAI
hatred............ODIUM, CONTEMPT
hautboy............................OBOE
haven ....ASYLUM, REFUGE;
................RETREAT; SANCTUARY ✺
Hawaiian bird, extinct....MAMO
Haw. bird, red-tailed............KOAE
Haw. dance ....HULA
Haw. farewell/greeting ....ALOHA
Haw. feast ....LUAU
Haw. food..............................POI

Haw. garland ....LEI   *c*
Haw. goddess of fire ....PELE
Haw. goose ....NENE
Haw. gooseberry....................POHA
Haw. governor, first...............DOLE
Haw. honeycreeper ....IIWI
Haw. loincloth ....MALO
Haw. porch ....LANAI
hawk ....KITE; PEDDLE
hawk, fish ....OSPREY
hawk, leash for a ....LUNE
hawk, unfledged ....EYAS
hawk-headed god of Egypt .HORUS
hawk's cage ....MEW
hawthorn, Eng. ....MAY
hay, spread to dry ....TED
haystack ....RICK
hazard ....RISK; PERIL;
....................CHANCE, DANGER
hazelnut............................FILBERT
head ....NOB; BEAN,
....................LEAD; BRAIN, CHIEF,
....................FROTH; LEADER,
....................NOGGIN, NOODLE
head, crown of the ....PATE
head-and-shoulders art ....BUST
head covering................CAP, HAT,
....................TAM; HOOD, VEIL;
................BERET, SCARF, SHAWL
headdress, bishop's..............MITER
headdress of hair, elaborate ..POUF   *d*
headgear, brimless..............TOQUE
headgear, clerical ....BERETTA,
....................BIRETTA
headgear, military.....KEPI; SHAKO;
....................HELMET
headgear, Muslim ....TARBOOSH
headgear, Turk. ....FEZ
headland........CAPE, NESS; POINT
headstrong ....TOUGH;
....................DOGGED, MULISH;
....................STUBBORN
health resort........................SPA
heap ....MASS, PILE; STACK
hear ....HEED; LISTEN
hear ye! ....OYES, OYEZ
heart....................CORE; CENTER
heart auricle(s).......ATRIA; ATRIUM
heart contraction............SYSTOLE
heartless ....CRUEL; CALLOUS
heart problem ....ANGINA
heat....................................WARM
heat, sexual ....ESTRUS
heath....................................MOOR
heathen ....PAGAN
heathen god............................IDOL
heather ....LING
heath evergreen....................ERICA
heating apparatus, old............ETNA
heavenly ....EDENIC, URANIC

58

heavenly being....................ANGEL;
....SERAPHIM
Hebrew alphabet........See alphabet.
Heb. descendant ....JEW
Heb. measure ....OMER; EPHAH
Heb. month, ancient.................ABIB
Heb. zitherlike instrument .....ASOR
heckle ....RAZZ; TAUNT
Hector, mother of ....HECUBA
Hecuba, husband of ....PRIAM
hedge plant ....PRIVET
heed..............CARE, HEAR, OBEY;
..............................LISTEN, NOTICE
heel of the foot.......................CALX
height..........APEX, PEAK; SUMMIT
heir.............................SON; SCION;
....................HERITOR, LEGATEE
Helen of Troy, lover of...........PARIS
Helen of Troy, mother of........LEDA
helical ....SPIRAL
Helios ....SUN
Helios, daughter of..............CIRCE
hell............................HADES, SHEOL
Hellespont swimmer.......LEANDER
helmet, 15th-century ....SALLET
helmet, medieval ....ARMET;
....HEAUME
helmet, Rom. ....GALEA
helmetshaped.................GALEATE
helm position.........................ALEE
helmsman ....PILOT
Heloise, husband of ....ABELARD
help ....AID; ABET, BACK,
...............................HAND; ASSIST,
............................RELIEF, SUCCOR
helper..............................CAD; AIDE
Helvetic................................SWISS
hem in ....BESET
hemp, broken fibers of.............TOW
hemp, Afr. bowstring ....IFE
hemp, Manila ....ABACA
hemp shrub..............................PUA
hemp stalk.............................HARL
hen ....BIDDY, LAYER
hence ....OFF, AWAY;
...............................THEREFORE
Henry IV, birthplace of ....PAU
hep ....ON TO
Hera, son of...........................ARES
herald...........................PRESAGE;
................ANNOUNCE, PROCLAIM
heraldic bearing........ORLE; FILLET
herald's coat ....TABARD
herb ....LEEK, MINT,
..................MOLY, WORT; TANSY;
.................YARROW; OREGANO
herb, aromatic ......BASIL; DITTANY
herb, bitter.....................RUE; ALOE
herb, umbel family.................ANISE
herb, forage ....SULLA

herb, medicinal.........ALOE; SENNA
herb, S. A. ....ANU
herbaceous plant, broad-leaved ......
....FORB
herb of grace ....RUE
Hercules, captive of ....IOLE
Hercules, father of ....ZEUS
Hercules, horse of ....ARION
Hercules, monster slain by ..HYDRA
Hercules, mother of ....ALCMENE
Hercules, wife of....................HEBE
herd ....PROD; DRIVE
hereditary factor.....................GENE
hereditary property ....UDAL
heretic, 4th-Century ....ARIUS
heretofore ....ERENOW
Hermes, mother of ....MAIA
Hermes, son of ....PAN
Hermes, wife of...................HERSE;
.................CHIONE; AGLAUCUS
hermit ....RECLUSE;
.................................ANCHORITE
hermit, pre-Islamic.................HANIF
Hero, love of...................LEANDER
heroic ....EPIC; EPICAL
heroic poem ....EPOS
heroic song of Iceland............EDDA
heron ....EGRET; BITTERN
herring, lake..........................CISCO
herring, small Eur. ....SPRAT
herring, young ....BRIT; BRITT
herring barrel..........................CADE
hesitate ....HALT; PAUSE,
.............................WAVER; DITHER,
..........................FALTER, TEETER
hesitation sounds.....................ERS
Hesperides, one of the.........AEGLE
Hezekiah, mother of ....ABI
Hi and Lois, child of .....DOT; DITTO
hiatus ....GAP; LACUNA
hickory tree.........................NOGAL
hidden..............ARCANE, BURIED,
.......................COVERT, SECRET,
..................VEILED; CLOAKED
hide..........................VEIL; CACHE
hide, undressed...........................KIP
hide of an animal ....PELT, SKIN
hide thong ....RIEM
Highlander...............................SCOT
high point..........TOP; APEX, PEAK;
................................CREST; ZENITH
highway ....PIKE; ROUTE
highwayman ..LADRON; LADRONE
"Highwayman, The" poet......NOYES
hike...........................CLIMB, TRAMP
hill, broad................LOMA, LOMITA
hill, crest of a.........................BROW
hill, flat-topped ....MESA
hill, isolated ....BUTTE
hill, S.Afr. ....KOP

a hill formed by a glacier ....PAHA,
....KAME
hillock: Brit. ....TUMP
hillside, Scot. ....BRAE
hilltop......................................KNAP
hilt of a sword........HAFT; HANDLE
Himalayan monkshood ....ATIS
hind..................ROE; BACK, REAR
hindrance...................BAR; SNAG;
.......................BLOCK; HURDLE;
...............................BARRICADE
Hindu, low caste ....KORI
Hindu ascetic............YOGI; FAKIR
Hindu breath of life ....PRANA
Hindu era ....YUGA
Hindu essence of being ....SAT
Hindu garment.......................SARI
Hindu gentleman ....BABU
Hindu god of love ....KAMA
Hindu good spirit ....DEVA
Hindu holy man ....SADHU;
....SADDHU
Hindu magic..........................MAYA
Hindu mendicant....................NAGA
Hindu philosophy ....YOGA
Hindu poet ....TAGORE
Hindu prince ....RAJA; RAJAH
Hindu princess ....RANA
Hindu queen..............RANI; RANEE
Hindu sacred writings ....VEDA
b Hindu sect..........JAIN, SIKH; JAINA
Hindu slave.............................DAS
Hindu scripture ....AGAMA;
....TANTRA
Hindustani language ..URDU; HINDI
Hindu stringed instrument.......BINA,
..............................VINA; SITAR
Hindu teacher.......................GURU
Hindu term of respect............SAHIB
Hindu title ....SRI
Hindu widow's suicide........SUTTEE
hint ....TIP; CLUE; POINTER
hip.............................COXA, ILIA
hip, of the ....ILIAC
hip, once ....HEP
Hippocrates, birthplace of.........KOS
hippodrome.........................ARENA
hipster ....CAT
hire..............................LET; RENT;
.......................ENGAGE; CHARTER
hired carriage ....HACK
history ....LORE, PAST
hit ....JAB; BASH, BIFF, CUFF,
.................WHAP, WHOP; PUNCH
hitherto ....YET
hit on the head............BOP; BEAN,
...............................CONK, COSH
hive of bees ....SKEP
hoard ....AMASS, STORE
hoarder ....MISER

hoarfrost................................RIME
hoary ....OLD; GRAY
hoax........RUSE; FRAUD; CANARD
hobgoblin ....PUCK; SPRITE
hock ....PAWN, WINE
hock of a horse ....GAMBREL
hodgepodge ....OLIO; JUMBLE,
.........................MEDLEY; VARIETY
hog, female ....GILT
hog, wild..................................BOAR
hog deer.....................................AXIS
hog plum, W. Indian...AMRA, JOBO
hog's guts............................HASLET
hoist ....HEAVE
hold...........................GRIP, KEEP;
.......................GRASP; CLUTCH;
..................CONTAIN, POSSESS
hold back ....DETER
hold fast: naut. ....BELAY
holding device ....VISE; TONGS
hole...........................FIX; LAIR,
................RENT, VENT; CAVITY;
...................ORIFICE, RUPTURE
hole for molten metal ....SPRUE
hole-in-one...............................ACE
holidays, Rom. ....FERIA
hollow ....IDLE, SINK; EMPTY;
...................CAVITY; CONCAVE
holly............ASSI, HOLM; YAUPON
holm oak ....ILEX; HOLLY
holy water font ....STOUP
homage................................HONOR
home ....ABODE, HAVEN,
........................HOUSE; REFUGE;
.............HABITAT; DWELLING
homestead: Brit. ....TOFT
homeopath school founder HERING
Homer.......................................KOR
Homer, epic by ....ILEAD;
....ODYSSEY
"Home Sweet Home" poet ...PAYNE
hominy ....SAMP
homosexuals........................GAYS
honey ....MEL; MELL
honey-badger ....RATEL
honeybee ....DESERET
honey buzzard ....PERN
honeycomb, like a ....FAVOSE
honey drink ....MEAD
honey-eater bird ....IAO; MOHO
honey possum.......................TAIT
honor ....HAIL; EXALT,
.......................KUDOS; ESTEEM,
...................HOMAGE, REPUTE
honorarium ....TIP
honorary commission ....BREVET
Honshu bay ....ISE
Honshu city..........................GIFU
Honshu seaport..........KOBE, KURE
hooded garment..................PARKA

c

d

a hoodoo ....JINX
hoodwinked ....HAD; CONNED;
..............................SWINDLED
hoofbeat ....CLOP
hook, large ....CLEEK
hooked ....HAMATE; FALCATE
Hoover Dam lake.................MEAD
hopscotch stone ....PEEVER
Horeb, Mount.......................SINAI
horizontal timber ....LINTEL
horn..................................CORNU
horn, crescent moon ....CUSP
horn, Heb. ....SHOFAR
hornblende ....EDENITE
hornless stag...................POLLARD
hors d'oeuvre ....CANAPE
horse ....COB, NAG;
......................MOUNT, STEED;
......................EQUINE, JENNET;
..................CHARGER, MUSTANG
horse, Australian ....WALER
horse, brown...............BAY; ROAN;
..............................SORREL
horse, draft..........................SHIRE
horse, female.......................MARE
horse, male....................STALLION
horse, piebald ....PINTO
horse, Polish wild ....TARPAN
horse, small ....PONY
horse, spirited ....STEED
b horse, young ....COLT, FOAL
horse blanket......................MANTA
horse-collar part...................HAME
horse disease ....SPAVIN
horsehair............................SETON
horse-mackerel ....SCAD
horsemanship..................MANEGE
horses, goddess of ....EPONA
horseshoe gripper.................CALK
horse-shoeing stall ....TRAVE
horse sound......................NEIGH;
.........................NICKER, WHINNY
horse's sideways tread ....VOLT
Horus, mother of ....ISIS
Hosea, wife of....................GOMER

host.........ARMY; HORDE, WAFER *c*
hostelry ....INN
hot-air chamber....................OVEN
hot spring, eruptive ....GEYSER
Hottentot ....NAMA
hourly....................................HORAL
house.......................HOME; VILLA;
.....................COTTAGE, MANSION;
..............................RESIDENCE
household gods....................LARES
housetop..............................ROOF
Howdy Doody's original name ....
..............................ELMER
howl ....BAY; WAIL; ULULATE
howler monkey ....MONO; ARABA
hubbub .....DIN; CLAMOR, TUMULT
hue ....COLOR,
..............................SHADE, TINGE
huge ....VAST; JUMBO; MASSIVE
Huguenot leader................ADRETS
hull.............................POD; HUSK
humble ......MEEK; ABASE, LOWLY
hummingbird ....AVA; TOPAZ
humorist..................................WIT
humpback salmon ..HADDO, HOLIA
Hung. dog ....PULI
Hung. hero ....NAGY
Hung. playwright...............MOLNAR
Hung. violinist.........................AUER
Huns, king of the ....ATLI; ETZEL;
..............................ATTILA *d*
hunter ....ORION; NIMROD
hunting cry ....TO-HO; YOICKS;
..............................TALLY-HO
huntress...........DIANA; ATALANTA
hup count ....ONE
hurry ....HIE; HASTEN
hurt...............HARM, PAIN; INJURE
hurtful ....MALEFIC
husk, cereal...........................BRAN
hut, crude Mex. ....JACAL
hymn...........................ODE; SONG
hypnotic state ....TRANCE
hypocritical remarks.......JAZZ, JIVE
hyson ....TEA

I

Iago, wife of..........................EMILIA
Ibsen character.............ASE; NORA
ice, slushy............SISH; LOLLY
ice block, glacial ....SERAC
Icelandic tale ....EDDA
ice mass ....BERG, FLOE
icy..GELID
idea, start of an ....GERM
ideal .... UTOPIAN

identical.......EVEN, SAME; EQUAL,
..........................EXACT; PRECISE
idiot......................FOOL; MORON;
..............................CRETIN
idle ....LAZE, LOAF
idolatrous............................PAGAN
Idumaea ....EDOM
if ever....................................ONCE
if not.....................................ELSE

a ignoble...............LOW; BASE, VILE;
.................COMMON, VULGAR
ignominy.......SHAME; DISHONOR
ignorant......................UNAWARE
ignore.................SNUB; SLIGHT;
..................................NEGLECT
illness.................FLU; COLD;
..................................DISEASE
illuminated............................LIT
illumination unit.......................LUX
illusion...........MIRAGE; CHIMERA,
..................FANTASY, FIGMENT
ill-will................SPITE; RANCOR
image.........COPY, IDOL; REPLICA
image, religious............ICON, IKON
imbibe......................NIP; DRINK
imitate......................APE; COPY,
....................MOCK; MIMIC
imitation................FAKE; MIMESIS
imitation gems......................PASTE
immature seed....................OVULE
immediately.....NOW; ANON, ASAP
immense..................HUGE, VAST;
....................GIANT; TITANIC;
..............................COLOSSAL
immerse.............DIP; DUCK, DUNK;
....................DOUSE, SOUSE
imou pine.......................RIMU
impair..................MAR; HARM,
....................HURT; BLEMISH,
b ....TARNISH, VITIATE
impart.........LEND, TELL; CONVEY,
....................................REPORT
impartial......................FAIR, JUST;
....................................NEUTRAL
impede..................BAR; BLOCK;
....................HAMPER, HINDER;
....................................OBSTRUCT
impel........MOVE; DRIVE; PROPEL
impertinent..........................PERT;
....................SASSY; BRAZEN;
.................FORWARD; IMPUDENT
implement, pounding..........PESTLE
implement, worker's.............TOOL
implied...................TACIT; UNSAID
import..............SENSE; MEANING
important..............VITAL; URGENT
importune.............BESET, HARRY,
....................HOUND; BADGER,
....................HARASS, PESTER
impose........LEVY; FOIST, WREAK
impost......................TAX
imposture.................RUSE; TRICK
impoverish..........RUIN; DEPLETE;
....................................BANKRUPT
Impressionist painter.........DEGAS,
.............MANET, MONET; RENOIR
imprison..................JAIL; IMMURE
improve.....HELP; AMEND, RALLY;
....................BETTER; UPGRADE

improvise music............VAMP *c*
impudence..........LIP; GUFF, SASS;
.................BRASS, CHEEK, NERVE
impudent person...................SNOT
impurities, layer of.............SCUM
inactive......................IDLE; INERT
inadequate.........WEAK; SCANTY,
....................SKIMPY; WANTING
in addition.........TOO; ALSO, PLUS
in agreement.......AS ONE; UNITED
inborn.................INBRED, NATIVE
incense................................JOSS
incense ingredient.....GUM; SPICE;
....................................STACTE
incentive.................PROD, SPUR;
....................FILLIP; IMPETUS
incessantly.....EVER; ENDLESSLY
inch, .001 of an.....................MIL
incinerate...........BURN; CREMATE
incite..........GOAD, SPUR; ROUSE
inclination..................BENT, CANT,
.................TILT; SLOPE; TALENT;
....................................GRADIENT
inclined................APT; PRONE
inclined way................RAMP
incompletely......................SEMI
inconsiderable.....PETTY; PALTRY;
....................TRIVIAL; PICAYUNE
increase...................HIKE, RISE;
....................BOOST, RAISE
incursion.................RAID; FORAY *d*
indentation, small........DING, POCK
India, minstrel of...................BHAT
Indian aborigine..................GOND
Indian coin, former.............PICE
Indian corn............................MAIZE
Indian dance drama................RAS
Indian deer....................SAMBAR
Indian fried wheat cake..........PURI
Indian ground salt.........REH; USAR
Indian intoxicant...................SOMA
Indian lady..............................BIBI
Indian nursemaid...................AYAH
Indian ox..............................ZEBU
Indian servant......................MATY
Indian tenant farmer..............RYOT
Indian wild ox......................GAUR
indict..............CHARGE; ARRAIGN
indifferent..............ALOOF; STOLID
indigo plant............................ANIL
indistinct, make....................BLUR
indite..........PEN; WRITE; SCRIBE
individual......................ONE; SELF
Indo-Chin. people.............LAO, TAI;
....................................SHAN
Indo-Eur. ....ARYAN
indolent..........IDLE, LAZY; OTIOSE
induce..................CAUSE, SPAWN
industrial arts class................SHOP
industrial fuel........................COKE

a ineffectual.................VAIN, WEAK;
...............FUTILE; IMPOTENT
inelastic......................................LIMP
inert ....IDLE
infatuation ....PASSION
infection's liquid matter.............PUS
inflexible ....RIGID; ADAMANT
inflict...........FOIST, VISIT, WREAK
inflorescence .....RACEME, SPADIX
influence ....SWAY;
...................AFFECT, EFFECT,
...................IMPACT, WEIGHT
information............................DATA
informer: slang ....NARK
ingenuous ....NAIVE; ARTLESS
inheritor...............HEIR; LEGATEE
initiate ....OPEN; BEGIN, START
injure...............MAR; HARM, HURT
injured remark......................OUCH
injury ....LESION, TRAUMA
inlaid decoration ....BUHL;
................BOULE; BOULLE
inlet.................BAY, RIA; FJORD
inlet, Dutch ....ZEE
inlet, Orkneys ....VOE
inn ....KHAN, SERAI; HOSTEL,
.......................POSADA; HOSPICE
inn, Turk. ....IMARET
in name only ....NOMINAL
innards ....GUTS
b inner ....INSIDE; VISCERAL
inn in *The Canterbury Tales*............
....TABARD
innkeeper ....PADRONE;
...............................BONIFACE
inquisitive ....NOSY
insane ....MAD; LOCO; CRAZY
insect ....ANT, BEE, BUG, DOR,
...............FLY; FLEA, GNAT, MITE;
...................APHID, EMESA;
...........BEETLE, CADDIS, CICADA,
...................MANTIS; PLOIARIA
insect, adult..........................IMAGO
insect, immature...................PUPA;
...................LARVA; INSTAR
insect, stinging....................WASP
insect body ....THORAX
insect order........................DIPTERA
insertion mark ....CARET
inset...................................PANEL
insidious ....SLY; ALLURING
insincere talk...............CANT, JIVE
insipid...........................DULL, FLAT;
.............BANAL, BLAND, INANE,
...............................VAPID; JEJUNE
insist............PROD, URGE; PRESS
inspire ....STIR; AROUSE,
...........INHALE, KINDLE, PROMPT
install ....SEAT; INSTATE
instance...............CASE; EXAMPLE

instant ....WINK; TRICE;   c
....MOMENT
instigate ....SPUR; ROUSE; KINDLE
instruct...............BRIEF; EDUCATE
instrument, ancient Chin. ....KIN
instrument, Heb. ....TIMBREL
instrument, Jap. 3-stringed ....
....SAMISEN
instrument, lyrelike Afr. ......KISSAR
instrument, naut. ....PELORUS,
....SEXTANT
instrument, Sp. ....CASTENET
instrument, surveying ....TRANSIT
instrument, three-stringed.............
....BANDORE
insulate ......SECLUDE; SEPARATE
insult ....CAG; OFFEND;
....AFFRONT
insurgent ....REBEL
intact ....SOUND, WHOLE
intellect ....MIND; REASON
inter...BURY
interdict ....BAN; FORBID
interferometer ....ETALON
interlock ....LINK, MESH
international pact.............ENTENTE
interpret................READ; RENDER
intersect...................MEET; CROSS
interstice, small.................AREOLA
intervening, in law ....MESNE
interweave ....TWINE; RADDLE   d
in the know.........................AWARE
in the matter of ....IN RE
in the past ....ONCE
in this place ....HERE
intimidate ....AWE, COW; DAUNT
intone ....CHANT
intoxicated ....DRUNK
intricate................................KNOTTY;
....................COMPLEX, TANGLED
intrigue ....CABAL
introduce........BROACH; PRESENT
Inuit boat ....KAYAK
Inuit boot ....MUKLUK
Inuit coat ....PARKA
Inuit house ....IGLOO
Inuit sealskin boot ....KAMIK
Inuit settlement ....ETAH
Inuit woman's knife ....ULU
inundation ....FLOOD, SPATE
....................DELUGE; CATARACT
inveigle......LURE; TEMPT; ENTICE
inventor, elevator......................OTIS
inventor, sewing machine .....HOWE
inventor, steam engine ....WATT
inventor's rights....................PATENT
invest ....ENDOW, ENDUE;
.......................CLOTHE, ORDAIN
investigate ....DELVE, PROBE
investigator.........................TRACER

invite / Italian family

a invite..................ASK, BID; COURT
involve..............ENTAIL; PERTAIN
Io, father of....................INACHUS
iodine source ....KELP
ion, negative ....ANION
ion, positive ....CATION
Ionian city ....TEOS
iota..............................JOT; MITE
Iranian, northern ....KURD
Iranian of central Asia...........SART
irascible ....SURLY, TESTY
irate ....ANGRY; ENRAGED
Ireland........................EIRE, ERIN
iridescent gem ....OPAL
iris, layer of the....................UVEA
iris root...............................ORRIS
Irish assembly ....DAIL
Irish church ....KIL
Irish clan, ancient..................SEPT
Irish competitive meet............FEIS;
................................AENACH
Irish crowning stone ....LIA FAIL
Irish dramatist ....SYNGE; BECKET
Irish-Gaelic............................ERSE
Irish king's home ....TARA
Irish nobleman ....AIRE
Irish poet ....COLUM,
....................MOORE, YEATS
Irish rebel group ....IRA
Irish sweetheart ....AGRA
b Irish writing.............OGAM, OGUM;
.............................OGHAM
iron, of.............................FERRIC
iron disulfide......................PYRITE
ironic ....WRY
iron lung ....CUIRASS
ironwood ....ACLE
irony ....SATIRE
irrigation ditch ....FLUME; SLUICE
irritate................VEX; GALL, RILE;
............ANNOY, CHAFE; NETTLE
irritating sensation ....ITCH
Irtysh, city on the ....OMSK
Isaac, son of.......................EDOM,
...........................ESAU; JACOB
Ishmael, mother of ....HAGAR
Ishmael, son of ....DUMAH
isinglass ....MICA
Isis, husband/brother of ....OSIRIS
island ....AIT, CAY, KEY;
..........HOLM, ISLE; ATOLL, ISLET
island, Aleutian....................ADAK,
................ATTU; KISKA, UMNAK;
..................................TANAGA
island, Argyll.........................IONA
island, Australian ....TASMANIA
island, Azores ....FAIAL
island, Baltic......................ALAND
island, Brit. ....MAN; SARK;
.....................WIGHT; JERSEY

island, Canadian ..DEVON, BANKS;
................BAFFIN; SOMERSET;
.............................VANCOUVER
island, Caribbean ....CUBA;
................ARUBA; TOBAGO;
................ANTIGUA; DOMINICA
island, Chin. ....HIANAN,
...............................QUEMOY
island, Cyclades............KEA; KEOS
island, Dodecanese..............KOS;
................CASO, LERO, SIMI
island, E. Indies.........BALI, JAVA;
........TIMOR; BORNEO, MADURA;
................CELEBES, SUMATRA
island, Fr. ....TAHITI; CORSICA
island, Great Barrier.............OTEA
island, Gr. ....CORFU, CRETE,
................NAXOS, PAROS;
................LESBOS, RHODES
island, Hawaiian ....MAUI, OAHU;
................KAUAI, LANAI; NIIHAU;
..................................MOLOKAI
island, Ionian ....ZANTE
island, Irish...........................ARAN
island, It. ......ELBA; CAPRI; SICILY
island, Jap. ...HONSHU, KYUSHU;
................IWO JIMA; OKINAWA
island, gulf of Riga ....OESEL
island, N. Z. ....NIUE
island, Pac. ....GUAM;
............NAURU, SAMOA, TONGA;
................BIKINI, EASTER, KODIAK,
................MIDWAY, TAHITI;
................VANUATU
island, Philippine........CEBU, JOLO;
................LEYTE, LUZON, PANAY,
......SAMAR; NEGROS; MINDORO,
................PALAWAN; MINDANAO
island, Rhode Island ....BLOCK
Island, Scot. ....HOY; SKYE,
................UIST, YELL; ARRAN,
..................................ISLAY, LEWIS
island, Tanzania ....PEMBA
island in the Firth of Clyde.......BUTE
isolate................................SECLUDE
Islamic leader's title ....SAYYID
Israelite tribe ....DAN, GAD; LEVI;
............ASHER, JUDAH; REUBEN;
.....SIMEON; EPHRAIM, ZEBULUN;
................ISSACHAR, BENJAMIN,
................MANASSEH, NAPHTALI
issue..............EMANATE, PUBLISH
isthmus.................................NECK
Italian, ancient......OSCAN; SABINE
It. actress ....DUSE
It. coins.................................LIRE
It. commune........................ESTE
It. composer ....VERDI; ROSSINI
It. family ....ESTE;
................CENCI, DORIA; MEDICI

c

d

64

a
It. finger-throwing game	MORA
It. painter	RENI; LIPPI; CRESPI, GIOTTO; DA VINCI
It. poet	DANTE, TASSO; ARIOSTO
It. violinmaker	AMATI
It. wine	ASTI

ITALIAN WORDS:
alley	CALLE
dear	CARA, CARO
dough	PASTA
eight	OTTO
enough	BASTA
evening	SERA
field	CAMPO
fly off, to	VOLARE
goat	CAPRA
hand	MANO
harbor	PORTO
harp	ARPA
hatred	ODIO
hello or good-by	CIAO
lady	DAMA; SIGNORA
lake	LAGO
leader	DUCE

c
love	AMORE
mother	MADRE
mountain summit	CIMA
nine	NOVE
one	UNO
Rome	ROMA
seven	SETTE
shore	LIDO
six	SEI
street	VIA; STRADA
three	TRE
time	ORA; TEMPO
today	OGGI
tomorrow	DOMANI
tour or drive	GIRO
two	DUE
very	MOLTO
voice	VOCE
well	BENE
with	CON
yesterday	IERI
itch	PSORA
itemize	LIST
ivory, elephant's	TUSK
ivory nut	TAGUA

J

b
jab	POKE, PROD; PUNCH
jackal, N. Afr.	DIEB
jackal genus	THOS
jackdaw, Scot.	KAE
jacket	ETON; BOLERO
jacket, armored	ACTON
jacket, Malay	BAJU
jacket, record	SLEEVE
jackfish	SCAD
jackfruit	JACA; KATHAL
jack in cribbage	NOB
jack-in-the-pulpit	ARAD; AROID
Jackson heroine	RAMONA
Jacob, brother of	EDOM, ESAU
Jacob, wife of	LEAH; RACHEL
jaeger gull	SKUA
jagged line	ZIG ZAG
jaguarundi's color phase	EYRA
jai alai	PELOTA
jai alai arena	FRONTON
jai alai racket	CESTA
Jamaican dance music	SKA
Japanese admiral	ITO
Jap.-Amer.	ISSEI, KIBEI, NISEI; SANSEI
Jap. apricot	UME
Jap. cedar	SUGI
Jap. cherry	FUJI
Jap. clogs	GETA

d
Jap. decorative alloy	MOKUM
Jap. deer	SIKA
Jap. drama	KABUKI
Jap. drink	SAKE
Jap. elder statesman	GENRO
Jap. Emperor's title	TENNO; MIKADO
Jap. festival	BON
Jap. fish	TAI
Jap. food paste	MISO
Jap. game of forfeits	KEN
Jap. garment	HAORI; KIMONO
Jap. hat material	TOYO
Jap. lute	BIWA
Jap. national park	ASO
Jap. news agency	DOMEI
Jap. parliament	DIET
Jap. persimmon	KAKI
Jap. plane	ZERO
Jap. plant, celerylike	UDO
Jap. poisonous fish	FUGU
Jap. prefecture	KEN
Jap. raw fish	SUSHI; SASHIMI
Jap. rural community	MURA
Jap. sash	OBI
Jap. self-defense	JUDO
Jap. Shinto deity	KAMI
Jap. ship	MARU
Jap. shrub	HAGI

a Jap. sliding door.................FUSUMA
Jap. stock exchange ....NIKKEI
Jap. sword ....CATAN; CATTAN
Jap. town ....MACHI
Jap. vegetable.............UDO; GOBO
Jap. volcano ....FUJI
Jap. wrestling ....SUMO
Jap. writing system................KANA
Jap. zither ....KOTO
Japheth, son of.................GOMER
jar.............BUMP, EWER, JOLT,
.................OLLA; CLASH, CRUSE
jargon ......CANT; ARGOT; PATOIS
jar ring...............................LUTE
Jason, father of..................AESON
Jason, first wife of ....MEDEA
Jason, second wife of ....CREUSA
Jason, teacher of ....CHIRON
Jason, uncle of ....PELIAS;
............................ATHAMAS
Jason's ship.......................ARGO
jaunty ....AIRY; DEBONAIR
Javanese carriage ....SADO
Javanese language, ancient...........
............................KAVI, KAWI
Javanese poison tree ....UPAS
javelin, Afr. ....ASSEGAI
javelin, Rom. ....PILUM
jazz.....................................JIVE
jazz solo ....LICK, RIFF
b jazz style ....BOP; SWING
jeer............MOCK; SCOFF, TAUNT
Jehoshaphat, father of..............ASA
Jehovah ....GOD
Jehovah, Heb. ....YAHWEH
jejune ....DULL; BANAL, BLAND,
.................INANE, VAPID; PUERILE
jelly, meat..............................ASPIC
jelly base..............................PECTIN
jelly fruit ....GUAVA
jeopardize.............RISK; MENACE;
...................IMPERIL; ENDANGER
Jericho, land opposite ....MOAB
jersey, woolen....................SINGLET
Jerusalem in poetry..............ARIEL
jest ....FUN; JOKE, JOSH, QUIP
jester ....MIME; BUFFOON
jet, fast ....SST
Jetsons, dog of the ....ASTRO
jetty.............PIER; BLACK, EBONY,
.....................SOOTY, WHARF
Jew ....HEBREW, SEMITE
jewelry setting.......................PAVE
jewels, adorn with ....BEGEM
jewfish ....MERO; GROUPER
Jewish ascetic, ancient......ESSENE
Jewish evil demon ....SHEDU
Jewish feast.......................SEDER
Jewish holiday ....PURIM;
...................SUKKOT; SUKKOTH

Jewish law........................TALMUD   *c*
Jewish marriage contract KETUBAH
Jewish offering.................CORBAN,
.................................KORBAN
Jewish prayer book ....MAHZOR,
.................SIDDUR; MACHZOR
Jewish scholar..........................RAB
Jewish teacher ....RABBI
Jewish title of honor..............GAON
Jezebel, husband of ....AHAB
jinx ....HEX; CURSE, SPELL
Joan of Arc's victory, site of ....
.................................ORLEANS
job, soft ....SNAP; SINECURE
Job's-tears..............................COIX
jog ....TROT; NUDGE
John, Gaelic ....IAN
John, Irish ....SEAN
John, Russ. ....IVAN
johnny-cake ....PONE
join ....WED; LINK,
.................SEAM, WELD; MERGE,
.................UNITE; ATTACH
joining bar ....YOKE
joint.....................HIP; KNEE,
.................................NODE; HINGE
joint, corner...............MITER, MITRE
joint, wood ....RABBET
joint part ....TENON; MORTISE
joke ....GAG; JAPE,
.................JEST, JOSH, QUIP;   *d*
.................................CAPER, PRANK
joker....................WAG, WIT; CARD
Jones, of Wall Street..............DOW
Joseph, father of ....JACOB
Joseph, nephew of ....TOLA
Joshua tree........................YUCCA
jostle..............JOG; BUMP; ELBOW
jot.....................IOTA; TITTLE
journey............RIDE, TOUR, TREK,
.................................TRIP; TRAVEL
joy ....CHEER; RELISH; DELIGHT
joyous.................................GLAD
Judah, city in..............ADAR, ENAM
Judah, son of ....ONAN
Judaism scriptures ....TORAH
judge ....DEEM, RATE;
.................................ARBITER
judge in Hades ....MINOS
judges' bench.......................BANC
judge's chambers ....CAMERA
judgment in Fr. law ....ARRET
judicial assembly ....COURT
jug, large beer ....RANTER
jug, wide-mouthed.................EWER
jug shaped like a man ....TOBY
juice ....SAP
jujitsu ....JUDO
Juliet, betrothed of................PARIS
Juliet, family of................CAPULET

a jumble ....MESS; CHAOS;
........................MUDDLE
jump ....HOP; BOLT,
....................LEAP; BOUND, VAULT;
....................HURDLE, SPRING
jumping rodent...................JERBOA
juncture, line of ....SEAM
June bug ....DOR
June 6, 1944 ....D-DAY
Jungle Book, The python ....KAA
Jungle Book, The boy ....MOWGLI
jungle clearing, temporary .....MILPA
junior's transportation ....BIKE
juniper ....GORSE, SAVIN
juniper, desert.....................RETEM

juniper, Eur. ....CADE *c*
juniper tree, Biblical ..EZEL; RETEM
Jupiter....................................JOVE
Jupiter, wife of ....HERA, JUNO
jurisdiction.............SWAY; POWER
jurisdiction, old-Eng. ....SOC; SOKE
jurisprudence...........................LAW
jury ....PANEL
jury list ....VENIRE
just..................EVEN, FAIR; VALID
just about............................MUCH
Jutland cape ....SKAW
Jutelander ....DANE
jutting rock..............................TOR
juxtapositon, place in........APPOSE

K

kangaroo, male ....BOOMER
kangaroo, young....................JOEY
Katzenjammer Kids....HANS; FRITZ
kava bowl............................TANOA
Keats poem ....LAMIA;
................HYPERION, ISABELLA
keel......................................CARINA
keel, at right angles to the ...ABEAM
keel, kind of ....FIN
b keel, part of a ....SKEG
keen.........................AVID; ACUTE;
...................SHARP; ASTUTE
keep ....HOLD, MIND,
....................OBEY, SAVE; CHECK,
...................STORE; COMPLY,
...................RETAIN; OBSERVE
keepsake ....TOKEN;
................MEMENTO; SOUVENIR
Kemo ____ ....SABE
Kentucky coffee tree ....CHICOT
kernel.....................................NUT
ketone, liquid ....ACETONE
kettledrum ....NAKER; ATABAL;
...................TIMPANI
key ....ISLE; MAIN; PIVOTAL
keyed up..............................AGOG
key fruit ....SAMARA
key notch............................WARD
key part................................BIT
Keystone ____ ....KOPS
Khond language ....KUI
kick.......................................BOOT
kid, undressed ....SUEDE
kidney bean ....BON
kidneys, of the.....................RENAL
killer whale...........................ORCA
kiln....................OAST, OVEN
kiloliter.................................STERE
kilt, drawers under a...........TREWS

kind ....ILK; SORT; GENRE;
....................HUMANE; SPECIES
kindly ....BENIGN
kindness ....LENITY
kindred......AKIN; AGNATE, ALLIED
...................CONNATE, RELATED
king.......................................REX
king, Amalekite ....AGAG
king, Midianite ....REBA
king, Phrygian.....................MIDAS *d*
king, rich ....CROESUS
king, Spartan ....AGIS; LEONIDAS
King Arthur, court of........CAMELOT
King Arthur, father of ....UTHER
King Arthur, fool of ....DAGONET
King Arthur, lance of ....RON
King Arthur, land of............AVALON
King Arthur, magician of ....MERLIN
King Arthur, mother of ......IGRAINE
King Arthur, queen of ..GUINEVERE
King Arthur, sword of ...EXCALIBUR
kingfish ....CERO
king of Crete ....MINOS
king of Athens ....CECROPS
king of elves ....ERLKING
king of Israel ....AHAB, ELAH,
................OMRI, SAUL; NADAB
king of Judah................ASA; AHAZ
...................AMON; UZZIAH
king of Judea................HEROD
king of Naples ....MURAT
king of Naples, Shak. ....ALONSO
king of Persia......................CYRUS
king of the Visigoths............ALARIC
king's bodyguard.................THANE
king's yellow ....ORPIMENT
Kipling hero...........................KIM
Kipling poem ....MANDALAY
____ Kippur ....YOM

a kismet ....FATE
kiss ....BUSS; SMACK; SMOOCH
kitchen, ship's ....GALLEY
kitchen tool ....CORER, RICER;
....GRATER
kitchen worker ....CHEF, COOK
kittiwake.................................GULL
kitty, feed the ....ANTE
knave ....JACK; ROGUE
knave of clubs ....PAM
kneecap............................PATELLA
Knievel, daredevil ....EVEL
knife..............SHIV, STAB; BLADE
................MACHETE; STILETTO
knife, Burmese................DAH, DAO
knife, Inuit woman's ....ULU
knife, P. I. ....BOLO
knife, Scot. ....SNEE
knife, single-edged..............BOWIE
knife, surgical ....SCALPEL
knife dealer........................CUTLER
knight..........See also Round Table.
knight ....SIR; RITTER;
...................................TEMPLAR
knight, heroic ....PALADIN
knight's mantel ....TABARD

c knight's wife ....DAME
knitting stitch.......................PURL
knob: anatomical.................CAPUT
knoblike ....NODAL
knoblike ornament ....KNOP
knockout..............................KAYO
knot......BOW; MILE, NODE, SNAG;
...........................GNARL, NODUS
knot, insecure ....GRANNY
knot in wood...........................KNAR
knots, types of ....HITCH; BOWLINE
...............................SHEEPSHANK
knot in fiber...................NEP; NOIL
knot in wood ....BURL, KNUR
knot lace ....TAT
know...............................KIN; WIST
kopecks, 100 ....RUBLE
Koran chapter..........SURA; SURAH
Koran scholars....................ULEMA
Korea, once ....CHOSEN
Korean apricot......................ANSU
Korean president, former ....RHEE
Korean soldier........................ROK
Kronos, wife of ....RHEA
kurrajong tree.....................CALOOL
Kwa language ......IBO; IGBO, AGNI

L

b Laban, daughter of ....LEAH
label ....TAG; BRAND; MARKER
La Boheme heroine..................MIMI
Labrador tea ....LEDUM
labyrinth ....MAZE
lac ....RESIN
lace, Fr. ....CLUNY; ALENCON
lace, square mesh background........
....FILET
lacerate.............................RIP; TEAR
laces' tip ....AGLET
lack ....NEED, WANT
lack of power ....ATONY
Laconian clan group ....OBE
ladderlike ....SCALAR
ladle......................................BAIL
Lady of the Lake outlaw ....DHU
lagoon ....LIMAN
lake ....MERE
lake, Afr. salt ....SHATT
lake, Blue Nile source.............TANA
lake, California-Nevada ....TAHOE
lake, Irish............................LOUGH
lake, Italian ....COMO; AVERNUS
lake, mountain.......................TARN
lake, Scot. ....LOCH
lake, Zaire-Rwanda ....KIVU
lake near Sea of Galilee .....MEROM

d Lakes, Great........................ERIE;
...................HURON; ONTARIO;
................MICHIGAN, SUPERIOR
Lake Tahoe trout ....POGY
lama, head..........................DALAI
lamb, birth a ....YEAN
lamb, holy ....AGNUS
lamb, young......................COSSET
Lamb's pen name...................ELIA
Lamb stew ....HARICOT
Lamech, ancestor of...............CAIN
Lamech, son of ....NOAH; JUBAL
lament............KEEN, WAIL, WEEP;
...........................GRIEVE, PLAINT
lamp black............................SOOT
lamprey ....EEL
lance, short.........................DART
lance head, blunted ....MORNE
Lancelot's beloved ....ELAINE
lancewood ....CIGUA
land, church ....GLEBE
landed ....LIT; ALIT
landfill area ....DUMP
landing place.........................KEY;
...................DOCK, PIER, QUAY;
...............................LEVEE, WHARF
land in law ....SOLUM
land measure ......ARE, ROD; ACRE

a landscape, home ....LAWN,
.........................YARD; GARDEN
language, Aramaic.............SYRIAC
language, Bantu.....................EFIK
language, early It. ....OSCAN
language, Eg. ....COPTIC
language, Finn. ....UGRIC
language, Gilgit ....SHINA
language, Indic.....................HINDI
language, Indo-Chin. ....LAI, LAO,
.........................MRU, PWO; AMOY,
...........................BODO, GARO,
.....................LOLO, NAGA, SHAN
language, Indo-Chin. extinct .AHOM
language, Kashmir ....SHINA
language, Mossi....................MOLE
language, Niger-Congo..........KWA;
....AKAN
language, N. Afr. ....BERBER
language, Semitic ....ARABIC
language, S. Afr. ....TAAL
language of Jesus ....ARAMAIC
language of the P. I. ......TAGALOG
languish ....FLAG, PINE, WANE;
...................WEAKEN, WITHER
langur, Ceylonese.................MAHA
Laomedon, father of...............ILUS
Laomedon, son of...............PRIAM;
...........................TITHONUS
Laos aborigine ....KHA, YUN
b lapel(s) ....REVER; REVERS
Lapp sled.............................PULKA
larboard ....APORT
large ....BIG; HUGE;
.....................JUMBO, BROAD;
.......................SIZABLE, WEIGHTY
large intestine beginning(s) ...CECA;
....CECUM
lariat ....ROPE; LASSO, RIATA
larva.....................................GRUB
larva, fly ....BOT
lascivious ....LEWD
lash ....TIE; WHIP
lasso ....ROPE; RIATA; LARIAT
last.........FINAL; OMEGA; ENDURE
last but one ....PENULTIMATE
Last Days of Pompeii character ....
....IONE
last Imam ....MAHDI
last section ....FINALE
late ....DEAD; TARDY; RECENT
lateen-rigged boat...............DHOW;
....MISTIC
latent ....ABEYANT, DORMANT
lateral....................................SIDE
lath ....SLAT; STRIP
LATIN WORDS:
  abbot............................ABBAS
  about ....CIRCA; CIRCITER
  above ....SUPER, SUPRA

c across.............................TRANS
after....................................POST
all ....OMNIS, TOTUS
alone ....UNUS; SOLUS
and others: Abbr. ....ET AL.
around ....CIRCA; CIRCUM
art...ARS
as far as ....QUA
at the age of ....AET; AETAT
backwards....................RETRO
before ....ANTE, PRAE
behold! ....ECCE
believe ....CREDO
below..............INFRA; SUBTER
bird ....AVIS
book................CODEX, LIBER
blessed ....BEATUS
bronze ....AES
but ....SED; PRAETER
cattle ....BOVES, PECUS
country ....RUS; RURI
cup ....CALIX
custom ....USUS
day ....DIES
divination by lots.............SORS
divine law...........................FAS
door ....IANUA; OSTIUM
earth ....SOLUM, TERRA
egg.....................................OVUM
eight ....OCTO
d error.................................LAPSUS
evil....................MALUM; MALUS
field ....AGER; CAMPUS
fire.....................................IGNIS
first....................................PRIMUS
fish ....PISCIS
force ....VIS
god.....................................DEUS
goddess.............................DEA
gold....................................AURUM
good ....BONA; BONUM, SALUS
grandfather ....AVUS
he ....ILLE
head ....CAPUT; VERTEX
high ....ALTE; ALTUS
himself ....IPSE
hours................................HORAE
ivory ....EBUR
journey................................ITER
knee ....GENU
lamb ....AGNUS
land....................................AGER
learned ....DOCTUS
life.......................VITA; ANIMA
lo ....ECCE
love.............AMO, AMAS, AMAT
man ....VIR; HOMO
mark.................................NOTA
mine ....MEUS
mountain ....MONS

a LATIN WORDS: *continued*
name ....NOMEN
not ....NON; HAUD
once ....SEMEL
or ....AUT
other ....ALIUS
over ....SUPER, SURPA
pardon............................VENIA
peace ....PAX; OTIUM
pin...................................ACUS
pledge ....PIGNUS
power...............................VIS
property ....BONA
quickly ....CITO
rate of interest ....USURA
right ....FAS, IUS; DEXTER
same ....IDEM; EADEM
same place, in the ....IBID
scarcely...............................VIX
see ....VIDERE
side ....LATUS
speaks, he or she...............LOQ
surety...................................VAS
table ....MENSA
tail ....CAUDA
that is (to say) ....ID EST
thing ....RES
this one............HIC, HOC; HAEC
thus ....ITA, SIC
throat............FAUCES, GUTTUR

b tooth...............................DENS
twice.....................................BIS
under................................SUB
unless ....NISI
use, to ....USUS
vein ....VENA
voice...................................VOX
water................................AQUA
we ....NOS
well ....BENE; PUTEUS
where.................................UBI
within...............................INTRA
without.............................SINE
wool...............................LANA
wrong ....MALE; FALSUS
year ....ANNO
laugh ....CACKLE, GUFFAW,
.......................HEEHAW, TITTER;
...................CHORTLE, CHUCKLE
laughable...........................RISIBLE
laughing...............................RIANT
laughing, of..................GELASTIC
laughter sound ....YUK; TEE-HEE
laughter sounds.HA'S, HO'S; YUKS
laurel ....BAY; DAPHNE
lava ....LATITE, SCORIA
lavender, Eur. ....ASPIC
law...........................JURE, RULE;
...............................CANON, EDICT
law, Rom. ....JUS, LEX

law excluding women from reign ......
....SALIC
lawful ....LEGAL, LICIT
lawgiver, Gr. ....DRACO, MINOS,
....SOLON
lawgiver, Heb. ....MOSES
law of Moses ....TORAH
lawyer...............................LEGIST
lay..........................PUT; DITTY
layer ....PLY; LAMINA;
......................PROVINE, STRATUM
layer of wood....................VENEER
layers ....STRATA
layman, of ....LAIC
lazar ....LEPER
lazy ....IDLE; OTIOSE;
..................INDOLENT, SLOTHFUL
LBJ's beagles ....HER, HIM
lead, pellets of ....SHOT
lead, pencil ....GRAPHITE
lead, white.......................CERUSE
lead-colored ....LIVID
leader, fishing ....SNELL
leader, Rom. ....DUX
lead ore ....GALENA
lead telluride ....ALTAITE
leaf, fern ....FROND
leaf, flower..........BRACT, SEPAL
leaf appendage.................STIPEL
leaf-cutting ant .....ATTA; PARASOL
leaf division.........................LOBE
leaf-miner beetle ....HISPA
leaf of a book.............PAGE; FOLIO
leaf vein...............................RIB
league, trading....................HANSE
Leah, father of.....................LABAN
Leah, son of ....LEVI
lean............CANT; GAUNT, SPARE
Leander's love ....HERO
Leaning Tower city.................PISA
lean-to ....SHED
leap ....LUNGE, VAULT
leap, horse's ....CURVET
leaping ....SALTANT
Lear, daughter of.............REGAN;
................GONERIL; CORDELIA
Lear, faithful follower of ....KENT
learned ....ERUDITE;
....LETTERED
learned person .....SAGE; PEDANT,
....SAVANT
learning ....LORE
least bit ....RAP
leather, glove ....KID; MOCHA,
....SUEDE
leather, kind of ....ELK; BOCK
leather, prepare ....TAN, TAW
leather, soft...............NAPA; ALUTA
leatherfish ....LIJA
leather flask, Gr. ....OLPE

c

d

a leatherneck ....MARINE
leather thong, hawk-restraining........
....BRAIL
leatherwood.........................TITI
leave ....QUIT, EXIT; DEPART
leave destitute ....STRAND
leaven...............................YEAST
leave of absence, school......EXEAT
leave-taking ....CONGE
leavings............DREGS; RESIDUE
Lebanese port ....TYRE
ledge, fort...............BERM; BERME
ledger entry ....ITEM;
......................DEBIT; CREDIT
lee, opposed to ....STOSS
leer...............................OGLE
Leeward island...................NEVIS
left, turn...........................HAW
left-hand page ....VERSO
leftover table scrap ....ORT
leg, front of the ....SHIN
legal action ....RES; CASE, SUIT
legal claim ....LIEN
legal delays.......................MORAE
legal injury ....TORT
legal offense.....................DELICT
legal order...........................WRIT
legal profession..............BAR, LAW
legal prosecution.....................SUIT
legal title................................DEED

b legatee................................HEIR
leg covering, ancient.........PEDULE
legend ....LORE, MYTH,
..................................SAGA, TALE
leg ends ....FEET
legion division, Rom. ....COHORT
legislate...............................ENACT
legislature ....DIET; SENATE
legislature, Sp. ....CORTES
leg joint, animal's ....HOCK
leglike part ....CRUS
leg of mutton or lamb............GIGOT
leg part.....................SHIN; SHANK
legs, shapely ....GAMS
legume ....PEA, POD; BEAN
leisure ....EASE, REST; REPOSE
lemur ....MAKI; INDRI,
..............................LORIS; AYE-AYE
lemur, Afr. ....GALAGO
lemur, flying ....COLUGO
lemur, ruffed ....VARI
lens-shaped aggregate ....AUGE
leopard's bane ....ARNICA
lepidopteran insect ....MOTH
lepton, charged ....MUON
Lesbos poet.........................ARION
less......................FEWER, MINUS
less: music ....MENO
lessen................ABATE; MITIGATE
let ....HIRE; LEASE; PERMIT

lethal ....FATAL; MORTAL
lethargic..................DOPY; DOPEY
lethargy ....COMA;
........................STUPOR, TORPOR
let it stand ....STET
letter ....NOTE; EPISTLE,
....MISSIVE
letter, curved ....CEE, ESS, GEE
letter, forked..............................WYE
letter, hooked...........................JAY
letter of resignation ....DEMIT
letters, slanted ....ITALICS
lettuce, kind of........COS; ICEBERG
....ROMAINE
let up ....ABATE, LAPSE
Levantine ketch ....SAIC
levee ....DIKE
level ....EVEN, RAZE; PLANE
leveling device ....SHIM
lever ....PRY; PEAVEY, TAPPET
levy ....TAX; CESS; IMPOST
liability..................................DEBT
liana ....CIPO, VINE
liang ....TAEL
liar ....ANANIAS
Liberal precursor, Brit. ....WHIG
library component ....BOOK
librettist von Hofmannsthal ....HUGO
lichen ....MOSS
lie............FIB; CANARD, REPOSE
liegeman ....VASSAL
lie in wait..............................LURK
lieu ....STEAD
life ....TERM; BIOTA;
..............................ENTITY, PERSON
life, brought to......................BORN
lifeless ....BLAH, DULL; AMORT,
..............................AZOIC, INERT
life prolonger.......................ELIXIR
life story, brief ....BIO; VITA
lifetime ....AGE
lifted and threw ....HOVE
ligament..............................BOND
light................AIRY, LAMP; KLIEG
light, as a line ....LEGER
light, circle of ....HALO; NIMBUS
light, science of ....OPTICS
light-bulb filler....................ARGON
light gas ....NEON
light ring............................CORONA
light unit ....LUMEN; HEFNER
lighter, lamp.........................SPILL
lighter, make ....LEAVEN
lighthouse ....PHAROS
ligulate ....LORATE
likely ....APT
likeness ....IMAGE; REPLICA
lily ....LYS; ALOE, ARUM,
................SEGO; CALLA; CAMASS
Lily Maid of Astolat..............ELAINE

c

d

71

a limb ....ARM, LEG; MANUS
limber......................................LITHE
limestone, grainy................OOLITE
limestone, soft ....MALM; CHALK
lime tree ....TEIL; LINDEN
limicoline bird........SNIPE; PLOVER
limit.............TERM; BOUND, STINT
limn ....DESCRIBE
line.........................ROW; RANK;
.............QUEUE, TRADE, WARES;
....WRINKLE
line, move in a ....FILE
line, naut. ....EARING; MARLINE
line, waiting ....QUEUE
linear measure, old Texas......VARA
line in mathematics ....VECTOR
linen, fine ....LAWN; TOILE
linen, household ....NAPERY
linen tape, braid....................INKLE
linen-thread fiber....................FLAX
line on a letter.......................SERIF
lines, marked with ....RULED;
....STRIATED
lines, of.................................LINEAR
lines, telescope-lens ....RETICLE
line with stone........STEEN, STEIN,
....................................STEYN
linger ....WAIT; TARRY; LOITER
lingo ....ARGOT; PATOIS
lingua.................................GLOSSA
b link.................TIE; BOND; BRIDGE
linnet ....TWITE
linseed oil source ....FLAX
lion ....LEO; SIMBA
lionet...CUB
lion group ....PRIDE
lion killed by Hercules.......NEMEAN
lion of God ....ALI
lip ornament ....LABRET
lips, of the ....LABIAL
liquefy ....MELT; THAW
liqueur ....CREME
liquid, lose ....DRIP, LEAK,
....OOZE, SEEP
liquid, without ....ANEROID
liquor ....GIN, RUM, RYE; GROG
liquor, malt................ALE; PORTER
liquor, Oriental....................ARRACK
liquor, P. I. ....VINO
liquor, Russ. ....VODKA
liquor, sugar-cane................TAFFIA
Lisbon's river ....TAGUS
lissome ....SVELTE
list ....TILT; ROSTER;
..............CATALOG; ENUMERATE
listed thing ....ITEM
listen...............HARK, HEAR, HEED
list-ending abbreviation ....ETC
listless..................MOPY; LANGUID
listlessness ....ENNUI; APATHY

list of candidates...................SLATE   *c*
list of persons ......PANEL; ROSTER
literary collection.....................ANA
literate ....LEARNED; LETTERED
little: music............................POCO
"Little Boy Blue" poet ....FIELD
Little Caesar gangster.............RICO
little casino ....TWO
little chief hare........................PIKA
Little Joe on dice...................FOUR
liturgy ....RITE
lively ....PERT, SPRY; BRISK;
.....................KINETIC; ANIMATED
lively: music..............VIVO; DESTO;
....ANIMATO
lively person ....GRIG
lively song ....LILT
live oak ....ENCINA
liver, of the........................HEPATIC
lixiviate ....LEACH
lizard ....GILA; GECKO,
.............GUANA, SKINK; IGUANA
lizard, Amer. ....ANOLE
lizard, Caribbean.......................UTA
lizard, large.......................MONITOR
lizard, myth. ....BASILISK
lizard, old world ....SEPS
lizard, small ....EFT
lizard, starred ....AGAMA
lizardlike ....SAURIAN
llamalike animal ....ALPACA   *d*
load ....LADE, ONUS
loam ....LOESS
loam, Indian ....REGUR
loath.....................................AVERSE
loathe.........................HATE; ABHOR
lobster box ....CAR
local ....NARROW; LIMITED
locale.......................................SITE
locality ....AREA; LOCUS, VENUE
location ....SITE, SPOT; PLACE
lock..........................CURL; TRESS
lockjaw ....TETANUS
locks, Panama Canal ....GATUN
locust...................ACACIA, CICADA
locust, N. Z. ....WETA
lodestone ....MAGNET
lodge, soldier's ....BILLET
lofty...TALL
log, spin a floating ....BIRL
loge ....STALL
logger's implement ....PEAVEY
logrolling tournament...........ROLEO
log splitter ....WEDGE
Lohengrin, wife of ....ELSA
loincloth, Polynesian ....MALO
Loire, city on the ....BLOIS
Loki, daughter of ....HEL
Loki, son of............................NARE
Loki, wife of.......................SIGYN

a lollapalooza............................LULU
London district.....................SO-HO
long.............PINE; CRAVE, YEARN
long ago..........................ELD; YORE
longing........................YEN; ACHE
long journey........TREK; ODYSSEY
long live!........................VIVA, VIVE
look...............................SEE; CAST,
...................FACE, VIEW; WATCH;
.....................REGARD; OBSERVE
look after.....................MIND, TEND
look at...............EYE; SCAN, VIEW
look narrowly...PEEK, PEEP, PEER
look slyly...................LEER, OGLE
loom, heddles of a...............CAAM
loon, kind of.........................DIVER
loop, edging.........................PICOT
Loop trains.............................ELS
loose........................LAX; FREE;
........................SLACK, UNTIE;
......................WANTON; RELEASE
loose coat................PALETOT
loosen.......................UNDO; UNTIE
loose robe..............SIMAR, SYMAR
lop.............................SNED; PRUNE
Lord High Executioner in *Mikado*.....
....KOKO
lord, Scot. ....LAIRD
lorica...............................CUIRASS
Lorna Doone character...........RIDD
b lot......................................FATE
Lot, father of.........................HARAN
Lot, son of............................MOAB
loud: music.........................FORTE
loudness measure.................PHON
loudspeaker, high...........TWEETER
loudspeaker, low..............WOOFER
loud-voiced person.........STENTOR
Louisiana county...............PARISH
Louisiana people..............CREOLE
lounge.........................LOAF, LOLL
love.......ZERO; AMORE; PASSION
love apple........................TOMATO
love feast.............................AGAPE
lover....................................ROMEO

Love's Labour's Lost constable........ *c*
....DULL
love song, dawn......................ALBA
loving.................FOND; AMATORY
low....................MOO; BASE, DEEP
Lowell, poetess.........................AMY
lower.................ABASE; DEBASE,
....NETHER
lower intestine(s).........ILEA; ILEUM
lowest deck.........................ORLOP
lowest part of a base...........PLINTH
lowest point...........................NADIR
low pasture.............................ING
loyal.............................LEAL; TRUE;
......................................STAUNCH
loyalist, Brit. ....TORY
lozenge.............PASTIL, ROTULA,
.....................TROCHE; PASTILLE
lucky stroke.........................FLUKE
lugubrious.................SAD; WOEFUL
lukewarm.............................TEPID
lumberman........................SAWYER
lumberman's boot....................PAC
lumberman's hook.............PEAVEY
luminaire..............................LAMP
luminary................................STAR
lump.................NUB, WAD; CLOT
luncheon.............................TIFFIN
luncheon meat, canned.........SPAM
lurch...............................CAREEN
lure..........................BAIT; DECOY *d*
luster.................GLOSS, SHEEN
lusterless.....................DIM; MATTE
lustrous................................NITID
lute, flat-backed.................CITOLE
luxuriant...............LUSH, RANK,
...............................RICH; PLUSH;
....................PROFUSE, RIOTOUS
luxuriate...............................BASK
Luzon people............................ATA
Lynette's knight.................GARETH
lynx, Afr. ....SYAGUSH
lynx, Pers. ....CARACAL
lyric muse...........................ERATO
Lytton heroine.......................IONE

M

macaque, crab-eating..............KRA
macaque, pigtailed.................BRUH
macaque monkey..............RHESUS
macaw, military...........ARA; ARARA
mace-bearer.....................BEADLE
macerate.....................RET; STEEP
machine, finishing...............EDGER
machine, hummeling..........AWNER
machine, ore-processing...VANNER

machine, rubber...........EXTRUDER
machine, sorting...............GRADER
machine gun...............BREN, STEN
machine part...............CAM; PAWL;
....TAPPET
mackerel...........................WAHOO
mackerel, young.................SPIKE
mackerel net......................SPILLER
Madagascar mammal.........LEMUR

a madam........................MUM; MA'AM
madder..................................RUBIA
madder, Indian...............MUNJEET
madness..........MANIA; DEMENTIA
mafura tree............................ROKA
magazine, cheap....................PULP
maggot..................................LARVA
Magi, gifts of the.....GOLD; MYRRH
Magi, the.....GASPAR; MELCHIOR;
...................................BALTHAZAR
magic.................................SORCERY
magic, of black..................GOETIC
magic, W. Indian..................OBEAH
magic dragon..........................PUFF
magician....................WIZ; MAGE;
....................MAGUS; WIZARD
magician, King Arthur's.......MERLIN
magic stone..........................AGATE
magic word.......................PRESTO,
...................SESAME, SHAZAM
magistrate, Athenian.........ARCHON
magistrate, It......................DOGE
magistrate, Orkney or Shetland......
...................................FOUD, FOWD
magistrate, Rom................AEDILE,
...................CONSUL; PRAETOR
magnanimous......BIG; GENEROUS
magnate............MOGUL; TYCOON
magnifying glass....................LENS
Magog, partner of....................GOG
b magpie.........................PIET; NINUT
____ Mahal..................................TAJ
Mahatma, the...................GANDHI
mah-jongg piece.....................TILE
mahogany, Sp......CAOBA; QUIRA
mahogany tree, Indian..........TOON
maid.........................LASS; BONNE
maid, lady's.......................ABIGAIL
maid, Oriental........................AMAH
maiden..................FIRST; DAMSEL
maiden name lead-in................NEE
maid-of-all-work.................SLAVEY
mail...........................POST, SEND
main point.....................NUB; CRUX,
.....................................GIST, PITH
maintain.....AVER, HOLD; ASSERT
maize..CORN
maize bread............................PIKI
major: music............................DUR
majority..................................MOST
major third: Gr. music........DITONE
make.................CREATE, RENDER
make fast: naut......................BELAY
make happy..........................ELATE
makeover..................................REDO
malarial fever..........................AGUE
Malay canoe..........................PROA
Malay dagger............................KRIS
Malay gibbon............................LAR
Malay law................................ADAT

c Malay sarong............................KAIN
Malay title of respect..............TUAN
male........MACHO, MANLY; VIRILE
male cat..............................GIB, TOM
malefic....................................EVIL
male person..........BOY, GUY, LAD,
..............MAN, SON; CHAP, JOCK,
.................STUD; BLOKE, HE-MAN
male swan................................COB
malic acid source...APPLE, GRAPE
malign..........................SLUR; VILIFY
malignant....................VILE; NASTY;
....DEADLY
malleable.............SOFT; DUCTILE
malleable metal........................TIN
mallet.......................MALL; GAVEL
maltreat..................................ABUSE
mammoth.............................GIANT
man.....................BUB, GUY, MAC;
....FELLOW
man, rich..........NABOB; CROESUS
manger..............CRIB; CRECHE
mangle..........IRON, MAUL; PRESS
mango fruit, wild.....................DIKA
mania......................RAGE; CRAZE;
....LUNACY
manifest.................SHOW; OVERT;
....EVINCE
Manila hemp..........................ABACA
manner.................AIR, HOW, WAY;
...................MIEN, MODE; METHOD
d manor................................DEMESNE
man's name: Abbr.......EDW, GEO,
.................JAS, JOS; CHAS, THOS
mantle....................................CAPE
manure....................................DUNG
Maori hen................................WEKA
map..CHART
map, builder's..........................PLAT
map collection.......................ATLAS
maple fruit or seed............SAMARA
maple genus..........................ACER
map on a map.......................INSET
mar..................DAMAGE; TARNISH
marble......MIB, MIG, TAW; AGATE,
.........................AGGIE; SHOOTER
marble, It.......CARRARA, CIPOLIN
March King..........................SOUSA
margin......................RIM; EDGE
marine snail..........................WHELK
mark.............DUPE, SIGN; BRAND,
.............GRADE; NOTICE, STIGMA
mark, diacritical.....................TILDE;
....MACRON
mark, short vowel.................BREVE
market............MART, SELL, VEND;
.........................STORE; RIALTO
market, Indonesian..............PASAR
market, Oriental..........SUQ; SOUK
marketplace.......................BAZAAR

a

marketplace(s), Rom. ....FORA; ....FORUM
mark of omission.................CARET
marmalade tree ....SAPOTE
marquisette ....LENO
marriage notice ....BANNS
marriage settlement............DOWRY
marriage vows ....TROTH
marrow..............................PITH
marry.....................WED; UNITE
Mars, Gr. ....ARES
marsh....................BOG, FEN; ....LIMAN, SWALE, SWAMP
marsh elder ....IVA
marsh gas.....................METHANE
marsh hen..................COOT, RAIL
marsh mallow ....ALTHAEA
marsh marigold.............COWSLIP
marsh plant.............REED; SEDGE
marsh tea ....LEDUM
marshy ....HELODES
marsupial ....KOALA; NUMBAT, ...WOMBAT; OPOSSUM; ....KANGAROO; PHALANGER
martyr, first Christian.......STEPHEN
marvel...........WONDER; MIRACLE
Marx Brothers.....................CHICO, ...GUMMO, HARPO, ZEPPO; ....GROUCHO
Mascagni heroine ....LOLA

b

mashie..........................CLUB, IRON
masjid............................MOSQUE
mask.......VEIL; COVER; SHROUD
mask, half........................DOMINO
mass..............GOB, WAD; BULK, ...HEAP; MOUND, SWARM
mass, amorphous......BLOB, GLOB, ...GLOP, PULP
mass book ....MISSAL
mass meeting ....RALLY
master stroke......................COUP
masticate............................CHEW
mastic bully ....ACOMA
mast support ....BIBB
mat, ornamental ....DOILY
match ....FIT; TWIN; EQUAL
match, friction.....................FUSEE
match, wax ....VESTA
matgrass............................NARD
mature.............AGE; RIPE; RIPEN
Mau Mau country ....KENYA
maxilla ....JAW
maxim.......SAW; ADAGE, GNOME, ...MOTTO; SAYING
Mayan year ....TUN; HAAB
meadow..............................LEA
meadow mouse ....VOLE
meager...............................SCANT
meal.................................REPAST
meal, boiled ....MUSH

c

meal, fine ....FARINA
meal, light ....BEVER
meal course ....SOUP; SALAD; ....ENTREE; DESSERT
meaning..............SENSE; IMPORT, ...INTENT; OBJECTIVE
meantime ....INTERIM
meat...................HAM, RIB; BEEF, ...CHOP, LOIN, PORK, RUMP, ...VEAL; FILET, STEAK
meat on a skewer................KEBAB
meat roll, fried..................RISSOLE
Mecca, pilgrimage to ....HAJJ
Mecca pilgrim...............HAJI; HAJJI
Mecca pilgrim's garb............IHRAM
Mecca shrine.......................KAABA
mechanical man ....ROBOT
mechanics, branch of........STATICS
mechanics of motion .....DYNAMICS
meddle ....TAMPER;
..................................INTERFERE
Medea, father of................AEETES
medical picture ....X-RAY
medicinal bark ....COTO
medicinal herb.........ALOE; IPECAC
medicinal plant....................SENNA
medicinal tablet................TROCHE
medicine man ....SHAMAN
medieval dawn love song ....ALBA
medieval poem ....LAY
medieval society ....GUILD
Mediterranean reedy grass......DISS
medlar...............................MISPEL
medley..............................OLIO
Medusa, father of ....PHORCYS
Medusa, mother of ....CETO
Medusa, slayer of ....PERSEUS
meet ....SIT; ABUT; GREET
meeting ....TRYST; SESSION
meeting, political ....CAUCUS
melancholy ....SAD; BLUE
melodious..........................ARIOSO
melody ....AIR; ARIA, TUNE
melon ....PEPO; CASSAVA
melted ....MOLTEN
melt together ....FUSE
membrane ......WEB; TELA; VELUM
memento ....RELIC
memorandum ....NOTE
memorial post, Indian ....TOTEM
memory, of ....MNEMONIC
memory method ....ROTE
Memphis, chief god of ....PTAH
Memphis, Tenn. street..........BEALE
mend ....FIX, SEW; ....DARN; REPAIR
mendacious person ....LIAR
mendicant friar.............CARMELITE
Menelaus, wife of ....HELEN
menhaden fish ....POGY

d

Menotti hero / Milton's rebel angel

a
Menotti hero......................AMAHL
Menotti heroine..................AMELIA
men's party........................STAG
mentally confused................GAGA
mention ....SITE
menu item..........................DISH
merchandise ....WARE; WARES
merchant ....TRADER
merchant, rich Indian..............SETH
merchant ship ....ARGOSY
Mercury, Gr. ....HERMES
Mercury's wand............CADUCEUS
mercy ....GRACE;
....CLEMENCY
mere.......................BARE; SCANT
merely ....JUST, ONLY
merganser duck...SMEW; GARBILL
merge.............MIX; FUSE; BLEND
merit ....EARN; VALUE;
....VIRTUE
merriment ....GLEE
Merry Widow composer ....LEHAR
mesh.........................NET, WEB;
....ENGAGE
Mesopotamian city ....URFA
mesquite bean flour ....PINOLE
metal, bar of........................INGOT
metal, coat with ......PLATE, TERNE
metal, white..................TIN; ZINC
metal alloy.............BRASS, INVAR;

b
...........................MONEL; BRONZE
metal-decorating art ....NIELLO
metal disk ....MEDAL
metal dross...........................SLAG
metal filings ....LEMEL
metal fissure ....LODE
metal leaf ....FOIL
metallic rock ....ORE
metallic sound ....DING, PING,
...............................TING; CLINK
metal mixture......................ALLOY
metal refuse ....SCORIA
metal spacer in printing ....SLUG
metal suit ....MAIL
metal sulfide, impure...........MATTE
metalware, lacquered ....TOLE
metalwork, god of ....VULCAN
meteor, exploding ....BOLIDE
meter, one-millionth of a ...MICRON
meters, one hundred square ....ARE
method.......................HOW, WAY;
...............................PLAN; ORDER
Methuselah, grandson of ....NOAH
Metis, lover of ....SELENE
metrical rhythm.....................ICTUS
metrical unit..........................MORA
metric measure......................ARE;
...................GRAM, KILO; LITER,
...........................METER, STERE;
.....................DECARE; HECTARE

c
metropolis ....CITY
metropolitan........................URBAN
mew ....GULL
Mex. Indian ....SERI
Mex. medicinal plant ....JALAP
Mex. mush...........................ATOLE
Mex. painter........................RIVERA
Mex. peninsula.......................BAJA
Mex. persimmon ....CHAPOTE
Mex. plant oil ....CHIA
Mex. president ....DIAZ;
....................ALEMAN, CALLES,
...............MADERO; GORTARI
Mex. resin tree ....DRAGO
Mex. slave.............................PEON
Mex. spiny tree.................RETAMA;
.................................PALOVERDE
Mex. wind instrument..........CLARIN
Mex. yucca...........................DATIL
MGM lion ....LEO
microbe ....GERM
microspores ....POLLEN
midday................................NOON
middle ....MEAN; MESNE;
..................CENTER, MEDIAN
middling ....SO-SO
Midgard Serpent, slayer of the.........
....THOR
midge ....GNAT
midwife, Indian ....DHAI
mien ....AIR; MANNER; ASPECT
might..........................MAY; SWAY;
...............................POWER, VIGOR
mignonette.........GREEN; RESEDA
migratory worker....................OKIE
Milanion, wife of............ATALANTA
mild..................MEEK, SOFT,
..............................TAME; BLAND;
.....................DOCILE, GENTLE
mile, naut. ....KNOT
milestone ....STELE
milfoil...............................YARROW
military cap.............................KEPI
military command..............AT EASE
military flag.......................GUIDON
military group ....CADRE, CORPS
military maneuvers............TACTICS
milk, coagulated....................CURD
milk, curdled ....CLABBER
milk, part of.......SERUM; LACTOSE
milk, of..............................LACTIC
milk, watery part of ....WHEY
milk coagulator ....RENNIN
milk protein ....CASEIN
mill, primitive hand ....QUERN
millrace ....LADE
millstone support.........RIND, RYND
millwheel bucket ....AWE
Milton, masque by ....COMUS
Milton's rebel angel..............ARIEL

d

a mime ....APER
mimosa ....ACACIA
mind ....CARE, TEND; BRAIN
mine, narrow vein of a ....RESUE
mine-cutter ....PARAVANE
mine entrance ....ADIT
mine incline ....DOOK
mine-laying soldier ....SAPPER
mine passageway....BORD; STULM
mineral, blue ....IOLITE
mineral, gun-powder ....NITER
mineral, lustrous ....SPAR
mineral, raw ....ORE
mineral, soft ....TALC
mineral, transparent ....MICA
mineral salt............................ALUM
mineral spring ....SPA
mineral tar ....BREA
mineral waste ....GANGUE
mine roof support...................NOG
Minerva, Gr. ....ATHENA
mine shaft drain pit ....SUMP
mine stair.....................LOB; LOBB
Ming's planet ....MONGO
minim ....DROP
mining tool............................GAD
minister, Muslim ....VIZIR
mink, Amer. ....VISON
minority, legal ....NONAGE
Minos, daughter of ....ARIADNE

b Minotaur, slayer of the ....THESEUS
minstrel..................................RIMER
minstrel, medieval ....GOLIARD
minstrel, Norse ....SKALD
mint......................COIN; FORTUNE
mint herb ....SAGE
minus ....LESS
minute...........................WEE; TINY;
.............................SMALL; LITTLE
mischievous sprite ....PUCK
misplaced ....LOST
misplay...........ERROR; RENEGE
misrepresent ....BELIE, COLOR;
...............FALSIFY, PERVERT
missile ....DART
missile, guided ....JUNO, NIKE;
..............SCUD, THOR; ATLAS,
..........TITAN; BOMARC; JUPITER;
................PERSHING, REGULUS
mist................FILM, HAZE, MURK
mistake ....BONER, ERROR
mistakes, list of ....ERRATA
mite.....................................ACARID
mitigate ....EASE; ABATE, ALLAY
mix ....STIR; BLEND;
....MINGLE
mixer....................................DANCE
mixture......................OLIO; BLEND
mixture, mineral ....MAGMA
mock..............APE; SHAM; FARCE

mock blow...........................FEINT
mock orange ....SYRINGA
model, perfect ....PARAGON
moderate.....................EASY, MILD;
...........................ABATE; EASE UP,
...........................GENTLE, RELENT
modernist ....NEO
modest......................SHY; MEEK;
......................TIMID; CHASTE,
......................DEMURE, HUMBLE
modify ....VARY; ALTER, EMEND;
........................CHANGE, TEMPER
Mogul emperor....................AKBAR
Mohammed, adopted son of.......ALI
Mohammed, birthplace of ...MECCA
Mohammed, daughter of.....FATIMA
Mohammed, mule of ....FADDA
Mohammed, supporters of...ANSAR
Mohammed, tomb city of....MEDINA
Mohammed, uncle of ....ABBAS
Mohammed, wife of...............AISHA
Mohammedanism...................ISLAM
Mohawk, city on the ....UTICA
Mohicans, last of the ....UNCAS
moiety ....HALF
moist ....WET; DAMP, DANK,
...........................DEWY; HUMID
moisture, morning....................DEW
molasses ....TREACLE
molasses rum ....TAFIA; TAFFIA
mold ....MODEL, SHAPE
molding.............OGEE; REEDING
molding, concave ....CONGE;
.....................SCOTIA; CAVETTO
molding, concave and convex........
...............CYMA, GOLA; DUCINE
molding, convex ....BEAK;
...........................OVOLO, TORUS;
....ASTRAGAL
molding, edge of ....ARRIS
molding, flat ....FILLET, REGLET
molding, square ....LISTEL
molding clay ....PUG
moldy....................................MUSTY
mole(s) ....NEVI; NEVUS;
....NAEVUS
mole, Old World ....TALPA
molelike mammal...............DESMAN
mollusk ....CLAM; CHITON,
...................MUSSEL; ABALONE
mollusk, bivalve ....SCALLOP
mollusk, chambered ....NAUTILUS
mollusk, gastropod ....SNAIL
mollusk, largest ....CHAMA
molt ....SHED
molten rock............LAVA; MAGMA
moment ....JIFF; TRICE
monad ....ATOM, UNIT
monastery church ....MINSTER
monetary units ....See page 213.

a money............CASH, GELT, JACK,
............KALE; BREAD,
............BUCKS, DOUGH; DINERO,
............MAZUMA, MOOLAH;
............CABBAGE; SIMOLEONS
money, borrowed ....LOAN
money, bronze........................AES
money, medieval ....ORA
money, Native Amer. ......WAMPUM
money, put in ....INVEST
money, shell......SEWAN; SEAWAN
money certificate .....BOND; SCRIP
money drawer........................TILL
money exchange fee..............AGIO
moneylender ....USERER
money reserve ....FUND
Mongol................................TARTAR
Mongol, Buddhist................ELEUT;
............KALMUCK
Mongol dynasty.....................YUAN
Mongol tent ....YURT
mongoose, crab-eating ....URVA
mongrel ....CUR; MUTT
monitor lizard ....URAN
monk ....FRA; FRIAR;
............CENOBITE
monk, Buddhist....................ARHAT
monk, Eng. ....BEDE
monk, head ....ABBOT
Monkees movie....................HEAD
b monkey ....APE, SAI;
........CHACMA, GIBBON, GRIVET,
............GUENON, RHESUS,
............SIMIAN; MACAQUE;
............CAPUCHIN, MANDRILL,
............MARMOSET; ORANGUTAN
monkey, Madagascar..........LEMUR
monkey, S. A. ....SAKI, TITI
monkey puzzle ....ARAUCARIA
monk settlement, E. Orthodox ....
............SKETE
monk's hood ....COWL
monolith ....MENHIR
monopoly ....TRUST
monopoly, international......CARTEL
monster....................OGRE; BEAST
monster, man-bull ....MINOTAUR
monster, 100-eyed ....ARGUS
monster in Gr. myth ....CHIMERA
monster slain by Hercules ...HYDRA
month, Hindu................PUS; ASIN,
............JETH, MAGH; AGHAN,
............ASARH, CHAIT;
............SAWAN; BHADON, KARTIK,
............PHAGUN; BAISAKH
month, Islamic ....RABI;
............RAJAB, SAFAR; JUMADA,
............SHA'BAN; RAMADAN,
............SHAWWAL; MUHARRAM;
............DHU'L-QA'DAH

month, Jewish ....ADAR, ELUL, *c*
............IYAR; NISAN, SIVAN;
............KISLEV, SHEBAT, TISHRI,
............TAMMUZ; HESHVAN
month, Muslim fast........RAMADAN
month abbreviation ....APR, AUG,
............DEC, FEB, JAN, JUL, JUN,
........MAR, NOV, OCT, SEP; SEPT
monument stone ....CAIRN;
............DOLMEN; CROMLECH
moons........See planets & satellites.
moon flower........................DAISY
moon goddess................ASTARTE
moon valley ....RILLE
moon vehicle: Abbr. ....LEM
mop ....SWAB
morass ....FEN; MIRE; MARSH;
............TANGLE; QUAGMIRE
moray ....EEL
more........ALSO; ADDED, EXTRA,
............STILL; BETTER
more!....................BIS; ENCORE
More's island ....UTOPIA
more than enough ...TOO; EXCESS
more than 50% ....MOST
morning glory ....IPOMOEA
morning prayer ....MATINS
morning song ....AUBADE
Moroccan Berber ....RIFF
Moroccan ....MOOR
moron ....FOOL; IDIOT; CRETIN *d*
morose ......DOUR, GLUM; SULLEN
morsel ....BIT; CRUMB; TIDBIT
mortar..................BOWL; CANNON
mortar ingredient ....LIME, SAND;
............WATER; CEMENT
mortar instrument ....PESTLE
mortar mixer..........................RAB
mortar tray............................HOD
mortise insert......................TENON
Mosaic law..........................TORAH
mosaic piece(s)................SMALTI,
............SMALTO; TESSERA
Moscow department store ....GUM
Moselle tributary....................SAAR
Moses, brother of ....AARON
Moses, father-in-law of ......JETHRO
Moses's death mountain........NEBO
Moses's spy in Canaan ....CALEB
Moslem......................See Muslim.
mosque ....MASJID
mosque in Jerusalem ....OMAR
mosque student ....SOFTA
mosquito genus ....AEDES
mossbunker fish ....POGY;
............MENHADEN
most................MAX; VERY; EXTRA
moth ....LUNA; EGGER, TINEA
motherless calf ....DOGIE
mother of gods ....RHEA

a mother-of-pearl....................NACRE
mother-of-pearl shell ....ABALONE
mother's side, related on......ENATE
motionless ....INERT, STILL
motive................CAUSE; REASON
motor, race the ....REV
mound ....HEAP, LUMP,
.................................PILE; STACK
mound, manmade protective ..TERP
mountain, Afr. ....JAJA;
..................................KILIMANJARO
mountain, Alps ....BLANC
mountain, Ant. ....SHINN, TYREE
mountain, Biblical..................NEBO;
................HOREB, SINAI; ARARAT
mountain, Canary Islands......TEIDE
mountain, fabled Hindu ....MERU
mountain, Gr. ....HELICON
mountain, N. Z. ....COOK
mountain, Sp. ....ANETO
mountain, Swiss ....DOM;
..................CASTOR; JUNGFRAU;
.........................MATTERHORN
mountain, Yukon ....LOGAN
mountain ash ....SORB; ROWAN
mountain climbing gear.........PITON
mountain crest ....ARETE
mountain in Thessaly ....OSSA;
....PELION
mountain lion ....PUMA
b mountain mint ....BASIL
mountain on Crete ....IDA
mountain pass ....COL
mountain pass in the Alps.....CENIS
mountain pass in India ....GHAT
mountain peak...........................ALP
mountain pool....................TARN
mountain range, Eur. ....ALPS
mountain range, Fr.-Swiss......JURA
mountain range, Ger. ....HARZ
mountain recess......................CWM
mountains, Asian ....ALTAI
mountain spinach ....ORACH
mountains, US ....BEAR, BONA,
...................HOOD, YALE; EVANS;
.........ANTERO, CASTLE, ELBERT,
........................HUNTER, WILSON;
..................FORAKER, HARVARD
....LA PLATA, RAINIER, WHITNEY
Mount of Olives ....OLIVET
mourn................GRIEVE; LAMENT
mournful ....SAD; RUEFUL,
......................WOEFUL; UNHAPPY
mourning band....................CRAPE
mouse, field ....VOLE
mousebird ....COLY; SHRIKE
mouse-spotter's cry ....EEK
mouth, away from the ....ABORAL
mouth, of the ....ORAL
mouth, river ....DELTA

mouth, tidal river ....FIRTH *c*
mouthlike orifice ....STOMA
mouth open.........................AGAPE
mouthpiece ....REED, BOCAL;
....................................LAWYER
move............STIR; SHIFT, TOUCH;
...................AFFECT; RELOCATE
move a camera........................PAN
move back ....EBB; RECEDE
move little by little...................INCH
movement, biological ....TAXIS
movement, capable of ....MOTILE
movement in music ....MOTO
move to and fro ....WAG;
............................FLAP, SWAY
move up and down ....BOB
movies.............................CINEMA
movies, XXX-rated.................PORN
moving part ....ROTOR
mow...CUT
mowed strip.........................SWATH
Mowgli, friend of ....BALOO
muck.....................GOO; OOZE;
............................GRIME, SLIME
mud, stick in the ....MIRE
mud deposit.............................SILT
muddle.................MESS; TURMOIL
muddy, make ....ROIL
mudfish ....AMIA; BOWFIN
mudhole.................................PULK
mud volcano ....SALSE *d*
mug.............................FACE; STEIN;
..................................NOGGIN
mug, small ....TOBY
mulberry-bark cloth................TAPA
mulberry-flavored wine........MORAT
mulberry of India ....AAL
mulct...................FINE; AMERCE
mullet, red................................SUR
multiform ....DIVERSE
multiplicand ....FACIEND
multiplier ....FACIENT
multitude ....HOST; HORDE
munch...............................CHOMP
mundane ....PROSAIC,
....................................WORLDLY
Munich's river ....ISAR
Munsters, dragon of the ....SPOT
murder...............OFF; KILL, SLAY
murder by suffocation ....BURKE
murderer, first ....CAIN
murmur ....BUZZ; GOSSIP,
......................MUMBLE, RUMBLE
muscle ....THEW; SINEW
muscle, kind of ....TENSOR;
....................ERECTOR, LEVATOR
muscle, like ....MYOID
muscular spasm ....TIC
Muse of astronomy.............URANIA
Muse of comedy ....THALIA

a Muse of dance ......TERPSICHORE
Muse of epic song ....CALLIOPE
Muse of erotic poetry ....ERATO
Muse of history ....CLIO
Muse of hymns ....POLYHYMNIA
Muse of lyric poetry........EUTERPE
Muse of tragedy ....MELPOMENE
Muses, nine ....PIERIDES
musette.................................OBOE
museum head ....CURATOR
mush......................ATOLE, SEPON
mushroom ....MOREL
mushroom cap ....PILEUS
mushroom stalk ....STIPE
music, as written in ....STA
music, choral ....MOTET;
....CANTATA
music, Indian...........................RAGA
musical beat............................TAKT
musical direction ....TACET
musical instrument (brass)....SAX;
........TUBA; BUGLE; CORNET;
....................ALPHORN, CLARION,
...................HELICON, TRUMPET;
...............................TROMBONE
musical instrument (keyboard)........
.................................ORGAN, PIANO;
...................CLAVIER; CALLIOPE
musical instrument (percussion) ......
.................DRUM, GONG; BELLS,
b ....CONGA, TABOR, VIBES;
........CHIMES, CYMBAL, NAGARA,
....................TAM-TAM; CELESTA;
...................MARACAS, MARIMBA,
....................TIMPANI; TRIANGLE
musical instrument (string)......OUD;
........BASS, HARP, LUTE, LYRE,
..................VIOL; BANJO, CELLO,
.............DOBRO, REBEC, SITAR,
..............VIOLA; FIDDLE, GUITAR,
.................................VIOLIN, ZITHER;
.................BANDORE, UKULELE;
..............DULCIMER, MANDOLIN

musical instrument (woodwind)........   *c*
...........FIFE, OBOE, PIPE; FLUTE,
....SHAWM; BASSOON, OCARINA,
.......................PANPIPE, PICCOLO,
.....................WHISTLE; CLARINET
musical work ....OPUS
music character .DOT; REST, CLEF
music drama......................OPERA
music for nine ....NONET
music for three......................TRIO
music for two ....DUET
music interval ....TRITONE
music lines............................STAFF
music student's piece ....ETUDE
music symbols, old..............NEUME
music terminology.....See page 233.
Musketeer...........ATHOS; ARAMIS;
...............PORTHOS; D'ARTAGNON
Muslim, branch of .....SHI'A; SUNNI
Muslim, strict....................WAHABI
Muslim call to prayer..............AZAN
Muslim deity..........................ALLAH
Muslim fast....................RAMADAN
Muslim festival....................BAIRAM
Muslim fiat..........................IRADE
Muslim fourth caliph.................ALI
Muslim guide in Pak. or India.....PIR
Muslim holy city...................MECCA
Muslim holy man....................IMAM
Muslim judge ....CADI,
...................................KADI, QADI   *d*
Muslim marriage, temporary ..MUTA
Muslim nymph ....HOURI
Muslim prayer ....SALAH, SALAT
Muslim pulpit......MIMBAR, MINBAR
Muslim sacred book ....KORAN
Muslim sect ....SUNNI; SHIITE
Muslim theologians..............ULEMA
mussel, freshwater................UNIO
musteline animal.OTTER, WEASEL
mutilate ....MAIM
muttonfish ....SAMA
mysterious........ARCANE, OCCULT

N

nab ....GRAB; ARREST
NaCl ....SALT
nail ....CLAW, TACK;
.................................SPIKE, TALON
nail, thin...................................BRAD
nail with a hole ....SPAD
nakedwood tree.......................MABI
namaycush ....TROUT
name ....DUB; TERM; TITLE
named ....CALLED, DUBBED,
....YCLEPT

namely....................................VIZ
Naomi, daughter-in-law of......RUTH
naos.....................................CELLA
nap-raising device ....TEASEL
nap-raising machine ....GIG
Napoleon, brother-in-law of .MURAT
Napoleon, isle of.....................ELBA
Napoleon, marshal of ....NEY
Napoleon, victory site of ....JANA,
....LODI
Narcissus, lover of ....ECHO

a narcotic..................DOPE, DRUG;
..................HEROINE, OPIATE
narcotic shrub...............COCA
narrate.............TELL; RECITE,
..............RELATE, REPORT
narrow.........TIGHT; INSULAR
nation, of a......................STATAL
National Socialist, Ger. ....NAZI
native......................RAW; CRUDE;
..........................ENDEMIC
natural..........................BORN
natural talent......................FLAIR
nature.............HUMOR; ESSENCE
nature goddess...............CYBELE
nature-story writer............SETON
nautical..........................MARINE
nautical cry.............AHOY; AVAST
Navaho dwelling...............HOGAN
navy jail......................BRIG
Navy mascot......................GOAT
near.........NIGH; ABOUT, CLOSE
nearest.............NEXT; PROXIMAL
nearsightedness...............MYOPIA
nearsighted person.........MYOPE
neat.............TIDY, TRIM;
..........................SPRUCE
necessitate......................ENTAIL;
..........................REQUIRE
neck, nape of the............NUCHA
neckline shape......................VEE;
b ....BOAT, CREW
necktie......................CRAVAT
neckwear......BOA; FICHU, STOLE
nee..........................BORN
need.............WANT; REQUIRE
needle.............PROD; BODKIN
needle case......................ETUI
needlefish......................GAR
needleshaped...............ACUATE
negation, particle of.............NOT
negative.............NAY; NOPE
nagatives......................NOES
neglect.............OMIT, SNUB;
..........SHIRK; IGNORE,
..........SLIGHT; DISREGARD
negligent.............LAX; REMISS
negotiate......................FIX, SET;
..........CLEAR; SETTLE;
..........................ARRANGE
neighborhood, dilapidated......SLUM
Nelson, victory site of.............NILE
nemesis..........................BANE
Neptune's spear.............TRIDENT
nerve cell.............AXON; NEURON
nerve layers, brain's.............ALVEI
nervous.............EDGY; JUMPY,
..........TENSE; UNEASY
nervous disease.............CHOREA
nest, eagle's......................AERIE
Nestor, mother of.............TYRO

c net..........................MESH;
..........................CLEAR, SEINE
netlike..........................RETIARY
network.............WEB; RETE
Nevada resort......................RENO
new......................NOVEL; RECENT
New Mexico art colony.........TAOS
News agency, Eng. ....REUTERS
News agency, Jap. ....DOMEI
News agency, Soviet.............TASS
newspaper.............RAG; POST;
..........PRESS; GAZETTE,
..........................JOURNAL
news piece......................ITEM
news service......................UPI
newt.............EFT; TRITON
new wine..........................MUST
New York harbor island.........ELLIS
New Zealand bird.........HUIA, KAKI,
..........................PEHO, RURU
N. Z. evergreen......................TAWA
N. Z. honeyeater.............TUI
N. Z. native people.............MAORI
N. Z. parrot......................KAKA
N. Z. rail bird......................WEKA
N. Z. tree.............KAURI, NGAIO;
..........................TOTARA
N. Z. woody vine......................AKA
niche.............ALCOVE, RECESS
Nichols' hero......................ABIE
d nickel-steel alloy...............INVAR
Nick's dog..........................ASTA
Nick's wife..........................NORA
nicotinic acid......................NIACIN
nictitate..........................WINK
niggardly.........MEAGER, STINGY
nigh..........................NEAR
nightingale, Pers. ....BULBUL
nightjar..........................POTOO
Nile island..........................RODA
Nile sailboat......................CANGIA
nimble.............SPRY; AGILE
nimbus..........................HALO
nimrod..........................HUNTER
nine, group of......................ENNEAD
nine, music for......................NONET
nine inches..........................SPAN
nipple..........................TEAT
Nisan, in old Hebrew............ABIB
niton..........................RADON
nitrogen, once......................AZOTE
No: Russ..........................NYET
Noah, landing place of.......ARARAT
Noah, son of.............HAM; SHEM;
..........................JAPHETH
noble, female......................DAME,
..........LADY; QUEEN;
..........DUCHESS; COUNTESS,
..........BARONESS, PRINCESS
noble, Ger. ....GRAF; RITTER

a noble, male ....DUKE, EARL,
.....................KING, LORD, PEER;
.............BARON, COUNT; KNIGHT,
....................PRINCE; BARONET,
.................MARQUIS; VISCOUNT
nocturnal mammal .....BAT; LEMUR
nod..............................BOW; BECK;
....................................ASSENT
Nod, land west of ....EDEN
node.........................KNOB, KNOT;
....NODUS
nod off.................................SLEEP
nomad ....WANDERER
nomadic people of the Nile .....BEJA
nomenclature ....NAMES
nominal value ....PAR
nominate................................NAME
non-cleric ....LAY; LAIC
nonchalant ....CALM, COOL,
.....................EVEN; COLLECTED
non-Jew(s) ....GOY; GOYIM
nonsense ....BOSH, BUNK,
.....................CRAP, GUFF, TOSH;
.........................BILGE; BUNKUM,
.........................PIFFLE; BLATHER
nonsensical talk ....BLAH
noose..................................LOOP
Normandy landing................D-DAY
Norse destiny goddess..........NORN
Norse epic............................EDDA
b Norse letter ....RUNE
Norseman ....DANE; SWEDE
Norse mythical hero ....EGIL
North, Mrs............................PAMELA
N. Afr. people ....BERBER
North Carolina college............ELON
North Carolinian ....TARHEEL
North Caucasian language.....UDI;
........................AVAR; UDIC; UDISH
northern ....BOREAL
northern Scand. ....LAPP
northernmost land ....THULE
North Sea, river into the...........DEE,
........................TAY; ELBE, TEES;
..........................FORTH; HUMBER
North Sea boat.....................COBLE
North Sea inlet ....WASH
North Star ....POLARIS
Northumberland river............TYNE
Norwegian coin ....ORE
Norwegian composer ....GRIEG
Norwegian king.....................OLAF
Norwegian novelist.........HAMSUN
nose ....SNOOP; SCHNOZ
nose, having a large ....NASUTE
nose, having a snub..........SIMOUS
nosegay ....POSY
nose opening(s)......NARES, NARIS
nostrils, of the....................NARIAL,
....................................NARINE

____ Nostrum (Mediterranean).........   *c*
....MARE
not at home ....OUT
notch...............KERF, NICK, NOCK
notched........................SERRATED
note ....CHIT, MEMO, TONE;
.......................REMARK, RENOWN
note, Guido's high ....E LA
note, Guido's low ....GAMUT
note, half............................MINIM
notes in Guido's scale ....ELAMI
not ever, in poetry ....NE'ER
nothing ....NIL, NIX; NULL,
............................ZERO; NIHIL
not in style ....OUT; PASSE
notion.....................................IDEA
notion, capricious ....WHIM
not long ago ....LATELY
not moving ....INERT; STATIC
not one.......................NARY, NONE
notorious ....INFAMOUS
not so great..............LESS; FEWER
notwithstanding ....YET
nought.....................ZERO, NULL
noun form ....CASE
nourish ....FEED; FOSTER
nourished ....FED
Nova Scotia ....ACADIA
novelty ....TOY; BAUBLE
novice ....TIRO, TYRO
nucha ....NAPE   *d*
nudge ....JOG; POKE, PROD
nuisance ....PEST; BOTHER
nullify ....NEGATE
nullify, legally ....VOID
number, irrational...................SURD
number, whole ....INTEGER
number under ten ....DIGIT
numerous................................MANY;
.........................LEGION, MYRIAD
nun, Franciscan ....CLARE
nun, head..........................ABBESS
nun's dress ....HABIT
nurse, Oriental ....AMAH
nurse, Slavic........................BABA
nursemaid, Indian.................AYAH
nut ....COLA, KOLA; ALMOND,
.........................CASHEW, LITCHI
nut, hickory ....PECAN
nut, pine ....PINON
nutlike drupe ....TRYMA
nutmeg husk ....MACE
nutria ....COYPU
nutriment ....FOOD; ALIMENT
nuts ....CRAZY; WHACKO
nymph, fountain ....EGERIA
nymph, laurel ....DAPHNE
nymph, mountain................OREAD
nymph, Muslim ....HOURI
nymph, water ....NAIAD

O

oaf.............CLOD, LOUT; LUMMOX
oak, California ....ENCINA
oak, dried fruit of ....CAMATA
oak, evergreen.......................HOLM
oak moss.........................EVERNIA
oakum, seal with ....CAULK
oar.............ROW; BLADE; PROPEL
oar at stern ....SCULL
oasis, N. Afr. ....WADI
oat genus ....AVENA
oath, euphemistic........GAD; DARN,
.............................DRAT; PHOOEY,
....SHUCKS
oath, old-fashioned ....EGAD
oath, say under ....DEPOSE
obeisance, show.......................BOW
obey ....HEED, MIND
object...........................ITEM; THING
objection, petty ....CAVIL
objective ....AIM; GOAL
object of art............................CURIO
obligation ....DEBT, DUTY, ONUS
oblique..............BIASED; SLANTED
obliterate ....ERASE; EFFACE
oblivion ....LETHE, LIMBO;
....................................ESCAPE
obscure ....DIM; FAINT,
.............MURKY, VAGUE; BLEARY
obscure, render ....DARKLE
observe ....SEE; NOTE; BEHOLD,
.................REMARK; CELEBRATE
obstinate ....TOUGH; STUBBORN
obtain ....GET; GAIN; PROCURE
obtained ....GOT; TOOK
obvious ....OPEN; PATENT
obvious, not.........................SUBTLE
occasional ....RARE; SCARCE;
.................UNUSUAL; SPORADIC
Occident ....WEST
occipital protuberance(s)..........INIA;
....INION
occupant........TENANT; RESIDENT
occupation ....TRADE
occupied................................BUSY
occupy.....FILL; ENGAGE, PEOPLE
occurrence ....EVENT
oceanic ....PELAGIC
oceanic tunicate ....SALP; SALPA
ocean motion...............TIDE, WAVE
octopus...........POULP; POULPE
Odin, brother of.........................VILI
Odin, grandfather of ....NANNA
Odin, home of ....VALHALLA
Odin, son of ....TYR; THOR, VALI
odor ....AROMA, SCENT
Odysseus ....ULYSSES
Odysseus, companion of ELPENOR

Odyssey beggar ....IRUS
Odyssey singer ....SIREN
Oedipus, father of ....LAIUS
Oedipus, mother of ....JOCASTA
off ....AWAY
offend ....AFFRONT
offense.........................SIN; CRIME
offer.............................BID; TENDER
offhand..............................CASUAL
office, R.C. curia ....DATARY
office holders............................INS
officer, church ....BEADLE
officer, Scot. court ....MACER
officer, Scot. municipal..........BAILIE
officer, minor Rom. ....LICTOR
officer, synagogue ....PARNAS
officer, university ...DEAN; BURSAR
office worker's skill................STENO
official, Muslim court ....HAJIB
official, Rom. ....EDILE; AEDILE;
....TRIBUNE
official, subordinate...........SATRAP
offspring ....BABY, CION, SONS;
.................................HEIRS; SCION
ogygian ....AGED;
...............ANCIENT; PRIMEVAL
Ohio college town ....ADA
oil ....FAT; LARD, SUET
oil, beetle ....MELOE
oil, cruet............................AMPULLA
oil, of.......................................OLEIC
oil, orange ....NEROLI
oil, put on ....ANOINT
oil, rose ....ATTAR
oil bottle ....CRUET
oilfish.................................ESCOLAR
oil-yielding tree.......................TUNG
oily ketone ....IRONE
ointment ....BALM, NARD;
..........SALVE; CERATE, POMADE
okay................ROGER; APPROVE
Okefenoke possum ....POGO
okra dish ....GUMBO
old...AGED
Old Curiosity Shop girl ....NELL
old Eng. militia.......................FYRD
old Eng. gold piece ....RYAL
old Eng. rune ....WEN
old Gr. coin........OBOL; OBOLUS
old Irish counterfeit coin...........RAP
old Pers. money ....DARIC
old Sp. gold coin ....DOBLA
old-timer....................COOT, FOGY;
....CODGER
old times ....ELD; YORE
old-womanish ....ANILE
oleaginous ....OILY

a oleic-acid salt ....OLEATE
oleoresin ....ANIME,
.......................ELEMI; BALSAM
olive color...............................DUNE;
........................TWINE; ANAMITE
olive genus ....OLEA
Olympus, mount near..............OSSA
Olympus, region near...........PIERIA
omen ....AUGURY; PORTENT
omentum, great ....CAUL
omission in a word............ELISION
omit ....DROP, PASS, SKIP
omit in pronunciation ....ELIDE
onager..ASS
one ....BUCK, UNIT; SINGLE
one, music for ....SOLO
one-base hit ....SINGLE
one behind another...........TANDEM
one-eighth troy ounce...........DRAM
one-eyed giant...............CYCLOPS
one-horse carriage ....SHAY
one hundred square meters .....ARE
one hundred thousand rupees ....
....LAKH
O'Neill heroine ....ANNA
one-spot...................................ACE
onion, Welsh ....CIBOL
onion, Sp. ....CIBOLA
onionlike plant...........LEEK; CHIVE;
....SHALLOT

b only ....MERE, SAVE, SOLE
onward ....AHEAD; FORWARD
ooze ....LEAK, SEEP; EXUDE
open ....AJAR; OVERT
opening..............GAP; HOLE, RIFT,
.....................SLOT, VENT; HIATUS
opening, skin........................PORE
opera, Beethoven...............FIDELIO
opera, Bellini ....NORMA
opera, Bizet ....CARMEN
opera, Delibes.....................LAKME
opera, Gounod.....................FAUST
opera, Massenet ....MANON, THAIS
opera, Puccini...................TOSCA;
..................................TURANDOT
opera, Strauss...................SALOME;
....ELEKTRA;
...................ARABELLA, CAPRICIO
opera, Verdi ....AIDA; ERNANI,
..............OTELLO; FALSTAFF;
.........DON CARLOS, RIGOLETTO
opera, Wagner ....RIENZI
opera hat................................GIBUS
opera heroine ....AIDA, ELSA,
..................MIMI; SENTA; ISOLDE
opera house, Milan ....LA SCALA
opera star ....DIVA
operate ....RUN; MANAGE
operated ....RAN
opium poppy seed..................MAW

opossum rat........................SELVA *c*
opponent ....FOE; ENEMY, RIVAL
opportune ....TIMELY
opportunity ....CHANCE
opposed, one ....ANTI
opposite.......................COUNTER,
...................REVERSE; CONTRARY
opposite extremities ....POLES
Ops, daughter of ....CERES
Ops, husband of...............SATURN
optical glass..........................LENS
optical illusion ....MIRAGE
optimistic.................................ROSY
oracle, Gr. ....DELOS; DELPHI
orange-red stone.....................SARD
orator ....RHETOR
orbit point ....APOGEE; PERIGEE
orchid tuber ....SALEP
ordain ....DECREE, IMPOSE
order...........................BID; FIAT;
...........................EDICT; DECREE
order, put in ....TIDY; SETTLE
ordinance ....LAW
ore deposit ....LODE
ore of iron ....OCHER
organ, seed-bearing..............PISTIL
organ control ....STOP
organism, one-celled ....AMOEBA
organism, simple.................MONAD
organization ....CLUB; GUILD,
............SETUP; LEAGUE; SOCIETY *d*
organ pipe ....REED
organ prelude ....VERSET
organ stop.............................SEXT;
........................DOLCAN; CELESTE,
...................MELODIA; DIAPASON
orgy ....BINGE, FLING,
.......................SPREE; RAMPAGE
Orient.......................................EAST
Oriental.................................ASIAN
Oriental nursemaid ....AMAH
Oriental plane tree.............CHINAR
Oriental potentate ....AGA
Oriental sailing ship ....DHOW
Oriental servant ....HAMAL
orifice ....PORE; STOMA
origin ....SEED; SOURCE
original ....NEW; FIRST, PRIME
original sinner ....ADAM
originate ....ARISE, BEGIN,
............................START; INVENT
Orinoco tributary.......................ARO
oriole, golden ....LORIOT
ornament.................TRIM; ADORN
ornament, curly ....SCROLL
ornamental border ....DADO
ornamental grass ....EULALIA
ornamental nailhead..............STUD
ornament in relief..............EMBOSS
Orpheus, destination of ....HADES

a | Orpheus, instrument of ....LYRE
orris ....IRIS
oscillate ....SWAY; SWING
osier...................................WITHE
Osiris, brother of ....SET
Osiris, wife/sister of ....ISIS
ostentation...............................POMP
ostrich, S. A. ....RHEA
ostrichlike bird ....EMU
Othello, foe of...........................IAGO
otherwise ....ELSE
otic ....AURAL
otter, common Indian...............NAIR
otter brown color...............LOUTRE
Ottoman ....TURK
ottoman ....POUF; HASSOCK
Ottoman court.....................PORTE
Ottoman official...................PASHA
Ottoman peasant..................RAYA;
....RAYAH
Our Gang dog ....PETE
Our Gang girl ....DARLA
Our Mutual Friend character.WEGG
oust ....EJECT, EVICT
out-and-out ....ARRANT
outbreak ....RIOT
outburst, sudden ....SPATE
outcast ....LEPER; PARIAH
outcome ....RESULT, UPSHOT
outcry ....CLAMOR

b | outer portion of Earth ....SIAL
outfit.............KIT, RIG; GEAR, SUIT
outfit, unusual ....GETUP
outlet.....................VENT; SOCKET
outline.................DRAFT; SKETCH;
..................CONTOUR, PROFILE
outlook ....VISTA; PROSPECT
outmoded ....PASSE
out of the way ....ASIDE

c | ova..EGGS
oval ....ELLIPTICAL
oven ....KILN, OAST
oven, annealing ....LEHR
over.........................ATOP, DONE;
................ABOVE, AGAIN, ENDED;
.......ACROSS, AROUND, UNDULY
overact ....EMOTE
overcoat..............LODEN; ULSTER;
....PALETOT
overdue payment...........ARREARS
overflow ....GLUT; SURPLUS
overjoy ....ELATE
overly fond of, act...................DOTE
overnice person.....................PRIG
overshadow.................TOP; BEST,
..................................PASS; EXCEL,
....................OUTDO; BETTER
overshoes.....................GALOSHES
overskirt...............................PANIER
overt.......................................OPEN
over there................YON; YONDER
overwhelm ....FLOOD;
........................DELUGE, ENGULF
ovule......................................SEED
ovum ....EGG
owl, horned ....BUBO
owl's cry ....HOOT
own up to ....AVOW
ox, extinct wild ....URUS

d | ox, forest ....ANOA
ox, long-haired ....YAK
Oxford...................................OXON
Oxford fellows ....DONS
oxide ....CALX
oxidize ....RUST
oyster, young ....SPAT
oysterfish........TAUTOG; TAUTAUG
Oz books author ....BAUM

P

pace ....WALK; SPEED, TEMPO
pachyderm ....ELEPHANT
pacify ....CALM; GENTLE,
......................SOOTHE; PLACATE
pack ....JAM, WAD; STOW
pack animal..............ASS; BURRO,
..........................LLAMA; SUMPTER
pack down..................RAM; TAMP
pad ....BLOCK; TABLET
padded jacket under armor .ACTON
padnag.................TROT; AMBLE
Padua, town near ....ESTE
pagan god...............................IDOL
page ....CALL, LEAF
pageantry ....POMP

page number ....FOLIO
Pagliacci characters............BEPPE,
..............................CANIO, NEDDA,
................................TONIO; SILVIO
pain ....ACHE, PANG; AGONY
pain, causing ....ALGETIC
pain reliever ....OPIATE; ANODYNE
paint ....COLOR; TEMPERA
paint, face ....ROUGE
painting, wall........................MURAL
painting style ....GENRE
pair.................DUO; DUAD, DUET,
............DYAD, MATE; TWOSOME
pairing ....MATING
pair of horses ....SPAN, TEAM

a Pakistani woman.................BEGUM
palanquin, Jap. ....KAGO
palanquin bearer.................HAMAL
palate, soft.........................VELUM
pale ....WAN; ASHY;
...................................ASHEN, PASTY
pale color.........................PASTEL
pale-colored.......................MEALY
Pallas...............................ATHENA
pallid......................................PALE
palm.....................COCO; TALIPOT
palm, Asian.........ARENGA, BETEL
palm, betel...........................ARECA
palm, book.........................TALIERA
palm, Braz. ....DATIL, ASSAI
palm, climbing.....................RATTAN
palm, N. Z. ....NIKAU
palm, nipa..........ATAP; ATTAP
palm, sago........................GOMUTI
palmetto..............................SABAL
palm fiber................DATIL; RAFFIA
palm juice, fermented............SURA
palm liquor................BENO, BINO,
................NIPA, TUBA; TODDY
palm starch........................SAGO
palp.....................................FEELER
pamper..............................COSSET
pamphlet..............................TRACT
pan, Chin. ....WOK
panacea............................ELIXIR
b Panama, former name of....DARIEN
panel of jurors....................VENIRE
pangolin, five-toed...............MANIS
panic.......................FEAR; ALARM;
....TERRIFY
pannier...............................DOSSER
pant.......................................GASP
pantry.................AMBRY; LARDER,
...................SPENCE; BUTTERY
papal cape.........................FANON
papal church...................LATERAN
papal court.............SEE; CURIA
papal letter............................BULL
papal scarf ....ORALE
papal seal.............................BULLA
paper, thin crisp.................PELURE
paper base............................PULP
paper folded once ....FOLIO
paper measure........REAM; QUIRE
paper mulberry.......................KOZO
paper mulberry bark ....TAPA
paper size..........................DEMY;
.......................FOLIO, SEXTO;
..................OCTAVO, QUARTO
papyrus...............................SEDGE
par ....NORM; AVERAGE
par, one under.....................BIRDIE
par, two under......................EAGLE
Para, Brazil, capital of..........BELEM
para-aminobenzoic acid ....PABA

parade.................MARCH, STRUT; c
...................FLAUNT, REVIEW
paradise, earthly ....EDEN
paradisiacal ....EDENIC
parasite ....LEECH
parasitic insect......................MITE;
...................LOUSE; ACARID
parasitic insects ....LICE
parasitic plant.......MOSS; DODDER
Parcae ....FATES
Parcae, the ....NONA; MORTA;
....................................DECUMA
parcel of land ....LOT
parchment, book ....FOREL;
...............................FORREL
pardon ....REMIT; CONDONE
pardon, general ....AMNESTY
pare..PEEL
pari-mutuel machine ....TOTE
Paris, father of ....PRIAM
Paris, first bishop of ....DENIS
Paris, wife of...................OENONE
Paris art exhibit ....SALON
parish head ....RECTOR
Paris subway.......................METRO
Paris thug...........................APACHE
Parkinson's disease drug ...L-DOPA
parlay..............................PALAVER
Parliamentary report......HANSARD
paroxysm ....FIT; SPASM
parrot...................EOS, KEA; LORY d
parrotfish................................LORO
parry ....FEND; EVADE;
.............................COUNTER
Parsee priest......................MOBED
Parsee scripture................AVESTA
parsley camphor.....APIOL; APIOLE
parsonage ....MANSE
parson bird ....POE, TUI; KOKO
part ....ROLE, SOME; BREAK,
................PIECE, SEVER, SHARE;
.......................CLEAVE; ELEMENT
participle ending ....-ING
particle.................BIT, JOT; DROP,
...................MITE; GRAIN; TITTLE
particle, electrically charged ......ION
particle in cosmic rays........MESON
particular...............................ITEM
partlet ....HEN; BIDDY
part of speech...........NOUN, VERB
party, wild ....BASH
parvenu ....UPSTART
pasha...................................DEY
pass....................SEND; THROW;
...................ELAPSE; OVERTAKE
passable ....OKAY, SO-SO
passage ....TEXT; SECTION;
.................................TRANSIT
passage, bastion ....POSTERN
passage, covered..............ARCADE

86

a passageway ....HALL; AISLE
pass a rope through ....REEVE
pass between peaks...............COL
pass on......................DIE; RELAY
pass over..........OMIT, SKIP; ELIDE
Passover.....................PASCH
Passover meal.....................SEDER
passport stamp ....VISA
past................AGO; OVER, YORE
pasteboard............................CARD
pastoral...........................IDYLLIC
pastry............FLAN, TART; ECLAIR
pasture........................LEA
pasture, low ....ING
pasty..................DOUGHY
patella............................ROTULA
path: mathematics ....LOCUS
path of a planet ....ORBIT
pathos ....PITY
pathos, false......................BATHOS
patriarch's title, Heb. ....NASI
patron ....CLIENT
patron saint of sailors..............ELMO
pattern ....HABIT, MOTIF;
...................DESIGN; EMULATE
pattern, large square..........DAMIER
pattern, recurring..................CYCLE
Paul, apostle......................SAUL
Paul, birthplace of..............TARSUS
paulownia tree.....................KIRI
b pause ....HALT, REST; BREAK
pause in poetry ....CAESURA
paver's mallet...........................TUP
pavilion ....TENT
paving stone ....FLAG, SETT
paw....................PUD; FOOT
pawl ....DETENT
pawn ....HOCK
pay................REMIT, WAGES
pay, fixed ....STIPEND
payable ....DUE
pay dirt ....ORE
pay for another ....TREAT
pay homage in feudal law .ATTORN
payment, press for ....DUN
pay out....................SPEND
pea..............................LEGUME
peaceful ....IRENIC, SERENE
peace of mind.........................REST
peacock blue.........................PAON
peacock constellation.............PAVO
peacock fish ....WRASSE
peak ....ALP, TOR; ACME;
..................APEX; PITON; ZENITH
peanut ....MANI; GOOBER
pear, autumn..........................BOSC
pear cider............................PERRY
pearl, imitation ....OLIVET
pearlweeds ....SAGINA
peat ....TURF

peat spade ....SLADE
pecan tree ....NOGAL
pedal.......................TREADLE
peddle............HAWK, SELL, VEND
pedestal for a bust ....GAINE
pedestal part ....DADO; PLINTH
peel ....PARE, RIND, SKIN
peep-show ....RAREE
peer........................PEEP; EQUAL
Peer Gynt, mother of ....ASE
peeve ....IRK, VEX;
..........................ANNOY; BOTHER
peg, golf ....TEE
peg, wooden ....NOG; TRENAIL
pellucid ....CLEAR; LIMPID
pelma.................................SOLE
pelota court ....FRONTON
pelt ....SKIN; STONE
pelvic bone, of the..................ILIAC
pelvic bones............................ILIA
penalty ....FINE
pendulum weight ....BOB
penetrate ....GORE; ENTER
penitential season....................LENT
penmanship ....HAND
pen name, Della Ramee.......OUIDA
pen name, Dickens..................BOZ
pen name, Lamb ....ELIA
pennant, ship's..................BURGEE
Pennsylvania sect................AMISH
pen point...........................NEB, NIB
Penrod dog ....DUKE
Pentateuch ....TORAH
people..............MEN; FOLK, ONES,
.............RACE; CROWD, DEMOS;
..................MASSES; POPULACE
pepper, climbing ....BETEL
Pequod, captain of the ....AHAB
perceive ....SEE; SENSE;
...........................DESCRY
perch...........................SIT; ROOST
perch, climbing ....ANABAS
perchlike fish ....DARTER
percolate ......OOZE, SEEP; LEACH
perfect........IDEAL, SHEER, TOTAL
perforate ....BORE; DRILL,
.........................PUNCH; RIDDLE
perform ....ACT; PLAY; STAGE
performer.................DOER; ACTOR
perfume ....AROMA; SMELL
perfume base.........................MUSK
perfumed pad ....SACHET
Pericles, consort of..........ASPASIA
period ....DOT, ERA; TIME
period, five-year...............LUSTRUM
periphery ......RIM; EDGE; MARGIN;
.................CIRCUIT, COMPASS
permission ....LEAVE
permit ....LET; ALLOW; LICENSE
perplex ....BAFFLE; CONFUSE

a Persephone, husband of ....HADES,
......................................PLUTO
Persia today ....IRAN
Persian, ancient....................MEDE
Per. coin, ancient ....DARIC
Per. fairy ....PERI
Per. governor....................SATRAP
Per. headdress....................TIARA
Per. king............DARIUS, XERXES
Per. lord ....KHAN
Per. mystic ....SUFI
Per. poet..............................OMAR
Per. potentate ....SHAH
Per. priestly caste ....MAGI
Per. province, ancient ....ELAM
Per. ruler ....SHAH
Per. sect............................BABISM
person, annoying........CUSS, PEST
person, contemptible............WORM
person, foolish ....BOZO, JERK,
................................TWIT, YOYO
person, impudent ....SNOT
person, insipid ....DRIP; LOSER
person, remarkable ....DARB
person, smugly superior ....SNOB
person, troublesome ....PEST
person, uncouth ....CAD; BOOR;
................YAHOO; GALOOT
person, very skilled ....WHIZ
person, wealthy ....NABOB

b personification of folly ....ATE
personnel................CREW; STAFF
perspiration ....SUDOR, SWEAT
perspire................................EGEST
pert girl....................CHIT, MINX
pertinent............................APT, PAT
perturb..............................UPSET;
..................BOTHER, RUFFLE;
..................FLUSTER; AGITATE
peruse ....READ, SCAN
peruser ....CONNER
Peruvian relic ......GUACO, HUACO
pervade ....FILL; IMBUE
peso, silver ....DURO
pester ....ANNOY, TEASE
pestle vessel....................MORTAR
Peter and the Wolf bird ....SASHA
Peter and the Wolf duck ....SONIA
Peter Pan children................JOHN;
................WENDY; MICHAEL
Peter Pan dog ....NANA
Peter Pan family name.....DARLING
Peter Pan pirate ....SMEE
petiole ....STIPE
pet lamb ....CADE
Petrarch, love of....................LAURA
petrol ....GAS
petty officer, ship's ....BO'S'N
peyote ....MESCAL
phantom(s) ....EIDOLA; EIDOLON

c Pharaoh ....SETI; RAMSES
phase ....FACET, STAGE
pheasant brood ....NIDE
Phidias, statue by ....ATHENA
philippic..............................TIRADE
Philippine Islands..See also islands.
P.I. ancestral spirit ....ANITO
P.I. dyewood tree ....TUI; IPIL
P.I. food..........................POI; SABA
P.I. Muslim ....MORO
P.I. peasant ....TAO
P.I. skirt ....SAYA
P.I. tree ....DITA
P.I. woody vine ....IYO
Philippines archipelago ....SULU
Philistine city ....GATH,
............................GAZA; EKRON
philosopher's stone.............ELIXIR
philosophy, of Zeno's........ELEATIC
phloem....................................BAST
phoebe..................PEWEE, PEWIT;
....................................LAPWING
Phoebe, daughter of ....LETO
Phoebe on dice ....FIVE
Phoebus....................SOL, SUN;
....................................APOLLO
Phoenician city ....TYRE
Phoenician port....................SIDON
Phoenician princess..........EUROPA
phosphate of lime..............APATITE
photo-developing powder ....METOL
photographer's solution ....BATH,
....................................HYPO
Phrygian god................MEN; ATTIS
physician ....GALEN, MEDIC
physician(s), for short....DOC, MDS;
....................................DOCS
physician's symbol ....CADUCEUS
physicist, noted.........RABI; BOYLE,
....................CURIE; EINSTEIN
picket ....PALE
pickled bamboo ....ACHAR
pickled meat ....SOUSE
pickling fluid ....BRINE
pickling herb ....DILL
pick out ....CULL; GLEAN
pickpocket ....DIP
Picnic playwright ....INGE
picture, composite..........MONTAGE
picture, medical....................X-RAY
picture border ....MAT
picturesque........................SCENIC
pie, meat ....PASTY
piebald pony........................PINTO
piece, large ....HUNK, SLAB
"Pied Piper" town ....HAMELIN
pier ....DOCK, QUAY
pierce ....GORE, STAB; SPEAR
pier support ....PILING
pig ....HOG, SOW; SHOAT

d

a pig, wild.................................BOAR
pig, young ....GRICE
pigeon ....NUN; BARB, DOVE;
....POUTER
pigeon hawk ....MERLIN
pigeon pea..........................TUR
piglike animal, S.A. ....PECCARY
pigment, blue-green................BICE
pigment, brown....................SEPIA;
....BISTRE
pigment, deep blue ....SMALT
pigment, red.........................LAKE
pigment, without.................ALBINO
pigmentation, lack of.....ACHROMIA
pigment test crystalline ....DOPA
pigs, litter of......................FARROW
pigs, red ....DUROC
pigtail................................QUEUE
pike, walleyed ....DORE
pilaster..................................ANTA
pilchard..............................SARDINE
pilchardlike fish ....SPRAT
pile.....................NAP; HEAP; SPILE
pile driver ....OLIVER
pile driver ram ....TUP
pile of hay ....RICK; STACK
pile wood.............................ALDER
pilfer..................................STEAL
pilgrim.................................PALMER
pilgrimage city ....MECCA

b pilgrimage to Mecca.....HADJ, HAJJ
pillage.....................LOOT, SACK;
.........................STEAL; PLUNDER
pillar, resembling a.............STELAR
pillar, tapering ....OBELISK
pill for an animal, large.........BOLUS
pillow ....BOLSTER
pilot ....GUIDE, STEER
pin ....BROOCH
pin, gunwale........................THOLE
pin, machine.......................COTTER
pin, metal ....RIVET
pin, old-time firing ....TIGE
pin, pivot ....PINTLE
pin, Rom. ....ACUS
pin, splicing ....FID
pin, very small LILL
pin, wooden.................NOG, PEG;
....DOWEL
pinafore................................TIER
pincer claw ....CHELA
pinch ....NIP
Pindar work ....ODE
pine, Mex. ....OCOTE, PINON
pinion....................................WING
pinnacle.......................TOP; APEX
pinnacle, ice.........................SERAC
pinniped.................SEAL; WALRUS
Pinocchio, carver of ....GEPETTO
pint, half....................................CUP

c pin wrench ....SPANNER
pioneered ....LED
pious biblical Jew ....TOBIT
pipe...........................TUBE; RISER
pipe, Irish clay ....DUDEEN
pipe, tobacco........................BRIER
pipelike...............................TUBATE
pique ....PEEVE
pirate ....ROVER; CORSAIR
pirate in War of 1812 ....LAFITTE
pismire ....ANT; EMMET
pistil part ....CARPEL
pistol ....MAUSER; SIDEARM
pit ....HOLE; ABYSS, STONE
pit, medical...........................FOSSA
pit, small ....FOVEA; LACUNA
pitch ....KEY, TAR;
.............................TONE; THROW
pitcher ....JUG; EWER
pitcher's false move ....BALK
pith ....NUB; GIST
pith helmet.................TOPI; TOPEE
pithy ....TERSE
pithy plant............................SOLA
pitiful quality ....PATHOS
pittance ....TRIFLE
pitted ....FOVEATE
pit viper, Jap. ....HABU
pity ....RUTH
placard ....POSTER

d place ....SET; LIEU;
.........................SPOT; STEAD
placid....................CALM; SERENE
plagiarize ....STEAL
plague ....PEST
plain, Arctic ....TUNDRA
plain, Argentine ....PAMPAS
plain, Russ. ....STEPPE
plain, S.A. ....LLANO
plain, treeless ....SAVANNAH
plait ....BRAID
plan ....DESIGN, LAYOUT,
.....................METHOD, SCHEME
plane, Fr. ....SPAD
plane, Ger. ....STUKA
plane, Jap. ....ZERO
plane, Russ. ....MIG
plane part ....FLAP, NOSE,
.................TAIL, WING; NACELLE
planetarium.......................ORRERY
planetary aspect........CUSP; TRINE
planets and satellites ....
.......................(in order from the sun)
.............................MERCURY,
...............VENUS, EARTH (LUNA),
...........MARS (DEIMOS, PHOBOS),
.................JUPITER (IO, EUROPA,
.............CALLISTO, GANYMEDE),
...............SATURN (RHEA, DIONE,
.............JANUS, MIMAS, PHOEBE,

a planets and satellites, *continued*......
................TETHYS, IAPETUS,
...........HYPERION, ENCELADUS),
..........URANUS (ARIEL, OBERON,
....................MIRANDA, TITANIA,
...................UMBRIEL), NEPTUNE
...........(NEREID, TRITON), PLUTO
plank's curve on a ship ....SNY
plant....................SOW; SEED
plant, any sea-bottom ....ENALID
plant, bayonet ....DATIL
plant, broom ....SPART
plant, bulb ....CAMASS
plant, medicinal ....ALOE; SENNA;
...............................IPECAC
plant, mustard family..............KALE;
...............................CRESS
plant, soap ....AMOLE
plant disease ....RUST, SMUT
plant growth ....LEAF
plant joined to another ....GRAFT
plant life..............................FLORA
plant louse..............................APHID
plant of the iris family ....IRID
plant pod ....BOLL
plant stem ....CAULIS
plant stem tissue ....PITH
plant used as a medicine ....HERB
plasterer's float ....DARBY
plaster of Paris ....GESSO

b plate, battery ....GRID
plate, Eucharist ....PATEN
plate, reptile's......................SCUTE
plateau ....MESA
plateau, Andes ....PUNA
platform ....DAIS; STAGE
platform, ancient church ....BEMA
platinum, of..........................OSMIC
play ....DRAMA
player..............................ACTOR
play on words ....PUN
play part......................ACT; SCENE
plead ....BEG, SUE;
...............................ENTREAT
pleasant..............................NICE
please ....SUIT
pleat..............................FOLD
pledge ....VOW; GAGE,
..................OATH, PAWN; TROTH
plexus ....RETE; RETIA
pliant ....LITHE
plinth ....ORLO; SOCLE
plot ....LOT; PLAT; CABAL
plow, sole of a......................SHARE
pluck ....PICK
plucky ....GAMY
plug..........CORK; STOPPER
plug, barrel..............................SPILE
plum ....GAGE, SLOE
plummet ....DROP; PLUNGE

c plunder............ROB; LOOT, SACK;
.............BOOTY; PILFER, RAVAGE
plunge ....DIVE, DROP
plus ....AND; ALSO; ASSET
Pluto ....DIS; HADES, ORCUS
Pluto, mother-in-law of....DEMETER
pneumonia, kind of ....LOBAR
pocket billiards ....POOL
pod, cotton ....BOLL
poem............ODE; ELEGY, EPODE
poem, Biblical ....PSALM
poem, eight-line ....TRIOLET
poem, heroic ....EPIC, EPOS
poem, love ....SONNET
poem, mournful ....ELEGY
poem, pastoral ....IDYL; IDYLL
poem division ....CANTO, VERSE
poet......................BARD; ODIST
poet, famous Bengal.........TAGORE
poet, Norse......................SKALD
poet, old English ....SCOP
poetry syllable, Gr. ....ARSIS
point ....END, TIP; BARB;
....................PUNTO; JUNCTURE
pointed ....SHARP; ACUATE
pointed arch ....OGEE
pointed end ....CUSP
pointed missile ....DART; SPEAR
pointed remark ....BARB
pointed staff ....PIKE
pointer..............................WAND
point of land ....SPIT
point of the crescent moon.....CUSP
point of view..........................ANGLE
point on a curve ....NODE
poison ....BANE; TAINT
poison, arrow ....UPAS; URALI;
........................CURARE, OORALI
poison, hemlock ....CONINE
poisonous protein ....RICIN
poisonous snakes, of ....ELAPINE
poisonous weed......................LOCO
poison tree ....UPAS
poi source ....TARO
poke ....JAB; PROD; NUDGE
poke fun at........KID; JOSH; TEASE
poker hand..............PAIR; FLUSH
poker stake..............................ANTE
poker winnings..............................POT
pokeweed ....POCAN, SCOKE
polar explorer ....BYRD
pole, boat........MAST, SPAR; SPRIT
polecat, Cape ....ZORIL;
...............................ZORILLE
pole in Gaelic games ....CABER
pole to pole, from ....AXIAL
police line ....CORDON
policeman ....COP
policeman, state ....TROOPER
polish ....RUB, WAX; SHINE

a Polish assembly ....SEJM
Polish rum cake.....................BABA
polished ....SHINY, SLEEK;
.......................URBANE; ELEGANT
polisher.................................EMERY
Polish general ....BOR; ANDERS
polishing material ....RABAT,
......................................ROUGE
polite......................CIVIL; GENTEEL
political booty ....GRAFT
political party..........DEM, GOP, IND
politition, veteran.....................POL
pollack fish ....SAITHE
pollen brush ....SCOPA
Pollux, mother of....................LEDA
Pollux, twin of....................CASTOR
polo stick ....MALLET
Polydorus, father of.............CREON
Polydorus, mother of.........HECUBA
Polynesian, N. Z. ....MAORI
Polynesian amulet ....TIKI
Polynesian cloth ....TAPA
Polynesian dance ....SIVA
Polynesian drink............AVA; KAVA
Polynesian god.........AKUA, ATUA
Polynesian spirit ....MANA
pome ....APPLE
"Pomp and Circumstances"
composer ....
....ELGAR

b pompous ....STUFFY, TURGID
poncho, Colombian ....RUANA
pond..........................MERE, POOL
ponder....................MULL, MUSE;
.............................THINK; REFLECT
pontiff ....POPE
pony, student's ....CRIB
pool ....POND, TARN;
.........................BAYOU; LAGOON
pool shot ....BANK, KISS;
.............BREAK, CAROM, MASSE
pool stick ....CUE
poor ....NEEDY
poorly ILL
poor-quality goods ....CRAP;
....SCHLOCK
Pope.......LEO; JOHN, PAUL, PIUS;
............................LINUS, URBAN
Pope, Eng. ....ADRIAN
Pope's triple crown ....TIARA
Popeye, foe of.....................BLUTO
Popeye, girlfriend of ......OLIVE OYL
poplar ....ALAMO, ASPEN
poplar, white ....ABELE
poppy red ......GRANAT; PONCEAU
poppy seed.............................MAW
populace, Gr. ....DEMOS
popular girl ....BELLE
porcelain..............CHINA; SEVRES;
....LIMOGES

porcelain, ancient Rom. .....MURRA
porcelain, Eng. ....SPODE
porch ....ANTA; LANAI, STOOP;
....VERANDA
porch, Gr. ....STOA
porch swing ....GLIDER
porcupine anteater...........ECHIDNA
pore ....STOMA
porgy, brown-and-white ....SCUP
porgy, Eur. ....PARGO
porgy, Jap. ....TAI
porous volcanic rock....TUFA, TUFF
porpoise ....DOLPHIN
porridge ....POBS; BROSE
porridge, cornmeal.................SAMP
porridge, S.A. ....ATOLE
port...........................LEFT, WINE;
............CARRY, HAVEN; HARBOR
port, Black Sea..................ODESSA
port, leave ....SAIL
port, Samoan ....APIA
port, Suez ....SAID
portable chair.......................SEDAN
portal ....DOOR, GATE
portend....................BODE; AUGUR;
....PRESAGE
portent ....OMEN, SIGN
porter, Oriental.....................HAMAL
Portia, handmaid of ....NERISSA
portico ....STOA
portion ....PART; SHARE
portion out.....DOLE, METE; ALLOT
port of Rome ....OSTIA
port opposite Gibraltar ....CEUTA
portray...............................DRAW,
..............................PLAY; DEPICT
Portuguese coin ....REI
Port. colony in India ....GOA
Port. explorer ....DIAS; DA GAMA
Port. folk tune ....FADO
Port. lady ....DONA
Port. man ....DOM
Port. port........................OPORTO
Port. Timor's capital................DILI
pose ....SIT; SHAM;
....STANCE
posed for a portrait....................SAT
Poseidon ....NEPTUNE
Poseidon, son of......................ARION,
............................ORION; TRITON
position.................PLACE; STATUS
positive terminal ....ANODE
possessed....................HAD; HELD;
....OWNED
possesses ....HAS; OWNS;
....KEEPS
possum of the comics ....POGO
post.........................MAIL, SEND;
....STAKE
postage stamp paper.........PELURE

c

d

a
post-crucifixion depiction ....PIETA
postpone ....DEFER
postulate...............POSIT; THEORY
posture ....STANCE
pot, small ....CRUSE
pot, Indian brass ....LOTAH
potassium chloride ....MURIATE
potassium nitrate ....NITER
potation, small ....DRAM
potato ....SPUD
potato, sweet...........YAM; BATATA
pother ....ADO; FUSS
pot herb...............................WORT
potpourri ....OLIO
pottage, beef.....................BREWIS
potter's blade ....PALLET
pottery, of ....CERAMIC
pottery, once ....CLAY
pottery fragment ....SHARD
pouch ....SAC
poultry ....HENS
poultry disease..............PIP; ROUP
pounce ....SWOOP
pound down ....RAM; TAMP
pour ....RAIN; TEEM
pour off gently ....DECANT
pour out ....LIBATE
poverty....................NEED, WANT
powder, astringent ....BORAL
powdered pumice ....TALC

b
power........DINT; FORCE; MIGHT
practical joke ....HOAX
practice ....WONT; DRILL,
..............HABIT, TRAIN; CUSTOM
practice exercise, musical....ETUDE
prairie copse......................MOTTE
praise.......................LAUD; EXTOL;
....TRIBUTE
prance...............................CAPER
prank ....DIDO
prate.........................GAB, YAP
pray: Yiddish ....DAVEN
prayer ....AVE; PLEA; ORISON
prayer, nine-day ....NOVENA
prayer book ....ORDO
prayer form ....LITANY
prayer position, Hindu..........ASANA
praying figure....................ORANT
preacher, Gospel ....EVANGEL
precept ....LAW; EDICT;
....DICTUM
precipitous....................STEEP
preclude ....AVERT, DETER
predicament..............FIX; SCRAPE
predicate ....BASE; FOUND;
....AFFIRM
predict...........AUGUR; FORECAST
predisposed........................PRONE
preen ....PLUME, PRINK
preface................................PROEM

PREFIXES:
abnormal ....DYS-
about ....PERI-
above ....HYPER-
acid...................ACET-; ACETO-
across.................DIA-; TRANS-
African...............................AFRO-
against...............................ANTI-
ahead ....PRE-
air ....AER-; AERI-, AERO-
angle ....GONI-; GONIO-
animal ....ZOO-
apart ....DIS-
away ....ABS-; CATA-
back ....NOTO-
backward ....RETRO-
bad ....MAL-; CACO-
badly ....MIS-
before ....PRE-; ANTE-
benzene, derived from.....PHEN-
bile ....CHOL-; CHOLE-
billionth ....NANO-
birds ....AVI-
bitter ....PICR-; PICRO-
blood ....VAS-; HEMA-,
.........................HEMO-, VASO-
bone ....OSSI-
both ....AMBI-
bromine.........BROM-; BROMO-
bull .....TAUR-; TAURI-, TAURO-
carbon ....CARB-; CARBO-
change ....MET-; META-
child ....PED-; PEDO-
Chinese ....SINO-
cloud.................NEPH-; NEPHO-
coil ....SPIR-; SPIRO-
common ....CEN-; CENO-
copper.............CUPR-; CUPRI-,
....CUPRO-
correct ....ORTH-; ORTHO-
current...............................RHEO-
custom...............................NOMO-
death ....NECR-; NECRO-
deputy ....VICE-
destroying ....PHAG-; PHAGO-
disease ....NOS-; NOSO-
distant ....TELE-, TELO-
down ....CATA-
dry.....................XER-; XERO-
dung.............COPR-; COPRO-
ear ....OTO-
earth ....GEO-
egg ....OVI-, OVO-
eight ....OCT-; OCTA-, OCTO-
end ....TELO-
equal ....ISO-; PARI-
everywhere ....OMNI-
eye....................OCUL-; OCULO-
fat .....LIP-; LIPO-, SEBI-, SEBO-
female ....GYN-; GYNO-

a PREFIXES: *continued*

fermentation ....ZYM-; ZYMO-
fever ....FEBR-; FEBRI-
few......................OLIG-; OLIGO-
fibrous ....FIBR-; FIBRO-
fire ....PYR-; IGNI-, PYRO-
fish ....PISC-; PISCI-
fluorine ....FLUO-;
................FLUOR-; FLUORO-
food ....SITO-
foot ....PED-; PEDI-
foreign.................XEN-; XENO-
four ....TETRA-
freeing....................LYS-; LYSI-
freezing ....CRYO-
fungus.FUNG-, MYCO-; FUNGI-
glass ....HYAL-; HYALO-
grain ....SITO-
ground ....PED-; PEDO-
gyrating ....GYR-; GYRO-
hair.................................PILI-
half...........DEMI-, HEMI-, SEMI-
hand..................CHIR-; CHIRO-
hatred ....MISO-
hearing...........ACOU-; ACOUO-
high ....ALTI-, ALTO-
highest ....ACRO-
horse.................HIPP-; HIPPO-
hundred..........HECT-; HECTO-
idea...............................IDEO-

b
ileum ....ILE-; ILEO-
India.............................INDO-
iodine ....IOD-; IODO-
kernel ....KARY-; KARYO-
ketone ....KET-; KETO-
kidney ....REN-; RENI-, RENO-
large ....MEG-; MEGA-
leftside ....LEV-; LEVO-
life.................................BIO-
lip........................CHIL-; CHILO-
main ....ARCH-
many ....POLY-
many times more than ....
...................MULT-; MULTI-
middle ....MESO-
moon ....LUNI-
mountain ....ORO-
movie ....CINE-
mucus ....MYX-; MUCO-, MYXO-
naked.GYMN-, NUDI-; GYMNO-
negative........................NON-
nerve ....NEUR-; NEURO-
new ....NEO-
night ....NOCT-; NOCTI-
nitrogen, containing...........AZO-;
...............NITR-; NITRO-
nose ....NAS-; NASO-,
...................RHIN-; RHINO-
numerous..........MYRI-; MYRIA-
oil ....OLEO-

c
one ....UNI-
one's own ....IDIO-
outer ....ECT-, ECTO-
outside ....EXO-
over...............................EPI-
oxygen ....OXA-, OXY-
pair.......................ZYG-; ZYGO-
partly ....SEMI-
pelvis ....PYEL-; PYELO-
people ....ETHN-; ETHNO-
physician...........MEDI-; MEDIO-
pointed.......ACU-, OXY-; ACRO-
power...............DYN-; DYNA-
pray ....ORA-
pressure............BARO-, TONO-
quintillionth ....ATTO-
rain ....HYET-; HYETO-
reproductive ....GON-; GONO-
root......................RHIZ-; RHIZO
sacred...............HIER-; HIERO-
same ....ISO-; EQUI-, HOMO-
scales.............CTEN-; CTENO-
serum.................SER-; SERO-
seven ....HEPT-; HEPTA-
sex ....SEX-; SEXI-
sexually united ....GAM-; GAMO-
single..HAPL-, MONO-; HAPLO-
six ....HEX-; HEXA-
sleep................NARC-; NARCO-
small.............................MINI-
snake ....OPHI-
sound ....PHON-; PHONO-
sound of a thump ....KER-
spinal cord ......MYEL-; MYELO-
spore ....SPOR-; SPORO-
star ....ASTR-; ASTRO-
starch ....AMYL-; AMYLO-
stone ....PETR-; PETRO-
sub-.............................SUS-
sulfur ....THIO-
sunlight ....HELI-; HELIO-
sword ....XIPH-
ten ....DEC-, DEK-;
.................DECA-, DEKA-
tendon ....TENO-
thin ....LEPT-; LEPTO-
thousand ....KILO-
three ....TER-, TRI-
to or from a distance ....TEL-;
...............................TELE-
trillion ....TERA-
two ....DUA-; DIPL-; DIPLO-
two, in................DICH-; DICHO-
under...............................SUB-
universe ....COSM-; COSMO-
uterus..............UTER-; UTERO-
variation ....ALLO-
vein ....VEN-; VENI-, VENO-
water ....HYDR-; HYDRO-
wax.....................CER-; CERO-

93

Prefixes: (weakly colored) / progeny

a PREFIXES: *continued*
weakly colored ...LEUC-, LEUK-;
..................LEUCO-, LEUKO-
wet ....HYGR-; HYGRO-
whole ....HOLO-, TOTI-
wide ....EURY-
wine ....OENO-, VINI-
wing................PTER-; PTERO-
with ....COM-, SYN-
within ....END-, ENT-;
.........................ENDO-, ENTO-
womb.............METR-; METRO-
wood...................HYL-, XYL-;
..................HYLO-, LIGN-,
.............XYLO-; LIGNI-; LIGNO-
wrong ....MIS-
prehistoric mound..................TERP
prejudice ....BIAS
prelate, high ....PRIMATE
premium exchange ....AGIO
prepare......................FIX; READY
prepare for publication ....EDIT
presage...............OMEN; AUGURY,
...................HERALD; PORTENT
prescribed ....THETIC
prescribed quantity ....DOSE
present ....NOW; GIFT, GIVE;
...............................DONATE
present, be...................ATTEND
presently ....ANON, SOON
b preserve.............CAN, JAM; KEEP,
.................SAVE; MAINTAIN
preserve in brine........CORN, SALT
presidential nickname ....ABE,
..............................CAL, IKE
presidents, US ....See page 190.
press coverage ....INK
press together.....................SERRY
pressure.........COERCE, DURESS,
.................STRESS; CONSTRAIN
pretend ....ACT; FAKE,
...................POSE; FEIGN;
............HAZARD; VENTURE
pretense........................SHAM
pretensions ....AIRS
prevail ....WIN
prevail on...................INDUCE
prevalent............................RIFE
prevent...........AVERT, DETER
prevent by law...................ESTOP
prey...............................VICTIM
prey upon...........................RAVINE
Priam, son of.......PARIS; HECTOR
Priam, wife of ....HECUBA
price ....FEE, TAB;
..............COST, RATE, TOLL
prickly plant ....BRIER; NETTLE
prickly seed coat ....BURR
pride ....EGO; VANITY
pride member ....LION

c priest ....FRA; ABBE,
..............................CURE; PADRE
priest, Celtic.........................DRUID
priest, Zoroastrian..............MAGUS
priestess, Rom. ....VESTAL
priest in the *Iliad*...........CALCHAS
priestly caste, Zoroastrian.......MAGI
prima donna...........................DIVA
primeval ....OLD; EARLY;
....................PRIMAL; PRISTINE
prince, Arabian ....EMIR; SAYID;
...............................SAYYID
prince, Indian....................RAJAH
prince, Oriental.....................KHAN
prince, petty ....SATRAP
prince, Slavic ....KNEZ
princely ....ROYAL
Prince of Darkness..............SATAN
princess, Indian.........RANI; RANEE
princess in Gr. myth................IOLE
principal....................HEAD, MAIN;
..........................CHIEF, PRIME
principal commodity ....STAPLE
principle, accepted ....AXIOM,
.......................PRANA, TENET
print.....................................STAMP
printer's direction ....DELE, STET
printer's mistake ....TYPO
printer's mistakes ....ERRATA
printing press handle ....ROUNCE
printing roller ....PLATEN
prison.................JUG; JAIL, STIR
prison: Brit. ....GAOL, QUOD
prison sentence..............RAP; LIFE
prison spy..........................MOUTON
privation ....LOSS
prize ....PRY; AWARD
pro.......................................FOR
probe, medical...................STYLET
problem.................ISSUE, POSER
proboscis ....SNOUT
proceed..........COME; ADVANCE
proceedings..........................ACTA
procession ....TRAIN; PARADE
proclaim.....................CRY; VOICE;
...............HERALD; DECLARE
procreation ....SEX
procurer...................................PIMP
prod.......................................URGE
produce ....BEGET, YIELD;
..................CREATE; GENERATE
profane..............................VIOLATE
profession ....ART; CAREER,
......................METIER; CALLING
professional, not.....................LAIC
profit ....GAIN; AVAIL
profit, to yield ....NET
profound ....DEEP
progenitor................SIRE; PARENT
progeny ....ISSUE

a prohibit..............BAN, BAR; VETO;
............................DEBAR, ESTOP
prohibition ....EMBARGO
project..................JUT; IDEA, PLAN
projectile.................DART; MISSILE
projecting edge ....RIM; FLANGE
projecting piece ....ARM; TENON
projecting tooth ....SNAG
projection ......EAR; BARB; PRONG
projection, fireplace ....HOB
promenade ....MALL
promise ....WORD
Promised Land ....ZION
promise to pay ....IOU; NOTE
promontory ....CAPE, NESS
promontory, rocky...................TOR
promote ....HYPE, TOUT;
.................FOSTER; ADVANCE
prompt...........SPUR, STIR; TIMELY
prone ....APT; FLAT
prong ....TINE; TOOTH
pronghorn ....CABRET
___ *pro nobis* ....ORA
pronoun ....HER, HIM, ONE, SHE,
.............YOU; THAT, THIS, THEM,
.................THEY; THESE, THOSE
pronoun, possessive ....HER, HIS,
.................ITS, OUR; HERS, MINE,
.......OURS, YOUR; THEIR, YOURS
pronoun, Quaker.....................THY;
b ....THEE, THOU; THINE
pronounce indistinctly ....SLUR
pronouncement ....DICTUM
pronounce strongly ....STRESS
proof, corrected...................REVISE
proof, legal ....IDS
proofreader's mark ....DELE,
...........................STET; CARET
prop ....HOLD, STAY; BRACE;
.................BOLSTER, SUSTAIN
propeller ....OAR
proper..................DUE, FIT; RIGHT
property, hold on ....LIEN
property, item of ....ASSET;
...............................CHATTEL
property, landed ....ESTATE
property, receiver of ....ALIENEE
prophesy ....AUGUR; DIVINE;
...............................FORETELL
prophet ....SEER
prophetess ....SIBYL; SEERESS
proportion ....RATIO
proportionally assess......PRORATE
proposition ....THESIS;
.................................PREMISE
proposition, logic ....LEMMA
proposition, math ....THEOREM
prosecutor ....SUER
proselyte to Judaism ....GER
prospect.....................VIEW; VISTA

prospects ....ODDS; FUTURE; *c*
..................................OUTLOOK
prosperity ....WEALTH
Prospero, servant of ....ARIEL
prostrate ....FLAT; PRONE;
...................................FLATTEN
protagonist.............................HERO
protected..........................HOUSED
protection ....AEGIS
prototype ....MASTER; ORIGINAL
protuberance......JAG, NUB; HUMP,
.................KNOB, NODE, WART
prove a claim by dueling..DERAIGN
proverb ....SAW; ADAGE,
.............AXIOM, MAXIM; SAYING
provide............................GIVE;
...........................OFFER; SUPPLY;
...................DELIVER, FURNISH
province, Rom. ....DACIA
provisional clause ....PROVISO
provoke ....RILE; ANGER
prow......................BOW; STEM
Prussian spa site....................EMS
pry ....NOSE; LEVER, SNOOP
Psalm, 51st ....MISERERE
Psalmist ....DAVID
Psalms, 113 to 118.............HALLEL
Psalms ending.....................SELAH
pseudonym ....ALIAS
pseudonym of H.H. Munro.......SAKI
pseudonym of Viaud ....LOTI *d*
psyche.....................................SOUL
psychiatrist, noted ....JUNG;
.............ADLER, FREUD; HORNEY
Ptah, embodiment of...............APIS
ptarmigan ....RYPE
pub fare ....ALE; BEER;
...........................LAGER, STOUT
public ....OPEN; CIVIL; PEOPLE
public, make ....AIR
publication style ....FORMAT
public esteem ....REPUTE
public gardens.......................PARK
public vehicle.........BUS, CAB; TAXI
publish ....ISSUE, PRINT
publish illegally ....PIRATE
Puccini heroine ....MIMI
puck material...................RUBBER
pudding ....DUFF, SAGO;
...........................TRIFLE; TAPIOCA
Pueblo Indian ....HOPI,
.................MOKI, TANO, ZUNI;
.................KERES, MOQUI
Pueblo sacred chamber...........KIVA
puffer fish........................TAMBOR
pull ....TOW, TUG; DRAG
pull abruptly................JERK, YANK
pulley wheel.......................SHEAVE
pulp, fruit...........................POMACE
pulpit.........................AMBO, BEMA

95

a pump handle........................SWIPE
pumpkin seed.....................PEPO
punch............................JAB; POKE,
.............SOCK; VIGOR; PUMMEL
punch, engraver's ....MATTOIR
Punch and Judy dog.........TOBY
punctuation mark....DASH; COLON,
...................COMMA; PERIOD
pungent................ACRID; BITING;
..............MORDANT, PIQUANT
punish by fine ....AMERCE
punishment, of.....................PENAL
punishment stick...............FERULE
Punjab inhabitant.....................JAT
punk ....AMADOU
punt......................................KICK
pupa....................................INSTAR
puppet....................................DOLL
purchase ....BUY; GRIP
pure thought ....NOESIS
purification, Rom. ....LUSTRUM

c purloin...............................STEAL
purple dye source ....MUREX
purplish-brown ....PUCE
purpose ....AIM, END;
........................GOAL; INTENT
purse net ....SEINE
pursy ....STOUT
push up.................................BOOST
put away ....STORE
put back...............................REPLACE
put down ....LAY; QUASH, WRITE
put off....................................DEFER
put out....................OUST; EJECT
puzzle...........POSER, REBUS;
....ENIGMA
Pygmalion's statue ....GALATEA
Pylos, kin of......................NESTOR
Pyramus, lover of...............THISBE
pyromaniac ....FIREBUG
Pythias, friend of................DAMON
python..................................BOA

Q

QED, part of..............ERAT, QUOD
quack..........................CHARLATAN
quack medicine ....NOSTRUM
b quadrant...................................ARC
quadrate.............................SQUARE
quaff....................................DRINK
quail.......................COLIN, COWER
quake................SHAKE; SHIVER,
.................TREMOR; TREMBLE
Quaker....................................FRIEND
Quaker poet ....WHITTIER
quaking ....TREPID
qualify ....MARK; ENABLE
qualified ....FIT; ABLE
quality ....CLASS, TRAIT,
................VALUE; CALIBER
___ qua non.............................SINE
quantity, indeterminate ....SOME
quantity, math ....SCALAR,
....VECTOR
quarrel ....ROW; FEUD,
...................SPAT; CLASH, FIGHT
quarrel, trivial...................MIFF, TIFF
quartz, green.......................PRASE
quartz, opaque reddish .....JASPER
quaternion....................TETRAD
quay ....LEVEE, WHARF
Quebec, patron saint of..........ANNE
Queen Boadicea's people .....ICENI
queenly ....REGAL, ROYAL;
................................REGINAL
Queen of Italy.....................ELENA
Queen of Ithaca ....PENELOPE

d Queen of Scots....................MARY
Queen of Spain, last................ENA
Queen of the fairies.................MAB
queen of the gods, Eg. ....SATI
queen of the gods, Rom. ....JUNO
Queen of the Nile ....CLEO
Queensland hemp plant ....SIDA
quell....................CRUSH, QUASH;
..............QUENCH, SQUASH
quench.................................SLAKE
quench steel ....AUSTEMPER
quern.....................................MILL
query.......................................ASK
queue.....................................LINE
question ....ASK; GRILL
question, hard......................POSER
question starter .HOW, WHO, WHY;
................WHAT, WHEN, WHOM;
............WHERE, WHICH, WHOSE
quetzal..............................TROGON
quibble....CARP; CAVIL; BICKER
quick.......................FAST; AGILE,
..............................ALIVE, RAPID
quicken ....HASTEN
quickly ....APACE; PRESTO,
....PRONTO
quickly, move ....SCAT, SCUD
quickly: music ....TOSTO
quicksilver....................MERCURY;
................................HEAUTARIT
quid....................................CUD
quid ___ quo ....PRO
quiescent........LATENT; DORMANT

_a_ quiet.....................CALM; STILL;
....................HUSHED, LOW-KEY,
....................PLACID; TRANQUIL
quill ....PEN; SPINE
quill feather(s) ....REMEX;
.................................REMIGES
quill for winding silk ....COP
quilt........................COVER, EIDER
quince yellow ....MELINE

quincunx...............................FIVE _c_
quinine ....CINCHONA
quintessence ....PITH; ELIXIR
quirt, cowboy's ....ROMAL
quit ....CEASE, LEAVE
quite ....JUST, WELL; FULLY;
.....................................WHOLLY
quod___ _demonstrandum_ .....ERAT
quote.....................................CITE

R

Ra, consort of ....MUT
Ra, son of ....SHU
rabbit, female ....DOE
rabbit, invisible ....HARVEY
rabbit, small S.A. ....TAPETI
rabbit cage..........................HUTCH
rabbit community.............WARREN
rabbit fur ....CONY;
.........................CONEY, LAPIN
rabble ....MOB
rabies.................................LYSSA
raccoon, briefly.....................COON
raccoonlike mammal ....COATI
race, boat ....REGATTA
race, segmented ....RELAY
_b_ race, short..........................SPRINT
racetrack circuit ....LAP
racetrack tipster......................TOUT
Rachel, father of...................LABAN
Radames, love of....................AIDA
radar screen ....SCOPE
radar signal ....BLIP
radiate................................EMANATE
radioactive ray ....GAMMA
radio wire ....LITZ
radium discoverer ....CURIE
radium emanation ....NITON;
......................................RADON
rag doll ....MOPPET
rage.............................FAD, IRE;
..............FURY; CRAZE, FUROR,
.................MANIA, WRATH
ragout, game ....SALMI
raid......................FORAY; INROAD
raiding soldier............COMMANDO
rail at ....REVILE
rail bird ....SORA, WEKA;
....CRAKE
railing.............................PARAPET
railroad bridge ....TRESTLE
railroad tie....................SLEEPER
railroad timber ....TIE
railroad warning light ....FLARE
railroad-yard signal..........TRIMMER
railway station: Fr. ....GARE

rain from a clear sky ....SEREIN
rainbow, of a ....IRIDAL
rainbow goddess.......................IRIS
raincoat ....MACK; PONCHO
rain forest ....SELVA, SILVA
rain gauge ....UDOMETER
rain tree ....SAMAN
rainy ....WET
raise.......................REAR; BREED;
.................................ELEVATE
raised ....BRED
raising device ....JACK
rake ....ROUE; LOTHARIO
rake with aerial gunfire.......STRAFE
rake with gunfire ....ENFILADE
ram ....TUP; TAMP; ARIES _d_
Ramachandra, wife of.............SITA
ramble ....GAD; ROVE
rampart ....AGGER; VALLUM
ran............BLED; OPERATED
range ....AREA; GAMUT, SCOPE
Rangoon's state.....................PEGU
ran into ....MET
rank ......ROW; RATE; DEGREE
rankle ....FESTER
ransom ....REDEEM
rapeseed ....COLZA
rapidly ....APACE
rapids, river ....SOO
rapier ....BILBO
rare-earth element ....CERIUM;
..................ERBIUM; HOLMIUM,
.................TERBIUM, THORIUM,
.................YTTRIUM; SCANDIUM
rascal ....IMP; ROGUE
rasp ....FILE; GRATE
raspberry variety ....BLACKCAP
rasse...................................CIVET
rat, Indian.................BANDICOOT
rate.........RANK; GRADE; ASSESS
rational ....SANE
rational integer ....NORM
rational principle ....LOGOS
ratite bird ....KIWI; OSTRICH;
...............................CASSOWARY

97

a rattan..CANE
rave.....................RANT; HARANGUE
"Raven, The" poet....................POE
"Raven, The" woman.........LENORE
ravine.......................DALE, GLEN,
........................WADI; GORGE
rawboned...............................LEAN
rawboned animal................SCRAG
ray..............BEAM; SHAFT, SKATE
rayon..........ACETATE; CELANESE
rays, like..............................RADIAL
raze..................LEVEL; DESTROY
razor-billed auk......................ALCA
reach....................RANGE, SCOPE;
.......................EXTENT; BREADTH
reach across........................SPAN
react...............................RESPOND
read, inability to...................ALEXIA
reader, first........................PRIMER
reading desk.......AMBO; LECTERN
read metrically.......................SCAN
read publicly....................PRELECT
reality..FACT
realm.......ARENA, ORBIT, SCOPE;
.......................DOMAIN; PURVIEW
real thing, the.....................MCCOY
rear...............BACK; ERECT, RAISE
rear, to the....................AFT; ABAFT;
......................................ASTERN
rearhorse............................MANTIS
b reasoning.............................LOGIC
reasoning, deductive........A PRIORI
Rebecca, son of.......ESAU; JACOB
rebound..........CAROM; RICOCHET
rebuff..........................SLAP, SNUB
rebuke...................CHIDE, SCOLD;
..............REPROVE, UPBRAID
recalcitrant.......UNRULY; DEFIANT
recant...............UNSAY; RETRACT
recede....................................EBB
recent...........................NEW; LATE
receptacle..............BIN, BOX, CUP;
......................................VESSEL
receptacle, shallow................TRAY
reception, morning.............LEVEE
recess.....................APSE; BREAK,
......................NICHE; ALCOVE
recipient..............................DONEE
reckless..................................RASH
reckon..................COUNT, TALLY;
.......................FIGURE; COMPUTE
reclaim...........................REDEEM
recline.............LIE; LOLL; REPOSE
recluse..............HERMIT; ASCETIC
recoil.............SHY; QUAIL, WINCE;
..................FLINCH; REBOUND
recombinant letters..................DNA
recompense....................FEE, PAY;
......................................REWARD
reconnaissance................PROBE

c reconnoiter.......SCOUT; EXPLORE
record.....LOG; DISC, NOTE, TAPE
recorded proceedings.............ACTA
records................................ANNALS
recover strength..................RALLY
recovery of goods, legal....TROVER
rectifier, current.....................DIODE
rectify..................AMEND, EMEND;
...............................SETTLE;
.................CORRECT, RESOLVE
red...............CARMINE, CRIMSON,
......................SCARLET, MAGENTA
red, Venetian.........................SIENA
redact....................................EDIT
redbreast.............................ROBIN
redcap...............................PORTER
red cedar...............................SAVIN
red deer, like a................ELAPHINE
reddish-yellow color...........ALOMA,
......................................SUDAN
red dye root.............CHAY, CHOY;
.......................CHAYA, CHOYA
redeem..........RANSOM; RECLAIM
redeye fish............................RUDD
red hog................................DUROC
red horse.....................BAY; ROAN
red ocher.............BOLE; RUDDLE
Red or White team...................SOX
red pigment.........................ROSET;
.........................BRAZIL; ASTACIN
red pine...................................RIMU
red planet.............................MARS
red powder, Indian.................ABIR
red squirrel..................CHICKAREE
reduce..........................CUT; PARE;
......................................DEVALUE
reduce sails............................REEF
reedbuck............................NAGOR
reek...........................FUG; STENCH
reef......................................SHOAL
reel, fishing............................PIRN
refer.................APPLY; MENTION,
...................PERTAIN; TRANSFER
refer to.....................................VIDE
reflection...............GLARE, IMAGE
refracting device....................LENS
refractor, light.....................PRISM
refrain..............................ABSTAIN,
....FORBEAR
refrain, musical........FA-LA; TRA-LA
refrigerant............................FREON
refuge...............HAVEN; ASYLUM;
.................SHELTER; RECOURSE
refugee...........................ESCAPEE,
......................................RUNAWAY
refuse...................DENY; SPURN;
....REJECT
refuse........SCUM; OFFAL, TRASH
refuse, piece of...................SCRAP
refuse, metal........DROSS; SCORIA

a refuse, wool ....COT
refute ....BELIE, REBUT;
................DISPROVE; DISCREDIT
regale ....ENTERTAIN
regalia.............FINERY; SYMBOLS
regard ....CARE, HEED; HONOR;
.....................ESTEEM; CONCERN
regarding ....IN RE; ANENT
regenerate ....RENEW
region ....AREA; TRACT;
....................SECTOR; QUARTER
region, Fr.-Ger. ....ALSACE
register ....FILE; ENROLL
regret ....RUE; REPENT;
....DEPLORE
regurgitate................PUKE; VOMIT
reign, of a ....REGNAL
reimbursed.............................PAID
reindeer, Santa's..............COMET,
.............CUPID, VIXEN; DANCER,
......DASHER, DONNER; BLITZEN,
....................PRANCER, RUDOLPH
reiterate..........REPEAT; RESTATE
reject...............SPURN; DECLINE
reject a lover ....JILT
relate ....TELL; RECITE;
...................REPORT; NARRATE
related ....AKIN, TOLD;
....COGNATE
related on father's side......AGNATE

b related on mother's side.......ENATE
relative ....KIN
relative, family.........BRO, SIB, SIS;
...................AUNT; NIECE, UNCLE
relative pronoun ....WHO; THAT,
....WHAT
relatives, favoring ....NEPOTISM
relative speed......................TEMPO
relax ....EASE, REST; LET UP
...........................LOOSE; UNWIND
relaxing of state tensions DETENTE
relay of horses.................REMUDA
release......EMIT, UNDO; LOOSE
relevant.........................GERMANE
reliable ....SURE; TRUSTY
relief ....DOLE; WELFARE
relieve ....EASE; ALLAY
religieuse ....NUN
religion ....FAITH
religion, Jap. ....SHINTO
religious festival ....EASTER
religious law, Rom. ....FAS
religious laywoman ....BEGUINE
religious sayings ....LOGIA
relinquish ....CEDE; FORGO,
.............WAIVE, YIELD; ABANDON
reliquary ....ARCA; CHEST
relish ....ZEST; GUSTO
reluctant...............LOATH; AVERSE
rely ....TRUST; DEPEND

c remain ....BIDE, STAY, WAIT;
................ABIDE, TARRY; LINGER
remainder ....REST
remaining ....LEFT; OVER;
....LEFTOVER
remark ....NOTE; COMMENT
remark, witty ....MOT; SALLY
remarks, defamatory......MUD; DIRT
remiss.........................LAX
remit ....SEND
remnant...................END; SHRED
remote ....FAR; ALOOF; DISTANT
remove ....DELETE
remove, legally ....ELOIGN
remove (one's hat) ....DOFF
remove the interior ....GUT
remunerate ....PAY
rend ....RIP; TEAR; WREST
rendezvous...........................TRYST
renegade.........REBEL; APOSTATE
renounce ....ABNEGATE
renown ....FAME, NOTE;
.................EMINENCE, PRESTIGE
rent...............................LET; HIRE,
...........................TORN; LEASE
renter ....LESSEE; TENANT
repair.................FIX; DARN, MEND
repartee ....COUNTER, RIPOSTE
repast ....MEAL
repay ....AVENGE; REQUITE

d repay in kind ....RETALIATE
repeat ....ECHO; ITERATE
repeat: music.............................BIS
repeatedly hit...................POMMEL
repeated phrase ....REPRISE
repeat performance ....ENCORE
repeat sign: music...............SEGNO
repetition ....ROTE
replete .....FULL; SATED; GORGED
report..................POP; ACCOUNT
repose ....LIE; EASE, REST
representative...................AGENT
reproach.............CHIDE; REBUKE
reptiles, of ....SAURIAN
Republican ...........................G.O.P.
repulse ....PARRY; DISGUST
reputation............FAME; RENOWN,
....................REPUTE; PRESTIGE
request ....ASK; SOLICIT
rescind...............CANCEL, REPEAL
resentment ....PIQUE; RANCOR
reserve supply ....STORE
residence ....HOME; ABODE
residence, church..........MANSE
residence, Irish chief's...........RATH
residence, rundown...DUMP, SLUM
resign ....QUIT; LEAVE
resin ....GUM, LAC; ANIME,
.................COPAL, ELEMI, JALAP,
...........MYRRH; BALSAM, MASTIC

a resin, fossil.......AMBER; GLESSITE
resist...............COMBAT, OPPOSE
resist authority.....................REBEL
resistor, current............RHEOSTAT
resort.................HAUNT; REFUGE
resort, Fr. ....PAU; NICE;
.....................CANNES; RIVIERA
resort, health.............................SPA
resources ....FUND;
.................MEANS; ASSETS
respect ....HONOR; ESTEEM
respiratory organ...................LUNG
respond.................REACT
rest ....EASE; REPOSE;
.................REMAINDER
restaurant, small................BISTRO
restive.....................EDGY; JUMPY;
.................FIDGETY
restore ....RENEW; REVIVE
restrain ....CURB, REIN;
.................BRAKE, CHECK
restrict...................LIMIT; CONFINE
retail business ....SHOP; STORE
retain...............KEEP, HIRE, HOLD
retaliate.........RETORT; COUNTER
retch ....KECK
retinue.....................SUITE, TRAIN
retract...........ABJURE; WITHDRAW
retreat...........HAVEN; SHELTER
retreat, cozy .....DEN; NEST, NOOK

b retreat house, female ......CENACLE
retribution ....REVENGE
retrograde.................BACKWARD
return....................RECUR; PROFIT
return on investment.............YIELD
revelry, drunken.....................ORGY
revelry cry ....EVOE
reverberate ....ECHO
revere...............ADORE; WORSHIP
reverence.............AWE; WORSHIP
reversion to type...............ATAVISM
revert (land) to state........ESCHEAT
revise ....EDIT; AMEND
revive wine ....STUM
revolve ....SPIN, TURN
revolver .....GAT, GUN, ROD; COLT
reward.................MEED; BONUS
Rhine, city on the ....KOLN;
.............ESSEN, MAINZ, WORMS
Rhine tributary ....AAR;
.................AARE, RUHR
rhinoceros, black ....BORELE;
.................NASICORN
rhinoceros beetle ....UANG
Rhone tributary...................SAONE
rhythm ....TIME; METER;
.................CADENCE
rhythmical accent.................BEAT
riata ....ROPE; LASSO; LARIAT
rib.................COSTA

ribbed fabric...............REP; CORDS; *c*
.................CORDUROY
ribbon, badge ....CORDON
ribs, having.....................COSTATE
rice bran ....DARAC
rice dish ....PIAF; PILAU, PILAF
rice field ....PADDY
rice in the husk ....PALAY
riches ....PELF; WEALTH
rich man ....MIDAS, NABOB;
.................CROESUS
richness ....LUXE
rid ....FREE
riddle ....ENIGMA
ridge ....ARETE
ridge, glacial.......................ESKAR
ridge created by a glacier ......KAME
ridge on cloth ....WALE
ridge on skin...........................WELT
ridicule ....MOCK; DERIDE
ridicule personified ....MOMUS
riding academy ....MANEGE
riding outfit...........................HABIT
rifle.................GARAND; CARBINE,
.................ENFIELD
rifle bullet, 19th-century..........MINIE
right, in law.........................DROIT
right, turn ....GEE
rightfully ....DULY
right-hand page ....RECTO
right to speak ....SAY *d*
Rigoletto, daughter of............GILDA
rigorous ....HARSH, STERN;
.......STRICT, SEVERE; AUSTERE
rim ....LIP; EDGE; FLANGE
ring ....PEAL, TOLL; KNELL
ring, naut. ....GROMMET
ring, rubber jar ....LUTE
ring, seal ....SIGNET
ring, stone of a ....CHATON
ring for reins.........................TERRET
ring inscription ....POSY
ringlet...................CURL; TRESS
ring of light.................AURA, HALO;
.................NIMBUS; AUREOLE
ring-shaped game-piece........QUOIT
ringworm.................TINEA; TETTER
ripening agent ....AGER
ripple...................LAP; WAVE
rise over...........................TOWER
risible...................COMIC, DROLL,
.................FUNNY; HUMOROUS
risky ....IFFY
rites, religious ....SACRA
river, Bremen's.....................WESER
river, Munich's ....ISAR
river, Polish border ....ODER
river, St. Petersburg's............NEVA
river, Southwest...................PECOS
___ Rivera, CA.......................PICO

a riverbank, growing by a..RIPARIAN;
....LITTORAL
river bed, dry Afr. ....WADI
river crossed by Caesar...RUBICON
river in Essex ....CAM
river in "Kubla Khan"...............ALPH
river into Tatar Strait......AMUR
river into the Caspian Sea......KURA
river into the Firth of Clyde ....DOON
river into the Humber ....OUSE;
....TRENT
river into the Moselle ....SAAR
river into the Rhone ....SAONE
river into the Yellow Sea ....LIAO
river islet ....AIT
river mouth ....DELTA
river nymph.................NAIS; NAIAD
river of Balmoral Castle ....DEE
River of Woe ....ACHERON
river through Florence and Pisa.......
....ARNO
river through Orleans ....LOIRE
river to the Sea of Azov............DON
rivulet.......................................RILL
RNA element ....CODON
road..........VIA, WAY; ITER, PATH;
.............................AVENUE, STREET
roadhouse ....INN
roam ....GAD; ROVE;
.........................TRAVEL, WANDER

b Roanoke Island message ....
....CROATOAN
roast ....BAKE, BURN;
.........................BROIL; SCORCH
roasted meat strip ....KABOB
roasting rod ....SPIT
rob......................DIVEST, HOLD UP
robber.....................THIEF; BANDIT
robe ....CLOAK; MANTLE
Roberta composer ....KERN
robot, Klaatu's........................GORT
robot in *Forbidden Planet*....ROBBY
robot of "The Jetsons" ....ROSEY
robot on "Captain Video" .....TOBOR
robot on "Get Smart"..............HYMIE
robot play ....RUR
rock, basic igneous ....SIMA
rock, dark volcanic ....BASALT
rock, fine grained igneous ......TRAP
rock, flintlike.........................CHERT
rock, granitoid ....DUNITE
rock, hard igneous..................WHIN
rock, jutting ....TOR
rock, laminated...................SHALE;
.............................SLATE; GNEISS
rock, melted ....LAVA
rock, mica-bearing..............DOMITE
rock, rugged..........................CRAG
rock cavity ....VUGG, VUGH;
....GEODE

c rock elm ....WAHOO
rockfish ....GOPHER, RASHER,
.....................TAMBOR; GROUPER
Rockies peak...........YALE; BROSS,
.............EOLUS, EVANS; ANTERO,
.........................CASTLE, ELBERT;
.........................LA PLATA, MAROON
Rockies range ....TETON, UINTA
rock oyster ....CHAMA
rockweed ....FUCUS
rod ....POLE, SPAR, WAND;
.............................BATON, STAFF
rod, pool ....CUE
rod, punishment ....FERULE
rodent......................RAT; HARE
rodent, rabbitlike ....PIKA
rodent, S. A. ....CAVY, DEGU,
.............................MARA, PACA;
.........................COYPU; AGOUTI
rogue ....IMP; SCAMP; RASCAL
roguish ....SLY; ARCH
roister..................RIOT; REVEL;
.....................FROLIC; CAROUSE
roll ....BUN, YAW; LIST, TILT;
.........................PITCH; ROSTER
roll-call response ....HERE
rolled meat......................ROULADE
roll of cloth ....BOLT
roll of paper........................SCROLL
roll up..................................FURL
romaine ....COS

d Roman assembly ....COMITIA
Rom. author ....CATO, LIVY,
.....................PLINY; CICERO,
.............SENECA, SILIUS; SALLUST
Rom. box ....CAPSA
Rom. boxing glove.............CESTUS
Rom. bronze ....AES
Rom. brooch ....FIBULA
romance, tale of ....GESTE
Rom. cloak...............................TOGA
Rom. Curia court....................ROTA
Rom. date ....IDES; NONES
Rom. dictator ....SULLA
Rom. dish ....PATERA
Rom. farce ....MIMUS
Rom. galley ....TRIREME
Rom. gaming cube ....TALUS
Rom. garment ....TOGA;
.............................STOLA, TUNIC
Rom. highway ....VIA; ITER
Rom. historian ....LIVY; NEPOS
Rom. house......................INSULA
Romanian money ....BAN; BANI
Rom. market(s) ....FORA; FORUM
Rom. numerals 1-I, 5-V, 10-X,
.............50-L, 100-C, 500-D, 1,00-M
Rom. official ....AEDILE;
.....................CONSUL; PRAETOR,
....TRIBUNE

Roman patriot / ruminant

a
Rom. patriot ....CATO
Rom. plate ....LANX
Rom. poet ....OVID; LUCAN;
...........................HORACE, VIRGIL
Rom. public games ....LUDI
Rom. public lands ....AGER
Rom. religious festivals ....VOTA
Rom. ruler....NERO, NUMA, OTHO;
.................GALBA, NERVA, TITUS
Rom. weapon ....FALX
Rome, conqueror of ....ALARIC
Rome, founders of ....REMUS;
.................................ROMULUS
Rome, fountain of ....TREVI
Rome, river of ....TIBER
Romulus, twin of ....REMUS
rood ....CROSS
rood screen ....JUBE
roof, rounded ....DOME; CUPOLA
roof, type of ....HIP: MANSARD
roof edge ....EAVES
roofing material ....TAR; TILE;
....SLATE
roofing slate...........................RAG
roofing timber.....................PURLIN
roof of the mouth ....PALATE
room ....CHAMBER
rooms, connecting...............SUITE
roomy ....WIDE; SPACIOUS
roost ....PERCH
b
rooster ....COCK
root.........................BASE; SOURCE
root, edible ....TARO
root, fragrant ....ORRIS
rope...........LASSO, RIATA, LARIAT
rope, naut. ....FOX, TYE; STAY,
.............VANG; HAWSER, RATLIN;
......................LANYARD, RATLINE
rope, weave ....REEVE
rope, yardarm ....SNOTTER
rope fiber ....COIR, HEMP, JUTE;
..............................ABACA, SISAL
rope for animals.................TETHER
rope loop ....BIGHT, NOOSE
rope-splicing tool ....FID
ropes, unite ....SPLICE
Rosalinda's maid..................ADELE
rosary bead............................AVE
Rosebud, e.g. ....SLED
rose fruit.....................................HIP
roselike plant........................AVENS
rose oil.....................................ATTAR
rose-shaped ornament....ROSETTE
roster ....LIST, ROTA
rotate ....TURN; GYRATE
rotating muscle ....EVERTOR
rotating part..............CAM; ROTOR
rotation producer ....TORQUE
rotten ....PUTRID
rouge ....RUDDLE

c
rough ......RUDE, CRUDE; UNEVEN
rough copy ....DRAFT
roulette bet ....RED; NOIR, TIER;
..............................BLACK, ROUGE
rounded projection.................LOBE
round room ....ROTUNDA
Round Table knights.................KAY,
.......TOR; BORS, MARK; FLOLL;
.......ACOLON, GARETH, GAWAIN,
......LIONEL, MODRED; GALAHAD;
.............LAMORACK, LANCELOT,
..............TRISTRAM; PALOMIDES,
....PERCIVALE
round-up event...................RODEO
rouse ....WAKE; WAKEN
Rousseau novel hero ....EMILE
route............WAY; PATH; COURSE
row......................LINE; SPAT, TIER
rower...OAR
rowing cadence caller ....COX
royal family, Fr. ....VALOIS
royal rod ....SCEPTER
royal treasury ....FISC
rub ....CHAFE; ABRADE,
....SCRAPE
rubber ....LATEX
rubber, black ....EBONITE
rubber, synthetic ....BUNA
rubber, wild ....CEARA
rubber tree.....................ULE; HULE
d
rubbery ....ELASTIC
rubbish....................JUNK; TRASH
rubbish: Brit. ....RAFF
rubella ....MEASLES
rub harshly ....GRATE
rub out ....KILL; ERASE
rub to shine ....POLISH
ruby red quartz...............RUBASSE
ruby spinel ....BALAS
rudder ....GUIDE
rudderfish ....CHOPA
rudder pivot pin...................PINTLE
ruddle ....RED ORE
rudiment ....BASE, ROOT
rue ....REGRET
ruff, female..............................REE
ruffle ....CRIMP
ruffle, neck ....JABOT, RUCHE
rug..................CARPET, RUNNER
ruin ....BANE; DESTROY
rule......................LAW; DOMINEER
"Rule Britannia" composer .....ARNE
ruler ....REGENT; MONARCH
ruler, Eastern ....EMIR;
..............................NAWAB, SHEIK;
........................CALIPH, SULTAN
rules, dueling ....DUELLO
rumen ....CUD
ruminant..............DEER, GOAT;
.........CAMEL, LLAMA; ANTELOPE

a

ruminate	MULL; PONDER
rumor	BUZZ; GOSSIP
rumor personified	FAMA
rumple	MUSS
run	RACE; OPERATE
run at top speed	SPRINT
run before the wind	SCUD
run into	RAM; MEET
runner, distance	MILER
run of the mill	PAR; AVERAGE
rupee, fraction of a	ANNA
rupee, legal weight of a	TOLA
rural	RUSTIC; PASTORAL
rush	HASTE, SPEED
rush, marsh	SPART
Russell's viper	DABOIA
Russ. beer, weak	KVASS
Russ. community farm	MIR
Russ. co-op	ARTEL
Russ. council, Czarist	DUMA

c

Russ. despot	CZAR, TSAR
Russ. distance measure	VERST;
	SAGENE
Russ. edict, Czarist	UKASE
Russ. emperor	IVAN; PETER
Russ. peninsula	KOLA
Russ. range	ALAI, URAL
Russ. sea, inland	ARAL, AZOV
Russ. secret police	KGB;
	NKVD, OGPU
Russ. three-stringed viol	GUDOK
Russ. urn	SAMOVAR
rust	UREDO
rustic	BOOR, RUBE;
	YOKEL; BUCOLIC
Ruth, husband of	BOAZ
Ruth, mother-in-law of	NAOMI
Ruth, son of	OBED
rye disease	ERGOT
Ryukyu Islands viper	HABU

S

b

sable	MARTEN
sack	LOOT; PILLAGE
sack fiber	JUTE
saclike cavity	BURSA
sacred asp symbol	URAEUS
sacred bull of Eg.	APIS
sacred chalice	GRAIL
sacred city of India	BENARES
sacred fig, Indian	PIPAL
sacred image	ICON
sacred lily	LOTUS
sacred lots, O.T.	URIM; THUMMIM
sacred place	SHRINE
sacrifice, place of	ALTAR
sad: music	MESTO
sad comment	ALAS; ALACK
saddle, rear of a	CANTLE
saddle horses, fresh	REMUDA
saddle knob	POMMEL
safe	VAULT; SECURE
safe place	HAVEN
safety lamp	DAVY
saga	TALE
saga, Icelandic	EDDA
sagacious	WISE; ASTUTE
sail, square	LUG
sail, triangular	JIB
sailboat	YAWL;
	KETCH, SLOOP
sail fastener	CLEW
sailing race	REGATTA
sail-line	EARING
sailor	GOB, TAR;
	SALT; SEADOG

d

sailor, Indian	LASCAR
sails of the constellation Argo	VELA
saint, Brit.	ALBAN
saint, Buddhist	ARHAT
St. Anthony's cross	TAU
St. Catherine, home of	SIENA
St. Francis, birthplace of	ASSISI
St. John's bread	CAROB
St. Johnswort tree	POON
"St. Louis Blues" composer	HANDY
St. Vitus dance	CHOREA
salacious	GAMY, LEWD;
	BAWDY
salad green	UDO; KALE;
	CRESS; ENDIVE;
	LETTUCE
salamander	EFT; NEWT
salary	PAY; WAGE; WAGES
salient angle	CANT
salientia	ANURA
salientian	ANURAN
sally	RETORT; SORTIE
salmon, smoked	LOX
salmon, female	HEN
salmon, male	COCK
salmon, second year	SMOLT
salmon, silver	COHO
salmon, young	PARR; GRILSE
salt, rock	HALITE
salt factory	SALTERN
saltpeter	NITER
salt pond	SALINA
salt solution	BRINE; SALINE
salt tax, Fr.	GABELLE

a salt tree, tamarisk....................ATLE
saltwort ....KALI; BARILLA
salutation ....AVE; HAIL; SALUTE;
....................WELCOME; GREETING
Salvation Army founder.......BOOTH
salver.....................................TRAY
sambar deer ....MAHA, RUSA
same again.............................DITTO
Samuel, king killed by............AGAG
Samuel, son of ....ABIA
Samuel, teacher of ....ELI
sanction......LET; ALLOW; PERMIT;
....................CONSENT, PENALTY
sanctuary.................FANE, NAOS;
....................CELLA; REFUGE
sand.......................................GRIT
sand, mound of ....DENE, DUNE
sandals, Mex. ....HUARACHES
sandalwood tree ....MAIRE
sandarac powder.............POUNCE
sandarac tree wood ....THYINE
sand bar ....REEF; SHOAL
sandbox tree ....HURA
sand-hill bird ....CRANE
sand island ....BAR
sandpiper, Eur. ....TEREK
sandpiper, red-backed...........STINT
sandstorm ....HABOOB,
....................................SIMOOM
sandwich, type of ....CLUB, HERO

b Sandwich Islands, discoverer of ......
....................................COOK
Sanskrit dialect.........................PALI
Sao Salvador's state ....BAHIA
sap spout ....SPILE
Saracen.....ARAB, MOOR; MUSLIM
Sarah, slave of ....HAGAR
sarcasm ....IRONY; MORDANCY
sartor ....TAILOR
sash, kimono...............................OBI
sassafras tree ....AGUE
Satan ....DEVIL; LUCIFER
satellite...................................MOON
satellites, Earth ....TIROS;
....................SKYLAB; SPUTNIK,
....................PIONEER; VANGUARD
satellite's path ....ORBIT
satiate................CLOY, FILL, GLUT
satisfy......................SUIT; PLEASE
saturate.......SOAK; IMBUE, STEEP
Saturn, wife of ....OPS
Saturnalia ....ORGY
satyr................LECHER, WANTON
sauce ....GRAVY; RAGOUT
sauce, fish ....ALEC
sauce, Oriental ....SOY
sauce, peppery ....TABASCO
sauce, tomato ....KETCHUP
sauce thickener ....ROUX
saucy ....PERT

c Saul, father of ....KISH
Saul, grandfather of......NER; ABIEL
Saul's army leader...............ABNER
Saul's successor ....DAVID
sausage, spicy ....SALAMI
savage.....................WILD; FERAL;
....................................FIERCE; VICIOUS
savanna, S. Afr. .....VELD; VELDT
save ....KEEP; RESCUE
savior ....REDEEMER
savory ....SAPID, TASTY
saw ....ADAGE, AXIOM,
....................MAXIM; SAYING
sawbill duck ....SMEW
say ....STATE, UTTER
say again ....ITERATE
sayings, religious ....LOGIA
scabbard, put into a ....SHEATHE
scale ....SKIN; CLIMB
scalloped.........................CRENATE
scamp ....ROGUE; RASCAL
scandalous material.....MUD; DIRT
Scandinavian ....DANE; SWEDE
Scand., old ....NORSE
Scand. chieftain, early.............JARL
Scand. legend ....SAGA
Scand. people ....GEAT; GEATS
scanty ....SPARSE
scarce ....RARE; SPORADIC
scarf ....BOA; ASCOT, STOLE

d Scarlett's home ....TARA
scatter ....STREW; DISPERSE
scene ....VIEW; TABLEAU
scenic view ....PANORAMA
scent ....ODOR; AROMA
schedule......................LIST, PLAN;
....................AGENDA, DOCKET,
....................LINE-UP, ROSTER
scheme ....PLOT
schism...................................SPLIT
scholar.................PUPIL; PUNDIT,
....................SAVANT; STUDENT
scholars, Islamic ....ULEMA
school, type of ....PREP
school grounds ....CAMPUS
school organization: Abbr. ....PTA
school residence ....DORM
schooner, three-masted ....TERN
schuss ....SKI
science class............................LAB
science fiction award............HUGO;
....................................NEBULA
scissors ....SHEARS
scoff ....MOCK; TAUNT; DERIDE
scold ....CHIDE; HARPY
scoop ....DIP
scope..........KEN; RANGE, REACH;
....................LEEWAY; PURVIEW
scorch ....CHAR; SINGE
score ....GOAL; TALLY; TWENTY

a scoria ....SLAG; DROSS
scoter......................................COOT
Scotland..............................SCOTIA
Scot. alderman.....................BAILIE
Scot. cake ....SCONE
Scot. cut of beef....................SEY
Scot. garb ....KILT
Scot. highlander ....GAEL
Scot. king...........................BRUCE
Scot. landholder................THANE
Scot. playwright ....BARRIE
Scot. poet ....BURNS
Scot. proprietor...................LAIRD
SCOTTISH WORDS:
　advise ....REDE
　breeches......................TREWS
　broth ....BREE, BROO
　brow of a hill.....................SNAB
　child ....BAIRN
　church ....KIRK
　devil ....DEIL
　dusty ....MOTTY
　enough ....ENOW
　family.................................ILK
　finely dressed..................BRAW
　fox.....................................TOD
　friends............................KITH
　from ....FRAE
　give...................................GIE
　have ....HAE
b 　hillside..............................BRAE
　kiss..................................PREE
　lake ....LOCH
　land under tenure ....FEU
　locker ....KIST
　loyal ....LEAL
　mountain ....BEN
　no.....................................NAE
　oatmeal ....BROSE
　old ....AULD
　out....................................OOT
　own ....AIN
　pantry ....SPENCE
　pipe.............................CUTTY
　quarter year ....RAITH
　river valley ....STRATH
　rowboat...........................COBLE
　scone ....FARL; FARLE
　scorn...............................GECK
　self.....................................SEL
　sheep walk......................SLAIT
　since ....SYNE
　small ....SMA, WEE
　snow...................................SNA
　song..............................STROUD
　son of ....MAC
　stupid one.........................CUIF
　to.......................................TAE
　turnip ....NEEP
　uncanny ....UNCO

uncle ....EME *c*
very ....VERA
young woman ....BURD
Scott poem, Sir Walter....MARMION
scoundrel ....ROGUE; VARLET
scout unit ....DEN; PACK; TROOP
scow...................BARGE; LIGHTER
scrape ....RASP; GRATE,
...........SCOUR, SCRUB; SCRIMP
scrape bottom ....DREDGE
scraps, table..........................ORTS
scratch...........MAR; RASP; SCORE
scratching ground for food ....
....RASORIAL
screed ....TIRADE
screen ....SIFT; SHADE
screen, altar ....REREDOS
screen, wind ....PARAVENT
script, upright ....RONDE
scrutinize ....STUDY; PERUSE
scuffle ....MELEE
scum, metal.......................DROSS
scup...................BREAM, PORGY
scuttle, coal ....HOD
scythe handle ......SNATH, SNEAD;
....SNATHE
Scythian people...................ALANS
sea anemone ....POLYP; OPELET
sea bass, Eur. ....LOUP
sea bird ....ERNE, GULL, SKUA, *d*
..............TERN; SCAUP; FULMAR,
..........GANNET, PETREL, PUFFIN,
....SCOTER
sea cow ....DUGONG; MANATEE
sea cucumber ....TREPANG
sea duck.............EIDER; SCOTER
sea green........................CELADON
sea gull, Pac. ....MEW
seal ....SIGIL; SIGNET
seal, eared.........................OTARY
seal, fur ....URSAL
seal, group of ....POD
seal, letter.........................CACHET
seal, official........................SIGNET
seal, papal ....BULLA
seal, young ....PUP
sea lettuce.......ALGA, NORI, ULVA;
....................LAVER; AMANORI
seamark ....BEACON
seamen: Brit. ....RATINGS
seamlike ridge; anat. ....RAPHE
seams of a boat, fill ....CAULK
sea nymph.........................NEREID
search ....GROPE
search for ....HUNT, SEEK
search for food..................FORAGE
sea serpent.........................ELOPS
sea shell ....TRITON
sea skeleton ....CORAL
sea snail ....WHELK

a

sea snake............................KERRIL
season ....AGE; FALL, SALT
season, church........LENT; ADVENT
seasoning herb ....SAGE;
...............................BASIL, THYME
seasons, goddesses of the .HORAE
seat, chancel.......................SEDILE
seat, long ....PEW; SETTEE
seat, Rom. ....SELLA
seaweed ....AGAR, KELP;
...............................LAVER, VAREC
seaweed, red ....DULCE, DULSE
secluded ....HIDDEN, REMOTE
second............AIDE, WINK; TRICE
secondary...........PETTY; LESSER
second brightest star ....BETA
second-growth crop..........ROWEN
Second Punic War's end, site of .....
....ZAMA
second team ....SCRUB
secret ....COVERT, HIDDEN;
....SUB-ROSA
secret agent.................SPY; MOLE;
....................................SLEEPER
secreted ....HID; HIDDEN
secret place ....MEW
secret police, Russ. ....CHEKA
secrets ....ARCANA
secrets, one learning ....EPOPT
sect...CULT

b

section of a journey.................LEG
secular............................LAY; LAIC
secure....................SAFE, SURE
secure firmly ....ANCHOR
secure with rope ....BELAY
security ....PLEDGE, SHIELD
sedate ......GRAVE, SOBER, STAID
sediment.......................LEES, SILT;
.......................DREGS; SILTAGE
see.............ESPY; LOOK; BEHOLD
see, church................BISHOPRIC
seed.................................PIP, PIT;
............................GRAIN, SPORE
seed, edible.................PEA; BEAN;
............................POPPY; LENTIL,
.........................PINOLE, SESAME
seed, immature ....OVULE
seedcase, prickly ....BUR
seed coat ....ARIL, HULL, HUSK;
.......................TESTA; TEGMEN
seedless plant ....FERN
seed plant, annual..................HERB
seeds, remove ....GIN
seek ....ASPIRE, STRIVE
seem.....................LOOK; APPEAR
seeping ....OOZY
seesaw ....TEETER
segment, circle ....ARC
segment, stinging ....TELSON
seine ....NET

c

seize ....NAB; GRAB; GRASP
Selene, lover of ....METIS
self...EGO
self-assurance...................APLOMB
self-reproach.................REMORSE
self-satisfied ....SMUG
sell.......................VEND; MARKET
seller ....VENDER; MERCHANT
selling price equivocation ....OBO
semblance ....GUISE
semester..............................TERM
semicircular room ....APSE
semi-diameter....................RADIUS
Seminole chief ....OSCEOLA
semi-precious stone...ONYX, SARD
Semitic deity ....BAAL
sen, tenth of a ....RIN
senate house of Rome..........CURIA
send ....PASS, SHIP;
.......................CONVEY; DISPATCH
send back...........REMIT; REMAND
send out......................EMIT; ISSUE
senility ....DOTAGE
senior ....ELDER
senna, source of ....CASSIA
sense ....FEEL
senseless ....INANE, SILLY
sensitive..............SORE; TOUCHY
sentence, analyze a.............PARSE
sentence part....................CLAUSE,
....PHRASE

d

Sentimental Journey author ....
......................................STERNE
sentinel ....GUARD; SENTRY
sentinel, mounted ....VEDETTE
separate ....PART, SORT;
...................APART, SPLIT; DIVIDE
separation ....SCHISM
sequence, three-card.........TIERCE
sequester ....ISOLATE
seraglio ....HAREM
Serbo-Croatian folk dance .....KOLO
serene ....CALM; PLACID
serf ....SLAVE
serf, A.-S. ....ESNE
serf, Spartan ....HELOT
sergeant fish ....COBIA, SNOOK;
......................................ROBALO
sergeant-major fish ....PINTANO
series..........SET; CHAIN, ROUND
series of tones.....................SCALE
serious................................GRAVE,
.......................SOBER; SEDATE;
.....................SEVERE, SOMBER
sermon ....HOMILY
serpent, Gr. ....SEPS
serpent, large ....BOA; PYTHON
serpentine...........................OPHITE
serpent monster...................ELOPS
serpent worship ....OPHISM

a servant.....................MAID; HAMAL;
....MENIAL
servant, man's ....VALET
servant at Cambridge, male .....GYP
server ....TRAY; SALVER
serve soup ....LADLE
service, Rom. Cath. ....MASS
service tree fruit ....SORB
servile ....MENIAL
serving boy.............................PAGE
sesame ....TIL; TEEL
session, held a ....MET, SAT
session, hold a ....SIT; MEET
set aside ....DEFER, TABLE
setback ....REVERSE
Seth, brother of ....ABEL, CAIN
Seth, parent of..............EVE; ADAM
Seth, son of.............................ENOS
set in type...............................PRINT
set price ....RATE
setting........SITE; SCENE; LOCALE
settled.......................................ALIT
seven, group of................HEPTAD,
..........................PLEIAD, SEPTET
Seven Deadly Sins..............ENVY,
...................LUST; ANGER, PRIDE,
.....................SLOTH; GLUTTONY,
........................COVETOUSNESS
Seven Dwarfs ....DOC; DOPEY,
..........HAPPY; GRUMPY, SLEEPY,
...........................SNEEZY; BASHFUL
b Seven Hills of Rome ....CAELIAN,
..................VIMINAL; AVENTINE,
..................PALATINE, QUIRINAL;
..............ESQUILINE; CAPITOLINE
Seven Pleiades ....MAIA;
..................MEROPE; ALCYONE,
..................CELAENO, ELECTRA,
..................TAYGATE; ASTEROPE
sever.............CUT; SPLIT; CLEAVE
severe ....DOUR; GRAVE,
....HARSH
Severn tributary ....WYE
sexes, both ....COED
sexual assault ....RAPE
shabby ....WORN
shabby woman ....DOWD
shackle ....BOND, GYVE;
..........................FETTER; MANACLE
shaddock ....POMELO
shade..............HUE; TINT; COLOR
shade of meaning ....NUANCE
shadow ....TAIL; GHOST
shadow, eclipse ....UMBRA
shaft ....BAR, RAY, ROD
shaft, wooden......................ARROW
shafter ....HORSE
shaft of a column ....FUST
shake ....JAR; CHURN, QUAKE;
.......................TREMOR; AGITATE

Shakespeare ....See page 192. *c*
Shakespeare, daughter of ..JUDITH;
....SUSANNA
Shakespeare, father of ....JOHN
Shakespeare, mother of ....MARY
Shakespeare, poem by ...LUCRECE
Shakespeare, river of ....AVON
Shakespeare, son of.........HAMNET
Shakespeare, wife of ....ANNE
Shak. clown ....BOTTOM,
....LAVACHE
Shak. contraction ....AS'T, E'EN,
..........................E'ER, IS'T, O'ER,
..........................ON'T, 'TIS; NE'ER,
..................TA'EN, 'TWAS; 'TWERE
Shak. forest ....ARDEN
Shak. king.............................LEAR
Shak. shepherdess ....MOPSA
Shak. shrew...........................KATE
Shak. sprite ....PUCK
Shak. villain ....IAGO
shaking table ....VANNER
sham ....FAKE; BOGUS;
....ERSATZ
Shang dynasty ....YIN
shank...........................CRUS, SHIN
shanty ....HUT
shape ....FORM, MOLD
shaping tool...........LATHE, SWAGE
share ....LOT; RATION
shark, long-nosed ....MAKO *d*
shark, nurse ....GATA
shark, small ....TOPE
shark parasite fish ....REMORA
sharp ....ACERB, ACUTE
sharpen ....HONE, WHET
sharpshooter ....ACE; SNIPER
shear ....CLIP
shed, sheep ....COTE
shed feathers...........MOLT; MOULT
sheen....................................GLOSS
sheep ....MERINO
sheep, Afr. ....AOUDAD
sheep, Asian ....ARGALI,
........................BHARAL, NAHOOR
sheep, black-faced ....LONK
sheep, female ....EWE
sheep, male ....RAM
sheep, of ....OVINE
sheep, two-year old ....TEG
sheep, young...........................LAMB
sheep disease ....COE, GID, ROT
sheep dog ....COLLIE
sheep's cry......................BAA, MAA
sheep shelter.........................FOLD
shelf ....LEDGE
shelf above an altar ....RETABLE
shell, exploding.....................BOMB
shell, large ....CONCH
shell, marine ....TRITON

a shellfish, edible ....CRAB;
.....................MUSSEL, ABALONE,
......................................SCALLOP
shell money.............KINA; COWRIE
shellac ....LAC; LAKH
shelter ....LEE; COTE, SHED;
......................HAVEN; SCREEN
shelter, hillside ....ABRI
shelter, toward ....ALEE
Shem, descendant of.........SEMITE
Shem, brother of....HAM; JAPHETH
Shem, son of ....LUD; ARAM,
.....................................ELAM
Sheol ....HELL; HADES
shepherd prophet ....AMOS
shepherd's song...........MADRIGAL
sheriff's men ....POSSE
sherry-wine coating ....FLOR
shield..................BLOCK; DEFEND
shield, Athena's....................AEGIS
shield, medieval.......................ECU
shield, Rom. ....SCUTUM
shield border ....ORLE
shield-shaped................PELTATE,
.................SCUTATE; SCUTIFORM
shield strap ....ENARME
shift............................TURN; STINT
shine ....GLOW; GLEAM, GLINT
shingles..................................ZONA
Shinto deity's power ....KAMI
b Shinto temple gate ....TORII
ship ....BOAT; LINER;
.....................TANKER, VESSEL
ship, ironclad.................MONITOR
ship, lowest part of a ....BILGE
ship, oar-propelled ....GALLEY
ship, one-masted ....SLOOP
ship, part of a ....DECK, KEEL
ship, to ....SEND
ship, two-masted ....BRIG
ship employee ....BURSAR;
...................................STEWARD
ship frame ....HULL
ship plank ....STRAKE
ship's deck ....POOP; ORLOP
ship's drainage hole ....SCUPPER
ship's front......BOW; FORE, PROW
ship-shaped clock ....NEF
ship's kitchen ....GALLEY
ship's mooring place ....DOCK;
......................................BERTH
ship's pole ....MAST, SPAR
ship's rear ....AFT; STERN
ship's wheel ....HELM
ship timber's curve...................SNY
shipworm............BORER; TEREDO
shirt, light long-sleeved ......CAMISE
shoal.......................................REEF
shoal water deposit...............CULM
shock..........JOLT, STUN; TRAUMA

shoe ....MULE, PUMP;
..........BUSKIN, GAITER, LOAFER,
.......................OXFORD, WEDGIE
shoe, armored ....SOLLERET
shoe, gym ....SNEAKER
shoe, heavy ....BROGAN, BROGUE
shoe, open ....ZORI, SANDAL
shoe, wooden..........GETA; SABOT
shoe, wooden-soled..............CLOG
shoe form ....LAST
shoe front...............................VAMP
shoe gripper ....CLEAT
shoemaker's saint ....CRISPIN
shoemaker's tool ....AWL
shoes, Mercury's winged ..TALARIA
shoe's interior ....INSOLE
shoot.........................FIRE; SPRIG
shoot, plant ....SOBOL; SOBOLE
shoot, sugar cane ....RATOON
shooter, hidden ....SNIPER
shooter marble............TAW; AGGIE
shoot from cover ....SNIPE
shooting match ....TIR
shoot wide ....MISS
shop ....STORE; MARKET
shopping center ....MALL
shop's nameplate ....FASCIA
shore ....COAST; STRAND
short ....CURT; BRIEF, TERSE;
...............CONCISE, WANTING
shortchange.........................GYP *d*
short comedy sketch ....SKIT
shortcut.................................ATAJO
shorten ....CUT, LOP; CROP
shortly ....ANON, SOON
short-spoken ....CURT; TERSE
short syllable indicator ....BREVE
Shoshonean ....UTE; KOSO
shoulder, road...........................BERM
shoulder blade.................SCAPULA
shoulder ornament............EPAULET
shoulder wrap.....................SHAWL
shout.................CRY; CALL, YELL
shove ....PUSH
shovel ....SPADE
Showboat playwright ....FERBER
show off................................FLAUNT
showroom model ....DEMO
showy...................VIVID; SPLASHY
shrew.................HARPY; VIRAGO
shrewd ....CAGEY, CANNY
shrill...................HIGH; TREBLE
shrimp, Brit. ....PRAWN
shrink ....SHY; QUAIL, WINCE;
...................RECOIL; CONTRACT
shrub, Amer. ....SALAL
shrub, Australian ....MULGA
shrub, berry-bearing.............ELDER
shrub, evergreen...................YEW;
....................HEATH; OLEANDER

c

108

a shrub, flowering ....AZALEA,
........................PRIVET, SPIREA;
......................................SYRINGA
shrub, Hawaiian....................OLONA
shrub, Med. ....CAPER
shrub, poisonous.................SUMAC
shrub, spiny........................GORSE
shrub, strong-scented...........BATIS
shrubbery ....BUSH
shun ....DUCK, SNUB;
................AVOID, DODGE, ELUDE
shy.............COY; TIMID; WANTING
Siamese ....THAI
Siamese garment ....PANUNG
Siamese twin.............ENG; CHANG
Siberian wild cat ....MANUL
Sicilian resort ....ENNA
sickle, curved like a..........FALCATE
side ....FACET, FLANK
side, pass to the ....LATERAL
sidearm ....GUN; PISTOL
side post ....JAMB
sideshow performer ....GEEK
sidetrack ....SHUNT
sidewalk's edge ....CURB
sidewalk's edge: Brit. ....KERB
sidewinder ....CROTALUS
sidle ....EDGE
Siegfried, murderer of ....HAGEN
siesta ....NAP

b sieve ....SIFT; BOLTER
sift...........................SORT; WINNOW
sifter......................................SIEVE
sigh ....SOUGH
sight, come into ....LOOM
sight, gun...............................BEAD
sight, of ....OCULAR
sign ....MARK, OMEN;
..........................TOKEN; SYMBOL
sign, music............PRESA, SEGNO
sign a contract..........................INK
signal, actor's ....CUE
signet ....SIGIL
signify ....MEAN; DENOTE,
.......................INTEND; CONNOTE
sign one's name ....ENDORSE
sign up ....ENROLL
Silas Marner author ....ELIOT
silence....................................HUSH;
............................QUIET, SHUSH
silence: music.......................TACET
silent ....DUMB, MUTE;
.................................QUIET, TACIT
silica...........................SAND; SILEX
silicate, complex.....................MICA
silk, Indian.............ROMAL, RUMAL
silk, old heavy ....CAMACA
silk, raw ....GREGE
silk, unravel ....SLEAVE
silk, watered ....MOIRE

silk-cotton tree ....CEIBA, KAPOK, *c*
....SIMAL
silk fabric.................GROS; PEKIN;
...............................SATIN, TULLE
silk substitute ....NYLON, ORLON,
.........................RAYON; DACRON
silk thread ....FLOSS
silk tree ....SIRIS; LEBBEK
silkworm disease ....UJI
silly ....MAD; ZANY; GIDDY
silver ingots ....SYCEE
silver-iron ore ....PACO
silvery...............................ARGENT
silvery-white metal ....COBALT
Simenon's detective ....MAIGRET
simian ....APE
similar..........................LIKE; ALIKE
simpatico ....NICE; CONGENIAL
simper...............................SMIRK
simple ....EASY; PLAIN; FACILE
simpleton............ASS, OAF; BOOB,
...................DOLT, FOOL, GABY,
...................GAWK, SIMP; GOOSE
simulate ....APE; SHAM;
.........................FEIGN; PRETEND
sin ....ERR; EVIL
sin, petty.................PECCADILLO
Sinai, Mount ....HOREB
Sinbad's bird ....ROC
sine ___ non...........................QUA

sinew.............................TENDON *d*
sinewy ....WIRY; BRAWNY
sing.................CAROL, CHANT
singe wood ....GENAPPE
singer, synagogue ....CANTOR
single ....ONE; BILL,
...................LONE, SOLE; UNWED
single out ....CHOOSE
singleton ....ACE
sing softly.............................CROON
sing Swiss style ....YODEL
sink a putt.............................HOLE
sinuous ....SNAKY; WINDING
sinus cavities ....ANTRA
Sioux tribe............................OTOE
siren, Rhine....................LORELEI
sister, religious ....NUN
Sistine Madonna painter .RAPHAEL
sitting on ....ASTRIDE
Siva, consort of ....DEVI, KALI, SATI
six, group of ....SESTET,
......................................SEXTET
six-line verse....................SESTINA
sixth: music.............................SEXT
sixth sense ....ESP
sixth sense, having a ....FEY
skate ....RAY
skating surface ....RINK
skeggar ....PARR
skein of yarn...........................HANK

a
skeletal.............................BONY
skeletal element..................BONE
skeleton, marine ....CORAL;
....SPONGE
skeptic ....DOUBTER
sketch.....................SKIT; DRAFT;
....OUTLINE
sketched...............................DREW
ski.......................................SCHUSS
skiing maneuver ....WEDELN
skiing position ....VORLAGE
skilled person ....ADEPT
skillful..............ABLE, DEFT; ADEPT
skin.........................FLAY; DERMA
skin design ....TATTOO
skin disease ....MANGE,
.............................PSORA; TETTER
skin eruption...............ACNE, RASH
skinflint................................MISER
skin infection ....LEPRA
skin layer ....CUTIS, DERMA;
...................CORIUM; ENDERON
skink, Eg. ....ADDA
skip..OMIT
skipjack ....BONITO, ELATER
skirmish ....CLASH, RUN-IN
skirt, ballet ....TUTU
ski run ....SLALOM
skittle......................................PIN
ski wax ....KLISTER

b
skulk.........LURK; CREEP; PROWL
skull, of the ....INIAC, INIAL
skullcap, Arabic...............CHECHIA
skull protuberance(s) ....INIA; INION
sky, highest point in the ......ZENITH
sky-blue ....AZURE
slab, engraved...................TABLET
slag.....................DROSS; SCORIA
slalom.....................................SKI
slam..........BANG, WHAM; WHACK
slam in cards ....VOLE
slander ....MUD; MALIGN;
..................................CALUMNY
slang...................................ARGOT
slant.......................BEVEL, SLOPE
slanted: naut. ....ARAKE
slanting...............................ASKEW
slantingly, hammer ....TOE
slanting type.........................ITALIC
slap ....CUFF, DRUB; SPANK
slash ....CUT; FLAY, GASH
slate-trimming tool.................ZAX
Slav in Saxony ....SORB, WEND
slave ....ESNE, SERF;
....THRALL
sled, type of...........................LUGE
sleep ....NAP, NOD;
..................DOZE; SNOOZE
sleep, deep ....SOPOR
sleeping ....ABED; DORMANT

c
sleeping location ....BED, COT;
.......................BUNK, CRIB; BERTH
sleeping sickness fly ....TSETSE
sleep state: Abbr. ....REM
sleep symbols........................ZEES
sleepy...................................DOZY
sleeve, large ....DOLMAN
sleigh ....PUNG
sleight-of-hand ....MAGIC
slender..........LEAN, THIN; GAUNT,
.........................SPARE; MEAGER
slender woman ....SYLPH
slice, thick ....SLAB
slice of bacon ....RASHER
slick ....SLY; GLIB, WILY;
..........................SHIFTY, SHREWD;
...................................SLIPPERY
slide...............SKID, SLIP; GLIDE
sliding piece ....CAM
sliding valve ....PISTON
slight............SLIM, SNUB; GENTLE
slimy....................................OOZY
slimy stuff ....GOOK, GOOP,
....................GUCK, GUNK, SCUM
sling around................SLEW, SLUE
slip ....ERR; BONER,
.................GLIDE, LAPSE, SLIDE
slip, plant.............SCION; CUTTING
slip by................................ELAPSE
slipknot...............................NOOSE
slipper ....MULE
slope ....RAMP; GRADIENT
slope, steep ....SCARP; ESCARP
slope of land........................VERSANT
sloping edge ....BEZEL
sloth, two-toed ....UNAU
sloths, S.A............................AIS
slow ....POKY; SLACK; RETARD
slow: music..........LARGO, LENTO;
..................ADAGIO; ANDANTE
slower: music ....RIT.
slow loris ....KOKAM
slugger's stat.............................RBI
sluggish..................SLOW; TORPID
sluice ....CLOW
slump...................DROP, SINK;
.............SLOUCH; RECESSION;
..................................DEPRESSION
slur over................................ELIDE
sly look..................................LEER
small ....WEE; TINY;
..................................PETIT, PETTY
small amount..............DRAM, DRIB,
...................................LICK; MINIM
small bottle ....VIAL
small cluster............................SPRIG
smallest ....LEAST
small number ....FEW
smallpox ....VARIOLA
small stream .....RUN; RILL; RILLET

d

110

a smaragd.......................EMERALD
smart ....CHIC, WISE; STING
smear on ....DAUB
smell.........ODOR; AROMA, SCENT
smell, bad................REEK; FETOR
smelting waste.........SLAG; DROSS
smile...GRIN
smirch ....SULLY
smock ....CAMISE
smoke ....FUME
smoke, wisp of........................FLOC
smoked beef ....PASTRAMI
smoking pipe ....BONG; BRIAR,
.....................BRIER; HOOKAH
smoky...............................FUMOUS
smooth ....EVEN; LEVEL
smooth feathers...................PREEN
smoothing tool.......................PLANE
smooth-spoken ....GLIB
smudge.....................................BLUR
snail, large.......................WHELK;
....ABALONE
snail, marine ....TRITON
snake...............ASP, BOA; ABOMA,
.................ADDER, COBRA, KRAIT,
.............MAMBA, RACER, URUTU,
.............VIPER; DABOIA, PYTHON;
.................RATTLER; ANACONDA
snakelike.........................SINUOUS
snakeroot, white ....STEVIA

b snare ....NET, WEB; TRAP
snarl ....MESH, MESS; JUMBLE
snatch ....GRAB; SEIZE
sneer.................SCORN; SNICKER
sneezewood ....ALANT
snoring..............................STERTOR
snow, watery ....SLOP
snow field.....................FIRN, NEVE
snow house ....IGLOO
snow leopard.......................OUNCE
snow mouse ....VOLE
snug ....COZY, TIDY; TIGHT
snuggery...................................NEST
so...................THUS, TRUE, VERY
so, about ....YAY
soak ....SOP; DOUSE,
.............................SOUSE, STEEP;
..................DRENCH; SATURATE
soak flax....................................RET
soap, fine ....CASTILE
soap-frame bar ....SESS
soap plant............................AMOLE
soapstone ....TALC
soap vine ....GOGO
so be it !..................................AMEN
sober...................GRAVE, STAID
social affair..............................TEA
social climber ....SNOB
social division ....CASTE
social unit ....SEPT; CLIQUE

society ....CLUB; GUILD; c
.....................LEAGUE; COMPANY
society, entrance into ....DEBUT
sod...TURF
sodium carbonate ....TRONA
sodium chloride ....NACL, SALT
sodium compound ....SODA
sodium nitrate.........................NITER
sofa ....COUCH, DIVAN
soft...............................LAX; EASY;
.....................QUIET; GENTLE,
.....................LOW-KEY, TENDER
soften ....CALM; PACIFY,
....SUBDUE
soft palate ....VELUM
soft palate lobe......................UVULA
soil, organic part of ....HUMUS
soil, rich..................LOAM; LOESS
solar-lunar year differential ..EPACT
soldier, Indian ....SEPOY
soldier, former ....VET
soldier from down under ......ANZAC
soldiers ....GIS
soldier's shelter...............FOXHOLE
solemn declaration ......VOW; OATH
sole of a plow ....SLADE
sole of the foot.........................VOLA
solicit ....ASK; REQUEST
solicitude............................REGARD;
....CONCERN
solid, become.................GEL, SET; d
...............................JELL; HARDEN
solid shape ...CONE, CUBE; PRISM
solitary ....LONE, ONLY, SOLE;
.......................SINGLE; SECLUDED
solo, opera ....ARIA
Solomon's temple, rebuilder of ....
....HIRAM
solution ....ANSWER
some......................ANY; SUNDRY;
....SEVERAL
so much: music...................TANTO
song..................LAY; TUNE; DITTY
song, Christmas ......NOEL; CAROL;
....WASSAIL
song, mournful ....DIRGE
song, nationalistic ....ANTHEM
song, religious ....HYMN; CHANT
song group ....GLEE
song of praise ....PAEAN
Song of the South uncle......REMUS
song thrush ....MAVIS
son-in-law ....GENER
son of, in Arabic names ....IBN
son of, in Gaelic names..MAC; FITZ
soon....................................ANON
soot...SMUT
soothe ....CALM; ALLAY, QUIET
soothsayer.................................SEER
sora ....RAIL

111

sorb / Spanish words (meadow)

a
sorb	WEND
sorceress	CIRCE, LAMIA
sore	ACHY; PAINFUL
sorghum variety	MILO
sorrel	DOCK
sorrow	WOE; DOLOR, GRIEF
sorrowful	SAD; BLUE
sort	KIND, TYPE; ASSORT
sortie	SALLY
so-so	OKAY
soul	ANIMA; SPIRIT
soul, Hindu	ATMAN
sound	FIT; HALE; NOISE, SOLID; COGENT; PRUDENT
sound, attention-getting	AHEM
sound, buzzing	WHIR, WHIZ; WHIRR, WHIZZ
sound, dull	THUD
sound, explosive	BOOM
sound, gagging	YECH, YUCH, YUCK
sound, monotonous	HUM; DRONE
sound, of	SONANT
sound, puffing	CHUG
sound, sibilant	HISS
sound, throat-clearing	AHEM
sound, vibratory	PURR
sound, whirring	BIRR

b
sound loudly	BLARE
sound of a horn	BEEP, HONK, TOOT
sound of pleasure or pain	MOAN
sound perception	EAR
sound reasoning	LOGIC
sound system	HI-FI; STEREO
sound waves	AUDIO
soup, thick	PUREE; BISQUE, POTAGE
soup spoon	LADLE
soup vessel	TUREEN
sour	GLUM, TART; ACRID
sour milk drink	LEBAN, LEBEN; KOUMISS
soursop	ANNONA
South African	BOER
S. Afr. assembly	RAAD
S. Afr. dialect	TAAL
S. Afr. hyrax	DAS; DASSIE
S. Afr. savanna	VELD; VELDT
S. Afr. town	STAD
S. Afr. village	KRAAL
Southern Cross constellation	CRUX
Southern France	MIDI
South Pacific hero	EMILE
sovereign	FREE
Soviet news agency	TASS
Soviet newspaper	PRAVDA
sow	PIG; GILT, SEED; PLANT

c
sower	SEEDER
soybean	SOYA
spa, Bohemian	BILIN
spa, Eng.	BATH
spa, Ger.	EMS; BADEN
spade	LOY; SHOVEL
spade, peat	SLANE
Sp. article	LAS, LOS, UNO
Sp. cellist	CASALS
Sp. coin, old	PISTOLE
Sp. cooking pot	OLLA
Sp. dance	JOTA; BOLERO; FLAMENCO
Sp. hero	EL CID
Sp. painter	GOYA, MIRO, SERT; PICASSO
Sp. peninsula	IBERIA
Sp. poet	ENCINA

SPANISH WORDS:
abbey	ABADIA
afternoon	TARDE
another	OTRO
aunt	TIA
bay	BAHIA
before	ANTES
black	NEGRO
blue	AZUL
boy	NINO
bravo	OLE
bull	TORO

d
but	MAS; PERO, SINO
canyon	CAJON
chaperon	DUENA
church	IGLESIA
city	CIUDAD
day	DIA
dove	PALOMA
evil	MAL; MALO
for	POR; PARA
friend	AMIGO
girl	NINA; CHICA
God	DIOS
gold	ORO
good-bye	ADIOS
gulch	ARROYO
gypsy	GITANO
hall	SALA
hamlet	ALDEA
here	AQUI
house	CASA
Indian	INDIO
inn	POSADA
king	REY
lady	DAMA; SENORA
lake	LAGO
land, plowed	ARADO
letter	CARTA
love	AMOR
man	VARON; HOMBRE
meadow	PRADO

a SPANISH WORDS: *continued*
mine ....MIA, MIO
mouth ....BOCA
other ....OTRO
pot ....OLLA
priest ....CURA; PADRE
queen ....REINA
red ....ROJO
river ....RIO
road ....CAMINO
room ....SALA; CUARTO
saint ....SAN; SANTO
saint, feminine ....SANTA
she ....ELLA
shortcut ....ATAJO
silver ....PLATA
six ....SEIS
south ....SUR
tall ....ALTO
this ....ESTA, ESTE
three ....TRES
tomorrow ....MANANA
uncle ....TIO
very ....MUY; MUCHO
water ....AGUA
work ....OBRA
spar ....BOX; BOOM,
.................MAST, POLE, YARD
spar, heavy ....BARITE
spar, loading ....STEEVE
b spar, small ....SPRIT
spare ....LEAN; EXTRA, GAUNT
spar for colors......................GAFF
sparkle ....GLITTER
sparrow, hedge ....DONEY
Sparta, queen of ....LEDA
Spartan magistrate ....EPHOR
spasm..................FIT, TIC; THROE
spawning ground ....REDD
speak ....SAY; TALK;
.................ORATE, UTTER
speak, inability to ....ALALIA,
.....................ALOGIA, MUTISM
speaker ....ORATOR; LOCUTOR
speaking, keep from.................GAG
speak theatrically ....EMOTE
spear.......................PIKE; LANCE;
.................ASSEGAI, JAVELIN
spear, three-pronged........TRIDENT
spear dance, Balinese...........BARIS
spear-shaped ....HASTATE
spear-thrower, Austral. WOOMERA
species................ILK; KIND, SORT,
.................TYPE; ORDER; VARIETY
specimen ....SAMPLE
speck ....DOT; MOTE; FLECK
speckle ....DAPPLE, MOTTLE,
.................PEPPER; STIPPLE
spectacle.........................PAGEANT
specter......BOGY; GHOST, SHADE

speech ....LECTURE, ORATION c
speech, art of ....RHETORIC
speech, local ....PATOIS
speech, long ....SPIEL
speech, loss of ....APHASIA
speech, violent...................TIRADE
speech defect.......LISP; STAMMER
speechless ....DUMB, MUTE
speech peculiarity.................IDIOM
speed ....PACE; HASTE,
.................HURRY, TEMPO;
.................VELOCITY
speed-of-sound number ....MACH
spelling contest ....BEE
spelunker's mecca ....CAVE
Spenser heroine ....UNA
Spenser's name for Ireland...IRENA
sphere......................ORB; SCOPE;
.................PURVIEW
sphere of action ....ARENA
Sphinx site ....GIZA
spicy ....RACY
spiders' nests.............................NIDI
spigot ....TAP
spin ....REEL; TWIRL;
.................ROTATE
spinal membrane ....DURA
spindle ....AXLE
spindle, yarn ....HASP
spine, slender ....SETA
spine bones ....SACRA d
spirit ....VIM; BRIO, ELAN, SOUL;
.............GHOST, VERVE; ANIMUS
spirited.....................FIERY; LIVELY
spirit of air..............................ARIEL
spirit of evil ....DEMON, DEVIL
spirits and water..................GROG
spirits of the dead...............MANES
spiritualist meeting ....SEANCE
splash....................LAP; SLOSH;
.................SPATTER
splash, large ....GOUT
splendid ....GRAND, REGAL;
.................SUPERB
splendor ....GLORY; MAJESTY
split ....RIFT; BREAK, SEVER
Splitsville............................RENO
spoil...........................ROT; DECAY;
.................MOLDER
spoil, as eggs ....ADDLE
spoils of war ....LOOT
spoken...................................ORAL
spokes, having ....RADIAL
sponge, bath ....LUFFA; LOOFAH
sponge, young.....................ASCON
sponsor ....PATRON
sponsorship............................AEGIS
spool ....REEL
spore ....SEED
spore cluster........................SORUS

113

a spore sac(s) ....ASCI; ASCUS
sport ....GAME, PLAY, WEAR
sports arena ....RINK; STADIUM
sports fig. ....STAT
sports hall ....GYM
spot on cards or dice..................PIP
spotted.............SAW; PIED; PINTO;
..................DAPPLED; MACULOSE
spotted eagle ray................OBISPO
spouse ....MATE, WIFE;
....HUSBAND
spray ....ATOMIZE
spray, sea...............................LIPPER
spread, as gossip ....BRUIT
spread (out) ....FAN
spread to dry................................TED
sprightly ....PERT
spring..................SPA; COIL;
...........................VAULT; VERNAL
spring, small ....SEEP
spring back ....RECOIL
spring rice, Indian ....BORO
sprinkle................DUST; DAPPLE;
....SPECKLE
sprint ....DART, DASH, RACE,
............RUSH; HASTEN, ROCKET
sprite ....ELF; PIXIE
sprout ....GROW; SCION
spruce ....TRIG, TRIM; NATTY
spume..........FOAM, SUDS; FROTH
b spun wool ....YARN
spur....................GOAD; CALCAR
spur, mountain ....ARETE
spur, wheel ....ROWEL
spurt ....JET; GUSH
squall ....HOWL, WAIL,
..................................WAUL, WAWL
squama ....ALULA; TEGULA
squander ....WASTE; DISSIPATE
square dance..........................REEL
squash....................CRUSH,
...........................GOURD; FLATTEN
squash bug ....ANASA
squirrel skin ....VAIR
squirrel's nest...............DRAY, DREY
stab............TRY; PANG; PRICK
stabilize................................STEADY
stable..........................FIRM; SOLID
stable compartment ....STALL
stableman ....OSTLER; HOSTLER
stables in London, royal........MEWS
stack of hay ....RICK
staff.................ROD; CANE; STICK;
....PERSONNEL
staff, bishop's................CROSIER
staff, royal ....SCEPTER, SCEPTRE
staff-bearer........................MACER
staff of office ....MACE
stag.................DEER, HART, MALE
stage ....ENACT, PHASE

c stage between molts..........INSTAR
stage direction ....EXUENT
stage equipment................PROPS
stage extra ....SUPER
stage horn signal ....SENNET
stage setting ....SCENE
stage whisper........................ASIDE
stagger.......................................REEL
stagnation ....TORPOR
stagnation, blood..................STASIS
stain ....DYE; SOIL, SPOT
stair part.................RISER, TREAD
stair post........................NEWEL
stake ....ANTE; WAGER
stake, pointed ....PALISADE
stale ....FLAT; BANAL, TRITE
stalk..............................STEM; SHAFT
stalk, flower ....SCAPE; PEDICEL;
....PEDUNCLE
stalk, frond ....STIPE
stalk, plant............................CAULIS
stalk, sugarcane ....RATOON
stammer........................HAW, HEM
stamp ....MARK, SIGN;
....IMPRESS
stamping device ....DIE
stamping machine................DATER
stamp-sheet segment.............PANE
stanch ....STEM
stand ....BEAR, RISE; ABIDE;
........................ENDURE; TOLERATE
stand, cuplike........................ZARF
stand, small ....TABORET
stand, three-legged ....TRIPOD
standard ....PAR; FLAG,
.........................NORM; ENSIGN
standing ....STATUS
stannum ....TIN
stanza, last ....ENVOY
stanza, part of a ....STAVE
star, blue ....VEGA
star, day..................................SUN
star, evening ......VENUS; HESPER
........................VESPER; HESPERUS
star, exploding ....NOVA
starch ....AMYL, ARUM, SAGO;
........................FARINA; CASSAVA
starchy rootstock ....TARO
star cluster ....NEBULA
stare fixedly ....GAZE
stare stupidly ....GAWK
star facet ....PANE
starfish ....ASTEROID
starnose ....MOLE
starred lizard ....AGAMA; HARDIM
stars, location of ....See page 207.
stars, look at............................GAZE
star-shaped....................STELLATE
start............JUMP; BEGIN, ONSET;
........................OUTSET; GENESIS

114

a starting with ....FROM
startling shout...........................BOO
Star Trek android...................DATA
starwort ....ASTER
state..........AIR, SAY; AVER, VENT;
.................UTTER, VOICE; NATION
station ....POST; DEPOT, PLACE
stationary ....FIXED; STATIC
stationary motor part ....STATOR
statistics....................................DATA
statute ....ACT, LAW
stave, barrel ....LAG
stay ....HOLD, WAIT; TARRY
stay rope ....GUY
stays...................................CORSET
steady look ....GAZE
steal ....COP, ROB; GLOM;
.............................SKULK; PILFER,
.............................SNITCH; PURLOIN
steal cattle..........................RUSTLE
steel: Ger. ....STAHL
steel: Russ. ....STALIN
steel beam ....GIRDER
steep ....SOAK; SHEER
steep in lime ....BOWK
steer......................GUIDE; CATTLE
stellar.................................STARRY
stem ....CORM; STALK;
....STAUNCH
stem, hollow ....CANE
b stem, jointed grass.................CULM
stem, ship's ....PROW
stem of hops ....BINE
stem-to-stern planking ....STRAKE
stench ....ODOR; FETOR
stentorian ....LOUD
step ....RUNG; PHASE, TREAD
step, dance ....PAS; CHASSE
step part.................RISER, TREAD
steppes storm ....BURAN
steps, outdoor...................PERRON
steps over a fence..................STILE
step up to the mark..................TOE
sterilize (a female animal) ......SPAY
stern ....AFT; BACK,
............................GRIM; HARSH
stick ....BAR, ROD;
....................................CANE, WAND
stick, conductor's ....BATON
sticks, bundle of ....FAGOT
stick to ....GLUE; PASTE;
....ADHERE
stick together ....COHERE
stick used in hurling ....CAMAN;
.....................................CAMMOCK
sticky stuff........GOO, GUM; PASTE
stiffly nice ....PRIM
stigma.........................BLOT; TAINT
still...................................BUT, YET;
....................................ALSO; QUIET

stimulant, coffee ....CAFFEINE *c*
stimulant, tea ....THEINE
stimulate................STIR; PROVOKE
sting......................BITE; SMART
stinging herb.......................NETTLE
stingy ....MEAN; TIGHT
stint.............TASK; CHORE, SHIFT,
.................SKIMP, SPELL; SCRIMP
stipend, church ....PREBEND
stipulation ....TERM; PROVISO
stir ....ADO, MIX;
.............................TO-DO; ROUSE
stir up ....RILE, ROIL
stitch ....SEW; PUNTO
stitchbird ....IHI
stitched fold ....TUCK
stithy ....ANVIL
stock.....................BREED, CARRY
.............................STORE; SUPPLY
stock exchange membership..SEAT
stock exchange, Paris.......BOURSE
stocking run: Brit. ....LADDER
stockings ....HOSE
stock market crash ....PANIC
stocky ....DUMPY, SQUAT
stolen goods..........................SWAG
stomach......................MAW, CRAW
stomach, first.......................RUMEN
stomach, ruminant's ....TRIPE;
....OMASUM
stone ....AGATE, LAPIS, SLATE *d*
stone, aquamarine ....BERYL
stone, breastplate ....JASPER
stone, fruit...........................DRUPE
stone, hollow ....GEODE
stone, monument ....MENHIR
stone, precious ....GEM; JEWEL
stone, red ....SARD; SPINEL
stone, square-cut ....ASHLAR
stone, woman turned to ....NIOBE
stone, yellow........TOPAZ; CITRINE
stone chest ....CIST
stone chip ....SPALL
stone-cutter's chisel ....DROVE
stone hammer.........................MASH
stone-hatchet, Austral. ....MOGO
stone heap............CAIRN, SCREE;
....RUBBLE
stone implement ....CELT;
.........................EOLITH; NEOLITH
stone pillar ....STELE
stone to death.................LAPIDATE
stone worker ....MASON
stool pigeon ....RAT; NARK
stop ....DAM, END; HALT, STEM,
............................WHOA; DESIST;
............................STATION, STAUNCH
stop: naut. ....AVAST, BELAY
stop an engine ....STALL
stoppage ....JAM; TIEUP

a stopper ....BUNG, CORK, PLUG
stop short ....BALK
storage battery plate ....GRID
storage place ....BIN; BARN, SILO
store fodder ....ENSILE
storehouse ....ETAPE
storehouse, army ....DEPOT
stork, type of ....MARABOU
storm ....FUME, FURY, RAGE
stout ....FAT; BURLY
stout, kind of.......................PORTER
stove.....................................RANGE
Stowe character ....EVA, TOM;
....TOPSY
Stowe villain ....LEGREE
straight ....NEAT; FRANK;
....DIRECT
straight-edge ....RULER
strain.......................TUNE; PAINS,
...........................TINGE; EFFORT,
..........................STRESS; TRAVAIL
strained ....TENSE
strainer ....SIEVE
strainer, wool cloth ....TAMIS
straining for effect...................CUTE
strange.......................ODD; ALIEN,
.......................WEIRD; PECULIAR
strap, falcon's ....JESS; JESSE
strass.....................................PASTE
stratagem.......PLOY, RUSE; TRICK

b stratum ....LAYER
straw braid..............................TAGAL
straw hat ....BAKU, TOYO;
...........................MILAN; PANAMA
stray ....ERR; SWERVE,
....WANDER
stray animal ....DOGIE
stray child.................................WAIF
streak ....RUN; LINE,
...................................VEIN; STRIA
stream ....RUN; FLOW,
.................................RILL; BROOK,
..........................CREEK; RIVULET
street, narrow.........................LANE
strength ....MIGHT, POWER
stress ....ACCENT, STRAIN
stretched out ....PROLATE
stretcher.................................LITTER
stretching frame....................TENTER
strife ....WAR; DISCORD
strike....................BOP, HIT, RAP;
......................CONK, SLUG, SOCK,
....................................SWAT; SMITE
stringed instrument, ancient.....DEL;
....NABLA
string of mules ....ATAJO
stringy ....ROPY
strip ....BARE; DIVEST;
....UNDRESS
stripe ....BAND, VEIN; VARIETY

c stripling ....BOY, LAD
strip off skin ....FLAY
strip of wood ....LATH
strive ....TRY; WORK; TRAVAIL
strobile ....CONE
stroke, successful ....COUP
stroll ....AMBLE
strong-arm man......................GOON
strongbox..............................SAFE
stronghold.........FORT; FORTRESS
strong man: Biblical ....SAMSON
strong man, Gr. ....ATLAS
strong point ....FORTE
strong-scented............OLID, RANK;
....FETID
structure, tall ....TOWER
struggle...................VIE; CONTEND
struggle helplessly........FLOUNDER
stud......................................BOSS
student in charge ....MONITOR
studio, art ....ATELIER
study............CON, DEN; READ
study group ....SEMINAR
study of numbers, briefly........MATH
stuff ....PAD; CRAM
stuffing, soft ....KAPOK
stum ....MUST
stunted trees........................SCRUB
stupefy ....DAZE, STUN;
....BENUMB
stupid..........SLOW; DENSE, THICK
stupid person ......ASS, OAF; CLOD,
........................DOLT, FOOL; IDIOT
stupor ....FOG; COMA, DAZE;
.............................SOPOR; TRANCE
sturgeon, small ....STERLET
style ....MODE; FASHION
style of art............................GENRE
stylet, surgical ....TROCAR
stymie ....FOIL; THWART
Styx ferryman ....CHARON
subbase...............................PLINTH
subdued shade...................PASTEL
subject ....THEME, TOPIC
subject in grammar...............NOUN
subject (to) ....LIABLE
subjoin.....................................ADD
sublime ....GRAND, ROYAL;
........................AUGUST, SUPERB
submit.........BOW; YIELD; TURN IN
subordinate ....MINOR; JUNIOR
subside ....EBB; WANE; ABATE,
.............................LET UP; RELENT
substantial ....BIG; REAL; LARGE;
...................COPIOUS; ABUNDANT
substantial amount...............MUCH
substantiate ....VERIFY
substantive word ....NOUN
substitute.........SWITCH; STAND-IN
subtle ....FINE; DELICATE

a
subtle variation..................NUANCE
subtract.................TAKE; DEDUCT
subway, London ....TUBE
subway, Paris ....METRO
subway entrance..................KIOSK
succinct ....BRIEF; TERSE
succor ....AID; HELP; RELIEF
suckling, stop ....WEAN
Sudan lake.............................CHAD
suet ....TALLOW
suffer ....LET; ALLOW; MOURN
sufficiently..............................DULY
SUFFIXES:
   action ....-ANCE
   adherent................................-IST
   adjective-forming..............-ARY,
   ....-ENT, -IAL, -INE, -ISH,
   ....-IST, -ITE, -ORY,
   ....-OUS; -EOUS, -IBLE,
   ....-ICAL, -IOUS
   belonging to ....-EAN
   blood disease ....-EMIA
   carbohydrate....................-OSE
   cavity ....-COEL; -COELE
   characterized by ....-IOUS
   comparative ....-IER, -IOR
   condition ....-ATE, -ISE;
   ....-ANCE, -OSIS, -SION,
   ....-STER, -TION
   decomposition ....-LYTE

b
   diminutive.....-ULA, -ULE; -ETTE
   disease, urinary ....-URIA
   dissolve ....-LYSE, -LYZE
   dividing............................-TOMY
   doctrine ....-ISM
   eye defect ....-OPIA
   females.........................-GYNY
   feminine.........-INA, -INE; -ELLA,
   ....-ETTA, -TRIX
   follower........................-IST, -ITE
   foot.................................-PEDE
   full of ....-OSE
   having ....-FUL
   indicating, in a way...........-ABLY
   inflammation ....-ITIS
   inhabitant of ....-ITE
   instrument.......................-TRON
   killer....................................-CIDE
   like....................................-OID
   little ....-OCK
   lizard..............................-SAUR
   mineral ....-ITE; -LITE
   noun-forming ....-ACY, -ARY,
   ....-ATE, -ENT, -ERY, -ESS,
   ....-IER, -IST, -ORY; -ANCY,
   ....-ENCE, -ENCY, -ENSE,
   ....-MENT, -STER,
   ....-TION, -TUDE
   number ....-ETH; -TEEN
   occasion of many ....-FEST

of the kind of......................-ATIC
one that eats ......-VORA, -VORE
one who is ....-NIK
ordinal ....-ETH
origin ....-GENY
pain ....-ALGY; -ALGIA
participle.............................-ING
quality ....-ANCE; -ILITY
recent ....-CENE
ruler.....................................-ARCH
sayings ....-ANA; -IANA
science of ....-ICS
scientific name................-ACEA,
..........................-IDAE, -PODA
skin ....-DERM
small ....-CULE
stabilizing instrument........-STAT
stone ....-LITE, -LITH
superlative ....-EST
supporter ....-CRAT
systematized knowledge -NOMY
teeth, animal ....-ODUS
teeth, having.................-ODONT
that which acts................-ATOR
times as many..................-FOLD
tumor ....-OMA; -CELE
verb-forming ....-ISE; -ESCE
vision......................-OPY; -OPIA
Sufi disciple ....MURID
sugar, crude..........GUR; JAGGERY
sugar, fruit ....KETOSE
sugarcane byproduct ......BAGASSE
sugarcane disease ....ILIAU
sugarcane shoot, new.............LALO
sugar source ....CANE
suggestion ....CUE; CLUE; HINT;
.........................TINGE, WHIFF
suitable ....APT, FIT; RIGHT
suitcase ....BAG; GRIP; VALISE
suit of mail ....ARMOR
suitor.........................BEAU; SWAIN
sullen.........................DOUR, GLUM;
.................GLOOMY; SATURNINE
sullen, act ....MOPE
sullen, be ....POUT, SULK
sully ....SOIL; DIRTY
sultan, Turk. ....SELIM
sultan's decree.......................IRADE
sultan's residence ....SERAI
sultry ....HOT; HUMID
summa ___ laude ....CUM
summary ....BRIEF, RECAP
summit ....TOP; PEAK
summon....................CALL; EVOKE
sun......................SOL; HELIOS
sun, halo around the ....CORONA
sun, of the ....SOLAR
Sunday in Lent, fourth .....LAETARE
sunder......................SPLIT; DIVIDE
sundial ....GNOMON

d

a sun disk................................ATON
sun-dried brick....................ADOBE
sunfish................................BREAM
sunken fence ....HA-HA
sun room ....SOLARIUM
superfluous: Fr. ....DE TROP
superintendent................MANAGER
superior ....PRIME; BETTER,
........................HIGHER, SENIOR
Superman, girlfriend of ....LOIS
Superman, real name of .....KAL-EL
supplication ....PLEA; PRAYER
supply ....STOCK; FURNISH
support ....PROP; BRACE
support structure ....WALL
suppose ....GUESS, INFER
suppress ....QUASH; STIFLE
surcoat ....TUNIC
surety agreement...................BOND
surf, sound of ....ROTE
surface ....TOP, FACE;
....VISAGE
surface, smooth..............VENEER
surfeit ....CLOY, GLUT, SATE
surge ....GUSH; SWELL
surgeon's instrument ....TREPAN,
.......................TROCAR; ABLATOR,
....SCALPEL
surgical thread ....SETON; SUTURE
surly ....GRUFF, TESTY

b surmise ....GUESS; THEORY
surpass....................TOP; BEST
surplus.................EXTRA; EXCESS
surrender ....CEDE; YIELD
surrender legally................REMISE
surround.....................HEM; GIRD;
.....................CIRCLE; ENCLOSE
surrounding area...................ZONE
survey ....EYE; LOOK;
....WATCH
surveyor's assistant..........RODMAN
surveyor's instrument ....ALIDADE
Susa inhabitant................ELAMITE
suspend ....HANG; DELAY,
.......................TABLE; SHELVE
suspenders...........................BRACES
suture ....STITCH
svelte ....SLIM, TRIM
swab ....MOP
swain..................BEAU; LOVER
swallow..................GULP; MARTIN
swallow, sea.........................TERN
swamp ....BOG, FEN; MARSH;
....MORASS
swamp gas........................MIASMA
swan, female ....PEN
swan, male ....COB
swan, whistling..................OLOR
swap ....TRADE
sward...........................SOD; TURF

swarm..........NEST, TEEM; HORDE *c*
swarthy...................................DARK
swastika ....FYLFOT
sway ....ROCK, ROLL
sway, hold ....RULE; DOMINATE
swear.......................AVER; CURSE
swear words, use ....CUSS
sweat ....PERSPIRE
Swed. coin................................ORE
Swed. county ....LAN
Swed. sculptor.....................MILLES
sweep, scythe's..................SWATH
sweet ....SUGARY
sweet flag ....CALAMUS
sweetheart, Irish ....AGRA
sweet liquid ....NECTAR
sweetness, with: music........SOAVE
sweet potato ....YAM; OCARINA
sweet red wine ....ALICANTE
sweet-smelling.............REDOLENT
sweetsop ....ATES; ANNONA
sweet spire...........................ITEA
swell ....WAX; GROW
swelling ....LUMP, NODE; EDEMA
swell of water......................WAVE
swerve ....SKEW, SLEW, SLUE
swift ....FAST; FLEET
swift, common.......................CRAN
swiftly, run ....DART, SCUD
swimming.............................NATANT
swindle ....CON, GYP; DUPE, *d*
..................GULL; CHEAT, COZEN,
..................FRAUD, MULCT, STING
swindler ....COZENER
swine.........HOG, PIG, SOW; BOAR
swing music...........................JAZZ
swinish ....PORCINE
swirl ....EDDY
Swiss card game....................JASS
Swiss state.........................CANTON
switch ....SHIFT, TRADE;
......................TOGGLE, WAGGLE
switch positions ....ONS; OFFS
swollen ....TURGID
swoon ....FAINT
sword........EPEE; BLADE, SABER;
....RAPIER
sword, King Arthur's ....EXCALIBUR
sword, matador's ....ESTOQUE
sword, medieval ....ESTOC
sword, put away a ....SHEATHE
syllable, last ....ULTIMA
syllable, short ....MORA
symbol ....TOKEN
symbol of authority ....MACE
synagogue ....SHUL; TEMPLE
syncopated music...........RAGTIME
syncope ....FAINT, SWOON
syphilis ....POX; LUES
Syria, ancient........................ARAM

a Syrian port, ancient.............SIDON
Syrian city ....ALEPPO
system of rules ....CODE

system of weights ....TROY   c
system of worship.................CULT
syzygy....................................PAIR

T

tab.............................FLAP; LABEL
tableland.............MESA; PLATEAU
tablet ....PAD; PILL;
...........................BLOCK, SLATE
tableware ....CUP; BOWL,
........DISH, FORK; GLASS, KNIFE,
..............PLATE, SPOON; SAUCER,
....................TUREEN; PLATTER
Tacoma's sound ....PUGET
tact....................................FINESSE
tag..LABEL
tail, of a..........CAUDAL; CAUDATE
tail, rabbit's ....SCUT
tail, thickly furred ....BUSH
tail of a coin ....VERSO
tailor ....SARTOR
Taj Mahal site ....AGRA
take away by force...............REAVE
take back words ....RECANT
take off a hat ....DOFF
take on cargo ....LADE, LOAD
b take out ....DELE; EXPUNGE
take part...................................SIDE
take up again ....RESUME
tale...........................YARN; STORY
tale, medieval..........GEST; GESTE
tale, medieval Fr. ....LAI
tale, Norse.............................SAGA
talent ....GIFT; FLAIR, KNACK
Tale of Two Cities, A girl ....LUCIE
talipot palm ....BURI
talisman..................JUJU; CHARM;
...................AMULET, FETISH
talisman, voodoo...............GRI-GRI
talk....................GAB, YAK; CHAT;
......................PRATE; PALAVER
talk, wildly ....RANT, RAVE;
.................................HARANGUE
talking horse ....MR. ED
talk pompously....................ORATE
talk stupidly................YAUP, YAWP
tall group of Afr. people ....SERER
tall tale ....LIE; YARN;
...................................WHOPPER
tally ....TAB; COUNT, SCORE
Talmud commentary.........GEMARA
talon.............................CLAW, NAIL
tamarack............................LARCH
tamarisk.....................ATLE; ATHEL
Tammany leader...............SACHEM
tan.............................BUFF; BEIGE

tanager, Asian ....YENI
tanager, S.A. ....LINDO
tanbark..................................ROSS
tangle ....SNARL; SLEAVE
tangled mass................MAT; SHAG
tanning, plant for ....ALDER
tanning gum ....KINO
tanning shrub ....SUMAC
tanning solution ....BATE
tan skins................................TAW
tantalize...................BAIT; TEASE;
....TORMENT
Tantalus, daughter of...........NIOBE
tantrum ....FIT; HUFF
tap..............................PAT; COCK;
.......................SPIGOT, FAUCET
tape, sample........................DEMO
tapering dagger ....ANLACE
tapering piece ....SHIM
tapestry ....ARRAS, TAPIS
tapeworm ....TAENIA
tapiocalike food ....SALEP   d
tapioca source.................CASSAVA
tapir, S.A. ....DANTA
taradiddle ....FIB, LIE
tarboosh ....FEZ
target ....AIM; GOAL
Tariff Act writer...................SMOOT;
....HAWLEY
Tarkington character ....SAM
tarnish..................................SULLY
taro ....GABI; DASHEEN
taro paste..............................POI
taro root ....KALO
tarpon ....SABALO
tarry ....BIDE, STAY, WAIT;
....LINGER
tarsus ....ANKLE
tart ....ACID, SOUR; WENCH
tartan pattern ....SETT
tartar, crude..........ARGAL, ARGOL
Tarzan's chimp ....CHETA
task...............................JOB; DUTY;
..........................CHORE, STINT
task, punishment ....PENSUM
taste ....SIP, SUP; SAPOR
tasteful ....SUBDUED; ARTISTIC
tasty.....................................SAPID
Tatar dynasty ....WEI
Tatler founder...................STEELE
tattle....................RAT; BLAB

a
taunt..........JEER, MOCK; HECTOR
taut ....TENSE, TIGHT
taut, pull ....STRETCH
tautomeric compound.............ENOL
tavern ....BAR, INN, PUB
tax ....CESS, GELD, LEVY;
............ASSESS, EXCISE, IMPOST
tax, church ....TITHE
tax, import ....OCTROI
tax group: Abbr. ....IRS
tea, black...............BOHEA, PEKOE
tea, green ....HYSON
tea, herbal ....PTISAN
tea, Indian...............................ASSAM
tea, marsh ....LEDUM
tea, Oriental ....CHA; OOLONG
tea, Paraguay ....MATE; YERBA
tea box ....CADDY; CANISTER
tea cake........................SCONE
teacher..........DOCENT, MENTOR
teacher, Heb. ....RABBI
teacher, Islamic ....ALIM; MULLA
teakettle: Fr. slang......SUKE, SUKY
team, three-horse ....RANDEM
team of horses ....SPAN
tear...................RIP; DROP, RENT
tease ....HARRY; HARASS,
....................PESTER; BEDEVIL
tedious writer ....PROSER
teem ....RAIN, POUR; SWARM

b
Telamon, son of ....AJAX
telegraph.................................WIRE
telegraph, underwater ....CABLE
telegraph inventor ....MORSE
telegraph key ....TAPPER
telegraph signal ....DOT; DASH
telegraph speed unit ....BAUD
telephone inventor...................BELL
telescope part ....LENS
television ....VIDEO
television alien ....ALF
television award ....EMMY
television cable ....COAXIAL
television channel ....See channel.
television station abbr. ....UHF, VHF
tell....................IMPART, RELATE;
...................NARRATE, RECOUNT
telling blow ....COUP
Tell legend site...........................URI
temper ....RAGE; ANNEAL
Tempest servant..............CALIBAN
Tempest sprite ....ARIEL
temple.......................................FANE
temple, Asian...................PAGODA
temple, inner part of a...........CELLA
temple chamber, Gr. ....NAOS
tempo: music ....TAKT
temporary decline ....SLUMP
temporary fashion ....FAD
temporary relief.............REPRIEVE

tempt....................LURE; COURT;
............ALLURE, ENTICE, SEDUCE
tenant ....LESSEE
tend........................MIND; SERVE
tennis, served perfectly in ......ACED
tennis score ....LOVE; DEUCE
tennis stroke ....ACE, LOB;
..........................SMASH; VOLLEY
tennis term ....LET, NET, SET
Tennyson character...............ENID;
............ARDEN, ENOCH; ELAINE
tenon...COG
tense ....EDGY, TAUT; UNEASY
tentacle ....FEELER
tent flap......................................FLY
tenth part....................DECI; TITHE
tentmaker, the ....OMAR
ten years ....DECADE
tepid ....MILD, WARM
Tereus, son of ....ITYS
term..........................SPAN, WORD;
..................................PERIOD
termagant ....SHREW
term in office ....TENURE
term of address ....SIR;
.............................SIRE; MADAM
terpene alcohol ....NEROL
terrapin ....EMYD;
..........................POTTER, SLIDER
terrible ....DIRE; AWFUL
terrier, kind of ....SKYE; CAIRN
terrified...............AFRAID, SCARED
..................................PANICKED
territory ....LAND, SOIL
territory, surrounded........ENCLAVE
terror.........................FEAR; PANIC
tessera.......................................TILE
test............EXAM; ASSAY, TEMPT;
....................TRIAL; EXAMINE
testament................................WILL
testifier ....DEPONENT
testify ....DEPONE
tetrad......................................FOUR
Teucer, half-brother of ....AJAX
Teutonic barbarian................GOTH
Texas shrine........................ALAMO
texture ....PITH; FIBER;
......................................ESSENCE
Thailand, once........................SIAM
Thames estuary ....NORE
thankless person ....INGRATE
thatcher's peg ....SCOB
thatching palm ....NIPA
thaw..MELT
theater ....ODEON, STAGE
theater box seat ....LOGE
theater district ....RIALTO
theater floor ....PIT
theater sign ....SRO
Theban bard......................PINDAR

c

d

a Thebes, king of ....CREON;
...............................OEDIPUS
theme ....ESSAY, MOTIF
theme: music...........................TEMA
theme-park thrill........................RIDE
then: music ....POI
therefore ....ERGO, THEN,
...........................THUS; HENCE
Theseus, father of ....AEGEUS
Theseus, killer of ....CREON
thesis, opposite of ....ARSIS
thespian...................................ACTOR
Thessaly, king of ....AEOLUS
Thessaly mountain ....OSSA
Thessaly valley ....TEMPE
thicket ....COPSE; COVERT
thick-lipped ....LABROSE
thickness ....PLY
thief, Yidd. ....GANEF
thigh, of the ....FEMORAL
thigh bone ....FEMUR
thin ....LANK, LEAN; GAUNT,
...........SHEER; DILUTE, PAPERY,
......................SPARSE; TENUOUS
thin cake................................WAFER
things added....................ADDENDA
things done ....ACTA
things to be done ....AGENDA
think..............DEEM, HOLD; OPINE;
....................PONDER; COGITATE

b think (over) ....MULL, MUSE
thin layer ....FILM
Thin Man, The, dog in............ASTA
thin out........................ATTENUATE
thin-toned................................REEDY
third day, every ....TERTIAN
thirsty ....DRY; PARCHED
thither....................................THERE
thong ....STRAP
thong, braided ....ROMAL
Thor, wife of................................SIF
thorax, organ in the ....LUNG
Thor in Ger. myth ....DONAR
thorn ....BRIER, SPINE
thorny plant ....BRIER
thoroughfare ....WAY; ROAD;
......................AVENUE, STREET
thoroughgoing ....ARRANT
thought....................IDEA; NOTION
thoughts, form ....IDEATE
thousand ....MIL
Thrace, ancient people of .....EDONI
thrall.........................ESNE; SLAVE
thrash ....BEAT, WHIP; POUND;
......................BATTER, PUMMEL
thread, cotton ....LISLE
thread, of a ....FILAR
threaded fastener ....NUT
threadlike ....FIBROUS;
......................................NEMALINE

c threadlike parts: anat. ....FILA
threads, cross ....RETICLE
threads crossed by woof ....WARP
threads crossing warp...........WEFT,
......................................WOOF
threaten.................COW; MENACE
Three Fates..CLOTHO; ATROPOS;
......................................LACHESIS
threefold ....TRINE; TREBLE;
.................TERNARY, TERNATE
Three Furies .ALECTO; MEGAERA;
......................................TISIPHONE
Three Graces ......AGLAIA, THALIA;
......................EUPHROSYNE
three-masted ship ....XEBEC;
......................................FRIGATE
three-spot ....TREY
Three Stooges ....MOE; CURLY,
....................LARRY, SHEMP
threshhold...............................SILL
thrifty....................................FRUGAL
thrive................................PROSPER
throat ....GORGE; GULLET
throat, of the ....GULAR
throb...................BEAT; PULSE;
......................................PULSATE
throe..PANG
throng....................MOB; HORDE
throw ....CAST, HURL, TOSS;
......................FLING, PITCH
throw, underhand....................LOB
throw back.............................REPEL
thrush, song ....MAVIS
thrust ....BUTT; PROD, PUSH;
....................LUNGE, SHOVE
thunderfish ....RAAD
thunder sound.........................CLAP
thurible ....CENSER
Thuringian city ....JENA
Thursday god........................THOR
thus ....SIC
thus far ....YET
thwart ....FOIL; DEFEAT,
.................STYMIE; TRAVERSE
Tiber tributary ....NERA
Tibetan priest ....LAMA
Tibeto-Burmese people ....KAW;
......................................AKHA
tibia ....CNEMIS
tick ....ACARID
ticket, half a ....STUB
tickets, sell illegally ....SCALP
tickle ....TITILLATE
Ticonderoga, commander at GATES
tidal flood.................BORE; EAGRE
tide, largest change in ....NEAP
tidings ....NEWS, WORD
tidings, Biblical ....GOSPEL
tidy ....NEAT, TRIM;
......................................ORDERED

a tie....................BIND, BOND, LASH;
......................TRUSS; CRAVAT
tie, kind of ....ASCOT
tie, railway ....SLEEPER
tie-breaking game ....RUBBER
tie off ....LIGATE
tier ....ROW; LEVEL
tight ....SNUG, TAUT
tighten: naut. ....FRAP
tightly stretched....................TENSE
tight spot...........FIX, JAM; SCRAPE
til ....SESAME
tiles, hexagonal ....FAVI
tile, roofing ....PANTILE
tilelike ....TEGULAR
tilled land ....ARADO
tiller ....HELM
till the earth...............FARM, PLOW
tilt ....TIP; CANT, LIST
tilting: naut. ....ALIST
timber, flooring ....BATTEN
timber bend.............................SNY
timber tree, Braz. ....ARACA
timber tree, Indian ....DAR
timber wolf.............................LOBO
time ....SPAN; CLOCK,
......................SPELL, TEMPO;
.................PERIOD; DURATION
time being ....NONCE
time gone by ....PAST
b *Time Machine, The* people .....ELOI;
...............................MORLOCKS
time off....................................LEAVE
time out ....RECESS
time period ....AGE, DAY,
.............EON, ERA; AEON, HOUR,
.................................WEEK, YEAR;
.........MONTH; DECADE, MINUTE,
.................SECOND; CENTURY
times, old ....ELD; YORE
timid ....SHY; BASHFUL
timorous ....TIMID
timothy ....HAY
tin.........................CAN; STANNUM
tin, containing...............STANNOUS
tine ....PRONG
tine of an antler.....................SNAG
tinge ....TAINT
tinge deeply ....IMBUE
tingle with feeling ....THRILL
tip ....END; CANT, LEAN;
.....................ADVICE; GRATUITY
tipping.......................ALIST, ATILT
tire ....PALL; WEARY;
.................................FATIGUE
tire casing ....SHOE
tire face ....TREAD
tire support ....RIM
tire tread groove......................SIPE
Titania, husband of ....OBERON

c Titans, The Twelve ....RHEA, THEA;
..........................COIUS, CRIUS;
.......CRONUS, PHOEBE, TETHYS;
....THEMIS; IAPETUS, OCEANUS;
.............HYPERION; MNEMOSYNE
Tithonus, brother of ....PRIAM
titlark ....PIPIT
title ....NAME
title, baronet's............................SIR
title, Benedictine ....DOM
title, Eth. ....RAS
title, knight's ....SIR
title, lady's....MRS.; DAME; MADAM
title, man's........SIR; SIRE; MISTER
title, Turk. ....PASHA
title of property ....DEED
titmouse ....CHICKADEE
tittle ....JOT; IOTA, WHIT
toad, tree ....HYLA
toasting word.........SALUD, SKOAL;
..................................PROSIT
tobacco, chewing ....CHAW, QUID
tobacco, coarse ....SHAG;
.................................CAPORAL
tobacco, fine Cuban ....CAPA
tobacco ash ....DOTTEL
toe ....DIGIT
toe, bump one's.....................STUB
toe, fifth ....MINIMUS
together.................................BOTH
d togs ....DUDS
Tokyo, old name of ....YEDO;
...................................YEDDO
Tokyo Bay, city on ....CHIBI
tolerable................................SO-SO
toll ....FEE; KNELL
Tolstoy heroine ....ANNA
tomboy ....HOYDEN
tomcat ....GIB
tone ....HUE; MOOD; NOTE;
......................SHADE; TIMBRE
tone, lack of ....ATONY
tone, of ....TONAL
tone down ....SOFTEN
tone quality ....TIMBRE
tones, series of..................OCTAVE
tongue, articulated with the .APICAL
tongue, of the ....GLOSSAL
tongue-clicking sound ......TSK, TUT
tongue of a wagon.................NEAP
tonic ....ROBORANT
tonic herb....................ALOE; TANSY
too early....................PREMATURE
took a chair ....SAT
tool, abrasive ....FILE, RASP
tool, boring....................AWL, BIT;
.....................AUGER; GIMLET
tool, cleaving ....FROE
tool, cutting ....ADZ, AXE;
..................................SAW; ADZE

a tool, engraver's ....BURIN;
....................................MATTOIR
tool, enlarging ....REAMER
tool, grass-cutting ....SCYTHE,
....................................SICKLE
tool, machine ....LATHE
tool, machine cutting ....HOB
tool, molding............................DIE
tool, pointed............................AWL;
....................BODKIN, BROACH
tool, post hole ....LOY
tool, splitting ....FROE, FROW
tool, stone ....CELT; EOLITH;
....................................NEOLITH
tool, threading ....CHASER
too much ....TROP
tooth..................COG; FANG, TINE;
............MOLAR; CANINE, CUSPID
tooth, long...................FANG, TUSK
tooth cover ....CAP
toothed formation.................SERRA
toothed wheel ....GEAR
toothless ....EDENTATE
toothlike ornament..............DENTIL
tooth pulp ....NERVE
top ....CAP, LID;
....................ACME, APEX; OUTDO
topaz hummingbird ....AVA
toper..........................SOT; SOUSE
topic...........................THEME

b topmast crossbar support...........FID
top-notch.............................A-ONE
topsail, triangular.................RAFFE;
....................................RAFFEE
torment ....BAIT; ANNOY,
..................DEVIL, HARRY, TEASE
torn place ....RENT
torrid zone ....TROPIC
tortoise, freshwater ....EMYDID
Tosca villain ....SCARPIA
toss ....CAST, FLIP, HURL;
....................FLING, PITCH
tosspot ....SOT; DRUNK
total....................ALL, SUM; TALLY
....................WHOLE; COMPLETE
totalitarian ruler..............DICTATOR
totem pole ....XAT
toucan, S.A. ....TOCO;
....................................ARACARI
touch............................ABUT, FEEL;
....................................CONTACT
touch, of ....HAPTIC, TACTIC;
....................TACTILE, TACTUAL
touch, organ of.......................PALP
touch lightly ....PAT, TAP
touchwood............................PUNK
tough ....HARD; SEVERE,
....................................STURDY
tour guide, museum ....DOCENT
tourmaline, colorless......ACHROITE

c tournament walkover ....BYE
tow ....DRAW, PULL
towel..................................WIPER
towel fabric...........................TERRY
tower, Biblical ....BABEL
tower, Indian ....MINAR
tower, little ....TURRET
tower, mosque ....MINARET
towering......................HIGH; LOFTY
towhead...........................BLONDE
toxic protein from jequirity .....ABRIN
toy (with) ....TRIFLE
trace ....TINGE; VESTIGE
track ....RAIL
track, animal ....RUN; SLOT;
....................................SPOOR
track, put off ....DERAIL
track, put on another..........SHUNT;
....................................SWITCH
track, ship's ....WAKE
track circuit ....LAP
tract..........................LOT; PLOT,
....................FIELD; PARCEL
trade...................SWAP; BARTER;
....................TRAFFIC; EXCHANGE
trader.............DEALER, MONGER
traduce ....SLUR; DEFAME
traffic..................................TRADE
trail ....TAIL; TRACK
train, stopping......................LOCAL
train of attendants ....RETINUE
trajectory.................................ARC
tramp..................HOBO; VAGRANT
trample ....TREAD
tranquil ....SERENE
transaction ....DEAL, SALE
transfer ....GRANT; CONFER
transform ....CONVERT
transgress......................ERR, SIN
___ *transit gloria mundi*..............SIC
transitional editing effect ....WIPE
transmit ....SEND
transom ....TRAVE
transparent as glass ....HYALINE
transpire...........................OCCUR;
....................................HAPPEN
transverse pin ....TOGGLE
trap ....SNARE
trappings...........................REGALIA
trapshooting ....SKEET
travel.......................ROAM, TREK;
....................WANDER; JOURNEY
tray ....SALVER, SERVER
tread softly ....PAD; SNEAK
treasure ....TROVE
treasurer, college ....BURSAR
treasury agents....................T-MEN
treat ....DOCTOR, MORSEL
treatment.............CARE; THERAPY
treat with malice....................SPITE

123

a tree..............ASH, BAY, ELM, FIG,
...................FIR, GUM, OAK, YEW;
.............LIME, PALM, PEAR, PINE,
.........PLUM, TEAK, UPAS; ALDER,
.................APPLE, ASPEN, BALSA,
...............BEECH, BIRCH, CACAO,
...............CEDAR, CLOVE, EBONY,
...............ELDER, GUAVA, HENNA,
...............HOLLY, LARCH, LEMON,
...............MANGO, MAPLE, OLIVE,
...............PAPAW, PEACH, PECAN,
...........PLANE, SENNA; ACACIA,
......ALMOND, BALSAM, BANYAN,
........CASHEW, CASSIA, CHERRY,
.........CITRON, LAUREL, LINDEN,
.........LITCHI, LOCUST, MEDLAR,
.....MIMOSA, NUTMEG, ORANGE,
........PAPAYA, POPLAR, QUINCE,
........SPRUCE, WALNUT, WILLOW
tree, Afr. ....AKEE, BAKU,
..................COLA, ROKA, SHEA;
.........................BUMBO; MAFURA
tree, black gum ....TUPELO
tree, body of a ....TRUNK
tree, Braz. gum ......ICICA; BALATA
tree, buckwheat ....TITI
tree, chicle ....SAPOTA;
....SAPODILLA
tree, Chin. ....GINKGO
tree, flowering ....CATALPA
b tree, Indian ....POON
tree, live oak ....ENCINA
tree, N.A. ....TAMARACK
tree, P.I. ....DITA
tree, pod ....CAROB
tree, trembling.....................ASPEN
tree, W. Afr. ....AFARA, LIMBA
tree cobra ....MAMBA
tree knot ....BURL
treeless plain ....PAMPAS,
.....................TUNDRA, STEPPE
tree moss..............................USNEA
trees of a region.....................SILVA
tree stump ....BOLE
tremble.....ROCK; QUAKE, SHAKE;
......................TWITTER, VIBRATE
trend...............FAD; TEND; VOGUE
trespass ....SIN; BREACH
trespass for game ....POACH
trespass to recover goods.TROVER
triad ....TRIO
trial ....TEST; ORDEAL;
....................................ENDEAVOR
triangle ....TRIGON;
..................................SCALENE
triangle, ancient..................TRIGON
triangle side ....LEG
triangular insert.....................GORE
tribal symbol ....TOTEM
tribe ....CLAN, FOLK, RACE

tribulation ....TRIAL; ORDEAL; c
....CRUCIBLE
tribunal ....FORUM
tribute ....PRAISE, SALUTE
trick............FEAT; PRANK, STUNT;
.......................SLEIGHT; ARTIFICE
tricks, game for no ....NULLO
tricks, win all ....SLAM; CAPOT
trifle...........TOY; FLIRT; WHATNOT
trifling.....................SMALL; SLIGHT
trig........................NEAT, TRIM
trigonometry function ....SINE;
...........................COSINE; SECANT
trim ....NEAT, TRIG;
.................ADORN; DECORATE
trimming, dress.........GIMP; RUCHE
trinket, worthless ....FICO, GAUD
triple ....TREBLE
tripod, six-footed ....CAT
Tristram's beloved ......ISOLDE
Tristram Shandy author.....STERNE
trite...........BANAL, STALE; CLICHE
triton..................................SNAIL
troche ....PASTIL, ROTULA;
....PASTILLE
Trojan hero ....PARIS; AENEAS,
.....................AGENOR, DARDAN,
.................HECTOR; ACHILLES
trolley ....TRAM
troops ....MEN
troops, spread ....DEPLOY d
trophy ....CUP
tropical fever ....DENGUE, NAGANA
trot ....JOG; AMBLE
trouble ....AIL; CARE; PAINS,
...................WORRY; TORMENT
troubles................................ILLS
trough, inclined ....CHUTE
trough, mining ....SLUICE
trout, Brit. ....SEWEN, SEWIN
trout, lake ....CISCO
trout, red-belly ....CHAR
trowel, plasterer's ....DARBY
Troy ....ILIUM
Troy, founder of.......................ILUS
Troy, land of.........................TROAS
Troy, last king of ......PARIS, PRIAM
truancy ....HOOKY
truck, Brit. ....LORRY
trudge ....PLOD, SLOG, TOIL
trumpet ....HORN; CLARION
trumpet shell ....CONCH; TRITON
trunkfish ....CHAPIN
trunk of a car: Brit. ....BOOT
trunk of the body ....TORSO
truss up.....................................TIE
trust ....RELY; RELIANCE
truth: Chin. ....TAO
truth drug...................PENTOTHAL
try ....TEST; ESSAY; ATTEMPT

a
try to equal	VIE; EMULATE
tsetse-fly disease	NAGANA
tub	VAT; BATH
tub, brewer's	KEEVE, KIEVE
tub, broad	KEELER
tube	DUCT, PIPE
tube, glass	PIPET
tuber, edible	YAM; TARO;
	POTATO
tuber, orchid	SALEP
tuber, S.A.	ANU, OCA, OKA
Tuesday god	TYR
tufted plant	MOSS
tulip tree	POPLAR
tumor, skin	WEN
tumult	FRAY, RIOT; BRAWL,
	MELEE; FRACAS
tune	AIR; ARIA, SONG;
	MELODY
tungstite	OCHER
tuning fork	DIAPASON
Tunis, ruler of	BEY, DEY
tunnel, Alps train	CENIS
tunny	TUNA; BLUEFIN
Turandot threesome	PANG,
	PING, PONG
turban, Oriental	MANDIL
turco	TAPACOLO
turf	SOD
turf, piece of	DIVOT

b
turkeys group of	RAFTER
Turkish caliph	ALI
Turk. government	PORTE
Turk. inn	IMARET
Turk. president, former	INONU
Turk. sultan	SELIM
Turk. title	AGA; AGHA;
	EMIR; PASHA
turmeric	MIMOSA
turmoil	CHAOS, SNARL
turn	BEND, MOVE;
	CROOK, SPOIL, STINT,
	WHIRL; DIVERT
turn aside	SKEW, VEER; SHUNT
turn back (to)	REVERT
turning point	CRISIS
turn inside out	EVERT
turnip	NEEP; SWEDE;
	RUTABAGA

c
turnover	PIE
turpentine, crude	GALIPOT
turtle, Amazon	ARRAU
turtle, edible	TERRAPIN
Tuscany town	SIENA
tusk, elephant	IVORY
twelve and one half cents	BIT
twenty-fourth part	CARAT,
	KARAT
twenty quires	REAM
twig, willow	WITHE
twilight	EVE; DUSK;
	GLOAM; EVENTIDE
twin crystal	MACLE
twine	COIL, WIND; TWIST
twins	GEMINI
twist	COIL, TURN, WARP;
	SPIRAL; CONTORT
twisted	WRY; AWRY;
	ASKEW; WARPED
twitch	TIC
two	DUO; DUAD, PAIR;
	COUPLE, DOUBLE
two, the	BOTH
two elements, having	BINARY
two feet, verse of	DIPODY
twofold	DUAL, TWIN; BINAL
two-footed	BIPEDAL
two-horse chariot	BIGA
two-hulled boat	CATAMARAN

d
two-spot	DEUCE
2001: A Space Odyssey computer	HAL
two-wheeled vehicle	GIG; CART
tycoon	NABOB
Tyndareus, wife of	LEDA
type, set of	FONT
type, conforming to	TYPICAL
type, five and one half point	AGATE
type, slanting	ITALIC
type separation	KERN
type size	PICA, AGATE, ELITE;
	BREVIER
typewriter roller	PLATEN
tyrant	DESPOT
Tyre, king of	HIRAM
Tyre, princess of	DIDO
Tyr in Ger. myth	TIU
tyro	NOVICE, ROOKIE

U

ukase	EDICT
Ulalume, author of	POE
Ulysses	ODYSSEUS
Ulysses author	JOYCE
umbrella, large	GAMP

umbrella part	RIB
umbrella tree	WAHOO
umpire	REFEREE
unable to hear	DEAF
unaccented vowel sound	SCHWA

a

unadulterated ....PURE
unaffected ....SIMPLE; ARTLESS
Unalaskan ....ALEUT
unaspirate ....LENIS
unassuming ....MEEK; LOWLY;
.....................HUMBLE, MODEST
unattractive ....UGLY
unbeliever ....HERETIC
unbleached shade ....ECRU; BEIGE
unburnt brick ....ADOBE
uncanny ....EERIE, WEIRD
Uncas, beloved of ....CORA
unceasing ....ENDLESS,
..................NONSTOP, ETERNAL;
.....................................PERPETUAL
uncivil ....RUDE
unclean in Jewish law ....TREF
"Uncle Remus" author ....HARRIS
"Uncle Remus" rabbit ....BR'ER
unclose ....OPE; OPEN
uncommon ....RARE; SCARCE
..................UNUSUAL; SINGULAR;
.....................................INFREQUENT
unconcerned ....ALOOF
unconscious state ....COMA
unction ....BALM
unctuous ....OILY; SMARMY
under ....NEATH; NETHER
under: naut. ....ALOW
underclothes ....CYMAR; CAMISE;

b

....SKIVVIES
underground growth ....BULB
underground reservoir ....CENOTE
underground space ....CAVE
underhanded ......SHIFTY, SNEAKY
understand ....GET; GRASP
understanding ....KEN; SENSE
under the weather ....SICK
underwear ....BRA; SLIP;
.........................CORSET, GIRDLE,
.........................SHORTS; PANTIES
underworld ....HADES, SHEOL
underworld god ....DIS; PLUTO
underworld god, Eg. ....OSIRIS;
....SERAPIS
underwrite ....ENSURE, INSURE
undeveloped ....LATENT
undraped ....NUDE
undulating ....WAVY
undulation ....CURL, WAVE
unequal angles, having ...SCALENE
uneven ....ROUGH; JAGGED
unevenly edged ....EROSE
unfair move ....FOUL
unfasten ....UNTIE; LOOSEN
unfavorable ....BAD, ILL
unfeeling ....NUMB; CALLOUS
unfold ....OPEN; EVOLVE
ungula ....CLAW, HOOF, NAIL
ungulate, S. A. ....TAPIR

unhappy ....SAD; BLUE;

c

.....................MOROSE, RUEFUL
unicorn fish ....NARWHAL
uniform ....EVEN; ALIKE;
....REGULAR
uninteresting ....DULL
union ....MERGER
union, political ....BLOC
unit ....ACE, ONE
unit, of a ....MONADIC
unite ....WED; ALLY, JOIN,
....................KNIT, WELD; MERGE
units, measurement ..See page 246.
unity ....ONE
universal ....GLOBAL; GENERAL
universe ....WORLD; COSMOS
universe, of the ....COSMIC
universities ....See page 200.
unkind ....ILL; NASTY
unless ....BUT; SAVE
unless, in law ....NISI
unload ....DUMP
unlock ....OPEN
unmarried ....SINGLE
unmatched ....ODD
unmixed ....PURE; SHEER
unnecessary ....NEEDLESS
unrelenting ....ADAMANT
unruffled ....CALM; SERENE
unsophisticated ....NAIF; NAIVE
unspoken ....TACIT

d

unstable ....FLUID; VOLATILE
unsuitable ....INAPT
untamed ....WILD; FERAL
untidy person ....SLOB
untrained ....RAW
unusual ....ODD; RARE;
....................QUAINT; SINGULAR
unwavering ....SURE; STEADY
unwieldy object ....HULK
unwilling ....LOATH; AVERSE
unwilling to listen ....DEAF
unyielding ....FIRM;
.........................FIXED; ADAMANT
unyielding: naut. ....FAST
upbraid ....CHIDE, SCOLD
upland plain ....WOLD
upon ....ATOP
upright ....ERECT; HONEST
upright column ....STELE
upright piece ....JAMB, STUD
uprising ....REVOLT
uproar ....DIN
uraeus ....ASP
urban center ....CITY
urban office holder ....MAYOR
urchin ....IMP; GAMIN
Urfa, today ....EDESSA
urge ....PROD; PRESS;
....EXHORT

a urticaria ....HIVES
usage ....WAY; FORM; HABIT;
.........................CUSTOM, PRAXIS
use, be of ....AVAIL
used to be ....WAS
used up ....DEPLETED
useful................GOOD; HANDY;
..................HELPFUL; SALUTARY
useless ....IDLE; FUTILE
u-shaped device ....CLEVIS

usual..............NORMAL; REGULAR   *c*
utensil ....TOOL
uterus ....WOMB
utmost ....TOP; SUPREME;
.............................ULTIMATE
utter ....SAY; SHEER, STARK
uttered ....ORAL, SAID; SPOKE
utter loudly ....VOCIFERATE
utterly................ALL; JUST; QUITE;
.........................PURELY, WHOLLY

V

vacant.......................BARE; CLEAR,
.........................EMPTY; HOLLOW,
.........................OTIOSE; VACUOUS
vacation spot ....SPA; CAMP;
....RESORT
vacuum.....................................VOID
vacuum, opposite of ....PLENUM
vacuum tube ....DIODE
vagabond....................BUM; HOBO;
.........................TRAMP; VAGRANT
vague ....HAZY; LOOSE
vainglorious ....PROUD
vair fur ....MINIVER
valance, decorative............PELMET
b vale ....VALLEY
valiant............BRAVE; STALWART
valley...............DALE, DELL, GLEN,
.........................VALE; GLADE
valley, deep ....COULEE
valley, Jordan ....GHOR
value ....RATE; PRIZE,
.........................WORTH; APPRAISE
valve ....COCK
vampire, female....................LAMIA
vandal..HUN
vanish ....FADE; EVAPORATE
vanity ....EGO; PRIDE; CONCEIT
vanity case ....ETUI
vantage, point of..................COIGN
vapid ....INANE, STALE
vapor ....HAZE, MIST; STEAM
vaporous ....FUMY
variable ....PROTEAN
variation, small....SHADE; NUANCE
variegated in color....PIED; CALICO
variety ....KIND, SORT
varnish, kind of ....SHELLAC
varnish ingredient..........LAC; KINO;
..................COPAL, ELEMI, RESIN
vase...URN
vat ....TUB; CISTERN
vat, brewer's ....KEEVE, KIEVE
vat, large ....KIER
vault ....JUMP, SAFE

vault, church ....CRYPT
vaulted alcove ....APSE
vaunt........................BRAG; BOAST
Vedic dialect............................PALI
veer.........................TURN; SHIFT
veer off ....SHEER
vegetable ....PEA; BEAN, BEET,
....................KALE, OKRA; CHARD;
.........CARROT, ENDIVE, TOMATO
vegetable fuel ....PEAT
vehicle ....CAR; CART; CYCLE
vehicle, exercise ....BIKE
vehicle, four-wheeled ....LANDAU
vehicle, moon: Abbr. ....LEM
vehicle, Native Amer. ......TRAVOIS   *d*
vehicle, rugged.......................JEEP
vehicle, Russ. ....TROIKA
vehicle, war ....TANK
vehicle compartment ..CAB; TRUNK
vein..CAVA
vein, throat ....JUGULAR
vein of ore ....LODE; SCRIN
velum.....................................PALATE
velvetlike cloth ....PANNE
velvet grass ....HOLCUS
vend ....SELL; PEDDLE
vendetta ....FEUD
venerable ....OLD; HOARY
"Venerable" monk....................BEDE
venerate........HAIL; LAUD; ADORE,
...............EXALT, EXTOL, HONOR;
.........PRAISE, REVERE; GLORIFY
veneration............AWE; WORSHIP
Venetian magistrate ....DOGE
Venetian red..........................SIENA
Venetian resort ....LIDO
Venetian traveler....................POLO
Venezuelan copper center.....AROA
Venice bridge ....RIALTO
Venice canals ....RII
venture ....RISK; WAGER;
.....................CHANCE, GAMBLE,
.....................HAZARD; PROJECT
Venus, island of...................MELOS

a

Venus, son of ....CUPID
Venus, youth loved by ....ADONIS
veranda, Hawaiian ....LANAI
verb, old-style............DOST, DOTH,
....................HAST, HATH, SHEW,
..........SMIT, WAST, WERT; DIDST
verbal ....ORAL
verbally ....ALOUD
verbal noun........................GERUND
verbal rhythm......................METER
verb form ....TENSE
Verdi heroine ....AIDA
verily ....YEA; AMEN
verity ....TRUTH
Verne's captain ....NEMO
versatile ....PROTEAN, VARIOUS
verse ....POEM; STICH
vertebral bones ....SACRA
vesicle, skin..................SAC; CYST;
....BLISTER
vessel ....ARK; SHIP; CRAFT
vessel, anatomical..................VASA
vessel, cooking .....PAN, POT, WOK
vessel, drinking.........MUG; GOURD
vessel, liquor........FLASK; FLAGON
vessel, shallow ....BASIN
vessel for liquors ....DECANTER
vestal ....CHASTE
vestige ....RELIC, TRACE
vestment ....ALB; COPE; AMICE,
....................................EPHOD, STOLE

b

vesuvianite, brown............EGERAN
vetch..TARE
vetch, bitter ....ERS
vex......................IRK; FRET, GALL;
..............ANNOY, CHAFE, PEEVE;
........BOTHER, NETTLE; IRRITATE
via ....PER
viands ....FOOD
vibrate ....SHAKE; TREMBLE
vibration: music ....TREMOLO
vice..SIN
vice presidents, US...See page 190.
Vichy premier ....LAVAL
victim ....PREY
victorious, was......................WON
victor's crown....................LAURELS
victuals....................................FOOD
vie ....RIVAL; CONTEND
Viennese park ....PRATER
view..........................SCENE, VISTA
vigilant ......WARY; ALERT, AWAKE
vigor ....PEP, VIM, ZIP; FORCE
Viking..............ERIC, OLAF; ROLLO
vilify..........SLUR; MALIGN, REVILE
village........DORP, TOWN; HAMLET
villain ....HEAVY; SCOUNDREL
vindicate ....AVENGE, EXCUSE
vine ....IVY; BINE
vine, woody..............ABUTA, LIANA

c

vinegar, of ....ACETIC
vinegar of ale ....ALEGAR
vinous ....WINY
viol, ancient............................REBEC
violent ....WILD; FIERCE
violin, famous........................STRAD
violin maker, Italian ....AMATI
viper ....ASP; ADDER
viper, horned..................CERASTES
Virgil's hero......................AENEAS
Virginia willow ....ITEA
visage ....FACE, LOOK
viscous ....SLIMY; VISCID
Vishnu, 7th incarnation of ......RAMA
Vishnu's bow ....SARAN
Vishnu's serpent ....NAGA
visible juncture ....SEAM
Visigoths, king of the..........ALARIC
vision......................DREAM, SIGHT
vision, of................................OPTIC
visionary ....SEER; UTOPIAN
visit ....CALL, STAY;
....SOJOURN
vison..MINK
vital fluid..................................SAP
vitalize ....ANIMATE
vital principle ....SOUL
vitamin A source ....CAROTENE
vitamin B ....BIOTIN, NIACIN;
....CHOLINE
vitamin B1 ....THIAMINE
vitamin B source ......LIVER, YEAST
vitamin B2....................RIBOFLAVIN
vitamin C deficiency ....SCURVY
vitamin D deficiency ....RICKETS
vitamin D source ....MILK, YOLK
vitamin H ....BIOTIN
vitamin K source.....FISH; ALFALFA
vitiate..........................SPOIL, TAINT;
....................NULLIFY, POLLUTE
Viti Levu Island seaport..........SUVA
vituperate ....ABUSE; ASSAIL,
....REVILE
vivacious................PERT; CHIPPER
vivacity ....VIM; BRIO,
....................DASH, ELAN; VERVE,
................................VIGOR; SPIRIT
vocal flourish..................ROULADE
vocation ....CAREER; CALLING
___ voce..............................SOTTO
voice..............SAY; VOTE; UTTER;
....................SINGER; DECLARE
voice, singing ....ALTO, BASS;
................TENOR; SOPRANO
voiced........................SONANT
voiced, not..................ASONANT
void ....NULL; ABYSS, SPACE
void, make..........ANNUL; CANCEL
volcanic crater, Jap. ....ASO
volcanic cinder ....SCORIA

d

volcanic rock...............TUFA, TUFF;
....LATITE
volcanic scoria matter .LAVA, SLAG
volcano, Caribbean ....PELEE
volcano, Mex. ....COLIMA
volcano, P. I. ....APO
volcano, Sicilian......................ETNA
volcano crater.......................MAAR
volcano hole ....CRATER
Volga tributary........................KAMA
volition ....WILL
Voltaire...............................AROUET
Voltaire play.............................ZAIRE
volt-ampere............................WATT
voluble.....................GLIB; FACILE
volume ....BOOK, BULK, MASS,
.........................OPUS, SIZE, TOME
vomiting ....EMESIS

voodoo charm ....MOJO; GRI-GRI
vote ....BALLOT
vote, negative ....NAY
vote, positive...................AYE, YEA
vote, right to ....FRANCHISE
vote, take a ....POLL
vote into office ....ELECT
votes ....AYES, NAYS, YEAS
voucher........................CHIT, NOTE
vouch for ....SPONSOR
vowel, line over a ....MACRON
vowel suppression ....ELISION
voyaging ....ASEA
V-shaped piece ....WEDGE
Vulcan, wife of........................MAIA
vulcanite ....EBONITE
vulgar ....COARSE, COMMON
vulture...............URUBU; CONDOR

W

W, old English...........................WEN
wade across.......................FORD
wading bird ....IBIS, RAIL; CRANE
.................EGRET, HERON, STILT;
....................AVOCET; FLAMINGO
wag..............WIT; JOKER; SWITCH
wages.........................PAY; SALARY
Wagner, son-in-law of ....LISZT
Wagner heroine ....ELSA; SENTA;
....ISOLDE
wagon ....CART, DRAY, WAIN
wagon, Russ. ....TELEGA
wagon-pin holder.................CLEVIS
wagon shaft............................THILL
wagon tongue ....NEAP, POLE
wahoo fish..............................PETO
wail ....BAWL, KEEN; LAMENT
waistcoat .....VEST; GILET; JERKIN
wait...............BIDE, STAY; PAUSE;
............TARRY; LINGER, REMAIN
waive ....CEDE; YIELD
waken................ROUSE; AROUSE
wale...WELT
Wales...............CYMRU; CAMBRIA
walk ....PACE, STEP; TREAD
walk, inability to ....ABASIA
walk affectedly......................MINCE
walk heavily ....PLOD; SLOG
walking stick...........................CANE
walk lamely.............................LIMP
walk purposefully ....STRIDE
walk through ....WADE
walkway, tree-lined ....ALAMEDA
wall...................FENCE; BARRIER,
..................ENCLOSE; PARTITION
wall, divided by a ....SEPTATE

wall, fortification ....RAMPART
wall, of a ....MURAL
walled city in Nigeria ....KANO
wallop ....SMASH; IMPACT
wallow ....LURCH;
.................................FLOUNDER
wall paneling.................WAINSCOT
wall section ....DADO; PANEL
walnut tree ....NOGAL
wampum ....PEAG; SEWAN;
....SEAWAN
wan ....ASHY, PALE; ASHEN
wand ....BATON, STICK
wander ....ROAM, ROVE; STRAY
wanderer...............................NOMAD
wane............................EBB; EASE;
.......................ABATE; LET UP
want.............LACK, NEED; DESIRE
wapiti ....ELK
war, religious......JIHAD; CRUSADE
war, Russ.-Eng. ....CRIMEA
warble.............SING; TRILL; YODEL
warclub, medieval ....MACE
warden, fire......................RANGER
ward off ....FEND; AVERT,
.................PARRY, REPEL, STAVE
warehouse ....DEPOT
warehouse area ....LOFT
war god ....TYR, ARES, MARS
war goddess ....ENYO
war horse ....CHARGER
warm ....HEAT; TEPID
warn.......................................ALERT
warning signal ....SIREN
warning system, early...........D.E.W.
warp yarn ....ABB

a warship ....CRUISER;
....DESTROYER
warship, sailing.................FRIGATE
wary ....CANNY, CHARY;
....PRUDENT
wash ....LAVE; BATHE, RINSE
wasp ....HORNET
waste................LOSS; SQUANDER
waste allowance ....TRET
waste away......................ATROPHY
wasted............................LOST
waste growth...................RUDERAL
wasteland.............................MOOR
waste matter ....SLAG; DROSS
waste silk............................FRISON
waste time ....IDLE, LOAF
watch ....SEE; GUARD, VIGIL
watch chain............................FOB
watchful ....WARY; ALERT
watchful guardian................ARGUS
watchtower .....TURRET; MIRADOR
water ....DILUTE;
....................IRRIGATE, SPRINKLE
water, body of ....BAY, SEA;
..........COVE, GULF, LAKE, LOCH,
.........MERE, POND, POOL, TARN;
.............BAYOU, BROOK, CANAL,
................CREEK, INLET, LOUGH,
.............OCEAN, RIVER, SOUND;
.......HARBOR, LAGOON, STREAM

b water, covered by ....AWASH
water, seek..........................DOUSE
water arum..........................CALLA
waterbuck ....KOB; KOBA;
....POKU, PUKU
water chestnut, Chin. ....LING
watercock.............................KORA
watercourse ....BROOK, CANAL,
.......................RIVER; STREAM
watered silk ....MOIRE
watering hole.........................OASIS
water lily............................LOTUS
water passage.....................CANAL,
.....................SOUND; SLUICE,
.....................STRAIT; CHANNEL
water pipe ...HOOKAH; NARGHILE,
...........................NARGILEH
waterproof canvas ....TARP
water reservoir, natural .....CENOTE
water sound............PLOP; SPLASH
water spirit ....ARIEL; SPRITE
water spirit, Gaelic..............KELPIE
water sprite, female ....NIXIE;
...........................UNDINE
water sprite, male......................NIX
waterthrush ....WAGTAIL
watertight, make...................CAULK
water vessel, Indian ....LOTAH
water wheel ....NORIA
watery ....SEROUS

wattle tree ....BOREE, MYALL   *c*
wave ....FLAP; FLUTTER;
....BRANDISH
waver..................SWAY; TEETER;
....VACILLATE
wax...CERE
wax, of...........................CERAL
wax, yellow or white ....CERESIN
wax for skis ....KLISTER
wax ointment ....CERATE
wax plant..............................HOYA
waxy chemical ....CERIN
way..............MODE, PATH, ROAD;
.........USAGE; AVENUE, METHOD,
...................STREET; TECHNIQUE
way of walking ....GAIT
way out...................EXIT; EGRESS
wayside.....................................EDGE
weak..........PUNY; FRAIL; FEEBLE
weaken ....SAP; FLAG, WANE;
................ENERVATE, ENFEEBLE
weakling ....WIMP
weakness...............................ATONY
weal ....WALE, WELT; BENEFIT
wealth................MEANS; ASSETS,
....RICHES
weapon ....GUN; BOMB;
...................KNIFE, LANCE, RIFLE,
.......................SPEAR, SWORD
weapon, gaucho's ....BOLAS
weapon, Maori ....PATU   *d*
weapon, P. I. ....BOLO
weapons ....ARMS
wear......................DON; SPORT
wear away ....ERODE; ABRADE
wear away slowly..........CORRODE
wear by friction ....RUB
wearing down...............ATTRITION
weary ....PALL; TIRED; FATIGUE
weasel ....ERMINE, FERRET
weasel, Eng. ....STOAT
weather.................LAST; PERSIST,
.....................RIDE OUT, SURVIVE
weather, inclement ....FOG;
.........................GALE, HAIL, RAIN,
.................SMOG, SNOW; SLEET
weathercock ....VANE
weather indicator.......BAROMETER
weaverbird .....BAYA, MAYA, TAHA;
.................WHYDAH; AVADAVAT
weaver's bobbin or shuttle.......PIRN
weaver's reed ....SLEY
weaving frame ....LOOM
weaving tool ....EVENER
web ....MESH, TELA
wed..........................MARRY, UNITE
wedge ....SHIM
wedge, steel............................FROE
wedgelike piece..................QUOIN
wedge-shaped ....CUNEATE

a Wednesday god ....WODEN
weed............BUR; TARE; DARNEL
weed, coarse ....DOCK; SORREL
week ....SENNIGHT
weekday, R.C. ....FERIA
weep ....CRY, SOB; BOOHOO,
....LAMENT
weeping statue......................NIOBE
weft ....WOOF
weight.......................HEFT, ONUS;
.....................................LEVERAGE
weight, ancient ....MINA; TALENT
weight, Asian...........................TAEL
weight, balance ....RIDER
weight, Eng. ....STONE
weight, heavy ....TON
weight allowance.........TARE, TRET
weights ....See page 246.
weight system ....TROY
weir ....DAM
weird ....EERIE; SPOOKY
welcome ....GREET
welfare ....DOLE, GOOD, SAKE
well-bred people..................GENTRY
Welsh ....CYMRIC; CAMBRIAN
Welsh capital ....CARDIFF
Welsh dog ....CORGI
Welsh people ....CYMRY
Welsh river...............................WYE
Welsh saint ....DAVID

b Welsh symbol ....LEEK
welt ....WALE, WEAL
W. Australia capital ....PERTH
Western shrub.......................SAGE
"Western Star" writer............BENET
W. Indies island....................CUBA;
............NEVIS; NASSAU, TOBAGO
W. Indies islands ....BAHAMAS;
.....................................ANTILLES
Westphalia, city in ....HERNE
West Pointer...........CADET; PLEBE
West Point mascot ....MULE
wet.........................DAMP; MOIST
whale ....ORC; BELUGA;
.....................................GRAMPUS
whalebone ....BALEEN
whales, group of.............GAM, POD
whale's tail ....FLUKES
wharf............................PIER, QUAY
whatever ....SUCH
whatnot shelf...................ETAGERE
wheat ....DURUM,
.............................EMMER, SPELT
wheat, Indian ....SUJI; SUJEE
wheat disease ....BUNT
wheat middlings.............SEMOLINA
wheedle ....COAX; CAJOLE
wheel........................RING; PIVOT;
.....................................GYRATE
wheel, furniture ....CASTER

c wheel, grooved ....SHEAVE
wheel center ....HUB; NAVE
wheel horse ....POLER
wheel part ......RIM; FELLY, SPOKE
wheel projection ....CAM
wheels, of..............................ROTAL
wheel shaft..............AXLE; ARBOR
wheel tread ....TIRE
whetstone ....BUHR, HONE
whiff ....SNIFF, TRACE
while ....WHEN
whimper ....MEWL, PULE
whin....................FURZE, GORSE
whine ....PULE; GROUCH
whinny ....NEIGH
whip ....BEAT, FLOG, LASH
whip, cowboy's..................CHICOTE
whip, Russ............................KNOUT
whip mark ......WALE, WEAL, WELT
whipsocket ....SNEAD
whirl ....REEL, SPIN
whirlpool ....EDDY; VORTEX
whiskers.............BEARD; GOATEE
whiskey, Irish....................POTEEN
whistle ....PIPE; SIREN
whist win..................................SLAM
whit ....BIT, JOT; ATOM, IOTA
white alkaline ....SODA
white ermine ......LASSET; MINIVER
white-flecked.........................ROAN
white matter of the brain ....ALBA
whiten ....ETIOLATE
white oak................................ROBLE
white poplar..........................ABELE
white with age ....HOAR
whitish ....HOARY
whitlow grass ....DRABA
Whittier heroine ....MAUD
whiz.......HUM; BUZZ; WHOOSH
whoa.........................STOP; HOLLA
whole amount.....................GROSS
wholesome ....HALE; SOUND;
wholly.................QUITE; UTTERLY
wicked ....BAD; EVIL; NASTY
wicker basket .....CESTA; PANNIER
wicker box.........................HANAPER
wickerwork..........................RATTAN
wicket, croquet ....HOOP
wide-mouthed vessel ....EWER,
.............................OLLA; PITCHER
wield ....PLY; EXERT; HANDLE
wife's property ....DOS
wig ....RUG; PERUKE
wigwam ....TEPEE
wild ....FERAL; SAVAGE
wild ass ....KIANG; ONAGER
wild buffalo ....ARNA
wildcat.....................................LYNX
wildcat, Afr. ....CHAUS
wildcat, Siberian ....MANUL

a
wild dog ....DHOLE
wild dog, Australian ....DINGO
Wild Duck playwright.............IBSEN
wildebeest.................................GNU
wild garlic...............................MOLY
wild ginger ....ASARUM
wild hog.................................BOAR
wildlife park ....ZOO
wild lime ....COLIMA
wild ox ....ANOA, GAUR
wild ox, extinct ....URUS
wild plum ....SLOE
wild plum, California.............ISLAY
wild sheep, Asian...............ARGALI
wild sheep, horned..........MUFLON;
..................................MOUFLON
wild sheep, Indian.................URIAL;
..................BHARAL, NAHOOR
wild sheep, N. Afr. ....AOUDAD
wild vanilla ....LIATRIS
will ....DESIRE; VOLITION
will, one making a ....DEVISOR
will addition.........................CODICIL
willingly ....LIEF
willow ....OSIER
willow twig.........................SALLOW
will power, loss of ....ABULIA
Wilson's thrush ....VEERY
wilt.................SAG; FLAG; DROOP
wily ....SLY; FOXY;

b
................CANNY; SLICK; CLEVER,
......................SHIFTY; CUNNING
wimple...................................TWIST
win ....GET; GAIN; VICTORY
winch.....................................HOIST
wind................COIL, GALE, TURN
wind, cold Adriatic.................BORA
wind, Andes ....PUNA, PUNO
wind, Australian ....BUSTER
wind, away from the...............ALEE
wind, cold alpine ....BISE
wind, cold Med. ....MISTRAL
wind, east ....EURUS
wind, god of the north ....BOREAS
wind, hot dry...SIMOOM; SIROCCO
wind, hot Med. ....SOLANO
wind, warm dry ....FOEHN
wind-blown loam ....LOESS
windborne.........................AEOLIAN
windflower......................ANEMONE
wind indicator ....SOCK, VANE
wind instrument, hole in a LILL
windlass ....CAPSTAN
windmill sail..............................AWE
window, bay ....ORIEL
window lead..........................CAME
window ledge...........................SILL
window part.............................SASH
window setter...................GLAZIER
windrow................................SWATH

c
windstorm...........GALE; CYCLONE,
....TORNADO
wine ....HOCK, PORT, SACK,
................VINO; MEDOC, TOKAY;
........CLARET, MALAGA, MUSCAT,
.....SHERRY; CHABLIS, MOSELLE
wine, Amer. ....CATAWBA
wine, dry ....SEC; SECCO
wine, golden ....BUAL
wine, honey and ....MULSE
wine, mulberry flavored.......MORAT
wine, new.............................MUST
wine, revived.........................STUM
wine, very dry ....BRUT
wine, white ....SAUTERNE
wine-and-lemon drink.........NEGUS
wine cask ....TUN, BUTT
wine container, Gr. ....OLPE
wine county, California ....NAPA
wine cup.....................AMA; AMULA
wine merchant.................VINTNER
wine region, It. ....ASTI
wine stopper ....CORK
wine vessel ....AMULA; CHALICE
wing ....ALA; PINION
wing, bastard ....ALULA
wing, beetle ....TEGUMEN
winged fruit ....SAMARA
winged god ....EROS; CUPID
winged victory ....NIKE
wing-footed....................ALIPED
wing-footed god ....MERCURY
wingless...........................APTERAL;
..................................APTEROUS
winglike..................................ALAR
wing movement.....................FLAP
wings.....................................ALAE
wings, having.......................ALATE
wink...............BLINK, GLINT;
....................................INSTANT
wink eyes rapidly ....BAT
Winnie the Pooh donkey ...EEYORE
Winnie the Pooh owl ....WOL
winnow ....SIFT, SORT;
....SEPARATE
winter, of ....BRUMAL,
..................HIEMAL; HIBERNAL
wipe out ....ERASE
wire measure ....MIL
wire service ....UPI; REUTERS
wisdom ....LORE; SENSE;
....GNOSIS
wise ....SAGE; SENSIBLE
wise advisor......................MENTOR
wisecrack ....JAB, DIG;
.............................QUIP; CRACK
wise man ....SAGE; SOLON;
....NESTOR
Wise Men ....MAGI; GASPAR;
...............MELCHIOR; BALTHAZAR

d

wish ....WANT, WILL; CRAVE,
............YEARN; DESIRE; HANKER
wish undone ....RUE
wisp ....HINT
wit................WAG; COMIC, SENSE
witch ....HAG; CRONE; HECATE;
................................SORCERESS
witch, male ....WARLOCK
witch city ....SALEM
witchcraft, W. Indies ....OBEAH
witch doctor ....SHAMAN
witch in *The Faerie Queene*.............
....DUESSA
with................................HAVING
withdraw..........RECALL, RECANT,
.....................REMOVE; RETREAT
wither ....SEAR; WIZEN;
..................MUMMIFY, SHRIVEL
withered ....DRY; SERE
within ....INTO; INSIDE
with joy.......................................FAIN
witless chatter........................GAB
witness..........SEE; MARK; ATTEST
witness, legal ....DEPONENT
witty remark ....MOT; QUIP
witty reply.......................REPARTEE
Wizard of Oz dog ....TOTO
Wizard of Oz witch ....GLINDA
wobble ......REEL, SWAY; FALTER,
.....................TEETER; STAGGER
Woden...................................ODIN
woe ....BANE; AGONY; MISERY
woe is me................................ALAS
wolf, gray.................................LOBO
wolfish.................................LUPINE
wolframite.................................CAL
woman, ill-tempered ....SHREW;
....VIRAGO
woman, loose .....BIM; DOXY, SLUT
woman: obs. ....FEME
Wonderland girl ....ALICE
wont....................................HABIT
wood....................................FOREST
wood, black ....EBONY
wood, flexible......................EDDER
wood, fragrant ....CEDAR
wood, light ....ANDA, CORK;
....BALSA
wood, long piece of...POLE; PLANK
wood, piece of.........................SLAT;
.....................SPRAG; BILLET
woodchuck ....MARMOT
wooded grove ....BOSK
wooden ....STOIC
wooden peg ....SKEG; DOWEL
wooden shoe ....SABOT; PATTEN
wood gum..............................XYLAN
woodland deity.............PAN; FAUN;
....SATYR
woodpecker, green ....HICKWALL

woodpecker, small ....PICULET
woodpeckers, of ....PICINE
wood sorrel ....OCA, OKA
woodwind..........OBOE; BASSOON,
....CLARINET
woodworm ....TERMITE
woody fiber ....BAST
woody plant ....TREE
woof......................................WEFT
wool.................ANGORA, MERINO
wool, reclaimed ....MUNGO
wool cluster..............................NEP
woolen cloth, coarse..........KERSEY
woolen thread ....YARN
wool fat ....LANOLIN
woolly ....LANATE, LANOSE
wool package, Australian.....FADGE
word, scrambled ....ANAGRAM
word blindness ....ALEXIA
word by word ....LITERAL
wording.......................................TEXT
word of God.........................LOGOS
word of mouth ....GOSSIP
work ....TOIL; LABOR; TRAVAIL
work, musical ....OPUS; OPERA;
....SONATA
work, piece of ....JOB; STINT
work, unit of..............................ERG
work aimlessly ....POTTER
work at steadily ....PLY
work basket, woman's...........CABA;
....CABAS
worker...............HAND; OPERATOR
work hard.........MOIL, TOIL; SLAVE
work unit..................................CREW
world holder ....ATLAS
World War I battle site ....MONS;
....MARNE
worm, eye-infesting...................LOA
wormwood paste ....MOXA
worn-out ....EFFETE
worn-out horse ....NAG; PLUG
worry ....CARE, CARK, FRET;
.....................ANGST; POTHER
worship ....ADORE; REVERE;
................................VENERATE;
................................REVERENCE
worship, form of..................RITUAL
worship, house of.............BETHEL,
.....................CHURCH, TEMPLE;
................................TABERNACLE
worship, object of ....GOD; IDOL
worship, place of ....ALTAR
worship of saints...................DULIA
worsted cloth ....ETAMINE
worthless ....NO-GOOD;
....USELESS
worthless mineral waste ...GANGUE
worthless trifle ....FICO, GAUD
wound ....HURT; INJURE

a
wound crust	SCAB
wound mark	SCAR
wrangle	BRAWL, FIGHT;
	BICKER; QUIBBLE
wrap	SWATHE; SWADDLE
wrath	IRE; ANGER
wrathful	IRATE
wreath	RING; CIRCLET
wreathe	COIL; TWINE; SPIRAL
wrest	WRING; WRENCH
wrestle	TUSSLE
wriggle	SQUIRM
wrinkle	RUCK, RUGA; RIMPLE
wrinkled	RUGATE, RUGOSE
wrist	CARPUS

c
wrist bone, of the	CARPAL
wrist guard	BRACER
writ, issue in a	MISE
write	PEN
write marginal comments	POSTIL
write music	NOTATE
writer	SCRIBE
writing table	DESK; ESCRITOIRE
writ of execution	ELEGIT
writ to arrest	CAPIAS
wrong	OFF, SIN; AWRY, EVIL;
	AMISS, FALSE; SPECIOUS
wrong, legal	TORT
wrongdoing	SIN; EVIL
wry face	MOUE

Y

b
yacht pennant	BURGEE
Yahi tribe survivor	ISHI
Yak's-tail fan	CHAMAR
Yale student	ELI
Yang, counterpart of	YIN
Yangtze River's other name	
	CHANG
Yangtze tributary	HAN
yarn	TALE; FABLE,
	STORY; WHOPPER
yarn count	TYPP
yarn lump	SLUB
yarn measure	LEA
yarn measure, old	HEER
yarn mop	SWAB
yarn quantity	SKEIN
yataghan	SABER
yaupon	CASSENA
yawn	GAPE
yearly	ANNUAL; ETESIAN
yearly church payment	ANNAT
yearn	ACHE, FEEL, PINE,
	PITY; CRAVE
yeast	LEAVEN
yeast, brewer's	BARM
yell	CRY; BAWL, CALL;
	SHOUT, WHOOP;
	BELLOW, HOLLER
yellow	AZO; BUFF,
	GOLD; AMBER, GREGE,
	OCHER; GOLDEN, MELINE,
	QUINCE; CITRINE;
	SAFFRON; PRIMROSE
yellow, sickly	SALLOW;
	JAUNDICE
yellow ide	ORF; ORFE
yellow ocher	SIL
yellow, pale	BEIGE, CREAM;
	FALLOW

d
yellow pigment	GAMBOGE;
	ORPIMENT
yellow quartz	TOPAZ
Yellow Sea arm	BO HAI
yellow wood	AVODIRE
yelp	YAP, YIP; SQUEAL
Yemen capital	SA'NA
yet	BUT; EVEN; STILL
yield	BEAR; OUTPUT;
	CONCEDE
yin, counterpart of	YANG
Yogi	SWAMI
Yogi's buddy	BOOBOO
yokel	OAF; HICK, RUBE
yolk of an egg	VITELLUS
yolky	EGGY
yon	THERE
Yorkshire city	LEEDS
Yorkshire river	ESK, URE;
	NIDD, OUSE; DERWENT
young animal	CUB, KID, PUP;
	CALF, COLT; WHELP
young bull: Brit.	STOT
younger son	CADET
young female pig	GILT
young kangaroo	JOEY
youngster	KID, TAD, TOT;
	SHAVER
young weaned pig	SHOAT,
	SHOTE
youth	LAD
youth shelter	HOSTEL
Yucatan people	MAYA
yuccalike plant	SOTOL
Yugoslavian	SERB; CROAT
Yugoslavian leader, former	TITO
Yum-yum's friend	KOKO;
	NANKIPOO
__ Yutang	LIN

Z

Z, Brit. ....ZED
zeal ....ELAN; ARDOR; FERVOR
zealous ....AVID
Zebedee, son of ....JOHN; JAMES
zebra, S. Afr. ....QUAGGA
zebra, young..........................COLT
zebra-ass hybrid..............ZEBRASS
zenith ....ACME, APEX,
.............................PEAK; CREST;
.............................CLIMAX, SUMMIT
zenith, opposite of.................NADIR
Zeno, follower of ....STOIC
zeppelin...................................BLIMP
zeppelin, famous...................GRAF
zero ....ZILCH; CIPHER
zest.......................TANG; GUSTO
Zeus, daughter of ....ATE;
.................HEBE; AEGLE, HELEN,
.............IRENE; AGLAIA, ATHENA,
.........................CLOTHO, THALIA
Zeus, epithet for ....AMMON
Zeus, maiden loved by ....LEDA;
....EUROPA

Zeus, mother of......................RHEA
Zeus, old Doric name of............ZAN
Zeus, sister of ....HERA
Zeus, son of ....ARES; ARCAS,
.............BELUS, MINOS; AEACUS,
.........................APOLLO, CASTOR,
.........HERMES, POLLUX, ZETHUS
Zeus, wife of.............HERA; METIS
Zilpah, son of ....GAD; ASHER
zinc in slabs ....SPELTER
zodiac sign ....LEO; ARIES,
.............LIBRA, VIRGO; CANCER,
............................GEMINI, PISCES,
.....................TAURUS; SCORPIO;
.............AQUARIUS; CAPRICORN;
.............................SAGITTARIUS
Zola novel ....NANA
zone ....AREA
zoophyte, marine ....CORAL
Zoroastrian ....PARSI; PARSEE
Zoroastrian scripture..........AVESTA
Zulu language ....BANTU
Zulu warriors..............................IMPI

SPECIAL SECTIONS

You will find the following sections very helpful when solving crossword puzzles. Use these sections in conjunction with the Clues & Definitions Section. Most of the information in the Special Sections is found only there, so you should familiarize yourself with these sections.

Information is presented in easy-to-understand lists in many categories. The order of presentation is; people, places, and things. You will find most of the lists from the original edition of this dictionary and many new ones. Lists are an efficient way to present information, therefore, this part of the book has been greatly expanded.

When the information presented is not straightforward, a brief introduction is given at the beginning of the Special Section.

All three- and four-letter words are cross-referenced from the Word Finder.

NAME FINDER

Many crossword puzzle clues involve the first and last names of famous people. When the clue tells you the last name, discovering the first name may be difficult but possible if you have a wide variety of reference sources available. For example, you can look up "Composer Khatchaturian" in an encyclopedia. However, many clues give you a first name and perhaps a profession. With the Name Finder either type of clue can be unravelled simply by looking up the first or last name. Thousands of names of famous people are cross-referenced here. If you have the clue, "Singer Bob," simply look up "Bob," listed alphabetically in the Name Finder, and you will see a listing of 32 people named Bob. Three of them, Dylan, Marley, and Seger are followed by the code letter "x." Code letters refer to the source of a person's fame. The chart below lists the meaning of each code letter. In this example, the code letter "x" indicates that the person is a singer.

Names are listed alphabetically, letter by letter, dictionary style. When there are instances of a name which is used as both a first and a last name, people with the first name are listed first followed by a separate list of people with the name used as a last name.

a ....ACTOR,	n ....HOCKEY PLAYER
.................................DANCER,	o ....JOURNALIST,
...............................MAGICIAN,	............TELEVISION REPORTER
.....................................MODEL	p....................MILITARY LEADER
b ....ARCHITECT	q ....MOVIE DIRECTOR,
c ....ARTIST,	...................................PRODUCER,
...................................DESIGNER	.......................STAGE DIRECTOR
d ....ASTRONAUT,	r.....................................MUSICIAN,
....PILOT	................................CONDUCTOR
e ....BASEBALL PLAYER	s ....OLYMPIC ATHLETE
f ....BASKETBALL PLAYER	t...POET
g.......................................BOXER	u.................................POLITICIAN,
h ....BUSINESS LEADER,	....LAWYER,
.........................LABOR LEADER,	....JUDGE
....................................GANGSTER	v....................RACE CAR DRIVER
i ....CARTOONIST	w ....SCIENTIST,
j ....COMEDIAN	............................PSYCHIATRIST,
k............................COMPOSER,	....................................INVENTOR
....................................LYRICIST	x ....SINGER
l....................FOOTBALL PLAYER	y ....TENNIS PLAYER
m......................................GOLFER	z.......................................WRITER

A.A. ....MILNE(z)
A.E. ....HOUSMAN(t)
A.J. ....FOYT(v)
Aaron ....BURR(u)
...............COPLAND(k)
.................SPELLING(q)
Aaron, ...HANK(e)
Abbott, ...BUD(j)
...................GEORGE(z)
Abby ....DALTON(a)
Abdul, ...PAULA(x)
Abdul-Jabbar, ...
...................KAREEM(f)
Abe ....BURROWS(z)
...................FORTAS(u)
.....................VIGODA(a
Abigail ....Van BUREN(o)
Abner...............................
............DOUBLEDAY(p)
Abraham .....LINCOLN(u)
Abraham, ...
............F. MURRAY(a)
Abramovitz, ...MAX(b)
Abrams, ...
..............CREIGHTON(p)
Abzug, ...BELLA(u)
Acheson, ...DEAN(u)
Acuff, ...ROY(r)
Ada ....REHAN(a)
Adam ....ANT(x)
.......SMITH(z), WEST(a)
Adams, ...ALICE(z)
....................BROOKE(a)
.......BRYAN(x), DON(a)
.................DOUGLAS(z)
.........EDIE(x), JOHN(u)
..........JOHN QUINCY(u)
....................MASON(a)
.....................MAUD(a)
...................SAMUEL(u)
Addams, ...CHARLES(i)
Adderley, ...JULIAN
............"Cannonball"(r)
Ade, ...GEORGE(z)
Adela...............ROGERS
..............ST. JOHN(z)
Adele..........ASTAIRE(a)
Adelina ....PATTI(x)
Adenauer, ..KONRAD(u)
Adjani, ...ISABELLE(a)
Adlai E. ....
............STEVENSON(u)
Adler, ...ALFRED(w)
.......CYRUS(z), FELIX(z)
......................LARRY(r)
Adolf ....HITLER(u)
Adolph ....GREEN(a)
......OCHS(o), ZUKOR(q)
Adolphe......MENJOU(a)
Adolphus........BUSCH(h)

Adoree, ...RENEE(a)
Adrian ....DANTLEY(f)
Adrienne....BARBEAU(a)
Agar, ...JOHN(a)
Agassi, ...ANDRE(y)
Agatha ......CHRISTIE(z)
Agee, ...JAMES(z)
Ager, ...MILTON(k)
Agnes ....De MILLE(a)
............MOOREHEAD(a)
Agnew, ...SPIRO(u)
Agutter, ...JENNY(a)
Aherne, ...BRIAN(a)
Ahmad ....RASHAD(l)
Aidan ....QUINN(a)
Aiello, ...DANNY(a)
Aiken, ...CONRAD(t)
Aikman, ...TROY(l)
Ailey, ...ALVIN(a)
Aimee, ...ANOUK(a)
Ainge, ...DANNY(f)
Akim........TAMIROFF(a)
Akira .....KUROSAWA(q)
Al ....ALBERT(o)
.....CAPONE(h), CAPP(i)
............GEIBERGER(m)
.....GORE(u), GREEN(x)
...............HIRSCHFELD(i)
...................JARREAU(x)
....................JOLSON(x)
....................KALINE(e)
...................MARTINO(x)
.................MICHAELS(o)
.................MOLINARO(a)
...................OERTER(s)
.....PACINO(a), RITZ(j)
...................STEWART(x)
.....................UNSER(v)
Alain ....DELON(a)
..................Le SAGE(z)
....................PROST(v)
Alan...................ALDA(a)
......ARKIN(a), BATES(a)
.................CRANSTON(t)
.............HALE(a), KING(j)
.................KULWICKI(v)
.......................LADD(a)
................MOWBRAY(a)
.....................PATON(z)
....................RACHINS(a)
.............SHEPARD, Jr.(d)
....................SILLITOE(z)
....................THICKE(a)
Alastair.................SIM(a)
Alban ....BERG(k)
Albee, ...EDWARD(z)
Alben ....BARKLEY(u)
Alberghetti, ...
.............ANNA MARIA(a)
Albert ....BROOKS(a)

........................CAMUS(z)
..................EINSTEIN(w)
.......................FINNEY(a)
..............MICHELSON(w)
Albert, ..AL(o), EDDIE(a)
......MARV(o), STEVE(o)
Alberto ....
............GIACOMETTI(c)
...................MORAVIA(z)
Albert Pinkham ....
........................RYDER(c)
Albertson, ...JACK(a)
Albrecht ....DURER(c)
Alcott, ...AMY(m)
............LOUISA MAY(z)
Alda, ...ALAN(a)
..................FRANCES(x)
......................ROBERT(a)
Aldiss, ...BRIAN W.(z)
Aldo.......................RAY(a)
Aldous ....HUXLEY(z)
Aldrin, ...EDWIN(d)
Alec...........BALDWIN(a)
..................GUINNESS(a)
Alejandro.............REY(a)
Aleksandr...BORODIN(k)
...................PUSHKIN(z)
...................SCRIABIN(k)
........SOLZHENITSYN(z)
Alessandro........................
..................SCARLATTI(k)
Alex.................CORD(a)
............DELVECCHIO(n)
................ENGLISH(f)
.......................HALEY(z)
.................RAYMOND(i)
....................TREBEK(a)
Alexander ....
............ARCHIPENKO(c)
....................CALDER(c)
..................FLEMING(w)
.........................HAIG(p)
..................HAMILTON(u)
.........................POPE(t)
..............WOOLLCOTT(z)
Alexander, .GROVER(e)
.......JANE(a), JASON(a)
Alexander Graham ....
.........................BELL(w)
Alexandre ......DUMAS(z)
Alexis ....SMITH(a)
Alf ....LANDON(u)
Alfonse ....D'AMATO(u)
Alfre.........WOODARD(a)
Alfred ....ADLER(w)
.....................DRAKE(a)
..................DREYFUS(p)
................HITCHCOCK(q)
.......................KRUPP(h)
.......LUNT(a), NOBEL(w)

Alfred *continued*......
............NOYES(t)
............TENNYSON(t)
Alfred A. ......KNOPF(h)
Alger ....HISS(u)
Alger, ...HORATIO(z)
Algernon ......
............SWINBURNE(t)
Ali............MacGRAW(a)
Ali, ...MUHAMMAD(g)
Alice............ADAMS(z)
....COOPER(x), FAYE(a)
............GHOSTLEY(a)
............MARBLE(y)
............WALKER(z)
Alighieri, ...DANTE(t)
Alison............LURIE(z)
Alistair............COOKE(z)
Alla ......NAZIMOVA(a)
Allan ......SHERMAN(x)
Allen............DRURY(z)
............GINSBERG(t)
............JENKINS(a)
Allen, ...DEBBIE(a)
......ETHAN(p), FRED(j)
....GRACIE(j), KAREN(a)
......MARCUS(l), MEL(o)
............NANCY(a)
............STEVE(a,j)
............WOODY(a,q)
Alley, ...KIRSTIE(a)
Allison, ...DAVEY(v)
Allman, ...DUANE(r)
............GREGG(r)
Ally............SHEEDY(a)
Allyce ......BEASLEY(a)
Allyson, ...JUNE(a)
Alma............GLUCK(x)
Alomar, ...ROBERTO(e)
............SANDY(e)
Alonso, ...
....MARIA CONCHITA(a)
Alonzo .....MOURNING(f)
Alou, ...FELIPE(e)
....JESUS(e), MATTY(e)
Alpert, ...HERB(r)
Althea ......GIBSON(y)
Alther, ...LISA(z)
Altman, ...ROBERT(q)
Alvin ....AILEY(a)
Alworth, ...LANCE(l)
Amanda....PLUMMER(a)
Ambler, ...ERIC(z)
Ambrose......BIERCE(z)
Ameche, ...DON(a)
Amedeo ......
............MODIGLIANI(c)
Amelia ......BLOOMER(u)
............EARHART(d)
Ames, ..ED(x), LEON(a)

Amilcare......
............PONCHIELLI(k)
Amis, ...KINGSLEY(z)
Amos ....OZ(z)
Amos, ...JOHN(a)
............TORI(x)
Amsterdam, ...MOREY(j)
Amy............ALCOTT(m)
...GRANT(x), IRVING(a)
............LOWELL(t)
............MADIGAN(a)
Anaïs............NIN(z)
Anatole ......FRANCE(z)
Andersen, ...
....HANS CHRISTIAN(z)
Anderson, ...HARRY(a)
............IAN(r,x), JACK(o)
....JON(x), JUDITH(a)
............LINDSAY(q)
............LONI(a), LYNN(x)
............MARIAN(x)
............MAXWELL(z)
............OTTIS(l)
........RICHARD DEAN(a)
............SHERWOOD(z)
Andersson, ...BIBI(a)
Andie....MacDOWELL(a)
André ....AGASSI(y)
............BRETON(z)
............CHENIER(t)
...DAWSON(a), GIDE(z)
........KOSTELANETZ(r)
............MALRAUX(z)
............NORTON(z)
...PREVIN(r), WATTS(r)
Andrea ....DORIA(u)
............McARDLE(a)
............MITCHELL(o)
Andrés ......SEGOVIA(r)
Andress, ...URSULA(a)
Andretti, ...MARIO(v)
Andrew ...CARNEGIE(h)
............JACKSON(u)
............JOHNSON(u)
............McCARTHY(a)
............MELLON(h)
............STEVENS(a)
............WYETH(c)
............YOUNG(u)
Andrew Lloyd......
............WEBBER(k)
Andrews, ..ANTHONY(a)
....DANA(a), JULIE(a)
............LA VERNE(x)
....MAXENE(x), PATTI(x)
Andric, ...IVO(z)
Andy............DEVINE(j)
......GARCIA(a), GIBB(x)
............GRIFFITH(a)
............NORTH(m)

............ROBUSTELLI(l)
............ROONEY(o)
............Van SLYKE(e)
............WARHOL(c)
............WILLIAMS(x)
Aneurin............BEVAN(u)
Angela ....DAVIS(u)
............LANSBURY(a)
Angelico, ...FRA(c)
Angelou,............MAYA(t)
Angie......DICKINSON(a)
Angus............WILSON(z)
Anita............BAKER(x)
............BROOKNER(z)
............EKBERG(a)
............GILLETTE(a)
........LOOS(z), O'DAY(x)
............POINTER(x)
Anjelica ......HUSTON(a)
Anka, ...PAUL(x)
Ann ....BEATTIE(z)
...BLYTH(a), JILLIAN(a)
............LANDERS(o)
............MILLER(a)
............REINKING(a)
............RICHARDS(u)
............SHERIDAN(a)
............SOTHERN(a)
............WILSON(x)
Ann B. ....DAVIS(a)
Anna............MAGNANI(a)
............MOFFO(x)
............NEAGLE(a)
............PAVLOVA(a)
............STEN(a)
Anna Maria ......
............ALBERGHETTI(a)
Anna May ......WONG(a)
Anne............ARCHER(a)
............BANCROFT(a)
............BAXTER(a)
............BOLEYN(u)
............BRONTE(z)
............De SALVO(a)
............FRANCIS(a)
............JACKSON(a)
............JEFFREYS(a)
............MEARA(a)
............MURRAY(x)
............SEXTON(t)
............TYLER(z)
Anne Morrow ......
............LINDBERGH(z)
Annenberg, ...
............WALTER(h)
Annette......BENING(a)
............FUNICELLO(a)
............O'TOOLE(a)
Annie ......LENNOX(x)
............POTTS(a)

Annunzio..............
.............MANTOVANI(r)
Anouk............AIMEE(a)
Ansara,......MICHAEL(a)
Anspach, ...SUSAN(a)
Ant, ...ADAM(x)
Anthony...ANDREWS(a)
.............BURGESS(z)
.............EDEN(u)
.............EDWARDS(a)
.............HOPKINS(a)
.............NEWLEY(x)
.............PERKINS(a)
.............QUINN(a)
.............TROLLOPE(z)
.............Van DYCK(c)
.............ZERBE(a)
Anthony, ...SUSAN B.(u)
Anthony M. ....
.............KENNEDY(u)
Antoine ...LAVOISIER(w)
Anton.....BRUCKNER(k)
.............CHEKHOV(z)
Anton, ...SUSAN(a)
Antonin.......DVORAK(k)
.............SCALIA(u)
Antonio........CANOVA(c)
....MORO(c), VIVALDI(k)
Anwar al-........SADAT(u)
Anya.............SETON(z)
Aoki, ...ISAO(m)
Aparicio, ...LUIS(e)
Applegate, ...
.............CHRISTINA(a)
Ara ....PARSEGHIAN(l)
Arafat, ...YASIR(u)
Aram ....
.......KHACHATURIAN(k)
Arbuckle, ...FATTY(j)
Archer, ...ANNE(a)
.............GEORGE(m)
Archibald ....MacLEISH(t)
Archibald, ...NATE(f)
Archie ....MOORE(g)
Archipenko, ...
.............ALEXANDER(c)
Arden, ...ELIZABETH(h)
.............EVE(a)
Arens, ...MOSHE(u)
Aretha ......FRANKLIN(x)
Ari.............MEYERS(a)
Arie.........LUYENDYK(v)
Ariel............SHARON(u)
Aristotle ......ONASSIS(h)
Arkin, ...ALAN(a)
Arledge, ...ROONE(h)
Arlen..........SPECTER(u)
Arlen, ...HAROLD(k)
Arlene ....DAHL(a)
.............FRANCIS(a)

Arliss, ...GEORGE(a)
Arlo............GUTHRIE(x)
Armand......ASSANTE(a)
.............HAMMER(h)
Armstrong, ...BESS(a)
.......LOUIS "Satchmo"(r)
.............NEIL(d)
Arnaz, ...DESI(a)
.............LUCIE(a)
Arne, ...THOMAS(k)
Arness, ...JAMES(a)
Arno............PENZIAS(w)
Arno, ...PETER(i)
Arnold ....PALMER(m)
.........SCHOENBERG(k)
.........SCHWARZEN-
.............EGGER(a)
.............STANG(j)
Arnold, ...BENEDICT(p)
.............EDDY(x)
.............MATTHEW(t)
.............ROSEANNE(a,j)
.............TOM(j)
Arquette, ...CLIFF(j)
.............ROSANNA(a)
Arsenio ....HALL(j)
Arshile ....GORKY(c)
Art ....BLAKEY(r)
.............BUCHWALD(o)
.............CARNEY(a)
.............DONOVAN(l)
.............GARFUNKEL(x)
.............LINKLETTER(j)
.......MONK(l), TATUM(r)
Arte ....JOHNSON(j)
Arthur.............ASHE(y)
.............BALFOUR(u)
.............FIEDLER(r)
.............GODFREY(j)
.......HAILEY(z), HILL(q)
.............HONEGGER(k)
.............KENNEDY(a)
.............MILLER(z)
.............O'CONNELL(a)
.............PENN(q)
.............RIMBAUD(t)
.............RUBINSTEIN(r)
.............TREACHER(a)
Arthur, ...BEATRICE(a)
.......CHESTER ALAN(u)
.............JEAN(a)
Arthur C. ....CLARKE(z)
Arthur Conan ....
.............DOYLE(z)
Arthur S. ...SULLIVAN(k)
Artie ....SHAW(r)
Artis ....GILMORE(f)
Arturo.......TOSCANINI(r)
Asa ....GRAY(w)
.............CANDLER(h)

Asch, ...SHOLEM(z)
Ashe, ...ARTHUR(y)
Asher............DURAND(c)
Ashford, ...EVELYN(s)
Ashley, ...ELIZABETH(a)
Asimov, ...ISAAC(z)
Asner, ...ED(a)
Aspin, ...LES(u)
Assante, ...ARMAND(a)
Astaire, ...ADELE(a)
.............FRED(a)
Astin, ...JOHN(a)
Astor, ..JOHN JACOB(h)
.............GERTRUDE(a)
.............MARY(a)
Astrud......GILBERTO(x)
Atherton, ...WILLIAM(a)
Athol.........FUGARD(z)
Atkins, ...CHET(r)
Attenborough, ...
.............DAVID(w)
.............RICHARD(a,q)
Attlee, ...CLEMENT(u)
Atwill, ...LIONEL(a)
Atwood, ...
.............MARGARET(z)
Auberjonois, ...RENE(a)
Aubrey ....
.............BEARDSLEY(c)
Auchincloss, ...LOUIS(z)
Auden, ...W.H.(t)
Audie ....MURPHY(a)
Audrey .....HEPBURN(a)
.............MEADOWS(a)
Audubon, ...
.......JOHN JAMES(c,w)
Auer, ...LEOPOLD(r)
Auerbach, ...RED(f)
August ....
.............STRINDBERG(z)
.............WILSON(z)
Auguste ....COMTE(z)
.............RODIN(c)
Aumont, ...
.............JEAN-PIERRE(a)
Austen, ...JANE(z)
Austin, ...TRACY(y)
Autry, ...GENE(a,h)
Ava ....GARDNER(a)
Avalon, ...FRANKIE(x)
Avery, ...TEX(i)
Axton, ...HOYT(x)
Aykroyd, ...DAN(a)
Ayn ....RAND(z)
Ayres, ...LEW(a)
Ayrton.........SENNA(v)
Aznavour, ..CHARLES(x)

B(ernard) ....KLIBAN(i)
B.F. ....SKINNER(w)

B.J. ....THOMAS(x)
Babe ....DIDRIKSON(s)
.................RUTH(e)
Babel, ...ISAAC(z)
Babilonia, ...TAI(s)
Bacall, ...LAUREN(a)
Bach, ...JOHANN
................CHRISTIAN(k)
.................JOHANN
.............SEBASTIAN(k)
Bacharach, ...BURT(k)
Backus, ...JIM(a)
Bacon, ...HENRY(b)
.................FRANCIS(u)
.................KEVIN(a)
Baer, ...MAX(g)
Baez, ...JOAN(x)
Bagnold, ...ENID(z)
Bahr, ...MATT(l)
Bailey, ...PEARL(x)
Bain, ...CONRAD(a)
Baio, ...SCOTT(a)
Baird, ...BIL(j)
Baker, ...ANITA(x)
.................CARROLL(a)
.................GEORGE(i)
.................HOWARD(u)
.................JAMES A.(u)
.................JOE DON(a)
.................JOSEPHINE(x)
.................RUSSELL(o)
Baker-Finch, ...IAN(m)
Bakula, ...SCOTT(a)
Baldwin, ...ALEC(a)
.................STANLEY(u)
.................WILLIAM(a)
Balfour, ...ARTHUR(u)
Balin, ...MARTY(x)
Ball, ...KENNY(r)
.................LUCILLE(j)
Ballard, ...J.G.(z)
.................KAYE(a)
Ballesteros, ...SEVE(m)
Balsam, ...MARTIN(a)
Balzac, ...
.........HONORE de(z)
Bancroft, ...ANNE(a)
Bankhead, ...
.................TALLULAH(a)
Banks, ...ERNIE(e)
.................TONY(r)
Bannister, ...ROGER(s)
Bara, ...THEDA(a)
Barbara........BARRIE(a)
.........BEL GEDDES(a)
.................BOSSON(a)
......BOXER(u), BUSH(u)
....EDEN(a), FELDON(a)
.................HALE(a)
.................HERSHEY(a)

.................MANDREL(x)
.................RUSH(a)
.................STANWYCK(a)
.................WALTERS(o)
Barbeau, ...
.................ADRIENNE(a)
Barber, ...RED(o)
Barbera, ...JOE(i)
Barbra....STREISAND(x)
Bardot, ...BRIGITTE(a)
Barenboim, ...DANIEL(r)
Barker, ...CLIVE(q, z)
Barkin, ...ELLEN(a)
Barkley, ...ALBEN(u)
.................CHARLES(f)
Barnard......HUGHES(a)
Barnard, ...ROBERT(z)
Barnes, ...CLIVE(o)
Barrie, ...BARBARA(a)
.................J.M.(z)
Barry.............BONDS(e)
.................BOSTWICK(a)
.........FITZGERALD(a)
.................GIBB(x)
.........GOLDWATER(u)
.................LEVINSON(q)
.................MANILOW(x)
.................MANN(k)
.................SULLIVAN(a)
.................WHITE(x)
Barry, ...DAVE(o)
.................GENE(a)
Barrymore, ...DREW(a)
......ETHEL(a), JOHN(a)
.................LIONEL(a)
Bart ....CONNER(s)
.................STARR(l)
Barth, ...JOHN(z)
Bartkowski, ...STEVE(l)
Bartók, ...BELA(k)
Bartolomé ....
.................MURILLO(c)
Barton, ...CLARA(h)
Barty, ...BILLY(a)
Baruch ....SPINOZA(z)
Baryshnikov, ...
.................MIKHAIL(a)
Basehart, ..RICHARD(a)
Basie, ...COUNT(r)
Basil ......RATHBONE(a)
Basinger, ...KIM(a)
Bassey, ...SHIRLEY(x)
Bateman, ...JASON(a)
.................JUSTINE(a)
Bates, ...ALAN(a)
.................KATHY(a)
Baudelaire, ...
.................CHARLES(t)
Baugh, ...SAMMY(l)
Baum, ...L. FRANK(z)

Baxter, ...ANNE(a)
.................MEREDITH(a)
.................WARNER(a)
Baylor, ...ELGIN(f)
Bea......BENADERET(a)
Beamon, ...BOB(s)
Bean, ...ORSON(a)
Beardsley, ...AUBREY(c)
Beasley, ...ALLYCE(a)
Beatrice ......ARTHUR(a)
.................LILLIE(j)
.................STRAIGHT(a)
Beatrix.........POTTER(z)
Beattie, ...ANN(z)
Beatty, ...NED(a)
.................WARREN(a)
Beau.........BRIDGES(a)
Bebe ....DANIELS(a)
.................NEUWIRTH(a)
Beck, ...C.C.(i), JEFF(r)
Becker, ...BORIS(y)
.................STEPHEN(z)
Beckett, ...SAMUEL(z)
Beckmann, ...MAX(c)
Bedrich ...SMETANA(k)
Beerbohm, ...MAX(z)
Beery, ...NOAH(a)
.................WALLACE(a)
Beethoven, ...
.........LUDWIG van(k)
Begin, ...MENACHEM(u)
Begley, ...ED(a)
Begley, Jr., ...ED(a)
Behan, ...BRENDAN(z)
Beiderbecke, ...BIX(r)
Bela ....BARTOK(k)
.................LUGOSI(a)
Belafonte, ...HARRY(x)
.................SHARI(a)
Bel Geddes, ...
.................BARBARA(a)
Belinda......CARLISLE(x)
Bell, ...ALEXANDER
.................GRAHAM(w)
.........GUS(e), RICKY(l)
.........ROBERT "Kool"(x)
Bella.............ABZUG(u)
Bellamy, ...RALPH(a)
Bellini, ...GENTILE(c)
.................GIOVANNI(c)
.................JACOPO(c)
.................VINCENZO(k)
Bellow, ...SAUL(z)
Bellows, ...
...GEORGE WESLEY(c)
Belluschi, ...PIETRO(b)
Belmondo, ...
.................JEAN-PAUL(a)
Belushi, ...~.JAMES(a)
.................JOHN(a)

Ben...................BLUE(j)
...............BRADLEE(o)
............CRENSHAW(m)
...................CROSS(a)
.................GAZZARA(a)
....................HECHT(z)
...................HOGAN(m)
..................JONSON(t)
...............KINGSLEY(a)
...................SHAHN(c)
...................TURPIN(a)
...................VEREEN(a)
Benaderet, ...BEA(a)
Benatar, ...PAT(x)
Benben, ...BRIAN(a)
Bench, ...JOHNNY(e)
Benchley, ...PETER(z)
..................ROBERT(z)
Bendix, ...WILLIAM(a)
Benedict .....ARNOLD(p)
Benedict, ...DIRK(a)
Benét, ...STEPHEN
....................VINCENT(t)
Ben-Gurion, ...DAVID(u)
Bening, ...ANNETTE(a)
Benito .....MUSSOLINI(u)
Benjamin .....BRITTEN(k)
..................CARDOZO(u)
...................DISRAELI(u)
..............FRANKLIN(u,w)
...............HARRISON(u)
.....................SPOCK(w)
.......................WEST(c)
Benjamin,
.................RICHARD(a,q)
Benjamin H.
...................LATROBE(b)
Bennett ....CERF(h, z)
Bennett,
...............CONSTANCE(a)
.........JOAN(a), TONY(x)
Ben Nighthorse..............
.................CAMPBELL(u)
Benny.......GOODMAN(r)
Benny, ...JACK(j)
Benoit, ...JOAN(s)
Benson, ...GEORGE(r)
....................ROBBY(a)
Benton, ...BROOK(x)
..................ROBERT(q)
.........THOMAS HART(c)
Bentsen, ...LLOYD(u)
Benvenuti, ...NINO(g)
Berenger, ...TOM(a)
Berg, ...ALBAN(k)
................GERTRUDE(j)
Bergen, ...CANDICE(a)
.......................EDGAR(j)
.........................POLLY(a)
Berger, ...THOMAS(z)

Bergman, ...INGMAR(q)
...................INGRID(a)
Berke ....BREATHED(i)
Berkeley, ...BUSBY(q)
Berle, ...MILTON(j)
Berlin, ...IRVING(k)
Berlioz, ...HECTOR(k)
Berman, ...CHRIS(o)
......LEN(o), SHELLEY(j)
Bernadette ...PETERS(a)
Bernard...............KING(f)
.................MALAMUD(z)
.......................SHAW(o)
Bernardi,
................HERSCHEL(a)
Bernardo
............BERTOLUCCI(q)
Bernhard....LANGER(m)
Bernhard, ...SANDRA(j)
Bernhardt, ...SARAH(a)
Bernie ....
...............GEOFFRION(n)
.....................KOPELL(a)
Bernini,
.........GIANLORENZO(c)
Bernsen, ...CORBIN(a)
Bernstein,
..................LEONARD(k)
Berra, ...YOGI(e)
Berry, ...CHUCK(x)
......................HALLE(a)
.............JIM(i), KEN(a)
Berryman, ...JOHN(t)
Bert ....BLYLEVEN(e)
.......LAHR(a), PARKS(a)
Bertinelli, ...VALERIE(a)
Bertolt ....BRECHT(z)
Bertolucci, ...
.................BERNARDO(q)
Bertrand
..............RUSSELL(w, z)
Bess....ARMSTRONG(a)
.................MYERSON(a)
Bessemer, ...HENRY(w)
Bessie ....SMITH(x)
Beth...............DANIEL(m)
.....................HENLEY(z)
Betjeman, ...JOHN(t)
Betsy ....KING(m)
......................PALMER(a)
Bette...............DAVIS(a)
..................MIDLER(a, x)
Betty ....BUCKLEY(a)
..........................FORD(u)
.....................FRIEDAN(z)
.....................GRABLE(a)
.....................HUTTON(a)
.......................WHITE(a)
Beulah.............BONDI(a)
Bevan, ...ANEURIN(u)

Beverly.....D'ANGELO(a)
...........................SILLS(x)
Bevin, ...ERNEST(u)
Bibi ......ANDERSSON(a)
Bickford, ...CHARLES(a)
Biden, Jr., ...JOSEPH(u)
Bierce, ...AMBROSE(z)
Bikel, ...THEODORE(a)
Bil ....BAIRD(j)
..........................KEANE(j)
Biletnikoff, ...FRED(l)
Bill ....BIXBY(a)
................BRADLEY(f,u)
....................CLINTON(u)
.........................COSBY(j)
.......................ELLIOTT(v)
....HALEY(r), HANNA(i)
....MACY(a), MEDLEY(x)
.......................MOYERS(o)
.........................MURRAY(j)
...........................RIPKEN(e)
.........................RUSSELL(f)
...........................TILDEN(y)
.........................TOOMEY(s)
.........................WALTON(f)
..............WATTERSON(i)
.........................WYMAN(r)
Billie ....BURKE(e)
.......................HOLIDAY(x)
Billie Jean ....KING(y)
Billy.....................BARTY(a)
....................CASPER(m)
.....................CRYSTAL(j)
................De WOLFE(a)
..........IDOL(x), JOEL(r,x)
..........................OCEAN(x)
.......................PRESTON(r)
.........................WILDER(q)
Billy Dee....WILLIAMS(a)
Bing.........CROSBY(a, x)
Bing, ...DAVE(f)
Bingham, ...
......GEORGE CALEB(c)
Biondi, ...MATT(s)
Bird, ...LARRY(f)
Birgit ....NILSSON(a)
Birney, ...DAVID(a)
Bishop, ...JOEY(j)
.....................STEPHEN(x)
Bisset,
.................JACQUELINE(a)
Bix .....BEIDERBECKE(r)
Bixby, ...BILL(a)
Bizet, ...GEORGES(k)
Björn ....BORG(y)
Black, ...CILLA(x)
......CLINT(x), KAREN(a)
Blackmun, ...HARRY(u)
Blades, ...RUBEN(a,x)
Blaine, ...VIVIAN(a,x)

141

STEVEN BOCHCO (handwritten)

Blair / Breathed

Blair ....BROWN(a)
..........UNDERWOOD(a)
Blair, ...LINDA(a)
Blaise..........PASCAL(w)
Blake........EDWARDS(q)
Blake, ...EUBIE(k)
..................ROBERT(a)
..............WILLIAM(c, t)
Blakely, ...SUSAN(a)
Blakey, ...ART(r)
Blanc, ...MEL(j)
Blanda, ...GEORGE(l)
Bledsoe,..TEMPESTT(a)
Blitzer, ...WOLF(o)
Block, ...HERB(i)
Blocker, ...DAN(a)
Blondell, ...JOAN(a)
Bloom, ...CLAIRE(a)
Bloomer, ...AMELIA(u)
Blore, ...ERIC(a)
Blount, ...MEL(l)
Blue, ...BEN(j), VIDA(e)
Bluford, ...GUION(d)
Blume, ...JUDY(z)
Bly, ...ROBERT(t)
Blyleven, ...BERT(e)
Blyth, ...ANN(a)
Blythe..........DANNER(a)
Bo ....DEREK(a)
..................DIDDLEY(r)
..............JACKSON(s)
Bob ....BEAMON(s)
......................CAIN(o)
..............CHARLES(m)
..................COSTAS(o)
....COUSY(f), CRANE(a)
...DENVER(a), DOLE(u)
....DYLAN(x), ELLIOTT(j)
..................ESTES(m)
..................FELLER(e)
..................FOSSE(q)
..................GIBSON(e)
..................GRAHAM(u)
..................GREENE(o)
....GRIESE(l), HAYES(s)
...HOPE(j), HOSKINS(a)
..............KEESHAN(a)
..................MARLEY(x)
..................MATHIAS(s)
..................MONTANA(i)
..................NEWHART(j)
..................PACKWOOD(u)
..................RICHARDS(s)
....SAGET(a), SEGER(x)
....THAVES(i), TWAY(m)
..................UECKER(e)
Bobby ....BONDS(e)
..................DARIN(x)
..................GOLDSBORO(x)
..................HATFIELD(x)

......HEBERT(l), HULL(n)
..................JONES(m)
..................McFERRIN(x)
.........ORR(n), RAHAL(v)
...RIGGS(y), RYDELL(x)
..............SHERMAN(x)
....SHORT(r), UNSER(v)
........VEE(x), VINTON(x)
..................WOMACK(x)
Boccaccio, ...
..................GIOVANNI(t)
Boccherini, ...LUIGI(k)
Bock, ...JERRY(k)
Bogarde, ...DIRK(a)
Bogart, ..HUMPHREY(a)
Bogdanovich, ...
..................PETER(q)
Boggs, ...WADE(e)
Bohr, ...NIELS(w)
Boitano, ...BRIAN(s)
Boleyn, ...ANNE(u)
Bolger, ...RAY(a)
Bolivar, ...SIMON(u)
Böll, ...HEINRICH(z)
Bolt, ...TOMMY(m)
Bombeck, ...ERMA(o)
Bonaparte, ...
..................NAPOLEON(p)
Bond, ...WARD(a)
Bondi, ...BEULAH(a)
Bonds, ...BARRY(e)
..................BOBBY(e)
Bonet, ...LISA(a)
Bonham-Carter, ...
..................HELENA(a)
Bonheur, ...ROSA(c)
Bon Jovi, ...JON(x)
Bonnard, ...PIERRE(c)
Bonnie .....FRANKLIN(a)
..................POINTER(x)
..................RAITT(x)
Bono, ...SONNY(j,x)
Boomer........ESIASON(l)
Boone, ...DEBBY(x)
....PAT(x), RICHARD(a)
Boosler, ...ELAYNE(j)
Booth ....
..........TARKINGTON(z)
Booth, ...EDWIN(a)
..........JOHN WILKES(a)
......JUNIUS BRUTUS(a)
..................SHIRLEY(a)
Borg, ...BJORN(y)
Borge, ...VICTOR(r)
Borges, ...
..............JORGE LUIS(z)
Borgia, ...CESARE(u)
..................LUCRETIA(u)
Borglum, ...GUTZON(c)
Borgnine, ...ERNEST(a)

Boris ....BECKER(y)
..................GODUNOV(u)
..................KARLOFF(a)
..............PASTERNAK(z)
..................YELTSIN(u)
Borman, ...FRANK(d)
Born, ...MAX(w)
Borodin, ...
..............ALEKSANDR(k)
Boros, ...JULIUS(m)
Boru, ...BRIAN(p)
Borzage, ...FRANK(q)
Borzov, ...VALERY(s)
Bosch, ...
..........HIERONYMUS(c)
Bosley, ...TOM(a)
Bosson, ...BARBARA(a)
Bostwick, ...BARRY(a)
Boswell, ...JAMES(z)
Botticelli, ...SANDRO(c)
Bottoms, ...TIMOTHY(a)
Bow, ...CLARA(a)
Bowe, ...RIDDICK(g)
Bowie, ...DAVID(a,x)
Boxer, ...BARBARA(u)
Boxleitner, ...BRUCE(a)
Boyd, ...STEPHEN(a)
..................WILLIAM(a)
Boyer, ...CHARLES(a)
..................CLETE(e)
Boyle, ...PETER(a)
Boz..............SCAGGS(x)
Bracken, ...EDDIE(a)
Brad ....FAXON(m)
Bradbury, ...RAY(z)
Bradford.....DILLMAN(a)
Bradlee, ...BEN(o)
Bradley, ...BILL(f,u)
..............ED(o), OMAR(p)
..................PAT(m)
Bradshaw, ...TERRY(l)
Brady, ...
..........DIAMOND JIM(h)
Braga, ...SONIA(a)
Brahe, ...TYCHO(w)
Brahms, JOHANNES(k)
Bram ....STOKER(z)
Branagh, ..KENNETH(q)
Branch ....RICKEY(e)
Brancusi, ...
..........CONSTANTIN(c)
Brandeis, ...LOUIS(u)
Brando, ...MARLON(a)
Brandon.....De WILDE(a)
Brandt, ...WILLY(u)
Branford....MARSALIS(r)
Branigan, ...LAURA(x)
Braque, ...GEORGES(c)
Brazzi, ...ROSSANO(a)
Breathed, ...BERKE(i)

Brecht, ...BERTOLT(z)
Brenda.................LEE(x)
...............VACCARO(a)
Brendan.......BEHAN(z)
Brennan, ...EILEEN(a)
................WALTER(a)
.........WILLIAM J.(u)
Brenner, ...DAVID(j)
Brent ...MUSBURGER(o)
.........SCOWCROFT(u)
.................SPINER(a)
Brent, ...GEORGE(a)
Breslin, ...JIMMY(o)
Bret.................HARTE(z)
.....................OGLE(m)
.........SABERHAGEN(e)
Breton, ...ANDRE(z)
Brett ....HULL(n)
Brett, ...GEORGE(e)
Brewer, ...TERESA(x)
Brezhnev, ...LEONID(u)
Brian............AHERNE(a)
..................BENBEN(a)
.................BOITANO(s)
.......................BORU(u)
.................DENNEHY(a)
................De PALMA(q)
.................DONLEVY(a)
....ENO(r), GARFIELD(z)
.................HOLLAND(k)
..................HYLAND(x)
.....JONES(r), KEITH(a)
................MULRONEY(u)
...................WILSON(r)
Brian Doyle ....
.......................MURRAY(j)
Brian W. ....ALDISS(z)
Brice, ...FANNY(j)
Brickell, ...EDIE(x)
Bridges, ...BEAU(a)
........JEFF(a), LLOYD(a)
Bridget ....FONDA(a)
Brigitte ....BARDOT(a)
Brimley, ...WILFORD(a)
Brinkley, ...CHRISTIE(a)
....................DAVID(o)
Britt ....EKLAND(a)
Britten, ...BENJAMIN(k)
Brock, ...LOU(e)
Broder, ...DAVID(o)
Broderick ....
..............CRAWFORD(a)
Broderick, ...JAMES(a)
.................MATTHEW(a)
Brodie, ...JOHN(l,m)
Brodsky, ...JOSEPH(t)
Brody, ...JANE(o)
Brokaw, ...TOM(o)
Brolin, ...JAMES(a)
Bronko ......NAGURSKI(l)

Bronson......PINCHOT(a)
Bronson, ...CHARLES(a)
Brontë, ...ANNE(z)
..............CHARLOTTE(z)
....................EMILY(z)
Brook ....BENTON(x)
Brook, ...PETER(q)
Brooke ....ADAMS(a)
....................SHIELDS(a)
Brooke, ...EDWARD(u)
....................RUPERT(t)
Brookner, ...ANITA(z)
Brooks....ROBINSON(e)
Brooks, ...ALBERT(a)
....................GARTH(x)
..................JAMES L.(q)
....................MEL(j,q)
Brosnan, ...PIERCE(a)
Brothers, ...JOYCE(o,w)
Brown, ...BLAIR(a)
..................BRYAN(a)
.....HELEN GURLEY(o)
.........JAMES(x), JIM(l)
..........JOE E.(j), LES(r)
..................ROBERT(w)
.......................RON(u)
Browne, ...DIK(i)
..................JACKSON(x)
.........ROSCOE LEE(a)
Browning, ...ELIZABETH
..................BARRETT(t)
.......ROBERT(t), TOD(q)
Brubeck, ...DAVE(r)
Bruce ...BOXLEITNER(a)
......................CABOT(a)
.............CRAMPTON(m)
....DERN(a), JENNER(s)
..........LEE(a), SMITH(l)
.........SPRINGSTEEN(x)
......WEITZ(a), WILLIS(a)
Bruce, ...LENNY(j)
.......................NIGEL(a)
....................VIRGINIA(a)
Bruckner, ...ANTON(k)
Bruegel, ...PIETER(c)
Brunner, ...JOHN(z)
Bruno............KIRBY(a)
Bryan ....ADAMS(x)
..................BROWN(a)
.......................FERRY(x)
Bryan, ...WILLIAM
..................JENNINGS(o)
Bryant...........GUMBLE(o)
Bryant, ...WILLIAM
..................CULLEN(t)
Brynner, ...YUL(a)
Bryson, ...PEABO(x)
Bubba..............SMITH(l)
Buber, ...MARTIN(z)
Buchan, ...JOHN(z)

Buchanan, ...EDGAR(a)
.........JAMES(u), PAT(o)
Buchwald, ...ART(o)
Buck..........HENRY(j,z)
Buck, ...PEARL S.(z)
Buckley, ...BETTY(a)
...........WILLIAM F.(o, z)
Bud...............ABBOTT(j)
Budd, ...ZOLA(s)
Buddy.............EBSEN(a)
...................HACKETT(j)
........HOLLY(x), RICH(r)
Budge, ...DON(y)
Bueno, ...MARIA(y)
Buffalo Bob .....SMITH(a)
Buffett, ...JIMMY(x)
Buffy ....
.........SAINTE-MARIE(x)
Bujold, ..GENEVIEVE(a)
Bulfinch, ...CHARLES(b)
Bumpers, ...DALE(y)
Bunche, ...RALPH(u)
Bunin, ...IVAN(z)
Buñuel..............LUIS(q)
Bunyan, ...JOHN(z)
Buono, ...VICTOR(a)
Burbank, ...LUTHER(w)
Burger, ...WARREN(u)
Burgess ...MEREDITH(a)
Burgess, ...ANTHONY(z)
Burghoff, ...GARY(a)
Burgoyne, ...JOHN(p)
Burke, ...BILLIE(a)
.......................DELTA(a)
...................EDMUND(z)
Burl.....................IVES(x)
Burnett, ...CAROL(j)
Burnham, ...
.................DANIEL H.(b)
Burns, ...GEORGE(j)
...................ROBERT(t)
Burr, ...AARON(u)
...................RAYMOND(a)
Burroughs, ...
..............EDGAR RICE(z)
Burrows, ...ABE(z)
Burstyn, ...ELLEN(a)
Burt ......BACHARACH(k)
................LANCASTER(a)
..............REYNOLDS(a)
.......................YOUNG(a)
Burton .....CUMMINGS(x)
Burton, ...LEVAR(a)
....................RICHARD(a)
Busby .....BERKELEY(q)
Busch, ...ADOLPHUS(h)
Busey, ...GARY(a)
Busfield, ...TIMOTHY(a)
Bush, ...BARBARA(u)
...................GEORGE(u)

Bushman / Cavendish

Bushman, ...
..............FRANCIS X.(a)
Buster..........CRABBE(a)
...............KEATON(a)
Butkus, ...DICK(l)
Butler, ...JERRY(x)
...............SAMUEL(c,k,z)
Butterfly ...McQUEEN(a)
Button, ...DICK(s)
Buttons, ...RED(a)
Buzzi, ...RUTH(j)
Byington, ...SPRING(a)
Byner, ...EARNEST(l)
Byrne, ...DAVID(x)
Byron ....NELSON(m)
.................WHITE(u)

C.C. ....BECK(i)
C.S. ....FORESTER(z)
................LEWIS(z)
C.Thomas ...HOWELL(a)
Caan, ...JAMES(a)
Cab ....CALLOWAY(r)
Cabot, ...BRUCE(a)
.............SEBASTIAN(a)
Caesar, ...SID(j)
Cage, ...JOHN(k)
.................NICOLAS(a)
Cagney, ...JAMES(a)
Cain, ...BOB(o)
.................JAMES M.(z)
Caine, ...MICHAEL(a)
Cal ....HUBBARD(l)
...........RIPKEN, Jr.(e)
Calcavecchia, ...
...................MARK(m)
Calder, ..ALEXANDER(c)
Caldwell, ...ERSKINE(z)
........SARAH(r), ZOE(x)
Cale ....
........YARBOROUGH(v)
Calhoun, ...JOHN C.(u)
.................RORY(a)
Calisher, ...
...........HORTENSE(z)
Callas, ...MARIA(x)
Calloway, ...CAB(r)
Calvé, ...EMMA(x)
Calvin ......COOLIDGE(u)
......KLEIN(h), PEETE(m)
.................TRILLIN(o)
Calvino, ...ITALO(z)
Camacho, ...HECTOR(g)
Cameron...MITCHELL(a)
Cameron, ...KIRK(a)
Camille ...PISSARRO(z)
........SAINT-SAENS(k)
Camp, ...HAMILTON(a)
Campanella, ...
.......JOSEPH(a), ROY(e)

Campbell, ...BEN
...........NIGHTHORSE(u)
...........EARL(l), GLEN(x)
Camus, ...ALBERT(z)
Canby, ...VINCENT(o)
Candice......BERGEN(a)
Candler, ...ASA(h)
Candy, ...JOHN(a)
Caniff, ...MILTON(i)
Cannon, ...DYAN(a)
...............FREDDY(x)
Canova, ...ANTONIO(c)
Canseco, ...JOSE(e)
Cantor, ...EDDIE(a)
Cantrell, ...LANA(x)
Capek, ...KAREL(z)
Capone, ...AL(h)
Caponi, ...DONNA(m)
Capote, ...TRUMAN(z)
Capp, ...AL(i)
Cappelletti, ...GINO(l)
Capra, ...FRANK(q)
Capriati, ...JENNIFER(y)
Cara, ...IRENE(x)
Cardozo, .BENJAMIN(u)
Carew, ...ROD(e)
Carey, ...
.............MacDONALD(a)
.................MARIAH(x)
Cariou, ...LEN(a)
Carl ....ELLER(l)
......ICAHN(h), JUNG(w)
....LEWIS(s), REINER(j)
.................SAGAN(w)
.................SANDBURG(t)
...............YASTRZEMSKI(e)
Carlin, ...GEORGE(j)
Carlisle, ...BELINDA(x)
.................KITTY(a)
Carlo............PONTI(q)
Carlos.........SANTANA(r)
Carlotta.........PATTI(x)
Carlton, ...STEVE(e)
Carly ....SIMON(x)
Carlyle, ...THOMAS(z)
Carmen .....MIRANDA(a)
Carmen, ...ERIC(x)
Carmichael, ..HOAGY(k)
.................IAN(a)
Carne, ...JUDY(j)
Carnegie, ...ANDREW(h)
Carner, ...JOANNE(m)
Carnera, ...PRIMO(g)
Carnes, ...KIM(x)
Carney, ...ART(a)
Carol ....BURNETT(j)
.............CHANNING(a)
.................KANE(a)
.............LAWRENCE(a)
.................REED(q)

Carole ....KING(x)
.................LANDIS(a)
...............LOMBARD(a)
Carolyn..........JONES(a)
Caron, ...LESLIE(a)
Carpenter, ...JOHN(q)
.................KAREN(x)
Carr, ...VIKKI(x)
Carradine, ...DAVID(a)
.......JOHN(a), KEITH(a)
Carrie ....FISHER(a)
Carrie Chapman ....
.................CATT(u)
Carrier, ...MARK(l)
Carrillo, ...LEO(a)
Carroll ....BAKER(a)
.................O'CONNOR(a)
Carroll, ...DIAHANN(a)
......LEO G.(a), LEWIS(z)
.................PAT(j)
Carson ....
............McCULLERS(z)
Carson, ...JACK(j)
.................JOHNNY(j)
Carter, ...JACK(j)
...........JIMMY(u), JOE(e)
.......JUNE(x), LYNDA(a)
.................NELL(a)
.................ROSALIND(u)
Caruso, ...ENRICO(x)
Carvel, ...TOM(h)
Carvey, ...DANA(j)
Cary ....ELWES(a)
.................GRANT(a)
.........MIDDLECOFF(m)
Casals, ...PABLO(r)
Casey ....KASEM(a)
.................STENGEL(e)
Cash, ...JOHNNY(x)
.................ROSANNE(x)
Casper, ...BILLY(m)
Cass ....ELLIOT(a)
.................GILBERT(b)
Cass, ...PEGGY(j)
Cassatt, ...MARY(c)
Cassavetes, ...JOHN(q)
Cassidy, ...DAVID(x)
.................SHAUN(x)
Castle, ...IRENE(a)
.................VERNON(a)
Castro, ...FIDEL(u)
Cat.............STEVENS(x)
Cather, ...WILLA(z)
Catherine ..DENEUVE(a)
Cathy......GUISEWITE(i)
.................RIGBY(s)
Catlin, ...GEORGE(c)
Catt, ...CARRIE
.................CHAPMAN(u)
Cavendish, ...HENRY(w)

Cavett, ...DICK(j)
Cazzie........RUSSELL(f)
Cecil............FIELDER(e)
................RHODES(h)
Cecil B........De MILLE(q)
Cedric...HARDWICKE(a)
Celeste............HOLM(a)
Cepeda, ...ORLANDO(e)
Cerf, ...BENNETT(h, z)
Cernan, ...EUGENE(d)
Cesar...........CHAVEZ(h)
...............ROMERO(a)
Cesare..........BORGIA(u)
Cetera, ...PETER(x)
Cezanne, ...PAUL(c)
Chad..........EVERETT(a)
Chagall, ...MARC(c)
Chaim ......HERZOG(u)
..............WEIZMANN(u)
Chaka............KHAN(x)
Chamberlain, ...
..............NEVILLE(u)
.....RICHARD(a), WILT(f)
Champion, ...GOWER(a)
..............MARGE(a)
Chance, ...DEAN(e)
..............FRANK(e)
Chancellor, ...JOHN(o)
Chandler, ...GENE(x)
..............JEFF(a)
..............RAYMOND(z)
Chaney, ...LON(a)
Chaney, Jr., ...LON(a)
Chang, ...MICHAEL(y)
Channing, ...CAROL(a)
..............STOCKARD(a)
Chapin, ...HARRY(x)
Chaplin, ...CHARLIE(j)
Chapman, ...GRAHAM(j)
..............TRACY(x)
Charisse, ...CYD(a)
Charles........ADDAMS(i)
..............AZNAVOUR(x)
..............BARKLEY(f)
..........BAUDELAIRE(t)
..............BICKFORD(a)
..............BOYER(a)
..............BRONSON(a)
..............BULFINCH(b)
..............COBURN(a)
..........CORNWALLIS(p)
..............DARWIN(w)
..De GAULLE(p, u)
..............DICKENS(z)
..............DURNING(a)
..............GIBSON(o)
..........GOODYEAR(w)
..............GOUNOD(k)
..............GRODIN(a)
..........HAID(a), IVES(k)

....KURALT(o), LAMB(z)
..............LAUGHTON(a)
..............LINDBERGH(d)
..............PATHE(q)
.....READE(z), ROBB(u)
..............SCHULZ(i)
Charles, ...BOB(m)
......EZZARD(g), RAY(x)
Charles Willson...............
..............PEALE(c)
Charley..........PRIDE(x)
Charlie ....CHAPLIN(j)
..............DANIELS(x)
......MINGUS(r), RICH(x)
..............ROSE(o)
..............RUGGLES(a)
.....SHEEN(a), WATTS(r)
Charlie "Bird" ....
..............PARKER(r)
Charlotte......BRONTE(z)
..............RAE(a)
Charlton......HESTON(a)
Chase, ...CHEVY(a)
..............ILKA(a)
..............SALMON P.(u)
Chast, ...ROZ(i)
Chaucer, ...
..............GEOFFREY(t)
Chavez, ...CESAR(h)
....JULIO CESAR(g)
Che (Ernesto) ....
..............GUEVARA(p,u)
Checker, ...CHUBBY(x)
Cheech ....MARIN(j)
Cheever, ...JOHN(z)
Chekhov, ...ANTON(z)
Cheney, ...RICHARD(u)
Chénier, ...ANDRE(t)
Cheryl ....LADD(a)
..............TIEGS(a)
Chester ....GOULD(i)
..............MORRIS(a)
..............NIMITZ(p)
Chester A. ..ARTHUR(u)
Chesterton, ...G.K.(z)
Chet ....ATKINS(r)
..............HUNTLEY(o)
Chevalier, .MAURICE(a)
Chevy..............CHASE(a)
Chic..............YOUNG(i)
Chick ....COREA(r)
Chico (Leonard)...............
..............MARX(j)
Childe ....HASSAM(c)
Chill ....WILLS(a)
Chita ....RIVERA(a)
Chomsky, ...NOAM(z)
Chong, ...RAE DAWN(a)
..............TOMMY(j)
Chopin, ...FREDERIC(k)

Chris ....BERMAN(o)
..............ELLIOTT(j)
..............EVERT(y)
......MULLIN(f), REA(x)
..............ROCK(j)
..............SCHENKEL(o)
Chrissie..........HYNDE(x)
Christensen, ...TODD(l)
Christian ....DIOR(c)
..............DOPPLER(w)
Christie .....BRINKLEY(a)
Christie, ...AGATHA(z)
..........JULIE(a), LOU(x)
Christina ....
..............APPLEGATE(a)
Christine...........LAHTI(a)
..............McVIE(x)
Christoph.......GLUCK(k)
Christopher....CROSS(x)
..........ISHERWOOD(z)
........LEE(a), LLOYD(a)
..............MARLOWE(t)
..............PLUMMER(a)
..............REEVE(a)
..............WALKEN(a)
..............WREN(b)
Christopher, ...
..............WARREN(u)
..............WILLIAM(a)
Christy ....
..............MATHEWSON(e)
Chubby .....CHECKER(x)
Chuck..............BERRY(x)
..............CONNORS(a)
..............JONES(i)
..............MANGIONE(r)
..............NORRIS(a)
..............YEAGER(d)
Chung, ...CONNIE(o)
Church,..FREDERICK(c)
Churchill, ..WINSTON(u)
Ciardi, ...JOHN(t)
Cicely ....TYSON(a)
Cierpinski, ...
..............WALDEMAR(s)
Cilla...............BLACK(x)
Cimabue, .GIOVANNI(c)
Cimino, ...MICHAEL(q)
Cindy.....CRAWFORD(a)
..............WILLIAMS(a)
Cissy.........HOUSTON(x)
Claes ...OLDENBURG(c)
Claiborne...........PELL(u)
Claiborne, ...LIZ(h)
Clair, ...RENE(q)
Claire..............BLOOM(a)
..............TREVOR(a)
Claire, ...INA(a)
Clancy, ...TOM(z)
Clapton, ...ERIC(r)

Clara / Costello

Clara............BARTON(h)
...................BOW(a)
Clarence ....DARROW(u)
...................THOMAS(u)
Clark...............GABLE(a)
Clark, ...DANE(a)
...................DICK(a)
............GARY(l), JIM(v)
........MARY HIGGINS(z)
........PETULA(x), ROY(r)
........SUSAN(a), WILL(e)
Clarke, ...ARTHUR C.(z)
Clary, ...ROBERT(a)
Claude.......DEBUSSY(k)
....MONET(c), RAINS(a)
Claudette...COLBERT(a)
Clavell, ...JAMES(z)
Clay...............HENRY(u)
Clayburgh, ...JILL(a)
Clayton ....MOORE(a)
Clayton ....MARK(l)
Cleavon ....LITTLE(a)
Cleese, ...JOHN(j)
Clemens, ...ROGER(a)
Clement ....ATTLEE(u)
Clement C. ....MOORE(t)
Clemente, ...
...................ROBERTO(e)
Cleo...............LAINE(x)
Clete ....BOYER(e)
Cleveland, ..GROVER(u)
Cliburn, ...VAN(r)
Cliff............ARQUETTE(j)
...............DRYSDALE(y)
...................RICHARD(x)
............ROBERTSON(a)
Clifford............ODETS(z)
Clift, ...
........MONTGOMERY(a)
Clifton ....WEBB(a)
Cline, ...PATSY(x)
Clint ....BLACK(x)
...............EASTWOOD(a)
Clinton, ...BILL(u)
...................De WITT(u)
...................HILLARY(u)
Clive.........BARKER(q, z)
...................BARNES(o)
Clooney, ...
............ROSEMARY(x)
Cloris.....LEACHMAN(a)
Close, ...GLENN(a)
Clu..........GULAGHER(a)
Clyde ....DREXLER(f)
.............McPHATTER(x)
Cobb, ...LEE J.(a)
...................TY(e)
Coburn, ...CHARLES(a)
...................JAMES(a)
Coca, ...IMOGENE(j)

Cocker, ...JOE(x)
Cocteau, ...JEAN(q,z)
Coe, ...SEBASTIAN(s)
Coen, ...ETHAN(q)
Cohan, ..GEORGE M.(q)
Cohen, ...LEONARD(t,x)
...................MYRON(j)
...................WILLIAM S.(u)
Cohn, ...MARC(r,x)
Colbert, ...JIM(m)
..............CLAUDETTE(a)
Cole ....PORTER(k)
Cole, ...COZY(r)
...............NAT "King"(x)
...................NATALIE(x)
...................THOMAS(a)
Coleman .....HAWKINS(r)
Coleman, ...CY(k)
....DABNEY(a), GARY(a)
...................ORNETTE(r)
Coleridge, ...
......SAMUEL TAYLOR(t)
Colette, ...SIDONIE
...............GABRIELLE(z)
Colgate, ...WILLIAM(h)
Colin ....POWELL(p)
Collins, ...JACKIE(z)
...................JOAN(a)
............JUDY(x), PHIL(x)
...................WILKIE(z)
Colm..........MEANEY(a)
Colman, ...RONALD(a)
Colter, ...JESSI(x)
Coltrane, ...JOHN(r)
Columbo, ...RUSS(r)
Comaneci, ...NADIA(s)
Como, ...PERRY(x)
Compton-Burnett ......
...................IVY(z)
Comte, ...AUGUSTE(z)
Conchata....FERRELL(a)
Condon, ...EDDIE(r)
Cone, ...DAVID(e)
Connelly, ...MARC(z)
Conner, ...BART(s)
Connery, ...SEAN(a)
Connick, Jr., ..HARRY(x)
Connie..........CHUNG(o)
...................FRANCIS(x)
...................HAWKINS(f)
...................MACK(e)
...............SELLECCA(a)
...................STEVENS(a)
Conniff, ...RAY(r)
Connolly, .MAUREEN(y)
Connors, ...CHUCK(a)
........JIMMY(y), MIKE(a)
Conrad........AIKEN(t)
.......BAIN(a), HILTON(h)
......NAGEL(a), VEIDT(a)

Conrad, ...JOSEPH(z)
...................ROBERT(a)
...................WILLIAM(a)
Conried, ...HANS(j)
Conroy, ...PAT(z)
Constable, ...JOHN(c)
Constance ....
...................BENNETT(a)
Constantin ....
...................BRANCUSI(c)
Conte, ...RICHARD(a)
Conti, ...TOM(a)
Conway ....TWITTY(x)
Conway, ...TIM(j)
Coogan, ...JACKIE(a)
Cook, ...JOHN(m)
...................PETER(j)
...................THOMAS(h)
Cooke, ...ALISTAIR(z)
...................SAM(x)
Coolidge, ...CALVIN(u)
...................RITA(x)
Cooper, ...ALICE(x)
......GARY(a), JACKIE(a)
....JAMES FENIMORE(z)
...................PETER(h)
...................L. GORDON(d)
Copernicus, ...
...................NICHOLAS(w)
Copland, ...AARON(k)
Copley, ...
....JOHN SINGLETON(c)
Coppola, ...
.......FRANCIS FORD(a)
Corbett, ...JAMES J.(g)
Corbin ....BERNSEN(a)
Corby, ...ELLEN(a)
Cord, ...ALEX(a)
Cordell...............HULL(u)
Corea, ...CHICK(r)
Coretta Scott .....KING(u)
Corey ....FELDMAN(a)
...................HAIM(a)
...................PAVIN(m)
Corey, ...WENDELL(a)
Corman, ...ROGER(q)
Cornelius ....
...................VANDERBILT(h)
Cornell, ...EZRA(h)
...................KATHARINE(a)
Cornwallis, ...
...................CHARLES(p)
Corot, ..JEAN-BAPTISTE
...................CAMILLE(c)
Cortés, ...HERNAN(p)
Cosby, ...BILL(j)
Cosell, ...HOWARD(o)
Costas, ...BOB(o)
Costello, ...ELVIS(x)
...................LOU(j)

Dennis, ...SANDY(a)
Denny, ...REGINALD(a)
................SANDY(x)
Dent, ...JIM(m)
................RICHARD(l)
Denver, ...BOB(a)
................JOHN(x)
Denzel
........WASHINGTON(a)
DePalma, ...BRIAN(q)
Depardieu, ..GERARD(a)
Depp, ...JOHNNY(a)
Derek............JACOBI(a)
Derek, ...BO(a)
................JOHN(a)
Dern, ...BRUCE(a)
................LAURA(a)
Des ....O'CONNOR(x)
De Salvo, ...ANNE(a)
Descartes, ...RENE(w)
DeShannon, ..JACKIE(x)
Desi.............ARNAZ(a)
De Sica, ...VITTORIO(a)
De Valera, ...EAMON(u)
Devane, ...WILLIAM(a)
Devers, ...GAIL(s)
Devine, ...ANDY(j)
DeVito, ...DANNY(a)
De Vries, ...PETER(z)
Dewey, ..THOMAS E.(u)
De Wilde, ...
................BRANDON(a)
De Witt........CLINTON(u)
DeWitt, ...JOYCE(a)
De Wolfe, ...BILLY(a)
Dexter ....GORDON(r)
Dey, ...SUSAN(a)
Diahann.....CARROLL(a)
Diamond, ...NEIL(x)
................SELMA(a)
Diamond Jim
................BRADY(h)
Diana ....DORS(a)
................MULDAUR(a)
.........RIGG(a), ROSS(x)
Diane ....KEATON(a)
.........LADD(a), LANE(a)
................SAWYER(o)
Dianne....FEINSTEIN(u)
................WIEST(a)
Dick.............BUTKUS(l)
................BUTTON(s)
....CAVETT(j), CLARK(a)
................FOSBURY(s)
................FRANCIS(z)
................GREGORY(j,u)
................MARTIN(j)
................POWELL(a)
................SMOTHERS(j)
................TIGER(g)

................TRICKLE(v)
................Van DYKE(a)
Dick (Night Train)............
................LANE(l)
Dickens, ...CHARLES(z)
Dickerson, ...ERIC(l)
Dickey, ...JAMES(z)
Dickinson, ...ANGIE(a)
................EMILY(t)
Diddley, ...BO(r)
Didion, ...JOAN(z)
Didrikson, ...BABE(s)
Diego.........RIVERA(c)
................VELAZQUEZ(c)
Diesel, ...RUDOLPH(w)
Dietrich, ...MARLENE(a)
Dik............BROWNE(i)
Diller, ...PHYLLIS(j)
Dillman, ...
................BRADFORD(a)
Dillon, ...MATT(a)
DiMaggio, ...DOM(e)
................JOE(e)
Di Muci, ...DION(x)
Dina ....MERRILL(a)
Dinah ....SHORE(x)
..........WASHINGTON(x)
Dinesen, ...ISAK(z)
Dinkins, ...DAVID(u)
Dion ....Di MUCI(x)
Dionne .....WARWICK(x)
Dionne, ...MARCEL(n)
Dior, ...CHRISTIAN(c)
Dirk............BENEDICT(a)
................BOGARDE(a)
Dirksen, ...EVERETT(u)
Disch, ...THOMAS M.(z)
Disney, ...WALT(i,q)
Disraeli, ...BENJAMIN(u)
Ditka, ...MIKE(l)
Dizzy ....DEAN(e)
................GILLESPIE(r)
Dmitri ....
.......SHOSTAKOVICH(k)
Dobson, ...KEVIN(a)
Doc ......SEVERINSEN(r)
Doctorow, ...E.L.(z)
Dodie ....STEVENS(a)
Dole, ...BOB(u)
................ELIZABETH(u)
Dolly ....PARTON(x)
Dolores ....DEL RIO(a)
Dom ....DeLUISE(a)
................DiMAGGIO(e)
Domingo, ...PLACIDO(x)
Domino, ...
................FATS(Antoine)(x)
Don.............ADAMS(a)
................AMECHE(a)
................BUDGE(y)

................DEFORE(a)
................DRYSDALE(e)
................EVERLY(x)
.......HENLEY(x), HO(x)
................JANUARY(m)
................JOHNSON(a)
................KNOTTS(a)
................LARSEN(e)
................MARQUIS(i)
................MATTINGLY(e)
................MAYNARD(l)
................McLEAN(x)
................MURRAY(a)
................NOVELLO(j)
................RICKLES(j)
................SHULA(l)
................WILLIAMS(x)
Donahue, ...PHIL(o)
................TROY(a)
Donald.............CRISP(a)
......FAGEN(x), MEEK(a)
................O'CONNOR(a)
................PLEASENCE(a)
................SUTHERLAND(a)
................TRUMP(h)
Donaldson, ...SAM(o)
Donat, ...ROBERT(a)
Donegan, ...LONNIE(x)
Donizetti, ..GAETANO(k)
Donleavy, ...J.P.(z)
Donlevy, ...BRIAN(a)
Donna ....CAPONI(m)
................FARGO(x)
................KELLEY(o)
......MILLS(a), REED(a)
................SUMMER(x)
Donne, ...JOHN(t)
Donny..........OSMOND(x)
Donovan.............ART(l)
Dooley, ...THOMAS(w)
Doppler, ...
................CHRISTIAN(w)
Doria, ...ANDREA(u)
Dorian ...HAREWOOD(a)
Doris................DAY(a, x)
................LESSING(z)
................ROBERTS(a)
Dorn, ...MICHAEL(a)
Dorothy ....
................DANDRIDGE(a)
.....GISH(a), LAMOUR(a)
................LOUDON(a)
................MALONE(a)
................McGUIRE(a)
................PARKER(z)
Dorothy L. ...SAYERS(z)
Dors, ...DIANA(a)
Dorsett, ...TONY(l)
Dorsey, ...JIMMY(r)
................TOMMY(r)

Edison, ...THOMAS(w)
Edith...............EVANS(a)
.................PIAF(x)
.........WHARTON(z)
Edmond ......O'BRIEN(a)
.............ROSTAND(z)
Edmund.........BURKE(z)
.............GWENN(a)
.............HALLEY(w)
.......KEAN(a), LOWE(u)
.............MUSKIE(u)
.............SPENSER(t)
.............WHITE(z)
.............WILSON(z)
Edna ....FERBER(z)
Edna St. Vincent.............
.............MILLAY(t)
Edouard...........LALO(k)
.............MANET(c)
Edvard ....GRIEG(k)
.............MUNCH(c)
Edward...........ALBEE(z)
.............BROOKE(u)
.............ELGAR(k)
.......FOX(a), HEATH(u)
.............HERRMANN(a)
.............HOPPER(c)
.............JENNER(w)
.............KENNEDY(u)
.............KOCH(u)
.............VILLELLA(u)
.............WOODWARD(a)
Edward Everett.............
.............HORTON(a)
Edward G. ....
.............ROBINSON(a)
Edward James.............
.............OLMOS(a)
Edward R. ....
.............MURROW(o)
Edwards, ..ANTHONY(a)
.............BLAKE(q)
Edwin ......ALDRIN, Jr.(d)
.............BOOTH(a)
.............HUBBLE(w)
......LAND(w), MOSES(s)
Edwin Arlington.............
.............ROBINSON(t)
Eero ....SAARINEN(b)
Efrem ....
.........ZIMBALIST, Jr.(a)
Ehrlich, ...PAUL(w)
Eichhorn, ...LISA(a)
Eikenberry, ...JILL(a)
Eileen........BRENNAN(a)
.............HECKART(a)
Einstein, ...ALBERT(w)
Eisenhower, ...
.....DWIGHT DAVID(p, u)
.............MAMIE(u)

Eisenstein, ...SERGEI(q)
Eisner, ...MICHAEL(h)
Ekberg, ...ANITA(a)
Ekland, ...BRITT(a)
Elaine.................MAY(j)
.............STRITCH(a)
Elam, ...JACK(a)
Elayne ....BOOSLER(j)
Eldra ....DEBARGE(x)
Eleanor........PARKER(a)
.............POWELL(a)
.........ROOSEVELT(u)
Eleonora...........DUSE(a)
Elgar, ...EDWARD(k)
Elgin.............BAYLOR(f)
Eli ....WALLACH(a)
.............WHITNEY(w)
Elia ....KAZAN(q, z)
Elias.............HOWE(w)
Elie.............WIESEL(z)
Eliel.........SAARINEN(b)
Elihu.............ROOT(u)
Elio.............VITTORINI(z)
Eliot, ...T.S.(z)
Eliot (Marian Evans), ...
.............GEORGE(z)
Elisha.............OTIS(w)
Elizabeth........ARDEN(h)
....ASHLEY(a), DOLE(u)
.........MONTGOMERY(a)
.............PERKINS(a)
.............TAYLOR(a)
Elizabeth Barrett.............
.............BROWNING(t)
Elke ....SOMMER(a)
Elkington, ...STEVE(m)
Ella ......FITZGERALD(x)
.............LOGAN(a)
Ellen.............BARKIN(a)
.............BURSTYN(a)
....CORBY(a), DREW(a)
.............GLASGOW(t)
.............TERRY(a)
Eller, ...CARL(l)
Elliman, ...YVONNE(x)
Ellington, ...DUKE(k, r)
Elliot, ...CASS(x)
Elliott.............GOULD(a)
Elliott, ...BILL(v)
.........BOB(j), CHRIS(j)
.............DENHOLM(a)
.............SAM(a)
Ellison, ...HARLAN(z)
.............RALPH(z)
Elman, ...MISCHA(r)
Elmer ....RICE(z)
Elmo ....LINCOLN(a)
Elmore......LEONARD(z)
Elroy (Crazy Legs)..........
.............HIRSCH(l)

Els, ...ERNIE(m)
Elsa...LANCHESTER(a)
.........SCHIAPARELLI(c)
Elton ....JOHN(x)
Elvis.........COSTELLO(x)
.............PRESLEY(x)
Elway, ...JOHN(l)
Elwes, ...CARY(a)
Emerson, ...
.........RALPH WALDO(t)
Emil ....JANNINGS(a)
.............ZATOPEK(s)
Emile.........GRIFFITH(g)
.............ZOLA(z)
Emiliano ......ZAPATA(u)
Emilio ......ESTEVEZ(a)
Emily ....BRONTE(z)
.............DICKINSON(t)
.............POST(z)
Emma ....CALVE(x)
.............LAZARUS(t)
.............SAMMS(a)
.............THOMPSON(a)
Emmett.............KELLY(j)
Emmylou......HARRIS(x)
Engelbert ....
.........HUMPERDINCK(k)
.........HUMPERDINCK(x)
Engels, ...
.............FRIEDRICH(u)
English, ...ALEX(f)
Englund, ...ROBERT(a)
Enid...........BAGNOLD(z)
Eno, ...BRIAN(r)
Enos...SLAUGHTER(e)
Enrico ....CARUSO(x)
.............FERMI(w)
Ephron, ...NORA(z)
Eric ....AMBLER(z)
.............BLORE(a)
.............CARMEN(x)
.............CLAPTON(r)
.............DICKERSON(l)
.............FROMM(z)
.........HEIDEN(s), IDLE(j)
.............ROBERTS(a)
.............ROHMER(q)
.............STOLTZ(a)
Erica ....JONG(z)
Erich ......LEINSDORF(r)
.........Von STROHEIM(a)
Erich Maria ....
.........REMARQUE(z)
Erik............ESTRADA(a)
.............SATIE(k)
Erin.................GRAY(a)
.............MORAN(a)
Erle Stanley ....
.............GARDNER(z)
Erma........BOMBECK(o)

Ernest / Fitzgerald

Ernest..............BEVIN(u)
..............BORGNINE(a)
..........HEMINGWAY(z)
..........RUTHERFORD(w)
..........................TRUEX(a)
Ernie..............BANKS(e)
......ELS(m), IRVAN(v)
..................KOVACS(j)
....NEVERS(l), PYLE(o)
Ernst..........LUBITSCH(q)
Ernst, ...MAX(c)
Errol..............FLYNN(a)
Errol, ...LEON(a)
Erroll ....GARNER(r)
Erskine ....CALDWELL(z)
Erving, ...JULIUS(f)
Erwin ....ROMMEL(p)
Erwin, ...STU(a)
Escher, ...M.C.(c)
Esiason, ...BOOMER(l)
Esposito, ...PHIL(n)
Estee ....LAUDER(h)
Estefan, ...GLORIA(x)
Estelle ....GETTY(a)
..................PARSONS(a)
..................WINWOOD(a)
Estes......KEFAUVER(u)
Estes, ...BOB(m)
Estevez, ...EMILIO(a)
Esther..............ROLLE(a)
..................WILLIAMS(a)
Estleman, .LOREN D.(z)
Estrada, ...ERIK(a)
Ethan ....ALLEN(p)
.....COEN(q), HAWKE(a)
Ethel....BARRYMORE(a)
..................KENNEDY(u)
..................MERMAN(x)
..................WATERS(x)
Etta ....JAMES(x)
Eubie..............BLAKE(k)
Eudora ....WELTY(z)
Eugene........CERNAN(d)
..........................DEBS(u)
..........DELACROIX(c)
..................IONESCO(z)
..............McCARTHY(u)
..................O'NEILL(z)
..................ORMANDY(r)
Euler, ...LEONHARD(w)
Eva..................GABOR(a)
..........Le GALLIENNE(a)
Eva (Evita).....PERON(u)
Eva Marie ....SAINT(a)
Evander ....
..................HOLYFIELD(g)
Evans, ...DALE(a)
..................DARRELL(e)
..................DWIGHT(e)
........EDITH(a), JANET(s)

..................LINDA(a)
..................ROBERT(o)
Eve ....ARDEN(a)
..................PLUMB(a)
Evelyn ......ASHFORD(s)
..................WAUGH(z)
Everett........DIRKSEN(u)
Everett, ...CHAD(a)
Everly, ...DON(x)
..........................PHIL(x)
Evers, ...JOHN(e)
Evert, ...CHRIS(y)
Evonne ....
..........GOOLAGONG(y)
Ewbank, ...WEEB(l)
Ewell, ...TOM(a)
Ewing, ...PATRICK(f)
Eydie ....GORME(x)
Ezio..................PINZA(x)
Ezra..........CORNELL(h)
..........................POUND(t)
Ezzard......CHARLES(g)

F. Murray ....
..................ABRAHAM(a)
F. Scott ....
..............FITZGERALD(z)
F.W. ..WOOLWORTH(h)
Fabares, ...SHELLEY(a)
Fabray, ...NANETTE(a)
Fagen, ...DONALD(x)
Fahey, ...JEFF(a)
Fahrenheit, ...
..................GABRIEL(w)
Fain, ...SAMMY(k)
Fairbanks, ...
..................DOUGLAS(a)
Fairbanks, Jr., ...
..................DOUGLAS(a)
Fairchild, ...MORGAN(a)
Faithful, ...MARIANNE(x)
Falana, ...LOLA(a)
Faldo, ...NICK(m)
Falk, ...PETER(a)
Fanny ....BRICE(j)
Faraday, ...MICHAEL(w)
Farentino, ...JAMES(a)
Fargo, ...DONNA(x)
Farley ...GRANGER(a)
Farmer, ...FRANCES(a)
..........PHILIP JOSE(z)
Farr, ...JAMIE(a)
Farragut, ...DAVID(p)
Farrah ......FAWCETT(a)
Farrell, ...MIKE(a)
Farrow, ...MIA(a)
Fats..............DOMINO(x)
..................WALLER(k)
Fatty (Roscoe) ....
..................ARBUCKLE(j)

Faulkner, ...WILLIAM(z)
Fawcett, ...FARRAH(a)
Faxon, ...BRAD(m)
Fay ....WRAY(a)
Faye........DUNAWAY(a)
Faye, ...ALICE(a)
Federico........FELLINI(q)
Feiffer, ...JULES(i)
Feinstein, ...DIANNE(u)
Feldman, ...COREY(a)
..................MARTY(a)
Feldon, ...BARBARA(a)
Feliciano, ...JOSE(x)
Felipe..............ALOU(e)
Felix ....ADLER(z)
......FRANKFURTER(u)
......MENDELSSOHN(k)
Fell, ...NORMAN(a)
Feller, ...BOB(e)
Fellini, ...FEDERICO(q)
Fender, ...FREDDY(x)
Feodor ....
........DOSTOYEVSKY(z)
Ferber, ...EDNA(z)
Ferde ....GROFE(k)
Ferdinand ...MARCOS(u)
Fermi, ...ENRICO(w)
Fernand..........LEGER(c)
Fernandez, ...GIGI(y)
..................MARY JOE(y)
Fernando........LAMAS(a)
..........VALENZUELA(e)
Ferrel, ...TYRA(a)
Ferrell, ...CONCHATA(a)
Ferrer, ...JOSE(a)
..........................MEL(a)
Ferry, ...BRYAN(x)
Fess............PARKER(a)
Fetchit,..........STEPIN(a)
Fidel ....CASTRO(u)
Fiedler, ...ARTHUR(r)
Field, ...SALLY(a)
Fielder, ...CECIL(e)
Fielding, ...HENRY(z)
Fields, ...GRACIE(a)
..........TOTIE(j), W.C.(j)
Filippino ....LIPPI(c)
Fillmore, ...MILLARD(u)
Finch, ...PETER(a)
Fine, ...LARRY(j)
Fingers, ...ROLLIE(e)
Finney, ...ALBERT(a)
Firth, ...PETER(a)
Fishburne, ...
..................LAWRENCE(a)
Fisher, ...CARRIE(a)
..................EDDIE(x)
Fitzgerald, ...BARRY(a)
....ELLA(x), F. SCOTT(z)
..................GERALDINE(a)

152

Flack, ...ROBERTA(x)
Flannery..........................
...........O'CONNOR(z)
Flaubert, ...GUSTAVE(z)
Fleetwood, ...MICK(r)
Fleming, ...
...........ALEXANDER(w)
.........IAN(z), PEGGY(s)
....................RHONDA(a)
....................VICTOR(q)
Fletcher, ...LOUISE(a)
Flip ....WILSON(j)
Florence..........................
........HENDERSON(a)
Florenz.....ZIEGFELD(q)
Floyd ...PATTERSON(a)
Floyd, ...RAYMOND (m)
Flynn, ...ERROL(a)
....................JOE(a)
Foch, ...NINA(a)
Fogelberg, ...DAN(x)
Fogerty, ...JOHN(x)
Fokine, ...MICHAEL(a)
Foley, ...THOMAS S.(u)
Follows, ...MEGAN(a)
Fonda, ...BRIDGET(a)
...................HENRY(a)
.......JANE(a), PETER(a)
Fontaine, ...JOAN(a)
Fonteyn, ...MARGOT(a)
Forbes, ...MALCOLM(h)
Ford, ...BETTY(u)
..........FORD MADOX(z)
...................GERALD(u)
...................GLENN(a)
...................HARRISON(a)
......HENRY(h), JOHN(q)
................TENNESSEE
...ERNIE(x), WHITEY(e)
Ford Madox ......FORD(z)
Foreman, ...GEORGE(g)
Forester, ...C.S.(z)
Forget, ...GUY(y)
Forman, ...MILOS(q)
Forrest.........TUCKER(a)
Forster, ...E.M.(z)
Forsythe, ...JOHN(a)
Fortas, ...ABE(u)
Fosbury, ...DICK(s)
Fosse, ...BOB(q)
Foster, ...JODIE(a)
...................PRESTON(a)
...................STEPHEN(k)
Foucault, ...JEAN(w)
Fountain, ...PETE(r)
Fouts, ...DAN(l)
Fowles, ...JOHN(z)
Fox, ...EDWARD(a)
...................JAMES(a)
...............MICHAEL J.(a)

Foxworth, ...ROBERT(a)
Foxx, ...JIMMY(e)
...................REDD(j)
Foy, ...EDDIE(a)
Foyt, ...A.J.(v)
Fra ....ANGELICO(c)
Fra Filippo...........LIPPI(c)
Frampton, ...PETER(x)
Fran......TARKENTON(l)
France, ...ANATOLE(z)
Frances.............ALDA(x)
...................FARMER(a)
...............STERNHAGEN(a)
Franchot..........TONE(a)
Franciosa, ...TONY(a)
Francis...........BACON(u)
...................POULENC(k)
Francis, ...ANNE(a)
...................ARLENE(a)
......CONNIE(x), DICK(z)
Francisco ....FRANCO(u)
Francis Ford ....
...................COPPOLA(q)
Francis Scott........KEY(t)
Francis X. ....
...................BUSHMAN(a)
Franco...........HARRIS(l)
.........ZEFFIRELLI(q)
Franco, ...
.........FRANCISCO(u)
François ...DUVALIER(u)
...................MAURIAC(z)
............MITTERRAND(u)
...................RABELAIS(z)
...................TRUFFAUT(q)
...................VILLON(t)
Frakes, ...JONATHAN(a)
Frank ....BORMAN(d)
...................BORZAGE(q)
...................CAPRA(q)
...................CHANCE(e)
...................DEFORD(o)
...................GIFFORD(l)
...................GORSHIN(a)
...................HERBERT(z)
...................HOWARD(e)
...................LANGELLA(a)
...................LLOYD(q)
...................LORENZO(h)
.....MUIR(z), PARKER(y)
...................ROBINSON(e)
...................SEDGMAN(s)
...................SESNO(o)
...................SHORTER(s)
...................SINATRA(x)
...................TASHLIN(q)
...................ZAPPA(r)
Frankenheimer, ...
...................JOHN(q)
Frankfurter, ...FELIX(u)

Frankie.........AVALON(x)
...................LAINE(x)
.........LYMON(x), VALLI(x)
Franklin.........PIERCE(u)
Franklin, ...ARETHA(x)
...........BENJAMIN(u, w)
....BONNIE(a), JOE(o)
Franklin Delano ....
...........ROOSEVELT(u)
Frank Lloyd.....................
...................WRIGHT(b)
Frann, ...MARY(a)
Frans................HALS(c)
Franz ....KAFKA(z)
......KLINE(c), LEHAR(k)
.........LISZT(k), MARC(c)
...................SCHUBERT(k)
Franz Joseph ....
...................HAYDN(k)
Fraser, ...DAWN(s)
...................NEALE(y)
Frawley, ...WILLIAM(a)
Frazier, ...JOE(g)
Fred.................ALLEN(j)
...................ASTAIRE(a)
...........BILETNIKOFF(l)
...................COUPLES(m)
...................DRYER(a,l)
...................GWYNNE(a)
...........MacMURRAY(a)
...................McGRIFF(e)
...................PERRY(y)
...................ROGERS(a)
...................SAVAGE(a)
...................STOLLE(y)
...................WARD(a)
...................ZINNEMANN(q)
Freda.............PAYNE(x)
Freddie .....MERCURY(x)
...................PRINZE(j)
Freddy.........CANNON(x)
...................FENDER(x)
Frederic ....CHOPIN(k)
...................MISTRAL(t)
...................REMINGTON(c)
Frederick.....CHURCH(c)
...................POHL(z)
Frederick L. ....
...................OLMSTED(b)
Fredric...........MARCH(a)
Freeman ......GOSDEN(j)
Freeman, ...MORGAN(a)
Freleng, ...FRIZ(i)
French, ...
....DANIEL CHESTER(c)
...................MARILYN(z)
Freud, ...SIGMUND(w)
Frey, ...GLEN(x)
Friedan, ...BETTY(z)
Friedkin, ...WILLIAM(q)

153

Friedrich / George Caleb

Friedrich.......ENGELS(u)
.............NIETZSCHE(z)
Friml, ...RUDOLF(k)
Fritz ....KREISLER(r)
..................LANG(q)
.................LEIBER(z)
.................WEAVER(a)
Friz ....FRELENG(i)
Fromm, ...ERIC(z)
Frost, ...DAVID(o)
.................ROBERT(t)
Fugard, ...ATHOL(z)
Fulbright, ...
...........J. WILLIAM(u)
Fuller, ...
....R.BUCKMINSTER(b)
Fulton, ...ROBERT(w)
Funicello, ..ANNETTE(a)
Fuzzy ....ZOELLER(m)

G.K. ...CHESTERTON(z)
Gabby ....HAYES(a)
Gable, ...CLARK(a)
Gabor, ...EVA(a)
......JOLIE(a), MAGDA(a)
.................ZSA ZSA(a)
Gabriel ....
............FAHRENHEIT(w)
Gabriel, ...PETER(x)
Gabriela ....MISTRAL(t)
.................SABATINI(y)
Gabriele ....
.............D'ANNUNZIO(t)
Gaddis, ...WILLIAM(z)
Gaetano ....
..........DONIZETTI(k)
Gagarin, ...YURI(d)
Gahan ....WILSON(i)
Gail ....DEVERS(s)
Gail, ...MAX(a)
Gainsborough, ...
.................THOMAS(c)
Galbraith, ...
......JOHN KENNETH(z)
Gale ....GORDON(a)
.................SAYERS(l)
.................STORM(x)
Galilei, ...GALILEO(w)
Galileo ....GALILEI(w)
Gallagher, ...MEGAN(a)
Galsworthy, ...JOHN(z)
Galway, ...JAMES(r)
Gam, ...RITA(a)
Gamal..........NASSER(u)
Gandhi, ...INDIRA(u)
.........MOHANDAS(u)
Garagiola, ...JOE(o)
Garbo, ...GRETA(a)
Garcia, ...ANDY(a)
Gardenia, ...VINCENT(a)

Gardner, ...AVA(a)
.........ERLE STANLEY(z)
Garfield, ...BRIAN(z)
.................JAMES A.(u)
.................JOHN(a)
Garfunkel, ...ART(x)
Garland, ...JUDY(a,x)
Garn, ...JAKE(d,u)
Garner, ...ERROLL(r)
.................JAMES(a)
.........JOHN NANCE(u)
Garo ....YEPREMIAN(l)
Garr, ...TERI(a)
Garrison ......KEILLOR(o)
Garry ......SHANDLING(j)
.................TRUDEAU(l)
Garson, ...GREER(a)
Garth ....BROOKS(x)
Garvey, ...STEVE(e)
Gary ......BURGHOFF(a)
......BUSEY(a), CLARK(l)
.................COLEMAN(a)
.................COOPER(a)
.....HART(u), LARSON(i)
.................MERRILL(a)
.................OLDMAN(a)
.................PLAYER(m)
.................SANDY(a)
.................SNYDER(t)
Gastineau, ...MARK(l)
Gates .....McFADDEN(a)
Gates, ...DAVID(x)
.................HORATIO(p)
Gauguin, ...PAUL(c)
Gavin ....MacLEOD(a)
Gay, ...JOHN(k,t)
Gaye, ...MARVIN(x)
Gayle ......CRYSTAL(x)
Gaylord ....PERRY(e)
Gaynor, ...JANET(a)
.................MITZI(a)
Gazzara, ...BEN(a)
Geddy.................LEE(x)
Geena.............DAVIS(a)
Geer, ...WILL(a)
Gehrig, ...LOU(e)
Geiberger, ...AL(m)
Gena......ROWLANDS(a)
Gene ......AUTRY(a,h)
.................BARRY(a)
.................CHANDLER(x)
.................HACKMAN(a)
.....KELLY(a), KRUPA(r)
.................LITTLER(m)
......PITNEY(x), SAKS(z)
.................SARAZEN(m)
.................SISKEL(o)
.................TIERNEY(a)
.................TUNNEY(g)
.................WILDER(a)

Genet, ...JEAN(z)
Genevieve ....BUJOLD(a)
Gentile..........BELLINI(c)
Geoffrey.....CHAUCER(t)
.................HOLDER(a)
Geoffrion, ...BERNIE(n)
Georg ....HEGEL(z)
.................SOLTI(r)
George ....ABBOTT(z)
.....ADE(z), ARCHER(m)
.....ARLISS(a), BAKER(i)
.................BENSON(r)
....BLANDA(l) BRENT(a)
.......BRETT(e), BURNS(j)
.......BUSH(u), CARLIN(j)
.................CATLIN(c)
.................CUKOR(q)
.................CUSTER(p)
.................DZUNDZA(a)
.................EASTMAN(h)
.................ELIOT(z)
.................FOREMAN(g)
.................GERSHWIN(k)
.................GRIZZARD(a)
.................HALAS(l)
.................HAMILTON(a)
.................HARRISON(r,x)
.................INNESS(c)
.....JESSEL(j), JONES(x)
.................KENNEDY(a)
.................LUCAS(q)
.................McGOVERN(u)
.................MEADE(u)
.................MEANY(h)
.................MICHAEL(x)
.................MURPHY(a)
.................ORWELL(z)
.................PATTON(p)
.................PEPPARD(a)
.................RAFT(a)
.................REEVES(a)
.................SAND(z)
.................SANDERS(a)
.................SANTAYANA(z)
.................SEGAL(a)
.................SHEARING(r)
.....STEINBRENNER(h)
.................STEVENS(q)
.................STRAIT(x)
.................SZELL(r)
.................WALLACE(u)
.................WASHINGTON(p)
.......WENDT(a), WILL(o)
George Bernard.............
.................SHAW(z)
George C.................
.................MARSHALL(p)
.................SCOTT(a)
George Caleb ....
.................BINGHAM(c)

Goulet / Hamilton

Goulet, ...ROBERT(x)
Gounod, ...CHARLES(k)
Gowdy, ...CURT(o)
Gower .....CHAMPION(a)
Grable, ...BETTY(a)
Grace............JONES(x)
......KELLY(a), SLICK(x)
Gracie ....ALLEN(j)
...................FIELDS(a)
Graf, ...STEFFI(y)
Grafton, ...SUE(z)
Graham .....CHAPMAN(j)
................GREENE(z)
..........HILL(v), NASH(x)
......................PARKER(x)
Graham, ...BOB(a)
...................DAVID(m)
.....MARTHA(a), OTTO(l)
...................VIRGINIA(a)
Grahame, ...GLORIA(a)
Graig.........NETTLES(e)
Gramm, ...LOU(x)
...................PHIL(u)
Grammer, ...KELSEY(a)
Grange, ...RED(l)
Granger, ...FARLEY(a)
...................STEWART(a)
Grant..............TINKER(h)
...................WOOD(c)
Grant, ...AMY(x)
...........CARY(a), LEE(a)
..........ULYSSES S.(p,u)
Grass, ...GUNTER(z)
Grau, .SHIRLEY ANN(z)
Graves, ...PETER(a)
...................ROBERT(z)
Gray, ...ASA(w)
..........ERIN(a), LINDA(a)
...................THOMAS(t)
Grayson, ..KATHRYN(a)
Graziano, ...ROCKY(g)
Greeley, ...HORACE(o)
Green, ...ADOLPH(a)
.......AL(x), HUBERT(m)
Greenberg, ...HANK(e)
Greene, ...BOB(o)
...................GRAHAM(z)
...................LORNE(a)
...................MICHELE(a)
...................SHECKY(j)
Greenfield, ...JEFF(o)
Greenstreet, ...
...................SYDNEY(a)
Greer ....GARSON(a)
Greg ....LAKE(x)
...................LOUGANIS(s)
...................MORRIS(a)
...................NORMAN(m)
Gregg...........ALLMAN(r)
Gregor ....MENDEL(w)

Gregory ...HARRISON(a)
.......HINES(a), PECK(a)
Gregory, ...DICK(j,u)
Greta ....GARBO(a)
Gretzky, ...WAYNE(n)
Grey, ...JENNIFER(a)
..........JOEL(a), ZANE(z)
Grieg, ...EDVARD(k)
Griese, ...BOB(l)
Griffin..............DUNNE(a)
Griffin, ...MERV(x)
Griffith, ...ANDY(a)
..........D.W.(q), EMILE(g)
...................HUGH(a)
...................MELANIE(a)
Grimes, ...MARTHA(z)
...................TAMMY(a)
Grimm, ...JAKOB(z)
...................WILHELM(z)
Gris, ...JUAN(c)
Grisham, ...JOHN(z)
Grissom, ...VIRGIL(d)
Grizzard, ...GEORGE(a)
Grodin, ...CHARLES(a)
Groening, ...MATT(i)
Grofe, ...FERDE(k)
Groh, ...DAVID(a)
Gropius, ...WALTER(b)
Grosbard, ...ULU(q)
Gross, ...MARY(j)
...................MICHAEL(a)
Groucho (Julius) ....
...................MARX(j)
Grove, ...LEFTY(e)
Grover ..ALEXANDER(e)
...................CLEVELAND(u)
Groza, ...LOU(l)
Guardino, ...HARRY(a)
Guest, ...EDGAR(t)
Guevara, ...CHE(p,u)
Guglielmo ....
...................MARCONI(w)
Guido ....RENI(c)
Guillaume, ..ROBERT(a)
Guillermo..........VILAS(y)
Guinness, ...ALEC(a)
Guion ....BLUFORD(a)
Guisewite, ...CATHY(i)
Guitry, ...SACHA(a, z)
Gulagher, ...CLU(a)
Gumble, ...BRYANT(o)
Gummo (Milton) ....
...................MARX(j)
Günter............GRASS(z)
Gus ....BELL(e)
Gustav ....HOLST(k)
...................KLIMT(c)
...................MAHLER(k)
Gustave ....COURBET(c)
...................FLAUBERT(z)

Guthrie, ...ARLO(x)
...................WOODY(x)
Guttenberg, ...STEVE(a)
Gutzon......BORGLUM(c)
Guy..............FORGET(y)
...................KIBBEE(a)
...................LOMBARDO(r)
Guy, ...JASMINE(a)
Gwen......TORRENCE(s)
...................VERDON(a)
Gwenn, ...EDMUND(a)
Gwynn, ...TONY(e)
Gwynne, ...FRED(a)
Gypsy Rose........LEE(a)

H.G. ....WELLS(z)
H.H. (Saki) ....MUNRO(z)
H.L. ....MENCKEN(z)
H.Ross.......PEROT(h, u)
H.Ryder....HAGGARD(z)
Hackett, ...BUDDY(j)
Hackman, ...GENE(a)
Hagar, ...SAMMY(x)
Hagen, ...UTA(a)
...................WALTER(m)
Haggard, ...H.RYDER(z)
...................MERLE(x)
Hagler, ...MARVIN(g)
Hagman, ...LARRY(a)
Hahn, ...OTTO(w)
Haid, ...CHARLES(a)
Haig, ...ALEXANDER(p)
...................DOUGLAS(p)
Haile..........SELASSIE(u)
Hailey, ...ARTHUR(z)
Haim, ...COREY(a)
Hal ....HOLBROOK(a)
...................LINDEN(a)
Halas, ...GEORGE(l)
Halberstam, ...DAVID(z)
Hale ....IRWIN(m)
Hale, ...ALAN(a)
...................BARBARA(a)
...................NATHAN(p)
Haley, ...ALEX(z)
...................BILL(r)
...................JACK(a)
Hall, ...ARSENIO(j)
...................DARYL(x)
...................DEIDRE(a)
...................HUNTZ(a)
...................MONTY(a)
...................TOM T.(x)
Halldór ....LAXNESS(z)
Halle...............BERRY(a)
Halley, ...EDMUND(w)
Hals, ...FRANS(c)
Hamel, ...VERONICA(a)
Hamill, ...MARK(a)
Hamilton...........CAMP(a)

Hamilton, ...
.............ALEXANDER(u)
...................GEORGE(a)
.....................LINDA(a)
................MARGARET(a)
........................SCOTT(s)
Hamlin, ...HARRY(a)
Hamlisch, ...MARVIN(k)
Hammarskjöld, ..DAG(u)
Hammer, ...ARMAND(h)
.........................JAN(r)
Hammerstein, ...
...................OSCAR(r)
Hammett, .DASHIELL(z)
Hampton, ...LIONEL(r)
Hamsun, ...KNUT(z)
Hana...MANDLIKOVA(y)
Hancock, ...HERBIE(r)
.........................JOHN(u)
Handel, ...GEORGE
....................FRIDERIC(k)
Handy, ...W.C.(k)
Hank..............AARON(e)
............GREENBERG(e)
.........................SNOW(x)
...................WILLIAMS(x)
.............WILLIAMS, Jr.(x)
Hanks, ...TOM(a)
Hanna, ...BILL(i)
Hannah, ...DARYL(a)
Hans ....CONRIED(j)
.............HOFMANN(c)
...............HOLBEIN(c)
Hans Christian..............
............ANDERSEN(z)
Harding, ...
..........WARREN G.(u)
Hardison, ...KADEEM(a)
Hardwicke, ...CEDRIC(a)
Hardy, ...OLIVER(j)
.................THOMAS(z)
Harewood, ...DORIAN(a)
Haring, ...KEITH(c)
Harlan.........ELLISON(z)
Harlow, ...JEAN(a)
Harmon.......................
................KILLEBREW(e)
Harmon, ...MARK(a)
.........................TOM(l)
Harold.............ARLEN(k)
.........................LLOYD(j)
...............MacMILLAN(u)
.....................PINTER(q)
.....................WILSON(u)
.........................UREY(w)
Harper.................LEE(z)
Harper, ...JESSICA(a)
....TESS(a), VALERIE(a)
Harpo (Arthur) ...MARX(j)
Harrelson, ...WOODY(a)

Harriet..........NELSON(a)
Harriet Beecher ....
......................STOWE(z)
Harriman,.....................
...........W. AVERELL(h)
Harrington, Jr., ...PAT(a)
Harris, ...ED(a)
.............EMMYLOU(x)
....FRANCO(l), JULIE(a)
......PHIL(j), RICHARD(a)
...............ROSEMARY(a)
Harrison ....FORD(a)
Harrison, .BENJAMIN(u)
....................GEORGE(r,x)
.................GREGORY(a)
..........NOEL(x), REX(a)
......WILLIAM HENRY(u)
Harry ......ANDERSON(a)
...............BELAFONTE(x)
.................BLACKMUN(u)
....................CHAPIN(a)
.........CONNICK, Jr.(x)
.................GUARDINO(a)
.......................HAMLIN(a)
.....................HOUDINI(a)
....JAMES(r), LAUDER(j)
...................MORGAN(a)
.....................NILSSON(x)
...................REASONER(o)
.....RITZ(j), Von ZELL(a)
Harry, ...DEBORAH(x)
Harry Dean ....
....................STANTON(a)
Harry S ....TRUMAN(u)
Hart, ...CRANE(r)
Hart, ...GARY(u)
.....JOHNNY(i), MOSS(a)
...............WILLIAM S.(a)
Harte, ...BRET(z)
Hartley, ...MARIETTE(a)
Hartman, ...DAVID(o)
.........LISA(a), PHIL(j)
Harvey ....KEITEL(a)
...................KORMAN(a)
Harvey, ..LAURENCE(a)
....PAUL(o), WILLIAM(w)
Haskell, ...PETER(a)
Hassam, ...CHILDE(c)
Hasso, ...SIGNE(a)
Hatch, ...ORRIN(u)
Hatfield, ...BOBBY(x)
Hattie ....McDANIEL(a)
Hauer, ...RUTGER(a)
Havens, ...RICHIE(x)
Haver, ...JUNE(a)
Havlicek, ...JOHN(f)
Havoc, ...JUNE(a)
Hawke, ...ETHAN(a)
Hawking,.....................
.............STEPHEN W.(w)

Hawkins, ...COLEMAN(r)
......CONNIE(f), JACK(a)
Hawn, ...GOLDIE(a)
Hawthorne, ...
...............NATHANIEL(z)
Haydn, ...
...FRANZ JOSEPH(k)
Hayes, ...BOB(s)
....................GABBY(a)
....HELEN(a), ISAAC(x)
......RUTHERFORD B.(u)
Hayley..............MILLS(a)
Haynie, ...SANDRA(m)
Hays, ...ROBERT(a)
Hayward, ...JUSTIN(x)
.........................SUSAN(a)
Hayworth, ...RITA(a)
Hearns, ...THOMAS(g)
Hearst, ...WILLIAM
.............RANDOLPH(h)
Heath, ...EDWARD(u)
Heather ...LOCKLEAR(a)
Hebert, ...BOBBY(l)
Hecht, ...BEN(z)
Heckart, ...EILEEN(a)
Hector ....BERLIOZ(k)
...................CAMACHO(g)
Hedy............LAMARR(a)
Heflin, ...VAN(a)
Hefner, ...HUGH(h)
Hefti, ...NEAL(r)
Hegel, ...GEORG(z)
Heiden, ...ERIC(s)
Heifetz, ...JASCHA(r)
Heine, ...HEINRICH(t)
Heinlein, ..ROBERT A.(z)
Heinrich ....BOLL(z)
.........................HEINE(t)
Heisenberg, ...
.......................WERNER(w)
Heitor ..VILLA-LOBOS(k)
Helen...............HAYES(a)
.........................HUNT(a)
.....................KELLER(z)
...................MENKEN(a)
.......................REDDY(x)
.......................SLATER(a)
........TWELVETREES(a)
Helena ....
...BONHAM-CARTER(a)
.....................SUKOVA(y)
Helen Gurley ....
.........................BROWN(o)
Heller, ...JOSEPH(z)
Hellman, ...LILLIAN(z)
Helm, ...LEVON(a,x)
Helmond,.......................
.............KATHERINE(a)
Helms, ...JESSE(u)
Helmut.............KOHL(u)

157

Hemingway,
...............ERNEST(z)
...............MARGAUX(a)
...............MARIEL(a)
Hemmings, ...DAVID(a)
Hemsley, ..SHERMAN(a)
Henderson,
...............FLORENCE(a)
...............RICKEY(e)
...............SKITCH(r)
Hendrix, ...JIMI(r,x)
Henie, ...SONJA(s)
Henley, ...BETH(z)
...............DON(x)
Henner, ...MARILU(a)
Henning, ...DOUG(a)
Henny.....YOUNGMAN(j)
Henri...........MATISSE(c)
...............POINCARE(w)
...............ROUSSEAU(z)
Henrik...........IBSEN(z)
Henry...........BACON(b)
...............BESSEMER(w)
...............CAVENDISH(w)
...............CLAY(u)
...............FIELDING(z)
......FONDA(a), FORD(f)
...GIBSON(j), JAMES(z)
...............KISSINGER(u)
...LEE(p), MANCINI(k, r)
...............MILLER(z)
...............MOORE(c)
...............MORGAN(j)
...............WINKLER(a)
Henry, ...BUCK(j,z)
...............PATRICK(u)
Henry Cabot ..LODGE(u)
Henry David...........
...............THOREAU(z)
Henry H. ....
...............RICHARDSON(b)
Henry J. ....KAISER(h)
Henry Wadsworth ....
...............LONGFELLOW(t)
Hepburn, ...AUDREY(a)
...............KATHARINE(a)
Herb ....ALPERT(r)
...............BLOCK(i)
Herbert...........HOOVER(u)
...............LOM(a)
...............MARSHALL(a)
Herbert, ...FRANK(z)
...............VICTOR(k,r)
Herbie ....HANCOCK(r)
...............MANN(r)
Herman .....MELVILLE(z)
...............WOUK(z)
Herman, ...JERRY(k)
...............PEE WEE(j)
...............WOODY(r)

Hermann ....HESSE(z)
Hermione ...GINGOLD(a)
Hernán ....CORTES(p)
Hernandez, ...KEITH(e)
Herrmann, ..EDWARD(a)
Herschel ..BERNARDI(a)
...............WALKER(l)
Hersey, ...JOHN(z)
Hershey, ...BARBARA(a)
Hershiser, ...OREL(e)
Herzog, ...CHAIM(u)
...............WERNER(q)
Hess, ...MYRA(a)
Hesse, ...HERMANN(z)
Hesseman,
...............HOWARD(a)
Heston, ..CHARLTON(a)
Heyerdahl, ...THOR(z)
Hieronymus ...BOSCH(c)
Hill, ...ARTHUR(q)
...............DAN(x), DAVE(m)
...............GEORGE ROY(q)
...............GRAHAM(v)
...............MIKE(m)
Hillary ....CLINTON(u)
Hiller, ...WENDY(a)
Hillerman, ...JOHN(a)
Hilton, ...CONRAD(h)
Hindemith, ...PAUL(k)
Hines, ...EARL "Fatha"(r)
...............GREGORY(a)
...............JEROME(a)
Hinton, ...S.E.(z)
Hirsch, ...ELROY
...............(Crazy Legs)(l)
...............JUDD(a)
Hirschfeld, ...AL(i)
Hiss, ...ALGER(u)
Hitchcock, ...ALFRED(q)
Hitler, ...ADOLF(u)
Ho, ...DON(x)
Hoagy ....
...............CARMICHAEL(k)
Hoban, ...JAMES(b)
Hockney, ...DAVID(c)
Hodges, ...GIL(e)
Hodiak, ...JOHN(a)
Hoffa, ...JAMES(h)
Hoffman, ...DUSTIN(a)
Hofmann, ...HANS(c)
Hofstadter, ...
...............DOUGLAS R.(w)
Hogan, ...BEN(m)
...............PAUL(a)
Hogarth, ...WILLIAM(c)
Holbein, ...HANS(c)
Holbrook, ...HAL(a)
Holden, ...WILLIAM(a)
Holder, ...GEOFFREY(a)
Holiday, ...BILLIE(x)

Holland, ...BRIAN(k)
...............EDDIE(k)
Holliday, ...JUDY(a)
...............POLLY(a)
Holliman,...........EARL(a)
Hollis ....STACY(m)
Holloway,..STERLING(a)
Holly ....HUNTER(a)
Holly, ...BUDDY(x)
Holm, ...CELESTE(a)
...............IAN(a)
Holmes, ...LARRY(g)
....OLIVER WENDELL(u)
Holst, ...GUSTAV(k)
Holt, ...JACK(a), TIM(a)
Holyfield, ..EVANDER(g)
Homer, ...WINSLOW(c)
Honegger, ...ARTHUR(k)
Honoré de.....BALZAC(z)
Honus.........WAGNER(e)
Hooks...........JAN(j)
...............ROBERT(a)
Hooper, ...TOBE(q)
Hoot...........GIBSON(a)
Hoover, ...HERBERT(u)
Hope ....LANGE(a)
Hope, ...BOB(j)
Hopkins, ...ANTHONY(a)
...............MIRIAM(a)
Hopper, ...DENNIS(a)
...............EDWARD(c)
Horace.......GREELEY(o)
Horatio..........ALGER(z)
...............GATES(p)
...............NELSON(p)
Horatio H. ....
...............KITCHENER(p)
Horne, ...LENA(x)
...............MARILYN(x)
Horney, ...KAREN(w)
Hornsby, ...ROGERS(e)
Hornung, ...PAUL(l)
Horowitz, ...VLADIMIR(r)
Horsley, ...LEE(a)
Hortense...CALISHER(z)
Horton, ...EDWARD
...............EVERETT(a)
Hoskins, ...BOB(a)
Hosni ....MUBARAK(u)
Houdini, ...HARRY(a)
Houseman, ...JOHN(a)
Housman, ...A.E.(t)
Houston, ...CISSY(x)
...............SAMUEL(u)
...............WHITNEY(x)
Howard...........BAKER(u)
...............COSELL(o)
...............HESSEMAN(a)
...............HUGHES(h)
...............JOHNSON(e)

Howard *continued*..........
.................JOHNSON(h)
.......JONES(x), KEEL(x)
.................ROLLINS(a)
.......................STERN(j)
Howard, ...CURLY(j)
.........FRANK(e), KEN(a)
.........LESLIE(a), MOE(j)
....RON(a, q), SHEMP(j)
..................TREVOR(a)
Howe, ...ELIAS(w)
...................GORDIE(n)
.......................STEVE(r)
Howell, ...C.THOMAS(a)
Howes, ..SALLY ANN(a)
Howie ....MANDEL(j)
Hoyt..................AXTON(x)
...............WILHELM(e)
Hubble, ...EDWIN(w)
Hubert.........GREEN(m)
............HUMPHREY(u)
Hudson, ...ROCK(a)
Huey.............LEWIS(x)
........................LONG(u)
Huff, ...SAM(l)
Hugh...........DOWNS(o)
..................GRIFFITH(a)
..................HEFNER(h)
................MASEKELA(r)
........................O'BRIAN(a)
Hughes, ..BARNARD(a)
................HOWARD(h)
....LANGSTON(t), TED(t)
Hugo, ...VICTOR(z)
Hulbert............MIKE(m)
Hulce, ...TOM(a)
Hull, ...BOBBY(n)
.........................BRETT(n)
...................CORDELL(u)
Hume ....CRONYN(a)
Hume, ...DAVID(z)
Humperdinck, ...
..............ENGELBERT(k)
..............ENGELBERT(x)
Humphrey ...BOGART(a)
Humphrey, ..HUBERT(u)
Humphry ....DAVY(w)
Hunt, ...HELEN(a)
........................LINDA(a)
.............RICHARD M.(b)
Hunter, ...HOLLY(a)
.......IAN(x), JEFFREY(a)
........KIM(a), RACHEL(a)
........ROSS(q), TAB(a, x)
Huntley, ...CHET(o)
Huntz................HALL(a)
Hurt, ...JOHN(a)
.............MARY BETH(a)
...............WILLIAM(a)
Hussein, ...SADDAM(u)

Huston, ...ANJELICA(a)
....JOHN(q), WALTER(a)
Hutton, ...BETTY(a)
.......JIM(a), LAUREN(a)
...................TIMOTHY(a)
Huxley, ...ALDOUS(z)
Hyland, ...BRIAN(x)
Hyman .....RICKOVER(p)
Hynde, ...CHRISSIE(x)

I(eoh) M(ing)........PEI(b)
Iacocca, ...LEE A.(h)
Ian........ANDERSON(r,x)
..........BAKER-FINCH(m)
............CARMICHAEL(a)
................FLEMING(z)
...HOLM(a), HUNTER(z)
................McKELLEN(a)
................WOOSNAM(m)
Ian, ...JANIS(x)
Ibsen, ...HENRIK(z)
Icahn, ...CARL(h)
Ida................LUPINO(a)
..................TARBELL(z)
Idle, ...ERIC(j)
Idol, ...BILLY(x)
Iglesias, ...JULIO(x)
Ignace ....
............PADEREWSKI(k)
Igor .....STRAVINSKY(k)
.................SIKORSKY(w)
Ike ....TURNER(r)
Ilie ....NASTASE(y)
Ilka ....CHASE(a)
Imelda.........MARCOS(u)
Immanuel ....KANT(z)
Imogene ....COCA(j)
Imre ....NAGY(u)
Ina ....CLAIRE(a)
Indira ....GANDHI(u)
Inge, ...WILLIAM(z)
Ingemar ....
...............JOHANSSON(g)
...............STENMARK(s)
Inger ....STEVENS(a)
Ingmar.....BERGMAN(q)
Ingram, ...JAMES(x)
Ingrid ....BERGMAN(a)
Inigo ....JONES(b)
Inkster, ...JULI(m)
Inness, ...GEORGE(c)
Inouye, ...DANIEL(u)
Ionesco, ...EUGENE(z)
Ira ....GERSHWIN(k)
........................LEVIN(z)
Irene ....CARA(x)
...CASTLE(a),DUNNE(a)
.......PAPAS(a), RYAN(a)
Iris............MURDOCH(z)
Irons, ...JEREMY(a)

Irvan, ...ERNIE(v)
Irving..............BERLIN(k)
Irving, ...AMY(a)
.......................JOHN(z)
..................WASHINGTON(z)
Irving R. ....LEVINE(o)
Irwin, ...HALE(m)
Isaac.............ASIMOV(z)
.....BABEL(z), HAYES(x)
....................NEWTON(w)
.......................STERN(r)
Isaac Bashevis ....
.......................SINGER(z)
Isabella ....
..............ROSSELLINI(a)
Isabelle ....ADJANI(a)
Isadora.......DUNCAN(a)
Isak.............DINESEN(z)
Isamu.........NOGUCHI(c)
Isao ....AOKI(m)
Isherwood, ...
.........CHRISTOPHER(z)
Isiah ....THOMAS(f)
Italo ....CALVINO(z)
Itzhak.........PERLMAN(r)
.......................RABIN(u)
Ivan ....BUNIN(z)
.......................LENDL(y)
.......................PAVLOV(w)
.................REITMAN(q)
.................TURGENEV(z)
Ives, ...BURL(x)
..................CHARLES(k)
.....................JAMES M.(c)
Ivey, ...JUDITH(a)
Ivo.................ANDRIC(z)
Ivor ....NOVELLO(a)
Ivory, ...JAMES(q)
Ivy ....COMPTON-
..................BURNETT(z)

J.C. ....SNEAD(m)
J.Carrol............NAISH(a)
J.D. ....SALINGER(z)
J.E.B. ....STUART(p)
J.G. ....BALLARD(z)
J.M. ....BARRIE(z)
J.M.W. ....TURNER(c)
J.P...........DONLEAVY(z)
J.R. ....SALAMANCA(z)
J.R.R. ....TOLKIEN(z)
J.Robert ....
........OPPENHEIMER(w)
J.Walter ....
...............THOMPSON(h)
J.William ....
...............FULBRIGHT(u)
Jack ......ALBERTSON(a)
................ANDERSON(o)
.......................BENNY(j)

Jean *continued* ....
..................SEBERG(a)
..............SHEPHERD(z)
...............SIBELIUS(k)
..............SIMMONS(a)
.............STAPLETON(a)
Jean-Antoine ....
.................WATTEAU(c)
Jean-Baptiste Camille.....
..................COROT(c)
Jean Baptiste ....
............MOLIERE(z)
Jean-Claude .....KILLY(s)
Jeane................
..........KIRKPATRICK(u)
Jeanette................
.............MacDONALD(x)
Jean-François................
...................MILLET(c)
Jean Jacques ....
..............ROUSSEAU(z)
Jean-Luc.....GODARD(q)
Jeanne ....CRAIN(a)
...................EAGELS(a)
.................MOREAU(a)
Jean-Paul ....
..............BELMONDO(a)
...................SARTRE(z)
Jean Paul ....GETTY(h)
..................MARAT(u)
Jean-Pierre ....
..................AUMONT(a)
...................RAMPAL(r)
Jeff ....BECK(r)
...............BRIDGES(a)
.............CHANDLER(a)
..............DANIELS(a)
...................FAHEY(a)
..............GOLDBLUM(a)
.............GREENFIELD(o)
...................LYNNE(r)
................MacNELLY(i)
...............SLUMAN(m)
Jefferson..........DAVIS(u)
Jefferson, ..THOMAS(u)
Jeffrey ....HUNTER(a)
..................TAMBOR(a)
Jeffreys, ...ANNE(a)
Jenkins, ...ALLEN(a)
Jenner, ...BRUCE(s)
..................EDWARD(w)
Jennifer......CAPRIATI(y)
.......GREY(a), JONES(a)
Jennifer Jason ....
..........................LEIGH(a)
Jennings, ...PETER(o)
..................WAYLON(x)
Jenny ....AGUTTER(a)
..........................LIND(x)
Jeremy ....IRONS(a)

Jermaine....JACKSON(x)
Jerome ....HINES(a)
.......................KERN(k)
...................ROBBINS(q)
Jerry ....BOCK(k)
..................BUTLER(x)
..................HERMAN(k)
.......LEWIS(j), LUCAS(f)
...................ORBACH(a)
..........PATE(m), REED(x)
....RICE(l), SEINFELD(j)
.....STILLER(j), VALE(x)
.................Van DYKE(a)
...........................WEST(f)
Jerry Lee ....LEWIS(x)
Jess............WILLARD(g)
Jesse ....HELMS(u)
..................JACKSON(u)
...................OWENS(s)
Jessel, ...GEORGE(j)
Jessi............COLTER(x)
Jessica ....HARPER(a)
....................LANGE(a)
.................MITFORD(z)
...................TANDY(a)
Jesus ....ALOU(e)
Jett, ...JOAN(x)
Jewison, ...NORMAN(x)
Jill........CLAYBURGH(a)
..............EIKENBERRY(a)
.................ST. JOHN(x)
Jillian, ...ANN(a)
Jim ....BACKUS(a)
....BERRY(i), BROWN(l)
.......................CLARK(v)
..................COLBERT(m)
..................COURIER(y)
.......CROCE(x), DALE(a)
........DAVIS(i), DENT(m)
.......HUTTON(a), KAAT(e)
....KELLY(l), LEHRER(o)
................McMAHON(l)
...................MORRISON(x)
..................NABORS(a)
..................NANCE(l,o)
..................PALMER(e)
..................PLUNKETT(l)
.....REEVES(x), RICE(e)
....RYUN(s), SEALS(x)
................STAFFORD(x)
................THOMPSON(z)
..................THORPE(s)
Jimi..........HENDRIX(r, x)
Jimmie.....RODGERS(x)
Jimmy ....BRESLIN(o)
..................BUFFETT(x)
..................CARTER(u)
..................CONNORS(y)
..................DEMARET(m)
..................DORSEY(r)

................DURANTE(j)
..........FOXX(e), PAGE(r)
...........RITZ(j), SMITS(a)
..........................WEBB(k)
Jo ....STAFFORD(x)
..................Van FLEET(a)
Joan ....BAEZ(x)
..................BENNETT(a)
..................BENOIT(s)
..................BLONDELL(a)
..................COLLINS(a)
..................CRAWFORD(a)
..................CUSACK(a)
.....DAVIS(a), DIDION(z)
..................FONTAINE(a)
..................JETT(x), MIRO(c)
..................PLOWRIGHT(a)
..................RIVERS(j)
..................SUTHERLAND(x)
..................Van ARK(a)
Joan D. ....VINGE(z)
Joanna ....KERNS(a)
JoAnne.....CARNER(m)
Joanne................DRU(a)
..................WOODWARD(a)
JoBeth.......WILLIAMS(a)
Jodie ....FOSTER(a)
Jody.....SCHECKTER(v)
Joe ....BARBERA(i)
..................CARTER(e)
..................COCKER(x)
..................DeLOACH(s)
..................DiMAGGIO(e)
..................DUMARS(f)
..................FLYNN(a)
..................FRANKLIN(o)
..................FRAZIER(g)
..................GARAGIOLA(e)
..................JACKSON(x)
..................LOUIS(g)
..................MONTANA(l)
..................MORGAN(e)
..................NAMATH(l)
.....ORTON(z), PESCI(a)
..................PISCOPO(j)
.......SPANO(a), TEX(x)
..................THEISMANN(l)
..................TINKER(e)
..................TURNER(x)
..................WALCOTT(g)
..................WALSH(r)
..................WILLIAMS(x)
Joe Don........BAKER(a)
Joe E. ....BROWN(j)
..................LEWIS(a)
Joel ....GREY(a)
..................McCREA(a)
Joel, ...BILLY(r,x)
Joey ....BISHOP(j)
..........................DEE(x)

Joffe, ...ROLAND(q)
Joffrey, ...ROBERT(a)
Johann.......STRAUSS(k)
Johanna...........SPYRI(z)
Johann Christian............
.................BACH(k)
Johannes ...BRAHMS(k)
.................KEPLER(w)
Johann Sebastian............
.................BACH(k)
Johansson, ...
.................INGEMAR(g)
John.................ADAMS(u)
.....AGAR(a), AMOS(a)
.................ASTIN(a)
..........BARRYMORE(a)
.................BARTH(z)
.................BELUSHI(a,j)
.................BERRYMAN(t)
.................BETJEMAN(t)
.................BRODIE(l,m)
.................BRUNNER(z)
.................BUCHAN(z)
.................BUNYAN(z)
.................BURGOYNE(p)
.....CAGE(k), CANDY(a)
..........CARPENTER(a)
..........CARRADINE(a)
..........CASSAVETES(q)
..........CHANCELLOR(o)
.................CHEEVER(z)
.................CIARDI(t)
.................CLEESE(j)
.................COLTRANE(r)
.................CONSTABLE(c)
.................COOK(m)
.................CUSACK(a)
.................DALY(m)
.................DAVIDSON(x)
.................DENVER(x)
....DEREK(a), DONNE(t)
....DOS PASSOS(z)
.................DRYDEN(t)
.........DUNS SCOTUS(z)
.....ELWAY(l), EVERS(e)
.........FOGERTY(x)
.................FORD(q)
.................FORSYTHE(a)
.................FOWLES(z)
....FRANKENHEIMER(q)
.....GALSWORTHY(z)
.................GARFIELD(a)
.................GAY(k,t)
.................GIELGUD(a)
.................GILBERT(a)
.................GLENN(d, u)
.................GOODMAN(a)
.................GRISHAM(z)
.................HANCOCK(u)
.................HAVLICEK(f)

.................HERSEY(z)
.................HILLERMAN(a)
.................HODIAK(a)
.................HOUSEMAN(a)
....HURT(a), HUSTON(q)
.........IRVING(z), JAY(u)
........KANDER(k), KAY(x)
.......KEATS(t), KERR(a)
.................KNOWLES(z)
.................La FARGE(c)
.................LANDIS(q)
........LARROQUETTE(a)
.................Le CARRE(z)
.................LEGUIZAMO(j)
.................LENNON(r)
.................LITHGOW(a)
.................LOCKE(z)
.................MADDEN(l)
.................MAJOR(u)
.........MALKOVICH(a)
.................MARIN(c)
.................MARSHALL(u)
.................MASEFIELD(t)
.................McENROE(y)
.................McGRAW(e)
........McVIE(r), MILLS(a)
....MILTON(t), MUIR(w)
.................NAPIER(w)
.........NEWCOMBE(y)
.................O'HARA(z)
.................OLERUD(e)
.................OSBORNE(z)
.................PERSHING(p)
.................RAITT(x)
....RATZENBERGER(a)
.................RIGGINS(l)
.................RITTER(a)
.................SAXON(a)
.................SAYLES(q)
......SCHLESINGER(q)
.................SEBASTIAN(x)
.................SHEA(a)
.................SINGLETON(q)
.................SLOAN(c)
.................STAMOS(a)
.................STEINBECK(z)
.................STOCKTON(f)
.................SUNUNU(u)
.................TRAVOLTA(a)
.................TRUMBULL(c)
....TYLER(u), UPDIKE(z)
.................VARLEY(z)
.................WAITE(x)
.............WANAMAKER(h)
.................WATERS(q)
.................WAYNE(a)
.................WILLIAMS(k)
.................WOODEN(f)
.................WYNDHAM(z)
John, ...ELTON(x)

John C. ......CALHOUN(u)
Johncock, ..GORDON(v)
John Cougar........................
..........MELLENCAMP(x)
John D. ....
.............MacDONALD(z)
.........ROCKEFELLER(h)
John F. .....KENNEDY(u)
John Foster......................
.................DULLES(u)
John Gregory.................
.................DUNNE(z)
John Jacob ....ASTOR(h)
John James ....
.............AUDUBON(c,w)
John Kenneth ....
.................GALBRAITH(z)
John L. .....SULLIVAN(g)
John M. ....SYNGE(t,z)
John Maynard.................
.................KEYES(z)
Johnnie ....RAY(x)
John Nance ....
.................GARNER(u)
Johnny ....BENCH(e)
.....CARSON(j), CASH(x)
.....DEPP(a), HART(i)
.................MATHIS(x)
.................MILLER(m)
.................PAYCHECK(x)
.................RIVERS(x)
.........RUTHERFORD(v)
.................TILLOTSON(x)
.................UNITAS(l)
......WEISSMULLER(a,s)
John Paul ....JONES(p)
.................STEVENS(u)
John Peter..ZENGER(o)
John Philip .....SOUSA(k)
John Pierpont ....
.................MORGAN(h)
John Quincy ..ADAMS(u)
Johns, ...GLYNIS(a)
.................JASPER(c)
John Singer ....
.................SARGENT(c)
John Singleton.................
.................COPLEY(c)
Johnson, ...ANDREW(u)
...........ARTE(j), DON(a)
.................HOWARD(e)
.................HOWARD(h)
.................LYNDON(u)
.......MAGIC(f), PHILIP(b)
.................SAMUEL(z)
.....VAN(a), WALTER(e)
John Steuart ..CURRY(c)
Johnston, ...LYNN(i)
John Stuart.........MILL(z)
John W. ......YOUNG(d)

Kavner, ...JULIE(a)
Kawabata,.....................
...............YASUNARI(z)
Kay...............KYSER(r)
..........MEDFORD(a)
.....................STARR(x)
Kay, ...JOHN(x)
Kaye.........BALLARD(a)
Kaye, ...DANNY(a)
Kazan, ...ELIA(q, z)
..................LAINIE(x)
Keach, ...STACY(a)
Kean, ...EDMUND(a)
Keane, ...BIL(i)
Keanu ....REEVES(a)
Keaton, ...BUSTER(a)
...................DIANE(a)
...............MICHAEL(a)
Keats, ...JOHN(t)
Keel, ...HOWARD(x)
Keeler, ...RUBY(a)
Keely ....SMITH(x)
Keenan...............WYNN(a)
Keenan Ivory ....
............WAYANS(j)
Keene ....CURTIS(a)
Keeshan, ...BOB(a)
Kefauver, ...ESTES(u)
Keillor, ...GARRISON(o)
Keir..............DULLEA(a)
Keitel, ...HARVEY(a)
Keith.....CARRADINE(a)
............HERNANDEZ(e)
................HARING(c)
.................JARRETT(r)
..............RICHARDS(r)
Keith, ...BRIAN(a)
.................DAVID(a)
Keller, ...HELEN(z)
Kellerman, ...SALLY(a)
Kelley, ...DeFOREST(a)
.................DONNA(o)
Kelly..........MCGILLIS(a)
Kelly, ...EMMETT(j)
.................GENE(a)
.........GRACE(a), JIM(l)
......................WALT(i)
Kelsey......GRAMMER(a)
Kemp, ...JACK(u)
Ken ....BERRY(a)
..................HOWARD(a)
....................KESEY(z)
.........KERCHEVAL(a)
.................NORTON(g)
....................OLIN(a)
..........ROSEWALL(y)
.............RUSSELL(q)
..................STABLER(l)
..............VENTURI(m)
Kendricks, ...EDDIE(x)

Kennedy, ...
..........ANTHONY M.(u)
....................ARTHUR(a)
.........EDWARD(Ted)(u)
......................ETHEL(u)
.................GEORGE(a)
...JAYNE(a), JOHN F.(u)
.................ROBERT F.(u)
.................WILLIAM(z)
Kenneth ...BRANAGH (q)
Kenny ....BALL(r)
.................LOGGINS(x)
..................ROGERS(x)
Kenton, ...STAN(r)
Kepler, ...JOHANNES(w)
Kercheval, ...KEN(a)
Kermit.........ZARLEY(m)
Kern, ...JEROME(x)
Kerns, ...JOANNA(a)
Kerouac, ...JACK(z)
Kerr, ...DEBORAH(a)
........................JOHN(a)
Kesey, ...KEN(z)
Kevin ....BACON(a)
..................COSTNER(a)
...................DOBSON(a)
.......................KLINE(a)
.............McCARTHY(a)
.................MCHALE(f)
.................MITCHELL(e)
.................NEALON(j)
Key, ...
.......FRANCIS SCOTT(t)
...........................TED(i)
Keyes, ...
......JOHN MAYNARD(z)
Khachaturian, ..ARAM(k)
Khan, ...CHAKA(x)
Khayyám, ...OMAR(t)
Khrushchev, ...NIKITA(u)
Kibbee, ...GUY(a)
Kidder, ...MARGOT(a)
Kidman, ...NICOLE(a)
Kierkegaard, ..SOREN(z)
Kiefer ....
.........SUTHERLAND(a)
Kiker, ...DOUGLAS(o)
Kiki ....DEE(x)
Kilbride, ...PERCY(a)
Kiley, ...RICHARD(x)
Killebrew, ...HARMON(e)
Killy, ..JEAN-CLAUDE(s)
Kilmer, ...JOYCE(t)
........................VAL(a)
Kim ....BASINGER(a)
..................CARNES(x)
...................DARBY(a)
....................HUNTER(a)
....................NOVAK(a)
.................STANLEY(a)

Kiner, ...RALPH(e)
King, ...ALAN(j)
....................BERNARD(f)
.......................BETSY(m)
..............BILLIE JEAN(y)
....................CAROLE(x)
.....CORETTA SCOTT(u)
........................LARRY(o)
.....MARTIN LUTHER(u)
.......................PERRY(a)
......................REGINA(a)
.................STEPHEN(z)
Kingdom, ...ROGER(s)
Kingman, ...DAVE(e)
Kingsley ....AMIS(z)
Kingsley, ...BEN(a)
Kinski, ...NASTASSIA(a)
Kinsley, ...MIKE(o)
Kipling, ...RUDYARD(z)
Kirby ....PUCKETT(e)
Kirby, ...BRUNO(a)
..................DURWARD(a)
Kiri ....Te KANAWA(x)
Kirk..........CAMERON(a)
.....................DOUGLAS(a)
Kirkland, ...LANE(h)
..........................SALLY(a)
Kirkpatrick, ...JEANE(u)
Kirstie..............ALLEY(a)
Kissinger, ...HENRY(u)
Kitchener, ...
.................HORATIO H.(p)
Kite, ...TOM(m)
Kitt, ...EARTHA(a)
Kitty.........CARLISLE(a)
.........................WELLS(x)
Klee, ...PAUL(c)
Klein, ...CALVIN(h)
.....................ROBERT(a)
Klemperer, ...OTTO(r)
.......................WERNER(a)
Kliban, ...B(ernard)(i)
Klimt, ...GUSTAV(c)
Kline, ...FRANZ(c)
.........................KEVIN(a)
Klugman, ...JACK(a)
Knight, ...GLADYS(x)
.............................TED(a)
Knopf, ...ALFRED A.(h)
Knopfler, ...MARK(r)
Knotts, ...DON(a)
Knowles, ...JOHN(z)
Knut ....HAMSUN(z)
Knute............ROCKNE(l)
Koch, ...EDWARD(u)
Kodály, ...ZOLTAN(k)
Kohl, ...HELMUT(u)
Kollwitz, ...KATHE(c)
Konrad....ADENAUER(u)
.....................LORENZ(w)

Lee / Locke

Lee, *continued*.....
.................MICHELE(a)
.....................PEGGY(x)
................ROBERT E.(p)
........SPIKE(q), STAN(i)
Lee A. ....IACOCCA(h)
Lee J. ....COBB(a)
Lefty ....GOMEZ(e)
.....................GROVE(e)
Le Gallienne, ...EVA(a)
Léger, ...FERNAND(c)
Legrand, ...MICHEL(r)
LeGuin, ...URSULA K.(z)
Leguizamo, ...JOHN(j)
Lehár, ...FRANZ(k)
Lehmann, ...LOTTE(x)
Lehrer, ...JIM(o)
Leiber, ...FRITZ(z)
Leibman, ...RON(a)
Leigh, ...JANET(a)
....JENNIFER JASON(a)
.....................VIVIEN(a)
Leinsdorf, ...ERICH(r)
Leisure, ...DAVID(j)
Lema, ...TONY(m)
Le May, ...CURTIS(p)
Lemieux, ...MARIO(n)
Lemmon, ...JACK(a)
Len.............BERMAN(o)
.....................CARIOU(a)
..................DAWSON(l)
.................DYKSTRA(e)
Lena ....HORNE(x)
..........................OLIN(a)
Lendl, ...IVAN(y)
L'Enfant, ...PIERRE(b)
Lenin,
....VLADIMIR ILYICH(u)
Lennon, ...JULIAN(x)
..........JOHN(r, x, z)
Lennox, ...ANNIE(x)
Lenny ....BRUCE(j)
Leno, ...JAY(j)
Lenya, ...LOTTE(a)
Leo ....CARRILLO(a)
.................DELIBES(k)
.................GORCEY(j)
..................SAYER(x)
.................TOLSTOY(z)
Leo G. ....CARROLL(a)
Leon ....AMES(a)
.....................ERROL(a)
.................RUSSELL(x)
..................SPINKS(g)
...TROTSKY(u), URIS(z)
Leonard ....
.............BERNSTEIN(k)
..................COHEN(t,x)
...................MALTIN(o)
....................NIMOY(a)

Leonard, ...ELMORE(z)
....RAY(g), SHELDON(j)
Leonardo......da VINCI(c)
Leoncavallo, ...
.................RUGGIERO(k)
Leonhard ....EULER(w)
Leonid.....BREZHNEV(u)
Leontyne..........PRICE(x)
Leopold ....AUER(r)
.................STOKOWSKI(r)
Leroy "Satchel".............
..........................PAIGE(e)
LeRoy, ...MERVYN(q)
Les.................ASPIN(u)
..................BROWN(r)
Le Sage, ...ALAIN(z)
Lesley ....GORE(x)
.........................STAHL(o)
Lesley Ann .....DOWN(a)
.................WARREN(a)
Leslie.............CARON(a)
.................HOWARD(a)
.................NIELSEN(a)
.................UGGAMS(x)
Lessing, ...DORIS(z)
Letterman, ...DAVID(j)
Levant, ...OSCAR(a)
LeVar ....BURTON(a)
Levin, ...IRA(z)
Levine, ...DAVID(l)
..................IRVING R.(o)
...................JAMES(r)
Levinson, ...BARRY(q)
Levon.............HELM(a,x)
Lew ....AYRES(a)
.................WALLACE(z)
Lewis ....CARROLL(z)
..............MILESTONE(q)
..................STONE(a)
Lewis, ...C.S.(z)
...................CARL(s)
......HUEY(x), JERRY(j)
...............JERRY LEE(x)
...................JOE E.(a)
...................RAMSEY(r)
...................RICHARD(j)
......................SHARI(j)
....SINCLAIR(z), TED(j)
Liam .....O'FLAHERTY(z)
Light, ...JUDITH(a)
Lightfoot, ...GORDON(x)
Lilli ....PALMER(a)
Lillian ....GISH(a)
.................HELLMAN(z)
.................RUSSELL(x)
Lillie ....LANGTRY(a)
Lillie, ...BEATRICE(j)
Lily ....PONS(x)
..................TOMLIN(j)
Lina ...WERTMULLER(a)

Lincoln, ...ABRAHAM(u)
.........................ELMO(a)
Lind, ...JENNY(x)
Linda ....BLAIR(a)
.................DARNELL(a)
......EVANS(a), GRAY(a)
.................HAMILTON(a)
........HUNT(a), LAVIN(a)
...................RONSTADT(x)
Lindbergh...........
.......ANNE MORROW(z)
..................CHARLES(d)
Linden, ...HAL(a)
Lindfors, ...VIVECA(a)
Lindsay ..ANDERSON(q)
..................CROUSE(a)
.................WAGNER(a)
Lindsay, ...VACHEL(t)
Linkletter, ...ART(j)
Linn-Baker, ...MARK(a)
Linus ....PAULING(w)
Lionel.............ATWILL(a)
.................BARRYMORE(a)
..................HAMPTON(r)
......................RICHIE(x)
..................STANDER(a)
Liotta, ...RAY(a)
Lipchitz, ...JACQUES(c)
Lippi, ...FILIPPINO(c)
..............FRA FILIPPO(c)
Lippmann, ..WALTER(o)
Lisa..........ALTHER(z)
.......................BONET(a)
.................EICHHORN(a)
.................HARTMAN(a)
Lise.............MEITNER(w)
Lisi, ...VIRNA(a)
Lister, ...JOSEPH(w)
Liston, ...SONNY(g)
Liszt, ...FRANZ(k)
Lithgow, ...JOHN(a)
Little, ...CLEAVON(a)
.................MALCOLM X(u)
..........................RICH(j)
Littler, ...GENE(m)
Liv ....ULLMANN(a)
Liz...........CLAIBORNE(h)
........................SMITH(o)
Liza ....MINNELLI(a,x)
Lizabeth ....SCOTT(a)
Lloyd...........BENTSEN(u)
.................BRIDGES(a)
......NOLAN(a), PRICE(x)
.....................WANER(e)
Lloyd,
.........CHRISTOPHER(a)
.....................FRANK(q)
.....................HAROLD(j)
Locke, ...JOHN(z)
...................SONDRA(a)

166

Lockhart, ...JUNE(a)
Locklear, ..HEATHER(a)
Lodge, ...
.........HENRY CABOT(u)
Logan, ...ELLA(a)
........................JOSH(q)
Loggia, ...ROBERT(a)
Loggins, ...KENNY(x)
Lola..............FALANA(x)
Lollobrigida, ...GINA(a)
Lom, ...HERBERT(a)
Lombard, ...CAROLE(a)
Lombardi, ...VINCE(l)
Lombardo, ...GUY(r)
Lon ....CHANEY(a)
.............CHANEY, Jr.(a)
London, ...JACK(z)
..........................JULIE(x)
Long, ...HUEY(u)
...................RICHARD(a)
...................SHELLEY(a)
Longfellow, ...HENRY
............WADSWORTH(t)
Loni ....ANDERSON(a)
Lonnie .....DONEGAN(x)
Loos, ...ANITA(z)
Lopez, ...NANCY(m)
..........................TRINI(x)
Lord, ...JACK(a)
Loren D. ..ESTLEMAN(z)
Loren, ...SOPHIA(a)
Lorenz, ...KONRAD(w)
Lorenzo..........LAMAS(a)
Lorenzo, ...FRANK(h)
Loretta...............LYNN(x)
......SWIT(a), YOUNG(a)
Lori.................PETTY(a)
Loring, ...GLORIA(a,x)
Lorna ....LUFT(x)
Lorne...........GREENE(a)
...................MICHAELS(q)
Lorre..............PETER(a)
Lott, ...RONNIE(l)
Lotte..........LEHMANN(x)
........................LENYA(a)
Lou ....BROCK(e)
...................CHRISTIE(x)
...................COSTELLO(j)
...................GEHRIG(e)
...GRAMM(x), GROZA(l)
.....RAWLS(x), REED(x)
Lou Diamond ....
.....................PHILLIPS(a)
Loudon, ...DOROTHY(a)
Louganis, ...GREG(s)
Louis ....ARMSTRONG(r)
.........AUCHINCLOSS(z)
...................BRANDEIS(u)
...........GOSSETT, Jr.(a)
...................JOURDAN(a)

...................LEAKEY(w)
.........................MALLE(q)
........MOUNTBATTEN(p)
...................PASTEUR(w)
.........................PRIMA(r)
.................RUKEYSER(o)
...................SULLIVAN(b)
Louis, ...JOE(g)
Louisa May...ALCOTT(z)
Louis B. ....MAYER(q)
Louis-Dreyfus, ...
.........................JULIA(a)
Louise......FLETCHER(a)
...................LASSER(a)
Louise, ...TINA(a)
Love, ...DARLENE(x)
Love III, ...DAVIS(m)
Lovelace, ..RICHARD(t)
Lovell, Jr., ...JAMES(d)
Lovett, ...LYLE(x)
Lovitz, ...JON(j)
Lowe, ...EDMUND(a)
...........NICK(x), ROB(a)
Lowell, ...AMY(t)
......JAMES RUSSELL(z)
...........................ROBERT(t)
Loy, ...MYRNA(a)
Lubitsch, ...ERNST(q)
Luca .....della ROBBIA(c)
Lucas ....CRANACH(c)
Lucas, ...GEORGE(q)
.........................JERRY(f)
Lucci, ...SUSAN(a)
Luchino......VISCONTI(q)
Luciano ..PAVAROTTI(x)
Lucie ....ARNAZ(a)
Lucille ....BALL(j)
Lucretia ....BORGIA(u)
..........................MOTT(u)
Luckman, ...SID(l)
Ludlum, ...ROBERT(z)
Ludwig ....MIES
............van der ROHE(b)
......van BEETHOVEN(k)
Luft, ...LORNA(x)
Luger, ...RICHARD(u)
Lugosi, ...BELA(a)
Luigi ...BOCCHERINI(k)
...........PIRANDELLO(z)
Luis ....APARICIO(e)
...................BUNUEL(q)
.........................TIANT(e)
Luise ....RAINER(a)
Lukas, ...PAUL(a)
Luke ....PERRY(a)
Lumet, ...SIDNEY(q)
Lunt, ...ALFRED(a)
Lupino, ...IDA(a)
Lupone, ...PATTI(a)
Lurie, ...ALISON(z)

Luther.......BURBANK(w)
..............VANDROSS(x)
Luyendyk, ...ARIE(v)
Lyle..............LOVETT(x)
Lyle, ...SANDY(m)
...................SPARKY(e)
Lymon, ...FRANKIE(x)
Lynch, ...DAVID(q)
Lynda..........CARTER(a)
Lynde, ...PAUL(j)
Lyndon......JOHNSON(u)
Lynn ....ANDERSON(x)
.................JOHNSTON(i)
........................MARTIN(u)
...............REDGRAVE(a)
...........................SWANN(l)
Lynn, ...LORETTA(x)
Lynne, ...JEFF(r)
Lytton ......STRACHEY(z)

M.C. ....ESCHER(c)
Mabel.......NORMAND(a)
Mac.................DAVIS(x)
MacArthur, ...
...................DOUGLAS(p)
Macaulay.......CULKIN(a)
Macchio, ...RALPH(a)
Macdonald ....CAREY(a)
Macdonald, ...
...........................RAMSAY(u)
MacDonald, ...
.................JEANETTE(x)
.....JOHN D.(z), ROSS(z)
MacDowell, ...ANDIE(a)
MacGraw, ...ALI(a)
Machiavelli, ...
...........................NICCOLO(z)
Mack..........SENNETT(q)
Mack, ...CONNIE(e)
MacKenzie.......................
...................PHILLIPS(a)
MacKenzie, ...GISELE(x)
MacLachlan, ...KYLE(a)
MacLaine, ..SHIRLEY(a)
MacLeish, ...
...................ARCHIBALD(t)
MacLeod, ...GAVIN(a)
Macmillan, ..HAROLD(u)
MacMurray, ...FRED(a)
MacNee, ...PATRICK(a)
MacNeil, ...ROBERT(o)
MacNelly, ...JEFF(i)
MacRae,..GORDON(a,x)
Macy, ...BILL(a)
Madden, ...JOHN(l)
Madeline...........KAHN(a)
Madigan, ...AMY(a)
Madison, ...JAMES(u)
Mae............MURRAY(a)
..........................WEST(a)

Magda / Martha

Magda .... GABOR(a)
Maggie .... SMITH(a)
Magic .... JOHNSON(f)
Magnani, ... ANNA(a)
Magritte, ... RENE(c)
Mahalia ..... JACKSON(x)
Mahler, ... GUSTAV(k)
Mahre, ... PHIL(s)
Mailer, ... NORMAN(z)
Main, ... MARJORIE(a)
Major, ... JOHN(u)
Majors, ... LEE(a)
Makeba, ... MIRIAM(x)
Malamud, .. BERNARD(z)
Malcolm .... FORBES(h)
.... McDOWELL(a)
Malcolm-Jamal ....
.... WARNER(a)
Malcolm X .... LITTLE(u)
Malden, ... KARL(a)
Malkovich, ... JOHN(a)
Mallarmé, ...
.... STEPHANE(t)
Malle, ... LOUIS(q)
Mallon, ... MEG(m)
Malone, ... DOROTHY(a)
.... KARL(f), MOSES(f)
Malory, ... THOMAS(z)
Malraux, ... ANDRE(z)
Maltin, ... LEONARD(o)
Mamet, ... DAVID(z)
Mamie ....
.... EISENHOWER(u)
.... Van DOREN(a)
Man .... RAY(c)
Manchester, ...
.... MELISSA(x)
Mancini, ... HENRY(k, r)
Mandel, ... HOWIE(j)
Mandela, ... NELSON(u)
Mandlikova, ... HANA(y)
Mandrel, .. BARBARA(x)
Mandy .... PATINKIN(a)
Manet, ... EDOUARD(c)
Mangione, ... CHUCK(r)
Manilow, ... BARRY(x)
Mankiewicz, ...
.... JOSEPH L.(q)
Mann, ... BARRY(k)
.... DELBERT(q)
.... HERBIE(r)
.... THOMAS(z)
Mansell, ... NIGEL(v)
Mansfield, ... JAYNE(a)
.... KATHERINE(z)
Mantle, ... MICKEY(e)
Mantovani, ...
.... ANNUNZIO(r)
Mapplethorpe, ...
.... ROBERT(c)

Marat, ... JEAN PAUL(u)
Maravich, ... PETE(f)
Marble, ... ALICE(y)
Marc .... CHAGALL(c)
.... COHN(r,x)
.... CONNELLY(z)
Marc, ... FRANZ(c)
Marceau, ... MARCEL(a)
Marcel .... DIONNE(n)
.... DUCHAMP(c)
.... MARCEAU(a)
.... PROUST(z)
Marcello ....
.... MASTROIANNI(a)
March, ... FREDRIC(a)
Marchand, ... NANCY(a)
Marciano, ... ROCKY(g)
Marconi, ...
.... GUGLIELMO(w)
Marcos, ...
.... FERDINAND(u)
.... IMELDA(u)
Marcus .... ALLEN(l)
Margaret ..... ATWOOD(z)
.... COURT(y)
.... DRABBLE(z)
.... DUMONT(a)
.... HAMILTON(a)
.... MEAD(z)
.... MITCHELL(z)
.... O'BRIEN(a)
.... RUTHERFORD(a)
.... SULLAVAN(a)
.... THATCHER(u)
Margaux ....
.... HEMINGWAY(a)
Marge ...... CHAMPION(a)
Margolin, ... JANET(a)
Margot ...... FONTEYN(a)
.... KIDDER(a)
Maria .... BUENO(y)
.... CALLAS(x)
.... MONTESSORI(w)
.... OUSPENSKAYA(a)
.... SCHELL(a)
.... SHRIVER(o)
Maria Conchita ....
.... ALONSO(a)
Mariah .... CAREY(x)
Marian .... ANDERSON(x)
.... MERCER(a)
Marianne ... FAITHFUL(x)
Marichal, ... JUAN(e)
Marie .... CURIE(w)
.... DRESSLER(a)
.... OSMOND(x)
.... WILSON(a)
Mariel ... HEMINGWAY(a)
Mariette ...... HARTLEY(a)
Marilu .... HENNER(a)

Marilyn .... FRENCH(z)
.... HORNE(x)
.... MONROE(a)
Marin, ... CHEECH(j)
.... JOHN(c)
Marina .... SIRTIS(a)
Marino, ... DAN(l)
Mario .... ANDRETTI(v)
.... CUOMO(u), LANZA(x)
.... LEMIEUX(n)
.... PUZO(z)
.... Van PEEBLES(a)
Marion .... ROSS(a)
Maris, ... ROGER(e)
Marjorie .... MAIN(a)
Mark ....
...... CALCAVECCHIA(m)
.... CARRIER(l)
.... CLAYTON(l)
.... DUPER(l)
.... GASTINEAU(l)
.... HAMILL(a)
.... HARMON(a)
.... KNOPFLER(r)
.... LINN-BAKER(a)
.... McGWIRE(e)
.... MESSIER(n)
.... O'MEARA(m)
.... ROTHKO(c)
.... RUSSELL(o)
.... RYPIEN(l), SPITZ(s)
.... TWAIN(z)
Markie .... POST(a)
Marla .... GIBBS(a)
Marlee .... MATLIN(a)
Marlene ..... DIETRICH(a)
Marley, ... BOB(x)
Marlo .... THOMAS(a)
Marlon .... BRANDO(a)
Marlowe, ...
.... CHRISTOPHER(t)
Marquis .... DON(i)
Marr, ... DAVE(m)
Marriner, ... NEVILLE(r)
Marsalis, ...
.... BRANFORD(r)
.... WYNTON(r)
Marsh, ... JEAN(a)
.... NGAIO(z)
Marsha .... MASON(a)
Marshall .... MCLUHAN(z)
Marshall, ... E.G.(a)
.... GEORGE C.(p)
.... HERBERT(a)
.... JOHN(u), PENNY(a)
.... PETER(a)
.... THURGOOD(u)
Martha .... GRAHAM(a)
.... GRIMES(z)
.... REEVES(x)

Marti, ...JOSE(t)
Martin...........BALSAM(a)
...................BUBER(z)
.................LANDAU(a)
.............LAWRENCE(j)
.......MILNER(a), MULL(j)
.............SCORSESE(q)
.....SHEEN(a), SHORT(j)
.............Van BUREN(u)
Martin, ...DEAN(a, x)
.........DICK(j), LYNN(u)
.......MARY(a), ROSS(a)
.......STEVE(a), TONY(x)
Martina.......................
.........NAVRATILOVA(y)
Martin Luther .....KING(u)
Martino, ...AL(x)
Marty ....BALIN(x)
.............FELDMAN(a)
...........ROBBINS(x)
Marv ....ALBERT(o)
Marvin............GAYE(x)
..............HAGLER(g)
.........HAMLISCH(k)
Marvin, ...LEE(a)
Marx, ...
....CHICO (Leonard)(j)
.....GROUCHO (Julius)(j)
.........GUMMO (Milton)(j)
.......HARPO (Arthur)(j)
.....................Karl(u)
........ZEPPO (Herbert)(j)
Mary..............ASTOR(a)
............CASSATT(c)
.....FRANN(a), GROSS(j)
................MARTIN(a)
.........McCARTHY(z)
.............PICKFORD(a)
................SHELLEY(z)
.......STEENBURGEN(a)
................TRAVERS(x)
.................WELLS(x)
Mary Beth.........HURT(a)
Mary Elizabeth..............
....MASTRANTONIO(a)
Mary Higgins ..CLARK(z)
Mary Joe.....................
...........FERNANDEZ(y)
Mary Lou......RETTON(s)
Mary Stuart..................
...........MASTERSON(a)
Mary Tyler.....MOORE(a)
Masefield, ...JOHN(t)
Masekela, ...HUGH(r)
Mason...........ADAMS(a)
.............WILLIAMS(r)
Mason, ...JACKIE(j)
.................JAMES(a)
.............MARSHA(a)
Massenet, ...JULES(k)

Massey, ..RAYMOND(a)
Masters, ...
.............EDGAR LEE(t)
Masterson, ...
.........MARY STUART(a)
Mastrantonio, ...
....MARY ELIZABETH(a)
Mastroianni, ...
.............MARCELLO(a)
Matheson, ...TIM(a)
Mathews, ...EDDIE(e)
Mathewson, ...
..................CHRISTY(e)
Mathias, ...BOB(s)
Mathis, ...JOHNNY(x)
Matisse, ...HENRI(c)
Matlin, ...MARLEE(a)
Mats.........WILANDER(y)
Matt ....BAHR(l)
.....................BIONDI(s)
..................DILLON(a)
...............GROENING(i)
.................WILLIAMS(e)
Mattea, ...KATHY(x)
Matthau, ...WALTER(a)
Matthew......ARNOLD(t)
.............BRODERICK(a)
................MODINE(a)
Mattingly, ...DON(e)
Matty..............ALOU(e)
Mature, ...VICTOR(a)
Maud ....ADAMS(a)
Maugham, ...
.........W. SOMERSET(z)
Maureen ....
.............CONNOLLY(y)
.............McGOVERN(x)
.................O'HARA(a)
.............O'SULLIVAN(a)
.............STAPLETON(a)
Mauriac, ..FRANCOIS(z)
Maurice..........................
.............CHEVALIER(a)
.......GIBB(x), RAVEL(k)
..................SENDAK(z)
...................UTRILLO(c)
Max.....ABRAMOVITZ(b)
.......................BAER(g)
...............BECKMANN(c)
.............BEERBOHM(z)
.....................BORN(w)
.....................ERNST(c)
......GAIL(a), PLANCK(w)
.............SCHMELING(g)
.............Von SYDOW(a)
.................WRIGHT(a)
Maxene ....ANDREWS(x)
Maxey..........................
.........ROSENBLOOM(g)
Maxfield ......PARRISH(c)

Maxim............GORKY(z)
Maximilian ....SCHELL(a)
Maxwell.......................
.............ANDERSON(z)
Maxwell, ...
.........JAMES CLERK(w)
May..............ROBSON(a)
.....................WHITTY(a)
May, ...ELAINE(j)
Maya...........ANGELOU(t)
Mayer, ...LOUIS B.(q)
Mayfield, ...CURTIS(x)
Maynard, ...DON(l)
Mayo, ...VIRGINIA(a)
Mays, ...WILLIE(e)
Mazursky, ...PAUL(q)
McArdle, ...ANDREA(a)
McBain ....ED(z)
McCallum, ...DAVID(a)
McCarthy, ..ANDREW(a)
.................EUGENE(u)
.................JOSEPH(u)
.......KEVIN(a), MARY(z)
McCartney, ...PAUL(r)
McCarver, ...TIM(e)
McClanahan, ...RUE(a)
McClure, ...DOUG(a)
McClurg, ...EDIE(a)
McCovey, ...WILLIE(e)
McCrea, ...JOEL(a)
McCullers, ..CARSON(z)
McDaniel, ...HATTIE(a)
McDonald, ...
.................MICHAEL(x)
McDowall, ...RODDY(a)
McDowell, ...
.................MALCOLM(a)
McEnroe, ...JOHN(y)
McEntire, ...REBA(x)
McFadden, ...GATES(a)
McFarland, ..SPANKY(a)
McFerrin, ...BOBBY(x)
McGavin, ...DARREN(a)
McGee, ...WILLIE(e)
McGillis, ...KELLY(a)
McGoohan, ...
.................PATRICK(a)
McGovern, ...
.................GEORGE(u)
.................MAUREEN(x)
McGraw, ...JOHN(e)
.....................TUG(e)
McGriff, ...FRED(e)
McGuinn, ...ROGER(x)
McGuire, ..DOROTHY(a)
McGwire, ...MARK(e)
McHale, ...KEVIN(f)
McKean, ...MICHAEL(a)
McKellen, ...IAN(a)
McKinley, ...WILLIAM(u)

MABEL NORMAND
MABEL MERCEL

McLaglen / Millet

McLaglen, ...VICTOR(a)
McLean,................................
............STEVENSON(a)
McLean, ...DON(x)
McLuhan,...............................
...............MARSHALL(z)
McMahon, ...ED(j)
........................JIM(l)
McMurtry, ...LARRY(z)
McNichol, ...KRISTY(a)
McPhatter, ...CLYDE(x)
McQueen, ...
.............BUTTERFLY(a)
.....................STEVE(a)
McRaney, ...GERALD(a)
McVie, ...CHRISTINE(x)
.......................JOHN(r)
Mead, ...MARGARET(z)
Meade, ...GEORGE(p)
Meadows, ...AUDREY(a)
.......................JAYNE(a)
Meaney, ...COLM(a)
Meany, ...GEORGE(h)
Meara, ...ANNE(a)
Mears, ...RICK(v)
Medford, ...KAY(a)
Medley, ...BILL(x)
Meek, ...DONALD(a)
Meg ....MALLON(m)
........RYAN(a), TILLY(a)
Megan.......FOLLOWS(a)
..........GALLAGHER(a)
Mehta, ...ZUBIN(r)
Meir, ...GOLDA(u)
Meitner, ...LISE(w)
Mel..................ALLEN(o)
.....BLANC(j), BLOUNT(l)
....................BROOKS(j,q)
.........................FERRER(a)
........GIBSON(a), OTT(e)
........STOTTLEMYRE(e)
......TILLIS(x), TORME(x)
Melanie......GRIFFITH(a)
Melba ....MOORE(x)
Melba, ...NELLIE(x)
Melina .....MERCOURI(a)
Melissa.......GILBERT(a)
.........MANCHESTER(x)
Mellencamp, ...
.........JOHN COUGAR(x)
Mellon, ...ANDREW(h)
Melville, ...HERMAN(z)
Melvyn ......DOUGLAS(a)
Menachem ......BEGIN(u)
Mencken, ...H.L.(z)
Mendel, ...GREGOR(w)
Mendelssohn, ..FELIX(k)
Mendes, ...SERGIO(r)
Menjou, ...ADOLPHE(a)
Menken, ...HELEN(a)

Menotti, ...
.............GIAN-CARLO(k)
Menuhin, ...YEHUDI(r)
Merce.......................................
.........CUNNINGHAM(a)
Mercer, ...MARIAN(a)
.............................RAY(g)
Mercouri, ...MELINA(a)
Mercury, ...FREDDIE(x)
Meredith.......BAXTER(a)
Meredith, ..BURGESS(a)
Mérimée, ..PROSPER(z)
Merle ....HAGGARD(x)
.................OBERON(a)
Merlin ....OLSEN(a,l)
Merman, ...ETHEL(x)
Merrick, ...DAVID(q)
Merrill, ...DINA(a)
.............................GARY(a)
.....................ROBERT(x)
Merv ....GRIFFIN(x)
Mervyn ....LEROY(q)
Meryl ....STREEP(a)
Messier, ...MARK(n)
Metcalf, ...LAURIE(a)
Meyerbeer, ...
.................GIACOMO(k)
Meyers, ...ARI(a)
Mia ....FARROW(a)
Michael ....ANSARA(a)
....CAINE(a), CHANG(y)
........................CIMINO(q)
.............CRAWFORD(a)
.............CRICHTON(z)
....CURTIZ(q), DORN(a)
.................DOUGLAS(a)
.................DUKAKIS(u)
.....................EISNER(h)
...................FARADAY(w)
........................GROSS(a)
.....................JACKSON(x)
.......................JORDAN(a)
.......................KEATON(a)
.....................LANDON(a)
.................LEARNED(a)
.............McDONALD(x)
.....................McKEAN(a)
.................MORIARTY(a)
.....................NESMITH(r)
.....................ONTKEAN(a)
............................PALIN(j)
.................REDGRAVE(a)
.......................RENNIE(a)
.....SPINKS(g), TODD(a)
.......................TUCKER(a)
...WILDING(a), YORK(a)
Michael, ...GEORGE(x)
Michael J. ....FOX(a)
Michaels, ...AL(o)
.....................LORNE(q)

Michel ....FOKINE(a)
.....LEGRAND(r), NEY(p)
Michele........GREENE(a)
.............................LEE(a)
Michelle.....PFEIFFER(a)
.....................PHILLIPS(a)
Michelson, ..ALBERT(w)
Michener, ..JAMES A.(z)
Mick......FLEETWOOD(x)
.........................JAGGER(x)
Mickey..........GILLEY(x)
.....................MANTLE(e)
.....................ROONEY(a)
.......................ROURKE(a)
.....................SPILLANE(z)
Middlecoff, ...CARY(m)
Midler, ...BETTE(a, x)
Miës van der Rohe ....
.....................LUDWIG(b)
Mifune, ...TOSHIRO(a)
Mike ....CONNORS(a)
...........................DITKA(l)
.....................FARRELL(a)
.............................HILL(m)
.....................HULBERT(m)
.....................KINSLEY(o)
.........................MYERS(j)
.....................NICHOLS(q)
.....................OLDFIELD(r)
.............................POST(r)
...........RUTHERFORD(r)
.....................SCHMIDT(e)
.........................TYSON(g)
.....................WALLACE(o)
Mikhail ....
.........BARYSHNIKOV(a)
.........GORBACHEV(u)
Mikita, ...STAN(n)
Milan ....KUNDERA(z)
Milburn ....STONE(a)
Mildred.......NATWICK(a)
Miles ....DAVIS(r)
Miles, ...SARAH(a)
...............................VERA(a)
Milestone, ...LEWIS(q)
Mill, ...JOHN STUART(z)
Milland, ...RAY(a)
Millard.......FILLMORE(u)
Millay, ...
....EDNA ST. VINCENT(t)
Miller, Mabel ....ANN(a)
.......................ARTHUR(z)
....DENNIS(j), GLENN(r)
.........................HENRY(z)
.....................JOHNNY(m)
.............JONATHAN(a,q,z)
.....MITCH(r), ROGER(x)
.............STEVE(r), SUE(z)
Millet, ...
.....JEAN-FRANCOIS(c)

Mills, ...DONNA(a)
.....HAYLEY(a), JOHN(a)
Milne, ...A.A.(z)
Milner, ...MARTIN(a)
Milo ....O'SHEA(a)
Milos ....FORMAN(q)
Milsap, ...RONNIE(x)
Milton...............AGER(k)
......BERLE(j), CANIFF(i)
Milton, ...JOHN(t)
Mimi ....ROGERS(a)
Mineo, ...SAL(a)
Mingus, ...CHARLIE(r)
Minnelli, ...LIZA(a,x)
.................VINCENTE(q)
Minnie ....PEARL(x)
.................RIPERTON(x)
Minuit, ...PETER(u)
Miranda, ...CARMEN(a)
Miriam ....HOPKINS(a)
...................MAKEBA(x)
Miró, ...JOAN(c)
Mischa ....ELMAN(r)
Mishima, ...YUKIO(z)
Mistral, ...FREDERIC(t)
................GABRIELA(t)
Mitch ....MILLER(r)
....................RYDER(r)
Mitchell, ...ANDREA(o)
................CAMERON(a)
..........JONI(x), KEVIN(e)
...........MARGARET(z)
Mitchum, ...ROBERT(a)
Mitford, ...JESSICA(z)
.....................NANCY(z)
Mitterrand, ...
.................FRANCOIS(u)
Mitzi ....GAYNOR(a)
Mix, ...TOM(a)
Mize, ...LARRY(m)
Mochrie, ...DOTTIE(m)
Modest..........................
.......MOUSSORGSKY(k)
Modigliani, ..AMEDEO(c)
Modine, ...MATTHEW(a)
Moe ....HOWARD(j)
Moffo, ...ANNA(x)
Mohandas ....GANDHI(u)
Moira ....SHEARER(a)
Molière, ...
.......JEAN BAPTISTE(z)
Molinaro, ...AL(a)
Moll, ...RICHARD(a)
Molly ......RINGWALD(a)
.......................YARD(u)
Mona.........Van DUYN(a)
..............WASHBURN(a)
Mondale ......WALTER(u)
Mondrian, ...PIET(c)
Monet, ...CLAUDE(c)

Money, ...EDDIE(x)
Monica ....SELES(y)
Monk, ...ART(l)
.............THELONIOUS(r)
Monroe, ...JAMES(u)
...................MARILYN(a)
....................VAUGHN(x)
Montalban, ...
....................RICARDO(a)
Montana, ...BOB(i)
...........................JOE(l)
Montessori, ...MARIA(w)
Montgomery .....CLIFT(a)
Montgomery, ...
.................ELIZABETH(a)
......ROBERT(a), WES(r)
Monty ....HALL(a)
..............WOOLLEY(a)
Moody, ...ORVILLE(m)
........................RON(a)
Moon, ...WARREN(l)
Moore, ...ARCHIE(g)
.................CLAYTON(a)
.............CLEMENT C.(t)
.....DEMI(a), DUDLEY(a)
.....................HENRY(c)
............MARY TYLER(a)
...MELBA(x), ROGER(a)
.....................THOMAS(t)
Moorehead, ..AGNES(a)
Moran ....ERIN(a)
Moranis, ...RICK(a)
Moravia, ...ALBERTO(z)
More, ...THOMAS(z)
Moreau, ...JEANNE(a)
Moreno, ...RITA(a)
Morey ...AMSTERDAM(j)
Morgan ....CHILDLIFA(a)
................FAIRCHILD(a)
.................FREEMAN(a)
Morgan, ...HARRY(a)
..........HENRY(j), JOE(e)
.....JOHN PIERPONT(h)
Moriarty, ...MICHAEL(a)
Morita, ...PAT(a)
Morley ....SAFER(o)
Moro, ...ANTONIO(c)
Morrall, ...EARL(l)
Morris, ...CHESTER(a)
........................GREG(a)
Morrison, ...JIM(x)
...........TONI(z), VAN(x)
Morrow, ...VIC(a)
Morse, ...ROBERT(a)
...................SAMUEL(w)
Mort ....DRUCKER(i)
.......SAHL(j), WALKER(i)
Moses ....MALONE(f)
Moses, ...EDWIN(s)
Moshe ....ARENS(u)
......................DAYAN(p)

Moss ....HART(z)
Mostel, ...ZERO(a)
Motherwell, ..ROBERT(c)
Mott, ...LUCRETIA(u)
Mountbatten, ..LOUIS(p)
Mourning, ...ALONZO(f)
Moussorgsky,.................
.........................MODEST(k)
Mowbray, ...ALAN(a)
Moyers, ...BILL(o)
Moynihan, ...
......DANIEL PATRICK(u)
Mozart, ...WOLFGANG
.................AMADEUS(k)
Muammar ...QADDAFI(u)
Mubarak, ...HOSNI(u)
Mudd, ...ROGER(o)
Muhammad.........ALI(g)
Muldaur, ...DIANA(a)
Mulgrew, ...KATE(a)
Muir, ...FRANK(z)
........................JOHN(w)
Mull, ...MARTIN(j)
Mullin, ...CHRIS(f)
Mulligan, ...GERRY(r)
...................RICHARD(a)
Mulroney, ...BRIAN(u)
Mumford, ...THAD(z)
Munch, ...EDVARD(c)
Muni, ...PAUL(a)
Munro,........H.H.(Saki)(z)
Murdoch, ...IRIS(z)
....................RUPERT(h)
Muriel ....SPARK(z)
Murillo, ...
.................BARTOLOME(c)
Murphy, ...AUDIE(a)
.......DALE(e), EDDIE(a,j)
.......................GEORGE(a)
Murray, ...ANNE(x)
...............................BILL(j)
..............BRIAN DOYLE(j)
..........DON(a), EDDIE(e)
...........................MAE(a)
Murrow,..EDWARD R.(o)
Musante, ...TONY(a)
Musburger, ...BRENT(o)
Musial, ...STAN(e)
Muskie, ...EDMUND(u)
Mussolini, ...BENITO(u)
Myers, ...MIKE(j)
Myerson, ...BESS(a)
Myra ....HESS(a)
Myrna.................LOY(a)
Myron ....COHEN(j)

N.C. ....WYETH(c)
Nabokov, ..VLADIMIR(z)
Nabors, ...JIM(a)
Nader, ...RALPH(o)

Nadia / Novello

Nadia.......COMANECI(s)
Nadine ...GORDIMER(z)
Nagel, ...CONRAD(a)
Nagurski, ...BRONKO(l)
Nagy, ...IMRE(u)
Naipaul, ...V.S.(z)
Naish, ...J.CARROL(a)
Naldi, ...NITA(a)
Namath, ...JOE(l)
Nance, ...JIM(l,o)
Nancy..............ALLEN(a)
..............DUSSAULT(a)
......KULP(a), LOPEZ(m)
..............MARCHAND(a)
..................MITFORD(z)
..................REAGAN(u)
..................WALKER(a)
....................WILSON(x)
Nanette ....FABRAY(a)
Naomi ....JUDD(x)
Napier, ...JOHN(w)
Napoleon ....
..........BONAPARTE(p)
Nash, ...GRAHAM(x)
....................OGDEN(t)
Nashe, ...THOMAS(z)
Nasser, ...GAMAL(u)
Nast, ...THOMAS(i)
Nastase, ...ILIE(y)
Nastassia........KINSKI(a)
Nat "King" ....COLE(x)
Natalie ....COLE(x)
......................WOOD(a)
Nate ....ARCHIBALD(f)
...........THURMOND(f)
Nathan ....HALE(p)
Nathanael........WEST(z)
Nathaniel....CURRIER(c)
..........HAWTHORNE(z)
Natwick, ...MILDRED(a)
Navratilova, ...
..................MARTINA(y)
Nazimova, ...ALLA(a)
Neagle, ...ANNA(a)
Neal ....HEFTI(r)
Neal, ...PATRICIA(a)
Neale ....FRASER(y)
Nealon, ...KEVIN(j)
Ned..............BEATTY(a)
....................ROREM(o)
....................SPARKS(a)
Negri, ...POLA(a)
Nehemiah ....
..................PERSOFF(a)
Nehru, ...
..........JAWAHARLAL(u)
Neil......ARMSTRONG(d)
..................DIAMOND(x)
....................SEDAKA(x)
....SIMON(z), YOUNG(x)

Neill, ...SAM(a)
Nell ....CARTER(a)
Nellie ....MELBA(x)
Nelligan, ...KATE(a)
Nelson ....EDDY(x)
..................MANDELA(a)
....................PIQUET(v)
....................RIDDLE(r)
Nelson, ...BYRON(m)
........ED(a), HARRIET(a)
..................HORATIO(p)
........JUDD(a), OZZIE(a)
....RICKY(x), WILLIE(x)
Nelson A. ....
........ROCKEFELLER(u)
Neruda, ...JAN(t)
....................PABLO(z)
Nesmith, ...MICHAEL(r)
Nettles, ...GRAIG(e)
Neuwirth, ...BEBE(a)
Nevers, ...ERNIE(l)
Neville ....
........CHAMBERLAIN(u)
..................MARRINER(r)
Newcombe, ...JOHN(y)
Newhart, ...BOB(j)
Newley, ...ANTHONY(x)
Newman, ...PAUL(a)
....................RANDY(x)
Newt........GINGRICH(u)
Newton, ...ISAAC(w)
....JUICE(x), WAYNE(x)
Newton-John, ...
....................OLIVIA(x)
Ney, ...MICHEL(z)
Ngaio ....MARSH(z)
Niccolo ....
............MACHIAVELLI(z)
....................PAGANINI(r)
Nicholas ....
........COPERNICUS(w)
Nichols, ...MIKE(q)
........................RED(r)
Nicholson, ...JACK(a)
Nick ....FALDO(m)
......LOWE(x), NOLTE(a)
....................PRICE(m)
Nicklaus, ...JACK(m)
Nicks, ...STEVIE(x)
Nicol.....WILLIAMSON(a)
Nicolai............RIMSKY-
..............KORSAKOV(k)
Nicolas ....CAGE(a)
....................ROEG(q)
Nicole ....KIDMAN(a)
Niekro, ...PHIL(e)
Niels ....BOHR(w)
Nielsen, ...LESLIE(a)
Nietzsche, ...
..............FRIEDRICH(z)

Nigel ....BRUCE(a)
..................MANSELL(v)
Nijinsky, ...VASLAV(a)
Niki ....LAUDA(v)
Nikita..........................
..............KHRUSHCHEV(u)
Nikola ....TESLA(w)
Nikolai ....GOGOL(z)
Nilsson, ...BIRGIT(a)
..........................HARRY(x)
Nimitz, ...CHESTER(p)
Nimoy, ...LEONARD(a)
Nin ....ANAIS(z)
Nina.................FOCH(a)
..................SIMONE(x)
Nino ....BENVENUTI(g)
Nipsey ....RUSSELL(j)
Nita ....NALDI(a)
Nitschke, ...RAY(l)
Niven, ...DAVID(a)
....................LARRY(z)
Nixon, ...OTIS(e)
....PAT(u), RICHARD(u)
Noah ....BEERY(a)
Noah, ...YANNICK(y)
Noam........CHOMSKY(z)
Nobel ....ALFRED(w)
Noel ....HARRISON(x)
..................COWARD(k,z)
Noguchi, ...ISAMU(c)
Nolan ....RYAN(e)
Nolan, ...LLOYD(a)
Nolte, ...NICK(a)
Noone, ...PETER(x)
Nora ....EPHRON(z)
Norbert ....WIENER(w)
Norm ....SNEAD(l)
.........Van BROCKLIN(l)
Norma ....SHEARER(a)
..................TALMADGE(a)
Norman ......COUSINS(z)
....FELL(a), JEWISON(q)
..................MAILER(z)
..................ROCKWELL(c)
........SCHWARZKOPF(p)
..................THOMAS(u)
Norman, ...GREG(m)
Normand, ...MABEL(a)
Norris, ...CHUCK(a)
North, ...ANDY(m)
..................OLIVER(p)
..................SHEREE(a)
Norton, ...ANDRE(z)
..........................KEN(g)
Norvo, ...RED(r)
Novak, ...KIM(a)
..................ROBERT(o)
Novarro, ...RAMON(a)
Novello, ...DON(j)
..........................IVOR(a)

Novotna, ...JANA(y)
Noyes, ...ALFRED(t)
Nugent, ...TED(r)
Nunn, ...SAM(u)
Nureyev, ...RUDOLF(a)
Nurmi, ...PAAVO(s)

O.J. ....SIMPSON(l)
Oakie, ...JACK(a)
Oates, ...
........JOYCE CAROL(z)
...............WARREN(a)
Oberon, ...MERLE(a)
O'Brian, ...HUGH(a)
O'Brien, ...EDMOND(a)
...............MARGARET(a)
.........................PAT(a)
Ocasek, ...RIC(x)
O'Casey, ...SEAN(z)
Ocean, ...BILLY(x)
Ochs, ...ADOLPH(o)
.........................PHIL(x)
O'Connell, ..ARTHUR(a)
O'Connor, ...
...............CARROLL(a)
.......DES(x), DONALD(a)
..............FLANNERY(z)
...........SANDRA DAY(u)
.......SINEAD(x), UNA(a)
Octavio ....PAZ(t)
O'Day, ...ANITA(x)
Odets, ...CLIFFORD(z)
Oerter, ...AL(s)
Offenbach, ...
...............JACQUES(k)
O'Flaherty, ...LIAM(z)
Ogden ....NASH(t)
Ogle, ...BRET(m)
O'Grady, ...SEAN(g)
O'Hara, ...JOHN(z)
................MAUREEN(a)
O'Keefe, ...DENNIS(a)
O'Keeffe, ...GEORGIA(c)
Okker, ...TOM(y)
Olaf.......STAPLEDON(z)
Oland, ...WARNER(a)
Oldenburg, ...CLAES(c)
Oldfield, ...MIKE(r)
Oldman, ...GARY(a)
Ole.................OLSEN(j)
Olerud, ...JOHN(e)
Olga...........KORBUT(s)
Olin, ...KEN(a), LENA(a)
Oliva, ...TONY(e)
Oliver.....CROMWELL(u)
.............GOLDSMITH(z)
.....HARDY(j), NORTH(p)
......REED(a), STONE(q)
Oliver Wendell ....
................HOLMES(u)

Olivia..........................
........De HAVILLAND(a)
.......NEWTON-JOHN(x)
Olivier, ...LAURENCE(a)
Olmos, ...
.....EDWARD JAMES(a)
Olmsted.......................
.........FREDERICK L.(b)
Olof ....PALME(u)
Olsen, ...MERLIN(a,l)
.............................OLE(j)
Olympia .....DUKAKIS(a)
Omar ....BRADLEY(p)
..............KHAYYAM(t)
.....................SHARIF(a)
O'Meara, ...MARK(m)
Onassis, ...
...............ARISTOTLE(h)
O'Neal, ...PATRICK(a)
.........................RYAN(a)
.............SHAQUILLE(f)
......................TATUM(a)
O'Neill, ...ED(a)
.....................EUGENE(z)
........................OONA(a)
Ono, ...YOKO(c, x)
Ontkean, ...MICHAEL(a)
Oona ....O'NEILL(a)
Oppenheimer, ...
................J. ROBERT(w)
Oprah........WINFREY(o)
Orbach, ...JERRY(a)
Orbison, ...ROY(x)
Orel ....HERSHISER(e)
Orlando........CEPEDA(e)
Orlando........TONY(x)
Ormandy, ...EUGENE(r)
Ornette ......COLEMAN(r)
Orozco, ...
.....JOSE CLEMENTE(c)
Orr, ...BOBBY(n)
Orrin, ...HATCH(u)
Orson................BEAN(a)
................WELLES(q)
Orton, ...JOE(z)
Orville ....MOODY(m)
.......................WRIGHT(w)
Orwell, ...GEORGE(z)
Osborne, ...JOHN(z)
Osbourne, ...OZZY(x)
Oscar ....
........HAMMERSTEIN(r)
..................LEVANT(a)
.............ROBERTSON(f)
......................WILDE(z)
O'Shea, ...MILO(a)
Oslin, ...K.T.(x)
Osmond, ...DONNY(x)
.......................MARIE(x)
Ossie ....DAVIS(a)

O'Sullivan, ...
...............MAUREEN(a)
Otis ....NIXON(e)
..................REDDING(x)
Otis, ...ELISHA(w)
O'Toole, ...ANNETTE(a)
.........................PETER(a)
Ott, ...MEL(e)
Ottis........ANDERSON(l)
Otto.............GRAHAM(l)
.........................HAHN(w)
............KLEMPERER(r)
..................KRUGER(a)
...............PREMINGER(q)
Ottorino .....RESPIGHI(k)
Ouspenskaya, ...
.........................MARIA(a)
Ovett, ...STEVE(s)
Owen, ...REGINALD(a)
Owens, ...JESSE(s)
Oz, ...AMOS(z)
Ozawa, ...SEIJI(r)
Ozzie ....NELSON(a)
.........................SMITH(e)
Ozzy.......OSBOURNE(x)

P.G. ....WODEHOUSE(z)
Paar, ...JACK(j)
Paavo ....NURMI(s)
Pablo............CASALS(r)
...................NERUDA(z)
....................PICASSO(c)
Pacino, ...AL(a)
Packwood, ...BOB(u)
Paderewski, ...
...........................IGNACE(k)
Paganini, ...NICCOLO(r)
Page, ...GERALDINE(a)
.......JIMMY(r), PATTI(x)
Paige, ...JANIS(a)
...LEROY"SATCHEL"(e)
Paine, ...THOMAS(z)
Palance, ...JACK(a)
Paley, ...WILLIAM S.(h)
Palin, ...MICHAEL(j)
Palme, ...OLOF(u)
Palmer, ...ARNOLD(m)
...........BETSY(a), JIM(e)
......LILLI(a), ROBERT(x)
......................SANDRA(m)
Pam ....DAWBER(a)
.........................SHRIVER(y)
Pancho...GONZALES(y)
.........................VILLA(u)
Paolo ....UCCELLO(c)
..................VERONESE(c)
Papas, ...IRENE(a)
Papp, ...JOSEPH(q)
Pär ....LAGERKVIST(z)
Parker ..STEVENSON(a)

Quayle, ...DAN(u)
Quentin.............CRISP(z)
Quincy..............JONES(r)
Quinn, ...AIDAN(u)
...............ANTHONY(a)
..........JANE BRYANT(o)

R. Buckminster ....
.................FULLER(b)
R.D. ....LAING(w)
Ra, ...SUN(r)
Rabbitt, ...EDDIE(x)
Rabe, ...DAVID(z)
Rabelais, ...
...............FRANCOIS(z)
Rabin, ...ITZHAK(u)
Rabindranath ....
...................TAGORE(z)
Rachel ....CROTHERS(z)
.................HUNTER(a)
......................WARD(a)
Rachins, ...ALAN(a)
Rachmaninoff, ...
...................SERGEI(k)
Racine, ...JEAN(z)
Radner, ...GILDA(a)
Rae, ...CHARLOTTE(a)
Rae Dawn .....CHONG(a)
Rafferty, ...GERRY(x)
Raft, ...GEORGE(a)
Rahal, ...BOBBY(v)
Rainer, ...LUISE(a)
Rainer Maria .....RILKE(t)
Raines, ...TIM(e)
Rains, ...CLAUDE(a)
Raisa ...GORBACHEV(u)
Raitt, ...BONNIE(x)
.......................JOHN(x)
Ralph ....BELLAMY(a)
................BUNCHE(u)
...................ELLISON(z)
.......................KINER(e)
...................LAUREN(c)
.................MACCHIO(a)
......................NADER(o)
.........RICHARDSON(a)
....WAITE(a), WENGE(o)
Ralph Waldo ....
.................EMERSON(t)
Ramon ....NOVARRO(a)
Rampal, ...
...........JEAN-PIERRE(r)
Ramsay ....
...........MacDONALD(u)
Ramsey............LEWIS(r)
Rand, ...AYN(z)
.......................SALLY(a)
Randall, ...TONY(a)
Randolph........SCOTT(a)
Randolph, ...JOYCE(a)

Randy.........NEWMAN(x)
....QUAID(a), TRAVIS(x)
Raoul ....DUFY(c)
......................WALSH(q)
Raphael ....SANTI(c)
Raquel...........WELCH(a)
Rashad, ...AHMAD(l)
......................PHYLICIA(a)
Rathbone, ...BASIL(a)
Rather, ...DAN(o)
Ratzenberger, ..JOHN(a)
Rauschenberg, ...
...................ROBERT(c)
Raul ....JULIA(a)
Ravel, ...MAURICE(k)
Ravi ....SHANKAR(r)
Rawls, ...LOU(x)
Ray..............BOLGER(a)
..............BRADBURY(z)
...................CHARLES(x)
......................CONNIFF(r)
.....DAVIES(x), KROC(h)
...................LEONARD(g)
.......................LIOTTA(a)
..................MERCER(g)
..................MILLAND(a)
....................NITSCHKE(l)
.........................PRICE(x)
...................STEVENS(x)
..................WALSTON(a)
Ray, ...ALDO(a)
....JOHNNIE(x), MAN(s)
Rayburn, ...SAM(u)
Raymond.........BURR(a)
................CHANDLER(z)
.......................FLOYD(m)
.......................MASSEY(a)
Raymond, ...ALEX(i)
Rea, ...CHRIS(x)
Reade, ...CHARLES(z)
Reagan, ...NANCY(u)
...................RONALD(u)
Reasoner, ...HARRY(o)
Reba.........McENTIRE(x)
Rebecca ....
................De MORNAY(a)
Red..........AUERBACH(f)
...................BARBER(o)
................BUTTONS(a)
...................GRANGE(l)
....................NICHOLS(r)
.......................NORVO(r)
...................SKELTON(i)
Redd.................FOXX(j)
Redding, ...OTIS(x)
Reddy, ...HELEN(x)
Redford, ...ROBERT(a)
Redgrave, ...LYNN(a)
...................MICHAEL(a)
..................VANESSA(a)

Reed, ...CAROL(q)
........................DONNA(a)
.........JERRY(x), LOU(x)
........OLIVER(a), REX(o)
......................ROBERT(a)
.....................WALTER(w)
..........................WILLIS(f)
Rees, ...ROGER(a)
Reese, ...DELLA(a,x)
......................PEE WEE(e)
Reeve, ...
.......CHRISTOPHER(a)
Reeves, ...GEORGE(a)
.................DAN(l), JIM(x)
.......................KEANU(a)
.....................MARTHA(x)
Reggie.......JACKSON(e)
.........ROBY(l), WHITE(l)
Regina ....KING(a)
........................RESNIK(x)
Reginald ....DENNY(a)
.........................OWEN(a)
Rehan, ...ADA(a)
Rehnquist, ..WILLIAM(u)
Reid, ...KATE(a), TIM(x)
Reiner, ...CARL(j)
..........................ROB(q)
Reinhold, ...JUDGE(a)
Reinking, ...ANN(a)
Reitman, ...IVAN(q)
Remarque, ...
.............ERICH MARIA(z)
Rembrandt......PEALE(c)
....................van RIJN(c)
Remick, ...LEE(a)
Remington, ...
...................FREDERIC(c)
Renata.........SCOTTO(x)
....................TEBALDI(x)
Rendell, ...RUTH(z)
René ....
.........AUBERJONOIS(a)
.......CLAIR(q), COTY(u)
.............DESCARTES(w)
.................LACOSTE(y)
.................MAGRITTE(c)
Renee ....ADOREE(a)
.......................TAYLOR(a)
Reni, ...GUIDO(c)
Rennie, ...MICHAEL(a)
Renoir, ...JEAN(q)
....PIERRE AUGUSTE(c)
Resnik, ...REGINA(x)
Respighi,.....................
................OTTORINO(k)
Reston, ...JAMES(o)
Retton, ...MARY LOU(s)
Rex.........HARRISON(a)
.......REED(o), STOUT(z)
Rey, ...ALEJANDRO(a)

Reynolds, ...BURT(a)
....................DEBBIE(a)
....................JOSHUA(c)
Rhea ....PERLMAN(a)
Rhee, ...SYNGMAN(u)
Rhodes, ...CECIL(h)
Rhonda.......FLEMING(a)
Ric ....OCASEK(x)
Ricardo ....
...........MONTALBAN(a)
Rice, ...ELMER(z)
..........JERRY(l), JIM(e)
Rich ....LITTLE(j)
Rich, ...BUDDY(r)
................CHARLIE(x)
Richard ....
.....ATTENBOROUGH(q)
..............BASEHART(a)
.............BENJAMIN(a,q)
...................BOONE(a)
..................BURTON(a)
.........CHAMBERLAIN(a)
..................CHENEY(u)
.....................CONTE(a)
..................CRENNA(a)
....DAWSON(a), DENT(l)
.........DREYFUSS(a)
....................DYSART(a)
.............GEPHARDT(u)
.....GERE(a), HARRIS(a)
....JORDAN(a), KILEY(x)
........LEWIS(j), LONG(a)
..............LOVELACE(t)
......LUGER(a), MOLL(a)
.................MULLIGAN(a)
.....NIXON(u), PETTY(v)
.....................PRYOR(j)
................RODGERS(k)
................SHERIDAN(z)
....................STEELE(o)
..................STRAUSS(k)
...................THOMAS(a)
.......................TODD(q)
.................WAGNER(k)
.................WIDMARK(a)
...................WILBUR(t)
...................WRIGHT(z)
Richard, ...CLIFF(x)
Richard Dean.................
..............ANDERSON(a)
Richard J. ......DALEY(u)
Richard M. .....DALEY(u)
........................HUNT(b)
Richards, ...ANN(u)
.........BOB(s), KEITH(r)
Richardson, ...
..................HENRY H.(b)
.......RALPH(a), TONY(q)
Richie...........HAVENS(x)
Richie, ...LIONEL(x)

Rick...............MEARS(v)
.................MORANIS(a)
.................SCHRODER(a)
.........SPRINGFIELD(x)
Rickey ....
..........HENDERSON(e)
Rickey, ...BRANCH(e)
Rickie Lee.......JONES(x)
Rickles, ...DON(j)
Rickover, ...HYMAN(p)
Ricky..................BELL(l)
...................NELSON(x)
Riddick ....BOWE(g)
Riddle, ...NELSON(r)
Ride, ...SALLY(d)
Rigby, ...CATHY(s)
Rigg, ...DIANA(a)
Riggins, ...JOHN(l)
Riggs, ...BOBBY(y)
Riis, ...JACOB(o)
Riley, ...PAT(f)
Rilke, ...
........RAINER MARIA(t)
Rimbaud, ...ARTHUR(t)
Rimsky-Korsakov, ...
....................NICOLAI(k)
Ring...........LARDNER(z)
Ringo ....STARR(r)
Ringwald, ...MOLLY(a)
Rip...............TAYLOR(j)
......................TORN(a)
Riperton, ...MINNIE(x)
Ripken, ...BILL(e)
Ripken, Jr., ...CAL(e)
Rita ....COOLIDGE(x)
...........DOVE(t), GAM(a)
.................HAYWORTH(a)
...................MORENO(a)
...................RUDNER(j)
Ritchard, ...CYRIL(a)
Ritchie ....VALENS(x)
Ritenour, ...LEE(r)
Ritter, ...JOHN(a)
.......TEX(x), THELMA(a)
Ritz, ...AL(j)
.......HARRY(j), JIMMY(j)
River...........PHOENIX(a)
Rivera, ...CHITA(a)
.....................DIEGO(c)
..................GERALDO(o)
Rivers, ...JOAN(j)
.................JOHNNY(x)
Roald ....DAHL(z)
Rob ....LOWE(a)
.....................REINER(q)
Robards, Jr., ...
.......................JASON(a)
Robb, ...CHARLES(u)
Robbie ....
.............ROBERTSON(x)

Robbins, ...JEROME(q)
....................MARTY(x)
Robby..........BENSON(a)
Robert ....ALDA(a)
....................ALTMAN(q)
................BARNARD(z)
.................BENCHLEY(z)
..................BENTON(q)
.......................BLAKE(a)
........BLY(t), BROWN(w)
..................BROWNING(t)
....BURNS(t), CLARY(a)
....................CONRAD(a)
.................CRIPPEN(d)
.......CRUMB(i), CULP(a)
.................CUMMINGS(a)
..................De NIRO(a)
.....................DONAT(a)
...................DOWNEY(q)
........DOWNEY, Jr.(a)
.......................DUVALL(a)
......................ENGLUND(a)
.......................EVANS(o)
.............FOXWORTH(a)
.........................FROST(t)
........................FULTON(w)
.....................GOULET(x)
....................GRAVES(z)
..................GUILLAUME(a)
.....HAYS(a), HOOKS(a)
.....................JOFFREY(a)
........................KLEIN(a)
....................LANSING(a)
.....................LOGGIA(a)
.......................LOWELL(t)
.....................LUDLUM(z)
.....................MacNEIL(o)
......MAPPLETHORPE(c)
.....................MERRILL(x)
...................MITCHUM(a)
.............MONTGOMERY(a)
.......................MORSE(i)
...............MOTHERWELL(c)
.......................NOVAK(o)
......................PALMER(x)
....PEEL(u), PLANT(x)
.....................PRESTON(a)
.......................PROSKY(a)
....RAUSCHENBERG(c)
.................REDFORD(a)
.........REED(a), RYAN(a)
.............SCHUMANN(k)
.........................SHAW(a)
...............SILVERBERG(z)
........................STACK(a)
.....................TAYLOR(a)
................TOWNSEND(q)
.........................URICH(a)
.....................VAUGHN(a)
....................WAGNER(a)

Roz.................CHAST(i)
Rozelle, ...PETE(l)
Rube ....GOLDBERG(i)
Ruben.......BLADES(a,x)
.................SIERRA(e)
Rubens, ...
.........PETER PAUL(c)
Rubinstein, ..ARTHUR(r)
Ruby ....DEE(a)
................KEELER(a)
Rudner, ...RITA(j)
Rudolf.............FRIML(k)
.............NUREYEV(a)
Rudolph ....DIESEL(w)
.............VALENTINO(a)
Rudolph, ...WILMA(s)
Rudy ....VALLEE(x)
Rudyard.......KIPLING(z)
Rue ...MCCLANAHAN(a)
Ruffin, ...DAVID(x)
Ruggiero ....
.........LEONCAVALLO(k)
Ruggles, ...CHARLIE(a)
Rukeyser, ...LOUIS(o)
Rumer........GODDEN(z)
Runyon, ...DAMON(z)
Rupert........BROOKE(t)
.............MURDOCH(h)
Rush, ...BARBARA(a)
Russ.........COLUMBO(r),
.................TAMBLYN(a)
Russell ....BAKER(o)
Russell, ...
.........BERTRAND(w, z)
.........BILL(f), CAZZIE(f)
.........JANE(a), KEN(q)
.........KURT(a), LEON(x)
.....LILLIAN(x), MARK(o)
.................NIPSEY(j)
.................ROSALIND(a)
.................THERESA(a)
Rusty ....WALLACE(v)
Rutger...........HAUER(a)
Ruth ....BUZZI(j)
.................GORDON(a)
.................POINTER(x)
.................RENDELL(z)
.................ROMAN(a)
.........WESTHEIMER(o)
Ruth, ...BABE(e)
Rutherford, ..ERNEST(w)
.................JOHNNY(v)
.................MARGARET(a)
.................MIKE(r)
Rutherford B...HAYES(u)
Ruttan, ...SUSAN(a)
Ryan.............O'NEAL(a)
Ryan, ...IRENE(a)
.........MEG(a), NOLAN(e)
.................ROBERT(a)

Rydell, ...BOBBY(x)
Ryder, ...
....ALBERT PINKHAM(c)
.................MITCH(r)
.................WINONA(a)
Ryne.......SANDBERG(e)
Rypien, ...MARK(l)
Ryun ....JIM(s)

S.E.................HINTON(z)
S.J. ....PERELMAN(z)
Saarinen, ...EERO(b)
.................ELIEL(b)
Sabatini, ..GABRIELA(y)
Saberhagen, ...BRET(e)
Sacha........GUITRY(a,z)
Sada .....THOMPSON(a)
Sadat, ...ANWAR al-(u)
Saddam.....HUSSEIN(u)
Safer, ...MORLEY(o)
Safire, ...WILLIAM(o)
Sagan, ...CARL(w)
Saget, ...BOB(a)
Sahl, ...MORT(j)
Saint, ...EVA MARIE(a)
Sainte-Marie, ..BUFFY(x)
St. James, ...SUSAN(a)
Saint-John.......PERSE(t)
St. John, ...JILL(a)
Saint-Saëns, ...
.................CAMILLE(k)
Sajak, ...PAT(j)
Saks, ...GENE(q)
Sal ....MINEO(a)
Salamanca, ...J.R.(z)
Sales, ...SOUPY(j)
Salinger, ...J.D.(z)
Salk, ...JONAS(w)
Sally ....FIELD(a)
.............KELLERMAN(a)
.................KIRKLAND(a)
.........RAND(a), RIDE(d)
.............STRUTHERS(a)
Sally Ann .....HOWES(a)
Salmon P. ......CHASE(u)
Salvador ....DALI(c)
Salvatore ....
.............QUASIMODO(t)
Sam ....COOKE(x)
.............DONALDSON(o)
.................ELLIOTT(a)
.........HUFF(l), JAFFE(a)
.......NEILL(a), NUNN(u)
.................RAYBURN(u)
.................SHEPARD(z)
.................SNEAD(m)
.................WALTON(h)
.............WANAMAKER(a)
.............WATERSTON(a)
Samms, ...EMMA(a)

Sammy ....BAUGH(l)
.................DAVIS, Jr.(x)
....FAIN(k), HAGAR(x)
Sampras, ...PETE(y)
Samuel ....ADAMS(u)
.................BECKETT(z)
.................BUTLER(c,k,z)
.................CUNARD(h)
.................GOLDWYN(q)
.................HOUSTON(u)
.................JOHNSON(z)
.................MORSE(w)
.................PEPYS(z)
Samuel R. ....DELANY(z)
Samuel Taylor ....
.............COLERIDGE(t)
Sand, ...GEORGE(z)
Sandberg, ...RYNE(e)
Sandburg, ...CARL(t)
Sanders, ...DEION(e)
.................GEORGE(a)
.................LAWRENCE(z)
Sandra....BERNHARD(j)
.......DEE(a), HAYNIE(m)
.................PALMER(m)
Sandra Day ....
.................O'CONNOR(u)
Sandro ...BOTTICELLI(c)
Sandy.........ALOMAR(e)
.................DENNIS(a)
.................DENNY(x)
.................DUNCAN(a)
.................KAUFAX(e)
.................LYLE(m)
Sandy, ...GARY(a)
Santana, ...CARLOS(r)
Santayana, ...
.................GEORGE(z)
Sara ....GILBERT(a)
.................TEASDALE(t)
Sarah ...BERNHARDT(a)
.................CALDWELL(r)
.................MILES(a)
.................VAUGHAN(x)
Sarah Jessica ....
.................PARKER(a)
Sarandon, ...SUSAN(a)
Sarazen, ...GENE(m)
Sargent, ...
.........JOHN SINGER(c)
Saroyan, ...WILLIAM(z)
Sartre, ...JEAN-PAUL(z)
Sassoon, ..SIEGFRIED(t)
Satie, ...ERIK(k)
Saul ....BELLOW(z)
Savage, ...FRED(a)
Savalas, ...TELLY(a)
Sawyer, ...DIANE(o)
Saxon, ...JOHN(a)
Sayer, ...LEO(x)

179

Sayers, ...
.............DOROTHY L.(z)
.........................GALE(l)
Sayles, ...JOHN(q)
Scaggs, ...BOZ(x)
Scalia, ...ANTONIN(u)
Scarlatti, ...
.........ALESSANDRO(k)
Scatman ....
.........CROTHERS(a)
Schallert, ...WILLIAM(a)
Scheckter, ...JODY(v)
Scheider, ...ROY(a)
Schell, ...MARIA(a)
.........MAXIMILIAN(a)
Schenkel, ...CHRIS(o)
Schiaparelli, ...ELSA(c)
Schirra, ...WALTER(d)
Schlesinger, ...JOHN(q)
Schmeling, ...MAX(g)
Schmidt, ...MIKE(e)
Schoenberg, ...
.........................ARNOLD(k)
Scholz, ...TOM(r)
Schroder, ...RICK(a)
Schubert, ...FRANZ(k)
Schulz, ...CHARLES(i)
Schumann, ..ROBERT(k)
Schwarzenegger, ...
.........................ARNOLD(a)
Schwarzkopf, ...
.........................NORMAN(p)
Scofield, ...PAUL(a)
Scolari, ...PETER(a)
Scorsese, ...MARTIN(q)
Scott ....BAIO(a)
...BAKULA(a),GLENN(a)
................HAMILTON(s)
.........................JOPLIN(k)
................SIMPSON(m)
Scott, ...GEORGE C.(a)
................LIZABETH(a)
................RANDOLPH(a)
...................WALTER(z)
................ZACHARY(a)
Scottie ....PIPPEN(f)
Scotto, ...RENATA(x)
Scowcroft, ...BRENT(u)
Scriabin, ...
.........ALEKSANDR(k)
Scully, ...VIN(o)
Seals, ...DAN(x), JIM(x)
Sean.........CONNERY(a)
................O'CASEY(z)
................O'GRADY(g)
.........................PENN(a)
Seau, ...JUNIOR(l)
Seaver, ...TOM(e)
Sebastian.......CABOT(a)
.........................COE(s)

Sebastian, ...JOHN(x)
Seberg, ...JEAN(a)
Sedaka, ...NEIL(x)
Sedgman, ...FRANK(y)
Seeger, ...PETE(x)
Segal, ...GEORGE(a)
Seger, ...BOB(x)
Segovia, ...ANDRES(r)
Seidelman, ...SUSAN(q)
Seiji ....OZAWA(r)
Seinfeld, ...JERRY(j)
Selassie, ...HAILE(u)
Seles, ...MONICA(y)
Sellecca, ...CONNIE(a)
Selleck, ...TOM(a)
Sellers, ...PETER(j)
Selma ....DIAMOND(a)
................LAGERLOF(z)
Selznick, ...DAVID O.(q)
Sendak, ...MAURICE(z)
Senna, ...AYRTON(v)
Sennett, ...MACK(q)
Serge ....
.......KOUSSEVITZKY(r)
Sergei ...EISENSTEIN(q)
.............PROKOFIEV(r)
......RACHMANINOFF(k)
Sergio ....MENDES(r)
Sesno, ...FRANK(o)
Seton, ...ANYA(z)
Seurat, ...GEORGES(c)
Seve ....
.......BALLESTEROS(m)
Severinsen, ...DOC(r)
Sexton, ...ANNE(t)
Seymour, ...JANE(a)
Shackelford, ...TED(a)
Shaffer, ...PAUL(r)
Shahn, ...BEN(c)
Shakespeare, ...
................WILLIAM(z)
Shamir, ...YITZHAK(u)
Shandling, ...GARRY(j)
Shane ....GOULD(s)
Shankar, ...RAVI(r)
Shannon, ...DEL(x)
Shaquille ....O'NEAL(f)
Shari .....BELAFONTE(a)
.........................LEWIS(j)
Sharif, ...OMAR(a)
Sharon ....GLESS(a)
Sharon, ...ARIEL(u)
Sharp, ...DEE DEE(x)
Shatner, ...WILLIAM(a)
Shaun ....CASSIDY(x)
Shaw, ...ARTIE(r)
................BERNARD(o)
.........................GEORGE
................BERNARD(z)
................ROBERT(a)

Shea, ...JOHN(a)
Shearer, ...MOIRA(a)
.........................NORMA(a)
Shearing, ...GEORGE(r)
Shecky ....GREENE(j)
Sheedy, ...ALLY(a)
Sheehan, ...PATTY(m)
Sheen, ...CHARLIE(a)
.........................MARTIN(a)
Sheena ....EASTON(x)
Sheldon......LEONARD(j)
Shelley ....BERMAN(j)
.........................DUVALL(a)
.........................FABARES(a)
.........................LONG(a)
.........................WINTERS(a)
Shelley, ...MARY(z)
......PERCY BYSSHE(t)
Shemp.........HOWARD(j)
Shepard, ...SAM(z)
Shepard, Jr., ...ALAN(d)
Shepherd, ...CYBILL(a)
.........................JEAN(z)
Sheree...........NORTH(a)
Sheridan, ...ANN(a)
.........................PHILIP(p)
.........................RICHARD(z)
Sherman ...HEMSLEY(a)
Sherman, ...ALLAN(x)
.........................BOBBY(x)
................WILLIAM T.(p)
Sherwood ....
................ANDERSON(z)
Sherwood, ...
................ROBERT E.(z)
Shields, ...BROOKE(a)
Shimon...........PERES(u)
Shire, ...TALIA(a)
Shirley ....BASSEY(x)
....BOOTH(a), JONES(a)
................MacLAINE(a)
.........................TEMPLE(a)
Shirley Ann.......GRAU(z)
Sholem ....ASCH(z)
Shore, ...DINAH(x)
Short, ...BOBBY(r)
.........................MARTIN(j)
Shorter, ...FRANK(s)
Shostakovich, ...
.........................DMITRI(k)
Shriver, ...MARIA(o)
.........................PAM(y)
Shula, ...DON(l)
Sibelius, ...JEAN(k)
Sid ....CAESAR(a)
................LUCKMAN(l)
Sidney ....LUMET(q)
.........................POITIER(a)
.........................TOLER(a)
Sidney, ...SYLVIA(a)

Sidonie Gabrielle ....
...............COLETTE(z)
Siegfried ....SASSOON(t)
Sierra, ...RUBEN(e)
Sigmund........FREUD(w)
Signe ....HASSO(a)
Signoret, ...SIMONE(a)
Sigourney ...WEAVER(a)
Sikorsky, ...IGOR(w)
Sillitoe, ...ALAN(z)
Sills, ...BEVERLY(x)
Silver, ...RON(a)
Silverberg, ..ROBERT(z)
Silvers, ...PHIL(j)
Sim, ...ALASTAIR(a)
Simmons, ...JEAN(a)
Simms, ...PHIL(l)
Simon ....BOLIVAR(p)
...............LEBON(x)
...............WARD(a)
Simon, ...CARLY(x)
...........NEIL(z), PAUL(u)
...............PAUL(x)
Simone ....SIGNORET(a)
Simone, ...NINA(x)
Simpson, ...O.J.(l)
...............SCOTT(m)
Sims, ...ZOOT(r)
Sinatra, ...FRANK(x)
Sinclair ....LEWIS(z)
Sinclair, ...UPTON(z)
Sinead....O'CONNOR(x)
Singer, ...
......ISAAC BASHEVIS(z)
Singh, ...VIJAY(m)
Singleton, ...JOHN(q)
Sirtis, ...MARINA(a)
Siskel, ...GENE(o)
Sissy ....SPACEK(a)
Skeeter ....DAVIS(x)
Skelton, ...RED(j)
Skerritt, ...TOM(a)
Skinner, ...B.F.(w)
Skitch ...HENDERSON(r)
Slater, ...HELEN(a)
Slaughter, ...ENOS(e)
Sledge, ...PERCY(x)
Slick, ...GRACE(x)
Slim ..SUMMERVILLE(a)
Sloan, ...JOHN(c)
Sluman, ...JEFF(m)
Sly.................STONE(r)
Smetana, ...BEDRICH(k)
Smith, ...ADAM(z)
...............ALEXIS(a)
...............BESSIE(x)
......BRUCE(l), BUBBA(l)
..........BUFFALO BOB(a)
...............DAVID(c)
......JACLYN(a), KATE(x)

...........KEELY(x), LIZ(o)
...............MAGGIE(a)
...............OZZIE(e)
........PATTI(x), STAN(y)
Smits, ...JIMMY(a)
Smokey ...ROBINSON(x)
Smothers, ...DICK(j)
...............TOM(j)
Smuts, ...JAN(u)
Snead, ...J.C.(m)
...........NORM(l), SAM(m)
Snell, ...PETER(s)
Sneva, ...TOM(v)
Snider, ...DUKE(a)
Snipes, ...WESLEY(a)
Snow, ...HANK(x)
...............PHOEBE(x)
Snyder, ...GARY(t)
...............TOM(o)
Solti, ...GEORG(r)
Solzhenitsyn, ...
............ALEKSANDR(z)
Somers, ...SUZANNE(a)
Sommer, ...ELKE(a)
Sondheim, ...
...............STEPHEN(k)
Sondra ....LOCKE(a)
Sonia ....BRAGA(a)
Sonja ....HENIE(s)
Sonny..............BONO(x)
...............JURGENSEN(l)
...............LISTON(g)
...............ROLLINS(r)
Sontag, ...SUSAN(z)
Soo, ...JACK(j)
Sophia.........LOREN(a)
Sophie ....TUCKER(x)
Soren ....
........KIERKEGAARD(z)
Sorvino, ...PAUL(a)
Sothern, ...ANN(a)
Soul, ...DAVID(a)
Soupy ....SALES(j)
Sousa, ..JOHN PHILIP(k)
Souter, ...DAVID(u)
Spacek, ...SISSY(a)
Spade, ...DAVID(j)
Spader, ...JAMES(a)
Spahn, ...WARREN(e)
Spanky...................
...............McFARLAND(a)
Spano, ...JOE(a)
...............VINCENT(a)
Spark, ...MURIEL(z)
Sparks, ...NED(a)
Sparky ....LYLE(a)
Speaker, ...TRIS(e)
Specter, ...ARLEN(u)
Spector, ...PHIL(r)
...............RONNIE(x)

Spelling, ...AARON(q)
Spencer..........TRACY(a)
Spender, ...STEPHEN(t)
Spenser, ...EDMUND(t)
Spielberg, ...STEVEN(q)
Spike ....JONES(r)
...............LEE(q)
Spillane, ...MICKEY(z)
Spiner, ...BRENT(a)
Spinks, ...LEON(g)
...............MICHAEL(g)
Spinoza, ...BARUCH(z)
Spiro ....AGNEW(u)
Spitz, ...MARK(s)
Spock, ...BENJAMIN(w)
Spring ......BYINGTON(a)
Springfield, ...DUSTY(x)
...............RICK(x)
Springsteen, ..BRUCE(x)
Spyri, ...JOHANNA(z)
Stabler, ...KEN(l)
Stack, ...ROBERT(a)
Stacy ....KEACH(a)
Stacy, ...HOLLIS(m)
Stadler, ...CRAIG(m)
Stafford, ...JIM(x), JO(x)
Stahl, ...LESLEY(o)
Stalin, ...JOSEPH(u)
Stallone, ...
...............SYLVESTER(a)
Stamos, ...JOHN(a)
Stamp, ...TERENCE(a)
Stan ....GETZ(r)
...............KENTON(r)
............LAUREL(j), LEE(i)
...............MIKITA(n)
....MUSIAL(e), SMITH(y)
Stander, ...LIONEL(a)
Stanford ....WHITE(b)
Stang, ...ARNOLD(j)
Stanley.......BALDWIN(u)
...............KRAMER(q)
...............KUBRICK(q)
Stanley, ...KIM(a)
Stanton, ...
...............HARRY DEAN(a)
Stanwyck, ...
...............BARBARA(a)
Stapledon, ...OLAF(z)
Stapleton, ...JEAN(a)
...............MAUREEN(a)
Stargell, ...WILLIE(e)
Starr, ...BART(l)
..........KAY(x), RINGO(r)
Staubach, ...ROGER(l)
Steele, ...RICHARD(o)
Steen, ...JAN(c)
Steenburgen, ..MARY(a)
Stefan..........EDBERG(y)
Stefanie ......POWERS(a)

Tom / Van Ark

Tom ....ARNOLD(j)
.............BERENGER(a)
.................BOSLEY(a)
.................BROKAW(o)
.................CARVEL(h)
...CLANCY(z), CONTI(a)
.....COURTENAY(a)
..................CRUISE(a)
....................EWELL(a)
.................GLAVINE(e)
...................HANKS(a)
.................HARMON(l)
.....HULCE(a), JONES(x)
.....KITE(m), LANDRY(l)
.........MIX(a), OKKER(y)
......................PETTY(x)
...................POSTON(j)
..................SCHOLZ(r)
..................SEAVER(e)
.................SELLECK(a)
.................SKERRITT(a)
................SMOTHERS(j)
.....................SNEVA(v)
..................SNYDER(o)
.................STOPPARD(z)
......................WAITS(x)
.................WATSON(m)
.............WEISKOPF(m)
....................WILSON(i)
....................WOLFE(z)
Tomlin, ...LILY(j)
Tommy.............BOLT(m)
.......................CHONG(j)
.....................DORSEY(r)
.......JAMES(x), TUNE(a)
Tommy Lee ....JONES(a)
Tom T. ....HALL(x)
Tone, ...FRANCHOT(a)
Toni.........MORRISON(z)
...................TENNILLE(x)
Tony................BANKS(r)
.................BENNETT(x)
...CURTIS(a), DANZA(a)
....DORSETT(l), DOW(a)
.............FRANCIOSA(a)
....................GWYNN(e)
...................JACKLIN(m)
......KUBEK(e), LEMA(m)
.....................MARTIN(x)
..................MUSANTE(a)
.......................OLIVA(e)
..................ORLANDO(x)
...PENA(e),RANDALL(a)
............RICHARDSON(q)
....................ROBERTS(a)
........................ROCHE(y)
...................TRABERT(y)
Toomey, ...BILL(s)
Tori....................AMOS(s)
Torme, ...MEL(x)

Torn, ...RIP(a)
Torquato..........TASSO(t)
Torrence, ...GWEN(s)
Toscanini, ...ARTURO(r)
Toshiro ....MIFUNE(a)
Totie.................FIELDS(j)
Townsend, ..ROBERT(q)
Townshend, ...PETE(x)
Trabert, ...TONY(y)
Tracey..........ULLMAN(a)
Tracy ....AUSTIN(y)
.....................CHAPMAN(x)
Tracy, ...SPENCER(a)
Travanti, ...DANIEL J.(a)
Travers, ...MARY(x)
Travis, ...RANDY(x)
Travolta, ...JOHN(a)
Traynor, ...PIE(e)
Treacher, ...ARTHUR(a)
Treat.........WILLIAMS(a)
Trebek, ...ALEX(a)
Trevino, ...LEE(m)
Trevor ....HOWARD(a)
Trevor, ...CLAIRE(a)
Trickle, ...DICK(v)
Trillin, ...CALVIN(o)
Trini..................LOPEZ(x)
Tris ....SPEAKER(e)
Trollope, ...ANTHONY(z)
Trotsky, ...LEON(u)
Troy ....AIKMAN(l)
.................DONAHUE(a)
Trudeau, ...GARRY(i)
.....PIERRE ELLIOTT(u)
Truex, ...ERNEST(a)
Truffaut, ..FRANCOIS(a)
Truman ....CAPOTE(z)
Truman, ...HARRY S(u)
Trumbull, ...JOHN(c)
Trump, ...DONALD(h)
Tryon, ...THOMAS(z)
Tschetter, ...KRIS(m)
Tucker, ...FORREST(a)
...................MICHAEL(a)
....SOPHIE(x), TANYA(x)
Tug ....McGRAW(e)
Tuesday ....WELD(a)
Tune, ...TOMMY(a)
Tunney, ...GENE(g)
Turgenev, ...IVAN(z)
Turner, ...IKE(r)
............J.M.W.(c), JOE(x)
................KATHLEEN(a)
.......................LANA(a)
............TED(h), TINA(x)
Turpin, ...BEN(a)
Twain, ...MARK(z)
Tway, ...BOB(m)
Tweed, ...WILLIAM M.
...................."Boss" (u)

Twelvetrees, ..HELEN(a)
Twitty, ...CONWAY(x)
Ty ....COBB(e)
Tycho ....BRAHE(w)
Tyler, ...ANNE(z)
............JOHN(u), WAT(u)
Tyne ....DALY(a)
Tyra..............FERREL(a)
Tyrone ....POWER(a)
Tyson, ...CICELY(a)
........................MIKE(g)
Tyus, ...WYOMIA(s)

U.....................THANT(u)
Ucccello, ...PAOLO(c)
Ueberroth, ...PETER(h)
Uecker, ...BOB(e)
Uggams, ...LESLIE(x)
Ullman, ...TRACEY(a)
Ullmann, ...LIV(a)
Ulu ....GROSBARD(q)
Ulysses S....GRANT(p,u)
Uma..........THURMAN(a)
Una ....O'CONNOR(a)
Underwood, ...BLAIR(a)
Unitas, ...JOHNNY(l)
Unser, ...AL(v)
.......................BOBBY(v)
Updike, ...JOHN(z)
Upton ....SINCLAIR(z)
Urey, ...HAROLD(w)
Urich, ...ROBERT(a)
Uris, ...LEON(z)
Ursula ....ANDRESS(a)
Ursula K. ......LEGUIN(z)
Ustinov, ...PETER(a)
Uta ....HAGEN(a)
Utrillo, ...MAURICE(c)

V.S. ....NAIPAUL(z)
Vaccaro, ...BRENDA(a)
Vachel..........LINDSAY(t)
Val.................KILMER(a)
Vale, ...JERRY(x)
Valens, ...RITCHIE(x)
Valentino, ...
..................RUDOLPH(a)
Valenzuela, ...
.................FERNANDO(e)
Valerie ...BERTINELLI(a)
.....................HARPER(a)
.......................PERRINE(a)
Valery ....BORZOV(s)
Vallee, ...RUDY(x)
Valli, ...FRANKIE(x)
Van ....CLIBURN(r)
.......................HEFLIN(a)
.................JOHNSON(a)
................MORRISON(x)
Van Ark, ...JOAN(a)

184

Van Brocklin, ...NORM(l)
Van Buren, ..ABIGAIL(o)
.................MARTIN(u)
Vance, ...VIVIAN(a)
Vanderbilt, ...
..............CORNELIUS(h)
.................GLORIA(h)
Van Doren, ...MAMIE(a)
Vandross, ...LUTHER(x)
Van Duyn, ...MONA(t)
Van Dyck, ...
................ANTHONY(c)
Van Dyke, ...DICK(a)
.................JERRY(a)
Vanessa.................
..............REDGRAVE(a)
...............WILLIAMS(x)
Van Fleet, ...JO(a)
Van Gogh, .VINCENT(c)
Vanna ....WHITE(a)
Van Peebles...MARIO(a)
Van Rijn, ...
..........REMBRANDT(c)
Van Slyke, ...ANDY(e)
Varley, ...JOHN(z)
Vaslav ....NIJINSKY(c)
Vaughan, ...SARAH(x)
Vaughn......MONROE(x)
Vaughn, ...ROBERT(a)
Vee, ...BOBBY(x)
Veidt, ...CONRAD(a)
Velázquez, ...DIEGO(c)
Ventura, ...ROBIN(e)
Venturi, ...KEN(m)
Vera................MILES(a)
Verdi, ...GIUSEPPE(k)
Verdon, ...GWEN(a)
Vereen, ...BEN(a)
Verlaine, ...PAUL(t)
Vermeer, ...JAN(c)
Verne, ...JULES(z)
Vernon..........CASTLE(a)
Veronese, ...PAOLO(c)
Veronica.........HAMEL(a)
.................LAKE(a)
Vic..............DAMONE(x)
.................MORROW(a)
Vicki ...LAWRENCE(a, x)
Victor.............BORGE(r)
.................BUONO(a)
.................FLEMING(q)
...............HERBERT(k,r)
........HUGO(z), JORY(a)
.................MATURE(a)
.................McLAGLEN(a)
Victoria ...JACKSON(j)
.................PRINCIPAL(a)
.................TENNANT(a)
Vida..................BLUE(e)
Vidal, ...GORE(z)

Vigoda, ...ABE(a)
Vijay ....SINGH(m)
Vikki................CARR(x)
Vilas, ...GUILLERMO(y)
Villa, ...PANCHO(u)
Villa-Lobos, ..HEITOR(k)
Villella, ...EDWARD(a)
Villon, ...FRANCOIS(t)
Vin ....SCULLY(o)
Vince........LOMBARDI(l)
Vincent..........CANBY(o)
.................GARDENIA(a)
.................PRICE(a)
.................SPANO(a)
.................Van GOGH(c)
Vincent, ...
.............JAN-MICHAEL(a)
Vincente.....MINNELLI(q)
Vincenzo ......BELLINI(k)
Vinge, ...JOAN D.(z)
Vinton, ...BOBBY(x)
Viren, ...LASSE(s)
Virgil ....GRISSOM(d)
Virginia..........BRUCE(a)
.................GRAHAM(a)
.......MAYO(a), WADE(y)
.................WOOLF(z)
Virna ....LISI(a)
Visconti, ...LUCHINO(q)
Vitas......GERULAITIS(y)
Vittorini, ...ELIO(z)
Vittorio..........De SICA(q)
Vivaldi, ...ANTONIO(k)
Viveca ......LINDFORS(a)
Vivian ......BLAINE(a,x)
.................VANCE(a)
Vivien..........LEIGH(a)
Vladimir ...HOROWITZ(r)
.................NABOKOV(z)
Vladimir Ilyich ....
.................LENIN(u)
Voight, ...JON(a)
Vonnegut, Jr., ..KURT(z)
Von Stroheim, ...
.................ERICH(a)
Von Sydow, ...MAX(a)
Von Zell, ...HARRY(a)

W. Averell ....
.................HARRIMAN(h)
W.C. ....FIELDS(j)
.................HANDY(k)
W.E.B. ......Du BOIS(u,z)
W.H. ....AUDEN(t)
W.Somerset.................
.................MAUGHAM(z)
Wade............BOGGS(e)
Wade, ...VIRGINIA(y)
Wadkins, ...LANNY(m)
Waggoner, ..PORTER(x)

Wagner, ...HONUS(e)
.................LINDSAY(a)
.................RICHARD(k)
.................ROBERT(a)
Waite, ...JOHN(x)
.................RALPH(a)
Waits, ...TOM(x)
Walcott, ...JOE(g)
Waldemar ....
.................CIERPINSKI(s)
Walden, ...ROBERT(a)
Waldheim, ...KURT(u)
Walesa, ...LECH(u)
Walken, ...
.........CHRISTOPHER(a)
Walker............PERCY(z)
Walker, ...ALICE(z)
.................HERSCHEL(l)
.......MORT(i), NANCY(a)
.................ROBERT(a)
Wallace ....BEERY(a)
.................STEGNER(z)
.................STEVENS(t)
Wallace ......GEORGE(u)
.........LEW(z), MIKE(o)
.................RUSTY(v)
Wallach, ...ELI(a)
Waller, ...
......THOMAS "Fats"(k, x)
Wally.................COX(j)
Walpole, ...ROBERT(u)
Walsh, ...JOE(r)
.................RAOUL(q)
Walston, ...RAY(a)
Walt...........DISNEY(i,q)
.................KELLY(i)
.................WHITMAN(t)
Walter ....
.................ANNENBERG(h)
.................BRENNAN(a)
.................CRONKITE(o)
.................de la MARE(z)
.................GROPIUS(b)
.................HAGEN(m)
.................HUSTON(a)
.................JOHNSON(e)
.................LANTZ(i)
.................LIPPMANN(o)
.................MATTHAU(a)
.................MONDALE(u)
.................PAYTON(l)
.................PIDGEON(a)
.................REED(w)
.................SCHIRRA(d)
.................SCOTT(z)
.................TEVIS(z)
Walters, ...BARBARA(o)
Walton, ...BILL(f)
.................SAM(h)
Waltrip, ...DARRELL(v)

EZER WEIZMAN

Wambaugh / William

Wambaugh, ...JOSEPH(z)
Wanamaker, ...JOHN(h)
.........................SAM(a)
Waner, ...LLOYD(e)
.........................PAUL(e)
Ward ....BOND(a)
Ward, ...FRED(a)
.................RACHEL (a)
.....................SIMON(a)
Warden, ...JACK(a)
Warhol, ...ANDY(c)
Warner.........BAXTER(a)
.....................OLAND(a)
Warner, ...CURT(l)
.....MALCOLM-JAMAL(a)
Warren ....BEATTY(a)
.................BURGER(u)
.........CHRISTOPHER(u)
.....MOON(l), OATES(a)
....SPAHN(e), ZEVON(x)
Warren, ...EARL(u)
.....LESLEY ANN(a)
......ROBERT PENN(t, z)
Warren G...HARDING(u)
Warwick, ...DIONNE(x)
Washburn, ...MONA(a)
Washington....IRVING(z)
Washington, ...
....DENZEL(a), DINAH(x)
.....................GEORGE(p)
Wasserstein, ...
.....................WENDY(z)
Wassily ..KANDINSKY(c)
Wat ....TYLER(u)
Waters, ...ETHEL(x)
.......JOHN(q), ROGER(r)
Waterston, ...SAM(a)
Watson, ...TOM(m)
Watt, ...JAMES(w)
Watteau, ...
.........JEAN-ANTOINE(c)
Watterson, ...BILL(i)
Watts, ...ANDRE(r)
.....................CHARLIE(r)
.....................GEORGE
.................FREDERIC(c)
Waugh, ...EVELYN(z)
Wayans, ...DAMON(j)
.........KEENAN IVORY(j)
Waylon .....JENNINGS(x)
Wayne ....GRETZKY(n)
.....................NEWTON(x)
Wayne, ...DAVID(a)
.........................JOHN(a)
Weaver, ...DENNIS(a)
.....................FRITZ(a)
.............SIGOURNEY(a)
Webb, ...CLIFTON(a)
.........JACK(a), JIMMY(k)

Webber, ...
.......ANDREW LLOYD(k)
Webster, ...DANIEL(u)
Weeb ....EWBANK(l)
Weil, ...CYNTHIA(k)
Weill, ...KURT(k)
Weir, ...PETER(q)
"Weird Al".....................
.................YANKOVIC(x)
Weiskopf, ...TOM(m)
Weissmuller, ...
.....................JOHNNY(a,s)
Weitz, ...BRUCE(a)
Weizmann........CHAIM(u)
Welch, ...RAQUEL(a)
Weld, ...TUESDAY(a)
Welk, ...LAWRENCE(r)
Welles, ...ORSON(q)
Wells, ...H.G.(z)
.........KITTY(x), MARY(x)
Welty, ...EUDORA(z)
Wendell ....COREY(a)
.....................WILLKIE(u)
Wenders, ...WIM(q)
Wendt, ...GEORGE(a)
Wendy ....HILLER(a)
.........WASSERSTEIN(z)
Wenge, ...RALPH(o)
Wenner, ...JANN(o)
Werner.........................
.............KLEMPERER(a)
.............HEISENBERG(w)
.....................HERZOG(q)
.............Von BRAUN(w)
Wertmuller, ...LINA(q)
Wes..MONTGOMERY(r)
Wesley ....SNIPES(a)
West, ...ADAM(a)
.................BENJAMIN(c)
.........JERRY(f), MAE(a)
.................NATHANAEL(z)
Westheimer, ...RUTH(o)
Weston, ...JACK(a)
Wharton, ...EDITH(z)
Wheaton, ...WIL(a)
Whistler, ...
.............JAMES ABBOTT
.................MCNEILL(c)
Whitaker, ...PERNELL(g)
White, ...BARRY(x)
....BETTY(a), BYRON(u)
.......E.B.(z), EDMUND(z)
.....................PATRICK(z)
.....................REGGIE(l)
.................STANFORD(b)
.....T.H.(z), VANNA(a)
Whiteman, ...PAUL(r)
Whitey ....FORD(e)
Whitman, ...WALT(t)
Whitmore, ...JAMES(a)

Whitney ....HOUSTON(x)
Whitney, ...ELI(w)
Whitty, ...MAY(a)
Whitworth, ...KATHY(m)
Whoopi...GOLDBERG(a)
Widmark, ...RICHARD(a)
Wiener, ...NORBERT(w)
Wiesel, ...ELIE(z)
Wiest, ...DIANNE(a)
Wil ....WHEATON(a)
Wilander, ...MATS(y)
Wilbur.........WRIGHT(w)
Wilbur, ...RICHARD(t)
Wilde, ...OSCAR(z)
Wilder, ...BILLY(q)
.....................GENE(a)
.................THORNTON(z)
Wilding, ...MICHAEL(a)
Wiley.................POST(d)
Wilford ....BRIMLEY(a)
Wilhelm ....GRIMM(z)
Wilhelm, ...HOYT(e)
.........................KATE(z)
Wilkie ....COLLINS(z)
Will ....CLARK(e)
....GEER(a), ROGERS(j)
Will, ...GEORGE(o)
Willa ....CATHER(z)
Willard, ...JESS(g)
Willem ....DAFOE(a)
.............de KOONING(c)
William....ATHERTON(a)
.....................BALDWIN(a)
.....................BENDIX(a)
.....BLAKE(c,t), BOYD(a)
.........CHRISTOPHER(a)
.....................COLGATE(h)
.....................CONRAD(a)
.....................DANIELS(a)
.................DEMAREST(a)
.....................DEVANE(a)
.................FAULKNER(z)
.................FRAWLEY(a)
.................FRIEDKIN(q)
.....................GADDIS(z)
.................GLADSTONE(u)
.....................GOLDING(z)
.....................HARVEY(w)
.................HOGARTH(c)
....HOLDEN(a), HURT(a)
.........INGE(z), JAMES(z)
.....................KENNEDY(z)
.................McKINLEY(u)
......PITT(u), POWELL(a)
.................REHNQUIST(u)
.....................SAFIRE(o)
.................SAROYAN(z)
.................SCHALLERT(a)
.........SHAKESPEARE(z)
.....................SHATNER(a)

186

ZELL MILLER

Youngman / Zukor

Youngman, ...HENNY(j)
Yount, ...ROBIN(e)
Yukio ....MISHIMA(z)
Yul ....BRYNNER(a)
Yuri ....GAGARIN(d)
Yuro, ...TIMI(x)
Yves ....TANGUY(c)
Yvonne......DECARLO(a)
....................ELLIMAN(x)

Zachary.........SCOTT(a)
................TAYLOR(u)
Zadora, ...PIA(x)
Zander, ...ROBIN(x)
Zane ....GREY(z)

Zanuck, ...
.................DARRYL F.(q)
Zapata, ...EMILIANO(u)
Zappa, ...FRANK(r)
Zarley, ...KERMIT(m)
Zasu ....PITTS(a)
Zatopek, ...EMIL(s)
Zeffirelli, ...FRANCO(q)
Zenger, ...
............JOHN PETER(o)
Zeppo ....
.........(Herbert) MARX (j)
Zerbe, ...ANTHONY(a)
Zero............MOSTEL(a)
Zevon, ...WARREN(x)

Ziegfeld, ...FLORENZ(q)
Zimbalist, Jr.,.....
.......................EFREM(a)
Zinnemann, ...FRED(q)
Zoe..........CALDWELL(a)
Zoeller, ...FUZZY(m)
Zola ....BUDD(s)
Zola, ...EMILE(z)
Zoltán..........KODALY(k)
Zoot................SIMS(r)
Zsa Zsa ....GABOR(a)
Zubin ....MEHTA(r)
Zuckerman, ,.....
.........................PINCHAS(r)
Zukor, ...ADOLPH(q)

KENTUCKY DERBY WINNERS

Year	Horse	Jockey
1920	Paul Jones	Rice
1921	Behave Yourself	Thompson
1922	Morvich	Johnson
1923	Zev	Sande
1924	Black Gold	Mooney
1925	Flying Ebony	Sande
1926	Bubbling Over	Johnson
1927	Whiskery	McAtee
1928	Reigh Count	Lang
1929	Clyde Van Dusen	McAtee
1930	* Gallant Fox	Sande
1931	Twenty Grand	Kurtsinger
1932	Burgoo King	James
1933	Brokers Tip	Meade
1934	Cavalcade	Garner
1935	* Omaha	Saunders
1936	Bold Venture	Hanford
1937	* War Admiral	Kurtsinger
1938	Lawrin	Arcaro
1939	Johnstown	Stout
1940	Gallahadion	Bierman
1941	* Whirlaway	Arcaro
1942	Shut Out	Wright
1943	* Count Fleet	Longden
1944	Pensive	McCreary
1945	Hoop, Jr.	Arcaro
1946	* Assault	Mehrtens
1947	Jet Pilot	Guerin
1948	* Citation	Arcaro
1949	Ponder	Brooks
1950	Middleground	Boland
1951	Count Turf	McCreary
1952	Hill Gail	Arcaro
1953	Dark Star	Moreno
1954	Determine	York
1955	Swaps	Shoemaker
1956	Needles	Erb
1957	Iron Liege	Hartack
1958	Tim Tam	Valenzuela
1959	Tomy Lee	Shoemaker
1960	Venetian Way	Hartack
1961	Carry Back	Sellers
1962	Decidedly	Hartack
1963	Chateaugay	Baeza
1964	Northern Dancer	Hartack
1965	Lucky Debonair	Shoemaker
1966	Kauai King	Brumfield
1967	Proud Clarion	Ussery
1968	Dancer's Image	Ussery
1969	Majestic Prince	Hartack
1970	Dust Commander	Manganello
1971	Canonero II	Avila
1972	Riva Ridge	Turcotte
1973	* Secretariat	Turcotte
1974	Cannonade	Cordero
1975	Foolish Pleasure	Vasquez
1976	Bold Forbes	Cordero
1977	* Seattle Slew	Cruguet
1978	* Affirmed	Cauthen
1979	Spectacular Bid	Franklin
1980	Genuine Risk	Vasquez
1981	Pleasant Colony	Velasquez
1982	Gato del Sol	Delahoussaye
1983	Sunny's Halo	Delahoussaye
1984	Swale	Pincay
1985	Spend a Buck	Cordero
1986	Ferdinand	Shoemaker
1987	Alysheba	McCarron
1988	Winning Colors	Stevens
1989	Sunday Silence	Valenzuela
1990	Unbridled	Perret
1991	Strike the Gold	Antley
1992	Lil E. Tee	Day
1993	Sea Hero	Bailey
1994	Go For Gin	McCarron

* Triple Crown Winner

NATIVE AMERICAN PEOPLE

Tribes are separated into groups based on the language spoken by members of the tribe. The language family is indicated at the beginning of each group of tribes.

Algonquin

ABENAKI
ARAPAHO
BLACKFOOT
CHEYENNE
CHIPPEWA
CREE
DELAWARE
FOX
GROS VENTRE
KICKAPOO
LENAPE
MAHICAN (MOHICAN)
MENOMINI
MIAMI
MOHEGAN
OJIBWA
OTTAWA
PIEGAN
POTAWATAMI
SAUK
SHAWNEE
YUROK

Athabaskan

APACHE
DENE
HUPA
NAVAHO

Caddoan

ARIKARA
CADDO
KIOWA
PAWNEE
REE

Coos

COOS

Haidan

HAIDA

Hokan

KAROK
POMO
YUMA

Inupiaq or Inuktitut

ALEUT
ESKIMO
INUIT
YUPIK

Iroquoian

CAYUGA
CHEROKEE
ERIE
HURON
IROQUOIS
MOHAWK
ONEIDA
ONONDAGA
SENECA

Muskhogean

CHICKASAW
CHOCTAW
CREEK
SEMINOLE

Penutian

CHINOOK
MAIDU

Pueblo

KERES
TANO
TEWA
ZUNI

Sahaptin

NEZ PERCE
UMATILLA
YAKIMA

Salish

FLATHEAD
KUTENAI (KUTENAY)
SALISH

Shoshonean

COMANCHE
HOPI
MISSION
PAIUTE
SHOSHONE
UINTA
UTE

Siouan

ASSINIBOINE
BILOXI
CATAWBA
CROW
DAKOTA
IOWA
MANDAN
MISSOURI
OGLALA
OMAHA
OSAGE
OTOE
PONCA
TETON
WINNEBAGO

Tlingit

TLINGIT

Uto-Aztecan

PAPAGO
PIMA

Wakashan

KWAKIUTL
NOOTKA

UNITED STATES PRESIDENTS

President & First Lady	Party	V.P.	Born	Term
1. WASHINGTON, George Martha Dandridge Custis	Fed.	Adams	VA	1789-1797
2. ADAMS, John Abigail Smith	Fed.	Jefferson	MA	1797-1801
3. JEFFERSON, Thomas Martha Wayles Skelton	Dem.-Rep.	Burr, Clinton	VA	1801-1809
4. MADISON, James Dorothea (Dolley) Payne Todd	Dem.-Rep.	Clinton, Gerry	VA	1809-1817
5. MONROE, James Elizabeth Kortright	Dem.-Rep.	Tompkins	VA	1817-1825
6. ADAMS, John Quincy Louise Catherine Johnson	Dem.-Rep.	Calhoun	MA	1825-1829
7. JACKSON, Andrew Rachel Donelson Robards	Dem.	Calhoun, Van Buren	SC	1829-1837
8. VAN BUREN, Martin Hannah Hoes	Dem.	Johnson	NY	1837-1841
9. HARRISON, William Henry Anna Symmes	Whig	Tyler	VA	1841
10. TYLER, John Letitia Christian and Julia Gardiner	Dem.		VA	1841-1845
11. POLK, James Knox Sarah Childress	Dem.	Dallas	NC	1845-1849
12. TAYLOR, Zachary Margaret Smith	Whig	Fillmore	VA	1849-1850
13. FILLMORE, Millard Abigail Powers and Caroline Carmichael McIntosh	Whig		NY	1850-1853
14. PIERCE, Franklin Jane Mears Appleton	Dem.	King	NH	1853-1857
15. BUCHANAN, James none	Dem.	Breckenridge	PA	1857-1861
16. LINCOLN, Abraham Mary Todd	Rep.	Hamlin, Johnson	KY	1861-1865
17. JOHNSON, Andrew Eliza McCardle	Dem.		NC	1865-1869
18. GRANT, Ulysses Simpson Julia Dent	Rep.	Colfax, Wilson	OH	1869-1877
19. HAYES, Rutherford Birchard Lucy Ware Webb	Rep.	Wheeler	OH	1877-1881
20. GARFIELD, James Abram Lucretia Rudolph	Rep.	Arthur	OH	1881
21. ARTHUR, Chester Alan Ellen Lewis Herndon	Rep.		VT	1881-1885

President & First Lady	Party	V.P.	Born	Term
22. CLEVELAND,Stephen Grover Frances Folsom	Dem.	Hendricks	NJ	1885-1889
23. HARRISON, Benjamin Caroline Lavinia Scott and Mary Scott Lord Dimmick	Rep.	Morton	OH	1889-1893
24. CLEVELAND,Stephen Grover Frances Folsom	Dem.	Stevenson	NJ	1893-1897
25. MCKINLEY, William Ida Saxton	Rep.	Hobart, Roosevelt	OH	1897-1901
26. ROOSEVELT, Theodore Alice Hathaway Lee and Edith Kermit Carow	Rep.	Fairbanks	NY	1901-1909
27. TAFT, William Howard Helen Herron	Rep.	Sherman	OH	1909-1913
28. WILSON, Thomas Woodrow Ellen Louise Axson and Edith Bolling Galt	Dem.	Marshall	VA	1913-1921
29. HARDING, Warren Gamaliel Florence Kling De Wolfe	Rep.	Coolidge	OH	1921-1923
30. COOLIDGE, John Calvin Grace Anna Goodhue	Rep.	Dawes	VT	1923-1929
31. HOOVER, Herbert Clark Lou Henry	Rep.	Curtis	IA	1929-1933
32. ROOSEVELT, Franklin Delano Anna Eleanor Roosevelt	Dem.	Garner, Wallace, Truman	NY	1933-1945
33. TRUMAN, Harry S Elizabeth (Bess) Wallace	Dem.	Barkley	MO	1945-1953
34. EISENHOWER, Dwight David Mamie Geneva Doud	Rep.	Nixon	TX	1953-1961
35. KENNEDY, John Fitzgerald Jacqueline Lee Bouvier	Dem.	Johnson	MA	1961-1963
36. JOHNSON, Lyndon Baines Claudia (Lady Bird) Alta Taylor	Dem.	Humphrey	TX	1963-1968
37. NIXON, Richard Milhous Thelma Catherine Patricia Ryan	Rep.	Agnew, Ford	CA	1968-1974
38. FORD, Gerald Rudolph ne, Leslie Lynch King, Jr. Elizabeth Bloomer Warren	Rep.	Rockefeller	NE	1974-1977
39. CARTER, James Earl, Jr. Rosalynn Smith	Dem.	Mondale	GA	1977-1981
40. REAGAN, Ronald Wilson Anne Frances Robbins Davis	Rep.	Bush	IL	1981-1989
41. BUSH, George Herbert Walker Barbara Pierce	Rep.	Quayle	MA	1989-1993
42. CLINTON, William Jefferson Hillary Rodham	Dem.	Gore	AR	1993-

191

SHAKESPEARE

1. *The First Part of King Henry the Sixth*
Sir William LUCY; King HENRY the Sixth; BASSET, Lord TALBOT, John TAL-BOT, VERNON; Duke of ALENÇON, Duke of BEDFORD, CHARLES, Duke of GLOSTER, Earl of SUFFOLK, Earl of WARWICK; Countess of AUVERGNE, Thomas, Henry, and John BEAUFORT, Duke of BURGUNDY, Sir John FAS-TOLFE, Sir Thomas GARGRAVE, MARGARET, Edmund MORTIMER, REIGNIER; Sir William GLANSDALE, Earl of SALISBURY, WOODVILLE; Richard PLANTAGENET; JOAN LA PUCELLE (Joan of Arc)

2. *The Second Part of King Henry the Sixth*
Lord SAY; Jack CADE, DICK the butcher, John HUME, Alexander IDEN, VAUX; George BEVIS, Matthew GOUGH, King HENRY the Sixth, PETER, SMITH the weaver; EDWARD, Thomas HORNER, Lord SCALES; ELEANOR, John HOLLAND, MICHAEL, MARGERY Jourdain, RICHARD, Saunder SIMP-COX, Sir John STANLEY, Duke of SUFFOLK, Earl of WARWICK; Cardinal BEAUFORT, Lord CLIFFORD and his son young CLIFFORD, HUMPHREY, MARGARET, Duke of SOMERSET, Sir Humphrey and William STAFFORD; Earl of SALISBURY, John SOUTHWELL; Duke of BUCKINGHAM; Roger BOLING-BROKE, Richard PLANTAGENET

3. *The Third Part of King Henry the Sixth*
BONA, Lady GRAY; King HENRY the Sixth; EDMUND, EDWARD, Duke of EXETER, GEORGE, Earl of OXFORD, Lord RIVERS; LOUIS XI, Duke of NOR-FOLK, RICHARD, Sir William STANLEY, Earl of WARWICK; Lord CLIFFORD, Lord HASTINGS, Queen MARGARET, Marquess of MONTAGUE, Sir John and Sir Hugh MORTIMER, Earl of PEMBROKE, Duke of SOMERSET, Lord STAFFORD; Sir John MONTGOMERY, Sir John SOMERVILLE; Richard PLAN-TAGENET; Earl of WESTMORELAND; Earl of NORTHUMBERLAND

4. *King Richard the Third*
Lady ANNE, Lord GREY, Duchess of YORK; HENRY, Lord LOVEL; Sir James BLOUNT, Marquess of DORSET, King EDWARD the Fourth, GEORGE, John MORTON, Earl of OXFORD, Earl RIVERS, Earl of SURREY, Sir James TYRREL; Sir William CATESBY, Sir Walter HERBERT, Duke of NORFOLK, King RICHARD the Third, Lord STANLEY, TRESSEL, Christopher URSWICK, Sir Thomas VAUGHAN; BERKELEY, Lord HASTINGS, MARGARET, Sir Richard RATCLIFF; Cardinal BOURCHIER, ELIZABETH, Thomas ROTHERHAM; Duke of BUCKINGHAM, Sir Robert BRAKENBURY

5. *Titus Andronicus*
AARON, CAIUS; CHIRON, LUCIUS, MUTIUS, TAMORA; ALARBUS, LAVINIA, MARTIUS, PUBLIUS, QUINTUS; AEMILIUS; BASSIANUS, DEMETRIUS, VALENTINE; SATURNINUS, SEMPRONIUS; TITUS ANDRONICUS; MARCUS ANDRONICUS

6. *The Comedy of Errors*
LUCE; PINCH; AEGEON, ANGELO, DROMIO (of Ephesus and of Syracuse, twin attendants); AEMILIA, ADRIANA, LUCIANA, SOLINUS; BALTHAZAR; ANTIPHOLUS (of Ephesus and of Syracuse, twins)

7. *The Two Gentlemen of Verona*
JULIA, SPEED; LAUNCE, SILVIA, THURIO; ANTONIO, LUCETTA, PROTEUS; EGLAMOUR, PANTHINO; VALENTINE

8. *Love's Labour's Lost*
DULL, MOTH; BOYET, MARIA; Don Adriano de ARMADO, BEROWNE, COSTARD, DUMAINE, MERCADE; PRINCESS of France, ROSALINE; FERDI-NAND, KATHERINE, Sir NATHANIEL; HOLOFERNES, JAQUENETTA, LON-GAVILLE

9. *Romeo and Juliet*
Friar JOHN; PARIS, PETER, ROMEO; JULIET, TYBALT; ABRAHAM, CAPULET, ESCALUS, GREGORY, SAMPSON; BENVOLIO, Friar LAURENCE, MERCUTIO, MONTAGUE; BALTHASAR

10. *A Midsummer Night's Dream*
LION, MOTH, PUCK, SNUG, WALL; EGEUS, FLUTE, SNOUT; BOTTOM, COB-WEB, HELENA, HERMIA, OBERON, QUINCE, THISBE; PYRAMUS, THESEUS, TITANIA; LYSANDER; DEMETRIUS, HIPPOLYTA, MOONSHINE; STARVELING; MUSTARD-SEED, PHILOSTRATE, PEAS-BLOSSOM

11. *King John*
King JOHN; Robert BIGOT, Prince HENRY, LOUIS, MELUN, PETER of Pomfret; ARTHUR, BLANCH, ELINOR, James GURNEY, King PHILIP of France; Hubert DE BURGH; Cardinal PANDULPH; CONSTANCE, CHATILLON, Geffrey FITZ-PETER, William LONGSWORD, William MARESHALL; Robert, Philip, and Lady FAULCONBRIDGE

12. *The Taming of the Shrew*
BIANCA, CURTIS, GREMIO, GRUMIO, PEDANT, TRANIO; BAPTISTA, LUCEN-TIO; BIONDELLO, HORTENSIO, KATHARINA, PETRUCHIO, VINCENTIO; CHRISTOPHER SLY

13. *King Richard the Second*
Lord ROSS, Duchess of YORK; BAGOT, BUSHY, GREEN, HENRY Bolingbroke, Henry PERCY; EDMUND of Langley, Sir PIERCE of Exton, Sir Stephen SCROOP, Duke of SURREY; Duke of AUMERLE, Lord BERKLEY, Duchess of GLOSTER, Thomas MOWBRAY, King RICHARD the Second; Lord FITZWA-TER, Earl of SALISBURY; Lord WILLOUGHBY; JOHN OF GAUNT; Earl of NORTHUMBERLAND

14. *The Merchant of Venice*
Launcelot GOBBO and his father, TUBAL; PORTIA; ANTONIO, Prince of ARRAGON, JESSICA, LORENZO, Prince of MOROCCO, NERISSA, SOLANIO, SHYLOCK; BASSANIO, GRATIANO, LEONARDO, SALARINO, STEPHANO; BALTHAZAR

15. *The First Part of King Henry the Fourth*
Prince JOHN, PETO; Sir Walter BLUNT, King HENRY the Fourth, Henry, and Lady PERCY; POINTZ, SCROOP, Sir Richard VERNON; HOTSPUR, Sir MICHAEL, Mistress QUICKLY; BARDOLPH, Sir John FALSTAFF, GADSHILL, Edmund and Lady MORTIMER; ARCHIBALD, Owen GLENDOWER; Earl of WESTMORELAND

16. *The Second Part of King Henry Fourth*
DAVY, FANG, Prince JOHN, PAGE, PETO, WART; BLUNT, GOWER, King HENRY the Fourth, SNARE; FEEBLE, MORTON, MOULDY, PISTOL, POINTZ, RUMOUR, SHADOW, SURREY, THOMAS of Clarence; MOWBRAY, Hostess QUICKLY, SHALLOW, SILENCE, TRAVERS, WARWICK; Lord BARDOLPH, BULLCALF, COLEVILE, FALSTAFF, HARCOURT, HASTINGS, HUMPHREY; WESTMORELAND; DOLL TEARSHEET; NORTHUMBERLAND

Shakespeare

17. *King Henry the Fifth*
NYM; Sir Thomas GREY, JAMY, Duke of YORK; ALICE, John BATES, Alexander COURT, GOWER, King HENRY the Fifth, LOUIS; Duke of EXETER, ISABEL, PISTOL, Lord SCROOP; Duke of BEDFORD, Duke of BOURBON, CHARLES the Sixth of France, Duke of GLOSTER, MONTJOY, Duke of ORLEANS, Mistress QUICKLY, Earl of WARWICK; BARDOLPH, Duke of BURGUNDY, FLUELLEN, GRANDPRE, RAMBURES, Michael WILLIAMS; Earl of CAMBRIDGE, Sir Thomas ERPINGHAM, KATHARINE, MACMORRIS, Earl of SALISBURY; Earl of WESTMORELAND

18. *Much Ado about Nothing*
HERO; URSULA, VERGES; ANTONIO, CLAUDIO, CONRADE, DON JOHN, Friar FRANCIS, LEONATO; BEATRICE, BENEDICK, BORACHIO, DOGBERRY, DON PEDRO, MARGARET; BALTHAZAR

19. *The Merry Wives of Windsor*
NYM; ANNE Page, FORD, PAGE; Doctor CAIUS, Sir Hugh EVANS, ROBIN, RUGBY; FENTON, PISTOL, SIMPLE; Mistress QUICKLY, SHALLOW, SLENDER, WILLIAM Page; BARDOLPH, Sir John FALSTAFF.

20. *Julius Caesar*
Young CATO; CASCA, CINNA, VARRO; CICERO, CLITUS, LUCIUS, PORTIA, STRATO; CASSIUS, FLAVIUS, MESSALA, PUBLIUS; CLAUDIUS, LIGARIUS, LUCILIUS, MARULLUS, PINDARUS, TITINIUS; DARDANIUS, TREBONIUS, VOLUMNIUS; CALPHURNIA; ARTEMIDORUS; DECIUS BRUTUS, JULIUS CAESAR, MARCUS BRUTUS, POPILIUS LENA; MARCUS ANTONIUS, METELLUS CIMBER, OCTAVIUS CAESAR; M. AEMILIUS LEPIDUS,

21. *As You Like It*
ADAM, DUKE; CELIA, CORIN, DENIS, HYMEN, PHEBE; AMIENS, AUDREY, JAQUES, LE BEAU, OLIVER; CHARLES, Sir Oliver MARTEXT, ORLANDO, SILVIUS, WILLIAM; ROSALIND; FREDERICK; TOUCHSTONE

22. *Twelfth Night; or, What You Will*
CLOWN, CURIO, MARIA, VIOLA; FABIAN, OLIVIA, ORSINO; ANTONIO; MALVOLIO; Andrew AGUECHEEK, SEBASTIAN, TOBY BELCH, VALENTINE

23. *Hamlet, Prince of Denmark*
OSRIC; HAMLET; HORATIO, LAERTES, OPHELIA; BERNARDO, CLAUDIUS, GERTRUDE, POLONIUS, REYNALDO; CORNELIUS, FRANCISCO, MARCELLUS, VOLTIMAND; FORTINBRAS; ROSENCRANTZ; GUILDENSTERN

24. *Troilus and Cressida*
AJAX; HELEN, PARIS, PRIAM; AENEAS, HECTOR, NESTOR; ANTENOR, CALCHAS, HELENUS, TROILUS, ULYSSES; ACHILLES, CRESSIDA, DIOMEDES, MENELAUS, PANDARUS; AGAMEMNON, ALEXANDER, CASSANDRA, DEIPHOBUS, PATROCLUS, THERSITES; ANDROMACHE, MARGARELON

25. *All's Well That Ends Well*
DIANA, LAFEU; HELENA; BERTRAM, LAVACHE, MARIANA, STEWARD; PAROLLES, VIOLENTA; Countess of ROUSILLON

26. *Measure for Measure*
ELBOW, FROTH, LUCIO, Friar PETER; ANGELO, JULIET, POMPEY, Friar THOMAS; CLAUDIO, ESCALUS, MARIANA, PROVOST, VARRIUS; ABHORSON, ISABELLA, OVERDONE; FRANCISCA, VINCENTIO; BARNARDINE

27. *Othello, the Moor of Venice*
IAGO; CLOWN; BIANCA, CASSIO, EMILIA; MONTANO, OTHELLO; GRA-
TIANO, LODOVICO, RODERIGO; BRABANTIO, DESDEMONA

28. *Macbeth*
ROSS; ANGUS; BANQUO, DUNCAN, HECATE, LENNOX, SEYTON, SIWARD;
FLEANCE, MACBETH, MACDUFF, MALCOLM; MENTEITH; CAITHNESS,
DONALBAIN; LADY MACBETH, LADY MACDUFF

29. *King Lear*
Earl of KENT, LEAR; CURAN, EDGAR, REGAN; Duke of ALBANY, EDMUND,
OSWALD; Earl of GLOSTER, GONERIL; CORDELIA, Duke of BURGUNDY,
Duke of CORNWALL

30. *Antony and Cleopatra*
EROS, IRAS; MENAS, PHILO; ALEXAS, GALLUS, SCARUS, SILIUS, TAURUS;
AGRIPPA, MARDIAN, OCTAVIA, THYREUS, VARRIUS; CANIDIUS, CHARMI-
AN, DERCETAS, DIOMEDES, MAECENAS, SELEUCUS; CLEOPATRA,
DEMETRIUS, DOLABELLA, VENTIDIUS; EUPHRONIUS, MARK ANTONY,
MENECRATES, PROCULEIUS; OCTAVIUS CAESAR, SEXTUS POMPEIUS; M.
AEMILIUS LEPIDUS; DOMITIUS ENOBARBUS

31. *Coriolanus*
VALERIA; COMINIUS, VIRGILIA, VOLUMNIA; CAIUS MARCIUS (Coriolanus),
JUNIUS BRUTUS, TITUS LARTIUS; TULLUS AUFIDIUS; MENENIUS AGRIP-
PA, SICINIUS VELUTUS

32. *Timon of Athens*
CUPID, TIMON, TITUS; CAPHIS, LUCIUS; FLAVIUS, PHRYNIA; LUCILIUS,
LUCULLUS, PHILOTUS, TIMANDRA; APEMANTUS, FLAMINIUS, SERVILIUS,
VENTIDIUS; ALCIBIADES, HORTENSIUS, SEMPRONIUS

33. *Pericles*
BOULT, CLEON, DIANA, GOWER; MARINA, THAISA; CERIMON, DIONYZA,
ESCANES, LEONINE; PERICLES, PHILEMON, THALIARD; ANTIOCHUS,
HELICANUS, LYCHORIDA, SIMONIDES; LYSIMACHUS

34. *Cymbeline*
HELEN, QUEEN; CLOTEN, IMOGEN; IACHIMO, PISANIO; BELARIUS, PHI-
LARIO; ARVIRAGUS, CORNELIUS, CYMBELINE, GUIDERIUS; CAIUS
LUCIUS; POSTHUMUS LEONATUS

35. *The Winter's Tale*
DION; CLOWN, MOPSA; DORCAS, EMILIA; CAMILLO, LEONTES, PAULINA,
PERDITA; FLORIZEL, HERMIONE; ANTIGONUS, AUTOLYCUS, CLEOMENES,
MAMILLIUS, POLIXENES; ARCHIDAMUS

36. *The Tempest*
IRIS, JUNO; ARIEL, CERES; ADRIAN, King ALONSO; ANTONIO, CALIBAN;
GONZALO, MIRANDA; PROSPERO, STEPHANO, TRINCULO; FERDINAND,
FRANCISCO, SEBASTIAN

37. *King Henry the Eighth*
Sir Nicholas VAUX; Doctor BUTTS, Sir Anthony DENNY, King HENRY the
Eighth, Lord SANDS; Sir Thomas LOVELL, Earl of SURREY, Cardinal WOLSEY;
BRANDON, CRANMER, Duke of NORFOLK, Duke of SUFFOLK; Cardinal
CAMPEIUS, CAPUCIUS, CROMWELL, GARDINER, GRIFFITH, PATIENCE; Sir
Henry GUILDFORD, KATHARINE; ANNE BULLEN, Duke of BUCKINGHAM;
Lord ABERGAVENNY

BIBLE CHARACTERS

OLD TESTAMENT
(Names used in the Douay Bible,
when different from the King James
Version, are in parentheses)

1. GENESIS
2. EXODUS
3. LEVITICUS
4. NUMBERS
5. DEUTERONOMY
6. JOSHUA
7. JUDGES
8. RUTH
9. I SAMUEL (I KINGS)
10. II SAMUEL (II KINGS)
11. I KINGS (III KINGS)
12. II KINGS (IV KINGS)
13. I CHRONICLES
    (I PARALIPOMENON)
14. II CHRONICLES
    (II PARALIPOMENON)
15. EZRA (I ESDRAS)
16. NEHEMIAH (II ESDRAS)
17. ESTHER
18. JOB
19. PSALMS
20. PROVERBS
21. ECCLESIASTES
22. SONG OF SOLOMON
    (CANTICLE OF CANTICLES)
23. ISAIAH (ISAIAS)
24. JEREMIAH (JEREMIAS)
25. LAMENTATIONS
26. EZEKIEL (EZECHIEL)
27. DANIEL
28. HOSEA (OSEE)
29. JOEL
30. AMOS
31. OBADIAH (ABDIAS)
32. JONAH (JONAS)
33. MICAH (MICHEAS)
34. NAHUM
35. HABAKKUK (HABACUC)
36. ZEPHANIAH
    (SOPHONIAS)
37. HAGGAI (AGGEUS)
38. ZECHARIAH (ZACHARIAS)
39. MALACHI (MALACHIAS)

BOOKS OF THE APOCRYPHA

I Esdras (III Esdras)
II Esdras (IV Esdras)
Tobit (Tobias)
Judith
Additions to Esther
Wisdom of Solomon
Ecclesiasticus
Baruch
Letter of Jeremiah
Additions to Daniel:
    Song of the Three Holy Children,
    Susanna, and
    Bel and the Dragon
Prayer of Manasses
I Maccabees (I Machabees)
II Maccabees (II Machabees)

NEW TESTAMENT

1. MATTHEW
2. MARK
3. LUKE
4. JOHN
5. THE ACTS
6. ROMANS
7. I CORINTHIANS
8. II CORINTHIANS
9. GALATIANS
10. EPHESIANS
11. PHILIPPIANS
12. COLOSSIANS
13. I THESSALONIANS
14. II THESSALONIANS
15. I TIMOTHY
16. II TIMOTHY
17. TITUS
18. PHILEMON
19. HEBREWS
20. JAMES
21. I PETER
22. II PETER
23. I JOHN
24. II JOHN
25. III JOHN
26. JUDE
27. REVELATION (APOCALYPSE)

<u>Prophets</u>

AMOS
EZRA
JOEL
HOSEA
JONAH
MICAH
MOSES
NAHUM
DANIEL
ELISHA
HAGGAI
ISAIAH
EZEKIEL
JEREMIAH

<u>Men of the Bible</u>

ARA
ASA
DAN
ELI
GOG
HAM
IRA
LOT
NUN
URI
ABEL
ADAM
AGAG
AHAB
AHAZ
AMOS
BOAZ
CAIN
CUSH
DOEG
ENOS
ESAU
HETH
IRAD
JADA
JEHU
JOAB
KISH
LEVI
MASH
MOAB
NOAH
OBAL

OBED
OMAR
OMRI
OREB
OZEM
SAUL
SETH
SHEM
SODI
ULAM
UNNI
URIA
AARON
ABIAH
ABIEL
AHIRA
AMASA
ANNAS
CALEB
CHUZA
CYRUS
DAVID
ENOCH
HAMAN
HARAN
HEROD
HIRAM
HOHAM
IBZAN
ISAAC
JACOB
JAMES
JARED
JORAM
LABAN
MASSA
MOREH
NABAL
NADAB
NAHBI
NAHOR
OPHIR
PELEG
REZON
SACAR
SERUG
TERAH
URIAH
ZAHAM
GIDEON
JOSHUA
LAMECH

REUBEN
SAMSON
ABRAHAM
ANANIAS
GOLIATH
ISHMAEL
JAPHETH
MESHACH
SOLOMON
ABEDNEGO
JEPHTHAH
JONATHAN
SHADRACH

<u>Women of the Bible</u>

EVE
ADAH
JAEL
LEAH
MARY
RUTH
DINAH
EGLAH
HAGAR
JULIA
JUNIA
LYDIA
MERAB
NAOMI
PHEBE
RAHAB
SARAH
TAMAR
BILHAH
DORCAS
ESTHER
HANNAH
HOGLAH
MAACAH
MAHLAH
MICHAL
MILCAH
MIRIAM
RACHEL
RIZPAH
SALOME
VASHTI
ZILLAH
ZILPAH
ABIGAIL
HAMUTAL

GODS & GODDESSES

GREEK MYTHOLOGY

chief god	ZEUS
demigod	SATYR; TRITON
goddess of agriculture	DEMETER
goddess of criminal folly	ATE
goddess of dawn	EOS
goddess of discord	ERIS
goddess of earth	GAEA
goddess of fate	MOIRA
goddess of love	APHRODITE
goddess of magic	HECATE
goddess of mischief	ATE
goddess of peace	IRENE
goddess of revenge	NEMESIS
goddess of the moon	HECATE, SELENE; ARTEMIS
goddess of the night	NYX
goddess of victory	NIKE
goddess of wisdom	ATHENA
goddess of youth	HEBE
god of fields, flocks, forests	PAN
god of love	EROS
god of mirth	COMUS
god of revelry	DIONYSUS
god of ridicule	MOMUS
god of the harvest	CRONUS
god of the north wind	BOREAS
god of the sea	NEREUS, TRITON; POSEIDON
god of the southeast wind	EURUS
god of the underworld	HADES, PLUTO
god of war	ARES
god of wealth	PLUTUS
god of wind	AEOLUS
god of youth	APOLLO
herald of the gods	HERMES
mother of the gods	RHEA
queen of the gods	HERA
Zeus, consort of	HERA, LEDA, LETO, MAIA; DANAE, METIS; AEGINA, CALYCE, EUROPA, SEMELE, SELENE, THEMIS; ALCMENE, ANTIOPE
Zeus, offspring of	ATE; ARES, HEBE; AEGLE, ARCAS, BELUS, HELEN, MINOS; AEACUS, AGLAIA, APOLLO, ATHENE, CLOTHO, HERMES, POLLUX, THALIA, ZETHUS

EGYPTIAN MYTHOLOGY

chief deity	AMON
goddess of the heavens	NUT
god of evil	BES, SET; SETH
god of fertility	AMON
god of magic	THOTH
god of Memphis	PTAH
god of pleasure	BES
god of the lower world	SERAPIS
god of the sun	AMON-RE
god of the underworld	OSIRIS
god of wisdom	THOTH
hawk-headed god	HORUS
Nile as a god	HAPI
Queen of the gods	SATI
serpent goddess	BUTO

NORSE MYTHOLOGY

chief god	ODIN
earlier race of gods	VANIR
fates	NORNS
goddess of beauty & love	FREYA
goddess of the earth	ERDA
goddess of the underworld	HEL
god of discord & mischief	LOKI
god of fertility	FREY
god of light	BALDER
god of poetry	BRAGI
god of the sea	AEGIR
god of the sky	TYR
god of thunder	THOR
home of the gods	ASGARD
Norse pantheon	AESIR

ROMAN MYTHOLOGY

chief god	JOVE
goddess of agriculture	CERES
goddess of crops	ANNONA
goddess of dawn	AURORA
goddess of faith	FIDES
goddess of grain	CERES
goddess of hope	SPES
goddess of horses	EPONA
goddess of love	VENUS
goddess of prosperity	SALUS
goddess of the earth	TERRA
goddess of the harvest	OPS
goddess of the hearth	VESTA
goddess of the moon	DIAN, LUNA
god of death	MORS
god of fields and herds	FAUN
god of fire	VULCAN
god of love	AMOR, CUPID
god of mirth and joy	COMUS
god of music	APOLLO
god of revelry	BACCHUS
god of the north wind	BOREAS

god of the sea ....NEPTUNE
god of the sun...............SOL; APOLLO
god of war ....MARS
gods of underworld..........DIS; ORCUS
queen of the gods........................JUNO

OTHER MYTHOLOGIES

Assyrian god of war ....ASHUR

Babylonian goddess of love ....ISHTAR
Babylonian god of earth ....DAGAN
Celtic chief god.......................DAGDA
Celtic god of the sea ....LER
Celtic queen of the gods ....DANU
Hindu goddess of evil ....KALI
Hindu god of love ....KAMA
Phoenician goddess, fertility ASTARTE
Welsh gods ....GWYN, LLEW

ACADEMY AWARD WINNERS

1994..........Tom Hanks, Jessica Lange	1961 ....Maximilian Schell,
1993.............Tom Hanks, Holly Hunter	....Sophia Loren
1992........Al Pacino, Emma Thompson	1960............................Burt Lancaster,
1991 ....Anthony Hopkins, Jodie Foster	................................Elizabeth Taylor
1990...........Jeremy Irons, Kathy Bates	1959 ....Charlton Heston,
1989 ....Daniel Day-Lewis,	..............................Simone Signoret
....Jessica Tandy	1958 ......David Niven, Susan Hayward
1988.......Dustin Hoffman, Jodie Foster	1957 ....Alec Guinness,
1987.................Michael Douglas, Cher	...............................Joanne Woodward
1986 ....Paul Newman, Marlee Matlin	1956........Yul Brynner, Ingrid Bergman
1985.......William Hurt, Geraldine Page	1955 ....Ernest Borgnine,
1984 ....F. Murray Abraham,	....Anna Magnani
....Sally Field	1954 ....Marlon Brando, Grace Kelly
1983 ....Robert Duvall,	1953..William Holden,Audrey Hepburn
.................................Shirley MacLaine	1952 ....Gary Cooper, Shirley Booth
1982..........Ben Kingsley, Meryl Streep	1951 ...Humphrey Bogart, Vivien Leigh
1981 ....Henry Fonda,	1950 ....Jose Ferrer, Judy Holliday
..............................Katharine Hepburn	1949 ....Broderick Crawford,
1980.......Robert DeNiro, Sissy Spacek	................................Olivia de Havilland
1979..........Dustin Hoffman, Sally Field	1948 ....Laurence Olivier, Jane Wyman
1978.............Jon Voight, Jane Fonda	1947....Ronald Colman, Loretta Young
1977.........................Richard Dreyfuss,	1946 ....Fredric March,
....Diane Keaton	................................Olivia de Havilland
1976....Peter Finch, Faye Dunaway	1945 ....Ray Milland, Joan Crawford
1975 ....Jack Nicholson,	1944 ....Bing Crosby, Ingrid Bergman
....Louise Fletcher	1943 ....Paul Lukas, Jennifer Jones
1974.............Art Carney, Ellen Burstyn	1942 .....James Cagney, Greer Garson
1973................................Jack Lemmon,	1941 ....Gary Cooper, Joan Fontaine
.................................Glenda Jackson	1940 ....James Stewart, Ginger Rogers
1972........Marlon Brando, Liza Minnelli	1939 ....Robert Donat, Vivien Leigh
1971 ....Gene Hackman, Jane Fonda	1938 ....Spencer Tracy, Bette Davis
1970 ....George C. Scott,	1937........Spencer Tracy, Luise Rainer
....Glenda Jackson	1936...............Paul Muni, Luise Rainer
1969 ....John Wayne, Maggie Smith	1935.......Victor McLaglen, Bette Davis
1968 ....Cliff Robertson,	1934 ....Clark Gable, Claudette Colbert
............................Katharine Hepburn &	1933.........................Charles Laughton,
......................................Barbra Streisand	................................Katharine Hepburn
1967 ....Rod Steiger,	1932............................Fredric March &
.................................Katharine Hepburn	...............Wallace Beery, Helen Hayes
1966 ....Paul Scofield, Elizabeth Taylor	1931 ....Lionel Barrymore,
1965.............Lee Marvin, Julie Christie	....Marie Dressler
1964........Rex Harrison, Julie Andrews	1930.....George Arliss, Norma Shearer
1963.........Sidney Poitier, Patricia Neal	1929......Warner Baxter, Mary Pickford
1962 ......Gregory Peck, Anne Bancroft	1928 ....Emil Jannings, Janet Gaynor

COLLEGES & UNIVERSITIES

The nickname of the sports teams of each college or university is indicated in parentheses. The location of the school follows the team nickname. The location is not given when the city and state are a part of the name of the school.

Adelphi U. (Panthers)
   Garden City, NY
Akron, U. of (Zips) Akron, OH
Alabama A&M U.(Bulldogs)
   Normal, AL
Alabama-Birmingham, U. of (Blazers)
Alabama-Huntsville, U. of (Chargers)
Alabama State U. (Hornets)
   Montgomery, AL
Alabama-Tuscaloosa, U. of
   (Crimson Tide)
Alaska-Anchorage, U. of (Seawolves)
Alaska-Fairbanks, U. of (Nanooks)
Alcorn State U. (Scalping Braves)
   Lorman, MS
Alfred U. (Saxons) Alfred, NY
Amherst Coll. (Lord Jeffs)
   Amherst, MA
Arizona, U. of (Wildcats) Tucson, AZ
Arizona State U. (Sun Devils)
   Tempe, AZ
Arkansas-Fayetteville, U. of
   (Razorbacks)
Arkansas-Little Rock, U. of (Trojans)
Arkansas-Monticello, U. of (Weevils)
Arkansas-Pine Bluff, U. of
   (Golden Lions)
Arkansas State U. (Indians)
   State University, AR
Auburn U. (Tigers) Auburn, AL
Augusta Coll. (Jaguars) Augusta, GA
Austin Peay State U. (Governors)
   Clarksville, TN

Babson Coll. (Beavers)
   Babson Park, MA
Ball State U. (Cardinals) Muncie, IN
Bard Coll. (Blazers)
   Annandale-on-Hudson, NY
Bates Coll. (Bobcats) Lewiston, ME
Baylor U. (Bears) Waco, TX
Belmont U. (Rebels) Nashville, TN
Beloit Coll. (Buccaneers) Beloit, WI
Bethune-Cookman Coll. (Wildcats)
   Daytona Beach, FL
Boise State U. (Broncos) Boise, ID
Boston Coll. (Eagles) Boston, MA
Boston U. (Terriers) Boston, MA
Bowdoin Coll. (Polar Bears)
   Brunswick, ME
Bowie State U. (Bulldogs) Bowie, MD

Bowling Green State U. (Falcons)
   Bowling Green, OH
Bradley U. (Braves) Peoria, IL
Brandeis U. (Judges) Waltham, MA
Brigham Young U. (Cougars)
   Provo, UT
Brown U. (Bears) Providence, RI
Bryant Coll. (Indians) Smithfield, RI
Bryn Mawr Coll. (Mawrters)
   Bryn Mawr, PA
Bucknell U. (Bison) Lewisburg, PA
Butler U. (Bulldogs) Indianapolis, IN

California-Berkeley, U. of
   (Golden Bears)
California-Davis, U. of (Aggies)
California-Irvine, U. of (Anteaters)
California-Los Angeles, U. of (Bruins)
California-Riverside, U. of
   (Highlanders)
California-San Diego, U. of (Tritons)
California-Santa Barbara, U. of
   (Gauchos)
California-Santa Cruz, U. of
   (Banana Slugs)
California State U. at Bakersfield
   (Roadrunners)
California State U. at Chico (Wildcats)
California State U. at Dominguez Hills
   (Toros)
California State U. at Fresno
   (Bulldogs)
California State U. at Fullerton
   (Titans)
California State U. at Hayward
   (Pioneers)
California State U. at Long Beach
   (49'ers)
California State U. at Los Angeles
   (Golden Eagles)
California State U. at Northridge
   (Matadors)
California State U. at Sacramento
   (Hornets)
California State U. at San Bernardino
   (Coyotes)
Campbell U. (Fighting Camels)
   Buies Creek, NC
Canisius Coll. (Griffs) Buffalo, NY
Carnegie Mellon U. (Tartans)
   Pittsburgh, PA

Case Western Reserve U. (Spartans)
Cleveland, OH
Catholic U. of America (Cardinals)
Washington, DC
Chicago, U. of (Maroons) Chicago, IL
Chicago State U. (Cougars)
Chicago, IL
Christian Brothers U. (Buccaneers)
Memphis, TN
Cincinnati, U. of (Bearcats)
Cincinnati, OH
Citadel, The (Bulldogs)
Charleston, SC
City College of New York (Beavers)
New York, NY
Clarkson, U. (Golden Knights)
Potsdam, NY
Clemson U. (Tigers) Clemson, SC
Cleveland State U. (Vikings)
Cleveland, OH
Coe Coll. (Kohawks)
Cedar Rapids, IA
Colby Coll. (White Mules)
Waterville, ME
Colgate U. (Red Raiders)
Hamilton, NY
Colorado-Boulder, U. of (Buffaloes)
Colorado-Colorado Springs, U. of
(Gold)
Colorado State U. (Rams)
Fort Collins, CO
Columbia U. (Lions) New York, NY
Concord Coll. (Mountain Lions)
Athens, WV
Concordia Coll. (Cobbers)
Moorhead, MN
Connecticut-Avery Point, U. of
(Pointers) Groton, CT
Connecticut Coll. (Camels)
New London, CT
Connecticut-Storrs, U. of (Huskies)
Cornell U. (Big Red) Ithaca, NY
Creighton U. (Bluejays) Omaha, NE

Dallas, U. of (Crusaders) Irving, TX
Dartmouth Coll. (The Big Green)
Hanover, NH
Davidson Coll. (Wildcats)
Davidson, NC
Delaware, U. of (Fightin' Blue Hens)
Newark, DE
Delaware State Coll. (Hornets)
Dover, DE
Denison U. (Big Red) Granville, OH
Denver, U. of (Pioneers) Denver, CO
DePaul U. (Blue Demons) Chicago, IL
DePauw U. (Tigers) Greencastle, IN
Detroit, U. of (Titans) Detroit, MI
Dickinson Coll. (Red Devils)
Carlisle, PA

Dillard U. (Blue Devils)
New Orleans, LA
Drake U. (Bulldogs) Des Moines, IA
Drew U. (Rangers) Madison, NJ
Drexel U. (Dragons) Philadelphia, PA
Dubuque, U. of (Spartans)
Dubuque, IA
Duke U. (Blue Devils) Durham, NC
Duquesne U. (Dukes) Pittsburgh, PA

Eckerd Coll. (Tritons)
St. Petersburg, FL
Elmira Coll. (Soaring Eagles)
Elmira, NY
Elon Coll. (Fighting Christians)
Elon, NC
Emerson Coll. (Lions) Boston, MA
Emory U. (Eagles) Atlanta, GA

Fairfield U. (Stags) Fairfield, CT
Fairleigh Dickinson U. (Knights)
Teaneck, NJ
Florida, U. of (Gators) Gainesville, FL
Florida A&M U. (Rattlers)
Tallahassee, FL
Florida State U. (Seminoles)
Tallahassee, FL
Fordham U. (Rams) Bronx, NY
Franklin & Marshall Coll. (Diplomats)
Lancaster, PA
Friends U. (Falcons) Wichita, KS
Furman U. (Paladins) Greenville, SC

Gallaudet U. (Bison) Washington, DC
Gannon U. (Golden Knights) Erie, PA
George Mason U. (Patriots)
Fairfax, VA
Georgetown U. (Hoyas)
Washington, DC
George Washington U. (Colonials)
Washington, DC
Georgia, U. of (Bulldogs) Athens, GA
Georgia Institute of Technology
(Yellow Jackets) Atlanta, GA
Georgia State U. (Panthers)
Atlanta, GA
Gonzaga U. (Bulldogs) Spokane, WA
Grambling State U. (Tigers)
Grambling, LA

Hampton U. (Pirates) Hampton, VA
Harding U. (Bison) Searcy, AR
Hartwick Coll. (Warriors) Oneonta, NY
Harvard U. (Crimson) Cambridge, MA
Haverford Coll. (The Red Wave)
Fords, PA
Hawaii, U. of (Rainbows) Honolulu, HI
Hawaii-Pacific U. (Sea Warriors)
Honolulu, HI
Hobart Coll. (Statesmen) Geneva, NY

Hofstra U. (Flying Dutchmen)
    Hempstead, NY
Houston, U. of (Cougars) Houston, TX
Howard U. (Bison) Washington, DC

Idaho, U. of (Vandals) Moscow, ID
Idaho State U. (Bengals) Pocatello, ID
Illinois-Champaign, U. of
    (Fighting Illini)
Illinois-Chicago, U. of (Flames)
Illinois State U. (Redbirds) Normal, IL
Illinois Wesleyan U. (Titans)
    Bloomington, IL
Indiana State U. (Sycamores)
    Terre Haute, IN
Indiana U. (Hoosiers) Bloomington, IN
Indiana U. at Kokomo (Knights)
Iona Coll. (Gaels) New Rochelle, NY
Iowa, U. of (Hawkeyes) Iowa City, IA
Iowa State U. (Cyclones) Ames, IA
Ithaca Coll. (Bombers) Ithaca, NY

Jackson State U. (Tigers)
    Jackson, MS
Jacksonville State U. (Gamecocks)
    Jacksonville, FL
Jacksonville U. (Dolphins)
    Jacksonville, FL
James Madison U. (Dukes)
    Harrisonburg, VA
John Brown U. (Golden Eagles)
    Siloam Springs, AR
John Jay Coll. (Bloodhounds)
    New York, NY
Johns Hopkins U. (Bluejays)
    Baltimore, MD
Johnson & Wales U. (Griffins)
    Providence, RI

Kalamazoo Coll. (Hornets)
    Kalamazoo, MI
Kansas, U. of (Jayhawks)
    Lawrence, KS
Kansas State U. (Wildcats)
    Manhattan, KS
Kent State U. (Golden Flashes)
    Kent, OH
Kentucky, U. of (Wildcats)
    Lexington, KY
Kentucky State U. (Thorobreds)
    Frankfort, KY
Kenyon Coll. (Lords) Gambier, OH
King's Coll. (Monarchs)
    Wilkes-Barre, PA

Lafayette Coll. (Leopards) Easton, PA
LaSalle U. (Explorers)
    Philadelphia, PA
Lawrence U. (Vikings) Appleton, WI
Lehigh U. (Engineers) Bethlehem, PA

LeMoyne Coll. (Dolphins)
    Syracuse, NY
Liberty U. (Flames) Lynchburg, VA
Lincoln U. (Blue Tigers)
    Jefferson City, MO
Long Island U, CW Post Campus
    (Pioneers) Brookville, NY
Long Island U. (Blackbirds)
    Brooklyn, NY
Long Island U. (Colonials)
    Southampton, NY
Louisiana State U. (Tigers)
    Baton Rouge, LA
Louisiana State U. (Pilots)
    Shreveport, LA
Louisville, U. of (Cardinals)
    Louisville, KY
Loyola, U (Ramblers) Chicago, IL

Maine-Farmington, U. of (Beavers)
Maine-Fort Kent, U. of (Bengals)
Maine-Machias, U. of (Clippers)
Maine-Orono, U. of (Black Bears)
Maine-Presque Isle, U. of (Owls)
Manhattan Coll. (Jaspers) Bronx, NY
Marist Coll. (Red Foxes)
    Poughkeepsie, NY
Marquette U. (Warriors)
    Milwaukee, WI
Marshall U. (Thundering Herd)
    Huntington, WV
Maryland-Baltimore, U. of (Retrievers)
Maryland-College Park, U. of
    (Terrapins)
Maryland-Eastern Shore, U. of
    (Hawks) Princess Anne, MD
Marywood Coll. (Pacers)
    Scranton, PA
Massachusetts-Amherst, U. of
    (Minutemen)
Massachusetts-Boston, U. of
    (Beacons)
Massachusetts-Dartmouth, U. of
    (Corsairs)
Massachusetts-Lowell, U. of (Chiefs)
Mass. Inst. of Tech. (Engineers)
    Cambridge, MA
Memphis State U. (Tigers)
    Memphis, TN
Mercer U. (Bears) Macon, GA
Mercy Coll. (Flyers) Dobbs Ferry, NY
Miami, U. of (Hurricanes)
    Coral Gables, FL
Miami U. (Redskins) Oxford, OH
Michigan-Ann Arbor, U. of
    (Wolverines)
Michigan-Dearborn, U. of (Wolves)
Michigan State U. (Spartans)
    East Lansing, MI
Minnesota-Duluth, U. of (Bulldogs)

Minnesota-Minneapolis, U. of
  (Golden Gophers)
Minnesota-Morris, U. of (Cougars)
Mississippi, U. of (Rebels)
  University, MS
Mississippi State U. (Bulldogs)
  Mississippi State, MS
Missouri-Columbia, U. of (Tigers)
Missouri-Kansas City, U. of
  (Kangaroos)
Missouri-Rolla, U of (Miners)
Missouri-St. Louis, U. of (Rivermen)
Molloy Coll. (Lions)
  Rockville Centre, NY
Monmouth Coll. (Hawks)
  West Long Branch, NJ
Montana, U. of (Grizzlies)
  Missoula, MT
Montana State U. (Bobcats)
  Bozeman, MT
Moorhead State U. (Dragons)
  Moorhead, MN
Moravian Coll. (Greyhounds)
  Bethlehem, PA
Morehead State U. (Eagles)
  Morehead, KY
Morehouse Coll. (Tigers) Atlanta, GA
Morgan State U. (Grizzly Bears)
  Baltimore, MD
Mount Holyoke Coll. (Lyons)
  South Hadley, MA
Murray State U. (Racers) Murray, KY

Nebraska-Kearney, U. of (Antelopes)
Nebraska-Lincoln, U. of(Cornhuskers)
Nebraska-Omaha, U. of (Mavericks)
Nevada-Las Vegas, U. of (Rebels)
Nevada-Reno, U. of (Wolf Pack)
New Hampshire, U. of (Wildcats)
  Durham, NH
New Mexico, U. of (Lobos)
  Albuquerque, NM
New Mexico State U. (Aggies)
  Las Cruces, NM
New Orleans, U. of (Privateers)
  New Orleans, LA
New York, State U. of, College at
  Binghamton (Colonials)
New York, State U. of, College at
  Brockport (Golden Eagles)
New York, State U. of, College at
  Cortland (Red Dragons)
New York, State U. of, College at
  Farmingdale (Rams)
New York, State U. of, College at
  Fredonia (Blue Devils)
New York, State U. of, College at
  Geneseo (Blue Knights)
New York, State U. of, College at
  New Paltz (Hawks)

New York, State U. of, College at
  Oneonta (Red Dragons)
New York, State U. of, College at
  Plattsburgh (Cardinals)
New York, State U. of, College at
  Purchase (Panthers)
New York-Albany, State U. of
  (Great Danes)
New York-Buffalo, State U. of (Bulls)
New York City U. of Lehman College
  (Lancers) New York, NY
New York-Potsdam, State U. of
  (Bears)
New York-Stony Brook, State U. of
  (Patriots)
New York U. (Violets) New York, NY
Niagara U. (Purple Eagles)
  Niagara, NY
Nicholls State U. (Colonels)
  Thibodaux, LA
Norfolk State U. (Spartans)
  Norfolk, VA
North Carolina-Ashville, U. of
  (Bulldogs)
North Carolina-Chapel Hill, U. of
  (Tar Heels)
North Carolina-Charlotte, U. of
  (49'ers)
North Carolina-Greensboro, U. of
  (Spartans)
North Carolina State U. (Wolfpack)
  Raleigh, NC
North Carolina-Wilmington, U. of
  (Seahawks)
North Dakota, U. of (Fighting Sioux)
  Grand Forks, ND
North Dakota State U. (Bison)
  Fargo, ND
Northeastern U. (Huskies)
  Boston, MA
Northwestern U. (Wildcats)
  Evanston, IL
Notre Dame. U. of (Fighting Irish)
  Notre Dame, IN
Nova U. (Knights) Ft. Lauderdale, FL

Oberlin Coll. (Yeomen) Oberlin, OH
Ohio State U. (Buckeyes)
  Columbus, OH
Ohio U. (Bobcats) Athens, OH
Oklahoma, U. of (Sooners)
  Norman, OK
Oklahoma State U. (Cowboys)
  Stillwater, OK
Old Dominion U. (Monarchs)
  Norfolk, VA
Oral Roberts U. (Titans) Tulsa, OK
Oregon, U. of (Ducks) Eugene, OR
Oregon State U. (Beavers)
  Corvallis, OR

Pace U. (Setters) Pleasantville, NY
Pennsylvania, U. of
(Quakers / Red & Blue)
Philadelphia, PA
Pennsylvania State U. (Nittany Lions)
University Park, PA
Pepperdine U. (Waves) Malibu, CA
Pittsburgh, U. of (Panthers)
Pittsburgh, PA
Portland, U. of (Pilots) Portland, OR
Portland State U. (Vikings)
Portland, OR
Pratt Institute (Cannoneers)
Brooklyn, NY
Princeton U. (Tigers) Princeton, NJ
Providence Coll. (Friars)
Providence, RI
Purdue U. (Boilermakers)
West Lafayette, IN

Queens Coll. (Knights) Flushing, NY

Radford U. (Highlanders) Radford, VA
Randolph-Macon Coll.
(Yellow Jackets) Ashland, VA
Reed Coll. (Griffins) Portland, OR
Regis Coll. (Beacons) Weston, MA
Rensselaer Inst. of Technology
(Engineers) Troy, NY
Rhode Island, U. of (Rams)
Kingston, RI
Rice U. (Owls) Houston, TX
Richmond, U. of (Spiders)
Richmond, VA
Rider Coll. (Broncs)
Lawrenceville, NJ
River Coll. (Raiders) Nashua, NH
Roanoke Coll. (Maroons) Salem, VA
Robert Morris Coll. (Colonials)
Coraopolis, PA
Rochester, U. of (Yellow Jackets)
Rochester, NY
Rochester Inst. of Technology
(Tigers) Rochester, NY
Rockhurst Coll. (Hawks)
Kansas City, MO
Roger Williams Coll. (Hawks)
Bristol, RI
Rollins Coll. (Tars) Winter Park, FL
Roosevelt U. (Lakers) Chicago, IL
Russell Sage Coll. (Gators) Troy, NY
Rutgers U. (Scarlet Knights)
New Brunswick, NJ

Sacred Heart U. (Pioneers)
Fairfield, CT
St. Cloud State U. (Huskies)
St. Cloud, MN
St. John's U. (Redmen) Jamaica, NY
St. Lawrence U. (Saints) Canton, NY

Samford U. (Bulldogs)
Birmingham, AL
Sam Houston State U. (Bearkats)
Huntsville, TX
San Diego, U. of (Toreros)
San Diego, CA
San Diego State U. (Aztecs)
San Diego, CA
San Francisco, U. of (Dons)
San Francisco, CA
San Francisco State U. (Gators)
San Francisco, CA
San Jose State U. (Spartans)
San Jose, CA
Santa Clara U. (Broncos)
Santa Clara, CA
Scranton, U. of (Royals) Scranton, PA
Seattle U. (Chieftains) Seattle, WA
Seton Hall U. (Pirates)
South Orange, NJ
Shaw U. (Bears) Raleigh, NC
Skidmore Coll. (Thoroughbreds)
Saratoga Springs, NY
Slippery Rock U. (The Rockets)
Slippery Rock, PA
Smith Coll. (Pioneers)
Northampton, MA
South Carolina, U. of
(Fighting Gamecocks)
Columbia, SC
South Carolina State U. (Bulldogs)
Orangeburg, SC
South Dakota, U of (Coyotes)
Vermillion, SD
South Dakota State U. (Jackrabbits)
Brookings, SD
Southern California, U. of (Trojans)
Los Angeles, CA
Southern Methodist U. (Mustangs)
Dallas, TX
South Florida, U. of (Bulls) Tampa, FL
Stanford U. (Cardinal) Stanford, CA
Stetson U. (Hatters) Deland, FL
Susquehanna U. (Crusaders)
Selinsgrove, PA
Swarthmore Coll. (Little Quakers)
Swarthmore, PA
Syracuse U. (Orangemen)
Syracuse, NY

Tampa, U. of (Spartans) Tampa, FL
Temple U. (Owls) Philadelphia, PA
Tennessee, U. of (Volunteers)
Knoxville, TN
Tennessee State U. (Tigers)
Nashville, TN
Texas A&M U. (Aggies)
College Station, TX
Texas-Arlington, U. of (Mavericks)
Texas-Austin, U. of (Longhorns)

Texas Christian U. (Horned Frogs)
    Fort Worth, TX
Texas-El Paso, U. of (Miners)
Texas-San Antonio, U. of
    (Roadrunners)
Texas-Tyler, U. of (Patriots)
Toledo, U. of (Rockets) Toledo, OH
Towson State U. (Tigers) Towson, MD
Transylvania U. (Pioneers)
    Lexington, KY
Trenton State Coll. (Lions)
    Trenton, NJ
Trinity Coll. (Bantams) Hartford, CT
Tufts U. (Jumbos) Medford, MA
Tulane U. (Green Wave)
    New Orleans, LA
Tulsa, U. of (Golden Hurricane)
    Tulsa, OK
Tuskegee U. (Golden Tigers)
    Tuskegee, AL

Union Coll. (Dutchmen)
    Schenectady, NY
US Air Force Academy (Falcons)
    Colorado Springs, CO
US International U. (Soaring Gulls)
    San Diego, CA
US Military Academy (Black Knights)
    West Point, NY
US Naval Academy (Midshipmen)
    Annapolis, MD
Ursinus Coll. (Grizzly Bears)
    Collegeville, PA
Utah, U. of (Utes) Salt Lake City, UT
Utah State U. (Aggies) Logan, UT

Vanderbilt U. (Commodores)
    Nashville, TN
Vassar Coll. (Brewers)
    Poughkeepsie, NY
Vermont, U. of (Catamounts)
    Burlington, VT
Villanova U. (Wildcats) Villanova, PA
Virginia, U. of (Cavaliers)
    Charlottesville, VA
Virginia Military Inst. (Keydets)
    Lexington, VA

Virginia State U. (Trojans)
    Petersburg, VA

Wake Forest U. (Demon Deacons)
    Winston-Salem, NC
Washington, U. of (Huskies)
    Seattle, WA
Washington & Jefferson Coll.
    (Presidents) Washington, PA
Washington & Lee U. (Generals)
    Lexington, VA
Washington State U. (Cougars)
    Pullman, WA
Wayne State U. (Tartars) Detroit, MI
Webster U. (Gorloks) St. Louis, MO
Wesleyan U. (Cardinals)
    Middletown, CT
West Virginia U. (Mountaineers)
    Morgantown, WV
Wheaton Coll. (Lyons) Norton, MA
Williams Coll. (Ephs)
    Williamstown, MA
Wisconsin-Eau Claire, U. of (Blugolds)
Wisconsin-Green Bay, U. of (Phoenix)
Wisconsin-Lacrosse, U. of (Eagles)
Wisconsin-Madison, U. of (Badgers)
Wisconsin-Milwaukee, U. of
    (Panthers)
Wisconsin-Oshkosh, U. of (Titans)
Wisconsin-Parkside, U. of (Rangers)
Wisconsin-Platteville, U. of (Pioneers)
Wisconsin-River Falls, U. of (Falcons)
Wisconsin-Stevens Point, U. of
    (Pointers)
Wisconsin-Stout, U. of (Blue Devils)
Wisconsin-Superior, U. of
    (Yellow Jackets)
Wisconsin-Whitewater, U. of
    (Warhawks)
Wyoming, U. of (Cowboys)
    Laramie, WY

Xavier U. (Musketeers) Cincinnati, OH

Yale U. (Bulldogs) New Haven, CT
Yeshiva U. (Maccabees)
    New York, NY

SPORTS TEAMS

LOCATION	BASEBALL	BASKETBALL	FOOTBALL	HOCKEY
ATLANTA	BRAVES	HAWKS	FALCONS	
BALTIMORE	ORIOLES			
BOSTON	RED SOX	CELTICS		BRUINS
BUFFALO			BILLS	SABRES
CALGARY				FLAMES
CALIFORNIA	ANGELS			
CAROLINA			PANTHERS	
CHARLOTTE		HORNETS		
CHICAGO	WHITE SOX	BULLS	BEARS	BLACKHAWKS
CHICAGO	CUBS			
CINCINNATI	REDS		BENGALS	
CLEVELAND	INDIANS	CAVALIERS	BROWNS	
COLORADO	ROCKIES			
DALLAS		MAVERICKS	COWBOYS	STARS
DENVER		NUGGETS	BRONCOS	
DETROIT	TIGERS	PISTONS	LIONS	REDWINGS
EDMONTON				OILERS
FLORIDA	MARLINS			
GOLDEN STATE		WARRIORS		
GREEN BAY			PACKERS	
HARTFORD				WHALERS
HOUSTON	ASTROS	ROCKETS	OILERS	
INDIANA		PACERS		
INDIANAPOLIS			COLTS	
JACKSONVILLE			JAGUARS	
KANSAS CITY	ROYALS		CHIEFS	
LOS ANGELES	DODGERS	LAKERS		KINGS
LOS ANGELES		CLIPPERS	RAIDERS	
MIAMI		HEAT	DOLPHINS	
MILWAUKEE	BREWERS	BUCKS		
MINNESOTA	TWINS	TIMBERWOLVES	VIKINGS	
MONTREAL	EXPOS			CANADIENS
NEW ENGLAND			PATRIOTS	
NEW JERSEY		NETS		DEVILS
NEW ORLEANS			SAINTS	
NEW YORK	YANKEES	KNICKS	GIANTS	RANGERS
NEW YORK	METS		JETS	ISLANDERS
OAKLAND	ATHLETICS			
ORLANDO		MAGIC		
OTTAWA				SENATORS
PHILADELPHIA	PHILLIES	76ERS	EAGLES	FLYERS
PHOENIX		SUNS	CARDINALS	
PITTSBURGH	PIRATES		STEELERS	PENGUINS
PORTLAND		TRAIL BLAZERS		
QUEBEC				NORDIQUES
SACRAMENTO		KINGS		
ST. LOUIS	CARDINALS		RAMS	BLUES
SAN ANTONIO		SPURS		
SAN DIEGO	PADRES		CHARGERS	
SAN FRANCISCO	GIANTS		49ERS	
SAN JOSE				SHARKS
SEATTLE	MARINERS	SUPERSONICS	SEAHAWKS	
TAMPA BAY			BUCCANEERS	LIGHTNING
TEXAS	RANGERS			
TORONTO	BLUE JAYS			MAPLE LEAFS
UTAH		JAZZ		
VANCOUVER				CANUCKS
WASHINGTON		BULLETS	REDSKINS	CAPITALS
WINNIPEG				JETS

CONSTELLATIONS & STARS

Andromeda.................................ROSS;
.........................ALMACH, MIRACH;
....ALPHERATZ
Antlia (Air Pump) ....
Apus (Bird of Paradise) ....
Aquarius (Water Bearer) ....LUYTEN
Aquila (Eagle) ....ALTAIR
Ara (Altar) ....
Aries (Ram).........................HAMAL;
.....................................SHERATAN
Auriga (Charioteer)..............CAPELLA
Boötes (Herdsman)..............NEKKAR;
.................................ARCTURUS
Caelum (Chisel)...............................
Camelopardalis (Giraffe) ....
Cancer (Crab) ....
Canes Venatici (Hunting Dogs) ....
.................................LALANDE
Canis Major (Greater Dog) ....
.........................WEZEN; ADHARA,
.........................MURZIM, SIRIUS
Canis Minor (Lesser Dog)...................
.................................PROCYON
Capricornus (Horned Goat) ......DABIH,
.........................DENEB, GAEDI
Carina (Keel).....................ARGUS;
.................CANOPUS, VELORUM
Cassiopeia............................CAPH;
.................RUCHBAH, SCHEDAR
Centaurus (Centaur) ....HADAR;
.....................................MENKENT;
.........................ALPHA CENTAURI
Cepheus ....ER RAI;
.................ALFIRK, KRUGER
Cetus (Whale).............MIRA; DIPHDA;
.................LUYTEN, MENKAR
Chamaeleon ....
Circinus (Dividers) ....
Columba (Noah's Dove) ....
Coma Berenices (Berenice's Hair) ....
Corona Australis (Southern Crown)......
Corona Borealis (Northern Crown).......
.................GEMMA; ALPHECCA
Corvus (Crow)........................GEINAH;
.................AL CHIBA, AL GORAH
Crater (Cup)......................................
Crux (Southern Cross)............ACRUX;
.........ALNAIR, GACRUX, MIMOSA
Cygnus (Swan).......................SADR;
.................CYGNI, DENEB; ALBIREO
Delphinus (Dolphin)............ROTANEV;
.................................SUALOCIN
Dorado (Swordfish)...........................
Draco (Dragon) ....THUBAN;
.................ELTANIN; RASTABAN
Equuleus (Colt)...............................

Eridanus (River) ....CURSA;
.... ACAMAR; ERIDANI;
.................................ACHERNAR
Fornax (Furnace).............................
Gemini (Twins).....................ALHENA,
.........................CASTOR, POLLUX,
.........................PROPUS; MEBSUTA,
.................................MEKBUDA
Grus (Crane).....................................
Hercules ....
Horologium (Clock)...........................
Hydra (Female Water Snake)...............
.................................ALPHARD
Hydrus (Male Water Snake).......ROSS
Indus (Indian)....................................
Lacerta (Lizard) ....
Leo (Lion) ....WOLF; ZOSMA;
.................CHERTAN, REGULUS;
.................RASSELAS; DENEBOLA
Leo Minor (Lesser Lion)....................
Lepus (Hare)...............ARNEB, NIHAL
Libra (Balance) ....
.................ZUBEN EL GENUBI;
.................ZUBENESCHAMALI
Lupus (Wolf) ....
Lynx ....
Lyra (Lyre) ....VEGA
Mensa (Table) ....
Microscopium (Microscope)...............
.................................LACAILLE
Monoceros (Unicorn) ....
Musca (Fly) ....
Norma (Ruler) ....
Octans (Octant) ....
Ophiuchus (Serpent Bearer) ....YED;
....SABIK;
.................BARNARD'S STAR
Orion (Hunter)........................RIGEL,
.................SAIPH; MINTAKA;
.................ALNILAM, ALNITAK;
.................................BELLATRIX;
.................................BETELGEUSE
Pavo (Peacock) ....
Pegasus (Winged Horse) ....ENIF;
.................BIHAM, HOMAM, MATAR;
.................MARKAB, SCHEAT
Perseus.....................ALGOL; MIRFAK
Phoenix ....ANKAA
Pictor (Painter)....................KAPTEYN
Pisces (Fish)................VAN MAANEN
Piscis Austrinus (Southern Fish) ....
.................LACAILLE; FOMALHAUT
Pleiades ....MAIA; MEROPE;
.................ALCYONE, CELAENO,
.................ELECTRA, PLEIONE,
.................TAYGETA; ASTEROPE

Constellations & Stars / Olympic Games Sites

Puppis (Deck) ....
Pyxis (Mariner's Compass)...................
Reticulum (Net)....................................
Sagitta (Arrow)....................................
Sagittarius (Bowman) ....KAUS,
.............................ROSS; NUNKI;
....................AL NASL; ASCELLA
Scorpio (Scorpion)................LESATH,
........................SHAULA; ANTARES;
...................GRAFFIAS; DSCHUBBA
Scutum (Shield)...................................
Serpens (Serpent) ....
Sextans (Sextant) ....
Taurus (Bull) ....EL NATH, HYADES;
..................................ALDEBARAN
Telescopium (Telescope) ....
Triangulum (Triangle) ....AVIOR

Triangulum Australe ....
.................................(Southern Triangle)
Tucana (Toucan) ....
Ursa Major (Greater Bear)...................
.................................ALCOR, DUBHE,
....................MERAK, MIZAR; ALIOTH,
.............ALKAID, MEGREZ, PHECDA;
...........................MUSCIDA, TALITHA;
...............................GROOMBRIDGE
Ursa Minor (Lesser Bear) ....
....KOCHAB;
.........................PHERKAD, POLARIS
Vela (Sails) ....SUHAIL
Virgo (Virgin) ....SPICA;
.........................PORRIMA; ZAVIJAVA
Volans (Flying Fish)............................
Vulpecula (Little Fox)..........................

OLYMPIC GAMES SITES

SUMMER GAMES

1896 ....Athens, Greece
1900 ....Paris, France
1904 ....St. Louis, MO, USA
1908 ....London, England
1912 ....Stockholm, Sweden
1916 ....not held
1920 ....Antwerp, Belgium
1924 ....Paris, France
1928 ....Amsterdam, Netherlands
1932 ....Los Angeles, CA, USA
1936 ....Berlin, Germany
1940 ....not held
1944 ....not held
1948 ....London, England
1952 ....Helsinki, Finland
1956 ....Melbourne, Australia
1960 ....Rome, Italy
1964 ....Tokyo, Japan
1968 ....Mexico City, Mexico
1972 ....Munich, West Germany
1976 ....Montreal, Canada
1980 ....Moscow, USSR
1984 ....Los Angeles, CA, USA
1988 ....Seoul, South Korea
1992 ....Barcelona, Spain
1996 ....Atlanta, GA, USA
2000 ....Sydney, Australia

WINTER GAMES

1924 ....Chamonix, France
1928 ....St. Moritz, Switzerland
1932 ....Lake Placid, NY, USA
1936 ....Garmisch-Partenkirchen,
....................................Germany
1940 ....not held
1944 ....not held
1948 ....St. Moritz, Switzerland
1952 ....Oslo, Norway
1956 ....Cortina d'Ampezzo, Italy
1960 ....Squaw Valley, CA, USA
1964 ....Innsbruck, Austria
1968 ....Grenoble, France
1972 ....Sapporo, Japan
1976 ....Innsbruck, Austria
1980 ....Lake Placid, NY, USA
1984 ....Sarajevo, Yugoslavia
1988 ....Calgary, Alberta, Canada
1992 ....Albertville, France
1994 ....Lillehammer, Norway
1998 ....Nagano, Japan

UNITED STATES INFORMATION

* Indicates one of the Thirteen Original States

ALABAMA: AL, Ala.; capital, MONTGOMERY; nicknames, COTTON, HEART OF DIXIE, YELLOWHAMMER; state flower, CAMELLIA; state bird, YELLOWHAMMER; motto, WE DARE DEFEND OUR RIGHTS.

ALASKA: AK, Alas.; capital, JUNEAU; nickname, THE LAST FRONTIER; state flower, FORGET-ME-NOT; state bird, WILLOW PTARMIGAN; motto, NORTH TO THE FUTURE.

ARIZONA: AZ, Ariz.; capital, PHOENIX; nickname GRAND CANYON; state flower, SAGUARO; state bird, SAGUARO CACTUS BLOSSOM; motto, *DITAT DEUS* (God enriches).

ARKANSAS: AR, Ark; capital, LITTLE ROCK; nickname, LAND OF OPPORTUNITY; state flower, APPLE BLOSSOM; state bird, MOCKINGBIRD; motto, *REGNAT POPULUS* (The people rule).

CALIFORNIA: CA, Cal., Calif.; capital, SACRAMENTO; nicknames, GOLDEN, EL DORADO; state flower; GOLDEN POPPY; state bird, CALIFORNIA VALLEY QUAIL; motto, EUREKA (I have found it).

COLORADO: CO, Colo.; capital, DENVER; nicknames CENTENNIAL, SILVER; state flower, COLUMBINE; state bird, LARK BUNTING; motto, *NIL SINE NUMINE* (Nothing without providence).

*CONNECTICUT: CT, Conn.; capital, HARTFORD; nicknames, CONSTITUTION, NUTMEG; state flower, MOUNTAIN LAUREL; state bird, ROBIN; motto, *QUI TRANSTULIT SUSTINET* (He who transplanted still sustains).

*DELAWARE: DE, Del., Dela.; capital, DOVER; nicknames FIRST, DIAMOND, BLUE HEN; state flower, PEACH BLOSSOM, AMERICAN BEAUTY ROSE; state bird, BLUE HEN CHICKEN; motto, LIBERTY AND INDEPENDENCE.

FLORIDA: FL, Fla.; capital, TALLAHASSEE; nickname, SUNSHINE; state flower, ORANGE BLOSSOM; state bird, MOCKINGBIRD; motto, IN GOD WE TRUST.

*GEORGIA: GA, Ga.; capital, ATLANTA; nicknames, PEACH, EMPIRE STATE OF THE SOUTH; state flower, CHEROKEE ROSE; state bird, BROWN THRASHER; motto, WISDOM, JUSTICE, AND MODERATION.

HAWAII: HI, Haw.; capital, HONOLULU; nicknames, ALOHA, PARADISE OF THE PACIFIC; state flower, HIBISCUS; state bird, NENE; motto, THE LIFE OF THE LAND IS PERPETUATED IN RIGHTEOUSNESS.

IDAHO: ID, Ida.; capital, BOISE; nickname, GEM; state flower, SYRINGA; state bird, MOUNTAIN BLUEBIRD; motto, *ESTO PERPETUA* (It is perpetual).

ILLINOIS: IL, Ill.; capital SPRINGFIELD; nicknames, PRAIRIE, SUCKER, THE INLAND EMPIRE; state flower, VIOLET; state bird, CARDINAL; motto, STATE SOVEREIGNTY—NATIONAL UNION.

INDIANA: IN, Ind.; capital, INDIANAPOLIS; nickname, HOOSIER; state flower, PEONY; state bird,CARDINAL; motto, CROSSROADS OF AMERICA.

IOWA: IA, Ia.; capital, DES MOINES; nickname, HAWKEYE; state flower, WILD ROSE; state bird, EASTERN GOLDFINCH; motto, OUR LIBERTIES WE PRIZE AND OUR RIGHTS WE WILL MAINTAIN.

KANSAS: KS, Kan., Kans.; capital, TOPEKA; nicknames, SUNFLOWER, JAY-HAWKER; state flower, SUNFLOWER; state bird, WESTERN MEADOWLARK; motto,*AD ASTRA PER ASPERA* (To the stars through difficulties).

KENTUCKY: KY, Ky.; capital, FRANKFORT; nickname, BLUEGRASS; state flower, GOLDENROD; state bird, CARDINAL; motto, UNITED WE STAND, DIVIDED WE FALL.

LOUISIANA: LA, La.; capital, BATON ROUGE; nicknames, PELICAN, CREOLE; state flower, MAGNOLIA; state bird, EASTERN BROWN PELICAN; motto, UNION, JUSTICE, AND CONFIDENCE.

MAINE: ME, Me.; capital, AUGUSTA; nicknames, PINE TREE, LUMBER; state flower, PINE CONE AND TASSEL; state bird, CHICKADEE; motto, *DIRIGO* (I direct).

*MARYLAND: MD, Md.; capital, ANNAPOLIS; nicknames, OLD LINE, FREE, COCKADE; state flower, BLACK-EYED SUSAN; state bird, BALTIMORE ORI-OLE; motto, *FATTI MASCHII, PAROLE FEMINE* (Manly deeds, womanly words).

*MASSACHUSETTS: MA, Mass.; capital, BOSTON; nicknames, BAY, OLD COLONY; state flower, MAYFLOWER; state bird, CHICKADEE; motto, *ENSE PETIT PLACIDAM SUB LIBERTATE QUIETEM* (By the sword we seek peace, but peace only under liberty).

MICHIGAN: MI, Mich.; capital, LANSING; nicknames, WOLVERINE, GREAT LAKE; state flower, APPLE BLOSSOM; state bird, ROBIN; motto, *SI QUAERIS PENINSULAM AMOENAM CIRCUMSPICE* (If you seek a pleasant peninsula, look about you).

MINNESOTA: MN, Minn.; capital, ST. PAUL; nicknames, NORTH STAR, GOPHER; state flower, LADY'S-SLIPPER; state bird, COMMON LOON; motto, *L'ETOILE DU NORD* (The star of the north).

MISSISSIPPI: MS, Miss.; capital, JACKSON; nicknames, MAGNOLIA, BAYOU; state flower, MAGNOLIA; state bird, MOCKINGBIRD; motto, *VIRTUTE ET ARMIS* (By valor and arms).

MISSOURI: MO, Mo.; capital, JEFFERSON CITY; nicknames, SHOW ME, BUL-LION; state flower, HAWTHORN; state bird, BLUEBIRD; motto, *SALUS POPULI SUPREMA LEX ESTO* (Will of the people shall be the supreme law).

MONTANA: MT, Mont.; capital, HELENA; nicknames, TREASURE, MOUNTAIN; state flower, BITTERROOT; state bird, WESTERN MEADOWLARK; motto, *ORO Y PLATA* (Gold and silver).

NEBRASKA: NE, Nebr.; capital, LINCOLN; nicknames, CORNHUSKER, BLACKWATER; state flower, GOLDENROD; state bird, WESTERN MEADOWLARK; motto, EQUALITY BEFORE THE LAW.

NEVADA: NV, Nev.; capital, CARSON CITY; nicknames, SAGE BRUSH, SILVER; state flower, SAGEBRUSH; state bird, MOUNTAIN BLUEBIRD; motto, ALL FOR OUR COUNTRY.

*NEW HAMPSHIRE: NH, N.H.; capital, CONCORD; nickname, GRANITE; state flower, PURPLE LILAC; state bird, PURPLE FINCH; motto, LIVE FREE OR DIE.

*NEW JERSEY: NJ, N.J.; capital, TRENTON; nickname, GARDEN; state flower, VIOLET; state bird, EASTERN GOLDFINCH; motto, LIBERTY AND PROSPERITY.

NEW MEXICO: NM, N.M.; capital, SANTA FE; nicknames, LAND OF ENCHANTMENT, SUNSHINE; state flower, YUCCA; state bird, ROADRUNNER; motto, *CRESCIT EUNDO* (It grows as it goes).

*NEW YORK: NY, N.Y.; capital, ALBANY; nickname, EMPIRE; state flower, ROSE; state bird, BLUEBIRD; motto, EXCELSIOR (Ever upward).

*NORTH CAROLINA: NC, N.C.; capital, RALEIGH; nicknames, TAR HEEL, OLD NORTH; state flower, DOGWOOD; state bird, CARDINAL; motto, *ESSE QUAM VIDERI* (To be rather than to seem).

NORTH DAKOTA: ND, N.D.; capital, BISMARCK; nicknames, PEACE GARDEN, SIOUX, FLICKERTAIL; state flower, WILD PRAIRIE ROSE; state bird, WESTERN MEADOWLARK; motto, LIBERTY AND UNION, NOW AND FOREVER, ONE AND INSEPARABLE.

OHIO: OH, O.; capital, COLUMBUS; nickname, BUCKEYE; state flower, SCARLET CARNATION; state bird, CARDINAL; motto, WITH GOD, ALL THINGS ARE POSSIBLE.

OKLAHOMA: OK, Okla.; capital, OKLAHOMA CITY; nickname, SOONER; state flower, MISTLETOE; state bird, SCISSOR-TAILED FLYCATCHER; motto, *LABOR OMNIA VINCIT* (Labor conquers all).

OREGON: OR, Ore.; capital, SALEM; nicknames, BEAVER, SUNSET, VALENTINE, WEBFOOT; state flower, OREGON GRAPE; state bird, WESTERN MEADOWLARK; motto, SHE FLIES WITH HER OWN WINGS.

*PENNSYLVANIA: PA, Penn., Penna.; capital, HARRISBURG; nickname, KEYSTONE; state flower, MOUNTAIN LAUREL; state bird, RUFFED GROUSE; motto, VIRTUE, LIBERTY, AND INDEPENDENCE.

U.S. Information (Rhode Island / Wyoming)

*RHODE ISLAND: RI, R.I.; capital, PROVIDENCE; nicknames, LITTLE RHODY, OCEAN; state flower, VIOLET; state bird, RHODE ISLAND RED; motto, HOPE.

*SOUTH CAROLINA: SC, S.C.; capital, COLUMBIA; nickname, PALMETTO; state flower, YELLOW JESSAMINE; state bird, CAROLINA WREN; motto, *DUM SPIRO SPERO* (While I breathe, I hope).

SOUTH DAKOTA: SD, S.D.; capital, PIERRE; nicknames, COYOTE, SUN-SHINE; state flower, PASQUE FLOWER; state bird, RINGNECKED PHEASANT; motto, UNDER GOD, THE PEOPLE RULE.

TENNESSEE: TN, Tenn.; capital, NASHVILLE; nickname, VOLUNTEER; state flower, IRIS; state bird, MOCKINGBIRD; motto, AGRICULTURE AND COM-MERCE..

TEXAS: TX, Tex.; capital, AUSTIN; nickname, LONE STAR; state flower, BLUE-BONNET; state bird, MOCKINGBIRD; motto, FRIENDSHIP.

UTAH: UT, Ut.; capital, SALT LAKE CITY; nicknames, BEEHIVE, MORMON; state flower, SEGO LILY; state bird, SEAGULL; motto, INDUSTRY.

VERMONT: VT, Vt.; capital, MONTPELIER; nickname, GREEN MOUNTAIN; state flower, RED CLOVER; state bird, HERMIT THRUSH; motto, FREEDOM AND UNITY.

*VIRGINIA: VA, Va.; capital, RICHMOND; nicknames, OLD DOMINION, MOTH-ER OF PRESIDENTS; state flower, DOGWOOD; state bird, CARDINAL; motto, *SIC SEMPER TYRANNIS* (Thus always to tyrants).

WASHINGTON: WA, Wash.; capital, OLYMPIA; nicknames, EVERGREEN, CHI-NOOK; state flower, WESTERN RHODODENDRON; state bird, WILLOW GOLDFINCH; motto, ALKI (By and by).

WEST VIRGINIA: WV, W.Va.; capital, CHARLESTON; nickname, MOUNTAIN; state flower, BIG RHODODENDRON; state bird, CARDINAL; motto, *MONTANI SEMPER LIBERI* (Mountaineers are always free).

WISCONSIN: WI, Wis., Wisc.; capital, MADISON; nickname, BADGER; state flower, WOOD VIOLET; state bird, ROBIN; motto, FORWARD.

WYOMING: WY, Wyo.; capital, CHEYENNE; nickname, EQUALITY; state flower, INDIAN PAINTBRUSH; state bird, MEADOWLARK; motto, EQUAL RIGHTS.

NATIONS INFORMATION

* Indicates official language.

AFGHANISTAN: capital, KABUL; ethnic groups, TAJIK, UZBEK, HAZARA, PUSHTUN; languages, UZBEK, PUSHTU, DARI PERSIAN; money, AFGHANI / PUL.

ALBANIA: capital, TIRANE; other cities, LEZHA, VLORA, DURRES; ethnic groups, GEG (GHEG), TOSK; languages, GREEK, ALBANIAN; money, LEK / QINTAR.

ALGERIA: capital, ALGIERS(El Djazair); other cities, ORAN, WAHRAN, QACENTINA; ethnic groups, ARAB, BERBER; languages, *ARABIC, BERBER; money, DINAR / CENTIME.

ANDORRA: capital, ANDORRA LA VELLA; ethnic groups, CATALAN, SPANISH, ANDORRAN, FRENCH; languages, *CATALAN, SPANISH, FRENCH; money, FRENCH FRANC and SPANISH PESETA.

ANGOLA: capital, LUANDA; ethnic groups, BAKONGO, KIMBUNDU, OVIMBUNDU; languages, PORTUGUESE, BANTU; money, KWANZA / LWEI.

ANTIGUA AND BARBUDA: capital, ST. JOHN'S; ethnic groups, AFRICANS; language, ENGLISH; money, DOLLAR / CENT.

ARGENTINA: capital, BUENOS AIRES; other cities, CORDOBA, MENDOZA, ROSARIO; ethnic groups, EUROPEANS, MESTIZOS, INDIANS; language, SPANISH; money, AUSTRAL / CENTAVO.

ARMENIA: capital, YEREVAN; ethnic groups, ARMENIAN, AZERBAIJAN; language, ARMENIAN; money, RUBLE / KOPECK.

AUSTRALIA: capital, CANBERRA; other cities, PERTH, SYDNEY, ADELAIDE, BRISBANE, MELBOURNE; states, VICTORIA, TASMANIA, QUEENSLAND, NEW SOUTH WALES; ethnic groups, EUROPEAN, ASIANS, ABORIGINES; language; ENGLISH; money, DOLLAR / CENT.

AUSTRIA: capital, VIENNA; other cities, INNSBRUCK, BREGENZ, LECH, GRAZ, LINZ, SALZBURG; ethnic groups, GERMAN, SLOVENE, CROATIAN; language, GERMAN; money, SCHILLING / GROSCHEN.

AZERBAIJAN: capital, BAKU; ethnic groups, AZERBAIJAN, RUSSIAN; languages, AZERI, TURKISH, RUSSIAN; money, RUBLE / KOPECK.

BAHAMAS, THE: capital, NASSAU; other cities, FREEPORT, NEW PROVIDENCE; ethnic groups, AFRICAN, CAUCASIAN; language, ENGLISH; money, DOLLAR / CENT.

BAHRAIN: capital, MANAMA; ethnic groups, BAHRAINI, ARAB, IRANIAN, ASIANS; language; ARABIC, FARSI, URDU; money, DINAR / FILS.

BANGLADESH: capital, DHAKA; other cities, KHULNA, CHITTAGONG; ethnic groups, BIHARI, BENGALI; languages, *BENGALI, MAGH, CHAKMA; money, TAKA / PAISA.

BARBADOS: capital, BRIDGETOWN; ethnic groups, AFRICAN, CAUCASIAN; language, ENGLISH; money, DOLLAR / CENT.

Nations (Belarus / Cameroon)

BELARUS: capital, MINSK; ethnic groups, BELARUS, POLES; language, BELORUSSIAN; money, RUBLE / KOPECK.

BELGIUM: capital, BRUSSELS; other cities, GHENT, LIEGE, ANTWERP; ethnic groups, FLEMING, WALLOON; languages, FRENCH, FLEMISH; money, FRANC / CENTIME.

BELIZE: capital, BELMOPAN; ethnic groups, MAYA, CREOLE, MESTIZO; languages, *ENGLISH, SPANISH, and CREOLE DIALECTS; money, DOLLAR / CENT.

BENIN: capital, PORTO-NOVO; other city, COTONOU; ethnic groups, FON, ADJA, BARIBA, YORUBA; languages, *FRENCH, FON, SOMBA, YORUBA; money, FRANC / CENTIME.

BHUTAN: capital, THIMPHU; other city, PARO DZONG; ethnic groups, BHOTE, NEPALESE; languages, *DZONGKHA, GURUNG, ASSAMESE; money, NGULTRUM / CHETRUM.

BOLIVIA: capitals, LA PAZ, SUCRE; other cities, SANTA CRUZ; ethnic groups, AYMARA, QUECHUA; languages, *AYMARA, *QUECHUA, *SPANISH; money, BOLIVIANO / PESO; river, BENI.

BOSNIA AND HERZEGOVINA: capital, SARAJEVO; other city, MOSTAR; ethnic groups, SERBIAN, MUSLIM-SLAV, CROATIAN; languages, SERBO-CROATIAN; money, DINAR / PARA.

BOTSWANA: capital, GABORONE; ethnic groups, TSWANA, KALANGA; languages, *ENGLISH, SHONA, TSWANA; money, PULA / THEBE.

BRAZIL: capital, BRASILIA; other cities, BELEM, RECIFE, SALVADOR, SAO PAULO, PORTO ALEGRE, RIO DE JANEIRO; states (selected), ACRE, PARA, AMAPA, BAHIA, CEARA, GOIAS, PIAUI, PARANA, ALAGOAS, GUAPORE, PARAIBA, SERGIPE, AMAZONAS; ethnic groups, PORTUGUESE, AFRICAN, MULATTO, AND OTHERS; language, PORTUGUESE; money, CRUZADO / CENTAVO.

BRUNEI DARUSSALAM: capital, BANDAR SERI BEGAWAN; ethnic groups, MALAY, CHINESE; languages, *MALAY, *ENGLISH, CHINESE; money, DOLLAR / CENT.

BULGARIA: capital, SOFIA; other cities, VARNA, PLOVDIV; ethnic groups, BULGARIAN, TURKS; languages, *BULGARIAN, TURKISH; money, LEV / STOTINKA.

BURKINA FASO: capital, OUAGADOUGOU; ethnic groups, BOBO, MANDE, MOSSI; languages, *FRENCH, VARIOUS TRIBAL LANGUAGES; money, FRANC / CENTIME.

BURMA (See **MYANMAR**).

BURUNDI: capital, BUJUMBURA; ethnic groups, TWA, HUTU, TUTSI; languages, *RUNDI, *FRENCH; money, FRANC / CENTIME.

CAMBODIA: capital, PHNOM PENH; ethnic groups, CAMBODIAN, VIETNAMESE, CHINESE; languages, *KHMER, FRENCH; money, RIEL / SEN.

CAMEROON: capital, YAOUNDE; other city, DOUALA; ethnic groups, FULANI, BAMILEKE; languages, *ENGLISH, *FRENCH; money, FRANC / CENTIME.

CANADA: capital, OTTAWA; other cities, QUEBEC, CALGARY, TORONTO, EDMONTON, MONTREAL, WINNIPEG, VANCOUVER; provinces, QUEBEC, ALBERTA, ONTARIO, MANITOBA, NOVA SCOTIA, NEW BRUNSWICK, NEW-FOUNDLAND, SASKATCHEWAN, BRITISH COLUMBIA, PRINCE EDWARD ISLAND; ethnic groups, BRITISH, FRENCH, EUROPEAN; language, *ENGLISH, *FRENCH; money, DOLLAR / CENT.

CAPE VERDE: capital, PRAIA; ethnic groups, CREOLE, SERER, AFRICAN; languages, *PORTUGUESE, CRIOULO; money, ESCUDO / CENTAVO.

CENTRAL AFRICAN REPUBLIC: capital, BANGUI; ethnic groups, BAYA, SARA, BANDA, MANDJA; language, FRENCH; money, FRANC / CENTIME.

CHAD: capital, N'DJAMENA; ethnic groups, VARIOUS TRIBAL; languages, *FRENCH, *ARABIC; money, FRANC / CENTIME.

CHILE: capital, SANTIAGO; ethnic groups, MESTIZOS, SPANISH, INDIAN; languages, SPANISH; money, PESO / CENTESIMO.

CHINA: capital, BEIJING; other cities, WUHAN, CANTON, TIANJIN, SHANGHAI; ethnic groups, HAN, LOLO, NOSU, MANCHU, MONGOL, KOREAN; languages, GAN, HUI, MIN, YUE, HAKKA, XIANG, ZHUANG, MANDARIN; Chinese provinces, ANHUI, GANSU, HEBEI, HENAN, HUBEI, HUNAN, JILIN, FUJIAN; money, YUAN / FEN.

COLOMBIA: capital, BOGOTA; other cities, CALI, MEDELLIN; ethnic groups, MESTIZOS, CAUCASIANS, MULATTO; language, SPANISH; money, PESO / CENTAVO.

COMOROS: capital, MORONI; ethnic groups, ARABS, AFRICANS, EAST INDIANS; languages, *ARABIC, *FRENCH; money, FRANC / CENTIME.

CONGO: capital, BRAZZAVILLE; other cities, LOUBOMO, POINT-NOIRE; ethnic groups, BATEKE, BAKONGO; languages, *FRENCH, TEKE, KONGO; money, FRANC / CENTIME.

COSTA RICA: capital, SAN JOSE; ethnic groups, SPANISH, MESTIZOS, language, SPANISH; money, COLON / CENTIMO.

COTE D'IVOIRE: capital, ABIDJAN; ethnic groups, BETE, BAULE, SENUFO, MALINKE; languages, *FRENCH, KRU, AKAN, MALINKE, VOLTAIC; money, FRANC / CENTIME.

CROATIA: capital, ZAGREB; other cities, CAMAGUEY; ethnic groups, CROATS, SERBIANS; languages, SERBO-CROATIAN; money, DINAR / PARA.

CUBA: capital, HAVANA; other city, GUANTANAMO; ethnic groups, SPANISH, AFRICAN; language, SPANISH; money, PESO / CENTAVO.

CYPRUS: capital, NICOSIA; ethnic groups, GREEKS, TURKS, ARMENIANS, MARONITES; languages, *GREEK, *TURKISH, ENGLISH; money, POUND / CENT.

CZECH REPUBLIC: capital, PRAGUE; other cities, BRNO, OSTRAVA, BRATISLAVA; ethnic group, CZECHS; language, CZECH; money, KORUNA / HALER.

DENMARK: capital, COPENHAGEN; ethnic group, SCANDINAVIAN; languages, DANISH; money, KRONE / ORE.

Nations (Djibouti / Ghana)

DJIBOUTI: capital, DJIBOUTI; ethnic groups, ISSA, AFAR, EUROPEAN; languages, *FRENCH, *ARABIC, AFAR, ISSA; money, FRANC / CENTIME.

DOMINICA: capital, ROSEAU; ethnic groups, AFRICAN, CARIB; languages, *ENGLISH, FRENCH CREOLE; money, DOLLAR / CENT.

DOMINICAN REPUBLIC: capital, SANTO DOMINGO; ethnic groups, CAUCASIAN, AFRICAN; languages, SPANISH; money, PESO / CENTAVO.

ECUADOR: capital, QUITO; other city, GUAYAQUIL; ethnic groups, MESTIZOS, AFRICAN, INDIANS, SPANISH; languages, *SPANISH, QUECHUAN, JIVAROAN; money, SUCRE / CENTAVO.

EGYPT: capital, CAIRO; other cities, GAZA, AL-JIZAH, ALEXANDRIA; ethnic groups, NUBIAN, BEDOUIN, HAMITIC; language, ARABIC; money, POUND / PIASTER; river, NILE.

EL SALVADOR: capital, SAN SALVADOR; ethnic groups, MESTIZO, INDIAN; language, SPANISH; money, COLON / CENTAVO.

EQUATORIAL GUINEA: capital, MALABO; ethnic groups, BUBI, FANG; languages, *SPANISH, BUBI, FANG; money, FRANC / CENTIME.

ESTONIA: capital, TALLINN; ethnic groups, ESTONIAN, RUSSIAN; languages, *ESTONIAN, RUSSIAN; money, RUBLE / KOPECK.

ETHIOPIA: capital, ADDIS ABABA; other cities, ASMERA, HARER, DESE, GONDER; ethnic groups, TIGRE, OROMO, AMHARA, SIDAMA, KAFA, SAHO, GALLA, KAFFA; languages, *AMHARIC, GALLA, TIGRE; money, BIRR / CENT; river, JUBA.

FIJI: capital, SUVA; ethnic groups, INDIAN, FIJIAN; languages, *ENGLISH, FIJIAN, HINDI; money, DOLLAR / CENT.

FINLAND: capital, HELSINKI; other cities, TURKU, TAMPERE; ethnic groups, FINNS, LAPPS, SWEDES; languages, *FINNISH, *SWEDISH; money, MARKKA / PENNI.

FRANCE: capital, PARIS; other cities, PAU, LYON, METZ, NICE, BREST, TOURS, NANCY, ROUEN, RENNES, TOULON; ethnic group, FRENCH; languages, *FRENCH, BASQUE, BRETON, CATALAN; money, FRANC / CENTIME; rivers, SEINE, SAONE, LOIRE.

GABON: capital, LIBREVILLE; ethnic groups, FANG, BAPOUNON; language, *FRENCH, BANTU; money, FRANC / CENTIME.

GAMBIA, THE: capital, BANJUL; ethnic groups, FULA, WOLOF, MANDINKA; languages, *ENGLISH, WOLOF, MALINKE; money, DALASI / BUTUT.

GEORGIA: capital, TBILISI; other cities, SUCHUMI, BATUMI; ethnic groups, GEORGIAN, RUSSIAN; languages, GEORGIAN, RUSSIAN; money, RUBLE / KOPECK.

GERMANY: capital, BERLIN; other cities, ULM, BONN, KOLN, ESSEN, BREMEN, ERFURT; ethnic group, GERMAN; language, GERMAN; money, DEUTSCHE MARK / PFENNIG; rivers, ISAR, RHINE, WESER, ELBE.

GHANA: capital, ACCRA; ethnic groups, AKAN, AKRA, MOSHI-DAGOMBA, EWE, GA; languages, *ENGLISH, MOSHI, EWE, AKAN; money, CEDI / PESEWA.

GREECE: capital, ATHENS; other cities, LARISA, PATRAS, CORINTH, PIRAEUS, THESSALONIKI; ethnic groups, GREEK; languages, GREEK; money, DRACHMA / LEPTON.

GRENADA: capital, ST. GEORGE'S; ethnic group, AFRICAN; language, *ENGLISH, FRENCH; money, DOLLAR / CENT.

GUATEMALA: capital, GUATEMALA CITY; other cities, ANTIGUA, QUEZALTE-NANGO; ethnic groups, MAYA, MESTIZOS; languages, *SPANISH, MAYAN; money, QUETZAL / CENTAVO.

GUINEA: capital, CONAKRY; other cities, LABE, KANKAN; ethnic groups, FOULAH, MALINKE, SOUSSOUS; languages, *FRENCH, PEUL, MANDE; money, FRANC / CENTIME.

GUINEA-BISSAU: capital, BISSAU; ethnic groups, BALANTA, FULA, MANDINKA, MANJACA; languages, *PORTUGUESE, CRIOULD; money, PESO / CENTAVO.

GUYANA: capital, GEORGETOWN; ethnic groups, EAST INDIAN, AFRICAN; language, ENGLISH; money, DOLLAR / CENT.

HAITI: capital, PORT-AU-PRINCE; ethnic group, AFRICAN; languages, *FRENCH, *CREOLE; money, GOURDE / CENTIME.

HONDURAS: capital, TEGUCIGALPA; ethnic groups, MESTIZO, INDIAN; languages, SPANISH; money, LEMPIRA / CENTAVO.

HUNGARY: capital, BUDAPEST; other cities, GYOR, PECS, MISKOLC, SZEGED, DEBRECEN; ethnic groups, MAGYAR, GERMAN, GYPSY; languages, HUNGARIAN; money, FORINT / FILLER.

ICELAND: capital, REYKJAVIK; ethnic groups, NORWEGIAN, CELT; languages, ISLENSKA (ICELANDIC); money, KRONA / EYRIR.

INDIA: capital, NEW DELHI; other cities, MADRAS, CALCUTTA, BOMBAY, AGRA, BENARES, AMRITSAR, PATNA, LUCKNOW, JAIPUR; states (selected) ASSAM, BIHAR, DELHI, BOMBAY, KERALA, MYSORE, ORISSA, PUNJAB; ethnic groups, INDO-ARYAN, DRAVIDIAN, MONGOLOID; languages, *HINDI; money, RUPEE / PAISA.

INDONESIA: capital, JAKARTA; other cities, DILI, SURABAYA, BANDUNG, MEDAN; ethnic groups, MAYAY, CHINESE, IRIANESE, DYAK; languages, *BAHASA, DAYAK (DYAK); money, RUPIAH / SEN.

IRAN: capital, TEHRAN; other cities, SHIRAZ, YAZD, ESFAHAN, MASHHAD, TABRIZ; ethnic groups, PERSIAN, AZERBAIJANI, KURD; languages, *FARSI, ARABIC, KURDISH, TURKISH; money, RIAL / DINAR.

IRAQ: capital, BAGHDAD; other cities, BASRA, MOSUL, IRBIL, KIRKUK; ethnic groups, ARAB, KURD, TURK; languages, *ARABIC, KURDISH; money, DINAR / FILS.

IRELAND, REPUBLIC OF: capital, DUBLIN; other cities, LIMERICK, CORK, GALWAY, WEXFORD; ethnic group, CELTIC; language, ENGLISH, IRISH-GAELIC; money, POUND / PENNY.

ISRAEL: capital, JERUSALEM; other cities, ACRE, TEL AVIV, HAIFA; ethnic groups, JEWISH, ARAB; languages, *HEBREW, *ARABIC; money, SHEKEL / AGORA.

Nations (Italy / Libya)

ITALY: capital, ROME (ROMA); other cities, MILAN (MILANO), FLORENCE (FIRENZE), VENICE (VENEZIA), PADUA (PADOVA), UDINE, TURIN (TORINO), GENOA (GENOVA), NAPLES (NAPOLI), BOLOGNA, LIVORNO, ANCONA, BRINDISI, TARANTO, BARI, SALERNO, PARMA, VERONA, TRIESTE, RIMINI, PALERMO (SICILY); ethnic groups, ITALIAN; languages, ITALIAN; money, LIRA / CENTESIMO.

JAMAICA: capital, KINGSTON; ethnic groups, various AFRICAN, CAU-CASIAN, CHINESE; languages, *ENGLISH, JAMAICAN CREOLE; money, DOL-LAR / CENT.

JAPAN: capital, TOKYO; other cities, OSAKA, HIROSHIMA, NAGASAKI, KOBE, KYOTO, YOKOHAMA, NAGOYA, SAPPORO, KAWASAKI, FUKUOKA; ethnic groups, JAPANESE; languages, JAPANESE; money, YEN / SEN.

JORDAN: capital, AMMAN; other cities, IRBID, AZ-ZARQA; ethnic groups, ARAB; languages, ARABIC; money, DINAR / FILS.

KAZAKHSTAN: capital, ALMA-ATA; ethnic groups, KAZAKH, RUSSIAN, GERMAN, UKRAINIAN; languages, KAZAKH, RUSSIAN; money, RUBLE / KOPECK.

KENYA: capital, NAIROBI; other city, MOMBASA; ethnic groups, KIKUYU, LUHYA, KELENJIN, LUO, KAMBA; languages, *SWAHILI, MERU, KIKUYU, LUHYA, LUO; money, SHILLING / CENT.

KIRIBATI: capital, TARAWA; ethnic groups, MICRONESIAN, POLYNESIAN; lan-guages, *ENGLISH, GILBERTESE; money, DOLLAR / CENT(Australian).

KOREA, NORTH: capital, PYONGYANG; ethnic group, KOREAN; language, KOREAN; money, WON / JEON or JUN.

KOREA, SOUTH: capital, SEOUL; other cities, TAEGU, PUSAN, KWANGJU, INCHON; ethnic group, KOREAN; language, KOREAN; money, WON.

KUWAIT: capital, KUWAIT; other city, HAWALLI; ethnic groups, KUWAITI, ARAB, IRANIAN, INDIAN, PAKISTANI; languages, ARABIC; money, DINAR / FILS.

KYRGYZSTAN: capital, BISHKEK; ethnic groups, KYRGHIZ, RUSSIAN, UZBEK; languages, KYRGHIZ, RUSSIAN; money, RUBLE / KOPECK

LAOS: capital, VIENTIANE; ethnic groups, LAO, MON-KHMER, THAI, MEO, YAO; languages, *LAO, TAI, PALAUNG-WA; money, KIP / AT.

LATVIA: capital, RIGA; ethnic groups, LATVIAN, RUSSIAN; languages, LAT-VIAN; money, RUBLE / KOPECK.

LEBANON: capital, BEIRUT; other cities, TRIPOLI, TYRE; ethnic groups, ARAB, PALESTINIAN, ARMENIAN; languages, *ARABIC, FRENCH; money, POUND / PIASTER.

LESOTHO: capital, MASERU; other cities, ; ethnic groups, SOTHO; languages, *ENGLISH, *SOTHO; money, LOTI / LISENTE.

LIBERIA: capital, MONROVIA; ethnic groups, KRU, VAI, VEI, GOLA, AMERICO-LIBERIAN; languages, ENGLISH; money, DOLLAR / CENT.

LIBYA: capital, TRIPOLI; other cities, BANGHAZI, TUBRUQ; ethnic groups, ARAB-BERBER; languages, ARABIC; money, DINAR / DIRHAM.

LIECHTENSTEIN: capital, VADUZ; other city, SCHAAN; ethnic groups, ALE-MANNIC, ITALIAN; languages, *GERMAN, ALEMANNIC; money, FRANC / CENTIME(Swiss).

LITHUANIA: capital, VILNIUS; other city, KAUNAS; ethnic groups, LITHUANIAN, RUSSIAN, POLISH; languages, LITHUANIAN, RUSSIAN; money, RUBLE / KOPECK.

LUXEMBOURG: capital, LUXEMBOURG; ethnic groups, FRENCH, GERMAN; languages, *FRENCH, *GERMAN, LUXEMBOURGISH; money, FRANC / CENTIME.

MADAGASCAR: capital, ANTANANARIVO; ethnic groups, HOVA, MERINA, MALAY, INDONESIAN, ARAB; languages, *MALAGASY, *FRENCH; money, FRANC / CENTIME.

MALAWI: capital, LILONGWE; other city, BLANTYRE; ethnic groups, CHEWA, NYANJA, LOMWE, BANTU; languages, *CHEWA, *ENGLISH, YAO, LOMWE; money, KWACHA / TAMBALA.

MALAYSIA: capital, KUALA LUMPUR; other cities, PINANG, KUCHING; ethnic groups, MALAY, CHINESE, INDIAN, DAYAK (DYAK); languages, *MALAY, ENGLISH, CHINESE; money, RINGGIT / SEN.

MALDIVES: capital, MALE; ethnic groups, SINHALESE, DRAVIDIAN, ARAB; languages, DIVEHI; money, RUFIYAA / LARI.

MALI: capital, BAMAKO; ethnic groups, MANDE, BAMBARA, MALINKE, SARAKOLE, PEUL, VOLTAIC, SONGHAI, TUAREG, MOOR; languages, *FRENCH, BAMBARA, SENUFO; money, FRANC / CENTIME.

MALTA: capital, VALLETTA; other cities, QORMI, BIRKIRKARA; ethnic groups, ITALIAN, ARAB, FRENCH; languages, *MALTESE, *ENGLISH; money, LIRA / CENT.

MARSHALL ISLANDS: capital, MAJURO; ethnic group, MARSHALLESE; languages, *ENGLISH, MARSHALLESE; money, DOLLAR / CENT (US).

MAURITANIA: capital, NOUAKCHOTT; other cities, NOUADHIBOU, KAEDI; ethnic groups, ARAB-BERBER, NEGROS; languages, ARABIC, FRENCH, HASSANYA; money, OUGUIYA / KHOUMS.

MAURITIUS: capital, PORT LOUIS; ethnic groups, INDO-MAURITIAN, CREOLE; languages, *ENGLISH, CREOLE, BHOJPURI; money, RUPEE / CENT.

MEXICO: capital, MEXICO CITY; other cities, GUADALAJARA, MONTERREY, TIJUANA, MEXICALI, JUAREZ, VERACRUZ, ACAPULCO, TAMPICO, DURANGO, MAZATLAN, CANCUN, PUEBLA, MATAMOROS; states (selected), COLIMA, DURANGO, HIDALGO, JALISCO, MORELOS, NAYARIT, OAXACA, PUEBLA, SONORA; ethnic groups, MESTIZO, NATIVE AMERICAN, CAUCASIAN; language, SPANISH ; money, PESO / CENTAVO.

MICRONESIA: capital, POHNPEI; ethnic groups, TRUKESE, POHNPEIAN; language, ENGLISH; money, DOLLAR / CENT (US).

MOLDOVA: capital, KISHINEV; ethnic groups, MOLDOVIAN, UKRAINIAN, RUSSIAN; languages, ROMANIAN, UKRAINIAN; money, RUBLE / KOPECK.

MONACO: capital, MONACO; ethnic groups, FRENCH, ITALIAN, MONEGASQUE; language, FRENCH; money, FRANC / CENTIME(French).

Nations (Mongolia / Panama)

MONGOLIA: capital, ULAANBAATAR; other city, DARHAN; ethnic group, MONGOL; language, MONGOLIAN; money, TUGRIK / MONGO.

MOROCCO: capital, RABAT; other cities, TANGER, FES, CASABLANCA, MARRAKECH, IFNI, AGADIR, MEKNES, SAFI; ethnic groups, ARAB-BERBER; languages, *ARABIC, BERBER; money, DIRHAM / CENTIME.

MOZAMBIQUE: capital, MAPUTO; other city, BEIRA; ethnic group, BANTU; languages, *PORTUGUESE, MAKUA, MALAWI, SHONA, TSONGA; money, METICAL / CENTAVO.

MYANMAR: capital, YANGON; other cities, KARBE, MANDALAY, MOULMEIN; ethnic groups, BURMANS, SHAN, LAI, KAREN, RAKHINE; languages, *BURMESE, KAREN, SHAN; money, KYAT / PYA.

NAMIBIA: capital, WINDHOEK; ethnic groups, OVAMBO, KAVANGO, HERERO, DAMARA; languages, *ENGLISH, AFRIKAANS; money, RAND / CENT (South African).

NAURU: capital, YAREN; ethnic groups, NAURUANS, PACIFIC ISLANDERS, CHINESE, EUROPEANS; language, NAURUAN; money, DOLLAR / CENT(Australian).

NEPAL: capital, KATMANDU; other cities, POKHARA, BIRGANI; ethnic groups, KIRANTI, INDIANS, TIBETANS; l anguage, NEPALI; money, RUPEE / PICE.

NETHERLANDS: capital, AMSTERDAM; other cities, ROTTERDAM, THE HAGUE, HAARLEM, BREDA, ARNHEM; ethnic group, DUTCH; language, DUTCH; money, GUILDER / CENT.

NEW ZEALAND: capital, WELLINGTON; other cities, AUCKLAND, MANUKAU, DUNEDIN, TIMARU; ethnic groups, EUROPEAN, POLYNESIAN, MAORI; languages, *ENGLISH, *MAORI; money, DOLLAR / CENT.

NICARAGUA: capital, MANAGUA; ethnic groups, MESTIZO, CAUCASIAN; languages, SPANISH; money, CORDOBA / CENTAVO.

NIGER: capital, NIAMEY; other cities, MARADI, ZINDER; ethnic groups, HAUSA, DJERMA, FULANI, TUAREG; languages, *FRENCH, HAUSA, FULANI; money, FRANC / CENTIME.

NIGERIA: capital, ABUJA; other cities, LAGOS, IBADAN; ethnic groups, HAUSA, FULANI, IBO, EDO, IGBO, EFIK, YORUBA; languages, *ENGLISH, HAUSA, IBO, YORUBA; money, NAIRA / KOBO.

NORWAY: capital, OSLO; other city, BERGEN; ethnic groups, GERMANIC, LAPPS; language, NORWEGIAN; money, KRONE / ORE.

OMAN: capital, MUSCAT; ethnic groups, OMANI ARAB, PAKISTANI; languages, ARABIC; money, RIAL / BAIZA.

PAKISTAN: capital, ISLAMABAD; other cities, LAHORE, KARACHI, HYDERABAD, RAWALPINDI; ethnic groups, PUNJABI, SINDHI, PUSHTUN, URDU, BALUCHI; languages, *URDU, PUNJABI, SINDHI, PUSHTU, BALUCHI, BRAHVI; money, RUPEE / PAISA.

PANAMA: capital, PANAMA; other cities, COLON, DAVID; ethnic groups, MESTIZO, CAUCASIAN, WEST INDIAN; languages, *SPANISH, ENGLISH; money, BALBOA / CENT.

PAPUA NEW GUINEA: capital, PORT MORESBY; other city, LAE; ethnic groups, PAPUAN, MELANESIAN, POLYNESIAN; languages, *ENGLISH, MELANESIAN; money, KINA / TOEA; river, SEPIK.

PARAGUAY: capital, ASUNCION; ethnic group, MESTIZOS; languages, *SPANISH, GUARANI; money, GUARANI / CENTIMO.

PERU: capital, LIMA; other cities, CALLAO, IQUITOS; ethnic groups, INDIANS, MESTIZOS, CAUCASIANS; languages, *SPANISH, *QUECHUA, AYMARA; money, INTI / SOL.

PHILIPPINES: capital, QUEZON CITY; other cities, CEBU, MANILA; ethnic groups, MALAYS, CHINESE, SPANISH; languages, *PILIPINO, *ENGLISH, TAGALOG, CEBUANO, BICOL, ILOCANO, PAMPANGO; money, PESO / CENTAVO.

POLAND: capital, WARSAW; other cities, LODZ, KRACOW, LUBLIN, POSNAN, WROCLAW; ethnic group, POLES; languages, POLISH; money, ZLOTY / GROSZ.

PORTUGAL: capital, LISBON; other cities, BRAGA, PORTO, COIMBRA, SETUBAL; ethnic group, PORTUGUESE; language, PORTUGUESE; money, ESCUDO / CENTAVO.

QATAR: capital, DOHA; ethnic groups, ARAB, IRANIAN, PAKISTANI, INDIAN; languages, ARABIC; money, RIYAL / DIRHAM.

ROMANIA: capital, BUCHAREST; other cities, ARAD, CLUJ, DEVA, IASI, BRASOV, GALATI, ORADEA, CONSTANTA ; ethnic groups, ROMANIANS, HUNGARIANS; languages, ROMANIAN; money, LEU / BAN; river, DANUBE.

RUSSIAN FEDERATION: capital, MOSCOW; other cities, ST. PETERSBURG, SAMARA; ethnic groups, RUSSIANS, TATARS; language, RUSSIAN; money, RUBLE / KOPECK.

RWANDA: capital, KIGALI; ethnic groups, HUTU, TUTSI, TWA; languages, *RWANDA, *FRENCH; money, FRANC / CENTIME.

ST. KITTS AND NEVIS: capital, BASSETERRE; ethnic groups, AFRICAN; languages, ENGLISH; money, E. CARIBBEAN DOLLAR.

SAINT LUCIA: capital, CASTRIES; ethnic groups, AFRICAN; languages, ENGLISH; money, DOLLAR / CENT.

SAINT VINCENT AND THE GRENADINES: capital, KINGSTOWN; ethnic groups, AFRICAN; languages, ENGLISH; money, DOLLAR / CENT.

SAN MARINO: capital, SAN MARINO; ethnic groups, SANMARINESE, ITALIANS; languages, ITALIAN; money, LIRA / CENTESIMO(Italian).

SAO TOME AND PRINCIPE: capital, SAO TOME; ethnic groups, PORTUGUESE, VARIOUS AFRICAN; languages, PORTUGUESE; money, DOBRA / CENTAVO.

SAUDI ARABIA: capital, RIYADH; other cities, JIDDA, MECCA; ethnic group, ARAB; language, ARABIC; money, RIYAL / HALALA.

SENEGAL: capital, DAKAR; other city, THIES; ethnic groups, WOLOF, SERER, FULANI, DIOLA, MANDINGO; languages, *FRENCH, WOLOF, SERER, PEUL, TUKULOR; money, FRANC / CENTIME.

SEYCHELLES: capital, VICTORIA; ethnic group, CREOLES; languages, *ENGLISH, *FRENCH; money, RUPEE / CENT.

SIERRA LEONE: capital, FREETOWN; other cities, KENEMA, MAKENI, BO; ethnic groups, TEMNE, MENDE; languages, *ENGLISH; money, LEONE / CENT.

SINGAPORE: capital, SINGAPORE; ethnic groups, CHINESE, MALAYS, INDIANS; languages, *CHINESE, *TAMIL, *ENGLISH, *MALAY; money, DOLLAR / CENT.

SLOVENIA: capital, LJUBLJANA; ethnic group, SLOVENES; languages, SLOVENIAN, YUGOSLAVIAN; money, DINAR / PARA.

SOLOMON ISLANDS: capital, HONIARA; ethnic groups, MELANESIAN, POLYNESIAN; languages, *ENGLISH, MELANESIAN, PAPUAN; money, DOLLAR / CENT.

SOMALIA: capital, MOGADISHU; ethnic group, HAMITIC; languages, *SOMALI, *ARABIC; money, SHILLING / CENT.

SOUTH AFRICA: capitals, CAPE TOWN (legislative), PRETORIA (administrative), and BLOEMFONTEIN (judicial); other cities, JOHANNESBURG, DURBAN; ethnic groups, EUROPEANS, BANTU, ZULU, SWAZI, SOTHO; languages, *AFRIKAANS, *ENGLISH, NGUNI, SOTHO; money, RAND / CENT; river, ORANGE.

SOVIET UNION (See under individual republics).

SPAIN: capital, MADRID; other cities, LEON, BILBAO, MALAGA, CORDOBA, GRANADA, VALENCIA, BARCELONA; ethnic groups, CASTILIAN, VALENCIAN, ANDALUSIAN, ASTURIAN; languages, *SPANISH, CATALAN, BASQUE, GALICIAN; money, PESETA / CENTIMO; river, EBRO.

SRI LANKA: capital, COLOMBO; other cities, GALLE, JAFFNA, KANDY; ethnic groups, SINHALESE, TAMILS, VEDDA, MOORS; languages, *SINHALESE, TAMIL; money, RUPEE / CENT.

SUDAN: capital, KHARTOUM; other cities, PORT SUDAN, OMDURMAN; ethnic groups, ARAB, BEJA, NUBIAN; languages, *ARABIC, DINKA, NUBIAN, NUER, BEJA; money, POUND / PIASTER; river, NILE.

SURINAM: capital, PARAMARIBO; ethnic groups, HINDUSTANIS, CREOLE; languages, DUTCH, ENGLISH, SRANANTONGA; money, GUILDER / CENT.

SWAZILAND: capital, MBABANE; other city, MANZINI; ethnic groups, SWAZI, ZULU, EUROPEAN; languages, *SWAZI, *ENGLISH; money, LILANGENI / CENT.

SWEDEN: capital, STOCKHOLM; other cities, MALMO, GOTEBORG; ethnic groups, SWEDISH, FINNISH, LAPP; languages, SWEDISH; money, KRONA / ORE.

SWITZERLAND: capital, BERN; other cities, BASEL, GENEVA, ZURICH; ethnic groups, MIXED EUROPEANS; languages, *FRENCH, *GERMAN, *ITALIAN; money, FRANC / CENTIME.

SYRIA: capital, DAMASCUS; other cities, HAMA, HOMS, ALEPPO; ethnic groups, ARAB, KURDS, ARMENIAN; languages, *ARABIC, KURDISH, ARMENIAN; money, POUND / PIASTER.

TAIWAN: capital, TAIPEI; other city, TAINAN; ethnic groups, TAIWANESE, CHINESE; languages, *MANDARIN, TAIWANESE, HAKKA; money, DOLLAR / CENT.

TAJIKSTAN: capital, DUSHANBE; ethnic groups, TAJIK, UZBEK, RUSSIAN; languages, TADZHIK, RUSSIAN; money, RUBLE / KOPECK.

TANZANIA: capital, DAR-ES-SALAAM; ethnic groups, VARIOUS; languages, *SWAHILI, *ENGLISH; money, SHILLING / CENT.

THAILAND: capital, BANGKOK; other cities, HAT YAI, KHON KAEN; ethnic groups, THAI, CHINESE; languages, *THAI, CHINESE, MALAY; money, BAHT / SATANG; river, CHAO PHRAYA.

TOGO: capital, LOME; ethnic groups, EWE, MINA, KABYE; languages, *FRENCH, GUR, KWA; money, FRANC / CENTIME.

TONGA: capital, NUKU'ALOFA; ethnic group, TONGAN; languages, TONGAN, ENGLISH; money, PA'ANGA / SENITI.

TRINIDAD AND TOBAGO: capital, PORT-OF-SPAIN; ethnic groups, AFRICANS, EAST INDIAN; languages, ENGLISH; money, DOLLAR / CENT.

TUNISIA: capital, TUNIS; other city, SFAX; ethnic group, ARAB; languages, *ARABIC, FRENCH; money, DINAR / MILLIME.

TURKEY: capital, ANKARA; other cities, ADANA, BURSA, IZMIR; ethnic groups, TURKS, KURDS; languages, *TURKISH, ARABIC, KURDISH; money, LIRA / KURUS.

TURKMENISTAN: capital, ASHKHABAD; ethnic groups, TURKMEN, UZBEK, RUSSIAN; languages, TURKMEN, RUSSIAN; money, RUBLE / KOPECK.

TUVALU: capital, FUNAFULI; ethnic group, POLYNESIAN; languages, TUVALUAN; money, DOLLAR / CENT(Australian).

UGANDA: capital, KAMPALA; other city, MASAKA; ethnic groups, BANTU, NILO-HAMITIC, NILOTIC; languages, *ENGLISH, SWAHILI, LUGANDA; money, SHILLING / CENT.

UKRAINE: capital, KIEV; other cities, LVOV, ODESSA, KHARKIV; ethnic groups, UKRAINIAN, RUSSIAN; languages, UKRAINIAN; money, RUBLE / KOPECK.

UNITED ARAB EMIRATES: capital, ABU DHABI; other city, DUBAVY; ethnic groups, ARAB, IRANIAN, PAKISTANI, INDIAN; languages, ARABIC; money, DIRHAM / FILS.

UNITED KINGDOM OF GREAT BRITAIN AND NORTHERN IRELAND: capital, LONDON; other cities, BELFAST, CARDIFF, EDINBURGH; ethnic groups, ENGLISH, SCOTTISH, IRISH, WELSH; languages, *ENGLISH, WELSH; money, POUND / PENCE; rivers, AIN, DEE, ESK, EXE, TAW, OUSE, TYNE, CLYDE, FORTH, TAMAR, TRENT, HUMBER, SEVERN, THAMES; possessions, BERMUDA, GIBRALTAR, HONG KONG, CHANNEL ISLANDS, ISLE OF MAN, PITCAIRN ISLAND, ASCENSION, TRISTAN DA CUNHA, ST. HELENA, FALKLAND ISLANDS, MONTSERRAT, BRITISH VIRGIN ISLANDS, CAYMAN ISLANDS, TURKS AND CAICOS ISLANDS.

UNITED STATES OF AMERICA: capital, WASHINGTON DC; languages, ENGLISH; money, DOLLAR / CENT.

Nations (Upper Volta / Zimbabwe)

UPPER VOLTA (See Burkina Faso).

URUGUAY: capital, MONTEVIDEO; ethnic groups, SPANISH, ITALIANS, MESTIZO; language, SPANISH; money, PESO / CENTESIMO; river, URUGUAY.

UZBEKISTAN: capital, TASHKENT; ethnic groups, UZBEK, RUSSIAN; language, UZBEK; money, RUBLE / KOPECK.

VANUATU: capital, PORT-VILA; other city, VILA; ethnic group, MELANESIAN; languages, BISLAMA, FRENCH, ENGLISH; money, VATU.

VATICAN CITY: ethnic groups, ITALIANS, SWISS; languages, LATIN, ITALIAN; money, LIRA / CENTESIMO(Italian).

VENEZUELA: capital, CARACAS; other city, MARACAIBO, VALENCIA; ethnic groups, MESTIZO, SPANISH; language, SPANISH; money, BOLIVAR / CENTIMO; river, ORINOCO.

VIETNAM: capital, HANOI; other city, HO CHI MINH CITY; ethnic groups, VIETNAMESE, MUONG, MEO, KHMER, MAN, CHAM; language, VIETNAMESE; money, DONG; rivers, RED, MEKONG.

WESTERN SAMOA: capital, APIA; ethnic group, SAMOAN; languages, *SAMOAN, *ENGLISH; money, TALA / SENE; islands, SAVAI'I, UPOLU, MANONO, APOLIMA.

YEMEN: capital, SANAA; other city, ADEN; ethnic groups, ARAB, INDIAN; language, ARABIC; money, DINAR/FILS, RIYAL / FILS.

YUGOSLAVIA (See also SLOVENIA, CROATIA, BOSNIA-HERZEGOVINA).

YUGOSLAVIA (SERBIA-MONTENEGRO): capital, BELGRADE; other cities, NIS, SKOPJE; ethnic group, SERBIANS; language, SERBO-CROATIAN, money, DINAR / PARA.

ZAIRE: capital, KINSHASA; other city, LUBUMBASHI; ethnic group, BANTU; languages, *FRENCH, KONGO, LUBA, MONGO, RWANDA; money, ZAIRE / LIKUTA; river, CONGO.

ZAMBIA: capital, LUSAKA; other cities, KITWE, NDOLA; ethnic group, BANTU; languages, *ENGLISH, BANTU; money, KWACHA / NGWEE; river, ZAMBESI.

ZIMBABWE: capital, HARARE; other city, BULAWAYO; ethnic groups, SHONA, NDEBELE; languages, *ENGLISH, SHONA, SINDE BELE; money, DOLLAR / CENT.

ANIMALS

AMPHIBIANS

BULLFROG
CAECILIAN
EEL, CONGO
EFT
FROG
FROG, GRASS
FROG, GREEN
FROG, LEOPARD
FROG, PICKEREL
FROG, SPRING
FROG, TREE
FROG, WOOD
HELLBENDER
MUD PUPPY
NEWT
SALAMANDER
SIREN
TOAD
TOAD, MIDWIFE
TOAD, SURINAM
WATER DOG

BIRDS

ADJUTANT BIRD
ALBATROSS
ARGALA
AUK
AVOCET
BALDPATE
BARBET
BIRD OF PARADISE
BITTERN
BLACKBIRD
BLACKCAP
BLUEBILL
BLUEBIRD
BLUE JAY
BOBOLINK
BOBWHITE
BOOBY
BRANT
BUDGERIGAR
BULLFINCH
BUNTING
BUNTING, INDIGO
BUNTING, SNOW
BUSTARD
BUTCHER BIRD
BUZZARD
CANARY
CAPERCAILLIE
CARACARA
CARDINAL

CASSOWARY
CATBIRD
CEDARBIRD
CEDAR WAXWING
CHAFFINCH
CHAT
CHEWINK
CHICKADEE
COCKATIEL
COCKATOO
CONDOR
COOT
CORMORANT
COWBIRD
CRAKE
CRANE
CREEPER
CROSSBILL
CROW
CUCKOO
CURLEW
CURLEW, STONE
CUSHAT
DABCHICK
DARTER
DIPPER
DODO
DOVE
DOVE, MOURNING
DOVE, ROCK
DUCK
DUCK, CANVASBACK
DUCK, FOOL
DUCK, RUDDY
DUCK, SCAUP
DUCK, SEA
DUCK, TEAL
DUCK, WILD
DUCK, WOOD
DUNLIN
EAGLE
EAGLE, BALD
EAGLE, GOLDEN
EAGLE, HARPY
EAGLE, SEA
EGRET
EGRET, CATTLE
EIDER DUCK
EMU
ERNE
FALCON
FALCON, PEREGRINE
FINCH
FINCH, HOUSE
FINCH, ZEBRA
FLAMINGO

FLICKER
FLYCATCHER
FRIGATE BIRD
FULMAR
GALLINULE
GANNET
GARGANEY
GOATSUCKER
GODWIT
GOLDENEYE
GOLDFINCH
GOOSE
GOOSE, BARNACLE
GOOSE, CANADA
GOOSE, SNOW
GOOSE, SOLAN
GOOSE, SWAN
GOSHAWK
GRACKLE
GREBE
GROSBEAK
GROUSE
GROUSE, BLACK
GROUSE, RED
GROUSE, RUFFED
GROUSE, SAGE
GUILLEMOT
GUINEA FOWL
GULL
GULL, SEA
GYRFALCON
HANGBIRD
HARRIER
HAWK
HAWK, CHICKEN
HAWK, FISH
HAWK, PIGEON
HAWK, SPARROW
HEN, MOOR
HEN, MUD
HEN, SAGE
HERON
HOBBY
HONKER
HOOPOE
HORNED SCREAMER
HUMMINGBIRD
IBIS
JACKDAW
JAY
JUNCO
JUNGLE FOWL
KEA
KESTREL
KILLDEER
KINGBIRD

Animals (birds / cetaceans)

KINGFISHER
KINGLET
KITE
KITTIWAKE
KIWI
KOOKABURRA
LAMMERGEIER
LAPWING
LARK
LARK, MEADOW
LINNET
LOON
LOVEBIRD
LYREBIRD
MACAW
MAGPIE
MALLARD
MAN-O'-WAR BIRD
MARTIN
MARTIN, HOUSE
MARTIN, PURPLE
MARTIN, SAND
MAVIS
MERGANSER
MERL
MEW
MOA
MOCKINGBIRD
MURRE
MYNA BIRD
NIGHTHAWK
NIGHT-HERON
NIGHTINGALE
NIGHTJAR
NUTCRACKER
NUTHATCH
ORIOLE
ORTOLAN
OSPREY
OSTRICH
OUZEL
OUZEL, RING
OWL
OWL, BARN
OWL, HAWK
OWL, HOOT
OWL, HORNED
OWL, SCREECH
OWL, WOOD
OYSTER CATCHER
PARAKEET
PARROT
PARTRIDGE
PEAFOWL
PEEWEE
PELICAN
PENGUIN
PETREL
PETREL, STORMY
PEWIT

PHALAROPE
PHEASANT
PHEASANT, RING-
NECKED
PHOEBE
PIGEON
PIGEON, PASSENGER
PIGEON, WOOD
PINTAIL
PIPIT
PLOVER
POCHARD
PTARMIGAN
PUFFIN
QUETZAL
RAIL
RAVEN
RAZORBILL
REDBIRD
REDHEAD
REDPOLL
REDSHANK
REDSTART
REDWING
REEDBIRD
RHEA
RICEBIRD
RINGDOVE
ROADRUNNER
ROBIN
ROOK
SANDPIPER
SAPSUCKER
SECRETARY BIRD
SHELDRAKE
SHOEBILL
SHOVELER
SHRIKE
SISKIN
SNIPE
SNOWBIRD
SONGBIRD
SPARROW
SPARROW, CHIPPING
SPARROW, ENGLISH
SPARROW, SONG
SPARROW, VESPER
SPOONBILL
SPRIG
STARLING
STILT
STILT PLOVER
STORK
STORK, MARABOU
SWALLOW
SWALLOW, BANK
SWALLOW, BARN
SWALLOW, CLIFF
SWALLOW, SEA
SWALLOW, TREE

SWAN
SWAN, MUTE
SWIFT
SWIFT, CHIMNEY
TANAGER
TANAGER, SCARLET
TEAL
TERN
THRASHER
THRASHER, BROWN
THRUSH
THRUSH, HERMIT
THRUSH, MISTLE
THRUSH, SONG
TIT
TITLARK
TITMOUSE
TOUCAN
TOWHEE
TRAGOPAN
TRUMPETER
TURKEY
TURKEY, BRUSH
TURKEY BUZZARD
TURKEY VULTURE
TURNSTONE
TURTLEDOVE
VEERY
VIREO
VULTURE
WARBLER
WARBLER, AUDUBON
WAXWING
WEAVERBIRD
WHEATEAR
WHIPPOORWILL
WHISTLER
WIDGEON
WILLET
WOODCOCK
WOODPECKER
WOODPECKER,
    RED-HEADED
WREN
WREN, BUSH
WREN-TIT
WRYNECK
YELLOWBIRD
YELLOWHAMMER
YELLOWLEGS
YELLOWTHROAT

CETACEANS

BELUGA
CACHALOT
DOLPHIN
FINBACK
GRAMPUS
NARWHAL

PORPOISE
RORQUAL
WHALE, BALEEN
WHALE, BLUE
WHALE, HUMPBACK
WHALE, KILLER
WHALE, RIGHT
WHALE, SPERM

DINOSAURS

ALLOSAUR(US)
AMMONITE
ARCHELON
AUROCHS
BRONTOPS
BRONTOSAUR(US)
CREODONT
DIPNOAN
EOHIPPUS
ERYOPSID
IGUANODON
MAMMOTH
MAMMOTH, WOOLLY
MASTODON
MEGATHERE
MERODUS
MIACIS
PTERODACTYL
SAUROPOD
SLOTH, GIANT
SMILODON
STEGOSAUR(US)
TIGER,
  SABER-TOOTHED
TYRANNOSAUR(US)
TYRANNOSAURUS
  REX
URUS

DOGS

AFFENPINSCHER
AFGHAN HOUND
AIREDALE TERRIER
ALSATIAN
BADGER DOG
BASENJI
BASSET HOUND
BEAGLE
BLOODHOUND
BOARHOUND
BORZOI
BOSTON BULL
BOUVIER
  DES FLANDRES
BOXER
BRIARD
BULLDOG
BULLDOG, ENGLISH

BULLDOG, FRENCH
BULL MASTIFF
CHIHUAHUA
CHOW
COCKER SPANIEL
COCKER SPANIEL,
  ENGLISH
COLLIE
COLLIE, BORDER
COLLIE, WELSH
COONHOUND
CORGI, WELSH
DACHSHUND
DALMATIAN,
  aka COACH DOG
DEERHOUND
DEERHOUND,
  SCOTTISH
DOBERMAN
  PINSCHER
ELKHOUND
ELKHOUND,
  NORWEGIAN
FOXHOUND
FOXHOUND,
  AMERICAN
FOXHOUND, ENGLISH
GERMAN SHEPHERD
GREAT DANE
GREAT PYRENEES
GREYHOUND
GREYHOUND, ITALIAN
HAIRLESS, MEXICAN
HARRIER
HOUND
HOUND, GAZELLE
HUSKY
HUSKY, SIBERIAN
KEESHOND
KOMONDOR
KUVASZ
LHASA APSO
MALAMUTE
MALAMUTE, ALASKAN
MALTESE
MASTIFF
NEWFOUNDLAND
OTTER HOUND
PAPILLON
PEKINGESE
PINSCHER,
  MINIATURE
POINTER
POINTER, GERMAN
  SHORT-HAIRED
POINTER, GERMAN
  WIRE-HAIRED
POMERANIAN
POODLE
POODLE, MINIATURE

POODLE, TOY
PUG
PULI
RETRIEVER
RETRIEVER,
  CHESAPEAKE BAY
RETRIEVER,
  FLAT-COATED
RETRIEVER, GOLDEN
RETRIEVER,
  LABRADOR
RIDGEBACK,
  RHODESIAN
ROTTWEILER
SAINT BERNARD
SALUKI
SAMOYED
SCHIPPERKE
SCHNAUZER
SCHNAUZER, GIANT
SCHNAUZER,
  MINIATURE
SETTER
SETTER, ENGLISH
SETTER, GORDON
SETTER, IRISH
SHEEP DOG, BELGIAN
SHEEP DOG,
  OLD ENGLISH
SHEEP DOG,
  SHETLAND
SHIH TZU
SPANIEL
SPANIEL, BLENHEIM
SPANIEL, BRITTANY
SPANIEL, CLUMBER
SPANIEL, ENGLISH
  SPRINGER
SPANIEL,
  ENGLISH TOY
SPANIEL,
  IRISH WATER
SPANIEL, JAPANESE
SPANIEL,
  KING CHARLES
SPANIEL, NORFOLK
SPANIEL, SPRINGER
SPANIEL, SUSSEX
SPANIEL, TOY
SPANIEL, WATER
SPANIEL, WELSH
  SPRINGER
SPITZ
STAGHOUND
TERRIER
TERRIER,
  AUSTRALIAN
TERRIER,
  BEDLINGTON
TERRIER, BORDER

Animals (dogs / fish)

TERRIER, BULL
TERRIER, CAIRN
TERRIER,
  CLYDESDALE
TERRIER, FOX
TERRIER, IRISH
TERRIER,
  KERRY BLUE
TERRIER, LAKELAND
TERRIER,
  MANCHESTER
TERRIER, NORWICH
TERRIER, RAT
TERRIER, SCOTTISH
TERRIER, SEALYHAM
TERRIER, SILKY
TERRIER, SKYE
TERRIER, TOY
TERRIER, WELSH
TERRIER, WEST
  HIGHLAND WHITE
TERRIER,
  WIRE-HAIRED
TERRIER, YORKSHIRE
TURNSPIT
VIZSLA
WATER SPANIEL,
  AMERICAN
WEIMARANER
WHIPPET
WOLFHOUND
WOLFHOUND, IRISH
WOLFHOUND,
  RUSSIAN

FISH

ALBACORE
ALEWIFE
AMBER JACK
ANCHOVY
ANGEL FISH
ARCHERFISH
BARBEL
BARRACUDA
BASS
BASS, BLACK
BASS, CHANNEL
BASS, SEA
BASS, STRIPED
BLACKFISH
BLEAK
BLIND FISH
BLOWFISH
BLUE FISH
BLUEGILL
BONEFISH
BONITO
BOWFIN
BREAM

BREAM, SEA
BUFFALO FISH
BULLHEAD
BURBOT
BUTTERFISH
CANDLEFISH
CAPELIN
CARP
CATFISH
CHAR
CHIMAERA
CHUB
CICHLID
CISCO
COBIA
COD
COELACANTH
CONGER EEL
CRAPPIE
CROAKER
CUTLASS FISH
DACE
DARTER
DEVILFISH
DOCTOR FISH
DOGFISH
DORADO
DRAGON FISH
DRUM
EEL
EEL, ELECTRIC
EEL, MORAY
EELPOUT
FILEFISH
FLATFISH
FLOUNDER
FLUKE
FLYING FISH
FLYING GURNARD
GAR
GLOBEFISH
GOATFISH
GOBY
GOLDFISH
GOURAMI
GRAYLING
GROUPER
GRUNION
GRUNT
GUDGEON
GUITARFISH
GUNNEL
GUPPY
HADDOCK
HAKE
HALIBUT
HERRING
HOGFISH
JEWFISH
KINGFISH

LAMPREY
LANTERN FISH
LING
LOACH
LUNG FISH
MACKEREL
MACKEREL, HORSE
MANTA
MARLIN
MENHADEN
MILLER'S-THUMB
MINNOW
MUDFISH
MUSKELLUNGE
PADDLEFISH
PERCH
PERCH, SEA
PICKEREL
PIKE
PIKE, WALLEYE
PILCHARD
PILOT FISH
PIRANHA
PLAICE
POMPANO
PORGY
PUFFER
RAY
RAY, ELECTRIC
RAY, STING
RAY, THORNBACK
REDFIN
REDFISH
ROACH
SAILFISH
SALMON
SALMON, CHINOOK
SALMON, SILVER
SARDINE
SAWFISH
SCUP
SEA HORSE
SERGEANT MAJOR
  FISH
SHARK
SHARK, BASKING
SHARK, BLUE
SHARK,
  HAMMERHEAD
SHARK, MAKO
SHARK, PORBEAGLE
SHARK, SHOVELHEAD
SHARK, THRESHER
SHINER
SKATE
SKATE, BARN DOOR
SMELT
SNAPPER
SNOOK
SOLE

SPRAT
STICKLEBACK
STURGEON
SUCKER
SUNFISH
SWORDFISH
TARPON
TAUTOG
TENCH
TETRA
TOADFISH
TOPE
TORPEDO FISH
TRIGGERFISH
TROUT
TROUT, BROOK
TROUT, BROWN
TROUT, CUTTHROAT
TROUT,
  DOLLY VARDEN
TROUT, GOLDEN
TROUT, LAKE
TROUT, RAINBOW
TROUT, SALMON
TROUT, SEA
TROUT, SPECKLED
TROUT, STEELHEAD
TUNA
TURBOT
WAHOO
WEAKFISH
WHITEFISH
WHITING
YELLOWTAIL

INSECTS

ANT
ANT LION
APHID
ASSASSIN BUG
BEDBUG
BEE
BEETLE
BEETLE, BUPRESTID
BEETLE, COLORADO
BEETLE,
  CUCUMBER FLEA
BEETLE, DUNG
BEETLE, ELM LEAF
BEETLE, FLEA
BEETLE, GRAIN
BEETLE, JAPANESE
BEETLE, ROSE
BEETLE, SCARAB
BEETLE, SNOUT
BEETLE, STAG
BILLBUG
BLOWFLY
BLUEBOTTLE

BOLL WEEVIL
BORER
BOTFLY
BRISTLETAIL
BUFFALO BUG
BUTTERFLY
CHAFER
CHIGOE
CHIGGER
CHINCH BUG
CICADA
COCKCHAFER
COCKROACH
CORN-NOSE
CRICKET
CRICKET, MOLE
CROTON BUG
CURCULIO
DAMSELFLY
DOBSONFLY
DRAGONFLY
DROSOPHILA
EARWIG
EPHEMERID
FIREBRAT
FIREFLY
FLEA
FLY
FLY, BEE
FLY, CADDIS
FLY, CRANE
FLY, DEER
FLY, FRUIT
FLY, HORN
FLY, LANTERN
FLY, ROBBER
FLY, SCORPION
FLY, SHAD
FLY, ST. MARK'S
FLY, STONE
FLY, SYRPHUS
FLY, TSETSE
GADFLY
GALLFLY
GLOWWORM
GNAT
GRASSHOPPER
HARLEQUIN
  CABBAGE BUG
HAWK, MOSQUITO
HAWK MOTH
HORNET
HORNTAIL
HORSEFLY
HOUSEFLY
JIGGER FLEA
JUNE BUG or BEETLE
KATYDID
KISSING BUG
LACEWING

LADYBUG
LEAFHOPPER
LOCUST
LOUSE
MANTIS
MANTIS, PRAYING
MAYFLY
MEALWORM
MEALYBUG
MIDGE
MILLER
MOSQUITO
MOTH
MOTH, CECROPIA
MOTH, CODLING
MOTH, FLOUR
MOTH, TIGER
PILL BUG
POTATO BUG
PUNKIE
ROACH
SAWFLY
SILVERFISH
SOW BUG
SPRINGTAIL
SQUASH BUG
STINK BUG
TERMITE
THRIPS
TICK, WOOD
TUMBLEBUG
WALKING STICK
WASP
WASP, WOOD
WATER BUG
WEEVIL
YELLOW JACKET

MAMMALS

AARDVARK
AARDWOLF
ADDAX
AGOUTI
ALPACA
ANOA
ANT BEAR
ANTEATER
ANTELOPE
ANTELOPE, GOAT
ANTELOPE,
  HARNESSED
ANTELOPE, SABLE
AOUDAD
ARGALI
ARMADILLO
ASS
ASS, WILD
AUROCHS
BADGER

Animals (mammals)

BANDICOOT
BANDICOOT, RABBIT
BARBIRUSA
BARONDUKI
BASSARISK
BAT
BEAR
BEAR, BLACK
BEAR, BROWN
BEAR, CINNAMON
BEAR, GRIZZLY
BEAR, ICE
BEAR, KODIAK
BEAR, POLAR
BEAR, SKUNK
BEAR, SYRIAN
BEAVER
BINTURONG
BISON
BOAR
BOAR, WILD
BOBCAT
BUCK, BLACK
BUFFALO
BUFFALO, CAPE
BUFFALO, INDIAN
BURRO
BUSH BABY
CACHALOT
CAMEL
CAMEL, BACTRIAN
CAMELOPARD
CAPYBARA
CARABAO
CARACAL
CARCAJOU
CARIBOU
CAT
CATAMOUNT
CATTALO
CAVY
CHAMOIS
CHEETAH
CHEVROTAIN
CHICKADEE
CHINCHILLA
CHIPMUNK
CIVET CAT
COATI
COUGAR
COW
COYOTE
COYPU
DEER
DEER, BRUSH
DEER, BURRO
DEER, FALLOW
DEER, MOUSE
DEER, MULE
DEER, MUSK

DEER, RED
DEER, VIRGINIA
DEER, WHITE-TAILED
DINGO
DOG
DOG, PRAIRIE
DONKEY
DORMOUSE
DROMEDARY
ECHIDNA
ELAND
ELEPHANT
ELK
ERMINE
FERRET
FITCH
FOX
FOX, ARCTIC
FOX, BLACK
FOX, BLUE
FOX, FLYING
FOX, GRAY
FOX, KIT
FOX, POLAR
FOX, PRAIRIE
FOX, RED
FOX, SILVER
FOX, WHITE
GAUR
GAZELLE
GEMSBOK
GENET
GERBIL
GIRAFFE
GNU
GOAT
GOAT, ANGORA
GOAT, CASHMERE
GOAT, GNU
GOAT, MOUNTAIN
GOAT,
    ROCKY MOUNTAIN
GOAT, WILD
GOPHER
GOPHER, POCKET
GROUNDHOG
GUANACO
GUINEA PIG
HAMSTER
HARE
HARE, ARCTIC
HARE, BELGIAN
HARTEBEEST
HEDGEHOG
HIPPOPOTAMUS
HOG
HOG, HERRING
HOG, MUSK
HORSE
HYENA

HYRAX
IBEX
JACKAL
JACKASS
JACKRABBIT
JAGUAR
JAGUARUNDI
JERBOA
KAAMA
KANGAROO
KANGAROO, JERBOA
KARAKUL
KIANG
KINKAJOU
KOALA
KUDU
LEMMING
LEMUR, FLYING
LEOPARD
LION
LION, MOUNTAIN
LLAMA
LORIS
LYNX
MARA
MARGAY
MARMOT
MARMOT, FLYING
MARTEN
MEERKAT
MINK
MOLE
MOLE, SHREW
MONGOOSE
MOOSE
MOUFLON
MOUSE
MOUSE, COTTON
MOUSE, DEER
MOUSE, FIELD
MOUSE,
    GRASSHOPPER
MOUSE, HARVEST
MOUSE, JUMPING
MOUSE, KANGAROO
MOUSE, MEADOW
MOUSE, PINE
MOUSE, POCKET
MOUSE, WOOD
MULE
MUNTJAC
MUSK-OX
MUSKRAT
NILGAI
NUTRIA
OCELOT
OKAPI
ONAGER
OONT
OPOSSUM

Animals (mammals / marine animals / primates / reptiles)

ORYX
OTTER
OUNCE
PANDA
PANGOLIN
PANTHER
PECCARY
PHALANGER
PHALANGER, FLYING
PIG
PIKA
PLATYPUS
POLECAT
PORCUPINE
POTTO
PRONGHORN
PUMA
RABBIT
RABBIT, COTTONTAIL
RABBIT, SNOWSHOE
RABBIT, SWAMP
RACCOON
RAT
RAT, COTTON
RAT, KANGAROO
RAT, PACK
RAT, POCKET
RAT, POUCHED
RAT, WHARF
RAT, WOOD
REINDEER
RHINOCEROS
ROEBUCK
SABLE
SAIGA
SAMBAR
SERVAL
SHEEP
SHEEP, BIGHORN
SHEEP, BLACK
SHEEP, MOUNTAIN
SHEEP, WILD
SHREW
SHREW, TREE
SIKA
SKUNK
SLOTH
SLOTH,
   GIANT GROUND
SPRINGBOK
SQUIRREL
SQUIRREL, FLYING
SQUIRREL, GROUND
SQUIRREL, RED
SQUIRREL, ROCK
STEENBOK
STOAT
SUSLIK
SWINE
TAKIN

TAMANDUA
TAMARIN
TAPIR
TATOUAY
TIGER
URUS
VOLE
WALLABY
WAPITI
WARTHOG
WATERBUCK
WATER BUFFALO
WEASEL
WILDCAT
WILDEBEEST
WOLF
WOLF, BRUSH
WOLF, BUFFALO
WOLF, GRAY
WOLF, PRAIRIE
WOLF, TIMBER
WOLF, WHITE
WOLVERINE
WOMBAT
WOODCHUCK
YAK
ZEBRA
ZEBU
ZORIL

MARINE ANIMALS

CRUSTACEANS
DUGONG
MANATEE
MOLLUSKS
OCTOPUS
SEA CALF
SEA COW
SEA DOG
SEA ELEPHANT
SEAL
SEAL, ELEPHANT
SEAL, FUR
SEAL, HARBOR
SEA LION
SEA URCHIN
SHELLFISH
SQUID
WALRUS

PRIMATES

ANGWANTIBO
APE
APE, ANTHROPOID
APE, BARBARY
AYE-AYE
BABOON
CAPUCHIN

CHACMA
CHIMPANZEE
COLOBUS
DRILL
ENTELLUS
GIBBON
GORILLA
GORILLA, MOUNTAIN
GRIVET
GUENON
HANUMAN
LANGUR
LEMUR
MACAQUE
MAN
MANDRILL
MARMOSET
ORANGUTAN,
   aka ORANG
PROBOSCIS MONKEY
RHESUS
SAKI
SIAMANG
SPIDER MONKEY

REPTILES

AGAMA
ALLIGATOR
ANOLE
BASILISK
BLINDWORM
CAYMAN
CHAMELEON
CROCODILE
GAVIAL
GECKO
GILA MONSTER
IGUANA
LEATHERBACK
LIZARD
LIZARD, ALLIGATOR
LIZARD, BEADED
LIZARD, BEARDED
LIZARD,
   GIRDLE-TAILED
LIZARD, SAND
LIZARD,
   STUMP-TAILED
MONITOR
SKINK
SLOW-WORM
SNAKE, GLASS
TERRAPIN
TOAD, HORNED
TORTOISE
TORTOISE, SEA
TUATARA
TURTLE
TURTLE, BOX

Animals / Groups of Animals

TURTLE, GREEN
TURTLE, HAWKSBILL
TURTLE,
   LOGGERHEAD
TURTLE, SEA
TURTLE, SNAPPING
TURTLE,
   SOFT-SHELLED

SNAKES

ADDER
ANACONDA
ASP
BLACK SNAKE
BLIND SNAKE
BOA
BOA CONSTRICTOR
BULL SNAKE
BUSHMASTER

COBRA
COBRA, KING
COBRA, SPECKLED
CONSTRICTOR
COPPERHEAD
CORAL SNAKE
COTTONMOUTH
DABOIA
FER-DE-LANCE
GARTER SNAKE
GOPHER SNAKE
HAMADRYAD
HARLEQUIN SNAKE
HOG-NOSE SNAKE
KING SNAKE
KRAIT
MAMBA
MILK SNAKE
MOCCASIN
PINE SNAKE

PUFF ADDER
PYTHON
RACER
RAT SNAKE
RATTLESNAKE,
   aka RATTLER
RATTLESNAKE,
   DIAMONDBACK
RATTLESNAKE,
   HORNED
SHOVEL-NOSE SNAKE
SIDEWINDER
THUNDER SNAKE
URUTU
VIPER
VIPER, HORNED
VIPER, RUSSELL'S
WATER MOCCASIN
WATER SNAKE
WORM SNAKE

GROUPS OF ANIMALS

ants	COLONY
badgers	CETE
bears	SLEUTH
bees	GRIST, SWARM
birds	FLIGHT, VOLERY
boars	SOUNDER
cats	CLOWDER, CLUTTER
cattle	DROVE
chicks	BROOD, CLUTCH
clams	BED
cranes	SIEGE
crows	MURDER
ducks	TEAM
elephants	HERD
elk	GANG
fish	SHOAL, SCHOOL
foxes	LEASH, SKULK
geese	FLOCK, SKEIN; GAGGLE
gnats	CLOUD, HORDE
goats	TRIP; TRIBE
goldfinches	CHARM
gorillas	BAND
greyhounds	LEASH
hares	DOWN, HUSK
hawks	CAST
horses	TEAM
hounds	CRY; MUTE, PACK
kangaroos	MOB; TROOP
kittens	KINDLE
larks	EXALTATION
leopards	LEAP
lions	PRIDE
monkeys	TROOP
mules	SPAN
nightingales	WATCH
oxen	YOKE
oysters	BED
partridge	COVEY
peacocks	MUSTER
pheasants	NEST, NIDE
pigs	LITTER
pilchards	SHOAL
plovers	WING; CONGREGATION
quail	BEVY; COVEY
rhinoceros	CRASH
seals	POD
sheep	DROVE; FLOCK
swans	BEVY
swine	DRIFT; SOUNDER
teals	SPRING
toads	KNOT
turtles	BALE
vipers	NEST
whales	GAM, POD
wolves	PACK

MUSIC TERMINOLOGY

andante, slightly faster then.................
....ANDANTINO
animatedly ....CON MOTO
animation, with ....ANIMATO
beats, pattern of.......................METER
brilliant flourish ....CADENZA
chant with Biblical lyrics......CANTICLE
composition, improvisational ....
.......................FANTASIA, RHAPSODY
composition, long dramatic...................
....ORATORIO
composition, musical..............FUGUE,
.............PIECE; SONATA; CANTATA;
..................CONCERTO, SYMPHONY
composition, playful ....SCHERZO
composition, section of a.....PASSAGE
composition, simple pastoral ....
....IDYL; IDYLL
composition, slow, sad.............DIRGE,
....ELEGY
composition especially for evening.......
....................NOCTURNE, SERENADE
composition for students ....ETUDE
concluding series of notes
    or chords........................CADENCE
conductor............................MAESTRO
conductor's stick.......................BATON
contrapuntal song.............MADRIGAL
dance, Bohemian......................POLKA
dance, lively ....RIGADOON
dance, lively round ....GALOP
dance, lively Spanish............BOLERO;
....FANDANGO
dance, minuetlike but faster.................
.............................GAVOT; GAVOTTE
dance, Polish folk...............MAZURKA
dance, Scottish ....REEL; FLING
dance, slow and solemn ....
....CHACONNE
dance, slow and stately ....MINUET;
....SARABAND
dance, slow Cuban ....HABANERA
dance, South American ....TANGO
dance, southern Italian ....
...................................TARANTELLA

dance, stately court ....
....................................PAVAN; PAVANE
dance, stately Polish........POLONAISE
dance in duple time, Brazilian..............
....SAMBA
effect, pulsating....................VIBRATO
effect, sliding...................GLISSANDO
effect, tremulous ....TREMOLO
end ....FINE
enthusiasm or devotion, with ....
.....................................CON AMORE
fast ....PRESTO; ALLEGRO
fast, moderately ....ALLEGRETTO
fast and with excitement ....AGITATO
fast as possible, as ......PRESTISSIMO
from the beginning................DA CAPO
gracefully ....LEGGIERO
gradually ....POCO A POCO
half ....MEZZO
half note: Brit. ....MINIM
harmonize................................CHORD
harmony, swelling burst of.................
....DIAPASON
hymn, funeral ....DIRGE, ELEGY
improvise a musical interlude .....VAMP
in the style of................................ALLA
keyboard ....CLAVIER
less ....MENO
little by little ....POCO A POCO
lively.................................GAI; VIVO
lively and spirited....................VIVACE
loud.......................................FORTE
loud, very.......................FORTISSIMO
loudness, gradual decrease in.............
....................................DIMINUENDO;
...................................DECRESCENDO
loudness, gradual increase in..............
....................................CRESCENDO
lullaby...............................BERCEUSE
measure, division of a ....BEAT
measured movement ....CADENCE
medley of familiar tunes......FANTASIA
moderate in tempo ....ANDANTE
moderately ....MEZZO
modulation ....CADENCE

233

Music Terminology

more ....PIU
much ....MOLTO
muffling device.........MUTE; SORDINO
notes, with no breaks between ....
....LEGATO
operatic solo.................................ARIA
part song...........................MADRIGAL
part song for 3 male voices.........GLEE
passage, concluding...........................
....CODA; FINALE
passage, concluding
   (with increasing speed)...STRETTO
passage, elaborate solo ......CADENZA
passage, slow and stately........LARGO
pause..................................FERMATA
pitch, half-step higher in ....SHARP
pitch, half-step lower in ....FLAT
pitch, standard of ....DIAPASON
pitch, vary the ....MODULATE
pitch symbol ....CLEF
plucked ....PIZZICATO
prolong, a tone or a rest ....HOLD
range...............................DIAPASON
repeat the passage...............DA CAPO
sign (esp. for end of a repeat) ....
....SEGNO
silence, measured interval of ......REST
singer, female professional.................
....CANTATRICE
singing style, pure ....BEL CANTO
sixteenth note ....SEMIQUAVER
slow and stately ....LARGO
slow............................LENTO, TARDO
slower, becoming gradually ....
....RITARDANDO
slower with more power,
   gradually ....ALLARGANDO
slowing down by degrees ....
....LENTANDO
slowly............................LENTAMENTE
slowly and leisurely.................ADAGIO
smooth ....LEGATO
softly...PIANO
softly, very ....PIANISSIMO
solo, opera ....ARIA

solo, short.............................ARIETTA;
....CAVATINA
sonata, last movement of a .....RONDO
song....................................CHANSON
song, contrapuntal ....MADRIGAL
song, German.............................LIED
songlike ....CANTABILE
song of praise ....ANTHEM
speed....................................TEMPO
spiritedly..............................CON BRIO
sung approximating speech.................
....PARLANDO
sweet......................................DOLCE
symbol on the staff ....CLEF, FLAT,
...........................NOTE, REST; SHARP
tempo (in increasing order).....LARGO,
.........................LARGHETTO, ADAGIO,
...................ANDANTE, ANDANTINO,
.................ALLEGRETTO, ALLEGRO,
...................PRESTO, PRESTISSIMO
tempo, with moderation in ....
....MODERATO
tempo determined by performer ....
....A CAPRICCIO
tenderly...........................CON AMORE
text of a musical work ....LIBRETTO
theme...TEMA
time signature indication ....METER
tone used as a standard............PITCH
tones, 3 or more
   sounded together ....CHORD
tones, with distinct
   breaks between...........STACCATO
too much.................................TANTO
tuning fork ....DIAPASON
vertical line dividing staff ....BAR
very ....MOLTO
vocal style ....ARIA; ARIOSO;
....RECITATIVE
voice ....VOCE
voice part ....CANTO
waltz...VALSE
without instrumental
   accompaniment ....A CAPPELLA
without varying ....SEMPRE

ABBREVIATIONS & ACRONYMS

AAA.................Amer. Automobile Assn.
AAM.............................air-to-air missile
AARP ....Amer. Assn.
.........................of Retired Persons
ABBR. ....abbreviation
ABA.................Amateur Boxing Assn.,
.........................Amer. Bar Assn.,
.........................Amer. Basketball Assn.
ABC.............Amer. Broadcasting Co.
ABD. ....abdomen, abdominal
ABM ....antiballistic missile
ABP. ....archbishop
ABR. ....abridged, abridgment
ABS................able-bodied seaman,
..................absent, absolute, abstract
ABT.................Amer. Ballet Theatre
ACAD. ....academy
ACC.................Atl. Coast Conference
ACCT. ....account, accountant
AC/DC ....alternating current/
..................................direct current
ACLU..........Amer. Civil Liberties Union
ACP ....Amer. Coll. of Physicians
ACS ....Amer. Cancer Society
ACTH.....adrenocorticotropic hormone
ADA.....................Amer. Dental Assn.
ADC...........Aid to Dependent Children,
.................................aide-de-camp
ADJ. ....adjacent, adjective
ADM. ....admiral
ADMIM. ....administration
ADP ....automatic data processing
ADV. ....adverb
AEC ....Atomic Energy Commission
AEF ....Amer. Expeditionary Forces
AERO. ....aeronautical, aeronautics
AFB..................................air force base
AFC ....Amer. Football Conference,
.........................automatic flight control,
.................automatic frequency control
AFDC....................Aid to Families with
.........................Dependent Children
AFG., AFGHAN. ....Afghanistan
AFL............Amer. Federation of Labor,
......................Amer. Football League
AFL-CIO...................Amer. Federation
.....................of Labor and Congress of
...................Industrial Organizations
AFR. ....Africa, African
AFTRA.................Amer. Federation of
.................Television and Radio Artists
AGCY. ....agency
AGI ....adjusted gross income
AGRI. ....agriculture, agricultural
AGT. ....agent, agreement
AHST.............Alaska Hawaii Std. Time

AIDS.........................acquired immune
.........................deficiency syndrome
AIM.................Amer. Indian Movement
AKA................................also known as
AKC.....................Amer. Kennel Club
ALA......................................Alabama
ALAS. ....Alaska
ALB. ....Albania, Albanian
ALG. ....algebra, Algeria, Algerian
ALS ....amyotrophic lateral sclerosis
ALTA. ....Alberta
ALUM. ....aluminum
AMA.................Amer. Medical Assn.
AMB. ....ambassador
AMER. ....American
AMESLAN.........Amer. Sign Language
AMEX..............Amer. Stock Exchange
AMP. ....amperage, ampere
AMPH. ....amphibian, amphibious
AMT. ....amount
ANAG. ....anagram
ANAT. ....anatomy
ANC. ....ancient
ANG. ....Angola
ANGL. ....Anglican
ANON. ....anonymous
ANSI ....Amer. Natl. Standards Inst.
ANTH. ....anthology
ANZAC ....Austral. and N. Z.
....Army Corps
APB................................all points bulletin
APO ....Army post office
APOC. ....Apocalypse, Apocrypha
APOS. ....apostrophe
APR........annual percentage rate, April
ARAB. ....Arabian, Arabic
ARC ....Amer. Red Cross
ARCH. ....archaic, archipelago,
.........................architect, architecture
ARG. ....Argentina
ARIZ. ....Arizona
ARK. ....Arkansas
ARR. ....arrangement, arrival
ARVN ....Army of the Rep. of Vietnam
ASAP ....as soon as possible
ASAT ....anti-satellite
ASB. ....asbestos
ASCAP...................Amer. Society of
......Composers, Authors, & Publishers
ASCII ....Amer. Standard Code
.................for Information Interchange
ASE..............Amer. Stock Exchange
ASI ....air-speed indicator
ASN ....Army service number
ASPCA...............Amer. Society for the
..........Prevention of Cruelty to Animals

235

ASSN. ....association
ASST. ....assistant
AST ....Atlantic standard time
ASV ....Amer. Standard Version
ATC ....air traffic control
ATF ....Bureau of Alcohol,
.......................Tobacco, and Firearms
ATL. ....Atlantic
ATM ....atmosphere,
.....................automated teller machine
AT.NO. ....atomic number
ATP ....Assn. of Tennis
.....................................Professionals
ATTN. ....attention
ATTY. ....attorney
ATV ....all-terrain vehicle
AT. WT. ....atomic weight
AUG. ....August
AUS ....Army of the United States,
..............................Austria, Austrian
AUSTRAL. ....Australia
AUTH. ....authentic, author, authority
AUX. ....auxiliary
AVDP. ....avoirdupois
AVE. ....avenue
AVG. ....average
AWACS....................airborne warning
........................and control system
AWOL ....absent without leave

BAPT. ....Baptist
BART. ....baronet
BASIC.............Beginner's All-purpose
.................Symbolic Instruction Code
BAV. ....Bavaria, Bavarian
BBB...............Better Business Bureau
BBC ....Brit. Broadcasting Corp.
BELG. ....Belgian, Belgium
BEV. ....beverage
BFA....................Bachelor of Fine Arts
B.GEN. ....brigadier general
BIA ....Bureau of Indian Affairs
BIBL. ....bibliography
BIO. ....biography
BIOL. ....biological, biologist, biology
BLDG. ....building
B.LIT....................Bachelor of Letters
BLS.............Bureau of Labor Statistics
BLT.............bacon, lettuce, and tomato
BLVD. ....boulevard
BMI ....Broadcast Music Inc.
BMOC ....big man on campus
BMX ....bicycle motocross
BOL. ....Bolivia, Bolivian
BOR. ....borough
BOT. ....botanical, botanist, botany
BPOE....................Benevolent and
.................Protective Order of Elks
BRAZ. ....Brazil, Brazilian
BRIT. ....Britain, British

BRO. ....brother
BROS. ....brothers
BSA................Boy Scouts of America
B.SC. ....Bachelor of Science
BTU.....................British thermal unit
BUL., BULG. ....Bulgaria, Bulgarian
BUR. ....bureau
BUS. ....business
B.V.I. ....Brit. Virgin Islands
B.V.M. ....Blessed Virgin Mary
BYOB ....bring your own bottle

CAB................Civil Aeronautics Board
CAD ....computer assisted design
CAM..............................computer-aided
....manufacturing
CAN. , CANAD. .....Canada, Canadian
CANC. ....canceled
CAPT. ....captain
CARE ....Cooperative for Amer.
.........................Relief to Everywhere
CATH. ....cathedral, Catholic
CAV. ....cavalry
CBC.............Can. Broadcasting Corp.
CBT ....Chicago Board of Trade
CCA....................circuit court of appeals
CCC ....Civilian Conservation Corps
CCW....................counterclockwise
CDC ....Centers for Disease Control
CDT ....central daylight time
CEA ....Council of Econ. Advisors
CEL. ....Celsius
CENT. ....central, center, centigrade,
.........................centime, century
CEO ....chief executive officer
CERN ....Eur. Center
.........................for Nuclear Research
CERT. ....certificate, certification,
.........................certified, certify
CETA....................Comprehensive
.............Employment and Training Act
CETI....................communication with
.................extraterrestrial intelligence
CFL ....Can. Football League
CFM ....cubic feet per minute
CFS ....cubic feet per second
CGI ....computer generated
....imagery
CHEM. ...chemical, chemist, chemistry
CHIN. ....Chinese
CHM. ....chairman, checkmate
CHOL. ....cholesterol
CHRON. ....Chronicles
CIA ....Central Intelligence Agcy.
.................Culinary Institute of Amer.
CID ....Criminal Investigative
.........................Dept. (Scotland Yard)
C.I.F. ....cost, insurance, and freight
C IN C.................Commander in Chief
CIO ....Congress of Industrial Org.

236

CIR., CIRC. ....circa, circle, circuit, ...circular, circulation, ...circumference
CIT. ....citation, citizen
CIV. ....civil, civilian
CKW............................clockwise
CLAR. ....clarinet
CLI...................cost of living index
CMDR. ....commander
CNO............chief of naval operations
CNS................central nervous system
COBOL..................Common Business ....Oriented Language
C.O.D. ....cash on delivery
COEF. ....coefficient
COLA.............cost-of-living adjustment
COLL. ....college, collegiate
COLO. ....Colorado
COMM. ....command, commandant, ...commander, commanding, ...commentary, commerce, ...commercial, commission, ...commissioned, committee, ...common, commoner, ...commonwealth, commune, ...communication, communist
COMP. ....companion, company, ...comparative, compare, compass, ...compensation, compilation, ...compiled, compiler, complement, ...complete, composer, composition, ...compound, comprehensive
COMR. ....commissioner
CONC. ......concentrate, concentrated, ...concentration, concentric, ...concerning, concrete, council
COND. ....condensed, condenser, ...condition, conduct, conductor
CONF. ....confederation, ...conference, confidential
CONG. ....congregation, congress, ...congressional
CONJ. ....conjugation, ...conjunction, conjunctive
CONN. ....Connecticut
CONT. ....containing, contemporary, ...contents, continental, continued, ...contract, control
COR. ....Corinthians
CORE.......Congress of Racial Equality
CORP. ....corporate, corporation
COS ....chief of staff, cosine
CPA...................Certified Public Acct.
CPB ....Corp. for Public Broadcasting
CPI ....consumer price index
CPL. ....corporal
CPO...........................chief petty officer
CPR ....cardiopulmonary ....resuscitation
CPU...............central processing unit

CRC..............Civil Rights Commission
CREEP........................Committee to ....Re-elect the President
CRIM. ....criminal
CRIT. ....critical, criticism
CROC. ....crocodile
CRT ....cathode-ray tube
C.S.A. ....Confederate States ....of America
CSC ....Civil Service Commission
C-Span ....Cable Satellite ....Public Affairs Network
CST ....central standard time
CTO ....concerto
CTS. ....cents
CVA...............Columbia Valley Auth.
CWO ....chief warrant officer
CYO........................Cath. Youth Org.

DAR ....Daughters of the Amer. Rev.
DAT ....digital audio tape
DAV ....Disabled Amer. Vet.
DBL. ....double
DDC ....Dewey Decimal ....Classification
DDS ....Doctor of Dental Surgery
DDT ....dichlorodiphenyltrichloroethane
DEA............Drug Enforcement Admin.
DEC. ....December
DECD. ....deceased, ...declared, decreased
DEF. ....defense, definition
DEG. ....degree
DEL. ....Delaware, delegate, delete
DEM. ....Democrat, Democratic
DEN. ....Denmark
DEPT. ....department, deputy
DESC. ....descendant
DEUT. ....Deuteronomy
DEW ....distant early warning
DFC.....Distinguished Flying Cross
DIAG. ....diagonal, diagram
DIAM. ....diameter
DICT. ....dictionary
DIF. ....difference
DIR. ....director
DISC. ....discharged, discontinue, ...discount, discovered
DIST. ....distance, district
DIV. ....dividend, division, divorced
DIY...............................do-it-yourself
D.L.O ....dead letter office
DMV ....Dept. of Motor Vehicles
DMZ........................demilitarized zone
DNA...................deoxyribonucleic acid
DNC ....Dem. Natl. Committee
D.O.A. ....dead on arrival
DOC. ....doctor, document
DOD...................Dept. of Defense
DOE...........................Dept. of Energy

237

DOL. ....dollar
DOM. ....domestic, dominion
DOS ....disk operating system
DOT ....Dept. of Transportation
DOZ. ....dozen
D.PH. ....Doctor of Philosophy
DPT ....diphtheria, pertussis, tetanus
DPW ....Department of Public Works
DSC ....Distinguished Service Cross
DST ....daylight saving time
D.TH. ....Doctor of Theology
DTS ....delirium tremens
DUI ....driving under the influence
DUP.......................duplex, duplicate
D.V.M. ...Doctor of Veterinary Medicine
DWI...............driving while intoxicated

ECCL. ....ecclesiastic, ecclesiastical
ECCLES. ....Ecclesiastes
ECG. ....electrocardiogram
ECOL. ....ecological, ecology
ECON. ....economic, economics,
..............................economist, economy
E-COM ....electronic computer-
................................originated mail
ECUA. ....Ecuador
EDP ....electronic data processing
EDT ....eastern daylight time
EDUC. ....educated, education,
................................educational
EEC...........Eur. Economic Community
EEG ....electroencephalogram
EEOC ....Equal Employment
....................Opportunity Commission
EFT ....electronic funds transfer
EKG ....electrocardiogram
ELEC. ...electric, electrical, electrician,
...........................electricity, electrified
ELEM. ....element, elementary
ELEV. ....elevation
ELIZ. ....Elizabeth
EMB. ....embargo, embassy
EMI.........electromagnetic interference
EMP. ....emperor, empire, employment
ENC., ENCL. ....enclosed, enclosure
ENCY. ....encyclopedia
ENG. ....England, English
ENGR. ....engineer, engraving
ENL. ....enlarged, enlisted
ENS...................................ensign
EOE..........equal opportunity employer
EPA ....Environmental
...............................Protection Agency
EPCOT...........Experimental Prototype
....................Community of Tomorrow
EPH. ....Ephesians
EPIS. ....Episcopal
EPIT. ....epitaph
EPROM ....erasable programmable
................................read-only memory

ERA....................earned run average
....................Equal Rights Amendment
ESL.......English as a second language
ESP...............extrasensory perception
ESQ. ....esquire
EST....................eastern standard time
.....................establishment, estimate
ESTH......................................Esther
ETA ....estimated time of arrival
ET AL. ....and elsewhere
ETC. ....et cetera
ETH. ....Ethiopia, Ethiopian
ETI ....extraterrestrial intelligence
ETO............Eur. theater of operations
ETV ....educational television
EUR. ....Europe, European
EVA.................extravehicular activity
EXCH. ....exchange, exchequer
EXCL. ....exclamation, exclude,
...........................excluding, exclusive
EXEC. ....executed, execution,
...........................executive, executor
EXP ....expense, experimental,
................exponent, export, express
EXOD. ....Exodus
EXT. ....extension, exterior
EZEK. ....Ezekiel

FAA ....Federal Aviation Admin.
FAHR. ....Fahrenheit
FAM. ....family
FBI ....Federal Bureau
................................of Investigation
FCC ....Federal Communications
....Commission
FDA ....Food and Drug Admin.
FDIC ......Fed. Deposit Insurance Corp.
FEB. ....February
FED. ....federal, federation
FEM. ....female, feminine
FEPA ....Fair Employment
...................................Practices Act
FEPC....................Fair Employment
.......................Practices Commission
FET ....Federal Excise Tax
FFF ....as loud as possible
FHA................Federal Housing Admin.
FICA ....Federal Insurance
.............................Contributions Act
FIG. ....figurative, figure
FINN. ....Finnish
FLA. ....Florida
FLEM. ....Flemish
FNMA.....Federal Natl. Mortgage Assn.
FOE............Fraternal Order of Eagles
F.O.I.A................Freedom of Info. Act
FORTRAN.............formula translation
FRB ....Federal Reserve Board
FREQ. ....frequency, frequent
FRI. ....Friday

FSLIC ....Federal Savings and
...................................Loan Corporation
FTC ....Federal Trade Commission
FUBAR ....fouled up beyond all
....................................recognition
FWD........................four-wheel drive
FYI..........................for your information

GAL. ....Galatians, gallon
GAO...........General Accounting Office
GARP..................Global Atmospheric
..............................Research Program
GATT.................General Agreement of
................................Tariffs and Trade
GED ....general equivalency diploma
GEN. ....Genesis
GENL. ....general
GEOG. ....geographic, geography
GEOL. ....geological, geology
GEOM. ....geometrical, geometry
GER. ....German, Germany, gerund
GHQ ....general headquarters
GIGO ....garbage in, garbage out
GLOS. ....glossary
GMT..................Greenwich mean time
GNP ....gross natl. product
GOES...........geostationary operational
.................environmental satellite
GOP...........................Grand Old Party
GOVT. ....government
GPA ....grade-point average
GPO ....general post office,
.................Government Printing Office
GRAD. ....gradient, graduate
GRE .....Graduate Record Examination
GRO. ....gross
G.R.U. ....Soviet Army Intelligence
GSA ....Girl Scouts of America
GSR ....galvanic skin response
GUAT. ....Guatemala
GUTS ....grand unification theories

HAB. ....Habakkuk
HAG. ....Haggai
HBO.........................Home Box Office
HCAP. ....handicap
HCL..........................high cost of living
HCP. ....handicap
HDBK. ....handbook
HDS .....Human Development Services
HDTV..............high definition television
HEB. ....Hebrew, Hebrews
HEW.................Department of Health,
.....................Education, and Welfare
HGT. ....height
HIST. ....historian, historical, history
HMO.....................health maintenance
....organization
HMS ....His (Her) Majesty's Service
.......................His (Her) Majesty's Ship

HNS ....Holy Name Society
HON. ....honor, honorable, honorary
HOND. ....Honduras
HOPE ....Health Opportunity for
...............................People Everywhere
HOR. ....horizon, horizontal
HORT. ....horticulture
HOS. ....Hosea
HOSP. ....hospital
HOV ....high-occupancy vehicle
HRA ....Health Resources Admin.
HRH ....His (Her) Royal Highness
HRIP ....here rests in peace
HRS. ....hours
HST ....Hawaiian standard time
HTS. ....heights
HUAC..................House Un-Amer.
.............................Activities Committee
HUD ....Department of Housing
.....................and Urban Development
HUNG. ....Hungarian, Hungary
HWY. ....highway

IAS........................indicated air speed
IBID. ....in the same place
ICBM ....Intercontinental
.................................ballistic missile
ICC ....Interstate Commerce
....Commission
ICE. ....Iceland
ICEL. ....Icelandic
ICU ....intensive care unit
IGN. ....ignition, unknown
IGY ....Intl. Geophysical Year
IHS ....Jesus
ILA...........Intl. Longshoreman's Assn.
ILGWU.........................Intl. Ladies'
.....................Garment Workers' Union
ILL. ....Illinois
ILO........................Intl. Labor Org.
IMF ....Intl. Monetary Fund
IMIT. ....imitation
IMP. ....imperative, imperfect,
.................import, in the first place
INC. ....incorporated
INCL. ......included, including, inclusive
IND. ....independent, Indian
.................................Indiana, industry
INFO. ....information
INIT. ....initial
INRI ....Jesus of Nazareth,
.................................King of the Jews
INS............................Immigration and
.............................Naturalization Service
INSP. ....inspector
INST. ....installment, institute,
..........institution, instruction, instructor,
...........................instrument, instrumental
INT. ....intelligence, interest
INTL. ....international

IOC...............Intl. Olympic Committee
I.O.M. ....Isle of Man
IOOF.................Independent Order of
....Odd Fellows
IOU..I owe you
I.O.W. ....Isle of Wight
IPA...............Intl. Phonetic Alphabet
IRA...............individual retirement acct.
I.R.A. ....Irish Republican Army
IRC........................Intl. Red Cross
IRE. ....Ireland
IRR. ....irregular
IRS...............Internal Revenue Service
ISA. ....Isaiah
ISBN........Intl. Standard Book Number
ISL. ....island
ISR. ....Israel
ITAL. ....italic, italicized
ITC.....................investment tax credit
ITO ....Intl. Trade Org.
IUD...........................intrauterine device
IWW....................Industrial Workers of
....the World

JAM. ....Jamaica
JAN. ....January
JAP.........................Japan, Japanese
JATO ....jet-assisted takeoff
JBS.........................John Birch Society
JCS........................Joint Chiefs of Staff
JCT. ....junction
JDL................Jewish Defense League
JER. ....Jeremiah
J.H.S.....................junior high school
JOBS ....Job Opportunities in the
....Business Sector
JUL. ....July
JUN. ....June

KAN., KANS. ....Kansas
KGB.....................Soviet State Security
....Committee
KIA ....killed in action
KJV ....King James Version
KPH ....kilometers per hour
KWH....................................kilowatt-hour

LAB. ....laboratory, Labrador
LAM....................................Lamentations
LANG. ....language
LASER...................Light Amplification
....by Stimulated
.............................Emission of Radiation
LAT. ....latent, lateral, Latvia, latitude
LAV. ....lavatory
LBS. ....pounds
LCD ....least common denominator,
.............................liquid crystal display
LCM ....least common multiple
LDS ....Ladder-day Saints

LEB. ....Lebanese, Lebanon
LED ....light-emitting diode
LEM...............lunar excursion module
LEV. ....Leviticus
LGE. ....large
LGTH. ....length
LIB. ....liberal, liberation
LIEUT. ....lieutenant
LITH. ....Lithuania, Lithuanian
LOC. ....in this place, local, location
LOG. ....logarithm
LON. ....longitude
LOQ. ....he/she speaks
LORAN...............long-range navigation
LOST ....Law of the Sea Treaty
LPGA ....Ladies Pro. Golf Assn.
LPN...............Licensed Practical Nurse
LSD...............................lysergic acid;
.....................pounds, shillings, pence
LTD. ....limited
LUTH. ....Lutheran
LUX. ....Luxembourg
LWV.............League of Women Voters

MAG. ....magazine, magnet
MAJ. ....major
MAL. ....Malachi
MAR. ....March
MASC. ....masculine
MASH ....mobile army surgical hosp.
MASS. ....Massachusetts
MATT. ....Matthew
MAX. ....maximum
M.B.A. ....Master of Bus. Admin.
MCP.....................male chauvinist pig
MDT................mountain daylight time
MED. ....medical, medicine,
.............................Mediterranean, medium
MET. ....metropolitan
METH. ....Methodist
MEX. ....Mexican, Mexico
MFD. ....manufactured
MFG. ....manufacturing
MFR. ....manufacture, manufacturer
MIA.....................missing in action
MIC. ....Micah
MICH. ....Michigan
MIL. ....military, million
MIN. ....mineral, minor, minute
MINN. ....Minnesota
MIRV...............multiple independently
.....................targeted reentry vehicle
MISC. ....miscellaneous, miscellany
MISS. ....Mississippi
MIXT. ....mixture
MLLE. ....mademoiselle
MME. ....Madame
MOD. ....modern
MON. ....Monday
MONT. ....Montana

MPG ....miles per gallon
MPH...............................miles per hour
MRS. ....mistress
MSGR. ....messenger, monseigneur,
....monsignor
M.SGT. ....master sergeant
MSS. ....manuscripts
MST ....mountain standard time
MTS. ....mountains
MUS. ....museum, music
MVP ....most valuable player

NAACP..............................Natl. Assn.
.........................for the Advancement of
....Colored People
NADA ....Natl. Automobile
......................................Dealers Assn.
NAH. ....Nahum
NAS ....Natl. Acad. of Sciences,
....naval air station
NASA ....Natl. Aeronautics
...................................and Space Admin.
NASCAR ....Natl. Assn.
.....................of Stock Car Auto Racing
NASDAQ ....Natl. Assn. of Securities
.............Dealers Automated Quotations
NASL........North Amer. Soccer League
NATL. ....national
NATO ....North Atl. Treaty Org.
NAUT. ....nautical
NAV. ....naval, navigable, navigate,
...................navigation, navigator, navy
NBA ....Natl. Basketball Assn.
NBC ....Natl. Broadcasting Co.
NBS.............Natl. Bureau of Standards
NCAA ....Natl. Coll. Athletic Assn.
NCO...........noncommissioned officer
NDA ....Natl. Dental Assn.
N. DAK. ....North Dakota
NEA................Natl. Educational Assn.,
...............Natl. Endowment for the Arts
NEB., NEBR. ....Nebraska
NEG. ....negative
NEH. ....Nehemiah
NETH. ....Netherlands
NEUT. ....neuter, neutral
NEV. ....Nevada
NFL ....Natl. Football League
N.H.I...............Natl. Health Insurance
NHL....................Natl. Hockey League
NHRA....................Natl. Hot Rod Assn.
NHS ....Natl. Health Service
NIRA........Natl. Industrial Recovery Act
NIT ....Natl. Invitational
....Tournament
NLRB........Natl. Labor Relations Board
N. Mex. ....New Mexico
NMI ....no middle initial
NOAA.....................Natl. Oceanic and
.............................Atmospheric Admin.

NOR. ....Norway, Norwegian
NORAD ....North Amer. Air
.............................Defense Command
NOS. ....numbers
NOV. ....November
NOW...............Natl. Org. for Women
NPR ....Natl. Public Radio
NRA ....Natl. Recovery Admin.,
...................................Natl. Rifle Assn.
NRC ....Natl. Research Council,
..........Nuclear Regulatory Commission
NSA...................Natl. Security Agency
NSC...................Natl. Security Council
NSF ....Natl. Science Foundation
N.S.W. ....New South Wales
NTSB ....Natl. Transportation
.....................................Safety Board
NT. WT. ....net weight
NUM. ....Numbers
NWT.................Northwest Territories
NYC ....New York City
NYSE ....New York Stock Exchange

OAS ....Org. of Amer. States
OAU ....Org. of African Unity
OBAD. ....Obadiah
O.B.E. ....Officer of the Order
...............................of the British Empire
OB-GYN.............obstetrics-gynecology
OBIT. ....obituary
OBJ. ....object, objection, objective
OBO ....or best offer
OBS. ....observation, obsolete
OCA.............Office of Consumer Affairs
OCS.............Officer Candidate School
OCT. ....October
OED ....Oxford English Dictionary
OEO ....Office of Econ. Opp.
OFF. ..offensive, office, officer, official
OKLA. ....Oklahoma
ONI ....Office of Naval Intelligence
ONO ....or nearest offer
ONT. ....Ontario
OOB ....off-off-Broadway
OP. CIT....................in the work cited
OPEC.....................Org. of Petroleum
.............................Exporting Countries
OPP. ....opportunities, opposite
ORCH. ....orchestra
ORE., OREG. ....Oregon
ORG. ....organization
ORIG. ....origin, original
ORK. ....Orkney
OSHA ....Occupational Safety and
......................................Health Admin.
OSS..........Office of Strategic Services
OTB ....off-track betting
OTC.........................over-the-counter
OXFAM....................Oxford Committee
...................................for Famine Relief

OZS. ....ounces

PAC...............................Pacific,
.................political action committee
PAK. ....Pakistan
PAL ....Police Athletic League
PAN. ....Panama
PAR. ....Paraguay
PAT ....point after touchdown
PBA...........Police Benevolent Assn.
.................Professional Bowlers Assn.
PBK ....Phi Beta Kappa
PBS........Public Broadcasting Service
PCT. ....percent, percentage
PDT...........Pacific daylight time
P.E.I. ....Prince Edward Island
PENN. ....Pennsylvania
PER. ....Persia, Persian
PERS. ......person, personal, personnel
PFC.......................private first class
PGA......................Pro. Golfers' Assn.
PHAR. ....pharmaceutical, pharmacy
PH.D. ....Doctor of Philosophy
PHIL. ....Philippians
PIC. ....picture
PIN ....pers. identification number
PIX. ....pictures
PLO.............Palestine Liberation Org.
PMS.............premenstrual syndrome
POL. ....Poland, Polish
POP. ....population
PORT. ....Portugal, Portuguese
POW ....prisoner of war
PPD. ....postpaid, prepaid
P.P.S...............additional postscript
PRES. ....president
PRO. ....professional
PROF. ....professor
PROM...............................programmable
.....................................read-only memory
PROT. ....Protestant
PROV. ....Proverbs
PSA....................................Psalms
PST ....Pacific standard time
PTA ....parent-teacher Assn.
PTO...........Patent & Trademark Office
PVT. ....private

Q.E.D. ....which was to be
.....................................demonstrated
Q.E.F...............which was to be done

RAAF ....Royal Australian Air Force
RAC ....Royal Automobile Club
RAF.......................Royal Air Force
RAM ....random access memory
RATO...............rocket-assisted takeoff
RBI.......................runs batted in
RCA...............Rodeo Cowboys Assn.
RCAF...........Royal Canadian Air Force

RCMP ....Royal Canadian
.....................................Mounted Police
RCN ....Royal Canadian Navy
RCT. ....receipt, recruit
RDA...............recommended daily
.....................................allowance
REA ....Rural Electrification Admin.
REF. ....referee
REG. ....regent, register,
.....................................regular, regulation
REM ....rapid eye movement
REP. ....representative, republic,
.....................................Republican
REQ. ....request, requisition
RET. ....retired
REV. ....Revelation, reverend
RFD ....rural free delivery
RFE...............Radio Free Europe
RHIP ....rank has its privileges
RIP ....may he/she rest in peace
RIT. ....ritardando
RMS. ....rooms
RNA ....ribonucleic acid
RNC ....Rep. Natl. Committee
R.O.C. ....Republic of China
R.O.K. ....Republic of Korea
ROM.........read-only memory, Roman,
.............Romania, Romanian, Romans
ROTC......................Reserve Officers'
.....................................Training Corps
RPM ....revolutions per minute
RSA..............Republic of South Africa
RSV ....Revised Standard Version
R.S.V.P. ....répondez s'il vous plait
RTE. ....route
RUSS. ....Russia, Russian
RWY. ....railway

SAC...............Strategic Air Command
SAE...............self-addressed envelope
S.AFR. ....South Africa, South African
SAG ....Screen Actors Guild
SALT ....Strategic Arms
.....................................Limitation Talks
SAM...............surface-to-air missile
SAR...............Sons of the Amer. Rev.
SASK. ....Saskatchewan
SAT...............Scholastic Aptitude Test
SBA...............Small Bus. Admin.
SCAND. ....Scandinavia, Scandinavian
SCH. ....school
SCI. ....science
SCI.-FI. ....science fiction
SCOT....................Scotland, Scottish
SCUBA........self-contained underwater
.....................................breathing apparatus
S.DAK. ....South Dakota
SDI...........Strategic Defense Initiative
SDS ....Students for a Dem. Society
SEATO ......Southeast Asia Treaty Org.

SEC ....Securities and Exchange
.....................................Commission
SECY. ....secretary
SEN. ....senate, senator
SEP., SEPT. ....September
SEQQ. ....in the following places
SER. ....serial, sermon, service
SESS. ....session
SGD. ....signed
SGT. ....sergeant
SHAK. ....Shakespearean
SKT. ....Sanskrit
S.L.C. ....Salt Lake City
SLR..........................single lens reflex
SNAFU ....situation normal,
....all fouled up
SNO...............Scottish Natl. Orchestra
SOC. ....socialist, society
SOP.......standard operating procedure
SOPH. ....sophomore
SOS........................(distress signal)
SOV. ....soviet
S.P.C.A........Society for the Prevention
............................of Cruelty to Animals
SPEC. ....special, specialist,
.............species, specific, specification
SPQR.........................the senate and
..............................the people of Rome
S.P.Q.R.......small profits, quick returns
SRA. ....señora
SRO..............single room occupancy,
................................standing room only
SRTA. ....señorita
SSA ....Social Security Admin.
S.SGT. ....staff sergeant
SSN ....Social Security number
SSR...............Soviet Socialist Republic
SSS.............Selective Service System
SST ....supersonic transport
START ....Strategic Arms
.............................Reduction Talks
STAT. ....immediately, statistic
STD ....standard
STE. ....saint (female Fr.)
STOL............short takeoff and landing
STR. ....strait, stringed
SUBJ. ....subject, subjective,
......................subjectively, subjunctive
SUN. ....Sunday
SUPT. ....superintendent, support
SURG. ....surgeon, surgery, surgical
SWAK............sealed with a kiss
SWAPO ....South-West African
..........................People's Organization
SWAT ....Special Weapons & Tactics
SWC................Southwest Conference
SWED. ....Sweden, Swedish
SYL., SYLL. ....syllable
SYM. ....symbol, symmetrical,
....symphony

SYR. ....Syria, Syrian
SYS. ....system

TAC ....Tactical Air Command
TASM. ....Tasmania
TAT............thematic apperception test
TBA...........................to be announced
TBS................................tablespoon,
.................Turner Broadcasting System
TEL. ....telegram, telephone
TEMP. ....temperance, temperature,
.............template, temporal, temporary
TENN. ....Tennessee
TER. ....terrace, territory
TEX. ....Texas
TGIF ....thank God it's Friday
THU., THUR., THURS. ....Thursday
TIROS ....television and infrared
.............................observation satellite
TIX...tickets
TKO.......................technical knockout
TLC.....................tender loving care
TNT.............................trinitrotoluene
TOPO. ....topographic, topographical
TRIG. ....trigonometry
TRIN. ....Trinidad
TUE., TUES. ....Tuesday
TURK. ....Turkey, Turkish
TVA..........Tennessee Valley Authority
TWIMC ....to whom it may concern
TWP. ....township

UAE ....United Arab Emirates
UAR ....United Arab Republic
UFO...............unidentified flying object
UFT......United Federation of Teachers
UFW ....United Farm Workers
UHF ....ultrahigh frequency
UMW...................United Mine Workers
UNCF ....United Negro College Fund
UNESCO.................United Nations
.................Educational, Scientific, and
..........................Cultural Organization
UNICEF.................United Nations Intl.
.................Children's Emergency Fund
UPC ....Universal Product Code
UPI ....United Press Intl.
UPS.................United Parcel Service
URU. ....Uruguay
USA ....United States Army
USAF.............United States Air Force
USCG ....United States Coast Guard
USDA ....United States Department
....of Agriculture
USIA.............United States Info. Agcy.
USMA.............United States Mil. Acad.
USMC .....United States Marines Corps
USN ....United States Navy
USNA ....United States Nav. Acad.
USNG ....United States Natl. Guard

USNR .....United States Naval Reserve
USO ....United Service Organizations
USOC...............United States Olympic
....Committee
USPO........United States Patent Office
USPS......United States Postal Service
USS.........................United States ship
USSR.........................Union of Soviet
......................Socialist Republics
USTA........United States Tennis Assn.
UXB......................unexploded bomb

VAT.........................value-added tax
VCR.................videocassette recorder
VDT....................video display terminal
VEN. ....Venezuela
VER. ....verse, version
VERT. ....vertical
VET. ....veteran, veterinarian
VFW............Veterans of Foreign Wars
VIP..................very important person
VISC. ....viscount
VISTA ....Volunteers in Service
...................................to America
VOA..........................Voice of America
VOL. ....volume, volunteer
VTOL ....vertical takeoff and landing

WAAC........Women's Army Aux. Corps
WAAF ....Women's Aux. Air Force
WAC ....Women's Army Corps
WAF...............Women in the Air Force
WASP............White Anglo-Saxon Prot.
WATS...............................Wide-area
...............Telecommunications Service

WBA.....................World Boxing Assn.
WBC...................World Boxing Council
WCT ....World Championship Tennis
WCTU.....................Women's Christian
...........................Temperance Union
WHA....................World Hockey Assn.
WHO..........World Health Organization
WIS., WISC. ....Wisconsin
WKLY. ....weekly
WPA...............Works Progress Admin.
WPM ....words per minute
WRAF ....Women's Royal Air Force
W.VA. ....West Virginia
WYO. ....Wyoming

X DIV. ....ex dividend
XING ....crossing

YDS. ....yards
YHWH....................................Yahweh
YMCA ....Young Men's
...............................Christian Assn.
YMHA.......Young Men's Hebrew Assn.
YRS. ....years
YWCA ....Young Women's
...............................Christian Assn.
YWHA ....Young Women's
...................................Hebrew Assn.

ZECH. ....Zechariah
ZEPH. ....Zephaniah
ZIP..................zone improvement plan
ZOOL. ....zoological, zoologist,
....zoology
ZPG................zero population growth

ELEMENTS

Elements are grouped according to length. Each element's two-letter abbreviation is given along with its atomic number.

gas. = gaseous
non. = nonmetallic
semi. = semimetallic
syn. = synthetic
all others are natural metallic elements

3 Letters
TIN-Sn-50

4 Letters
GOLD-Au-79
IRON-Fe-26
LEAD-Pb-82
NEON-Ne-10 (gas.)
ZINC-Zn-30

5 Letters
ARGON-Ar-18 (gas.)
BORON-B-5 (non.)
RADON-Rn-86 (gas.)
XENON-Xe-54 (gas.)

6 Letters
BARIUM-Ba-56
CARBON-C-6 (non.)
CERIUM-Ce-58
CESIUM-Cs-55
COBALT-Co-27
COPPER-Cu-29
CURIUM-Cm-96 (syn.)
ERBIUM-Er-68
HELIUM-He-2 (gas.)
INDIUM-In-49
IODINE-I-53 (non.)
NICKEL-Ni-28
OSMIUM-Os-76
OXYGEN-O-8 (gas.)
RADIUM-Ra-88
SILVER-Ag-47
SODIUM-Na-11
SULFUR-S-16 (non.)

7 Letters
ARSENIC-As-33
  (semi.)
BISMUTH-Bi-83
BROMINE-Br-35 (non.)
CADMIUM-Cd-48
CALCIUM-Ca-20
FERMIUM-Fm-100
  (syn.)

GALLIUM-Ga-31
HAFNIUM-Hf-72
HOLMIUM-Ho-67
IRIDIUM-Ir-77
KRYPTON-Kr-36 (gas.)
LITHIUM-Li-3
MERCURY-Hg-80
NIOBIUM-Nb-41
RHENIUM-Re-75
RHODIUM-Rh-45
SILICON-Si-14 (non.)
TERBIUM-Tb-65
THORIUM-Th-90
THULIUM-Tm-69
URANIUM-U-92
YTTRIUM-Y-39

8 Letters
ACTINIUM-Ac-89
ALUMINUM-Al-13
ANTIMONY-Sb-51
ASTATINE-At-85
  (semi.)
CHLORINE-Cl-17 (gas.)
CHROMIUM-Cr-24
EUROPIUM-Eu-63
FLUORINE-F-9 (gas.)
FRANCIUM-Fr-87
HYDROGEN-H-1 (gas.)
LUTETIUM-Lu-71
NITROGEN-N-7 (gas.)
NOBELIUM-No-102
  (syn.)
PLATINUM-Pt-78
POLONIUM-Po-84
RUBIDIUM-Rb-37
SAMARIUM-Sm-62
SCANDIUM-Sc-21
SELENIUM-Se-34
  (non.)
TANTALUM-Ta-73
THALLIUM-Tl-81
TITANIUM-Ti-22
TUNGSTEN-W-74
VANADIUM-V-23

9 Letters
AMERICIUM-Am-95
  (syn.)
BERKELIUM-Bk-97
  (syn.)
BERYLLIUM-Be-4
GERMANIUM-Ge-32
LANTHANUM-La-57
MAGNESIUM-Mg-12
MANGANESE-Mn-25
NEODYMIUM-Nd-60
NEPTUNIUM-Np-93
  (syn.)
PALLADIUM-Pd-46
PLUTONIUM-Pu-94
POTASSIUM-K-19
RUTHENIUM-Ru-44
STRONTIUM-Sr-38
TELLURIUM-Te-52
  (non.)
YTTERBIUM-Yb-70
ZIRCONIUM-Zr-40

10 Letters
DYSPROSIUM-Dy-66
GADOLINIUM-Gd-64
LAWRENCIUM-Lr-103
  (syn.)
MOLYBDENUM-Mo-42
PHOSPHORUS-P-15
  (non.)
PROMETHIUM-Pm-61
TECHNETIUM-Tc-43

11 Letters
CALIFORNIUM-Cf-98
  (syn.)
EINSTEINIUM-Es-99
  (syn.)
MENDELEVIUM-Md-101
  (syn.)

12 Letters
PRASEODYMIUM-Pr-59
PROTACTINIUM-Pa-91

WEIGHTS & MEASURES

AREA

Intl. ....ARE; ACRE; DECARE

China ....MOU; CHUO
Jap. ....CHO
Thailand..RAI

DISTANCE

Intl. ....ROD; METER; MICRON

Belgium..AUNE
China..........................CH'IH, TSUN
Czech Republic ....LATRO
Denmark ....FOD
Egypt.............................PIK; DIRAA
France.......................................TOISE
Greece ....PICKI
India..KOSS
Iran ....GUZ, ZER; GUEZA
Japan ....KEN, SUN
Netherlands ....DUIM
Russ. ....FUT; FOUTE, VERST
Sweden......................................FOT
Thailand...........KUP, NIN, NIU, SEN
UK ....ELL; POLE; PERCH
US ....MIL; FOOT, HAND,
............................INCH, MILE, YARD;
....FURLONG

VOLUME

Intl. ....DRAM, KILO

China..TOU
Cyprus...OKE
Denmark.......................................POT
Egypt ....KELA
Germany ....EIMER
Israel................CAB, COR, HIN, LOG;
.....................................BATH; EPHAH
Japan ....SHO; KOKU, KWAN
Netherlands....................KAN, MUD,
......................................VAT, ZAK
Scottish ....FOU
S. Afr..AUM
Switzerland ....ELLE, IMMI
UK ....PIN, TUN;
......................BUTT, GILL; MINIM
US ....GILL, PECK, PINT; MINIM

WEIGHT

Intl. ....KIP, TON; GRAM, KILO;
...................................CARAT, GRAIN

Bulgaria...OKE
China...TAN
Egypt...OKA
Germany ....LOT
Greece ....MNA; OBOLE
Japan ....KIN, RIO
Korea ....KON
Malaysia ....GIN; CHEE,
...............................HOON, KATI;
...............................CATTY, TAHIL
Netherlands ....ONS
Portugal ....ONCA; LIBRA
Russia ....POOD
Thailand ....BAT; BAHT; TICAL
Turkey..OCK
UK............TOD, WEY; PACK; STONE
US............................OUNCE, POUND

OTHER

unit, power ratio ....BEL
unit of capacity ....FARAD
unit of conductance ....MHO
unit of electrical intensity ......AMPERE
unit of electrical reluctance ....REL
unit of electricity ....OHM; WATT;
...................................FARAD, WEBER
unit of electromotive force ....VOLT
unit of energy ....ERG
unit of fluidity ....RHE
unit of force ....DYNE
unit of heat ....CALORIE
unit of illumination ....PHOT
unit of light....................LUX; LUMEN;
....HEFNER
unit of loudness ....SONE
unit of luminance...........................NIT
unit of power...............................OHM;
...............................DYNE, WATT;
...............................FARAD, WEBER
unit of pressure........................TORR
unit of radiation ....RAD, REM
unit of resistance ....OHM
unit of viscosity ....POISE
unit of work ....ERG

WORD FINDER

When solving a crossword puzzle, you may reach the point where there remain a few three- or four-letter words you are unable to fill in. You may have tried unsuccessfully to find the clue for a word, and its crossing words, in the other sections of this book. The Word Finder gives you another option to resolve this dilemma.

When you know only the first and last letters, or any two adjoining letters, of a three- or four-letter word, you can use the Word Finder to find a list of all the words which have the two letters you know in the correct letter positions. Two-letter words have not been included in this book because their use in contemporary puzzles is frowned upon.

In the left column of each page are letter-position guides. They are listed alphabetically by the first known letter. If, for example, you are looking for a four-letter word with the second letter "J" and third letter "A," you should scan the letter-position guide until you find the combination "_ J A _". You will see an alphabetical listing of all four-letter words with "J" and "A" in those positions in boldface capital letters.

When two or more words are spelled the same, they are listed separately. They are listed in the following order: proper nouns, abbreviations of proper nouns, common nouns, suffixes, prefixes, and all other abbreviations.

The numbers in parentheses following each word are page numbers for cross-reference to all of the other sections in this book. Many words have several cross-references. They are listed in numerical order. Cross-references to pages in the Special Sections consist of page numbers only. Cross-references to the Clues & Definitions section also include a lower case "a," "b," "c," or "d." These letters refer to the four quadrants of each Clues & Definitions page. They are indicated by those same letters on the Clues & Definitions pages.

Some listed words are not followed by cross-reference page numbers. These words are plurals and various verb cases for the most part. In the case of plurals, you will find cross-references with listings of the singular forms of words. Clues for verbs are most often in the present tense. If, for example, you find no cross-references listed for a word which is a verb in the past tense, try looking up the present tense of the verb.

THREE-LETTER WORDS

A A _   AAA (235), aal (79d), AAM (235), Aar (18c, 100b)

A _ A   AAA (235), ABA (235), aba (13d, 23c, 52d), ADA (235), Ada (83c, 137), aga (84d, 125b), a-ha (42c), aka (81c, 235), Ala. (209, 235), ala (16c, 132c), a la (9c), AMA (235), ama (23d, 25d, 27b, 29b, 32b, 132c), ana (12c, 29a, 72c), -ana (117c), Apa (12b), apa (21c), Ara (12a, 139, 197, 207), ara (73b), Asa (9a, 56a, 66b, 67d, 139, 197), Ata (73d), Ava (22d, 139), ava (61c, 91a, 123a)

_ A A   AAA (235), baa (107d), FAA (238), Kaa (67a), maa (107d)

A B _   ABA (235), aba (13d, 23c, 52d), abb (129d), ABC (26a, 235), abd. (235), Abe (94b, 137), Abi (59d), ABM (235), abp. (235), abr. (235), ABS (235), abs- (92c), ABT (33b, 235), abu (44d)

A _ B   abb (129d), AFB (235), Alb. (235), alb (52d, 128a), amb. (235), APB (235), asb. (235)

_ A B   Bab (16a), CAB (236), Cab (144), cab (95d, 127d, 246), dab (38b, 46d, 47d), gab (26b, 92b, 119b, 133a), Hab. (239), jab (60b, 90d, 96a, 132d), Lab. (240), lab (104d), Mab (44a, 96c), nab (14c, 24a, 24d, 106c), Rab (37b), rab (18a, 66c, 78d), Tab (183), tab (47b, 94b, 119b)

A C _   ACC (235), ace (24a, 46c, 60c, 84a, 107d, 109d, 120c, 126c), ach (11a, 42c, 53d), ACP (235), ACS (235), act (34b, 45a, 87d, 90b, 94b, 115a), acu- (93c), -acy (117b)

A _ C   ABC (26a, 235), ACC (235), ADC (15b, 235), AEC (235), AFC (235), AKC (235), AMC (26a), anc. (235), ARC (235), arc (27b, 32d, 96b, 106b, 123d), ATC (236)

_ A C   bac (27b), lac (43c, 99d, 108a, 127b), Mac (167), mac (45b, 74c, 105b, 111d), Pac. (242), pac (57b, 73c), RAC (242), SAC (242), sac (92a, 128a), TAC (243), WAC (244)

A D _   ADA (235), Ada (83c, 137), ADC (15b, 235), add (12d, 13c, 116d), Ade (43b, 137), ade (38a), adj. (235), Adm. (235), ado (21b, 22d, 29b, 52c, 92a, 115c), ADP (235), ads (27d), adv. (235), adz (33c, 122d)

A _ D   abd. (235), add (12d, 13c, 116d), aid (15a, 57d, 59b, 117a), and (30a, 90c)

_ A D   bad (42b, 44d, 126b, 131d), CAD (236), cad (21b, 59b, 88a), dad (11d, 44b, 44d), fad (31d, 97b, 120b, 124b), Gad (64d, 135c), gad (47c, 77a, 83a, 97d, 101a), had (61a, 91d), lad (21c, 45b, 74c, 116c, 134d), mad (12d, 63b, 109c), pad (32d, 47d, 48b, 116c, 119a, 123d), rad (40d, 246), sad (11d, 20a, 26b, 35a, 36c, 37c, 73c, 75d, 79b, 112a, 126c), tad (134d), wad (55a, 73c, 75b, 85b)

A E _   AEC (235), AEF (235), aer (25d), aer- (92c), aes (22a, 69c, 78a, 101d), aet (69c)

A _ E   Abe (94b, 137), ace (24a, 46c, 60c, 84a, 107d, 109d, 120c, 126c), Ade (43b, 137), ade (38a), age (41b, 41c, 41d, 53b, 71d, 75b, 106a, 122b), ale (18a, 72b, 95d), ame (51a), ane (50b), ape (30d, 62a, 77b, 78b, 109c, 231), are (68d, 76b, 84a, 246), ASE (235), Ase (61b, 87c), Ate (88b, 135a, 198), ate, -ate (117a, 117b), Ave. (236), ave (44b, 56c, 57b, 92b, 102b, 104a), awe (63d, 76d, 100b, 127d, 132b), axe (27a, 33c, 36c, 122d), aye (10b, 44d, 129c)

_ A E   hae (105a), kae (65b), Lae (221), Mae (167), nae (105b), Rae (176), sae (242), tae (105b), UAE (243)

A F _   AFB (235), AFC (235), Afg. (235), AFL (235), Afr. (235), aft (15b, 18b, 98a, 108b, 115b)

A _ F   AEF (235), Alf (120b, 137), ATF (236)

_ A F   kaf (11d, 12a), oaf (21a, 37b, 38c, 109c, 116d, 134d), qaf (11d), RAF (242), WAF (244)

A G _   aga (84d, 125b), age (41b, 41c, 41d, 53b, 71d, 75b, 106a, 122b), AGI (235), ago (23a, 55b, 87a), agt. (235)

A _ G   Afg. (235), Alg. (235), alg. (31b), Ang. (235), Arg. (235), Aug. (78c, 236), avg. (236)

_ A G   bag (24a, 117d), cag (63c), Dag (147), fag (27b), gag (26d, 66c, 113b), Hag. (239), hag (133a), jag (95c), lag (34c, 115a), mag (57c), mag. (240), nag (21b, 58a, 61a, 133d), rag (28b, 81c, 102a), SAG (242), sag (38a, 132a), tag (52b, 68b), wag (66d, 79c, 133a)

A H _   a-ha (42c), ahs (42c), ahu (53b)

A _ H   ach (11a, 42c, 53d), ash (40c, 58a, 124a)

_ A H   bah (42c), dah (68a), hah (42c), Nah. (241), pah (42c), rah (26b), yah (34c)

A I _   aid (15a, 57d, 59b, 117a), ail (124d), AIM (235), aim (54d, 83a, 96c, 119d), Ain (223), ain (105b), air (14b, 22a, 34d, 36c, 43a, 45a, 74c, 75d, 76d, 95d, 115a, 125a), ais (110d), ait (64b, 101a)

A _ I   Abi (59d), AGI (235), Ali (23b, 44d, 72b, 77c, 80c, 125b, 138), ami (50b), ani (19b, 19d, 32c), Ari (139), ASI (235), avi- (92c)

_ A I   gal (50c, 233), Kai (163), Lai (69a, 220), lai (119b), mai (49d), rai (246), sai (78b), Tai (62d, 183, 218), tai (65d, 91c), Vai (218), Yai (223)

A _ J   adj. (235)

_ A J   Maj. (240), raj (41a), Taj (74b)

A K _   **aka** (81c, 235), **AKC** (235), **aku** (46d)

A _ K   **Ark.** (209, 235), **ark** (20b, 128a), **ask** (31d, 64a, 96d, 99d, 111c), **auk** (19a, 225)

_ A K   **oak** (58a, 124a), **Pak.** (242), **yak** (85d, 119b, 231), **zak** (246)

A L _   **Ala.** (209, 235), **ala** (16c, 132c), **a la** (9c), **Alb.** (235), **alb** (52d, 128a), **ale** (18a, 72b, 95d), **Alf** (120b, 137), **Alg.** (235), **alg.** (31b), **Ali** (23b, 44d, 72b, 77c, 80c, 125b, 138), **all** (10d, 29c, 123b, 127c), **alp** (79b, 87b), **ALS** (235), **als** (54a), **alt** (54a)

A _ L   **aal** (79d), **AFL** (235), **ail** (124d), **all** (10d, 29c, 123b, 127c), **Atl.** (236), **awl** (108c, 122d, 123a)

_ A L   **aal** (79d), **bal** (50a), **Cal** (94b, 144), **Cal.** (209), **cal** (46c, 133b), **dal** (11d), **Gal.** (239), **gal** (45b, 54c), **Hal** (125d, 156), **-ial** (117a), **kal** (46c), **Mal.** (240), **mal** (42b, 50b, 112d), **mal-** (92c), **PAL** (242), **pal** (29b, 32a, 45b), **Sal** (52b, 179), **sal** (39b), **Val** (184)

A M _   **AMA** (235), **ama** (23d, 25d, 27b, 29b, 32b, 132c), **amb.** (235), **AMC** (26a), **ame** (51a), **ami** (50b), **amo** (69d), **amp.** (40a, 235), **amt** (31b), **amt.** (235), **Amu** (33d), **Amy** (11a, 73c, 138)

A _ M   **AAM** (235), **ABM** (235), **Adm.** (235), **AIM** (235), **aim** (54d, 83a, 96c, 119d), **arm** (13c, 21c, 49a, 72a, 95a), **ATM** (236), **aum** (246)

_ A M   **AAM** (235), **CAM** (236), **cam** (39c, 73d, 101a, 102b, 110c, 131c), **dam** (40b, 115d, 131a), **fam.** (238), **Gam** (154), **gam** (131b, 232), **gam-** (93c), **Ham** (81d, 108a, 197), **ham** (9d, 75c), **Jam.** (240), **jam** (35d, 85b, 94b, 115d, 122a), **Lam.** (240), **lam** (11d, 47c), **Pam** (173), **pam** (68a), **RAM** (242), **ram** (17c, 32c, 85b, 92a, 103a, 107d), **SAM** (242), **Sam** (24c, 119d, 179), **tam** (58b, 58c), **yam** (39c, 92a, 118c, 125a)

A N _   **ana** (12c, 29a, 72c), **-ana** (117c), **anc.** (235), **and** (30a, 90c), **ane** (50b), **Ang.** (235), **ani** (19b, 19d, 32c), **Ann** (138), **Ant** (139), **ant** (40c, 49a, 63b, 89c, 229), **anu** (59c, 125a), **any** (111d)

A _ N   **Ain** (223), **ain** (105b), **Ann** (138), **arn** (11b), **ASN** (235), **awn** (14b, 17d), **Ayn** (139), **ayn** (11d)

_ A N   **ban** (63c, 95a, 101d, 221), **Can.** (236), **can** (9a, 22c, 30b, 36c, 94b, 122b), **Dan** (64d, 147, 197), **-ean** (117a), **fan** (35c, 114a), **Gan** (215), **Han** (26d, 134a, 215), **Ian** (66c, 159), **Jan** (160), **Jan.** (78c, 240), **Kan.** (210, 240), **kan** (246), **lan** (31b, 118c), **Man** (64b, 168, 224), **man** (49a, 52c, 74c, 231), **Nan** (20c, **Pan** (45d, 55a, 59c, 133b, 198), **Pan.** (242), **pan** (18d, 79c, 128a), **ran** (19d, 29c, 84b), **san** (113a), **tan** (22b, 70d, 246), **Van** (184), **van** (48d), **wan** (57b, 86a), **Zan** (135c)

A _ O   **ado** (21b, 22d, 29b, 52c, 92a, 115c), **ago** (23a, 55b, 87a), **amo** (69d), **APO** (235), **Apo** (129a), **Aro** (84d), **Aso** (65d, 128d), **azo** (38d, 134b), **azo-** (93b)

_ A O   dao (68a), **GAO** (239), iao (60d), **Lao** (62d, 69a, 218), **Mao** (26d), tao (88c, 124d), **Yao** (218, 219)

A P _   Apa (12b), apa (21c), **APB** (235), ape (30d, 62a, 77b, 78b, 109c, 231), **APO** (235), **Apo** (129a), **APR** (235), **Apr.** (78c), apt (13d, 22a, 28a, 36c, 47b, 62c, 71d, 88b, 95a, 117d)

A _ P   abp. (235), **ACP** (235), **ADP** (235), alp (79b, 87b), **amp.** (40a, 235), **Arp** (33a), asp (10a, 28a, 111a, 126d, 128c, 232), **ATP** (236)

_ A P   cap (19b, 32b, 35b, 55c, 58c, 123a), dap (35d, 47a), gap (13b, 21d, 59d, 84b), hap (18b, 25d), **Jap.** (240), lap (26c, 27b, 31b, 97b, 100d, 113d, 123c), map (24c, 26b), nap (89a, 109a, 110b), pap (48b), rap (70d, 83d, 94d, 116b), sap (37d, 42d, 56d, 66d, 128c, 130c), tap (44d, 113c, 123b), yap (17b, 26b, 92b, 134c)

A R _   Ara (12a, 139, 197, 207), ara (73b), **ARC** (235), arc (27b, 32d, 96b, 106b, 123d), are (68d, 76b, 84a, 246), **Arg.** (235), **Ari** (139), **Ark.** (209, 235), ark (20b, 128a), arm (13c, 21c, 49a, 72a, 95a), arn (11b), **Aro** (84d), **Arp** (33a), arr. (235), ars (69c), **Art** (139), art (31d, 46a, 94d), -ary (117a, 117b)

A _ R   Aar (18c, 100b), abr. (235), aer (25d), aer- (92c), **Afr.** (235), air (14b, 22a, 34d, 36c, 43a, 45a, 74c, 75d, 76d, 95d, 115a, 125a), **APR** (235), **Apr.** (78c), arr. (235)

_ A R   Aar (18c, 100b), bar (20a, 31b, 32b, 42c, 60a, 62b, 71a, 95a, 104a, 107b, 115b, 120a, 234), car (72d, 127c), **DAR** (237), dar (53a, 122a), ear (15d, 25c, 51d, 57d, 95a, 112b), far (36d, 99c), gar (46c, 46d, 81b, 228), jar (27d, 30b, 56a, 107b), lar (54b, 74b), **Mar.** (78c, 240), mar (36b, 62a, 63a, 105c), oar (95b, 102c), **Pär** (173), **Par.** (242), par (16a, 41b, 41d, 55b, 82a, 103a, 114d), **SAR** (242), tar (55a, 89c, 102a, 103b), **UAR** (243), war (116b)

A S _   Asa (9a, 56a, 66b, 67d, 139, 197), asb. (235), **ASE** (235), **Ase** (61b, 87c), ash (40c, 58a, 124a), **ASI** (235), ask (31d, 64a, 96d, 99d, 111c), **ASN** (235), **Aso** (65d, 128d), asp (10a, 28a, 111a, 126d, 128c, 232), ass (17d, 20a, 37b, 37c, 41b, 48b, 84a, 85b, 109c, 116d, 229), **AST** (236), as't (107c), **ASV** (236)

A _ S   **ABS** (235), abs- (92c), **ACS** (235), ads (27d), aes (22a, 69c, 78a, 101d), ahs (42c), ais (110d), **ALS** (235), als (54a), ars (69c), ass (17d, 20a, 37b, 37c, 41b, 48b, 84a, 85b, 109c, 116d, 229), **AUS** (236), aus (54a)

_ A S   bas (50c), das (53c, 54a, 60b, 112b), fas (69c, 70a, 99b), gas (12c, 52a, 88b), has (91d), ha's (70b), **IAS** (239), **Jas.** (74d), las (50a, 112c), mas (112d), **NAS** (241), nas- (93b), **OAS** (241), pas (33b, 115b), ras (41d, 62d, 122c), vas (38c, 70a), vas- (92c), was (57a, 127a)

A T _   Ata (73d), **ATC** (236), **Ate** (88b, 135a, 198), ate, -ate (117a, 117b), **ATF** (236), **Atl.** (236), **ATM** (236), **ATP** (236), **ATV** (236)

A _ T   **ABT** (33b, 235), **act** (34b, 45a, 87d, 90b, 94b, 115a), **aet** (69c), **aft** (15b, 18b, 98a, 108b, 115b), **agt.** (235), **ait** (64b, 101a), **alt** (54a), **amt** (31b), **amt.** (235), **Ant** (139), **ant** (40c, 49a, 63b, 89c, 229), **apt** (13d, 22a, 28a, 36c, 47b, 62c, 71d, 88b, 95a, 117d), **Art** (139), **art** (31d, 46a, 94d), **AST** (236), **as't** (107c), **aut** (70a)

_ A T   **bat** (17b, 82a, 132d, 230, 246), **Cat** (144), **cat** (45a, 56c, 60b, 124c, 230), **DAT** (237), **eat** (31a), **fat** (31a, 83d, 116a), **gat** (57c, 100b), **Hat** (223), **hat** (58c), **Jat** (96a), **Lat.** (240), **lat** (29a), **mat** (47d, 88d, 119c), **Nat** (172), **oat** (16a, 25c, 55c), **PAT** (242), **Pat** (174), **pat** (88b, 119c, 123b), **rat** (16d, 35b, 101c, 115d, 119d, 231), **SAT** (242), **sat** (60a, 91d, 107a, 122d), **TAT** (243), **tat** (39c, 68c), **VAT** (244), **vat** (27b, 30b, 125a, 246), **Wat** (186), **xat** (123b)

A U _   **Aug.** (78c, 236), **auk** (19a, 225), **aum** (246), **AUS** (236), **aus** (54a), **aut** (70a), **aux.** (236)

A _ U   **abu** (44d), **acu-** (93c), **ahu** (53b), **aku** (46d), **Amu** (33d), **anu** (59c, 125a)

_ A U   **eau** (51b), **gau** (53c), **OAU** (241), **Pau** (39c, 59b, 100a, 216), **tau** (11d, 103d)

A V _   **Ava** (22d, 139), **ava** (61c, 91a, 123a), **Ave.** (236), **ave** (44b, 56c, 57b, 92b, 102b, 104a), **avg.** (236), **avi-** (92c)

A _ V   **adv.** (235), **ASV** (236), **ATV** (236)

_ A V   **Bav.** (236), **cav.** (236), **DAV** (237), **lav.** (240), **nav.** (241), **tav** (12a), **vav** (12a)

A W _   **awe** (63d, 76d, 100b, 127d, 132b), **awl** (108c, 122d, 123a), **awn** (14b, 17d)

_ A W   **caw** (19b), **daw** (55c), **Haw.** (209), **haw** (29b, 71a, 114c), **jaw** (75b), **Kaw** (121d), **law** (23d, 28d, 33a, 39c, 67c, 71a, 84c, 92b, 102d, 115a), **maw** (31d, 32a, 56d, 84b, 91b, 115c), **paw** (48b, 57d), **raw** (32b, 81a, 126d), **saw** (9d, 13b, 33c, 75b, 95c, 114a, 122d), **Taw** (223), **taw** (70d, 74d, 108c, 119c), **waw** (11d), **yaw** (101c)

A X _   **axe** (27a, 33c, 36c, 122d)

A _ X   **aux.** (236)

_ A X   **fax** (30d), **lax** (39b, 73a, 81b, 99c, 111c), **Max** (169), **Max.** (240), **max** (78d), **pax** (70a), **sax** (80a), **tax** (15a, 62b, 71c), **wax** (15d, 56d, 90d, 118c), **zax** (110b)

A Y _   **aye** (10b, 44d, 129c), **Ayn** (139), **ayn** (11d)

A _ Y   **-acy** (117b), **Amy** (11a, 73c, 138), **any** (111d), **-ary** (117a, 117b)

_ A Y   **bay** (12d, 17b, 58a, 61a, 61c, 63a, 70b, 98c, 124a, 130a), **cay** (64b), **Day** (148), **day** (33d, 122b), **Fay** (152), **fay** (44a), **Gay** (154), **gay**

(18b), **hay** (122b), **Jay** (160), **jay** (19b, 71c, 225), **Kay** (14d, 102c, 164), **lay** (16c, 75c, 82a, 96c, 106b, 111d), **May** (24a, 169), **may** (58c, 76d), **nay** (22d, 34d, 81b, 129c), **pay** (29c, 36a, 98b, 99c, 103d, 129b), **Ray** (176), **ray** (17d, 46d, 107b, 109d, 228), **Say** (192), **say** (100d, 113b, 115a, 127c, 128d), **Tay** (82b), **way** (31b, 74c, 76b, 101a, 102c, 121b, 127a), **yay** (9b, 111b), **zay** (11d)

A Z _   **azo** (38d, 134b), **azo-** (93b)

A _ Z   **adz** (33c, 122d)

_ A Z   **laz** (25a), **Paz** (174)

B A _   **baa** (107d), **Bab** (16a), **bac** (27b), **bad** (42b, 44d, 126b, 131d), **bag** (24a, 117d), **bah** (42c), **bal** (50a), **ban** (63c, 95a, 101d, 221), **bar** (20a, 31b, 32b, 42c, 60a, 62b, 71a, 95a, 104a, 107b, 115b, 120a, 234), **bas** (50c), **bat** (17b, 82a, 132d, 230, 246), **Bav.** (236), **bay** (12d, 17b, 58a, 61a, 61c, 63a, 70b, 98c, 124a, 130a)

B _ A   **baa** (107d), **Bea** (140), **BFA** (236), **BIA** (236), **boa** (30b, 45a, 81b, 96c, 104c, 106d, 111a, 232), **bra** (18d, 126b), **BSA** (236)

_ B A   **ABA** (235), **aba** (13d, 23c, 52d), **MBA** (240), **NBA** (241), **PBA** (242), **SBA** (242), **tba** (243), **WBA** (244)

B B _   **BBB** (236), **BBC** (26a, 236)

B _ B   **Bab** (16a), **BBB** (236), **bib** (28b), **Bob** (142), **bob** (47a, 79c, 87c), **bub** (45a, 74c)

_ B B   **abb** (129d), **BBB** (236), **ebb** (9a, 34b, 35d, 79c, 98b, 116d, 129d)

B _ C   **bac** (27b), **BBC** (26a, 236), **B.Sc.** (236)

_ B C   **ABC** (26a, 235), **BBC** (26a, 236), **CBC** (26a, 236), **NBC** (26a, 241), **WBC** (244)

B _ D   **bad** (42b, 44d, 126b, 131d), **bed** (21b, 52d, 110c, 232), **bid** (21d, 64a, 83c, 84c), **Bud** (143), **bud** (45a, 47d)

_ B D   **abd.** (235)

B E _   **Bea** (140), **bed** (21b, 52d, 110c, 232), **bee** (38a, 63b, 113c, 229), **beg** (31d, 90b), **bel** (34a, 246), **Ben** (141), **ben** (105b), **Bes** (39d, 198), **bet** (52b), **bev.** (236), **bey** (55c, 125a)

B _ E   **bee** (38a, 63b, 113c, 229), **bye** (32a, 123c)

_ B E   **Abe** (94b, 137), **NbE** (29c), **OBE** (241), **obe** (68b), **SbE** (29c)

B F _   **BFA** (236)

B _ G   **bag** (24a, 117d), **beg** (31d, 90b), **big** (69b, 74a, 116d), **bog** (39a, 75a, 118b), **bug** (21b, 53c, 63b)

B _ H   **bah** (42c)

B I _   **BIA** (236), **bib** (28b), **bid** (21d, 64a, 83c, 84c), **big** (69b, 74a, 116d), **Bil** (141), **bim** (133b), **bin** (21b, 98b, 116a), **bio** (71d), **bio-** (93b), **bio.** (31b, 236), **bis** (10c, 50b, 70b, 78c, 99d), **bit** (23d, 37d, 67b, 78d, 86d, 122d, 125c, 131c), **Bix** (141)

B _ I   **BMI** (236), **B.V.I.** (236)

_ B I   **Abi** (59d), **FBI** (238), **obi** (45c, 54c, 65d, 104b), **RBI** (110d, 242), **ubi** (70b)

_ B J   **obj.** (241)

_ B K   **PBK** (242)

B L _   **BLS** (236), **blt** (236), **Bly** (142)

B _ L   **bal** (50a), **bel** (34a, 246), **Bil** (141), **Bol.** (236), **Bul.** (236)

_ B L   **dbl.** (237)

B M _   **BMI** (236), **BMX** (236)

B _ M   **bim** (133b), **bum** (38a, 127a), **BVM** (236)

_ B M   **ABM** (235)

B _ N   **ban** (63c, 95a, 101d, 221), **Ben** (141), **ben** (105b), **bin** (21b, 98b, 116a), **bon** (45a, 50b, 65d, 67b), **bun** (57b, 101c)

_ B N   **EbN** (29c), **ibn** (111d), **WbN** (29c)

B O _   **boa** (30b, 45a, 81b, 96c, 104c, 106d, 111a, 232), **Bob** (142), **bob** (47a, 79c, 87c), **bog** (39a, 75a, 118b), **Bol.** (236), **bon** (45a, 50b, 65d, 67b), **boo** (36a, 115a), **bop** (60b, 66b, 116b), **Bor** (91a), **bor.** (236), **bot** (69b), **bot.** (236), **Bow** (142), **bow** (20c, 32d, 48d, 68c, 82a, 83a, 95c, 108b, 116d), **box** (30b, 98b, 113a), **boy** (74c, 116c), **Boz** (35c, 87c, 142)

B _ O   **bio** (71d), **bio-** (93b), **bio.** (31b, 236), **boo** (36a, 115a), **bro.** (99b, 236)

_ B O   **HBO** (26a, 239), **Ibo** (68c, 220), **obo** (106c, 241)

B _ P   **bop** (60b, 66b, 116b)

_ B P   **abp.** (235)

B R _   **bra** (18d, 126b), **bro.** (99b, 236)

B _ R   **bar** (20a, 31b, 32b, 42c, 60a, 62b, 71a, 95a, 104a, 107b, 115b, 120a, 234), **Bor** (91a), **bor.** (236), **bur** (106b, 131a), **bur.** (236)

_ B R   **abr.** (235)

B S _   **BSA** (236), **B.Sc.** (236)

B _ S   **bas** (50c), **Bes** (39d, 198), **bis** (10c, 50b, 70b, 78c, 99d), **BLS** (236), **bus** (95d), **bus.** (236)

_ B S   **ABS** (235), **abs-** (92c), **CBS** (26a), **EbS** (29c), **GBS** (43a), **JBS** (240), **lbs.** (240), **NBS** (241), **obs.** (241), **PBS** (26a, 242), **TBS** (26a), **tbs.** (243), **WbS** (29c)

B T _   **BTU** (10d, 236)

B _ T   **bat** (17b, 82a, 132d, 230, 246), **bet** (52b), **bit** (23d, 37d, 67b, 78d, 86d, 122d, 125c, 131c), **blt** (236), **bot** (69b), **bot.** (236), **but** (11d, 30a, 42b, 115b, 126c, 134c)

_ B T   **ABT** (33b, 235), **CBT** (236)

B U _   **bub** (45a, 74c), **Bud** (143), **bud** (45a, 47d), **bug** (21b, 53c, 63b), **Bul.** (236), **bum** (38a, 127a), **bun** (57b, 101c), **bur** (106b, 131a), **bur.** (236), **bus** (95d), **bus.** (236), **but** (11d, 30a, 42b, 115b, 126c, 134c), **buy** (17b, 96a)

B _ U   **BTU** (10d, 236)

_ B U   **abu** (44d)

B V _   **B.V.I.** (236), **BVM** (236)

B _ V   **Bav.** (236), **bev.** (236)

B _ W   **Bow** (142), **bow** (20c, 32d, 48d, 68c, 82a, 83a, 95c, 108b, 116d)

_ B W   **NbW** (29c), **SbW** (29c)

B _ X   **Bix** (141), **BMX** (236), **box** (30b, 98b, 113a)

B Y _   **bye** (32a, 123c)

B _ Y   **bay** (12d, 17b, 58a, 61a, 61c, 63a, 70b, 98c, 124a, 130a), **bey** (55c, 125a), **Bly** (142), **boy** (74c, 116c), **buy** (17b, 96a)

B _ Z   **Boz** (35c, 87c, 142)

C A _   **CAB** (236), **Cab** (144), **cab** (95d, 127d, 246), **CAD** (236), **cad** (21b, 59b, 88a), **cag** (63c), **Cal** (94b, 144), **Cal.** (209), **cal** (46c, 133b), **CAM** (236), **cam** (39c, 73d, 101a, 102b, 110c, 131c), **Can.** (236), **can** (9a, 22c, 30b, 36c, 94b, 122b), **cap** (19b, 32b, 35b, 55c, 58c, 123a), **car** (72d, 127c), **Cat** (144), **cat** (45a, 56c, 60b, 124c, 230), **cav.** (236), **caw** (19b), **cay** (64b)

C _ A   **CCA** (236), **CEA** (236), **cha** (120a), **CIA** (236), **CPA** (237), **CSA** (237), **CVA** (237)

_ C A   **CCA** (236), **Ica** (12b), **OCA** (241), **oca** (39c, 125a, 133c), **RCA** (242), **uca** (45d)

C B _   **CBC** (26a, 236), **CBS** (26a), **CBT** (236)

C _ B   **CAB** (236), **Cab** (144), **cab** (95d, 127d, 246), **cob** (25c, 61a, 74c, 118b), **CPB** (237), **cub** (72b, 134d)

C C _   **CCA** (236), **CCC** (236), **ccw** (236)

C _ C   **CBC** (26a, 236), **CCC** (236), **CDC** (236), **CRC** (237), **CSC** (237)

_ C C   **ACC** (235), **CCC** (236), **FCC** (238), **ICC** (239)

C D _   **CDC** (236), **CDT** (236)

C _ D   **CAD** (236), **cad** (21b, 59b, 88a), **CID** (236), **COD** (237), **Cod** (24a), **cod** (46d, 228), **cud** (96d, 102d), **Cyd** (147)

_ C D   **LCD** (240)

C E _   **CEA** (236), **cee** (55c, 71c), **Cel.** (236), **cen-** (92d), **CEO** (236), **cer-** (93d), **ces** (49d)

C _ E   **cee** (55c, 71c), **Che** (145), **cie** (49c), **Coe** (146, 201), **coe** (107d), **cue** (9d, 24d, 91b, 101c, 109b, 117d)

_ C E   **ace** (24a, 46c, 60c, 84a, 107d, 109d, 120c, 126c), **Ice.** (239), **ice** (30c, 51c)

C F _   **CFL** (236), **cfm** (236), **cfs** (236)

C _ F   **CIF** (236)

C G _   **CGI** (236)

C _ G   **cag** (63c), **cog** (53b, 120c, 123a)

_ C G   **ECG** (238)

C H _   **cha** (120a), **Che** (145), **chi** (11d), **chm.** (236), **cho** (246)

_ C H   **ach** (11a, 42c, 53d), **ich** (53d), **och** (11a, 42c), **sch.** (242), **tch** (42c)

C I _   **CIA** (236), **CID** (236), **Cie.** (49c), **CIF** (236), **CIO** (236), **cir.** (237), **cit.** (237), **civ.** (237)

C _ I   **CGI** (236), **chi** (11d), **CLI** (237), **CPI** (237)

_ C I   **ici** (50c), **sci.** (31b, 242)

C K _   **ckw** (237)

_ C K   **ock** (246), **-ock** (117b)

C L _   CLI (237), Clu (146)

C _ L   Cal (94b, 144), Cal. (209), cal (46c, 133b), Cel. (236), CFL (236), col (79b, 87a), Cpl. (237)

_ C L   HCL (239)

C _ M   CAM (236), cam (39c, 73d, 101a, 102b, 110c, 131c), cfm (236), chm. (236), com- (94a), cum (117d), cwm (79b)

_ C M   LCM (240)

C N _   CNN (26a), CNO (237), CNS (237)

C _ N   Can. (236), can (9a, 22c, 30b, 36c, 94b, 122b), cen- (92d), CNN (26a), con (10c, 26b, 65c, 116c, 118d)

_ C N   RCN (242)

C O _   cob (25c, 61a, 74c, 118b), COD (237), Cod (24a), cod (46d, 228), Coe (146, 201), coe (107d), cog (53b, 120c, 123a), col (79b, 87a), com- (94a), con (10c, 26b, 65c, 116c, 118d), coo (19b), cop (90d, 97a, 115a), coq (50a), Cor. (237), cor (246), cos (71c, 101d), cos. (237), cot (18a, 99a, 110c), cow (21b, 63d, 121c, 230), Cox (147), cox (102c), coy (17c, 109a)

C _ O   CEO (236), cho (246), CIO (236), CNO (237), coo (19b), CPO (237), cto. (237), CWO (237), CYO (237)

_ C O   NCO (241)

C P _   CPA (237), CPB (237), CPI (237), Cpl. (237), CPO (237), CPR (237), CPU (237)

C _ P   cap (19b, 32b, 35b, 55c, 58c, 123a), cop (90d, 97a, 115a), cup (38a, 55b, 89b, 98b, 119a, 124d)

_ C P   ACP (235), hcp. (239), MCP (240)

C _ Q   coq (50a)

C R _   CRC (237), CRT (237), cru (50d), cry (23b, 94d, 108d, 131a, 134b, 232)

C _ R   car (72d, 127c), cer- (93d), cir. (237), Cor. (237), cor (246), CPR (237), cur (78a)

_ C R   VCR (244)

C S _   CSA (237), CSC (237), CST (237)

C _ S   CBS (26a), ces (49d), cfs (236), CNS (237), cos (71c, 101d), cos. (237), cts. (237)

_ C S   ACS (235), -ics (117c), JCS (240), OCS (241)

C T _   cto. (237), cts. (237)

C _ T   Cat (144), cat (45a, 56c, 60b, 124c, 230), CBT (236), CDT (236), cit. (237), cot (18a, 99a, 110c), CRT (237), CST (237), cut (27a, 28a, 79c, 98d, 107b, 108d, 110b)

_ C T   act (34b, 45a, 87d, 90b, 94b, 115a), ect- (93c), jct. (240), Oct. (78c, 241), oct- (92d), pct. (242), rct. (242), WCT (244)

C U _   cub (72b, 134d), cud (96d, 102d), cue (9d, 24d, 91b, 101c, 109b, 117d), cum (117d), cup (38a, 55b, 89b, 98b, 119a, 124d), cur (78a), cut (27a, 28a, 79c, 98d, 107b, 108d, 110b)

C _ U   Clu (146), CPU (237), cru (50d)

_ C U   acu- (93c), ecu (47b, 108a), ICU (239)

C V _   CVA (237)

C _ V   cav. (236), civ. (237)

C W _   cwm (79b), CWO (237)

C _ W   caw (19b), ccw (236), ckw (237), cow (21b, 63d, 121c, 230)

_ C W   ccw (236)

C _ X   Cox (147), cox (102c)

C Y _   Cyd (147), CYO (237)

C _ Y   cay (64b), coy (17c, 109a), cry (23b, 94d, 108d, 131a, 134b, 232)

_ C Y   -acy (117b), icy (19c, 53b)

D A _   dab (38b, 46d, 47d), dad (11d, 44b, 44d), Dag (147), dah (68a), dal (11d), dam (40b, 115d, 131a), Dan (64d, 147, 197), dao (68a), dap (35d, 47a), DAR (237), dar (53a, 122a), das (53c, 54a, 60b, 112b), DAT (237), DAV (237), daw (55c), Day (148), day (33d, 122b)

D _ A   DEA (237), dea (69d), dia (112d), dia- (92c), DNA (53b, 98b, 237), DOA (237), dua- (93d)

_ D A   ADA (235), Ada (83c, 137), FDA (238), Ida (79b, 159), Ida. (209), NDA (241), oda (58a), RDA (242)

D B _   dbl. (237)

D _ B   dab (38b, 46d, 47d), deb (31a), dib (47a), dub (23b, 80b)

D _ C   DDC (237), Dec. (78c, 237), dec- (93d), DFC (237), DNC (237), Doc (88d, 107a, 149), doc. (237), DSC (238), duc (50b)

_ D C   ADC (15b, 235), CDC (236), DDC (237)

D D _   DDC (237), DDS (237), DDT (45c, 237)

D _ D   dad (11d, 44b, 44d), did (9c), DOD (237), dod (27d), dud (44a)

_ D D   add (12d, 13c, 116d), odd (116a, 126c, 126d)

D E _   DEA (237), dea (69d), deb (31a), dec- (93d), Dec. (78c, 237), Dee (82b, 101a, 148, 223), def. (237), deg. (237), dek- (93d), Del (148), Del. (209, 237), del (116b), Dem. (91a, 237), Den. (237), den (31c, 36d, 100a, 105c, 116c), der (53c, 54a), Des (149), des (51a), DEW (129d, 237), dew (77c), Dey (149), dey (11b, 86d, 125a)

D _ E   Dee (82b, 101a, 148, 223), die (24d, 34d, 43d, 54a, 87a, 114c, 123a), DOE (237), doe (34b, 97a), due (65c, 87b, 95b), dye (29a, 114c)

_ D E   Ade (43b, 137), ade (38a), Ede (29b, 38d, 53b), ide (46d), ode (61d, 89b, 90c)

D F _   DFC (237)

D _ F   def. (237), dif. (237)

D _ G   Dag (147), deg. (237), dig (42b, 132d), dog (12c, 23d, 32d, 48b, 230), dug (42b)

D H _   Dhu (68b)

D _ H   dah (68a), D.Ph. (238), D.Th. (238)

_ D H   edh (12c)

D I _   dia (112d), dia- (92c), dib (47a), did (9c), die (24d, 34d, 43d, 54a, 87a, 114c, 123a), dif. (237), dig (42b, 132d), Dik (149), dim (33d, 38d, 43d, 73d, 83a), din (27d, 61c, 126d), dip (23d, 62a, 88d, 104d), dir. (237), Dis (57a, 90c, 126b, 199), dis- (92c), div. (237), Dix (49a), DIY (237)

D _ I   DUI (38b, 238), DWI (38b, 238)

_ D I   SDI (242), Udi (82b)

_ D J   adj. (235)

D _ K   dek- (93d), Dik (149)

D L _   DLO (237)

D _ L   dal (11d), dbl. (237), Del (148), Del. (209, 237), del (116b), dol. (238)

_ D L   JDL (240)

D M _ DMV (237), DMZ (237)

D _ M dam (40b, 115d, 131a), **Dem.** (91a, 237), **dim** (33d, 38d, 43d, 73d, 83a), **Dom** (79a, 149), **dom** (91d, 122c), **dom.** (238), **DVM** (238)

_ D M Adm. (235)

D N _ DNA (53b, 98b, 237), DNC (237)

D _ N Dan (64d, 147, 197), **Den.** (237), **den** (31c, 36d, 100a, 105c, 116c), **din** (27d, 61c, 126d), **Don** (101a, 149), **don** (50b, 130d), **dun** (18d, 38c, 56a, 87b), **dyn-** (93c)

D O _ DOA (237), **Doc** (88d, 107a, 149), **doc.** (237), **DOD** (237), **dod** (27d), **DOE** (237), **doe** (34b, 97a), **dog** (12c, 23d, 32d, 48b, 230), **dol.** (238), **Dom** (79a, 149), **dom** (91d, 122c), **dom.** (238), **Don** (101a, 149), **don** (50b, 130d), **dop** (32d), **dor** (18b, 38a, 38d, 63b, 67a), **DOS** (238), **dos** (50a, 131d), **DOT** (238), **dot** (59d, 80c, 87d, 113b, 120b), **Dow** (66d, 150), **doz.** (238)

D _ O dao (68a), DLO (237), **duo** (85d, 125c)

_ D O ado (21b, 22d, 29b, 52c, 92a, 115c), **Edo** (220), **ido** (14d, 41c), **udo** (26d, 65d, 66a, 103d)

D P _ D.Ph. (238), DPT (238), DPW (238)

D _ P dap (35d, 47a), **dip** (23d, 62a, 88d, 104d), **dop** (32d), **dup.** (238)

_ D P ADP (235), EDP (238)

D R _ Dru (150), **dry** (38c, 121b, 133a)

D _ R DAR (237), **dar** (53a, 122a), **der** (53c, 54a), **dir.** (237), **dor** (18b, 38a, 38d, 63b, 67a), **dur** (74b)

D S _ DSC (238), DST (238)

D _ S das (53c, 54a, 60b, 112b), **DDS** (237), **Des** (149), **des** (51a), **Dis** (57a, 90c, 126b, 199), **dis-** (92c), **DOS** (238), **dos** (50a, 131d), **DTs** (238), **dys-** (92c)

_ D S ads (27d), DDS (237), HDS (239), IDs (95b), ids (51b), LDS (240), MDs (88d), SDS (242), yds. (244)

D T _ D.Th. (238), DTs (238)

D _ T DAT (237), DDT (45c, 237), DOT (238), dot (59d, 80c, 87d, 113b, 120b), DPT (238), DST (238)

_ D T CDT (236), DDT (45c, 237), EDT (238), MDT (240), PDT (242), VDT (244)

D U _ dua- (93d), **dub** (23b, 80b), **duc** (50b), **dud** (44a), **due** (65c, 87b,

95b), **dug** (42b), **DUI** (38b, 238), **dun** (18d, 38c, 56a, 87b), **duo** (85d, 125c), **dup.** (238), **dur** (74b), **dux** (52a, 70c)

D _ U   **Dhu** (68b), **Dru** (150)

D V _   **DVM** (238)

D _ V   **DAV** (237), **div.** (237), **DMV** (237)

_ D V   **adv.** (235)

D W _   **DWI** (38b, 238)

D _ W   **daw** (55c), **DEW** (129d, 237), **dew** (77c), **Dow** (66d, 150), **DPW** (238)

_ D W   **Edw.** (74d)

D _ X   **Dix** (49a), **dux** (52a, 70c)

D Y _   **dye** (29a, 114c), **dyn-** (93c), **dys-** (92c)

D _ Y   **Day** (148), **day** (33d, 122b), **Dey** (149), **dey** (11b, 86d, 125a), **DIY** (237), **dry** (38c, 121b, 133a)

D _ Z   **DMZ** (237), **doz.** (238)

_ D Z   **adz** (33c, 122d)

E A _   **-ean** (117a), **ear** (15d, 25c, 51d, 57d, 95a, 112b), **eat** (31a), **eau** (51b)

E _ A   **ela** (56d, 82c), **Ena** (11b, 96c), **EPA** (238), **ERA** (238), **era** (10d, 41b, 87d, 122b), **ETA** (238), **eta** (11d), **EVA** (238), **Eva** (116a, 152)

_ E A   **Bea** (140), **CEA** (236), **DEA** (237), **dea** (69d), **Kea** (64c), **kea** (19a, 86d, 225), **Lea** (21c, 165), **lea** (45d, 75b, 87a, 134b), **NEA** (241), **pea** (28c, 71b, 106b, 127c), **REA** (242), **Rea** (176), **sea** (42d, 47c, 130a), **tea** (61d, 111b), **yea** (10b, 128a, 129c)

E B _   **ebb** (9a, 34b, 35d, 79c, 98b, 116d, 129d), **EbN** (29c), **EbS** (29c)

E _ B   **ebb** (9a, 34b, 35d, 79c, 98b, 116d, 129d), **emb.** (238)

_ E B   **deb** (31a), **Feb.** (78c, 238), **Heb.** (239), **J.E.B.** (159), **Leb.** (240), **Neb.** (241), **neb** (17d, 18d, 19b, 87d), **reb** (30a), **W.E.B.** (185), **web** (41a, 75d, 76a, 81c, 111b)

E C _   **ECG** (238), **ect-** (93c), **ecu** (47b, 108a)

E _ C   **EEC** (238), **enc.** (238), **etc.** (72b, 238)

_ E C   **AEC** (235), **Dec.** (78c, 237), **dec-** (93d), **EEC** (238), **SEC** (242), **sec** (38b, 132c), **tec** (35b)

E D _ Ede (29b, 38d, 53b), **edh** (12c), **Edo** (220), **EDP** (238), **EDT** (238), **Edw.** (74d)

E _ D **eld** (12c, 73a, 83d, 122b), **end** (10d, 32c, 54d, 90c, 96c, 99c, 115d, 122b), **end-** (94a)

_ E D **bed** (21b, 52d, 110c, 232), **Fed.** (238), **fed** (82c), **GED** (239), **he'd** (30c), **LED** (240), **led** (46c, 89c), **Med.** (240), **Ned** (172), **OED** (241), **ped-** (92d, 93a), **QED** (242), **Red** (176, 224), **red** (32a, 48a, 102c), **sed** (69c), **Ted** (183), **ted** (58c, 114a), **wed** (66c, 75a, 126c), **we'd** (30c), **Yed** (207), **zed** (135a)

E E _ **EEC** (238), **EEG** (238), **eek** (79b), **eel** (30a, 46d, 68d, 78c, 228), **e'en** (30b, 107c), **e'er** (12a, 107c)

E _ E **Ede** (29b, 38d, 53b), **eke** (54b), **eme** (105c), **ENE** (29c), **EOE** (238), **'ere** (18b, 30b), **ESE** (29c), **ete** (51a), **Eve** (9a, 107a, 152, 197), **eve** (38d, 125c), **Ewe** (216, 223), **ewe** (107d), **Exe** (35c, 223), **eye** (73a, 118b)

_ E E **bee** (38a, 63b, 113c, 229), **cee** (55c, 71c), **Dee** (82b, 101a, 148, 223), **fee** (26a, 47b, 94b, 98b, 122d), **gee** (29b, 71c, 100c), **Lee** (27c, 165), **lee** (108a), **nee** (19b, 21a, 74b), **Ree** (14b, 23a, 189), **ree** (102d), **see** (19c, 36a, 41c, 43c, 55d, 73a, 83b, 86b, 87d, 130a, 133a), **tee** (55a, 55b, 87c), **Vee** (185), **vee** (47b, 81a), **wee** (77b, 105b, 110d), **zee** (63a)

E F _ **EFT** (238), **eft** (72c, 81c, 103d, 225)

E _ F **elf** (44a, 114a)

_ E F **AEF** (235), **def.** (237), **kef** (13d, 58b), **nef** (28b, 108b), **QEF** (242), **ref.** (242)

E G _ **egg** (28c, 85c), **ego** (94b, 106c, 127b)

E _ G **ECG** (238), **EEG** (238), **egg** (28c, 85c), **EKG** (238), **Eng** (109a), **Eng.** (238), **erg** (40d, 133c, 246)

_ E G **beg** (31d, 90b), **deg.** (237), **EEG** (238), **Geg** (213), **keg** (24c), **leg** (31b, 72a, 106b, 124b), **Meg** (11a, 170), **meg-** (93b), **neg.** (241), **peg** (32a, 38a, 44c, 89b), **reg.** (242), **teg** (107d)

E _ H **edh** (12c), **Eph.** (238), **Eth.** (238), **eth** (12c), **-eth** (117b, 117c)

_ E H **Neh.** (241), **reh** (11b, 62d)

E I _ **ein** (53c, 53d, 54a), **eis** (53d)

E _ I **Eli** (104a, 134a, 151, 197), **EMI** (238), **epi-** (93c), **ETI** (238)

_ E I **fei** (16d), **lei** (52d, 58c), **P.E.I.** (242), **Pei** (174), **rei** (91d), **sei** (65c), **Vei** (218), **Wei** (119d)

E K _   **eke** (54b), **EKG** (238)

E _ K   **eek** (79b), **elk** (21c, 70d, 129d, 230), **Esk** (134d, 223)

_ E K   **dek-** (93d), **eek** (79b), **lek** (31c, 36c, 213)

E L _   **ela** (56d, 82c), **eld** (12c, 73a, 83d, 122b), **elf** (44a, 114a), **Eli** (104a, 134a, 151, 197), **elk** (21c, 70d, 129d, 230), **ell** (12d, 22c, 28b, 246), **elm** (124a), **Els** (151), **els** (73a), **Ely** (25a)

E _ L   **eel** (30a, 46d, 68d, 78c, 228), **ell** (12d, 22c, 28b, 246), **enl.** (238), **ESL** (238)

_ E L   **bel** (34a, 246), **Cel.** (236), **Del** (148), **Del.** (209, 237), **del** (116b), **eel** (30a, 46d, 68d, 78c, 228), **gel** (28c, 58a, 111d), **Hel** (72d, 198), **Mel** (170), **mel** (60d), **rel** (40a, 246), **sel** (51a, 105b), **Tel** (16a), **Tel.** (243), **tel-** (93d)

E M _   **emb.** (238), **eme** (105c), **EMI** (238), **emp.** (238), **Ems** (95c, 112c), **emu** (19b, 85a, 225)

E _ M   **elm** (124a)

_ E M   **Dem.** (91a, 237), **fem.** (238), **Gem** (209), **gem** (115d), **hem** (39c, 40d, 114c, 118b), **LEM** (78c, 127c, 240), **mem** (12a), **REM** (110c, 242), **rem** (246)

E N _   **Ena** (11b, 96c), **enc.** (238), **end** (10d, 32c, 54d, 90c, 96c, 99c, 115d, 122b), **end-** (94a), **ENE** (29c), **Eng** (109a), **Eng.** (238), **enl.** (238), **Eno** (151), **ens** (18b), **ens.** (238), **-ent** (117a, 117b), **ent-** (94a)

E _ N   **-ean** (117a), **EbN** (29c), **e'en** (30b, 107c), **ein** (53c, 53d, 54a), **eon** (10d, 41d, 122b), **ern** (39a)

_ E N   **Ben** (141), **ben** (105b), **cen-** (92d), **Den.** (237), **den** (31c, 36d, 100a, 105c, 116c), **e'en** (30b, 107c), **fen** (20c, 75a, 78c, 118b, 215), **Gen.** (239), **gen** (27d), **hen** (18d, 49b, 86d, 103d), **Ken** (17a, 164), **ken** (65d, 104d, 126b, 246), **Len** (166), **Men** (88d), **men** (87d, 124c), **pen** (30a, 40d, 62d, 97a, 118b, 134c), **ren-** (93b), **Sen.** (243), **sen** (214, 217, 218, 219, 246), **ten** (18d, 34a, 34d), **Ven.** (244), **ven-** (93d), **wen** (33c, 83d, 125a, 129a), **xen-** (93a), **yen** (35b, 58a, 73a, 218), **Zen** (22b)

E O _   **EOE** (238), **eon** (10d, 41d, 122b), **Eos** (15d, 33d, 198), **eos** (86d)

E _ O   **Edo** (220), **ego** (94b, 106c, 127b), **Eno** (151), **ETO** (238), **exo-** (93c)

_ E O   **CEO** (236), **Geo.** (74d), **geo-** (92d), **Leo** (76c, 91b, 135c, 166, 207), **leo** (72b), **Meo** (218, 224), **neo** (77c), **neo-** (93b), **OEO** (241), **Reo** (24a)

E P _   **EPA** (238), **Eph.** (238), **epi-** (93c)

E _ P   **EDP** (238), **emp.** (238), **ESP** (109d, 238), **exp.** (238)

_ E P   **hep** (23a, 60b), **nep** (28c, 45d, 68c, 133c), **Pep** (174), **pep** (40d, 128b), **Rep.** (242), **rep** (10d, 43b, 100c), **Sep.** (78c, 243), **yep** (10b)

E _ Q   **Esq.** (238)

_ E Q   **req.** (242)

E R _   **ERA** (238), **era** (10d, 41b, 87d, 122b), **'ere** (18b, 30b), **erg** (40d, 133c, 246), **ern** (39a), **err** (20b, 35c, 109c, 110c, 116b, 123d), **ers** (19c, 59d, 128b), **-ery** (117b)

E _ R   **ear** (15d, 25c, 51d, 57d, 95a, 112b), **e'er** (12a, 107c), **err** (20b, 35c, 109c, 110c, 116b, 123d), **Eur.** (238)

_ E R   **aer** (25d), **aer-** (92c), **cer-** (93d), **der** (53c, 54a), **e'er** (12a, 107c), **Ger.** (239), **ger** (30c, 95b), **her** (70c, 95a), **-ier** (40d, 117a, 117b), **Jer.** (240), **ker-** (93d), **Ler** (22b, 199), **mer** (51a), **Ner** (104c), **o'er** (30b, 107c), **Per.** (242), **per** (128b), **ser-** (93c), **ser.** (243), **ter-** (93d), **ter.** (243), **ver.** (244), **xer-** (92d), **zer** (246)

E S _   **ESE** (29c), **Esk** (134d, 223), **ESL** (238), **ESP** (109d, 238), **Esq.** (238), **ess** (32d, 71c), **-ess** (117b), **EST** (238), **est** (50b, 50c), **-est** (40d, 117c)

E _ S   **EbS** (29c), **eis** (53d), **Els** (151), **els** (73a), **Ems** (95c, 112c), **ens** (18b), **ens.** (238), **Eos** (15d, 33d, 198), **eos** (86d), **ers** (19c, 59d, 128b), **ess** (32d, 71c), **-ess** (117b)

_ E S   **aes** (22a, 69c, 78a, 101d), **Bes** (39d, 198), **ces** (49d), **Des** (149), **des** (51a), **Fes** (220), **he's** (30c), **Les** (166), **les** (50a), **mes** (49d), **pes** (48c), **res** (70a, 71a), **ses** (50c), **Wes** (186), **yes** (10b, 44d)

E T _   **ETA** (238), **eta** (11d), **etc.** (72b, 238), **ete** (51a), **Eth.** (238), **eth** (12c), **-eth** (117b, 117c), **ETI** (238), **ETO** (238), **ETV** (238)

E _ T   **eat** (31a), **ect-** (93c), **EDT** (238), **EFT** (238), **eft** (72c, 81c, 103d, 225), **-ent** (117a, 117b), **ent-** (94a), **EST** (238), **est** (50b, 50c), **-est** (40d, 117c), **ext.** (238)

_ E T   **aet** (69c), **bet** (52b), **FET** (238), **get** (9d, 29b, 52a, 83b, 126b, 132b), **het** (12a), **jet** (11a, 19d, 114b), **ket-** (93b), **let** (11c, 60b, 87d, 99c, 104a, 117a, 120c), **Met.** (240), **met** (40d, 97d, 107a), **met-** (92d), **net** (24a, 27d, 41a, 43b, 76a, 94d, 106b, 111b, 120c), **pet** (24b, 31a, 44d, 48b), **ret** (47c, 73b, 111b), **ret.** (242), **Set** (42b, 198), **set** (10a, 14c, 15c, 28a, 31a, 47b, 58a, 81b, 85a, 89d, 106d, 111d, 120c), **vet** (111c), **vet.** (244), **wet** (33b, 33c, 37d, 77c, 97c), **yet** (18c, 22d, 60b, 82c, 115b, 121d)

E U _   **Eur.** (238)

E _ U   **eau** (51b), **ecu** (47b, 108a), **emu** (19b, 85a, 225)

_ E U   **feu** (45c, 50b, 105b), **heu** (11a), **jeu** (50b), **leu** (221), **neu** (54a), **peu** (50c)

264

E V _   **EVA** (238), **Eva** (116a, 152), **Eve** (9a, 107a, 152, 197), **eve** (38d, 125c)

E _ V   **ETV** (238)

_ E V   **bev.** (236), **Lev.** (240), **lev** (214), **lev-** (93b), **Nev.** (211, 241), **Rev.** (242), **rev** (41a, 79a)

E W _   **Ewe** (216, 223), **ewe** (107d)

E _ W   **Edw.** (74d)

_ E W   **DEW** (129d, 237), **dew** (77c), **few** (110d), **HEW** (239), **hew** (27a, 33a), **Jew** (59a), **Lew** (166), **mew** (19a, 25a, 45a, 56d, 58c, 105d, 106a, 226), **new** (13a, 43c, 51b, 84d, 98b), **pew** (18c, 27a, 47a, 106a), **sew** (75d, 115c), **yew** (30a, 42a, 108d, 124a)

E X _   **Exe** (35c, 223), **exo-** (93c), **exp.** (238), **ext.** (238)

_ E X   **hex** (66c), **hex-** (93c), **lex** (70b), **Mex.** (240), **Rex** (176), **rex** (67c), **sex** (53b, 94d), **sex-** (93c), **Tex** (31c, 183), **Tex.** (212, 243), **vex** (12d, 21b, 36d, 64b, 87c)

E Y _   **eye** (73a, 118b)

E _ Y   **Ely** (25a), **-ery** (117b)

_ E Y   **bey** (55c, 125a), **Dey** (149), **dey** (11b, 86d, 125a), **fey** (109d), **hey** (42c), **Key** (164), **key** (25c, 28d, 64b, 68d, 89c), **Ney** (49d, 80d, 172), **Rey** (176), **rey** (112d), **sey** (105a), **wey** (246)

_ E Z   **fez** (58b, 58d, 119d), **nez** (50d)

F A _   **FAA** (238), **fad** (31d, 97b, 120b, 124b), **fag** (27b), **fam.** (238), **fan** (35c, 114a), **far** (36d, 99c), **fas** (69c, 70a, 99b), **fat** (31a, 83d, 116a), **fax** (30d), **Fay** (152), **fay** (44a)

F _ A   **FAA** (238), **FDA** (238), **FHA** (238), **Fla.** (209, 238), **Fra** (153), **fra** (22a, 51c, 78a, 94c)

_ F A   **BFA** (236), **ufa** (42c)

F B _   **FBI** (238)

F _ B   **Feb.** (78c, 238), **fib** (71c, 119d), **fob** (48a, 130a), **FRB** (238)

_ F B   **AFB** (235)

F C _   **FCC** (238)

F _ C   **FCC** (238), **FTC** (239)

_ F C   **AFC** (235), **DFC** (237), **pfc** (242)

F D _   **FDA** (238)

F _ D   **fad** (31d, 97b, 120b, 124b), **Fed.** (238), **fed** (82c), **fid** (17a, 44c, 89b, 102b, 123b), **fod** (246), **fwd** (239)

_ F D   **Mfd.** (240), **RFD** (242)

F E _   **Feb.** (78c, 238), **Fed.** (238), **fed** (82c), **fee** (26a, 47b, 94b, 98b, 122d), **fei** (16d), **fem.** (238), **fen** (20c, 75a, 78c, 118b, 215), **Fes** (220), **FET** (238), **feu** (45c, 50b, 105b), **few** (110d), **fey** (109d), **fez** (58b, 58d, 119d)

F _ E   **fee** (26a, 47b, 94b, 98b, 122d), **fie** (42c, 49a), **FOE** (238), **foe** (84c)

_ F E   **ife** (59b), **RFE** (242)

F F _   **fff** (238)

F _ F   **fff** (238)

_ F F   **fff** (238), **off** (9b, 59b, 79d, 134c), **off.** (241)

F _ G   **fag** (27b), **fig** (51d, 124a), **fig.** (238), **fog** (28b, 116d, 130d), **fug** (98d)

_ F G   **Afg.** (235), **Mfg.** (240)

F H _   **FHA** (238)

F I _   **fib** (71c, 119d), **fid** (17a, 44c, 89b, 102b, 123b), **fie** (42c, 49a), **fig** (51d, 124a), **fig.** (238), **fin** (11a, 47b, 67a), **fir** (16d, 30a, 42a, 124a), **fit** (9c, 10a, 13d, 41b, 75b, 86c, 95b, 96b, 112a, 113b, 117d, 119c), **fix** (10a, 12c, 14c, 15c, 31a, 35d, 55c, 60c, 75d, 81b, 92b, 94a, 99c, 122a)

F _ I   **FBI** (238), **fei** (16d), **Fri.** (238), **fyi** (239)

F L _   **Fla.** (209, 238), **Flo** (12c), **flu** (62a), **fly** (47c, 63b, 120c, 229)

F _ L   **-ful** (117b)

_ F L   **AFL** (235), **CFL** (236), **NFL** (241)

F _ M   **fam.** (238), **fem.** (238)

_ F M   **cfm** (236)

F _ N   **fan** (35c, 114a), **fen** (20c, 75a, 78c, 118b, 215), **fin** (11a, 47b, 67a), **Fon** (214), **fun** (52b, 66b)

F O _   **fob** (48a, 130a), **fod** (246), **FOE** (238), **foe** (84c), **fog** (28b, 116d, 130d), **Fon** (214), **fop** (31c, 33c, 38c, 44b), **for** (94d), **fot** (246), **fou** (246), **Fox** (153, 189), **fox** (23a, 23d, 54c, 102b, 230), **Foy** (153)

F _ O   Flo (12c), fro (16b)

_ F O   UFO (48a, 243)

F _ P   fop (31c, 33c, 38c, 44b)

F R _   Fra (153), fra (22a, 51c, 78a, 94c), FRB (238), Fri. (238), fro (16b),
         fry (30c, 47a)

F _ R   far (36d, 99c), fir (16d, 30a, 42a, 124a), for (94d), fur (28c, 57b)

_ F R   Afr. (235), Mfr. (240)

F _ S   fas (69c, 70a, 99b), Fes (220)

_ F S   cfs (236), ifs (30b)

F T _   FTC (239)

F _ T   fat (31a, 83d, 116a), FET (238), fit (9c, 10a, 13d, 41b, 75b, 86c,
         95b, 96b, 112a, 113b, 117d, 119c), fot (246), fut (246)

_ F T   aft (15b, 18b, 98a, 108b, 115b), EFT (238), eft (72c, 81c, 103d,
         225), oft' (30b), UFT (243)

F U _   fug (98d), -ful (117b), fun (52b, 66b), fur (28c, 57b), fut (246)

F _ U   feu (45c, 50b, 105b), flu (62a), fou (246)

F W _   fwd (239)

F _ W   few (110d)

_ F W   UFW (243), VFW (244)

F _ X   fax (30d), fix (10a, 12c, 14c, 15c, 31a, 35d, 55c, 60c, 75d, 81b, 92b,
         94a, 99c, 122a), Fox (153, 189), fox (23a, 23d, 54c, 102b, 230)

F Y _   fyi (239)

F _ Y   Fay (152), fay (44a), fey (109d), fly (47c, 63b, 120c, 229), Foy
         (153), fry (30c, 47a)

F _ Z   fez (58b, 58d, 119d)

G A _   gab (26b, 92b, 119b, 133a), Gad (64d, 135c), gad (47c, 77a, 83a,
         97d, 101a), gag (26d, 66c, 113b), gai (50c, 233), Gal. (239), gal
         (45b, 54c), Gam (154), gam (131b, 232), gam- (93c), Gan (215),
         GAO (239), gap (13b, 21d, 59d, 84b), gar (46c, 46d, 81b, 228), gas
         (12c, 52a, 88b), gat (57c, 100b), gau (53c), Gay (154), gay (18b)

G _ A   Goa (91d), goa (53b), GPA (239), GSA (239)

_ G A   aga (84d, 125b), PGA (242)

G B _   **GBS** (43a)

G _ B   **gab** (26b, 92b, 119b, 133a), **gib** (17d, 24d, 51c, 74c, 122d), **gob** (75b, 103b)

_ G B   **KGB** (103c, 240)

G _ D   **Gad** (64d, 135c), **gad** (47c, 77a, 83a, 97d, 101a), **GED** (239), **gid** (107d), **God** (66b), **god** (34c, 133d)

_ G D   **sgd.** (243)

G E _   **GED** (239), **gee** (29b, 71c, 100c), **Geg** (213), **gel** (28c, 58a, 111d), **Gem** (209), **gem** (115d), **Gen.** (239), **gen** (27d), **Geo.** (74d), **geo-** (92d), **Ger.** (239), **ger** (30c, 95b), **get** (9d, 29b, 52a, 83b, 126b, 132b)

G _ E   **gee** (29b, 71c, 100c), **gie** (105a), **GRE** (239)

_ G E   **age** (41b, 41c, 41d, 53b, 71d, 75b, 106a, 122b), **lge.** (240)

G_ G   **gag** (26d, 66c, 113b), **Geg** (213), **Gig** (155), **gig** (24a, 24c, 25d, 46d, 80d, 125d), **Gog** (74a, 197)

_ G G   **egg** (28c, 85c)

G H _   **GHQ** (239)

_ G H   **ugh** (42c)

G I _   **gib** (17d, 24d, 51c, 74c, 122d), **gid** (107d), **gie** (105a), **Gig** (155), **gig** (24a, 24c, 25d, 46d, 80d, 125d), **Gil** (155), **gin** (11a, 24a, 31b, 72b, 106b, 246), **Gls** (111c)

G _ I   **gai** (50c, 233)

_ G I   **AGI** (235), **CGI** (236)

G _ L   **Gal.** (239), **gal** (45b, 54c), **gel** (28c, 58a, 111d), **Gil** (155)

G M _   **GMT** (239)

G _ M   **Gam** (154), **gam** (131b, 232), **gam-** (93c), **Gem** (209), **gem** (115d), **gum** (10a, 43c, 62c, 78d, 99d, 115b, 124a), **gym** (114a)

G N _   **GNP** (239), **gnu** (13a, 132a, 230)

G _ N   **Gan** (215), **gen** (27d), **Gen.** (239), **gin** (11a, 24a, 31b, 72b, 106b, 246), **gon-** (93c), **gun** (46b, 100b, 109a, 130c), **gyn-** (92d)

_ G N   **ign.** (239)

G O _   **Goa** (91d), **goa** (53b), **gob** (75b, 103b), **God** (66b), **god** (34c, 133d), **Gog** (74a, 197), **gon-** (93c), **goo** (79c, 115b), **GOP** (91a, 99d, 239), **got** (23b, 83b), **goy** (82a)

G _ O   **GAO** (239), **Geo.** (74d), **geo-** (92d), **goo** (79c, 115b), **GPO** (239), **gro.** (239)

_ G O   **ago** (23a, 55b, 87a), **ego** (94b, 106c, 127b)

G P _   **GPA** (239), **GPO** (239)

G _ P   **gap** (13b, 21d, 59d, 84b), **GNP** (239), **GOP** (91a, 99d, 239), **gyp** (107a, 108d, 118d)

G _ Q   **GHQ** (239)

G R _   **GRE** (239), **gro.** (239), **GRU** (239)

G _ R   **gar** (46c, 46d, 81b, 228), **Ger.** (239), **ger** (30c, 95b), **Gur** (223), **gur** (117c), **gyr-** (93a)

G S _   **GSA** (239)

G _ S   **gas** (12c, 52a, 88b), **GBS** (43a), **Gls** (111c), **Gus** (156)

G _ T   **gat** (57c, 100b), **get** (9d, 29b, 52a, 83b, 126b, 132b), **GMT** (239), **got** (23b, 83b), **gut** (99c)

_ G T   **agt.** (235), **hgt.** (239), **Sgt.** (243)

G U _   **gum** (10a, 43c, 62c, 78d, 99d, 115b, 124a), **gun** (46b, 100b, 109a, 130c), **Gur** (223), **gur** (117c), **Gus** (156), **gut** (99c), **Guy** (156), **guy** (45a, 74c, 115a), **guz** (246)

G _ U   **gau** (53c), **gnu** (13a, 132a, 230), **GRU** (239)

G Y _   **gym** (114a), **gyn-** (92d), **gyp** (107a, 108d, 118d), **gyr-** (93a)

G _ Y   **Gay** (154), **gay** (18b), **goy** (82a), **Guy** (156), **guy** (45a, 74c, 115a)

_ G Y   **IGY** (239)

G _ Z   **guz** (246)

H A _   **Hab.** (239), **had** (61a, 91d), **hae** (105a), **Hag.** (239), **hag** (133a), **hah** (42c), **Hal** (125d, 156), **Ham** (81d, 108a, 197), **ham** (9d, 75c), **Han** (26d, 134a, 215), **hap** (18b, 25d), **has** (91d), **ha's** (70b), **Hat** (223), **hat** (58c), **Haw.** (209), **haw** (29b, 71a, 114c), **hay** (122b)

H _ A   **HRA** (239)

_ H A   **a-ha** (42c), **cha** (120a), **FHA** (238), **Kha** (69a), **kha** (11d), **tha** (11d), **WHA** (244)

H B _   **HBO** (26a, 239)

H _ B   **Hab.** (239), **Heb.** (239), **hob** (33c, 46b, 95a, 123a), **hub** (25c, 131c)

H C _   **HCL** (239), **hcp.** (239)

H _ C   hic (70a), hoc (70a)

H D _   HDS (239)

H _ D   had (61a, 91d), he'd (30c), hid (31c, 106a), hod (21d, 28c, 78d, 105c), HUD (239)

_ H D   Ph.D. (242)

H E _   Heb. (239), he'd (30c), Hel (72d, 198), hem (39c, 40d, 114c, 118b), hen (18d, 49b, 86d, 103d), hep (23a, 60b), her (70c, 95a), he's (30c), het (12a), heu (11a), HEW (239), hew (27a, 33a), hex (66c), hex- (93c), hey (42c)

H _ E   hae (105a), hie (61d), hoe (32c, 52d), hue (29a, 107b, 122d)

_ H E   Che (145), rhe (47d, 246), She (57b), she (95a), the (14d)

_ H F   UHF (120b, 243), VHF (120b)

H G _   hgt. (239)

H _ G   Hag. (239), hag (133a), hog (88d, 118d, 230), hug (40c)

H _ H   hah (42c), HRH (239), huh (42c)

H I _   hic (70a), hid (31c, 106a), hie (61d), him (70c, 95a), hin (246), hip (44a, 66c, 102a, 102b), his (95a), hit (15a, 15c, 18c, 28b, 116b)

H _ I   hoi (42c), Hui (215), hui (15a)

_ H I   chi (11d), ihi (46d, 115c), NHI (241), phi (11d)

H _ L   Hal (125d, 156), HCL (239), Hel (72d, 198), hyl- (94a)

_ H L   NHL (241)

H M _   HMO (239), HMS (239)

H _ M   Ham (81d, 108a, 197), ham (9d, 75c), hem (39c, 40d, 114c, 118b), him (70c, 95a), hum (38a, 112a, 131d)

_ H M   chm. (236), ohm (40a, 53d, 246)

H N _   HNS (239)

H _ N   Han (26d, 134a, 215), hen (18d, 49b, 86d, 103d), hin (246), Hon. (239), hon (40d), Hun (127b)

H O _   hob (33c, 46b, 95a, 123a), hoc (70a), hod (21d, 28c, 78d, 105c), hoe (32c, 52d), hog (88d, 118d, 230), hoi (42c), Hon. (239), hon (40d), hop (33b, 67a), hor. (239), Hos. (239), ho's (70b), hot (12d, 117d), HOV (239), how (74c, 76b, 96c), Hoy (64d), hoy (17b, 20b)

H _ O   HBO (26a, 239), HMO (239)

_ H O	cho (246), mho (40a, 246), o-ho (42c), rho (11d), sho (246), WHO (244), who (96d, 99b)
H _ P	hap (18b, 25d), hcp. (239), hep (23a, 60b), hip (44a, 66c, 102a, 102b), hop (33b, 67a), hup (23a, 29b)
_ H Q	GHQ (239)
H R _	HRA (239), HRH (239), hrs. (239)
H _ R	her (70c, 95a), hor. (239)
_ H R	ihr (54b)
H S _	HST (239)
H _ S	has (91d), ha's (70b), HDS (239), he's (30c), his (95a), HMS (239), HNS (239), Hos. (239), ho's (70b), hrs. (239), hts. (239)
_ H S	ahs (42c), IHS (239), JHS (240), NHS (241), ohs (42c)
H T _	hts. (239)
H _ T	Hat (223), hat (58c), het (12a), hgt. (239), hit (15a, 15c, 18c, 28b, 116b), hot (12d, 117d), HST (239), hut (107c)
H U _	hub (25c, 131c), HUD (239), hue (29a, 107b, 122d), hug (40c), huh (42c), Hui (215), hui (15a), hum (38a, 112a, 131d), Hun (127b), hup (23a, 29b), hut (107c)
H _ U	heu (11a)
_ H U	ahu (53b), Dhu (68b), Shu (97a), Thu. (243)
H _ V	HOV (239)
H W _	hwy. (239)
H _ W	Haw. (209), haw (29b, 71a, 114c), HEW (239), hew (27a, 33a), how (74c, 76b, 96d)
H _ X	hex (66c), hex- (93c)
H Y _	hyl- (94a)
H _ Y	hay (122b), hey (42c), Hoy (64d), hoy (17b, 20b), hwy. (239)
_ H Y	shy (17c, 31c, 77c, 98b, 108d, 122b), thy (95a), why (96d)
I A _	-ial (117a), Ian (66c, 159), iao (60d), IAS (239)
I _ A	Ica (12b), Ida (79b, 159), Ida. (209), ILA (239), Ila (17a), Ina (159), -ina (117b), ioa (51c), IPA (240), IRA (64a, 240), Ira (159, 197), Isa. (240), ita (70a), iva (75a), iwa (51c)

_ I A   **BIA** (236), **CIA** (236), **dia** (112d), **dia-** (92c), **KIA** (240), **MIA** (240), **Mia** (170), **mia** (113a), **Pia** (175), **pia** (14d, 39b), **ria** (41d, 63a), **tia** (112c), **via** (65c, 101a, 101d)

I B _   **ibn** (111d), **Ibo** (68c, 220)

_ I B   **bib** (28b), **dib** (47a), **fib** (71c,119d), **gib** (17d, 24d, 51c, 74c, 122d), **jib** (103b), **Lib.** (240), **lib** (49b), **mib** (11c, 74d), **nib** (17d, 19b, 87d), **rib** (31a, 33a, 70d, 75c, 125d), **sib** (99b)

I C _   **Ica** (12b), **ICC** (239), **Ice.** (239), **ice** (30c, 51c), **ich** (53d), **ici** (50c), **-ics** (117c), **ICU** (239), **icy** (19c, 53b)

I _ C   **ICC** (239), **Inc.** (239), **IOC** (240), **IRC** (240), **ITC** (240)

_ I C   **hic** (70a), **Mic.** (240), **pic.** (242), **Ric** (177), **sic** (70a, 121d, 123d), **tic** (79d, 113b, 125c), **Vic** (32d, 185)

I D _   **Ida** (79b, 159), **Ida.** (209), **ide** (46d), **ido** (14d,41c), **IDs** (95b), **ids** (51b)

I _ D   **Ind.** (91a, 210, 239), **iod-** (93b), **IUD** (240)

_ I D   **aid** (15a, 57d, 59b, 117a), **bid** (21d, 64a, 83c, 84c), **CID** (236), **did** (9c), **fid** (17a, 44c, 89b, 102b, 123b), **gid** (107d), **hid** (31c, 106a), **kid** (26c, 54d, 70d, 90d, 134d), **lid** (123a), **mid** (12b, 25c, 57c), **-oid** (117b), **rid** (27d, 36b, 40b, 49b), **Sid** (180)

I E _   **-ier** (40d, 117a, 117b)

I _ E   **Ice.** (239), **ice** (30c, 51c), **ide** (46d), **ife** (59b), **Ike** (94b, 159), **ile** (50c), **ile-** (93b), **Ine** (12c), **-ine** (117a, 117b), **Ire.** (240), **ire** (12c, 26d, 52c, 97b, 134a), **Ise** (60d), **-ise** (117a, 117c), **-ite** (117a, 117b), **I've** (30c)

_ I E   **cie** (49c), **die** (24d, 34d, 43d, 54a, 87a, 114c, 123a), **fie** (42c, 49a), **gie** (105a), **hie** (61d), **lie** (44a, 55a, 98b, 99d, 119b, 119d), **nie** (54a), **Pie** (175), **pie** (35b, 125c), **sie** (54b), **tie** (12c, 20d, 31d, 37d, 41b, 42a, 69b, 72b, 97b, 124d), **vie** (30b, 116c, 125a)

I F _   **ife** (59b), **ifs** (30b)

I _ F   **IMF** (239)

_ I F   **CIF** (236), **dif.** (237), **Sif** (121b), **vif** (50c)

I G _   **ign.** (239), **IGY** (239)

I _ G   **Ing** (12c), **ing** (73c, 87a), **-ing** (86d, 117c)

_ I G   **big** (69b, 74a, 116d), **dig** (42b, 132d), **fig** (51d, 124a), **fig.** (238), **Gig** (155), **gig** (24a, 24c, 25d, 46d, 80d, 125d), **jig** (33b), **mig** (11c, 74d, 89d), **nig** (28d), **pig** (112b, 118d, 231), **rig** (41b, 53b, 85b), **wig** (57b)

I H _   **ihi** (46d, 115c), **ihr** (54b), **IHS** (239)

I _ H   **ich** (53d), **-ish** (117a), **Ith** (25c)

I _ I   **ici** (50c), **ihi** (46d, 115c)

_ I I   **rii** (127d)

I K _   **Ike** (94b, 159)

I _ K   **ilk** (27d, 67c, 105a, 113b), **ink** (33c, 94b, 109b), **irk** (12d, 87c, 128b)

_ I K   **Dik** (149), **-nik** (117c), **pik** (246)

I L _   **ILA** (239), **Ila** (17a), **ile** (50c), **ile-** (93b), **ilk** (27d, 67c, 105a, 113b), **Ill.** (210, 239), **I'll** (30c), **ill** (91b, 126b, 126c), **ILO** (239), **ils** (49d, 51a)

I _ L   **-ial** (117a), **Ill.** (210, 239), **I'll** (30c), **ill** (91b, 126b, 126c), **isl.** (240)

_ I L   **ail** (124d), **Bil** (141), **Gil** (155), **kil** (64a), **Li'l** (9a), **mil** (62c, 121b, 132d, 246), **mil.** (240), **nil** (82c), **oil** (13a, 52a, 56a), **sil** (26d, 134b), **til** (107a), **'til** (30b), **Wil** (186)

I M _   **IMF** (239), **imp** (34d, 97d, 101c, 126d), **imp.** (239)

I _ M   **I.O.M.** (240), **-ism** (117b)

_ I M   **AIM** (235), **aim** (54d, 83a, 96c, 119d), **bim** (133b), **dim** (33d, 38d, 43d, 73d, 83a), **him** (70c, 95a), **Jim** (161), **jim** (11d), **Kim** (67d, 164), **mim** (11d), **rim** (21a, 39c, 74d, 87d, 95a, 122b, 131c), **Sim** (181), **Tim** (35c, 183), **vim** (40d, 48c, 113d, 128b, 128d), **Wim** (187)

I N _   **Ina** (159), **-ina** (117b), **Inc.** (239), **Ind.** (91a, 210, 239), **Ine** (12c), **-ine** (117a, 117b), **Ing** (12c), **ing** (73c, 87a), **-ing** (86d, 117c), **ink** (33c, 94b, 109b), **Inn** (33c), **inn** (56d, 61c, 101a, 120a), **Ino** (15b, 23a), **INS** (239), **ins** (83c), **int.** (239)

I _ N   **Ian** (66c, 159), **ibn** (111d), **ign.** (239), **Inn** (33c), **inn** (56d, 61c, 101a, 120a), **Ion** (13b, 26a, 40a, 86d)

_ I N   **Ain** (223), **ain** (105b), **bin** (21b, 98b, 116a), **din** (27d, 61c, 126d), **ein** (53c, 53d, 54a), **fin** (11a, 47b, 67a), **gin** (11a, 24a, 31b, 72b, 106b, 246), **hin** (246), **kin** (26d, 63c, 68c, 99b, 246), **Lin** (134d), **Min** (215), **min.** (240), **Nin** (172), **nin** (246), **PIN** (242), **pin** (37c, 44c, 110a, 246), **rin** (106c), **sin** (11d, 12a, 83c, 123d, 124b, 128b, 134c), **tin** (30b, 74c, 76a, 114d, 245), **Vin** (185), **vin** (51b), **win** (9d, 52a, 94b), **Yin** (26d), **yin** (107c, 134a)

I O _   **ioa** (51c), **IOC** (240), **iod-** (93b), **I.O.M.** (240), **Ion** (13b, 26a, 40a, 86d), **-ior** (40d, 117a), **IOU** (95a, 240), **I.O.W.** (240)

I _ O   **iao** (60d), **Ibo** (68c, 220), **ido** (14d, 41c), **ILO** (239), **Ino** (15b, 23a), **iso-** (92d, 93c), **ITO** (240), **Ito** (65b), **Ivo** (159), **iyo** (10b, 88c)

_ I O   **bio** (71d), **bio-** (93b), **bio.** (31b, 236), **CIO** (236), **mio** (113a), **rio** (113a, 246), **tio** (113a)

I P _   **IPA** (240)

I _ P   **imp** (34d, 97d, 101c, 126d), **imp.** (239)

_ I P   **dip** (23d, 62a, 88d, 104d), **hip** (44a, 66c, 102a, 102b), **kip** (18a, 57c, 59d, 218, 246), **lip** (39c, 47b, 62c, 100d), **lip-** (92d), **nip** (19c, 38a, 62a, 89b), **Pip** (35c), **pip** (13c, 92a, 106b, 114a), **RIP** (242), **Rip** (177), **rip** (68b, 99c, 120a), **sip** (37d, 38a, 119d), **tip** (40d, 56a, 60b, 60d, 90c, 122a), **VIP** (35d, 244), **yip** (17b, 37b, 134c), **zip** (40d, 128b, 244)

I R _   **IRA** (64a, 240), **Ira** (159, 197), **IRC** (240), **Ire.** (240), **ire** (12c, 26d, 52c, 97b, 134a), **irk** (12d, 87c, 128b), **irr.** (240), **IRS** (120a, 240)

I _ R   **-ier** (40d, 117a, 117b), **ihr** (54b), **-ior** (40d, 117a), **irr.** (240), **Isr.** (240)

_ I R   **air** (14b, 22a, 34d, 36c, 43a, 45a, 74c, 75d, 76d, 95d, 115a, 125a), **cir.** (237), **dir.** (237), **fir** (16d, 30a, 42a, 124a), **mir** (103a), **pir** (80c), **sir** (68a, 120c, 122c), **tir** (51a, 108c), **vir** (69d)

I S _   **Isa.** (240), **Ise** (60d), **-ise** (117a, 117c), **-ish** (117a), **isl.** (240), **-ism** (117b), **iso-** (92d, 93c), **Isr.** (240), **-ist** (117a, 117b), **is't** (107c)

I _ S   **IAS** (239), **-ics** (117c), **IDs** (95b), **ids** (51b), **ifs** (30b), **IHS** (239), **ils** (49d, 51a), **INS** (239), **ins** (83c), **IRS** (120a, 240), **its** (95a), **it's** (30c), **ius** (70a)

_ I S   **ais** (110d), **bis** (10c, 50b, 70b, 78c, 99d), **Dis** (57a, 90c, 126b, 199), **dis-** (92c), **eis** (53d), **Gls** (111c), **his** (95a), **lis** (49a, 50c), **mis-** (92c, 94a), **Nis** (30b), **sis** (44b, 54c, 99b), **'tis** (30b, 107c), **vis** (69d, 70a), **Wis.** (212, 244)

I T _   **-ite** (117a, 117b), **ita** (70a), **ITC** (240), **Ith** (25c), **ITO** (240), **Ito** (65b), **its** (95a), **it's** (30c), **Itt** (10a)

I _ T   **int.** (239), **is't** (107c), **-ist** (117a, 117b), **Itt** (10a)

_ I T   **ait** (64b, 101a), **bit** (23d, 37d, 67b, 78d, 86d, 122d, 125c, 131c), **cit.** (237), **fit** (9c, 10a, 13d, 41b, 75b, 86c, 95b, 96b, 112a, 113b, 117d, 119c), **hit** (15a, 15c, 18c, 28b, 116b), **kit** (85b), **lit** (62a, 68d), **lit.** (31b), **mit** (54a), **NIT** (241), **nit** (39d, 246), **pit** (42b, 106b, 120d), **rit.** (110d, 242), **sit** (75d, 87d, 91d, 107a), **tit** (19a, 226), **wit** (36a, 61c, 66d, 129a)

I U _   **IUD** (240), **ius** (70a)

I _ U   **ICU** (239), **IOU** (95a, 240)

_ I U   **niu** (246), **piu** (234), **Tiu** (53c, 125d)

I V _   **iva** (75a), **I've** (30c), **Ivo** (159), **Ivy** (159), **ivy** (28a, 31d, 128b)

_ I V	**civ.** (237), **div.** (237), **Liv** (166)
I W _	**iwa** (51c), **IWW** (240)
I _ W	**I.O.W.** (240), **IWW** (240)
_ I X	**Bix** (141), **Dix** (49a), **fix** (10a, 12c, 14c, 15c, 31a, 35d, 55c, 60c, 75d, 81b, 92b, 94a, 99c, 122a), **Mix** (171), **mix** (11c, 76a, 115c), **nix** (82c, 130b), **pix** (242), **six** (57c), **tix** (243), **vix** (70a)
I Y _	**iyo** (10b, 88c)
I _ Y	**icy** (19c, 53b), **IGY** (239), **Ivy** (159), **ivy** (28a, 31d, 128b)
_ I Y	**DIY** (237)
_ I Z	**Liz** (166), **viz** (80d), **wiz** (74a)
J A _	**jab** (60b, 90d, 96a, 132d), **jag** (95c), **Jam.** (240), **jam** (35d, 85b, 94b, 115d, 122a), **Jan** (160), **Jan.** (78c, 240), **Jap.** (240), **jar** (27d, 30b, 56a, 107b), **Jas.** (74d), **Jat** (96a), **jaw** (75b), **Jay** (160), **jay** (19b, 71c, 225)
J B _	**JBS** (240)
J _ B	**jab** (60b, 90d, 96a, 132d), **J.E.B.** (159), **jib** (103b), **Job** (196), **job** (27a, 119d, 133c)
J C _	**JCS** (240), **jct.** (240)
J D _	**JDL** (240)
J E _	**J.E.B.** (159), **Jer.** (240), **jet** (11a, 19d, 114b), **jeu** (50b), **Jew** (59a)
J _ E	**Joe** (161), **joe** (45a)
J _ G	**jag** (95c), **jig** (33b), **jog** (66d, 82d, 124d), **jug** (89c, 94d)
J H _	**JHS** (240)
J I _	**jib** (103b), **jig** (33b), **Jim** (161), **jim** (11d)
_ J I	**uji** (109c)
J _ L	**JDL** (240), **Jul.** (78c, 240)
J M _	**J.M.W.** (159)
J _ M	**Jam.** (240), **jam** (35d, 85b, 94b, 115d, 122a), **Jim** (161), **jim** (11d)
J _ N	**Jan** (160), **Jan.** (78c, 240), **Jon** (163), **Jun.** (78c, 240), **jun** (218)
J O _	**Job** (196), **job** (27a, 119d, 133c), **Joe** (161), **joe** (45a), **jog** (66d, 82d, 124d), **Jon** (163), **Jos.** (74d), **jot** (64a, 86d, 122c, 131c), **joy** (34c)

J _ P   Jap. (240)

J R _   J.R.R. (159)

J _ R   jar (27d, 30b, 56a, 107b), Jer. (240), J.R.R. (159)

J _ S   Jas. (74d), JBS (240), JCS (240), JHS (240), Jos. (74d), jus (50c, 70b)

J _ T   Jat (96a), jct. (240), jet (11a, 19d, 114b), jot (64a, 86d, 122c, 131c), jut (95a)

J U _   jug (89c, 94d), Jul. (78c, 240), Jun. (78c, 240), jun (218), jus (50c, 70b), jut (95a)

J _ U   jeu (50b)

_ J V   KJV (240)

J _ W   jaw (75b), Jew (59a), J.M.W. (159)

J _ Y   Jay (160), jay (19b, 71c, 225), joy (34c)

K A _   Kaa (67a), kae (65b), kaf (11d, 12a), Kai (163), kal (46c), Kan. (210, 240), kan (246), Kaw (121d), Kay (14d, 102c, 164)

K _ A   Kaa (67a), Kea (64c), kea (19a, 86d, 225), Kha (69a), kha (11d), KIA (240), kra (73b), Kwa (69a, 223)

_ K A   aka (81c, 235), oka (125a, 133c, 246), ska (65b)

K _ B   KGB (103c, 240), kob (13a, 130b)

_ K C   AKC (235)

K _ D   kid (26c, 54d, 70d, 90d, 134d)

_ K D   ok'd (13d)

K E _   Kea (64c), kea (19a, 86d, 225), kef (13d, 58b), keg (24c), Ken (17a, 164), ken (65d, 104d, 126b, 246), ker- (93d), ket- (93b), Key (164), key (25c, 28d, 64b, 68d, 89c)

K _ E   kae (65b)

_ K E   eke (54b), Ike (94b, 159), oke (246)

K _ F   kaf (11d, 12a), kef (13d, 58b)

K G _   KGB (103c, 240)

K _ G   keg (24c)

_ K G   EKG (238)

K H _	Kha (69a), kha (11d)
K _ H	kph (240), kwh (240)
K I _	KIA (240), kid (26c, 54d, 70d, 90d, 134d), kil (64a), Kim (67d, 164), kin (26d, 63c, 68c, 99b, 246), kip (18a, 57c, 59d, 218, 246), kit (85b)
K _ I	Kai (163), koi (24b, 46d), Kui (67b)
_ K I	ski (104d, 110b)
K J _	KJV (240)
K _ L	kal (46c), kil (64a), Kol (18c)
K _ M	Kim (67d, 164)
K _ N	Kan. (210, 240), kan (246), Ken (17a, 164), ken (65d, 104d, 126b, 246), kin (26d, 63c, 68c, 99b, 246), kon (246)
K O _	kob (13a, 130b), koi (24b, 46d), Kol (18c), kon (246), kop (59d), Kor (60d), Kos (60b, 64c)
_ K O	TKO (21b, 243)
K P _	kph (240)
K _ P	kip (18a, 57c, 59d, 218, 246), kop (59d), kup (246)
K R _	kra (73b), Kru (215, 218)
_ K R	ker- (93d), Kor (60d)
K _ S	Kos (60b, 64c)
_ K S	ok's (13d)
K _ T	ket- (93b), kit (85b)
_ K T	Skt. (243)
K U _	Kui (67b), kup (246)
K _ U	Kru (215, 218)
_ K U	aku (46d)
K _ V	KJV (240)
K W _	Kwa (69a, 223), kwh (240)
K _ W	Kaw (121d)
_ K W	ckw (237)

277

K _ Y   Kay (14d, 102c, 164), Key (164), key (25c, 28d, 64b, 68d, 89c)

_ K Y   sky (46c)

L A _   Lab. (240), lab (104d), lac (43c, 99d, 108a, 127b), lad (21c, 45b, 74c, 116c, 134d), Lae (221), lag (34c, 115a), Lai (69a, 220), lai (119b), Lam. (240), lam (11d, 47c), lan (31b, 118c), Lao (62d, 69a, 218), lap (26c, 27b, 31b, 97b, 100d, 113d, 123c), lar (54b, 74b), las (50a, 112c), Lat. (240), lat (29a), lav. (240), law (23d, 28d, 33a, 39c, 67c, 71a, 84c, 92b, 102d, 115a), lax (39b, 73a, 81b, 99c, 111c), lay (16c, 75c, 82a, 96c, 106b, 111d), laz (25a)

L _ A   Lea (21c, 165), lea (45d, 75b, 87a, 134b), Loa (57b), loa (10c, 43c, 133d)

_ L A   Ala. (209, 235), ala (16c, 132c), a la (9c), ela (56d, 82c), Fla. (209, 238), ILA (239), lla (17a), -ula (117b)

L B _   lbs. (240)

L _ B   Lab. (240), lab (104d), Leb. (240), Lib. (240), lib (49b), lob (77a, 120c, 121d)

_ L B   Alb. (235), alb (52d, 128a)

L C _   LCD (240), LCM (240)

L _ C   lac (43c, 99d, 108a, 127b), loc. (240)

_ L C   SLC (243), TLC (243)

L D _   LDS (240)

L _ D   lad (21c, 45b, 74c, 116c, 134d), LCD (240), LED (240), led (46c, 89c), lid (123a), LSD (240), LTD (240), Lud (108a)

_ L D   eld (12c, 73a, 83d, 122b), old (10d, 12c, 60c, 94c, 127d)

L E _   Lea (21c, 165), lea (45d, 75b, 87a, 134b), Leb. (240), LED (240), led (46c, 89c), Lee (27c, 165), lee (108a), leg (31b, 72a, 106b, 124b), lei (52d, 58c), lek (31c, 36c, 213), LEM (78c, 127c, 240), Len (166), Leo (76c, 91b, 135c, 166, 207), leo (72b), Ler (22b, 199), Les (166), les (50a), let (11c, 60b, 87d, 99c, 104a, 117a, 120c), leu (221), Lev. (240), lev (214), lev- (93b), Lew (166), lex (70b)

L _ E   Lae (221), Lee (27c, 165), lee (108a), lge. (240), lie (44a, 55a, 98b, 99d, 119b, 119d), lye (11b)

_ L E   ale (18a, 72b, 95d), ile (50c), ile- (93b), Ole (173), ole (22c, 26b, 112c), ule (21c, 25a, 102c), -ule (117b)

_ L F   Alf (120b, 137), elf (44a, 114a)

L G _   lge. (240)

L _ G	**lag** (34c, 115a), **leg** (31b, 72a, 106b, 124b), **log** (52a, 98c, 246), **log.** (240), **lug** (24c, 37c, 39a, 57d, 103b)
_ L G	**Alg.** (235), **alg.** (31b)
L I _	**Lib.** (240), **lib** (49b), **lid** (123a), **lie** (44a, 55a, 98b, 99d, 119b, 119d), **Li'l** (9a), **Lin** (134d), **lip** (39c, 47b, 62c, 100d), **lip-** (92d), **lis** (49a, 50c), **lit** (62a, 68d), **lit.** (31b), **Liv** (166), **Liz** (166)
L _ I	**Lai** (69a, 220), **lai** (119b), **lei** (52d, 58c), **loi** (50c)
_ L I	**Ali** (23b, 44d, 72b, 77c, 80c, 125b, 138), **CLI** (237), **Eli** (104a, 134a, 151, 197)
L _ K	**lek** (31c, 36c, 213)
_ L K	**elk** (21c, 70d, 129d, 230), **ilk** (27d, 67c, 105a, 113b)
L _ L	**Li'l** (9a)
_ L L	**all** (10d, 29c, 123b, 127c), **ell** (12d, 22c, 28b, 246), **I'll** (30c), **Ill.** (210, 239), **ill** (91b, 126b, 126c)
L _ M	**Lam.** (240), **lam** (11d, 47c), **LCM** (240), **LEM** (78c, 127c, 240), **Lom** (167)
_ L M	**elm** (124a), **Ulm** (33c, 216)
L _ N	**Ian** (31b, 118c), **Len** (166), **Lin** (134d), **Lon** (167), **Ion.** (240), **LPN** (240)
L O _	**Loa** (57b), **loa** (10c, 43c, 133d), **lob** (77a, 120c, 121d), **loc.** (240), **log** (52a, 98c, 246), **log.** (240), **loi** (50c), **Lom** (167), **Lon** (167), **Ion.** (240), **loo** (24a), **lop** (27a, 33a, 108d), **loq** (70a), **loq.** (240), **los** (112c), **Lot** (9b, 58a, 197), **lot** (11c, 14c, 25d, 44d, 86c, 90b, 107c, 123c, 246), **Lou** (167), **low** (12d, 17b, 35a, 54c, 62a), **lox** (52a, 103d), **Loy** (167), **loy** (112c, 123a)
L _ O	**Lao** (62d, 69a, 218), **Leo** (76c, 91b, 135c, 166, 207), **leo** (72b), **loo** (24a), **Luo** (218)
_ L O	**DLO** (237), **Flo** (12c), **ILO** (239), **PLO** (242)
L P _	**LPN** (240)
L _ P	**lap** (26c, 27b, 31b, 97b, 100d, 113d, 123c), **lip** (39c, 47b, 62c, 100d), **lip-** (92d), **lop** (27a, 33a, 108d)
_ L P	**alp** (79b, 87b)
L _ Q	**loq** (70a), **loq.** (240)
L _ R	**lar** (54b, 74b), **Ler** (22b, 199)
_ L R	**SLR** (243)

L S _   **LSD** (240)

L _ S   **las** (50a, 112c), **lbs.** (240), **LDS** (240), **Les** (166), **les** (50a), **lis** (49a, 50c), **los** (112c), **lys** (71d), **lys-** (93a)

_ L S   **ALS** (235), **als** (54a), **BLS** (236), **Els** (151), **els** (73a), **ils** (49d, 51a)

L T _   **Ltd.** (240)

L _ T   **Lat.** (240), **lat** (29a), **let** (11c, 60b, 87d, 99c, 104a, 117a, 120c), **lit** (62a, 68d), **lit.** (31b), **Lot** (9b, 58a, 197), **lot** (11c, 14c, 25d, 44d, 86c, 90b, 107c, 123c, 246), **Lut** (35a)

_ L T   **alt** (54a), **blt** (236), **Olt** (33c)

L U _   **Lud** (108a), **lug** (24c, 37c, 39a, 57d, 103b), **Luo** (218), **Lut** (35a), **Lux** (240), **lux** (62a, 246)

L _ U   **leu** (221), **Lou** (167)

_ L U   **Clu** (146), **flu** (62a), **Ulu** (184), **ulu** (63d, 68a)

L _ V   **lav.** (240), **Lev.** (240), **lev** (214), **lev-** (93b), **Liv** (166), **LWV** (240)

L W _   **LWV** (240)

L _ W   **law** (23d, 28d, 33a, 39c, 67c, 71a, 84c, 92b, 102d, 115a), **Lew** (166), **low** (12d, 17b, 35a, 54c, 62a)

L _ X   **lax** (39b, 73a, 81b, 99c, 111c), **lex** (70b), **lox** (52a, 103d), **Lux** (240), **lux** (62a, 246)

L Y _   **lye** (11b), **lys** (71d), **lys-** (93a)

L _ Y   **lay** (16c, 75c, 82a, 96c, 106b, 111d), **Loy** (167), **loy** (112c, 123a)

_ L Y   **Bly** (142), **Ely** (25a), **fly** (47c, 63b, 120c, 229), **ply** (48a, 70c, 121a, 131d, 133c), **Sly** (181), **sly** (14d, 31d, 32c, 52c, 63b, 101c, 110c, 132a)

L _ Z   **laz** (25a), **Liz** (166)

M A _   **maa** (107d), **Mab** (44a, 96c), **Mac** (167), **mac** (45b, 74c, 105b, 111d), **mad** (12d, 63b, 109c), **Mae** (167), **mag** (57c), **mag.** (240), **mai** (49d), **Maj.** (240), **Mal.** (240), **mal** (42b, 50b, 112d), **mal-** (92c), **Man** (64b, 168, 224), **man** (49a, 52c, 74c, 231), **Mao** (26d), **map** (24c, 26b), **Mar.** (78c, 240), **mar** (36b, 62a, 63a, 105c), **mas** (112d), **mat** (47d, 88d, 119c), **maw** (31d, 32a, 56d, 84b, 91b, 115c), **Max** (169), **Max.** (240), **max** (78d), **May** (24a, 169), **may** (58c, 76d)

M _ A   **maa** (107d), **MBA** (240), **MIA** (240), **Mia** (170), **mia** (113a), **mna** (246), **moa** (19b, 226)

_ M A   **AMA** (235), **ama** (23d, 25d, 27b, 29b, 32b, 132c), **-oma** (117c), **sma** (105b), **Uma** (184), **Yma** (187)

M B _   **MBA** (240)

M _ B   **Mab** (44a, 96c), **mib** (11c, 74d), **mob** (97a, 121c, 232)

_ M B   **amb.** (235), **emb.** (238)

M C _   **MCP** (240)

M _ C   **Mac** (167), **mac** (45b, 74c, 105b, 111d), **Mic.** (240)

_ M C   **AMC** (26a)

M D _   **MDs** (88d), **MDT** (240)

M _ D   **mad** (12d, 63b, 109c), **Med.** (240), **Mfd.** (240), **mid** (12b, 25c, 57c), **mod** (30b), **mod.** (240), **mud** (39a, 99c, 104c, 110b, 246)

M E _   **Med.** (240), **Meg** (11a, 170), **meg-** (93b), **Mel** (170), **mel** (60d), **mem** (12a), **Men** (88d), **men** (87d, 124c), **Meo** (218, 224), **mer** (51a), **mes** (49d), **Met.** (240), **met** (40d, 97d, 107a), **met-** (92d), **mew** (19a, 25a, 45a, 56d, 58c, 105d, 106a, 226), **Mex.** (240)

M _ E   **Mae** (167), **Mme.** (240), **Moe** (121c, 171)

_ M E   **ame** (51a), **eme** (105c), **Mme.** (240), **ume** (13d, 65b)

M F _   **Mfd.** (240), **Mfg.** (240), **Mfr.** (240)

_ M F   **IMF** (239)

M _ G   **mag** (57c), **mag.** (240), **Meg** (11a, 170), **meg-** (93b), **Mfg.** (240), **mig** (11c, 74d, 89d), **mpg** (241), **mug** (38a, 52c, 128a)

M H _   **mho** (40a, 246)

M _ H   **mph** (241)

M I _   **MIA** (240), **Mia** (170), **mia** (113a), **mib** (11c, 74d), **Mic.** (240), **mid** (12b, 25c, 57c), **mig** (11c, 74d, 89d), **mil** (62c, 121b, 132d, 246), **mil.** (240), **mim** (11d), **Min** (215), **min.** (240), **mio** (113a), **mir** (103a), **mis-** (92c, 94a), **mit** (54a), **Mix** (171), **mix** (11c, 76a, 115c)

M _ I   **mai** (49d), **moi** (50d)

_ M I   **ami** (50b), **BMI** (236), **EMI** (238), **NMI** (241)

M _ J   **Maj.** (240)

M _ L   **Mal.** (240), **mal** (42b, 50b, 112d), **mal-** (92c), **Mel** (170), **mel** (60d), **mil** (62c, 121b, 132d, 246), **mil.** (240)

M M _	**Mme.** (240)
M _ M	**mem** (12a), **mim** (11d), **mom** (44b), **mum** (27a, 74a)
M N _	**mna** (246)
M _ N	**Man** (64b, 168, 224), **man** (49a, 52c, 74c, 231), **Men** (88d), **men** (87d, 124c), **Min** (215), **min.** (240), **Mon.** (240), **mon** (16b)
M O _	**moa** (19b, 226), **mob** (97a, 121c, 232), **mod** (30b), **mod.** (240), **Moe** (121c, 171), **moi** (50d), **mom** (44b), **Mon.** (240), **mon** (16b), **moo** (12d, 73c), **mop** (118b), **mot** (99c, 133a), **mou** (246), **mow** (28a, 33a)
M _ O	**Mao** (26d), **Meo** (218, 224), **mho** (40a, 246), **mio** (113a), **moo** (12d, 73c)
_ M O	**amo** (69d), **HMO** (239)
M P _	**mpg** (241), **mph** (241)
M _ P	**map** (24c, 26b), **MCP** (240), **mop** (118b), **MVP** (241)
_ M P	**amp.** (40a, 235), **emp.** (238), **imp** (34d, 97d, 101c, 126d), **imp.** (239)
M R _	**Mrs.** (122c, 241), **Mru** (69a)
M _ R	**Mar.** (78c, 240), **mar** (36b, 62a, 63a, 105c), **mer** (51a), **Mfr.** (240), **mir** (103a), **mur** (51b)
M S _	**mss.** (241), **MST** (241)
M _ S	**mas** (112d), **MDs** (88d), **mes** (49d), **mis-** (92c, 94a), **Mrs.** (122c, 241), **mss.** (241), **Mts.** (241), **mus.** (241)
_ M S	**Ems** (95c, 112c), **HMS** (239), **PMS** (242), **rms.** (242)
M T _	**Mts.** (241), **MTV** (26a)
M _ T	**mat** (47d, 88d, 119c), **MDT** (240), **Met.** (240), **met** (40d, 97d, 107a), **met-** (92d), **mit** (54a), **mot** (99c, 133a), **MST** (241), **Mut** (12b, 97a)
_ M T	**amt** (31b), **amt.** (235), **GMT** (239)
M U _	**mud** (39a, 99c, 104c, 110b, 246), **mug** (38a, 52c, 128a), **mum** (27a, 74a), **mur** (51b), **mus.** (241), **Mut** (12b, 97a), **muy** (113a)
M _ U	**mou** (246), **Mru** (69a)
_ M U	**Amu** (33d), **emu** (19b, 85a, 225), **SMU** (33a)
M V _	**MVP** (241)
M _ V	**MTV** (26a)

_ M V	**DMV** (237)
M _ W	**maw** (31d, 32a, 56d, 84b, 91b, 115c), **mew** (19a, 25a, 45a, 56d, 58c, 105d, 106a, 226), **mow** (28a, 33a)
_ M W	**J.M.W.** (159), **UMW** (243)
M _ X	**Max** (169), **Max.** (240), **max** (78d), **Mex.** (240), **Mix** (171), **mix** (11c, 76a, 115c), **myx-** (93b)
_ M X	**BMX** (236)
M Y _	**myx-** (93b)
M _ Y	**May** (24a, 169), **may** (58c, 76d), **muy** (113a)
_ M Y	**Amy** (11a, 73c, 138)
_ M Z	**DMZ** (237)
N A _	**nab** (14c, 24a, 24d, 106c), **nae** (105b), **nag** (21b, 58a, 61a, 133d), **Nah.** (241), **Nan** (20c), **nap** (89a, 109a, 110b), **NAS** (241), **nas-** (93b), **Nat** (172), **nav.** (241), **nay** (22d, 34d, 81b, 129c)
N _ A	**NBA** (241), **NDA** (241), **NEA** (241), **NRA** (20b, 241), **NSA** (241)
_ N A	**ana** (12c, 29a, 72c), **-ana** (117c), **DNA** (53b, 98b, 237), **Ena** (11b, 96c), **Ina** (159), **-ina** (117b), **mna** (246), **RNA** (53b, 242), **sna** (105b), **Una** (43d, 113c, 184)
N B _	**NBA** (241), **NBC** (26a, 241), **NbE** (29c), **NBS** (241), **NbW** (29c)
N _ B	**nab** (14c, 24a, 24d, 106c), **Neb.** (241), **neb** (17d, 18d, 19b, 87d), **nib** (17d, 19b, 87d), **nob** (32a, 58c, 65b), **nub** (54c, 73c, 74b, 89c, 95c)
N C _	**NCO** (241)
N _ C	**NBC** (26a, 241), **NRC** (241), **NSC** (241), **NYC** (18d, 241)
_ N C	**anc.** (235), **DNC** (237), **enc.** (238), **Inc.** (239), **RNC** (242)
N D _	**NDA** (241)
N _ D	**Ned** (172), **Nod** (23a, 39b), **nod** (38b, 110b)
_ N D	**and** (30a, 90c), **end** (10d, 32c, 54d, 90c, 96c, 99c, 115d, 122b), **end-** (94a), **Ind.** (91a, 210, 239), **und** (53c)
N E _	**NEA** (241), **Neb.** (241), **neb** (17d, 18d, 19b, 87d), **Ned** (172), **nee** (19b, 21a, 74b), **nef** (28b, 108b), **neg.** (241), **Neh.** (241), **neo** (77c), **neo-** (93b), **nep** (28c, 45d, 68c, 133c), **Ner** (104c), **net** (24a, 27d, 41a, 43b, 76a, 94d, 106b, 111b, 120c), **neu** (54a), **Nev.** (211, 241), **new** (13a, 43c, 51b, 84d, 98b), **Ney** (49d, 80d, 172), **nez** (50d)

N _ E   nae (105b), NbE (29c), nee (19b, 21a, 74b), nie (54a), NNE (29c), nue (50a)

_ N E   ane (50b), ENE (29c), Ine (12c), -ine (117a, 117b), NNE (29c), one (61d, 62d, 95a, 109d, 126c), une (49d, 50a, 50d)

N F _   NFL (241)

N _ F   nef (28b, 108b), NSF (241)

N _ G   nag (21b, 58a, 61a, 133d), neg. (241), nig (28d), nog (11b, 20a, 37d, 39d, 77a, 87c, 89b)

_ N G   Ang. (235), Eng (109a), Eng. (238), Ing (12c), ing (73c, 87a), -ing (86d, 117c)

N H _   NHI (241), NHL (241), NHS (241)

N _ H   Nah. (241), Neh. (241), nth (34c)

N I _   nib (17d, 19b, 87d), nie (54a), nig (28d), -nik (117c), nil (82c), Nin (172), nin (246), nip (19c, 38a, 62a, 89b), Nis (30b), NIT (241), nit (39d, 246), niu (246), nix (82c, 130b)

N _ I   NHI (241), NMI (241)

_ N I   ani (19b, 19d, 32c), ONI (241), uni- (93c)

N _ K   -nik (117c)

_ N K   ink (33c, 94b, 109b)

N _ L   NFL (241), NHL (241), nil (82c)

_ N L   enl. (238)

N M _   NMI (241)

N _ M   nom (50d), Num. (241), Nym (44a, 194)

N N _   NNE (29c), NNW (29c)

N _ N   Nan (20c), Nin (172), nin (246), non (50d, 70a), non- (93b), Nun (197), nun (11d, 12a, 22c, 89a, 99b, 109d)

_ N N   Ann (138), CNN (26a), Inn (33c), inn (56d, 61c, 101a, 120a)

N O _   nob (32a, 58c, 65b), Nod (23a, 39b), nod (38b, 110b), nog (11b, 20a, 37d, 39d, 77a, 87c, 89b), nom (50d), non (50d, 70a), non- (93b), Nor. (241), nor (12c, 30a, 31a), nos (70b), nos- (92d), nos. (241), not (81b), Nov. (78c, 241), NOW (241), now (49a, 62a, 94a)

N _ O   NCO (241), neo (77c), neo- (93b)

_ N O   CNO (237), **Eno** (151), **Ino** (15b, 23a), **Ono** (173), **ono** (241), **SNO** (243), **uno** (65c, 112c)

N P _   NPR (241)

N _ P   nap (89a, 109a, 110b), **nep** (28c, 45d, 68c, 133c), **nip** (19c, 38a, 62a, 89b)

_ N P   GNP (239)

N R _   NRA (20b, 241), **NRC** (241)

N _ R   Ner (104c), **Nor.** (241), **nor** (12c, 30a, 31a), **NPR** (241)

N S _   NSA (241), **NSC** (241), **NSF** (241), **NSW** (241)

N _ S   NAS (241), **nas-** (93b), **NBS** (241), **NHS** (241), **Nis** (30b), **nos** (70b), **nos-** (92d), **nos.** (241)

_ N S   CNS (237), **ens** (18b), **ens.** (238), **HNS** (239), **INS** (239), **ins** (83c), **ons** (32a, 118d, 246), **uns** (54a)

N T _   nth (34c)

N _ T   Nat (172), **net** (24a, 27d, 41a, 43b, 76a, 94d, 106b, 111b, 120c), **NIT** (241), **nit** (39d, 246), **not** (81b), **Nut** (198), **nut** (22c, 28c, 31d, 44c, 51d, 67b, 121b), **NWT** (241)

_ N T   Ant (139), **ant** (40c, 49a, 63b, 89c, 229), **ent-** (94a), **-ent** (117a, 117b), **int.** (239), **Ont.** (241), **on't** (107c), **TNT** (26a, 43a, 243)

N U _   nub (54c, 73c, 74b, 89c, 95c), **nue** (50a), **Num.** (241), **Nun** (197), **nun** (11d, 12a, 22c, 89a, 99b, 109d), **Nut** (198), **nut** (22c, 28c, 31d, 44c, 51d, 67b, 121b)

N _ U   neu (54a), **niu** (246)

_ N U   anu (59c, 125a), **gnu** (13a, 132a, 230)

N _ V   nav. (241), **Nev.** (211, 241), **Nov.** (78c, 241)

N W _   NWT (241)

N _ W   NbW (29c), **new** (13a, 43c, 51b, 84d, 98b), **NNW** (29c), **NOW** (241), **now** (49a, 62a, 94a), **NSW** (241)

_ N W   NNW (29c), **WNW** (29c)

N _ X   nix (82c, 130b), **Nyx** (56b, 198)

N Y _   NYC (18d, 241), **Nym** (44a, 194), **Nyx** (56b, 198)

N _ Y   nay (22d, 34d, 81b, 129c), **Ney** (49d, 80d, 172)

_ N Y   any (111d), **sny** (18c, 32d, 90a, 108b, 122a)

N _ Z   **nez** (50d)

O A _   **oaf** (21a, 37b, 38c, 109c, 116d, 134d), **oak** (58a, 124a), **oar** (95b, 102c), **OAS** (241), **oat** (16a, 25c, 55c), **OAU** (241)

O _ A   **OCA** (241), **oca** (39c, 125a, 133c), **oda** (58a), **oka** (125a, 133c, 246), **-oma** (117c), **ora** (65c, 78a, 95a), **ora-** (93c), **ova** (39d), **oxa-** (93c)

_ O A   **boa** (30b, 45a, 81b, 96c, 104c, 106d, 111a, 232), **DOA** (237), **Goa** (91d), **goa** (53b), **ioa** (51c), **Loa** (57b), **loa** (10c, 43c, 133d), **moa** (19b, 226), **poa** (20b, 55d), **toa** (18a), **VOA** (244), **zoa** (39d)

O B _   **OBE** (241), **obe** (68b), **obi** (45c, 54c, 65d, 104b), **obj.** (241), **obo** (106c, 241), **obs.** (241)

O _ B   **OOB** (241), **orb** (43c, 54d, 113c), **OTB** (52b, 241)

_ O B   **Bob** (142), **bob** (47a, 79c, 87c), **cob** (25c, 61a, 74c, 118b), **fob** (48a, 130a), **gob** (75b, 103b), **hob** (33c, 46b, 95a, 123a), **Job** (196), **job** (27a, 119d, 133c), **kob** (13a, 130b), **lob** (77a, 120c, 121d), **mob** (97a, 121c, 232), **nob** (32a, 58c, 65b), **OOB** (241), **Rob** (177), **rob** (36c, 37a, 90c, 115a), **sob** (32b, 131a), **tob** (10c)

O C _   **OCA** (241), **oca** (39c, 125a, 133c), **och** (11a, 42c), **ock** (246), **-ock** (117b), **OCS** (241), **Oct.** (78c, 241), **oct-** (92d)

O _ C   **orc** (25d, 55d, 131b), **OTC** (241)

_ O C   **Doc** (88d, 107a, 149), **doc.** (237), **hoc** (70a), **IOC** (240), **loc.** (240), **ROC** (242), **Roc** (19b, 109c), **soc** (67c), **soc.** (243)

O D _   **oda** (58a), **odd** (116a, 126c, 126d), **ode** (61d, 89b, 90c)

O _ D   **odd** (116a, 126c, 126d), **OED** (241), **-oid** (117b), **ok'd** (13d), **old** (10d, 12c, 60c, 94c, 127d), **Ord** (23b, 49a), **oud** (80b)

_ O D   **COD** (237), **Cod** (24a), **cod** (46d, 228), **DOD** (237), **dod** (27d), **fod** (246), **God** (66b), **god** (34c, 133d), **hod** (21d, 28c, 78d, 105c), **iod-** (93b), **mod** (30b), **mod.** (240), **Nod** (23a, 39b), **nod** (38b, 110b), **pod** (61c, 71b, 105d, 131b, 232), **Rod** (178), **rod** (17a, 57c, 68d, 100b, 107b, 114b, 115b, 246), **sod** (118b, 125a), **Tod** (183), **tod** (22d, 105a, 246), **Vod** (16d), **yod** (12a)

O E _   **OED** (241), **OEO** (241), **o'er** (30b, 107c)

O _ E   **OBE** (241), **obe** (68b), **ode** (61d, 89b, 90c), **oke** (246), **Ole** (173), **ole** (22c, 26b, 112c), **one** (61d, 62d, 95a, 109d, 126c), **ope** (126a), **Ore.** (211, 241), **ore** (32b, 35a, 76b, 77a, 82b, 87b, 118c, 215, 220, 222), **-ose** (117a, 117b), **owe** (34a)

_ O E   **Coe** (146, 201), **coe** (107d), **DOE** (237), **doe** (34b, 97a), **EOE** (238), **FOE** (238), **foe** (84c), **hoe** (32c, 52d), **Joe** (161), **joe** (45a), **Moe**

(121c, 171), **Poe** (98a, 125b, 175), **poe** (86d), **roe** (25b, 34b, 34c, 39d, 47a, 60a), **toe** (55b, 110b, 115b), **voe** (63a), **woe** (23a, 56c, 112a), **Zoe** (188)

O F _   **off** (9b, 59b, 79d, 134c), **off.** (241), **oft'** (30b)

O _ F   **oaf** (21a, 37b, 38c, 109c, 116d, 134d), **off** (9b, 59b, 79d, 134c), **off.** (241), **orf** (134b)

O _ G   **org.** (241)

_ O G   **bog** (39a, 75a, 118b), **cog** (53b, 120c, 123a), **dog** (12c, 23d, 32d, 48b, 230), **fog** (28b, 116d, 130d), **Gog** (74a, 197), **hog** (88d, 118d, 230), **jog** (66d, 82d, 124d), **log** (52a, 98c, 246), **log.** (240), **nog** (11b, 20a, 37d, 39d, 77a, 87c, 89b), **tog** (28b)

O H _   **ohm** (40a, 53d, 246), **o-ho** (42c), **ohs** (42c)

O _ H   **och** (11a, 42c)

O I _   **-oid** (117b), **oil** (13a, 52a, 56a)

O _ I   **obi** (45c, 54c, 65d, 104b), **ONI** (241), **oui** (51b), **ovi-** (92d)

_ O I   **hoi** (42c), **koi** (24b, 46d), **loi** (50c), **moi** (50d), **poi** (36b, 58b, 88c, 119d, 121a), **roi** (50c), **toi** (49d, 51b)

O _ J   **obj.** (241)

O K _   **oka** (125a, 133c, 246), **ok'd** (13d), **oke** (246), **ok's** (13d)

O _ K   **oak** (58a, 124a), **ock** (246), **-ock** (117b), **Ork.** (241)

_ O K   **ROK** (68c, 242), **wok** (86a, 128a)

O L _   **old** (10d, 12c, 60c, 94c, 127d), **Ole** (173), **ole** (22c, 26b, 112c), **Olt** (33c)

O _ L   **oil** (13a, 52a, 56a), **owl** (19a, 226)

_ O L   **Bol.** (236), **col** (79b, 87a), **dol.** (238), **Kol** (18c), **Pol.** (242), **pol** (91a), **Sol** (88c, 199), **sol** (117d, 221), **vol.** (244), **wol** (132d)

O M _   **-oma** (117c)

O _ M   **ohm** (40a, 53d, 246)

_ O M   **com-** (94a), **Dom** (79a, 149), **dom** (91d, 122c), **dom.** (238), **I.O.M.** (240), **Lom** (167), **mom** (44b), **nom** (50d), **ROM** (29c, 242), **Rom** (57c), **Tom** (116a, 184), **tom** (74c), **yom** (33d, 67d)

O N _   **one** (61d, 62d, 95a, 109d, 126c), **ONI** (241), **Ono** (173), **ono** (241), **ons** (32a, 118d, 246), **Ont.** (241), **on't** (107c)

O _ N   **own** (9d, 29d)

_ O N bon (45a, 50b, 65d, 67b), con (10c, 26b, 65c, 116c, 118d), Don (101a, 149), don (50b, 130d), eon (10d, 41d, 122b), Fon (214), gon- (93c), Hon. (239), hon (40d), Ion (13b, 26a, 40a, 86d), Jon (163), kon (246), Lon (167), Ion. (240), Mon. (240), mon (16b), non (50d, 70a), non- (93b), Ron (67d, 178), son (59a, 74c), ton (131a, 246), von (53d), won (46c, 128b, 218), yon (36d, 85c)

O O _ OOB (241), oot (105b)

O _ O obo (106c, 241), OEO (241), o-ho (42c), Ono (173), ono (241), oro (112d), oro- (93b), oto- (92d), ovo- (92d)

_ O O boo (36a, 115a), coo (19b), goo (79c, 115b), loo (24a), moo (12d, 73c), Soo (181), soo (97d), too (12c, 18c, 62c, 78c), woo (31b), zoo (132a), zoo- (92c)

O P _ ope (126a), opp. (241), Ops (25c, 58b, 104b, 198), opt (27a), -opy (117c)

O _ P opp. (241)

_ O P bop (60b, 66b, 116b), cop (90d, 97a, 115a), dop (32d), fop (31c, 33c, 38c, 44b), GOP (91a, 99d, 239), hop (33b, 67a), kop (59d), lop (27a, 33a, 108d), mop (118b), pop (38a, 42d, 44b, 44d, 99d), pop. (242), SOP (243), sop (9b, 21d, 29d, 111b), top (31d, 42b, 59d, 85c, 89b, 117d, 118a, 118b, 127c)

_ O Q coq (50a), loq (70a), loq. (240)

O R _ ora (65c, 78a, 95a), ora- (93c), orb (43c, 54d, 113c), orc (25d, 55d, 131b), Ord (23b, 49a), Ore. (211, 241), ore (32b, 35a, 76b, 77a, 82b, 87b, 118c, 215, 220, 222), orf (134b), org. (241), Ork. (241), oro (112d), oro- (93b), Orr (173), ors (12a), ort (48b, 71a), -ory (117a, 117b)

O _ R oar (95b, 102c), o'er (30b, 107c), Orr (173), our (95a)

_ O R Bor (91a), bor. (236), Cor. (237), cor (246), dor (18b, 38a, 38d, 63b, 67a), for (94d), hor. (239), -ior (40d, 117a), Kor (60d), Nor. (241), nor (12c, 30a, 31a), por (112d), Tor (102c), tor (31d, 67c, 87b, 95a, 101b)

O S _ -ose (117a, 117b), OSS (241)

O _ S OAS (241), obs. (241), OCS (241), ohs (42c), ok's (13d), ons (32a, 118d, 246), Ops (25c, 58b, 104b, 198), ors (12a), OSS (241), -ous (117a), ozs. (242)

_ O S cos (71c, 101d), cos. (237), DOS (238), dos (50a, 131d), Eos (15d, 33d, 198), eos (86d), Hos. (239), ho's (70b), Jos. (74d), Kos (60b, 64c), los (112c), nos (70b), nos- (92d), nos. (241), SOS (36d, 243)

O T _ OTB (52b, 241), OTC (241), oto- (92d), Ott (173)

O _ T   oat (16a, 25c, 55c), Oct. (78c, 241), oct- (92d), oft' (30b), Olt (33c),
         Ont. (241), on't (107c), oot (105b), opt (27a), ort (48b, 71a), Ott
         (173), out (9b, 49a, 55b, 82c)

_ O T   bot (69b), bot. (236), cot (18a, 99a, 110c), DOT (238), dot (59d,
         80c, 87d, 113b, 120b), fot (246), got (23b, 83b), hot (12d, 117d), jot
         (64a, 86d, 122c, 131c), Lot (9b, 58a, 197), lot (11c, 14c, 25d, 44d,
         86c, 90b, 107c, 123c, 246), mot (99c, 133a), not (81b), oot (105b),
         pot (90d, 128a, 246), rot (21a, 34a, 45c, 107d, 113d), sot (38b,
         123a, 123b), tot (26c, 134d)

O U _   oud (80b), oui (51b), our (95a), -ous (117a), out (9b, 49a, 55b, 82c)

O _ U   OAU (241)

_ O U   fou (246), IOU (95a, 240), Lou (167), mou (246), sou (49c), tou
         (246), you (95a)

O V _   ova (39d), ovi- (92d), ovo- (92d)

_ O V   HOV (239), Nov. (78c, 241), Sov. (243)

O W _   owe (34a), owl (19a, 226), own (9d, 29d)

_ O W   Bow (142), bow (20c, 32d, 48d, 68c, 82a, 83a, 95c, 108b, 116d),
         cow (21b, 63d, 121c, 230), Dow (66d, 150), how (74c, 76b, 96d),
         I.O.W. (240), low (12d, 17b, 35a, 54c, 62a), mow (28a, 33a), NOW
         (241), now (49a, 62a, 94a), POW (242), row (14b, 46a, 72a, 83a,
         96b, 97d, 122a), sow (88d, 90a, 118d), tow (37c, 59b, 95d), vow
         (90b, 111c), wow (42c), yow (42c)

O X _   oxa- (93c), oxy- (93c)

_ O X   box (30b, 98b, 113a), Cox (147), cox (102c), Fox (153, 189), fox
         (23a, 23d, 54c, 102b, 230), lox (52a, 103d), pox (36a, 118d), sox
         (17c, 98c), vox (70b)

O _ Y   -opy (117c), -ory (117a, 117b), oxy- (93c)

_ O Y   boy (74c, 116c), coy (17c, 109a), Foy (153), goy (82a), Hoy (64d),
         hoy (17b, 20b), joy (34c), Loy (167), loy (112c, 123a), Roy (178),
         soy (17d, 104b), toy (82c, 124c)

O Z _   ozs. (242)

_ O Z   Boz (35c, 87c, 142), doz. (238), Roz (179)

P A _   Pac. (242), pac (57b, 73c), pad (32d, 47d, 48b, 116c, 119a, 123d),
         pah (42c), Pak. (242), PAL (242), pal (29b, 32a, 45b), Pam (173),
         pam (68a), Pan (45d, 55a, 59c, 133b, 198), Pan. (242), pan (18d,
         79c, 128a), pap (48b), Pär (173), Par. (242) par (16a, 41b, 41d,
         55b, 82a, 103a, 114d), pas (33b, 115b), PAT (242), Pat (174), pat
         (88b, 119c, 123b), Pau (39c, 59b, 100a, 216), paw (48b, 57d), pax
         (70a), pay (29c, 36a, 98b, 99c, 103d, 129b), Paz (174)

P _ A   PBA (242), **pea** (28c, 71b, 106b, 127c), **PGA** (242), **Pia** (175), **pia** (14d, 39b), **poa** (20b, 55d), **Psa.** (242), **PTA** (104d, 242), **pua** (59b), **pya** (220)

_ P A   **Apa** (12b), **apa** (21c), **CPA** (237), **EPA** (238), **GPA** (239), **IPA** (240), **spa** (58d, 77a, 100a, 114a, 127a), **WPA** (244)

P B _   PBA (242), **PBK** (242), **PBS** (26a, 242)

P _ B   **pub** (120a)

_ P B   **APB** (235), **CPB** (237)

P C _   **pct.** (242)

P _ C   **Pac.** (242), **pac** (57b, 73c), **pfc** (242), **pic.** (242)

_ P C   **UPC** (243)

P D _   **PDT** (242)

P _ D   **pad** (32d, 47d, 48b, 116c, 119a, 123d), **ped-** (92d, 93a), **Ph.D.** (242), **pod** (61c, 71b, 105d, 131b, 232), **ppd.** (242), **pud** (57d, 87b)

_ P D   **ppd.** (242)

P E _   **pea** (28c, 71b, 106b, 127c), **ped-** (92d, 93a), **peg** (32a, 38a, 44c, 89b), **P.E.I.** (242), **Pei** (174), **pen** (30a, 40d, 62d, 97a, 118b, 134c), **Pep** (174), **pep** (40d, 128b), **Per.** (242), **per** (128b), **pes** (48c), **pet** (24b, 31a, 44d, 48b), **peu** (50c), **pew** (18c, 27a, 47a, 106a)

P _ E   **Pie** (175), **pie** (35b, 125c), **Poe** (98a, 125b, 175), **poe** (86d), **pre** (18b), **pre-** (92c)

_ P E   **ape** (30d, 62a, 77b, 78b, 109c, 231), **ope** (126a)

P F _   **pfc** (242)

P G _   **PGA** (242)

P _ G   **peg** (32a, 38a, 44c, 89b), **pig** (112b, 118d, 231), **pug** (37a, 77d, 227)

_ P G   **mpg** (241), **ZPG** (244)

P H _   **Ph.D.** (242), **phi** (11d)

P _ H   **pah** (42c)

_ P H   **D.Ph.** (238), **Eph.** (238), **kph** (240), **mph** (241)

P I _   **Pia** (175), **pia** (14d, 39b), **pic.** (242), **Pie** (175), **pie** (35b, 125c), **pig** (112b, 118d, 231), **pik** (246), **PIN** (242), **pin** (37c, 44c, 110a, 246), **Pip** (35c), **pip** (13c, 92a, 106b, 114a), **pir** (80c), **pit** (42b, 106b, 120d), **piu** (234), **pix** (242)

P _ I   P.E.I. (242), **Pei** (174), **phi** (11d), **poi** (36b, 58b, 88c, 119d, 121a), **psi** (11d)

_ P I   CPI (237), **epi-** (93c), UPI (81c, 132d, 243)

P _ K   **Pak.** (242), PBK (242), **pik** (246)

P L _   PLO (242), **ply** (48a, 70c, 121a, 131d, 133c)

P _ L   PAL (242), **pal** (29b, 32a, 45b), **Pol.** (242), **pol** (91a), **pul** (213)

_ P L   **Cpl.** (237)

P M _   PMS (242)

P _ M   **Pam** (173), **pam** (68a)

_ P M   **rpm** (242), **wpm** (244)

P _ N   **Pan** (45d, 55a, 59c, 133b, 198), **Pan.** (242), **pan** (18d, 79c, 128a), **pen** (30a, 40d, 62d, 97a, 118b, 134c), PIN (242), **pin** (37c, 44c, 110a, 246), **pun** (90b)

_ P N   LPN (240)

P O _   **poa** (20b, 55d), **pod** (61c, 71b, 105d, 131b, 232), **Poe** (98a, 125b, 175), **poe** (86d), **poi** (36b, 58b, 88c, 119d, 121a), **Pol.** (242), **pol** (91a), **pop** (38a, 42d, 44b, 44d, 99d), **pop.** (242), **por** (112d), **pot** (90d, 128a, 246), POW (242), **pox** (36a, 118d)

P _ O   PLO (242), **pro** (48c, 96d), **pro.** (242), PTO (242), **Pwo** (69a)

_ P O   APO (235), **Apo** (129a), CPO (237), GPO (239)

P P _   **ppd.** (242), PPS (242)

P _ P   **pap** (48b), **Pep** (174), **pep** (40d, 128b), **Pip** (35c), **pip** (13c, 92a, 106b, 114a), **pop** (38a, 42d, 44b, 44d, 99d), **pop.** (242), **pup** (105d, 134d)

_ P P   **opp.** (241)

P R _   **pre** (18b), **pre-** (92c), **pro** (48c, 96d), **pro.** (242), **pry** (71c, 94d)

P _ R   **Pär** (173), **Par.** (242), **par** (16a, 41b, 41d, 55b, 82a, 103a, 114d), **Per.** (242), **per** (128b), **pir** (80c), **por** (112d), **pyr-** (93a)

_ P R   APR (235), **Apr.** (78c), CPR (237), NPR (241)

P S _   **Psa.** (242), **psi** (11d), PST (242)

P _ S   **pas** (33b, 115b), PBS (26a, 242), **pes** (48c), PMS (242), PPS (242), **pus** (63a, 78b)

_ P S   **Ops** (25c, 58b, 104b, 198), PPS (242), UPS (243), **ups** (21a)

P T _   **PTA** (104d, 242), **PTO** (242)

P _ T   **PAT** (242), **Pat** (174), **pat** (88b, 119c, 123b), **pct.** (242), **PDT** (242), **pet** (24b, 31a, 44d, 48b), **pit** (42b, 106b, 120d), **pot** (90d, 128a, 246), **PST** (242), **put** (70c), **Pvt.** (242)

_ P T   **apt** (13d, 22a, 28a, 36c, 47b, 62c, 71d, 88b, 95a, 117d), **DPT** (238), **opt** (27a)

P U _   **pua** (59b), **pub** (120a), **pud** (57d, 87b), **pug** (37a, 77d, 227), **pul** (213), **pun** (90b), **pup** (105d, 134d), **pus** (63a, 78b), **put** (70c)

P _ U   **Pau** (39c, 59b, 100a, 216), **peu** (50c), **piu** (234)

_ P U   **CPU** (237)

P V _   **Pvt.** (242)

P W _   **Pwo** (69a)

P _ W   **paw** (48b, 57d), **pew** (18c, 27a, 47a, 106a), **POW** (242)

_ P W   **DPW** (238)

P _ X   **pax** (70a), **pix** (242), **pox** (36a, 118d), **pyx** (27b, 42a)

P Y _   **pya** (220), **pyr-** (93a), **pyx** (27b, 42a)

P _ Y   **pay** (29c, 36a, 98b, 99c, 103d, 129b), **ply** (48a, 70c, 121a, 131d, 133c), **pry** (71c, 94d)

_ P Y   **-opy** (117c), **spy** (36a, 41c, 106a)

P _ Z   **Paz** (174)

Q A _   **qaf** (11d)

Q _ A   **qua** (69c, 109c)

Q _ D   **QED** (242)

Q E _   **QED** (242), **QEF** (242)

Q _ F   **qaf** (11d), **QEF** (242)

Q U _   **qua** (69c, 109c)

R A _   **Rab** (37b), **rab** (18a, 66c, 78d), **RAC** (242), **rad** (40d, 246), **Rae** (176), **RAF** (242), **rag** (28b, 81c, 102a), **rah** (26b), **rai** (246), **raj** (41a), **RAM** (242), **ram** (17c, 32c, 85b, 92a, 103a, 107d), **ran** (19d, 29c, 84b), **rap** (70d, 83d, 94d, 116b), **ras** (41d, 62d, 122c), **rat** (16d, 35b, 101c, 115d, 119d, 231), **raw** (32b, 81a, 126d), **Ray** (176), **ray** (17d, 46d, 107b, 109d, 228)

R _ A   **RCA** (242), **RDA** (242), **REA** (242), **Rea** (176), **ria** (41d, 63a), **RNA** (53b, 242), **RSA** (242)

_ R A   Ara (12a, 139, 197, 207), ara (73b), **bra** (18d, 126b), **ERA** (238), **era** (10d, 41b, 87d, 122b), **Fra** (153), **fra** (22a, 51c, 78a, 94c), **HRA** (239), **IRA** (64a, 240), **Ira** (159, 197), **kra** (73b), **NRA** (20b, 241), **ora** (65c, 78a, 95a), **ora-** (93c), **Sra.** (243)

R B _   RBI (110d, 242)

R _ B   Rab (37b), rab (18a, 66c, 78d), **reb** (30a), **rib** (31a, 33a, 70d, 75c, 125d), **Rob** (177), **rob** (36c, 37a, 90c, 115a), **rub** (9b, 22d, 25d, 35d, 90d, 130d)

_ R B   FRB (238), orb (43c, 54d, 113c)

R C _   RCA (242), RCN (242), rct. (242)

R _ C   RAC (242), Ric (177), RNC (242), ROC (242), Roc (19b, 109c)

_ R C   ARC (235), arc (27b, 32d, 96b, 106b, 123d), **CRC** (237), **IRC** (240), **NRC** (241), **orc** (25d, 55d, 131b)

R D _   RDA (242)

R _ D   rad (40d, 246), Red (176, 224), red (32a, 48a, 102c), **RFD** (242), **rid** (27d, 36b, 40b, 49b), **Rod** (178), **rod** (17a, 57c, 68d, 100b, 107b, 114b, 115b, 246)

_ R D   Ord (23b, 49a), urd (17d)

R E _   REA (242), Rea (176), **reb** (30a), **Red** (176, 224), **red** (32a, 48a, 102c), **Ree** (14b, 23a, 189), **ree** (102d), **ref.** (242), **reg.** (242), **reh** (11b, 62d), **rei** (91d), **rel** (40a, 246), **REM** (110c, 242), **rem** (246), **ren-** (93b), **Reo** (24a), **Rep.** (242), **rep** (10d, 43b, 100c), **req.** (242), **res** (70a, 71a), **ret** (47c, 73b, 111b), **ret.** (242), **Rev.** (242), **rev** (41a, 79a), **Rex** (176), **rex** (67c), **Rey** (176), **rey** (112d)

R _ E   Rae (176), Ree (14b, 23a, 189), **ree** (102d), **RFE** (242), **rhe** (47d, 246), **roe** (25b, 34b, 34c, 39d, 47a, 60a), **rte.** (242), **Rue** (179), **rue** (35a, 59b, 59c, 99a, 133a), **rye** (11a, 25c, 55c, 72b)

_ R E   are (68d, 76b, 84a, 246), 'ere (18b, 30b), **GRE** (239), **Ire.** (240), **ire** (12c, 26d, 52b, 97b, 134a), **Ore.** (211, 241), **ore** (32b, 35a, 76b, 77a, 82b, 87b, 118c, 215, 220, 222), **pre** (18b), **pre-** (92c), **tre** (65c), **Ure** (134d)

R F _   RFD (242), RFE (242)

R _ F   RAF (242), ref. (242)

_ R F   orf (134b)

R _ G   rag (28b, 81c, 102a), reg. (242), **rig** (41b, 53b, 85b), **rug** (47d, 57b, 131d)

_ R G   Arg. (235), erg (40d, 133c, 246), org. (241)

293

R H _   rhe (47d, 246), rho (11d)

R _ H   rah (26b), reh (11b, 62d)

_ R H   HRH (239)

R I _   ria (41d, 63a), rib (31a, 33a, 70d, 75c, 125d), Ric (177), rid (27d, 36b, 40b, 49b), rig (41b, 53b, 85b), rii (127d), rim (21a, 39c, 74d, 87d, 95a, 122b, 131c), rin (106c), rio (113a, 246), RIP (242), Rip (177), rip (68b, 99c, 120a), rit. (110d, 242)

R _ I   rai (246), RBI (110d, 242), rei (91d), rii (127d), roi (50c)

_ R I   Ari (139), Fri. (238), sri (60b), tri- (93d), Uri (120b, 197)

R _ J   raj (41a)

R _ K   ROK (68c, 242)

_ R K   Ark. (209, 235), ark (20b, 128a), irk (12d, 87c, 128b), Ork. (241)

R _ L   rel (40a, 246)

R M _   rms. (242)

R _ M   RAM (242), ram (17c, 32c, 85b, 92a, 103a, 107d), REM (110c, 242), rem (246), rim (21a, 39c, 74d, 87d, 95a, 122b, 131c), ROM (29c, 242), Rom (57c), rpm (242), rum (11a, 72b)

_ R M   arm (13c, 21c, 49a, 72a, 95a)

R N _   RNA (53b, 242), RNC (242)

R _ N   ran (19d, 29c, 84b), RCN (242), ren- (93b), rin (106c), Ron (67d, 178), run (12d, 20d, 38a, 47c, 47d, 54d, 84b, 110d, 116b, 123c)

_ R N   arn (11b), ern (39a), urn (30b, 127b)

R O _   Rob (177), rob (36c, 37a, 90c, 115a), ROC (242), Roc (19b, 109c), Rod (178), rod (17a, 57c, 68d, 100b, 107b, 114b, 115b, 246), roe (25b, 34b, 34c, 39d, 47a, 60a), roi (50c), ROK (68c, 242), ROM (29c, 242), Rom (57c), Ron (67d, 178), rot (21a, 34a, 45c, 107d, 113d), row (14b, 46a, 72a, 83a, 96b, 97d, 122a), Roy (178), Roz (179)

R _ O   Reo (24a), rho (11d), rio (113a, 246)

_ R O   Aro (84d), bro. (99b, 236), fro (16b), gro. (239), oro (112d), oro- (93b), pro (48c, 96d), pro. (242), SRO (120d, 243)

R P _   rpm (242)

R _ P   rap (70d, 83d, 94d, 116b), Rep. (242), rep (10d, 43b, 100c), RIP (242), Rip (177), rip (68b, 99c, 120a)

_ R P   **Arp** (33a)

R _ Q   **req.** (242)

R _ R   **RUR** (101b)

_ R R   **arr.** (235), **err** (20b, 35c, 109c, 110c, 116b, 123d), **irr.** (240), **J.R.R.** (159), **Orr** (173)

R S _   **RSA** (242), **RSV** (242)

R _ S   **ras** (41d, 62d, 122c), **res** (70a, 71a), **rms.** (242), **rus** (69c)

_ R S   **ars** (69c), **ers** (19c, 59d, 128b), **hrs.** (239), **IRS** (120a, 240), **Mrs.** (122c, 241), **ors** (12a), **yrs.** (244)

R T _   **rte.** (242)

R _ T   **rat** (16d, 35b, 101c, 115d, 119d, 231), **rct.** (242), **ret** (47c, 73b, 111b), **ret.** (242), **rit.** (110d, 242), **rot** (21a, 34a, 45c, 107d, 113d), **rut** (56c, 57a)

_ R T   **Art** (139), **art** (31d, 46a, 94d), **CRT** (237), **ort** (48b, 71a)

R U _   **rub** (9b, 22d, 25d, 35d, 90d, 130d), **Rue** (179), **rue** (35a, 59b, 59c, 99a, 133a), **rug** (47d, 57b, 131d), **rum** (11a, 72b), **run** (12d, 20d, 38a, 47c, 47d, 54d, 84b, 110d, 116b, 123c), **RUR** (101b), **rus** (69c), **rut** (56c, 57a)

_ R U   **Dru** (150), **GRU** (239), **Kru** (215, 218), **Mru** (69a), **Uru.** (243)

R _ V   **Rev.** (242), **rev** (41a, 79a), **RSV** (242)

R W _   **rwy.** (242)

R _ W   **raw** (32b, 81a, 126d), **row** (14b, 46a, 72a, 83a, 96b, 97d, 122a)

R _ X   **Rex** (176), **rex** (67c)

R Y _   **rye** (11a, 25c, 55c, 72b)

R _ Y   **Ray** (176), **ray** (17d, 46d, 107b, 109d, 228), **Rey** (176), **rey** (112d), **Roy** (178), **rwy.** (242)

_ R Y   **-ary** (117a, 117b), **cry** (23b, 94d, 108d, 131a, 134b, 232), **dry** (38c, 121b, 133a), **-ery** (117b), **fry** (30c, 47a), **-ory** (117a, 117b), **pry** (71c, 94d), **try** (12d, 15c, 40d, 41d, 114b, 116c), **wry** (64b, 125c)

R _ Z   **Roz** (179)

S A _   **SAC** (242), **sac** (92a, 128a), **sad** (11d, 20a, 26b, 35a, 36c, 37c, 73c, 75d, 79b, 112a, 126c), **sae** (242), **SAG** (242), **sag** (38a, 132a), **sai** (78b), **Sal** (52b, 179), **sal** (39b), **SAM** (242), **Sam** (24c, 119d, 179), san (113a), sap (37d, 42d, 56d, 66d, 128c, 130c), **SAR** (242), **SAT** (242), sat (60a, 91d, 107a, 122d), saw (9d, 13b, 33c, 75b, 95c, 114a, 122d), sax (80a), Say (192), say (100d, 113b, 115a, 127c, 128d)

S _ A	SBA (242), sea (42d, 47c, 130a), ska (65b), sma (105b), sna (105b), spa (58d, 77a, 100a, 114a, 127a), Sra. (243), SSA (243), sta (80a)
_ S A	Asa (9a, 56a, 66b, 67d, 139, 197), BSA (236), CSA (237), GSA (239), Isa. (240), NSA (241), Psa. (242), RSA (242), SSA (243), USA (26a, 243)
S B _	SBA (242), SbE (29c), SbW (29c)
S _ B	sib (99b), sob (32b, 131a), sub (70b), sub- (93d)
_ S B	asb. (235)
S C _	sch. (242), sci. (31b, 242)
S _ C	SAC (242), sac (92a, 128a), SEC (242), sec (38b, 132c), sic (70a, 121d, 123d), SLC (243), soc (67c), soc. (243), SWC (243)
_ S C	B.Sc. (236), CSC (237), DSC (238), NSC (241)
S D _	SDI (242), SDS (242)
S _ D	sad (11d, 20a, 26b, 35a, 36c, 37c, 73c, 75d, 79b, 112a, 126c), sed (69c), sgd. (243), Sid (180), sod (118b, 125a), std. (243)
_ S D	LSD (240)
S E _	sea (42d, 47c, 130a), SEC (242), sec (38b, 132c), sed (69c), see (19c, 36a, 41c, 43c, 55d, 73a, 83b, 86b, 87d, 130a, 133a), sei (65c), sel (51a, 105b), Sen. (243), sen (214, 217, 218, 219, 246), Sep. (78c, 243), ser- (93c), ser. (243), ses (50c), Set (42b, 198), set (10a, 14c, 15c, 28a, 31a, 47b, 58a, 81b, 85a, 89d, 106d, 111d, 120c), sew (75d, 115c), sex (53b, 94d), sex- (93c), sey (105a)
S _ E	sae (242), SbE (29c), see (19c, 36a, 41c, 43c, 55d, 73a, 83b, 86b, 87d, 130a, 133a), She (57b), she (95a), sie (54b), SSE (29c), Ste. (243), Sue (182), sue (49c, 90b)
_ S E	ASE (235), Ase (61b, 87c), ESE (29c), Ise (60d), -ise (117a, 117c), -ose (117a, 117b), SSE (29c), use (38d, 40c, 43a, 52a)
S _ F	Sif (121b)
_ S F	NSF (241)
S G _	sgd. (243), Sgt. (243)
S _ G	SAG (242), sag (38a, 132a)

S H _   She (57b), she (95a), sho (246), Shu (97a), shy (17c, 31c, 77c, 98b, 108d, 122b)

S _ H   sch. (242)

_ S H   ash (40c, 58a, 124a), -ish (117a)

S I _   sib (99b), sic (70a, 121d, 123d), Sid (180), sie (54b), Sif (121b), sil (26d, 134b), Sim (181), sin (11d, 12a, 83c, 123d, 124b, 128b, 134c), sip (37d, 38a, 119d), sir (68a, 120c, 122c), sis (44b, 54c, 99b), sit (75d, 87d, 91d, 107a), six (57c)

S _ I   sai (78b), sci. (31b, 242), SDI (242), sei (65c), ski (104d, 110b), sri (60b), Sui (26d)

_ S I   ASI (235), psi (11d)

S K _   ska (65b), ski (104d, 110b), Skt. (243), sky (46c)

_ S K   ask (31d, 64a, 96d, 99d, 111c), Esk (134d, 223), tsk (42c, 122d)

S L _   SLC (243), SLR (243), Sly (181), sly (14d, 31d, 32c, 52c, 63b, 101c, 110c, 132a)

S _ L   Sal (52b, 179), sal (39b), sel (51a, 105b), sil (26d, 134b), Sol (88c, 199), sol (117d, 221), syl. (243)

_ S L   ESL (238), isl. (240)

S M _   sma (105b), SMU (33a)

S _ M   SAM (242), Sam (24c, 119d, 179), Sim (181), sum (10d, 123b), sym. (243)

_ S M   -ism (117b)

S N _   sna (105b), SNO (243), sny (18c, 32d, 90a, 108b, 122a)

S _ N   san (113a), Sen. (243), sen (214, 217, 218, 219, 246), sin (11d, 12a, 83c, 123d, 124b, 128b, 134c), son (59a, 74c), SSN (243), Sun (182), Sun. (243), sun (59a, 88c, 114d, 246), syn- (94a)

_ S N   ASN (235), SSN (243), USN (243)

S O _   sob (32b, 131a), soc (67c), soc. (243), sod (118b, 125a), Sol (88c, 199), sol (117d, 221), son (59a, 74c), Soo (181), soo (97d), SOP (243), sop (9b, 21d, 29d, 111b), SOS (36d, 243), sot (38b, 123a, 123b), sou (49c), Sov. (243), sow (88d, 90a, 118d), sox (17c, 98c), soy (17d, 104b)

S _ O   sho (246), SNO (243), Soo (181), soo (97d), SRO (120d, 243)

_ S O   Aso (65d, 128d), iso- (92d, 93c), USO (244)

S P _   spa (58d, 77a, 100a, 114a, 127a), spy (36a, 41c, 106a)

S _ P   **sap** (37d, 42d, 56d, 66d, 128c, 130c), **Sep.** (78c, 243), **sip** (37d, 38a, 119d), **SOP** (243), **sop** (9b, 21d, 29d, 111b), **sup** (39b, 119d)

_ S P   **asp** (10a, 28a, 111a, 126d, 128c, 232), **ESP** (109d, 238)

S _ Q   **suq** (74d)

_ S Q   **Esq.** (238)

S R _   **Sra.** (243), **sri** (60b), **SRO** (120d, 243)

S _ R   **SAR** (242), **ser-** (93c), **ser.** (243), **sir** (68a, 120c, 122c), **SLR** (243), **SSR** (243), **str.** (243), **sur** (50d, 51b, 79d, 113a), **Syr.** (243)

_ S R   **Isr.** (240), **SSR** (243)

S S _   **SSA** (243), **SSE** (29c), **SSN** (243), **SSR** (243), **SSS** (243), **SST** (66b, 243), **SSW** (29c)

S _ S   **SDS** (242), **ses** (50c), **sis** (44b, 54c, 99b), **SOS** (36d, 243), **SSS** (243), **sus-** (93d), **sys.** (243)

_ S S   **ass** (17d, 20a, 37b, 37c, 41b, 48b, 84a, 85b, 109c, 116d, 229), **ess** (32d, 71c), **-ess** (117b), **mss.** (241), **OSS** (241), **SSS** (243), **USS** (244)

S T _   **sta** (80a), **std.** (243), **Ste.** (243), **str.** (243), **Stu** (182), **sty** (43c)

S _ T   **SAT** (242), **sat** (60a, 91d, 107a, 122d), **Set** (42b, 198), **set** (10a, 14c, 15c, 28a, 31a, 47b, 58a, 81b, 85a, 89d, 106d, 111d, 120c), **Sgt.** (243), **sit** (75d, 87d, 91d, 107a), **Skt.** (243), **sot** (38b, 123a, 123b), **SST** (66b, 243)

_ S T   **AST** (236), **as't** (107c), **CST** (237), **DST** (238), **EST** (238), **est** (50b, 50c), **-est** (40d, 117c), **HST** (239), **is't** (107c), **-ist** (117a, 117b), **MST** (241), **PST** (242), **SST** (66b, 243)

S U _   **sub** (70b), **sub-** (93d), **Sue** (182), **sue** (49c, 90b), **Sui** (26d), **sum** (10d, 123b), **Sun** (182), **Sun.** (243), **sun** (59a, 88c, 114d, 246), **sup** (39b, 119d), **suq** (74d), **sur** (50d, 51b, 79d, 113a), **sus-** (93d)

S _ U   **Shu** (97a), **SMU** (33a), **sou** (49c), **Stu** (182)

S _ V   **Sov.** (243)

_ S V   **ASV** (236), **RSV** (242)

S W _   **SWC** (243)

S _ W   **saw** (9d, 13b, 33c, 75b, 95c, 114a, 122d), **SbW** (29c), **sew** (75d, 115c), **sow** (88d, 90a, 118d), **SSW** (29c)

_ S W   **NSW** (241), **SSW** (29c), **WSW** (29c)

S _ X   **sax** (80a), **sex** (53b, 94d), **sex-** (93c), **six** (57c), **sox** (17c, 98c)

S Y _   **syl.** (243), **sym.** (243), **syn-** (94a), **Syr.** (243), **sys.** (243)

S _ Y   **Say** (192), **say** (100d, 113b, 115a, 127c, 128d), **sey** (105a), **shy** (17c, 31c, 77c, 98b, 108d, 122b), **sky** (46c), **Sly** (181), **sly** (14d, 31d, 32c, 52c, 63b, 101c, 110c, 132a), **sny** (18c, 32d, 90a, 108b, 122a), **soy** (17d, 104b), **spy** (36a, 41c, 106a), **sty** (43c)

T A _   **Tab** (183), **tab** (47b, 94b, 119b), **TAC** (243), **tad** (134d), **tae** (105b), **tag** (52b, 68b), **Tai** (62d, 183, 218), **tai** (65d, 91c), **Taj** (74b), **tam** (58b, 58c), **tan** (22b, 70d, 246), **tao** (88c, 124d), **tap** (44d, 113c, 123b), **tar** (55a, 89c, 102a, 103b), **TAT** (243), **tat** (39c, 68c), **tau** (11d, 103d), **tav** (12a), **Taw** (223), **taw** (70d, 74d, 108c, 119c), **tax** (15a, 62b, 71c), **Tay** (82b)

T _ A   **tba** (243), **tea** (61d, 111b), **tha** (11d), **tia** (112c), **toa** (18a), **TVA** (243), **Twa** (214, 221)

_ T A   **Ata** (73d), **ETA** (238), **eta** (11d), **ita** (70a), **PTA** (104d, 242), **sta** (80a), **Uta** (184), **uta** (72c)

T B _   **tba** (243), **TBS** (26a), **tbs.** (243)

T _ B   **Tab** (183), **tab** (47b, 94b, 119b), **tob** (10c), **tub** (20b, 24c, 30b, 127b)

_ T B   **OTB** (52b, 241)

T C _   **tch** (42c)

T _ C   **TAC** (243), **tec** (35b), **tic** (79d, 113b, 125c), **TLC** (243)

_ T C   **ATC** (236), **etc.** (72b, 238), **FTC** (239), **ITC** (240), **OTC** (241)

T _ D   **tad** (134d), **Ted** (183), **ted** (58c, 114a), **Tod** (183), **tod** (22d, 105a, 246)

_ T D   **Ltd.** (240), **std.** (243)

T E _   **tea** (61d, 111b), **tec** (35b), **Ted** (183), **ted** (58c, 114a), **tee** (55a, 55b, 87c), **teg** (107d), **Tel** (16a), **Tel.** (243), **tel-** (93d), **ten** (18d, 34a, 34d), **ter-** (93d), **ter.** (243), **Tex** (31c, 183), **Tex.** (212, 243)

T _ E   **tae** (105b), **tee** (55a, 55b, 87c), **the** (14d), **tie** (12c, 20d, 31d, 37d, 41b, 42a, 69b, 72b, 97b, 124d), **toe** (55b, 110b, 115b), **tre** (65c), **Tue.** (243), **tye** (25d, 102b)

_ T E   **Ate** (88b, 135a, 198), **ate, -ate** (117a, 117b), **ete** (51a), **-ite** (117a, 117b), **rte.** (242), **Ste.** (243), **Ute** (108d, 189)

_ T F   **ATF** (236)

T _ G   **tag** (52b, 68b), **teg** (107d), **tog** (28b), **Tug** (184), **tug** (20b, 28d, 37c, 95d)

T H _   **tha** (11d), **the** (14d), **Thu.** (243), **thy** (95a)

T _ H	**tch** (42c)
_ T H	**D.Th.** (238), **Eth.** (238), **eth** (12c), **-eth** (117b, 117c), **lth** (25c), **nth** (34c)
T I _	**tia** (112c), **tic** (79d, 113b, 125c), **tie** (12c, 20d, 31d, 37d, 41b, 42a, 69b, 72b, 97b, 124d), **til** (107a), **'til** (30b), **Tim** (35c, 183), **tin** (30b, 74c, 76a, 114d, 245), **tio** (113a), **tip** (40d, 56a, 60b, 60d, 90c, 122a), **tir** (51a, 108c), **'tis** (30b, 107c), **tit** (19a, 226), **Tiu** (53c, 125d), **tix** (243)
T _ I	**Tai** (62d, 183, 218), **tai** (65d, 91c), **toi** (49d, 51b), **tri-** (93d), **tui** (38d, 81c, 86d, 88c), **Twi** (216)
_ T I	**ETI** (238)
T _ J	**Taj** (74b)
T K _	**TKO** (21b, 243)
T _ K	**tsk** (42c, 122d)
T L _	**TLC** (243)
T _ L	**Tel** (16a), **Tel.** (243), **tel-** (93d), **til** (107a), **'til** (30b)
_ T L	**Atl.** (236)
T _ M	**tam** (58b, 58c), **Tim** (35c, 183), **Tom** (116a, 184), **tom** (74c), **tum** (24b)
_ T M	**ATM** (236)
T N _	**TNT** (26a, 43a, 243)
T _ N	**tan** (22b, 70d, 246), **ten** (18d, 34a, 34d), **tin** (30b, 74c, 76a, 114d, 245), **ton** (131a, 246), **tun** (21d, 24c, 75b, 132c, 246)
T O _	**toa** (18a), **tob** (10c), **Tod** (183), **tod** (22d, 105a, 246), **toe** (55b, 110b, 115b), **tog** (28b), **toi** (49d, 51b), **Tom** (116a, 184), **tom** (74c), **ton** (131a, 246), **too** (12c, 18c, 62c, 78c), **top** (31d, 42b, 59d, 85c, 89b, 117d, 118a, 118b, 127c), **Tor** (102c), **tor** (31d, 67c, 87b, 95a, 101b), **tot** (26c, 134d), **tou** (246), **tow** (37c, 59b, 95d), **toy** (82c, 124c)
T _ O	**tao** (88c, 124d), **tio** (113a), **TKO** (21b, 243), **too** (12c, 18c, 62c, 78c), **two** (21c, 31b, 72c)
_ T O	**cto.** (237), **ETO** (238), **ITO** (240), **Ito** (65b), **oto-** (92d), **PTO** (242)
T _ P	**tap** (44d, 113c, 123b), **tip** (40d, 56a, 60b, 60d, 90c, 122a), **top** (31d, 42b, 59d, 85c, 89b, 117d, 118a, 118b, 127c), **tup** (32c, 87b, 89a, 97d), **twp.** (243)
_ T P	**ATP** (236)

T R _   tre (65c), tri- (93d), try (12d, 15c, 40d, 41d, 114b, 116c)

T _ R   tar (55a, 89c, 102a, 103b), ter- (93d), ter. (243), tir (51a, 108c), Tor (102c), tor (31d, 67c, 87b, 95a, 101b), tur (25a, 89a), Tyr (10b, 83b, 125a, 129d, 198)

_ T R   str. (243)

T S _   tsk (42c, 122d)

T _ S   TBS (26a), tbs. (243), 'tis (30b, 107c)

_ T S   cts. (237), DTs (238), hts. (239), its (95a), it's (30c), Mts. (241)

T _ T   TAT (243), tat (39c, 68c), tit (19a, 226), TNT (26a, 43a, 243), tot (26c, 134d), Tut (21c, 40a), tut (42c, 122d)

_ T T   ltt (10a), Ott (173)

T U _   tub (20b, 24c, 30b, 127b), Tue. (243), Tug (184), tug (20b, 28d, 37c, 95d), tui (38d, 81c, 86d, 88c), tum (24b), tun (21d, 24c, 75b, 132c, 246), tup (32c, 87b, 89a, 97d), tur (25a, 89a), Tut (21c, 40a), tut (42c, 122d), tux (35d)

T _ U   tau (11d, 103d), Thu. (243), Tiu (53c, 125d), tou (246)

_ T U   BTU (10d, 236), cru (50d), Stu (182)

T V _   TVA (243)

T _ V   tav (12a)

_ T V   ATV (236), ETV (238), MTV (26a)

T W _   Twa (214, 221), Twi (216), two (21c, 31b, 72c), twp. (243)

T _ W   Taw (223), taw (70d, 74d, 108c, 119c), tow (37c, 59b, 95d)

T _ X   tax (15a, 62b, 71c), Tex (31c, 183), Tex. (212, 243), tix (243), tux (35d)

T Y _   tye (25d, 102b), Tyr (10b, 83b, 125a, 129d, 198)

T _ Y   Tay (82b), thy (95a), toy (82c, 124c), try (12d, 15c, 40d, 41d, 114b, 116c)

_ T Y   sty (43c)

U A _   UAE (243), UAR (243)

U _ A   uca (45d), ufa (42c), -ula (117b), Uma (184), Una (43d, 113c, 184), USA (26a, 243), Uta (184), uta (72c), uva (51d, 55d)

_ U A   dua- (93d), pua (59b), qua (69c, 109c)

U B _   ubi (70b)

U _ B   **uxb** (244)

_ U B   **bub** (45a, 74c), **cub** (72b, 134d), **dub** (23b, 80b), **hub** (25c, 131c), **nub** (54c, 73c, 74b, 89c, 95c), **pub** (120a), **rub** (9b, 22d, 25d, 35d, 90d, 130d), **sub** (70b), **sub-** (93d), **tub** (20b, 24c, 30b, 127b)

U C _   **uca** (45d)

U _ C   **UPC** (243)

_ U C   **duc** (50b)

U D _   **Udi** (82b), **udo** (26d, 65d, 66a, 103d)

U _ D   **und** (53c), **urd** (17d)

_ U D   **Bud** (143), **bud** (45a, 47d), **cud** (96d, 102d), **dud** (44a), **HUD** (239), **IUD** (240), **Lud** (108a), **mud** (39a, 99c, 104c, 110b, 246), **oud** (80b), **pud** (57d, 87b)

U _ E   **UAE** (243), **ule** (21c, 25a, 102c), **-ule** (117b), **ume** (13d, 65b), **une** (49d, 50a, 50d), **Ure** (134d), **use** (38d, 40c, 43a, 52a), **Ute** (108d, 189)

_ U E   **cue** (9d, 24d, 91b, 101c, 109b, 117d), **due** (65c, 87b, 95b), **hue** (29a, 107b, 122d), **nue** (50a), **Rue** (179), **rue** (35a, 59b, 59c, 99a, 133a), **Sue** (182), **sue** (49c, 90b), **Tue.** (243), **Yue** (215)

U F _   **ufa** (42c), **UFO** (48a, 243), **UFT** (243), **UFW** (243)

U _ F   **UHF** (120b, 243)

U G _   **ugh** (42c)

_ U G   **Aug.** (78c, 236), **bug** (21b, 53c, 63b), **dug** (42b), **fug** (98d), **hug** (40c), **jug** (89c, 94d), **lug** (24c, 37c, 39a, 57d, 103b), **mug** (38a, 52c, 128a), **pug** (37a, 77d, 227), **rug** (47d, 57b, 131d), **Tug** (184), **tug** (20b, 28d, 37c, 95d), **vug** (25b, 53c)

U H _   **UHF** (120b, 243)

U _ H   **ugh** (42c)

_ U H   **huh** (42c)

U _ I   **ubi** (70b), **Udi** (82b), **uji** (109c), **uni-** (93c), **UPI** (81c, 132d, 243), **Uri** (120b, 197)

_ U I   **DUI** (38b, 238), **Hui** (215), **hui** (15a), **Kui** (67b), **oui** (51b), **Sui** (26d), **tui** (38d, 81c, 86d, 88c)

U J _   **uji** (109c)

_ U K   **auk** (19a, 225), **yuk** (70b)

U L _   -ula (117b), **ule** (21c, 25a, 102c), -ule (117b), **Ulm** (33c, 216), **Ulu** (184), **ulu** (63d, 68a)

_ U L   **Bul.** (236), -ful (117b), **Jul.** (78c, 240), **pul** (213), **Yul** (188)

U M _   **Uma** (184), **ume** (13d, 65b), **UMW** (243)

U _ M   **Ulm** (33c, 216)

_ U M   **aum** (246), **bum** (38a, 127a), **cum** (117d), **gum** (10a, 43c, 62c, 78d, 99d, 115b, 124a), **hum** (38a, 112a, 131d), **mum** (27a, 74a), **Num.** (241), **rum** (11a, 72b), **sum** (10d, 123b), **tum** (24b)

U N _   **Una** (43d, 113c, 184), **und** (53c), **une** (49d, 50a, 50d), **uni-** (93c), **uno** (65c, 112c), **uns** (54a)

U _ N   **urn** (30b, 127b), **USN** (243)

_ U N   **bun** (57b, 101c), **dun** (18d, 38c, 56a, 87b), **fun** (52b, 66b), **gun** (46b, 100b, 109a, 130c), **Hun** (127b), **Jun.** (78c, 240), **jun** (218), **Nun** (197), **nun** (11d, 12a, 22c, 89a, 99b, 109d), **pun** (90b), **run** (12d, 20d, 38a, 47c, 47d, 54d, 84b, 110d, 116b, 123c), **Sun** (182), **Sun.** (243), **sun** (59a, 88c, 114d, 246), **tun** (21d, 24c, 75b, 132c, 246), **Yun** (69a)

U _ O   **udo** (26d, 65d, 66a, 103d), **UFO** (48a, 243), **uno** (65c, 112c), **USO** (244)

_ U O   **duo** (85d, 125c), **Luo** (218)

U P _   **UPC** (243), **UPI** (81c, 132d, 243), **UPS** (243), **ups** (21a)

_ U P   **cup** (38a, 55b, 89b, 98b, 119a, 124d), **dup.** (238), **hup** (23a, 29b), **kup** (246), **pup** (105d, 134d), **sup** (39b, 119d), **tup** (32c, 87b, 89a, 97d)

_ U Q   **suq** (74d)

U R _   **urd** (17d), **Ure** (134d), **Uri** (120b, 197), **urn** (30b, 127b), **Uru.** (243)

U _ R   **UAR** (243)

_ U R   **bur** (106b, 131a), **bur.** (236), **cur** (78a), **dur** (74b), **Eur.** (238), **fur** (28c, 57b), **Gur** (223), **gur** (117c), **mur** (51b), **our** (95a), **RUR** (101b), **sur** (50d, 51b, 79d, 113a), **tur** (25a, 89a)

U S _   **USA** (26a, 243), **use** (38d, 40c, 43a, 52a), **USN** (243), **USO** (244), **USS** (244)

U _ S   **uns** (54a), **UPS** (243), **ups** (21a), **USS** (244)

_ U S   **AUS** (236), **aus** (54a), **bus** (95d), **bus.** (236), **Gus** (156), **ius** (70a), **jus** (50c, 70b), **mus.** (241), -**ous** (117a), **pus** (63a, 78b), **rus** (69c), **sus-** (93d)

U T _   **Uta** (184), **uta** (72c), **Ute** (108d, 189)

U _ T   UFT (243)

_ U T   aut (70a), **but** (11d, 30a, 42b, 115b, 126c, 134c), **cut** (27a, 28a, 79c, 98d, 107b, 108d, 110b), **fut** (246), **gut** (99c), **hut** (107c), **jut** (95a), **Lut** (35a), **Mut** (12b, 97a), **Nut** (198), **nut** (22c, 28c, 31d, 44c, 51d, 67b, 121b), **out** (9b, 49a, 55b, 82c), **put** (70c), **rut** (56c, 57a), **Tut** (21c, 40a), **tut** (42c, 122d

U _ U   Ulu (184), **ulu** (63d, 68a), **Uru.** (243)

U V _   uva (51d, 55d)

U _ W   UFW (243), **UMW** (243)

U X _   uxb (244)

_ U X   aux. (236), **dux** (52a, 70c), **Lux** (240), **lux** (62a, 246), **tux** (35d)

_ U Y   buy (17b, 96a), **Guy** (156), **guy** (45a, 74c, 115a), **muy** (113a)

_ U Z   guz (246)

V A _   Vai (218), **Val** (184), **Van** (184), **van** (48d), **vas** (38c, 70a), **vas-** (92c), **VAT** (244), **vat** (27b, 30b, 125a, 246), **vav** (12a)

V _ A   via (65c, 101a, 101d), **VOA** (244)

_ V A   Ava (22d, 139), **ava** (61c, 91a, 123a), **CVA** (237), **EVA** (238), **Eva** (116a, 152), **iva** (75a), **ova** (39d), **TVA** (243), **uva** (51d, 55d), **W.Va.** (212, 244)

V C _   VCR (244)

V _ C   Vic (32d, 185)

V D _   VDT (244)

V _ D   Vod (16d)

V E _   Vee (185), **vee** (47b, 81a), **Vei** (218), **ven-** (93d), **Ven.** (244), **ver.** (244), **vet** (111c), **vet.** (244), **vex** (12d, 21b, 36d, 64b, 87c)

V _ E   Vee (185), **vee** (47b, 81a), **vie** (30b, 116c, 125a), **voe** (63a)

_ V E   Ave. (236), **ave** (44b, 56c, 57b, 92b, 102b, 104a), **Eve** (9a, 107a, 152, 197), **eve** (38d, 125c), **I've** (30c)

V F _   VFW (244)

V _ F   VHF (120b), **vif** (50c)

V _ G   vug (25b, 53c)

_ V G   avg. (236)

V H _   VHF (120b)

V I _   **via** (65c, 101a, 101d), **Vic** (32d, 185), **vie** (30b, 116c, 125a), **vif** (50c), **vim** (40d, 48c, 113d, 128b, 128d), **Vin** (185), **vin** (51b), **VIP** (35d, 244), **vir** (69d), **vis** (69d, 70a), **vix** (70a), **viz** (80d)

V _ I   **Vai** (218), **Vei** (218)

_ V I   **avi-** (92c), **B.V.I.** (236), **ovi-** (92d)

V _ L   **Val** (184), **vol.** (244)

V _ M   **vim** (40d, 48c, 113d, 128b, 128d)

_ V M   **BVM** (236), **DVM** (238)

V _ N   **Van** (184), **van** (48d), **Ven.** (244), **ven-** (93d), **Vin** (185), **vin** (51b), **von** (53d)

V O _   **VOA** (244), **Vod** (16d), **voe** (63a), **vol.** (244), **von** (53d), **vow** (90b, 111c), **vox** (70b)

_ V O   **Ivo** (159), **ovo-** (92d)

V _ P   **VIP** (35d, 244)

_ V P   **MVP** (241)

V _ R   **VCR** (244), **ver.** (244), **vir** (69d)

V _ S   **vas** (38c, 70a), **vas-** (92c), **vis** (69d, 70a)

V _ T   **VAT** (244), **vat** (27b, 30b, 125a, 246), **VDT** (244), **vet** (111c), **vet.** (244)

_ V T   **Pvt.** (242)

V U _   **vug** (25b, 53c)

V _ V   **vav** (12a)

V _ W   **VFW** (244), **vow** (90b, 111c)

V _ X   **vex** (12d, 21b, 36d, 64b, 87c), **vix** (70a), **vox** (70b)

_ V Y   **Ivy** (159), **ivy** (28a, 31d, 128b)

V _ Z   **viz** (80d)

W A _   **WAC** (244), **wad** (55a, 73c, 75b, 85b), **WAF** (244), **wag** (66d, 79c, 133a), **wan** (57b, 86a), **war** (116b), **was** (57a, 127a), **Wat** (186), **waw** (11d), **wax** (15d, 56d, 90d, 118c), **way** (31b, 74c, 76b, 101a, 102c, 121b, 127a)

W _ A   **WBA** (244), **WHA** (244), **WPA** (244), **W.Va.** (212, 244)

_ W A   **iwa** (51c), **Kwa** (69a, 223), **Twa** (214, 221)

W B _   **WBA** (244), **WBC** (244), **WbN** (29c), **WbS** (29c)

W _ B   **W.E.B.** (185), **web** (41a, 75d, 76a, 81c, 111b)

W C _   **WCT** (244)

W _ C   **WAC** (244), **WBC** (244)

_ W C   **SWC** (243)

W _ D   **wad** (55a, 73c, 75b, 85b), **wed** (66c, 75a, 126c), **we'd** (30c)

_ W D   **fwd** (239)

W E _   **W.E.B.** (185), **web** (41a, 75d, 76a, 81c, 111b), **wed** (66c, 75a, 126c), **we'd** (30c), **wee** (77b, 105b, 110d), **Wei** (119d), **wen** (33c, 83d, 125a, 129a), **Wes** (186), **wet** (33b, 33c, 37d, 77c, 97c), **wey** (246)

W _ E   **wee** (77b, 105b, 110d), **woe** (23a, 56c, 112a), **Wye** (107b, 131a), **wye** (71c)

_ W E   **awe** (63d, 76d, 100b, 127d, 132b), **Ewe** (216, 223), **ewe** (107d), **owe** (34a)

W _ F   **WAF** (244)

W _ G   **wag** (66d, 79c, 133a), **wig** (57b)

W H _   **WHA** (244), **WHO** (244), **who** (96d, 99b), **why** (96d)

_ W H   **kwh** (240)

W I _   **wig** (57b), **Wil** (186), **Wim** (187), **win** (9d, 52a, 94b), **Wis.** (212, 244), **wit** (36a, 61c, 66d, 129a), **wiz** (74a)

W _ I   **Wei** (119d)

_ W I   **DWI** (38b, 238), **Twi** (216)

W _ K   **wok** (86a, 128a)

W _ L   **Wil** (186), **wol** (132d)

_ W L   **awl** (108c, 122d, 123a), **owl** (19a, 226)

W _ M   **Wim** (187), **wpm** (244)

_ W M   **cwm** (79b)

W N _   **WNW** (29c)

W _ N   **wan** (57b, 86a), **WbN** (29c), **wen** (33c, 83d, 125a, 129a), **win** (9d, 52a, 94b), **won** (46c, 128b, 218)

_ W N   **awn** (14b, 17d), **own** (9d, 29d)

W O _	**woe** (23a, 56c, 112a), **wok** (86a, 128a), **wol** (132d), **won** (46c, 128b, 218), **woo** (31b), **wow** (42c)
W _ O	**WHO** (244), **who** (96d, 99b), **woo** (31b), **Wyo.** (212, 244)
_ W O	**CWO** (237), **Pwo** (69a), **two** (21c, 31b, 72c)
W P _	**WPA** (244), **wpm** (244)
_ W P	**twp.** (243)
W R _	**wry** (64b, 125c)
W _ R	**war** (116b)
W S _	**WSW** (29c)
W _ S	**was** (57a, 127a), **WbS** (29c), **Wes** (186), **Wis.** (212, 244)
W _ T	**Wat** (186), **WCT** (244), **wet** (33b, 33c, 37d, 77c, 97c), **wit** (36a, 61c, 66d, 129a)
_ W T	**NWT** (241)
W V _	**W.Va.** (212, 244)
_ W V	**LWV** (240)
W _ W	**waw** (11d), **WNW** (29c), **wow** (42c), **WSW** (29c)
_ W W	**IWW** (240)
W _ X	**wax** (15d, 56d, 90d, 118c)
W Y _	**Wye** (107b, 131a), **wye** (71c), **Wyo.** (212, 244)
W _ Y	**way** (31b, 74c, 76b, 101a, 102c, 121b, 127a), **wey** (246), **why** (96d), **wry** (64b, 125c)
_ W Y	**hwy.** (239), **rwy.** (242)
W _ Z	**wiz** (74a)
X A _	**xat** (123b)
_ X A	**oxa-** (93c)
_ X B	**uxb** (244)
X E _	**xen-** (93a), **xer-** (92d)
_ X E	**axe** (27a, 33c, 36c, 122d), **Exe** (35c, 223)
X _ L	**xyl-** (94a)
X _ N	**xen-** (93a)

_ X O	**exo-** (93c)
_ X P	**exp.** (238)
X _ R	**xer-** (92d)
X _ T	**xat** (123b)
_ X T	**ext.** (238)
X Y _	**xyl-** (94a)
_ X Y	**oxy-** (93c)
Y A _	**yah** (34c), **Yai** (223), **yak** (85d, 119b, 231), **yam** (39c, 92a, 118c, 125a), **Yao** (218, 219), **yap** (17b, 26b, 92b, 134c), **yaw** (101c), **yay** (9b, 111b)
Y _ A	**yea** (10b, 128a, 129c), **Yma** (187)
_ Y A	**pya** (220)
_ Y C	**NYC** (18d, 241)
Y D _	**yds.** (244)
Y _ D	**Yed** (207), **yod** (12a)
_ Y D	**Cyd** (147)
Y E _	**yea** (10b, 128a, 129c), **Yed** (207), **yen** (35b, 58a, 73a, 218), **yep** (10b), **yes** (10b, 44d), **yet** (18c, 22d, 60b, 82c, 115b, 121d), **yew** (30a, 42a, 108d, 124a)
Y _ E	**Yue** (215)
_ Y E	**aye** (10b, 44d, 129c), **bye** (32a, 123c), **dye** (29a, 114c), **eye** (73a, 118b), **lye** (11b), **rye** (11a, 25c, 55c, 72b), **tye** (25d, 102b), **Wye** (107b, 131a), **wye** (71c)
Y _ G	**zyg-** (93c)
Y _ H	**yah** (34c)
Y I _	**Yin** (26d), **yin** (107c, 134a), **yip** (17b, 37b, 134c)
Y _ I	**Yai** (223)
_ Y I	**fyi** (239)
Y _ K	**yak** (85d, 119b, 231), **yuk** (70b)
Y _ L	**Yul** (188)
_ Y L	**hyl-** (94a), **syl.** (243), **xyl-** (94a)

Y M _	Yma (187)
Y _ M	yam (39c, 92a, 118c, 125a), yom (33d, 67d)
_ Y M	gym (114a), Nym (44a, 194), sym. (243), zym- (93a)
Y _ N	yen (35b, 58a, 73a, 218), Yin (26d), yin (107c, 134a), yon (36d, 85c), Yun (69a)
_ Y N	Ayn (139), ayn (11d), dyn- (93c), gyn- (92d), syn- (94a)
Y O _	yod (12a), yom (33d, 67d), yon (36d, 85c), you (95a), yow (42c)
Y _ O	Yao (218, 219)
_ Y O	CYO (237), iyo (10b, 88c), Wyo. (212, 244)
Y _ P	yap (17b, 26b, 92b, 134c), yep (10b), yip (17b, 37b, 134c)
_ Y P	gyp (107a, 108d, 118d)
Y R _	yrs. (244)
_ Y R	gyr- (93a), pyr- (93a), Syr. (243), Tyr (10b, 83b, 125a, 129d, 198)
Y _ S	yds. (244), yes (10b, 44d), yrs. (244)
_ Y S	dys- (92c), lys (71d), lys- (93a), sys. (243)
Y _ T	yet (18c, 22d, 60b, 82c, 115b, 121d)
Y U _	Yue (215), yuk (70b), Yul (188), Yun (69a)
Y _ U	you (95a)
Y _ W	yaw (101c), yew (30a, 42a, 108d, 124a), yow (42c)
_ Y X	myx- (93b), Nyx (56b, 198), pyx (27b, 42a)
Y _ Y	yay (9b, 111b)
Z A _	zak (246), Zan (135c), zax (110b), zay (11d)
Z _ A	zoa (39d)
Z _ D	zed (135a)
Z E _	zed (135a), zee (63a), Zen (22b), zer (246)
Z _ E	zee (63a), Zoe (188)
Z _ G	ZPG (244), zyg- (93c)
Z I _	zip (40d, 128b, 244)
Z _ K	zak (246)

Z _ M	zym- (93a)
Z _ N	Zan (135c), Zen (22b)
Z O _	zoa (39d), Zoe (188), zoo (132a), zoo- (92c)
Z _ O	zoo (132a), zoo- (92c)
_ Z O	azo (38d, 134b), azo- (93b)
Z P _	ZPG (244)
Z _ P	zip (40d, 128b, 244)
Z _ R	zer (246)
_ Z S	ozs. (242)
Z _ X	zax (110b)
Z Y _	zyg- (93c), zym- (93a)
Z _ Y	zay (11d)

FOUR-LETTER WORDS

A A _ _ Aare (18c, 100b), AARP (235)

_ A A _ Baal (106c), baas, caam (73a), Caan (144), haab (75b), Kaat (163), laap (41d), ma'am (74a), maar (129a), Paar (173), raad (15a, 40a, 112b, 121d), RAAF (242), saal (53d), Saar (49c, 78d, 101a), Taal (10c, 69a, 112b), WAAC (244), WAAF (244)

_ _ A A NCAA (241), NOAA (241)

A _ _ A abba (19c, 44d), Abia (104a), -acea (117c), acta (34b, 94d, 98c, 121a), adda (110a), Adja (214), agha (125b), Agra (24c, 119a), agra (64a, 118c), agua (113a), Aïda (84b, 97b, 128a), Akha (121d), Akra (216), akua (91a), alba (73c, 75c, 131d), alca (15d, 98a), Alda (137), Alea (15b), alga (105d), Alla (138), alla (233), Alma (138), alma (32a, 33b), Alta. (235), Alva (39c), amia (21b, 79c), amla (39b), amma (9a), amra (60c), anba (28a), anda (21c, 133b), Anka (138), Anna (84a, 122d, 138), anna (103a), anoa (48d, 85d, 132a, 229), ansa (57d), anta (89a, 91c), Anya (139), Apia (91c, 224), aqua (20b, 70b), arca (11d, 21b, 99b), area (36d, 37b, 45d, 72d, 97d, 99a, 135c), aria (75d, 111d, 125a, 234), arna (22b, 131d), Aroa (127d), arpa (65a), Arta (56d), asea (32b, 129c), Asia (39b), Asta (37b, 81d, 121b), atta (70c), atua (91a), aula (53d), aura (10d, 36d, 39d, 40b, 57c, 100d)

A B _ _ a bas (50b), abba (19c, 44d), abbe (28a, 49d, 94c), abbr. (235), Abby (137), abcs (46c), abed (110b), Abel (10a, 23a, 107a, 197), Abes, abet (10d, 48b, 59b), Abia (104a), abib (59a, 81d), Abie (81c), abir (98d), able (10a, 29c, 96b, 110a), -ably (117b), abou (44d), abri (51a, 108a), abut (21a, 75d, 123b)

_ A B _ baba (82d, 91a), Babe (140), babe (26c, 40d), Babi (16a), Babs, babu (60a), baby (26c, 40d, 83c), caba (133d), cabs, dabs, fabe (55b), gabi (119d), gabs, gaby (109c), habu (89c, 103c), jabs, Labe (217), labs, mabi (47d, 80b), nabs, PABA (86b), Rabe (176), Rabi (15c, 88d), rabi (78b), saba (45d, 88c), Sabe (67b), tabs, tabu (48c)

_ _ A B Ahab (24a, 66c, 67d, 87d, 197), Arab (104b, 213, 217, 218, 219, 221, 222, 223, 224), Arab. (235), blab (119d), crab (32b, 108a), drab (22b, 26b, 29a, 38c, 43d, 47b), grab (80b, 106c, 111b), haab (75b), Joab (33d, 197), Moab (66b, 73b, 197), scab (134a), slab (88d, 110c), snab (22b, 105a), stab (15c, 68a, 88d), swab (57c, 78c, 134b)

A _ _ B abib (59a, 81d), Agib (13d), Ahab (24a, 66c, 67d, 87d, 197), Arab (104b, 213, 217, 218, 219, 221, 222, 223, 224), Arab. (235)

A C _ _ acad. (235), acct. (235), AC/DC (235), -acea (117c), aced (120c), acer (74d), aces, acet- (92c), ache (73a, 85d, 134b), acht (53d), achy (112a), acid (119d), Acis (52b), acle (64b), ACLU (235), acme (32c, 87b, 123a, 135a), acne (110a), acou- (93a), Acre (214), acre (45d, 68d, 246), acro- (93a, 93c), acta (34b, 94d, 98c, 121a), ACTH (235), acts, acus (70a, 89b)

_ A C _ Bach (140), back (14c, 59b, 60a, 98a, 115b), caco- (92c), dace (46c, 228), each (13b), face (15a, 30a, 73a, 79d, 118a, 128c), fact (9d, 35b, 98a), hack (24c, 33a, 60b), jaca (65b), Jack (159), jack (17a, 24a, 68a, 78a, 97c), lace (47b), lack (34c, 129d), lacy (34c), mace (40c, 82d, 114b, 118d, 129d), mach (113c), Mack (167), mack (97c), Macy (167), NaCL (111c), paca (25b, 101c), Pace (204), pace (52a, 113c, 129b), pack (16d, 22c, 105c, 232, 246), paco (11d, 109c), pact (10d, 11c, 17b, 20d), race (87d, 103a, 114a, 124b), rack (10b, 28b), racy (20a, 113c), sack (30b, 36a, 89b, 90c, 132c), sacs, tack (13d, 15c, 31b, 44c, 80b), tact (35d), Waco (21d), WACs

_ _ A C HUAC (239), WAAC (244)

A _ _ C AC/DC (235), AFDC (235), Alec (137), alec (12c, 47a, 104b), Apoc. (235), -atic (117c), avec (51b)

A D _ _ adad (42c), Adah (41c, 197), Adak (64b), Adam (23d, 84d, 107a, 137, 194, 197), Adar (66d, 78c), Adas, adat (74b), adda (110a), adds, Aden (13d, 224), adit (41b, 77a), Adja (214), admi (53b), adze (122d)

_ A D _ bade, Cade (192), cade (59d, 67c, 88b), cadi (13d, 80c), cads, Dada (14d, 49c), dado (34b, 84d, 87c, 129d), dads, Eads (21d), fade (35c, 36a, 127b), fado (91d), fads, gads, hade (53c), hadj (89b), Jada (197), jade (53b, 56c), kadi (13d, 80d), Ladd (165), lade (24b, 35d, 72d, 76d, 119a), lads, lady (45b, 81d), made (31d), NADA (241), pads, qadi (13d, 80d), rads, Sada (179), sado (24c, 66a), Sadr (207), tads, Wade (185), wade (129b), wadi (38b, 83a, 98a, 101a), wads

_ _ A D   acad. (235), adad (42c), Arad (221), arad (65b), bead (17d, 109b), Brad (142), brad (44c, 54d, 80b), Chad (117a, 145, 215), clad (37d), dead (69b), duad (85d, 125c), dyad (85d), egad (83a), Fuad (44c), glad (66d), goad (62c, 114b), grad (25c), grad. (239), head (21a, 25d, 26c, 51c, 78a, 94c), Irad (197), Joad (55d), lead (29d, 35d, 56d, 58c, 245), load (10b, 22d, 24b, 119a), Mead (61a, 170), mead (18a, 37d, 60d), Obad. (241), quad (29a), raad (15a, 40a, 112b, 121d), read (63c, 88b, 116c), road (31b, 38a, 121b, 130c), scad (24d, 27b, 61b, 65b), shad (25b, 46d), spad (80b, 89d), stad (112b), Thad (183), toad (17c, 225), woad (20a, 38d)

A _ _ D   abed (110b), acad. (235), aced (120c), acid (119d), adad (42c), aged (12c, 83c, 83d), amid (12b), aped, apod (48c), Arad (221), arad (65b), arid (38b), Arnd (53d), auld (105b), avid (39a, 41b, 56b, 67b, 135a), awed, axed

A E _ _   aeon (122b), aeri- (92c), aero- (92c), aero. (235), aery (39a)

_ A E _   Baer (140), Baez (140), Caen (17c), Gaea (39b, 198), Gael (25c, 105a), haec (70a), Jael (197), Kael (163), Kaen (223), laet (49b), Maes, Raes, tael (71c, 131a), ta'en (107c)

_ _ A E   alae (132d), brae (60a, 105b), frae (105a), -idae (117c), irae (35c), koae (58b), prae (69c)

A _ _ E   Aare (18c, 100b), abbe (28a, 49d, 94c), Abie (81c), able (10a, 29c, 96b, 110a), ache (73a, 85d, 134b), acle (64c), acme (32c, 87b, 123a, 135a), acne (110a), Acre (214), acre (45d, 68d, 246), adze (122d), Agee (137), ague (26c, 45c, 74b, 104b), aide (10a, 15b, 59b, 106a), aine (51a), aire (64a), akee (51d, 124a), alae (132d), alee (59a, 108a, 132b), aloe (10c, 19c, 59b, 59c, 71d, 75c, 90a, 122d), alte (69d), amie (50b), -ance (117a, 117c), Anne (96b, 107c, 138, 192, 194), anse (50c), ante (68a, 69c, 90d, 114c), ante- (92c), a-one (42b, 46c, 123b), apse (12a, 27a, 98b, 106c, 127c), Arie (139), Arne (102d, 139), Arte (139), Ashe (139), asse (49b), atle (104a, 119b), aube (11a), auge (71b), aune (246), axle (113c, 131c)

A F _ _   Afar (41d, 216), afar (36d), AFDC (235), affy (18d), Afro (57b), Afro- (92c)

_ A F _   baff (55b), baft (43b), cafe (19c), daft (48b), gaff (46d, 47a, 113b), haft (60a), Kafa (32d, 216), oafs, raff (102d), Raft (176), raft (47c), S.Afr. (242), safe (106b, 116c, 127b), Safi (220), Taft (183, 191), waft (47c)

_ _ A F   deaf (125d, 126d), Graf (135a, 156), graf (53d, 81d), leaf (85b, 90a), loaf (61d, 73b, 130a), neaf (47b), Olaf (82b, 128b, 173), Piaf (49d, 100c, 175), RAAF (242), RCAF (242), USAF (243), WAAF (244), WRAF (244)

A _ _ F   alif (11d), atef (32b, 39d)

A G _ _   Agag (67c, 104a, 197), agal (18a, 30d), Agao (57c), Agar (137), agar (32c, 106a), **agas**, **Agau** (57c), **agcy.** (235), **aged** (12c, 83c, 83d), **Agee** (137), **Ager** (137), **ager** (69d, 100d, 102a), **ages**, **agha** (125b), **Agib** (13d), **agio** (42c, 48d, 78a, 94a), **Agis** (67d), **Agni** (68c), **agog** (39a, 42c, 67b), **agon** (30b, 45c, 56b), **Agra** (24c, 119a), **agra** (64a, 118c), **agri.** (235), **agua** (113a), **ague** (26c, 45c, 74b, 104b)

_ A G _   **bago** (15a), **bags**, **Cage** (144), **cage** (30a, 40d), **cagy** (31d), **gaga** (24c, 76a), **gage** (90b), **gags**, **hagi** (65d), **hags**, **Iago** (44a, 85a, 107c, 195), **jags**, **kago** (86a), **Iago** (65a, 112d), **lags**, **mage** (74a), **Magh** (213), **magh** (78b), **magi** (88a, 94c, 132d), **Naga** (15a, 69a, 128c), **naga** (23c, 28c, 60a), **nags**, **Nagy** (61c, 172), **Page** (173, 193, 194), **page** (12d, 41c, 48b, 70d, 107a), **raga** (80a), **rage** (26d, 74c, 116a, 120b), **ragi** (25c), **rags**, **saga** (71b, 104c, 119b), **sage** (14c, 70d, 77b, 106a, 131b, 132d), **sago** (44b, 86a, 95d, 114d), **sags**, **tags**, **vagi** (31d), **wage** (103d), **wags**

_ _ A G   **Agag** (67c, 104a, 197), **anag.** (235), **brag** (20b, 24a, 32b, 127c), **crag** (101b), **diag.** (237), **drag** (30d, 95d), **flag** (17a, 38a, 41a, 69a, 87b, 114d, 130c, 132a), **peag** (129d), **phag-** (92d), **quag** (20c), **shag** (57b, 119c, 122c), **slag** (28c, 38b, 76b, 105a, 111a, 129a, 130a), **snag** (13a, 24d, 60a, 68c, 95a, 122b), **stag** (34c, 52b, 76a), **swag** (115c)

A _ _ G   **Agag** (67c, 104a, 197), **agog** (39a, 42c, 67b), **anag.** (235)

A H _ _   **Ahab** (24a, 66c, 67d, 87d, 197), **Ahaz** (67d, 197), **ahem** (15c, 112a), **ahey** (42c), **ahir** (24d), **Ahom** (69a), **ahoy** (57b, 81a), **AHST** (235)

_ A H _   **Bahr** (140), **baht** (223, 246), **Dahl** (147), **Fahr.** (238), **ha-ha** (45b, 118a), **Hahn** (156), **hahs** (42c), **Kahn** (163), **kahu** (15d), **Lahr** (165), **maha** (25d, 69a, 104a), **Oahe** (33b), **Oahu** (64c), **paha** (60a), **rahs**, **Sahl** (179), **Saho** (32d, 57c, 216), **taha** (130d), **tahr** (55a)

_ _ A H   **Adah** (41c, 197), **amah** (74b, 82d, 84d), **ayah** (62d, 82d), **blah** (82a, 71d), **Elah** (67d), **Etah** (56c, 63d), **Leah** (65b, 68b, 197), **Noah** (68d, 76b, 172, 197), **opah** (22a, 46d), **Ptah** (75d, 198), **shah** (16c, 88a), **Utah** (212), **yeah** (10b)

A _ _ H   **ACTH** (235), **Adah** (41c, 197), **Alph** (101a), **amah** (74b, 82d, 84d), **amph.** (235), **ankh** (32a), **anth.** (235), **arch** (28a, 41b, 101c), **-arch** (117c), **arch-** (93b), **arch.** (235), **Asch** (139), **auth.** (236), **ayah** (62d, 82d)

A I _ _   **Aïda** (84b, 97b, 128a), **aide** (10a, 15b, 59b, 106a), **AIDS** (235), **aids**, **ails**, **aims**, **aine** (51a), **ains**, **ain't**, **aire** (64a), **airs** (94b), **airy** (41d, 66a, 71d)

_ A I _   **bail** (20d, 68b), **Bain** (140), **bain** (50a), **Baio** (140), **bait** (16b, 41b, 73d, 119c, 123b), **Cain** (9a, 10a, 41a, 68d, 79d, 107a, 144, 197), **dail** (40a, 64a), **dais** (41d, 90b), **fail** (35c, 44a, 48a), **Fain** (152), **fain** (35b, 54c, 133a), **fair** (10a, 17d, 41b, 45c, 62b, 67c), **fait** (9c, 50b), **Gaia** (39b), **Gail** (154), **gain** (9d, 44d, 83b, 94d, 132b), **gait**

313

(130c), **Haid** (156), **Haig** (156), **haik** (52d), **hail** (9c, 16a, 56c, 60d, 104a, 127d, 130d), **Haim** (156), **hair** (46a), **jail** (62b), **jain** (60b), **kail** (23a), **kain** (74c), **laic** (28a, 70c, 82a, 94d, 106b), **laid, lain, lair** (34d, 60c), **lait** (50d), **Maia** (59c, 107b, 129c, 198, 207), **maid** (37b, 54c, 107a), **mail** (14c, 76b, 91d), **maim** (80d), **Main** (168), **main** (26c, 29d, 67b, 94c), **mais** (50a), **naid** (51b), **naif** (126c), **nail** (27d, 44c, 119b, 126b), **Nair** (37d), **nair** (85a), **nais** (51b, 101a), **paid** (99a), **pail** (30b), **pain** (10b, 61d), **pair** (21c, 31b, 90d, 119c, 125c), **raid** (48c, 62d), **rail** (9c, 19a, 30d, 75a, 111d, 123c, 129a, 226), **rain** (92a, 120a, 130d), **rais** (24a), **saic** (71c), **Said** (91c), **said** (127c), **sail** (91c), **sain** (19d, 32b), **Sais** (39d), **sais** (56c), **tail** (13c, 25a, 40d, 48b, 89d, 107b, 123c), **tait** (15d, 60d), **vain** (40c, 63a), **vair** (52c, 114b), **waif** (116b), **wail** (32b, 61c, 68d, 114b), **wain** (129b), **wait** (24b, 72a, 99c, 115a, 119d)

_ _ A I   **Alai** (103c), **dhai** (76c), **Thai** (109a, 218, 223)

A _ _ I   **abri** (51a, 108a), **admi** (53b), **aeri-** (92c), **Agni** (68c), **agri.** (235), **Alai** (103c), **alti-** (93a), **ambi-** (92c), **a moi** (50d), **Andi** (25a), **ANSI** (235), **anti** (10c, 84c), **anti-** (92c), **Aoki** (139), **aqui** (112d), **arui** (13b), **asci** (114a), **assi** (60c), **Asti** (65a, 132c), **Atli** (15c, 56d, 61c)

A J _ _   **ajar** (84b), **Ajax** (56b, 120b, 120d, 194)

_ A J _   **Baja** (23b, 76c), **baju** (65b), **haje** (28c, 39d), **haji** (75c), **hajj** (75c, 89b), **Jaja** (79a), **maja** (31d), **raja** (60a)

A K _ _   **Akan** (69a, 215, 216), **akee** (51d, 124a), **Akha** (121d), **Akim** (137), **akin** (67c, 99a), **Akra** (216), **akua** (91a)

_ A K _   **bake** (30c, 101b), **Baku** (24b, 213), **baku** (116b, 124a), **cake** (35b), **fake** (45a, 62a, 94b, 107c), **hake** (46d, 228), **Jake** (160), **jako** (56a), **kaka** (81c), **kaki** (65d, 81c), **Lake** (165), **lake** (89a, 130a), **lakh** (84a, 108a), **laky** (65d, 81c), **make** (13c, 29c, 30c, 40d, 43d, 44c), **maki** (71b), **mako** (20b, 107d), **oaks, rake** (34a, 52d), **raki** (11a), **sake** (10b, 65d, 131a), **Saki** (95c), **saki** (78b, 231), **Saks** (179), **taka** (213), **take** (117a), **takt** (80a, 120b), **waka** (23d), **wake** (102c, 123c), **yaks**

_ _ A K   **Adak** (64b), **anak** (54b), **beak** (18d, 77d), **dhak** (39b), **Dyak** (217, 219), **flak** (13a), **Isak** (159), **leak** (72b, 84b), **N.Dak.** (241), **peak** (11d, 31d, 32c, 59a, 59d, 117d, 135a), **S.Dak.** (242), **Shak.** (243), **soak** (9b, 37d, 104b, 115a), **SWAK** (243), **teak** (39b, 124a), **weak** (45a, 62c, 63a)

A _ _ K   **Adak** (64b), **amok** (18c, 51b), **anak** (54b)

A L _ _   **alae** (132d), **Alai** (103c), **Alan** (137), **alar** (16c, 132d), **Alas.** (209, 235), **alas** (42c, 103b, 133b), **alba** (73c, 75c, 131d), **albs, alca** (15d, 98a), **Alda** (137), **Aldo** (137), **Alea** (15b), **Alec** (137), **alec** (12c, 47a, 104b), **alee** (59a, 108a, 132b), **ales, Alex** (137), **Alfs, alga** (105d), **-algy** (117c), **alif** (11d), **alim** (120a), **alit** (36c, 68d, 107a), **Alla** (138), **alla** (233), **allo-** (93d), **Ally** (138), **ally** (11b, 15b, 29d, 30a, 126c), **Alma** (138), **alma** (32a, 33b), **alms** (26a), **aloe**

314

(10c, 19c, 59b, 59c, 71d, 75c, 90a, 122d), **alop** (38a), **Alou** (138), **alow** (18c, 126a), **Alph** (101a), **Alps** (79b), **also** (12c, 18c, 62c, 78c, 90c, 115b), **Alta.** (235), **alte** (69d), **alti-** (93a), **alto** (113a, 128d), **alto-** (93a), **alum** (37c, 77a), **alum.** (235), **Alva** (39c)

_ A L _   **Bala** (53c), **bald** (17b), **bale** (22c, 232), **Bali** (64c), **balk** (16b, 89c, 116a), **Ball** (140), **ball** (17b), **balm** (83d, 126a), **Cale** (144), **calf** (134d), **Cali** (215), **calk** (61b), **call** (12d, 15a, 85b, 108d, 117d, 128c, 134b), **calm** (11c, 13c, 15b, 82a, 85b, 89d, 97a, 106d, 111c, 111d, 126c), **calx** (59a, 85d), **Dale** (26d, 147), **dale** (35d, 98a, 127b), **Dali** (147), **Daly** (147), **Fala** (44d), **fa-la** (98d), **Falk** (152), **fall** (38b, 57b, 106a), **falx** (102a), **gala** (45c), **Gale** (154), **gale** (130d, 132b, 132c), **gall** (18d, 25d, 64b, 128b), **gals, Hale** (12b, 156), **hale** (112a, 131d), **half** (77c), **Hall** (156), **hall** (31a, 87a), **halo** (27b, 71d, 81d, 100d), **Hals** (38d, 156), **halt** (14c, 25b, 32a, 59d, 87b, 115d), **kale** (23a, 78a, 90a, 103d, 127c), **Kali** (109d, 199), **kali** (104a), **kalo** (119d), **Lalo** (165), **lalo** (117d), **Male** (37d, 219), **male** (53b, 70b, 114b), **Mali** (219), **mali** (24d), **mall** (74c, 95a, 108c), **malm** (27d, 72a), **malo** (21d, 58c, 72d, 112d), **malt** (18a), **pale** (19d, 86a, 88d, 129d), **Pali** (22b, 104b, 127c), **pall** (28b, 122b, 130d), **palm** (124a), **palp** (13a, 45a, 123b), **pals, rale** (21d, 26c, 34a), **sala** (112d, 113a), **sale** (15c, 17b, 50b, 51a, 123d), **Salk** (179), **salp** (83b), **SALT** (242), **salt** (29d, 80b, 94b, 103b, 106a, 111c), **tala** (17c), **talc** (25d, 49c, 77a, 92a, 111b), **tale** (43a, 71b, 103b, 134a), **talk** (29d, 36a, 113b), **tall** (72d), **Vale** (184), **vale** (44b, 127b), **Vali** (83b), **wale** (55c, 100c, 130c, 131b, 131c), **walk** (85b), **Wall** (193), **wall** (118a), **Walt** (185), **Yale** (79b, 101c, 205)

_ _ A L   **agal** (18a, 30d), **anal** (51c), **Aral** (103c), **Baal** (106c), **bual** (132c), **coal** (13a, 40c, 52a), **deal** (17b, 36a, 36d, 123d), **dhal** (11d), **dial** (43d), **dual** (37c, 125c), **egal** (50b), **et al.** (69c, 238), **foal** (61b), **goal** (10d, 17c, 40d, 83a, 96c, 104d, 119d), **heal** (32d), **hyal-** (93a), **-ical** (117a), **ital.** (240), **leal** (73c, 105b), **meal** (56c, 99c), **Neal** (172), **Obal** (197), **opal** (19c, 53b, 54c, 64a), **oral** (79b, 113d, 127c, 128a), **oval** (39d, 40b), **peal** (100d), **real** (9d, 116d), **rial** (220), **ryal** (83d), **saal** (53d), **seal** (28b, 44c, 89b, 231), **sial** (85b), **Taal** (10c, 69a, 112b), **teal** (19a, 20b, 38c, 226), **udal** (59c), **Ural** (103c), **veal** (23b, 75c), **vial** (110d), **weal** (131b, 131c), **zeal** (14b, 45c)

A _ _ L   **Abel** (10a, 23a, 107a, 197), **agal** (18a, 30d), **amyl** (114d), **amyl-** (93d), **anal** (51c), **Angl.** (235), **anil** (38d, 62d), **Aral** (103c), **aril** (106b), **aryl** (14b), **AWOL** (236), **axil** (12c), **azul** (112c)

A M _ _   **amah** (74b, 82d, 84d), **amas** (69d), **amat** (69d), **ambi-** (92c), **ambo** (95d, 98a), **amen** (111b, 128a), **Amer.** (235), **amer** (50a), **Ames** (138), **AMEX** (235), **amia** (21b, 79c), **amid** (12b), **amie** (50b), **amir** (10b, 13d), **Amis** (138), **amis** (50b), **amla** (39b), **amma** (9a), **ammo** (12b), **a moi** (50d), **amok** (18c, 51b), **Amon** (67d, 198), **Amor** (32d, 198), **amor** (112d), **Amos** (108a, 138, 196, 197), **Amoy** (69a), **amph.** (235), **amps, amra** (60c), **Amur** (101a), **amyl** (114d), **amyl-** (93d), **Amys**

_ A M _   **came** (132b), **Camp** (144), **camp** (19c, 39d, 127a), **cams, dama** (65a, 112d), **dame** (45b, 54c, 68c, 81d, 122c), **damp** (33c, 77c,

131b), **dams**, **Fama** (103a), **fame** (99c, 99d), **gamb** (12d), **game** (114a), **gamo-** (93c), **Gamp** (35c), **gamp** (125b), **gams** (71b), **gamy** (90b, 103d), **Hama** (222), **hame** (61b), **hams**, **iamb** (48c), **jamb** (37c, 109a, 126d), **jams**, **Jamy** (194), **Kama** (199), **kama** (60a, 129a), **kame** (60a, 100c), **kami** (65d, 108a), **lama** (22b, 121d), **Lamb** (40b, 165), **lamb** (107d), **lame** (32a, 57c), **lamp** (71d, 73c), **lams**, **mama** (44b), **mamo** (58b), **Nama** (61c), **name** (10d, 13c, 28d, 38b, 82a, 122c), **Pams**, **Rama** (128c), **rami** (21c), **ramp** (52c, 62c, 110d), **Rams** (206), **rams**, **sama** (80d), **same** (36d, 61d), **samp** (55c, 60d, 91c), **Sams**, **tame** (37a, 37b, 53c), **tamp** (76d, 85b, 92a, 97d), **tams**, **vamp** (62c, 108c, 233), **yams**, **Zama** (106a)

_ _ A M   **Adam** (23d, 84d, 107a, 137, 194, 197), **Aram** (108a, 118d, 139), **beam** (98a), **Bram** (142), **caam** (73a), **Cham** (224), **clam** (19c, 77d), **cram** (116c), **diam.** (237), **dram** (38a, 38b, 84a, 92a, 110d, 246), **Edam** (26b, 38d), **Elam** (88a, 108a, 151), **Enam** (66d), **exam** (120d), **flam** (38b), **foam** (51c, 114a), **gram** (76b, 246), **Guam** (64c), **imam** (23b, 80c), **Liam** (166), **loam** (39a, 111c), **ma'am** (74a), **Noam** (172), **ogam** (64b), **pram** (16a, 24c), **ream** (18d, 31b, 41a, 86b, 125c), **roam** (123d, 129d), **seam** (66c, 67a, 128c), **sham** (9d, 34a, 45a, 49b, 77b, 91d, 94b, 109c), **Siam** (120d), **slam** (124c, 131c), **Spam** (73c), **swam**, **team** (32a, 48c, 56c, 85d, 232), **tram** (124c), **Ulam** (197), **wham** (110b)

A _ _ M   **Adam** (23d, 84d, 107a, 137, 194, 197), **ahem** (15c, 112a), **Ahom** (69a), **Akim** (137), **alim** (120a), **alum** (37c, 77a), **alum.** (235), **Aram** (108a, 118d, 139), **arum** (32c, 71d, 114d), **atom** (77d, 131c)

A N _ _   **anag.** (235), **anak** (54b), **anal** (51c), **anas**, **anat.** (235), **anba** (28a), **-ance** (117a, 117c), **-ancy** (117b), **anda** (21c, 133b), **Andi** (25a), **Andy** (138), **anew** (10b, 10c), **Angl.** (235), **anil** (38d, 62d), **anis**, **Anka** (138), **ankh** (32a), **Anna** (84a, 122d, 138), **anna** (103a), **Anne** (96b, 107c, 138, 192, 194), **anno** (70b), **Anns**, **anoa** (48d, 85d, 132a, 229), **anon** (10c, 15d, 62a, 94a, 108d, 111d), **anon.** (235), **ansa** (57d), **anse** (50c), **ANSI** (235), **ansu** (13d, 68c), **anta** (89a, 91c), **ante** (68a, 69c, 90d, 114c), **ante-** (92c), **anth.** (235), **anti** (10c, 84c), **anti-** (92c), **ants**, **Anya** (139)

_ A N _   **banc** (66d), **band** (56c, 116b, 232), **bane** (58a, 81b, 90d, 102d, 133b), **bang** (110b), **bani** (101d), **bank** (19a, 47c, 91b), **bans**, **Cana** (46c, 52b), **canc.** (236), **cane** (98a, 114b, 115a, 115b, 117d, 129b), **cans**, **cant** (62c, 63b, 66a, 70d, 103d, 122a, 122b), **Dana** (147), **Dane** (67c, 82b, 104c, 147), **dang** (42a), **dank** (33b, 77c), **Dans**, **dans** (50c), **Danu** (199), **fane** (104a, 120b), **Fang** (193, 216), **fang** (123a), **fans**, **gang** (16d, 32a, 232), **Hana** (157), **hand** (10d, 15a, 59b, 87c, 133d, 246), **hang** (118b), **Hank** (157), **hank** (57b, 109d), **Hans** (17b, 53d, 67a, 157), **-iana** (117c), **Ians**, **Jana** (80d, 160), **Jane** (160), **Jann** (160), **Jans**, **kana** (66a), **Kane** (163), **Kano** (129c), **Kans.** (210, 240), **Kant** (53d, 163), **Lana** (165), **lana** (70b), **Land** (165), **land** (9d, 36b, 120d), **Lane** (165), **lane** (11c, 21b, 116b), **Lang** (165), **lang.** (240), **lank** (121a), **lanx** (102a), **mana** (91a), **mand** (25c), **mane** (57b), **mani** (87b), **Mann** (168), **mano** (65a), **Manx** (25c), **manx** (24d), **many** (82d), **Nana** (88b, 135c), nano- (92c), **Nans, pane** (114c, 114d), **Pang** (125a), **pang** (85d, 114b, 121c), **pans, pant** (18a, 21d), **rana** (51c, 60a), **Rand** (176), **rand** (220, 222), **rang, rani** (60a, 94c), **rank** (27d, 46a, 55c, 72a, 73d, 97d, 116c), **rant** (34b, 58a, 98a, 119b), **Sa'na** (134c), **Sand** (179), **sand** (78d, 109b), **sane** (97d), **sang, sank, sans** (51b), **Tana** (68b), **T'ang** (26d), **tang** (22a, 47b, 135a), **tank** (127d), **Tano** (95d, 189), **tans, uang** (100b), **vane** (130d, 132b), **vang** (57c, 102b), **vans, wand** (90d, 101c, 115b), **wane** (9a, 34b, 69a, 116d), **want** (34a, 35b, 68b, 81b, 92a, 133a), **yang** (134d), **Yank** (12b), **yank** (95d), **Zana** (58a), **Zane** (188), **zany** (28b, 38a, 48b, 109c)

_ _ **A N**   **Akan** (69a, 215, 216), **Alan** (137), **Aran** (52b, 64c), **azan** (80c), **Bean** (140), **bean** (58c, 60b, 71b, 106b, 127c), **bran** (22a, 22b, 55d, 61d), **Caan** (144), **clan** (124b), **cran** (118c), **Dean** (148), **dean** (83c), **Dian** (198), **duan** (52a), **Dyan** (150), **elan** (33d, 41b, 113d, 128d, 135a), **flan** (32d, 87a), **Fran** (153), **G-man** (45a), **guan** (19b), **Iban** (33d), **Iran** (88a, 217), **Ivan** (66c, 103c, 159), **Jean** (160), **Joan** (161), **Juan** (163), **Kean** (164), **Khan** (164), **khan** (10b, 63a, 88a, 94c), **kwan** (246), **Lean** (165), **lean** (24b, 29b, 98a, 110c, 113b, 121a, 122b), **loan** (17a, 78a), **mean** (9a, 16a, 17b, 34d, 76c, 109b, 115c), **moan** (32b, 112b), **Oman** (220), **Onan** (66d), **Oran** (213), **plan** (13d, 15c, 35b, 76b, 95a, 104d), **roan** (61a, 98c, 131c), **Ryan** (179), **scan** (47c, 73a, 88b, 98a), **Sean** (66c, 180), **Shan** (62d, 69a, 220), **span** (21d, 32a, 38d, 49a, 81d, 85d, 98a, 120a, 120c, 122a, 232), **Stan** (181), **Svan** (25a), **swan** (19a, 28c, 226), **than** (29b), **T-man** (45a), **tuan** (74c), **uran** (78a), **wean** (117a), **yean** (68d), **Yüan** (26d, 78a), **yuan** (215)

A _ _ **N**   **Aden** (13d, 224), **aeon** (122b), **agon** (30b, 45c, 56b), **Akan** (69a, 215, 216), **akin** (67c, 99a), **Alan** (137), **amen** (111b, 128a), **Amon** (67d, 198), **anon** (10c, 15d, 62a, 94a, 108d, 111d), **anon.** (235), **Aran** (52b, 64c), **ARVN** (235), **asin** (78b), **assn.** (236), **aton** (118a), **attn.** (236), **Avon** (107c), **axon** (81b), **ayin** (12a), **azan** (80c), **azon** (10b)

A O _ _   **Aoki** (139), **a-one** (42b, 46c, 123b), **aout** (49d)

_ **A O** _   faon (44d), **gaol** (94d), **gaon** (66c), **Laos** (218), **naos** (25b, 104a, 120b), **paon** (87b), **Taos** (81c)

_ _ **A O**   **Agao** (57c), **ciao** (65a), **Isao** (159), **Liao** (101a)

A _ _ **O**   acro- (93a, 93c), aero- (92c, aero. (235, **Afro** (57b), **Afro-** (92c), **Agao** (57c), **agio** (42c, 48d, 78a, 94a), **Aldo** (137), **allo-** (93d), **also** (12c, 18c, 62c, 78c, 90c, 115b), **alto** (113a, 128d), **alto-** (93a), **ambo** (95d, 98a), **ammo** (12b), **anno** (70b), **Argo** (14b, 66a), **Arlo** (139), **Arno** (101a, 139), **at. no.** (236), **atto-** (93c), **auto** (24a)

A P _ _   apar (14b), **aped, aper** (28b, 77a), **apes, apex** (32c, 59a, 59d, 87b, 89b, 123a, 135a), **Apia** (91c, 224), **Apis** (22c, 40a, 95d, 103b), **Apoc.** (235), **apod** (48c), **apos.** (235), **apse** (12a, 27a, 98b, 106c, 127c), **Apus** (207)

_ **A P** _   **Bapt.** (236), **capa** (122c), **cape** (37c, 58d, 74d, 95a), **Caph** (207),

317

Capp (144), **caps, Capt.** (236), **daps, gape** (134b), **gaps, Hapi** (198), **hapi** (53b), **hapl-** (93c), **jape** (66c), **Lapp** (82b, 222), **laps, mapo** (55a), **maps, Napa** (23b, 132c), **napa** (54d, 70d), **nape** (16b, 82d), **naps, papa** (12a, 44b), **Papp** (173), **paps, rape** (107b), **raps, rapt** (9b, 41a), **sapa** (55d), **saps, tapa** (17b, 28b, 43b, 45c, 79d, 86b, 91a), **tape** (19a, 98c), **taps, yapp** (20d), **yaps**

_ _ **A P**   **asap** (62a, 235), **atap** (86a), **chap** (45b, 74c), **clap** (13c, 121d), **crap** (82a, 91b), **flap** (48a, 79c, 89d, 119a, 130c, 132d), **frap** (37d, 122a), **hcap.** (239), **heap** (17a, 75b, 79a, 89a), **knap** (60a), **laap** (41d), **leap** (24a, 67a, 232), **neap** (121d, 122d, 129b), **reap** (9d, 33a, 58b), **slap** (22c, 98b), **snap** (17b, 21d, 31d, 39b, 44c, 66c), **soap** (17c), **swap** (123c), **trap** (24c, 24d, 41a, 54b, 55b, 101b, 111b), **whap** (60b), **wrap** (19a, 28a, 41b)

A _ _ P   **AARP** (235), **alop** (38a), **asap** (62a, 235), **atap** (86a), **atop** (85c, 126d), **avdp.** (236)

A Q _ _   **aqua** (20b, 70b), **aqui** (112d)

_ _ **A Q**   **Iraq** (217)

A R _ _   **Arab** (104b, 213, 217, 218, 219, 221, 222, 223, 224), **Arab.** (235), **Arad** (221), **arad** (65b), **Aral** (103c), **Aram** (108a, 118d, 139), **Aran** (52b, 64c), **Aras, arca** (11d, 21b, 99b), **arch** (28a, 41b, 101c), **-arch** (117c), **arch-** (93b), **arch.** (235), **arcs, area** (36d, 37b, 45d, 72d, 97d, 99a, 135c), **Ares** (13b, 41c, 59b, 75a, 129d, 135c, 198), **Argo** (14b, 66a), **aria** (75d, 111d, 125a, 234), **arid** (38b), **Arie** (139), **aril** (106b), **Ariz.** (209, 235), **arks, Arlo** (139), **arms** (130d), **army** (61c), **arna** (22b, 131d), **Arnd** (53d), **Arne** (102d, 139), **Arno** (101a, 139), **arns, Aroa** (127d), **arpa** (65a), **Arta** (56d), **Arte** (139), **arts, arty, arui** (13b), **arum** (32c, 71d, 114d), **ARVN** (235), **aryl** (14b)

_ **A R _**   **Aare** (18c, 100b), **AARP** (235), **Bara** (140), **barb** (47a, 89a, 90c, 95a), **Bard** (200), **bard** (14c, 16b, 90c), **bare** (36a, 40c, 43a, 76a, 116b, 127a), **Bari** (10a, 218), **bark** (12d, 37b), **barm** (134b), **barn** (116a), **baro-** (93c), **bars, Bart** (140), **Bart.** (236), **Cara** (144), **cara** (65a), **carb-** (92d), **card** (29a, 66d, 87a), **CARE** (236), **care** (13a, 25b, 29d, 59a, 77a, 99a, 123d, 124d, 133d), **cark** (24b, 133d), **Carl** (144), **caro** (65a), **carp** (25b, 32a, 46a, 46c, 96d, 228), **Carr** (144), **cars, cart** (125d, 127c, 129b), **Cary** (144), **darb** (88a), **dare** (25d, 34c), **dark** (38d, 54d, 118c), **darn** (42a, 75d, 83a, 99c), **dart** (14c, 33d, 68d, 77b, 90c, 95a, 114a, 118c), **Earl** (150), **earl** (82a), **earn** (35b, 52a, 76a), **ears, fare** (35c, 48b), **farl** (105b), **farm** (21d, 32a, 55d, 122a), **faro** (24b), **Farr** (152), **garb** (28b, 37d), **gare** (50d, 97b), **Garn** (154), **Garo** (69a, 154), **GARP** (239), **Garr** (154), **gars, Gary** (154), **hard** (123b), **hare** (101c, 230), **hark** (72b), **harl** (46a, 48a, 59b), **harm** (33b, 61d, 62a, 63a), **harp** (80b), **Hart** (157), **hart** (34c, 114b), **Harz** (79b), **jarl** (104c), **jars, kari** (15d), **Karl** (163), **kary-** (93b), **Lara** (23c), **lard** (44c, 50a, 56a, 83d), **lari** (219), **lark** (19a, 51c, 226), **mara** (101c, 230), **Marc** (168), **marc** (55d), **mare** (61a, 82c), **Mari** (16d), **mari** (50c), **Mark** (42a, 102c, 168, 196), **mark** (10d, 15c, 55c, 96b, 109b, 114c, 133a), **marl** (27d, 35a, 45c), **Marr** (168), **Mars** (89d, 98d, 129d, 199), **mars** (49d), **mart** (40c,

74d), **maru** (65d), **Marv** (169), **Marx** (169), **Mary** (96c, 107c, 169, 197), **narc-** (93c), **nard** (75b, 83d), **Nare** (72d), **nark** (63a, 115d), **nary** (82c), **oars**, **Para** (18b, 214), **para** (112d, 214, 215, 222, 224), **pard** (24d), **pare** (87c, 98d), **pari-** (92d), **park** (53b, 95d), **parr** (103d, 109d), **pars**, **part** (11c, 43d, 49b, 57b, 91d, 106d), **rare** (83b, 104c, 126a, 126d), **Sara** (179, 215), **sard** (24b, 25d, 53b, 84c, 106c, 115d), **sari** (52d, 60a), **Sark** (26a, 64b), **Sart** (64a), **Tara** (104d), **tara** (45b, 64a), **tare** (128b, 131a), **tarn** (68b, 79b, 91b, 130a), **taro** (14d, 39c, 52a, 90d, 102b, 114d, 125a), **tarp** (23d, 130b), **tars**, **tart** (87a, 112b), **vara** (72a), **vari** (71b), **vary** (26a, 35c, 77c), **Ward** (186), **ward** (27c, 35a, 67b), **ware** (76a), **warm** (10b, 58d, 120c), **warn** (11b, 25b), **warp** (30b, 121c, 125c), **wars**, **Wart** (193), **wart** (95c), **wary** (25b, 128b, 130a), **Yard** (187), **yard** (40d, 69a, 113a, 246), **yarn** (43a, 114b, 119b, 133c), **zarf** (28d, 32d, 114d)

_ _ **A R**   **Adar** (66d, 78c), **Afar** (41d, 216), **afar** (36d), **Agar** (137), **agar** (32c, 106a), **ajar** (84b), **alar** (16c, 132d), **apar** (14b), **Avar** (25a, 82b), **Bear** (79b), **bear** (40d, 114c, 134c, 230), **boar** (60c, 89a, 118d, 132a, 230), **char** (104d, 124d, 228), **clar.** (237), **czar** (103c), **dear** (40d), **fear** (11a, 51c, 86b, 120d), **gear** (13c, 28b, 41b, 85b, 123a), **gnar** (56d), **guar** (38b, 48c), **hear** (59a, 72b), **hoar** (51c, 131d), **Isar** (33d, 79d, 100d, 216), **iyar** (78c), **izar** (52d), **knar** (68c), **Lear** (30d, 107c, 195), **liar** (75d), **maar** (129a), **near** (13d, 28b, 81d), **Omar** (41c, 78d, 88a, 120c, 173, 197), **Paar** (173), **pear** (51d, 124a), **Phar.** (242), **rear** (10c, 21d, 40d, 41c, 60a, 97c), **roar** (12d, 13c), **Saar** (49c, 78d, 101a), **scar** (27b, 134a), **sear** (25b, 133a), **soar** (48a), **spar** (21b, 22c, 52a, 77a, 90d, 101c, 108b), **star** (15b, 73c), **tear** (68b, 99c), **Thar** (35a), **thar** (55a), **tsar** (103c), **usar** (11b, 17b, 62d), **wear** (114a), **year** (122b)

A _ _ R   **abbr.** (235), **abir** (98d), **acer** (74d), **Adar** (66d, 78c), **Afar** (41d, 216), **afar** (36d), **Agar** (137), **agar** (32c, 106a), **Ager** (137), **ager** (69d, 100d, 102a), **ahir** (24d), **ajar** (84b), **alar** (16c, 132d), **Amer.** (235), **amer** (50a), **amir** (10b, 13d), **Amor** (32d, 198), **amor** (112d), **Amur** (101a), **apar** (14b), **aper** (28b, 77a), **asor** (59a), **astr-** (93d), **-ator** (117c), **Auer** (61c, 139), **Avar** (25a, 82b), **aver** (10b, 15a, 16c, 34b, 74b, 115a, 118c), **azur** (50a)

A S _ _   **asap** (62a, 235), **Asas**, **ASAT** (235), **Asch** (139), **asci** (114a), **asea** (32b, 129c), **Ashe** (139), **ashy** (86a, 129d), **Asia** (39b), **asin** (78b), **asks**, **asor** (59a), **asps**, **asse** (49b), **assi** (60c), **assn.** (236), **asst.** (236), **Asta** (37b, 81d, 121b), **Asti** (65a, 132c), **astr-** (93d)

_ **A S _**   **base** (9a, 41d, 49a, 62a, 73c, 92b, 102b, 102d), **bash** (60b, 86d), **bask** (46d, 73d, 80b, 128d, 228), **bast** (17b, 45d, 88c, 133c), **casa** (112d), **case** (14b, 30b, 63b, 71a, 82c), **Cash** (144), **cash** (15a, 78a), **cask** (30b), **Caso** (64c), **Cass** (144), **cast** (15a, 73a, 121c, 123b, 232), **dash** (20a, 96a, 114a, 120b, 128d), **ease** (10b, 11c, 15b, 29b, 42d, 71b, 77b, 99b, 99d, 100a, 129d), **east** (84d), **easy** (43d, 53c, 55c, 77c, 109c, 111c), **fast** (46b, 47c, 96d, 118c, 126d), **gash** (33a, 110b), **gasp** (21d, 86b), **hash** (21b), **hasp** (44c, 113c), **hast** (128a), **lasi** (221), **jass** (118d), **lash** (42d, 47c, 122a, 131c), **lass** (45b, 74b), **last** (30b, 40d, 108c, 130d), **masa** (30d), **masc.** (240), **MASH** (240), **Mash** (197), **mash** (32b, 115d), **mask** (29d,

36b, 37c), **Mass.** (210, 240), **mass** (9c, 10d, 17a, 22c, 53a, 58d, 107a, 129a), **mast** (18a, 90d, 108b, 113a), **NASA** (241), **Nash** (172), **nasi** (87a), **NASL** (241), **naso-** (93b), **Nast** (172), **oast** (16b, 67b, 85c), **pass** (13d, 21d, 84a, 85c, 106c), **past** (55b, 60b, 122a), **rase** (34d), **rash** (98b, 110a), **rasp** (46a, 56a, 105c, 122d), **sash** (18c, 37c, 54c, 132b), **Sask.** (242), **sass** (16b, 62c), **task** (115c), **Tasm.** (243), **TASS** (81c, 112b), **vasa** (38c, 128a), **vase** (30b, 47d), **vaso-** (92c), **vast** (61c, 62a), **Wash** (82b), **Wash.** (212), **wash** (14d), **WASP** (244), **wasp** (63b, 229), **wast** (128a), **Zasu** (188)

_ _ A S   a bas (50b), **Adas, agas, Alas.** (209, 235), **alas** (42c, 103b, 133b), **amas** (69d), **anas, Aras, Asas, Avas, baas, Beas, bias** (12c, 35c, 94a), **boas, bras** (49d), **Chas.** (74d), **Dias** (91d), **eras, Evas, eyas** (19b, 58c), **fras, goas, Idas** (24d), **Iras** (28a, 195), **keas, leas, Lias** (53c), **moas, okas, peas, seas, spas, teas, 'twas** (30b, 107c), **Unas, upas** (66a, 90d, 124a), **utas** (40a), **Xmas** (27a), **yeas** (129c)

A _ _ S   a bas (50b), **abcs** (46c), **Abes, aces, Acis** (52b), **acts, acus** (70a, 89b), **Adas, adds, agas, ages, Agis** (67d), **AIDS** (235), **aids, ails, aims, ains, airs** (94b), **Alas.** (209, 235), **alas** (42c, 103b, 133b), **albs, ales, Alfs, alms** (26a), **Alps** (79b), **amas** (69d), **Ames** (138), **Amis** (138), **amis** (50b), **Amos** (108a, 138, 196, 197), **amps, Amys, anas, anis, Anns, ants, apes, Apis** (22c, 40a, 95d, 103b), **apos.** (235), **Apus** (207), **Aras, arcs, Ares** (13b, 41c, 59b, 75a, 129d, 135c, 198), **arks, arms** (130d), **arns, arts, Asas, asks, asps, ates** (118c), **atis** (60a), **auks, Avas, aves, avis** (69c), **avus** (69d), **awes, awls, awns, axes, axis** (25c, 34c, 60c), **ayes** (129c)

A T _ _   **atap** (86a), **atef** (32b, 39d), **ates** (118c), **-atic** (117c), **atis** (60a), **atle** (104a, 119b), **Atli** (15c, 56d, 61c), **at. no.** (236), **atom** (77d, 131c), **aton** (118a), **atop** (85c, 126d), **-ator** (117c), **atta** (70c), **attn.** (236), **atto-** (93c), **Attu** (64b), **atty.** (236), **atua** (91a), **at. wt.** (236)

_ A T _   **bate** (119c), **Bath** (41a, 112c), **bath** (35d, 88d, 125a, 246), **bats, batt** (16d), **cata-** (92c, 92d), **Cath.** (236), **Cato** (101d, 102a, 194), **cats, Catt** (144), **data** (29c, 63a, 115a), **date** (33d, 51d), **eats** (48b), **fate** (35b, 68a, 73b), **Fats** (152), **gata** (107d), **gate** (15c, 41b, 91c), **Gath** (88c), **gats, GATT** (239), **hate** (35b, 72d), **hath** (128a), **hats, JATO** (240), **Kate** (107c, 163), **kati** (246), **Kato** (56c), **late** (33d, 98b), **lath** (116c), **mate** (15b, 18d, 26c, 29b, 34c, 85d, 114a, 120a), **math** (116c), **Mats** (169), **Matt** (169, 240), **maty** (62d), **Nate** (172), **Natl.** (241), **NATO** (11c, 241), **Nats, oath** (90b, 111c), **oats, Pate** (174), **pate** (32b, 58c), **path** (101a, 102c, 130c), **pats, patu** (130d), **rata** (46a), **rate** (13d, 27d, 30b, 41d, 42a, 55c, 66d, 94b, 97d, 107a, 127b), **rath** (99d), **RATO** (242), **rats, sate** (28b, 54d, 56a, 118a), **Sati** (96d, 109d, 198), **SATs** (29a), **ta-ta** (44b), **tats, tatu** (14b), **vats, vatu** (224), **WATS** (244), **Watt** (63d, 186), **watt** (129a, 246), **yate** (41d)

_ _ A T   **adat** (74b), **amat** (69d), **anat.** (235), **ASAT** (235), **beat** (17c, 30a, 47c, 100b, 121b, 121c, 131c, 233), **bhat** (62d), **blat** (20b), **boat** (81b, 108b), **brat** (26c), **chat** (19a, 29d, 119b, 225), **coat** (52d), **-crat** (117c), **drat** (42a, 83a), **erat** (96a, 97c), **etat** (51a), **feat** (9d, 43a, 124c), **fiat** (34b, 84c), **flat** (42a, 63b, 95a, 95c, 114c, 234), **frat**

(29a), **Geat** (104c), **ghat** (28c, 79b), **gnat** (48a, 63b, 76c, 229), **goat** (81a, 102d, 230), **Guat.** (239), **Heat** (206), **heat** (129d), **Kaat** (163), **khat** (58b), **kyat** (220), **meat** (48b), **moat** (36d), **neat** (10a, 116a, 121d, 124c), **peat** (52a, 127c), **plat** (74d, 90b), **prat** (23a), **scat** (54b, 96d), **seat** (25d, 63b, 115c), **skat** (24b), **slat** (69b, 133b), **spat** (14b, 85d, 96b, 102c), **stat** (15c, 114a), -**stat** (117c), **stat.** (243), **SWAT** (243), **swat** (20a, 28b, 116b), **teat** (81d), **that** (34d, 95a, 99b), **what** (96d, 99b)

A _ _ T   **abet** (10d, 48b, 59b), **abut** (21a, 75d, 123b), **acct.** (235), **acet-** (92c), **acht** (53d), **adat** (74b), **adit** (41b, 77a), **AHST** (235), **ain't**, **alit** (36c, 68d, 107a), **amat** (69d), **anat.** (235), **aout** (49d), **ASAT** (235), **asst.** (236), **at. wt.** (236), **aunt** (44b, 99b)

A U _ _   **aube** (11a), **Auer** (61c, 139), **auge** (71b), **auks, aula** (53d), **auld** (105b), **aune** (246), **aunt** (44b, 99b), **aura** (10d, 36d, 39d, 40b, 57c, 100d), **auth.** (236), **auto** (24a)

_ A U _   **baud** (120b), **Baum** (85d, 140), **caul** (45c, 84a), **daub** (111a), **dauw** (22d), **eaux** (51b), **Faun** (45d, 133b, 198), **gaud** (124c, 133d), **Gaul** (49b), **gaur** (25a, 62d, 132a, 230), **haud** (70a), **haul** (37c), **Kaus** (208), **laud** (57b, 92b, 127d), **Maud** (131d, 169), **maud** (43b, 56a), **Maui** (64c), **maul** (17c, 57d, 74c), **naut.** (241), **Paul** (18a, 91b, 174), **Raul** (176), **Sauk** (49b, 56c, 189), **Saul** (67d, 87a, 179, 197), -**saur** (117b), **taur-** (92c), **taus, taut** (120c, 122a), **Vaux** (192, 195), **vaux** (49c), **waul** (114b), **yaup** (119b)

_ _ A U   **Agau** (57c), **Beau** (140), **beau** (117d, 118b), **Esau** (64b, 65b, 98b, 197), **frau** (54a), **Grau** (156), **luau** (58b), **Seau** (180), **unau** (110d)

A _ _ U   **abou** (44d), **ACLU** (235), **acou-** (93a), **Agau** (57c), **Alou** (138), **ansu** (13d, 68c), **Attu** (64b)

A V _ _   **Avar** (25a, 82b), **Avas, avdp.** (236), **avec** (51b), **aver** (10b, 15a, 16c, 34b, 74b, 115a, 118c), **aves, avid** (39a, 41b, 56b, 67b, 135a), **avis** (69c), **Avon** (107c), **avow** (9d, 15a, 16c, 29d, 30a, 34b, 85c), **avus** (69d)

_ A V _   **cava** (127d), **cave** (113c, 126b), **cavy** (56d, 101c, 230), **Dave** (148), **Davy** (148, 193), **davy** (103b), **favi** (122a), **gave, have** (20b), **Java** (64c), **java** (28d), **kava** (18d, 91a), **kavi** (66a), **lava** (77d, 101b, 129a), **lave** (130a), **nave** (27a, 131c), **navy** (20a, 47c), **pave** (66b), **Pavo** (87b, 207), **rave** (34b, 58a, 119b), **Ravi** (176), **save** (42b, 67b, 84b, 94b, 126c), **wave** (48a, 83b, 100d, 118c, 126b), **wavy** (126b)

_ _ A V   **Muav** (53c), **Slav** (14d)

A _ _ V   **Azov** (19d, 103c)

A W _ _   **away** (9b, 55b, 59b, 83c), **awed, awes, awls, awns, awny, AWOL** (236), **awry** (15a, 32a, 125c, 134c)

321

_ A W _   **bawd** (22a), **bawl** (18c, 129b, 134b), **caws, Dawn** (148), **dawn** (14b, 15d, 33d), **fawn** (32a, 34c), **gawk** (109c, 114d), **hawk** (19a, 87c, 225), **Hawn** (157), **haws, jaws, kawi** (66a), **lawn** (31a, 43b, 69a, 72a), **laws, maws, pawl** (73d), **pawn** (26c, 60c, 90b), **paws, sawn, saws, tawa** (81c), **taws, wawl** (114b), **yawl** (20b, 103b), **yawn** (21a), **yawp** (12d, 119b), **yaws**

_ _ A W   **braw** (105a), **chaw** (122c), **claw** (26b, 80b, 119b, 126b), **craw** (32a, 56d, 115c), **draw** (11d, 43c, 91d, 123c), **flaw** (19d, 34c), **gnaw** (19c, 26c), **Shaw** (41a, 43a, 180, 204), **skaw** (67c), **slaw** (28d), **thaw** (72b)

A _ _ W   **alow** (18c, 126a), **anew** (10b, 10c), **avow** (9d, 15a, 16c, 29d, 30a, 34b, 85c)

A X _ _   **axed, axes, axil** (12c), **axis** (25c, 34c, 60c), **axle** (113c, 131c), **axon** (81b)

_ A X _   **taxi** (95d), **waxy**

_ _ A X   **Ajax** (56b, 120b, 120d, 194), **coax** (131b), **flax** (72a, 72b), **hoax** (34a, 92b), **olax** (42b), **Sfax** (223)

A _ _ X   **Ajax** (56b, 120b, 120d, 194), **Alex** (137), **AMEX** (235), **apex** (32c, 59a, 59d, 87b, 89b, 123a, 135a)

A Y _ _   **ayah** (62d, 82d), **ayes** (129c), **ayin** (12a)

_ A Y _   **Baya** (215), **baya** (130d), **bays, cays, days, Faye** (152), **Fays, Gaya** (18d), **Gaye** (154), **gays** (60d), **Hays** (157), **jays, Kaye** (164), **kayo** (68c), **Kays, lays, Maya** (134d, 169, 214, 217), **maya** (60a, 130d), **Mayo** (169), **Mays** (169), **nays** (129c), **pays, raya** (85a), **rays, saya** (88c), **says, ways**

_ _ A Y   **away** (9b, 55b, 59b, 83c), **bray** (12d, 37c), **chay** (39b, 98c), **Clay** (146), **clay** (39a, 92a), **D-Day** (67a, 82a), **dray** (24c, 114b, 129b), **flay** (110a, 110b, 116c), **fray** (45d, 49b, 125a), **Gray** (21a, 41a, 156, 192), **gray** (60c), **O'Day** (173), **okay** (10b, 13d, 86d, 112a), **play** (51c, 52b, 87d, 91d, 114a), **pray** (18c, 41b), **quay** (68d, 88d, 131b), **shay** (84a), **slay** (36c, 79d), **spay** (115b), **stay** (34c, 57c, 95b, 99c, 102b, 119d, 128c, 129b), **sway** (29b, 37b, 63a, 67c, 76d, 79c, 85a, 130c, 133a), **tray** (98b, 104a, 107a), **Tway** (184), **Wray** (187), **x-ray** (12a, 75c, 88d)

A _ _ Y   **Abby** (137), **-ably** (117b), **achy** (112a), **aery** (39a), **affy** (18d), **agcy.** (235), **ahey** (42c), **ahoy** (57b, 81a), **airy** (41d, 66a, 71d), **-algy** (117c), **Ally** (138), **ally** (11b, 15b, 29d, 30a, 126c), **Amoy** (69a), **-ancy** (117b), **Andy** (138), **army** (61c), **arty, ashy** (86a, 129d), **atty.** (236), **away** (9b, 55b, 59b, 83c), **awny, awry** (15a, 32a, 125c, 134c)

A Z _ _   **azan** (80c), **azon** (10b), **Azov** (19d, 103c), **azul** (112c), **azur** (50a)

_ A Z _   daze (48a, 116c, 116d), **faze** (36a), **Gaza** (88c, 216), **gaze** (114d, 115a), **haze** (28b, 48a, 77b, 127b), **hazy** (127a), **Jazz** (206), **jazz** (61d, 118d), **laze** (61d), **lazy** (62d), **maze** (68b), **mazy, nazi** (81a), **raze** (34d, 35b, 36c, 71c), **razz** (59a), **Yazd** (217)

_ _ A Z   Ahaz (67d, 197), **Boaz** (103c, 197), **Braz.** (236), **Diaz** (76c), **Graz** (213)

A _ _ Z   Ahaz (67d, 197), **Ariz.** (209, 235)

B A _ _   Baal (106c), **baas, baba** (82d, 91a), **Babe** (140), **babe** (26c, 40d), **Babi** (16a), **Babs, babu** (60a), **baby** (26c, 40d, 83c), **Bach** (140), **back** (14c, 59b, 60a, 98a, 115b), **bade, Baer** (140), **Baez** (140), **baff** (55b), **baft** (43b), **bago** (15a), **bags, Bahr** (140), **baht** (223, 246), **bail** (20d, 68b), **Bain** (140), **bain** (50a), **Baio** (140), **bait** (16b, 41b, 73d, 119c, 123b), **Baja** (23b, 76c), **baju** (65b), **bake** (30c, 101b), **Baku** (24b, 213), **baku** (116b, 124a), **Bala** (53c), **bald** (17b), **bale** (22c, 232), **Bali** (64c), **balk** (16b, 89c, 116a), **Ball** (140), **ball** (17b), **balm** (83d, 126a), **banc** (66d), **band** (56c, 116b, 232), **bane** (58a, 81b, 90d, 102d, 133b), **bang** (110b), **bani** (101d), **bank** (19a, 47c, 91b), **bans, Bapt.** (236), **Bara** (140), **barb** (47a, 89a, 90c, 95a), **Bard** (200), **bard** (14c, 16b, 90c), **bare** (36a, 40c, 43a, 76a, 116b, 127a), **Bari** (10a, 218), **bark** (12d, 37b), **barm** (134b), **barn** (116a), **baro-** (93c), **bars, Bart** (140), **Bart.** (236), **base** (9a, 41d, 49a, 62a, 73c, 92b, 102b, 102d), **bash** (60b, 86d), **bask** (46d, 73d, 80b, 128d, 228), **bast** (17b, 45d, 88c, 133c), **bate** (119c), **Bath** (41a, 112c), **bath** (35d, 88d, 125a, 246), **bats, batt** (16d), **baud** (120b), **Baum** (85d, 140), **bawd** (22a), **bawl** (18c, 129b, 134b), **Baya** (215), **baya** (130d), **bays**

_ B A _   a bas (50b), **Iban** (33d), **Obad.** (241), **Obal** (197)

_ _ B A   abba (19c, 44d), **alba** (73c, 75c, 131d), **anba** (28a), **baba** (82d, 91a), **caba** (133d), **Cuba** (64c, 131b, 215), **Elba** (64c, 80d), **Juba** (216), **koba** (13a, 130b), **Kuba** (24b), **Luba** (224), **PABA** (86b), **peba** (14b), **Reba** (67c, 176), **saba** (45d, 88c), **tuba** (80a, 86a)

B _ _ A   baba (82d, 91a), **Baja** (23b, 76c), **Bala** (53c), **Bara** (140), **Baya** (215), **baya** (130d), **Beja** (82a, 222), **Bela** (18c, 39c, 140), **bema** (90b, 95d), **beta** (11d, 106a), **biga** (125c), **bina** (60b), **biwa** (65d), **boca** (113a), **bola** (53a), **boma** (10c), **Bona** (79b, 192), **bona** (69d, 70a), **bora** (132b), **bosa** (13d), **boza** (13d), **brea** (77a), **buna** (102c)

_ B B _   abba (19c, 44d), **abbe** (28a, 49d, 94c), **abbr.** (235), **Abby** (137), **ebbs**

_ _ B B   bibb (75b), **Cobb** (146), **Gibb** (155), **lobb** (77a), **Robb** (177), **Webb** (186)

B _ _ B   barb (47a, 89a, 90c, 95a), **bibb** (75b), **blab** (119d), **bleb** (20a, 22b, 54c), **blob** (29a, 75b), **bomb** (107d, 130c), **boob** (109c), **bulb** (30d, 126b), **BYOB** (236)

_ B C _   abcs (46c)

B _ _ C   banc (66d), bloc (126c), BMOC (236), bosc (87b)

B _ _ D   bald (17b), band (56c, 116b, 232), Bard (200), bard (14c, 16b, 90c), baud (120b), bawd (22a), bead (17d, 109b), bend (12c, 32d, 125b), bind (122a), Bird (141), bird (16a), bled (97d), Blvd. (236), bold (33d), Bond (142), bond (10a, 28d, 71d, 72b, 78a, 107b, 118a, 122a), bord (77a), Boyd (142), Brad (142), brad (44c, 54d, 80b), bred (97c), Budd (143), bund (40b), burd (105c), Byrd (90d)

B E _ _   bead (17d, 109b), beak (18d, 77d), beam (98a), Bean (140), bean (58c, 60b, 71b, 106b, 127c), Bear (79b), bear (40d, 114c, 134c, 230), Beas, beat (17c, 30a, 47c, 100b, 121b, 121c, 131c, 233), Beau (140), beau (117d, 118b), Bebe (140), bebe (50a), Beck (140), beck (82a), Bede (78a, 127d), beds, beef (29c, 75c), been, beep (112b), beer (18d, 95d), bees, beet (127c), begs, Beja (82a, 222), Bela (18c, 39c, 140), Belg. (236), Bell (140), bell (22c, 120b), bels, belt (16d, 27b), bema (90b, 95d), bend (12c, 32d, 125b), bene (65c, 70b), Beni (214), beno (86a), Bens, bent (13d, 32a, 55d, 62c), Berg (141), berg (61b), berm (23c, 71a, 108d), Bern (9a, 222), Bert (20c, 141), Bess (141), best (26d, 30a, 34c, 42b, 85c, 118b), beta (11d, 106a), Bete (215), bete (50a), Beth (11a, 141), beth (12a), bets, Bevs, bevy (16d, 31c, 47c, 232), beys

_ B E _   abed (110b), Abel (10a, 23a, 107a, 197), Abes, abet (10d, 48b, 59b), ibex (54d, 230), Obed (103c, 197), obex (21c), obey (29c, 59a, 67b, 10a)

_ _ B E   abbe (28a, 49d, 94c), aube (11a), Babe (140), babe (26c, 40d), Bebe (140), bebe (50a), cube (53c, 111d), Elbe (82b, 216), fabe (55b), gibe (10d, 35a), Hebe (32d, 59c, 135a, 198), imbe (30d, 45c), jibe (28d, 29d, 31a), jube (102a), kibe (26c), Kobe (60d, 218), Labe (217), lobe (70d, 102c), Rabe (176), robe (52d), Rube (179), rube (31b, 103c, 134d), Sabe (67b), Tobe (183), tobe (10c), tube (33c, 89c, 117a)

B _ _ E   Babe (140), babe (26c, 40d), bade, bake (30c, 101b), bale (22c, 232), bane (58a, 81b, 90d, 102d, 133b), bare (36a, 40c, 43a, 76a, 116b, 127a), base (9a, 41d, 49a, 62a, 73c, 92b, 102b, 102d), bate (119c), Bebe (140), bebe (50a), Bede (78a, 127d), bene (65c, 70b), Bete (215), bete (50a), bice (20b, 56c, 89a), bide (38d, 99c, 119d, 129b), bike (67a, 127c), bile (26d), bine (115b, 128b), bise (132b), bite (26c, 115c), Blue (142), blue (75d, 112a, 126c), boce (22a, 46d), bode (48d, 91c), bole (27d, 98c, 124b), bone (46a, 110a), bore (23b, 37d, 87d, 121d), Bowe (142), BPOE (236), brae (60a, 105b), bree (105a), brie (26b), Bute (64d), byre (31c)

B _ _ F   baff (55b), beef (29c, 75c), biff (60b), buff (119b, 134b)

B G _ _   B. Gen. (236)

B _ _ G   bang (110b), Belg. (236), Berg (141), berg (61b), Bing (141), bldg. (236), bong (111a), Borg (142), brag (20b, 24a, 32b, 127c), brig (81a, 108b), Bulg. (236), bung (116a), burg (21a, 57c)

B H _ _   **bhat** (62d), **bhut** (54b)

_ _ B H   **Cobh** (30d)

B _ _ H   **Bach** (140), **bash** (60b, 86d), **Bath** (41a, 112c), **bath** (35d, 88d, 125a, 246), **Beth** (11a, 141), **beth** (12a), **blah** (82a, 71d), **bosh** (82a), **both** (122c, 125c), **bruh** (73b), **Bush** (143, 191), **bush** (109a, 119a)

B I _ _   **bias** (12c, 35c, 94a), **bibb** (75b), **Bibi** (141), **bibi** (62d), **bibl.** (236), **bibs, bice** (20b, 56c, 89a), **bide** (38d, 99c, 119d, 129b), **bids, bien** (51b), **bier** (28d, 53d), **biff** (60b), **biga** (125c), **bike** (67a, 127c), **bile** (26d), **bilk** (26b, 34a, 34c), **Bill** (141), **bill** (17d, 109d), **bina** (60b), **bind** (122a), **bine** (115b, 128b), **Bing** (141), **bino** (86a), **bins, biol.** (236), **Bion** (56b), **Bird** (141), **bird** (16a), **birl** (72d), **birn** (27d), **birr** (112a, 216), **bise** (132b), **bite** (26c, 115c), **bito** (10c, 35b, 47a), **bits** (19a), **bitt** (44c), **biwa** (65d)

_ B I _   **Abia** (104a), **abib** (59a, 81d), **Abie** (81c), **abir** (98d), **ibid.** (70a, 239), **ibis** (19a, 39d, 40a, 129a, 225), **obia** (45c), **obis, obit.** (34a, 52c, 241)

_ _ B I   **ambi-** (92c), **Babi** (16a), **Bibi** (141), **bibi** (62d), **Bubi** (216), **gabi** (119d), **Gobi** (35a), **mabi** (47d, 80b), **Rabi** (15c, 88d), **rabi** (78b)

B _ _ I   **Babi** (16a), **Bali** (64c), **bani** (101d), **Bari** (10a, 218), **Beni** (214), **Bibi** (141), **bibi** (62d), **Bubi** (216), **buri** (119b)

_ _ B J   **subj.** (243)

_ _ B K   **hdbk.** (239)

B _ _ K   **back** (14c, 59b, 60a, 98a, 115b), **balk** (16b, 89c, 116a), **bank** (19a, 47c, 91b), **bark** (12d, 37b), **bask** (46d, 73d, 80b, 128d, 228), **beak** (18d, 77d), **Beck** (140), **beck** (82a), **bilk** (26b, 34a, 34c), **Bock** (142), **bock** (18a, 70d), **book** (71c, 129a), **bosk** (133b), **bowk** (115a), **Buck** (23b, 31c, 143), **buck** (34c, 84a), **bulk** (20c, 75b, 129a), **bunk** (82a, 110c), **busk** (20c, 31a, 45c)

B L _ _   **blab** (119d), **blah** (82a, 71d), **blat** (20b), **bldg.** (236), **bleb** (20a, 22b, 54c), **bled** (97d), **blet** (51d), **bleu** (26b, 50a), **blew, blip** (97b), **B. Lit.** (236), **blob** (29a, 75b), **bloc** (126c), **blot** (115b), **blow** (42d), **Blue** (142), **blue** (75d, 112a, 126c), **blur** (62d, 111a), **blut** (53d), **Blvd.** (236)

_ B L _   **able** (10a, 29c, 96b, 110a), **-ably** (117b), **-ible** (117a)

_ _ B L   **bibl.** (236)

B _ _ L   **Baal** (106c), **bail** (20d, 68b), **Ball** (140), **ball** (17b), **bawl** (18c, 129b, 134b), **Bell** (140), **bell** (22c, 120b), **bibl.** (236), **Bill** (141), **bill** (17d, 109d), **biol.** (236), **birl** (72d), **boil** (30c), **Böll** (142), **boll** (90a, 90c), **bowl** (78d, 119a), **bual** (132c), **buhl** (63a), **bull** (21b, 86b), **Burl** (143), **burl** (68c, 124b)

B M _ _   BMOC (236)

_ _ B M   ICBM (239)

B _ _ M   balm (83d, 126a), barm (134b), Baum (85d, 140), beam (98a), berm (23c, 71a, 108d), boom (43a, 112a, 113a), Bram (142), brim (21a), brom- (92c)

_ _ B N   ISBN (240)

B _ _ N   Bain (140), bain (50a), barn (116a), Bean (140), bean (58c, 60b, 71b, 106b, 127c), been, Bern (9a, 222), B. Gen. (236), bien (51b), Bion (56b), birn (27d), Bonn (18b, 216), boon (18c, 20a), Born (142), born (71d, 81a, 81b), bo's'n (20c, 88b), bran (22a, 22b, 55d, 61d), bren (73d), burn (62c, 101b)

B O _ _   boar (60c, 89a, 118d, 132a, 230), boas, boat (81b, 108b), Boaz (103c, 197), Bobo (214), boca (113a), boce (22a, 46d), Bock (142), bock (18a, 70d), bode (48d, 91c), Bodo (69a), body (56c), Boer (10c, 112b), bogs, bogy (13c, 113b), Bohr (15c, 33c, 142), boil (30c), bois (51b), bola (53a), bold (33d), bole (27d, 98c, 124b), Böll (142), boll (90a, 90c), bolo (68a, 130d), Bolt (142), bolt (44c, 47c, 67a, 101c), boma (10c), bomb (107d, 130c), Bona (79b, 192), bona (69d, 70a), Bond (142), bond (10a, 28d, 71d, 72b, 78a, 107b, 118a, 122a), bone (46a, 110a), bong (111a), Bonn (18b, 216), Bono (142), bony (110a), boob (109c), book (71c, 129a), boom (43a, 112a, 113a), boon (18c, 20a), boor (17a, 38c, 88a, 103c), boos, boot (29c, 67b, 124d), bops, bora (132b), bord (77a), bore (23b, 37d, 87d, 121d), Borg (142), Born (142), born (71d, 81a, 81b), boro (114a), Bors (102c), bort (35c), Boru (142), bosa (13d), bosc (87b), bosh (82a), bosk (133b), bo's'n (20c, 88b), boss (40c, 116c), both (122c, 125c), bots, bott (27d), bout (30b), Bowe (142), bowk (115a), bowl (78d, 119a), bows, Boyd (142), boys, boza (13d), bozo (38d, 88a)

_ B O _   abou (44d), ebon (19d), oboe (58b, 80a, 80c, 133c), obol (26b, 83d)

_ _ B O   ambo (95d, 98a), Bobo (214), bubo (85c), Gobo (16d), gobo (66a), hobo (123d, 127a), Igbo (68c, 220), jobo (60c), kobo (220), lobo (122a, 133b), Nebo (78d, 79a), sebo- (92d), umbo (21a)

B _ _ O   bago (15a), Baio (140), baro- (93c), beno (86a), bino (86a), bito (10c, 35b, 47a), Bobo (214), Bodo (69a), bolo (68a, 130d), Bono (142), boro (114a), bozo (38d, 88a), brio (33d, 113d, 128d), Brno (215), broo (105a), bubo (85c), Buto (198), buyo (18d)

B P _ _   BPOE (236)

B _ _ P   beep (112b), blip (97b), bump (66a, 66d), burp (18b)

B R _ _   Brad (142), brad (44c, 54d, 80b), brae (60a, 105b), brag (20b, 24a, 32b, 127c), Bram (142), bran (22a, 22b, 55d, 61d), bras (49d), brat (26c), braw (105a), bray (12d, 37c), Braz. (236), brea (77a), bred

(97c), **bree** (105a), **bren** (73d), **br'er** (126a), **Bret** (143), **brew** (29d), **brie** (26b), **brig** (81a, 108b), **brim** (21a), **brio** (33d, 113d, 128d), **Brit.** (236), **brit** (59d), **Brno** (215), **brom-** (92c), **broo** (105a), **Bros.** (236), **brow** (48d, 59d), **bruh** (73b), **brut** (38b, 132c)

_ **B R** _   **abri** (51a, 108a), **Ebro** (222), **obra** (113a)

_ _ **B R**   **abbr.** (235), **febr-** (93a), **fibr-** (93a), **Nebr.** (211, 241)

B _ _ **R**   **Baer** (140), **Bahr** (140), **Bear** (79b), **bear** (40d, 114c, 134c, 230), **beer** (18d, 95d), **bier** (28d, 53d), **birr** (112a, 216), **blur** (62d, 111a), **boar** (60c, 89a, 118d, 132a, 230), **Boer** (10c, 112b), **Bohr** (15c, 33c, 142), **boor** (17a, 38c, 88a, 103c), **br'er** (126a), **buhr** (131c), **Burr** (143, 190), **burr** (94b)

_ _ **B S**   **albs, Babs, bibs, bubs, cabs, cobs, Cubs** (206), **cubs, dabs, Debs** (148), **debs, dibs** (55d), **dubs, ebbs, fibs, fobs, gabs, gibs, gobs, hobs, hubs, jabs, jibs, JOBS** (240), **jobs, labs, mobs, nabs, nebs, nibs, nobs** (32a), **nubs, orbs, pobs** (91c), **pubs, rebs, ribs, robs, rubs, sibs, sobs, subs, tabs, tubs, webs**

B _ _ **S**   **baas, Babs, bags, bans, bars, bats, bays, Beas, beds, bees, begs, bels, Bens, Bess** (141), **bets, Bevs, beys, bias** (12c, 35c, 94a), **bibs, bids, bins, bits** (19a), **boas, bogs, bois** (51b), **boos, bops, Bors** (102c), **boss** (40c, 116c), **bots, bows, boys, bras** (49d), **Bros.** (236), **bubs, buds, bugs, bums, buns, burs, buss** (68a), **buts, buys, byes**

_ _ **B T**   **debt** (71c, 83a)

B _ _ **T**   **baft** (43b), **baht** (223, 246), **bait** (16b, 41b, 73d, 119c, 123b), **Bapt.** (236), **Bart** (140), **Bart.** (236), **bast** (17b, 45d, 88c, 133c), **batt** (16d), **beat** (17c, 30a, 47c, 100b, 121b, 121c, 131c, 233), **beet** (127c), **belt** (16d, 27b), **bent** (13d, 32a, 55d, 62c), **Bert** (20c, 141), **best** (26d, 30a, 34c, 42b, 85c, 118b), **bhat** (62d), **bhut** (54b), **bitt** (44c), **blat** (20b), **blet** (51d), **B. Lit.** (236), **blot** (115b), **blut** (53d), **boat** (81b, 108b), **Bolt** (142), **bolt** (44c, 47c, 67a, 101c), **boot** (29c, 67b, 124d), **bort** (35c), **bott** (27d), **bout** (30b), **brat** (26c), **Bret** (143), **Brit.** (236), **brit** (59d), **brut** (38b, 132c), **bunt** (17c, 131b), **Burt** (143), **bust** (14c, 17a, 21d, 44a, 58c), **butt** (121d, 132c, 246)

B U _ _   **bual** (132c), **Bubi** (216), **bubo** (85c), **bubs, Buck** (23b, 31c, 143), **buck** (34c, 84a), **Budd** (143), **buds, buff** (119b, 134b), **bugs, buhl** (63a), **buhr** (131c), **bulb** (30d, 126b), **Bulg.** (236), **bulk** (20c, 75b, 129a), **bull** (21b, 86b), **bump** (66a, 66d), **bums, buna** (102c), **bund** (40b), **bung** (116a), **bunk** (82a, 110c), **buns, bunt** (17c, 131b), **buoy** (26a, 47c), **burd** (105c), **burg** (21a, 57c), **buri** (119b), **Burl** (143), **burl** (68c, 124b), **burn** (62c, 101b), **burp** (18b), **Burr** (143, 190), **burr** (94b), **burs, Burt** (143), **bury** (63c), **Bush** (143, 191), **bush** (109a, 119a), **busk** (20c, 31a, 45c), **buss** (68a), **bust** (14c, 17a, 21d, 44a, 58c), **busy** (40d, 83b), **Bute** (64d), **Buto** (198), **buts, butt** (121d, 132c, 246), **buyo** (18d), **buys, buzz** (79d, 103a, 131d)

_ **B U** _   **abut** (21a, 75d, 123b), **ebur** (69d)

_ _ B U babu (60a), Cebu (64d, 221), habu (89c, 103c), imbu (51d), tabu (48c), zebu (21c, 62d, 231)

B _ _ U babu (60a), baju (65b), Baku (24b, 213), baku (116b, 124a), Beau (140), beau (117d, 118b), bleu (26b, 50a), Boru (142)

B _ _ W blew, blow (42d), braw (105a), brew (29d), brow (48d, 59d)

B Y _ _ byes, BYOB (236), Byrd (90d), byre (31c)

_ _ B Y Abby (137), baby (26c, 40d, 83c), gaby (109c), goby (46d, 228), Roby (178), Ruby (179), ruby (19c, 53b), toby (11b, 38a, 66d, 79d, 96a)

B _ _ Y baby (26c, 40d, 83c), bevy (16d, 31c, 47c, 232), body (56c), bogy (13c, 113b), bony (110a), bray (12d, 37c), buoy (26a, 47c), bury (63c), busy (40d, 83b)

B _ _ Z Baez (140), Boaz (103c, 197), Braz. (236), buzz (79d, 103a, 131d)

C A _ _ caam (73a), Caan (144), caba (133d), cabs, caco- (92c), Cade (192), cade (59d, 67c, 88b), cadi (13d, 80c), cads, Caen (17c), cafe (19c), Cage (144), cage (30a, 40d), cagy (31d), Cain (9a, 10a, 41a, 68d, 79d, 107a, 144, 197), cake (35b), Cale (144), calf (134d), Cali (215), calk (61b), call (12d, 15a, 85b, 108d, 117d, 128c, 134b), calm (11c, 13c, 15b, 82a, 85b, 89d, 97a, 106d, 111c, 111d, 126c), calx (59a, 85d), came (132b), Camp (144), camp (19c, 39d, 127a), cams, Cana (46c, 52b), canc. (236), cane (98a, 114b, 115a, 115b, 117d, 129b), cans, cant (62c, 63b, 66a, 70d, 103d, 122a, 122b), capa (122c), cape (37c, 58d, 74d, 95a), Caph (207), Capp (144), caps, Capt. (236), Cara (144), cara (65a), carb- (92d), card (29a, 66d, 87a), CARE (236), care (13a, 25b, 29d, 59a, 77a, 99a, 123d, 124d, 133d), cark (24b, 133d), Carl (144), caro (65a), carp (25b, 32a, 46a, 46c, 96d, 228), Carr (144), cars, cart (125d, 127c, 129b), Cary (144), casa (112d), case (14b, 30b, 63b, 71a, 82c), Cash (144), cash (15a, 78a), cask (30b), Caso (64c), Cass (144), cast (15a, 73a, 121c, 123b, 232), cata- (92c, 92d), Cath. (236), Cato (101d, 102a, 194), cats, Catt (144), caul (45c, 84a), cava (127d), cave (113c, 126b), cavy (56d, 101c, 230), caws, cays

_ C A _ acad. (235), hcap. (239), -ical (117a), NCAA (241), RCAF (242), scab (134a), scad (24d, 27b, 61b, 65b), scan (47c, 73a, 88b, 98a), scar (27b, 134a), scat (54b, 96d)

_ _ C A alca (15d, 98a), arca (11d, 21b, 99b), boca (113a), caco- (92c), ceca (69b), Coca (146), coca (28c, 81a), deca- (93d), Ecca (53c), esca (19d, 36a, 55d), FICA (238), Inca (15b), jaca (65b), juca (24c), Luca (167), mica (64b, 77a, 109b), onca (246), orca (67b), paca (25b, 101c), pica (53c, 125d), SPCA (243), YMCA (244), yuca (24c), YWCA (244)

C _ _ A caba (133d), Cana (46c, 52b), capa (122c), Cara (144), cara (65a), casa (112d), cata- (92c, 92d), cava (127d), ceca (69b), CETA (236), chia (18d, 76c), cima (65c), Coca (146), coca (28c, 81a),

coda (28b, 29d, 46a, 234), **COLA** (237), **cola** (82d, 124a), **coma** (71c, 116d, 126a), **Cora** (34d, 126a), **cora** (53b), **coxa** (60b), **Cuba** (64c, 131b, 215), **cura** (113a), **cyma** (37c, 77d)

_ C B _   **ICBM** (239)

C _ _ B   **carb-** (92d), **chub** (46c, 228), **club** (21c, 32c, 75b, 84c, 104a, 111c), **Cobb** (146), **comb** (31d), **crab** (32b, 108a), **crib** (26b, 74c, 91b, 110c), **curb** (100a, 109a)

_ C C _   **acct.** (235), **Ecca** (53c), **ecce** (18b, 69c, 69d), **eccl.** (238)

C _ _ C   **canc.** (236), **Chic** (145), **chic** (111a), **C in C** (236), **circ.** (237), **conc.** (237), **croc.** (237)

_ C D _   **AC/DC** (235)

_ _ C D   **decd.** (237)

C _ _ D   **card** (29a, 66d, 87a), **Chad** (117a, 145, 215), **clad** (37d), **clod** (21a, 37b, 83a, 116d), **coed** (107b), **cold** (53b, 62a), **cond.** (237), **Cord** (146), **cord** (32c, 43b), **crud** (28c, 35a, 36a), **cued, curd** (76d)

C E _ _   **Cebu** (64d, 221), **ceca** (69b), **cede** (54c, 55d, 99b, 118b, 129b), **cedi** (216), **cees, ceil** (25b), **-cele** (117c), **cell** (32c), **Celt** (22a, 217), **celt** (115d, 123a), **-cene** (117c), **ceno-** (92d), **cent** (30c, 213-224), **cent.** (236), **cepe** (39c), **cere** (18d, 130c), **Cerf** (145), **CERN** (236), **cero** (46d, 67d), **cero-** (93d), **cert.** (236), **cess** (71c, 120a), **cest** (54c), **CETA** (236), **cete** (232), **CETI** (236), **Ceto** (55c, 75d), **Ceyx** (57b)

_ C E _   **-acea** (117c), **aced** (120c), **acer** (74d), **aces, acet-** (92c), **iced, Icel.** (239), **icer, ices**

_ _ C E   **-ance** (117a, 117c), **bice** (20b, 56c, 89a), **boce** (22a, 46d), **dace** (46c, 228), **dice** (52c), **duce** (65a), **ecce** (18b, 69c, 69d), **-ence** (117b), **-esce** (117c), **face** (15a, 30a, 73a, 79d, 118a, 128c), **lace** (47b), **lice** (86c), **Luce** (10a, 29b, 192), **mace** (40c, 82d, 114b, 118d, 129d), **mice, Nice** (49c, 100a, 216), **nice** (90b, 109c), **once** (18b, 49a, 61d, 63d), **Pace** (204), **pace** (52a, 113c, 129b), **pice** (62d, 220), **puce** (42a, 96c), **race** (87d, 103a, 114a, 124b), **Rice** (177, 204), **rice** (37d), **sice** (56c), **syce** (56c), **vice** (35a), **vice-** (92d), **voce** (65c, 234)

C _ _ E   **Cade** (192), **cade** (59d, 67c, 88b), **cafe** (19c), **Cage** (144), **cage** (30a, 40d), **cake** (35b), **Cale** (144), **came** (132b), **cane** (98a, 114b, 115a, 115b, 117d, 129b), **cape** (37c, 58d, 74d, 95a), **CARE** (236), **care** (13a, 25b, 29d, 59a, 77a, 99a, 123d, 124d, 133d), **case** (14b, 30b, 63b, 71a, 82c), **cave** (113c, 126b), **cede** (54c, 55d, 99b, 118b, 129b), **-cele** (117c), **-cene** (117c), **cepe** (39c), **cere** (18d, 130c), **cete** (232), **chee** (246), **-cide** (117b), **cine-** (93b), **cite** (97c), **clue** (60b, 117d), **code** (20c, 23d, 27b, 119a), **coke** (28c, 52a, 62d), **Cole** (146), **come** (94d), **Cone** (146), **cone** (53c, 116c, 111d), **cope** (23d, 30b, 30d, 52d, 128a), **CORE** (237), **core** (25c, 41d, 58d), **cote**

(19b, 107d, 108a), **cove** (17d, 58a, 130a), **Cree** (11b, 189), **cube** (53c, 111d), **cuke** (32c), **-cule** (117c), **cure** (94c), **cute** (10a, 32c, 116a), **cyme** (47d)

_ _ **C F**   **UNCF** (243)

C _ _ F   **calf** (134d), **Cerf** (145), **chef** (30c, 50c, 68a), **clef** (80c, 234), **coef.** (237), **coif** (57b), **conf.** (237), **corf** (28c), **cuff** (21b, 60b, 105b, 110b)

_ _ **C G**   **USCG** (243)

C _ _ G   **chug** (112a), **clog** (20a, 108c), **cong.** (237), **crag** (101b)

C H _ _   **Chad** (117a, 145, 215), **Cham** (224), **chap** (45b, 74c), **char** (104d, 124d, 228), **Chas.** (74d), **chat** (19a, 29d, 119b, 225), **chaw** (122c), **chay** (39b, 98c), **chee** (246), **chef** (30c, 50c, 68a), **chem.** (31b, 236), **cher** (50b), **Chet** (145), **chew** (75b), **chez** (50a), **chia** (18d, 76c), **Chic** (145), **chic** (111a), **ch'ih** (246), **chil-** (93b), **Ch'in** (26d), **Chin.** (236), **chin** (29d), **Chip** (26d), **chip** (55b), **chir-** (93a), **chis**, **chit** (54c, 82c, 88b, 129c), **chol-** (92c), **chol.** (236), **chop** (75c), **Chou** (26d), **chou** (50a), **chow** (37a, 227), **choy** (39b, 98c), **chub** (46c, 228), **chug** (112a), **chum** (15b, 32a, 45b), **chuo** (246)

_ **C H _**   **ache** (73a, 85d, 134b), **acht** (53d), **achy** (112a), **echo** (12a, 99d, 100b), **Echo** (80d), **echt** (54a), **icho** (54b), **ichu** (12c, 55d), **Ochs** (173)

_ _ **C H**   **arch** (28a, 41b, 101c), **-arch** (117c), **arch-** (93b), **arch.** (235), **Asch** (139), **Bach** (140), **dich** (54b), **dich-** (93d), **each** (13b), **etch** (14d, 35a), **euch** (54b), **exch.** (238), **Foch** (49c, 153), **hoch** (42c, 53d), **inch** (31d, 79c, 246), **itch** (58a, 64b), **Koch** (53c, 164), **Lech** (165, 213), **loch** (68b, 105b, 130a), **mach** (113c), **Mich.** (210, 240), **much** (67c, 116d), **orch.** (241), **ouch** (42c, 63a), **Rich** (177), **rich** (73d), **such** (131b), **yech** (112a), **yuch** (112a), **Zech.** (244)

C _ _ H   **Caph** (207), **Cash** (144), **cash** (15a, 78a), **Cath.** (236), **ch'ih** (246), **Cobh** (30d), **cosh** (60b), **Cush** (57c, 197)

C I _ _   **ciao** (65a), **-cide** (117b), **cima** (65c), **C in C** (236), **cine-** (93b), **cinq** (50b), **cion** (83c), **cipo** (71c), **circ.** (237), **cist** (115d), **cite** (97c), **cito** (70a), **city** (76c, 126d)

_ **C I _**   **acid** (119d), **Acis** (52b)

_ _ **C I**   **asci** (114a), **deci** (120c), **foci** (25c), **fuci** (38d), **loci** (27a)

C _ _ I   **cadi** (13d, 80c), **Cali** (215), **cedi** (216), **CETI** (236)

C _ _ J   **Cluj** (221), **conj.** (237)

_ _ **C K**   **back** (14c, 59b, 60a, 98a, 115b), **Beck** (140), **beck** (82a), **Bock** (142), **bock** (18a, 70d), **Buck** (23b, 31c, 143), **buck** (34c, 84a), **cock** (26a, 44d, 102b, 103d, 119c, 127b), **deck** (34b, 108b), **Dick**

(149, 192), **dick** (35b), **dock** (33a, 68d, 88d, 108b, 112a, 131a), **duck** (16c, 19a, 19b, 23d, 43b, 62a, 109a, 225), **geck** (105b), **guck** (110c), **hack** (24c, 33a, 60b), **heck** (42a), **hick** (134d), **hock** (71b, 87b, 132c), **Jack** (159), **jack** (17a, 24a, 68a, 78a, 97c), **jock** (74c), **keck** (100a), **kick** (21a, 96a), **lack** (34c, 129d), **lick** (18a, 66a, 110d), **lock** (44c, 57b), **luck** (25d), **Mack** (167), **mack** (97c), **Mick** (170), **mock** (35a, 62a, 66b, 100c, 104d, 120a), **muck** (39a), **neck** (64d), **Nick** (172), **nick** (26d, 82c), **nock** (14c, 82c), **pack** (16d, 22c, 105c, 232, 246), **Peck** (174), **peck** (22d, 246), **pick** (27a, 90b), **pock** (62d), **Puck** (107c, 193), **puck** (36b, 55a, 60c, 77b), **rack** (10b, 28b), **reck** (24b), **Rick** (24c, 177), **rick** (58c, 89a, 114b), **Rock** (178), **rock** (118c, 124b), **ruck** (134a), **sack** (30b, 36a, 89b, 90c, 132c), **sick** (126b), **sock** (96a, 116b, 132b), **suck** (9b), **tack** (13d, 15c, 31b, 44c, 80b), **tick** (14a, 20a, 229), **tock** (10c), **tuck** (115c), **wick** (23d), **yuck** (112a)

C _ _ K   **calk** (61b), **cark** (24b, 133d), **cask** (30b), **cock** (26a, 44d, 102b, 103d, 119c, 127b), **conk** (60b, 116b), **Cook** (79a, 104b, 146), **cook** (68a), **Cork** (217), **cork** (90b, 116a, 132c, 133b), **cusk** (46d)

C L _ _   **clad** (37d), **clam** (19c, 77d), **clan** (124b), **clap** (13c, 121d), **clar.** (237), **claw** (26b, 80b, 119b, 126b), **Clay** (146), **clay** (39a, 92a), **clef** (80c, 234), **Cleo** (96d, 146), **clew** (16c, 103b), **Clio** (29b, 80a), **clip** (15c, 44c, 107d), **clod** (21a, 37b, 83a, 116d), **clog** (20a, 108c), **clop** (61a), **clot** (28c, 73c), **clou** (50d), **clow** (47c, 110d), **cloy** (54d, 104b, 118a), **club** (21c, 32c, 75b, 84c, 104a, 111c), **clue** (60b, 117d), **Cluj** (221), **Clym** (14a)

_ C L _   **acle** (64b), **ACLU** (235)

_ _ C L   **eccl.** (238), **encl.** (238), **excl.** (238), **incl.** (239), **NaCL** (111c)

C _ _ L   **call** (12d, 15a, 85b, 108d, 117d, 128c, 134b), **Carl** (144), **caul** (45c, 84a), **ceil** (25b), **cell** (32c), **chil-** (93b), **chol-** (92c), **chol.** (236), **coal** (13a, 40c, 52a), **-coel** (117a), **coil** (32d, 114a, 125c, 132b, 134a), **coll.** (237), **cool** (23b, 82a), **cowl** (78b), **cull** (88d), **curl** (32a, 57b, 72d, 100d, 126b)

C M _ _   **Cmdr.** (237)

_ C M _   **acme** (32c, 87b, 123a, 135a), **RCMP** (242)

C _ _ M   **caam** (73a), **calm** (11c, 13c, 15b, 82a, 85b, 89d, 97a, 106d, 111c, 111d, 126c), **Cham** (224), **chem.** (31b, 236), **chum** (15b, 32a, 45b), **clam** (19c, 77d), **Clym** (14a), **Colm** (146), **comm.** (237), **coom** (28c), **corm** (22c, 115a), **cosm-** (93d), **cram** (116c), **crim.** (237), **culm** (13a, 28c, 56a, 108b, 115b)

_ C N _   **acne** (110a)

C _ _ N   **Caan** (144), **Caen** (17c), **Cain** (9a, 10a, 41a, 68d, 79d, 107a, 144, 197), **CERN** (236), **Ch'in** (26d), **Chin.** (236), **chin** (29d), **cion** (83c), **clan** (124b), **Coen** (146), **Cohn** (146), **coin** (77b), **Conn.** (209, 237), **conn** (35d), **coon** (97a), **corn** (74b, 94b), **cran** (118c), **cten-** (93c)

C O _ _　　coal (13a, 40c, 52a), coat (52d), coax (131b), Cobb (146), Cobh (30d), cobs, Coca (146), coca (28c, 81a), cock (26a, 44d, 102b, 103d, 119c, 127b), coco (86a), coda (28b, 29d, 46a, 234), code (20c, 23d, 27b, 119a), coed (107b), coef. (237), -coel (117a), Coen (146), cogs, Cohn (146), coho (103d), coif (57b), coil (32d, 114a, 125c, 132b, 134a), coin (77b), coir (28d, 30d, 45c, 102b), coix (66c), coke (28c, 52a, 62d), COLA (237), cola (82d, 124a), cold (53b, 62a), Cole (146), coll. (237), Colm (146), Colo. (209, 237), colp (25c), cols, colt (61b, 100b, 134d, 135a), coly (79b), coma (71c, 116d, 126a), comb (31d), come (94d), comm. (237), Como (68b, 146), Comp. (237), comr. (237), conc. (237), cond. (237), Cone (146), cone (53c, 116c, 111d), conf. (237), cong. (237), conj. (237), conk (60b, 116b), Conn. (209, 237), conn (35d), cons, cont. (237), cony (97a), Cook (79a, 104b, 146), cook (68a), cool (23b, 82a), coom (28c), coon (97a), coop (40d), Coos (189), coos, coot (19a, 38c, 56d, 75a, 83d, 105a, 225), cope (23d, 30b, 30d, 52d, 128a), copr- (92d), cops, Copt (39d), copy (40c, 62a), Cora (34d, 126a), cora (53b), Cord (146), cord (32c, 43b), CORE (237), core (25c, 41d, 58d), corf (28c), Cork (217), cork (90b, 116a, 132c, 133b), corm (22c, 115a), corn (74b, 94b), Corp. (237), cosh (60b), cosm- (93d), cost (26a, 94b), cote (19b, 107d, 108a), coto (17b, 75c), cots, Coty (49d, 147), coup (75b, 116c, 120b), cove (17d, 58a, 130a), cowl (78b), cows (21b), coxa (60b), coyo (16a, 26d), Cozy (147), cozy (39b, 111b)

_ C O _　　acou- (93a), ecol. (238), E-COM (238), econ. (238), icon (62a, 103b), scob (120d), scop (90c), Scot (59d), Scot. (242), scow (20c, 47b)

_ _ C O　　coco (86a), fico (124c, 133d), loco (31d, 63b, 90d), muco- (93b), myco- (93a), paco (11d, 109c), Pico (100d), poco (72c), Rico (72c), soco (21c), toco (123b), unco (105b), Waco (21d)

C _ _ O　　caco- (92c), caro (65a), Caso (64c), Cato (101d, 102a, 194), ceno- (92d), cero (46d, 67d), cero- (93d), Ceto (55c, 75d), chuo (246), ciao (65a), cipo (71c), cito (70a), Cleo (96d, 146), Clio (29b, 80a), coco (86a), coho (103d), Colo. (209, 237), Como (68b, 146), coto (17b, 75c), coyo (16a, 26d), cryo- (93a)

C _ _ P　　Camp (144), camp (19c, 39d, 127a), Capp (144), carp (25b, 32a, 46a, 46c, 96d, 228), chap (45b, 74c), Chip (26d), chip (55b), chop (75c), clap (13c, 121d), clip (15c, 44c, 107d), clop (61a), colp (25c), Comp. (237), coop (40d), Corp. (237), coup (75b, 116c, 120b), crap (82a, 91b), crop (31d, 108d), Culp (147), cusp (31d, 61a, 89d, 90c, 90d)

C _ _ Q　　cinq (50b)

C R _ _　　crab (32b, 108a), crag (101b), cram (116c), cran (118c), crap (82a, 91b), -crat (117c), craw (32a, 56d, 115c), Cree (11b, 189), crew (48c, 56c, 81b, 88b, 133d), crib (26b, 74c, 91b, 110c), crim. (237), crit. (237), croc. (237), crop (31d, 108d), Crow (189), crow (19b, 19d, 20b, 43c, 225), crud (28c, 35a, 36a), crus (71b, 107c), Crux (207), crux (32b, 74b, 112b), cryo- (93a)

_ C R _   Acre (214), acre (45d, 68d, 246), acro- (93a, 93c), ecru (18b, 22b, 126a)

_ _ C R   necr- (92d), picr- (92c)

C _ _ R   Carr (144), char (104d, 124d, 228), cher (50b), chir- (93a), clar. (237), Cmdr. (237), coir (28d, 30d, 45c, 102b), comr. (237), copr- (92d), cuir (37c, 50c), cupr- (92d), czar (103c)

_ _ C S   abcs (46c), arcs, docs (88d), orcs, Pecs (217), sacs, tics, WACs

C _ _ S   cabs, cads, cams, cans, caps, cars, Cass (144), cats, caws, cays, cees, cess (71c, 120a), Chas. (74d), chis, cobs, cogs, cols, cons, Coos (189), coos, cops, cots, cows (21b), crus (71b, 107c), Cubs (206), cubs, cues, cups, curs, cuss (32d, 88a, 118c), cuts

C T _ _   cten- (93c)

_ C T _   acta (34b, 94d, 98c, 121a), ACTH (235), acts, ecto- (93c), octa- (92d), octo (69c), octo- (92d), WCTU (244)

_ _ C T   acct. (235), dict. (237), duct (125a), fact (9d, 35b, 98a), hect- (93a), noct- (93b), pact (10d, 11c, 17b, 20d), Pict (22a), sect (34d, 43d), tact (35d)

C _ _ T   cant (62c, 63b, 66a, 70d, 103d, 122a, 122b), Capt. (236), cart (125d, 127c, 129b), cast (15a, 73a, 121c, 123b, 232), Catt (144), Celt (22a, 217), celt (115d, 123a), cent (30c, 213-224), cent. (236), cert. (236), cest (54c), chat (19a, 29d, 119b, 225), Chet (145), chit (54c, 82c, 88b, 129c), cist (115d), clot (28c, 73c), coat (52d), colt (61b, 100b, 134d, 135a), cont. (237), coot (19a, 38c, 56d, 75a, 83d, 105a, 225), Copt (39d), cost (26a, 94b), -crat (117c), crit. (237), cult (106a, 119c), Curt (147), curt (20b, 22a, 108c, 108d), cyst (128a)

C U _ _   Cuba (64c, 131b, 215), cube (53c, 111d), Cubs (206), cubs, cued, cues, cuff (21b, 60b, 105b, 110b), cuir (37c, 50c), cuke (32c), -cule (117c), cull (88d), culm (13a, 28c, 56a, 108b, 115b), Culp (147), cult (106a, 119c), cupr- (92d), cups, cura (113a), curb (100a, 109a), curd (76d), cure (94c), curl (32a, 57b, 72d, 100d, 126b), curs, Curt (147), curt (20b, 22a, 108c, 108d), Cush (57c, 197), cusk (46d), cusp (31d, 61a, 89d, 90c, 90d), cuss (32d, 88a, 118c), cute (10a, 32c, 116a), cuts

_ C U _   acus (70a, 89b), Ecua. (238), ocul- (92d), Scud (77b), scud (96d, 103a, 118c), scum (62c, 98d, 110c), scup (91c, 228), scut (119a)

C _ _ U   Cebu (64d, 221), Chou (26d), chou (50a), clou (50d)

C _ _ W   chaw (122c), chew (75b), chow (37a, 227), claw (26b, 80b, 119b, 126b), clew (16c, 103b), clow (47c, 110d), craw (32a, 56d, 115c), crew (48c, 56c, 81b, 88b, 133d), Crow (189), crow (19b, 19d, 20b, 43c, 225)

C _ _ X   **calx** (59a, 85d), **Ceyx** (57b), **coax** (131b), **coix** (66c), **Crux** (207), **crux** (32b, 74b, 112b)

C Y _ _   **cyma** (37c, 77d), **cyme** (47d), **cyst** (128a)

_ _ C Y   **agcy.** (235), **-ancy** (117b), **-ency** (117b), **ency.** (238), **lacy** (34c), **Lucy** (192), **Macy** (167), **racy** (20a, 113c), **secy.** (243)

C _ _ Y   **cagy** (31d), **Cary** (144), **cavy** (56d, 101c, 230), **chay** (39b, 98c), **choy** (39b, 98c), **city** (76c, 126d), **Clay** (146), **clay** (39a, 92a), **cloy** (54d, 104b, 118a), **coly** (79b), **cony** (97a), **copy** (40c, 62a), **Coty** (49d, 147), **Cozy** (147), **cozy** (39b, 111b)

C Z _ _   **czar** (103c)

C _ _ Z   **chez** (50a)

D A _ _   **dabs**, **dace** (46c, 228), **Dada** (14d, 49c), **dado** (34b, 84d, 87c, 129d), **dads**, **daft** (48b), **Dahl** (147), **dail** (40a, 64a), **dais** (41d, 90b), **Dale** (26d, 147), **dale** (35d, 98a, 127b), **Dali** (147), **Daly** (147), **dama** (65a, 112d), **dame** (45b, 54c, 68c, 81d, 122c), **damp** (33c, 77c, 131b), **dams**, **Dana** (147), **Dane** (67c, 82b, 104c, 147), **dang** (42a), **dank** (33b, 77c), **Dans**, **dans** (50c), **Danu** (199), **daps**, **darb** (88a), **dare** (25d, 34c), **dark** (38d, 54d, 118c), **darn** (42a, 75d, 83a, 99c), **dart** (14c, 33d, 68d, 77b, 90c, 95a, 114a, 118c), **dash** (20a, 96a, 114a, 120b, 128d), **data** (29c, 63a, 115a), **date** (33d, 51d), **daub** (111a), **dauw** (22d), **Dave** (148), **Davy** (148, 193), **davy** (103b), **Dawn** (148), **dawn** (14b, 15d, 33d), **days**, **daze** (48a, 116c, 116d)

_ D A _   **adad** (42c), **Adah** (41c, 197), **Adak** (64b), **Adam** (23d, 84d, 107a, 137, 194, 197), **Adar** (66d, 78c), **Adas**, **adat** (74b), **D-Day** (67a, 82a), **Edam** (26b, 38d), **-idae** (117c), **Idas** (24d), **N.Dak.** (241), **O'Day** (173), **S.Dak.** (242), **udal** (59c)

_ _ D A   **adda** (110a), **Aïda** (84b, 97b, 128a), **Alda** (137), **anda** (21c, 133b), **coda** (28b, 29d, 46a, 234), **Dada** (14d, 49c), **edda** (59c, 61b, 82a, 103b), **Erda** (22b, 198), **Jada** (197), **Leda** (24d, 59a, 91a, 113b, 125d, 135a, 198), **NADA** (241), **-poda** (117c), **Roda** (81d), **Sada** (179), **sida** (30d, 96d), **soda** (18d, 38a, 111c, 131c), **Toda** (37d), **USDA** (243), **veda** (60a), **Vida** (185)

D _ _ A   **Dada** (14d, 49c), **dama** (65a, 112d), **Dana** (147), **data** (29c, 63a, 115a), **deca-** (93d), **deka-** (93d), **Dela.** (209), **Deva** (60a, 221), **dika** (74c), **Dina** (149), **dita** (88c, 124b), **diva** (84b, 94c), **Doha** (221), **dona** (91d), **dopa** (89a), **Dora** (30c, 33d, 35c), **duma** (103a), **dura** (113c), **dyna-** (93c)

_ D B _   **hdbk.** (239)

D _ _ B   **darb** (88a), **daub** (111a), **dieb** (65b), **doob** (18c), **drab** (22b, 26b, 29a, 38c, 43d, 47b), **drib** (110d), **drub** (17c, 32c, 42c, 110b), **dumb** (109b, 113c)

_ _ D C   **AC/DC** (235), **AFDC** (235)

D _ _ C   **desc.** (237), **disc** (58b, 98c), **disc.** (237)

D D _ _   **D-Day** (67a, 82a)

_ D D _   **adda** (110a), **adds**, **edda** (59c, 61b, 82a, 103b), **Eddy** (150), **eddy** (31b, 118d, 131c), **odds** (10b, 11c, 26a, 95c)

_ _ D D   **Budd** (143), **Judd** (163), **Ladd** (165), **Mudd** (171), **Nidd** (134d), **Redd** (176), **redd** (113b), **Ridd** (73a), **rudd** (24b, 46c, 98c), **sudd** (47c), **Todd** (183)

D _ _ D   **dead** (69b), **decd.** (237), **deed** (9d, 43a, 71a, 122c), **died**, **dowd** (107b), **duad** (85d, 125c), **dyad** (85d), **dyed**

D E _ _   **dead** (69b), **deaf** (125d, 126d), **deal** (17b, 36a, 36d, 123d), **Dean** (148), **dean** (83c), **dear** (40d), **Debs** (148), **debs**, **debt** (71c, 83a), **deca-** (93d), **decd.** (237), **deci** (120c), **deck** (34b, 108b), **deed** (9d, 43a, 71a, 122c), **deem** (30b, 66d, 121a), **deep** (9b, 41c, 73c, 94d), **deer** (25d, 102d, 114b, 230), **dees**, **deft** (10a, 14d, 110a), **defy** (25d), **degu** (101c), **deil** (105a), **dein** (54b), **deka-** (93d), **Dela.** (209), **dele** (23c, 40b, 43a, 94c, 95b, 119b), **dell** (35d, 127b), **deme** (56b), **Demi** (148), **demi-** (93a), **demo** (108d, 119c), **demy** (86b), **Dene** (189), **dene** (104a), **dens** (70b), **Dent** (149), **dent** (35a), **deny** (30c, 36a, 98d), **Depp** (149), **dept.** (237), **-derm** (117c), **Dern** (149), **desc.** (237), **Dese** (216), **Desi** (149), **desk** (134c), **deus** (42d, 69d), **Deut.** (237), **Deva** (60a, 221), **Devi** (109d), **dewy** (77c), **deys**

_ D E _   **Aden** (13d, 224), **edel** (54a), **Eden** (41a, 82a, 86c, 150), **idea** (35b, 44b, 82c, 95a, 121b), **idee** (50c), **idem** (70a), **Iden** (192), **ideo-** (93a), **ides** (33d, 101d), **odea** (29d), **Oder** (100d), **odes**

_ _ D E   **aide** (10a, 15b, 59b, 106a), **bade**, **Bede** (78a, 127d), **bide** (38d, 99c, 119d, 129b), **bode** (48d, 91c), **Cade** (192), **cade** (59d, 67c, 88b), **cede** (54c, 55d, 99b, 118b, 129b), **-cide** (117b), **code** (20c, 23d, 27b, 119a), **dude** (27c, 33c, 44b), **Erde** (22b), **fade** (35c, 36a, 127b), **Gide** (49c, 155), **hade** (53c), **hide** (29d, 31c, 43a), **Hyde** (37a), **jade** (53b, 56c), **Jude** (13b, 196), **lade** (24b, 35d, 72d, 76d, 119a), **lode** (35a, 76b, 84c, 127d), **made** (31d), **Mede** (14d, 88a), **mode** (44c, 74d, 116d, 130c), **nide** (88c, 232), **node** (66c, 68c, 90d, 95c, 118c), **nude** (17b, 126b), **onde** (51b), **-pede** (117b), **rede** (31b, 105a), **Ride** (177), **ride** (29b, 66d, 121a), **rode** (38b), **rude** (102c, 126a), **side** (43d, 47b, 69b, 119b), **tide** (83b), **-tude** (117b), **vide** (98d), **Wade** (185), **wade** (129b), **wide** (102a)

D _ _ E   **dace** (46c, 228), **Dale** (26d, 147), **dale** (35d, 98a, 127b), **dame** (45b, 54c, 68c, 81d, 122c), **Dane** (67c, 82b, 104c, 147), **dare** (25d, 34c), **date** (33d, 51d), **Dave** (148), **daze** (48a, 116c, 116d), **dele** (23c, 40b, 43a, 94c, 95b, 119b), **deme** (56b), **Dene** (189), **dene** (104a), **Dese** (216), **dice** (52c), **dike** (40b, 71c), **dime** (44d), **dine** (39b), **dire** (37d, 44d, 45a, 54b, 56a, 120c), **dive** (34d, 90c), **doge** (74a, 127d), **Dole** (58c, 149), **dole** (91d, 99b, 131a), **dome** (32d, 102a), **done** (85c), **dope** (10b, 38b, 81a), **Dore** (49c), **dore** (54b,

89a), **dose** (94a), **dote** (85c), **Dove** (150), **dove** (19a, 89a, 225), **doze** (110b), **duce** (65a), **dude** (27c, 33c, 44b), **Duke** (87d, 150, 194, 201), **duke** (82a), **dune** (84a, 104a), **dupe** (25a, 34a, 48b, 56d, 74d, 118d), **Duse** (64d, 150), **dyne** (48c, 246)

D _ _ F **deaf** (125d, 126d), **doff** (99c, 119a), **duff** (95d)

_ D G _ **edge** (10b, 19c, 21a, 21b, 74d, 87d, 100d, 109a, 130c), **edgy** (81b, 100a, 120c)

_ _ D G **bldg.** (236)

D _ _ G **dang** (42a), **diag.** (237), **ding** (62d, 76b), **Doeg** (197), **dong** (224), **Doug** (150), **drag** (30d, 95d), **drug** (81a), **dung** (42d, 74d)

D H _ _ **dhai** (76c), **dhak** (39b), **dhal** (11d), **dhow** (69b, 84d)

D _ _ H **dash** (20a, 96a, 114a, 120b, 128d), **dich** (54b), **dich-** (93d), **dish** (76a, 119a), **doth** (128a)

D I _ _ **diag.** (237), **dial** (43d), **diam.** (237), **Dian** (198), **Dias** (91d), **Diaz** (76c), **dibs** (55d), **dice** (52c), **dich** (54b), **dich-** (93d), **Dick** (149, 192), **dick** (35b), **dict.** (237), **Dido** (24c, 125d), **dido** (13a, 24a, 52b, 92b), **didy** (35c), **dieb** (65b), **died**, **dies** (69c), **diet** (44b, 65d, 71b), **dieu** (50b), **digs**, **dika** (74c), **dike** (40b, 71c), **Dili** (91d, 217), **dill** (14c, 88d), **dime** (44d), **dims**, **Dina** (149), **dine** (39b), **ding** (62d, 76b), **Dino** (47c), **dins**, **dint** (42d, 92b), **Dion** (149, 195), **Dior** (149), **dios** (112d), **dipl-** (93d), **dips**, **dire** (37d, 44d, 45a, 54b, 56a, 120c), **Dirk** (149), **dirk** (33a), **dirt** (39a, 99c, 104c), **disc** (58b, 98c), **disc.** (237), **dish** (76a, 119a), **disk** (27b), **diss** (75d), **dist.** (237), **dita** (88c, 124b), **diva** (84b, 94c), **dive** (34d, 90c)

_ D I _ **adit** (41b, 77a), **Edie** (150), **edit** (20b, 40c, 94a, 98c, 100b), **FDIC** (238), **idio-** (93c), **Odin** (10b, 51c, 133b, 198), **odio** (65a), **Udic** (82b), **XDIV** (244)

_ _ D I **Andi** (25a), **cadi** (13d, 80c), **cedi** (216), **kadi** (13d, 80d), **Lodi** (80d), **ludi** (102a), **medi-** (93c), **Midi** (112b), **nidi** (113c), **nudi-** (93b), **pedi-** (93a), **qadi** (13d, 80d), **Sodi** (197), **wadi** (38b, 83a, 98a, 101a)

D _ _ I **Dali** (147), **deci** (120c), **Demi** (148), **demi-** (93a), **Desi** (149), **Devi** (109d), **dhai** (76c), **Dili** (91d, 217), **doni** (25d), **drei** (54a)

_ D J _ **Adja** (214)

_ _ D J **hadj** (89b)

D _ _ K **dank** (33b, 77c), **dark** (38d, 54d, 118c), **deck** (34b, 108b), **desk** (134c), **dhak** (39b), **Dick** (149, 192), **dick** (35b), **Dirk** (149), **dirk** (33a), **disk** (27b), **dock** (33a, 68d, 88d, 108b, 112a, 131a), **dook** (77a), **duck** (16c, 19a, 19b, 23d, 43b, 62a, 109a, 225), **dunk** (35d, 62a), **dusk** (125c), **Dyak** (217, 219)

_ D L _ **Idle** (159), **idle** (40c, 60c, 62c, 62d, 63a, 70c, 127a, 130a), **idly**

D _ _ L **Dahl** (147), **dail** (40a, 64a), **deal** (17b, 36a, 36d, 123d), **deil** (105a), **dell** (35d, 127b), **dhal** (11d), **dial** (43d), **dill** (14c, 88d), **dipl-** (93d), **doll** (45b, 96a), **dual** (37c, 125c), **duel** (45d), **Dull** (193), **dull** (20b, 28b, 47b, 63b, 66b, 71d, 73c, 126c)

_ D M _ **admi** (53b)

D _ _ M **deem** (30b, 66d, 121a), **-derm** (117c), **diam.** (237), **doom** (35b, 44d, 54b), **dorm** (104d), **dram** (38a, 38b, 84a, 92a, 110d, 246), **drum** (80a, 228), **duim** (246)

_ D N _ **Edna** (151)

D _ _ N **darn** (42a, 75d, 83a, 99c), **Dawn** (148), **dawn** (14b, 15d, 33d), **Dean** (148), **dean** (83c), **dein** (54b), **Dern** (149), **Dian** (198), **Dion** (149, 195), **Doon** (101a), **Dorn** (149), **Down** (150), **down** (35a, 45a, 232), **duan** (52a), **Dyan** (150)

D O _ _ **dock** (33a, 68d, 88d, 108b, 112a, 131a), **docs** (88d), **dodo** (19b, 38c, 225), **Doeg** (197), **doer** (87d), **does**, **doff** (99c, 119a), **doge** (74a, 127d), **dogs**, **dogy** (38c), **Doha** (221), **doit** (38d), **Dole** (58c, 149), **dole** (91d, 99b, 131a), **doll** (45b, 96a), **dolt** (20a, 48b, 109c, 116d), **dome** (32d, 102a), **doms**, **dona** (91d), **done** (85c), **dong** (224), **doni** (25d), **dons** (85d), **don't**, **doob** (18c), **dook** (77a), **doom** (35b, 44d, 54b), **Doon** (101a), **door** (41b, 91c), **dopa** (89a), **dope** (10b, 38b, 81a), **dopp** (32d), **dopy** (71c), **Dora** (30c, 33d, 35c), **Dore** (49c), **dore** (54b, 89a), **dorm** (104d), **Dorn** (149), **dorp** (57c, 128b), **dorr** (54c), **Dors** (149), **dory** (20b, 47b), **dose** (94a), **doss** (18a), **dost** (128a), **dote** (85c), **doth** (128a), **dots**, **Doug** (150), **dour** (54d, 78d, 107b, 117d), **Dove** (150), **dove** (19a, 89a, 225), **dowd** (107b), **Down** (150), **down** (35a, 45a, 232), **doxy** (133b), **doze** (110b), **dozy** (110c)

_ D O _ **Edom** (41c, 61d, 64b, 65b), **Idol** (159), **idol** (39d, 44a, 44d, 58d, 62a, 85b, 133d), **odor** (104d, 111a, 115b), **udos**

_ _ D O **Aldo** (137), **Bodo** (69a), **dado** (34b, 84d, 87c, 129d), **Dido** (24c, 125d), **dido** (13a, 24a, 52b, 92b), **dodo** (19b, 38c, 225), **endo-** (94a), **fado** (91d), **Indo-** (93b), **iodo-** (93b), **judo** (65d, 66d), **lido** (65c, 127d), **ludo** (52b), **ordo** (21a, 27a, 92b), **pedo-** (92d, 93a), **redo** (26a, 74b), **sado** (24c, 66a), **to-do** (21b, 22d, 29b, 52c, 115c), **undo** (12d, 41c, 73a, 99b), **Yedo** (122d)

D _ _ O **dado** (34b, 84d, 87c, 129d), **demo** (108d, 119c), **Dido** (24c, 125d), **dido** (13a, 24a, 52b, 92b), **Dino** (47c), **dodo** (19b, 38c, 225), **Dr. No** (20d), **duro** (88b)

_ _ D P **avdp.** (236)

D _ _ P **damp** (33c, 77c, 131b), **deep** (9b, 41c, 73c, 94d), **Depp** (149), **dopp** (32d), **dorp** (57c, 128b), **drip** (72b, 88a), **drop** (44a, 48d, 77a, 84a, 86d, 90b, 90c, 110d, 120a), **dump** (68d, 99d, 126c)

D R _ _ **drab** (22b, 26b, 29a, 38c, 43d, 47b), **drag** (30d, 95d), **dram** (38a, 38b, 84a, 92a, 110d, 246), **drat** (42a, 83a), **draw** (11d, 43c, 91d,

123c), **dray** (24c, 114b, 129b), **drei** (54a), **Drew** (150, 201), **drew** (110a), **drey** (114b), **drib** (110d), **drip** (72b, 88a), **Dr. No** (20d), **drop** (44a, 48d, 77a, 84a, 86d, 90b, 90c, 110d, 120a), **drub** (17c, 32c, 42c, 110b), **drug** (81a), **drum** (80a, 228)

_ _ D R   **Cmdr.** (237), **hydr-** (93d), **Sadr** (207)

D _ _ R   **dear** (40d), **deer** (25d, 102d, 114b, 230), **Dior** (149), **doer** (87d), **door** (41b, 91c), **dorr** (54c), **dour** (54d, 78d, 107b, 117d), **dyer**

_ _ D S   **adds**, **AIDS** (235), **aids**, **beds**, **bids**, **buds**, **cads**, **dads**, **duds** (28b, 122d), **Eads** (21d), **ends**, **fads**, **fids**, **gads**, **gods**, **hods**, **kids**, **lads**, **lids**, **muds**, **Neds**, **nods**, **odds** (10b, 11c, 26a, 95c), **pads**, **pods**, **rads**, **Reds** (206), **reds**, **rids**, **rods**, **Sids**, **sods**, **suds** (18a, 48a, 114a), **tads**, **Teds**, **tods**, **wads**, **weds**, **zeds**

D _ _ S   **dabs**, **dads**, **dais** (41d, 90b), **dams**, **Dans**, **dans** (50c), **daps**, **days**, **Debs** (148), **debs**, **dees**, **dens** (70b), **deus** (42d, 69d), **deys**, **Dias** (91d), **dibs** (55d), **dies** (69c), **digs**, **dims**, **dins**, **dios** (112d), **dips**, **diss** (75d), **docs** (88d), **does**, **dogs**, **doms**, **dons** (85d), **Dors** (149), **doss** (18a), **dots**, **dubs**, **duds** (28b, 122d), **dues**, **duos**, **dyes**

_ D T _   **HDTV** (239)

D _ _ T   **daft** (48b), **dart** (14c, 33d, 68d, 77b, 90c, 95a, 114a, 118c), **debt** (71c, 83a), **deft** (10a, 14d, 110a), **Dent** (149), **dent** (35a), **dept.** (237), **Deut.** (237), **dict.** (237), **diet** (44b, 65d, 71b), **dint** (42d, 92b), **dirt** (39a, 99c, 104c), **dist.** (237), **doit** (38d), **dolt** (20a, 48b, 109c, 116d), **don't**, **dost** (128a), **drat** (42a, 83a), **duct** (125a), **duet** (80c, 85d), **dust** (114a)

D U _ _   **duad** (85d, 125c), **dual** (37c, 125c), **duan** (52a), **dubs**, **duce** (65a), **duck** (16c, 19a, 19b, 23d, 43b, 62a, 109a, 225), **duct** (125a), **dude** (27c, 33c, 44b), **duds** (28b, 122d), **duel** (45d), **dues**, **duet** (80c, 85d), **duff** (95d), **Dufy** (49c, 150), **duim** (246), **Duke** (87d, 150, 194, 201), **duke** (82a), **Dull** (193), **dull** (20b, 28b, 47b, 63b, 66b, 71d, 73c, 126c), **duly** (100c, 117a), **duma** (103a), **dumb** (109b, 113c), **dump** (68d, 99d, 126c), **dune** (84a, 104a), **dung** (42d, 74d), **dunk** (35d, 62a), **duos**, **dupe** (25a, 34a, 48b, 56d, 74d, 118c), **dura** (113c), **duro** (88b), **Duse** (64d, 150), **dusk** (125c), **dust** (114a), **duty** (27a, 83a, 119d)

_ D U _   **educ.** (238), **-odus** (117c)

_ _ D U   **kudu** (13a, 230), **pudu** (34b), **Urdu** (60b, 213, 220)

D _ _ U   **Danu** (199), **degu** (101c), **dieu** (50b)

D _ _ W   **dauw** (22d), **dhow** (69b, 84d), **draw** (11d, 43c, 91d, 123c), **Drew** (150, 201), **drew** (110a)

D Y _ _   **dyad** (85d), **Dyak** (217, 219), **Dyan** (150), **dyed**, **dyer**, **dyes**, **dyna-** (93c), **dyne** (48c, 246)

_ D Y _   idyl (90c, 233)

_ _ D Y   Andy (138), body (56c), didy (35c), Eddy (150), eddy (31b, 118d, 131c), Hedy (157), Jody (161), Judy (163), lady (45b, 81d), Rudy (179), tidy (81a, 84c, 111b), tody (19b)

D _ _ Y   Daly (147), Davy (148, 193), davy (103b), D-Day (67a, 82a), defy (25d), demy (86b), deny (30c, 36a, 98d), dewy (77c), didy (35c), dogy (38c), dopy (71c), dory (20b, 47b), doxy (133b), dozy (110c), dray (24c, 114b, 129b), drey (114b), Dufy (49c, 150), duly (100c, 117a), duty (27a, 83a, 119d)

_ D Z _   adze (122d)

_ _ D Z   Lodz (221)

D _ _ Z   Diaz (76c)

E A _ _   each (13b), Eads (21d), Earl (150), earl (82a), earn (35b, 52a, 76a), ears, ease (10b, 11c, 15b, 29b, 42d, 71b, 77b, 99b, 99d, 100a, 129d), east (84d), easy (43d, 53c, 55c, 77c, 109c, 111c), eats (48b), eaux (51b)

_ E A _   bead (17d, 109b), beak (18d, 77d), beam (98a), Bean (140), bean (58c, 60b, 71b, 106b, 127c), Bear (79b), bear (40d, 114c, 134c, 230), Beas, beat (17c, 30a, 47c, 100b, 121b, 121c, 131c, 233), Beau (140), beau (117d, 118b), dead (69b), deaf (125d, 126d), deal (17b, 36a, 36d, 123d), Dean (148), dean (83c), dear (40d), fear (11a, 51c, 86b, 120d), feat (9d, 43a, 124c), gear (13c, 28b, 41b, 85b, 123a), Geat (104c), head (21a, 25d, 26c, 51c, 78a, 94c), heal (32d), heap (17a, 75b, 79a, 89a), hear (59a, 72b), Heat (206), heat (129d), Jean (160), Kean (164), keas, lead (29d, 35d, 56d, 58c, 245), leaf (85b, 90a), Leah (65b, 68b, 197), leak (72b, 84b), leal (73c, 105b), Lean (165), lean (24b, 29b, 98a, 110c, 113b, 121a, 122b), leap (24a, 67a, 232), Lear (30d, 107c, 195), leas, Mead (61a, 170), mead (18a, 37d, 60d), meal (56c, 99c), mean (9a, 16a, 17b, 34d, 76c, 109b, 115c), meat (48b), neaf (47b), Neal (172), neap (121d, 122d, 129b), near (13d, 28b, 81d), neat (10a, 116a, 121d, 124c), peag (129d), peak (11d, 31d, 32c, 59a, 59d, 117d, 135a), peal (100d), pear (51d, 124a), peas, peat (52a, 127c), read (63c, 88b, 116c), real (9d, 116d), ream (18d, 31b, 41a, 86b, 125c), reap (9d, 33a, 58b), rear (10c, 21d, 40d, 41c, 60a, 97c), seal (28b, 44c, 89b, 231), seam (66c, 67a, 128c), Sean (66c, 180), sear (25b, 133a), seas, seat (25d, 63b, 115c), Seau (180), teak (39b, 124a), teal (19a, 20b, 38c, 226), team (32a, 48c, 56c, 85d, 232), tear (68b, 99c), teas, teat (81d), veal (23b, 75c), weak (45a, 62c, 63a), weal (131b, 131c), wean (117a), wear (114a), yeah (10b), yean (68d), year (122b), yeas (129c), zeal (14b, 45c)

_ _ E A   -acea (117c), Alea (15b), area (36d, 37b, 45d, 72d, 97d, 99a, 135c), asea (32b, 129c), brea (77a), flea (63b, 229), Gaea (39b, 198), idea (35b, 44b, 82c, 95a, 121b), ilea (73c), itea (118c, 128c), odea (29d), olea (84a), Otea (64c), plea (42d, 92b, 118a), Rhea

(68c, 78d, 89d, 122c, 135c, 177, 198), **rhea** (19b, 26c, 85a, 226), **Shea** (180), **shea** (22d, 124a), **Thea** (122c), **toea** (221), **urea** (45c), **uvea** (43c, 64a)

E _ _ A   **Ecca** (53c), **Ecua.** (238), **edda** (59c, 61b, 82a, 103b), **Edna** (151), **Elba** (64c, 80d), **Elia** (68d, 87c, 151), **Ella** (151), **ella** (113a), **-ella** (117b), **Elsa** (55c, 72d, 84b, 129b, 151), **-emia** (117a), **Emma** (21b, 151), **Enna** (109a), **Erda** (22b, 198), **Erma** (151), **esca** (19d, 36a, 55d), **esta** (113a), **Etna** (129a), **etna** (58d), **Etta** (152), **-etta** (117b), **eyra** (65b), **Ezra** (152, 196, 197)

E B _ _   **ebbs, ebon** (19d), **Ebro** (222), **ebur** (69d)

_ E B _   **Bebe** (140), **bebe** (50a), **Cebu** (64d, 221), **Debs** (148), **debs, debt** (71c, 83a), **febr-** (93a), **Hebe** (32d, 59c, 135a, 198), **Nebo** (78d, 79a), **Nebr.** (211, 241), **nebs, peba** (14b), **Reba** (67c, 176), **rebs, sebi-** (92d), **sebo-** (92d), **Webb** (186), **webs, zebu** (21c, 62d, 231)

_ _ E B   **bleb** (20a, 22b, 54c), **dieb** (65b), **Oreb** (197), **pleb** (29b), **Weeb** (186)

E C _ _   **Ecca** (53c), **ecce** (18b, 69c, 69d), **eccl.** (238), **Echo** (80d), **echo** (12a, 99d, 100b), **echt** (54a), **ecol.** (238), **E-COM** (238), **econ.** (238), **ecru** (18b, 22b, 126a), **ecto-** (93c), **Ecua.** (238)

_ E C _   **Beck** (140), **beck** (82a), **ceca** (69b), **deca-** (93d), **decd.** (237), **deci** (120c), **deck** (34b, 108b), **geck** (105b), **heck** (42a), **hect-** (93a), **keck** (100a), **Lech** (165, 213), **neck** (64d), **necr-** (92d), **Peck** (174), **peck** (22d, 246), **Pecs** (217), **reck** (24b), **sect** (34d, 43d), **secy.** (243), **yech** (112a), **Zech.** (244)

_ _ E C   **Alec** (137), **alec** (12c, 47a, 104b), **avec** (51b), **elec.** (238), **exec.** (238), **haec** (70a), **OPEC** (241), **spec.** (243)

E _ _ C   **educ.** (238), **EEOC** (238), **elec.** (238), **epic** (59c, 90c), **Eric** (128b, 151), **eruc** (30d, 45d), **exec.** (238)

E D _ _   **Edam** (26b, 38d), **edda** (59c, 61b, 82a, 103b), **Eddy** (150), **eddy** (31b, 118d, 131c), **edel** (54a), **Eden** (41a, 82a, 86c, 150), **edge** (10b, 19c, 21a, 21b, 74d, 87d, 100d, 109a, 130c), **edgy** (81b, 100a, 120c), **Edie** (150), **edit** (20b, 40c, 94a, 98c, 100b), **Edna** (151), **Edom** (41c, 61d, 64b, 65b), **educ.** (238)

_ E D _   **Bede** (78a, 127d), **beds, cede** (54c, 55d, 99b, 118b, 129b), **cedi** (216), **Hedy** (157), **Leda** (24d, 59a, 91a, 113b, 125d, 135a, 198), **Mede** (14d, 88a), **medi-** (93c), **Neds, -pede** (117b), **pedi-** (93a), **pedo-** (92d, 93a), **Redd** (176), **redd** (113b), **rede** (31b, 105a), **redo** (26a, 74b), **Reds** (206), **reds, Teds, veda** (60a), **weds, Yedo** (122d), **zeds**

_ _ E D   **abed** (110b), **aced** (120c), **aged** (12c, 83c, 83d), **aped, awed, axed, bled** (97d), **bred** (97c), **coed** (107b), **cued, deed** (9d, 43a, 71a, 122c), **died, dyed, eked, eyed, feed** (82c), **fled, Fred** (47c,

340

153), **gled** (42a), **heed** (15c, 25b, 58d, 72b, 83a, 99a), **hied**, **hoed**, **hued**, **iced**, **lied** (54a, 234), **meed** (100b), **Mr. Ed** (119b), **need** (34d, 42d, 68b, 92a, 129d), **Obed** (103c, 197), **owed**, **pied** (114a, 127b), **pled**, **Reed** (176, 204), **reed** (16d, 55d, 75a, 79c, 84d), **rued**, **seed** (55c, 84d, 85c, 90a, 112b, 113d), **shed** (24d, 70d, 77d, 108a), **she'd** (30c), **sled** (102b), **sned** (73a), **sped**, **sued**, **Swed.** (243), **teed**, **tied**, **toed**, **used** (9c, 57a), **vied**, **weed** (52d)

E _ _ D   **egad** (83a), **eked**, **emyd** (120c), **Enid** (14d, 23c, 53c, 120c, 151), **Exod.** (238), **eyed**

E E _ _   **eels**, **eely**, **EEOC** (238), **Eero** (151)

_ E E _   **beef** (29c, 75c), **been**, **beep** (112b), **beer** (18d, 95d), **bees**, **beet** (127c), **cees**, **deed** (9d, 43a, 71a, 122c), **deem** (30b, 66d, 121a), **deep** (9b, 41c, 73c, 94d), **deer** (25d, 102d, 114b, 230), **dees**, **feed** (82c), **feel** (56c, 106c, 123b, 134b), **fees**, **feet** (71b), **geek** (109a), **Geer** (154), **gees**, **Geez** (41d), **heed** (15c, 25b, 58d, 72b, 83a, 99a), **heel** (55b), **Heep** (33d, 35c), **heer** (134b), **jeep** (127d), **jeer** (120a), **jeez** (42a), **keef** (58b), **Keel** (164), **keel** (108b), **keen** (16a, 45c, 68d, 129b), **keep** (10a, 60c, 94b, 100a, 104c), **keet** (56d), **leek** (59b, 84a, 131b), **leer** (12b, 73a, 110d), **lees** (37d, 106b), **leet** (31c), **meed** (100b), **Meek** (170), **meek** (37a, 53c, 61c, 76d, 77c, 126a), **meet** (9c, 15a, 30a, 40d, 43d, 63c, 103a, 107a), **need** (34d, 42d, 68b, 92a, 129d), **neep** (105b, 125b), **ne'er** (30b, 82c, 107c), **peek** (73a), **Peel** (174), **peel** (43a, 86c), **peen** (57d), **peep** (73a, 87c), **peer** (41b, 73a, 82a), **Reed** (176, 204), **reed** (16d, 55d, 75a, 79c, 84d), **reef** (98d, 104a, 108b), **reek** (43c, 52a, 111a), **reel** (20c, 33b, 113c, 113d, 114b, 114c, 131c, 133a, 233), **Rees** (176), **seed** (55c, 84d, 85c, 90a, 112b, 113d), **seek** (105d), **seel** (20a), **seem** (13c), **seen**, **seep** (72b, 84b, 87d, 114a), **seer** (95b, 111d, 128c), **sees**, **teed**, **teel** (107a), **teem** (9b, 92a, 118c), **-teen** (117b), **Tees** (82b), **tees**, **veer** (35c, 125b), **vees**, **Weeb** (186), **weed** (52d), **week** (122b), **weep** (32b, 68d), **zees** (110c)

_ _ E E   **Agee** (137), **akee** (51d, 124a), **alee** (59a, 108a, 132b), **bree** (105a), **chee** (246), **Cree** (11b, 189), **epee** (45b, 118d), **flee** (9b, 41c), **free** (36b, 56a, 73a, 100c, 112b), **ghee** (22d), **glee** (76a, 111d, 234), **idee** (50c), **Klee** (164), **knee** (66c), **ogee** (14a, 77d, 90c), **pree** (105b), **Rhee** (68c, 177), **Smee** (88b), **snee** (33a, 35d, 68a), **Spee** (53c, 55c), **thee** (95b), **tree** (30d, 53b, 133c), **tyee** (26d)

E _ _ E   **ease** (10b, 11c, 15b, 29b, 42d, 71b, 77b, 99b, 99d, 100a, 129d), **ecce** (18b, 69c, 69d), **edge** (10b, 19c, 21a, 21b, 74d, 87d, 100d, 109a, 130c), **Edie** (150), **eine** (53d, 54a), **Eire** (64a), **Elbe** (82b, 216), **Elie** (151), **Elke** (151), **elle** (49d, 51a, 246), **else** (18c, 61d, 85a), **-ence** (117b), **-ense** (117b), **epee** (45b, 118d), **Erde** (22b), **Erie** (23c, 68d, 189), **Erle** (151), **erne** (19a, 39a, 105c, 225), **Erse** (25c, 52a, 64a), **-esce** (117c), **esne** (12c, 106d, 110b, 121b), **esse** (9d, 18b), **Este** (44b, 45b, 64d, 85b), **este** (113a), **etre** (50a), **-ette** (117b), **eure** (54b), **evoe** (16a, 100b), **Eyre** (22a)

E F _ _   **Efik** (69a, 220), **efts**

_ E F _   **deft** (10a, 14d, 110a), **defy** (25d), **heft** (22c, 131a), **Jeff** (161), **left** (9a, 34d, 91c, 99c), **teff** (10c), **weft** (32b, 121c, 133c)

_ _ E F   **atef** (32b, 39d), **beef** (29c, 75c), **chef** (30c, 50c, 68a), **clef** (80c, 234), **coef.** (237), **fief** (45c), **keef** (58b), **lief** (132a), **reef** (98d, 104a, 108b), **tref** (48b, 126a)

E _ _ F   **Enif** (207)

E G _ _   **egad** (83a), **egal** (50b), **Eger** (40a), **eggs** (85c), **eggy** (134d), **Egil** (82b), **egos**

_ E G _   **begs**, **degu** (101c), **kegs**, **legs**, **mega-** (93b), **Megs**, **pega** (46d), **pegs**, **Pegu** (97d), **sego** (22c, 71d), **tegs**, **Vega** (114d, 207), **Wegg** (85a), **yegg** (22d)

_ _ E G   **Doeg** (197), **Gheg** (213), **Greg** (156), **Oreg.** (241), **Roeg** (178), **skeg** (67b, 133b)

_ E H _   **Jehu** (197), **jehu** (38a), **lehr** (54c, 85c), **peho** (81c), **sehr** (54a), **wehe** (53d)

E _ _ H   **each** (13b), **Elah** (67d), **Esth.** (16d, 238), **Etah** (56c, 63d), **etch** (14d, 35a), **euch** (54b), **exch.** (238)

E I _ _   **eine** (53d, 54a), **Eire** (64a)

_ E I _   **ceil** (25b), **deil** (105a), **dein** (54b), **feis** (64a), **hein** (42c, 49c), **heir** (63a, 71b), **Keir** (164), **Leif** (43a), **leis**, **mein** (26d), **Meir** (170), **Neil** (172), **nein** (54a), **Reid** (176), **rein** (26b, 30c, 100a), **reis** (24a), **Seir** (41c), **seis** (113a), **teil** (72a), **veil** (29d, 36b, 58c, 59d, 75b), **vein** (20a, 116b), **Weil** (186), **Weir** (186), **weir** (33b, 47a), **zein** (30d)

_ _ E I   **drei** (54a), **Iwei** (213), **Omei** (22b)

E _ _ I   **Eloi** (122b), **equi-** (93c), **etui** (24c, 50a, 51a, 81b, 127b)

E J _ _   **ejoo** (45a)

_ E J _   **Beja** (82a, 222), **sejm** (91a)

E K _ _   **eked**, **ekes**

_ E K _   **deka-** (93d), **leks**, **Reki** (16d), **Teke** (215), **weka** (19b, 74d, 81c, 97b)

_ _ E K   **Ezek.** (238), **geek** (109a), **leek** (59b, 84a, 131b), **Meek** (170), **meek** (37a, 53c, 61c, 76d, 77c, 126a), **peek** (73a), **reek** (43c, 52a, 111a), **seek** (105d), **trek** (66d, 73a, 123d), **week** (122b)

E _ _ K   **Efik** (69a, 220), **Erik** (151), **Ezek.** (238)

E L _ _   **Elah** (67d), **Elam** (88a, 108a, 151), **elan** (33d, 41b, 113d, 128d, 135a), **Elba** (64c, 80d), **Elbe** (82b, 216), **elec.** (238), **elem.** (238), **elev.** (238), **Elia** (68d, 87c, 151), **Elie** (151), **Elio** (151), **Elis** (56b),

Eliz. (238), **Elke** (151), **elks**, **Ella** (151), **ella** (113a), **-ella** (117b), **elle** (49d, 51a, 246), **ells**, **Elmo** (21a, 87a, 151), **elms**, **elmy**, **Eloi** (122b), **Elon** (41c, 82b, 201), **Elsa** (55c, 72d, 84b, 129b, 151), **else** (18c, 61d, 85a), **elul** (78c)

_ E L _ **Bela** (18c, 39c, 140), **Belg.** (236), **Bell** (140), **bell** (22c, 120b), **bels**, **belt** (16d, 27b), **-cele** (117c), **cell** (32c), **Celt** (22a, 217), **celt** (115d, 123a), **Dela.** (209), **dele** (23c, 40b, 43a, 94c, 95b, 119b), **dell** (35d, 127b), **eels**, **eely**, **Fell** (152), **fell** (33a), **felt** (42d, 43b, 43d), **geld** (120a), **gels**, **gelt** (78a), **held** (91d), **heli-** (93d), **Hell** (9a, 16a, 34a, 57a, 108a), **he'll** (30c), **Helm** (157), **helm** (108b, 122a), **help** (10d, 15a, 62b, 117a), **jell** (111d), **kela** (246), **kelp** (64a, 106a), **meld** (23c, 34b), **mell** (60d), **Mels**, **melt** (72b, 120d), **Nell** (83d, 172), **Pele** (58c), **pelf** (21a, 46a, 100c), **Pell** (174), **pelt** (28c, 43a, 57b, 59d), **pelu** (26c), **rely** (124d), **self** (39d, 62d), **sell** (74d, 87c, 127d), **tela** (21c, 75d, 130d), **tele-** (92d, 93d), **Tell** (14a), **tell** (13d, 62b, 81a, 99a), **telo-** (92d), **Vela** (103c, 208), **veld** (104c, 112b), **Weld** (186), **weld** (38d, 66c, 126c), **Welk** (186), **well** (25c, 97c), **we'll** (30c), **welt** (100c, 129b, 130c, 131c), **Yell** (64d), **yell** (18c, 108d), **yelp** (12d, 37b)

_ _ E L **Abel** (10a, 23a, 107a, 197), **-coel** (117a), **duel** (45d), **edel** (54a), **esel** (53d), **Evel** (68a), **ezel** (67c), **feel** (56c, 106c, 123b, 134b), **fuel** (53a), **Gael** (25c, 105a), **goel** (16a), **heel** (55b), **Icel.** (239), **Jael** (197), **Joel** (161, 196, 197), **Kael** (163), **Keel** (164), **keel** (108b), **Kiel** (23c), **koel** (32c), **myel-** (93d), **Noel** (172), **noel** (24b, 27a, 111d), **Orel** (173), **Peel** (174), **peel** (43a, 86c), **pyel-** (93c), **reel** (20c, 33b, 113c, 113d, 114b, 114c, 131c, 133a, 233), **riel** (214), **seel** (20a), **tael** (71c, 131a), **teel** (107a)

E _ _ L **Earl** (150), **earl** (82a), **eccl.** (238), **ecol.** (238), **edel** (54a), **egal** (50b), **Egil** (82b), **elul** (78c), **Emil** (151), **encl.** (238), **enol** (120a), **esel** (53d), **et al.** (69c, 238), **Evel** (68a), **evil** (74c, 109c, 131d, 134c), **excl.** (238), **ezel** (67c)

E M _ _ **emeu** (19b), **-emia** (117a), **Emil** (151), **emim** (54b), **emir** (13d, 94c, 102d, 125b), **emit** (36a, 40a, 43c, 47d, 99b, 106c), **Emma** (21b, 151), **Emmy** (120b), **emus**, **emyd** (120c)

_ E M _ **bema** (90b, 95d), **deme** (56b), **Demi** (148), **demi-** (93a), **demo** (108d, 119c), **demy** (86b), **feme** (133b), **gems**, **hema-** (92c), **heme** (20a), **hemi-** (93a), **hemo-** (92c), **hemp** (23d, 30d, 45c, 55d, 102b), **hems**, **Kemp** (164), **Lema** (166), **memo** (82c), **nema** (39d), **Nemo** (128a), **remi** (53b), **seme** (37c), **semi** (62c), **semi-** (93a, 93c), **tema** (121a, 234), **temp.** (243), **xema** (14a, 56d), **zemi** (45c)

_ _ E M **ahem** (15c, 112a), **chem.** (31b, 236), **deem** (30b, 66d, 121a), **elem.** (238), **Flem.** (238), **idem** (70a), **item** (9c, 14d, 35b, 41b, 71a, 72b, 81c, 83a, 86d), **Ozem** (197), **poem** (128a), **riem** (59d), **seem** (13c), **Shem** (81d, 197), **stem** (26b, 95c, 114c, 115d), **teem** (9b, 92a, 118c), **them** (95a)

E _ _ M **E-COM** (238), **Edam** (26b, 38d), **Edom** (41c, 61d, 64b, 65b), **Elam** (88a, 108a, 151), **elem.** (238), **emim** (54b), **Enam** (66d), **exam** (120d)

343

E N _ _ Enam (66d), -ence (117b), encl. (238), -ency (117b), ency. (238), endo- (94a), ends, engr. (238), Enid (14d, 23c, 53c, 120c, 151), Enif (207), Enna (109a), enol (120a), Enos (9d, 42a, 107a, 151, 197), enow (105a), -ense (117b), ento- (94a), envy (34a, 107a), Enyo (129d)

_ E N _ bend (12c, 32d, 125b), bene (65c, 70b), Beni (214), beno (86a), Bens, bent (13d, 32a, 55d, 62c), -cene (117c), ceno- (92d), cent (30c, 213-224), cent. (236), Dene (189), dene (104a), dens (70b), Dent (149), dent (35a), deny (30c, 36a, 98d), fend (44b, 86d, 129d), fens, Gena (154), Gene (154), gene (59c), Genl. (239), gens (35a), gent (45b), genu (18c, 69d), -geny (117c), hens (92a), Jena (121d), keno (52b), Kens, Kent (70d, 195, 202), Lena (30b, 52a, 166), lend (62b), Leno (166), leno (43b, 75a), lens (54c, 74a, 84c, 98d, 120b), Lent (44c, 87c, 106a), lent, mend (99c), mene (57d), meno (71b, 233), -ment (117b), menu (19a, 24c, 29c, 48b, 51a), nene (58c), oeno- (94a), Peña (174), pend (16c, 58a), Penn (174), Penn. (211, 242), pens, pent (30a), rend (28a), René (176), Reni (65a, 176), reni- (93b), Reno (15c, 81c, 113d), reno- (93b), rent (60b, 60c, 120a, 123b), send (36c, 74b, 86d, 91d, 99c, 108b, 123d), sens (49c), sent, tend (24b, 73a, 77a, 124b), Tenn. (212, 243), teno- (93d), tens, tent (24a, 87b), vena (70b), vend (74d, 87c, 106c), veni- (93d), veno- (93d), vent (11a, 13b, 40c, 60c, 84b, 85b, 115a), wend (54d, 110b, 112a), wens, went (34d), xeno- (93a), yeni (119c), yens, Zeno (56b)

_ _ E N Aden (13d, 224), amen (111b, 128a), been, B. Gen. (236), bien (51b), bren (73d), Caen (17c), Coen (146), cten- (93c), Eden (41a, 82a, 86c, 150), even (23b, 41b, 42b, 47b, 61d, 67c, 71c, 82a, 111a, 126c, 134c), Glen (155), glen (35d, 98a, 127b), G-men (45a), Gwen (156), Iden (192), Kaen (223), keen (16a, 45c, 68d, 129b), lien (53a, 71a, 95b), mien (13c, 17d, 24c, 34d, 36d, 74d), omen (15d, 48c, 48d, 91c, 94a, 109b), open (18b, 23c, 49b, 63a, 83b, 85c, 95d, 126a, 126b, 126c), oven (61c, 67b), oxen (12d, 21b), peen (57d), phen- (92c), pien (14c), rien (50d), seen, Sten (182), sten (73d), Sven, ta'en (107c), -teen (117b), then (10c, 121a), T-men (45a, 123d), when (96d, 131c), Wien (33c), Wren (187), wren (19a, 226)

E _ _ N earn (35b, 52a, 76a), ebon (19d), econ. (238), Eden (41a, 82a, 86c, 150), elan (33d, 41b, 113d, 128d, 135a), Elon (41c, 82b, 201), Erin (64a, 151), ESPN (26a), ethn- (93c), Eton (58b, 65b), even (23b, 41b, 42b, 47b, 61d, 67c, 71c, 82a, 111a, 126c, 134c)

E O _ _ eons, -eous (117a)

_ E O _ aeon (122b), EEOC (238), geog. (239), geol. (239), geom. (239), jeon (218), Keos (64c), Leon (166, 222), Leos, meow (25a), neon (53a, 71d, 245), peon (48c, 76c), Teos (64a)

_ _ E O Cleo (96d, 146), ideo- (93a), ileo- (93b), oleo- (93b), rheo- (92d), skeo (47a)

E _ _ O Ebro (222), Echo (80d), echo (12a, 99d, 100b), ecto- (93c), Eero (151), ejoo (45a), Elio (151), Elmo (21a, 87a, 151), endo- (94a), ento- (94a), Enyo (129d), ergo (121a), Ezio (152)

E P _ _ epee (45b, 118d), epic (59c, 90c), Epis. (238), epit. (238), epos (41b, 59c, 90c)

_ E P _ cepe (39c), Depp (149), dept. (237), FEPA (238), FEPC (238), hept- (93c), kepi (58d, 76d), kept, lept- (93d), neph- (92d), pepo (32c, 75d, 96a), peps, repp (43b), reps, seps (72c, 106d), Sept. (78c, 243), sept (27d, 64a, 111b), wept, Zeph. (244)

_ _ E P beep (112b), deep (9b, 41c, 73c, 94d), Heep (33d, 35c), jeep (127d), keep (10a, 60c, 94b, 100a, 104c), neep (105b, 125b), peep (73a, 87c), prep (104d), seep (72b, 84b, 87d, 114a), skep (18a, 60b), step (55c, 129b), weep (32b, 68d)

E Q _ _ equi- (93c)

_ E Q _ seqq. (243)

_ _ E Q freq. (238)

E R _ _ eras, erat (96a, 97c), Erda (22b, 198), Erde (22b), ergo (121a), ergs, Eric (128b, 151), Erie (23c, 68d, 189), Erik (151), Erin (64a, 151), Eris (14b, 198), Erle (151), Erma (151), erne (19a, 39a, 105c, 225), erns, Eros (32d, 132c, 195, 198), errs, Erse (25c, 52a, 64a), erst (49a), eruc (30d, 45d)

_ E R _ aeri- (92c), aero- (92c), aero. (235), aery (39a), Berg (141), berg (61b), berm (23c, 71a, 108d), Bern (9a, 222), Bert (20c, 141), cere (18d, 130c), Cerf (145), CERN (236), cero (46d, 67d), cero- (93d), cert. (236), -derm (117c), Dern (149), Eero (151), fern (106b), feru (30d, 45c), gerb (46b), Gere (155), germ (36b, 61b, 76c), Hera (14b, 67c, 135c, 198), Herb (158), herb (90a, 106b), herd (38b, 232), here (63d, 101c), herl (14d, 17a), Hero (70d, 194), hero (34d, 95c, 104a), herr (53d), hers (95a), ieri (65c), jerk (20a, 38d, 48b, 88a, 95d), kerb (109a), kerf (33a, 82c), Kern (164), kern (48c, 101b, 125d), Kerr (164), Lero (64c), lerp (41d), mere (17b, 50d, 68b, 84b, 91b, 130a), merl (19a, 19d, 226), mero (56c, 66b), Meru (79a, 218), Merv (170), Nera (121d), Nero (10d, 102a), pere (49d, 50b), peri (44a, 88a), peri- (92c), perk (28d, 51c), pern (60d), pero (112d), Pers. (242), pert (49a, 62b, 72c, 104b, 114a, 128d), Peru (221), sera (13a, 47d, 65a), Serb (134d), sere (37d, 133a), serf (20d, 110b), Seri (76c), sero- (93c), Sert (112c), tera- (93d), Teri (183), term (71d, 72a, 80b, 106c, 115c), tern (19a, 28c, 56d, 104d, 105d, 118b, 226), terp (79a, 94a), Vera (185), vera (105c), verb (86d), vers (51b), vert (56c), vert. (244), very (43c, 78d, 111b), were, we're (30c), werf (44c), weri (16c, 25a), wert (128a), xero- (92c), Zero (188), zero (27b, 65d, 73b, 82c, 89d)

_ _ E R acer (74d), Ager (137), ager (69d, 100d, 102a), Amer. (235), amer (50a), aper (28b, 77a), Auer (61c, 139), aver (10b, 15a, 16c, 34b, 74b, 115a, 118c), Baer (140), beer (18d, 95d), bier (28d, 53d),

Boer (10c, 112b), **br'er** (126a), **cher** (50b), **deer** (25d, 102d, 114b, 230), **doer** (87d), **dyer**, **Eger** (40a), **euer** (54b), **ever** (12a, 18b, 62c), **ewer** (66a, 66d, 89c, 131d), **Geer** (154), **gier** (39a), **goer**, **heer** (134b), **hier** (51b), **hier-** (93c), **hoer**, **icer**, **Iser** (40a), **iter** (69d, 101a, 101d), **jeer** (120a), **kier** (19d, 127b), **leer** (12b, 73a, 110d), **ne'er** (30b, 82c, 107c), **Nuer** (222), **Oder** (100d), **omer** (59a), **over** (9b, 9d, 14c, 32a, 87a, 99c), **oyer** (31c), **peer** (41b, 73a, 82a), **Pier** (175), **pier** (21d, 66b, 68d, 131b), **pter-** (94a), **ruer**, **seer** (95b, 111d, 128c), **-ster** (117a, 117b), **suer** (95b), **tier** (46a, 89b, 102c), **user** (10a, 29c, 40c), **uter-** (93d), **veer** (35c, 125b), **vier** (53d)

E _ _ R   **ebur** (69d), **Eger** (40a), **emir** (13d, 94c, 102d, 125b), **engr.** (238), **euer** (54b), **ever** (12a, 18b, 62c), **ewer** (66a, 66d, 89c, 131d)

E S _ _   **Esau** (64b, 65b, 98b, 197), **esca** (19d, 36a, 55d), **-esce** (117c), **esel** (53d), **esne** (12c, 106d, 110b, 121b), **ESPN** (26a), **espy** (106b), **esse** (9d, 18b), **esta** (113a), **Este** (44b, 45b, 64d, 85b), **este** (113a), **Esth.** (16d, 238)

_ E S _   **Bess** (141), **best** (26d, 30a, 34c, 42b, 85c, 118b), **cess** (71c, 120a), **cest** (54c), **desc.** (237), **Dese** (216), **Desi** (149), **desk** (134c), **Fess** (152), **fess** (41c), **-fest** (117b), **gest** (119b), **Hess** (158), **Jess** (161), **jess** (116a), **jest** (17a, 66d), **less** (77b, 82c), **lest** (48d), **mesa** (40b, 59d, 90b, 119a), **mesh** (40d, 63c, 81c, 111b, 130d), **meso-** (93b), **mess** (21b, 26a, 30a, 36c, 67a, 79c, 111b), **ness** (24a, 58d, 95a), **nest** (31c, 100a, 111b, 118c, 232), **peso** (215 - 217, 219, 221, 224), **pest** (82d, 88a, 89d), **resh** (12a), **rest** (16b, 21d, 71b, 80c, 87b, 99b, 99c, 99d, 234), **sess** (111b), **sess.** (243), **Tess** (58a, 183), **test** (23d, 41d, 42b, 124b, 124d), **vest** (28b, 129b), **West** (186), **west** (83b), **zest** (45c, 57c, 99b)

_ _ E S   **Abes**, **aces**, **ages**, **ales**, **Ames** (138), **apes**, **Ares** (13b, 41c, 59b, 75a, 129d, 135c, 198), **ates** (118c), **aves**, **awes**, **axes**, **ayes** (129c), **bees**, **byes**, **cees**, **cues**, **dees**, **dies** (69c), **does**, **dues**, **dyes**, **ekes**, **Eves**, **eves**, **ewes**, **exes**, **eyes**, **fees**, **foes**, **gees**, **GOES** (239), **goes**, **hies**, **hoes**, **hues**, **ices**, **ides** (33d, 101d), **Ikes**, **Ives** (159), **Joes**, **lees** (37d, 106b), **lies**, **lues** (118d), **lyes**, **Maes**, **Moes**, **noes** (81b), **odes**, **ones** (87d), **ores**, **owes**, **oyes** (31c, 32c, 58d), **pies**, **Pres.** (242), **pres** (50d), **pyes**, **Raes**, **Rees** (176), **roes**, **rues**, **sees**, **she's** (30c), **Spes** (198), **sues** (82b), **tees**, **ties**, **toes**, **tres** (42b, 51b, 113a), **Tues.** (243), **uses**, **Utes**, **vees**, **vies**, **woes**, **Yves** (188), **zees** (110c), **Zoes**

E _ _ S   **Eads** (21d), **ears**, **eats** (48b), **ebbs**, **eels**, **efts**, **eggs** (85c), **egos**, **ekes**, **Elis** (56b), **elks**, **ells**, **elms**, **emus**, **ends**, **Enos** (9d, 42a, 107a, 151, 197), **eons**, **-eous** (117a), **Epis.** (238), **epos** (41b, 59c, 90c), **eras**, **ergs**, **Eris** (14b, 198), **erns**, **Eros** (32d, 132c, 195, 198), **errs**, **Evas**, **Eves**, **eves**, **ewes**, **exes**, **eyas** (19b, 58c), **eyes**

E T _ _   **Etah** (56c, 63d), **et al.** (69c, 238), **etat** (51a), **etch** (14d, 35a), **ethn-** (93c), **Etna** (129a), **etna** (58d), **Eton** (58b, 65b), **etre** (50a), **Etta** (152), **-etta** (117b), **-ette** (117b), **etui** (24c, 50a, 51a, 81b, 127b)

_ E T _   **beta** (11d, 106a), **Bete** (215), **bete** (50a), **Beth** (11a, 141), **beth**

(12a), **bets**, **CETA** (236), **cete** (232), **CETI** (236), **Ceto** (55c, 75d), **fete** (45c), **geta** (65b, 108c), **gets**, **Getz** (155), **Heth** (197), **jete** (16c), **jeth** (78b), **Jets** (206), **jets**, **Jett** (161), **keta** (37b), **keto-** (93b), **Leto** (13b, 14d, 28d, 88c, 198), **lets**, **Lett** (16d), **meta-** (92d), **mete** (11c, 13d, 91d), **Meth.** (240), **metr-** (94a), **Mets** (206), **Metz** (216), **Neth.** (241), **Nets** (206), **nets**, **Pete** (85a, 174), **Peto** (193), **peto** (129b), **petr-** (93d), **pets**, **rete** (81c, 90b), **rets**, **seta** (22a, 57b, 113c), **Seth** (10a, 42b, 197, 198), **seth** (76a), **Seti** (88c), **sets**, **sett** (87b, 119d), **tete** (50c), **teth** (12a), **veto** (95a), **vets**, **weta** (72d), **wets**, **Yeti** (9b), **zeta** (11d)

_ _ E T   **abet** (10d, 48b, 59b), **acet-** (92c), **beet** (127c), **blet** (51d), **Bret** (143), **Chet** (145), **diet** (44b, 65d, 71b), **duet** (80c, 85d), **feet** (71b), **fret** (22a, 25d, 36d, 42c, 128b, 133d), **hyet-** (93c), **keet** (56d), **laet** (49b), **leet** (31c), **meet** (9c, 15a, 30a, 40d, 43d, 63c, 103a, 107a), **nyet** (81d), **Piet** (175), **piet** (26b, 74b), **poet** (40b), **spet** (17b), **stet** (71c, 94c, 95b), **suet** (44c, 83d), **tret** (130a, 131a), **whet** (39c, 107d)

E _ _ T   **east** (84d), **echt** (54a), **edit** (20b, 40c, 94a, 98c, 100b), **emit** (36a, 40a, 43c, 47d, 99b, 106c), **epit.** (238), **erat** (96a, 97c), **erst** (49a), **etat** (51a), **exit** (71a, 130c)

E U _ _   **euch** (54b), **euer** (54b), **eure** (54b), **eury-** (94a)

_ E U _   **deus** (42d, 69d), **Deut.** (237), **feud** (45c, 96b, 127d), **jeux** (50b), **leuc-** (94a), **leuk-** (94a), **meus** (69d), **neur-** (93b), **neut.** (241), **oeuf** (50b), **Peul** (217, 219, 221), **peur** (50b), **Zeus** (55c, 59c, 198)

_ _ E U   **bleu** (26b, 50a), **dieu** (50b), **emeu** (19b), **lieu** (89d)

E _ _ U   **ecru** (18b, 22b, 126a), **emeu** (19b), **Esau** (64b, 65b, 98b, 197)

E V _ _   **Evas**, **Evel** (68a), **even** (23b, 41b, 42b, 47b, 61d, 67c, 71c, 82a, 111a, 126c, 134c), **ever** (12a, 18b, 62c), **Eves**, **eves**, **evil** (74c, 109c, 131d, 134c), **evoe** (16a, 100b)

_ E V _   **Bevs**, **bevy** (16d, 31c, 47c, 232), **Deva** (60a, 221), **Devi** (109d), **Levi** (13b, 64d, 70d, 197), **levo-** (93b), **levy** (15a, 62b, 120a), **Neva** (100d), **neve** (46c, 54c, 55d, 111b), **nevi** (19c, 77d), **reve** (50b), **revs**, **Seve** (180), **we've** (30c)

_ _ E V   **elev.** (238), **Kiev** (223)

E _ _ V   **elev.** (238)

E W _ _   **ewer** (66a, 66d, 89c, 131d), **ewes**

_ E W _   **dewy** (77c), **hewn** (27a), **hews**, **Jews**, **lewd** (69b, 103d), **mewl** (131c), **mews** (114b), **news** (121d), **Newt** (172), **newt** (39d, 103d, 225) **pews**, **sewn**, **sews**, **Tewa** (189), **yews**

_ _ E W   **anew** (10b, 10c), **blew**, **brew** (29d), **chew** (75b), **clew** (16c, 103b), **crew** (48c, 56c, 81b, 88b, 133d), **Drew** (150, 201), **drew** (110a), flew, grew, knew, Llew (199), phew (42c), plew (18a), shew (128a), skew (118c, 125b), slew (110c, 118c), smew (19a, 38c, 76a, 104c), spew (40a), stew (20c, 30c), thew (79d), view (12c, 15a, 42b, 73a, 95b, 104d), whew (42c)

E _ _ W   enow (105a)

E X _ _   exam (120d), exch. (238), excl. (238), exec. (238), exes, exit (71a, 130c), Exod. (238)

_ E X _   hexa- (93c), next (81a), sexi- (93c), sext (23d, 84d, 109d), sexy (41c), text (86d, 133c)

_ _ E X   Alex (137), AMEX (235), apex (32c, 59a, 59d, 87b, 89b, 123a, 135a), flex (18c), ibex (54d, 230), ilex (60c), N. Mex. (241), obex (21c)

E _ _ X   eaux (51b)

E Y _ _   eyas (19b, 58c), eyed, eyes, eyra (65b), Eyre (22a), eyry (39a)

_ E Y _   beys, Ceyx (57b), deys, keys

_ _ E Y   ahey (42c), drey (114b), Frey (10b, 153, 198), Grey (156, 192, 194), Huey (159), Ivey (159), Joey (161), joey (67a, 134d), obey (29c, 59a, 67b, 10a), prey (128b), sley (130d), they (95a), trey (24a, 121c), Urey (15c, 184), whey (76d)

E _ _ Y   easy (43d, 53c, 55c, 77c, 109c, 111c), Eddy (150), eddy (31b, 118d, 131c), edgy (81b, 100a, 120c), eely, eggy (134d), elmy, Emmy (120b), -ency (117b), ency. (238), envy (34a, 107a), espy (106b), eury- (94a), eyry (39a)

E Z _ _   Ezek. (238), ezel (67c), Ezio (152), Ezra (152, 196, 197)

_ _ E Z   Baez (140), chez (50a), Geez (41d), Inez (37c), jeez (42a), knez (94c), oyez (31c, 32c, 58d), Suez (23c)

E _ _ Z   Eliz. (238)

F A _ _   fabe (55b), face (15a, 30a, 73a, 79d, 118a, 128c), fact (9d, 35b, 98a), fade (35c, 36a, 127b), fado (91d), fads, Fahr. (238), fail (35c, 44a, 48a), Fain (152), fain (35b, 54c, 133a), fair (10a, 17d, 41b, 45c, 62b, 67c), fait (9c, 50b), fake (45a, 62a, 94b, 107c), Fala (44d), fa-la (98d), Falk (152), fall (38b, 57b, 106a), falx (102a), Fama (103a), fame (99c, 99d), fane (104a, 120b), Fang (193, 216), fang (123a), fans, faon (44d), fare (35c, 48b), farl (105b), farm (21d, 32a, 55d, 122a), faro (24b), Farr (152), fast (46b, 47c, 96d, 118c, 126d), fate (35b, 68a, 73b), Fats (152), Faun (45d, 133b, 198), favi (122a), fawn (32a, 34c), Faye (152), Fays, faze (36a)

_ F A _   Afar (41d, 216), afar (36d), Sfax (223)

_ _ F A   Kafa (32d, 216), sofa (36d), tufa (91c, 129a), Urfa (76a)

F _ _ A   **Fala** (44d), **fa-la** (98d), **Fama** (103a), **FEPA** (238), **FICA** (238), **fila** (121c), **flea** (63b, 229), **FNMA** (238), **FOIA** (238), **fora** (75a, 101d), **Fula** (216, 217)

F _ _ B   **flub** (21b), **forb** (59c), **frib** (35d)

F _ _ C   **FDIC** (238), **FEPC** (238), **fisc** (42c, 102c), **floc** (111a)

F D _ _   **FDIC** (238)

_ F D _   **AFDC** (235)

F _ _ D   **feed** (82c), **fend** (44b, 86d, 129d), **feud** (45c, 96b, 127d), **find** (36a), **fled**, **fold** (57d, 90b, 107d), **-fold** (117c), **fond** (10b, 73c), **food** (44b, 56d, 82d, 128b), **Ford** (153, 191, 194), **ford** (129a), **foud** (44c, 74a), **fowd** (44c, 74a), **Fred** (47c, 153), **Fuad** (44c), **fund** (9c, 78a, 100a), **fyrd** (83d)

F E _ _   **fear** (11a, 51c, 86b, 120d), **feat** (9d, 43a, 124c), **febr-** (93a), **feed** (82c), **feel** (56c, 106c, 123b, 134b), **fees**, **feet** (71b), **feis** (64a), **Fell** (152), **fell** (33a), **felt** (42d, 43b, 43d), **feme** (133b), **fend** (44b, 86d, 129d), **fens**, **FEPA** (238), **FEPC** (238), **fern** (106b), **feru** (30d, 45c), **Fess** (152), **fess** (41c), **-fest** (117b), **fete** (45c), **feud** (45c, 96b, 127d)

_ _ F E   **cafe** (19c), **fife** (48a, 80c), **life** (19a, 57a, 94d), **orfe** (46d, 134b), **rife** (9b, 94b), **safe** (106b, 116c, 127b), **wife** (114a)

F _ _ E   **fabe** (55b), **face** (15a, 30a, 73a, 79d, 118a, 128c), **fade** (35c, 36a, 127b), **fake** (45a, 62a, 94b, 107c), **fame** (99c, 99d), **fane** (104a, 120b), **fare** (35c, 48b), **fate** (35b, 68a, 73b), **Faye** (152), **faze** (36a), **feme** (133b), **fete** (45c), **fife** (48a, 80c), **file** (72a, 97d, 99a, 122d), **Fine** (152), **fine** (26d, 34c, 40b, 40d, 79d, 87c, 116d, 233), **fire** (14b, 36a, 36c, 108c), **five** (17c, 88c, 97c), **flee** (9b, 41c), **floe** (61b), **flue** (11a, 26c), **fore** (51c, 108b), **frae** (105a), **free** (36b, 56a, 73a, 100c, 112b), **froe** (28a, 122d, 123a, 130d), **fume** (111a, 116a), **fuse** (75d, 76a), **fuze** (35b), **fyke** (16b)

_ F F _   **affy** (18d), **iffy** (26a, 100d), **offs** (32a, 118d)

_ _ F F   **baff** (55b), **biff** (60b), **buff** (119b, 134b), **cuff** (21b, 60b, 105b, 110b), **doff** (99c, 119a), **duff** (95d), **gaff** (46d, 47a, 113b), **guff** (16b, 62c, 82a), **Huff** (159), **huff** (47b, 119c), **Jeff** (161), **jiff** (77d), **luff** (48a), **miff** (96b), **Muff** (17b), **muff** (17c, 21b, 22c), **puff** (20a, 74a), **raff** (102d), **riff** (66a, 78c), **ruff** (34d, 37b, 51c), **teff** (10c), **tiff** (96b), **toff** (33c), **tuff** (91c, 129a)

F _ _ F   **fief** (45c)

F _ _ G   **Fang** (193, 216), **fang** (123a), **flag** (17a, 38a, 41a, 69a, 87b, 114d, 130c, 132a), **flog** (131c), **frog** (17c, 225), **frug** (33b), **fung-** (93a)

F _ _ H   **fish** (128d), **Foch** (49c, 153)

349

F I _ _ fiat (34b, 84c), fibr- (93a), fibs, FICA (238), fico (124c, 133d), fids, fief (45c), fife (48a, 80c), figs, Fiji (216), fila (121c), file (72a, 97d, 99a, 122d), fill (83b, 88b, 104b), film (28b, 77b, 121b), fils (51a, 213, 217, 218, 223, 224), find (36a), Fine (152), fine (26d, 34c, 40b, 40d, 79d, 87c, 116d, 233), fink (46a), Finn. (238), fins, fire (14b, 36a, 36c, 108c), firm (29b, 29d, 114b, 126d), firn (54c, 55d, 111b), firs, fisc (42c, 102c), fish (128d), fisk (42c), fist (21c, 57d), fits, fitz (111d), five (17c, 88c, 97c), fizz (39d)

_ F I _ Efik (69a, 220)

_ _ F I hi-fi (112b), Safi (220), sufi (88a)

F _ _ I favi (122a), Fiji (216), foci (25c), fuci (38d), Fuji (66a), fuji (65b)

F _ _ K Falk (152), fink (46a), fisk (42c), flak (13a), folk (87d, 124b), fork (13c, 36d, 37a, 119a), funk (10d, 35a, 47b)

F L _ _ flag (17a, 38a, 41a, 69a, 87b, 114d, 130c, 132a), flak (13a), flam (38b), flan (32d, 87a), flap (48a, 79c, 89d, 119a, 130c, 132d), flat (42a, 63b, 95a, 95c, 114c, 234), flaw (19d, 34c), flax (72a, 72b), flay (110a, 110b, 116c), flea (63b, 229), fled, flee (9b, 41c), Flem. (238), flew, flex (18c), Flip (153), flip (123b), flit (33d), floc (111a), floe (61b), flog (131c), flop (44a), flor (46a, 108a), flow (14b, 37d, 116b), flub (21b), flue (11a, 26c), fluo- (93a), flux (26a, 47d)

F _ _ L fail (35c, 44a, 48a), fall (38b, 57b, 106a), farl (105b), feel (56c, 106c, 123b, 134b), Fell (152), fell (33a), fill (83b, 88b, 104b), foal (61b), foil (16b, 45b, 76b, 116d, 121d), fool (20b, 22c, 34a, 38d, 61d, 78d, 109c, 116d), foul (9a, 126b), fowl (19b), fuel (53a), full (29c, 99d), furl (101c)

F _ _ M farm (21d, 32a, 55d, 122a), film (28b, 77b, 121b), firm (29b, 29d, 114b, 126d), flam (38b), Flem. (238), foam (51c, 114a), form (44c, 107c, 127a), from (18b, 115a)

F N _ _ FNMA (238)

_ F N _ Ifni (220)

F _ _ N Fain (152), fain (35b, 54c, 133a), faon (44d), Faun (45d, 133b, 198), fawn (32a, 34c), fern (106b), Finn. (238), firn (54c, 55d, 111b), flan (32d, 87a), Fran (153)

F O _ _ foal (61b), foam (51c, 114a), fobs, Foch (49c, 153), foci (25c), foes, fogs, fogy (83d), FOIA (238), foil (16b, 45b, 76b, 116d, 121d), Foix (49c), fold (57d, 90b, 107d), -fold (117c), folk (87d, 124b), fond (10b, 73c), font (17a, 125d), food (44b, 56d, 82d, 128b), fool (20b, 22c, 34a, 38d, 61d, 78d, 109c, 116d), foot (17b, 87b, 246), fops, fora (75a, 101d), forb (59c), Ford (153, 191, 194), ford (129a), fore (51c, 108b), fork (13c, 36d, 37a, 119a), form (44c, 107c, 127a), fort (51c, 116c), foss (36d), foud (44c, 74a), foul (9a, 126b), four (72c, 120d), fowd (44c, 74a), fowl (19b), Foxx (153), foxy (14d, 31d, 132a), Foyt (153)

_ _ F O	**info.** (239)
F _ _ O	**fado** (91d), **faro** (24b), **fico** (124c, 133d), **fluo-** (93a)
F _ _ P	**flap** (48a, 79c, 89d, 119a, 130c, 132d), **Flip** (153), **flip** (123b), **flop** (44a), **frap** (37d, 122a)
F _ _ Q	**freq.** (238)
F R _ _	**frae** (105a), **Fran** (153), **frap** (37d, 122a), **fras, frat** (29a), **frau** (54a), **fray** (45d, 49b, 125a), **Fred** (47c, 153), **free** (36b, 56a, 73a, 100c, 112b), **freq.** (238), **fret** (22a, 25d, 36d, 42c, 128b, 133d), **Frey** (10b, 153, 198), **frib** (35d), **frit** (54c), **Friz** (154), **friz** (32d), **froe** (28a, 122d, 123a, 130d), **frog** (17c, 225), **from** (18b, 115a), **frow** (123a), **frug** (33b)
_ F R _	**Afro** (57b), **Afro-** (92c)
_ _ F R	**S. Afr.** (242)
F _ _ R	**Fahr.** (238), **fair** (10a, 17d, 41b, 45c, 62b, 67c), **Farr** (152), **fear** (11a, 51c, 86b, 120d), **febr-** (93a), **fibr-** (93a), **flor** (46a, 108a), **four** (72c, 120d)
_ _ F S	**Alfs, oafs, offs** (32a, 118d)
F _ _ S	**fads, fans, Fats** (152), **Fays, fees, feis** (64a), **fens, Fess** (152), **fess** (41c), **fibs, fids, figs, fils** (51a, 213, 217, 218, 223, 224), **fins, firs, fits, fobs, foes, fogs, fops, foss** (36d), **fras, furs, fuss** (21b, 36d, 92a)
_ F T _	**efts**
_ _ F T	**baft** (43b), **daft** (48b), **deft** (10a, 14d, 110a), **gift** (13d, 94a, 119b), **haft** (60a), **heft** (22c, 131a), **left** (9a, 34d, 91c, 99c), **lift** (40b), **loft** (15c, 55b, 129d), **Luft** (167), **raft** (176), **raft** (47c), **rift** (21d, 47a, 84b, 113d), **sift** (105c, 109b, 132d), **soft** (39b, 74c, 76d), **Taft** (183, 191), **toft** (60d), **tuft** (22c, 28c), **waft** (47c), **weft** (32b, 121c, 133c)
F _ _ T	**fact** (9d, 35b, 98a), **fait** (9c, 50b), **fast** (46b, 47c, 96d, 118c, 126d), **feat** (9d, 43a, 124c), **feet** (71b), **felt** (42d, 43b, 43d), **-fest** (117b), **fiat** (34b, 84c), **fist** (21c, 57d), **flat** (42a, 63b, 95a, 95c, 114c, 234), **flit** (33d), **font** (17a, 125d), **foot** (17b, 87b, 246), **fort** (51c, 116c), **Foyt** (153), **frat** (29a), **fret** (22a, 25d, 36d, 42c, 128b, 133d), **frit** (54c), **fust** (107b)
F U _ _	**Fuad** (44c), **fuci** (38d), **fuel** (53a), **fugu** (65d), **Fuji** (66a), **fuji** (65b), **Fula** (216, 217), **full** (29c, 99d), **fume** (111a, 116a), **fumy** (127b), **fund** (9c, 78a, 100a), **fung-** (93a), **funk** (10d, 35a, 47b), **furl** (101c), **furs, fury** (97b, 116a), **fuse** (75d, 76a), **fuss** (21b, 36d, 92a), **fust** (107b), **fuze** (35b), **fuzz** (37c)
_ _ F U	**Gifu** (60d)
F _ _ U	**feru** (30d, 45c), **frau** (54a), **fugu** (65d)

F _ _ W   **flaw** (19d, 34c), **flew, flow** (14b, 37d, 116b), **frow** (123a)

F _ _ X   **falx** (102a), **flax** (72a, 72b), **flex** (18c), **flux** (26a, 47d), **Foix** (49c), **Foxx** (153)

F Y _ _   **fyke** (16b), **fyrd** (83d)

_ _ F Y   **affy** (18d), **defy** (25d), **Dufy** (49c, 150), **iffy** (26a, 100d)

F _ _ Y   **flay** (110a, 110b, 116c), **fogy** (83d), **foxy** (14d, 31d, 132a), **fray** (45d, 49b, 125a), **Frey** (10b, 153, 198), **fumy** (127b), **fury** (97b, 116a)

F _ _ Z   **fitz** (111d), **fizz** (39d), **Friz** (154), **friz** (32d), **fuzz** (37c)

G A _ _   **gabi** (119d), **gabs, gaby** (109c), **gads, Gaea** (39b, 198), **Gael** (25c, 105a), **gaff** (46d, 47a, 113b), **gaga** (24c, 76a), **gage** (90b), **gags, Gaia** (39b), **Gail** (154), **gain** (9d, 44d, 83b, 94d, 132b), **gait** (130c), **gala** (45c), **Gale** (154), **gale** (130d, 132b, 132c), **gall** (18d, 25d, 64b, 128b), **gals, gamb** (12d), **game** (114a), **gamo-** (93c), **Gamp** (35c), **gamp** (125b), **gams** (71b), **gamy** (90b, 103d), **gang** (16d, 32a, 232), **gaol** (94d), **gaon** (66c), **gape** (134b), **gaps, garb** (28b, 37d), **gare** (50d, 97b), **Garn** (154), **Garo** (69a, 154), **GARP** (239), **Garr** (154), **gars, Gary** (154), **gash** (33a, 110b), **gasp** (21d, 86b), **gata** (107d), **gate** (15c, 41b, 91c), **Gath** (88c), **gats, GATT** (239), **gaud** (124c, 133d), **Gaul** (49b), **gaur** (25a, 62d, 132a, 230), **gave, gawk** (109c, 114d), **Gaya** (18d), **Gaye** (154), **gays** (60d), **Gaza** (88c, 216), **gaze** (114d, 115a)

_ G A _   **Agag** (67c, 104a, 197), **agal** (18a, 30d), **Agao** (57c), **Agar** (137), **agar** (32c, 106a), **agas, Agau** (57c), **egad** (83a), **egal** (50b), **ogam** (64b)

_ _ G A   **alga** (105d), **biga** (125c), **gaga** (24c, 76a), **giga** (45d), **juga** (24c), **LPGA** (240), **mega-** (93b), **Naga** (15a, 69a, 128c), **naga** (23c, 28c, 60a), **Olga** (173), **pega** (46d), **raga** (80a), **Riga** (218), **ruga** (48a, 134a), **saga** (71b, 104c, 119b), **soga** (52c), **toga** (101d), **Vega** (114d, 207), **yoga** (14d, 60a), **yuga** (60a)

G _ _ A   **Gaea** (39b, 198), **gaga** (24c, 76a), **Gaia** (39b), **gala** (45c), **gata** (107d), **Gaya** (18d), **Gaza** (88c, 216), **Gena** (154), **geta** (65b, 108c), **giga** (45d), **gila** (72c), **Gina** (155), **Giza** (113c), **Gola** (218), **gola** (33c, 37c, 77d), **Goya** (112c)

_ G B _   **Igbo** (68c, 220)

G _ _ B   **gamb** (12d), **garb** (28b, 37d), **gerb** (46b), **Gibb** (155), **glib** (47d, 110c, 111a, 129a), **glob** (75b), **grab** (80b, 106c, 111b), **grub** (35d, 69b), **guib** (13a)

_ G C _   **agcy.** (235)

G _ _ D   **gaud** (124c, 133d), **geld** (120a), **gild** (40b), **gird** (16d, 18c, 40c,

118b), **glad** (66d), **gled** (42a), **goad** (62c, 114b), **gold** (74a, 134b, 245), **Gond** (62d), **good** (127a, 131a), **grad** (25c), **grad.** (239), **grid** (17c, 90b, 116a)

G E _ _   **gear** (13c, 28b, 41b, 85b, 123a), **Geat** (104c), **geck** (105b), **geek** (109a), **Geer** (154), **gees, Geez** (41d), **geld** (120a), **gels, gelt** (78a), **gems, Gena** (154), **Gene** (154), **gene** (59c), **Genl.** (239), **gens** (35a), **gent** (45b), **genu** (18c, 69d), **-geny** (117c), **geog.** (239), **geol.** (239), **geom.** (239), **gerb** (46b), **Gere** (155), **germ** (36b, 61b, 76c), **gest** (119b), **geta** (65b, 108c), **gets, Getz** (155)

_ G E _   **aged** (12c, 83c, 83d), **Agee** (137), **Ager** (137), **ager** (69d, 100d, 102a), **ages, B. Gen.** (236), **Eger** (40a), **ogee** (14a, 77d, 90c)

_ _ G E   **auge** (71b), **Cage** (144), **cage** (30a, 40d), **doge** (74a, 127d), **edge** (10b, 19c, 21a, 21b, 74d, 87d, 100d, 109a, 130c), **gage** (90b), **huge** (54b, 62a, 69b), **Inge** (22d, 54d, 88d, 159), **loge** (120d), **luge** (110b), **mage** (74a), **Page** (173, 193, 194), **page** (12d, 41c, 48b, 70d, 107a), **rage** (26d, 74c, 116a, 120b), **sage** (14c, 70d, 77b, 106a, 131b, 132d), **tige** (89b), **urge** (35b, 54d, 63b, 94d), **wage** (103d)

G _ _ E   **gage** (90b), **Gale** (154), **gale** (130d, 132b, 132c), **game** (114a), **gaon** (66c), **gape** (134b), **gare** (50d, 97b), **gate** (15c, 41b, 91c), **gave, Gaye** (154), **gaze** (114d, 115a), **Gene** (154), **gene** (59c), **Gere** (155), **ghee** (22d), **gibe** (10d, 35a), **Gide** (49c, 155), **gite** (50c), **give** (11c, 13d, 29d, 94a, 95c), **glee** (76a, 111d, 234), **glue** (10a, 115b), **gone** (9b, 34d, 36c), **Gore** (155, 191), **gore** (87c, 88d, 124b), **gyle** (21d), **gyne** (45b), **gyre** (27b), **gyve** (45c, 107b)

G _ _ F   **gaff** (46d, 47a, 113b), **golf** (12a), **goof** (28b), **Graf** (135a, 156), **graf** (53d, 81d), **guff** (16b, 62c, 82a), **gulf** (9c, 130a)

_ G G _   **eggs** (85c), **eggy** (134d), **oggi** (65c)

_ _ G G   **nogg** (11b), **Rigg** (177), **vugg** (25b, 53c, 101b), **Wegg** (85a), **yegg** (22d)

G _ _ G   **gang** (16d, 32a, 232), **geog.** (239), **Gheg** (213), **gong** (80a), **Greg** (156), **grig** (32a, 39c, 56a, 72c), **grog** (11a, 72b, 113d)

G H _ _   **ghat** (28c, 79b), **ghee** (22d), **Gheg** (213), **ghor** (127b)

_ G H _   **agha** (125b)

_ _ G H   **high** (108d, 123c), **Hugh** (159), **Magh** (213), **magh** (78b), **nigh** (28b, 81a), **sigh** (21d), **vugh** (25b, 53c, 101b), **yogh** (12c)

G _ _ H   **gash** (33a, 110b), **Gath** (88c), **Gish** (155), **gosh** (42a, 53b), **Goth** (120d), **Groh** (156), **gush** (114b, 118a)

G I _ _   **Gibb** (155), **gibe** (10d, 35a), **gibs, Gide** (49c, 155), **gier** (39a), **gift** (13d, 94a, 119b), **Gifu** (60d), **giga** (45d), **Gigi** (155), **GIGO** (239),

gigs, **gila** (72c), **gild** (40b), **gill** (21c, 246), **Gils**, **gilt** (60c, 112b, 134d), **gimp** (124c), **Gina** (155), **gink** (39c), **Gino** (155), **gins**, **gird** (16d, 18c, 40c, 118b), **girl** (45b), **giro** (31d, 65c), **girt** (27b), **Gish** (155), **gist** (74b, 89c), **gite** (50c), **give** (11c, 13d, 29d, 94a, 95c), **Giza** (113c)

_ G I _   **Agib** (13d), **agio** (42c, 48d, 78a, 94a), **Agis** (67d), **Egil** (82b), **TGIF** (243)

_ _ G I   **Gigi** (155), **hagi** (65d), **magi** (88a, 94c, 132d), **oggi** (65c), **ragi** (25c), **sugi** (65b), **vagi** (31d), **Yogi** (187), **yogi** (60a)

G _ _ I   **gabi** (119d), **Gigi** (155), **Gobi** (35a), **goni-** (92c), **gyri** (21c)

G _ _ K   **gawk** (109c, 114d), **geck** (105b), **geek** (109a), **gink** (39c), **gook** (110c), **guck** (110c), **gunk** (110c)

G L _ _   **glad** (66d), **gled** (42a), **glee** (76a, 111d, 234), **Glen** (155), **glen** (35d, 98a, 127b), **glib** (47d, 110c, 111a, 129a), **glim** (23d, 43c), **glob** (75b), **glom** (115a), **glop** (75b), **glos.** (239), **glow** (108a), **glue** (10a, 115b), **glum** (54d, 78d, 112b, 117d), **glut** (42b, 55b, 85c, 104b, 118a)

_ G L _   **Ogle** (173), **ogle** (43c, 71a, 73a), **ugli** (51d), **ugly** (126a)

_ _ G L   **Angl.** (235)

G _ _ L   **Gael** (25c, 105a), **Gail** (154), **gall** (18d, 25d, 64b, 128b), **gaol** (94d), **Gaul** (49b), **Genl.** (239), **geol.** (239), **gill** (21c, 246), **girl** (45b), **goal** (10d, 17c, 40d, 83a, 96c, 104d, 119d), **goel** (16a), **gull** (19a, 28c, 34a, 34c, 68a, 76c, 105c, 118d, 225)

G M _ _   **G-man** (45a), **G-men** (45a)

G _ _ M   **geom.** (239), **germ** (36b, 61b, 76c), **glim** (23d, 43c), **glom** (115a), **glum** (54d, 78d, 112b, 117d), **gram** (76b, 246), **grim** (19d, 54b, 115b), **grum** (54d), **Guam** (64c)

G N _ _   **gnar** (56d), **gnat** (48a, 63b, 76c, 229), **gnaw** (19c, 26c), **gnus**

_ G N _   **Agni** (68c), **igni-** (93a)

_ _ G N   **lign-** (94a), **sign** (74d, 91c, 114c)

G _ _ N   **gain** (9d, 44d, 83b, 94d, 132b), **Garn** (154), **Glen** (155), **glen** (35d, 98a, 127b), **G-man** (45a), **G-men** (45a), **goon** (116c), **gown** (37d), **grin** (111a), **guan** (19b), **Gwen** (156), **Gwyn** (199), **gymn-** (93b)

G O _ _   **goad** (62c, 114b), **goal** (10d, 17c, 40d, 83a, 96c, 104d, 119d), **goas**, **goat** (81a, 102d, 230), **Gobi** (35a), **Gobo** (16d), **gobo** (66a), **gobs**, **goby** (46d, 228), **goel** (16a), **gods**, **goer**, **GOES** (239), **goes**, **Gogo** (17a), **gogo** (111b), **Gola** (218), **gola** (33c, 37c, 77d), **gold** (74a, 134b, 245), **golf** (12a), **Gond** (62d), **gone** (9b, 34d, 36c), gong (80a), goni- (92c), gono- (93c), good (127a, 131a), goof (28b), gook (110c), goon (116c), goop (110c), Gore (155, 191), gore (87c, 88d, 124b), Gort (101b), gory (20a), gosh (42a, 53b), Goth (120d), gout (14d, 113d), govt. (239), gown (37d), Goya (112c)

_ G O _   agog (39a, 42c, 67b), agon (30b, 45c, 56b), egos, Igor (49b, 159)

_ _ G O   Argo (14b, 66a), bago (15a), ergo (121a), GIGO (239), Gogo (17a), gogo (111b), Hugo (49c, 71c, 104d, 159), Iago (44a, 85a, 107c, 195), kago (86a), lago (65a, 112d), logo (22d, 29b), mogo (115d), Pogo (83d, 91d), sago (44b, 86a, 95d, 114d), sego (22c, 71d), Togo (223), zygo- (93c)

G _ _ O   gamo- (93c), Garo (69a, 154), GIGO (239), Gino (155), giro (31d, 65c), Gobo (16d), gobo (66a), Gogo (17a), gogo (111b), gono- (93c), gyno- (92d), gyro- (93a)

_ G P _   OGPU (103c)

G _ _ P   Gamp (35c), gamp (125b), GARP (239), gasp (21d, 86b), gimp (124c), glop (75b), goop (110c), grip (27d, 55d, 60c, 96a, 117d), gulp (20d, 37d, 118b)

G R _ _   grab (80b, 106c, 111b), grad (25c), grad. (239), Graf (135a, 156), graf (53d, 81d), gram (76b, 246), Grau (156), Gray (21a, 41a, 156, 192), gray (60c), Graz (213), Greg (156), grew, Grey (156, 192, 194), grid (17c, 90b, 116a), grig (32a, 39c, 56a, 72c), grim (19d, 54b, 115b), grin (111a), grip (27d, 55d, 60c, 96a, 117d), Gris (156), gris (50c), grit (104a), grog (11a, 72b, 113d), Groh (156), Gros (49c), gros (38c, 43d, 109c), grow (15d, 41a, 42d, 43a, 114a, 118c), grub (35d, 69b), grum (54d), Grus (207)

_ G R _   Agra (24c, 119a), agra (64a, 118c), agri. (235), ogre (78b)

_ _ G R   engr. (238), hygr- (94a), Msgr. (241)

G _ _ R   Garr (154), gaur (25a, 62d, 132a, 230), gear (13c, 28b, 41b, 85b, 123a), Geer (154), ghor (127b), gier (39a), gnar (56d), goer, guar (38b, 48c), guhr (39a), Gyor (217)

_ _ G S   bags, begs, bogs, bugs, cogs, digs, dogs, eggs (85c), ergs, figs, fogs, gags, gigs, hags, hogs, hugs, jags, jigs, jogs, jugs, kegs, lags, legs, logs, lugs, Megs, mugs, nags, nogs, pegs, pigs, pugs, rags, rigs, rugs, sags, tags, tegs, togs (28b), tugs, wags, wigs

G _ _ S   gabs, gads, gags, gals, gams (71b), gaps, gars, gats, gays (60d), gees, gels, gems, gens (35a), gets, gibs, gigs, Gils, gins, glos. (239), gnus, goas, gobs, gods, GOES (239), goes, Gris (156), gris (50c), Gros (49c), gros (38c, 43d, 109c), Grus (207), gums, guns, GUTS (239), guts (63a), guys, gyms, gyps

_ G T _   lgth. (240)

_ _ G T   M.Sgt. (241), S.Sgt. (243)

G _ _ T   gait (130c), GATT (239), Geat (104c), gelt (78a), gent (45b), gest (119b), ghat (28c, 79b), gift (13d, 94a, 119b), gilt (60c, 112b, 134d), girt (27b), gist (74b, 89c), glut (42b, 55b, 85c, 104b, 118a), gnat (48a, 63b, 76c, 229), goat (81a, 102d, 230), Gort (101b), gout (14d, 113d), govt. (239), grit (104a), Guat. (239), gust (20a)

G U _ _   Guam (64c), guan (19b), guar (38b, 48c), Guat. (239), guck (110c), guff (16b, 62c, 82a), guhr (39a), guib (13a), gulf (9c, 130a), gull (19a, 28c, 34a, 34c, 68a, 76c, 105c, 118d, 225), gulp (20d, 37d, 118b), gums, gunk (110c), guns, guru (60b), gush (114b, 118a), gust (20a), GUTS (239), guts (63a), guys

_ G U _   agua (113a), ague (26c, 45c, 74b, 104b), ogum (64b)

_ _ G U   degu (101c), fugu (65d), Pegu (97d)

G _ _ U   genu (18c, 69d), Gifu (60d), Grau (156), guru (60b)

G W _ _   Gwen (156), Gwyn (199)

G _ _ W   glow (108a), gnaw (19c, 26c), grew, grow (15d, 41a, 42d, 43a, 114a, 118c)

G Y _ _   gyle (21d), gymn- (93b), gyms, gyne (45b), gyno- (92d), -gyny (117b), Gyor (217), gyps, gyre (27b), gyri (21c), gyro- (93a), gyve (45c, 107b)

_ _ G Y   -algy (117c), bogy (13c, 113b), cagy (31d), dogy (38c), edgy (81b, 100a, 120c), eggy (134d), fogy (83d), logy (38c), Nagy (61c, 172), orgy (24b, 100b, 104b), pogy (68d, 75d, 78d)

G _ _ Y   gaby (109c), gamy (90b, 103d), Gary (154), -geny (117c), goby (46d, 228), gory (20a), Gray (21a, 41a, 156, 192), gray (60c), Grey (156, 192, 194), -gyny (117b)

G _ _ Z   Geez (41d), Getz (155), Graz (213)

H A _ _   haab (75b), habu (89c, 103c), hack (24c, 33a, 60b), hade (53c), hadj (89b), haec (70a), haft (60a), hagi (65d), hags, ha-ha (45b, 118a), Hahn (156), hahs (42c), Haid (156), Haig (156), haik (52d), hail (9c, 16a, 56c, 60d, 104a, 127d, 130d), Haim (156), hair (46a), haje (28c, 39d), haji (75c), hajj (75c, 89b), hake (46d, 228), Hale (12b, 156), hale (112a, 131d), half (77c), Hall (156), hall (31a, 87a), halo (27b, 71d, 81d, 100d), Hals (38d, 156), halt (14c, 25b, 32a, 59d, 87b, 115d), Hama (222), hame (61b), hams, Hana (157), hand (10d, 15a, 59b, 87c, 133d, 246), hang (118b), Hank (157), hank (57b, 109d), Hans (17b, 53d, 67a, 157), Hapi (198), hapi (53b), hapl- (93c), hard (123b), hare (101c, 230), hark (72b), harl (46a, 48a, 59b), harm (33b, 61d, 62a, 63a), harp (80b), Hart (157), hart (34c, 114b), Harz (79b), hash (21b), hasp (44c, 113c), hast (128a), hate (35b, 72d), hath (128a), hats, haud (70a), haul (37c),

have (20b), **hawk** (19a, 87c, 225), **Hawn** (157), **haws**, **Hays** (157), **haze** (28b, 48a, 77b, 127b), **hazy** (127a)

_ H A _ **Ahab** (24a, 66c, 67d, 87d, 197), **Ahaz** (67d, 197), **bhat** (62d), **Chad** (117a, 145, 215), **Cham** (224), **chap** (45b, 74c), **char** (104d, 124d, 228), **Chas.** (74d), **chat** (19a, 29d, 119b, 225), **chaw** (122c), **chay** (39b, 98c), **dhai** (76c), **dhak** (39b), **dhal** (11d), **ghat** (28c, 79b), **Khan** (164), **khan** (10b, 63a, 88a, 94c), **khat** (58b), **phag-** (92d), **Phar.** (242), **shad** (25b, 46d), **shag** (57b, 119c, 122c), **shah** (16c, 88a), **Shak.** (243), **sham** (9d, 34a, 45a, 49b, 77b, 91d, 94b, 109c), **Shan** (62d, 69a, 220), **Shaw** (41a, 43a, 180, 204), **shay** (84a), **Thad** (183), **Thai** (109a, 218, 223), **than** (29b), **Thar** (35a), **thar** (55a), **that** (34d, 95a, 99b), **thaw** (72b), **wham** (110b), **whap** (60b), **what** (96d, 99b)

_ _ H A **agha** (125b), **Akha** (121d), **Doha** (221), **ha-ha** (45b, 118a), **maha** (25d, 69a, 104a), **OSHA** (241), **paha** (60a), **poha** (58c), **taha** (130d), **YMHA** (244), **YWHA** (244)

H _ _ A **ha-ha** (45b, 118a), **Hama** (222), **Hana** (157), **hema-** (92c), **Hera** (14b, 67c, 135c, 198), **hexa-** (93c), **hora** (21a, 33b), **Hova** (219), **hoya** (12c, 15d, 130c), **Hsia** (26d, 38d), **huia** (81c), **hula** (58b), **Hupa** (15b, 189), **hura** (104a), **hyla** (12b, 122c)

H _ _ B **haab** (75b), **Herb** (158)

H C _ _ **hcap.** (239)

H _ _ C **haec** (70a), **HUAC** (239)

H D _ _ **hdbk.** (239), **HDTV** (239)

H _ _ D **Haid** (156), **hand** (10d, 15a, 59b, 87c, 133d, 246), **hard** (123b), **haud** (70a), **head** (21a, 25d, 26c, 51c, 78a, 94c), **heed** (15c, 25b, 58d, 72b, 83a, 99a), **held** (91d), **herb** (90a, 106b), **herd** (38b, 232), **hied**, **hind** (34b, 37a), **hoed**, **hold** (9c, 15a, 16c, 27d, 67b, 74b, 95b, 100a, 115a, 121a, 234), **Hond.** (239), **Hood** (79b), **hood** (19c, 31c, 52c, 58c), **hued**

H E _ _ **head** (21a, 25d, 26c, 51c, 78a, 94c), **heal** (32d), **heap** (17a, 75b, 79a, 89a), **hear** (59a, 72b), **Heat** (206), **heat** (129d), **Hebe** (32d, 59c, 135a, 198), **heck** (42a), **hect-** (93a), **Hedy** (157), **heed** (15c, 25b, 58d, 72b, 83a, 99a), **heel** (55b), **Heep** (33d, 35c), **heer** (134b), **heft** (22c, 131a), **hein** (42c, 49c), **heir** (63a, 71b), **held** (91d), **heli-** (93d), **Hell** (9a, 16a, 34a, 57a, 108a), **he'll** (30c), **Helm** (157), **helm** (108b, 122a), **help** (10d, 15a, 62b, 117a), **hema-** (92c), **heme** (20a), **hemi-** (93a), **hemo-** (92c), **hemp** (23d, 30d, 45c, 55d, 102b), **hems**, **hens** (92a), **hept-** (93c), **Hera** (14b, 67c, 135c, 198), **Herb** (158), **herb** (90a, 106b), **herd** (38b, 232), **here** (63d, 101c), **herl** (14d, 17a), **Hero** (70d, 194), **hero** (34d, 95c, 104a), **herr** (53d), **hers** (95a), **Hess** (158), **Heth** (197), **hewn** (27a), **hews**, **hexa-** (93c)

_ H E _ **ahem** (15c, 112a), **ahey** (42c), **chee** (246), **chef** (30c, 50c, 68a), **chem.** (31b, 236), **cher** (50b), **Chet** (145), **chew** (75b), **chez** (50a), ghee (22d), Gheg (213), phen- (92c), phew (42c), Rhea (68c, 78d, 89d, 122c, 135c, 177, 198), rhea (19b, 26c, 85a, 226), Rhee (68c, 177), rheo- (92d), Shea (180), shea (22d, 124a), shed (24d, 70d, 77d, 108a), she'd (30c), Shem (81d, 197), she's (30c), shew (128a), Thea (122c), thee (95b), them (95a), then (10c, 121a), thew (79d), they (95a), when (96d, 131c), whet (39c, 107d), whew (42c), whey (76d)

_ _ H E   ache (73a, 85d, 134b), Ashe (139), Oahe (33b), wehe (53d)

H _ _ E   hade (53c), haje (28c, 39d), hake (46d, 228), Hale (12b, 156), hale (112a, 131d), hame (61b), hare (101c, 230), hate (35b, 72d), have (20b), haze (28b, 48a, 77b, 127b), Hebe (32d, 59c, 135a, 198), heme (20a), here (63d, 101c), hide (29d, 31c, 43a), hike (62c), hire (40c, 40d, 71b, 99c, 100a), hive (18a), hole (9c, 13b, 84b, 89c, 109d), home (61c, 99d), hone (39c, 107d, 131c), HOPE (239), Hope (158), hope (42d), hose (115c), hove (71d), Howe (17c, 63d, 159), huge (54b, 62a, 69b), hule (21c, 25a, 102c), Hume (159, 192), Hyde (37a), hype (95a)

H _ _ F   half (77c), hoof (126b), Huff (159), huff (47b, 119c)

H _ _ G   Haig (156), hang (118b), hing (14d), hong (26d), Hung. (239), hung

H _ _ H   hash (21b), hath (128a), Heth (197), high (108d, 123c), hoch (42c, 53d), Hoth (20a), Hugh (159), hush (109b)

H I _ _   hick (134d), hide (29d, 31c, 43a), hied, hier (51b), hier- (93c), hies, hi-fi (112b), high (108d, 123c), hike (62c), Hill (158), hill (17a), hilt (57d), hind (34b, 37a), hing (14d), hint (11d, 32c, 33d, 117d, 133a), hipp- (93a), hips, hire (40c, 40d, 71b, 99c, 100a), Hiss (158), hiss (36a, 112a), hist. (239), hits, hive (18a)

_ H I _   ahir (24d), chia (18d, 76c), Chic (145), chic (111a), ch'ih (246), chil- (93b), Ch'in (26d), Chin. (236), chin (29d), Chip (26d), chip (55b), chir- (93a), chis, chit (54c, 82c, 88b, 129c), Ohio (211), Phil (175), Phil. (242), phis, Phiz (35c), rhin- (93b), RHIP (242), rhiz- (93c), shi'a (80c), shim (71c, 119c, 130d), shin (11d, 12a, 71a, 71b, 107c), ship (106c, 128a), shiv (68a), thin (35c, 35d, 53b, 110c), thio- (93d), this (34d, 95a), whig (71c), whim (24a, 44b, 82c), whin (55c, 101b), whip (18a, 47c, 69b, 121b), whir (112a), whit (122c), whiz (88a, 112a)

_ _ H I   Ishi (134a), ophi- (93d)

H _ _ I   hagi (65d), haji (75c), Hapi (198), hapi (53b), heli- (93d), hemi- (93a), hi-fi (112b), Hopi (95d, 189)

H _ _ J   hadj (89b), hajj (75c, 89b)

H _ _ K   hack (24c, 33a, 60b), haik (52d), Hank (157), hank (57b, 109d), hark (72b), hawk (19a, 87c, 225), hdbk. (239), heck (42a), hick

(134d), **hock** (71b, 87b, 132c), **honk** (55b, 112b), **hook** (24d, 27d, 55b), **hulk** (126d), **hunk** (57d, 88d), **husk** (43a, 61c, 106b, 232)

_ _ H L **buhl** (63a), **Dahl** (147), **Kohl** (18c, 164), **kohl** (43c), **Pohl** (175), **Sahl** (179)

H _ _ L **hail** (9c, 16a, 56c, 60d, 104a, 127d, 130d), **Hall** (156), **hall** (31a, 87a), **hapl-** (93c), **harl** (46a, 48a, 59b), **haul** (37c), **heal** (32d), **heel** (55b), **Hell** (9a, 16a, 34a, 57a, 108a), **he'll** (30c), **herl** (14d, 17a), **Hill** (158), **hill** (17a), **howl** (12d, 17d, 32b, 114b), **Hull** (159), **hull** (106b, 108b), **hurl** (121c, 123b), **hyal-** (93a)

_ H M _ **ohms**

H _ _ M **Haim** (156), **harm** (33b, 61d, 62a, 63a), **Helm** (157), **helm** (108b, 122a), **Holm** (158), **holm** (60c, 64b, 83a)

_ H N _ **ohne** (54a)

_ _ H N **Cohn** (146), **ethn-** (93c), **Hahn** (156), **John** (13b, 18a, 88b, 91b, 107c, 135a, 162, 193, 196), **Kahn** (163)

H _ _ N **Hahn** (156), **Hawn** (157), **hein** (42c, 49c), **hewn** (27a), **hoon** (246), **Horn** (24a), **horn** (13a, 31a, 124d), **hymn** (111d)

H O _ _ **hoar** (51c, 131d), **hoax** (34a, 92b), **hobo** (123d, 127a), **hobs**, **hoch** (42c, 53d), **hock** (71b, 87b, 132c), **hods**, **hoed**, **hoer**, **hoes**, **hogs**, **hold** (9c, 15a, 16c, 27d, 67b, 74b, 95b, 100a, 115a, 121a, 234), **hole** (9c, 13b, 84b, 89c, 109d), **Holm** (158), **holm** (60c, 64b, 83a), **holo-** (94a), **Holt** (158), **holt** (30c), **holy** (30b), **home** (61c, 99d), **homo** (69d), **homo-** (93c), **Homs** (222), **Hond.** (239), **hone** (39c, 107d, 131c), **hong** (26d), **honk** (55b, 112b), **Hood** (79b), **hood** (19c, 31c, 52c, 58c), **hoof** (126b), **hook** (24d, 27d, 55b), **hoon** (246), **hoop** (131d), **Hoot** (158), **hoot** (85c), **HOPE** (239), **Hope** (158), **hope** (42d), **Hopi** (95d, 189), **hops** (18a), **hora** (21a, 33b), **Horn** (24a), **horn** (13a, 31a, 124d), **hors** (50d), **hort.** (239), **hose** (115c), **hosp.** (239), **host** (14c, 42a, 79d), **Hoth** (20a), **hour** (122b), **Hova** (219), **hove** (71d), **Howe** (17c, 63d, 159), **howl** (12d, 17d, 32b, 114b), **hoya** (12c, 15d, 130c), **Hoyt** (159)

_ H O _ **Ahom** (69a), **ahoy** (57b, 81a), **chol-** (92c), **chol.** (236), **chop** (75c), **Chou** (26d), **chou** (50a), **chow** (37a, 227), **choy** (39b, 98c), **dhow** (69b, 84d), **ghor** (127b), **Khon** (223), **mhos**, **phon** (73b), **phon-** (93d), **phot** (246), **rhos**, **shod**, **shoe** (122b), **shoo** (38a, 54b), **shop** (62d, 100a), **shot** (12b, 70c), **shou** (26d), **show** (9d, 34d, 35a, 36c, 43a, 74c), **Thor** (10b, 76c, 77b, 83b, 121d, 183, 198), **Thos.** (74d), **thos** (65b), **thou** (95b), **whoa** (42c, 115d), **whom** (34d, 96d), **whop** (60b)

_ _ H O **coho** (103d), **Echo** (80d), **echo** (12a, 99d, 100b), **icho** (54b), **moho** (60d), **Otho** (102a), **peho** (81c), **Saho** (32d, 57c, 216), **So-Ho** (73a), **to-ho** (61d)

H _ _ O   **halo** (27b, 71d, 81d, 100d), **hemo-** (92c), **Hero** (70d, 194), **hero** (34d, 95c, 104a), **hobo** (123d, 127a), **holo-** (94a), **homo** (69d), **homo-** (93c), **Hugo** (49c, 71c, 104d, 159), **hylo-** (94a), **hypo** (88d)

H _ _ P   **harp** (80b), **hasp** (44c, 113c), **hcap.** (239), **heap** (17a, 75b, 79a, 89a), **Heep** (33d, 35c), **help** (10d, 15a, 62b, 117a), **hemp** (23d, 30d, 45c, 55d, 102b), **hipp-** (93a), **hoop** (131d), **hosp.** (239), **hrip** (239), **hump** (95c)

H R _ _   **hrip** (239)

_ H R _   **ihre** (54b), **NHRA** (241), **thru**

_ _ H R   **Bahr** (140), **Bohr** (15c, 33c, 142), **buhr** (131c), **Fahr.** (238), **guhr** (39a), **Lahr** (165), **lehr** (54c, 85c), **mohr** (53b), **Ruhr** (53d, 100b), **sehr** (54a), **tahr** (55a)

H _ _ R   **hair** (46a), **hear** (59a, 72b), **heer** (134b), **heir** (63a, 71b), **herr** (53d), **hier** (51b), **hier-** (93c), **hoar** (51c, 131d), **hoer, hour** (122b), **hydr-** (93d), **hygr-** (94a)

H S _ _   **Hsia** (26d, 38d)

_ H S _   **AHST** (235)

_ _ H S   **hahs** (42c), **Ochs** (173), **rahs**

H _ _ S   **hags, hahs** (42c), **Hals** (38d, 156), **hams, Hans** (17b, 53d, 67a, 157), **hats, haws, Hays** (157), **hems, hens** (92a), **hers** (95a), **Hess** (158), **hews, hies, hips, Hiss** (158), **hiss** (36a, 112a), **hits, hobs, hods, hoes, hogs, Homs** (222), **hops** (18a), **hors** (50d), **hubs, hues, hugs, hums, Huns** (15c), **huts**

_ _ H T   **acht** (53d), **baht** (223, 246), **echt** (54a)

H _ _ T   **haft** (60a), **halt** (14c, 25b, 32a, 59d, 87b, 115d), **Hart** (157), **hart** (34c, 114b), **hast** (128a), **Heat** (206), **heat** (129d), **hect-** (93c), **heft** (22c, 131a), **hept-** (93c), **hilt** (57d), **hint** (11d, 32c, 33d, 117d, 133a), **hist.** (239), **Holt** (158), **holt** (30c), **Hoot** (158), **hoot** (85c), **hort.** (239), **host** (14c, 42a, 79d), **Hoyt** (159), **Hunt** (159), **hunt** (105d), **Hurt** (159), **hurt** (33b, 58a, 62a, 63a, 133d), **hyet-** (93c)

H U _ _   **HUAC** (239), **hubs, hued, hues, Huey** (159), **Huff** (159), **huff** (47b, 119c), **huge** (54b, 62a, 69b), **Hugh** (159), **Hugo** (49c, 71c, 104d, 159), **hugs, huia** (81c), **hula** (58b), **hule** (21c, 25a, 102c), **hulk** (126d), **Hull** (159), **hull** (106b, 108b), **Hume** (159, 192), **hump** (95c), **hums, Hung.** (239), **hung, hunk** (57d, 88d), **Huns** (15c), **Hunt** (159), **hunt** (105d), **Hupa** (15b, 189), **hura** (104a), **hurl** (121c, 123b), **Hurt** (159), **hurt** (33b, 58a, 62a, 63a, 133d), **hush** (109b), **husk** (43a, 61c, 106b, 232), **huts, Hutu** (214, 221)

_ H U _   **bhut** (54b), **chub** (46c, 228), **chug** (112a), **chum** (15b, 32a, 45b), **chuo** (246), **shul** (118d), **shun** (16c, 41c), **shut** (28b), **thud** (20a, 112a), **thug** (52c), **Thur.** (243), **thus** (111b, 121a)

_ _ H U   ichu (12c, 55d), Jehu (197), jehu (38a), kahu (15d), Oahu (64c)

H _ _ U   habu (89c, 103c), Hutu (214, 221)

H _ _ V   HDTV (239)

_ H W _   YHWH (244)

H _ _ X   hoax (34a, 92b)

H Y _ _   hyal- (93a), Hyde (37a), hydr- (93d), hyet- (93c), hygr- (94a), hyla (12b, 122c), hylo- (94a), hymn (111d), hype (95a), hypo (88d)

_ H Y _   whys

_ _ H Y   achy (112a), ashy (86a, 129d)

H _ _ Y   hazy (127a), Hedy (157), holy (30b), Huey (159)

H _ _ Z   Harz (79b)

I A _ _   Iago (44a, 85a, 107c, 195), Ians, iamb (48c), -iana (117c), Iasi (221)

_ I A _   bias (12c, 35c, 94a), ciao (65a), diag. (237), dial (43d), diam. (237), Dian (198), Dias (91d), Diaz (76c), fiat (34b, 84c), Liam (166), Liao (101a), liar (75d), Lias (53c), Piaf (49d, 100c, 175), rial (220), sial (85b), Siam (120d), vial (110d)

_ _ I A   Abia (104a), amia (21b, 79c), Apia (91c, 224), aria (75d, 111d, 125a, 234), Asia (39b), chia 18d, 76c), Elia (68d, 87c, 151), -emia (117a), FOIA (238), Gaia (39b), Hsia (26d, 38d), huia (81c), ilia (60b, 87c), inia (12b, 83b, 110b), ixia (30d), Maia (59c, 107b, 129c, 198, 207), obia (45c), -opia (117b, 117c), shi'a (80c), Uria (197), -uria (117b), USIA (243)

I _ _ A   -iana (117c), idea (35b, 44b, 82c, 95a, 121b), ilea (73c), ilia (60b, 87c), Ilka (159), Ilsa (24c), Inca (15b), inia (12b, 83b, 110b), Iona (25c, 64b, 202), iota (11d, 66d, 122c, 131c), Iowa (189, 210), Issa (216), itea (118c, 128c), ixia (30d)

I B _ _   Iban (33d), ibex (54d, 230), ibid. (70a, 239), ibis (19a, 39d, 40a, 129a, 225), -ible (117a)

_ I B _   bibb (75b), Bibi (141), bibi (62d), bibl. (236), bibs, dibs (55d), fibr- (93a), fibs, Gibb (155), gibe (10d, 35a), gibs, jibe (28d, 29d, 31a), jibs, kibe (26c), nibs, ribs, sibs

_ _ I B   abib (59a, 81d), Agib (13d), crib (26b, 74c, 91b, 110c), drib (110d), frib (35d), glib (47d, 110c, 111a, 129a), guib (13a), stib (38d)

I _ _ B   iamb (48c)

361

I C _ _   -ical (117a), ICBM (239), iced, Icel. (239), icer, ices, icho (54b), ichu (12c, 55d), icon (62a, 103b)

_ I C _   bice (20b, 56c, 89a), dice (52c), dich (54b), dich- (93d), Dick (149, 192), dick (35b), dict. (237), FICA (238), fico (124c, 133d), hick (134d), kick (21a, 96a), lice (86c), lick (18a, 66a, 110d), mica (64b, 77a, 109b), mice, Mich. (210, 240), Mick (170), Nice (49c, 100a, 216), nice (90b, 109c), Nick (172), nick (26d, 82c), pica (53c, 125d), pice (62d, 220), pick (27a, 90b), Pico (100d), picr- (92c), Pict (22a), Rice (177, 204), rice (37d), Rich (177), rich (73d), Rick (24c, 177), rick (58c, 89a, 114b), Rico (72c), sice (56c), sick (126b), tick (14a, 20a, 229), tics, vice (35a), vice- (92d), wick (23d)

_ _ I C   -atic (117c), Chic (145), chic (111a), epic (59c, 90c), Eric (128b, 151), FDIC (238), laic (28a, 70c, 82a, 94d, 106b), otic (15d, 39a), saic (71c), Udic (82b)

I D _ _   -idae (117c), Idas (24d), idea (35b, 44b, 82c, 95a, 121b), idee (50c), idem (70a), Iden (192), ideo- (93a), ides (33d, 101d), idio- (93c), Idle (159), idle (40c, 60c, 62c, 62d, 63a, 70c, 127a, 130a), idly, Idol (159), idol (39d, 44a, 44d, 58d, 62a, 85b, 133d), idyl (90c, 233)

_ I D _   Aïda (84b, 97b, 128a), aide (10a, 15b, 59b, 106a), AIDS (235), aids, bide (38d, 99c, 119d, 129b), bids, -cide (117b), Dido (24c, 125d), dido (13a, 24a, 52b, 92b), didy (35c), fids, Gide (49c, 155), hide (29d, 31c, 43a), kids, lido (65c, 127d), lids, Midi (112b), Nidd (134d), nide (88c, 232), nidi (113c), Ridd (73a), Ride (177), ride (29b, 66d, 121a), rids, sida (30d, 96d), side (43d, 47b, 69b, 119b), Sids, tide (83b), tidy (81a, 84c, 111b), Vida (185), vide (98d), wide (102a)

_ _ I D   acid (119d), amid (12b), arid (38b), avid (39a, 41b, 56b, 67b, 135a), Enid (14d, 23c, 53c, 120c, 151), grid (17c, 90b, 116a), Haid (156), ibid. (70a, 239), irid (90a), laid, maid (37b, 54c, 107a), naid (51b), olid (49a, 116c), Ovid (102a), paid (99a), quid (32c, 122c), raid (48c, 62d), Reid (176), Said (91c), said (127c), skid (110c), slid, void (12d, 40c, 82d, 127a)

I _ _ D   ibid. (70a, 239), iced, Irad (197), irid (90a)

I E _ _   ieri (65c)

_ I E _   bien (51b), bier (28d, 53d), dieb (65b), died, dies (69c), diet (44b, 65d, 71b), dieu (50b), fief (45c), gier (39a), hied, hier (51b), hier- (93c), hies, Kiel (23c), kier (19d, 127b), Kiev (223), lied (54a, 234), lief (132a), lien (53a, 71a, 95b), lies, lieu (89d), mien (13c, 17d, 24c, 34d, 36d, 74d), pied (114a, 127b), pien (14c), Pier (175), pier (21d, 66b, 68d, 131b), pies, Piet (175), piet (26b, 74b), riel (214), riem (59d), rien (50d), tied, tier (46a, 89b, 102c), ties, vied, vier (53d), vies, view (12c, 15a, 42b, 73a, 95b, 104d), Wien (33c)

_ _ I E   Abie (81c), amie (50b), Arie (139), brie (26b), Edie (150), Elie (151), Erie (23c, 68d, 189), Ilie (159), Okie (76d), soie (51a)

I _ _ E   -ible (117a), -idae (117c), idee (50c), Idle (159), idle (40c, 60c, 62c, 62d, 63a, 70c, 127a, 130a), ihre (54b), Ilie (159), ille (69d), imbe (30d, 45c), Imre (159), Inge (22d, 54d, 88d, 159), in re (29d, 63d, 99a), Iole (42a, 59c, 94c), Ione (22c, 69b, 73d), ipse (37a, 69d), irae (35c), isle (11a, 64b, 67b)

I F _ _   iffy (26a, 100d), Ifni (220)

_ I F _   biff (60b), fife (48a, 80c), gift (13d, 94a, 119b), Gifu (60d), hi-fi (112b), jiff (77d), life (19a, 57a, 94d), lift (40b), miff (96b), rife (9b, 94b), riff (66a, 78c), rift (21d, 47a, 84b, 113d), sift (105c, 109b, 132d), tiff (96b), wife (114a)

_ _ I F   alif (11d), coif (57b), Enif (207), Leif (43a), naif (126c), TGIF (243), waif (116b)

I _ _ F   IOOF (240)

I G _ _   Igbo (68c, 220), igni- (93a), Igor (49b, 159)

_ I G _   biga (125c), digs, figs, giga (45d), Gigi (155), GIGO (239), gigs, high (108d, 123c), jigs, lign- (94a), nigh (28b, 81a), pigs, Riga (218), Rigg (177), rigs, sigh (21d), sign (74d, 91c, 114c), tige (89b), wigs

_ _ I G   brig (81a, 108b), grig (32a, 39c, 56a, 72c), Haig (156), olig- (93a), orig. (241), prig (85c), swig (37d, 57a), trig (114a, 124c), trig. (31b, 243), twig (21c), whig (71c)

I H _ _   ihre (54b)

_ _ I H   ch'ih (246)

I _ _ H   inch (31d, 79c, 246), itch (58a, 64b)

I I _ _   iiwi (58c)

_ I I _   Riis (177)

I _ _ I   Iasi (221), ieri (65c), Ifni (220), igni- (93a), iiwi (58c), immi (246), Impi (135c), INRI (32b, 239), inti (221), Ishi (134a)

_ I J _   Fiji (216), lija (46a, 70d)

I K _ _   Ikes, ikon (62a)

_ I K _   bike (67a, 127c), dika (74c), dike (40b, 71c), hike (62c), Kiki (164), kiku (27a), like (24b, 109c), Mike (170), mike (12a), Nike (77b, 132c, 198), Niki (172), pika (30c, 72c, 101c, 231), pike (46d, 59d, 90c, 113b, 228), piki (74b), sika (34c, 65d, 231), Sikh (60b), tiki (91a)

_ _ I K   Efik (69a, 220), Erik (151), haik (52d)

I _ _ K   Isak (159)

I L _ _ ilea (73c), ileo- (93b), ilex (60c), ilia (60b, 87c), llie (159), Ilka (159), ille (69d), ills (124d), illy, Ilsa (24c), Ilus (69a, 124d)

_ I L _ ails, bile (26d), bilk (26b, 34a, 34c), Bill (141), bill (17d, 109d), Dili (91d, 217), dill (14c, 88d), fila (121c), file (72a, 97d, 99a, 122d), fill (83b, 88b, 104b), film (28b, 77b, 121b), fils (51a, 213, 217, 218, 223, 224), gila (72c), gild (40b), gill (21c, 246), Gils, gilt (60c, 112b, 134d), Hill (158), hill (17a), hilt (57d), Jill (161), jilt (99a), kill (31d, 79d, 102d), kiln (16b, 85c), kilo (12a, 76b, 246), kilo- (93d), kilt (105a), lill (16b, 89b, 132b), lilt (72c), Lily (166), lily (47c, 47d), mild (28a, 53c, 77c, 120c), mile (52c, 68c, 246), milk (128d), Mill (170), mill (96d), Milo (171), milo (112a), mils, milt (47a), Nile (81b, 216, 222), oils, oily (44c, 83d, 126a), pile (17a, 58d, 79a), pili- (93a), pill (119a), rile (12d, 64b, 95c, 115c), rill (22a, 31d, 101a, 110d, 116b), silk (43b), Sill (49a), sill (37c, 121c, 132b), silo (48a, 116a), silt (79c, 106b), tile (27d, 46b, 74b, 102a, 120d), till (32c), tilt (23d, 24b, 62c, 72b, 101c), Vila (224), vile (9a, 17b, 46a, 62a, 74c), Vili (83b), wild (18c, 31d, 104c, 126d, 128c), wile (34a), Will (186), will (18c, 35b, 120d, 129a, 133a), Wilt (187), wilt (38a), wily (14d, 31d, 32c, 110c)

_ _ I L anil (38d, 62d), aril (106b), axil (12c), bail (20d, 68b), boil (30c), ceil (25b), chil- (93b), coil (32d, 114a, 125c, 132b, 134a), dail (40a, 64a), deil (105a), Egil (82b), Emil (151), evil (74c, 109c, 131d, 134c), fail (35c, 44a, 48a), foil (16b, 45b, 76b, 116d, 121d), Gail (154), hail (9c, 16a, 56c, 60d, 104a, 127d, 130d), ipil (88c), jail (62b), kail (23a), koil (32c), mail (14c, 76b, 91d), moil (20c, 133d), nail (27d, 44c, 119b, 126b), Neil (172), noil (45d, 68c), pail (30b), Phil (175), Phil. (242), rail (9c, 19a, 30d, 75a, 111d, 123c, 129a, 226), roil (79c, 115c), sail (91c), soil (39a, 114c, 117d, 120d), tail (13c, 25a, 40d, 48b, 89d, 107b, 123c), teil (72a), toil (38b, 124d, 133c, 133d), veil (29d, 36b, 58c, 59d, 75b), wail (32b, 61c, 68d, 114b), Weil (186)

I _ _ L -ical (117a), Icel. (239), Idol (159), idol (39d, 44a, 44d, 58d, 62a, 85b, 133d), idyl (90c, 233), incl. (239), Intl. (239), ipil (88c), ital. (240), it'll (30c)

I M _ _ imam (23b, 80c), imbe (30d, 45c), imbu (51d), imit. (239), immi (246), Impi (135c), imps, Imre (159)

_ I M _ aims, cima (65c), dime (44d), dims, gimp (124c), Jimi (161), Jims, Lima (27c, 221), lima (12a, 17d), limb (13c, 21c), lime (23b, 27c, 51d, 78d, 124a), limn (35a), limp (47b, 63a, 129b), limy, mime (66b), Mimi (68b, 84b, 95d, 171), Pima (189), pima (31a), pimp (94d), Rima (56c), rima (47a), rime (30a, 51c, 60c), rims, rimu (62a, 98d), rimy, sima (101b), Simi (64c), simp (48b, 109c), Sims (181), time (38d, 41b, 41c, 87d, 100b), Timi (183), Tims, wimp (130c)

_ _ I M Akim (137), alim (120a), brim (21a), crim. (237), duim (246), emim (54b), glim (23d, 43c), grim (19d, 54b, 115b), Haim (156), maim (80d), prim (115b), shim (71c, 119c, 130d), skim (47c, 54d,

56a), **Slim** (181), **slim** (110c, 118b), **swim** (37a), **trim** (81a, 84d, 114a, 118b, 121d, 124c), **urim** (103b), **whim** (24a, 44b, 82c)

I _ _ M   **ICBM** (239), **idem** (70a), **imam** (23b, 80c), **item** (9c, 14d, 35b, 41b, 71a, 72b, 81c, 83a, 86d)

I N _ _   **Inca** (15b), **inch** (31d, 79c, 246), **incl.** (239), **Indo-** (93b), **Inez** (37c), **info.** (239), **Inge** (22d, 54d, 88d, 159), **inia** (12b, 83b, 110b), **init.** (239), **inks, inky** (19d, 33d), **inns, in re** (29d, 63d, 99a), **INRI** (32b, 239), **Insp.** (239), **Inst.** (239), **inti** (221), **Intl.** (239), **into** (133a)

_ I N _   **ain't, aine** (51a), **ains, bina** (60b), **bind** (122a), **bine** (115b, 128b), **Bing** (141), **bino** (86a), **bins, C in C** (236), **cine-** (93b), **cinq** (50b), **Dina** (149), **dine** (39b), **ding** (62d, 76b), **Dino** (47c), **dins, dint** (42d, 92b), **eine** (53d, 54a), **find** (36a), **Fine** (152), **fine** (26d, 34c, 40b, 40d, 79d, 87c, 116d, 233), **fink** (46a), **Finn.** (238), **fins, Gina** (155), **gink** (39c), **Gino** (155), **gins, hind** (34b, 37a), **hing** (14d), **hint** (11d, 32c, 33d, 117d, 133a), **jink** (40b), **jinx** (61a), **kina** (108a, 221), **kind** (112a, 113b, 127b), **kine** (31c), **King** (164, 190), **king** (24a, 26c, 82a), **kink** (31d), **kino** (38d, 57a, 119c, 127b), **Lina** (166), **Lind** (166), **line** (11b, 30d, 46a, 96d, 102c, 116b), **ling** (22c, 46d, 58d, 130b, 228), **link** (30a, 63c, 66c), **lint** (47d), **liny, Linz** (33c, 213), **Mina** (223), **mina** (131a), **mind** (29c, 63c, 67b, 73a, 83a, 120c), **mine** (55a, 95a), **Ming** (26d), **mini-** (93c), **mink** (128c, 230), **Minn.** (210, 240), **mint** (14c, 28d, 59b), **minx** (88b), **Nina** (24a, 29a, 172), **nina** (112d), **nine** (17c), **Nino** (172), **nino** (112c), **pina** (29d), **pine** (30a, 42a, 69a, 73a, 124a, 134b), **Ping** (125a), **ping** (76b), **pink** (24b), **pins, pint** (54b, 246), **piny, rind** (43a, 76d, 87c), **rine** (36d), **Ring** (177), **ring** (16d, 27b, 40c, 40d, 131b, 134a), **rink** (109d, 114a), **sine** (52a, 70b, 96b, 124c), **sing** (129d), **sink** (34b, 60c, 110d), **Sino-** (92d), **sino** (112d), **sins, Tina** (183), **tine** (13a, 95a, 123a), **ting** (76b), **tins, tint** (29a, 107b), **tiny** (77b, 110d), **vina** (60b), **vine** (28a, 71c), **vini-** (94a), **vino** (72b, 132c), **viny, wind** (10d, 28d, 32d, 125c), **wine** (60c, 91c), **wing** (12d, 47c, 48a, 89b, 89d, 232), **wink** (63c, 81d, 106a), **wino** (38b), **wins, winy** (128c), **Xing.** (244), **zinc** (20b, 76a, 245), **zing** (32a)

_ _ I N   **akin** (67c, 99a), **asin** (78b), **ayin** (12a), **Bain** (140), **bain** (50a), **Cain** (9a, 10a, 41a, 68d, 79d, 107a, 144, 197), **Ch'in** (26d), **Chin.** (236), **chin** (29d), **coin** (77b), **dein** (54b), **Erin** (64a, 151), **Fain** (152), **fain** (35b, 54c, 133a), **gain** (9d, 44d, 83b, 94d, 132b), **grin** (111a), **hein** (42c, 49c), **jain** (60b), **join** (30a, 126c), **juin** (49d), **kain** (74c), **lain, loin** (33a, 75c), **Main** (168), **main** (26c, 29d, 67b, 94c), **mein** (26d), **nein** (54a), **Odin** (10b, 51c, 133b, 198), **Olin** (173), **pain** (10b, 61d), **rain** (92a, 120a, 130d), **rein** (26b, 30c, 100a), **rhin-** (93b), **ruin** (34d, 35b, 62b), **sain** (19d, 32b), **shin** (11d, 12a, 71a, 71b, 107c), **skin** (43a, 59d, 87c, 104c), **spin** (100b, 131c), **thin** (35c, 35d, 53b, 110c), **Trin.** (243), **Tsin** (26d), **twin** (37c, 75b, 125c), **vain** (40c, 63a), **vein** (20a, 116b), **wain** (129b), **whin** (55c, 101b), **zein** (30d)

I _ _ N   **Iban** (33d), **icon** (62a, 103b), **Iden** (192), **ikon** (62a), **Iran** (88a,

217), **iron** (45b, 45c, 55a, 57c, 74c, 75b, 245), **ISBN** (240), **Ivan** (66c, 103c, 159)

I O _ _   **iodo-** (93b), **Iole** (42a, 59c, 94c), **Iona** (25c, 64b, 202), **Ione** (22c, 69b, 73d), **ions**, **IOOF** (240), **iota** (11d, 66d, 122c, 131c), **-ious** (117a), **Iowa** (189, 210)

_ I O _   **biol.** (236), **Bion** (56b), **cion** (83c), **Dion** (149, 195), **Dior** (149), **dios** (112d), **Lion** (193), **lion** (94b, 230), **pion** (42b), **riot** (85a, 101c, 125a), **-sion** (117a), **-tion** (117a, 117b), **viol** (80b), **zion** (95a)

_ _ I O   **agio** (42c, 48d, 78a, 94a), **Baio** (140), **brio** (33d, 113d, 128d), **Clio** (29b, 80a), **Elio** (151), **Ezio** (152), **idio-** (93c), **odio** (65a), **Ohio** (211), **olio** (36b, 60c, 75d, 77b, 92a), **thio-** (93d), **trio** (80c, 124b), **unio** (80d)

I _ _ O   **Iago** (44a, 85a, 107c, 195), **icho** (54b), **ideo-** (93a), **idio-** (93c), **Igbo** (68c, 220), **ileo-** (93b), **Indo-** (93b), **info.** (239), **into** (133a), **iodo-** (93b), **Isao** (159)

I P _ _   **ipil** (88c), **ipse** (37a, 69d)

_ I P _   **cipo** (71c), **dipl-** (93d), **dips**, **hipp-** (93a), **hips**, **kips**, **Li Po** (26d), **lipo-** (92d), **lips**, **nipa** (15b, 38a, 39b, 86a, 120d), **nips**, **pipe** (80c, 125a, 131c), **pips**, **ripe** (47b, 75b), **rips**, **sipe** (122b), **sips**, **tips**, **VIPs**, **wipe** (123d), **xiph-** (93d), **yipe** (42c), **yips**, **zips**

_ _ I P   **blip** (97b), **Chip** (26d), **chip** (55b), **clip** (15c, 44c, 107d), **drip** (72b, 88a), **Flip** (153), **flip** (123b), **grip** (27d, 55d, 60c, 96a, 117d), **hrip** (239), **quip** (66b, 66d, 132d, 133a), **RHIP** (242), **ship** (106c, 128a), **skip** (9b, 56a, 84a, 87a), **slip** (36b, 41c, 52d, 54d, 110c, 126b), **snip** (28a), **trip** (66d, 232), **whip** (18a, 47c, 69b, 121b)

I _ _ P   **Insp.** (239)

I _ _ Q   **Iraq** (217)

I R _ _   **Irad** (197), **irae** (35c), **Iran** (88a, 217), **Iraq** (217), **Iras** (28a, 195), **irid** (90a), **Iris** (159, 195), **iris** (20b, 43c, 85a, 97c), **irks**, **iron** (45b, 45c, 55a, 57c, 74c, 75b, 245), **Irus** (83c)

_ I R _   **aire** (64a), **airs** (94b), **airy** (41d, 66a, 71d), **Bird** (141), **bird** (16a), **birl** (72d), **birn** (27d), **birr** (112a, 216), **circ.** (237), **dire** (37d, 44d, 45a, 54b, 56a, 120c), **Dirk** (149), **dirk** (33a), **dirt** (39a, 99c, 104c), **Eire** (64a), **fire** (14b, 36a, 36c, 108c), **firm** (29b, 29d, 114b, 126d), **firn** (54c, 55d, 111b), **firs**, **gird** (16d, 18c, 40c, 118b), **girl** (45b), **giro** (31d, 65c), **girt** (27b), **hire** (40c, 40d, 71b, 99c, 100a), **Kiri** (164), **kiri** (87a), **Kirk** (164), **kirk** (27a, 105a), **lira** (25c, 218, 219, 221, 223, 224), **lire** (50d, 64d), **Mira** (207), **mire** (20c, 39a, 78c, 79c), **Miró** (112c, 171), **MIRV** (240), **NIRA** (241), **pirn** (20c, 98d, 130d), **sire** (18b, 21d, 44d, 48d, 94d, 120c, 122c), **sirs**, **tire** (21a, 42d, 44d, 47b, 131c), **tiro** (18b, 82c), **wire** (30d, 120b), **wiry** (109d)

_ _ I R   **abir** (98d), **ahir** (24d), **amir** (10b, 13d), **chir-** (93a), **coir** (28d, 30d, 45c, 102b), **cuir** (37c, 50c), **emir** (13d, 94c, 102d, 125b), **fair** (10a, 17d, 41b, 45c, 62b, 67c), **hair** (46a), **heir** (63a, 71b), **Keir** (164), **lair** (34d, 60c), **loir** (37c), **Meir** (170), **Muir** (11a, 171), **Nair** (37d), **nair** (85a), **noir** (50a, 102c), **pair** (21c, 31b, 90d, 119c, 125c), **Seir** (41c), **soir** (50b), **spir-** (92d), **stir** (10d, 14c, 29b, 36d, 63b, 77b, 79c, 94d, 95a, 115c), **vair** (52c, 114b), **Weir** (186), **weir** (33b, 47a), **whir** (112a), **ymir** (54b)

I _ _ R   **icer, Igor** (49b, 159), **Isar** (33d, 79d, 100d, 216), **Iser** (40a), **iter** (69d, 101a, 101d), **Ivor** (159), **iyar** (78c), **izar** (52d)

I S _ _   **Isak** (159), **Isao** (159), **Isar** (33d, 79d, 100d, 216), **ISBN** (240), **Iser** (40a), **Ishi** (134a), **Isis** (61b, 85a), **isle** (11a, 64b, 67b), **isn't, Issa** (216)

_ I S _   **bise** (132b), **cist** (115d), **disc** (58b, 98c), **disc.** (237), **dish** (76a, 119a), **disk** (27b), **diss** (75d), **dist.** (237), **fisc** (42c, 102c), **fish** (128d), **fisk** (42c), **fist** (21c, 57d), **Gish** (155), **gist** (74b, 89c), **Hiss** (158), **hiss** (36a, 112a), **hist.** (239), **Kish** (197), **kish** (55d, 104c), **kiss** (22d, 91b), **kist** (105b), **Lisa** (166), **Lise** (166), **Lisi** (166), **lisp** (113c), **liss** (49a), **list** (24d, 41b, 65c, 101c, 102b, 104d, 122a), **misc.** (240), **mise** (10d, 134c), **miso** (65d), **miso-** (93a), **Miss.** (210, 240), **miss** (54c, 108c), **mist** (28b, 38a, 48a, 127b), **nisi** (70b, 126c), **Pisa** (70d), **pisc-** (93a), **pish** (42c), **pisk** (12b), **rise** (62c, 114c), **risk** (52b, 58c, 66b, 127d), **sish** (61b), **Uist** (64d), **visa** (87a), **Visc.** (244), **vise** (60c), **Wisc.** (212, 244), **Wise** (187), **wise** (103b, 111a), **wish** (35b), **wisp** (49b), **wist** (68c)

_ _ I S   **Acis** (52b), **Agis** (67d), **Amis** (138), **amis** (50b), **anis, Apis** (22c, 40a, 95d, 103b), **atis** (60a), **avis** (69c), **axis** (25c, 34c, 60c), **bois** (51b), **chis, dais** (41d, 90b), **Elis** (56b), **Epis.** (238), **Eris** (14b, 198), **feis** (64a), **Gris** (156), **gris** (50c), **ibis** (19a, 39d, 40a, 129a, 225), **Iris** (159, 195), **iris** (20b, 43c, 85a, 97c), **Isis** (61b, 85a), **-itis** (117b), **Kris** (165), **kris** (74b), **leis, Lois** (118a), **Luis** (167), **mais** (50a), **nais** (51b, 101a), **obis, -osis** (117a), **Otis** (12b, 63d, 173), **phis, psis, rais** (24a), **reis** (24a), **Riis** (177), **Sais** (39d), **sais** (56c), **seis** (113a), **skis, this** (34d, 95a), **Tris** (184), **Uris** (184)

I _ _ S   **Ians, ibis** (19a, 39d, 40a, 129a, 225), **ices, Idas** (24d), **ides** (33d, 101d), **Ikes, ills** (124d), **Ilus** (69a, 124d), **imps, inks, inns, ions, -ious** (117a), **Iras** (28a, 195), **Iris** (159, 195), **iris** (20b, 43c, 85a, 97c), **irks, Irus** (83c), **Isis** (61b, 85a), **-itis** (117b), **Itys** (120c), **Ives** (159)

I T _ _   **ital.** (240), **itch** (58a, 64b), **itea** (118c, 128c), **item** (9c, 14d, 35b, 41b, 71a, 72b, 81c, 83a, 86d), **iter** (69d, 101a, 101d), **-itis** (117b), **it'll** (30c), **Itys** (120c)

_ I T _   **bite** (26c, 115c), **bito** (10c, 35b, 47a), **bits** (19a), **bitt** (44c), **cite** (97c), **cito** (70a), **city** (76c, 126d), **dita** (88b, 124b), **fits, fitz** (111d), **gite** (50c), **hits, Kite** (164), **kite** (19a, 58c, 226), **kith** (105a), **kits, Kitt** (164), **-lite** (117b, 117c), **Lith.** (240), **-lith** (117c), **litz** (97b), mite (14a, 63b, 64a, 86c, 86d), mitt (17b, 46b, 54d), mitu (32d), Nita (172), nito (45b), nitr- (93b), nits, pita (11d, 25c, 45c), pith (30d, 41d, 51d, 54c, 74b, 75a, 90a, 97c, 120d), pits, Pitt (41a, 175), pity (29b, 87a, 134b), Rita (177), rite (72c), Ritz (177), Sita (97d), site (72d, 76a, 107a), sito- (93a), sits, titi (20b, 71a, 78b, 124a), Tito (183, 134d), tits, vita (69d, 71d), vite (50d), with (11d, 12c), wits, Witt (187)

_ _ I T   adit (41b, 77a), alit (36c, 68d, 107a), bait (16b, 41b, 73d, 119c, 123b), B. Lit. (236), Brit. (236), brit (59d), chit (54c, 82c, 88b, 129c), crit. (237), doit (38d), edit (20b, 40c, 94a, 98c, 100b), emit (36a, 40a, 43c, 47d, 99b, 106c), epit. (238), exit (71a, 130c), fait (9c, 50b), flit (33d), frit (54c), gait (130c), grit (104a), imit. (239), init. (239), knit (126c), lait (50d), nuit (50d), obit. (34a, 52c, 241), omit (40b, 81b, 87a, 110a), quit (9a, 34d, 71a, 99d), skit (108d, 110a), slit (33a), smit (128a), snit (10d, 12c, 47b), spit (90d, 101b), suit (9c, 10a, 31c, 47b, 71a, 85b, 90b, 104b), Swit (182), tait (15d, 60d), twit (88a), unit (77d, 84a), wait (24b, 72a, 99c, 115a, 119d), whit (122c), writ (71a)

I _ _ T   imit. (239), init. (239), Inst. (239), isn't

_ I U _   Niue (64c), Pius (91b)

I _ _ U   ichu (12c, 55d), imbu (51d)

I V _ _   Ivan (66c, 103c, 159), Ives (159), Ivey (159), Ivor (159)

_ I V _   diva (84b, 94c), dive (34d, 90c), five (17c, 88c, 97c), give (11c, 13d, 29d, 94a, 95c), hive (18a), jive (61d, 63b, 66a), kiva (25c, 95d), Kivu (68b), live (38d, 42d), Livy (101d), rive (28a), Siva (91a), viva (73a), vive (73a), vivo (72c, 233)

_ _ I V   shiv (68a), XDIV (244)

_ I W _   biwa (65d), iiwi (58c), kiwi (13d, 19a, 19b, 97d, 226)

I X _ _   ixia (30d)

_ I X _   mixt. (240)

_ _ I X   coix (66c), Foix (49c), -trix (117b)

I _ _ X   ibex (54d, 230), ilex (60c)

I Y _ _   iyar (78c)

I _ _ Y   idly, iffy (26a, 100d), illy, inky (19d, 33d), Ivey (159)

I Z _ _   izar (52d)

_ I Z _   fizz (39d), Giza (113c), Liza (166), Mize (171), size (129a)

_ _ I Z   Ariz. (209, 235), Eliz. (238), Friz (154), friz (32d), Phiz (35c), quiz (42b), rhiz- (93c), whiz (88a, 112a)

I _ _ Z   Inez (37c)

J A _ _   jabs, jaca (65b), Jack (159), jack (17a, 24a, 68a, 78a, 97c), Jada (197), jade (53b, 56c), Jael (197), jags, jail (62b), jain (60b), Jaja (79a), Jake (160), jako (56a), jamb (37c, 109a, 126d), jams, Jamy (194), Jana (80d, 160), Jane (160), Jann (160), Jans, jape (66c), jarl (104c), jars, jass (118d), JATO (240), Java (64c), java (28d), jaws, jays, Jazz (206), jazz (61d, 118d)

_ J A _   ajar (84b), Ajax (56b, 120b, 120d, 194)

_ _ J A   Adja (214), Baja (23b, 76c), Beja (82a, 222), Jaja (79a), lija (46a, 70d), maja (31d), raja (60a), soja (56c)

J _ _ A   jaca (65b), Jada (197), Jaja (79a), Jana (80d, 160), Java (64c), java (28d), Jena (121d), jota (112c), Juba (216), juca (24c), juga (24c), Jura (79b)

J _ _ B   jamb (37c, 109a, 126d), Joab (33d, 197)

J _ _ D   Joad (55d), Judd (163)

J E _ _   Jean (160), jeep (127d), jeer (120a), jeez (42a), Jeff (161), Jehu (197), jehu (38a), jell (111d), Jena (121d), jeon (218), jerk (20a, 38d, 48b, 88a, 95d), Jess (161), jess (116a), jest (17a, 66c), jete (16c), jeth (78b), Jets (206) jets, Jett (161), jeux (50b), Jews

_ _ J E   haje (28c, 39d)

J _ _ E   jade (53b, 56c), Jake (160), Jane (160), jape (66c), jete (16c), jibe (28d, 29d, 31a), jive (61d, 63b, 66a), joke (66b), José (163), Jove (67c, 198), jube (102a), Jude (13b, 196), Jule (163), June (163), jure (70b), jute (30d, 45c, 102b, 103a)

J _ _ F   Jeff (161), jiff (77d)

J _ _ G   Jong (163), Jung (95d, 163)

J _ _ H   jeth (78b), Josh (163), josh (17a, 6b, 66d, 90d)

J I _ _   jibe (28d, 29d, 31a), jibs, jiff (77d), jigs, Jill (161), jilt (99a), Jimi (161), Jims, jink (40b), jinx (61a), jive (61d, 63b, 66a)

_ _ J I   Fiji (216), Fuji (66a), fuji (65b), haji (75c), suji (131b)

J _ _ I   Jimi (161), joli (50d), Joni (163), Juli (163)

_ _ J J   hajj (75c, 89b)

J _ _ K   Jack (159), jack (17a, 24a, 68a, 78a, 97c), jerk (20a, 38d, 48b, 88a, 95d), jink (40b), jock (74c), junk (26c, 102d)

J _ _ L   Jael (197), jail (62b), jarl (104c), jell (111d), Jill (161), Joel (161, 196, 197), jowl (26b, 35c)

369

_ _ J M   sejm (91a)

J _ _ N   jain (60b), Jann (160), Jean (160), jeon (218), Joan (161), John (13b, 18a, 88b, 91b, 107c, 135a, 162, 193, 196), join (30a, 126c), Juan (163), juin (49d)

J O _ _   Joab (33d, 197), Joad (55d), Joan (161), jobo (60c), JOBS (240), jobs, jock (74c), Jody (161), Joel (161, 196, 197), Joes, Joey (161), joey (67a, 134d), jogs, John (13b, 18a, 88b, 91b, 107c, 135a, 162, 193, 196), join (30a, 126c), joke (66b), joli (50d), Jolo (64d), jolt (20a, 66a, 108b), Jong (163), Joni (163), Jons, Jory (163), José (163), Josh (163), josh (17a, 66b, 66d, 90d), joss (26d, 62c), jota (112c), jots, Jove (67c, 198), jowl (26b, 35c), joys

_ J O _   ejoo (45a)

_ _ J O   mojo (129c), rojo (113a)

J _ _ O   jako (56a), JATO (240), jobo (60c), Jolo (64d), judo (65d, 66d), Juno (67c, 77b, 96d, 195, 199)

J _ _ P   jeep (127d), Jump (163), jump (10b, 114d, 127b)

J _ _ R   jeer (120a)

J _ _ S   jabs, jags, jams, Jans, jars, jass (118d), jaws, jays, Jess (161), jess (116a), Jets (206), jets, Jews, jibs, jigs, Jims, JOBS (240), jobs, Joes, jogs, Jons, joss (26d, 62c), jots, joys, jugs, juts

J _ _ T   jest (17a, 66d), Jett (161), jilt (99a), jolt (20a, 66a, 108b), just (41b, 44a, 62b, 76a, 97c, 127c)

J U _ _   Juan (163), Juba (216), jube (102a), juca (24c), Judd (163), Jude (13b, 196), judo (65d, 66d), Judy (163), juga (24c), jugs, juin (49d), juju (26b, 45c, 119b), Jule (163), Juli (163), July, Jump (163), jump (10b, 114d, 127b), June (163), Jung (95d, 163), junk (26c, 102d), Juno (67c, 77b, 96d, 195, 199), Jura (79b), jure (70b), jury (31c), just (41b, 44a, 62b, 76a, 97c, 127c), jute (30d, 45c, 102b, 103a), juts

_ _ J U   baju (65b), juju (26b, 45c, 119b)

J _ _ U   Jehu (197), jehu (38a), juju (26b, 45c, 119b)

J _ _ X   jeux (50b), jinx (61a)

J _ _ Y   Jamy (194), Jody (161), Joey (161), joey (67a, 134d), Jory (163), Judy (163), July, jury (31c)

J _ _ Z   Jazz (206), jazz (61d, 118d), jeez (42a)

K A _ _   Kaat (163), kadi (13d, 80d), Kael (163), Kaen (223), Kafa (32d, 216), kago (86a), Kahn (163), kahu (15d), kail (23a), kain (74c), kaka (81c), kaki (65d, 81c), kale (23a, 78a, 90a, 103d, 127c), Kali (109d, 199), kali (104a), kalo (119d), Kama (199), kama (60a, 129a), kame (60a, 100c), kami (65d, 108a), kana (66a), Kane (163), Kano (129c), Kans. (210, 240), Kant (53d, 163), kari (15d), Karl (163), kary- (93b), Kate (107c, 163), kati (246), Kato (56c), Kaus (208), kava (18d, 91a), kavi (66a), kawi (66a), Kaye (164), kayo (68c), Kays

_ K A _   Akan (69a, 215, 216), okas, okay (10b, 13d, 86d, 112a), skat (24b), skaw (67c)

_ _ K A   Anka (138), deka- (93d), dika (74c), Ilka (159), kaka (81c), pika (30c, 72c, 101c, 231), roka (74a, 124a), sika (34c, 65d, 231), taka (213), waka (23d), weka (19b, 74d, 81c, 97b)

K _ _ A   Kafa (32d, 216), kaka (81c), Kama (199), kama (60a, 129a), kana (66a), kava (18d, 91a), kela (246), keta (37b), kina (108a, 221), kiva (25c, 95d), koba (13a, 130b), Kola (103c), kola (82d), kora (130b), Kuba (24b), Kura (101a)

K _ _ B   kerb (109a), knob (57d, 82a, 95c)

K _ _ C   Kroc (165)

K _ _ D   kind (112a, 113b, 127b), Kurd (64a, 217)

K E _ _   Kean (164), keas, keck (100a), keef (58b), Keel (164), keel (108b), keen (16a, 45c, 68d, 129b), keep (10a, 60c, 94b, 100a, 104c), keet (56d), kegs, Keir (164), kela (246), kelp (64a, 106a), Kemp (164), keno (52b), Kens, Kent (70d, 195, 202), Keos (64c), kepi (58d, 76d), kept, kerb (109a), kerf (33a, 82c), Kern (164), kern (48c, 101b, 125d), Kerr (164), keta (37b), keto- (93b), keys

_ K E _   akee (51d, 124a), eked, ekes, Ikes, skeg (67b, 133b), skeo (47a), skep (18a, 60b), skew (118c, 125b)

_ _ K E   bake (30c, 101b), bike (67a, 127c), cake (35b), coke (28c, 52a, 62d), cuke (32c), dike (40b, 71c), Duke (87d, 150, 194, 201), duke (82d), Elke (151), fake (45a, 62a, 94b, 107c), fyke (16b), hake (46d, 228), hike (62c), Jake (160), joke (66b), Lake (165), lake (89a, 130a), like (24b, 109c), Luke (42a, 167, 196), make (13c, 29c, 30c, 40d, 43d, 44c), Mike (170), mike (12a), moke (37c), Nike (77b, 132c, 198), pike (46d, 59d, 90c, 113b, 228), poke (65b, 82d, 96a), puke (99a), rake (34a, 52d), sake (10b, 65d, 131a), soke (67c), suke (120a), take (117a), Teke (215), tuke (23d, 43b), tyke (21c, 26c), wake (102c, 123c), woke, yoke (66c, 232)

K _ _ E   kale (23a, 78a, 90a, 103d, 127c), kame (60a, 100c), Kane (163), Kate (107c, 163), Kaye (164), kibe (26c), kine (31c), Kite (164), kite (19a, 58c, 226), Klee (164), knee (66c), koae (58b), Kobe (60d, 218), Kure (60d), Kyle (165)

K _ _ F   keef (58b), kerf (33a, 82c)

K _ _ G   King (164, 190), king (24a, 26c, 82a)

K H _ _   Khan (164), khan (10b, 63a, 88a, 94c), khat (58b), Khon (223)

_ K H _   Akha (121d)

_ _ K H   ankh (32a), lakh (84a, 108a), Sikh (60b)

K _ _ H   Kish (197), kish (55d, 104c), kith (105a), Koch (53c, 164), koph (12a)

K I _ _   kibe (26c), kick (21a, 96a), kids, Kiel (23c), kier (19d, 127b), Kiev (223), Kiki (164), kiku (27a), kill (31d, 79d, 102d), kiln (16b, 85c), kilo (12a, 76b, 246), kilo- (93d), kilt (105a), kina (108a, 221), kind (112a, 113b, 127b), kine (31c), King (164, 190), king (24a, 26c, 82a), kink (31d), kino (38d, 57a, 119c, 127b), kips, Kiri (164), kiri (87a), Kirk (164), kirk (27a, 105a), Kish (197), kish (55d, 104c), kiss (22d, 91b), kist (105b), Kite (164), kite (19a, 58c, 226), kith (105a), kits, Kitt (164), kiva (25c, 95d), Kivu (68b), kiwi (13d, 19a, 19b, 97d, 226)

_ K I _   Akim (137), akin (67c, 99a), Okie (76d), skid (110c), skim (47c, 54d, 56a), skin (43a, 59d, 87c, 104c), skip (9b, 56a, 84a, 87a), skis, skit (108d, 110a)

_ _ K I   Aoki (139), kaki (65d, 81c), Kiki (164), Loki (10b, 16c, 198), maki (71b), Moki (95d), Niki (172), piki (74b), raki (11a), Reki (16d), Saki (95c), saki (78b, 231), tiki (91a)

K _ _ I   kadi (13d, 80d), kaki (65d, 81c), Kali (109d, 199), kali (104a), kami (65d, 108a), kari (15d), kati (246), kavi (66a), kawi (66a), kepi (58d, 76d), Kiki (164), Kiri (164), kiri (87a), kiwi (13d, 19a, 19b, 97d, 226), koli (24d), kori (10b, 60a)

K _ _ K   keck (100a), kick (21a, 96a), kink (31d), Kirk (164), kirk (27a, 105a), kook (39c)

K L _ _   Klee (164)

_ K L _   Okla. (211, 241), wkly. (244)

K _ _ L   Kael (163), kail (23a), Karl (163), Keel (164), keel (108b), Kiel (23c), kill (31d, 79d, 102d), koel (32c), Kohl (18c, 164), kohl (43c), koil (32c)

K N _ _   knap (60a), knar (68c), knee (66c), knew, knez (94c), knit (126c), knob (57d, 82a, 95c), knop (68c), knot (76d, 82a, 232), know (13a, 16c), Knox (49a), knur (54d, 68c), Knut (33c, 164)

K _ _ N   Kaen (223), Kahn (163), kain (74c), Kean (164), keen (16a, 45c, 68d, 129b), Kern (164), kern (48c, 101b, 125d), Khan (164), khan (10b, 63a, 88a, 94c), Khon (223), kiln (16b, 85c), Koln (100b, 216), kwan (246)

K O _ _ koae (58b), koba (13a, 130b), Kobe (60d, 218), kobo (220), Koch (53c, 164), koel (32c), Kohl (18c, 164), kohl (43c), koil (32c), Koko (73a, 134d), koko (86d), koku (246), Kola (103c), kola (82d), koli (24d), Koln (100b, 216), kolo (48b, 106d), kook (39c), koph (12a), Kops (67b), kora (130b), kori (10b, 60a), Koso (108d), koss (246), koto (66a), kozo (86b)

_ K O _ ikon (62a)

_ _ K O jako (56a), Koko (73a, 134d), koko (86d), mako (20b, 107d), Yoko (187)

K _ _ O kago (86a), kalo (119d), Kano (129c), Kato (56c), kayo (68c), keno (52b), keto- (93b), kilo (12a, 76b, 246), kilo- (93d), kino (38d, 57a, 119c, 127b), kobo (220), Koko (73a, 134d), koko (86d), kolo (48b, 106d), Koso (108d), koto (66a), kozo (86b)

K _ _ P keep (10a, 60c, 94b, 100a, 104c), kelp (64a, 106a), Kemp (164), knap (60a), knop (68c), Kulp (165)

K R _ _ Kris (165), kris (74b), Kroc (165)

_ K R _ Akra (216), okra (57a, 127c)

K _ _ R Keir (164), Kerr (164), kier (19d, 127b), knar (68c), knur (54d, 68c)

_ _ K S arks, asks, auks, elks, inks, irks, leks, oaks, Saks (179), yaks, yuks (70b)

K _ _ S Kans. (210, 240), Kaus (208), Kays, keas, kegs, Kens, Keos (64c), keys, kids, kips, kiss (22d, 91b), kits, Kops (67b), koss (246), Kris (165), kris (74b)

_ _ K T takt (80a, 120b)

K _ _ T Kaat (163), Kant (53d, 163), keet (56d), Kent (70d, 195, 202), kept, khat (58b), kilt (105a), kist (105b), Kitt (164), knit (126c), knot (76d, 82a, 232), Knut (33c, 164), Kurt (165), kyat (220)

K U _ _ Kuba (24b), kudu (13a, 230), Kulp (165), Kura (101a), Kurd (64a, 217), Kure (60d), Kurt (165)

_ K U _ akua (91a), skua (56d, 65b, 105c)

_ _ K U Baku (24b, 213), baku (116b, 124a), kiku (27a), koku (246), poku (13a, 130b), puku (13a, 130b)

K _ _ U kahu (15d), kiku (27a), Kivu (68b), koku (246), kudu (13a, 230)

_ K V _ NKVD (103c)

K _ _ V Kiev (223)

K W _ _ kwan (246)

373

K _ _ W   knew, know (13a, 16c)

K _ _ X   Knox (49a)

K Y _ _   kyat (220), Kyle (165)

_ K Y _   Skye (64d, 120d), skyr (20d)

_ _ K Y   inky (19d, 33d), laky, poky (110d), suky (120a)

K _ _ Y   kary- (93b)

K _ _ Z   knez (94c)

L A _ _   laap (41d), Labe (217), labs, lace (47b), lack (34c, 129d), lacy (34c), Ladd (165), lade (24b, 35d, 72d, 76d, 119a), lads, lady (45b, 81d), laet (49b), lago (65a, 112d), lags, Lahr (165), laic (28a, 70c, 82a, 94d, 106b), laid, lain, lair (34d, 60c), lait (50d), Lake (165), lake (89a, 130a), lakh (84a, 108a), laky, Lalo (165), lalo (117d), lama (22b, 121d), Lamb (40b, 165), lamb (107d), lame (32a, 57c), lamp (71d, 73c), lams, Lana (165), lana (70b), land (9d, 36b, 120d), Lane (165), lane (11c, 21b, 116b), Lang (165), lang. (240), lank (121a), lanx (102a), Laos (218), Lapp (82b, 222), laps, Lara (23c), lard (44c, 50a, 56a, 83d), lari (219), lark (19a, 51c, 226), lash (42d, 47c, 122a, 131c), lass (45b, 74b), last (30b, 40d, 108c, 130d), late (33d, 98b), lath (116c), laud (57b, 92b, 127d), lava (77d, 101b, 129a), lave (130a), lawn (31a, 43b, 69a, 72a), laws, lays, laze (61d), lazy (62d)

_ L A _   alae (132d), Alai (103c), Alan (137), alar (16c, 132d), Alas. (209, 235), alas (42c, 103b, 133b), blab (119d), blah (82a, 71d), blat (20b), clad (37d), clam (19c, 77d), clan (124b), clap (13c, 121d), clar. (237), claw (26b, 80b, 119b, 126b), Clay (146), clay (39a, 92a), Elah (67d), Elam (88a, 108a, 151), elan (33d, 41b, 113d, 128d, 135a), flag (17a, 38a, 41a, 69a, 87b, 114d, 130c, 132a), flak (13a), flam (38b), flan (32d, 87a), flap (48a, 79c, 89d, 119a, 130c, 132d), flat (42a, 63b, 95a, 95c, 114c, 234), flaw (19d, 34c), flax (72a, 72b), flay (110a, 110b, 116c), glad (66d), Olaf (82b, 128b, 173), olax (42b), plan (13d, 15c, 35b, 76b, 95a, 104d), plat (74d, 90b), play (51c, 52b, 87d, 91d, 114a), slab (88d, 110c), slag (28c, 38b, 76b, 105a, 111a, 129a, 130a), slam (124c, 131c), slap (22c, 98b), slat (69b, 133b), Slav (14d), slaw (28d), slay (36c, 79d), Ulam (197)

_ _ L A   Alla (138), alla (233), amla (39b), aula (53d), Bala (53c), Bela (18c, 39c, 140), bola (53a), COLA (237), cola (82d, 124a), Dela. (209), Ella (151), ella (113a), -ella (117b), Fala (44d), fa-la (98d), fila (121c), Fula (216, 217), gala (45c), gila (72c), Gola (218), gola (33c, 37c, 77d), hula (58b), hyla (12b, 122c), kela (246), Kola (103c), kola (82d), Lola (25b, 75a, 167), Okla. (211, 241), olla (30c, 36b, 66a, 112c, 113a, 131d), Oola (11c), Pola (175), pula (214), pyla (21c), sala (112d, 113a), sola (11d, 39b, 89c), tala (17c), tela (21c, 75d, 130d), tola (66d, 103a), tula (10d, 11d), Vela (103c, 208), Vila (224), vola (111c), Zola (49c, 188)

L _ _ A lama (22b, 121d), Lana (165), lana (70b), Lara (23c), lava (77d, 101b, 129a), Leda (24d, 59a, 91a, 113b, 125d, 135a, 198), Lema (166), Lena (30b, 52a, 166), lija (46a, 70d), Lima (27c, 221), lima (12a, 17d), Lina (166), lira (25c, 218, 219, 221, 223, 224), Lisa (166), Liza (166), Lola (25b, 75a, 167), loma (59d), LPGA (240), Luba (224), Luca (167), Luna (89d, 198), luna (78d), Lyra (58a, 207)

_ L B _ alba (73c, 75c, 131d), albs, Elba (64c, 80d), Elbe (82b, 216)

_ _ L B bulb (30d, 126b)

L _ _ B Lamb (40b, 165), lamb (107d), limb (13c, 21c), lobb (77a)

_ L C _ alca (15d, 98a)

_ _ L C talc (25d, 49c, 77a, 92a, 111b)

L _ _ C laic (28a, 70c, 82a, 94d, 106b), leuc- (94a)

_ L D _ Alda (137), Aldo (137), bldg. (236)

_ _ L D auld (105b), bald (17b), bold (33d), cold (53c, 62a), fold (57d, 90b, 107d), -fold (117c), geld (120a), gild (40b), gold (74a, 134b, 245), held (91d), hold (9c, 15a, 16c, 27d, 67b, 74b, 95b, 100a, 115a, 121a, 234), meld (23c, 34b), mild (28a, 53c, 77c, 120c), mold (44c, 107c), sold, told (99a), veld (104c, 112b), Weld (186), weld (38d, 66c, 126c), wild (18c, 31d, 104c, 126d, 128c), wold (38d, 126d)

L _ _ D Ladd (165), laid, Land (165), land (9d, 36b, 120d), lard (44c, 50a, 56a, 83d), laud (57b, 92b, 127d), lead (29d, 35d, 56d, 58c, 245), lend (62b), lewd (69b, 103d), lied (54a, 234), Lind (166), load (10b, 22d, 24b, 119a), Lord (167), lord (82a), loud (115b)

L E _ _ lead (29d, 35d, 56d, 58c, 245), leaf (85b, 90a), Leah (65b, 68b, 197), leak (72b, 84b), leal (73c, 105b), Lean (165), lean (24b, 29b, 98a, 110c, 113b, 121a, 122b), leap (24a, 67a, 232), Lear (30d, 107c, 195), leas, Lech (165, 213), Leda (24d, 59a, 91a, 113b, 125d, 135a, 198), leek (59b, 84a, 131b), leer (12b, 73a, 110d), lees (37d, 106b), leet (31c), left (9a, 34d, 91c, 99c), legs, lehr (54c, 85c), Leif (43a), leis, leks, Lema (166), Lena (30b, 52a, 166), lend (62b), Leno (166), leno (43b, 75a), lens (54c, 74a, 84c, 98d, 120b), Lent (44c, 87c, 106a), lent, Leon (166, 222), Leos, lept- (93d), Lero (64c), lerp (41d), less (77b, 82c), lest (48d), Leto (13b, 14d, 28d, 88c, 198), lets, Lett (16d), leuc- (94a), leuk- (94a), Levi (13b, 64d, 70d, 197), levo- (93b), levy (15a, 62b, 120a), lewd (69b, 103d)

_ L E _ Alea (15b), Alec (137), alec (12c, 47a, 104b), alee (59a, 108a, 132b), ales, Alex (137), bleb (20a, 22b, 54c), bled (97d), blet (51d), bleu (26b, 50a), blew, clef (80c, 234), Cleo (96d, 146), clew (16c, 103b), elec. (238), elem. (238), elev. (238), flea (63b, 229), fled, flee (9b, 41c), Flem. (238), flew, flex (18c), gled (42a), glee

(76a, 111d, 234), **Glen** (155), **glen** (35d, 98a, 127b), **ilea** (73c), **ileo-** (93b), **ilex** (60c), **Klee** (164), **Llew** (199), **olea** (84a), **oleo-** (93b), **plea** (42d, 92b, 118a), **pleb** (29b), **pled, plew** (18a), **sled** (102b), **slew** (110c, 118c), **sley** (130d)

_ _ **L E** **able** (10a, 29c, 96b, 110a), **acle** (64b), **atle** (104a, 119b), **axle** (113c, 131c), **bale** (22c, 232), **bile** (26d), **bole** (27d, 98c, 124b), **Cale** (144), **-cele** (117c), **Cole** (146), **-cule** (117c), **Dale** (26d, 147), **dale** (35d, 98a, 127b), **dele** (23c, 40b, 43a, 94c, 95b, 119b), **Dole** (58c, 149), **dole** (91d, 99b, 131a), **elle** (49d, 51a, 246), **Erle** (151), **file** (72a, 97d, 99a, 122d), **Gale** (154), **gale** (130d, 132b, 132c), **gyle** (21d), **Hale** (12b, 156), **hale** (112a, 131d), **hole** (9c, 13b, 84b, 89c, 109d), **hule** (21c, 25a, 102c), **-ible** (117a), **Idle** (159), **idle** (40c, 60c, 62c, 62d, 63a, 70c, 127a, 130a), **ille** (69d), **lole** (42a, 59c, 94c), **isle** (11a, 64b, 67b), **Jule** (163), **kale** (23a, 78a, 90a, 103d, 127c), **Kyle** (165), **Lyle** (167), **Male** (37d, 219), **male** (53b, 70b, 114b), **mile** (52c, 68c, 246), **Mlle.** (240), **Mole** (69a), **mole** (19b, 22d, 106a, 114d, 230), **mule** (108c, 110d, 131b, 230), **Nile** (81b, 216, 222), **Ogle** (173), **ogle** (43c, 71a, 73a), **orle** (46a, 59b, 108a), **pale** (19d, 86a, 88d, 129d), **Pele** (58c), **pile** (17a, 58d, 79a), **pole** (101c, 113a, 129b, 133b, 246), **pule** (131c), **Pyle** (175), **rale** (21d, 26c, 34a), **rile** (12d, 64b, 95c, 115c), **role** (52a, 86d), **rule** (13b, 35b, 37b, 70b, 118c), **sale** (15c, 17b, 50b, 51a, 123d), **sole** (42c, 46d, 47d, 84b, 87c, 109d, 111d, 228), **tale** (43a, 71b, 103b, 134a), **tele-** (92d, 93d), **tile** (27d, 46b, 74b, 102a, 120d), **tole** (41b, 76b), **tule** (22c, 25a), **Vale** (184), **vale** (44b, 127b), **vile** (9a, 17b, 46a, 62a, 74c), **vole** (75b, 79b, 110b, 111b, 231), **wale** (55c, 100c, 130c, 131b, 131c), **wile** (34a), **Yale** (79b, 101c, 205), **yule** (27a)

L _ _ **E** **Labe** (217), **lace** (47b), **lade** (24b, 35d, 72d, 76d, 119a), **Lake** (165), **lake** (89a, 130a), **lame** (32a, 57c), **Lane** (165), **lane** (11c, 21b, 116b), **late** (33d, 98b), **lave** (130a), **laze** (61d), **lice** (86c), **life** (19a, 57a, 94d), **like** (24b, 109c), **lime** (23b, 27c, 51d, 78d, 124a), **line** (11b, 30d, 46a, 96d, 102c, 116b), **lire** (50d, 64d), **Lise** (166), **-lite** (117b, 117c), **live** (38d, 42d), **lobe** (70d, 102c), **lode** (35a, 76b, 84c, 127d), **loge** (120d), **Lome** (223), **lone** (109d, 111d), **lope** (39b, 52a, 52b), **lore** (60b, 70d, 71b, 132d), **lose** (48d), **Love** (167), **love** (24b, 120c), **Lowe** (167), **Luce** (10a, 29b, 192), **luge** (110b), **Luke** (42a, 167, 196), **lune** (31d, 58c), **lure** (34b, 41b, 63d, 120c), **lute** (25c, 66a, 80b, 100d), **luxe** (100c), **Lyle** (167), **lyre** (80b, 85a), **-lyse** (117b), **-lyte** (117a), **-lyze** (117b)

_ **L F** _ **Alfs**

_ _ **L F** **calf** (134d), **golf** (12a), **gulf** (9c, 130a), **half** (77c), **pelf** (21a, 46a, 100c), **self** (39d, 62d), **Wolf** (187, 207), **wolf** (23d, 231)

L _ _ **F** **leaf** (85b, 90a), **Leif** (43a), **lief** (132a), **loaf** (61d, 73b, 130a), **luff** (48a)

L G _ _ **lgth.** (240)

_ **L G** _ **alga** (105d), **-algy** (117c), **Olga** (173)

_ _ L G	**Belg.** (236), **Bulg.** (236)
L _ _ G	**Lang** (165), **lang.** (240), **ling** (22c, 46d, 58d, 130b, 228), **Long** (167), **long** (31d), **lung** (100a, 121b)
L _ _ H	**lakh** (84a, 108a), **lash** (42d, 47c, 122a, 131c), **lath** (116c), **Leah** (65b, 68b, 197), **Lech** (165, 213), **lgth.** (240), **Lith.** (240), **-lith** (117c), **loch** (68b, 105b, 130a), **losh** (40b), **lush** (38b, 73d), **Luth.** (240)
L I _ _	**Liam** (166), **Liao** (101a), **liar** (75d), **Lias** (53c), **lice** (86c), **lick** (18a, 66a, 110d), **lido** (65c, 127d), **lids**, **lied** (54a, 234), **lief** (132a), **lien** (53a, 71a, 95b), **lies**, **lieu** (89d), **life** (19a, 57a, 94d), **lift** (40b), **lign-** (94a), **lija** (46a, 70d), **like** (24b, 109c), **lill** (16b, 89b, 132b), **lilt** (72c), **Lily** (166), **lily** (47c, 47d), **Lima** (27c, 221), **lima** (12a, 17d), **limb** (13c, 21c), **lime** (23b, 27c, 51d, 78d, 124a), **limn** (35a), **limp** (47b, 63a, 129b), **limy**, **Lina** (166), **Lind** (166), **line** (11b, 30d, 46a, 96d, 102c, 116b), **ling** (22c, 46d, 58d, 130b, 228), **link** (30a, 63c, 66c), **lint** (47d), **liny**, **Linz** (33c, 213), **Lion** (193), **lion** (94b, 230), **Li Po** (26d), **lipo-** (92d), **lips**, **lira** (25c, 218, 219, 221, 223, 224), **lire** (50d, 64d), **Lisa** (166), **Lise** (166), **Lisi** (166), **lisp** (113c), **liss** (49a), **list** (24d, 41b, 65c, 101c, 102b, 104d, 122a), **-lite** (117b, 117c), **Lith.** (240), **-lith** (117c), **litz** (97b), **live** (38d, 42d), **Livy** (101d), **Liza** (166)
_ L I _	**alif** (11d), **alim** (120a), **alit** (36c, 68d, 107a), **B. Lit.** (236), **blip** (97b), **Clio** (29b, 80a), **clip** (15c, 44c, 107d), **Elia** (68d, 87c, 151), **Elie** (151), **Elio** (151), **Elis** (56b), **Eliz.** (238), **Flip** (153), **flip** (123b), **flit** (33d), **glib** (47d, 110c, 111a, 129a), **glim** (23d, 43c), **ilia** (60b, 87c), **Ilie** (159), **olid** (49a, 116c), **olig-** (93a), **Olin** (173), **olio** (36b, 60c, 75d, 77b, 92a), **slid**, **Slim** (181), **slim** (110c, 118b), **slip** (36b, 41c, 52d, 54d, 110c, 126b), **slit** (33a)
_ _ L I	**Atli** (15c, 56d, 61c), **Bali** (64c), **Cali** (215), **Dali** (147), **Dili** (91d, 217), **heli-** (93d), **joli** (50d), **Juli** (163), **Kali** (109d, 199), **kali** (104a), **koli** (24d), **Mali** (219), **mali** (24d), **Pali** (22b, 104b, 127c), **pili-** (93a), **puli** (37b, 61c, 227), **soli** (14b), **ugli** (51d), **Vali** (83b), **Vili** (83b)
L _ _ I	**lari** (219), **Levi** (13b, 64d, 70d, 197), **Lisi** (166), **loci** (27a), **Lodi** (80d), **Loki** (10b, 16c, 198), **Loni** (167), **Lori** (167), **Loti** (49c, 95d), **loti** (218), **ludi** (102a), **luni-** (93b), **lwei** (213), **lysi-** (93a)
_ L K _	**Elke** (151), **elks**, **Ilka** (159)
_ _ L K	**balk** (16b, 89c, 116a), **bilk** (26b, 34a, 34c), **bulk** (20c, 75b, 129a), **calk** (61b), **Falk** (152), **folk** (87d, 124b), **hulk** (126d), **milk** (128d), **Polk** (175, 190), **pulk** (79c), **Salk** (179), **silk** (43b), **sulk** (117d), **talk** (29d, 36a, 113b), **volk** (54a), **walk** (85b), **Welk** (186), **yolk** (128d)
L _ _ K	**lack** (34c, 129d), **lank** (121a), **lark** (19a, 51c, 226), **leak** (72b, 84b), **leek** (59b, 84a, 131b), **leuk-** (94a), **lick** (18a, 66a, 110d), **link** (30a, 63c, 66c), **lock** (44c, 57b), **lonk** (107d), **look** (13c, 15a, 22b, 43d, 106b, 118b, 128c), **luck** (25d), **lurk** (71d, 110b)

377

L L _ _   Llew (199)

_ L L _   Alla (138), alla (233), allo- (93d), Ally (138), ally (11b, 15b, 29d, 30a, 126c), Ella (151), ella (113a), -ella (117b), elle (49d, 51a, 246), ells, ille (69d), ills (124d), illy, Mlle. (240), olla (30c, 36b, 66a, 112c, 113a, 131d)

_ _ L L   Ball (140), ball (17b), Bell (140), bell (22c, 120b), Bill (141), bill (17d, 109d), Böll (142), boll (90a, 90c), bull (21b, 86b), call (12d, 15a, 85b, 108d, 117d, 128c, 134b), cell (32c), coll. (237), cull (88d), dell (35d, 127b), dill (14c, 88d), doll (45b, 96a), Dull (193), dull (20b, 28b, 47b, 63b, 66b, 71d, 73c, 126c), fall (38b, 57b, 106a), Fell (152), fell (33a), fill (83b, 88b, 104b), full (29c, 99d), gall (18d, 25d, 64b, 128b), gill (21c, 246), gull (19a, 28c, 34a, 34c, 68a, 76c, 105c, 118d, 225), Hall (156), hall (31a, 87a), Hell (9a, 16a, 34a, 57a, 108a), he'll (30c), Hill (158), hill (17a), Hull (159), hull (106b, 108b), it'll (30c), jell (111d), Jill (161), kill (31d, 79d, 102d), lill (16b, 89b, 132b), loll (38a, 73b, 98b), lull (11c), mall (74c, 95a, 108c), mell (60d), Mill (170), mill (96d), Moll (171), moll (52d), Mull (171), mull (43b, 91b, 103a, 121b), Nell (83d, 172), null (82c, 128d), pall (28b, 122b, 130d), Pell (174), pill (119a), poll (129c), pull (11d, 37d, 123c), rill (22a, 31d, 101a, 110d, 116b), roll (118c), sell (74d, 87c, 127d), Sill (49a), sill (37c, 121c, 132b), syll. (243), tall (72d), Tell (14a), tell (13d, 62b, 81a, 99a), till (32c), toll (18c, 94b, 100d), Wall (193), wall (118a), well (25c, 97c), we'll (30c), Will (186), will (18c, 35b, 120d, 129a, 133a), Yell (64d), yell (18c, 108d)

L _ _ L   leal (73c, 105b), lill (16b, 89b, 132b), loll (38a, 73b, 98b), lull (11c)

_ L M _   Alma (138), alma (32a, 33b), alms (26a), Elmo (21a, 87a, 151), elms, elmy

_ _ L M   balm (83d, 126a), calm (11c, 13c, 15b, 82a, 85b, 89d, 97a, 106d, 111c, 111d, 126c), Colm (146), culm (13a, 28c, 56a, 108b, 115b), film (28b, 77b, 121b), Helm (157), helm (108b, 122a), Holm (158), holm (60c, 64b, 83a), malm (27d, 72a), palm (124a)

L _ _ M   Liam (166), loam (39a, 111c), loom (13c, 40c, 57d, 109b, 130d)

_ L N _   ulna (32c, 20d)

_ _ L N   kiln (16b, 85c), Koln (100b, 216)

L _ _ N   lain, lawn (31a, 43b, 69a, 72a), Lean (165), lean (24b, 29b, 98a, 110c, 113b, 121a, 122b), Leon (166, 222), lien (53a, 71a, 95b), lign- (94a), limn (35a), Lion (193), lion (94b, 230), loan (17a, 78a), loin (33a, 75c), loon (19a, 19b, 226), lorn (49a), Lynn (167), Lyon (216)

L O _ _   load (10b, 22d, 24b, 119a), loaf (61d, 73b, 130a), loam (39a, 111c), loan (17a, 78a), lobb (77a), lobe (70d, 102c), lobo (122a, 133b), lobs, loch (68b, 105b, 130a), loci (27a), lock (44c, 57b), loco (31d, 63b, 90d), lode (35a, 76b, 84c, 127d), Lodi (80d), Lodz (221), loft (15c, 55b, 129d), loge (120d), logo (22d, 29b), logs, logy (38c), loin (33a, 75c), loir (37c), Lois (118a), Loki (10b, 16c, 198), Lola (25b, 75a, 167), loll (38a, 73b, 98b), Lolo (69a, 215), loma (59d), Lome (223), lone (109d, 111d), Long (167), long (31d), Loni (167), lonk (107d), look (13c, 15a, 22b, 43d, 106b, 118b, 128c), loom (13c, 40c, 57d, 109b, 130d), loon (19a, 19b, 226), loop (27b, 82a), Loos (167), loot (21a, 58b, 89b, 90c, 103a, 113d), lope (39b, 52a, 52b), lops, Lord (167), lord (82a), lore (60b, 70d, 71b, 132d), Lori (167), lorn (49a), loro (86d), lory (86d), lose (48d), losh (40b), loss (35a, 94d, 130a), LOST (240), lost (77b, 130a), Loti (49c, 95d), loti (218), lots (26a), Lott (167), loud (115b), loup (50d, 51b, 105c), lour (33d, 54d), lout (21a, 83a), Love (167), love (24b, 120c), Lowe (167), lows

_ L O _   aloe (10c, 19c, 59b, 59c, 71d, 75c, 90a, 122d), alop (38a), Alou (138), alow (18c, 126a), blob (29a, 75b), bloc (126c), blot (115b), blow (42d), clod (21a, 37b, 83a, 116d), clog (20a, 108c), clop (61a), clot (28c, 73c), clou (50d), clow (47c, 110d), cloy (54d, 104b, 118a), Eloi (122b), Elon (41c, 82b, 201), floc (111a), floe (61b), flog (131c), flop (44a), flor (46a, 108a), flow (14b, 37d, 116b), glob (75b), glom (115a), glop (75b), glos. (239), glow (108a), Olof (173), olor (118b), plod (124d, 129b), plop (44a, 130b), plot (23a, 30b, 104d, 123c), plow (32c, 122a), ploy (14d, 116a), slob (126d), sloe (15b, 19d, 51d, 90b, 132a), slog (38b, 124d, 129b), slop (48b, 111b), slot (12d, 13b, 34c, 84b, 123c), slow (34a, 35d, 58a, 110d, 116d)

_ _ L O   allo- (93d), Arlo (139), bolo (68a, 130d), Colo. (209, 237), halo (27b, 71d, 81d, 100d), holo- (94a), hylo- (94a), Jolo (64d), kalo (119d), kilo (12a, 76b, 246), kilo- (93d), kolo (48b, 106d), Lalo (165), lalo (117d), Lolo (69a, 215), malo (21d, 58c, 72d, 112d), Milo (171), milo (112a), orlo (46a, 90b), Oslo (220), Polo (127d), silo (48a, 116a), solo (11d, 14b, 84a), telo- (92d), xylo- (94a)

L _ _ O   lago (65a, 112d), Lalo (165), lalo (117d), Leno (166), leno (43b, 75a), Lero (64c), Leto (13b, 14d, 28d, 88c, 198), levo- (93b), Liao (101a), lido (65c, 127d), Li Po (26d), lipo- (92d), lobo (122a, 133b), loco (31d, 63b, 90d), logo (22d, 29b), Lolo (69a, 215), loro (86d), ludo (52b)

L P _ _   LPGA (240)

_ L P _   Alph (101a), Alps (79b), olpe (70d, 132c)

_ _ L P   colp (25c), Culp (147), gulp (20d, 37d, 118b), help (10d, 15a, 62b, 117a), kelp (64a, 106a), Kulp (165), palp (13a, 45a, 123b), pulp (51d, 74a, 75b, 86b), salp (83b), yelp (12d, 37b)

L _ _ P   laap (41d), lamp (71d, 73c), Lapp (82b, 222), leap (24a, 67a, 232), lerp (41d), limp (47b, 63a, 129b), lisp (113c), loop (27b, 82a), loup (50d, 51b, 105c), lump (17a, 55a, 79a, 118c)

_ L R _   NLRB (241)

L _ _ R Lahr (165), lair (34d, 60c), Lear (30d, 107c, 195), leer (12b, 73a, 110d), lehr (54c, 85c), liar (75d), loir (37c), lour (33d, 54d)

_ L S _ also (12c, 18c, 62c, 78c, 90c, 115b), Elsa (55c, 72d, 84b, 129b, 151), else (18c, 61d, 85a), Ilsa (24c)

_ _ L S ails, awls, bels, cols, eels, ells, fils (51a, 213, 217, 218, 223, 224), gals, gels, Gils, Hals (38d, 156), ills (124d), Mels, mils, oils, owls, pals, Sols

L _ _ S labs, lads, lags, lams, Laos (218), laps, lass (45b, 74b), laws, lays, leas, lees (37d, 106b), legs, leis, leks, lens (54c, 74a, 84c, 98d, 120b), Leos, less (77b, 82c), lets, Lias (53c), lids, lies, lips, liss (49a), lobs, logs, Lois (118a), Loos (167), lops, loss (35a, 94d, 130a), lots (26a), lows, lues (118d), lugs, Luis (167), lyes

_ L T _ Alta. (235), alte (69d), alti- (93a), alto (113a, 128d), alto- (93a)

_ _ L T belt (16d, 27b), Bolt (142), bolt (44c, 47c, 67a, 101c), Celt (22a, 217), celt (115d, 123a), colt (61b, 100b, 134d, 135a), cult (106a, 119c), dolt (20a, 48b, 109c, 116d), felt (42d, 43b, 43d), gelt (78a), gilt (60c, 112b, 134d), halt (14c, 25b, 32a, 59d, 87b, 115d), hilt (57d), Holt (158), holt (30c), jilt (99a), jolt (20a, 66a, 108b), kilt (105a), lilt (72c), malt (18a), melt (72b, 120d), milt (47a), molt (24d, 107d), mult- (93b), pelt (28c, 43a, 57b, 59d), SALT (242), salt (29d, 80b, 94b, 103b, 106a, 111c), silt (79c, 106b), tilt (23d, 24b, 62c, 72b, 101c), volt (40a, 61b, 246), Walt (185), welt (100c, 129b, 130c, 131c), Wilt (187), wilt (38a)

L _ _ T laet (49b), lait (50d), last (30b, 40d, 108c, 130d), leet (31c), left (9a, 34d, 91c, 99c), Lent (44c, 87c, 106a), lent, lept- (93d), lest (48d), Lett (16d), lift (40b), lilt (72c), lint (47d), list (24d, 41b, 65c, 101c, 102b, 104d, 122a), loft (15c, 55b, 129d), loot (21a, 58b, 89b, 90c, 103a, 113d), LOST (240), lost (77b, 130a), Lott (167), lout (21a, 83a), Luft (167), Lunt (167), lust (34a, 107a)

L U _ _ luau (58b), Luba (224), Luca (167), Luce (10a, 29b, 192), luck (25d), Lucy (192), ludi (102a), ludo (52b), lues (118d), luff (48a), Luft (167), luge (110b), lugs, Luis (167), Luke (42a, 167, 196), lull (11c), lulu (73a), lump (17a, 55a, 79a, 118c), Luna (89d, 198), luna (78d), lune (31d, 58c), lung (100a, 121b), luni- (93b), Lunt (167), lure (34b, 41b, 63d, 120c), lurk (71d, 110b), lush (38b, 73d), lust (34a, 107a), lute (25c, 66a, 80b, 100d), Luth. (240), luxe (100c)

_ L U _ alum (37c, 77a), alum. (235), Blue (142), blue (75d, 112a, 126c), blur (62d, 111a), blut (53d), club (21c, 32c, 75b, 84c, 104a, 111c), clue (60b, 117d), Cluj (221), elul (78c), flub (21b), flue (11a, 26c), fluo- (93a), flux (26a, 47d), glue (10a, 115b), glum (54d, 78d, 112b, 117d), glut (42b, 55b, 85c, 104b, 118a), Ilus (69a, 124d), plug (116a, 133d), plum (51d, 124a), plus (12c, 62c), slub (134b), slue (110c, 118c), slug (38a, 76b, 116b), slum (81b, 99d), slur (36c, 40b, 74c, 95b, 123c, 128b), slut (133b)

_ _ L U   **ACLU** (235), **lulu** (73a), **pelu** (26c), **Sulu** (88c), **sulu** (46a), **tolu** (16d), **Zulu** (12a, 222)

L _ _ U   **lieu** (89d), **luau** (58b), **lulu** (73a)

L V _ _   **Lvov** (223)

_ L V _   **Alva** (39c), **Blvd.** (236), **ulva** (105d)

L _ _ V   **Lvov** (223)

L W _ _   **lwei** (213)

L _ _ W   **Llew** (199)

_ _ L X   **calx** (59a, 85d), **falx** (102a)

L _ _ X   **lanx** (102a), **Lynx** (207), **lynx** (24a, 131d, 230)

L Y _ _   **lyes**, **Lyle** (167), **Lynn** (167), **Lynx** (207), **lynx** (24a, 131d, 230), **Lyon** (216), **Lyra** (58a, 207), **lyre** (80b, 85a), **-lyse** (117b), **lysi-** (93a), **-lyte** (117a), **-lyze** (117b)

_ L Y _   **Clym** (14a)

_ _ L Y   **-ably** (117b), **Ally** (138), **ally** (11b, 15b, 29d, 30a, 126c), **coly** (79b), **Daly** (147), **duly** (100c, 117a), **eely**, **holy** (30b), **idly**, **illy**, **July**, **Lily** (166), **lily** (47c, 47d), **moly** (59b, 132a), **oily** (44c, 83d, 126a), **only** (11d, 22d, 42c, 76a, 111d), **poly-** (93b), **rely** (124d), **ugly** (126a), **wily** (14d, 31d, 32c, 110c), **wkly.** (244)

L _ _ Y   **lacy** (34c), **lady** (45b, 81d), **laky**, **lazy** (62d), **levy** (15a, 62b, 120a), **Lily** (166), **lily** (47c, 47d), **limy**, **liny**, **Livy** (101d), **logy** (38c), **Lucy** (192)

L _ _ Z   **Linz** (33c, 213), **litz** (97b), **Lodz** (221)

M A _ _   **ma'am** (74a), **maar** (129a), **mabi** (47d, 80b), **mace** (40c, 82d, 114b, 118d, 129d), **mach** (113c), **Mack** (167), **mack** (97c), **Macy** (167), **made** (31d), **Maes**, **mage** (74a), **Magh** (213), **magh** (78b), **magi** (88a, 94c, 132d), **maha** (25d, 69a, 104a), **Maia** (59c, 107b, 129c, 198, 207), **maid** (37b, 54c, 107a), **mail** (14c, 76b, 91d), **maim** (80d), **Main** (168), **main** (26c, 29d, 67b, 94c), **mais** (50a), **maja** (31d), **make** (13c, 29c, 30c, 40d, 43d, 44c), **maki** (71b), **mako** (20b, 107d), **Male** (37d, 219), **male** (53b, 70b, 114b), **Mali** (219), **mali** (24d), **mall** (74c, 95a, 108c), **malm** (27d, 72a), **malo** (21d, 58c, 72d, 112d), **malt** (18a), **mama** (44b), **mamo** (58b), **mana** (91a), **mand** (25c), **mane** (57b), **mani** (87b), **Mann** (168), **mano** (65a), **Manx** (25c), **manx** (24d), **many** (82d), **mapo** (55a), **maps**, **mara** (101c, 230), **Marc** (168), **marc** (55d), **mare** (61a, 82c), **Mari** (16d), **mari** (50c), **Mark** (42a, 102c, 168, 196), **mark** (10d, 15c, 55c, 96b, 109b, 114c, 133a), **marl** (27d, 35a, 45c), **Marr** (168), **Mars** (89d, 98d, 129d, 199), **mars** (49d), **mart** (40c, 74d), **maru** (65d), **Marv** (169), **Marx** (169), **Mary** (96c, 107c, 169, 197), **masa** (30d), **masc.** (240),

MASH (240), Mash (197), mash (32b, 115d), mask (29d, 36b, 37c), Mass. (210, 240), mass (9c, 10d, 17a, 22c, 53a, 58d, 107a, 129a), mast (18a, 90d, 108b, 113a), mate (15b, 18d, 26c, 29b, 34c, 85d, 114a, 120a), math (116c), Mats (169), Matt (169, 240), maty (62d), Maud (131d, 169), maud (43b, 56a), Maui (64c), maul (17c, 57d, 74c), maws, Maya (134d, 169, 214, 217), maya (60a, 130d), Mayo (169), Mays (169), maze (68b), mazy

_ M A _   amah (74b, 82d, 84d), amas (69d), amat (69d), G-man (45a), imam (23b, 80c), Oman (220), Omar (41c, 78d, 88a, 120c, 173, 197), T-man (45a), Xmas (27a)

_ _ M A   Alma (138), alma (32a, 33b), amma (9a), bema (90b, 95d), boma (10c), cima (65c), coma (71c, 116d, 126a), cyma (37c, 77d), dama (65a, 112d), duma (103a), Emma (21b, 151), Erma (151), Fama (103a), FNMA (238), Hama (222), hema- (92c), Kama (199), kama (60a, 129a), lama (22b, 121d), Lema (166), Lima (27c, 221), lima (12a, 17d), loma (59d), mama (44b), Nama (61c), nema (39d), noma (52c), Numa (102a), Pima (189), pima (31a), puma (24d, 31b, 79a, 231), Rama (128c), Rima (56c), rima (47a), Roma (65c, 218), sama (80d), sima (101b), soma (12d, 20c, 62d), tema (121a, 234), USMA (243), xema (14a, 56d), Yuma (189), Zama (106a)

M _ _ A   maha (25d, 69a, 104a), Maia (59c, 107b, 129c, 198, 207), maja (31d), mama (44b), mana (91a), mara (101c, 230), masa (30d), Maya (134d, 169, 214, 217), maya (60a, 130d), mega- (93b), mesa (40b, 59d, 90b, 119a), meta- (92d), mica (64b, 77a, 109b), Mina (223), mina (131a), Mira (207), Mona (171), mona (56d), mora (46b, 48c, 52b, 56d, 65a, 76b, 118d), moxa (25b, 26d, 133d), mura (65d), musa (16d), muta (26a, 80d), Myra (15a, 171), myna (19b)

_ M B _   ambi- (92c), ambo (95d, 98a), imbe (30d, 45c), imbu (51d), umbo (21a)

_ _ M B   bomb (107d, 130c), comb (31d), dumb (109b, 113c), gamb (12d), iamb (48c), jamb (37c, 109a, 126d), Lamb (40b, 165), lamb (107d), limb (13c, 21c), numb (33d, 126b), tomb (22d), womb (127c)

M _ _ B   Moab (66b, 73b, 197)

_ M C _   YMCA (244)

_ _ M C   USMC (243)

M _ _ C   Marc (168), marc (55d), masc. (240), misc. (240)

_ M D _   Cmdr. (237)

M _ _ D   maid (37b, 54c, 107a), mand (25c), Maud (131d, 169), maud (43b, 56a), Mead (61a, 170), mead (18a, 37d, 60d), meed (100b), meld (23c, 34b), mend (99c), mild (28a, 53c, 77c, 120c), mind (29c, 63c, 67b, 73a, 83a, 120c), mold (44c, 107c), mood (10d, 36c, 122d), Mr. Ed (119b), Mudd (171)

M E _ _   Mead (61a, 170), mead (18a, 37d, 60d), meal (56c, 99c), mean (9a, 16a, 17b, 34d, 76c, 109b, 115c), meat (48b), Mede (14d, 88a), medi- (93c), meed (100b), Meek (170), meek (37a, 53c, 61c, 76d, 77c, 126a), meet (9c, 15a, 30a, 40d, 43d, 63c, 103a, 107a), mega- (93b), Megs, mein (26d), Meir (170), meld (23c, 34b), mell (60d), Mels, melt (72b, 120d), memo (82c), mend (99c), mene (57d), meno (71b, 233), -ment (117b), menu (19a, 24c, 29c, 48b, 51a), meow (25a), mere (17b, 50d, 68b, 84b, 91b, 130a), merl (19a, 19d, 226), mero (56c, 66b), Meru (79a, 218), Merv (170), mesa (40b, 59d, 90b, 119a), mesh (40d, 63c, 81c, 111b, 130d), meso- (93b), mess (21b, 26a, 30a, 36c, 67a, 79c, 111b), meta- (92d), mete (11c, 13d, 91d), Meth. (240), metr- (94a), Mets (206), Metz (216), meus (69d), mewl (131c), mews (114b)

_ M E _   amen (111b, 128a), Amer. (235), amer (50a), Ames (138), AMEX (235), emeu (19b), G-men(45a), N.Mex.(241), Omei (22b), omen (15d, 48c, 48d, 91c, 94a, 109b), omer (59a), Smee (88b), smew (19a, 38c, 76a, 104c), T-men (45a, 123d)

_ _ M E   acme (32c, 87b, 123a, 135a), came (132b), come (94d), cyme (47d), dame (45b, 54c, 68c, 81d, 122c), deme (56b), dime (44d), dome (32d, 102a), fame (99c, 99d), feme (133b), fume (111a, 116a), game (114a), hame (61b), heme (20a), home (61c, 99d), Hume (159, 192), kame (60a, 100c), lame (32a, 57c), lime (23b, 27c, 51d, 78d, 124a), Lome (223), mime (66b), name (10d, 13c, 28d, 38b, 82a, 122c), pome (51d), rime (30a, 51c, 60c), Rome (13c, 27c, 41d, 218), same (36d, 61d), seme (37c), some (86d, 96b), tame (37a, 37b, 53c), time (38d, 41b, 41c, 87d, 100b), tome (20d, 129a)

M _ _ E   mace (40c, 82d, 114b, 118d, 129d), made (31d), mage (74a), make (13c, 29c, 30c, 40d, 43d, 44c), Male (37d, 219), male (53b, 70b, 114b), mane (57b), mare (61a, 82c), mate (15b, 18d, 26c, 29b, 34c, 85d, 114a, 120a), maze (68b), Mede (14d, 88a), mene (57d), mere (17b, 50d, 68b, 84b, 91b, 130a), mete (11c, 13d, 91d), mice, Mike (170), mike (12a), mile (52c, 68c, 246), mime (66b), mine (55a, 95a), mire (20c, 39a, 78c, 79c), mise (10d, 134c), mite (14a, 63b, 64a, 86c, 86d), Mize (171), Mlle. (240), mode (44c, 74d, 116d, 130c), moke (37c), Mole (69a), mole (19b, 22d, 106a, 114d, 230), mope (22a, 117d), More (171), more (43c, 56a), mote (113b), moue (50d, 134c), move (10d, 36b, 62b, 125b), mule (108c, 110d, 131b, 230), muse (52d, 91b, 121b), mute (109b, 113c, 232, 234)

M _ _ F   miff (96b), Muff (17b), muff (17c, 21b, 22c)

M _ _ G   Ming (26d)

M H _ _   mhos

_ M H _   YMHA (244)

M _ _ H   mach (113c), Magh (213), magh (78b), MASH (240), Mash (197), mash (32b, 115d), math (116c), mesh (40d, 63c, 81c, 111b, 130d),

Meth. (240), **Mich.** (210, 240), **Moth** (193), **moth** (22d, 71b, 229), **much** (67c, 116d), **mush** (75b), **myth** (43a, 71b)

M I _ _ **mica** (64b, 77a, 109b), **mice**, **Mich.** (210, 240), **Mick** (170), **Midi** (112b), **mien** (13c, 17d, 24c, 34d, 36d, 74d), **miff** (96b), **Mike** (170), **mike** (12a), **mild** (28a, 53c, 77c, 120c), **mile** (52c, 68c, 246), **milk** (128d), **Mill** (170), **mill** (96d), **Milo** (171), **milo** (112a), **mils**, **milt** (47a), **mime** (66b), **Mimi** (68b, 84b, 95d, 171), **Mina** (223), **mina** (131a), **mind** (29c, 63c, 67b, 73a, 83a, 120c), **mine** (55a, 95a), **Ming** (26d), **mini-** (93c), **mink** (128c, 230), **Minn.** (210, 240), **mint** (14c, 28d, 59b), **minx** (88b), **Mira** (207), **mire** (20c, 39a, 78c, 79c), **Miró** (112c, 171), **MIRV** (240), **misc.** (240), **mise** (10d, 134c), **miso** (65d), **miso-** (93a), **Miss.** (210, 240), **miss** (54c, 108c), **mist** (28b, 38a, 48a, 127b), **mite** (14a, 63b, 64a, 86c, 86d), **mitt** (17b, 46b, 54d), **mitu** (32d), **mixt.** (240), **Mize** (171)

_ M I _ **amia** (21b, 79c), **amid** (12b), **amie** (50b), **amir** (10b, 13d), **Amis** (138), **amis** (50b), **-emia** (117a), **Emil** (151), **emim** (54b), **emir** (13d, 94c, 102d, 125b), **emit** (36a, 40a, 43c, 47d, 99b, 106c), **imit.** (239), **omit** (40b, 81b, 87a, 110a), **smit** (128a), **ymir** (54b)

_ _ M I **admi** (53b), **Demi** (148), **demi-** (93a), **hemi-** (93a), **immi** (246), **Jimi** (161), **kami** (65d, 108a), **Mimi** (68b, 84b, 95d, 171), **rami** (21c), **remi** (53b), **semi** (62c), **semi-** (93a, 93c), **Simi** (64c), **Timi** (183), **zemi** (45c)

M _ _ I **mabi** (47d, 80b), **magi** (88a, 94c, 132d), **maki** (71b), **Mali** (219), **mali** (24d), **mani** (87b), **Mari** (16d), **mari** (50c), **Maui** (64c), **medi-** (93c), **Midi** (112b), **Mimi** (68b, 84b, 95d, 171), **mini-** (93c), **Moki** (95d), **Muni** (171), **myri-** (93b)

M _ _ K **Mack** (167), **mack** (97c), **Mark** (42a, 102c, 168, 196), **mark** (10d, 15c, 55c, 96b, 109b, 114c, 133a), **mask** (29d, 36b, 37c), **Meek** (170), **meek** (37a, 53c, 61c, 76d, 77c, 126a), **Mick** (170), **milk** (128d), **mink** (128c, 230), **mock** (35a, 62a, 66b, 100c, 104d, 120a), **Monk** (171), **monk** (25c, 51c), **muck** (39a), **murk** (28b, 48a, 77b), **musk** (87d)

M L _ _ **Mlle.** (240)

_ M L _ **amla** (39b)

M _ _ L **mail** (14c, 76b, 91d), **mall** (74c, 95a, 108c), **marl** (27d, 35a, 45c), **maul** (17c, 57d, 74c), **meal** (56c, 99c), **mell** (60d), **merl** (19a, 19d, 226), **mewl** (131c), **Mill** (170), **mill** (96d), **moil** (20c, 133d), **Moll** (171), **moll** (52d), **Mull** (171), **mull** (43b, 91b, 103a, 121b), **myel-** (93d)

_ M M _ **amma** (9a), **ammo** (12b), **Emma** (21b, 151), **Emmy** (120b), **immi** (246)

_ _ M M **comm.** (237)

M _ _ M **ma'am** (74a), **maim** (80d), **malm** (27d, 72a)

_ M N _ omni- (92d)

_ _ M N gymn- (93b), hymn (111d), limn (35a)

M _ _ N Main (168), main (26c, 29d, 67b, 94c), Mann (168), mean (9a, 16a, 17b, 34d, 76c, 109b, 115c), mein (26d), mien (13c, 17d, 24c, 34d, 36d, 74d), Minn. (210, 240), moan (32b, 112b), Moon (171), moon (33a, 104b), morn (33d), mown, muon (71b)

M O _ _ Moab (66b, 73b, 197), moan (32b, 112b), moas, moat (36d), mobs, mock (35a, 62a, 66b, 100c, 104d, 120a), mode (44c, 74d, 116d, 130c), Moes, mogo (115d), moho (60d), mohr (53b), moil (20c, 133d), mojo (129c), moke (37c), Moki (95d), mold (44c, 107c), Mole (69a), mole (19b, 22d, 106a, 114d, 230), Moll (171), moll (52d), molt (24d, 107d), moly (59b, 132a), moms, Mona (171), mona (56d), Monk (171), monk (25c, 51c), mono (61c), mono- (93c), mons (69d, 133d), Mont. (211, 240), mont (50d), mood (10d, 36c, 122d), Moon (171), moon (33a, 104b), Moor (78c, 104b, 219), moor (12c, 15c, 58d, 130a), moos, moot (36d), mope (22a, 117d), mops, mopy (72b), mora (46b, 48c, 52b, 56d, 65a, 76b, 118d), More (171), more (43c, 56a), morn (33d), Moro (171), moro (88c), Mors (34a, 198), Mort (171), Moss (171), moss (71c, 86c, 125a), most (74b, 78c), mote (113b), Moth (193), moth (22d, 71b, 229), moto (79c), mots, Mott (171), moue (50d, 134c), move (10d, 36b, 62b, 125b), mown, mows, moxa (25b, 26d, 133d)

_ M O _ a moi (50d), amok (18c, 51b), Amon (67d, 198), Amor (32d, 198), amor (112d), Amos (108a, 138, 196, 197), Amoy (69a), BMOC (236), smog (130d)

_ _ M O ammo (12b), Como (68b, 146), demo (108d, 119c), Elmo (21a, 87a, 151), gamo- (93c), hemo- (92c), homo (69d), homo- (93c), mamo (58b), memo (82c), Nemo (128a), nomo- (92d), Pomo (189), sumo (66a), zymo- (93a)

M _ _ O mako (20b, 107d), malo (21d, 58c, 72c, 112d), mamo (58b), mano (65a), mapo (55a), Mayo (169), memo (82c), meno (71b, 233), mero (56c, 66b), meso- (93b), Milo (171), milo (112a), Miró (112c, 171), miso (65d), miso- (93a), mogo (115d), moho (60d), mojo (129c), mono (61c), mono- (93c), Moro (171), moro (88c), moto (79c), muco- (93b), myco- (93a), myxo- (93b)

_ M P _ amph. (235), amps, Impi (135c), imps

_ _ M P bump (66a, 66d), Camp (144), camp (19c, 39d, 127a), Comp. (237), damp (33c, 77c, 131b), dump (68d, 99d, 126c), Gamp (35c), gamp (125b), gimp (124c), hemp (23d, 30d, 45c, 55d, 102b), hump (95c), Jump (163), jump (10b, 114d, 127b), Kemp (164), lamp (71d, 73c), limp (47b, 63a, 129b), lump (17a, 55a, 79a, 118c), pimp (94d), pomp (85a, 85b), pump (108c), ramp (52c, 62c, 110d), RCMP (242), romp (51c), rump (23a, 33a, 75c), samp (55c, 60d, 91c), simp (48b, 109c), sump (25d, 77a), tamp (76d, 85b, 92a, 97d), temp. (243), tump (60a), tymp (19d), vamp (62c, 108c, 233), wimp (130c)

M R _ _   **Mr. Ed** (119b)

_ M R _   **amra** (60c), **Imre** (159), **Omri** (67d, 197)

_ _ M R   **comr.** (237)

M _ _ R   **maar** (129a), **Marr** (168), **Meir** (170), **metr-** (94a), **mohr** (53b), **Moor** (78c, 104b, 219), **moor** (12c, 15c, 58d, 130a), **Msgr.** (241), **Muir** (11a, 171)

M S _ _   **Msgr.** (241), **M.Sgt.** (241)

_ M S _   **Omsk** (64b)

_ _ M S   **aims, alms** (26a), **arms** (130d), **bums, cams, dams, dims, doms, elms, gams** (71b), **gems, gums, gyms, hams, hems, Homs** (222), **hums, jams, Jims, lams, moms, mums, ohms, Pams, Rams** (206), **rams, rims, rums, Sams, Sims** (181), **sums, tams, Tims, Toms, yams**

M _ _ S   **Maes, mais** (50a), **maps, Mars** (89d, 98d, 129d, 199), **mars** (49d), **Mass.** (210, 240), **mass** (9c, 10d, 17a, 22c, 53a, 58d, 107a, 129a), **Mats** (169), **maws, Mays** (169), **Megs, Mels, mess** (21b, 26a, 30a, 36c, 67a, 79c, 111b), **Mets** (206), **meus** (69d), **mews** (114b), **mhos, mils, Miss.** (210, 240), **miss** (54c, 108c), **moas, mobs, Moes, moms, mons** (69d, 133d), **moos, mops, Mors** (34a, 198), **Moss** (171), **moss** (71c, 86c, 125a), **mots, mows, muds, mugs, mums, muss** (103a)

M _ _ T   **malt** (18a), **mart** (40c, 74d), **mast** (18a, 90d, 108b, 113a), **Matt** (169, 240), **meat** (48b), **meet** (9c, 15a, 30a, 40d, 43d, 63c, 103a, 107a), **melt** (72b, 120d), **-ment** (117b), **milt** (47a), **mint** (14c, 28d, 59b), **mist** (28b, 38a, 48a, 127b), **mitt** (17b, 46b, 54d), **mixt.** (240), **moat** (36d), **molt** (24d, 107d), **Mont.** (211, 240), **mont** (50d), **moot** (36d), **Mort** (171), **most** (74b, 78c), **Mott** (171), **M.Sgt.** (241), **mult-** (93b), **must** (55d, 81c, 116c, 132c), **mutt** (32d, 78a), **myst** (56b)

M U _ _   **Muav** (53c), **much** (67c, 116d), **muck** (39a), **muco-** (93b), **Mudd** (171), **muds, Muff** (17b), **muff** (17c, 21b, 22c), **mugs, Muir** (11a, 171), **mule** (108c, 110d, 131b, 230), **Mull** (171), **mull** (43b, 91b, 103a, 121b), **mult-** (93b), **mums, Muni** (171), **muon** (71b), **mura** (65d), **murk** (28b, 48a, 77b), **musa** (16d), **muse** (52d, 91b, 121b), **mush** (75b), **musk** (87d), **muss** (103a), **must** (55d, 81c, 116c, 132c), **muta** (26a, 80d), **mute** (109b, 113c, 232, 234), **mutt** (32d, 78a)

_ M U _   **Amur** (101a), **emus, smug** (29c, 106c), **smur** (38a), **smut** (28c, 36a, 90a, 111d)

_ _ M U   **rimu** (62a, 98d)

M _ _ U   **maru** (65d), **menu** (19a, 24c, 29c, 48b, 51a), **Meru** (79a, 218), **mitu** (32d)

M _ _ V   Marv (169), Merv (170), MIRV (240), Muav (53c)

M _ _ W   meow (25a)

M _ _ X   Manx (25c), manx (24d), Marx (169), minx (88b)

M Y _ _   myco- (93a), myel- (93d), myna (19b), Myra (15a, 171), myri-(93b), myst (56b), myth (43a, 71b), myxo- (93b)

_ M Y _   amyl (114d), amyl- (93d), Amys, emyd (120c)

_ _ M Y   army (61c), demy (86b), elmy, Emmy (120b), fumy (127b), gamy (90b, 103d), Jamy (194), limy, -nomy (117c), rimy, -tomy (117b)

M _ _ Y   Macy (167), many (82d), Mary (96c, 107c, 169, 197), maty (62d), mazy, moly (59b, 132a), mopy (72b)

M _ _ Z   Metz (216)

N A _ _   nabs, NaCL (111c), NADA (241), Naga (15a, 69a, 128c), naga (23c, 28c, 60a), nags, Nagy (61c, 172), naid (51b), naif (126c), nail (27d, 44c, 119b, 126b), Nair (37d), nair (85a), nais (51b, 101a), Nama (61c), name (10d, 13c, 28d, 38b, 82a, 122c), Nana (88b, 135c), nano- (92c), Nans, naos (25b, 104a, 120b), Napa (23b, 132c), napa (54d, 70d), nape (16b, 82d), naps, narc- (93c), nard (75b, 83d), Nare (72d), nark (63a, 115d), nary (82c), NASA (241), Nash (172), nasi (87a), NASL (241), naso- (93b), Nast (172), Nate (172), Natl. (241), NATO (11c, 241), Nats, naut. (241), nave (27a, 131c), navy (20a, 47c), nays (129c), nazi (81a)

_ N A _   anag. (235), anak (54b), anal (51c), anas, anat. (235), Enam (66d), gnar (56d), gnat (48a, 63b, 76c, 229), gnaw (19c, 26c), knap (60a), knar (68c), Onan (66d), snab (22b, 105a), snag (13a, 24d, 60a, 68c, 95a, 122b), snap (17b, 21d, 31d, 39b, 44c, 66c), Unas, unau (110d)

_ _ N A   Anna (84a, 122d, 138), anna (103a), arna (22b, 131d), bina (60b), Bona (79b, 192), bona (69d, 70a), buna (102c), Cana (46c, 52b), Dana (147), Dina (149), dona (91d), dyna- (93c), Edna (151), Enna (109a), Etna (129a), etna (58d), Gena (154), Gina (155), Hana (157), -iana (117c), Iona (25c, 64b, 202), Jana (80d, 160), Jena (121d), kana (66a), kina (108a, 221), Lana (165), lana (70b), Lena (30b, 52a, 166), Lina (166), Luna (89d, 198), luna (78d), mana (91a), Mina (223), mina (131a), Mona (171), mona (56d), myna (19b), Nana (88b, 135c), Nina (24a, 29a, 172), nina (112d), Nona (86c), Oona (173), Peña (174), pina (29d), Puna (12c), puna (28d, 90b, 132b), rana (51c, 60a), Sa'na (134c), Tana (68b), Tina (183), tuna (125a, 229), ulna (32c, 20d), USNA (243), vena (70b), vina (60b), Zana (58a), zona (108a)

N _ _ A   NADA (241), Naga (15a, 69a, 128c), naga (23c, 28c, 60a), Nama (61c), Nana (88b, 135c), Napa (23b, 132c), napa (54d, 70d), NASA (241), NCAA (241), nema (39d), Nera (121d), Neva (100d), NHRA

(241), **Nina** (24a, 29a, 172), **nina** (112d), **nipa** (15b, 38a, 39b, 86a, 120d), **NIRA** (241), **Nita** (172), **NOAA** (241), **noma** (52c), **Nona** (86c), **Nora** (61b, 81d, 172), **nota** (69d), **Nova** (203), **nova** (114d), **Numa** (102a)

_ N B _   **anba** (28a)

N _ _ B   **NLRB** (241), **NTSB** (241), **numb** (33d, 126b)

N C _ _   **NCAA** (241)

_ N C _   **-ance** (117a, 117c), **-ancy** (117b), **-ence** (117b), **encl.** (238), **-ency** (117b), **ency.** (238), **Inca** (15b), **inch** (31d, 79c, 246), **incl.** (239), **onca** (246), **once** (18b, 49a, 61d, 63d), **UNCF** (243), **unco** (105b)

_ _ N C   **banc** (66d), **canc.** (236), **C in C** (236), **conc.** (237), **zinc** (20b, 76a, 245)

N _ _ C   **narc-** (93c)

N D _ _   **N.Dak.** (241)

_ N D _   **anda** (21c, 133b), **Andi** (25a), **Andy** (138), **endo-** (94a), **ends**, **Indo-** (93b), **onde** (51b), **undo** (12d, 41c, 73a, 99b)

_ _ N D   **Arnd** (53d), **band** (56c, 116b, 232), **bend** (12c, 32d, 125b), **bind** (122a), **Bond** (142), **bond** (10a, 28d, 71d, 72b, 78a, 107b, 118a, 122a), **bund** (40b), **cond.** (237), **fend** (44b, 86d, 129d), **find** (36a), **fond** (10b, 73c), **fund** (9c, 78a, 100a), **Gond** (62d), **hand** (10d, 15a, 59b, 87c, 133d, 246), **hind** (34b, 37a), **Hond.** (239), **kind** (112a, 113b, 127b), **Land** (165), **land** (9d, 36b, 120d), **lend** (62b), **Lind** (166), **mand** (25c), **mend** (99c), **mind** (29c, 63c, 67b, 73a, 83a, 120c), **pend** (16c, 58a), **pond** (91b, 130a), **Rand** (176), **rand** (220, 222), **rend** (28a), **rind** (43a, 76d, 87c), **rynd** (76d), **Sand** (179), **sand** (78d, 109b), **send** (36c, 74b, 86d, 91d, 99c, 108b, 123d), **tend** (24b, 73a, 77a, 124b), **vend** (74d, 87c, 106c), **wand** (90d, 101c, 115b), **wend** (54d, 110b, 112a), **wind** (10d, 28d, 32d, 125c), **yond** (36d)

N _ _ D   **naid** (51b), **nard** (75b, 83d), **need** (34d, 42d, 68b, 92a, 129d), **Nidd** (134d), **NKVD** (103c)

N E _ _   **neaf** (47b), **Neal** (172), **neap** (121d, 122d, 129b), **near** (13d, 28b, 81d), **neat** (10a, 116a, 121d, 124c), **Nebo** (78d, 79a), **Nebr.** (211, 241), **nebs**, **neck** (64d), **necr-** (92d), **Neds**, **need** (34d, 42d, 68b, 92a, 129d), **neep** (105b, 125b), **ne'er** (30b, 82c, 107c), **Neil** (172), **nein** (54a), **Nell** (83d, 172), **nema** (39d), **Nemo** (128a), **nene** (58c), **neon** (53a, 71d, 245), **neph-** (92d), **Nera** (121d), **Nero** (10d, 102a), **ness** (24a, 58d, 95a), **nest** (31c, 100a, 111b, 118c, 232), **Neth.** (241), **Nets** (206), **nets**, **neur-** (93b), **neut.** (241), **Neva** (100d), **neve** (46c, 54c, 55d, 111b), **nevi** (19c, 77d), **news** (121d), **Newt** (172), **newt** (39d, 103d, 225), **next** (81a)

_ N E _   **anew** (10b, 10c), **Inez** (37c), **knee** (66c), **knew**, **knez** (94c), **ones** (87d), **sned** (73a), **snee** (33a, 35d, 68a)

_ _ N E acne (110a), aine (51a), **Anne** (96b, 107c, 138, 192, 194), **a-one** (42b, 46c, 123b), **Arne** (102d, 139), aune (246), **bane** (58a, 81b, 90d, 102d, 133b), **bene** (65c, 70b), **bine** (115b, 128b), **bone** (46a, 110a), **cane** (98a, 114b, 115a, 115b, 117d, 129b), -**cene** (117c), **cine-** (93b), **Cone** (146), cone (53c, 116c, 111d), **Dane** (67c, 82b, 104c, 147), **Dene** (189), dene (104a), **dine** (39b), **done** (85c), **dune** (84a, 104a), **dyne** (48c, 246), **eine** (53d, 54a), **erne** (19a, 39a, 105c, 225), **esne** (12c, 106d, 110b, 121b), **fane** (104a, 120b), **Fine** (152), **fine** (26d, 34c, 40b, 40d, 79d, 87c, 116d, 233), **Gene** (154), **gene** (59c), **gone** (9b, 34d, 36c), **gyne** (45b), **hone** (39c, 107d, 131c), **Ione** (22c, 69b, 73d), **Jane** (160), **June** (163), **Kane** (163), **kine** (31c), **Lane** (165), **lane** (11c, 21b, 116b), **line** (11b, 30d, 46a, 96d, 102c, 116b), **lone** (109d, 111d), **lune** (31d, 58c), **mane** (57b), **mene** (57d), **mine** (55a, 95a), **nene** (58c), **nine** (17c), **none** (82c), **ohne** (54a), **Orne** (23a), **pane** (114c, 114d), **pine** (30a, 42a, 69a, 73a, 124a, 134b), **pone** (30d, 66c), **René** (176), **rine** (36d), **rune** (82b), **Ryne** (179), **sane** (97d), **sine** (52a, 70b, 96b, 124c), **sone** (246), **syne** (105b), **tine** (13a, 95a, 123a), **Tone** (184), **tone** (9c, 82c, 89c), **Tune** (184), **tune** (9c, 10a, 10d, 14b, 58a, 75d, 111d, 116a), **Tyne** (82b, 184, 223), **vane** (130d, 132b), **vine** (28a, 71c), **wane** (9a, 34b, 69a, 116d), **wine** (60c, 91c), **Zane** (188), **zone** (18c, 36d, 40d, 118b)

N _ _ E **name** (10d, 13c, 28d, 38b, 82a, 122c), **nape** (16b, 82d), **Nare** (72d), **Nate** (172), **nave** (27a, 131c), **nene** (58c), **neve** (46c, 54c, 55d, 111b), **Nice** (49c, 100a, 216), **nice** (90b, 109c), **nide** (88c, 232), **Nike** (77b, 132c, 198), **Nile** (81b, 216, 222), **nine** (17c), **Niue** (64c), **node** (66c, 68c, 90d, 95c, 118c), **none** (82c), **nope** (81b), **Nore** (120d), **nose** (89d, 95c), **note** (15c, 71c, 75d, 83b, 95a, 98c, 99c, 122d, 129c, 234), **nove** (65c), **nude** (17b, 126b), **NYSE** (241)

_ N F _ info. (239)

_ _ N F conf. (237)

N _ _ F naif (126c), neaf (47b)

_ N G _ Angl. (235), engr. (238), Inge (22d, 54d, 88d, 159)

_ _ N G **bang** (110b), **Bing** (141), **bong** (111a), **bung** (116a), cong. (237), **dang** (42a), **ding** (62d, 76b), **dong** (224), **dung** (42d, 74d), **Fang** (193, 216), **fang** (123a), **fung-** (93a), **gang** (16d, 32a, 232), **gong** (80a), **hang** (118b), **hing** (14d), **hong** (26d), **Hung.** (239), **hung**, **Jong** (163), **Jung** (95d, 163), **King** (164, 190), **king** (24a, 26c, 82a), **Lang** (165), **lang.** (240), **ling** (22c, 46d, 58d, 130b, 228), **Long** (167), **long** (31d), **lung** (100a, 121b), **Ming** (26d), **Pang** (125a), **pang** (85d, 114b, 121c), **Ping** (125a), **ping** (76b), **Pong** (125a), **pung** (21c, 110c), **rang**, **Ring** (177), **ring** (16d, 27b, 40c, 40d, 131b, 134a), **rung** (25d, 32b, 115b), **sang**, **sing** (129d), **song** (14b, 61d, 125a), **Sung** (26d), **sung**, **T'ang** (26d), **tang** (22a, 47b, 135a), **ting** (76b), **tong** (26d), **tung** (83d), **uang** (100b), **USNG** (243), **vang** (57c, 102b), **wing** (12d, 47c, 48a, 89b, 89d, 232), **Wong** (187), **Xing.** (244), **yang** (134d), **zing** (32a)

N _ _ G   **nogg** (11b)

N H _ _   **NHRA** (241)

N _ _ H   **Nash** (172), **neph-**(92d), **Neth.**(241), **nigh** (28b, 81a), **Noah** (68d, 76b, 172, 197)

N I _ _   **nibs**, **Nice** (49c, 100a, 216), **nice** (90b, 109c), **Nick** (172), **nick** (26d, 82c), **Nidd** (134d), **nide** (88c, 232), **nidi** (113c), **nigh** (28b, 81a), **Nike** (77b, 132c, 198), **Niki** (172), **Nile** (81b, 216, 222), **Nina** (24a, 29a, 172), **nina** (112d), **nine** (17c), **Nino** (172), **nino** (112c), **nipa** (15b, 38a, 39b, 86a, 120d), **nips**, **NIRA** (241), **nisi** (70b, 126c), **Nita** (172), **nito** (45b), **nitr-** (93b), **nits**, **Niue** (64c)

_ N I _   **anil** (38d, 62d), **anis**, **Enid** (14d, 23c, 53c, 120c, 151), **Enif** (207), **inia** (12b, 83b, 110b), **init.** (239), **knit** (126c), **snip** (28a), **snit** (10d, 12c, 47b), **unio** (80d), **unit** (77d, 84a)

_ _ N I   **Agni** (68c), **bani** (101d), **Beni** (214), **doni** (25d), **goni-** (92c), **Ifni** (220), **igni-** (93a), **Joni** (163), **Loni** (167), **luni-** (93b), **mani** (87b), **mini-** (93c), **Muni** (171), **omni-** (92d), **rani** (60a, 94c), **Reni** (65a, 176), **reni-** (93b), **sebi-** (92d), **Toni** (184), **Unni** (197), **veni-** (93d), **vini-** (94a), **yeni** (119c), **Zuni** (95d, 189)

N _ _ I   **nasi** (87a), **nazi** (81a), **nevi** (19c, 77d), **nidi** (113c), **Niki** (172), **nisi** (70b, 126c), **nori** (11b, 105d), **nudi-** (93b)

_ _ N J   **conj.** (237)

N K _ _   **NKVD** (103c)

_ N K _   **Anka** (138), **ankh** (32a), **inks**, **inky** (19d, 33d)

_ _ N K   **bank** (19a, 47c, 91b), **bunk** (82a, 110c), **conk** (60b, 116b), **dank** (33b, 77c), **dunk** (35d, 62a), **fink** (46a), **funk** (10d, 35a, 47b), **gink** (39c), **gunk** (110c), **Hank** (157), **hank** (57b, 109d), **honk** (55b, 112b), **hunk** (57d, 88d), **jink** (40b), **junk** (26c, 102d), **kink** (31d), **lank** (121a), **link** (30a, 63c, 66c), **lonk** (107d), **mink** (128c, 230), **Monk** (171), **monk** (25c, 51c), **pink** (24b), **punk** (12a, 123b), **rank** (27d, 46a, 55c, 72a, 73d, 97c, 116c), **rink** (109d, 114a), **sank**, **sink** (34b, 60c, 110d), **sunk**, **tank** (127d), **wink** (63c, 81d, 106a), **Yank** (12b), **yank** (95d)

N _ _ K   **nark** (63a, 115d), **N.Dak.** (241), **neck** (64d), **Nick** (172), **nick** (26d, 82c), **nock** (14c, 82c), **nook** (30d, 100a)

N L _ _   **NLRB** (241)

_ N L _   **only** (11d, 22d, 42c, 76a, 111d)

_ _ N L   **Genl.** (239)

N _ _ L   **NaCL** (111c), **nail** (27d, 44c, 119b, 126b), **NASL** (241), **Natl.** (241), **Neal** (172), **Neil** (172), **Nell** (83d, 172), **Noel** (172), **noel** (24b, 27a, 111d), **noil** (45d, 68c), **null** (82c, 128d)

N M _ _   **N.Mex.** (241)

_ N M _   **FNMA** (238)

N _ _ M   **Noam** (172), **Norm** (172), **norm** (16a, 86b, 97d, 114d)

_ N N _   **Anna** (84a, 122d, 138), **anna** (103a), **Anne** (96b, 107c, 138, 192, 194), **anno** (70b), **Anns, Enna** (109a), **inns, Unni** (197)

_ _ N N   **Bonn** (18b, 216), **Conn.** (209, 237), **conn** (35d), **Finn.** (238), **Jann** (160), **Lynn** (167), **Mann** (168), **Minn.** (210, 240), **Nunn** (173), **Penn** (174), **Penn.** (211, 242), **sunn** (45d), **Tenn.** (212, 243), **Wynn** (187)

N _ _ N   **nein** (54a), **neon** (53a, 71d, 245), **noon** (76c), **Norn** (82a), **noun** (86d, 116d), **Nunn** (173)

N O _ _   **NOAA** (241), **Noah** (68d, 76b, 172, 197), **Noam** (172), **nobs** (32a), **nock** (14c, 82c), **noct-** (93b), **node** (66c, 68c, 90d, 95c, 118c), **nods, Noel** (172), **noel** (24b, 27a, 111d), **noes** (81b), **nogg** (11b), **nogs, noil** (45d, 68c), **noir** (50a, 102c), **noma** (52c), **nomo-** (92d), **-nomy** (117c), **Nona** (86c), **none** (82c), **nook** (30d, 100a), **noon** (76c), **nope** (81b), **Nora** (61b, 81d, 172), **Nore** (120d), **nori** (11b, 105d), **Norm** (172), **norm** (16a, 86b, 97d, 114d), **Norn** (82a), **nose** (89d, 95c), **noso-** (92d), **Nosu** (215), **nosy** (63b), **nota** (69d), **note** (15c, 71c, 75d, 83b, 95a, 98c, 99c, 122d, 129c, 234), **noto-** (92c), **noun** (86d, 116d), **nous** (50d, 51b), **Nova** (203), **nova** (114d), **nove** (65c)

_ N O _   **anoa** (48d, 85d, 132a, 229), **anon** (10c, 15d, 62a, 94a, 108d, 111d), **anon.** (235), **enol** (120a), **Enos** (9d, 42a, 107a, 151, 197), **enow** (105a), **knob** (57d, 82a, 95c), **knop** (68c), **knot** (76d, 82a, 232), **know** (13a, 16c), **Knox** (49a), **snob** (88a, 111b), **snot** (62c, 88a), **Snow** (181), **snow** (130d)

_ _ N O   **anno** (70b), **Arno** (101a, 139), **at. no.** (236), **beno** (86a), **bino** (86a), **Bono** (142), **Brno** (215), **ceno-** (92d), **Dino** (47c), **Dr. No** (20d), **Gino** (155), **gono-** (93c), **gyno-** (92d), **Juno** (67c, 77b, 96d, 195, 199), **Kano** (129c), **keno** (52b), **kino** (38d, 57a, 119c, 127b), **Leno** (166), **leno** (43b, 75a), **mano** (65a), **meno** (71b, 233), **mono** (61c), **mono-** (93c), **nano-** (92c), **Nino** (172), **nino** (112c), **oeno-** (94a), **puno** (132b), **Reno** (15c, 81c, 113d), **reno-** (93b), **Sino-** (92d), **sino** (112d), **Tano** (95d, 189), **teno-** (93d), **tono-** (93c), **tuno** (57c), **veno-** (93d), **vino** (72b, 132c), **wino** (38b), **xeno-** (93a), **Zeno** (56b)

N _ _ O   **nano-** (92c), **naso-** (93b), **NATO** (11c, 241), **Nebo** (78d, 79a), **Nemo** (128a), **Nero** (10d, 102a), **Nino** (172), **nino** (112c), **nito** (45b), **nomo-** (92d), **noso-** (92d), **noto-** (92c)

N _ _ P   **neap** (121d, 122d, 129b), **neep** (105b, 125b)

_ _ N Q   **cinq** (50b)

_ N R _   in re (29d, 63d, 99a), INRI (32b, 239)

_ _ N R   USNR (244)

N _ _ R   Nair (37d), nair (85a), near (13d, 28b, 81d), Nebr. (211, 241), necr- (92d), ne'er (30b, 82c, 107c), neur- (93b), nitr- (93b), noir (50a, 102c), Nuer (222)

_ N S _   ansa (57d), anse (50c), ANSI (235), ansu (13d, 68c), -ense (117b), Insp. (239), Inst. (239)

_ _ N S   ains, Anns, arns, awns, bans, Bens, bins, buns, cans, cons, Dans, dans (50c), dens (70b), dins, dons (85d), eons, erns, fans, fens, fins, gens (35a), gins, guns, Hans (17b, 53d, 67a, 157), hens (92a), Huns (15c), Ians, inns, ions, Jans, Jons, Kans. (210, 240), Kens, lens (54c, 74a, 84c, 98d, 120b), mons (69d, 133d), Nans, nuns, owns (91d), pans, pens, pins, Pons (49d, 175), puns, runs, sans (51b), sens (49c), sins, sons (83c), Suns (206), suns, tans, tens, tins, tons, tuns, urns, vans, wens, wins, yens

N _ _ S   nabs, nags, nais (51b, 101a), Nans, naos (25b, 104a, 120b), naps, Nats, nays (129c), nebs, Neds, ness (24a, 58d, 95a), Nets (206), nets, news (121d), nibs, nips, nits, nobs (32a), nods, noes (81b), nogs, nous (50d, 51b), nubs, nuns, nuts

N T _ _   NTSB (241), Nt. Wt. (241)

_ N T _   anta (89a, 91c), ante (68a, 69c, 90d, 114c), ante- (92c), anth. (235), anti (10c, 84c), anti- (92c), ants, ento- (94a), inti (221), Intl. (239), into (133a), on to (59b), unto

_ _ N T   ain't, aunt (44b, 99b), bent (13d, 32a, 55d, 62c), bunt (17c, 131b), cant (62c, 63b, 66a, 70d, 103d, 122a, 122b), cent (30c, 213-224), cent. (236), cont. (237), Dent (149), dent (35a), dint (42d, 92b), don't, font (17a, 125d), gent (45b), hint (11d, 32c, 33d, 117d, 133a), Hunt (159), hunt (105d), isn't, Kant (53d, 163), Kent (70d, 195, 202), Lent (44c, 87c, 106a), lent, lint (47d), Lunt (167), -ment (117b), mint (14c, 28d, 59b), Mont. (211, 240), mont (50d), oont (23c, 230), pant (18a, 21d), pent (30a), pint (54b, 246), pont (50a), punt (20b, 47b), rant (34b, 58a, 98a, 119b), rent (60b, 60c, 120a, 123b), runt (12d, 38d), sent, tent (24a, 87b), tint (29a, 107b), vent (11a, 13b, 40c, 60c, 84b, 85b, 115a), want (34a, 35b, 68b, 81b, 92a, 133a), went (34d), wont (9c, 33a, 57a, 92b)

N _ _ T   Nast (172), naut. (241), neat (10a, 116a, 121d, 124c), nest (31c, 100a, 111b, 118c, 232), neut. (241), Newt (172), newt (39d, 103d, 225), next (81a), noct- (93b), Nt. Wt. (241), nuit (50d), nyet (81d)

N U _ _   nubs, nude (17b, 126b), nudi- (93b), Nuer (222), nuit (50d), null (82c, 128d), Numa (102a), numb (33d, 126b), Nunn (173), nuns, nuts

_ N U _   gnus, knur (54d, 68c), Knut (33c, 164), onus (22d, 72d, 83a, 131a), snub (62a, 81b, 98b, 109a, 110c), Snug (193), snug (31c, 122a), unus (69c)

_ _ N U   Danu (199), **genu** (18c, 69d), **menu** (19a, 24c, 29c, 48b, 51a)

N _ _ U   Nosu (215)

_ N V _   envy (34a, 107a)

_ _ N X   jinx (61a), **lanx** (102a), **Lynx** (207), **lynx** (24a, 131d, 230), **Manx** (25c), **manx** (24d), **minx** (88b)

N _ _ X   N.Mex. (241)

N Y _ _   nyet (81d), **NYSE** (241)

_ N Y _   Anya (139), **Enyo** (129d), **onyx** (23c, 25d, 53b, 106c)

_ _ N Y   awny, **bony** (110a), **cony** (97a), **deny** (30c, 36a, 98d), **-geny** (117c), **-gyny** (117b), **liny, many** (82d), **piny, pony** (26b, 33b, 61a), **puny** (45a, 130c), **tiny** (77b, 110d), **Tony** (184), **viny, winy** (128c), **zany** (28b, 38a, 48b, 109c)

N _ _ Y   Nagy (61c, 172), **nary** (82c), **navy** (20a, 47c), **-nomy** (117c), **nosy** (63b)

_ _ N Z   Linz (33c, 213)

O A _ _   oafs, **Oahe** (33b), **Oahu** (64c), **oaks, oars, oast** (16b, 67b, 85c), **oath** (90b, 111c), **oats**

_ O A _   boar (60c, 89a, 118d, 132a, 230), **boas, boat** (81b, 108b), **Boaz** (103c, 197), **coal** (13a, 40c, 52a), **coat** (52d), **coax** (131b), **foal** (61b), **foam** (51c, 114a), **goad** (62c, 114b), **goal** (10d, 17c, 40d, 83a, 96c, 104d, 119d), **goas, goat** (81a, 102d, 230), **hoar** (51c, 131d), **hoax** (34a, 92b), **Joab** (33d, 197), **Joad** (55d), **Joan** (161), **koae** (58b), **load** (10b, 22d, 24b, 119a), **loaf** (61d, 73b, 130a), **loam** (39a, 111c), **loan** (17a, 78a), **Moab** (66b, 73b, 197), **moan** (32b, 112b), **moas, moat** (36d), **NOAA** (241), **Noah** (68d, 76b, 172, 197), **Noam** (172), **road** (31b, 38a, 121b, 130c), **roam** (123d, 129d), **roan** (61a, 98c, 131c), **roar** (12d, 13c), **soak** (9b, 37d, 104b, 115a), **soap** (17c), **soar** (48a), **toad** (17c, 225), **woad** (20a, 38d)

_ _ O A   anoa (48d, 85d, 132a, 229), **Aroa** (127d), **proa** (20c, 23d, 74b), **stoa** (29a, 91c), **whoa** (42c, 115d)

O _ _ A   obia (45c), **obra** (113a), **octa-** (92d), **odea** (29d), **Okla.** (211, 241), **okra** (57a, 127c), **olea** (84a), **Olga** (173), **olla** (30c, 36b, 66a, 112c, 113a, 131d), **onca** (246), **Oola** (11c), **Oona** (173), **-opia** (117b, 117c), **orca** (67b), **OSHA** (241), **Ossa** (79a, 84a, 121a), **ossa** (20d), **Otea** (64c)

O B _ _   Obad. (241), **Obal** (197), **Obed** (103c, 197), **obex** (21c), **obey** (29c, 59a, 67b, 10a), **obia** (45c), **obis, obit.** (34a, 52c, 241), **oboe** (58b, 80a, 80c, 133c), **obol** (26b, 83d), **obra** (113a)

_ O B _   Bobo (214), **Cobb** (146), **Cobh** (30d), **cobs, fobs, Gobi** (35a), **Gobo** (16d), **gobo** (66a), **gobs, goby** (46d, 228), **hobo** (123d,

127a), **hobs**, **jobo** (60c), **JOBS** (240), **jobs**, **koba** (13a, 130b), **Kobe** (60d, 218), **kobo** (220), **lobb** (77a), **lobe** (70d, 102c), **lobo** (122a, 133b), **lobs**, **mobs**, **nobs** (32a), **pobs** (91c), **Robb** (177), **robe** (52d), **robs**, **Roby** (178), **sobs**, **Tobe** (183), **tobe** (10c), **toby** (11b, 38a, 66d, 79d, 96a)

_ _ O B   **blob** (29a, 75b), **boob** (109c), **BYOB** (236), **doob** (18c), **glob** (75b), **knob** (57d, 82a, 95c), **scob** (120d), **slob** (126d), **snob** (88a, 111b)

O _ _ B   **Oreb** (197)

O C _ _   **Ochs** (173), **octa-** (92d), **octo** (69c), **octo-** (92d), **ocul-** (92d)

_ O C _   **boca** (113a), **boce** (22a, 46d), **Bock** (142), **bock** (18a, 70d), **Coca** (146), **coca** (28c, 81a), **cock** (26a, 44d, 102b, 103d, 119c, 127b), **coco** (86a), **dock** (33a, 68d, 88d, 108b, 112a, 131a), **docs** (88d), **Foch** (49c, 153), **foci** (25c), **hoch** (42c, 53d), **hock** (71b, 87b, 132c), **jock** (74c), **Koch** (53c, 164), **loch** (68b, 105b, 130a), **loci** (27a), **lock** (44c, 57b), **loco** (31d, 63b, 90d), **mock** (35a, 62a, 66b, 100c, 104d, 120a), **nock** (14c, 82c), **noct-** (93b), **pock** (62d), **poco** (72c), **Rock** (178), **rock** (118c, 124b), **sock** (96a, 116b, 132b), **soco** (21c), **tock** (10c), **toco** (123b), **voce** (65c, 234)

_ _ O C   **Apoc.** (235), **bloc** (126c), **BMOC** (236), **croc.** (237), **EEOC** (238), **floc** (111a), **Kroc** (165), **USOC** (244)

O _ _ C   **OPEC** (241), **otic** (15d, 39a)

O D _ _   **O'Day** (173), **odds** (10b, 11c, 26a, 95c), **odea** (29d), **Oder** (100d), **odes**, **Odin** (10b, 51c, 133b, 198), **odio** (65a), **odor** (104d, 111a, 115b), **-odus** (117c)

_ O D _   **bode** (48d, 91c), **Bodo** (69a), **body** (56c), **coda** (28b, 29d, 46a, 234), **code** (20c, 23d, 27b, 119a), **dodo** (19b, 38c, 225), **gods**, **hods**, **iodo-** (93b), **Jody** (161), **lode** (35a, 76b, 84c, 127d), **Lodi** (80d), **Lodz** (221), **mode** (44c, 74d, 116d, 130c), **node** (66c, 68c, 90d, 95c, 118c), **nods**, **-poda** (117c), **pods**, **Roda** (81d), **rode** (38b), **rods**, **soda** (18d, 38a, 111c, 131c), **Sodi** (197), **sods**, **Toda** (37d), **Todd** (183), **to-do** (21b, 22d, 29b, 52c, 115c), **tods**, **tody** (19b)

_ _ O D   **apod** (48c), **clod** (21a, 37b, 83a, 116d), **Exod.** (238), **food** (44b, 56d, 82d, 128b), **good** (127a, 131a), **Hood** (79b), **hood** (19c, 31c, 52c, 58c), **mood** (10d, 36c, 122d), **plod** (124d, 129b), **pood** (246), **prod** (38a, 46a, 54d, 59c, 62c, 63b, 65b, 81b, 82d, 90d, 121d, 126d), **quod** (94d, 96a), **rood** (32a), **shod**, **trod**, **Wood** (187), **wood** (55a)

O _ _ D   **Obad.** (241), **Obed** (103c, 197), **olid** (49a, 116c), **Ovid** (102a), **owed**

O E _ _   **oeno-** (94a), **oeuf** (50b)

_ O E _   Boer (10c, 112b), coed (107b), coef. (237), -coel (117a), Coen (146), Doeg (197), doer (87d), does, foes, goel (16a), goer, GOES (239), goes, hoed, hoer, hoes, Joel (161, 196, 197), Joes, Joey (161), joey (67a, 134d), koel (32c), Moes, Noel (172), noel (24b, 27a, 111d), noes (81b), poem (128a), poet (40b), Roeg (178), roes, toea (221), toed, toes, woes, Zoes

_ _ O E   aloe (10c, 19c, 59b, 59c, 71d, 75c, 90a, 122d), BPOE (236), evoe (16a, 100b), floe (61b), froe (28a, 122d, 123a, 130d), oboe (58b, 80a, 80c, 133c), Otoe (109d, 189), shoe (122b), sloe (15b, 19d, 51d, 90b, 132a)

O _ _ E   Oahe (33b), oboe (58b, 80a, 80c, 133c), ogee (14a, 77d, 90c), Ogle (173), ogle (43c, 71a, 73a), ogre (78b), ohne (54a), Okie (76d), olpe (70d, 132c), once (18b, 49a, 61d, 63d), onde (51b), ooze (43c, 72b, 79c, 87d), orfe (46d, 134b), orle (46a, 59b, 108a), Orne (23a), oste (20d), Otoe (109d, 189), Ouse (101a, 134d, 223)

O F _ _   offs (32a, 118d)

_ O F _   doff (99c, 119a), loft (15c, 55b, 129d), sofa (36d), soft (39b, 74c, 76d), toff (33c), toft (60d)

_ _ O F   goof (28b), hoof (126b), IOOF (240), Olof (173), Prof. (242), roof (61c), woof (32b, 37b, 121c, 131a)

O _ _ F   oeuf (50b), Olaf (82b, 128b, 173), Olof (173)

O G _ _   ogam (64b), ogee (14a, 77d, 90c), oggi (65c), Ogle (173), ogle (43c, 71a, 73a), OGPU (103c), ogre (78b), ogum (64b)

_ O G _   bogs, bogy (13c, 113b), cogs, doge (74a, 127d), dogs, dogy (38c), fogs, fogy (83d), Gogo (17a), gogo (111b), hogs, jogs, loge (120d), logo (22d, 29b), logs, logy (38c), mogo (115d), nogg (11b), nogs, Pogo (83d, 91d), pogy (68d, 75d, 78d), soga (52c), toga (101d), Togo (223), togs (28b), yoga (14d, 60a), yogh (12c), Yogi (187), yogi (60a)

_ _ O G   agog (39a, 42c, 67b), clog (20a, 108c), flog (131c), frog (17c, 225), geog. (239), grog (11a, 72b, 113d), slog (38b, 124d, 129b), smog (130d)

O _ _ G   olig- (93a), Oreg. (241), orig. (241)

O H _ _   Ohio (211), ohms, ohne (54a)

_ O H _   Bohr (15c, 33c, 142), Cohn (146), coho (103d), Doha (221), John (13b, 18a, 88b, 91b, 107c, 135a, 162, 193, 196), Kohl (18c, 164), kohl (43c), moho (60d), mohr (53b), poha (58c), Pohl (175), So-Ho (73a), to-ho (61d)

_ _ O H   Groh (156), pooh (42c)

O _ _ H   oath (90b, 111c), opah (22a, 46d), orch. (241), orth- (92d), ouch (42c, 63a)

O I _ _   oils, oily (44c, 83d, 126a)

_ O I _   boil (30c), bois (51b), coif (57b), coil (32d, 114a, 125c, 132b, 134a), coin (77b), coir (28d, 30d, 45c, 102b), coix (66c), doit (38d), FOIA (238), foil (16b, 45b, 76b, 116d, 121d), Foix (49c), join (30a, 126c), koil (32c), loin (33a, 75c), loir (37c), Lois (118a), moil (20c, 133d), noil (45d, 68c), noir (50a, 102c), roil (79c, 115c), soie (51a), soil (39a, 114c, 117d, 120d), soir (50b), toil (38b, 124d, 133c, 133d), void (12d, 40c, 82d, 127a)

_ _ O I   a moi (50d), Eloi (122b)

O _ _ I   oggi (65c), Omei (22b), omni- (92d), Omri (67d, 197), ophi- (93d), ossi- (92c)

_ O J _   mojo (129c), rojo (113a), soja (56c)

O K _ _   okas, okay (10b, 13d, 86d, 112a), Okie (76d), Okla. (211, 241), okra (57a, 127c)

_ O K _   Aoki (139), coke (28c, 52a, 62d), joke (66b), Koko (73a, 134d), koko (86d), koku (246), Loki (10b, 16c, 198), moke (37c), Moki (95d), poke (65b, 82d, 96a), poku (13a, 130b), poky (110d), roka (74a, 124a), soke (67c), woke, yoke (66c, 232), Yoko (187)

_ _ O K   amok (18c, 51b), book (71c, 129a), Cook (79a, 104b, 146), cook (68a), dook (77a), gook (110c), hook (24d, 27d, 55b), kook (39c), look (13c, 15a, 22b, 43d, 106b, 118b, 128c), nook (30d, 100a), rook (19b, 26c, 32b, 226), sook (23b), took (83b)

O _ _ K   Omsk (64b)

O L _ _   Olaf (82b, 128b, 173), olax (42b), olea (84a), oleo- (93b), Olga (173), olid (49a, 116c), olig- (93a), Olin (173), olio (36b, 60c, 75d, 77b, 92a), olla (30c, 36b, 66a, 112c, 113a, 131d), Olof (173), olor (118b), olpe (70d, 132c)

_ O L _   bola (53a), bold (33d), bole (27d, 98c, 124b), Böll (142), boll (90a, 90c), bolo (68a, 130d), Bolt (142), bolt (44c, 47c, 67a, 101c), COLA (237), cola (82d, 124a), cold (53b, 62a), Cole (146), coll. (237), Colm (146), Colo. (209, 237), colp (25c), cols, colt (61b, 100b, 134d, 135a), coly (79b), Dole (58c, 149), dole (91d, 99b, 131a), doll (45b, 96a), dolt (20a, 48b, 109c, 116d), fold (57d, 90b, 107d), -fold (117c), folk (87d, 124b), Gola (218), gola (33c, 37c, 77d), gold (74a, 134b, 245), golf (12a), hold (9c, 15a, 16c, 27d, 67b, 74b, 95b, 100a, 115a, 121a, 234), hole (9c, 13b, 84b, 89c, 109d), Holm (158), holm (60c, 64b, 83a), holo- (94a), Holt (158), holt (30c), holy (30b), lole (42a, 59c, 94c), joli (50d), Jolo (64d), jolt (20a, 66a, 108b), Kola (103c), kola (82d), koli (24d), Koln (100b, 216), kolo (48b, 106d), Lola (25b, 75a, 167), loll (38a, 73b, 98b), Lolo (69a, 215), mold (44c, 107c), Mole (69a), mole (19b, 22d, 106a, 114d, 230), Moll (171), moll (52d), molt (24d, 107d), moly (59b, 132a), Oola (11c), Pola (175), pole (101c, 113a, 129b,

133b, 246), **Polk** (175, 190), **poll** (129c), **Polo** (127d), **poly-** (93b), **role** (52a, 86d), **roll** (118c), **sola** (11d, 39b, 89c), **sold, sole** (42c, 46d, 47d, 84b, 87c, 109d, 111d, 228), **soli** (14b), **solo** (11d, 14b, 84a), **Sols, tola** (66d, 103a), **told** (99a), **tole** (41b, 76b), **toll** (18c, 94b, 100d), **tolu** (16d), **vola** (111c), **vole** (75b, 79b, 110b, 111b, 231), **volk** (54a), **volt** (40a, 61b, 246), **wold** (38d, 126d), **Wolf** (187, 207), **wolf** (23d, 231), **yolk** (128d), **Zola** (49c, 188)

_ _ O L   **AWOL** (236), **biol.** (236), **chol-** (92c), **chol.** (236), **cool** (23b, 82a), **ecol.** (238), **enol** (120a), **fool** (20b, 22c, 34a, 38d, 61d, 78d, 109c, 116d), **gaol** (94d), **geol.** (239), **Idol** (159), **idol** (39d, 44a, 44d, 58d, 62a, 85b, 133d), **obol** (26b, 83d), **pool** (52b, 90c, 91b, 130a), **STOL** (243), **tool** (25a, 62b, 127c), **viol** (80b), **VTOL** (244), **wool** (47c), **zool.** (244)

O _ _ L   **Obal** (197), **obol** (26b, 83d), **ocul-** (92d), **opal** (19c, 53b, 54c, 64a), **oral** (79b, 113d, 127c, 128a), **Orel** (173), **oval** (39d, 40b)

O M _ _   **Oman** (220), **Omar** (41c, 78d, 88a, 120c, 173, 197), **Omei** (22b), **omen** (15d, 48c, 48d, 91c, 94a, 109b), **omer** (59a), **omit** (40b, 81b, 87a, 110a), **omni-** (92d), **Omri** (67d, 197), **Omsk** (64b)

_ O M _   **boma** (10c), **bomb** (107d, 130c), **coma** (71c, 116d, 126a), **comb** (31d), **come** (94d), **comm.** (237), **Como** (68b, 146), **Comp.** (237), **comr.** (237), **dome** (32d, 102a), **doms, home** (61c, 99d), **homo** (69d), **homo-** (93c), **Homs** (222), **loma** (59d), **Lome** (223), **moms, noma** (52c), **nomo-** (92d), **-nomy** (117c), **pome** (51d), **Pomo** (189), **pomp** (85a, 85b), **Roma** (65c, 218), **Rome** (13c, 27c, 41d, 218), **romp** (51c), **soma** (12d, 20c, 62d), **some** (86d, 96b), **tomb** (22d), **tome** (20d, 129a), **Toms, -tomy** (117b), **womb** (127c)

_ _ O M   **Ahom** (69a), **atom** (77d, 131c), **boom** (43a, 112a, 113a), **brom-** (92c), **coom** (28c), **doom** (35b, 44d, 54b), **E-COM** (238), **Edom** (41c, 61d, 64b, 65b), **from** (18b, 115a), **geom.** (239), **glom** (115a), **loom** (13c, 40c, 57d, 109d, 130d), **PROM** (29c, 242), **prom** (33b), **room** (25d), **whom** (34d, 96d), **zoom** (23c)

O _ _ M   **ogam** (64b), **ogum** (64b), **ovum** (39d, 69c), **Ozem** (197)

O N _ _   **Onan** (66d), **onca** (246), **once** (18b, 49a, 61d, 63d), **onde** (51b), **ones** (87d), **only** (11d, 22d, 42c, 76a, 111d), **on to** (59b), **onus** (22d, 72d, 83a, 131a), **onyx** (23c, 25d, 53b, 106c)

_ O N _   **a-one** (42b, 46c, 123b), **Bona** (79b, 192), **bona** (69d, 70a), **Bond** (142), **bond** (10a, 28d, 71d, 72b, 78a, 107b, 118a, 122a), **bone** (46a, 110a), **bong** (111a), **Bonn** (18b, 216), **Bono** (142), **bony** (110a), **conc.** (237), **cond.** (237), **Cone** (146), **cone** (53c, 116c, 111d), **conf.** (237), **cong.** (237), **conj.** (237), **conk** (60b, 116b), **Conn.** (209, 237), **conn** (35d), **cons, cont.** (237), **cony** (97a), **don't, dona** (91d), **done** (85c), **dong** (224), **doni** (25d), **dons** (85d), **eons, fond** (10b, 73c), **font** (17a, 125d), **Gond** (62d), **gone** (9b, 34d, 36c), **gong** (80a), **goni-** (92c), **gono-** (93c), **Hond.** (239), **hone** (39c, 107d, 131c), **hong** (26d), **honk** (55b, 112b), **Iona** (25c, 64b,

397

202), **lone** (22c, 69b, 73d), **ions**, **Jong** (163), **Joni** (163), **Jons**, **lone** (109d, 111d), **Long** (167), **long** (31d), **Loni** (167), **lonk** (107d), **Mona** (171), **mona** (56d), **Monk** (171), **monk** (25c, 51c), **mono** (61c), **mono-** (93c), **mons** (69d, 133d), **Mont.** (211, 240), **mont** (50d), **Nona** (86c), **none** (82c), **Oona** (173), **oont** (23c, 230), **pond** (91b, 130a), **pone** (30d, 66c), **Pong** (125a), **Pons** (49d, 175), **pont** (50a), **pony** (26b, 33b, 61a), **sone** (246), **song** (14b, 61d, 125a), **sons** (83c), **Tone** (184), **tone** (9c, 82c, 89c), **tong** (26d), **Toni** (184), **tono-** (93c), **tons**, **Tony** (184), **Wong** (187), **wont** (9c, 33a, 57a, 92b), **yond** (36d), **zona** (108a), **zone** (18c, 36d, 40d, 118b)

_ _ O N   **aeon** (122b), **agon** (30b, 45c, 56b), **Amon** (67d, 198), **anon** (10c, 15d, 62a, 94a, 108d, 111d), **anon.** (235), **aton** (118a), **Avon** (107c), **axon** (81b), **azon** (10b), **Bion** (56b), **boon** (18c, 20a), **cion** (83c), **coon** (97a), **Dion** (149, 195), **Doon** (101a), **ebon** (19d), **econ.** (238), **Elon** (41c, 82b, 201), **Eton** (58b, 65b), **faon** (44d), **gaon** (66c), **goon** (116c), **hoon** (246), **icon** (62a, 103b), **ikon** (62a), **iron** (45b, 45c, 55a, 57c, 74c, 75b, 245), **jeon** (218), **Khon** (223), **Leon** (166, 222), **Lion** (193), **lion** (94b, 230), **loon** (19a, 19b, 226), **Lyon** (216), **Moon** (171), **moon** (33a, 104b), **muon** (71b), **neon** (53a, 71d, 245), **noon** (76c), **Oxon** (85d), **paon** (87b), **peon** (48c, 76c), **phon** (73b), **phon-** (93d), **pion** (42b), **poon** (103d, 124b), **-sion** (117a), **soon** (94a, 108d), **-tion** (117a, 117b), **toon** (74b), **-tron** (117b), **upon** (9b), **zion** (95a), **zoon** (39d)

O _ _ N   **Odin** (10b, 51c, 133b, 198), **Olin** (173), **Oman** (220), **omen** (15d, 48c, 48d, 91c, 94a, 109b), **Onan** (66d), **open** (18b, 23c, 49b, 63a, 83b, 85c, 95d, 126a, 126b, 126c), **Oran** (213), **oven** (61c, 67b), **oxen** (12d, 21b), **Oxon** (85d)

O O _ _   **Oola** (11c), **Oona** (173), **oont** (23c, 230), **ooze** (43c, 72b, 79c, 87d), **oozy** (106b, 110c)

_ O O _   **boob** (109c), **book** (71c, 129a), **boom** (43a, 112a, 113a), **boon** (18c, 20a), **boor** (17a, 38c, 88a, 103c), **boos**, **boot** (29c, 67b, 124d), **Cook** (79a, 104b, 146), **cook** (68a), **cool** (23b, 82a), **coom** (28c), **coon** (97a), **coop** (40d), **Coos** (189), **coos**, **coot** (19a, 38c, 56d, 75a, 83d, 105a, 225), **doob** (18c), **dook** (77a), **doom** (35b, 44d, 54b), **Doon** (101a), **door** (41b, 91c), **food** (44b, 56d, 82d, 128b), **fool** (20b, 22c, 34a, 38d, 61d, 78d, 109c, 116d), **foot** (17b, 87b, 246), **good** (127a, 131a), **goof** (28b), **gook** (110c), **goon** (116c), **goop** (110c), **Hood** (79b), **hood** (19c, 31c, 52c, 58c), **hoof** (126b), **hook** (24d, 27d, 55b), **hoon** (246), **hoop** (131d), **Hoot** (158), **hoot** (85c), **IOOF** (240), **kook** (39c), **look** (13c, 15a, 22b, 43d, 106b, 118b, 128c), **loom** (13c, 40c, 57d, 109b, 130d), **loon** (19a, 19b, 226), **loop** (27b, 82a), **Loos** (167), **loot** (21a, 58b, 89b, 90c, 103a, 113d), **mood** (10d, 36c, 122d), **Moon** (171), **moon** (33a, 104b), **Moor** (78c, 104b, 219), **moor** (12c, 15c, 58d, 130a), **moos**, **moot** (36d), **nook** (30d, 100a), **noon** (76c), **pood** (246), **pooh** (42c), **pool** (52b, 90c, 91b, 130a), **poon** (103d, 124b), **poop** (20c, 34b, 108b), **poor** (28d), **rood** (32a), **roof** (61c), **rook** (19b, 26c, 32b, 226), **room** (25d), **Roos** (53d), **Root** (178), **root** (17b, 17c, 102d), **sook** (23b), **soon** (94a, 108d), **soot** (24a, 28c, 68d), **took**

(83b), **tool** (25a, 62b, 127c), **toon** (74b), **toot** (112b), **Wood** (187), **wood** (55a), **woof** (32b, 37b, 121c, 131a), **wool** (47c), **woos, zool.** (244), **zoom** (23c), **zoon** (39d), **zoos, Zoot** (188)

_ _ O O   **broo** (105a), **ejoo** (45a), **shoo** (38a, 54b)

O _ _ O   **octo** (69c), **octo-** (92d), **odio** (65a), **oeno-** (94a), **Ohio** (211), **oleo-** (93b), **olio** (36b, 60c, 75d, 77b, 92a), **on to** (59b), **ordo** (21a, 27a, 92b), **orlo** (46a, 90b), **Oslo** (220), **Otho** (102a), **otro** (112c, 113a), **Otto** (53c, 173), **otto** (65a), **ouzo** (11a)

O P _ _   **opah** (22a, 46d), **opal** (19c, 53b, 54c, 64a), **OPEC** (241), **open** (18b, 23c, 49b, 63a, 83b, 85c, 95d, 126a, 126b, 126c), **ophi-** (93d), **-opia** (117b, 117c), **opts, opus** (29c, 80c, 129a, 133c)

_ O P _   **bops, cope** (23d, 30b, 30d, 52d, 128a), **copr-** (92d), **cops, Copt** (39d), **copy** (40c, 62a), **dopa** (89a), **dope** (10b, 38b, 81a), **dopp** (32d), **dopy** (71c), **fops, HOPE** (239), **Hope** (158), **hope** (42d), **Hopi** (95d, 189), **hops** (18a), **koph** (12a), **Kops** (67b), **lope** (39b, 52a, 52b), **lops, mope** (22a, 117d), **mops, mopy** (72b), **nope** (81b), **Pope** (27c, 175), **pope** (19c, 27a, 91b), **pops, rope** (30d, 69b, 100b), **ropy** (116b), **soph.** (243), **sops, tope** (107d, 229), **topi** (30d, 89c), **topo.** (243), **tops**

_ _ O P   **alop** (38a), **atop** (85c, 126d), **chop** (75c), **clop** (61a), **coop** (40d), **crop** (31d, 108d), **drop** (44a, 48d, 77a, 84a, 86d, 90b, 90c, 110d, 120a), **flop** (44a), **glop** (75b), **goop** (110c), **hoop** (131d), **knop** (68c), **loop** (27b, 82a), **plop** (44a, 130b), **poop** (20c, 34b, 108b), **prop** (118a), **scop** (90c), **shop** (62d, 100a), **slop** (48b, 111b), **stop** (9a, 14c, 17a, 25b, 40d, 57c, 84c, 131d), **trop** (51b, 123a), **whop** (60b)

O R _ _   **oral** (79b, 113d, 127c, 128a), **Oran** (213), **orbs, orca** (67b), **orch.** (241), **orcs, ordo** (21a, 27a, 92b), **Oreb** (197), **Oreg.** (241), **Orel** (173), **ores, orfe** (46d, 134b), **orgy** (24b, 100b, 104b), **orig.** (241), **orle** (46a, 59b, 108a), **orlo** (46a, 90b), **Orne** (23a), **orth-** (92d), **orts** (105c), **oryx** (13a, 231)

_ O R _   **bora** (132b), **bord** (77a), **bore** (23b, 37d, 87d, 121d), **Borg** (142), **Born** (142), **born** (71d, 81a, 81b), **boro** (114a), **Bors** (102c), **bort** (35c), **Boru** (142), **Cora** (34d, 126a), **cora** (53b), **Cord** (146), **cord** (32c, 43b), **CORE** (237), **core** (25c, 41d, 58d), **corf** (28c), **Cork** (217), **cork** (90b, 116a, 132c, 133b), **corm** (22c, 115a), **corn** (74b, 94b), **Corp.** (237), **Dora** (30c, 33d, 35c), **Dore** (49c), **dore** (54b, 89a), **dorm** (104d), **Dorn** (149), **dorp** (57c, 128b), **dorr** (54c), **Dors** (149), **dory** (20b, 47b), **fora** (75a, 101d), **forb** (59c), **Ford** (153, 191, 194), **ford** (129a), **fore** (51c, 108b), **fork** (13c, 36d, 37a, 119a), **form** (44c, 107c, 127a), **fort** (51c, 116c), **Gore** (155, 191), **gore** (87c, 88d, 124b), **Gort** (101b), **gory** (20a), **hora** (21a, 33b), **Horn** (24a), **horn** (13a, 31a, 124d), **hors** (50d), **hort.** (239), **Jory** (163), **kora** (130b), **kori** (10b, 60a), **Lord** (167), **lord** (82a), **lore** (60b, 70d, 71b, 132d), **Lori** (167), **lorn** (49a), **loro** (86d), **lory** (86d), **mora** (46b, 48c, 52b, 56d, 65a, 76b, 118d), **More** (171), **more** (43c, 56a),

morn (33d), **Moro** (171), **moro** (88c), **Mors** (34a, 198), **Mort** (171),
Nora (61b, 81d, 172), **Nore** (120d), **nori** (11b, 105d), **Norm** (172),
norm (16a, 86b, 97d, 114d), **Norn** (82a), **porc** (50d), **pore** (48c,
84b, 84d), **pork** (55c, 75c), **porn** (79c), **Port.** (242), **port** (58a,
132c), **Rory** (178), **sora** (19a, 97b), **sorb** (13c, 79a, 107a, 110b),
sore (12d, 106c), **sori** (45b), **sors** (69c), **sort** (27d, 36d, 67c, 106d,
109b, 113b, 127b, 132d), **tora** (13a, 58b), **tore**, **Tori** (184), **tori**
(30c), **Torn** (184), **torn** (99c), **toro** (31c, 112c), **torr** (246), **tors**, **tort**
(27c, 71a, 134c), **tory** (22a, 30b, 73c), **-vora** (117c), **-vore** (117c),
word (95a, 120c, 121d), **wore**, **work** (52a, 116c), **worm** (88a),
worn (107b), **wort** (59b, 92a), **yore** (12c, 23a, 55b, 73a, 83d, 87a,
122b), **York** (41a, 187, 192, 193, 194), **zori** (108c)

_ _ O R amor (112d), **Amor** (32d, 198), **asor** (59a), **-ator** (117c), **boor** (17a,
38c, 88a, 103c), **Dior** (149), **door** (41b, 91c), **flor** (46a, 108a), **ghor**
(127b), **Gyor** (217), **Igor** (49b, 159), **Ivor** (159), **Moor** (78c, 104b,
219), **moor** (12c, 15c, 58d, 130a), **odor** (104d, 111a, 115b), **olor**
(118b), **poor** (28d), **spor-** (93d), **Thor** (10b, 76c, 77c, 83b, 121d,
183, 198)

O _ _ R Oder (100d), **odor** (104d, 111a, 115b), **olor** (118b), **Omar** (41c,
78d, 88a, 120c, 173, 197), **omer** (59a), **over** (9b, 9d, 14c, 32a, 87a,
99c), **oyer** (31c)

O S _ _ OSHA (241), **-osis** (117a), **Oslo** (220), **Ossa** (79a, 84a, 121a),
ossa (20d), **ossi-** (92c), **oste** (20d)

_ O S _ bosa (13d), **bosc** (87b), **bosh** (82a), **bosk** (133b), **bo's'n** (20c,
88b), **boss** (40c, 116c), **cosh** (60b), **cosm-** (93d), **cost** (26a, 94b),
dose (94a), **doss** (18a), **dost** (128a), **foss** (36d), **gosh** (42a, 53b),
hose (115c), **hosp.** (239), **host** (14c, 42a, 79d), **José** (163), **Josh**
(163), **josh** (17a, 66b, 66d, 90d), **joss** (26d, 62c), **Koso** (108d),
koss (246), **lose** (48d), **losh** (40b), **loss** (35a, 94d, 130a), **LOST**
(240), **lost** (77b, 130a), **Moss** (171), **moss** (71c, 86c, 125a), **most**
(74b, 78c), **nose** (89d, 95c), **noso-** (92d), **Nosu** (215), **nosy** (63b),
pose (9d, 15c, 94b), **posh** (21a, 40b), **Post** (175), **post** (69c, 74b,
81c, 115a), **posy** (82b, 100d), **Rosa** (178), **Rose** (9a, 178), **Ross**
(178, 193, 195, 207, 208), **ross** (17b, 119c), **rosy** (54d, 84c), **so-so**
(76c, 86d, 122d), **tosh** (82a), **Tosk** (213), **toss** (22c, 47c, 121c)

_ _ O S Amos (108a, 138, 196, 197), **apos.** (235), **boos**, **Bros.** (236), **Coos**
(189), **coos**, **dios** (112d), **duos**, **egos**, **Enos** (9d, 42a, 107a, 151,
197), **epos** (41b, 59c, 90c), **Eros** (32d, 132c, 195, 198), **glos.** (239),
Gros (49c), **gros** (38c, 43d, 109c), **Keos** (64c), **Laos** (218), **Leos**,
Loos (167), **mhos**, **moos**, **naos** (25b, 104a, 120b), **pros**, **rhos**,
Roos (53d), **Taos** (81c), **Teos** (64a), **Thos.** (74d), **thos** (65b),
twos, **udos**, **woos**, **zoos**

O _ _ S oafs, **oaks**, **oars**, **oats**, **obis**, **Ochs** (173), **odds** (10b, 11c, 26a,
95c), **odes**, **-odus** (117c), **offs** (32a, 118d), **ohms**, **oils**, **okas**, **ones**
(87d), **onus** (22d, 72c, 83a, 131a), **opts**, **opus** (29c, 80c, 129a,
133c), **orbs**, **orcs**, **ores**, **orts** (105c), **-osis** (117a), **Otis** (12b, 63d,
173), **otus** (54b), **ours** (95a), **outs**, **owes**, **owls**, **owns** (91d), **oyes**
(31c, 32c, 58d)

O T _ _   Otea (64c), Otho (102a), otic (15d, 39a), Otis (12b, 63d, 173), Otoe (109d, 189), otro (112c, 113a), Otto (53c, 173), otto (65a), otus (54b)

_ O T _   both (122c, 125c), bots, bott (27d), cote (19b, 107d, 108a), coto (17b, 75c), cots, Coty (49d, 147), dote (85c), doth (128a), dots, Goth (120d), Hoth (20a), iota (11d, 66d, 122c, 131c), jota (112c), jots, koto (66a), Loti (49c, 95d), loti (218), lots (26a), Lott (167), mote (113b), Moth (193), moth (22d, 71b, 229), moto (79c), mots, Mott (171), nota (69d), note (15c, 71c, 75d, 83b, 95a, 98c, 99c, 122d, 129c, 234), noto- (92c), pots, rota (25a, 27a, 31c, 101d, 102b), ROTC (242), Rote (178), rote (75d, 99d, 118a), Roth (178), roti (51a), rots, sots, tote (22a, 24c, 86c), toti- (94a), Toto (37b, 133a), tots, vota (102a), vote (49b, 128d)

_ _ O T   blot (115b), boot (29c, 67b, 124d), clot (28c, 73c), coot (19a, 38c, 56d, 75a, 83d, 105a, 225), foot (17b, 87b, 246), Hoot (158), hoot (85c), knot (76d, 82a, 232), loot (21a, 58b, 89b, 90c, 103a, 113d), moot (36d), phot (246), plot (23a, 30b, 104d, 123c), Prot. (242), riot (85a, 101c, 125a), Root (178), root (17b, 17c, 102d), ryot (62d), Scot (59d), Scot. (242), shot (12b, 70c), slot (12d, 13b, 34c, 84b, 123c), snot (62c, 88a), soot (24a, 28c, 68d), spot (35d, 72d, 79d, 89d, 114c), stot (134d), toot (112b), trot (66c, 85b), Zoot (188)

O _ _ T   oast (16b, 67b, 85c), obit. (34a, 52c, 241), omit (40b, 81b, 87a, 110a), oont (23c, 230), oust (35b, 40a, 42b, 96c)

O U _ _   ouch (42c, 63a), ours (95a), Ouse (101a, 134d, 223), oust (35b, 40a, 42b, 96c), outs, ouzo (11a)

_ O U _   aout (49d), bout (30b), coup (75b, 116c, 120b), Doug (150), dour (54d, 78d, 107b, 117d), -eous (117a), foud (44c, 74a), foul (9a, 126b), four (72c, 120d), gout (14d, 113d), hour (122b), -ious (117a), loud (115b), loup (50d, 51b, 105c), lour (33d, 54d), lout (21a, 83a), moue (50d, 134c), noun (86d, 116d), nous (50d, 51b), pouf (48c, 58d, 85a), pour (120a), pout (117d), roue (34a, 97c), roup (92a), rout (34c, 36c), roux (104b), souk (17d, 74d), Soul (181), soul (95d, 113d, 128c), soup (75c), sour (15b, 119d), sous (51b), tour (66d), tous (49d), tout (49d, 95a, 97b), vous (51b), Wouk (187), you'd (30c), your (95a)

_ _ O U   abou (44d), acou- (93a), Alou (138), Chou (26d), chou (50a), clou (50d), shou (26d), thou (95b)

O _ _ U   Oahu (64c), OGPU (103c)

O V _ _   oval (39d, 40b), oven (61c, 67b), over (9b, 9d, 14c, 32a, 87a, 99c), Ovid (102a), ovum (39d, 69c)

_ O V _   cove (17d, 58a, 130a), Dove (150), dove (19a, 89a, 225), govt. (239), Hova (219), hove (71d), Jove (67c, 198), Love (167), love (24b, 120c), move (10d, 36b, 62b, 125b), Nova (203), nova (114d), nove (65c), rove (97d, 101a, 129d), wove

401

_ _ O V   Azov (19d, 103c), Lvov (223), Prov. (242)

O W _ _   owed, owes, owls, owns (91d)

_ O W _   Bowe (142), bowk (115a), bowl (78d, 119a), bows, cowl (78b), cows (21b), dowd (107b), Down (150), down (35a, 45a, 232), fowd (44c, 74a), fowl (19b), gown (37d), Howe (17c, 63d, 159), howl (12d, 17d, 32b, 114b), Iowa (189, 210), jowl (26b, 35c), Lowe (167), lows, mown, mows, rows, sown, sows, town (57c, 128b), tows, vows, wows, yowl (12d, 32b)

_ _ O W   alow (18c, 126a), avow (9d, 15a, 16c, 29d, 30a, 34b, 85c), blow (42d), brow (48d, 59d), chow (37a, 227), clow (47c, 110d), Crow (189), crow (19b, 19d, 20b, 43c, 225), dhow (69b, 84d), enow (105a), flow (14b, 37d, 116b), frow (123a), glow (108a), grow (15d, 41a, 42d, 43a, 114a, 118c), know (13a, 16c), meow (25a), plow (32c, 122a), prow (20c, 108b, 115b), scow (20c, 47b), show (9d, 34d, 35a, 36c, 43a, 74c), slow (34a, 35d, 58a, 110d, 116d), Snow (181), snow (130d), stow (85b), trow (18b)

O X _ _   oxen (12d, 21b), Oxon (85d)

_ O X _   coxa (60b), doxy (133b), Foxx (153), foxy (14d, 31d, 132a), moxa (25b, 26d, 133d)

_ _ O X   Knox (49a)

O _ _ X   obex (21c), olax (42b), onyx (23c, 25d, 53b, 106c), oryx (13a, 231)

O Y _ _   oyer (31c), oyes (31c, 32c, 58d), oyez (31c, 32c, 58d)

_ O Y _   Boyd (142), boys, coyo (16a, 26d), Foyt (153), Goya (112c), hoya (12c, 15d, 130c), Hoyt (159), joys, Roys, soya (112c), soys, toyo (58b, 65d, 116b), toys, yoyo (88a)

_ _ O Y   ahoy (57b, 81a), Amoy (69a), buoy (26a, 47c), choy (39b, 98c), cloy (54d, 104b, 118a), ploy (14d, 116a), Troy (184), troy (119c, 131a)

O _ _ Y   obey (29c, 59a, 67b, 10a), O'Day (173), oily (44c, 83d, 126a), okay (10b, 13d, 86d, 112a), only (11d, 22c, 42c, 76a, 111d), oozy (106b, 110c), orgy (24b, 100b, 104b), Ozzy (173)

O Z _ _   Ozem (197), Ozzy (173)

_ O Z _   boza (13d), bozo (38d, 88a), Cozy (147), cozy (39b, 111b), doze (110b), dozy (110c), kozo (86b), ooze (43c, 72b, 79c, 87d), oozy (106b, 110c)

O _ _ Z   oyez (31c, 32c, 58d)

P A _ _   Paar (173), PABA (86b), paca (25b, 101c), Pace (204), pace (52a, 113c, 129b), pack (16d, 22c, 105c, 232, 246), paco (11d, 109c),

pact (10d, 11c, 17b, 20d), **pads**, **Page** (173, 193, 194), **page** (12d, 41c, 48b, 70d, 107a), **paha** (60a), **paid** (99a), **pail** (30b), **pain** (10b, 61d), **pair** (21c, 31b, 90d, 119c, 125c), **pale** (19d, 86a, 88d, 129d), **Pali** (22b, 104b, 127c), **pall** (28b, 122b, 130d), **palm** (124a), **palp** (13a, 45a, 123b), **pals**, **Pams**, **pane** (114c, 114d), **Pang** (125a), **pang** (85d, 114b, 121c), **pans**, **pant** (18a, 21d), **paon** (87b), **papa** (12a, 44b), **Papp** (173), **paps**, **Para** (18b, 214), **para** (112d, 214, 215, 222, 224), **pard** (24d), **pare** (87c, 98d), **pari-** (92d), **park** (53b, 95d), **parr** (103d, 109d), **pars**, **part** (11c, 43d, 49b, 57b, 91d, 106d), **pass** (13d, 21d, 84a, 85c, 106c), **past** (55b, 60b, 122a), **Pate** (174), **pate** (32b, 58c), **path** (101a, 102c, 130c), **pats**, **patu** (130d), **Paul** (18a, 91b, 174), **pave** (66b), **Pavo** (87b, 207), **pawl** (73d), **pawn** (26c, 60c, 90b), **paws**, **pays**

_ **P A** _   **apar** (14b), **opah** (22a, 46d), **opal** (19c, 53b, 54c, 64a), **spad** (80b, 89d), **Spam** (73c), **span** (21d, 32a, 38d, 49a, 81d, 85d, 98a, 120a, 120c, 122a, 232), **spar** (21b, 22c, 52a, 77a, 90d, 101c, 108b), **spas**, **spat** (14b, 85d, 96b, 102c), **spay** (115b), **upas** (66a, 90d, 124a)

_ _ **P A**   **arpa** (65a), **capa** (122c), **dopa** (89a), **FEPA** (238), **Hupa** (15b, 189), **Napa** (23b, 132c), **napa** (54d, 70d), **nipa** (15b, 38a, 39b, 86a, 120d), **papa** (12a, 44b), **pupa** (27a, 28d, 63b), **sapa** (55d), **tapa** (17b, 28b, 43b, 45c, 79d, 86b, 91a)

P _ _ **A**   **PABA** (86b), **paca** (25b, 101c), **paha** (60a), **papa** (12a, 44b), **Para** (18b, 214), **para** (112d, 214, 215, 222, 224), **peba** (14b), **pega** (46d), **Peña** (174), **pica** (53c, 125d), **pika** (30c, 72c, 101c, 231), **Pima** (189), **pima** (31a), **pina** (29d), **Pisa** (70d), **pita** (11d, 25c, 45c), **plea** (42d, 92b, 118a), **-poda** (117c), **poha** (58c), **Pola** (175), **proa** (20c, 23d, 74b), **pula** (214), **puma** (24d, 31b, 79a, 231), **Puna** (12c), **puna** (28d, 90b, 132b), **pupa** (27a, 28d, 63b), **pyla** (21c)

P _ _ **B**   **pleb** (29b)

_ **P C** _   **SPCA** (243)

_ _ **P C**   **FEPC** (238)

P _ _ **C**   **pisc-** (93a), **porc** (50d)

P _ _ **D**   **paid** (99a), **pard** (24d), **pend** (16c, 58a), **pied** (114a, 127b), **pled**, **plod** (124d, 129b), **pond** (91b, 130a), **pood** (246), **prod** (38a, 46a, 54d, 59c, 62c, 63b, 65b, 81b, 82d, 90d, 121d, 126d)

P E _ _   **peag** (129d), **peak** (11d, 31d, 32c, 59a, 59d, 117d, 135a), **peal** (100d), **pear** (51d, 124a), **peas**, **peat** (52a, 127c), **peba** (14b), **Peck** (174), **peck** (22d, 246), **Pecs** (217), **-pede** (117b), **pedi-** (93a), **pedo-** (92d, 93a), **peek** (73a), **Peel** (174), **peel** (43a, 86c), **peen** (57d), **peep** (73a, 87c), **peer** (41b, 73a, 82a), **pega** (46d), **pegs**, **Pegu** (97d), **peho** (81c), **Pele** (58c), **pelf** (21a, 46a, 100c), **Pell** (174), **pelt** (28c, 43a, 57b, 59d), **pelu** (26c), **Peña** (174), **pend** (16c, 58a), **Penn** (174), **Penn.** (211, 242), **pens**, **pent** (30a), **peon** (48c, 76c), **pepo** (32c, 75d, 96a), **peps**, **pere** (49d, 50b), **peri** (44a, 88a),

peri- (92c), **perk** (28d, 51c), **pern** (60d), **pero** (112d), **Pers.** (242), **pert** (49a, 62b, 72c, 104b, 114a, 128d), **Peru** (221), **peso** (215, 216, 217, 219, 221, 224), **pest** (82d, 88a, 89d), **Pete** (85a, 174), **Peto** (193), **peto** (129b), **petr-** (93d), **pets, Peul** (217, 219, 221), **peur** (50b), **pews**

_ P E _   **aped, aper** (28b, 77a), **apes, apex** (32c, 59a, 59d, 87b, 89b, 123a, 135a), **epee** (45b, 118d), **OPEC** (241), **open** (18b, 23c, 49b, 63a, 83b, 85c, 95d, 126a, 126b, 126c), **spec.** (243), **sped, Spee** (53c, 55c), **Spes** (198), **spet** (17b), **spew** (40a)

_ _ P E   **cape** (37c, 58d, 74d, 95a), **cepe** (39c), **cope** (23d, 30b, 30d, 52d, 128a), **dope** (10b, 38b, 81a), **dupe** (25a, 34a, 48b, 56d, 74d, 118d), **gape** (134b), **HOPE** (239), **Hope** (158), **hope** (42d), **hype** (95a), **jape** (66c), **lope** (39b, 52a, 52b), **mope** (22a, 117d), **nape** (16b, 82d), **nope** (81b), **olpe** (70d, 132c), **pipe** (80c, 125a, 131c), **Pope** (27c, 175), **pope** (19c, 27a, 91b), **rape** (107b), **ripe** (47b, 75b), **rope** (30d, 69b, 100b), **rype** (95d), **sipe** (122b), **tape** (19a, 98c), **tope** (107d, 229), **type** (27d, 112a, 113b), **wipe** (123d), **yipe** (42c)

P _ _ E   **Pace** (204), **pace** (52a, 113c, 129b), **Page** (173, 193, 194), **page** (12d, 41c, 48b, 70d, 107a), **pale** (19d, 86a, 88d, 129d), **pane** (114c, 114d), **pare** (87c, 98d), **Pate** (174), **pate** (32b, 58c), **pave** (66b), **-pede** (117b), **Pele** (58c), **pere** (49d, 50b), **Pete** (85a, 174), **pice** (62d, 220), **pike** (46d, 59d, 90c, 113b, 228), **pile** (17a, 58d, 79a), **pine** (30a, 42a, 69a, 73a, 124a, 134b), **pipe** (80c, 125a, 131c), **poke** (65b, 82d, 96a), **pole** (101c, 113a, 129b, 133b, 246), **pome** (51d), **pone** (30d, 66c), **Pope** (27c, 175), **pope** (19c, 27a, 91b), **pore** (48c, 84b, 84d), **pose** (9d, 15c, 94b), **prae** (69c), **pree** (105b), **puce** (42a, 96c), **puke** (99a), **pule** (131c), **pure** (9b, 26b, 126a, 126c), **Pyle** (175), **pyre** (52c)

P _ _ F   **pelf** (21a, 46a, 100c), **Piaf** (49d, 100c, 175), **pouf** (48c, 58d, 85a), **Prof.** (242), **puff** (20a, 74a)

_ P G _   **LPGA** (240)

P _ _ G   **Pang** (125a), **pang** (85d, 114b, 121c), **peag** (129d), **phag-** (92d), **Ping** (125a), **ping** (76b), **plug** (116a, 133d), **Pong** (125a), **prig** (85c), **pung** (21c, 110c)

P H _ _   **phag-** (92d), **Phar.** (242), **phen-** (92c), **phew** (42c), **Phil** (175), **Phil.** (242), **phis, Phiz** (35c), **phon** (73b), **phon-** (93d), **phot** (246)

_ P H _   **ophi-** (93d)

_ _ P H   **Alph** (101a), **amph.** (235), **Caph** (207), **koph** (12a), **neph-** (92d), **soph.** (243), **xiph-** (93d), **Zeph.** (244)

P _ _ H   **path** (101a, 102c, 130c), **pish** (42c), **pith** (30d, 41d, 51d, 54c, 74b, 75a, 90a, 97c, 120d), **pooh** (42c), **posh** (21a, 40b), **Ptah** (75d, 198), **push** (38a, 46a, 108d, 121d)

P I _ _   **Piaf** (49d, 100c, 175), **pica** (53c, 125d), **pice** (62d, 220), **pick** (27a,

90b), **Pico** (100d), **picr-** (92c), **Pict** (22a), **pied** (114a, 127b), **pien** (14c), **Pier** (175), **pier** (21d, 66b, 68d, 131b), **pies, Piet** (175), **piet** (26b, 74b), **pigs, pika** (30c, 72c, 101c, 231), **pike** (46d, 59d, 90c, 113b, 228), **piki** (74b), **pile** (17a, 58d, 79a), **pili-** (93a), **pill** (119a), **Pima** (189), **pima** (31a), **pimp** (94d), **pina** (29d), **pine** (30a, 42a, 69a, 73a, 124a, 134b), **Ping** (125a), **ping** (76b), **pink** (24b), **pins, pint** (54b, 246), **piny, pion** (42b), **pipe** (80c, 125a, 131c), **pips, pirn** (20c, 98d, 130d), **Pisa** (70d), **pisc-** (93a), **pish** (42c), **pisk** (12b), **pita** (11d, 25c, 45c), **pith** (30d, 41d, 51d, 54c, 74b, 75a, 90a, 97c, 120d), **pits, Pitt** (41a, 175), **pity** (29b, 87a, 134b), **Pius** (91b)

_ P I _   **Apia** (91c, 224), **Apis** (22c, 40a, 95d, 103b), **epic** (59c, 90c), **Epis.** (238), **epit.** (238), **ipil** (88c), **-opia** (117b, 117c), **spin** (100b, 131c), **spir-** (92d), **spit** (90d, 101b)

_ _ P I   **Hapi** (198), **hapi** (53b), **Hopi** (95d, 189), **Impi** (135c), **kepi** (58d, 76d), **topi** (30d, 89c), **Tupi** (12b)

P _ _ I   **Pali** (22b, 104b, 127c), **pari-** (92d), **pedi-** (93a), **peri** (44a, 88a), **peri-** (92c), **piki** (74b), **pili-** (93a), **puli** (37b, 61c, 227), **puri** (62d)

P _ _ K   **pack** (16d, 22c, 105c, 232, 246), **park** (53b, 95d), **peak** (11d, 31d, 32c, 59a, 59d, 117d, 135a), **Peck** (174), **peck** (22d, 246), **peek** (73a), **perk** (28d, 51c), **pick** (27a, 90b), **pink** (24b), **pisk** (12b), **pock** (62d), **Polk** (175, 190), **pork** (55c, 75c), **Puck** (107c, 193), **puck** (36b, 55a, 60c, 77b), **pulk** (79c), **punk** (12a, 123b)

P L _ _   **plan** (13d, 15c, 35b, 76b, 95a, 104d), **plat** (74d, 90b), **play** (51c, 52b, 87d, 91d, 114a), **plea** (42d, 92b, 118a), **pleb** (29b), **pled, plew** (18a), **plod** (124d, 129b), **plop** (44a, 130b), **plot** (23a, 30b, 104d, 123c), **plow** (32c, 122a), **ploy** (14d, 116a), **plug** (116a, 133d), **plum** (51d, 124a), **plus** (12c, 62c)

_ _ P L   **dipl-** (93d), **hapl-** (93c)

P _ _ L   **pail** (30b), **pall** (28b, 122b, 130d), **Paul** (18a, 91b, 174), **pawl** (73d), **peal** (100d), **Peel** (174), **peel** (43a, 86c), **Pell** (174), **Peul** (217, 219, 221), **Phil** (175), **Phil.** (242), **pill** (119a), **Pohl** (175), **poll** (129c), **pool** (52b, 90c, 91b, 130a), **pull** (11d, 37d, 123c), **purl** (68c), **pyel-** (93c)

P _ _ M   **palm** (124a), **plum** (51d, 124a), **poem** (128a), **pram** (16a, 24c), **prim** (115b), **PROM** (29c, 242), **prom** (33b)

_ _ P N   **ESPN** (26a)

P _ _ N   **pain** (10b, 61d), **paon** (87b), **pawn** (26c, 60c, 90b), **peen** (57d), **Penn** (174), **Penn.** (211, 242), **peon** (48c, 76c), **pern** (60d), **phen-** (92c), **phon** (73b), **phon-** (93d), **pien** (14c), **pion** (42b), **pirn** (20c, 98d, 130d), **plan** (13d, 15c, 35b, 76b, 95a, 104d), **poon** (103d, 124b), **porn** (79c)

P O _ _   **pobs** (91c), **pock** (62d), **poco** (72c), **-poda** (117c), **pods, poem** (128a), **poet** (40b), **Pogo** (83d, 91d), **pogy** (68d, 75d, 78d), **poha**

(58c), **Pohl** (175), **poke** (65b, 82d, 96a), **poku** (13a, 130b), **poky** (110d), **Pola** (175), **pole** (101c, 113a, 129b, 133b, 246), **Polk** (175, 190), **poll** (129c), **Polo** (127d), **poly-** (93b), **pome** (51d), **Pomo** (189), **pomp** (85a, 85b), **pond** (91b, 130a), **pone** (30d, 66c), **Pong** (125a), **Pons** (49d, 175), **pont** (50a), **pony** (26b, 33b, 61a), **pood** (246), **pooh** (42c), **pool** (52b, 90c, 91b, 130a), **poon** (103d, 124b), **poop** (20c, 34b, 108b), **poor** (28d), **Pope** (27c, 175), **pope** (19c, 27a, 91b), **pops**, **porc** (50d), **pore** (48c, 84b, 84d), **pork** (55c, 75c), **porn** (79c), **Port.** (242), **port** (58a, 132c), **pose** (9d, 15c, 94b), **posh** (21a, 40b), **Post** (175), **post** (69c, 74b, 81c, 115a), **posy** (82b, 100d), **pots**, **pouf** (48c, 58d, 85a), **pour** (120a), **pout** (117d)

_ **P O** _   **Apoc.** (235), **apod** (48c), **apos.** (235), **BPOE** (236), **epos** (41b, 59c, 90c), **spor-**(93d), **spot** (35d, 72d, 79d, 89d, 114c), **upon** (9b)

_ _ **P O**   **cipo** (71c), **hypo** (88d), **Li Po** (26d), **lipo-** (92d), **mapo** (55a), **pepo** (32c, 75d, 96a), **topo.** (243), **typo** (41c, 94c), **USPO** (244)

P _ _ **O**   **paco** (11d, 109c), **Pavo** (87b, 207), **pedo-** (92d, 93a), **peho** (81c), **pepo** (32c, 75d, 96a), **pero** (112d), **peso** (215, 216, 217, 219, 221, 224), **Peto** (193), **peto** (129b), **Pico** (100d), **poco** (72c), **Pogo** (83d, 91d), **Polo** (127d), **Pomo** (189), **puno** (132b), **Puzo** (175), **pyro-** (93a)

_ _ **P P**   **Capp** (144), **Depp** (149), **dopp** (32d), **hipp-** (93a), **Lapp** (82b, 222), **Papp** (173), **repp** (43b), **typp** (134b), **yapp** (20d)

P _ _ **P**   **palp** (13a, 45a, 123b), **Papp** (173), **peep** (73a, 87c), **pimp** (94d), **plop** (44a, 130b), **pomp** (85a, 85b), **poop** (20c, 34b, 108b), **prep** (104d), **prop** (118a), **pulp** (51d, 74a, 75b, 86b), **pump** (108c)

_ **P Q** _   **SPQR** (243)

P R _ _   **prae** (69c), **pram** (16a, 24c), **prat** (23a), **pray** (18c, 41b), **pree** (105b), **prep** (104d), **Pres.** (242), **pres** (50d), **prey** (128b), **prig** (85c), **prim** (115b), **proa** (20c, 23d, 74b), **prod** (38a, 46a, 54d, 59c, 62c, 63b, 65b, 81b, 82d, 90d, 121d, 126d), **Prof.** (242), **PROM** (29c, 242), **prom** (33b), **prop** (118a), **pros**, **Prot.** (242), **Prov.** (242), **prow** (20c, 108b, 115b), **Prut** (33d)

_ **P R** _   **spry** (9d, 72c, 81d)

_ _ **P R**   **copr-** (92d), **cupr-** (92d)

P _ _ **R**   **Paar** (173), **pair** (21c, 31b, 90d, 119c, 125c), **parr** (103d, 109d), **pear** (51d, 124a), **peer** (41b, 73a, 82a), **petr-** (93d), **peur** (50b), **Phar.** (242), **picr-** (92c), **Pier** (175), **pier** (21d, 66b, 68d, 131b), **poor** (28d), **pour** (120a), **pter-** (94a), **purr** (112a)

P S _ _   **psis**

_ **P S** _   **apse** (12a, 27a, 98b, 106c, 127c), **ipse** (37a, 69d)

_ _ P S   **Alps** (79b), **amps, asps, bops, caps, cops, cups, daps, dips, fops, gaps, gyps, hips, hops** (18a), **imps, kips, Kops** (67b), **laps, lips, lops, maps, mops, naps, nips, paps, peps, pips, pops, pups, raps, reps, rips, saps, seps** (72c, 106d), **sips, sops, sups, taps, tips, tops, tups, USPS** (244), **VIPs, yaps, yips, zips**

P _ _ S   **pads, pals, Pams, pans, paps, pars, pass** (13d, 21d, 84a, 85c, 106c), **pats, paws, pays, peas, Pecs** (217), **pegs, pens, peps, Pers.** (242), **pets, pews, phis, pies, pigs, pins, pips, pits, Pius** (91b), **plus** (12c, 62c), **pobs** (91c), **pods, Pons** (49d, 175), **pops, pots, Pres.** (242), **pres** (50d), **pros, pubs, pugs, puns, pups, puss** (24d), **puts, pyes**

P T _ _   **Ptah** (75d, 198), **pter-** (94a)

_ P T _   **opts**

_ _ P T   **Bapt.** (236), **Capt.** (236), **Copt** (39d), **dept.** (237), **hept-** (93c), **kept, lept-** (93d), **rapt** (9b, 41a), **Sept.** (78c, 243), **sept** (27d, 64a, 111b), **supt.** (243), **wept**

P _ _ T   **pact** (10d, 11c, 17b, 20d), **pant** (18a, 21d), **part** (11c, 43d, 49b, 57b, 91d, 106d), **past** (55b, 60b, 122a), **peat** (52a, 127c), **pelt** (28c, 43a, 57b, 59d), **pent** (30a), **pert** (49a, 62b, 72c, 104b, 114a, 128d), **pest** (82d, 88a, 89d), **phot** (246), **Pict** (22a), **Piet** (175), **piet** (26b, 74b), **pint** (54b, 246), **Pitt** (41a, 175), **plat** (74d, 90b), **plot** (23a, 30b, 104d, 123c), **poet** (40b), **pont** (50a), **Port.** (242), **port** (58a, 132c), **Post** (175), **post** (69c, 74b, 81c, 115a), **pout** (117d), **prat** (23a), **Prot.** (242), **Prut** (33d), **punt** (20b, 47b), **putt** (55b)

P U _ _   **pubs, puce** (42a, 96c), **Puck** (107c, 193), **puck** (36b, 55a, 60c, 77b), **pudu** (34b), **puff** (20a, 74a), **pugs, puke** (99a), **puku** (13a, 130b), **pula** (214), **pule** (131c), **puli** (37b, 61c, 227), **pulk** (79c), **pull** (11d, 37d, 123c), **pulp** (51d, 74a, 75b, 86b), **puma** (24d, 31b, 79a, 231), **pump** (108c), **Puna** (12c), **puna** (28d, 90b, 132b), **pung** (21c, 110c), **punk** (12a, 123b), **puno** (132b), **puns, punt** (20b, 47b), **pupa** (27a, 28d, 63b), **pups, pure** (9b, 26b, 126a, 126c), **puri** (62d), **purl** (68c), **purr** (112a), **push** (38a, 46a, 108d, 121d), **puss** (24d), **puts, putt** (55b), **Puzo** (175)

_ P U _   **Apus** (207), **opus** (29c, 80c, 129a, 133c), **spud** (92a), **spun, spur** (46a, 54d, 62c, 63c, 95a)

_ _ P U   **OGPU** (103c)

P _ _ U   **patu** (130d), **Pegu** (97d), **pelu** (26c), **Peru** (221), **poku** (13a, 130b), **pudu** (34b), **puku** (13a, 130b)

P _ _ V   **Prov.** (242)

P _ _ W   **phew** (42c), **plew** (18a), **plow** (32c, 122a), **prow** (20c, 108b, 115b)

P Y _ _   **pyel-** (93c), **pyes, pyla** (21c), **Pyle** (175), **pyre** (52c), **pyro-** (93a)

_ _ P Y   copy (40c, 62a), dopy (71c), espy (106b), mopy (72b), ropy (116b)

P _ _ Y   piny, pity (29b, 87a, 134b), play (51c, 52b, 87d, 91d, 114a), ploy (14d, 116a), pogy (68d, 75d, 78d), poky (110d), poly- (93b), pony (26b, 33b, 61a), posy (82b, 100d), pray (18c, 41b), prey (128b), puny (45a, 130c)

P _ _ Z   Phiz (35c)

Q A _ _   qadi (13d, 80d)

Q _ _ D   quad (29a), quid (32c, 122c), quod (94d, 96a)

Q _ _ G   quag (20c)

Q _ _ I   qadi (13d, 80d)

Q _ _ P   quip (66b, 66d, 132d, 133a)

_ _ Q Q   seqq. (243)

_ _ Q R   SPQR (243)

Q _ _ T   quit (9a, 34d, 71a, 99d)

Q U _ _   quad (29a), quag (20c), quay (68d, 88d, 131b), quid (32c, 122c), quip (66b, 66d, 132d, 133a), quit (9a, 34d, 71a, 99d), quiz (42b), quod (94d, 96a)

_ Q U _   aqua (20b, 70b), aqui (112d), equi- (93c)

Q _ _ Y   quay (68d, 88d, 131b)

Q _ _ Z   quiz (42b)

R A _ _   raad (15a, 40a, 112b, 121d), RAAF (242), Rabe (176), Rabi (15c, 88d), rabi (78b), race (87d, 103a, 114a, 124b), rack (10b, 28b), racy (20a, 113c), rads, Raes, raff (102d), Raft (176), raft (47c), raga (80a), rage (26d, 74c, 116a, 120b), ragi (25c), rags, rahs, raid (48c, 62d), rail (9c, 19a, 30d, 75a, 111d, 123c, 129a, 226), rain (92a, 120a, 130d), rais (24a), raja (60a), rake (34a, 52d), raki (11a), rale (21d, 26c, 34a), Rama (128c), rami (21c), ramp (52c, 62c, 110d), Rams (206), rams, rana (51c, 60a), Rand (176), rand (220, 222), rang, rani (60a, 94c), rank (27d, 46a, 55c, 72a, 73d, 97d, 116c), rant (34b, 58a, 98a, 119b), rape (107b), raps, rapt (9b, 41a), rare (83b, 104c, 126a, 126d), rase (34d), rash (98b, 110a), rasp (46a, 56a, 105c, 122d), rata (46a), rate (13d, 27d, 30b, 41d, 42a, 55c, 66d, 94b, 97d, 107a, 127b), rath (99d), RATO (242), rats, Raul (176), rave (34b, 58a, 119b), Ravi (176), raya (85a), rays, raze (34d, 35b, 36c, 71c), razz (59a)

_ R A _   Arab (104b, 213, 217, 218, 219, 221, 222, 223, 224), Arab. (235), Arad (221), arad (65b), Aral (103c), Aram (108a, 118d, 139), Aran

(52b, 64c), **Aras**, **Brad** (142), **brad** (44c, 54d, 80b), **brae** (60a, 105b), **brag** (20b, 24a, 32b, 127c), **Bram** (142), **bran** (22a, 22b, 55d, 61d), **bras** (49d), **brat** (26c), **braw** (105a), **bray** (12d, 37c), **Braz.** (236), **crab** (32b, 108a), **crag** (101b), **cram** (116c), **cran** (118c), **crap** (82a, 91b), **-crat** (117c), **craw** (32a, 56d, 115c), **drab** (22b, 26b, 29a, 38c, 43d, 47b), **drag** (30d, 95d), **dram** (38a, 38b, 84a, 92a, 110d, 246), **drat** (42a, 83a), **draw** (11d, 43c, 91d, 123c), **dray** (24c, 114b, 129b), **eras**, **erat** (96a, 97c), **frae** (105a), **Fran** (153), **frap** (37d, 122a), **fras**, **frat** (29a), **frau** (54a), **fray** (45d, 49b, 125a), **grab** (80b, 106c, 111b), **grad** (25c), **grad.** (239), **Graf** (135a, 156), **graf** (53d, 81d), **gram** (76b, 246), **Grau** (156), **Gray** (21a, 41a, 156, 192), **gray** (60c), **Graz** (213), **Irad** (197), **irae** (35c), **Iran** (88a, 217), **Iraq** (217), **Iras** (28a, 195), **oral** (79b, 113d, 127c, 128a), **Oran** (213), **prae** (69c), **pram** (16a, 24c), **prat** (23a), **pray** (18c, 41b), **tram** (124c), **trap** (24c, 24d, 41a, 54b, 55b, 101b, 111b), **tray** (98b, 104a, 107a), **Ural** (103c), **uran** (78a), **WRAF** (244), **wrap** (19a, 28a, 41b), **Wray** (187), **x-ray** (12a, 75c, 88d)

_ _ R A   **Agra** (24c, 119a), **agra** (64a, 118c), **Akra** (216), **amra** (60c), **aura** (10d, 36d, 39d, 40b, 57c, 100d), **Bara** (140), **bora** (132b), **Cara** (144), **cara** (65a), **Cora** (34d, 126a), **cora** (53b), **cura** (113a), **Dora** (30c, 33d, 35c), **dura** (113c), **eyra** (65b), **Ezra** (152, 196, 197), **fora** (75a, 101d), **Hera** (14b, 67c, 135c, 198), **hora** (21a, 33b), **hura** (104a), **Jura** (79b), **kora** (130b), **Kura** (101a), **Lara** (23c), **lira** (25c, 218, 219, 221, 223, 224), **mara** (101c, 230), **Mira** (207), **mora** (46b, 48c, 52b, 56d, 65a, 76b, 118d), **mura** (65d), **Myra** (15a, 171), **Nera** (121d), **NHRA** (241), **NIRA** (241), **Nora** (61b, 81d, 172), **obra** (113a), **okra** (57a, 127c), **Para** (18b, 214), **para** (112d, 214, 215, 222, 224), **Sara** (179, 215), **sera** (13a, 47d, 65a), **sora** (19a, 97b), **sura** (68c, 86a), **Tara** (104d), **tara** (45b, 64a), **tera-** (93d), **tora** (13a, 58b), **Tyra** (184), **vara** (72a), **Vera** (185), **vera** (105c), **-vora** (117c)

R _ _ A   **raga** (80a), **raja** (60a), **Rama** (128c), **rana** (51c, 60a), **rata** (46a), **raya** (85a), **Reba** (67c, 176), **Rhea** (68c, 78d, 89d, 122c, 135c, 177, 198), **rhea** (19b, 26c, 85a, 226), **Riga** (218), **Rima** (56c), **rima** (47a), **Rita** (177), **Roda** (81d), **roka** (74a, 124a), **Roma** (65c, 218), **Rosa** (178), **rota** (25a, 27a, 31c, 101d, 102b), **ruga** (48a, 134a), **rusa** (104a)

_ R B _   **orbs**

_ _ R B   **barb** (47a, 89a, 90c, 95a), **carb-** (92d), **curb** (100a, 109a), **darb** (88a), **forb** (59c), **garb** (28b, 37d), **gerb** (46b), **Herb** (158), **herb** (90a, 106b), **kerb** (109a), **NLRB** (241), **Serb** (134d), **sorb** (13c, 79a, 107a, 110b), **verb** (86d)

R _ _ B   **Robb** (177)

R C _ _   **RCAF** (242), **RCMP** (242)

_ R C _   **arca** (11d, 21b, 99b), **arch** (28a, 41b, 101c), **-arch** (117c), **arch-** (93b), **arch.** (235), **arcs**, **orca** (67b), **orch.** (241), **orcs**

_ _ R C   circ. (237), **Marc** (168), **marc** (55d), **narc-** (93c), **porc** (50d)

R _ _ C   **ROTC** (242)

_ R D _   **Erda** (22b, 198), **Erde** (22b), **ordo** (21a, 27a, 92b), **Urdu** (60b, 213, 220)

_ _ R D   **Bard** (200), **bard** (14c, 16b, 90c), **Bird** (141), **bird** (16a), **bord** (77a), **burd** (105c), **Byrd** (90d), **card** (29a, 66d, 87a), **Cord** (146), **cord** (32c, 43b), **curd** (76d), **Ford** (153, 191, 194), **ford** (129a), **fyrd** (83d), **gird** (16d, 18c, 40c, 118b), **hard** (123b), **herd** (38b, 232), **Kurd** (64a, 217), **lard** (44c, 50a, 56a, 83d), **Lord** (167), **lord** (82a), **nard** (75b, 83d), **pard** (24d), **sard** (24b, 25d, 53b, 84c, 106c, 115d), **surd** (30b, 82d), **Ward** (186), **ward** (27c, 35a, 67b), **word** (95a, 120c, 121d), **Yard** (187), **yard** (40d, 69a, 113a, 246)

R _ _ D   **raad** (15a, 40a, 112b, 121d), **raid** (48c, 62d), **Rand** (176), **rand** (220, 222), **read** (63c, 88b, 116c), **Redd** (176), **redd** (113b), **Reed** (176, 204), **reed** (16d, 55d, 75a, 79c, 84d), **Reid** (176), **rend** (28a), **Ridd** (73a), **rind** (43a, 76d, 87c), **road** (31b, 38a, 121b, 130c), **rood** (32a), **rudd** (24b, 46c, 98c), **rued, rynd** (76d)

R E _ _   **read** (63c, 88b, 116c), **real** (9d, 116d), **ream** (18d, 31b, 41a, 86b, 125c), **reap** (9d, 33a, 58b), **rear** (10c, 21d, 40d, 41c, 60a, 97c), **Reba** (67c, 176), **rebs, reck** (24b), **Redd** (176), **redd** (113b), **rede** (31b, 105a), **redo** (26a, 74b), **Reds** (206), **reds, Reed** (176, 204), **reed** (16d, 55d, 75a, 79c, 84d), **reef** (98d, 104a, 108b), **reek** (43c, 52a, 111a), **reel** (20c, 33b, 113c, 113d, 114b, 114c, 131c, 133a, 233), **Rees** (176), **Reid** (176), **rein** (26b, 30c, 100a), **reis** (24a), **Reki** (16d), **rely** (124d), **remi** (53b), **rend** (28a), **René** (176), **Reni** (65a, 176), **reni-** (93b), **Reno** (15c, 81c, 113d), **reno-** (93b), **rent** (60b, 60c, 120a, 123b), **repp** (43b), **reps, resh** (12a), **rest** (16b, 21d, 71b, 80c, 87b, 99b, 99c, 99d, 234), **rete** (81c, 90b), **rets, reve** (50b), **revs**

_ R E _   **area** (36d, 37b, 45d, 72d, 97d, 99a, 135c), **Ares** (13b, 41c, 59b, 75a, 129d, 135c, 198), **brea** (77a), **bred** (97c), **bree** (105a), **bren** (73d), **br'er** (126a), **Bret** (143), **brew** (29d), **Cree** (11b, 189), **crew** (48c, 56c, 81b, 88b, 133d), **drei** (54a), **Drew** (150, 201), **drew** (110a), **drey** (114b), **Fred** (47c, 153), **free** (36b, 56a, 73a, 100c, 112b), **freq.** (238), **fret** (22a, 25d, 36d, 42c, 128b, 133d), **Frey** (10b, 153, 198), **Greg** (156), **grew, Grey** (156, 192, 194), **Mr. Ed** (119b), **Oreb** (197), **Oreg.** (241), **Orel** (173), **ores, pree** (105b), **prep** (104d), **Pres.** (242), **pres** (50d), **prey** (128b), **tree** (30d, 53b, 133c), **tref** (48b, 126a), **trek** (66d, 73a, 123d), **tres** (42b, 51b, 113a), **tret** (130a, 131a), **trey** (24a, 121c), **urea** (45c), **Urey** (15c, 184), **Wren** (187), **wren** (19a, 226)

_ _ R E   **Aare** (18c, 100b), **Acre** (214), **acre** (45d, 68d, 246), **aire** (64a), **bare** (36a, 40c, 43b, 76a, 116b, 127a), **bore** (23b, 37d, 87d, 121d), **byre** (31c), **CARE** (236), **care** (13a, 25b, 29d, 59a, 77a, 99a, 123d, 124d, 133d), **cere** (18d, 130c), **CORE** (237), **core** (25c, 41d, 58d), **cure** (94c), **dare** (25d, 34c), **dire** (37d, 44d, 45a, 54b, 56a, 120c), **Dore**

410

(49c), **dore** (54b, 89a), **Eire** (64a), **etre** (50a), **eure** (54b), **Eyre** (22a), **fare** (35c, 48b), **fire** (14b, 36a, 36c, 108c), **fore** (51c, 108b), **gare** (50d, 97b), **Gere** (155), **Gore** (155, 191), **gore** (87c, 88d, 124b), **gyre** (27b), **hare** (101c, 230), **here** (63d, 101c), **hire** (40c, 40d, 71b, 99c, 100a), **ihre** (54b), **Imre** (159), **in re** (29d, 63d, 99a), **jure** (70b), **Kure** (60d), **lire** (50d, 64d), **lore** (60b, 70d, 71b, 132d), **lure** (34b, 41b, 63d, 120c), **Lyra** (58a, 207), **lyre** (80b, 85a), **mare** (61a, 82c), **mere** (17b, 50d, 68b, 84b, 91b, 130a), **mire** (20c, 39a, 78c, 79c), **More** (171), **more** (43c, 56a), **Nare** (72d), **Nore** (120d), **ogre** (78b), **pare** (87c, 98d), **pere** (49d, 50b), **pore** (48c, 84b, 84d), **pure** (9b, 26b, 126a, 126c), **pyre** (52c), **rare** (83b, 104c, 126a, 126d), **rire** (50c), **sere** (37d, 133a), **sire** (18b, 21d, 44d, 48d, 94d, 120c, 122c), **sore** (12d, 106c), **sure** (10b, 99b, 106b, 126d), **tare** (128b, 131a), **tire** (21a, 42d, 44d, 47b, 131c), **tore**, **Tyre** (71a, 88c, 218), **-vore** (117c), **ware** (76a), **were**, **we're** (30c), **wire** (30d, 120b), **wore**, **yore** (12c, 23a, 55b, 73a, 83d, 87a, 122b)

R _ _ E   **Rabe** (176), **race** (87d, 103a, 114a, 124b), **rage** (26d, 74c, 116a, 120b), **rake** (34a, 52d), **rale** (21d, 26c, 34a), **rape** (107b), **rare** (83b, 104c, 126a, 126d), **rase** (34d), **rate** (13d, 27d, 30b, 41d, 42a, 55c, 66d, 94b, 97d, 107a, 127b), **rave** (34b, 58a, 119b), **raze** (34d, 35b, 36c, 71c), **rede** (31b, 105a), **René** (176), **rete** (81c, 90b), **reve** (50b), **Rhee** (68c, 177), **Rice** (177, 204), **rice** (37d), **Ride** (177), **ride** (29b, 66d, 121a), **rife** (9b, 94b), **rile** (12d, 64b, 95c, 115c), **rime** (30a, 51c, 60c), **rine** (36d), **ripe** (47b, 75b), **rire** (50c), **rise** (62c, 114c), **rite** (72c), **rive** (28a), **robe** (52d), **rode** (38b), **role** (52a, 86d), **Rome** (13c, 27c, 41d, 218), **rope** (30d, 69b, 100b), **Rose** (9a, 178), **Rote** (178), **rote** (75d, 99d, 118a), **roue** (34a, 97c), **rove** (97d, 101a, 129d), **Rube** (179), **rube** (31b, 103c, 134d), **rude** (102c, 126a), **rule** (13b, 35b, 37b, 70b, 118c), **rune** (82b), **ruse** (60c, 62b, 116a), **Ryne** (179), **rype** (95d)

_ R F _   **orfe** (46d, 134b), **Urfa** (76a)

_ _ R F   **Cerf** (145), **corf** (28c), **kerf** (33a, 82c), **serf** (20d, 110b), **surf** (21d), **turf** (87b, 111c, 118b), **werf** (44c), **zarf** (28d, 32d, 114d)

R _ _ F   **RAAF** (242), **raff** (102d), **RCAF** (242), **reef** (98d, 104a, 108b), **riff** (66a, 78c), **roof** (61c), **ruff** (34d, 37b, 51c)

_ R G _   **Argo** (14b, 66a), **ergo** (121a), **ergs**, **orgy** (24b, 100b, 104b), **urge** (35b, 54d, 63b, 94d)

_ _ R G   **Berg** (141), **berg** (61b), **Borg** (142), **burg** (21a, 57c), **surg.** (243)

R _ _ G   **rang**, **Rigg** (177), **Ring** (177), **ring** (16d, 27b, 40c, 40d, 131b, 134a), **Roeg** (178), **rung** (25d, 32b, 115b)

R H _ _   **Rhea** (68c, 78d, 89d, 122c, 135c, 177, 198), **rhea** (19b, 26c, 85a, 226), **Rhee** (68c, 177), **rheo-** (92d), **rhin-** (93b), **RHIP** (242), **rhiz-** (93c), **rhos**

R _ _ H   **rash** (98b, 110a), **rath** (99d), **resh** (12a), **Rich** (177), **rich** (73d),

Roth (178), **Rush** (179), **rush** (114a), **Ruth** (80d, 179, 196, 197), **ruth** (29b, 89c)

R I _ _   **rial** (220), **ribs**, **Rice** (177, 204), **rice** (37d), **Rich** (177), **rich** (73d), **Rick** (24c, 177), **rick** (58c, 89a, 114b), **Rico** (72c), **Ridd** (73a), **Ride** (177), **ride** (29b, 66d, 121a), **rids**, **riel** (214), **riem** (59d), **rien** (50d), **rife** (9b, 94b), **riff** (66a, 78c), **rift** (21d, 47a, 84b, 113d), **Riga** (218), **Rigg** (177), **rigs**, **Riis** (177), **rile** (12d, 64b, 95c, 115c), **rill** (22a, 31d, 101a, 110d, 116b), **Rima** (56c), **rima** (47a), **rime** (30a, 51c, 60c), **rims**, **rimu** (62a, 98d), **rimy**, **rind** (43a, 76d, 87c), **rine** (36d), **Ring** (177), **ring** (16d, 27b, 40c, 40d, 131b, 134a), **rink** (109d, 114a), **riot** (85a, 101c, 125a), **ripe** (47b, 75b), **rips**, **rire** (50c), **rise** (62c, 114c), **risk** (52b, 58c, 66b, 127d), **Rita** (177), **rite** (72c), **Ritz** (177), **rive** (28a)

_ R I _   **aria** (75d, 111d, 125a, 234), **arid** (38b), **Arie** (139), **aril** (106b), **Ariz.** (209, 235), **brie** (26b), **brig** (81a, 108b), **brim** (21a), **brio** (33d, 113d, 128d), **Brit.** (236), **brit** (59d), **crib** (26b, 74c, 91b, 110c), **crim.** (237), **crit.** (237), **drib** (110d), **drip** (72b, 88a), **Eric** (128b, 151), **Erie** (23c, 68d, 189), **Erik** (151), **Erin** (64a, 151), **Eris** (14b, 198), **frib** (35d), **frit** (54c), **Friz** (154), **friz** (32d), **grid** (17c, 90b, 116a), **grig** (32a, 39c, 56a, 72c), **grim** (19d, 54b, 115b), **grin** (111a), **grip** (27d, 55d, 60c, 96a, 117d), **Gris** (156), **gris** (50c), **grit** (104a), **hrip** (239), **irid** (90a), **Iris** (159, 195), **iris** (20b, 43c, 85a, 97c), **Kris** (165), **kris** (74b), **orig.** (241), **prig** (85c), **prim** (115b), **trig** (114a, 124c), **trig.** (31b, 243), **trim** (81a, 84d, 114a, 118b, 121d, 124c), **Trin.** (243), **trio** (80c, 124b), **trip** (66d, 232), **Tris** (184), **-trix** (117b), **Uria** (197), **-uria** (117b), **urim** (103b), **Uris** (184), **writ** (71a)

_ _ R I   **abri** (51a, 108a), **aeri-** (92c), **agri.** (235), **Bari** (10a, 218), **buri** (119b), **gyri** (21c), **ieri** (65c), **INRI** (32b, 239), **kari** (15d), **Kiri** (164), **kiri** (87a), **kori** (10b, 60a), **lari** (219), **Lori** (167), **Mari** (16d), **mari** (50c), **myri-** (93b), **nori** (11b, 105d), **Omri** (67d, 197), **pari-** (92d), **peri** (44a, 88a), **peri-** (92c), **puri** (62d), **ruri** (69c), **sari** (52d, 60a), **Seri** (76c), **sori** (45b), **Teri** (183), **Tori** (184), **tori** (30c), **vari** (71b), **weri** (16c, 25a), **Yuri** (188), **zori** (108c)

R _ _ I   **Rabi** (15c, 88d), **rabi** (78b), **ragi** (25c), **raki** (11a), **rami** (21c), **rani** (60a, 94c), **Ravi** (176), **Reki** (16d), **remi** (53b), **Reni** (65a, 176), **reni-** (93b), **roti** (51a), **ruri** (69c)

_ R K _   **arks**, **irks**

_ _ R K   **bark** (12d, 37b), **cark** (24b, 133d), **Cork** (217), **cork** (90b, 116a, 132c, 133b), **dark** (38d, 54d, 118c), **Dirk** (149), **dirk** (33a), **fork** (13c, 36d, 37a, 119a), **hark** (72b), **jerk** (20a, 38d, 48b, 88a, 95d), **Kirk** (164), **kirk** (27a, 105a), **lark** (19a, 51c, 226), **lurk** (71d, 110b), **Mark** (42a, 102c, 168, 196), **mark** (10d, 15c, 55c, 96b, 109b, 114c, 133a), **murk** (28b, 48a, 77b), **nark** (63a, 115d), **park** (53b, 95d), **perk** (28d, 51c), **pork** (55c, 75c), **Sark** (26a, 64b), **Turk** (85a, 217), **Turk.** (243), **work** (52a, 116c), **York** (41a, 187, 192, 193, 194)

R _ _ K   **rack** (10b, 28b), **rank** (27d, 46a, 55c, 72a, 73d, 97d, 116c), **reck**

(24b), **reek**(43c, 52a, 111a), **Rick**(24c, 177), **rick**(58c, 89a, 114b), **rink** (109d, 114a), **risk** (52b, 58c, 66b, 127d), **Rock** (178), **rock** (118c, 124b), **rook** (19b, 26c, 32b, 226), **ruck** (134a), **rusk** (21d)

_ R L _   **Arlo** (139), **Erle** (151), **orle** (46a, 59b, 108a), **orlo** (46a, 90b)

_ _ R L   **birl** (72d),**Burl** (143),**burl** (68c,124b),**Carl** (144),**curl** (32a, 57b, 72d, 100d,126b),**Earl** (150),**earl** (82a), **farl** (105b), **furl** (101c), **girl** (45b), **harl** (46a, 48a, 59b), **herl** (14d, 17a), **hurl** (121c, 123b), **jarl** (104c), **Karl** (163), **marl** (27d, 35a, 45c), **merl** (19a, 19d, 226), **purl** (68c)

R _ _ L   **rail** (9c, 19a, 30d, 75a, 111d, 123c, 129a, 226), **Raul** (176), **real** (9d, 116d), **reel** (20c, 33b, 113c, 113d, 114b, 114c, 131c, 133a, 233), **rial** (220), **riel** (214), **rill** (22a, 31d, 101a, 110d, 116b), **roil** (79c, 15c), **roll** (118c), **ryal** (83d)

_ R M _   **arms** (130d), **army** (61c), **Erma** (151)

_ _ R M   **barm** (134b), **berm** (23c, 71a, 108d), **corm** (22c, 115a), **-derm** (117c), **dorm** (104d), **farm** (21d, 32a, 55d, 122a), **firm** (29b, 29d, 114b, 126d), **form** (44c, 107c, 127a), **germ** (36b, 61b, 76c), **harm** (33b, 61d, 62a, 63a), **Norm** (172), **norm** (16a, 86b, 97d, 114d), **term** (71d, 72a, 80b, 106c, 115c), **warm** (10b, 58d, 120c), **worm** (88a), **wurm** (54c)

R _ _ M   **ream** (18d, 31b, 41a, 86b, 125c), **riem** (59d), **roam** (123d, 129d), **room** (25d)

_ R N _   **arna** (22b, 131d), **Arnd** (53d), **Arne** (102d, 139), **Arno** (101a, 139), **arns, Brno** (215), **Dr. No** (20d), **erne** (19a, 39a, 105c, 225), **erns, Orne** (23a), **urns**

_ _ R N   **barn** (116a), **Bern** (9a, 222), **birn** (27d), **Born** (142), **born** (71d, 81a, 81b), **burn** (62c, 101b), **CERN** (236), **corn** (74b, 94b), **darn** (42a, 75d, 83a, 99c), **Dern** (149), **Dorn** (149), **earn** (35b, 52a, 76a), **fern** (106b), **firn** (54c, 55d, 111b), **Garn** (154), **Horn** (24a), **horn** (13a, 31a, 124d), **Kern** (164), **kern** (48c, 101b, 125d), **lorn** (49a), **morn** (33d), **Norn** (82a), **pern** (60d), **pirn** (20c, 98d, 130d), **porn** (79c), **tarn** (68b, 79b, 91b, 130a), **tern** (19a, 28c, 56d, 104d, 105d, 118b, 226), **Torn** (184), **torn** (99c), **turn** (12c, 100b, 102b, 108a, 125c, 127c, 132b), **warn** (11b, 25b), **worn** (107b), **yarn** (43a, 114b, 119b, 133c)

R _ _ N   **rain** (92a, 120a, 130d), **rein** (26b, 30c, 100a), **rhin-** (93b), **rien** (50d), **roan** (61a, 98c, 131c), **ruin** (34d, 35b, 62b), **Ryan** (179), **Ryun** (179)

R O _ _   **road** (31b, 38a, 121b, 130c), **roam** (123d, 129d), **roan** (61a, 98c, 131c), **roar** (12d, 13c), **Robb** (177), **robe** (52d), **robs, Roby** (178), **Rock** (178), **rock** (118c, 124b), **Roda** (81d), **rode** (38b), **rods, Roeg** (178), **roes, roil** (79c, 115c), **rojo** (113a), **roka** (74a, 124a), **role** (52a, 86d), **roll** (118c), **Roma** (65c, 218), **Rome** (13c, 27c, 41d, 218), **romp** (51c), **rood** (32a), **roof** (61c), **rook** (19b, 26c, 32b,

226), **room** (25d), **Roos** (53d), **Root** (178), **root** (17b, 17c, 102d), **rope** (30d, 69b, 100b), **ropy** (116b), **Rory** (178), **Rosa** (178), **Rose** (9a, 178), **Ross** (178, 193, 195, 207, 208), **ross** (17b, 119c), **rosy** (54d, 84c), **rota** (25a, 27a, 31c, 101d, 102b), **ROTC** (242), **Rote** (178), **rote** (75d, 99d, 118a), **Roth** (178), **roti** (51a), **rots, roue** (34a, 97c), **roup** (92a), **rout** (34c, 36c), **roux** (104b), **rove** (97d, 101a, 129d), **rows, Roys**

_ R O _   **Aroa** (127d), **brom-** (92c), **broo** (105a), **Bros.** (236), **brow** (48d, 59d), **croc.** (237), **crop** (31d, 108d), **Crow** (189), **crow** (19b, 19d, 20b, 43c, 225), **drop** (44a, 48d, 77a, 84a, 86d, 90b, 90c, 110d, 120a), **Eros** (32d, 132c, 195, 198), **froe** (28a, 122d, 123a, 130d), **frog** (17c, 225), **from** (18b, 115a), **frow** (123a), **grog** (11a, 72b, 113d), **Groh** (156), **Gros** (49c), **gros** (38c, 43d, 109c), **grow** (15d, 41a, 42d, 43a, 114a, 118c), **iron** (45b, 45c, 55a, 57c, 74c, 75b, 245), **Kroc** (165), **proa** (20c, 23d, 74b), **prod** (38a, 46a, 54d, 59c, 62c, 63b, 65b, 81b, 82d, 90d, 121d, 126d), **Prof.** (242), **PROM** (29c, 242), **prom** (33b), **prop** (118a), **pros, Prot.** (242), **Prov.** (242), **prow** (20c, 108b, 115b), **trod, -tron** (117b), **trop** (51b, 123a), **trot** (66c, 85b), **trow** (18b), **Troy** (184), **troy** (119c, 131a)

_ _ R O   **acro-** (93a, 93c), **aero-** (92c), **aero.** (235), **Afro** (57b), **Afro-** (92c), **baro-** (93c), **boro** (114a), **caro** (65a), **cero** (46d, 67d), **cero-** (93d), **duro** (88b), **Ebro** (222), **Eero** (151), **faro** (24b), **Garo** (69a, 154), **giro** (31d, 65c), **gyro-** (93a), **Hero** (70d, 194), **hero** (34d, 95c, 104a), **Lero** (64c), **loro** (86d), **mero** (56c, 66d), **Miró** (112c, 171), **Moro** (171), **moro** (88c), **Nero** (10d, 102a), **otro** (112c, 113a), **pero** (112d), **pyro-** (93a), **sero-** (93c), **taro** (14d, 39c, 52a, 90d, 102b, 114d, 125a), **tiro** (18b, 82c), **toro** (31c, 112c), **Tyro** (81b), **tyro** (12b, 18b, 82c), **xero-** (92d), **Yuro** (188), **Zero** (188), **zero** (27b, 65d, 73b, 82c, 89d)

R _ _ O   **RATO** (242), **redo** (26a, 74b), **Reno** (15c, 81c, 113d), **reno-** (93b), **rheo-** (92d), **Rico** (72c), **rojo** (113a)

_ R P _   **arpa** (65a)

_ _ R P   **AARP** (235), **burp** (18b), **carp** (25b, 32a, 46a, 46c, 96d, 228), **Corp.** (237), **dorp** (57c, 128b), **GARP** (239), **harp** (80b), **lerp** (41d), **tarp** (23d, 130b), **terp** (79a, 94a), **warp** (30b, 121c, 125c)

R _ _ P   **ramp** (52c, 62c, 110d), **rasp** (46a, 56a, 105c, 122d), **RCMP** (242), **reap** (9d, 33a, 58b), **repp** (43b), **RHIP** (242), **romp** (51c), **roup** (92a), **RSVP** (242), **rump** (23a, 33a, 75c)

_ R R _   **errs**

_ _ R R   **birr** (112a, 216), **Burr** (143, 190), **burr** (94b), **Carr** (144), **dorr** (54c), **Farr** (152), **Garr** (154), **herr** (53d), **Kerr** (164), **Marr** (168), **parr** (103d, 109d), **purr** (112a), **torr** (246)

R _ _ R   **rear** (10c, 21d, 40d, 41c, 60a, 97c), **roar** (12d, 13c), **ruer, Ruhr** (53d, 100b)

R S _ _   **RSVP** (242)

_ R S _   **Erse** (25c, 52a, 64a), **erst** (49a), **Ursa** (17d)

_ _ R S   **airs** (94b), **bars**, **Bors** (102c), **burs**, **cars**, **curs**, **Dors** (149), **ears**, **errs**, **firs**, **furs**, **gars**, **hers** (95a), **hors** (50d), **jars**, **Mars** (89d, 98d, 129d, 199), **mars** (49d), **Mors** (34a, 198), **oars**, **ours** (95a), **pars**, **Pers.** (242), **sirs**, **sors** (69c), **tars**, **tors**, **vers** (51b), **wars**

R _ _ S   **rads**, **Raes**, **rags**, **rahs**, **rais** (24a), **Rams** (206), **rams**, **raps**, **rats**, **rays**, **rebs**, **Reds** (206), **reds**, **Rees** (176), **reis** (24a), **reps**, **rets**, **revs**, **rhos**, **ribs**, **rids**, **rigs**, **Riis** (177), **rims**, **rips**, **robs**, **rods**, **roes**, **Roos** (53d), **Ross** (178, 193, 195, 207, 208), **ross** (17b, 119c), **rots**, **rows**, **Roys**, **rubs**, **rues**, **rugs**, **rums**, **runs**, **Russ** (179), **Russ.** (242), **ruts**

_ R T _   **Arta** (56d), **Arte** (139), **arts**, **arty**, **orth-** (92d), **orts** (105c), **Srta.** (243)

_ _ R T   **Bart** (140), **Bart.** (236), **Bert** (20c, 141), **bort** (35c), **Burt** (143), **cart** (125d, 127c, 129b), **cert.** (236), **Curt** (147), **curt** (20b, 22a, 108c, 108d), **dart** (14c, 33d, 68d, 77b, 90c, 95a, 114a, 118c), **dirt** (39a, 99c, 104c), **fort** (51c, 116c), **girt** (27b), **Gort** (101b), **Hart** (157), **hart** (34c, 114b), **hort.** (239), **Hurt** (159), **hurt** (33b, 58a, 62a, 63a, 133d), **Kurt** (165), **mart** (40c, 74d), **Mort** (171), **part** (11c, 43d, 49b, 57b, 91d, 106d), **pert** (49a, 62b, 72c, 104b, 114a, 128d), **Port.** (242), **port** (58a, 132c), **Sart** (64a), **Sert** (112c), **sort** (27d, 36d, 67c, 106d, 109b, 113b, 127b, 132d), **tart** (87a, 112b), **tort** (27c, 71a, 134c), **vert** (56c), **vert.** (244), **Wart** (193), **wart** (95c), **wert** (128a), **wort** (59b, 92a), **yurt** (78a)

R _ _ T   **Raft** (176), **raft** (47c), **rant** (34b, 58a, 98a, 119b), **rapt** (9b, 41a), **rent** (60b, 60c, 120a, 123b), **rest** (16b, 21d, 71b, 80c, 87b, 99b, 99c, 99d, 234), **rift** (21d, 47a, 84b, 113d), **riot** (85a, 101c, 125a), **Root** (178), **root** (17b, 17c, 102d), **rout** (34c, 36c), **runt** (12d, 38d), **rust** (31a, 85d, 90a), **ryot** (62d)

R U _ _   **Rube** (179), **rube** (31b, 103c, 134d), **rubs**, **Ruby** (179), **ruby** (19c, 53b), **ruck** (134a), **rudd** (24b, 46c, 98c), **rude** (102c, 126a), **Rudy** (179), **rued**, **ruer**, **rues**, **ruff** (34d, 37b, 51c), **ruga** (48a, 134a), **rugs**, **Ruhr** (53d, 100b), **ruin** (34d, 35b, 62b), **rule** (13b, 35b, 37b, 70b, 118c), **rump** (23a, 33a, 75c), **rums**, **rune** (82b), **rung** (25d, 32b, 115b), **runs**, **runt** (12d, 38d), **ruri** (69c), **ruru** (81c), **rusa** (104a), **ruse** (60c, 62b, 116a), **Rush** (179), **rush** (114a), **rusk** (21d), **Russ** (179), **Russ.** (242), **rust** (31a, 85d, 90a), **Ruth** (80d, 179, 196, 197), **ruth** (29b, 89c), **ruts**

_ R U _   **arui** (13b), **arum** (32c, 71d, 114d), **bruh** (73b), **brut** (38b, 132c), **crud** (28c, 35a, 36a), **crus** (71b, 107c), **Crux** (207), **crux** (32b, 74b, 112b), **drub** (17c, 32c, 42c, 110b), **drug** (81a), **drum** (80a, 228), **eruc** (30d, 45d), **frug** (33b), **grub** (35d, 69b), **grum** (54d), **Grus** (207), **Irus** (83c), **Prut** (33d), **true** (9d, 15d, 31a, 42b, 44a, 73c, 111b), **Truk** (24b), **urus** (15d, 85c, 132a, 227, 231)

_ _ R U   Boru (142), ecru (18b, 22b, 126a), feru (30d, 45c), guru (60b), maru (65d), Meru (79a, 218), Peru (221), ruru (81c), thru

R _ _ U   rimu (62a, 98d), ruru (81c)

_ R V _   ARVN (235), urva (78a)

_ _ R V   Marv (169), Merv (170), MIRV (240)

_ _ R X   Marx (169)

R _ _ X   roux (104b)

R Y _ _   ryal (83d), Ryan (179), rynd (76d), Ryne (179), ryot (62d), rype (95d), Ryun (179)

_ R Y _   aryl (14b), cryo- (93a), oryx (13a, 231)

_ _ R Y   aery (39a), airy (41d, 66a, 71d), awry (15a, 32a, 125c, 134c), bury (63c), Cary (144), dory (20b, 47b), eury- (94a), eyry (39a), fury (97b, 116a), Gary (154), gory (20a), Jory (163), jury (31c), kary- (93b), lory (86d), Mary (96c, 107c, 169, 197), nary (82c), Rory (178), spry (9d, 72c, 81d), tory (22a, 30b, 73c), vary (26a, 35c, 77c), very (43c, 78d, 111b), wary (25b, 128b, 130a), wiry (109d)

R _ _ Y   racy (20a, 113c), rely (124d), rimy, Roby (178), ropy (116b), Rory (178), rosy (54d, 84c), Ruby (179), ruby (19c, 53b), Rudy (179)

_ _ R Z   Harz (79b)

R _ _ Z   razz (59a), rhiz- (93c), Ritz (177)

S A _ _   saal (53d), Saar (49c, 78d, 101a), saba (45d, 88c), Sabe (67b), sack (30b, 36a, 89b, 90c, 132c), sacs, Sada (179), sado (24c, 66a), Sadr (207), safe (106b, 116c, 127b), Safi (220), S.Afr. (242), saga (71b, 104c, 119b), sage (14c, 70d, 77b, 106a, 131b, 132d), sago (44b, 86a, 95d, 114d), sags, Sahl (179), Saho (32d, 57c, 216), saic (71c), Said (91c), said (127c), sail (91c), sain (19d, 32b), Sais (39d), sais (56c), sake (10b, 65d, 131a), Saki (95c), saki (78b, 231), Saks (179), sala (112d, 113a), sale (15c, 17b, 50b, 51a, 123d), Salk (179), salp (83b), SALT (242), salt (29d, 80b, 94b, 103b, 106a, 111c), sama (80d), same (36d, 61d), samp (55c, 60d, 91c), Sams, Sa'na (134c), Sand (179), sand (78d, 109b), sane (97d), sang, sank, sans (51b), sapa (55d), saps, Sara (179, 215), sard (24b, 25d, 53b, 84c, 106c, 115d), sari (52d, 60a), Sark (26a, 64b), Sart (64a), sash (18c, 37c, 54c, 132b), Sask. (242), sass (16b, 62c), sate (28b, 54d, 56a, 118a), Sati (96d, 109d, 198), SATs (29a), Sauk (49b, 56c, 189), Saul (67d, 87a, 179, 197), -saur (117b), save (42b, 67b, 84b, 94b, 126c), sawn, saws, saya (88c), says

_ S A _   asap (62a, 235), Asas, ASAT (235), Esau (64b, 65b, 98b, 197), Isak (159), Isao (159), Isar (33d, 79d, 100a, 216), tsar (103c), USAF (243), usar (11b, 17b, 62d)

_ _ S A   **ansa** (57d), **bosa** (13d), **casa** (112d), **Elsa** (55c, 72d, 84b, 129b, 151), **Ilsa** (24c), **Issa** (216), **Lisa** (166), **masa** (30d), **mesa** (40b, 59d, 90b, 119a), **musa** (16d), **NASA** (241), **Ossa** (79a, 84a, 121a), **ossa** (20d), **Pisa** (70d), **Rosa** (178), **rusa** (104a), **Susa** (40a), **Ursa** (17d), **vasa** (38c, 128a), **visa** (87a)

S _ _ A   **saba** (45d, 88c), **Sada** (179), **saga** (71b, 104c, 119b), **sala** (112d, 113a), **sama** (80d), **Sa'na** (134c), **sapa** (55d), **Sara** (179, 215), **saya** (88c), **sera** (13a, 47d, 65a), **seta** (22a, 57b, 113c), **Shea** (180), **shea** (22d, 124a), **shi'a** (80c), **sida** (30d, 96d), **sika** (34c, 65d, 231), **sima** (101b), **Sita** (97d), **Siva** (91a), **skua** (56d, 65b, 105c), **soda** (18d, 38a, 111c, 131c), **sofa** (36d), **soga** (52c), **soja** (56c), **sola** (11d, 39b, 89c), **soma** (12d, 20c, 62d), **sora** (19a, 97b), **soya** (112c), **SPCA** (243), **Srta.** (243), **stoa** (29a, 91c), **sura** (68c, 86a), **Susa** (40a), **Suva** (128d, 216)

_ S B _   **ISBN** (240)

_ _ S B   **NTSB** (241)

S _ _ B   **scab** (134a), **scob** (120d), **Serb** (134d), **slab** (88d, 110c), **slob** (126d), **slub** (134b), **snab** (22b, 105a), **snob** (88a, 111b), **snub** (62a, 81b, 98b, 109a, 110c), **sorb** (13c, 79a, 107a, 110b), **stab** (15c, 68a, 88d), **stib** (38d), **stub** (121d, 122c), **swab** (57c, 78c, 134b)

S C _ _   **scab** (134a), **scad** (24d, 27b, 61b, 65b), **scan** (47c, 73a, 88b, 98a), **scar** (27b, 134a), **scat** (54b, 96d), **scob** (120d), **scop** (90c), **Scot** (59d), **Scot.** (242), **scow** (20c, 47b), **Scud** (77b), **scud** (96d, 103a, 118c), **scum** (62c, 98d, 110c), **scup** (91c, 228), **scut** (119a)

_ S C _   **Asch** (139), **asci** (114a), **esca** (19d, 36a, 55d), **-esce** (117c), **USCG** (243)

_ _ S C   **bosc** (87b), **desc.** (237), **disc** (58b, 98c), **disc.** (237), **fisc** (42c, 102c), **masc.** (240), **misc.** (240), **pisc-** (93a), **Visc.** (244), **Wisc.** (212, 244)

S _ _ C   **saic** (71c), **spec.** (243)

S D _ _   **S.Dak.** (242)

_ S D _   **USDA** (243)

S _ _ D   **Said** (91c), **said** (127c), **Sand** (179), **sand** (78d, 109b), **sard** (24b, 25d, 53b, 84c, 106c, 115d), **scad** (24d, 27b, 61b, 65b), **Scud** (77b), **scud** (96d, 103a, 118c), **seed** (55c, 84d, 85c, 90a, 112b, 113d), **send** (36c, 74b, 86d, 91d, 99c, 108b, 123d), **shad** (25b, 46d), **shed** (24d, 70d, 77d, 108a), **she'd** (30c), **shod**, **skid** (110c), **sled** (102b), **slid**, **sned** (73a), **sold**, **spad** (80b, 89d), **sped**, **spud** (92a), **stad** (112b), **stud** (23a, 44c, 74c, 84d, 126d), **sudd** (47c), **sued**, **surd** (30b, 82d), **Swed.** (243)

417

S E _ _ seal (28b, 44c, 89b, 231), **seam** (66c, 67a, 128c), **Sean** (66c, 180), **sear** (25b, 133a), **seas, seat** (25d, 63b, 115c), **Seau** (180), **sebi-** (92d), **sebo-** (92d), **sect** (34d, 43d), **secy.** (243), **seed** (55c, 84d, 85c, 90a, 112b, 113d), **seek** (105d), **seel** (20a), **seem** (13c), **seen, seep** (72b, 84b, 87d, 114a), **seer** (95b, 111d, 128c), **sees, sego** (22c, 71d), **sehr** (54a), **Seir** (41c), **seis** (113a), **sejm** (91a), **self** (39d, 62d), **sell** (74d, 87c, 127d), **seme** (37c), **semi** (62c), **semi-** (93a, 93c), **send** (36c, 74b, 86d, 91d, 99c, 108b, 123d), **sens** (49c), **sent, seps** (72c, 106d), **Sept.** (78c, 243), **sept** (27d, 64a, 111b), **seqq.** (243), **sera** (13a, 47d, 65a), **Serb** (134d), **sere** (37d, 133a), **serf** (20d, 110b), **Seri** (76c), **sero-** (93c), **Sert** (112c), **sess** (111b), **sess.** (243), **seta** (22a, 57b, 113c), **Seth** (10a, 42b, 197, 198), **seth** (76a), **Seti** (88c), **sets, sett** (87b, 119d), **Seve** (180), **sewn, sews, sexi-** (93c), **sext** (23d, 84d, 109d), **sexy** (41c)

_ S E _ asea (32b, 129c), **esel** (53d), **Iser** (40a), **used** (9c, 57a), **user** (10a, 29c, 40c), **uses**

_ _ S E anse (50c), **apse** (12a, 27a, 98b, 106c, 127c), **asse** (49b), **base** (9a, 41d, 49a, 62a, 73c, 92b, 102b, 102d), **bise** (132b), **case** (14b, 30b, 63b, 71a, 82c), **Dese** (216), **dose** (94a), **Duse** (64d, 150), **ease** (10b, 11c, 15b, 29b, 42d, 71b, 77b, 99b, 99d, 100a, 129d), **else** (18c, 61d, 85a), **-ense** (117b), **Erse** (25c, 52a, 64a), **esse** (9d, 18b), **fuse** (75d, 76a), **hose** (115c), **ipse** (37a, 69d), **José** (163), **Lise** (166), **lose** (48d), **-lyse** (117b), **mise** (10d, 134c), **muse** (52d, 91b, 121b), **nose** (89d, 95c), **NYSE** (241), **Ouse** (101a, 134d, 223), **pose** (9d, 15c, 94b), **rase** (34d), **rise** (62c, 114c), **Rose** (9a, 178), **ruse** (60c, 62b, 116a), **vase** (30b, 47d), **vise** (60c), **Wise** (187), **wise** (103b, 111a)

S _ _ E Sabe (67b), **safe** (106b, 116c, 127b), **sage** (14c, 70d, 77b, 106a, 131b, 132d), **sake** (10b, 65d, 131a), **sale** (15c, 17b, 50b, 51a, 123d), **same** (36d, 61d), **sane** (97d), **sate** (28b, 54d, 56a, 118a), **save** (42b, 67b, 84b, 94b, 126c), **seme** (37c), **sere** (37d, 133a), **Seve** (180), **shoe** (122b), **sice** (56c), **side** (43d, 47b, 69b, 119b), **sine** (52a, 70b, 96b, 124c), **sipe** (122b), **sire** (18b, 21d, 44d, 48d, 94d, 120c, 122c), **site** (72d, 76a, 107a), **size** (129a), **Skye** (64d, 120d), **sloe** (15b, 19d, 51d, 90b, 132a), **slue** (110c, 118c), **Smee** (88b), **snee** (33a, 35d, 68a), **soie** (51a), **soke** (67c), **sole** (42c, 46d, 47d, 84b, 87c, 109d, 111d, 228), **some** (86d, 96b), **sone** (246), **sore** (12d, 106c), **Spee** (53c, 55c), **suke** (120a), **sure** (10b, 99b, 106b, 126d), **syce** (56c), **syne** (105b)

S F _ _ Sfax (223)

S _ _ F self (39d, 62d), **serf** (20d, 110b), **surf** (21d)

_ S G _ Msgr. (241), **M.Sgt.** (241), **S.Sgt.** (243)

S _ _ G sang, **shag** (57b, 119c, 122c), **sing** (129d), **skeg** (67b, 133b), **slag** (28c, 38b, 76b, 105a, 111a, 129a, 130a), **slog** (38b, 124d, 129b), **slug** (38a, 76b, 116b), **smog** (130d), **smug** (29c, 106c), **snag** (13a, 24d, 60a, 68c, 95a, 122b), **Snug** (193), **snug** (31c, 122a), **song**

(14b, 61d, 125a), **stag** (34c, 52b, 76a), **Sung** (26d), **sung, surg.**
(243), **swag** (115c), **swig** (37d, 57a)

S H _ _   **shad** (25b, 46d), **shag** (57b, 119c, 122c), **shah** (16c, 88a), **Shak.**
(243), **sham** (9d, 34a, 45a, 49b, 77b, 91d, 94b, 109c), **Shan** (62d,
69a, 220), **Shaw** (41a, 43a, 180, 204), **shay** (84a), **Shea** (180),
shea (22d, 124a), **shed** (24d, 70d, 77d, 108a), **she'd** (30c), **Shem**
(81d, 197), **she's** (30c), **shew** (128a), **shi'a** (80c), **shim** (71c, 119c,
130d), **shin** (11d, 12a, 71a, 71b, 107c), **ship** (106c, 128a), **shiv**
(68a), **shod, shoe** (122b), **shoo** (38a, 54b), **shop** (62d, 100a), **shot**
(12b, 70c), **shou** (26d), **show** (9d, 34d, 35a, 36c, 43a, 74c), **shul**
(118d), **shun** (16c, 41c), **shut** (28b)

_ S H _   **Ashe** (139), **ashy** (86a, 129d), **Ishi** (134a), **OSHA** (241)

_ _ S H   **bash** (60b, 86d), **bosh** (82a), **Bush** (143, 191), **bush** (109a, 119a),
Cash (144), **cash** (15a, 78a), **cosh** (60b), **Cush** (57c, 197), **dash**
(20a, 96a, 114a, 120b, 128d), **dish** (76a, 119a), **fish** (128d), **gash**
(33a, 110b), **Gish** (155), **gosh** (42a, 53b), **gush** (114b, 118a), **hash**
(21b), **hush** (109b), **Josh** (163), **josh** (17a, 66b, 66d, 90d), **Kish**
(197), **kish** (55d, 104c), **lash** (42d, 47c, 122a, 131c), **losh** (40b),
lush (38b, 73d), **MASH** (240), **Mash** (197), **mash** (32b, 115d),
mesh (40d, 63c, 81c, 111b, 130d), **mush** (75b), **Nash** (172), **pish**
(42c), **posh** (21a, 40b), **push** (38a, 46a, 108d, 121d), **rash** (98b,
110a), **resh** (12a), **Rush** (179), **rush** (114a), **sash** (18c, 37c, 54c,
132b), **sish** (61b), **tosh** (82a), **tush** (23a), **Wash** (82b), **Wash.**
(212), **wash** (14d), **wish** (35b)

S _ _ H   **sash** (18c, 37c, 54c, 132b), **Seth** (10a, 42b, 197, 198), **seth** (76a),
shah (16c, 88a), **sigh** (21d), **Sikh** (60b), **sish** (61b), **soph.** (243),
such (131b)

S I _ _   **sial** (85b), **Siam** (120d), **sibs, sice** (56c), **sick** (126b), **sida** (30d,
96d), **side** (43d, 47b, 69b, 119b), **Sids, sift** (105c, 109b, 132d),
sigh (21d), **sign** (74d, 91c, 114c), **sika** (34c, 65d, 231), **Sikh** (60b),
silk (43b), **Sill** (49a), **sill** (37c, 121c, 132b), **silo** (48a, 116a), **silt**
(79c, 106b), **sima** (101b), **Simi** (64c), **simp** (48b, 109c), **Sims**
(181), **sine** (52a, 70b, 96b, 124c), **sing** (129d), **sink** (34b, 60c,
110d), **Sino-** (92d), **sino** (112d), **sins, -sion** (117a), **sipe** (122b),
sips, sire (18b, 21d, 44d, 48d, 94d, 120c, 122c), **sirs, sish** (61b),
Sita (97d), **site** (72d, 76a, 107a), **sito-** (93a), **sits, Siva** (91a), **size**
(129a)

_ S I _   **Asia** (39b), **asin** (78b), **Hsia** (26d, 38d), **Isis** (61b, 85a), **-osis**
(117a), **psis, Tsin** (26d), **USIA** (243)

_ _ S I   **ANSI** (235), **assi** (60c), **Desi** (149), **Iasi** (221), **Lisi** (166), **lysi-**
(93a), **nasi** (87a), **nisi** (70b, 126c), **ossi-** (92c)

S _ _ I   **Safi** (220), **Saki** (95c), **saki** (78b, 231), **sari** (52d, 60a), **Sati** (96d,
109d, 198), **sebi-** (92d), **semi** (62c), **semi-** (93a, 93c), **Seri** (76c),
Seti (88c), **sexi-** (93c), **Simi** (64c), **Sodi** (197), **soli** (14b), **sori**
(45b), **sufi** (88a), **sugi** (65b), **suji** (131b)

S _ _ J subj. (243)

S K _ _ skat (24b), skaw (67c), skeg (67b, 133b), skeo (47a), skep (18a, 60b), skew (118c, 125b), skid (110c), skim (47c, 54d, 56a), skin (43a, 59d, 87c, 104c), skip (9b, 56a, 84a, 87a), skis, skit (108d, 110a), skua (56d, 65b, 105c), Skye (64d, 120d), skyr (20d)

_ S K _ asks

_ _ S K bask (46d, 73d, 80b, 128d, 228), bosk (133b), busk (20c, 31a, 45c), cask (30b), cusk (46d), desk (134c), disk (27b), dusk (125c), fisk (42c), husk (43a, 61c, 106b, 232), mask (29d, 36b, 37c), musk (87d), Omsk (64b), pisk (12b), risk (52b, 58c, 66b, 127d), rusk (21d), Sask. (242), task (115c), Tosk (213), tusk (46d, 65c, 123a)

S _ _ K sack (30b, 36a, 89b, 90c, 132c), Salk (179), sank, Sark (26a, 64b), Sask. (242), Sauk (49b, 56c, 189), S.Dak. (242), seek (105d), Shak. (243), sick (126b), silk (43b), sink (34b, 60c, 110d), soak (9b, 37d, 104b, 115a), sock (96a, 116b, 132b), sook (23b), souk (17d, 74d), suck (9b), sulk (117d), sunk, SWAK (243)

S L _ _ slab (88d, 110c), slag (28c, 38b, 76b, 105a, 111a, 129a, 130a), slam (124c, 131c), slap (22c, 98b), slat (69b, 133b), Slav (14d), slaw (28d), slay (36c, 79d), sled (102b), slew (110c, 118c), sley (130d), slid, Slim (181), slim (110c, 118b), slip (36b, 41c, 52d, 54d, 110c, 126b), slit (33a), slob (126d), sloe (15b, 19d, 51d, 90b, 132a), slog (38b, 124d, 129b), slop (48b, 111b), slot (12d, 13b, 34c, 84b, 123c), slow (34a, 35d, 58a, 110d, 116d), slub (134b), slue (110c, 118c), slug (38a, 76b, 116b), slum (81b, 99d), slur (36c, 40b, 74c, 95b, 123c, 128b), slut (133b)

_ S L _ isle (11a, 64b, 67b), Oslo (220)

_ _ S L NASL (241)

S _ _ L saal (53d), Sahl (179), sail (91c), Saul (67d, 87a, 179, 197), seal (28b, 44c, 89b, 231), seel (20a), sell (74d, 87c, 127d), shul (118d), sial (85b), Sill (49a), sill (37c, 121c, 132b), soil (39a, 114c, 117d, 120d), Soul (181), soul (95d, 113d, 128c), STOL (243), syll. (243)

S M _ _ Smee (88b), smew (19a, 38c, 76a, 104c), smit (128a), smog (130d), smug (29c, 106c), smur (38a), smut (28c, 36a, 90a, 111d)

_ S M _ USMA (243), USMC (243)

_ _ S M cosm- (93d), Tasm. (243)

S _ _ M scum (62c, 98d, 110c), seam (66c, 67a, 128c), seem (13c), sejm (91a), sham (9d, 34a, 45a, 49b, 77b, 91d, 94b, 109c), Shem (81d, 197), shim (71c, 119c, 130d), Siam (120d), skim (47c, 54d, 56a), slam (124c, 131c), Slim (181), slim (110c, 118b), slum (81b, 99d), Spam (73c), stem (26b, 95c, 114c, 115d), stum (55d, 100b, 132c), swam, swim (37a), swum

S N _ _   snab (22b, 105a), snag (13a, 24d, 60a, 68c, 95a, 122b), snap (17b, 21d, 31d, 39b, 44c, 66c), sned (73a), snee (33a, 35d, 68a), snip (28a), snit (10d, 12c, 47b), snob (88a, 111b), snot (62c, 88a), Snow (181), snow (130d), snub (62a, 81b, 98b, 109a, 110c), Snug (193), snug (31c, 122a)

_ S N _   esne (12c, 106d, 110b, 121b), isn't, USNA (243), USNG (243), USNR (244)

_ _ S N   assn. (236), bo's'n (20c, 88b)

S _ _ N   sain (19d, 32b), sawn, scan (47c, 73a, 88b, 98a), Sean (66c, 180), seen, sewn, Shan (62d, 69a, 220), shin (11d, 12a, 71a, 71b, 107c), shun (16c, 41c), sign (74d, 91c, 114c), -sion (117a), skin (43a, 59d, 87c, 104c), soon (94a, 108d), sown, span (21d, 32a, 38d, 49a, 81d, 85d, 98a, 120a, 120c, 122a, 232), spin (100b, 131c), spun, Stan (181), Sten (182), sten (73d), stun (108b, 116c), sunn (45d), Svan (25a), Sven, swan (19a, 28c, 226)

S O _ _   soak (9b, 37d, 104b, 115a), soap (17c), soar (48a), sobs, sock (96a, 116b, 132b), soco (21c), soda (18d, 38a, 111c, 131c), Sodi (197), sods, sofa (36d), soft (39b, 74c, 76d), soga (52c), So-Ho (73a), soie (51a), soil (39a, 114c, 117d, 120d), soir (50b), soja (56c), soke (67c), sola (11d, 39b, 89c), sold, sole (42c, 46d, 47d, 84b, 87c, 109d, 111d, 228), soli (14b), solo (11d, 14b, 84a), Sols, soma (12d, 20c, 62d), some (86d, 96b), sone (246), song (14b, 61d, 125a), sons (83c), sook (23b), soon (94a, 108d), soot (24a, 28c, 68d), soph. (243), sops, sora (19a, 97b), sorb (13c, 79a, 107a, 110b), sore (12d, 106c), sori (45b), sors (69c), sort (27d, 36d, 67c, 106d, 109b, 113b, 127b, 132d), so-so (76c, 86d, 122d), sots, souk (17d, 74d), Soul (181), soul (95d, 113d, 128c), soup (75c), sour (15b, 119d), sous (51b), sown, sows, soya (112c), soys

_ S O _   asor (59a), USOC (244)

_ _ S O   also (12c, 18c, 62c, 78c, 90c, 115b), Caso (64c), Koso (108d), meso- (93b), miso (65d), miso- (93a), naso- (93b), noso- (92d), peso (215, 216, 217, 219, 221, 224), so-so (76c, 86d, 122d), vaso- (92c)

S _ _ O   sado (24c, 66a), sago (44b, 86a, 95d, 114d), Saho (32d, 57c, 216), sebo- (92d), sego (22c, 71d), sero- (93c), shoo (38a, 54b), silo (48a, 116a), Sino- (92d), sino (112d), sito- (93a), skeo (47a), soco (21c), So-Ho (73a), solo (11d, 14b, 84a), so-so (76c, 86d, 122d), sumo (66a)

S P _ _   spad (80b, 89d), Spam (73c), span (21d, 32a, 38d, 49a, 81d, 85d, 98a, 120a, 120c, 122a, 232), spar (21b, 22c, 52a, 77a, 90d, 101c, 108b), spas (93b), spat (14b, 85d, 96b, 102c), spay (115b), SPCA (243), spec. (243), sped, Spee (53c, 55c), Spes (198), spet (17b), spew (40a), spin (100b, 131c), spir- (92d), spit (90d, 101b), spor- (93d), spot (35d, 72d, 79d, 89d, 114c), SPQR (243), spry (9d, 72c, 81d), spud (92a), spun, spur (46a, 54d, 62c, 63c, 95a)

_ S P _   **asps**, **ESPN** (26a), **espy** (106b), **USPO** (244), **USPS** (244)

_ _ S P   **cusp** (31d, 61a, 89d, 90c, 90d), **gasp** (21d, 86b), **hasp** (44c, 113c), **hosp.** (239), **Insp.** (239), **lisp** (113c), **rasp** (46a, 56a, 105c, 122d), **WASP** (244), **wasp** (63b, 229), **wisp** (49b)

S _ _ P   **salp** (83b), **samp** (55c, 60d, 91c), **scop** (90c), **scup** (91c, 228), **seep** (72b, 84b, 87d, 114a), **ship** (106c, 128a), **shop** (62d, 100a), **simp** (48b, 109c), **skep** (18a, 60b), **skip** (9b, 56a, 84a, 87a), **slap** (22c, 98b), **slip** (36b, 41c, 52d, 54d, 110c, 126b), **slop** (48b, 111b), **snap** (17b, 21d, 31d, 39b, 44c, 66c), **snip** (28a), **soap** (17c), **soup** (75c), **step** (55c, 129b), **stop** (9a, 14c, 17a, 25b, 40d, 57c, 84c, 131d), **sump** (25d, 77a), **swap** (123c)

S _ _ Q   **seqq.** (243)

S R _ _   **Srta.** (243)

_ _ S R   **USSR** (244)

S _ _ R   **Saar** (49c, 78d, 101a), **Sadr** (207), **S.Afr.** (242), **-saur** (117b), **scar** (27b, 134a), **sear** (25b, 133a), **seer** (95b, 111d, 128c), **sehr** (54a), **Seir**(41c), **skyr**(20d), **slur** (36c, 40b, 74c, 95b, 123c, 128b), **smur** (38a), **soar** (48a), **soir** (50b), **sour** (15b, 119d), **spar** (21b, 22c, 52a, 77a, 90d, 101c, 108b), **spir-** (92d), **spor-** (93d), **SPQR** (243), **spur** (46a, 54d, 62c, 63c, 95a), **star** (15b, 73c), **-ster** (117a, 117b), **stir** (10d, 14c, 29b, 36d, 63b, 77b, 79c, 94d, 95a, 115c), **suer** (95b)

S S _ _   **S.Sgt.** (243)

_ S S _   **asse** (49b), **assi** (60c), **assn.** (236), **asst.** (236), **esse** (9d, 18b), **Issa** (216), **Ossa** (79a, 84a, 121a), **ossa** (20d), **ossi-** (92c), **USSR** (244)

_ _ S S   **Bess** (141), **boss** (40c, 116c), **buss** (68a), **Cass** (144), **cess** (71c, 120a), **cuss** (32d, 88a, 118c), **diss** (75d), **doss** (18a), **Fess** (152), **fess** (41c), **foss** (36d), **fuss** (21b, 36d, 92a), **Hess** (158), **Hiss** (158), **hiss** (36a, 112a), **jass** (118d), **Jess** (161), **jess** (116a), **joss** (26d, 62c), **kiss** (22d, 91b), **koss** (246), **lass** (45b, 74b), **less** (77b, 82c), **liss** (49a), **loss** (35a, 94d, 130a), **Mass.** (210, 240), **mass** (9c, 10d, 17a, 22c, 53a, 58d, 107a, 129a), **mess** (21b, 26a, 30a, 36c, 67a, 79c, 111b), **Miss.** (210, 240), **miss** (54c, 108c), **Moss** (171), **moss** (71c, 86c, 125a), **muss** (103a), **ness** (24a, 58d, 95a), **pass** (13d, 21d, 84a, 85c, 106c), **puss** (24d), **Ross** (178, 193, 195, 207, 208), **ross** (17b, 119c), **Russ** (179), **Russ.** (242), **sass** (16b, 62c), **sess** (111b), **sess.** (243), **TASS** (81c, 112b), **Tess** (58a, 183), **toss** (22c, 47c, 121c)

S _ _ S   **sacs**, **sags**, **Sais** (39d), **sais** (56c), **Saks** (179), **Sams**, **sans** (51b), **saps**, **sass** (16b, 62c), **SATs** (29a), **saws**, **says**, **seas**, **sees**, **seis** (113a), **sens** (49c), **seps** (72c, 106d), **sess** (111b), **sess.** (243), **sets**, **sews**, **she's** (30c), **sibs**, **Sids**, **Sims** (181), **sins**, **sips**, **sirs**, **sits**, **skis**, **sobs**, **sods**, **Sols**, **sons** (83c), **sops**, **sors** (69c), **sots**,

sous (51b), **sows, soys, spas, Spes** (198), **Stus, subs, suds** (18a, 48a, 114a), **sues, sums, Suns** (206), **suns, sups**

S T _ _   **stab** (15c, 68a, 88d), **stad** (112b), **stag** (34c, 52b, 76a), **Stan** (181), **star** (15b, 73c), **stat** (15c, 114a), **-stat** (117c), **stat.** (243), **stay** (34c, 57c, 95b, 99c, 102b, 119d, 128c, 129b), **stem** (26b, 95c, 114c, 115d), **Sten** (182), **sten** (73d), **step** (55c, 129b), **-ster** (117a, 117b), **stet** (71c, 94c, 95b), **stew** (20c, 30c), **stib** (38d), **stir** (10d, 14c, 29b, 36d, 63b, 77b, 79c, 94d, 95a, 115c), **stoa** (29a, 91c), **STOL** (243), **stop** (9a, 14c, 17a, 25b, 40d, 57c, 84c, 131d), **stot** (134d), **stow** (85b), **stub** (121d, 122c), **stud** (23a, 44c, 74c, 84d, 126d), **stum** (55d, 100b, 132c), **stun** (108b, 116c), **Stus, Styx** (26b, 57a)

_ S T _   **Asta** (37b, 81d, 121b), **Asti** (65a, 132c), **astr-** (93d), **esta** (113a), **Este** (44b, 45b, 64d, 85b), **este** (113a), **Esth.** (16d, 238), **oste** (20d), **USTA** (244)

_ _ S T   **AHST** (235), **asst.** (236), **bast** (17b, 45d, 88c, 133c), **best** (26d, 30a, 34c, 42b, 85c, 118b), **bust** (14c, 17a, 21d, 44a, 58c), **cast** (15a, 73a, 121c, 123b, 232), **cest** (54c), **cist** (115d), **cost** (26a, 94b), **cyst** (128a), **dist.** (237), **dost** (128a), **dust** (114a), **east** (84d), **erst** (49a), **fast** (46b, 47c, 96d, 118c, 126d), **-fest** (117b), **fist** (21c, 57d), **fust** (107b), **gest** (119b), **gist** (74b, 89c), **gust** (20a), **hast** (128a), **hist.** (239), **host** (14c, 42a, 79d), **Inst.** (239), **jest** (17a, 66d), **just** (41b, 44a, 62b, 76a, 97c, 127c), **kist** (105b), **last** (30b, 40d, 108c, 130d), **lest** (48d), **list** (24d, 41b, 65c, 101c, 102b, 104d, 122a), **LOST** (240), **lost** (77b, 130a), **lust** (34a, 107a), **mast** (18a, 90d, 108b, 113a), **mist** (28b, 38a, 48a, 127b), **most** (74b, 78c), **must** (55d, 81c, 116c, 132c), **myst** (56b), **Nast** (172), **nest** (31c, 100a, 111b, 118c, 232), **oast** (16b, 67b, 85c), **oust** (35b, 40a, 42b, 96c), **past** (55b, 60b, 122a), **pest** (82d, 88a, 89d), **Post** (175), **post** (69c, 74b, 81c, 115a), **rest** (16b, 21d, 71b, 80c, 87b, 99b, 99c, 99d, 234), **rust** (31a, 85d, 90a), **test** (23d, 41d, 42b, 124b, 124d), **Uist** (64d), **vast** (61c, 62a), **vest** (28b, 129b), **wast** (128a), **West** (186), **west** (83b), **wist** (68c), **zest** (45c, 57c, 99b)

S _ _ T   **SALT** (242), **salt** (29d, 80b, 94b, 103b, 106a, 111c), **Sart** (64a), **scat** (54b, 96d), **Scot** (59d), **Scot.** (242), **scut** (119a), **seat** (25d, 63b, 115c), **sect** (34d, 43d), **sent, Sept.** (78c, 243), **sept** (27d, 64a, 111b), **Sert** (112c), **sett** (87b, 119d), **sext** (23d, 84d, 109d), **shot** (12b, 70c), **shut** (28b), **sift** (105c, 109b, 132d), **silt** (79c, 106b), **skat** (24b), **skit** (108d, 110a), **slat** (69b, 133b), **slit** (33a), **slot** (12d, 13b, 34c, 84b, 123c), **slut** (133b), **smit** (128a), **smut** (28c, 36a, 90a, 111d), **snit** (10d, 12c, 47b), **snot** (62c, 88a), **soft** (39b, 74c, 76d), **soot** (24a, 28c, 68d), **sort** (27d, 36d, 67c, 106d, 109b, 113b, 127b, 132d), **spat** (14b, 85d, 96b, 102c), **spet** (17b), **spit** (90d, 101b), **spot** (35d, 72d, 79d, 89d, 114c), **S.Sgt.** (243), **stat** (15c, 114a), **-stat** (117c), **stat.** (243), **stet** (71c, 94c, 95b), **stot** (134d), **suet** (44c, 83d), **suit** (9c, 10a, 31c, 47b, 71a, 85b, 90b, 104b), **supt.** (243), **SWAT** (243), **swat** (20a, 28b, 116c), **Swit** (182)

S U _ _   **subj.** (243), **subs, such** (131b), **suck** (9b), **sudd** (47c), **suds** (18a, 48a, 114a), **sued, suer** (95b), **sues, suet** (44c, 83d), **Suez** (23c), sufi (88a), **sugi** (65b), **suit** (9c, 10a, 31c, 47b, 71a, 85b, 90b, 104b), **suji** (131b), **suke** (120a), **suky** (120a), **sulk** (117d), **Sulu** (88c), **sulu** (46a), **sumo** (66a), **sump** (25d, 77a), **sums, Sung** (26d), **sung, sunk, sunn** (45d), **Suns** (206), **suns, sups, supt.** (243), **sura** (68c, 86a), **surd** (30b, 82d), **sure** (10b, 99b, 106b, 126d), **surf** (21d), **surg.** (243), **Susa** (40a), **susu** (20a), **Suva** (128d, 216)

_ S U _   **tsun** (246), **usus** (69c, 70b)

_ _ S U   **ansu** (13d, 68c), **Nosu** (215), **susu** (20a), **Zasu** (188)

S _ _ U   **Seau** (180), **shou** (26d), **Sulu** (88c), **sulu** (46a), **susu** (20a)

S V _ _   **Svan** (25a), **Sven**

_ S V _   **RSVP** (242)

S _ _ V   **shiv** (68a), **Slav** (14d)

S W _ _   **swab** (57c, 78c, 134b), **swag** (115c), **SWAK** (243), **swam, swan** (19a, 28c, 226), **swap** (123c), **SWAT** (243), **swat** (20a, 28b, 116b), **sway** (29b, 37b, 63a, 67c, 76d, 79c, 85a, 130c, 133a), **Swed.** (243), **swig** (37d, 57a), **swim** (37a), **Swit** (182), **swum**

S _ _ W   **scow** (20c, 47b), **Shaw** (41a, 43a, 180, 204), **shew** (128a), **show** (9d, 34d, 35a, 36c, 43a, 74c), **skaw** (67c), **skew** (118c, 125b), **slaw** (28d), **slew** (110c, 118c), **slow** (34a, 35d, 58a, 110d, 116d), **smew** (19a, 38c, 76a, 104c), **Snow** (181), **snow** (130d), **spew** (40a), **stew** (20c, 30c), **stow** (85b)

S _ _ X   **Sfax** (223), **Styx** (26b, 57a)

S Y _ _   **syce** (56c), **syll.** (243), **syne** (105b)

_ _ S Y   **busy** (40d, 83b), **easy** (43d, 53c, 55c, 77c, 109c, 111c), **nosy** (63b), **posy** (82b, 100d), **rosy** (54d, 84c)

S _ _ Y   **secy.** (243), **sexy** (41c), **shay** (84a), **slay** (36c, 79d), **sley** (130d), **spay** (115b), **spry** (9d, 72c, 81d), **stay** (34c, 57c, 95b, 99c, 102b, 119d, 128c, 129b), **suky** (120a), **sway** (29b, 37b, 63a, 67c, 76d, 79c, 85a, 130c, 133a)

S _ _ Z   **Suez** (23c)

T A _ _   **Taal** (10c, 69a, 112b), **tabs, tabu** (48c), **tack** (13d, 15c, 31b, 44c, 80b), **tact** (35d), **tads, tael** (71c, 131a), **ta'en** (107c), **Taft** (183, 191), **tags, taha** (130d), **tahr** (55a), **tail** (13c, 25a, 40d, 48b, 89d, 107b, 123c), **tait** (15d, 60d), **taka** (213), **take** (117a), **takt** (80a, 120b), **tala** (17c), **talc** (25d, 49c, 77a, 92a, 111b), **tale** (43a, 71b, 103b, 134a), **talk** (29d, 36a, 113b), **tall** (72d), **tame** (37a, 37b, 53c), **tamp** (76d, 85b, 92a, 97d), **tams, Tana** (68b), **T'ang** (26d), **tang** (22a, 47b, 135a), **tank** (127d), **Tano** (95d, 189), **tans, Taos** (81c),

tapa (17b, 28b, 43b, 45c, 79d, 86b, 91a), **tape** (19a, 98c), **taps**, **Tara** (104d), **tara** (45b, 64a), **tare** (128b, 131a), **tarn** (68b, 79b, 91b, 130a), **taro** (14d, 39c, 52a, 90d, 102b, 114d, 125a), **tarp** (23d, 130b), **tars, tart** (87a, 112b), **task** (115c), **Tasm.** (243), **TASS** (81c, 112b), **ta-ta** (44b), **tats, tatu** (14b), **taur-** (92c), **taus, taut** (120c, 122a), **tawa** (81c), **taws, taxi** (95d)

_ T A _   **atap** (86a), **Etah** (56c, 63d), **et al.** (69c, 238), **etat** (51a), **ital.** (240), **Ptah** (75d, 198), **stab** (15c, 68a, 88d), **stad** (112b), **stag** (34c, 52b, 76a), **Stan** (181), **star** (15b, 73c), **stat** (15c, 114a), **-stat** (117c), **stat.** (243), **stay** (34c, 57c, 95b, 99c, 102b, 119d, 128c, 129b), **Utah** (212), **utas** (40a)

_ _ T A   **acta** (34b, 94d, 98c, 121a), **Alta.** (235), **anta** (89a, 91c), **Arta** (56d), **Asta** (37b, 81d, 121b), **atta** (70c), **beta** (11d, 106a), **cata-** (92c, 92d), **CETA** (236), **data** (29c, 63a, 115a), **dita** (88c, 124b), **esta** (113a), **Etta** (152), **-etta** (117b), **gata** (107d), **geta** (65b, 108c), **iota** (11d, 66d, 122c, 131c), **jota** (112c), **keta** (37b), **meta-** (92d), **muta** (26a, 80d), **Nita** (172), **nota** (69d), **octa-** (92d), **pita** (11d, 25c, 45c), **rata** (46a), **Rita** (177), **rota** (25a, 27a, 31c, 101d, 102b), **seta** (22a, 57b, 113c), **Sita** (97d), **Srta.** (243), **ta-ta** (44b), **USTA** (244), **vita** (69d, 71d), **vota** (102a), **weta** (72d), **zeta** (11d)

T _ _ A   **taha** (130d), **taka** (213), **tala** (17c), **Tana** (68b), **tapa** (17b, 28b, 43b, 45c, 79d, 86b, 91a), **Tara** (104d), **tara** (45b, 64a), **ta-ta** (44b), **tawa** (81c), **tela** (21c, 75d, 130d), **tema** (121a, 234), **tera-** (93d), **Tewa** (189), **Thea** (122c), **Tina** (183), **Toda** (37d), **toea** (221), **toga** (101d), **tola** (66d, 103a), **tora** (13a, 58b), **tuba** (80a, 86a), **tufa** (91c, 129a), **tula** (10d, 11d), **tuna** (125a, 229), **Tyra** (184)

T _ _ B   **tomb** (22d)

_ T C _   **etch** (14d, 35a), **itch** (58a, 64b)

_ _ T C   **ROTC** (242)

T _ _ C   **talc** (25d, 49c, 77a, 92a, 111b)

T _ _ D   **teed, tend** (24b, 73a, 77a, 124b), **Thad** (183), **thud** (20a, 112a), **tied, toad** (17c, 225), **Todd** (183), **toed, told** (99a), **trod**

T E _ _   **teak** (39b, 124a), **teal** (19a, 20b, 38c, 226), **team** (32a, 48c, 56c, 85d, 232), **tear** (68b, 99c), **teas, teat** (81d), **Teds, teed, teel** (107a), **teem** (9b, 92a, 118c), **-teen** (117b), **Tees** (82b), **tees, teff** (10c), **tegs, teil** (72a), **Teke** (215), **tela** (21c, 75d, 130d), **tele-** (92d, 93d), **Tell** (14a), **tell** (13d, 62b, 81a, 99a), **telo-** (92d), **tema** (121a, 234), **temp.** (243), **tend** (24b, 73a, 77a, 124b), **Tenn.** (212, 243), **teno-** (93d), **tens, tent** (24a, 87b), **Teos** (64a), **tera-** (93d), **Teri** (183), **term** (71d, 72a, 80b, 106c, 115c), **tern** (19a, 28c, 56d, 104d, 105d, 118b, 226), **terp** (79a, 94a), **Tess** (58a, 183), **test** (23d, 41d, 42b, 124b, 124d), **tete** (50c), **teth** (12a), **Tewa** (189), **text** (86d, 133c)

_ T E _   **atef** (32b, 39d), **ates** (118c), **cten-** (93c), **itea** (118c, 128c), **item** (9c, 14d, 35b, 41b, 71a, 72b, 81c, 83a, 86d), **iter** (69d, 101a, 101d),

Otea (64c), pter- (94a), **stem** (26b, 95c, 114c, 115d), **Sten** (182), **sten** (73d), **step** (55c, 129b), -ster (117a, 117b), **stet** (71c, 94c, 95b), **stew** (20c, 30c), uter- (93d), **Utes**

_ _ T E   alte (69d), ante (68a, 69c, 90d, 114c), ante- (92c), **Arte** (139), **bate** (119c), **Bete** (215), bete (50a), bite (26c, 115c), **Bute** (64d), cete (232), **cite** (97c), **cote** (19b, 107d, 108a), **cute** (10a, 32c, 116a), date (33d, 51d), dote (85c), **Este** (44b, 45b, 64d, 85b), este (113a), -ette (117b), fate (35b, 68a, 73b), fete (45c), gate (15c, 41b, 91c), gite (50c), hate (35b, 72d), jete (16c), jute (30d, 45c, 102b, 103a), **Kate** (107c, 163), **Kite** (164), kite (19a, 58c, 226), late (33d, 98b), -lite (117b, 117c), lute (25c, 66a, 80b, 100d), -lyte (117a), **mate** (15b, 18d, 26c, 29b, 34c, 85d, 114a, 120a), mete (11c, 13d, 91d), mite (14a, 63b, 64a, 86c, 86d), **mote** (113b), **mute** (109b, 113c, 232, 234), **Nate** (172), note (15c, 71c, 75d, 83b, 95a, 98c, 99c, 122d, 129c, 234), oste (20d), **Pate** (174), pate (32b, 58c), **Pete** (85a, 174), rate (13d, 27d, 30b, 41d, 42a, 55c, 66d, 94b, 97d, 107a, 127b), rete (81c, 90b), rite (72c), **Rote** (178), rote (75d, 99d, 118a), sate (28b, 54d, 56a, 118a), site (72d, 76a, 107a), tete (50c), **tote** (22a, 24c, 86c), vite (50d), **vote** (49b, 128d), yate (41d)

T _ _ E   take (117a), tale (43a, 71b, 103b, 134a), tame (37a, 37b, 53c), tape (19a, 98c), tare (128b, 131a), **Teke** (215), tele- (92d, 93d), tete (50c), thee (95b), tide (83b), tige (89b), tile (27d, 46b, 74b, 102a, 120d), time (38d, 41b, 41c, 87d, 100b), tine (13a, 95a, 123a), tire (21a, 42d, 44d, 47b, 131c), **Tobe** (183), tobe (10c), tole (41b, 76b), tome (20d, 129a), **Tone** (184), tone (9c, 82c, 89c), tope (107d, 229), tore, tote (22a, 24c, 86c), tree (30d, 53b, 133c), true (9d, 15d, 31a, 42b, 44a, 73c, 111b), tube (33c, 89c, 117a), -tude (117b), tuke (23d, 43b), tule (22c, 25a), **Tune** (184), tune (9c, 10a, 10d, 14b, 58a, 75d, 111d, 116a), tyee (26d), tyke (21c, 26c), **Tyne** (82b, 184, 223), **type** (27d, 112a, 113b), **Tyre** (71a, 88c, 218)

T _ _ F   teff (10c), **TGIF** (243), tiff (96b), toff (33c), tref (48b, 126a), **tuff** (91c, 129a), turf (87b, 111c, 118b)

T G _ _   **TGIF** (243)

T _ _ G   T'ang (26d), tang (22a, 47b, 135a), thug (52c), ting (76b), **tong** (26d), trig (114a, 124c), trig. (31b, 243), tung (83d), twig (21c)

T H _ _   **Thad** (183), **Thai** (109a, 218, 223), than (29b), **Thar** (35a), thar (55a), that (34d, 95a, 99b), thaw (72b), **Thea** (122c), thee (95b), them (95a), then (10c, 121a), thew (79d), they (95a), thin (35c, 35d, 53b, 110c), thio- (93d), this (34d, 95a), **Thor** (10b, 76c, 77b, 83b, 121d, 183, 198), **Thos.** (74d), thos (65b), thou (95b), thru, thud (20a, 112a), thug (52c), **Thur.** (243), thus (111b, 121a)

_ T H _   ethn- (93c), **Otho** (102a)

_ _ T H   **ACTH** (235), anth. (235), auth. (236), **Bath** (41a, 112c), bath (35d, 88d, 125a, 246), **Beth** (11a, 141), beth (12a), both (122c, 125c), **Cath.** (236), doth (128a), **Esth.** (16d, 238), **Gath** (88c), **Goth**

(120d), **hath** (128a), **Heth** (197), **Hoth** (20a), **jeth** (78b), **kith** (105a), **lath** (116c), **lgth.** (240), **Lith.** (240), **-lith** (117c), **Luth.** (240), **math** (116c), **Meth.** (240), **Moth** (193), **moth** (22d, 71b, 229), **myth** (43a, 71b), **Neth.** (241), **oath** (90b, 111c), **orth-** (92d), **path** (101a, 102c, 130c), **pith** (30d, 41d, 51d, 54c, 74b, 75a, 90a, 97c, 120d), **rath** (99d), **Roth** (178), **Ruth** (80d, 179, 196, 197), **ruth** (29b, 89c), **Seth** (10a, 42b, 197, 198), **seth** (76a), **teth** (12a), **with** (11d, 12c)

T _ _ H   **teth** (12a), **tosh** (82a), **tush** (23a)

T I _ _   **tick** (14a, 20a, 229), **tics**, **tide** (83b), **tidy** (81a, 84c, 111b), **tied**, **tier** (46a, 89b, 102c), **ties**, **tiff** (96b), **tige** (89b), **tiki** (91a), **tile** (27d, 46b, 74b, 102a, 120d), **till** (32c), **tilt** (23d, 24b, 62c, 72b, 101c), **time** (38d, 41b, 41c, 87d, 100b), **Timi** (183), **Tims**, **Tina** (183), **tine** (13a, 95a, 123a), **ting** (76b). **tins**, **tint** (29a, 107b), **tiny** (77b, 110d), **-tion** (117a, 117b), **tips**, **tire** (21a, 42d, 44d, 47b, 131c), **tiro** (18b, 82c), **titi** (20b, 71a, 78b, 124a), **Tito** (183, 134d), **tits**

_ T I _   **-atic** (117c), **atis** (60a), **-itis** (117b), **otic** (15d, 39a), **Otis** (12b, 63d, 173), **stib** (38d), **stir** (10d, 14c, 29b, 36d, 63b, 77b, 79c, 94d, 95a, 115c)

_ _ T I   **alti-** (93a), **anti** (10c, 84c), **anti-** (92c), **Asti** (65a, 132c), **CETI** (236), **inti** (221), **kati** (246), **Loti** (49c, 95d), **loti** (218), **roti** (51a), **Sati** (96d, 109d, 198), **Seti** (88c), **titi** (20b, 71a, 78b, 124a), **toti-** (94a), **Yeti** (9b)

T _ _ I   **taxi** (95d), **Teri** (183), **Thai** (109a, 218, 223), **tiki** (91a), **Timi** (183), **titi** (20b, 71a, 78b, 124a), **Toni** (184), **topi** (30d, 89c), **Tori** (184), **tori** (30c), **toti-** (94a), **Tupi** (12b)

T _ _ K   **tack** (13d, 15c, 31b, 44c, 80b), **talk** (29d, 36a, 113b), **tank** (127d), **task** (115c), **teak** (39b, 124a), **tick** (14a, 20a, 229), **tock** (10c), **took** (83b), **Tosk** (213), **trek** (66d, 73a, 123d), **Truk** (24b), **tuck** (115c), **Turk** (85a, 217), **Turk.** (243), **tusk** (46d, 65c, 123a)

_ T L _   **atle** (104a, 119b), **Atli** (15c, 56d, 61c), **it'll** (30c)

_ _ T L   **Intl.** (239), **Natl.** (241)

T _ _ L   **Taal** (10c, 69a, 112b), **tael** (71c, 131a), **tail** (13c, 25a, 40d, 48b, 89d, 107b, 123c), **tall** (72d), **teal** (19a, 20b, 38c, 226), **teel** (107a), **teil** (72a), **Tell** (14a), **tell** (13d, 62b, 81a, 99a), **till** (32c), **toil** (38b, 124d, 133c, 133d), **toll** (18c, 94b, 100d), **tool** (25a, 62b, 127c)

T M _ _   **T-man** (45a), **T-men** (45a, 123d)

T _ _ M   **Tasm.** (243), **team** (32a, 48c, 56c, 85d, 232), **teem** (9b, 92a, 118c), **term** (71d, 72a, 80b, 106c, 115c), **them** (95a), **tram** (124c), **trim** (81a, 84d, 114a, 118b, 121d, 124c)

_ T N _   **at. no.** (236), **Etna** (129a), **etna** (58d)

_ _ T N attn. (236)

T _ _ N ta'en (107c), tarn (68b, 79b, 91b, 130a), -teen (117b), Tenn. (212, 243), tern (19a, 28c, 56d, 104d, 105d, 118b, 226), than (29b), then (10c, 121a), thin (35c, 35d, 53b, 110c), -tion (117a, 117b), T-man (45a), T-men (45a, 123d), toon (74b), Torn (184), torn (99c), town (57c, 128b), Trin. (243), -tron (117b), Tsin (26d), tsun (246), tuan (74c), turn (12c, 100b, 102b, 108a, 125c, 127c, 132b), twin (37c, 75b, 125c)

T O _ _ toad (17c, 225), Tobe (183), tobe (10c), toby (11b, 38a, 66d, 79d, 96a), tock(10c), toco (123b), Toda (37d), Todd (183), to-do (21b, 22d, 29b, 52c, 115c), tods, tody (19b), toea (221), toed, toes, toff (33c), toft (60d), toga (101d), Togo (223), togs (28b), to-ho (61d), toil (38b, 124d, 133c, 133d), tola (66d, 103a), told (99a), tole (41b, 76b), toll (18c, 94b, 100d), tolu (16d), tomb (22d), tome (20d, 129a), Toms, -tomy (117b), Tone (184), tone (9c, 82c, 89c), tong (26d), Toni (184), tono- (93c), tons, Tony (184), took (83b), tool (25a, 62b, 127c), toon (74b), toot (112b), tope (107d, 229), topi (30d, 89c), topo. (243), tops, tora (13a, 58b), tore, Tori (184), tori (30c), Torn (184), torn (99c), toro (31c, 112c), torr (246), tors, tort (27c, 71a, 134c), tory (22a, 30b, 73c), tosh (82a), Tosk (213), toss (22c, 47c, 121c), tote (22a, 24c, 86c), toti- (94a), Toto (37b, 133a), tots, tour (66d), tous (49d), tout (49d, 95a, 97b), tows, town (57c, 128b), toyo (58b, 65d, 116b), toys

_ T O _ atom (77d, 131c), aton (118a), atop (85c, 126d), -ator (117c), Eton (58b, 65b), Otoe (109d, 189), stoa (29a, 91c), STOL (243), stop (9a, 14c, 17a, 25b, 40d, 57c, 84c, 131d), stot (134d), stow (85b), VTOL (244)

_ _ T O alto (113a, 128d), alto- (93a), atto- (93c), auto (24a), bito (10c, 35b, 47a), Buto (198), Cato (101d, 102a, 194), Ceto (55c, 75d), cito (70a), coto (17b, 75c), ecto- (93c), ento- (94a), into (133a), JATO (240), Kato (56c), keto- (93b), koto (66a), Leto (13b, 14d, 28d, 88c, 198), moto (79c), NATO (11c, 241), nito (45b), noto- (92c), octo (69c), octo- (92d), on to (59b), Otto (53c, 173), otto (65a), Peto (193), peto (129b), RATO (242), sito- (93a), Tito (183, 134d), Toto (37b, 133a), unto, veto (95a)

T _ _ O Tano (95d, 189), taro (14d, 39c, 52a, 90d, 102b, 114d, 125a), telo- (92d), teno- (93d), thio- (93d), tiro (18b, 82c), Tito (183, 134d), toco (123b), to-do (21b, 22d, 29b, 52c, 115c), Togo (223), to-ho (61d), tono- (93c), topo. (243), toro (31c, 112c), Toto (37b, 133a), toyo (58b, 65d, 116b), trio (80c, 124b), tuno (57c), typo (41c, 94c), Tyro (81b), tyro (12b, 18b, 82c)

T _ _ P tamp (76d, 85b, 92a, 97d), tarp (23d, 130b), temp. (243), terp (79a, 94a), trap (24c, 24d, 41a, 54b, 55b, 101b, 111b), trip (66d, 232), trop (51b, 123a), tump (60a), tymp (19d), typp (134b)

T R _ _ tram (124c), trap (24c, 24d, 41a, 54b, 55b, 101b, 111b), tray (98b, 104a, 107a), tree (30d, 53b, 133c), tref (48b, 126a), trek (66d, 73a,

123d), **tres** (42b, 51b, 113a), **tret** (130a, 131a), **trey** (24a, 121c), **trig** (114a, 124c), **trig.** (31b, 243), **trim** (81a, 84d, 114a, 118b, 121d, 124c), **Trin.** (243), **trio** (80c, 124b), **trip** (66d, 232), **Tris** (184), **-trix** (117b), **trod**, **-tron** (117b), **trop** (51b, 123a), **trot** (66c, 85b), **trow** (18b), **Troy** (184), **troy** (119c, 131a), **true** (9d, 15d, 31a, 42b, 44a, 73c, 111b), **Truk** (24b)

_ T R _   **etre** (50a), **otro** (112c, 113a)

_ _ T R   **astr-** (93d), **metr-** (94a), **nitr-** (93b), **petr-** (93d)

T _ _ R   **tahr** (55a), **taur-** (92c), **tear** (68b, 99c), **Thar** (35a), **thar** (55a), **Thor** (10b, 76c, 77b, 83b, 121d, 183, 198), **Thur.** (243), **tier** (46a, 89b, 102c), **torr** (246), **tour** (66d), **tsar** (103c)

T S _ _   **tsar** (103c), **Tsin** (26d), **tsun** (246)

_ T S _   **NTSB** (241)

_ _ T S   **acts**, **ants**, **arts**, **bats**, **bets**, **bits** (19a), **bots**, **buts**, **cats**, **cots**, **cuts**, **dots**, **eats** (48b), **efts**, **Fats** (152), **fits**, **gats**, **gets**, **GUTS** (239), **guts** (63a), **hats**, **hits**, **huts**, **Jets** (206), **jets**, **jots**, **juts**, **kits**, **lets**, **lots** (26a), **Mats** (169), **Mets** (206), **mots**, **Nats**, **Nets** (206), **nets**, **nits**, **nuts**, **oats**, **opts**, **orts** (105c), **outs**, **pats**, **pets**, **pits**, **pots**, **puts**, **rats**, **rets**, **rots**, **ruts**, **SATs** (29a), **sets**, **sits**, **sots**, **tats**, **tits**, **tots**, **vats**, **vets**, **WATS** (244), **wets**, **wits**

T _ _ S   **tabs**, **tads**, **tags**, **tams**, **tans**, **Taos** (81c), **taps**, **tars**, **TASS** (81c, 112b), **tats**, **taus**, **taws**, **teas**, **Teds**, **Tees** (82b), **tees**, **tegs**, **tens**, **Teos** (64a), **Tess** (58a, 183), **this** (34d, 95a), **Thos.** (74d), **thos** (65b), **thus** (111b, 121a), **tics**, **ties**, **Tims**, **tins**, **tips**, **tits**, **tods**, **toes**, **togs** (28b), **Toms**, **tons**, **tops**, **tors**, **toss** (22c, 47c, 121c), **tots**, **tous** (49d), **tows**, **toys**, **tres** (42b, 51b, 113a), **Tris** (184), **tubs**, **Tues.** (243), **tugs**, **tuns**, **tups**, **'twas** (30b, 107c), **twos**, **Tyus** (184)

_ T T _   **atta** (70c), **attn.** (236), **atto-** (93c), **Attu** (64b), **atty.** (236), **Etta** (152), **-etta** (117b), **-ette** (117b), **Otto** (53c, 173), **otto** (65a)

_ _ T T   **batt** (16d), **bitt** (44c), **bott** (27d), **butt** (121d, 132c, 246), **Catt** (144), **GATT** (239), **Jett** (161), **Kitt** (164), **Lett** (16d), **Lott** (167), **Matt** (169, 240), **mitt** (17b, 46b, 54d), **Mott** (171), **mutt** (32d, 78a), **Pitt** (41a, 175), **putt** (55b), **sett** (87b, 119d), **Watt** (63d, 186), **watt** (129a, 246), **Witt** (187)

T _ _ T   **tact** (35d), **Taft** (183, 191), **tait** (15d, 60d), **takt** (80a, 120b), **tart** (87a, 112b), **taut** (120c, 122a), **teat** (81d), **tent** (24a, 87b), **test** (23d, 41d, 42b, 124b, 124d), **text** (86d, 133c), **that** (34d, 95a, 99b), **tilt** (23d, 24b, 62c, 72b, 101c), **tint** (29a, 107b), **toft** (60d), **toot** (112b), **tort** (27c, 71a, 134c), **tout** (49d, 95a, 97b), **tret** (130a, 131a), **trot** (66c, 85b), **tuft** (22c, 28c), **twit** (88a)

T U _ _   **tuan** (74c), **tuba** (80a, 86a), **tube** (33c, 89c, 117a), **tubs**, **tuck** (115c), **-tude** (117b), **Tues.** (243), **tufa** (91c, 129a), **tuff** (91c,

129a), **tuft** (22c, 28c), **tugs**, **tuke** (23d, 43b), **tula** (10d, 11d), **tule** (22c, 25a), **tump** (60a), **tuna** (125a, 229), **Tune** (184), **tune** (9c, 10a, 10d, 14b, 58a, 75d, 111d, 116a), **tung** (83d), **tuno** (57c), **tuns**, **Tupi** (12b), **tups**, **turf** (87b, 111c, 118b), **Turk** (85a, 217), **Turk.** (243), **turn** (12c, 100b, 102b, 108a, 125c, 127c, 132b), **tush** (23a), **tusk** (46d, 65c, 123a), **tutu** (16d, 110a)

_ **T U** _   **atua** (91a), **etui** (24c, 50a, 51a, 81b, 127b), **otus** (54b), **stub** (121d, 122c), **stud** (23a, 44c, 74c, 84d, 126d), **stum** (55d, 100b, 132c), **stun** (108b, 116c), **Stus**

_ _ **T U**   **Attu** (64b), **Hutu** (214, 221), **mitu** (32d), **patu** (130d), **tatu** (14b), **tutu** (16d, 110a), **vatu** (224), **WCTU** (244)

T _ _ **U**   **tabu** (48c), **tatu** (14b), **thou** (95b), **thru**, **tolu** (16d), **tutu** (16d, 110a)

_ _ **T V**   **HDTV** (239)

T W _ _   **'twas** (30b, 107c), **Tway** (184), **twig** (21c), **twin** (37c, 75b, 125c), **twit** (88a), **twos**

_ **T W** _   **at. wt.** (236), **Nt. Wt.** (241)

T _ _ **W**   **thaw** (72b), **thew** (79d), **trow** (18b)

T _ _ **X**   **-trix** (117b)

T Y _ _   **tyee** (26d), **tyke** (21c, 26c), **tymp** (19d), **Tyne** (82b, 184, 223), **type** (27d, 112a, 113b), **typo** (41c, 94c), **typp** (134b), **Tyra** (184), **Tyre** (71a, 88c, 218), **Tyro** (81b), **tyro** (12b, 18b, 82c), **Tyus** (184)

_ **T Y** _   **ltys** (120c), **Styx** (26b, 57a)

_ _ **T Y**   **arty, atty.** (236), **city** (76c, 126d), **Coty** (49d, 147), **duty** (27a, 83a, 119d), **maty** (62d), **pity** (29b, 87a, 134b)

T _ _ **Y**   **they** (95a), **tidy** (81a, 84c, 111b), **tiny** (77b, 110d), **toby** (11b, 38a, 66d, 79d, 96a), **tody** (19b), **-tomy** (117b), **Tony** (184), **tory** (22a, 30b, 73c), **tray** (98b, 104a, 107a), **trey** (24a, 121c), **Troy** (184), **troy** (119c, 131a), **Tway** (184)

_ _ **T Z**   **fitz** (111d), **Getz** (155), **litz** (97b), **Metz** (216), **Ritz** (177)

U A _ _   **uang** (100b)

_ **U A** _   **bual** (132c), **duad** (85d, 125c), **dual** (37c, 125c), **duan** (52a), **Fuad** (44c), **Guam** (64c), **guan** (19b), **guar** (38b, 48c), **Guat.** (239), **HUAC** (239), **Juan** (163), **luau** (58b), **Muav** (53c), **quad** (29a), **quag** (20c), **quay** (68d, 88d, 131b), **tuan** (74c), **Yüan** (26d, 78a), **yuan** (215)

_ _ **U A**   **agua** (113a), **akua** (91a), **aqua** (20b, 70b), **atua** (91a), **Ecua.** (238), **roue** (34a, 97c), **skua** (56d, 65b, 105c)

U _ _ A   ulna(32c, 20d), ulva(105d), urea(45c), Urfa(76a), Uria(197), -uria (117b), Ursa (17d), urva (78a), USDA (243), USIA (243), USMA (243), USNA (243), USTA (244), uvea (43c, 64a)

_ U B _   aube (11a), Bubi (216), bubo (85c), bubs, Cuba (64c,131b,215), cube (53c, 111d), Cubs (206), cubs, dubs, hubs, Juba (216), jube (102a), Kuba (24b), Luba (224), nubs, pubs, Rube (179), rube (31b, 103c, 134d), rubs, Ruby (179), ruby (19c, 53b), subj. (243), subs, tuba (80a, 86a), tube (33c, 89c, 117a), tubs

_ _ U B   chub (46c, 228), club (21c, 32c, 75b, 84c, 104a, 111c), daub (111a), drub (17c, 32c, 42c, 110b), flub (21b), grub (35d, 69b), slub (134b), snub (62a, 81b, 98b, 109a, 110c), stub (121d, 122c)

_ U C _   Buck (23b, 31c, 143), buck (34c, 84a), duce (65a), duck (16c, 19a, 19b, 23d, 43b, 62a, 109a, 225), duct (125a), euch (54b), fuci (38d), guck (110c), juca (24c), Luca (167), Luce (10a, 29b, 192), luck (25d), Lucy (192), much (67c, 116d), muck (39a), muco- (93b), ouch (42c, 63a), puce (42a, 96c), Puck (107c, 193), puck (36b, 55a, 60c, 77b), ruck (134a), such (131b), suck (9b), tuck (115c), yuca (24c), yuch (112a), yuck (112a)

_ _ U C   educ. (238), eruc (30d, 45d), leuc- (94a)

U _ _ C   Udic (82b), USMC (243), USOC (244)

U D _ _   udal (59c), Udic (82b), udos

_ U D _   Budd (143), buds, dude (27c, 33c, 44b), duds (28b, 122d), Judd (163), Jude (13b, 196), judo (65d, 66d), Judy (163), kudu (13a, 230), ludi (102a), ludo (52b), Mudd (171), muds, nude (17b, 126b), nudi- (93b), pudu (34b), rudd (24b, 46c, 98c), rude (102c, 126a), Rudy (179), sudd (47c), suds (18a, 48a, 114a), -tude (117b)

_ _ U D   baud (120b), crud (28c, 35a, 36a), feud (45c, 96b, 127d), foud (44c, 74a), gaud (124c, 133d), haud (70a), laud (57b, 92b, 127d), loud (115b), Maud (131d, 169), maud (43b, 56a), Scud (77b), scud (96d, 103a, 118c), spud (92a), stud (23a, 44c, 74c, 84d, 126d), thud (20a, 112a), you'd (30c)

U _ _ D   used (9c, 57a)

_ U E _   Auer (61c, 139), cued, cues, duel (45d), dues, duet (80c, 85d), euer (54b), fuel (53a), hued, hues, Huey (159), lues (118d), Nuer (222), rued, ruer, rues, sued, suer (95b), sues, suet (44c, 83d), Suez (23c), Tues. (243)

_ _ U E   ague (26c, 45c, 74c, 104b), Blue (142), blue (75d, 112a, 126c), clue (60b, 117d), flue (11a, 26c), glue (10a, 115b), moue (50d, 134c), Niue (64c), slue (110c, 118c), true (9d, 15d, 31a, 42b, 44a, 73c, 111b)

U _ _ E   urge (35b, 54d, 63b, 94d)

_ U F _   **buff** (119b, 134b), **cuff** (21b, 60b, 105b, 110b), **duff** (95d), **Dufy** (49c, 150), **guff** (16b, 62c, 82a), **Huff** (159), **huff** (47b, 119c), **luff** (48a), **Luft** (167), **Muff** (17b), **muff** (17c, 21b, 22c), **puff** (20a, 74a), **ruff** (34d, 37b, 51c), **sufi** (88a), **tufa** (91c, 129a), **tuff** (91c, 129a), **tuft** (22c, 28c)

_ _ U F   **oeuf** (50b), **pouf** (48c, 58d, 85a)

U _ _ F   **UNCF** (243), **USAF** (243)

U G _ _   **ugli** (51d), **ugly** (126a)

_ U G _   **auge** (71b), **bugs**, **fugu** (65d), **huge** (54b, 62a, 69b), **Hugh** (159), **Hugo** (49c, 71c, 104d, 159), **hugs**, **juga** (24c), **jugs**, **luge** (110b), **lugs**, **mugs**, **pugs**, **ruga** (48a, 134a), **rugs**, **sugi** (65b), **tugs**, **vugg** (25b, 53c, 101b), **vugh** (25b, 53c, 101b), **yuga** (60a)

_ _ U G   **chug** (112a), **Doug** (150), **drug** (81a), **frug** (33b), **plug** (116a, 133d), **slug** (38a, 76b, 116b), **smug** (29c, 106c), **Snug** (193), **snug** (31c, 122a), **thug** (52c)

U _ _ G   **uang** (100b), **USCG** (243), **USNG** (243)

_ U H _   **buhl** (63a), **buhr** (131c), **guhr** (39a), **Ruhr** (53d, 100b)

_ _ U H   **bruh** (73b)

U _ _ H   **Utah** (212)

U I _ _   **Uist** (64d)

_ U I _   **cuir** (37c, 50c), **duim** (246), **guib** (13a), **huia** (81c), **juin** (49d), **Luis** (167), **Muir** (11a, 171), **nuit** (50d), **quid** (32c, 122c), **quip** (66b, 66d, 132d, 133a), **quit** (9a, 34d, 71a, 99d), **quiz** (42b), **ruin** (34d, 35b, 62b), **suit** (9c, 10a, 31c, 47b, 71a, 85b, 90b, 104b)

_ _ U I   **aqui** (112d), **arui** (13b), **equi-** (93c), **etui** (24c, 50a, 51a, 81b, 127b), **Maui** (64c)

U _ _ I   **ugli** (51d), **Unni** (197)

_ U J _   **Fuji** (66a), **fuji** (65b), **juju** (26b, 45c, 119b), **suji** (131b)

_ _ U J   **Cluj** (221)

_ U K _   **auks**, **cuke** (32c), **Duke** (87d, 150, 194, 201), **duke** (82a), **Luke** (42a, 167, 196), **puke** (99a), **puku** (13a, 130b), **suke** (120a), **suky** (120a), **tuke** (23d, 43b), **yuks** (70b)

_ _ U K   **leuk-** (94a), **Sauk** (49b, 56c, 189), **souk** (17d, 74d), **Truk** (24b), **Wouk** (187)

U L _ _   **Ulam** (197), **ulna** (32c, 20d), **ulva** (105d)

_ U L _ aula (53d), auld (105b), bulb (30d, 126b), Bulg. (236), bulk (20c, 75b, 129a), bull (21b, 86b), -cule (117c), cull (88d), culm (13a, 28c, 56a, 108b, 115b), Culp (147), cult (106a, 119c), Dull (193), dull (20b, 28b, 47b, 63b, 66b, 71d, 73c, 126c), duly (100c, 117a), Fula (216, 217), full (29c, 99d), gulf (9c, 130a), gull (19a, 28c, 34a, 34c, 68a, 76c, 105c, 118d, 225), gulp (20d, 37d, 118b), hula (58b), hule (21c, 25a, 102c), hulk (126d), Hull (159), hull (106b, 108b), Jule (163), Juli (163), July, Kulp (165), lull (11c), lulu (73a), mule (108c, 110d, 131b, 230), Mull (171), mull (43b, 91b, 103a, 121b), mult- (93b), null (82c, 128d), pula (214), pule (131c), puli (37b, 61c, 227), pulk (79c), pull (11d, 37d, 123c), pulp (51d, 74a, 75b, 86b), rule (13b, 35b, 37b, 70b, 118c), sulk (117d), Sulu (88c), sulu (46a), tula (10d, 11d), tule (22c, 25a), yule (27a), Zulu (12a, 222)

_ _ U L azul (112c), caul (45c, 84a), elul (78c), foul (9a, 126b), Gaul (49b), haul (37c), maul (17c, 57d, 74c), ocul- (92d), Paul (18a, 91b, 174), Peul (217, 219, 221), Raul (176), Saul (67d, 87a, 179, 197), shul (118d), Soul (181), soul (95d, 113d, 128c), waul (114b)

U _ _ L udal (59c), Ural (103c)

U M _ _ umbo (21a)

_ U M _ bump (66a, 66d), bums, duma (103a), dumb (109b, 113c), dump (68d, 99d, 126c), fume (111a, 116a), fumy (127b), gums, Hume (159, 192), hump (95c), hums, Jump (163), jump (10b, 114d, 127b), lump (17a, 55a, 79a, 118c), mums, Numa (102a), numb (33d, 126b), puma (24d, 31b, 79a, 231), pump (108c), rump (23a, 33a, 75c), rums, sumo (66a), sump (25d, 77a), sums, tump (60a), Yuma (189)

_ _ U M alum (37c, 77a), alum. (235), arum (32c, 71d, 114d), Baum (85d, 140), chum (15b, 32a, 45b), drum (80a, 228), glum (54d, 78d, 112b, 117d), grum (54d), ogum (64b), ovum (39d, 69c), plum (51d, 124a), scum (62c, 98d, 110c), slum (81b, 99d), stum (55d, 100b, 132c), swum

U _ _ M Ulam (197), urim (103b)

U N _ _ Unas, unau (110d), UNCF (243), unco (105b), undo (12d, 41c, 73a, 99b), unio (80d), unit (77d, 84a), Unni (197), unto, unus (69c)

_ U N _ aune (246), aunt (44b, 99b), buna (102c), bund (40b), bung (116a), bunk (82a, 110c), buns, bunt (17c, 131b), dune (84a, 104a), dung (42d, 74d), dunk (35d, 62a), fund (9c, 78a, 100a), fung- (93a), funk (10d, 35a, 47b), gunk (110c), guns, Hung. (239), hung, hunk (57d, 88d), Huns (15c), Hunt (159), hunt (105d), June (163), Jung (95d, 163), junk (26c, 102d), Juno (67c, 77b, 96d, 195, 199), Luna (89d, 198), luna (78d), lune (31d, 58c), lung (100a, 121b), luni- (93b), Lunt (167), Muni (171), Nunn (173), nuns, Puna (12c), puna (28d, 90b, 132b), pung (21c, 110c), punk (12a, 123b), puno (132b), puns, punt (20b, 47b), puny (45a, 130c), rune

(82b), **rung** (25d, 32b, 115b), **runs, runt** (12d, 38d), **Sung** (26d), **sung, sunk, sunn** (45d), **Suns** (206), **suns, tuna** (125a, 229), **Tune** (184), **tune** (9c, 10a, 10d, 14b, 58a, 75d, 111d, 116a), **tung** (83d), **tuno** (57c), **tuns, Zuni** (95d, 189)

_ _ U N   **Faun** (45d, 133b, 198), **noun** (86d, 116d), **Ryun** (179), **shun** (16c, 41c), **spun, stun** (108b, 116c), **tsun** (246)

U _ _ N   **upon** (9b), **uran** (78a)

_ U O _   **buoy** (26a, 47c), **duos, muon** (71b), **quod** (94d, 96a)

_ _ U O   **chuo** (246), **fluo-** (93a)

U _ _ O   **umbo** (21a), **unco** (105b), **undo** (12d, 41c, 73a, 99b), **unio** (80d), **unto, USPO** (244)

U P _ _   **upas** (66a, 90d, 124a), **upon** (9b)

_ U P _   **cupr-** (92d), **cups, dupe** (25a, 34a, 48b, 56d, 74d, 118d), **Hupa** (15b, 189), **pupa** (27a, 28d, 63b), **pups, sups, supt.** (243), **Tupi** (12b), **tups**

_ _ U P   **coup** (75b, 116c, 120b), **loup** (50d, 51b, 105c), **roup** (92a), **scup** (91c, 228), **soup** (75c), **yaup** (119b)

U R _ _   **Ural** (103c), **uran** (78a), **Urdu** (60b, 213, 220), **urea** (45c), **Urey** (15c, 184), **Urfa** (76a), **urge** (35b, 54d, 63b, 94d), **Uria** (197), **-uria** (117b), **urim** (103b), **Uris** (184), **urns, Ursa** (17d), **urus** (15d, 85c, 132a, 227, 231), **urva** (78a)

_ U R _   **aura** (10d, 36d, 39d, 40b, 57c, 100d), **burd** (105c), **burg** (21a, 57c), **buri** (119b), **Burl** (143), **burl** (68c, 124b), **burn** (62c, 101b), **burp** (18b), **Burr** (143, 190), **burr** (94b), **burs, Burt** (143), **bury** (63c), **cura** (113a), **curb** (100a, 109a), **curd** (76d), **cure** (94c), **curl** (32a, 57b, 72d, 100d, 126b), **curs, Curt** (147), **curt** (20b, 22a, 108c, 108d), **dura** (113c), **duro** (88b), **eure** (54b), **eury-** (94a), **furl** (101c), **furs, fury** (97b, 116a), **guru** (60b), **hura** (104a), **hurl** (121c, 123b), **Hurt** (159), **hurt** (33b, 58a, 62a, 63a, 133d), **Jura** (79b), **jure** (70b), **jury** (31c), **Kura** (101a), **Kurd** (64a, 217), **Kure** (60d), **Kurt** (165), **lure** (34b, 41b, 63d, 120c), **lurk** (71d, 110b), **mura** (65d), **murk** (28b, 48a, 77b), **ours** (95a), **pure** (9b, 26b, 126a, 126c), **puri** (62d), **purl** (68c), **purr** (112a), **ruri** (69c), **ruru** (81c), **sura** (68c, 86a), **surd** (30b, 82d), **sure** (10b, 99b, 106b, 126d), **surf** (21d), **surg.** (243), **turf** (87b, 111c, 118b), **Turk** (85a, 217), **Turk.** (243), **turn** (12c, 100b, 102b, 108a, 125c, 127c, 132b), **wurm** (54c), **Yuri** (188), **Yuro** (188), **yurt** (78a)

_ _ U R   **Amur** (101a), **azur** (50a), **blur** (62d, 111a), **dour** (54d, 78d, 107b, 117d), **ebur** (69d), **four** (72c, 120d), **gaur** (25a, 62d, 132a, 230), **hour** (122b), **knur** (54d, 68c), **lour** (33d, 54d), **neur-** (93b), **peur** (50b), **pour** (120a), **-saur** (117b), **slur** (36c, 40b, 74c, 95b, 123c, 128b), **smur** (38a), **sour** (15b, 119d), **spur** (46a, 54d, 62c, 63c, 95a), **taur-** (92c), **Thur.** (243), **tour** (66d), **your** (95a)

434

U _ _ R usar (11b, 17b, 62d), **user** (10a, 29c, 40c), **USNR** (244), **USSR** (244), **uter-** (93d)

U S _ _ USAF (243), **usar** (11b, 17b, 62d), **USCG** (243), **USDA** (243), **used** (9c, 57a), **user** (10a, 29c, 40c), **uses**, **USIA** (243), **USMA** (243), **USMC** (243), **USNA** (243), **USNG** (243), **USNR** (244), **USOC** (244), **USPO** (244), **USPS** (244), **USSR** (244), **USTA** (244), **usus** (69c, 70b)

_ U S _ Bush (143, 191), **bush** (109a, 119a), **busk** (20c, 31a, 45c), **buss** (68a), **bust** (14c, 17a, 21d, 44a, 58c), **busy** (40d, 83b), **Cush** (57c, 197), **cusk** (46d), **cusp** (31d, 61a, 89d, 90c, 90d), **cuss** (32d, 88a, 118c), **Duse** (64d, 150), **dusk** (125c), **dust** (114a), **fuse** (75d, 76a), **fuss** (21b, 36d, 92a), **fust** (107b), **gush** (114b, 118a), **gust** (20a), **hush** (109b), **husk** (43a, 61c, 106b, 232), **just** (41b, 44a, 62b, 76a, 97c, 127c), **lush** (38b, 73d), **lust** (34a, 107a), **musa** (16d), **muse** (52d, 91b, 121b), **mush** (75b), **musk** (87d), **muss** (103a), **must** (55d, 81c, 116c, 132c), **Ouse** (101a, 134d, 223), **oust** (35b, 40a, 42b, 96c), **push** (38a, 46a, 108d, 121d), **puss** (24d), **rusa** (104a), **ruse** (60c, 62b, 116a), **Rush** (179), **rush** (114a), **rusk** (21d), **Russ** (179), **Russ.** (242), **rust** (31a, 85d, 90a), **Susa** (40a), **susu** (20a), **tush** (23a), **tusk** (46d, 65c, 123a)

_ _ U S acus (70a, 89b), **Apus** (207), **avus** (69d), **crus** (71b, 107c), **deus** (42d, 69d), **emus**, **-eous** (117a), **gnus**, **Grus** (207), **Ilus** (69a, 124d), **-ious** (117a), **Irus** (83c), **Kaus** (208), **meus** (69d), **nous** (50d, 51b), **-odus** (117c), **onus** (22d, 72d, 83a, 131a), **opus** (29c, 80c, 129a, 133c), **otus** (54b), **Pius** (91b), **plus** (12c, 62c), **sous** (51b), **Stus**, **taus**, **thus** (111b, 121a), **tous** (49d), **Tyus** (184), **unus** (69c), **urus** (15d, 85c, 132a, 227, 231), **usus** (69c, 70b), **vous** (51b), **Zeus** (55c, 59c, 198)

U _ _ S udos, **Unas**, **unus** (69c), **upas** (66a, 90d, 124a), **Uris** (184), **urns**, **urus** (15d, 85c, 132a, 227, 231), **uses**, **USPS** (244), **usus** (69c, 70b), **utas** (40a), **Utes**

U T _ _ Utah (212), **utas** (40a), **uter-** (93d), **Utes**

_ U T _ auth. (236), **auto** (24a), **Bute** (64d), **Buto** (198), **buts**, **butt** (121d, 132c, 246), **cute** (10a, 32c, 116a), **cuts**, **duty** (27a, 83a, 119d), **GUTS** (239), **guts** (63a), **huts**, **Hutu** (214, 221), **jute** (30d, 45c, 102b, 103a), **juts**, **lute** (25c, 66a, 80b, 100d), **Luth.** (240), **muta** (26a, 80d), **mute** (109b, 113c, 232, 234), **mutt** (32d, 78a), **nuts**, **outs**, **puts**, **putt** (55b), **Ruth** (80d, 179, 196, 197), **ruth** (29b, 89c), **ruts**, **tutu** (16d, 110a)

_ _ U T abut (21a, 75d, 123b), **aout** (49d), **bhut** (54b), **blut** (53d), **bout** (30b), **brut** (38b, 132c), **Deut.** (237), **glut** (42b, 55b, 85c, 104b, 118a), **gout** (14d, 113d), **Knut** (33c, 164), **lout** (21a, 83a), **naut.** (241), **neut.** (241), **pout** (117d), **Prut** (33d), **rout** (34c, 36c), **scut** (119a), **shut** (28b), **slut** (133b), **smut** (28c, 36a, 90a, 111d), **taut** (120c, 122a), **tout** (49d, 95a, 97b)

U _ _ T Uist (64d), **unit** (77d, 84a)

U _ _ U   **unau** (110d), **Urdu** (60b, 213, 220)

U V _ _   **uvea** (43c, 64a)

_ U V _   **Suva** (128d, 216)

_ _ U W   **dauw** (22d)

_ U X _   **luxe** (100c)

_ _ U X   **Crux** (207), **crux** (32b, 74b, 112b), **eaux** (51b), **flux** (26a, 47d), **jeux** (50b), **roux** (104b), **Vaux** (192, 195), **vaux** (49c)

_ U Y _   **buyo** (18d), **buys, guys**

U _ _ Y   **ugly** (126a), **Urey** (15c, 184)

_ U Z _   **buzz** (79d, 103a, 131d), **fuze** (35b), **fuzz** (37c), **ouzo** (11a), **Puzo** (175)

V A _ _   **vagi** (31d), **vain** (40c, 63a), **vair** (52c, 114b), **Vale** (184), **vale** (44b, 127b), **Vali** (83b), **vamp** (62c, 108c, 233), **vane** (130d, 132b), **vang** (57c, 102b), **vans, vara** (72a), **vari** (71b), **vary** (26a, 35c, 77c), **vasa** (38c, 128a), **vase** (30b, 47d), **vaso-** (92c), **vast** (61c, 62a), **vats, vatu** (224), **Vaux** (192, 195), **vaux** (49c)

_ V A _   **Avar** (25a, 82b), **Avas, Evas, Ivan** (66c, 103c, 159), **oval** (39d, 40b), **Svan** (25a)

_ _ V A   **Alva** (39c), **cava** (127d), **Deva** (60a, 221), **diva** (84b, 94c), **Hova** (219), **Java** (64c), **java** (28d), **kava** (18d, 91a), **kiva** (25c, 95d), **lava** (77d, 101b, 129a), **Neva** (100d), **Nova** (203), **nova** (114d), **Siva** (91a), **Suva** (128d, 216), **ulva** (105d), **urva** (78a), **viva** (73a)

V _ _ A   **vara** (72a), **vasa** (38c, 128a), **veda** (60a), **Vega** (114d, 207), **Vela** (103c, 208), **vena** (70b), **Vera** (185), **vera** (105c), **Vida** (185), **Vila** (224), **vina** (60b), **visa** (87a), **vita** (69d, 71d), **viva** (73a), **vola** (111c), **-vora** (117c), **vota** (102a)

V _ _ B   **verb** (86d)

V _ _ C   **Visc.** (244)

_ V D _   **avdp.** (236)

_ _ V D   **Blvd.** (236), **NKVD** (103c)

V _ _ D   **veld** (104c, 112b), **vend** (74d, 87c, 106c), **vied, void** (12d, 40c, 82d, 127a)

V E _ _   **veal** (23b, 75c), **veda** (60a), **veer** (35c, 125b), **vees, Vega** (114d, 207), **veil** (29d, 36b, 58c, 59d, 75b), **vein** (20a, 116b), **Vela** (103c, 208), **veld** (104c, 112b), **vena** (70b), **vend** (74d, 87c, 106c), **veni-**

(93d), **veno-** (93d), **vent** (11a, 13b, 40c, 60c, 84b, 85b, 115a), **Vera** (185), **vera** (105c), **verb** (86d), **vers** (51b), **vert** (56c), **vert.** (244), **very** (43c, 78d, 111b), **vest** (28b, 129b), **veto** (95a) **vets**

_ V E _   **avec** (51b), **aver** (10b, 15a, 16c, 34b, 74b, 115a, 118c), **aves**, **Evel** (68a), **even** (23b, 41b, 42b, 47b, 61d, 67c, 71c, 82a, 111a, 126c, 134c), **ever** (12a, 18b, 62c), **Eves**, **eves**, **Ives** (159), **Ivey** (159), **oven** (61c, 67b), **over** (9b, 9d, 14c, 32a, 87a, 99c), **Sven**, **uvea** (43c, 64a), **Yves** (188)

_ _ V E   **cave** (113c, 126b), **cove** (17d, 58a, 130a), **Dave** (148), **dive** (34d, 90c), **Dove** (150), **dove** (19a, 89a, 225), **five** (17c, 88c, 97c), **gave**, **give** (11c, 13d, 29d, 94a, 95c), **gyve** (45c, 107b), **have** (20b), **hive** (18a), **hove** (71d), **jive** (61d, 63b, 66a), **Jove** (67c, 198), **lave** (130a), **live** (38d, 42d), **Love** (167), **love** (24b, 120c), **move** (10d, 36b, 62b, 125b), **nave** (27a, 131c), **neve** (46c, 54c, 55d, 111b), **nove** (65c), **pave** (66b), **rave** (34b, 58a, 119b), **reve** (50b), **rive** (28a), **rove** (97d, 101a, 129d), **save** (42b, 67b, 84b, 94b, 126c), **Seve** (180), **vive** (73a), **wave** (48a, 83b, 100d, 118c, 126b), **we've** (30c), **wove**

V _ _ E   **Vale** (184), **vale** (44b, 127b), **vane** (130d, 132b), **vase** (30b, 47d), **vice** (35a), **vice-** (92d), **vide** (98d), **vile** (9a, 17b, 46a, 62a, 74c), **vine** (28a, 71c), **vise** (60c), **vite** (50d), **vive** (73a), **voce** (65c, 234), **vole** (75b, 79b, 110b, 111b, 231), **-vore** (117c), **vote** (49b, 128d)

V _ _ G   **vang** (57c, 102b), **vugg** (25b, 53c, 101b)

V _ _ H   **vugh** (25b, 53c, 101b)

V I _ _   **vial** (110d), **vice** (35a), **vice-** (92d), **Vida** (185), **vide** (98d), **vied**, **vier** (53d), **vies**, **view** (12c, 15a, 42b, 73a, 95b, 104d), **Vila** (224), **vile** (9a, 17b, 46a, 62a, 74c), **Vili** (83b), **vina** (60b), **vine** (28a, 71c), **vini-** (94a), **vino** (72b, 132c), **viny**, **viol** (80b), **VIPs**, **visa** (87a), **Visc.** (244), **vise** (60c), **vita** (69d, 71d), **vite** (50d), **viva** (73a), **vive** (73a), **vivo** (72c, 233)

_ V I _   **avid** (39a, 41b, 56b, 67b, 135a), **avis** (69c), **evil** (74c, 109c, 131d, 134c), **Ovid** (102a)

_ _ V I   **Devi** (109d), **favi** (122a), **kavi** (66a), **Levi** (13b, 64d, 70d, 197), **nevi** (19c, 77d), **Ravi** (176)

V _ _ I   **vagi** (31d), **Vali** (83b), **vari** (71b), **veni-** (93d), **Vili** (83b), **vini-** (94a)

V _ _ K   **volk** (54a)

V _ _ L   **veal** (23b, 75c), **veil** (29d, 36b, 58c, 59d, 75b), **vial** (110d), **viol** (80b), **VTOL** (244)

_ _ V N   **ARVN** (235)

V _ _ N   **vain** (40c, 63a), **vein** (20a, 116b)

V O _ _   voce(65c, 234), void(12d, 40c, 82d, 127a), vola(111c), vole (75b, 79b, 110b, 111b, 231), volk (54a), volt (40a, 61b, 246), -vora (117c), -vore (117c), vota (102a), vote (49b, 128d), vous (51b), vows

_ V O _   Avon (107c), avow (9d, 15a, 16c, 29d, 30a, 34b, 85c), evoe (16a, 100b), Ivor (159), Lvov (223)

_ _ V O   levo- (93b), Pavo (87b, 207), vivo (72c, 233)

V _ _ O   vaso- (92c), veno- (93d), veto (95a), vino (72b, 132c), vivo (72c, 233)

_ _ V P   RSVP (242)

V _ _ P   vamp (62c, 108c, 233)

V _ _ R   vair (52c, 114b), veer (35c, 125b), vier (53d)

_ _ V S   Bevs, revs

V _ _ S   vans, vats, vees, vers (51b), vies, VIPs, vous (51b), vows

V T _ _   VTOL (244)

_ _ V T   govt. (239)

V _ _ T   vast (61c, 62a), vent (11a, 13b, 40c, 60c, 84b, 85b, 115a), vert (56c), vert. (244), vest (28b, 129b), volt (40a, 61b, 246)

V U _ _   vugg (25b, 53c, 101b), vugh (25b, 53c, 101b)

_ V U _   avus (69d), ovum (39d, 69c)

_ _ V U   Kivu (68b)

V _ _ U   vatu (224)

V _ _ W   view (12c, 15a, 42b, 73a, 95b, 104d)

V _ _ X   Vaux (192, 195), vaux (49c)

_ _ V Y   bevy (16d, 31c, 47c, 232), cavy (56d, 101c, 230), Davy (148, 193), davy (103b), envy (34a, 107a), levy (15a, 62b, 120a), Livy (101d), navy (20a, 47c), wavy (126b)

V _ _ Y   vary (26a, 35c, 77c), very (43c, 78d, 111b), viny

W A _ _   WAAC (244), WAAF (244), Waco (21d), WACs, Wade (185), wade (129b), wadi (38b, 83a, 98a, 101a), wads, waft (47c), wage (103d), wags, waif (116b), wail (32b, 61c, 68d, 114b), wain (129b), wait (24b, 72a, 99c, 115a, 119d), waka (23d), wake (102c, 123c), wale (55c, 100c, 130c, 131b, 131c), walk (85b), Wall (193), wall (118a),

Walt (185), **wand** (90d, 101c, 115b), **wane** (9a, 34b, 69a, 116d), **want** (34a, 35b, 68b, 81b, 92a, 133a), **Ward** (186), **ward** (27c, 35a, 67b), **ware** (76a), **warm** (10b, 58d, 120c), **warn** (11b, 25b), **warp** (30b, 121c, 125c), **wars**, **Wart** (193), **wart** (95c), **wary** (25b, 128b, 130a), **Wash** (82b), **Wash.** (212), **wash** (14d), **WASP** (244), **wasp** (63b, 229), **wast** (128a), **WATS** (244), **Watt** (63d, 186), **watt** (129a, 246), **waul** (114b), **wave** (48a, 83b, 100d, 118c, 126b), **wavy** (126b), **wawl** (114b), **waxy**, **ways**

_ **W A** _   **away** (9b, 55b, 59b, 83c), **kwan** (246), **swab** (57c, 78c, 134b), **swag** (115c), **SWAK** (243), **swam**, **swan** (19a, 28c, 226), **swap** (123c), **SWAT** (243), **swat** (20a, 28b, 116b), **sway** (29b, 37b, 63a, 67c, 76d, 79c, 85a, 130c, 133a), **'twas** (30b, 107c), **Tway** (184)

_ _ **W A**   **biwa** (65d), **Iowa** (189, 210), **tawa** (81c), **Tewa** (189)

W _ _ **A**   **waka** (23d), **weka** (19b, 74d, 81c, 97b), **weta** (72d), **whoa** (42c, 115d)

W _ _ **B**   **Webb** (186), **Weeb** (186), **womb** (127c)

W C _ _   **WCTU** (244)

_ **W C** _   **YWCA** (244)

W _ _ **C**   **WAAC** (244), **Wisc.** (212, 244)

_ _ **W D**   **bawd** (22a), **dowd** (107b), **fowd** (44c, 74a), **lewd** (69b, 103d)

W _ _ **D**   **wand** (90d, 101c, 115b), **Ward** (186), **ward** (27c, 35a, 67b), **weed** (52d), **Weld** (186), **weld** (38d, 66c, 126c), **wend** (54d, 110b, 112a), **wild** (18c, 31d, 104c, 126d, 128c), **wind** (10d, 28d, 32d, 125c), **woad** (20a, 38d), **wold** (38d, 126d), **Wood** (187), **wood** (55a), **word** (95a, 120c, 121d)

W E _ _   **weak** (45a, 62c, 63a), **weal** (131b, 131c), **wean** (117a), **wear** (114a), **Webb** (186), **webs**, **weds**, **Weeb** (186), **weed** (52d), **week** (122b), **weep** (32b, 68d), **weft** (32b, 121c, 133c), **Wegg** (85a), **wehe** (53d), **Weil** (186), **Weir** (186), **weir** (33b, 47a), **weka** (19b, 74d, 81c, 97b), **Weld** (186), **weld** (38d, 66c, 126c), **Welk** (186), **well** (25c, 97c), **we'll** (30c), **welt** (100c, 129b, 130c, 131c), **wend** (54d, 110b, 112a), **wens**, **went** (34d), **wept**, **were**, **we're** (30c), **werf** (44c), **weri** (16c, 25a), **wert** (128a), **West** (186), **west** (83b), **weta** (72d), **wets**, **we've** (30c)

_ **W E** _   **awed**, **awes**, **ewer** (66a, 66d, 89c, 131d), **ewes**, **Gwen** (156), **Iwei** (213), **owed**, **owes**, **Swed.** (243)

_ _ **W E**   **Bowe** (142), **Howe** (17c, 63d, 159), **Lowe** (167)

W _ _ **E**   **Wade** (185), **wade** (129b), **wage** (103d), **wake** (102c, 123c), **wale** (55c, 100c, 130c, 131b, 131c), **wane** (9a, 34b, 69a, 116d), **ware** (76a), **wave** (48a, 83b, 100d, 118c, 126b), **wehe** (53d), **were**, **we're**

(30c), **we've** (30c), **wide** (102a), **wife** (114a), **wile** (34a), **wine** (60c, 91c), **wipe** (123d), **wire** (30d, 120b), **Wise** (187), **wise** (103b, 111a) **woke, wore, wove**

W _ _ F   **WAAF** (244), **waif** (116b), **werf** (44c), **Wolf** (187, 207), **wolf** (23d, 231), **woof** (32b, 37b, 121c, 131a), **WRAF** (244)

W _ _ G   **Wegg** (85a), **whig** (71c), **wing** (12d, 47c, 48a, 89b, 89d, 232), **Wong** (187)

W H _ _   **wham** (110b), **whap** (60b), **what** (96d, 99b), **when** (96d, 131c), **whet** (39c, 107d), **whew** (42c), **whey** (76d), **whig** (71c), **whim** (24a, 44b, 82c), **whin** (55c, 101b), **whip** (18a, 47c, 69b, 121b), **whir** (112a), **whit** (122c), **whiz** (88a, 112a), **whoa** (42c, 115d), **whom** (34d, 96d), **whop** (60b), **whys**

_ W H _   **YWHA** (244)

_ _ W H   **YHWH** (244)

W _ _ H   **Wash** (82b), **Wash.** (212), **wash** (14d), **wish** (35b), **with** (11d, 12c)

W I _ _   **wick** (23d), **wide** (102a), **Wien** (33c), **wife** (114a), **wigs, wild** (18c, 31d, 104c, 126d, 128c), **wile** (34a), **Will** (186), **will** (18c, 35b, 120d, 129a, 133a), **Wilt** (187), **wilt** (38a), **wily** (14d, 31d, 32c, 110c), **wimp** (130c), **wind** (10d, 28d, 32d, 125c), **wine** (60c, 91c), **wing** (12d, 47c, 48a, 89b, 89d, 232), **wink** (63c, 81d, 106a), **wino** (38b), **wins, winy** (128c), **wipe** (123d), **wire** (30d, 120b), **wiry** (109d), **Wisc.** (212, 244), **Wise** (187), **wise** (103b, 111a), **wish** (35b), **wisp** (49b), **wist** (68c), **with** (11d, 12c), **wits, Witt** (187)

_ W I _   **swig** (37d, 57a), **swim** (37a), **Swit** (182), **twig** (21c), **twin** (37c, 75b, 125c), **twit** (88a)

_ _ W I   **iiwi** (58c), **kawi** (66a), **kiwi** (13d, 19a, 19b, 97d, 226)

W _ _ I   **wadi** (38b, 83a, 98a, 101a), **weri** (16c, 25a)

W K _ _   **wkly.** (244)

_ _ W K   **bowk** (115a), **gawk** (109c, 114d), **hawk** (19a, 87c, 225)

W _ _ K   **walk** (85b), **weak** (45a, 62c, 63a), **week** (122b), **Welk** (186), **wick** (23d), **wink** (63c, 81d, 106a), **work** (52a, 116c), **Wouk** (187)

_ W L _   **awls, owls**

_ _ W L   **bawl** (18c, 129b, 134b), **bowl** (78d, 119a), **cowl** (78b), **fowl** (19b), **howl** (12d, 17d, 32b, 114b), **jowl** (26b, 35c), **mewl** (131c), **pawl** (73d), **wawl** (114b), **yawl** (20b, 103b), **yowl** (12d, 32b)

W _ _ L   **wail** (32b, 61c, 68d, 114b), **Wall** (193), **wall** (118a), **waul** (114b), **wawl** (114b), **weal** (131b, 131c), **Weil** (186), **well** (25c, 97c), **we'll** (30c), **Will** (186), **will** (18c, 35b, 120d, 129a, 133a), **wool** (47c)

W _ _ M warm (10b, 58d, 120c), wham (110b), whim (24a, 44b, 82c), whom (34d, 96d), worm (88a), wurm (54c)

_ W N _ awns, awny, owns (91d)

_ _ W N Dawn (148), dawn (14b, 15d, 33d), Down (150), down (35a, 45a, 232), fawn (32a, 34c), gown (37d), Hawn (157), hewn (27a), lawn (31a, 43b, 69a, 72a), mown, pawn (26c, 60c, 90b), sawn, sewn, sown, town (57c, 128b), yawn (21a)

W _ _ N wain (129b), warn (11b, 25b), wean (117a), when (96d, 131c), whin (55c, 101b), Wien (33c), worn (107b), Wren (187), wren (19a, 226), Wynn (187)

W O _ _ woad (20a, 38d), woes, woke, wold (38d, 126d), Wolf (187, 207), wolf (23d, 231), womb (127c), Wong (187), wont (9c, 33a, 57a, 92b), Wood (187), wood (55a), woof (32b, 37b, 121c, 131a), wool (47c), woos, word (95a, 120c, 121d), wore, work (52a, 116c), worm (88a), worn (107b), wort (59b, 92a), Wouk (187), wove, wows

_ W O _ AWOL (236), twos

W _ _ O Waco (21d), wino (38b)

_ _ W P yawp (12d, 119b)

W _ _ P warp (30b, 121c, 125c), WASP (244), wasp (63b, 229), weep (32b, 68d), whap (60b), whip (18a, 47c, 69b, 121b), whop (60b), wimp (130c), wisp (49b), wrap (19a, 28a, 41b)

W R _ _ WRAF (244), wrap (19a, 28a, 41b), Wray (187), Wren (187), wren (19a, 226), writ (71a)

_ W R _ awry (15a, 32a, 125c, 134c)

W _ _ R wear (114a), Weir (186), weir (33b, 47a), whir (112a)

_ _ W S bows, caws, cows (21b), haws, hews, jaws, Jews, laws, lows, maws, mews (114b), mows, news (121d), paws, pews, rows, saws, sews, sows, taws, tows, vows, wows, yaws, yews

W _ _ S WACs, wads, wags, wars, WATS (244), ways, webs, weds, wens, wets, whys, wigs, wins, wits, woes, woos, wows

_ _ W T at. wt. (236), Newt (172), newt (39d, 103d, 225), Nt. Wt. (241)

W _ _ T waft (47c), wait (24b, 72a, 99c, 115a, 119d), Walt (185), want (34a, 35b, 68b, 81b, 92a, 133a), Wart (193), wart (95c), wast (128a), Watt (63d, 186), watt (129a, 246), weft (32b, 121c, 133c), welt (100c, 129b, 130c, 131c), went (34d), wept, wert (128a), West (186), west (83b), what (96d, 99b), whet (39c, 107d), whit (122c), Wilt (187), wilt (38a), wist (68c), Witt (187), wont (9c, 33a, 57a, 92b), wort (59b, 92a), writ (71a)

W U _ _   **wurm** (54c)

_ W U _   **swum**

W _ _ U   **WCTU** (244)

W _ _ W   **whew** (42c)

W Y _ _   **Wynn** (187)

_ W Y _   **Gwyn** (199)

_ _ W Y   **dewy** (77c)

W _ _ Y   **wary** (25b, 128b, 130a), **wavy** (126b), **waxy**, **whey** (76d), **wily** (14d, 31d, 32c, 110c), **winy** (128c), **wiry** (109d), **wkly.** (244), **Wray** (187)

W _ _ Z   **whiz** (88a, 112a)

_ X A _   **exam** (120d)

_ _ X A   **coxa** (60b), **hexa-** (93c), **moxa** (25b, 26d, 133d)

X _ _ A   **xema** (14a, 56d)

_ X C _   **exch.** (238), **excl.** (238)

X D _ _   **XDIV** (244)

X E _ _   **xema** (14a, 56d), **xeno-** (93a), **xero-** (92d)

_ X E _   **axed**, **axes**, **exec.** (238), **exes**, **oxen** (12d, 21b)

_ _ X E   **luxe** (100c)

X _ _ G   **Xing.** (244)

X _ _ H   **xiph-** (93d)

X I _ _   **Xing.** (244), **xiph-** (93d)

_ X I _   **axil** (12c), **axis** (25c, 34c, 60c), **exit** (71a, 130c), **ixia** (30d)

_ _ X I   **sexi-** (93c), **taxi** (95d)

_ X L _   **axle** (113c, 131c)

X M _ _   **Xmas** (27a)

_ X O _   **axon** (81b), **Exod.** (238), **Oxon** (85d)

_ _ X O   **myxo-** (93b)

X _ _ O	xeno- (93a), xero- (92d), xylo- (94a)
X R _ _	x-ray (12a, 75c, 88d)
X _ _ S	Xmas (27a)
_ _ X T	mixt. (240), next (81a), sext (23d, 84d, 109d), text (86d, 133c)
X _ _ V	XDIV (244)
_ _ X X	Foxx (153)
X Y _ _	xylo- (94a)
_ _ X Y	doxy (133b), foxy (14d, 31d, 132a), sexy (41c), waxy
X _ _ Y	x-ray (12a, 75c, 88d)
Y A _ _	yaks, Yale (79b, 101c, 205), yams, yang (134d), Yank (12b), yank (95d), yapp (20d), yaps, Yard (187), yard (40d, 69a, 113a, 246), yarn (43a, 114b, 119b, 133c), yate (41d), yaup (119b), yawl (20b, 103b), yawn (21a), yawp (12d, 119b), yaws, Yazd (217)
_ Y A _	ayah (62d, 82d), dyad (85d), Dyak (217, 219), Dyan (150), eyas (19b, 58c), hyal- (93a), iyar (78c), kyat (220), ryal (83d), Ryan (179)
_ _ Y A	Anya (139), Baya (215), baya (130d), Gaya (18d), Goya (112c), hoya (12c, 15d, 130c), Maya (134d, 169, 214, 217), maya (60a, 130d), raya (85a), saya (88c), soya (112c)
Y _ _ A	YMCA (244), YMHA (244), yoga (14d, 60a), yuca (24c), yuga (60a), Yuma (189), YWCA (244), YWHA (244)
_ Y C _	myco- (93a), syce (56c)
_ Y D _	Hyde (37a), hydr- (93d)
_ _ Y D	Boyd (142), emyd (120c)
Y _ _ D	Yard (187), yard (40d, 69a, 113a, 246), Yazd (217), yond (36d), you'd (30c)
Y E _ _	yeah (10b), yean (68d), year (122b), yeas (129c), yech (112a), Yedo (122d), yegg (22d), Yell (64d), yell (18c, 108d), yelp (12d, 37b), yeni (119c), yens, Yeti (9b), yews
_ Y E _	ayes (129c), byes, dyed, dyer, dyes, eyed, eyes, hyet- (93c), lyes, myel- (93d), nyet (81d), oyer (31c), oyes (31c, 32c, 58d), oyez (31c, 32c, 58d), pyel- (93c), pyes, tyee (26d)
_ _ Y E	Faye (152), Gaye (154), Kaye (164), Skye (64d, 120d)
Y _ _ E	Yale (79b, 101c, 205), yate (41d), yipe (42c), yoke (66c, 232), yore (12c, 23a, 55b, 73a, 83d, 87a, 122b), yule (27a)

443

_ Y G _	hygr- (94a), zygo- (93c)
Y _ _ G	yang (134d), yegg (22d)
Y H _ _	YHWH (244)
Y _ _ H	yeah (10b), yech (112a), YHWH (244), yogh (12c), yuch (112a)
Y I _ _	yipe (42c), yips
_ Y I _	ayin (12a)
Y _ _ I	yeni (119c), Yeti (9b), Yogi (187), yogi (60a), Yuri (188)
_ Y K _	fyke (16b), tyke (21c, 26c)
Y _ _ K	Yank (12b), yank (95d), yolk (128d), York (41a, 187, 192, 193, 194), yuck (112a)
_ Y L _	gyle (21d), hyla (12b, 122c), hylo- (94a), Kyle (165), Lyle (167), pyla (21c), Pyle (175), syll. (243), xylo- (94a)
_ _ Y L	amyl (114d), amyl- (93d), aryl (14b), idyl (90c, 233)
Y _ _ L	yawl (20b, 103b), Yell (64d), yell (18c, 108d), yowl (12d, 32b)
Y M _ _	YMCA (244), YMHA (244), ymir (54b)
_ Y M _	cyma (37c, 77d), cyme (47d), gymn- (93b), gyms, hymn (111d), tymp (19d), zymo- (93a)
_ _ Y M	Clym (14a)
_ Y N _	dyna- (93c), dyne (48c, 246), gyne (45b), gyno- (92d), -gyny (117b), Lynn (167), Lynx (207), lynx (24a, 131d, 230), myna (19b), rynd (76d), Ryne (179), syne (105b), Tyne (82b, 184, 223), Wynn (187)
_ _ Y N	Gwyn (199)
Y _ _ N	yarn (43a, 114b, 119b, 133c), yawn (21a), yean (68d), Yüan (26d, 78a), yuan (215)
Y O _ _	yoga (14d, 60a), yogh (12c), Yogi (187), yogi (60a), yoke (66c, 232), Yoko (187), yolk (128d), yond (36d), yore (12c, 23a, 55b, 73a, 83d, 87a, 122b), York (41a, 187, 192, 193, 194), you'd (30c), your (95a), yowl (12d, 32b), yoyo (88a)
_ Y O _	BYOB (236), Gyor (217), Lyon (216), ryot (62d)
_ _ Y O	buyo (18d), coyo (16a, 26d), cryo- (93a), Enyo (129d), kayo (68c), Mayo (169), toyo (58b, 65d, 116b), yoyo (88a)
Y _ _ O	Yedo (122d), Yoko (187), yoyo (88a), Yuro (188)

_ Y P _   **gyps, hype** (95a), **hypo** (88d), **rype** (95d), **type** (27d, 112a, 113b), **typo** (41c, 94c), **typp** (134b)

Y _ _ P   **yapp** (20d), **yaup** (119b), **yawp** (12d, 119b), **yelp** (12d, 37b)

_ Y R _   **Byrd** (90d), **byre** (31c), **eyra** (65b), **Eyre** (22a), **eyry** (39a), **fyrd** (83d), **gyre** (27b), **gyri** (21c), **gyro-** (93a), **Lyra** (58a, 207), **lyre** (80b, 85a), **Myra** (15a, 171), **myri-** (93b), **pyre** (52c), **pyro-** (93a), **Tyra** (184), **Tyre** (71a, 88c, 218), **Tyro** (81b), **tyro** (12b, 18b, 82c)

_ _ Y R   **skyr** (20d)

Y _ _ R   **year** (122b), **ymir** (54b), **your** (95a)

_ Y S _   **cyst** (128a), **-lyse** (117b), **lysi-** (93a), **myst** (56b), **NYSE** (241)

_ _ Y S   **Amys, bays, beys, boys, buys, cays, days, deys, Fays, gays** (60d), **guys, Hays** (157), **ltys** (120c), **jays, joys, Kays, keys, lays, Mays** (169), **nays** (129c), **pays, rays, Roys, says, soys, toys, ways, whys**

Y _ _ S   **yaks, yams, yaps, yaws, yeas** (129c), **yens, yews, yips, yuks** (70b), **Yves** (188)

_ Y T _   **-lyte** (117a), **myth** (43a, 71b)

_ _ Y T   **Foyt** (153), **Hoyt** (159)

Y _ _ T   **yurt** (78a)

Y U _ _   **Yüan** (26d, 78a), **yuan** (215), **yuca** (24c), **yuch** (112a), **yuck** (112a), **yuga** (60a), **yuks** (70b), **yule** (27a), **Yuma** (189), **Yuri** (188), **Yuro** (188), **yurt** (78a)

_ Y U _   **Ryun** (179), **Tyus** (184)

Y V _ _   **Yves** (188)

_ Y V _   **gyve** (45c, 107b)

Y W _ _   **YWCA** (244), **YWHA** (244)

_ Y X _   **myxo-** (93b)

_ _ Y X   **Ceyx** (57b), **onyx** (23c, 25d, 53b, 106c), **oryx** (13a, 231), **Styx** (26b, 57a)

_ Y Z _   **-lyze** (117b)

Z A _ _   **Zama** (106a), **Zana** (58a), **Zane** (188), **zany** (28b, 38a, 48b, 109c), **zarf** (28d, 32d, 114d), **Zasu** (188)

_ Z A _   **azan** (80c), **czar** (103c), **izar** (52d)

_ _ Z A   **boza** (13d), **Gaza** (88c, 216), **Giza** (113c), **Liza** (166)

Z _ _ A   **Zama** (106a), **Zana** (58a), **zeta** (11d), **Zola** (49c, 188), **zona**(108a)

Z _ _ C   **zinc** (20b, 76a, 245)

_ _ Z D   **Yazd** (217)

Z E _ _   **zeal** (14b, 45c), **zebu** (21c, 62d, 231), **Zech.** (244), **zeds, zees** (110c), **zein** (30d), **zemi** (45c), **Zeno** (56b), **Zeph.** (244), **Zero** (188), **zero** (27b, 65d, 73b, 82c, 89d), **zest** (45c, 57c, 99b), **zeta** (11d), **Zeus** (55c, 59c, 198)

_ Z E _   **Ezek.** (238), **ezel** (67c), **Ozem** (197)

_ _ Z E   **adze** (122d), **daze** (48a, 116c, 116d), **doze** (110b), **faze** (36a), **fuze** (35b), **gaze** (114d, 115a), **haze** (28b, 48a, 77b, 127b), **laze** (61d), **-lyze** (117b), **maze** (68b), **Mize** (171), **ooze** (43c, 72b, 79c, 87d), **raze** (34d, 35b, 36c, 71c), **size** (129a)

Z _ _ E   **Zane** (188), **zone** (18c, 36d, 40d, 118b)

Z _ _ F   **zarf** (28d, 32d, 114d)

Z _ _ G   **zing** (32a)

Z _ _ H   **Zech.** (244), **Zeph.** (244)

Z I _ _   **zinc** (20b, 76a, 245), **zing** (32a), **zion** (95a), **zips**

_ Z I _   **Ezio** (152)

_ _ Z I   **nazi** (81a)

Z _ _ I   **zemi** (45c), **zori** (108c), **Zuni** (95d, 189)

Z _ _ L   **zeal** (14b, 45c), **zool.** (244)

Z _ _ M   **zoom** (23c)

Z _ _ N   **zein** (30d), **zion** (95a), **zoon** (39d)

Z O _ _   **Zoes, Zola** (49c, 188), **zona** (108a), **zone** (18c, 36d, 40d, 118b), **zool.** (244), **zoom** (23c), **zoon** (39d), **zoos, Zoot** (188), **zori**(108c)

_ Z O _   **azon** (10b), **Azov** (19d, 103c)

_ _ Z O   **bozo** (38d, 88a), **kozo** (86b), **ouzo** (11a), **Puzo** (175)

Z _ _ O   **Zeno** (56b), **Zero** (188), **zero** (27b, 65d, 73b, 82c, 89d), **zygo-** (93c), **zymo-** (93a)

_ Z R _   **Ezra** (152, 196, 197)

Z _ _ S   **zeds**, **zees** (110c), **Zeus** (55c, 59c, 198), **zips**, **Zoes**, **zoos**

Z _ _ T   **zest** (45c, 57c, 99b), **Zoot** (188)

Z U _ _   **Zulu** (12a, 222), **Zuni** (95d, 189)

_ Z U _   **azul** (112c), **azur** (50a)

Z _ _ U   **Zasu** (188), **zebu** (21c, 62d, 231), **Zulu** (12a, 222)

Z Y _ _   **zygo-** (93c), **zymo-** (93a)

_ _ Z Y   **Cozy** (147), **cozy** (39b, 111b), **dozy** (110c), **hazy** (127a), **lazy** (62d), **mazy**, **oozy** (106b, 110c), **Ozzy** (173)

Z _ _ Y   **zany** (28b, 38a, 48b, 109c)

_ Z Z _   **Ozzy** (173)

_ _ Z Z   **buzz** (79d, 103a, 131d), **fizz** (39d), **fuzz** (37c), **Jazz** (206), **jazz** (61d, 118d), **razz** (59a)